SAS/STAT® User's Guide, Release 6.03 Edition

SAS Institute Inc.
SAS Campus Drive
Cary, NC 27513

The correct bibliographic citation for this manual is as follows: SAS Institute Inc., *SAS/STAT® User's Guide, Release 6.03 Edition.* Cary, NC: SAS Institute Inc., 1988. 1028 pp.

SAS/STAT® User's Guide, Release 6.03 Edition

Contents

APPENDICES

Tables

Credits

Documentation

Composition	Gail C. Freeman, Kelly W. Godfrey
Graphics	Jesse C. Chavis, Michael J. Pezzoni
Proofreading	Rebecca A. Fritz, Reid J. Hardin, Drew Saunders, Michael H. Smith
Technical Review	Gerardo I. Hurtado, Jeanne Martin, Nancy Miles-McDermott, John P. Sall, Warren S. Sarle, David C. Schlotzhauer, Maura Stokes
Writing and Editing	Kathryn P. Ingraham, Regina C. Luginbuhl, Sandra D. Schlotzhauer, Harriet Watts

Software

The procedures in SAS/STAT software were implemented by the Statistics section of the Applications Division under the leadership of David M. DeLong. Substantial contributions and support were given to the project by the members of the Applications Division, the Core Division, and the Host Systems Division.

Program development includes design, programming, debugging, support, and preliminary documentation. Many procedures in SAS/STAT software were converted from Version 5 procedures (in PL/I). Other procedures had been previously converted and were documented in Release 6.02 of the *SAS/STAT Guide for Personal Computers, Version 6 Edition*. Several procedures were greatly enhanced, and some were made interactive. In the list below, asterisks follow the names of developers currently supporting the procedure. Other developers listed worked on the procedure previously. (Developers no longer with SAS Institute are listed in the Acknowledgments.)

ACECLUS	Warren S. Sarle, Donna Lucas Watts*
ANOVA	Randall D. Tobias*, Yang C. Yuan
CANCORR	Warren S. Sarle, Donna Lucas Watts*
CANDISC	Warren S. Sarle, Yang C. Yuan*
CATMOD	John P. Sall, William M. Stanish*
CLUSTER	Warren S. Sarle*
DISCRIM	Warren S. Sarle, Yang C. Yuan*
FACTOR	Wolfgang M. Hartmann*, Warren S. Sarle
FASTCLUS	Warren S. Sarle, Donna Lucas Watts*
FREQ	William M. Stanish*
GLM	James H. Goodnight, John P. Sall, Warren S. Sarle, Randall D. Tobias* Yang C. Yuan

LIFEREG	David M. DeLong*
NESTED	Leigh A. Ihnen, Randall D. Tobias*
NLIN	James H. Goodnight, Leigh A. Ihnen*
NPAR1WAY	Jane Pierce*, John P. Sall
ORTHOREG	Wolfgang M. Hartmann*, John P. Sall
PLAN	Leigh A. Ihnen, Randall D. Tobias*
PRINCOMP	Warren S. Sarle*
REG	Leigh A. Ihnen, Charles Lin*, John P. Sall
RSREG	John P. Sall, Randall D. Tobias*
SCORE	John P. Sall, Donna Lucas Watts*
STEPDISC	Warren S. Sarle, Yang C. Yuan*
TREE	Heman Robinson*, Warren S. Sarle
TTEST	James H. Goodnight, William M. Stanish*
VARCLUS	Wolfgang M. Hartmann*, Warren S. Sarle
VARCOMP	James H. Goodnight, Randall D. Tobias*
Probability Routines	David M. DeLong
Multiple Comparisons and Multivariate Routines	Wolfgang M. Hartmann, Warren S. Sarle
Other Numerical Routines	Wolfgang M. Hartmann, Ken Howell, Richard D. Langston, Katherine Ng, Jane Pierce, John P. Sall, Brian T. Schellenberger
Quality Assurance Testing	Brett Chapman, Gerardo I. Hurtado, Jeanne Martin, David M. Price, Kathy Roggenkamp, Maura Stokes, Charles W. Wakeford
Statistical Consulting and Technical Support	John C. Boling, John C. Brocklebank, Donna Fulenwider, Bart Killam, Herbert J. Kirk, Dale Moffett, Eddie Routten

The following staff members made special contributions in the form of leadership and support for other SAS/STAT procedure developers: Ken Howell, Leigh A. Ihnen, Richard D. Langston, Jeffrey A. Polzin, Jack J. Rouse, Warren S. Sarle.

The PC version of the SAS System was developed on an Apollo domain network, as well as on IBM PCs.

A final and most important credit is given to Margaret Lois Adair who died on May 1, 1987, at the age of 41. As Technical Support Manager, Statistical Group, she made many contributions to technical support and documentation that will not be forgotten by her colleagues and friends.

Acknowledgments

Hundreds of people have helped the SAS System in many ways since its inception. The individuals that we acknowledge here have been especially helpful in the development of statistical procedures.

Anthony James Barr	Barr Systems, Gainesville, FL
Mary Butler Moore	University of Florida at Gainesville
Wilbert P. Byrd	Clemson University
George Chao	Arnar-Stone Laboratories
Daniel M. Chilko	West Virginia University
Richard E. Cooper	USDA
Sandra Donaghy	North Carolina State University
David B. Duncan	Johns Hopkins University
Rudolf J. Freund	Texas A & M University
Wayne Fuller	Iowa State University
A. Ronald Gallant	North Carolina State University
Charles Gates	Texas A & M University
Thomas M. Gerig	North Carolina State University
Francis Giesbrecht	North Carolina State University
Harvey J. Gold	North Carolina State University
Harold W. Gugel	General Motors Corporation
Donald Guthrie	University of California, Los Angeles
Gerald Hajian	Burroughs Wellcome Company
Frank E. Harrell, Jr.	Duke University Medical Center
Walter Harvey	Ohio State University
Ronald Helms	University of North Carolina at Chapel Hill
Jane T. Helwig	Seasoned Systems Inc., Chapel Hill, NC
Donald J. Henderson	ORI, Inc.
Ronald R. Hocking	Texas A & M University
Harold Huddleston	Data Collection & Analysis, Inc., Falls Church, Virginia
David Hurst	University of Alabama at Birmingham
Emilio A. Icaza	Louisiana State University
William Kennedy	Iowa State University
Gary Koch	University of North Carolina at Chapel Hill
Kenneth L. Koonce	Louisiana State University
Clyde Y. Kramer (deceased)	Virginia Polytechnic Institute and State University, University of Kentucky, and The Upjohn Company
Ardell C. Linnerud	North Carolina State University
Ramon C. Littell	University of Florida at Gainesville

H.L. Lucas (deceased)	North Carolina State University
David D. Mason	North Carolina State University
J. Philip Miller	Washington University Medical Center
Robert J. Monroe	North Carolina State University
Robert D. Morrison	Oklahoma State University
Kenneth Offord	Mayo Clinic
Robert Parks	Washington University Medical Center
Richard M. Patterson	Auburn University
Virginia Patterson	University of Tennessee
C.H. Proctor	North Carolina State University
Dana Quade	University of North Carolina at Chapel Hill
William L. Sanders	University of Tennessee
Robert Schechter	Scott Paper Company
Shayle Searle	Cornell University
Jolayne Service	University of California at Irvine
Roger Smith	USDA
Phil Spector	University of California, Berkeley
Michael Speed	formerly of Louisiana State University
Robert Teichman	ICI Americas Inc.
Glenn Ware	University of Georgia
Love Casanova	Nissan Motor Corporation
Edward W. Whitehorne	Family Health International
William Wigton	USDA
Forrest W. Young	University of North Carolina at Chapel Hill

The final responsibility for the SAS System lies with SAS Institute alone. We hope that you will always let us know your opinions about the SAS System and its documentation. It is through your participation that the progress of SAS software has been accomplished.

The Staff of SAS Institute Inc.

Preface

What Is the SAS System?

The SAS System is a software system for data analysis. The goal of SAS Institute is to provide data analysts with one system to meet all their computing needs. When your computing needs are met, you are free to concentrate on results rather than on the mechanics of getting them. Instead of learning programming languages, several statistical packages, and utility programs, you only need to learn the SAS System.

The SAS System is available on many mainframes, minicomputers, and personal computers under a variety of operating systems. Not all products in the SAS System are available for all operating systems. For more information about how to license products under your operating system, see **Licensing the SAS System** later in this section.

Base SAS Software

Base SAS software provides tools for

- information storage and retrieval
- data modification and programming
- report writing
- descriptive statistics
- file handling.

Each of these tools is briefly summarized in the paragraphs below.

Information storage and retrieval   The SAS System reads data values in virtually any form and then organizes the values into a SAS data set. The data can be combined with other SAS data sets using the file-handling operations described below. You can analyze the data and produce reports. SAS data sets are automatically self-documenting since they contain both the data values and their descriptions. The special structure of a SAS data library minimizes maintenance.

Data modification and programming   A complete set of SAS statements and functions is available for modifying data. Some program statements perform standard operations such as creating new variables, accumulating totals, and checking for errors; others are powerful programming tools such as DO/END and IF-THEN/ELSE statements. The data-handling features are so valuable that many people use base SAS software as a data base management system.

Report writing   Just as base SAS software reads data in almost any form, it can write data in almost any form. In addition to the preformatted reports that SAS procedures produce, you can design and produce printed reports in any form, including output files on disk.

Descriptive Statistics   Procedures available in base SAS software

- provide simple descriptive statistics, such as averages and standard deviations
- produce bar charts, pie charts, and plots
- produce and analyze contingency tables
- rank and standardize data.

You can supplement these basic procedures with the powerful tools available in SAS/STAT software.

File handling   Combining values and observations from several data sets is often necessary for data analysis. Base SAS software has tools for editing, subsetting, concatenating, merging, and updating data sets. Multiple input files can be processed simultaneously, and several reports can be produced in one pass of the data.

Other SAS System Products

To base SAS software, you can add tools for statistical analysis, graphics, forecasting, data entry, operations research, quality control, interactive matrix applications, data base management, and interfaces to other data bases to provide one total system. With base SAS software, you can integrate other SAS software products to provide one total system. The other products currently available for Release 6.03 are

SAS/STAT software
   a powerful set of statistical analysis procedures

SAS/AF software
   a full-screen, interactive applications facility

SAS/FSP software
   interactive, menu-driven facilities for data entry, editing, retrieval of SAS files, and text processing

SAS/GRAPH software
   device-intelligent color graphics for business and research applications

SAS/IML software
   an interactive matrix facility for advanced mathematical, engineering, and statistical needs.

Documentation for the SAS System

This book documents Release 6.03 of SAS/STAT software. The statistical analysis procedures in SAS/STAT software are among the finest available. They range from simple descriptive statistics to complex multivariate techniques. Their designs are based on our belief that you should never need to tell the SAS System anything it can figure out by itself. Statistical integrity is thus accompanied by ease of use. For more information on how to use this book, read the section titled "Using This Book."

Other manuals and technical reports are available for base SAS software and for the other products available for Release 6.03. In addition, other versions of the SAS System are documented in other manuals not listed here. Release 6.03 manuals are

SAS Introductory Guide, Release 6.03 Edition
SAS Language Guide, Release 6.03 Edition
SAS Procedures Guide, Release 6.03 Edition
SAS/AF User's Guide, Release 6.03 Edition
SAS/FSP User's Guide, Release 6.03 Edition
SAS/GRAPH User's Guide, Release 6.03 Edition
SAS/IML User's Guide, Release 6.03 Edition
SAS Guide to Macro Processing, Version 6 Edition
SAS Guide to TABULATE Processing, Second Edition
Master Index to SAS System Documentation, Version 6 Edition.

You can write the Institute's Book Sales Department for a current publications catalog, which describes the manuals and technical reports and lists their prices.

SAS Services to Users

Technical support   SAS Institute supports users through the Technical Support Department. If you have a problem running a SAS job, you should contact your site's SAS Software Consultant. If the problem cannot be resolved locally, your local support personnel should call the Institute's Technical Support Department at (919) 677-8008 on weekdays between 9:00 a.m. and 8:00 p.m. Eastern Time. A brochure describing the services provided by the Technical Support Department is available from SAS Institute.

Training   SAS Institute sponsors a comprehensive training program, including programs of study for novice data processors, statisticians, applications programmers, systems programmers, and local support personnel. *SAS Training*, a semi-annual training publication available from the Education Division, describes the total training program and each course currently being offered by SAS Institute.

News magazine   *SAS Communications* is the quarterly news magazine of SAS Institute. Each issue contains ideas for more effective use of the SAS System, information about research and development underway at SAS Institute, the current training schedule, new publications, and news of the SAS Users Group International (SUGI).

To subscribe to *SAS Communications*, send your name and complete address to

SAS Institute Mailing List
SAS Institute Inc.
SAS Campus Drive
Cary, NC 27513

Sample library   Both base SAS and SAS/STAT software contain a directory of sample SAS applications illustrating features of SAS statistical procedures and creative SAS programming techniques that can help you gain an in-depth knowledge of the capabilities of the software. Check with your SAS Software Consultant to find out how to access the sample library.

SAS Users Group International (SUGI)

The SAS Users Group International (SUGI) is a nonprofit association of professionals who are interested in how others are using the SAS System. Although SAS Institute provides administrative support, SUGI is independent from the Institute. Membership is open to all users at SAS sites, and there is no membership fee.

Annual conferences are structured to allow many avenues of discussion. Users present invited and contributed papers on various topics.

Proceedings of the annual conferences are distributed free to SUGI registrants. Extra copies can be purchased from SAS Institute.

SASware Ballot   SAS users provide valuable input toward the direction of future SAS development by ranking their priorities on the annual SASware Ballot. The top vote-getters are announced at the SUGI conference. Complete results of the SASware Ballot are also printed in the *SUGI Proceedings*.

Licensing the SAS System

The SAS System is licensed to customers in the Western Hemisphere from the Institute's headquarters in Cary, NC. To serve the needs of our international customers, the Institute maintains many international subsidiaries. In addition, agents in other countries are licensed distributors for the SAS System. For a complete list of offices, write or call

SAS Institute Inc.
SAS Campus Drive
Cary, NC 27513
(919) 677-8000

Using This Book

Purpose of This Book

This book documents all of the procedures available in Release 6.03 of SAS/STAT software and supersedes the *SAS/STAT Guide for Personal Computers, Version 6 Edition*. To find out which release of SAS/STAT software you are using, look at the notes at the beginning of the SAS log.

How This Book Is Organized

Chapters 1 through 8 of this book provide an overview and introduce you to the eight groups of procedures in SAS/STAT software. These introductory chapters briefly describe the procedures available in a given group and compare and contrast procedures. The final introductory chapter, Chapter 9, contains detailed information about the four types of estimable functions that are used by many regression and analysis-of-variance procedures.

After the nine introductory chapters, the next twenty-six chapters describe individual SAS/STAT procedures in alphabetical order. Each procedure description is self-contained; you need to be familiar with only the most basic features of the SAS System and SAS terminology to use most procedures. The statements and syntax necessary to run each procedure are presented in a uniform format throughout this book. You can duplicate the examples by copying the statements and data and running the SAS program. The examples are also useful as models for writing your own programs.

Each procedure description is divided into the following major parts:

ABSTRACT a short paragraph describing what the procedure does.

INTRODUCTION introductory and background material, including definitions and occasional introductory examples.

SPECIFICATIONS reference section for the syntax for the procedure. The statement syntax is summarized, then the PROC statement is described, and then all other statements are described in alphabetical order. Options for a statement are described in alphabetical order, or they are grouped and described in alphabetical order within each group.

DETAILS expanded descriptions of features, internal operations, statistical background, treatment of missing values, computational methods, required computational resources, and input and output data sets.

EXAMPLES examples using the procedure, including data, SAS statements, and printed output. You can reproduce these examples by copying the statements and data and running the job.

REFERENCES a selected bibliography.

Following the chapters that describe SAS/STAT procedures, there are two appendices. The first appendix summarizes the changes and enhancements to SAS/STAT procedures, and the second appendix contains a discussion of special SAS data sets.

How to Use This Book

If you have not used the SAS System before, you should read the *SAS Introductory Guide*. You can also refer to the *SAS Language Guide* and the *SAS Procedures Guide*. Next, read the introductory chapter that corresponds to your area of interest. The introductory chapter will help you choose the procedure that best meets your needs. Once you have chosen a procedure, you can turn to the chapter on the procedure. First, read the **ABSTRACT** and **INTRODUCTION** to get an overview of how the procedure works. Next, look at the first part of the **SPECIFICATIONS** section to get a summary of which statements can be used with the procedure and what each statement does. At this point, you may know exactly what statements you need to use for your situation. If not, there may be an example in the **EXAMPLES** section that closely matches your problem and can guide you in selecting statements to use. Otherwise, you may need to read the **SPECIFICATIONS** section in more detail. Finally, the **DETAILS** section contains information on advanced topics and details of analysis.

If you are familiar with the SAS System and with the procedures in SAS/STAT software, first turn to Appendix 1, which summarizes the changes and enhancements to the statistical procedures. Next, review specific chapters to learn more about the changes to a particular procedure. Many procedures have expanded introductions, new or expanded details sections, and new examples, so even if the procedure has not changed very much, the chapter on the procedure may have new information.

Typographical Conventions

In this book, you will see several type styles used. Style conventions are summarized below:

roman type   is the basic type style used for most text.

italic type   is used to define new terms and to indicate items in statement syntax that you need to supply.

bold type   is used in **SPECIFICATIONS** sections to indicate that you must use the exact spelling and form shown, to refer to matrices and vectors, and to refer you to other sections (either in the same or in other chapters). In addition, sentences of extreme importance are entirely in bold type.

code   is used to show examples of SAS statements. In most cases, this book uses lowercase type for SAS code. You can enter your own SAS code in lowercase, uppercase, or a mixture of the two. The SAS System always changes your variable names to uppercase, but character variable values remain in lowercase if you have entered them that way. Enter any titles and footnotes exactly as you want them to appear on your output.

How the Output Is Shown

Output from procedures is enclosed in boxes. Within a chapter, the output is numbered consecutively starting with 1, and each output is given a title. Most of the programs in this book were run using the SAS system options LINESIZE=120, PAGESIZE=60, and NODATE. In situations where other options were used, these are usually indicated in the SAS code that accompanies the output. In some cases, if you run the examples, you will get slightly different output. This is a function of whether a floating-point processor is used in your computer, rather than a problem with the software. In all situations, the difference should be very small.

Chapter 1

Introduction to Regression Procedures

Introduction

This chapter reviews SAS/STAT software procedures that are used for regression analysis: REG, CATMOD, GLM, NLIN, ORTHOREG, and RSREG. REG provides the most general analysis capabilities; the other procedures give more specialized analyses. This chapter also briefly mentions several procedures in SAS/ETS software.

Many SAS/STAT procedures, each with special features, perform regression analysis. The following procedures perform at least one type of regression analysis:

CATMOD   analyzes data that can be represented by a contingency table. CATMOD fits linear models to functions of response frequencies and can be used for linear and logistic regression. The CATMOD procedure is discussed in detail in Chapter 3, "Introduction to Categorical Data Analysis Procedures."

GLM   uses the method of least squares to fit general linear models. In addition to many other analyses, GLM can perform simple, multiple, polynomial and weighted regression. GLM has many of the same input/output capabilities as REG but does not provide as many diagnostic tools or allow interactive changes in the model or data. The GLM procedure is discussed in detail in Chapter 2, "Introduction to Analysis-of-Variance Procedures."

LIFEREG   fits parametric models to failure-time data that may be right-censored. These types of models are commonly used in survival analysis. The LIFEREG procedure is discussed in detail in Chapter 8, "Introduction to Survival Analysis Procedures."

NLIN   builds nonlinear regression models. Several different iterative methods are available.

ORTHOREG   performs regression using the Gentleman-Givens computational method. For ill-conditioned data, ORTHOREG can produce more accurate parameter estimates than other procedures such as GLM and REG.

REG   performs linear regression with many diagnostic capabilities, selects models using one of nine methods, produces scatter plots of raw data and statistics, highlights scatter plots to identify particular observations, and allows interactive changes in both the regression model and the data used to fit the model.

RSREG   builds quadratic response-surface regression models. RSREG analyzes the fitted response surface to determine the factor levels of optimum response and performs a ridge analysis to search for the region of optimum response.

Several SAS/ETS procedures also perform regression. The procedures listed below are documented in the *SAS/ETS User's Guide, Version 5 Edition*:

AUTOREG   implements regression models using time-series data where the errors are autocorrelated.

PDLREG   performs regression analysis with polynomial distributed lags.

SYSLIN   handles linear simultaneous systems of equations, such as econometric models.

SYSNLIN   handles nonlinear simultaneous systems of equations, such as econometric models.

Regression analysis is the analysis of the relationship between one variable and another set of variables. The relationship is expressed as an equation that predicts a *response variable* (also called a *dependent variable* or *criterion*) from a function of *regressor variables* (also called *independent variables, predictors, explanatory variables, factors,* or *carriers*) and *parameters*. The parameters are adjusted so that a measure of fit is optimized. For example, the equation for the *i*th observation might be

$$y_i = \beta_0 + \beta_1 x_i + \varepsilon_i$$

where y_i is the response variable, x_i is a regressor variable, β_0 and β_1 are unknown parameters to be estimated, and ε_i is an error term.

You might use regression analysis to find out how well you can predict a child's weight if you know that child's height. Suppose you collect your data by measuring heights and weights of nineteen school children. You want to estimate the intercept β_0 and the slope β_1 of a line described by the equation

$$\text{WEIGHT} = \beta_0 + \beta_1 \text{HEIGHT} + \varepsilon$$

where

WEIGHT	is the response variable.
β_0, β_1	are the unknown parameters.
HEIGHT	is the regressor variable.
ε	is the unknown error.

The data are included in the program below. The results are shown in **Output 1.1**, which shows a regression analysis and a plot of the data.

```
data class;
   input name $ height weight age;
   cards;
Alfred  69.0 112.5 14
Alice   56.5  84.0 13
Barbara 65.3  98.0 13
Carol   62.8 102.5 14
Henry   63.5 102.5 14
James   57.3  83.0 12
Jane    59.8  84.5 12
Janet   62.5 112.5 15
Jeffrey 62.5  84.0 13
John    59.0  99.5 12
Joyce   51.3  50.5 11
Judy    64.3  90.0 14
Louise  56.3  77.0 12
Mary    66.5 112.0 15
Philip  72.0 150.0 16
Robert  64.8 128.0 12
Ronald  67.0 133.0 15
Thomas  57.5  85.0 11
William 66.5 112.0 15
;
proc reg;
   model weight=height;
   plot weight*height;
run;
```

Output 1.1   Regression for Weight and Height Data

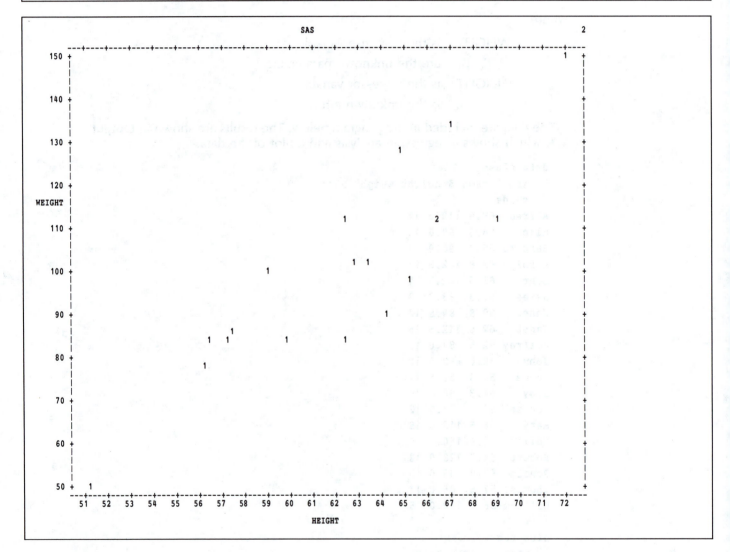

Estimates of β_0 and β_1 for these data are $b_0 = -143.0$ and $b_1 = 3.9$, so the line is described by the equation

WEIGHT $= -143.0 + 3.9*$HEIGHT

Regression is often used in an exploratory fashion to look for empirical relationships, such as the relationship between HEIGHT and WEIGHT. In this example, HEIGHT is not the cause of WEIGHT. You would need a controlled experiment to scientifically confirm the relationship. See **Comments on Interpreting Regression Statistics** later in this chapter for more information.

The method most commonly used to estimate the parameters is to minimize the sum of squares of the differences between the actual response value and the value predicted by the equation. The estimates are called *least-squares estimates,* and the criterion value is called the *error sum of squares*

$$SSE = \Sigma (y_i - b_0 - b_1 x_i)^2$$

where b_0 and b_1 are the estimates of β_0 and β_1 that minimize SSE.

For a general discussion of the theory of least-squares estimation of linear models and its application to regression and analysis of variance, see one of the applied regression texts, including Draper and Smith (1981), Daniel and Wood (1980), Johnston (1972), and Weisberg (1985).

SAS/STAT regression procedures produce the following information for a typical regression analysis:

- parameter estimates using the least-squares criterion
- estimates of the variance of the error term
- estimates of the variance or standard deviation of the sampling distribution of the parameter estimates
- tests of hypotheses about the parameters
- predicted values and residuals using the estimates
- statistics for evaluating the fit or lack of fit.

Besides the usual statistics of fit produced for a regression, SAS/STAT regression procedures can produce many other specialized diagnostic statistics, including

- collinearity diagnostics to measure how strongly regressors are related to other regressors and how this affects the stability and variance of the estimates (REG).
- influence diagnostics to measure how each individual observation contributes to determining the parameter estimates, the SSE, and the fitted values (REG, RSREG).
- lack-of-fit diagnostics that measure the lack of fit of the regression model by comparing the error variance estimate to another pure error variance that is not dependent on the form of the model (RSREG).
- diagnostic scatter plots that check the fit of the model, and highlighted scatter plots that identify particular observations or groups of observations (REG).
- predicted and residual values, and confidence intervals for the mean and for an individual value (GLM, REG).
- time-series diagnostics for equally spaced time-series data that measure how much errors may be related across neighboring observations. These diagnostics can also measure functional goodness of fit for data sorted by regressor or response (REG, SAS/ETS procedures).

Other diagnostic statistics can be produced by programming a sequence of runs. For example, tests to measure structural change in a model over time can be performed by calculating items from several regressions or by writing a program with SAS/IML software.

General Regression Using PROC REG

PROC REG is a general-purpose procedure for regression that

- handles multiple regression models
- provides nine model-selection methods
- allows interactive changes both in the model and in the data used to fit the model
- allows linear inequality restrictions on parameters
- tests linear hypotheses and multivariate hypotheses
- produces collinearity diagnostics, influence diagnostics, and partial regression leverage plots
- saves estimates, predicted values, residuals, confidence limits, and other diagnostic statistics in output SAS data sets
- generates scatter plots of data and of various statistics
- "paints" or highlights scatter plots to identify particular observations or groups of observations
- can use correlations or crossproducts for input.

Model-selection Methods in PROC REG

The nine methods of model selection implemented in PROC REG are

NONE   no selection. This method is the default and uses the full model given in the MODEL statement to fit the linear regression.

FORWARD   forward selection. This method starts with no variables in the model and adds variables one by one to the model. At each step, the variable added is the one that maximizes the fit of the model. An option allows you to specify the criterion for inclusion.

BACKWARD   backward elimination. This method starts with a full model and eliminates variables one by one from the model. At each step, the variable with the smallest contribution to the model is deleted. An option allows you to specify the criterion for exclusion.

STEPWISE   stepwise regression, forward and backward. This method is a modification of the forward-selection method in that variables already in the model do not necessarily stay there. Again, options allow you to specify criteria for entry into the model and for remaining in the model.

MAXR   maximum R^2 improvement. This method tries to find the best one-variable model, the best two-variable model, and so on. MAXR differs from STEPWISE in that many more models are evaluated with MAXR, which considers all switches before making any switch. The STEPWISE method may remove the "worst" variable without considering what the "best" remaining variable might accomplish, whereas MAXR would consider what the "best" remaining variable might accomplish. Consequently, MAXR typically takes much longer to run than STEPWISE.

MINR   minimum R^2 improvement. This method closely resembles MAXR, but the switch chosen is the one that produces the smallest increase in R^2.

RSQUARE   finds a specified number of models having the highest R^2 in each of a range of model sizes.

CP   finds a specified number of models with the lowest C_p within a range of model sizes.

ADJRSQ   finds a specified number of models having the highest adjusted R^2 within a range of model sizes.

Nonlinear Regression Using PROC NLIN

PROC NLIN implements iterative methods that attempt to find least-squares estimates for nonlinear models. The default method is Gauss-Newton, although several other methods are available. You must specify parameter names, starting values, and expressions for the model. For some iterative methods, you also need to specify expressions for derivatives of the model with respect to the parameters. A grid search is also available to select starting values for the parameters. Since nonlinear models are often difficult to estimate, NLIN may not always find the globally optimal least-squares estimates.

Fitting Quadratic Response Surfaces Using PROC RSREG

RSREG fits a quadratic response-surface model, which is useful in searching for factor values that optimize a response. The following features in RSREG make it preferable to other regression procedures for analyzing response surfaces:

- automatic generation of quadratic effects
- a lack-of-fit test
- solutions for critical values of the surface
- eigenvalues of the associated quadratic form
- a ridge analysis to search for the direction of optimum response.

Regression for Ill-conditioned Data Using PROC ORTHOREG

The ORTHOREG procedure performs linear least-squares regression using the Gentleman-Givens computational method and can produce more accurate parameter estimates for ill-conditioned data. PROC GLM and PROC REG produce very accurate estimates for most problems. However, if you have very ill-conditioned data, consider using the ORTHOREG procedure. The collinearity diagnostics in PROC REG can help you to determine whether PROC ORTHOREG would be useful.

Regression Using PROC GLM, PROC CATMOD, and PROC LIFEREG

PROC GLM fits general linear models to data, and it can perform regression, analysis of variance, analysis of covariance, and many other analyses. Certain of its features for regression distinguish GLM from other regression procedures:

- direct specification of polynomial effects
- ease of specifying categorical effects (GLM automatically generates dummy variables for class variables).

Most of the statistics based on predicted and residual values that are available in PROC REG are also available in GLM. However, GLM does not produce collinearity diagnostics, influence diagnostics, or scatter plots. In addition, GLM allows only one model and fits the full model.

See Chapter 2, "Introduction to Analysis-of-Variance Procedures," and the chapter on the GLM procedure for more detail.

PROC CATMOD can perform linear regression and logistic regression of response functions for data that can be represented in a contingency table. See Chapter 3, "Introduction to Categorical Data Analysis Procedures," and the chapter on the CATMOD procedure for more detail.

PROC LIFEREG is useful in fitting equations to data that may be right-censored. See Chapter 8, "Introduction to Survival Analysis Procedure," and the chapter on the LIFEREG procedure for more detail.

Interactive Features in the CATMOD, GLM, and REG Procedures

The CATMOD, GLM, and REG procedures do not stop after processing a RUN statement. More statements can be submitted as a continuation of the previous statements. Many new features in these procedures are useful to request after you have reviewed the result from previous statements. The procedures stop if a DATA step or another procedure is requested or if a QUIT statement is submitted.

Statistical Background

The rest of this chapter outlines the way many SAS/STAT regression procedures calculate various regression quantities. Exceptions and further details are documented with individual procedures.

In matrix algebra notation, a linear model is written as

$$y = X\beta + \varepsilon$$

where X is the $n \times k$ design matrix (rows are observations and columns are the regressors), β is the $k \times 1$ vector of unknown parameters, and ε is the $n \times 1$ vector of unknown errors. The first column of X is usually a vector of 1s used in estimating the intercept term.

The statistical theory of linear models is based on strict classical assumptions. Ideally, the response is measured with all the factors controlled in an experimentally determined environment. Or, if you cannot control the factors experimentally, some tests must be interpreted as being conditional on the observed values of the regressors.

Other assumptions are that

- the form of the model is correct
- regressor variables are measured without error
- the expected value of the errors is zero
- the variance of the errors (and thus the dependent variable) is a constant across observations (called σ^2)
- the errors are uncorrelated across observations.

When hypotheses are tested, the additional assumption is made that

- the errors are normally distributed.

Statistical Model

If the model satisfies all the necessary assumptions, the least-squares estimates are the best linear unbiased estimates (BLUE). In other words, the estimates have minimum variance among the class of estimators that are unbiased and are linear functions of the responses. If the additional assumption that the error term is normally distributed is also satisfied, then

- the statistics that are computed have the proper sampling distributions for hypothesis testing
- parameter estimates are normally distributed
- various sums of squares are distributed proportional to chi-square, at least under proper hypotheses
- ratios of estimates to standard errors are distributed as Student's t under certain hypotheses
- appropriate ratios of sums of squares are distributed as F under certain hypotheses.

When regression analysis is used to model data that do not meet the assumptions, the results should be interpreted in a cautious, exploratory fashion, with discounted credence in the significance probabilities.

Box (1966) and Mosteller and Tukey (1977, chapters 12–13) discuss the problems that are encountered with regression data, especially when the data are not under experimental control.

Parameter Estimates and Associated Statistics

Parameter estimates are formed using least-squares criteria by solving the normal equations

$$(\mathbf{X'X})\mathbf{b} = \mathbf{X'y}$$

for the parameter estimates $\mathbf{b}$, yielding

$$\mathbf{b} = (\mathbf{X'X})^{-1}\mathbf{X'y} \ \ .$$

Assume for the present that $(\mathbf{X'X})$ is full rank (this assumption is relaxed later). The variance of the error σ^2 is estimated by the mean square error

$$s^2 = MSE = SSE \ / \ (n - k) = \Sigma \ (y_i - \mathbf{x}_i\mathbf{b})^2 \ / \ (n - k)$$

where $\mathbf{x}_i$ is the ith row of regressors.
The parameter estimates are unbiased:

$$E \ (\mathbf{b}) = \beta$$

$$E \ (s^2) = \sigma^2 \ \ .$$

The estimates have the variance-covariance matrix:

$$Var \ (\mathbf{b}) = (\mathbf{X'X})^{-1} \ \sigma^2 \ \ .$$

The estimate of the variance matrix replaces σ^2 with s^2 in the formula above:

$$COVB = (\mathbf{X'X})^{-1}s^2 \ \ .$$

The correlations of the estimates are derived by scaling to 1s on the diagonal.

Let

$$S = \text{diag} ((\mathbf{X'X})^{-1})^{-0.5}$$

$$\text{CORRB} = S(\mathbf{X'X})^{-1}S$$

Standard errors of the estimates are computed using the equation

$$\text{STDERR} (b_i) = \sqrt{(\mathbf{X'X})^{ii}s^2}$$

where $(\mathbf{X'X})^{ii}$ is the ith diagonal element of $(\mathbf{X'X})^{-1}$. The ratio

$$t = b_i \, / \, \text{STDERR} (b_i)$$

is distributed as Student's t under the hypothesis that β_i is zero. Regression procedures print the t ratio and the significance probability, the probability under the hypothesis $\beta_i=0$ of a larger absolute t value than was actually obtained. When the probability is less than some small level, the event is considered so unlikely that the hypothesis is rejected.

Type I SS and Type II SS measure the contribution of a variable to the reduction in SSE. Type I SS measure the reduction in SSE as that variable is entered into the model in sequence. Type II SS are the increment in SSE that results from removing the variable from the full model. Type II SS are equivalent to the Type III and Type IV SS reported in the GLM procedure. If Type II SS are used in the numerator of an F test, the test is equivalent to the t test for the hypothesis that the parameter is zero. In polynomial models, Type I SS measure the contribution of each polynomial term after it is orthogonalized to the previous terms in the model. The four types of SS are described in Chapter 9, "The Four Types of Estimable Functions."

Standardized estimates are defined as the estimates that result when all variables are standardized to a mean of 0 and a variance of 1. Standardized estimates are computed by multiplying the original estimates by the sample standard deviation of the regressor variable and dividing by the sample standard deviation of the dependent variable.

R^2 is an indicator of how much of the variation in the data is explained by the model. It is defined as

$$R^2 = 1 - (\text{SSE} \, / \, \text{TSS})$$

where SSE is the Sum of Squares for Error and TSS is the Corrected Total Sum of Squares. The Adjusted R^2 statistic is an alternative to R^2 that is adjusted for the number of parameters in the model. This is calculated as

$$\text{ADJRSQ} = 1 - [((n - i)(1 - R^2)) \, / \, (n - p)]$$

where n is the number of observations used to fit the model, p is the number of parameters in the model (including the intercept), and i is 1 if the model includes an intercept term, and 0 otherwise.

Tolerances and variance inflation factors measure the strength of interrelationships among the regressor variables in the model. If all variables are orthogonal to each other, both tolerance and variance inflation are 1. If a variable is very closely related to other variables, the tolerance goes to 0 and the variance inflation gets very large. Tolerance (TOL) is 1 minus the R^2 that results from the regression of the other variables in the model on that regressor. Variance inflation (VIF) is the diagonal of $(\mathbf{X'X})^{-1}$ if $(\mathbf{X'X})$ is scaled to correlation form. The statistics are related as

$$VIF = 1 \, / \, TOL \quad .$$

Models Not of Full Rank

If the model is not full rank, then a generalized inverse can be used to solve the normal equations to minimize the SSE:

$$\mathbf{b} = (\mathbf{X'X})^{-}\mathbf{X'y} \quad .$$

However, these estimates are not unique since there are an infinite number of solutions using different generalized inverses. REG and other regression procedures choose a nonzero solution for all variables that are linearly independent of previous variables and a zero solution for other variables. This corresponds to using a generalized inverse in the normal equations, and the expected values of the estimates are the Hermite normal form of $\mathbf{X'X}$ multiplied by the true parameters:

$$E\,(\mathbf{b}) = (\mathbf{X'X})^{-}(\mathbf{X'X})\boldsymbol{\beta} \quad .$$

Degrees of freedom for the zeroed estimates are reported as zero. The hypotheses that are not testable have t tests printed as missing. The message that the model is not full rank includes a printout of the relations that exist in the matrix.

Comments on Interpreting Regression Statistics

In most applications, regression models are merely useful approximations. Reality is often so complicated that you cannot know what the true model is. You may have to choose a model more on the basis of what variables can be measured and what kinds of models can be estimated than on a rigorous theory that explains how the universe really works. However, even in cases where theory is lacking, a regression model may be an excellent predictor of the response if the model is carefully formulated from a large sample. The interpretation of statistics such as parameter estimates may nevertheless be highly problematical.

Statisticians usually use the word "prediction" in a technical sense. *Prediction* in this sense does not refer to "predicting the future" (statisticians call that *forecasting*) but rather to guessing the response from the values of the regressors in an observation taken under the same circumstances as the sample from which the regression equation was estimated. If you developed a regression model for predicting consumer preferences in 1958, it may not give very good predictions in 1988 no matter how well it did in 1958. If it is the future you want to predict, your model must include whatever relevant factors may change over time. If the process you are studying does in fact change over time, you must take observations at several, perhaps many, different times. Analysis of such data is the province of SAS/ETS procedures such as AUTOREG and STATESPACE. See the *SAS/ETS User's Guide* for more information on these procedures.

The comments in the rest of this section are directed toward linear least-squares regression. Nonlinear regression and non-least-squares regression often introduce further complications.

For more detailed discussions of the interpretation of regression statistics, see Darlington (1968), Mosteller and Tukey (1977), Weisberg (1985), and Younger (1979).

Interpreting Parameter Estimates from a Controlled Experiment

Parameter estimates are easiest to interpret in a controlled experiment in which the regressors are manipulated independently of each other. In a well-designed experiment, such as a randomized factorial design with replications in each cell, you can use lack-of-fit tests and estimates of the standard error of prediction to determine whether the model describes the experimental process with adequate precision. If so, a regression coefficient estimates the amount by which the mean response changes when the regressor is changed by one unit while all the other regressors are unchanged. However, if the model involves interactions or polynomial terms, it may not be possible to interpret individual regression coefficients. For example, if the equation includes both linear and quadratic terms for a given variable, you cannot physically change the value of the linear term without also changing the value of the quadratic term. Sometimes it may be possible to recode the regressors, for example by using orthogonal polynomials, to make the interpretation easier.

If the nonstatistical aspects of the experiment are also treated with sufficient care (including such things as use of placebos and double blinds), then you can state conclusions in causal terms; that is, this change in a regressor causes that change in the response. Causality can never be inferred from statistical results alone or from an observational study.

If the model that you fit is not the true model, then the parameter estimates may depend strongly on the particular values of the regressors used in the experiment. For example, if the response is actually a quadratic function of a regressor but you fit a linear function, the estimated slope may be a large negative value if you use only small values of the regressor, a large positive value if you use only large values of the regressor, or near zero if you use both large and small regressor values. In reporting the results of an experiment, it is important to include the values of the regressors. It is also important to avoid extrapolating the regression equation outside the range of regressors in the sample.

Interpreting Parameter Estimates from an Observational Study

In an observational study, parameter estimates can be interpreted as the expected difference in response of two observations that differ by one unit on the regressor in question and that have the same values for all other regressors. You cannot make inferences about "changes" in an observational study since you have not actually changed anything. It may not be possible even in principle to change one regressor independently of all the others. Neither can you draw conclusions about causality without experimental manipulation.

If you conduct an observational study and if you do not know the true form of the model, interpretation of parameter estimates becomes even more convoluted. A coefficient must then be interpreted as an average over the sampled population of expected differences in response of observations that differ by one unit on only one regressor. The considerations that were discussed under controlled experiments for which the true model is not known also apply.

Comparing Parameter Estimates

Two coefficients in the same model can be directly compared only if the regressors are measured in the same units. You can make any coefficient large or small just by changing the units. If you convert a regressor from feet to miles, the parameter estimate is multiplied by 5280.

Sometimes standardized regression coefficients are used to compare the effects of regressors measured in different units. Standardizing the variables effectively makes the standard deviation the unit of measurement. This makes sense only if the standard deviation is a meaningful quantity, which usually is the case only if the observations are sampled from a well-defined population. In a controlled experiment, the standard deviation of a regressor depends on the values of the regressor selected by the experimenter. Thus, you can make a standardized regression coefficient large by using a large range of values for the regressor.

In some applications you may be able to compare regression coefficients in terms of the practical range of variation of a regressor. Suppose that each independent variable in an industrial process can be set to values only within a certain range. You can rescale the variables so that the smallest possible value is zero and the largest possible value is one. Then the unit of measurement for each regressor is the maximum possible range of the regressor, and the parameter estimates are comparable in that sense. Another possibility is to scale the regressors in terms of the cost of setting a regressor to a particular value, so comparisons can be made in monetary terms.

Correlated Regressors

In an experiment, you can often select values for the regressors such that the regressors are orthogonal (not correlated with each other). Orthogonal designs have enormous advantages in interpretation. With orthogonal regressors, the parameter estimate for a given regressor does not depend on which other regressors are included in the model, although other statistics such as standard errors and p values may change.

If the regressors are correlated, it becomes difficult to disentangle the effects of one regressor from another, and the parameter estimates may be highly dependent on which regressors are used in the model. Two correlated regressors may be nonsignificant when tested separately but highly significant when considered together. If two regressors have a correlation of 1.0, it is impossible to separate their effects.

It may be possible to recode correlated regressors to make interpretation easier. For example, if X and Y are highly correlated, they could be replaced in a linear regression by X+Y and X−Y without changing the fit of the model or statistics for other regressors.

Errors in the Regressors

If there is error in the measurements of the regressors, the parameter estimates must be interpreted with respect to the measured values of the regressors, not the true values. A regressor may be statistically nonsignificant when measured with error even though it would have been highly significant if measured accurately.

Probability Values (*p* values)

P values do not necessarily measure the importance of a regressor. An important regressor can have a large (nonsignificant) p value if the sample is small, if the regressor is measured over a narrow range, if there are large measurement errors, or if another closely related regressor is included in the equation. An unimportant regressor can have a very small p value in a large sample. Computing a confidence interval for a parameter estimate gives you more useful information than just looking at the p value, but confidence intervals do not solve problems of measurement errors in the regressors or highly correlated regressors.

P values are always approximations. The assumptions required to compute exact p values are never satisfied in practice.

Interpreting R^2

R^2 is usually defined as the proportion of variance of the response that is predictable from (that can be explained by) the regressor variables. It may be easier to interpret $\sqrt{1-R^2}$, which is approximately the factor by which the standard error of prediction is reduced by the introduction of the regressor variables.

R^2 is easiest to interpret when the observations, including the values of both the regressors and response, are randomly sampled from a well-defined population. Nonrandom sampling can greatly distort R^2. For example, excessively large values of R^2 can be obtained by omitting from the sample observations with regressor values near the mean.

In a controlled experiment, R^2 depends on the values chosen for the regressors. A wide range of regressor values generally yields a larger R^2 than a narrow range. In comparing the results of two experiments on the same variables but with different ranges for the regressors, you should look at the standard error of prediction (root mean square error) rather than R^2.

Whether a given R^2 value is considered to be large or small depends on the context of the particular study. A social scientist might consider an R^2 of 0.30 to be large, while a physicist might consider 0.98 to be small.

You can always get an R^2 arbitrarily close to 1.0 by including a large number of completely unrelated regressors in the equation. If the number of regressors is close to the sample size, R^2 is very biased. In such cases the adjusted R^2 and related statistics discussed by Darlington (1968) are less misleading.

If you fit many different models and choose the model with the largest R^2, all the statistics are biased and the p values for the parameter estimates are not valid.

Incorrect Data Values

All regression statistics can be seriously distorted by a single incorrect data value. A decimal point in the wrong place can completely change the parameter estimates, R^2, and other statistics. It is important to check your data for outliers and influential observations. The diagnostics in PROC REG are particularly useful in this regard.

Predicted and Residual Values

After the model has been fit, predicted and residual values are usually calculated and output. The predicted values are calculated from the estimated regression equation; the residuals are calculated as actual minus predicted. Some procedures can calculate standard errors of residuals, predicted mean values, and individual predicted values.

Consider the ith observation where $\mathbf{x}_i$ is the row of regressors, $\mathbf{b}$ is the vector of parameter estimates, and s^2 is the mean squared error.

Let

$$h_i = \mathbf{x}_i(\mathbf{X'X})^{-1}\mathbf{x}_i' \quad \text{(the leverage)}.$$

Then

$$\hat{y}_i = \mathbf{x}_i\mathbf{b} \quad \text{(the predicted mean value)}$$

$$\text{STDERR}(\hat{y}_i) = \sqrt{h_i\,s^2} \quad \text{(the standard error of the predicted mean)}.$$

The standard error of the individual (future) predicted value y_i is

$$\text{STDERR}(y_i) = \sqrt{(1 + h_i)s^2}$$

The residual is defined as

$$\text{RESID}_i = y_i - \mathbf{x}_i\mathbf{b} \quad \text{(the residual)}$$

$$\text{STDERR}(\text{RESID}_i) = \sqrt{(1 - h_i)s^2} \quad \text{(the standard error of the residual)}.$$

The ratio of the residual to its standard error, called the *studentized residual*, is sometimes shown as

$$\text{STUDENT}_i = \text{RESID}_i / \text{STDERR}(\text{RESID}_i)$$

There are two kinds of confidence intervals for predicted values. One type of confidence interval is an interval for the mean value of the response. The other type, sometimes called a *prediction* or *forecasting interval*, is an interval for the actual value of a response, which is the mean value plus error.

For example, you can construct for the *i*th observation a confidence interval that contains the true mean value of the response with probability $1-\alpha$. The upper and lower limits of the confidence interval for the mean value are

$$\text{LowerM} = \mathbf{x}_i\mathbf{b} - t_{a/2}\sqrt{h_i s^2}$$

$$\text{UpperM} = \mathbf{x}_i\mathbf{b} + t_{a/2}\sqrt{h_i s^2}$$

where $t_{a/2}$ is the tabulated *t* statistic with degrees of freedom equal to the degrees of freedom for Mean Square Error.

The limits for the confidence interval for an actual individual response are

$$\text{LowerI} = \mathbf{x}_i\mathbf{b} - t_{a/2}\sqrt{(1 + h_i)s^2}$$

$$\text{UpperI} = \mathbf{x}_i\mathbf{b} + t_{a/2}\sqrt{(1 + h_i)s^2} \quad .$$

Influential observations are those that, according to various criteria, appear to have a large influence on the parameter estimates. One measure of influence, Cook's *D*, measures the change to the estimates that results from deleting each observation:

$$\text{COOKD} = \text{STUDENT}^2 \, (\text{STDERR}(\hat{y}) / \text{STDERR}(\text{RESID}))^2 / k$$

where *k* is the number of parameters in the model (including the intercept). For more information, see Cook (1977, 1979).

The *predicted residual* for observation *i* is defined as the residual for the *i*th observation that results from dropping the *i*th observation from the parameter estimates. The sum of squares of predicted residual errors is called the *PRESS statistic*:

$$\text{PRESID}_i = \text{RESID}_i / (1 - h_i)$$

$$\text{PRESS} = \Sigma \, \text{PRESID}_i^2 \quad .$$

Testing Linear Hypotheses

The general form of a linear hypothesis for the parameters is

$$H_0: L\beta = c$$

where L is $q \times k$, β is $k \times 1$, and c is $q \times 1$. To test this hypothesis, the linear function is taken with respect to the parameter estimates:

$$(Lb - c) \quad .$$

This has variance

$$\text{Var} (Lb - c) = L\text{Var} (b)L' = L(X'X)^- L'\sigma^2$$

where b is the estimate of β.

A quadratic form called the *sum of squares due to the hypothesis* is calculated:

$$\text{SS} (Lb - c) = (Lb - c)'(L(X'X)^- L')^{-1}(Lb - c) \quad .$$

Assuming that this is testable, the SS can be used as a numerator of the F test:

$$F = [\text{SS} (Lb - c) / q] / s^2 \quad .$$

This is referred to an F distribution with q and dfe degrees of freedom, where dfe is the degrees of freedom for residual error.

Multivariate Tests

Multivariate hypotheses involve several dependent variables in the form

$$H_0: L\beta M = d$$

where L is a linear function on the regressor side, β is a matrix of parameters, M is a linear function on the dependent side, and d is a matrix of constants.

The special case (handled by REG) where the constants are the same for each dependent variable is written

$$(L\beta - cj)M = 0$$

where c is a column vector of constants and j is a row vector of 1s. The special case where the constants are 0 is

$$L\beta M = 0 \quad .$$

These multivariate tests are covered in detail in Morrison (1976); Timm (1975); Mardia, Kent, and Bibby (1979); Bock (1975); and other works cited in Chapter 4, "Introduction to Multivariate Procedures."

To test this hypothesis, construct two matrices, H and E, that correspond to the numerator and denominator of a univariate F test:

$$H = M'(LB - cj)'(L(X'X)^- L')^{-1}(LB - cj)M$$

$$E = M'(Y'Y - B'(X'X)B)M$$

Four test statistics, based on the eigenvalues of $\mathbf{E}^{-1}\mathbf{H}$ or $(\mathbf{E}+\mathbf{H})^{-1}\mathbf{H}$, are formed. Let λ_i be the ordered eigenvalues of $\mathbf{E}^{-1}\mathbf{H}$ (if the inverse exists), and let ξ_i be the ordered eigenvalues of $(\mathbf{E}+\mathbf{H})^{-1}\mathbf{H}$. It happens that $\xi_i = \lambda_i/(1+\lambda_i)$ and $\lambda_i = \xi_i/(1-\xi_i)$, and it turns out that $\rho_i = \sqrt{\xi_i}$ is the ith canonical correlation.

Let p be the rank of $(\mathbf{H}+\mathbf{E})$, which is less than or equal to the number of columns of $\mathbf{M}$. Let q be the rank of $\mathbf{L}(\mathbf{X}'\mathbf{X})^-\mathbf{L}'$. Let v be the error degrees of freedom and $s = \min(p,q)$. Let $m = 0.5(\,|\,p-q\,|\,-1)$, and let $n = 0.5(v-p-1)$. Then the statistics below have the approximate F statistics as shown:

Wilks' Lambda

$$\Lambda = \det(\mathbf{E})\,/\,\det(\mathbf{H}+\mathbf{E}) = \Pi[1/(1+\lambda_i)] = \Pi(1-\xi_i)\quad.$$

$F = [(1-\Lambda^{1/t})/(\Lambda^{1/t})][(rt-2u)/pq]$ is approximately F, where

$$r = v - (p-q+1)\,/\,2$$

$$u = (pq-2)\,/\,4$$

$$t = \sqrt{(p^2q^2-4)\,/\,(p^2+q^2-5)}\quad\text{if }(p^2+q^2-5)>0$$

or 1 otherwise.

The degrees of freedom are pq and $rt-2u$. This approximation is exact if $\min(p,q)\le 2$. (See Rao 1973, 556.)

Pillai's Trace

$$\mathbf{V} = \text{trace}\,(\mathbf{H}(\mathbf{H}+\mathbf{E})^{-1}) = \Sigma\lambda_i\,/\,(1+\lambda_i) = \Sigma\,\xi_i\quad.$$

$F = [(2n+s+1)/(2m+s+1)]\,[\mathbf{V}/(s-\mathbf{V})]$ is approximately F with $s(2m+s+1)$ and $s(2n+s+1)$ degrees of freedom.

Hotelling-Lawley Trace

$$\mathbf{U} = \text{trace}\,(\mathbf{E}^{-1}\mathbf{H}) = \Sigma\,\lambda_i = \Sigma\,\xi_i\,/\,(1-\xi_i)\quad.$$

$F = [2(sn+1)\mathbf{U}]/(s^2(2m+s+1))$ is approximately F with $s(2m+s+1)$ and $2(sn+1)$ degrees of freedom.

Roy's Maximum Root

$$\Theta = \lambda_1\quad.$$

$F = \Theta(v-r+q)/r$ where $r = \max(p, q)$ is an upper bound on F that yields a lower bound on the significance level. Degrees of freedom are r for the numerator and $v-r+q$ for the denominator.

Tables of critical values for these statistics are found in Pillai (1960).

References

Allen, D.M. (1971), "Mean Square Error of Prediction as a Criterion for Selecting Variables," *Technometrics*, 13, 469–475.

Allen, D.M. and Cady, F.B. (1982), *Analyzing Experimental Data by Regression*, Belmont, CA: Lifetime Learning Publications.

Belsley, D.A., Kuh, E., and Welsch, R.E. (1980), *Regression Diagnostics*, New York: John Wiley & Sons, Inc.

Bock, R.D. (1975), *Multivariate Statistical Methods in Behavioral Research*, New York: McGraw-Hill Book Co.

Box, G.E.P. (1966), "The Use and Abuse of Regression," *Technometrics*, 8, 625–629.

Cook, R.D. (1977), "Detection of Influential Observations in Linear Regression," *Technometrics*, 19, 15–18.

Cook, R.D. (1979), "Influential Observations in Linear Regression," *Journal of the American Statistical Association*, 74, 169–174.

Daniel, C. and Wood, F. (1980), *Fitting Equations to Data*, Revised Edition, New York: John Wiley & Sons, Inc.

Darlington, R.B. (1968), "Multiple Regression in Psychological Research and Practice," *Psychological Bulletin*, 69, 161–182.

Draper, N. and Smith, H. (1981), *Applied Regression Analysis*, 2d Edition, New York: John Wiley & Sons, Inc.

Durbin, J. and Watson, G.S. (1951), "Testing for Serial Correlation in Least Squares Regression," *Biometrika*, 37, 409–428.

Freund, R.J., Littell, R.C., and Spector P.C. (1986), *SAS System for Linear Models, 1986 Edition*, Cary, NC: SAS Institute Inc.

Freund, R.J. and Littell, R.C. (1986), *SAS System for Regression, 1986 Edition*, Cary, NC: SAS Institute Inc.

Goodnight, J.H. (1979), "A Tutorial on the SWEEP Operator," *The American Statistician*, 33, 149–158. (Also available as *The Sweep Operator: Its Importance in Statistical Computing*, SAS Technical Report R-106, Cary, NC: SAS Institute Inc.)

Johnston, J. (1972), *Econometric Methods*, New York: McGraw-Hill Book Co.

Kennedy, W.J. and Gentle, J.E. (1980), *Statistical Computing*, New York: Marcel Dekker, Inc.

Mallows, C.L. (1973), "Some Comments on Cp," *Technometrics*, 15, 661–675.

Mardia, K.V., Kent, J.T., and Bibby, J.M. (1979), *Multivariate Analysis*, London: Academic Press.

Morrison, D.F. (1976), *Multivariate Statistical Methods*, 2d Edition, New York: McGraw-Hill Book Co.

Mosteller, F. and Tukey, J.W. (1977), *Data Analysis and Regression*, Reading, MA: Addison-Wesley Publishing Co., Inc.

Neter, J. and Wasserman, W. (1974), *Applied Linear Statistical Models*, Homewood, IL: Irwin.

Pillai, K.C.S. (1960), *Statistical Table for Tests of Multivariate Hypotheses*, Manila: The Statistical Center, University of Philippines.

Pindyck, R.S. and Rubinfeld, D.L. (1981), *Econometric Models and Econometric Forecasts*, 2d Edition, New York: McGraw-Hill Book Co.

Rao, C.R. (1973), *Linear Statistical Inference and Its Applications*, 2d Edition, New York: John Wiley & Sons, Inc.

Sall, J.P. (1981), *SAS Regression Applications*, Revised Edition, SAS Technical Report A-102, Cary, NC: SAS Institute Inc.

Timm, N.H. (1975), *Multivariate Analysis with Applications in Education and Psychology*, Monterey, CA : Brooks-Cole Publishing Co.

Weisberg, S. (1985), *Applied Linear Regression*, 2d Edition. New York: John Wiley & Sons, Inc.

Younger, M.S. (1979), *Handbook for Linear Regression*, North Scituate, MA: Duxbury Press.

Chapter 2

Introduction to Analysis-of-Variance Procedures

Introduction

This chapter reviews the SAS/STAT software procedures that are used for analysis of variance: GLM, ANOVA, CATMOD, NESTED, NPAR1WAY, PLAN, TTEST, and VARCOMP.

The most general analysis-of-variance procedure is PROC GLM, which can handle most problems. GLM and other procedures that are used for special cases are described below:

ANOVA   handles analysis of variance, multivariate analysis of variance, and repeated measures analysis of variance for balanced designs. ANOVA also performs several multiple comparison tests.

CATMOD   fits linear models to functions of categorical data and performs analysis of variance and repeated measures analysis of variance for categorical data.

GLM   performs analysis of variance, regression, analysis of covariance, repeated measures analysis, and multivariate analysis of variance. GLM gives several diagnostic measures, performs tests for random effects, provides contrasts and estimates for customized hypothesis tests, performs several multiple comparison tests, and provides tests for means adjusted for covariates.

NESTED   performs analysis of variance and analysis of covariance for purely nested random models.

NPAR1WAY   performs nonparametric one-way analysis of rank scores.

PLAN   constructs designs and randomizes plans for nested and crossed experiments.

TTEST   compares the means of two groups of observations.

VARCOMP   estimates variance components for random or mixed models.

These procedures perform *analysis of variance*, which is a technique for analyzing experimental data. A continuous response variable, called a *dependent variable*, is measured under various experimental conditions identified by classification variables, called *independent variables*. The combinations of levels for the classification variables form the cells of an experimental design. For example, an experiment may measure weight change (the dependent variable) for men and women who participated in three different weight-loss programs. The six cells of the design are formed by the six combinations of sex (men, women) and program (A, B, C).

Classification variables may represent fixed or random effects. The levels of a classification variable for a fixed effect give all the levels of interest, while the levels of a classification variable for a random effect are a subset of levels selected from a population of levels. For example, three levels that represent three types of drugs comprise a fixed effect, but levels that represent a selection of fields on a large farm comprise a random effect.

In an analysis of variance, the variation in the response is separated into variation due to the classification variables and variation due to random error. An analysis of variance constructs tests to determine the significance of the classification variables. A typical goal in an analysis of variance is to compare means of the response variable for various combinations of the classification variables.

An analysis of variance may be written as a linear model. Analysis of variance procedures in SAS/STAT software use the model to predict the response for each observation. The difference between the actual and predicted response is the *residual error*. The various procedures fit model parameters that minimize the sum of squares of residual errors. Thus, the method is called *least squares*. The variance due to the random error, σ^2, is estimated by the mean squared error (MSE or s^2).

Analysis of variance was pioneered by R.A. Fisher (1925). For a general introduction to analysis of variance, see an intermediate statistical methods textbook such as Steel and Torrie (1980), Snedecor and Cochran (1980), Mendenhall (1968), John (1971), Ott (1977), or Kirk (1968). A classic source is Scheffe (1959). Freund, Littell, and Spector (1986) bring together a treatment of these statistical methods and SAS/STAT software procedures. Linear models texts include Searle (1971), Graybill (1976), and Hocking (1984). Kennedy and Gentle (1980) survey the computing aspects.

The remaining sections of this chapter assume a basic understanding of analysis of variance and give brief descriptions of how this analysis is performed with procedures in SAS/STAT software. For more detail, see the chapters for the individual procedures or Freund, Littell, and Spector (1986). References for analysis of variance are described above.

PROC ANOVA for Balanced Designs

In choosing a SAS/STAT procedure to perform an analysis of variance, you first need to decide whether your data are balanced or unbalanced. When you design an experiment, you choose how many experimental units to assign to each combination of levels (or cells) in the classification. In order to achieve good statistical properties and simplify the statistical arithmetic, you typically attempt to assign the same number of units to every cell in the design. These designs are called *balanced*.

If you have balanced data, the arithmetic for calculating sums of squares can be greatly simplified. In SAS/STAT software, you can use the ANOVA procedure, which is more efficient than the GLM procedure for balanced data. Generalizations of the balanced concept can be made to use the arithmetic for balanced designs even though the design does not contain an equal number of observations per cell. You can use balanced arithmetic for all one-way models regardless of how unbalanced the cell counts are. You can even use the balanced arithmetic for Latin squares that do not always have data in all cells. **However, if you use the ANOVA procedure to analyze a design that is not balanced, you may get incorrect results, including negative values reported for the sums of squares**.

Analysis-of-variance procedures construct ANOVA tests by comparing mean squares relative to their expected values under the null hypothesis. In an analysis-of-variance model with fixed effects only, each mean square has an expected value that is composed of two components: quadratic functions of fixed parameters and random variation. For a fixed effect called A, the expected value of its mean square is written as

$$E(MS(A)) = Q(\beta) + \sigma_e^2 \quad .$$

The mean square is constructed so that under the hypothesis to be tested (null hypothesis), the fixed portion $Q(\beta)$ of the expected value is zero. This mean square is then compared to another mean square, say MS(E), that is independent of the first, yet has the expected value σ_e^2. The ratio of the two mean squares is an F statistic that has the F distribution under the null hypothesis:

$$F = MS(A)/MS(E) \quad .$$

When the null hypothesis is false, the numerator term has a larger expected value, but the expected value of the denominator remains the same. Thus, large F values lead to rejection of the null hypothesis. The probability of getting an even larger F value given that the null hypothesis is true is called the *significance probability value*. If this probability is small, say below 0.05 or 0.01, you are wrong in rejecting the null hypothesis less than 5 or 1 percent of the time, respectively. If you are unable to reject the hypothesis, you conclude that either the null hypothesis was true or that you do not have enough data to detect the differences to be tested.

PROC GLM for Unbalanced Designs

General Linear Models

If your data do not fit into a balanced design, then you probably need the framework of linear models in the GLM procedure.

An analysis-of-variance model can be written as a linear model, which is an equation that predicts the response as a linear function of parameters and design variables. In general,

$$y_i = \beta_0 x_{0i} + \beta_1 x_{1i} + \ldots + \beta_k x_{ki} + \varepsilon_i \qquad i = 1, 2, \ldots, n$$

where y_i is the response for the ith observation, β_k are unknown parameters to be estimated, and x_{ij} are design variables. Design variables for analysis of variance are indicator variables; that is, they are always either 0 or 1.

The simplest model is to fit a single mean to all observations. In this case there is only one parameter, β_0, and one design variable, x_{0i}, which always has the value of 1:

$$\begin{aligned} y_i &= \beta_0 x_{0i} + \varepsilon_i \\ &= \beta_0 + \varepsilon_i \end{aligned}$$

The least-squares estimator of β_0 is the mean of the y_i. This simple model underlies all more complex models, and all larger models are compared to this simple mean model. In writing the parameterization of a linear model, β_0 is usually referred to as the intercept.

A one-way model is written by introducing an indicator variable for each level of the classification variable. Suppose that a variable A has four levels, with two observations per level. The indicator variables are created as shown below:

Intercept	A1	A2	A3	A4
1	1	0	0	0
1	1	0	0	0
1	0	1	0	0
1	0	1	0	0
1	0	0	1	0
1	0	0	1	0
1	0	0	0	1
1	0	0	0	1

The linear model for this example is

$$y_i = \beta_0 + A1_i\beta_1 + A2_i\beta_2 + A3_i\beta_3 + A4_i\beta_4$$

To construct crossed and nested effects, you can simply multiply out all combinations of the main-effect columns. This is described in detail in the section **Parameterization of GLM Models** in "The GLM Procedure."

Linear Hypotheses

When models are expressed in the framework of linear models, hypothesis tests are expressed in terms of a linear function of the parameters. For example, you may want to test that $\beta_2 - \beta_3 = 0$. In general, the coefficients for linear hypotheses are some set of Ls:

$$H_0: \quad L_0\beta_0 + L_1\beta_1 + \ldots + L_k\beta_k = 0 \quad .$$

Several of these linear functions can be combined to make one joint test. These tests can be expressed in one matrix equation:

$$H_0: \; \mathbf{L\beta} = 0 \; .$$

For each linear hypothesis, a sum of squares due to that hypothesis can be constructed. These sums of squares can be calculated either as a quadratic form of the estimates:

$$SS(\mathbf{L\beta} = 0) = (Lb)'(L(X'X)^{-}L')^{-1}(Lb)$$

or equivalently as the increase in SSE for the model constrained by the hypothesis

$$SS(\mathbf{L\beta} = 0) = SSE(constrained) - SSE(full) \; .$$

This SS is then divided by degrees of freedom and used as a numerator of an F statistic.

Comparison of Means with PROC ANOVA and PROC GLM

When you have more than two means to compare, an F test in ANOVA or GLM tells you if the means are significantly different from each other, but it does not tell you which means differ from which other means.

If you have specific comparisons in mind, you can use the CONTRAST statement in PROC GLM to make these comparisons. However, if you make many comparisons using some alpha level to judge significance, you are more likely to make a type 1 error (rejecting incorrectly a hypothesis that the means are equal) simply because you have more chances to make the error.

Multiple comparison methods give you more detailed information about the differences among the means and allow you to control error rates for a multitude of comparisons. A variety of multiple comparison methods are available with the MEANS statement in both the ANOVA and GLM procedures. These are described in detail in the section **Comparisons of Means** in the chapter on the GLM procedure.

Comparing Two Groups with PROC TTEST

If you want to perform an analysis of variance and have only one classification variable with two levels, you can use PROC TTEST. In this special case, the results generated by TTEST are equivalent to the results generated by ANOVA or GLM. In addition to testing for differences between two groups, TTEST performs a test for unequal variances. You can use TTEST with balanced or unbalanced groups.

GLM, NESTED, and VARCOMP for Random and Mixed Models

A *random effect* is an effect whose values are drawn from a normally distributed random process with mean zero and common variance. Effects are declared random when the levels are randomly selected from a large population of possible levels. Inferences are made using only a few levels but can be generalized across the whole population of random effects levels.

In agricultural experiments, it is common to declare locations (or plots) as random because the levels are chosen randomly from a large population of locations and you assume fertility to vary normally across locations. In repeated-measures experiments with people or animals as subjects, subjects are declared random because they are selected from the larger population to which you want to generalize.

For models consisting entirely of random effects, you can use either the GLM or the NESTED procedure to perform an analysis of variance. You can use the VARCOMP procedure to produce estimates of variance components associated with the random effects. For mixed models, which are models containing both random and fixed effects, use GLM for analysis of variance and VARCOMP to estimate variance components.

When effects are declared random in GLM, the expected mean square of each effect is calculated. For completely random models, each expected mean square is a function of variances of random effects. For mixed models, each expected mean square is a function of variances of random effects and quadratic functions of parameters of fixed effects. To test a given effect, you can either let GLM construct tests, or you can construct your own tests. The TEST option in the RANDOM statement in GLM constructs exact tests for random effects if possible and constructs approximate tests if exact tests are not possible. To construct your own test, you must search for a denominator term. This term must have the same expectation as your numerator term, except for the portion of the expectation that you want to test. If the two mean squares are independent, then the resulting F test is valid. Sometimes, however, you may not be able to find a proper denominator term. In these cases, you must construct an approximate test. See Milliken and Johnson (1984) for more information.

PROC CATMOD for Categorical Data

A *categorical variable* is defined as one that can assume only a limited number of values. For example, a person's sex is a categorical variable that can assume one of two values. Variables whose levels simply name a group are said to be measured on a *nominal scale*. Categorical variables can also be measured using an *ordinal scale*, which means that the levels of the variable are ordered in some way. For example, responses to an opinion poll are usually measured on an ordinal scale, with levels ranging from "strongly disagree" to "no opinion" to "strongly agree."

For two categorical variables, one measured on an ordinal scale and one measured on a nominal scale, you may assign scores to the levels of the ordinal variable and test if the mean scores for the different levels of the nominal variable are significantly different. This process is analogous to performing an analysis of variance on continuous data, which can be performed by CATMOD. If there are n nominal variables, rather than 1, then CATMOD can do an n-way analysis of variance of the mean scores.

For two categorical variables measured on a nominal scale, you can test whether the distribution of the first variable is significantly different for the levels of the second variable. This process is an analysis of variance of proportions, rather than means, and can be performed by CATMOD. The corresponding n-way analysis of variance can also be performed by CATMOD.

See Chapter 3, "Introduction to Categorical Data Analysis Procedures," and the chapter on the CATMOD procedure for more information.

Nonparametric Analysis

Analysis of variance is sensitive to the distribution of the error term. If the error term is not normally distributed, the statistics based on normality can be misleading. The traditional test statistics are called *parametric tests* because they depend on the specification of a certain probability distribution except for a set of free parameters. Parametric tests are said to depend on distributional assumptions.

Nonparametric methods perform the tests without making any strict distributional assumptions. Even if the data are distributed normally, nonparametric methods are often almost as powerful as parametric methods.

Most nonparametric methods are based on taking the ranks of a variable and analyzing these ranks (or transformations of them) instead of the original values. The NPAR1WAY procedure performs a nonparametric one-way analysis of variance. Other nonparametric tests can be performed by taking ranks of the data (using PROC RANK) and using a regular parametric procedure (such as GLM or ANOVA) to perform the analysis. Some of these techniques are outlined in the description of PROC RANK in the *SAS Procedures Guide, Release 6.03 Edition* and in Conover and Iman (1981).

Constructing Designs

Analysis of variance is most often used for data from designed experiments. You can use PROC PLAN to construct designs for many experiments. For example, PLAN constructs designs for completely randomized experiments, randomized blocks, Latin squares, factorial experiments, and balanced incomplete block designs.

Randomization, or randomly assigning experimental units to cells in a design and to treatments within a cell, is another important aspect of experimental design. For either a new or an existing design, you can use PLAN to randomize the experimental plan.

References

Conover, W.J. and Iman, R.L. (1981), "Rank Transformations as a Bridge Between Parametric and Nonparametric Statistics," *The American Statistician*, 35, 124–129.

Fisher, R.A. (1925), *Statistical Methods for Research Workers*, Edinburgh: Oliver & Boyd.

Freund, R.J., Littell, R.C., and Spector, P.C. (1986), *SAS System for Linear Models, 1986 Edition*, Cary, NC: SAS Institute Inc.

Graybill, F.A. (1976), *Theory and Applications of the Linear Model*, North Scituate, MA: Duxbury Press.

Hocking, R.R. (1984), *Analysis of Linear Models*, Monterey, CA: Brooks-Cole Publishing Co.

John, P. (1971), *Statistical Design and Analysis of Experiments*, New York: Macmillan Publishing Co.

Kennedy, W.J., Jr. and Gentle, J.E. (1980), *Statistical Computing*, New York: Marcel Dekker, Inc.

Kirk, R.E. (1968), *Experimental Design: Procedures for the Behavioral Sciences*, Monterey, CA: Brooks-Cole Publishing Co.

Mendenhall, W. (1968), *Introduction to Linear Models and the Design and Analysis of Experiments*, Belmont, CA: Duxbury Press.

Milliken, G.A. and Johnson, D.E. (1984), *Analysis of Messy Data Volume I: Designed Experiments*, Belmont, CA: Lifetime Learning Publications.

Ott, L. (1977), *Introduction to Statistical Methods and Data Analysis*, 2d Edition, Belmont, CA: Duxbury Press.

Scheffe, H. (1959), *The Analysis of Variance*, New York: John Wiley & Sons, Inc.

Searle, S.R. (1971), *Linear Models*, New York: John Wiley & Sons, Inc.

Snedecor, G.W. and Cochran, W.G. (1980), *Statistical Methods*, 7th Edition, Ames, IA: Iowa State University Press.

Steel R.G.D. and Torrie, J.H. (1980), *Principles and Procedures of Statistics*, 2d Edition, New York: McGraw-Hill Book Co.

26

Chapter 3

Introduction to Categorical Data Analysis Procedures

Introduction

Two procedures in SAS/STAT software are designed for the analysis of categorical data:

FREQ   builds frequency tables or contingency tables and produces a number of tests and measures of association such as chi-square (χ^2) statistics, odds ratios, correlation statistics, and Fisher's exact test for any two-way table. In addition, it does stratified analysis, computing Cochran-Mantel-Haenszel statistics and estimates of the common relative risk.

CATMOD   fits linear models to functions of categorical data, facilitating such analyses as regression, analysis of variance, linear modeling, log-linear modeling, logistic regression, and repeated measures analysis.

For a comparison of the procedures with respect to their capabilities, assumptions, and sample size requirements, see **Comparison of Procedures** later in this chapter.

A *categorical variable* is defined as one that can assume only a limited number of discrete values. The measurement scale for such a variable is unrestricted. It can be *nominal*, which means that the observed levels are not ordered. It can be *ordinal*, which means that the observed levels are ordered in some way. Or it can be *interval*, which means that the observed levels are ordered and numeric and that any interval of one unit on the scale of measurement represents the same amount, regardless of its location on the scale. One example of such a categorical variable is litter size; another is the number of times a subject has been married. A variable that lies on a nominal scale is sometimes called a *qualitative* or *classification variable*.

Categorical data result from observations on multiple subjects where one or more categorical variables are observed for each subject. If there is only one categorical variable, then the data are generally represented by a *frequency table*, which lists each observed value of the variable and its frequency of occurrence.

If there are two or more categorical variables, then a subject's *profile* is defined as the subject's observed values for each of the variables. Such categorical data can be represented by a frequency table that lists each observed profile and its frequency of occurrence.

If there are exactly two categorical variables, then the data are often represented by a two-dimensional *contingency table*, which has one row for each level of variable 1 and one column for each level of variable 2. The intersections of rows and columns, called *cells*, correspond to variable profiles, and each cell contains the frequency of occurrence of the corresponding profile.

If there are more than two categorical variables, then the data can be represented by a *multidimensional contingency table*. There are two commonly used methods for displaying such tables, and both require that the variables be divided into two sets.

In the first method, one set contains a row variable and a column variable for a two-dimensional contingency table, and the second set contains all of the other variables. The variables in the second set are used to form a set of profiles. Then the data are represented as a series of two-dimensional contingency tables, one for each profile. This is the data representation used by PROC FREQ.

In the second method, one set contains the independent variables, and the other set contains the dependent variables. Profiles based on the independent variables are called *population profiles*, whereas those based on the dependent variables are called *response profiles*. A two-dimensional contingency table is then formed, with one row for each population profile and one column for each response profile. Since any subject can have only one population profile and one response profile, the contingency table is uniquely defined. This is the data representation used by PROC CATMOD.

Simple Random Sampling: One Population

Suppose you take a simple random sample of 100 people and ask each person the following question: Of the three colors red, blue, and green, which is your favorite? You then tabulate the results in a frequency table as shown in **Table 3.1**.

Table 3.1   One-Way Frequency Table

	Favorite Color			
	Red	Blue	Green	Total
Frequency	52	31	17	100
Proportion	0.52	0.31	0.17	1.00

In the population you are sampling, there is an unknown probability that a population member, selected at random, would choose any given color. In order to estimate that probability, you use the sample proportion

$$p_j = n_j / n$$

where n_j is the frequency of the jth response and n is the total frequency.

Because of the random variation inherent in any random sample, the frequencies have a probability distribution representing their relative frequency of occurrence in a hypothetical series of samples. For a simple random sample, the distribution of frequencies for a frequency table with three levels is as follows. The probability that the first frequency is n_1, the second frequency is n_2, and the third is $n_3 = n - n_1 - n_2$ is

$$\text{Prob}(n_1, n_2, n_3) = n!\, \pi_1^{n_1} \pi_2^{n_2} \pi_3^{n_3} / (n_1! n_2! n_3!)$$

where π_j is the true probability of observing the jth response level in the population. This distribution, called the *multinomial distribution*, can be generalized to any number of response levels. The special case of two response levels is called the *binomial distribution*.

Simple random sampling is the type of sampling required by PROC CATMOD when there is one population. CATMOD uses the multinomial distribution to estimate a probability vector and its covariance matrix. If the sample size is sufficiently large, then the probability vector is approximately normally distributed as a result of central limit theory, and CATMOD uses this result to compute appropriate test statistics for the specified statistical model.

Stratified Simple Random Sampling: Multiple Populations

Suppose you take two simple random samples, fifty men and fifty women, and ask the same question as before. You are now sampling two different populations that may have different response probabilities. The data can be tabulated as shown in **Table 3.2**.

Table 3.2   Two-Way Contingency Table: Sex by Color

Sex	Favorite Color Red	Blue	Green	Total
Male	30	10	10	50
Female	20	10	20	50
Total	50	20	30	100

Note that the row marginal totals (50, 50) of the contingency table are fixed by the sampling design, but the column marginal totals (50, 20, 30) are random. There are six probabilities of interest for this table, and they are estimated by the sample proportions

$$p_{ij} = n_{ij} / n_i$$

where n_{ij} denotes the frequency for the ith population and the jth response, and n_i is the total frequency for the ith population. For this contingency table, the sample proportions are shown in **Table 3.3**.

Table 3.3 Table of Sample Proportions by Sex

Sex	Favorite Color			Total
---	Red	Blue	Green	
Male	0.60	0.20	0.20	1.00
Female	0.40	0.20	0.40	1.00

The probability distribution of the six frequencies is the *product multinomial distribution*

$$\text{Prob}\,(n_{11},\, n_{12},\, n_{13},\, n_{21},\, n_{22},\, n_{23}) = \frac{n_1!\; n_2!\; \pi_{11}{}^{n_{11}}\; \pi_{12}{}^{n_{12}}\; \pi_{13}{}^{n_{13}}\; \pi_{21}{}^{n_{21}}\; \pi_{22}{}^{n_{22}}\; \pi_{23}{}^{n_{23}}}{n_{11}!n_{12}!n_{13}!n_{21}!n_{22}!n_{23}!}$$

where π_{ij} is the true probability of observing the jth response level in the ith population. The product multinomial distribution is simply the product of two or more individual multinomial distributions since the populations are independent. This distribution can be generalized to any number of populations and response levels.

Stratified simple random sampling is the type of sampling required by PROC CATMOD when there is more than one population. CATMOD uses the product multinomial distribution to estimate a probability vector and its covariance matrix. If the sample sizes are sufficiently large, then the probability vector is approximately normally distributed as a result of central limit theory, and CATMOD uses this result to compute appropriate test statistics for the specified statistical model. The statistics are known as Wald statistics, and they are approximately distributed as chi-square when the null hypothesis is true.

Observational Data: Analyzing the Entire Population

Sometimes the observed data do not come from a random sample but instead represent a complete set of observations on some population. For example, suppose a class of 100 students is classified according to sex and favorite color. The results are shown in **Table 3.4**.

In this case, you could argue that all of the frequencies are fixed since the entire population is observed; therefore, there is no sampling error. On the other hand, you could hypothesize that the observed table has only fixed marginals and that the cell frequencies represent one realization of a conceptual process of assigning color preferences to individuals. The assignment process is open to hypothesis, which means that you can hypothesize restrictions on the joint probabilities.

Table 3.4   Two-Way Contingency Table: Sex by Color

Sex	Favorite Color			Total
	Red	Blue	Green	
Male	16	21	20	57
Female	12	20	11	43
Total	28	41	31	100

The usual hypothesis (sometimes called *randomness*) is that the distribution of the column variable (Favorite Color) does not depend on the row variable (Sex). This implies that, for each row of the table, the assignment process corresponds to a simple random sample (without replacement) from the finite population represented by the column marginal totals (or by the column marginal subtotals that remain after sampling other rows). The hypothesis of randomness induces a probability distribution on the frequencies in the table; it is called the *hypergeometric distribution*.

If the same row and column variables are observed for each of several populations, then the probability distribution of all the frequencies can be called the *multiple hypergeometric distribution*. Each population is called a *stratum*, and an analysis that draws information from each stratum and then summarizes across them is called a *stratified analysis* (or a *blocked analysis* or a *matched analysis*). PROC FREQ does such a stratified analysis, computing test statistics and measures of association. In general, the populations are formed on the basis of cross-classifications of independent variables. Stratified analysis is a method of adjusting for the effect of these variables without being forced to estimate parameters for them.

The multiple hypergeometric distribution is the one used by PROC FREQ for the computation of Cochran-Mantel-Haenszel statistics. These statistics are in the class of *randomization model test statistics*, which require minimal assumptions for their validity. PROC FREQ uses the multiple hypergeometric distribution to compute the mean and the covariance matrix of a function vector in order to measure the deviation between the observed and expected frequencies with respect to a particular type of alternative hypothesis. If the cell frequencies are sufficiently large, then the function vector is approximately normally distributed as a result of central limit theory, and FREQ uses this result to compute a quadratic form that has a chi-square distribution when the null hypothesis is true.

Randomized Experiments

Consider a *randomized experiment* in which patients are assigned to one of two treatment groups according to a randomization process that allocates fifty patients to each group. After a specified period of time, each patient's status (cured or uncured) is recorded. Suppose the data shown in **Table 3.5** give the results of the experiment. The null hypothesis is that the two treatments are equally effective. Under this hypothesis, treatment is a randomly assigned label that has no effect on the cure rate of the patients. But this implies that each row of the table represents a simple random sample from the finite population whose cure rate is described by the column marginal totals. Therefore, the column marginals (58, 42) are fixed under the hypothesis. Since the row marginals (50, 50) are fixed by the allocation process, the hypergeometric distribution is induced on the cell frequencies. Randomized experiments can also be specified in a stratified framework, and Cochran-Mantel-Haenszel statistics can be computed relative to the corresponding multiple hypergeometric distribution.

Table 3.5 Two-Way Contingency Table: Treatment by Status

Treatment	Status		Total
	Cured	Uncured	
1	36	14	50
2	22	28	50
Total	58	42	100

Relaxation of Sampling Assumptions

As indicated above, the CATMOD procedure assumes that the data are from a stratified simple random sample, so it uses the product multinomial distribution. If the data are not from such a sample, then in many cases it is still possible to use CATMOD by arguing that each row of the contingency table *does* represent a simple random sample from some hypothetical population. The extent to which the inferences are generalizable depends on the extent to which the hypothetical population is perceived to resemble the target population.

Similarly, the Cochran-Mantel-Haenszel statistics use the multiple hypergeometric distribution, which requires fixed row and column marginal totals in each contingency table. If the sampling process does not yield a table with fixed margins, then it is usually possible to fix the margins through conditioning arguments similar to the ones used by Fisher when he developed the Exact Test for 2×2 tables. In other words, if you want fixed marginal totals, you can generally make your analysis conditional on those observed totals.

For more information on sampling models for categorical data, see Bishop, Fienberg, and Holland (1975, Chapter 13).

Comparison of Procedures

CATMOD is the only available procedure for categorical data modeling. FREQ is used primarily to investigate the relationship between two variables; any confounding variables are taken into account by stratification rather than by parameter estimation. CATMOD is used to investigate the relationship among many variables, all of which are integrated into a parametric model.

When CATMOD estimates the covariance matrix of the frequencies, it assumes that the frequencies were obtained by a stratified simple random sampling procedure. However, CATMOD can also analyze input data that consist of a function vector and a covariance matrix. Therefore, if the sampling procedure is different, you can estimate the covariance matrix of the frequencies in the appropriate manner before submitting the data to CATMOD.

For the FREQ procedure, Fisher's Exact Test and Cochran-Mantel-Haenszel statistics are based on the hypergeometric distribution, which corresponds to fixed marginal totals. However, by conditioning arguments, these tests are generally applicable to a wide range of sampling procedures. Similarly, the Pearson and likelihood-ratio chi-square statistics can be derived under a variety of sampling situations.

FREQ can do some traditional nonparametric analysis (such as the Kruskal-Wallis test and Spearman's correlation) since it can generate rank scores internally. Fisher's Exact Test and the Cochran-Mantel-Haenszel statistics are also inherently nonparametric. CATMOD does not perform nonparametric analysis.

A large sample size is required for the validity of the chi-square distributions, the standard errors, and the covariance matrices for both FREQ and CATMOD. If sample size is a problem, then FREQ has the advantage with its CMH statistics because it does not use any degrees of freedom to estimate parameters for confounding variables. In addition, FREQ can compute exact p values for any two-way table, provided that the sample size is sufficiently small in relation to the size of the table. The measures of association printed by FREQ are also valid for any sample size.

References

Bishop, Y., Fienberg, S.E., and Holland, P.W. (1975), *Discrete Multivariate Analysis: Theory and Practice*, Cambridge, MA: MIT Press.

Grizzle, J.E., Starmer, C.F., and Koch, G.G. (1969), "Analysis of Categorical Data by Linear Models," *Biometrics*, 25, 489–504.

Chapter 4

Introduction to Multivariate Procedures

Introduction

The procedures discussed in this chapter investigate relationships among variables without designating some as independent and others as dependent. Principal component analysis and common factor analysis examine relationships within a single set of variables, whereas canonical correlation looks at the relationship between two sets of variables. The following is a brief description of SAS/STAT multivariate procedures:

PRINCOMP   performs a principal component analysis and outputs standardized or unstandardized principal component scores.

FACTOR   performs principal component and common factor analyses with rotations and outputs component scores or estimates of common factor scores.

CANCORR   performs a canonical correlation analysis and outputs canonical variable scores.

Many other SAS/STAT procedures can also analyze multivariate data, for example, CATMOD, GLM, REG, and procedures for cluster and discriminant analysis.

The purpose of *principal component analysis* (Rao 1964) is to derive a small number of linear combinations (principal components) of a set of variables that retain as much of the information in the original variables as possible. Often a small number of principal components can be used in place of the original variables for plotting, regression, clustering, and so on. Principal component analysis can also be viewed as an attempt to uncover approximate linear dependencies among variables.

The purpose of *common factor analysis* (Mulaik 1972) is to explain the correlations or covariances among a set of variables in terms of a limited number of unobservable, latent variables. The latent variables are not generally computable as linear combinations of the original variables. In common factor analysis it is assumed that the variables would be linearly related were it not for uncorrelated random error or *unique variation* in each variable; both the linear relations and the amount of unique variation can be estimated.

Principal component and common factor analysis are often followed by rotation of the components or factors. *Rotation* is the application of a nonsingular linear transformation to components or common factors to aid interpretation.

The purpose of *canonical correlation analysis* (Mardia, Kent, and Bibby 1979) is to explain or summarize the relationship between two sets of variables by finding a small number of linear combinations from each set of variables that have the highest possible between-set correlations. Plots of the canonical variables can be useful in examining multivariate dependencies. With appropriate input, the CANCORR procedure can be used for maximum redundancy analysis (Van den Wollenberg 1977) or principal components of instrumental variables (Rao 1964); contingency table analysis and optimal scaling (Mardia, Kent, and Bibby 1979, 290–295; Kshirsagar 1972; Nishisato 1980); orthogonal Procrustes rotation (Mulaik 1972; Hanson and Norris 1981); and finding a polynomial transformation of the dependent variable to minimize interaction in an analysis of variance.

Comparison of the PRINCOMP and FACTOR Procedures

Although PROC FACTOR can be used for common factor analysis, the default method is principal components. PROC FACTOR produces the same results as PROC PRINCOMP except that scoring coefficients from FACTOR are normalized to give principal component scores with unit variance, whereas PRINCOMP by default produces principal component scores with variance equal to the corresponding eigenvalue. PRINCOMP can also compute scores standardized to unit variance.

PRINCOMP has the following advantages over FACTOR:

- PRINCOMP is slightly faster if a small number of components is requested.
- PRINCOMP can analyze somewhat larger problems in a fixed amount of memory.
- PRINCOMP can output scores from an analysis of a partial correlation or covariance matrix.
- PRINCOMP is simpler to use.

FACTOR has the following advantages over PRINCOMP for principal component analysis:

- FACTOR produces more output, including the scree (eigenvalue) plot, pattern matrix, and residual correlations.
- FACTOR has options for printing matrices in more easily interpretable forms.
- FACTOR does rotations.

If you want to do a common factor analysis, you must use FACTOR instead of PRINCOMP. Principal component analysis should never be used if a common factor solution is desired (Dziuban and Harris 1973; Lee and Comrey 1979).

References

Dziuban, C.D. and Harris, C.W. (1973), "On the Extraction of Components and the Applicability of the Factor Model," *American Educational Research Journal*, 10, 93–99.

Hanson, R.J. and Norris, M.J. (1981), "Analysis of Measurements Based on the Singular Value Decomposition," *SIAM Journal on Scientific and Statistical Computing*, 2, 363–373.

Kshirsagar, A.M. (1972), *Multivariate Analysis*, New York: Marcel Dekker, Inc.

Lee, H.B. and Comrey, A.L. (1979), "Distortions in a Commonly Used Factor Analytic Procedure," *Multivariate Behavioral Research*, 14, 301–321.

Mardia, K.V., Kent, J.T., and Bibby, J.M. (1979), *Multivariate Analysis*, London: Academic Press.

Mulaik, S.A. (1972), *The Foundations of Factor Analysis*, New York: McGraw-Hill Book Co.

Nishisato, S. (1980), *Analysis of Categorical Data: Dual Scaling and Its Applications,* Toronto: University of Toronto Press.

Rao, C.R. (1964), "The Use and Interpretation of Principal Component Analysis in Applied Research," *Sankhya A,* 26, 329–358.

Van den Wollenberg, A.L. (1977), "Redundancy Analysis—An Alternative to Canonical Correlation Analysis," *Psychometrika,* 42, 207–219.

Chapter 5

Introduction to Discriminant Procedures

Introduction

The SAS procedures for discriminant analysis treat data with one classification variable and several quantitative variables. The purpose of discriminant analysis can be to find one or more of the following:

- a mathematical rule, or *discriminant function*, for guessing to which class an observation belongs, based on knowledge of the quantitative variables only
- a set of linear combinations of the quantitative variables that best reveals the differences among the classes
- a subset of the quantitative variables that best reveals the differences among the classes.

The SAS discriminant procedures are as follows:

DISCRIM   computes various discriminant functions for classifying observations. Linear or quadratic discriminant functions can be used for data with approximately multivariate normal within-class distributions. Nonparametric methods can be used without making any assumptions about these distributions.

CANDISC   performs a canonical analysis to find linear combinations of the quantitative variables that best summarize the differences among the classes.

STEPDISC   uses forward selection, backward elimination, or stepwise selection to try to find a subset of quantitative variables that best reveals differences among the classes.

The term *discriminant analysis* (Fisher 1936; Cooley and Lohnes 1971; Tatsuoka 1971; Kshirsagar 1972; Lachenbruch 1975, 1979; Gnanadesikan 1977; Klecka 1980; Hand 1981,1982; Silverman, 1986) refers to several different types of analysis. *Classificatory discriminant analysis* is used to classify observations into two or more known groups on the basis of one or more quantitative variables. Classification can be done by either a parametric method or a nonparametric method in the DISCRIM procedure. A parametric method is appropriate only for approximately normal within-class distributions. The method generates either a linear discriminant function (the within-class covariance matrices are assumed equal) or a quadratic discriminant function (the within-class covariance matrices are assumed unequal).

When the distribution within each group is not assumed to have any specific distribution or is assumed to have a distribution different from the multivariate normal distribution, nonparametric methods can be used to derive classification criteria. These methods include the kernel method and nearest-neighbor methods. The kernel method uses uniform, normal, Epanechnikov, biweight, or triweight kernels in estimating the group-specific density at each observation. The within-group covariance matrices or the pooled covariance matrix can be used to scale the data.

The performance of a discriminant function can be evaluated by estimating error rates (probabilities of misclassification). Error count estimates and posterior probability error rate estimates can be evaluated with DISCRIM. When the input data set is an ordinary SAS data set, the error rates can also be estimated by cross-validation.

In multivariate statistical applications, the data collected are largely from distributions different from the normal distribution. Various forms of non-normality can arise, such as qualitative variables or variables with underlying continuous but non-normal distributions. If the multivariate normality assumption is violated, the use of parametric discriminant analysis may not be appropriate. When a parametric classification criterion (linear or quadratic discriminant function) is derived from a non-normal population, the resulting error rate estimates may be biased.

If your quantitative variables are not normally distributed, or if you want to classify observations on the basis of categorical variables, you should consider using the CATMOD procedure to fit a categorical linear model with the classification variable as the dependent variable. Press and Wilson (1978) compare logistic regression and parametric discriminant analysis and conclude that logistic regression is preferable to parametric discriminant analysis in cases for which the variables do not have multivariate normal distributions within classes. However, if you should have normal within-class distributions, logistic regression is less efficient than parametric discriminant analysis. Efron (1975) shows that with two normal populations having a common covariance matrix, logistic regression is between one half and two thirds as effective as the linear discriminant function to achieve asymptotically the same error rate.

Do not confuse discriminant analysis with cluster analysis. All varieties of discriminant analysis require prior knowledge of the classes, usually in the form of a sample from each class. In *cluster analysis*, the data do not include information on class membership; the purpose is to construct a classification. See Chapter 6, "Introduction to Clustering Procedures."

Canonical discriminant analysis is a dimension-reduction technique related to principal components and canonical correlation and can be performed by both the CANDISC and DISCRIM procedures. *Stepwise discriminant analysis* is a variable-selection technique implemented by the STEPDISC procedure. After selecting a subset of variables with STEPDISC, use any of the other discriminant procedures to obtain more detailed analyses. CANDISC and STEPDISC perform hypothesis tests that require the within-class distributions to be approximately normal, but these procedures can be used descriptively with non-normal data.

Another alternative to discriminant analysis is to perform a series of univariate one-way *ANOVAs*. All three discriminant procedures provide summaries of the univariate *ANOVAs*. The advantage of the multivariate approach is that two or more classes that overlap considerably when each variable is viewed separately may be more distinct when examined from a multivariate point of view. Consider the two classes indicated by 'H' and 'O' in the following example. The results are shown in **Output 5.1**.

```
data random;
   drop n;
   group='H';
   do n=1 to 20;
       x=4.5+2*rannor(57391);
       y=x+.5+rannor(57391);
       output;
       end;
   group='O';
   do n=1 to 20;
       x=6.25+2*rannor(57391);
       y=x-1.+rannor(57391);
       output;
       end;
run;
proc plot; plot y*x=group;
run;
proc candisc anova;
   class group;
   var x y;
run;
```

Output 5.1 Contrasting Univariate and Multivariate Analyses

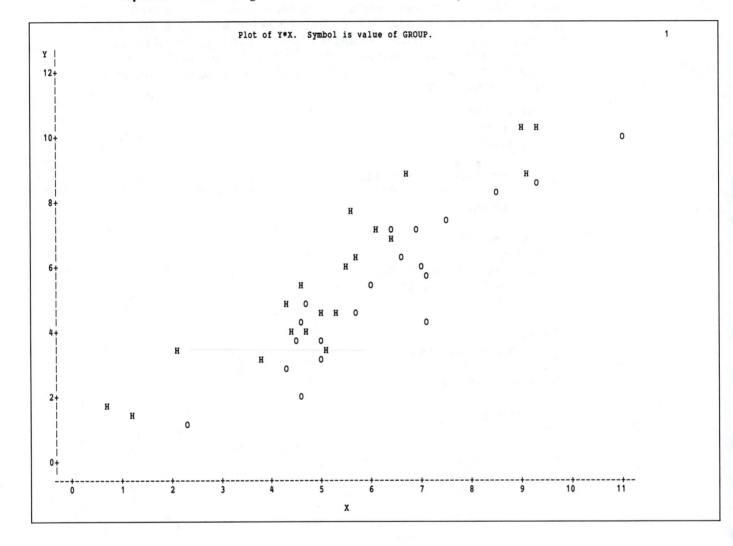

```
                    CANONICAL DISCRIMINANT ANALYSIS                              2

              40 Observations         39 DF Total
               2 Variables            38 DF Within Classes
               2 Classes               1 DF Between Classes


                        Class Level Information

           GROUP    Frequency        Weight      Proportion

           H               20       20.0000        0.500000
           O               20       20.0000        0.500000
```

```
                    CANONICAL DISCRIMINANT ANALYSIS                              3

                        Univariate Test Statistics

                    F Statistics,    Num DF= 1   Den DF= 38

               Total     Pooled     Between                 RSQ/
 Variable       STD        STD        STD     R-Squared    (1-RSQ)        F        Pr > F

 X             2.1776     2.1498     0.6820    0.050307     0.0530      2.0129     0.1641
 Y             2.4215     2.4486     0.2047    0.003667     0.0037      0.1398     0.7105

         Average R-Squared:  Unweighted = 0.0269868      Weighted by Variance = 0.0245201


                 Multivariate Statistics and Exact F Statistics

                          S=1    M=0    N=17.5

           Statistic                  Value        F      Num DF   Den DF   Pr > F

           Wilks' Lambda           0.64203704   10.3145      2       37     0.0003
           Pillai's Trace          0.35796296   10.3145      2       37     0.0003
           Hotelling-Lawley Trace  0.55754252   10.3145      2       37     0.0003
           Roy's Greatest Root     0.55754252   10.3145      2       37     0.0003
```

```
                    CANONICAL DISCRIMINANT ANALYSIS                              4

                                                   Eigenvalues of INV(E)*H
               Adjusted     Approx    Squared         = CanRsq/(1-CanRsq)
    Canonical  Canonical   Standard  Canonical
    Correlation Correlation  Error   Correlation  Eigenvalue  Difference  Proportion  Cumulative

 1    0.598300   0.589467  0.102808   0.357963      0.5575                  1.0000      1.0000

      Test of HO: The canonical correlations in the current row and all that follow are zero

               Likelihood
                 Ratio          F        Num DF   Den DF   Pr > F

           1   0.64203704   10.3145        2        37     0.0003


                        Total Canonical Structure

                                CAN1

                      X      -0.374883
                      Y       0.101206
```

(continued on next page)

(continued from previous page)

```
                          Between Canonical Structure

                                        CAN1

                          X          -1.000000
                          Y           1.000000


                       Pooled Within Canonical Structure

                                        CAN1

                          X          -0.308237
                          Y           0.081243


                       Standardized Canonical Coefficients

                                        CAN1

                          X          -2.625596855
                          Y           2.446680169


                          Raw Canonical Coefficients

                                        CAN1

                          X          -1.205756217
                          Y           1.010412967
```

```
                    CANONICAL DISCRIMINANT ANALYSIS                        5

                    Class Means on Canonical Variables

                  GROUP              CAN1

                    H           0.7277811475
                    O          -.7277811475
```

The univariate R^2s are very small, 0.050307 for X and 0.003667 for Y, and neither variable shows a significant difference between the classes at the 0.10 level.

The multivariate test for differences between the classes is significant at the 0.0003 level. Thus, the multivariate analysis has found a highly significant difference, whereas the univariate analyses failed to achieve even the 0.10 level. The canonical coefficients for the first canonical variable, CAN1, show that the classes differ most widely on the linear combination $-1.205756217X + 1.010412967Y$, or approximately $Y - 1.2X$. The R^2 between CAN1 and the class variable is 0.357963 as given by the Squared Canonical Correlation, which is much higher than either univariate R^2.

In this example the variables are highly correlated within classes. If the within-class correlation were smaller, there would be greater agreement between the univariate and multivariate analyses.

References

Cooley, W.W. and Lohnes, P.R. (1971), *Multivariate Data Analysis*, New York: John Wiley & Sons, Inc.

Efron, B. (1975), "The Efficiency of Logistic Regression Compared to Normal Discriminant Analysis," *Journal of the American Statistical Association*, 70, 892-898.

Fisher, R.A. (1936), "The Use of Multiple Measurements in Taxonomic Problems," *Annals of Eugenics*, 7, 179-188.

Gnanadesikan, R. (1977), *Methods for Statistical Data Analysis of Multivariate Observations*, New York: John Wiley & Sons, Inc.

Hand, D.J. (1981), *Discrimination and Classification*, New York: John Wiley & Sons, Inc.

Hand, D.J. (1982), *Kernel Discriminant Analysis*, New York: Research Studies Press.

Hora, S.C. and Wilcox, J.B. (1982), "Estimation of Error Rates in Several-Population Discriminant Analysis," *Journal of Marketing Research*, XIX, 57-61.

Klecka, W.R. (1980), *Discriminant Analysis*, Sage University Paper Series on Quantitative Applications in the Social Sciences, 07-019. Beverly Hills, CA: Sage Publications.

Kshirsagar, A.M. (1972), *Multivariate Analysis*, New York: Marcel Dekker, Inc.

Lachenbruch, P.A. (1975), *Discriminant Analysis*, New York: Hafner.

Lachenbruch, P.A. (1979), "Discriminant Analysis," *Biometrics*, 35, 69-85.

Press, S.J. and Wilson, S. (1978), "Choosing Between Logistic Regression and Discriminant Analysis," *Journal of the American Statistical Association*, 73, 699-705.

Silverman, B.W. (1986), *Density Estimation for Statistics and Data Analysis*, New York: Chapman and Hall.

Tatsuoka, M.M. (1971), *Multivariate Analysis*, New York: John Wiley & Sons, Inc.

Chapter 6

Introduction to Clustering Procedures

Introduction

SAS clustering procedures can be used to cluster the observations or the variables in a SAS data set. Both hierarchical and disjoint clusters can be obtained. Only numeric variables are permitted.

The purpose of cluster analysis is to place objects into groups or clusters suggested by the data, not defined a priori, such that objects in a given cluster tend to be similar to each other in some sense, and objects in different clusters tend to be dissimilar. Cluster analysis can also be used for summarizing data rather than for finding "natural" or "real" clusters; this use of clustering is sometimes called *dissection* (Everitt 1980).

Any generalization about cluster analysis must be vague because a vast number of clustering methods have been developed in several different fields, with different definitions of clusters and similarity among objects. The variety of clustering techniques is reflected by the variety of terms used for cluster analysis: botryology, classification, clumping, morphometrics, nosography, nosology, numerical taxonomy, partitioning, Q-analysis, systematics, taximetrics, taxonorics, typology, and unsupervised pattern recognition. Good (1977) has also suggested aciniformics and agminatics.

Several types of clusters are possible:

- Disjoint clusters place each object in one and only one cluster.
- Hierarchical clusters are organized so that one cluster may be entirely contained within another cluster, but no other kind of overlap between clusters is allowed.
- Overlapping clusters can be constrained to limit the number of objects that belong simultaneously to two clusters, or they can be unconstrained, allowing any degree of overlap in cluster membership.
- Fuzzy clusters are defined by a probability or grade of membership of each object in each cluster. Fuzzy clusters can be disjoint, hierarchical, or overlapping.

The data representations of objects to be clustered also take many forms. The most common are

- a square distance or similarity matrix, in which both rows and columns correspond to the objects to be clustered. A correlation matrix is an example of a similarity matrix.
- a coordinate matrix, in which the rows are observations and the columns are variables, as in the usual SAS multivariate data set. The observations, the variables, or both may be clustered.

The SAS procedures for clustering are oriented toward disjoint or hierarchical clusters from coordinate data, distance data, or a correlation or covariance matrix. The following procedures are used for clustering:

CLUSTER   does hierarchical clustering of observations using eleven agglomerative methods applied to coordinate data or distance data.

FASTCLUS   finds disjoint clusters of observations using a *k*-means method applied to coordinate data. PROC FASTCLUS is especially suitable for large data sets containing as many as 100,000 observations.

VARCLUS   is for both hierarchical and disjoint clustering of variables by oblique multiple-group component analysis.

TREE   draws tree diagrams, also called *dendrograms* or *phenograms*, using output from the CLUSTER or VARCLUS procedures. PROC TREE can also create a data set indicating cluster membership at any specified level of the cluster tree.

In addition, the following procedures are described in the *SUGI Supplemental Library User's Guide, Version 5 Edition*:

HIER   draws hierarchical diagrams and can be used instead of PROC TREE with the output data sets from the CLUSTER and VARCLUS procedures.

IPFPHC   hierarchically clusters the units of a transaction flow table (an asymmetric similarity matrix) and can be used for single linkage clustering.

OVERCLUS   finds overlapping clusters from similarity data.

The following procedures are useful for processing data prior to the actual cluster analysis:

ACECLUS   attempts to estimate the pooled within-cluster covariance matrix from coordinate data without knowledge of the number or the membership of the clusters (Art, Gnanadesikan, and Kettenring 1982). PROC ACECLUS outputs a data set containing canonical variable scores to be used in the cluster analysis proper.

PRINCOMP   performs a principal component analysis and outputs principal component scores.

STANDARD   standardizes variables to a specified mean and variance.

Excellent introductions to cluster analysis are Everitt (1980) and Massart and Kaufman (1983). Other important texts are Anderberg (1973), Sneath and Sokal (1973), Duran and Odell (1974), and Hartigan (1975). Hartigan (1975) and Spath (1980) give numerous FORTRAN programs for clustering. Any prospective user of cluster analysis should study the Monte Carlo results of Milligan (1980), Milligan and Cooper (1985), and Cooper and Milligan (1984). Essential references on the statistical aspects of clustering include MacQueen (1967), Wolfe (1970), Scott and Symons (1971), Hartigan (1977; 1978; 1981), Binder (1978; 1981), Symons (1981), Wong and Schaack (1982), Wong and Lane (1983), and Sarle (1983). See also SAS Technical Report P-175, "Changes and Enhancements to the SAS System, Release 5.18, under OS and CMS." See Blashfield and Aldenderfer (1978) for a discussion of the fragmented state of the literature on cluster analysis.

Clustering Variables

Factor rotation is often used to cluster variables, but the resulting clusters are fuzzy. It is preferable to use PROC VARCLUS if you want hard (non-fuzzy), disjoint clusters. Factor rotation is better if you want to be able to find overlapping clusters. It is often a good idea to try both VARCLUS and FACTOR with an oblique rotation, compare the amount of variance explained by each, and see how fuzzy the factor loadings are and whether there seem to be overlapping clusters.

You can use PROC VARCLUS to harden a fuzzy factor rotation; use PROC FACTOR to create an output data set containing scoring coefficients and initialize VARCLUS with this data set:

```
proc factor rotate=promax score outstat=fact;
proc varclus initial=input proportion=0;
```

Any rotation method can be used instead of PROMAX. The SCORE and OUTSTAT= options are necessary in the PROC FACTOR statement. VARCLUS reads the correlation matrix from the data set created by FACTOR. The INITIAL=INPUT option tells VARCLUS to read initial scoring coefficients from the data set. PROPORTION=0 keeps VARCLUS from splitting any of the clusters.

Clustering Observations

PROC CLUSTER is easier to use than PROC FASTCLUS because one run produces results from one cluster up to as many as you like. You must run FASTCLUS once for each number of clusters.

The time required by FASTCLUS is roughly proportional to the number of observations, whereas the time required by CLUSTER with most methods varies with the square or cube of the number of observations. Therefore, FASTCLUS can be used with much larger data sets than CLUSTER.

If you want to hierarchically cluster a data set that is too large to use with CLUSTER directly, you can have FASTCLUS produce, for example, fifty clusters, and let CLUSTER analyze these fifty clusters instead of the entire data set. The MEAN= data set produced by FASTCLUS contains two special variables:

- _FREQ_ gives the number of observations in the cluster.
- _RMSSTD_ gives the root-mean-square across variables of the cluster standard deviations.

These variables are automatically used by CLUSTER to give the correct results when clustering clusters. For example, you could use Ward's minimum variance method (Ward 1963):

```
proc fastclus maxclusters=50 mean=temp;
   var x y z;
proc cluster method=ward outtree=tree;
   var x y z;
```

or Wong's hybrid method (Wong 1982):

```
proc fastclus maxclusters=50 mean=temp;
   var x y z;
```

```
proc cluster method=density hybrid outtree=tree;
   var x y z;
```

More detailed examples are given in "The CLUSTER Procedure."

Characteristics of Methods for Clustering Observations

Many simulation studies comparing various methods of cluster analysis have been performed. In these studies, artificial data sets containing known clusters are produced using pseudo-random-number generators. The data sets are analyzed by a variety of clustering methods, and the degree to which each clustering method recovers the known cluster structure is evaluated. See Milligan (1981) for a review of such studies. In most of these studies, the clustering method with the best overall performance has been either average linkage or Ward's minimum variance method. The method with the poorest overall performance has almost invariably been single linkage. However, in many respects, the results of simulation studies are inconsistent and confusing.

In attempting to evaluate clustering methods, it is essential to realize that most methods are biased toward finding clusters possessing certain characteristics related to size (number of members), shape, or dispersion. Methods based on the least-squares criterion (Sarle 1982), such as k-means and Ward's minimum variance method, tend to find clusters with roughly the same number of observations in each cluster. Average linkage is somewhat biased toward finding clusters of equal variance. Many clustering methods tend to produce compact, roughly hyperspherical clusters and are incapable of detecting clusters with highly elongated or irregular shapes. The methods with the least bias are those based on nonparametric density estimation such as single linkage and density linkage.

Most simulation studies have generated compact (often multivariate-normal) clusters of roughly equal size or dispersion. Such studies naturally favor average linkage and Ward's method over most other hierarchical methods, especially single linkage. It would be easy, however, to design a study using elongated or irregular clusters in which single linkage would perform much better than average linkage or Ward's method (see some of the examples below). Even studies that compare clustering methods using "realistic" data may unfairly favor particular methods. For example, in all the data sets used by Mezzich and Solomon (1980), the clusters established by field experts are of equal size. When interpreting simulation or other comparative studies, you must therefore decide whether the artificially generated clusters in the study resemble the clusters you suspect may exist in your data in terms of size, shape, and dispersion. If, like many people doing exploratory cluster analysis, you have no idea what kinds of clusters to expect, you should include at least one of the relatively unbiased methods, such as density linkage, in your analysis.

If the population clusters are sufficiently well separated, almost any clustering method will perform well, as demonstrated in the following example using single linkage. In this and subsequent examples, the output from the clustering procedures is not shown, but cluster membership is displayed in scatter plots. The following SAS statements produce **Output 6.1**:

```
data compact;
   keep x y;
   n=50; scale=1;
   mx=0; my=0; link generate;
   mx=8; my=0; link generate;
   mx=4; my=8; link generate;
   stop;
generate:
   do i=1 to n;
      x=rannor(1)*scale+mx;
      y=rannor(1)*scale+my;
```

```
        output;
       end;
    return;
proc cluster data=compact outtree=tree method=single noprint;
proc tree noprint out=out n=3;
   copy x y;
proc plot; plot y*x=cluster;
   title 'Single Linkage Cluster Analysis';
   title2 'of Data Containing Well-Separated, Compact Clusters';
run;
```

Output 6.1   Data Containing Well-Separated, Compact Clusters: PROC
CLUSTER with METHOD=SINGLE and PROC PLOT

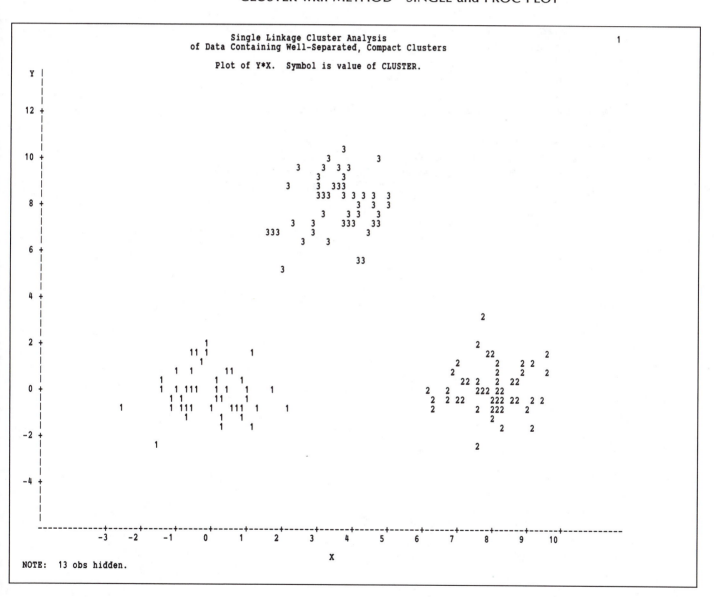

To see how various clustering methods differ, it is necessary to pose a more difficult problem. The following data set is similar to the first except that the three clusters are much closer together. FASTCLUS and five hierarchical methods described in "The CLUSTER Procedure" are used. Also included is a plot of the density estimates obtained in conjunction with two-stage density linkage in PROC CLUSTER. The following SAS statements produce **Output 6.2**:

```
data closer;
   keep x y;
   n=50; scale=1;
   mx=0; my=0; link generate;
   mx=3; my=0; link generate;
   mx=1; my=2; link generate;
   stop;
generate:
   do i=1 to n;
      x=rannor(9)*scale+mx;
      y=rannor(9)*scale+my;
      output;
      end;
   return;
proc fastclus data=closer out=out maxc=3 noprint;
proc plot;
   plot y*x=cluster;
   title 'FASTCLUS Analysis';
   title2 'of Data Containing Poorly Separated, Compact Clusters';
run;
```

Output 6.2   Data Containing Poorly Separated, Compact Clusters: PROC
FASTCLUS and PROC PLOT

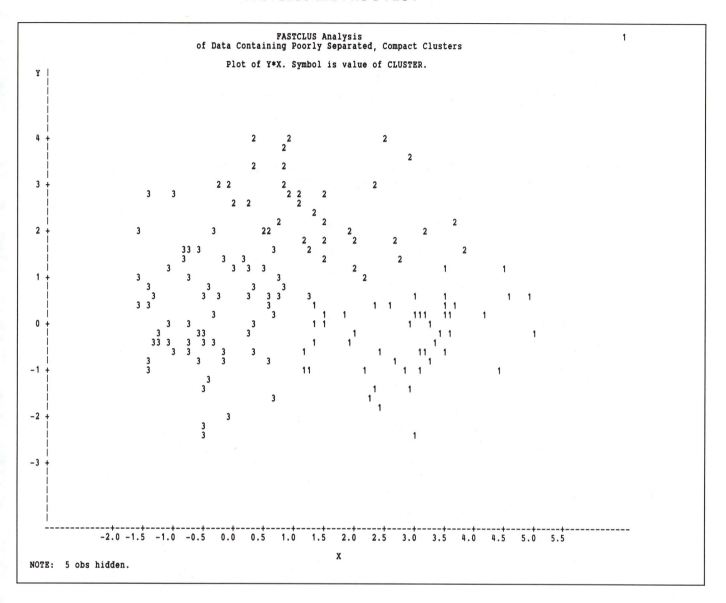

The following SAS statements produce **Output 6.3**:

```
proc cluster data=closer outtree=tree method=ward noprint;
proc tree noprint out=out n=3;
   copy x y;
proc plot;
   plot y*x=cluster;
   title 'Ward''s Minimum Variance Cluster Analysis';
   title2 'of Data Containing Poorly Separated, Compact Clusters';
run;
```

Output 6.3   Data Containing Poorly Separated, Compact Clusters: PROC
CLUSTER with METHOD=WARD and PROC PLOT

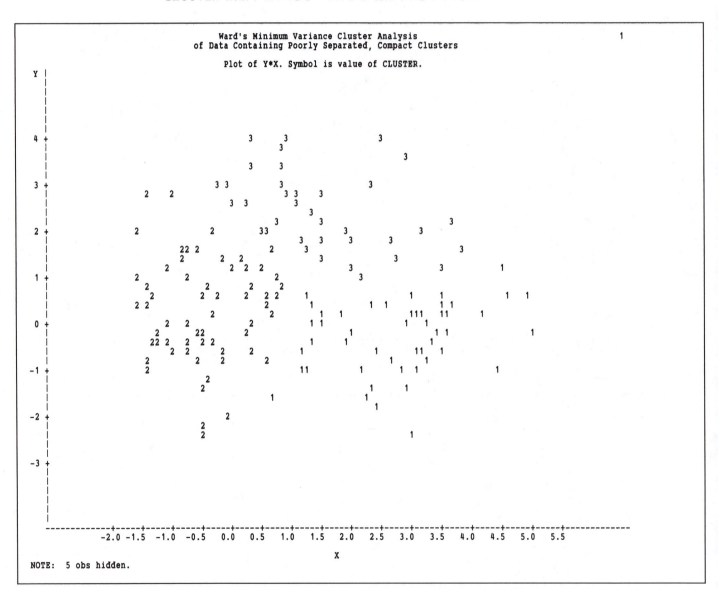

The following SAS statements produce **Output 6.4**:

```
proc cluster data=closer outtree=tree method=average noprint;
proc tree noprint out=out n=3 dock=5;
   copy x y;
proc plot;
   plot y*x=cluster;
   title 'Average Linkage Cluster Analysis';
   title2 'of Data Containing Poorly Separated, Compact Clusters';
run;
```

Output 6.4   Data Containing Poorly Separated, Compact Clusters: PROC
CLUSTER with METHOD=AVERAGE and PROC PLOT

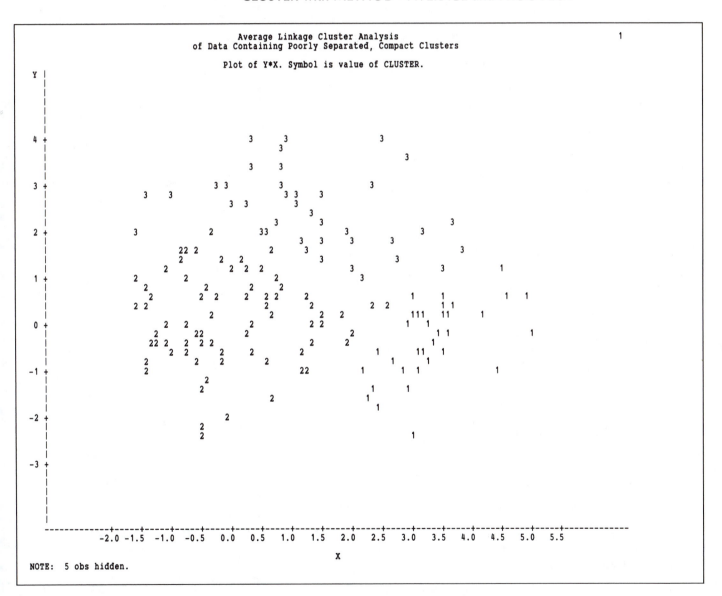

The following SAS statements produce **Output 6.5**:

```
proc cluster data=closer outtree=tree method=centroid noprint;
proc tree noprint out=out n=3 dock=5;
   copy x y;
proc plot;
   plot y*x=cluster;
   title 'Centroid Cluster Analysis';
   title2 'of Data Containing Poorly Separated, Compact Clusters';
run;
```

Output 6.5   Data Containing Poorly Separated, Compact Clusters: PROC
CLUSTER with METHOD=CENTROID and PROC PLOT

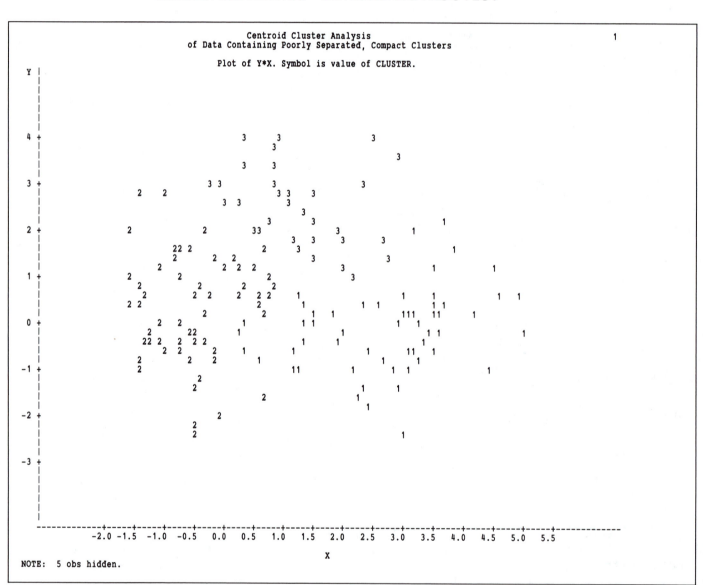

The following SAS statements produce **Output 6.6**:

```
proc cluster data=closer outtree=tree method=twostage k=10 noprint;
proc tree noprint out=out n=3;
   copy x y _dens_;
proc plot;
   plot y*x=cluster;
   title 'Two-Stage Density Linkage Cluster Analysis';
   title2 'of Data Containing Poorly Separated, Compact Clusters';
proc plot;
   plot y*x=_dens_ / contour=6;
   title 'Estimated Densities';
   title2 'for Data Containing Poorly Separated, Compact Clusters';
run;
```

Output 6.6   Data Containing Poorly Separated, Compact Clusters: PROC CLUSTER with METHOD=TWOSTAGE and PROC PLOT

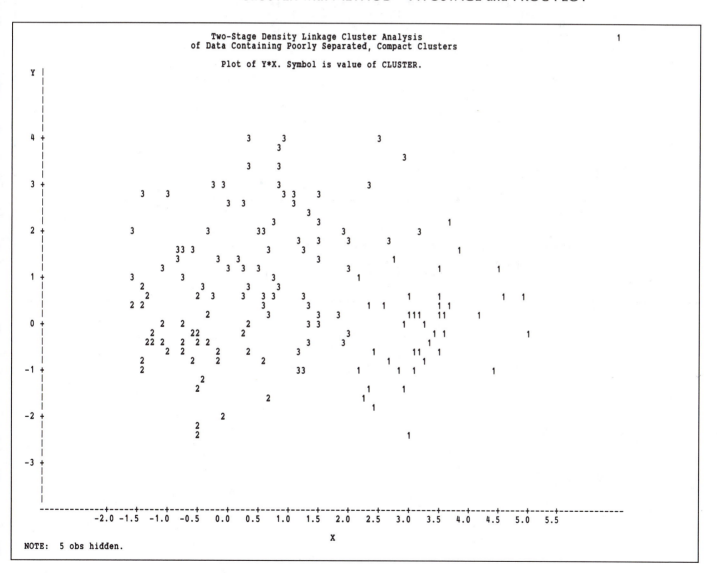

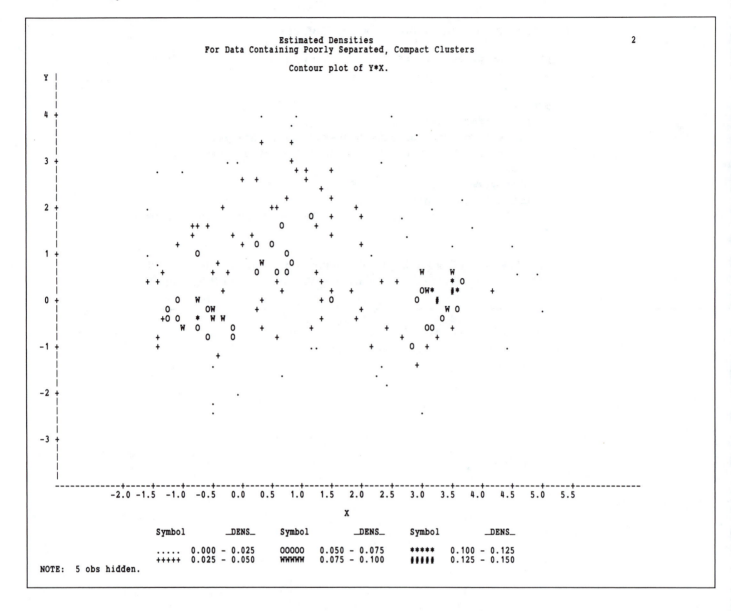

The following SAS statements produce **Output 6.7**:

```
proc cluster data=closer outtree=tree method=single noprint;
proc tree data=tree noprint out=out n=3 dock=5;
   copy x y;
proc plot;
   plot y*x=cluster;
   title 'Single Linkage Cluster Analysis';
   title2 'of Data Containing Poorly Separated, Compact Clusters';
run;
```

Output 6.7   Data Containing Poorly Separated, Compact Clusters: PROC
CLUSTER with METHOD=SINGLE and PROC PLOT

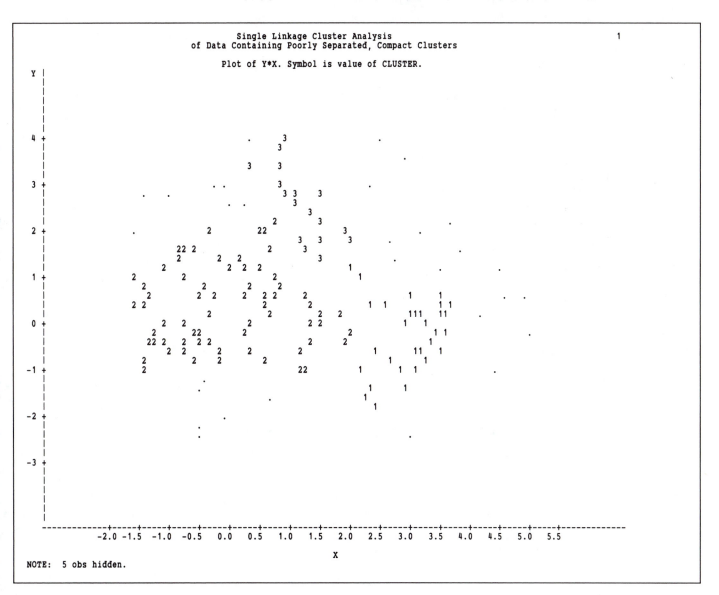

The two least-squares methods, FASTCLUS and Ward's, yield the most uniform cluster sizes and the best recovery of the true clusters. This result was expected since these two methods are biased toward recovering compact clusters of equal size. With average linkage, the lower-left cluster is too large; with the centroid method, the lower-right cluster is too large; and with two-stage density linkage, the top cluster is too large. The single linkage analysis resembles average linkage except for the large number of outliers resulting from the DOCK= option in the PROC TREE statement; the outliers are plotted as dots (missing values).

In the next example, there are three multinormal clusters that differ in size and dispersion. The following SAS statements produce **Output 6.8**:

```
data unequal;
   keep x y;
   mx=1; my=0; n=20; scale=.5; link generate;
   mx=6; my=0; n=80; scale=2.; link generate;
   mx=3; my=4; n=40; scale=1.; link generate;
   stop;
generate:
   do i=1 to n;
      x=rannor(1)*scale+mx;
      y=rannor(1)*scale+my;
      output;
      end;
   return;
proc fastclus data=unequal out=out maxc=3 noprint;
proc plot;
   plot y*x=cluster;
   title 'FASTCLUS Analysis';
   title2 'of Data Containing Compact Clusters of Unequal Size';
run;
```

Output 6.8   Data Containing Compact Clusters of Unequal Size: PROC
FASTCLUS and PROC PLOT

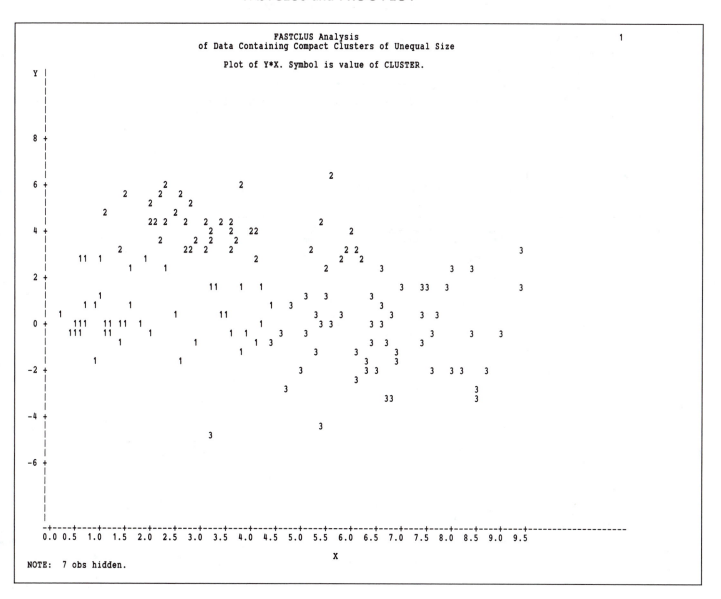

NOTE: 7 obs hidden.

The following SAS statements produce **Output 6.9**:

```
proc cluster data=unequal outtree=tree method=ward noprint;
proc tree noprint out=out n=3;
   copy x y;
proc plot;
   plot y*x=cluster;
   title 'Ward''s Minimum Variance Cluster Analysis';
   title2 'of Data Containing Compact Clusters of Unequal Size';
run;
```

Output 6.9   Data Containing Compact Clusters of Unequal Size: PROC
CLUSTER with METHOD=WARD and PROC PLOT

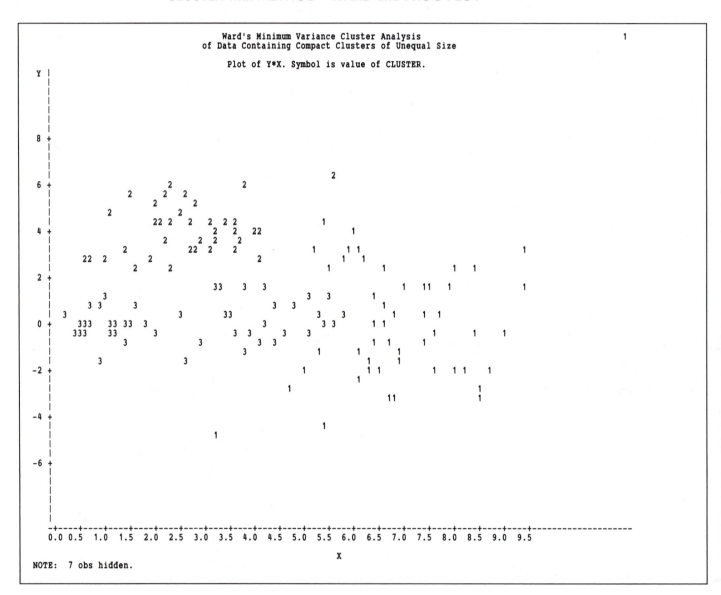

The following SAS statements produce **Output 6.10**:

```
proc cluster data=unequal outtree=tree method=average noprint;
proc tree noprint out=out n=3 dock=5;
   copy x y;
proc plot;
   plot y*x=cluster;
   title 'Average Linkage Cluster Analysis';
   title2 'of Data Containing Compact Clusters of Unequal Size';
run;
```

Output 6.10   Data Containing Compact Clusters of Unequal Size: PROC CLUSTER with METHOD=AVERAGE and PROC PLOT

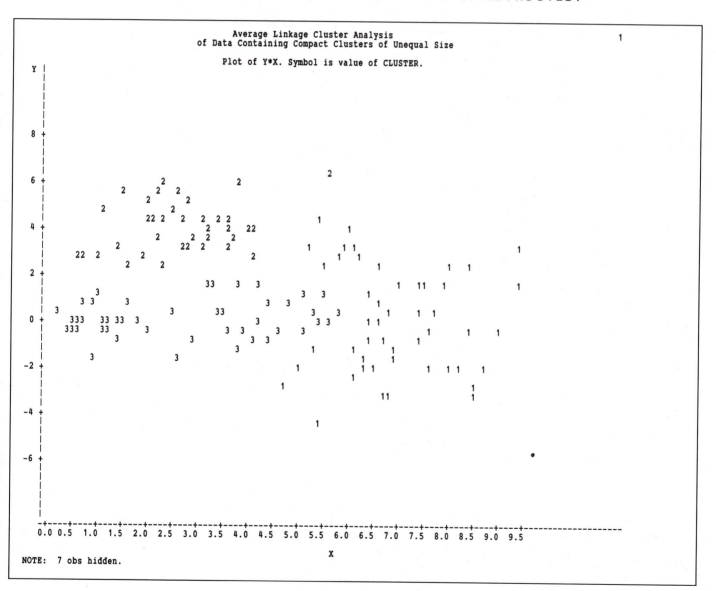

The following SAS statements produce **Output 6.11**:

```
proc cluster data=unequal outtree=tree method=centroid noprint;
proc tree noprint out=out n=3 dock=5;
   copy x y;
proc plot;
   plot y*x=cluster;
   title 'Centroid Cluster Analysis';
   title2 'of Data Containing Compact Clusters of Unequal Size';
run;
```

Output 6.11 Data Containing Compact Clusters of Unequal Size: PROC
CLUSTER with METHOD=CENTROID and PROC PLOT

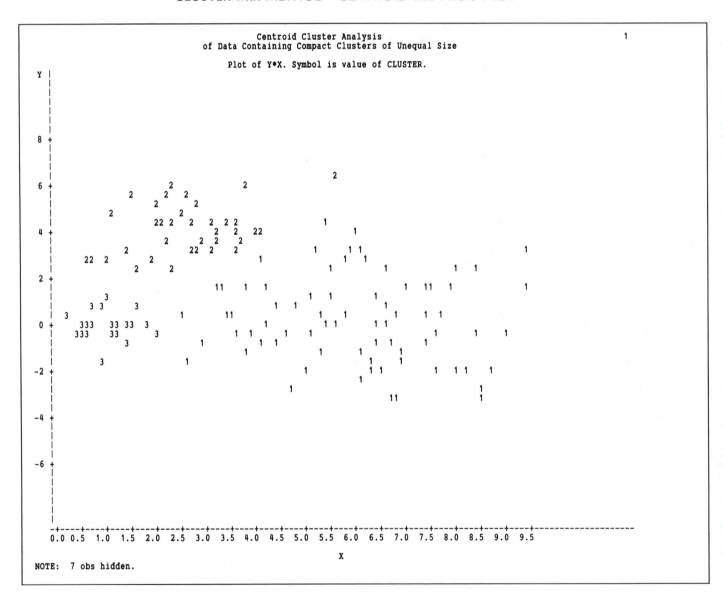

The following SAS statements produce **Output 6.12**:

```
proc cluster data=unequal outtree=tree method=twostage k=10 noprint;
proc tree noprint out=out n=3;
   copy x y _dens_;
proc plot;
   plot y*x=cluster;
   title 'Two-Stage Density Linkage Cluster Analysis';
   title2 'of Data Containing Compact Clusters of Unequal Size';
proc plot;
   plot y*x=_dens_ / contour=6;
   title 'Estimated Densities';
   title2 'for Data Containing Compact Clusters of Unequal Size';
run;
```

Output 6.12   Data Containing Compact Clusters of Unequal Size: PROC
CLUSTER with METHOD=TWOSTAGE and PROC PLOT

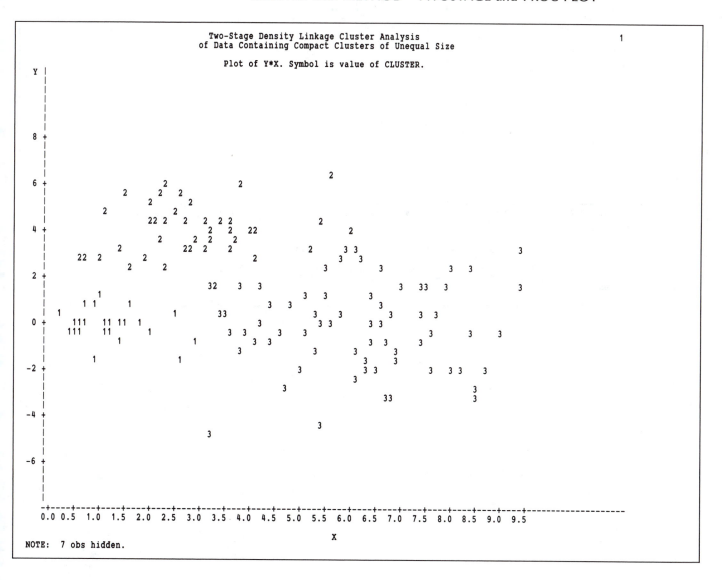

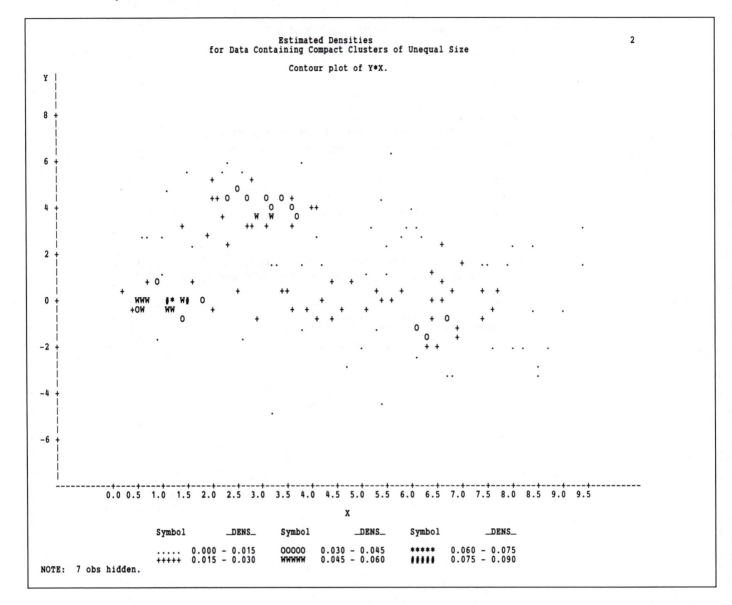

The following SAS statements produce **Output 6.13**:

```
proc cluster data=unequal outtree=tree method=single noprint;
proc tree data=tree noprint out=out n=3 dock=5;
   copy x y;
proc plot;
   plot y*x=cluster;
   title 'Single Linkage Cluster Analysis';
   title2 'of Data Containing Compact Clusters of Unequal Size';
run;
```

Output 6.13 Data Containing Compact Clusters of Unequal Size: PROC
CLUSTER with METHOD=SINGLE and PROC PLOT

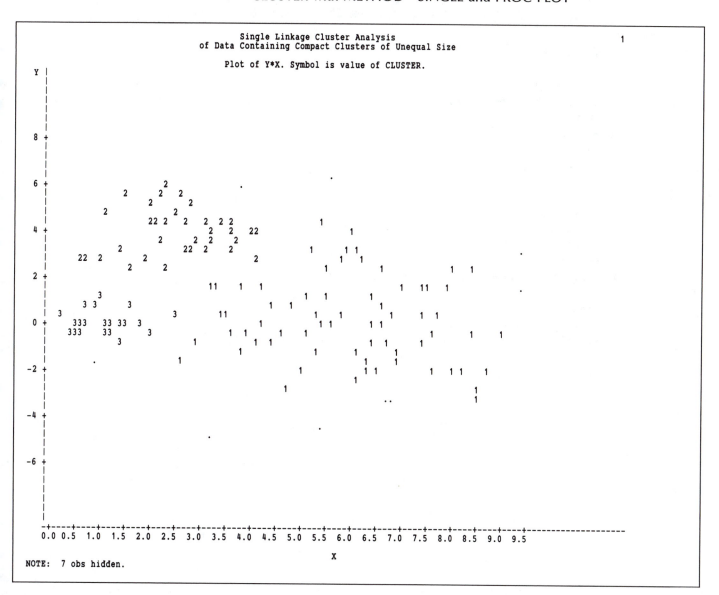

In the FASTCLUS analysis, the smallest cluster, in the bottom left of the plot, has stolen members from the other two clusters, and the upper-left cluster has also acquired some observations that rightfully belong to the larger, lower-right cluster. With Ward's method, the upper-left cluster is separated correctly, but the lower-left cluster has taken a large bite out of the lower-right cluster. For both of these methods, the clustering errors are in accord with the biases of the methods to produce clusters of equal size. In the average linkage analysis, both the upper- and lower-left clusters have encroached on the lower-right cluster, thereby making the variances more nearly equal than in the true clusters. The centroid method, which lacks the size and dispersion biases of the previous methods, obtains an essentially correct partition. Two-stage density linkage does almost as well even though the compact shapes of these clusters favor the traditional methods. Single linkage also produces excellent results.

In the next example, the data are sampled from two highly elongated multinormal distributions with equal covariance matrices. The following SAS statements produce **Output 6.14**:

```
data elongate;
   keep x y;
   ma=8; mb=0; link generate;
   ma=6; mb=8; link generate;
   stop;
generate:
   do i=1 to 50;
      a=rannor(7)*6+ma;
      b=rannor(7)+mb;
      x=a-b;
      y=a+b;
      output;
      end;
   return;
proc fastclus data=elongate out=out maxc=2 noprint;
proc plot;
   plot y*x=cluster;
   title 'FASTCLUS Analysis';
   title2 'of Data Containing Parallel Elongated Clusters';
run;
```

Output 6.14   Data Containing Parallel Elongated Clusters: PROC FASTCLUS
and PROC PLOT

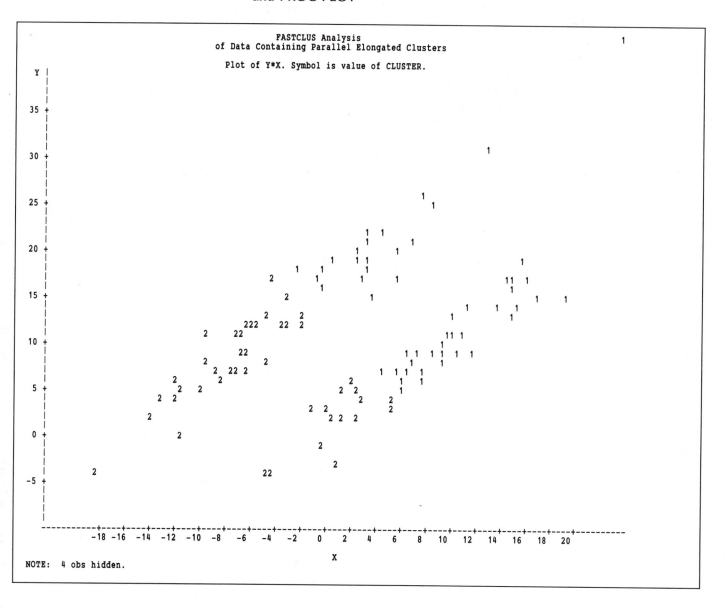

NOTE: 4 obs hidden.

The following SAS statements produce **Output 6.15**:

```
proc cluster data=elongate outtree=tree method=average noprint;
proc tree noprint out=out n=2 dock=5;
   copy x y;
proc plot;
   plot y*x=cluster;
   title 'Average Linkage Cluster Analysis';
   title2 'of Data Containing Parallel Elongated Clusters';
run;
```

Output 6.15   Data Containing Parallel Elongated Clusters: PROC CLUSTER
with METHOD=AVERAGE and PROC PLOT

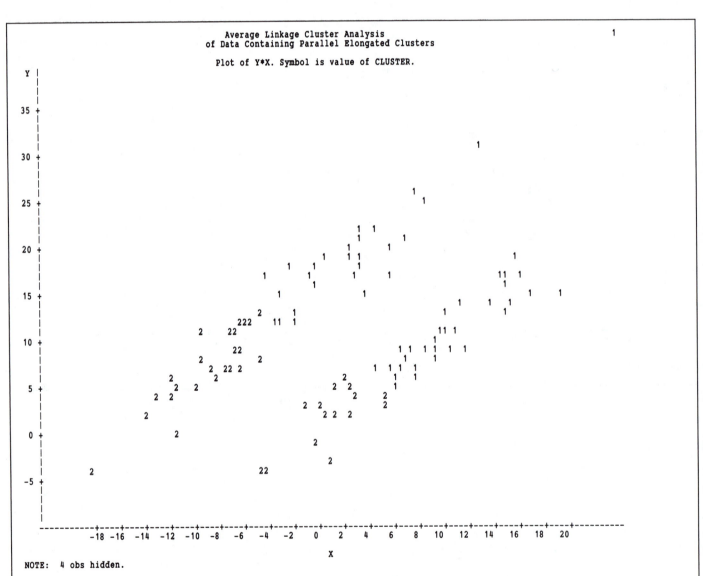

The following SAS statements produce **Output 6.16**:

```
proc cluster data=elongate outtree=tree method=twostage k=10 noprint;
proc tree noprint out=out n=2;
   copy x y;
proc plot;
   plot y*x=cluster;
   title 'Two-Stage Density Linkage Cluster Analysis';
   title2 'of Data Containing Parallel Elongated Clusters';
run;
```

Output 6.16   Data Containing Parallel Elongated Clusters: PROC CLUSTER
with METHOD=TWOSTAGE and PROC PLOT

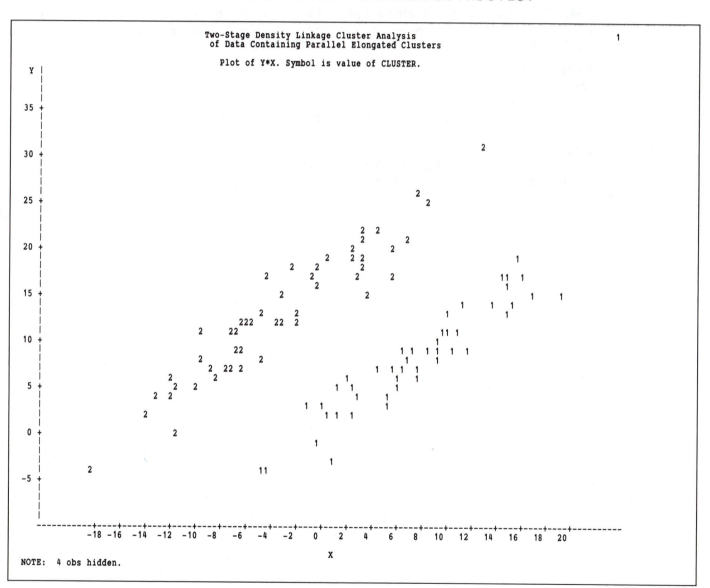

FASTCLUS and average linkage fail miserably. Ward's method and the centroid method, not shown, produce almost the same results. Two-stage density linkage, however, recovers the correct clusters. Single linkage, not shown, finds the same clusters as two-stage density linkage except for some outliers.

In this example, the population clusters have equal covariance matrices. If the within-cluster covariances were known, the data could be transformed to make the clusters spherical so that any of the clustering methods could find the correct clusters. But when you are doing a cluster analysis, you do not know what the true clusters are, so you cannot calculate the within-cluster covariance matrix. Nevertheless, it is sometimes possible to estimate the within-cluster covariance matrix without knowing the cluster membership or even the number of clusters, using an approach invented by Art, Gnanadesikan, and Kettenring (1982). A method for obtaining such an estimate is available in the ACECLUS procedure.

In the following analysis, ACECLUS transforms the variables X and Y into canonical variables CAN1 and CAN2. The latter are plotted and then used in a cluster analysis by Ward's method. The clusters are then plotted with the original variables X and Y. The following SAS statements produce **Output 6.17**:

```
proc aceclus data=elongate out=ace p=.1;
   var x y;
   title 'ACECLUS Analysis';
   title2 'of Data Containing Parallel Elongated Clusters';
proc plot;
plot can2*can1;
   title 'Data Containing Parallel Elongated Clusters';
   title2 'After Transformation by ACECLUS';
run;
```

Output 6.17 Data Containing Parallel Elongated Clusters: PROC ACECLUS and PROC PLOT

```
                      ACECLUS Analysis                                    1
          of Data Containing Parallel Elongated Clusters

       Approximate Covariance Estimation for Cluster Analysis

            100 Observations   Proportion = 0.1
              2 Variables      Converge =  0.001

                   Means and Standard Deviations

          Variable          Mean          Std Dev

            X            2.640588         8.349440
            Y           10.648822         6.842021


                 COV: Total Sample Covariances

                     69.71315    24.24269
                     24.24269    46.81325


    Initial Within-Cluster Covariance Estimate = Full Covariance Matrix

                     Threshold = 0.328478

                                        Pairs
                       RMS     Distance  Within   Convergence
          Iteration  Distance   Cutoff   Cutoff     Measure

              1       2.000      0.657     672      0.673685
              2       9.382      3.082     716      0.006963
              3       9.339      3.068     760      0.008362
              4       9.437      3.100     824      0.009656
              5       9.359      3.074     889      0.010269
              6       9.267      3.044     955      0.011276
              7       9.208      3.025     999      0.009230
              8       9.230      3.032    1052      0.011394
              9       9.226      3.030    1091      0.007924
             10       9.173      3.013    1121      0.007993

                    Iteration Limit Exceeded

      ACE: Approximate Covariance Estimate Within Clusters

                     9.29933     8.215363
                     8.215363    8.937754

              Eigenvalues of Inv(ACE)*(COV-ACE)

          Eigenvalue   Difference   Proportion   Cumulative

   CAN1    36.7091      33.1672      0.912003     0.91200
   CAN2     3.5420         .         0.087997     1.00000
```

```
                      ACECLUS Analysis                                    2
          of Data Containing Parallel Elongated Clusters

                        Eigenvectors

                     CAN1        CAN2

                   -.748392    0.109547
                   0.736349    0.230272
```

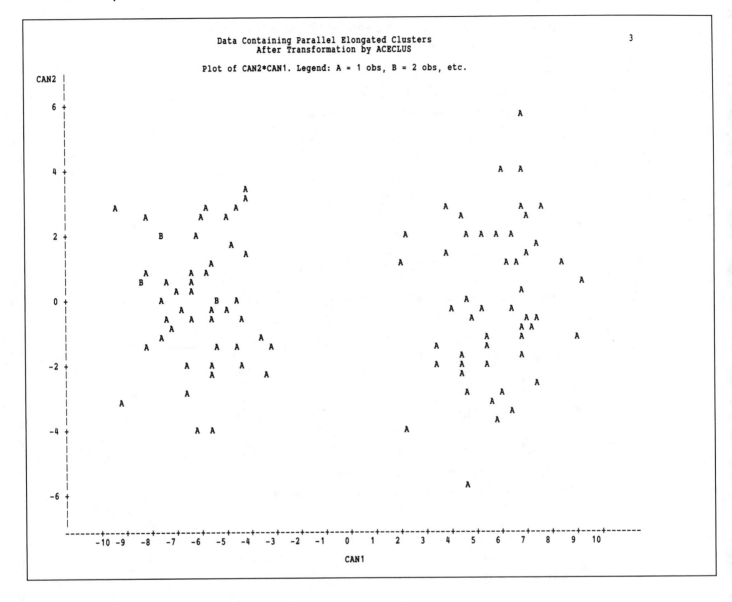

Data Containing Parallel Elongated Clusters
After Transformation by ACECLUS

Plot of CAN2*CAN1. Legend: A = 1 obs, B = 2 obs, etc.

The following SAS statements produce **Output 6.18**:

```
proc cluster data=ace outtree=tree method=ward noprint;
   var can1 can2;
   copy x y;
proc tree noprint out=out n=2;
   copy x y;
proc plot;
   plot y*x=cluster;
   title 'Ward''s Minimum Variance Cluster Analysis';
   title2 'of Data Containing Parallel Elongated Clusters';
   title3 'After Transformation by ACECLUS';
run;
```

Output 6.18   Transformed Data Containing Parallel Elongated Clusters: PROC
CLUSTER with METHOD=WARD and PROC PLOT

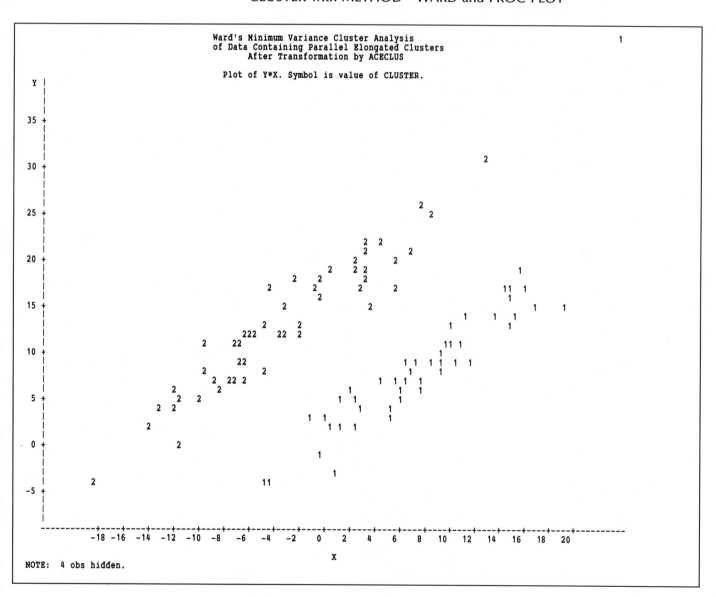

If the population clusters have very different covariance matrices, ACECLUS is of no avail. Although methods exist for estimating multinormal clusters with unequal covariance matrices (Wolfe 1970; Symons 1981; Everitt and Hand 1981), these methods tend to have serious problems with initialization and may converge to degenerate solutions. For unequal covariance matrices or radically non-normal distributions, the best approach to cluster analysis is through nonparametric density estimation, as in density linkage. The next example illustrates population clusters with nonconvex density contours. The following SAS statements produce **Output 6.19**:

```
data noncon;
   keep x y;
   do i=1 to 100;
      a=i*.0628319;
      x=cos(a)+(i>50)+rannor(7)*.1;
      y=sin(a)+(i>50)*.3+rannor(7)*.1;
      output;
      end;
proc fastclus data=noncon out=out maxc=2 noprint;
proc plot;
   plot y*x=cluster;
   title 'FASTCLUS Analysis';
   title2 'of Data Containing Nonconvex Clusters';
run;
```

Output 6.19   Data Containing Nonconvex Clusters: PROC FASTCLUS and PROC PLOT

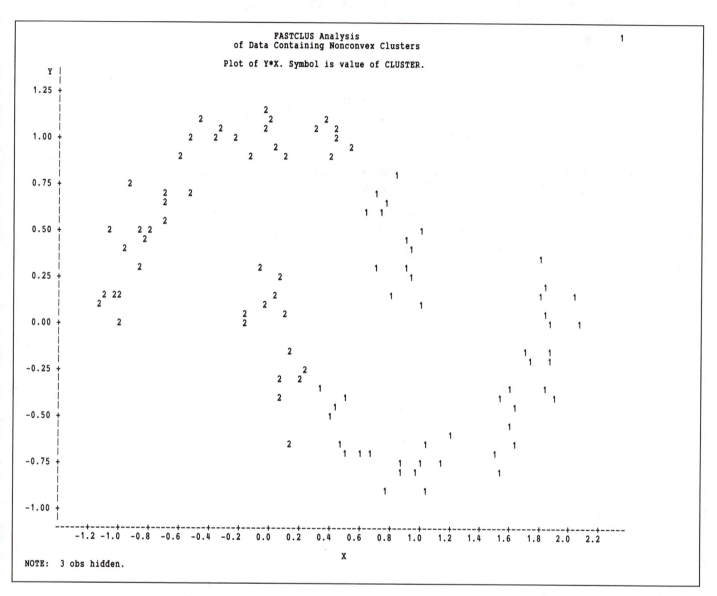

The following SAS statements produce **Output 6.20**.

```
proc cluster data=noncon outtree=tree method=centroid noprint;
proc tree noprint out=out n=2 dock=5;
   copy x y;
proc plot;
   plot y*x=cluster;
   title 'Centroid Cluster Analysis';
   title2 'of Data Containing Nonconvex Clusters';
run;
```

Output 6.20   Data Containing Nonconvex Clusters: PROC CLUSTER with
METHOD=CENTROID and PROC PLOT

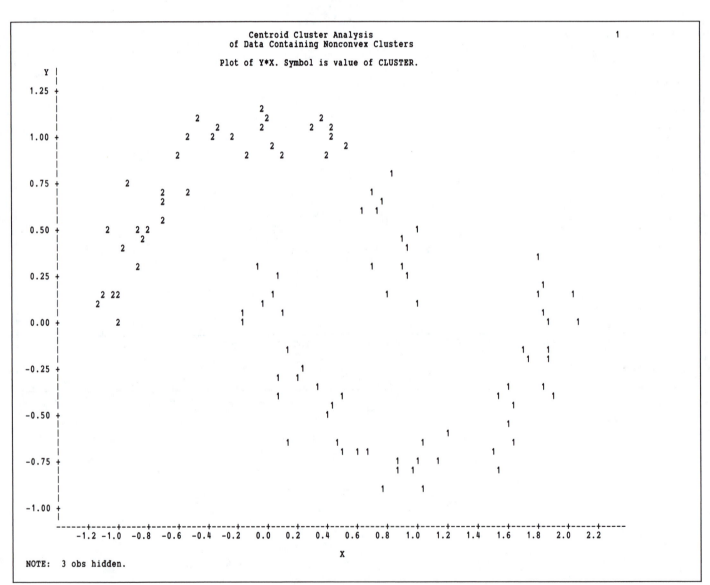

The following SAS statements produce **Output 6.21**.

```
proc cluster data=noncon outtree=tree method=twostage k=10 noprint;
proc tree noprint out=out n=2;
   copy x y;
proc plot;
   plot y*x=cluster;
   title 'Two-Stage Density Linkage Cluster Analysis';
   title2 'of Data Containing Nonconvex Clusters';
run;
```

Output 6.21   Data Containing Nonconvex Clusters: PROC CLUSTER with
METHOD=TWOSTAGE and PROC PLOT

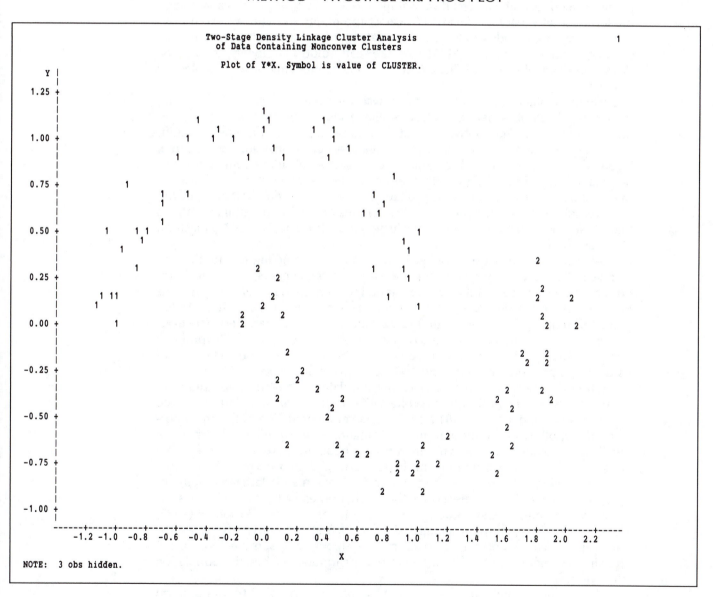

Ward's method and average linkage, not shown, do better than FASTCLUS but not as well as the centroid method. Two-stage density linkage recovers the correct clusters, as does single linkage, which is not shown.

The examples above are intended merely to illustrate some of the properties of clustering methods in common use. If you intend to perform a cluster analysis, you should consult more systematic and rigorous studies of the properties of clustering methods, such as Milligan (1980).

The Number of Clusters

There are no satisfactory methods for determining the number of population clusters for any type of cluster analysis (Everitt 1979, 1980). The number-of-clusters problem is, if anything, more difficult than the number-of-factors problem.

If your purpose in clustering is dissection, that is, to summarize the data without trying to uncover real clusters, it may suffice to look at R^2 for each variable and pooled over all variables. Plots of R^2 against the number of clusters are useful.

It is always a good idea to look at your data graphically. If you have only two or three variables, use PROC PLOT to make scatterplots identifying the clusters. With more variables, use PROC CANDISC to compute canonical variables for plotting.

Ordinary significance tests, such as analysis-of-variance F tests, are not valid for testing differences between clusters. Since clustering methods attempt to maximize the separation between clusters, the assumptions of the usual significance tests, parametric or nonparametric, are drastically violated. For example, if you take a sample of 100 observations from a single univariate normal distribution, have PROC FASTCLUS divide it into two clusters, and run a t test between the clusters, you usually obtain a probability level of less than 0.0001. For the same reason, methods that purport to test for clusters against the null hypothesis that objects are assigned randomly to clusters (McClain and Rao 1975; Klastorin 1983) are useless.

Most valid tests for clusters either have intractable sampling distributions or involve null hypotheses for which rejection is uninformative. For clustering methods based on distance matrices, a popular null hypothesis is that all permutations of the values in the distance matrix are equally likely (Ling 1973; Hubert 1974). Using this null hypothesis, you can do a permutation test or a rank test. The trouble with the permutation hypothesis is that with any real data, the null hypothesis is implausible even if the data do not contain clusters. Rejecting the null hypothesis does not provide any useful information (Hubert and Baker 1977).

Another common null hypothesis is that the data are a random sample from a multivariate normal distribution (Wolfe 1970, 1978; Duda and Hart 1973; Lee 1979; see also Binder 1978, 1981 for a Bayesian approach). The multivariate normal null hypothesis is better than the permutation null hypothesis, but it is not satisfactory because there is typically a high probability of rejection if the data are sampled from a distribution with lower kurtosis than a normal distribution, such as a uniform distribution. The tables in Englemann and Hartigan (1969), for example, generally lead to rejection of the null hypothesis when the data are sampled from a uniform distribution. Hawkins, Muller, and ten Krooden (1982, 337–340) discuss a highly conservative Bonferroni method for hypothesis testing. The conservativeness of this approach may compensate to some extent for the liberalness exhibited by tests based on normal distributions when the population is uniform.

Perhaps a better null hypothesis is that the data are sampled from a uniform distribution (Hartigan 1978; Arnold 1979; Sarle 1983). The uniform null hypothesis leads to conservative error rates when the data are sampled from a strongly unimodal distribution such as the normal. However, in two or more dimensions and depending on the test statistic, the results can be very sensitive to the shape of the region of support of the uniform distribution. Sarle (1983) suggests using a hyperbox with sides proportional in length to the singular values of the centered coordinate matrix.

Given that the uniform distribution provides an appropriate null hypothesis, there are still serious difficulties in obtaining sampling distributions. Hartigan (1978) has obtained asymptotic distributions for the within-cluster sum of squares, the criterion that PROC FASTCLUS and Ward's minimum variance method attempt to optimize, but only in one dimension. Hartigan's results are very liberal when applied to small samples. No distributional theory for finite sample sizes has yet appeared. Currently, the only practical way to obtain sampling distributions for realistic sample sizes is by computer simulation.

Arnold (1979) used simulation to derive tables of the distribution of a criterion based on the determinant of the within-cluster sum of squares matrix $|\mathbf{W}|$. Both normal and uniform null distributions were used. Having obtained clusters with either FASTCLUS or CLUSTER, you can compute Arnold's criterion with the ANOVA or CANDISC procedure. Arnold's tables provide a conservative test because FASTCLUS and CLUSTER attempt to minimize the trace of $\mathbf{W}$ rather than the determinant. Marriott (1971, 1975) also gives useful information on $|\mathbf{W}|$ as a criterion for the number of clusters.

Sarle (1983) used extensive simulations to develop the cubic clustering criterion (CCC), which can be used for crude hypothesis testing and estimating the number of population clusters. The CCC is based on the assumption that a uniform distribution on a hyperrectangle will be divided into clusters shaped roughly like hypercubes. In large samples that can be divided into the appropriate number of hypercubes, this assumption gives very accurate results. In other cases the approximation is generally conservative. For details about the interpretation of the CCC, consult Sarle (1983).

Milligan and Cooper (1985) and Cooper and Milligan (1984) compared thirty methods for estimating the number of population clusters using four hierarchical clustering methods. The three criteria that performed best in these simulation studies with a high degree of error in the data were a pseudo F statistic developed by Calinski and Harabasz (1974), a statistic referred to as $J_e(2)/J_e(1)$ by Duda and Hart (1973) that can be transformed into a pseudo t^2 statistic, and the cubic clustering criterion. The pseudo F statistic and the CCC are printed by FASTCLUS; these two statistics and the pseudo t^2 statistic, which can be applied only to hierarchical methods, are printed by CLUSTER. It may be advisable to look for consensus among the three statistics, that is, local peaks of the CCC and pseudo F statistic combined with a small value of the pseudo t^2 statistic and a larger pseudo t^2 for the next cluster fusion. It must be emphasized that these criteria are appropriate only for compact or slightly elongated clusters, preferably clusters that are roughly multivariate normal.

Perhaps the best approach to the number-of-clusters problem that has yet appeared is provided by Wong and Schaack (1982). The kth-nearest-neighbor clustering method developed by Wong and Lane (1983) is applied with varying values of k. Each value of k yields an estimate of the number of modal clusters. If the estimated number of modal clusters is constant for a wide range of k values, there is strong evidence of at least that many modes in the population. A plot of the estimated number of modes against k can be highly informative. Hypothesis testing requires bootstrapping or simulation. This method requires much weaker assumptions than any of the other approaches discussed above, namely, that the observations are sampled independently and that each cluster corresponds to a mode of the population density. The kth-nearest-neighbor clustering method is implemented in the CLUSTER procedure as METHOD=DENSITY with the K= option. The SAS macro language provides a convenient way to run

CLUSTER with a range of K= values. Sarle (1986) has developed a less expensive approximate nonparametric test for the number of clusters.

References

Anderberg, M.R. (1973), *Cluster Analysis for Applications*, New York: Academic Press, Inc.

Arnold, S.J. (1979), "A Test for Clusters," *Journal of Marketing Research*, 16, 545–551.

Art, D., Gnanadesikan, R., and Kettenring, R. (1982), "Data-based Metrics for Cluster Analysis," *Utilitas Mathematica*, 21A, 75–99.

Binder, D.A. (1978), "Bayesian Cluster Analysis," *Biometrika*, 65, 31–38.

Binder, D.A. (1981), "Approximations to Bayesian Clustering Rules," *Biometrika*, 68, 275–285.

Blashfield, R.K. and Aldenderfer, M.S. (1978), "The Literature on Cluster Analysis," *Multivariate Behavioral Research*, 13, 271–295.

Calinski, T. and Harabasz, J. (1974), "A Dendrite Method for Cluster Analysis," *Communications in Statistics*, 3, 1–27.

Cooper, M.C. and Milligan, G.W. (1984), "The Effect of Error on Determining the Number of Clusters," *College of Administrative Science Working Paper Series 84-2*, Columbus, OH: The Ohio State University.

Duda, R.O. and Hart, P.E. (1973), *Pattern Classification and Scene Analysis*, New York: John Wiley & Sons, Inc.

Duran, B.S. and Odell, P.L. (1974), *Cluster Analysis*, New York: Springer-Verlag.

Englemann, L. and Hartigan, J.A. (1969), "Percentage Points of a Test for Clusters," *Journal of the American Statistical Association*, 64, 1647–1648.

Everitt, B.S. (1979), "Unresolved Problems in Cluster Analysis," *Biometrics*, 35, 169–181.

Everitt, B.S. (1980), *Cluster Analysis*, 2d Edition, London: Heineman Educational Books Ltd.

Everitt, B.S. and Hand, D.J. (1981), *Finite Mixture Distributions*, New York: Chapman and Hall.

Good, I.J. (1977), "The Botryology of Botryology," in *Classification and Clustering*, ed. J. Van Ryzin, New York: Academic Press, Inc.

Harman, H.H. (1976), *Modern Factor Analysis*, 3d Edition, Chicago: University of Chicago Press.

Hartigan, J.A. (1975), *Clustering Algorithms*, New York: John Wiley & Sons, Inc.

Hartigan, J.A. (1977), "Distribution Problems in Clustering," in *Classification and Clustering*, ed. J. Van Ryzin, New York: Academic Press, Inc.

Hartigan, J.A. (1978), "Asymptotic Distributions for Clustering Criteria," *Annals of Statistics*, 6, 117–131.

Hartigan, J.A. (1981), "Consistency of Single Linkage for High-Density Clusters," *Journal of the American Statistical Association*, 76, 388–394.

Hawkins, D.M., Muller, M.W., and ten Krooden, J.A. (1982), "Cluster Analysis," in *Topics in Applied Multivariate Analysis*, ed. D.M. Hawkins, Cambridge: Cambridge University Press.

Hubert, L. (1974), "Approximate Evaluation Techniques for the Single-Link and Complete-Link Hierarchical Clustering Procedures," *Journal of the American Statistical Association*, 69, 698–704.

Hubert, L.J. and Baker, F.B. (1977), "An Empirical Comparison of Baseline Models for Goodness-of-Fit in r-Diameter Hierarchical Clustering," in *Classification and Clustering*, ed. J. Van Ryzin, New York: Academic Press, Inc.

Klastorin, T.D. (1983), "Assessing Cluster Analysis Results," *Journal of Marketing Research*, 20, 92–98.

Lee, K.L. (1979), "Multivariate Tests for Clusters," *Journal of the American Statistical Association*, 74, 708–714.

Ling, R.F (1973), "A Probability Theory of Cluster Analysis," *Journal of the American Statistical Association*, 68, 159–169.

MacQueen, J.B. (1967), "Some Methods for Classification and Analysis of Multivariate Observations," *Proceedings of the Fifth Berkeley Symposium on Mathematical Statistics and Probability*, 1, 281–297.

Marriott, F.H.C. (1971), "Practical Problems in a Method of Cluster Analysis," *Biometrics*, 27, 501–514.

Marriott, F.H.C. (1975), "Separating Mixtures of Normal Distributions," *Biometrics*, 31, 767–769.

Massart, D.L. and Kaufman, L. (1983), *The Interpretation of Analytical Chemical Data by the Use of Cluster Analysis*, New York: John Wiley & Sons, Inc.

McClain, J.O. and Rao, V.R. (1975), "CLUSTISZ: A Program to Test for the Quality of Clustering of a Set of Objects," *Journal of Marketing Research*, 12, 456–460.

Mezzich, J.E and Solomon, H. (1980), *Taxonomy and Behavioral Science*, New York: Academic Press, Inc.

Milligan, G.W. (1980), "An Examination of the Effect of Six Types of Error Perturbation on Fifteen Clustering Algorithms," *Psychometrika*, 45, 325–342.

Milligan, G.W. (1981), "A Review of Monte Carlo Tests of Cluster Analysis," *Multivariate Behavioral Research*, 16, 379–407.

Milligan, G.W. and Cooper, M.C. (1985), "An Examination of Procedures for Determining the Number of Clusters in a Data Set," *Psychometrika*, 50, 159–179.

Sarle, W.S. (1982), "Cluster Analysis by Least Squares," *Proceedings of the Seventh Annual SAS Users Group International Conference*, 651–653.

Sarle, W.S. (1983), *Cubic Clustering Criterion*, SAS Technical Report A-108, Cary, NC: SAS Institute Inc.

SAS Institute Inc. (1988), *Changes and Enhancements to the SAS System, Release 5.18, under OS and CMS*, SAS Technical Report P-175, Cary, NC: SAS Institute Inc.

Scott, A.J. and Symons, M.J. (1971), "Clustering Methods Based on Likelihood Ratio Criteria," *Biometrics*, 27, 387–397.

Sneath, P.H.A. and Sokal, R.R. (1973), *Numerical Taxonomy*, San Francisco: W.H. Freeman.

Spath, H. (1980), *Cluster Analysis Algorithms*, Chichester, England: Ellis Horwood.

Symons, M.J. (1981), "Clustering Criteria and Multivariate Normal Mixtures," *Biometrics*, 37, 35–43.

Ward, J.H. (1963), "Hierarchical Grouping to Optimize an Objective Function," *Journal of the American Statistical Association*, 58, 236–244.

Wolfe, J.H. (1970), "Pattern Clustering by Multivariate Mixture Analysis," *Multivariate Behavioral Research*, 5, 329–350.

Wolfe, J.H. (1978), "Comparative Cluster Analysis of Patterns of Vocational Interest," *Multivariate Behavioral Research*, 13, 33–44.

Wong, M.A. (1982), "A Hybrid Clustering Method for Identifying High-Density Clusters," *Journal of the American Statistical Association*, 77, 841–847.

Wong, M.A. and Lane, T. (1983), "A *k*th Nearest Neighbor Clustering Procedure," *Journal of the Royal Statistical Society*, Series B, 45, 362–368.

Wong, M.A. and Schaack, C. (1982), "Using the *k*th Nearest Neighbor Clustering Procedure to Determine the Number of Subpopulations," *American Statistical Association 1982 Proceedings of the Statistical Computing Section*, 40–48.

Chapter 7

Introduction to Scoring Procedures

Scoring procedures are utilities that produce an output data set with new variables that are transformations of data in the old data set. PROC STANDARD transforms each variable individually. PROC SCORE constructs functions across the variables. PROC RANK produces rank scores across observations. All three procedures produce an output data set but no printed output.

STANDARD   standardizes variables to a given mean and standard deviation. For a complete discussion of the STANDARD procedure, see the *SAS Procedures Guide, Release 6.03 Edition*.

RANK   ranks the observations of each numeric variable from low to high and outputs ranks or rank scores. For a complete discussion of the RANK procedure, see the *SAS Procedures Guide*.

SCORE   constructs new variables that are a linear combination of old variables according to a scoring data set. This procedure is used with PROC FACTOR and other procedures that output scoring coefficients.

Chapter 8

Introduction to Survival Analysis Procedure

Introduction

Data that measure lifetimes or the length of time to the occurrence of an event are often called *survival data*. For example, a variable of interest might be the lifetime of diesel engines or the length of time a person stayed at a job. Such kinds of data have special features that can complicate their analyses.

Background

The LIFEREG procedure fits parametric accelerated failure time or regression models while allowing for data that may be right-, left-, or interval-censored. The baseline distribution can be specified as one of several possibilities including the log normal, log logistic, exponential, and Weibull distributions. The parameter estimates and their estimated covariance matrix are available in an output data set if no classification variables are used in the model.

A key feature of lifetime or survival data is the presence of *censored observations*, those observations that are due to either the withdrawal of the item under observation or to the termination of the period of observation. Because the response is usually a duration, some of the possible events may not yet have occurred when the data collection is terminated. Also, some of the possible responses may be lost to observation before the event occurs. In either case, only a lower bound for the event time is known for some of the observations. These observations are said to be *right-censored*. Thus, an additional censoring variable is incorporated into the analysis indicating which observations are observed event times and which are censored event times. These kinds of data cannot be analyzed by ignoring the censored observations because, among other considerations, the longer-lived units are more likely to be the right-censored ones. The analysis methodology must correctly use the censored observations as well as the noncensored observations. More generally, the variable may only be known to be smaller than a given value (*left-censoring*) or known to be within an interval (*interval-censoring*). Censoring can arise with data other than survival data. In particular, choice related data in econometrics often contain censored data. The monograph by Maddala (1983) discusses several related types of censoring situations.

Another characteristic feature of survival data is that the response variable cannot be negative. This suggests that a transformation such as a log transformation may be necessary before standard statistical methods can be applied or that specialized methods may be more appropriate than those that assume a normal distribution of error. It is especially important to check any distributional and model assumptions as a part of the analysis.

Although survival data may consist solely of a response variable that measures the time until a specified event, say, the failure of a system, often there are other variables thought to be associated with the response variable. The system may be biological, as with most medical data, or it may be a physical system, as with engineering data. The primary purpose of survival analysis is to describe the distribution of the event-time variable and its relation to the other variables. The other variables may be either discrete classification variables, such as race and gender, or continuous variables, such as temperature and age.

If appropriate, the effects of the covariates on the response time can be modeled. One class of parametric models, called accelerated failure time models, is of the form

$$y = \mathbf{x}'\boldsymbol{\beta} + \varepsilon$$

where y is usually the log of the event time, $\mathbf{x}$ is the vector of covariate values, $\boldsymbol{\beta}$ is a vector of unknown parameters to be fit, and ε is a value from some baseline distribution. The LIFEREG procedure fits this type of model allowing some of the more common distributions for ε. After the model is fit, the predicted values, residuals, and other computed values should be used to assess the model adequacy. Cox and Oakes (1984) and Lawless (1982) suggest some plots and other methods to examine the quality of fit for these and other types of models.

References

Cox, D.R. and Oakes, D. (1984), *Analysis of Survival Data*, London: Chapman and Hall.

Elandt-Johnson, R.C. and Johnson, N.L. (1980), *Survival Models and Data Analysis*, New York: John Wiley & Sons, Inc.

Gross, A.J. and Clark, V.A. (1975), *Survival Distributions: Reliability Applications in the Biomedical Sciences*, New York: John Wiley & Sons, Inc.

Kalbfleisch, J.D. and Prentice, R.L. (1980), *The Statistical Analysis of Failure Time Data*, New York: John Wiley & Sons, Inc.

Lawless, J.E. (1982), *Statistical Models and Methods for Lifetime Data*, New York: John Wiley & Sons, Inc.

Lee, E.T. (1980), *Statistical Methods for Survival Data Analysis*, Belmont, CA: Lifetime Learning Publications.

Maddala, G.S. (1983) *Limited-Dependent and Qualitative Variables in Econometrics*, New York: Cambridge University Press.

Chapter 9

The Four Types
of Estimable
Functions

INTRODUCTION

PROC GLM, PROC VARCOMP, and other SAS/STAT procedures label the Sums of Squares (SS) associated with the various effects in the model as Type I, Type II, Type III, and Type IV. The four types of hypotheses available in GLM may not always be sufficient for a statistician to perform all desired hypothesis tests, but they should suffice for the vast majority of analyses. The purpose of this chapter is to explain the hypotheses tested by each of the four types of SS. For additional discussion, see Freund, Littell, and Spector (1986).

ESTIMABILITY

For linear models such as

$$\mathbf{Y} = \mathbf{X}\boldsymbol{\beta} + \boldsymbol{\varepsilon}$$

that have $E(\mathbf{Y}) = \mathbf{X}\boldsymbol{\beta}$, a primary analytical goal is to estimate or test (where possible) the elements of $\boldsymbol{\beta}$ or certain linear combinations of the elements of $\boldsymbol{\beta}$. This is accomplished by computing linear combinations of the observed $\mathbf{Y}$s. To estimate a specific linear function of the individual βs, say $\mathbf{L}\boldsymbol{\beta}$, you must be able to find a linear combination of the **Y**s that has an expected value of **Lβ**. Hence the following definition:

> **Lβ** is estimable if and only if a linear combination of the **Y**s exists that has an expected value of **Lβ**.

Any linear combination of the **Y**s that is computed, for instance **KY**, will have $E(\mathbf{KY}) = \mathbf{KX}\boldsymbol{\beta}$. Thus, the expected value of any linear combination of the **Y**s is equal to that same linear combination of the rows of **X** multiplied by **β**. Therefore,

> **Lβ** is estimable if and only if a linear combination of the rows of **X** that is equal to **L** can be found.

Thus, the rows of **X** form a generating set from which an **L** can be constructed. Since **X** can be reconstructed from the rows of **X′X**, that is, $\mathbf{X} = [\mathbf{X}(\mathbf{X'X})^{-}(\mathbf{X'X})]$, the rows of **X′X** also form a generating set from which all **L**s can be constructed. Similarly, the rows of $(\mathbf{X'X})^{-}\mathbf{X'X}$ also form a generating set for **L**.

Therefore, if **L** is generated as a linear combination of the rows of **X**, **X′X**, or $(\mathbf{X'X})^{-}\mathbf{X'X}$, **Lβ** is estimable. Furthermore, any number of row operations that do not destroy the row rank can be performed on **X**, **X′X**, or $(\mathbf{X'X})^{-}\mathbf{X'X}$. The rows of the resulting matrices also form a generating set for **L**.

Once an **L** of full row rank has been formed from a generating set, **Lβ** can be estimated by computing **Lb**, where $\mathbf{b} = (\mathbf{X'X})^{-}\mathbf{X'Y}$. From the general theory of linear models, **Lb** is the best linear unbiased estimator of **Lβ**. To test the hypothesis that **Lβ**=0, compute SS (H0: $\mathbf{L}\boldsymbol{\beta}=0$) $= (\mathbf{Lb})'(\mathbf{L}(\mathbf{X'X})^{-}\mathbf{L'})^{-1}\mathbf{Lb}$ and form an F test using the appropriate error term.

General Form of an Estimable Function

Although any generating set for **L**, such as **X**, **X′X**, or $(\mathbf{X'X})^{-}\mathbf{X'X}$, could be printed to inform you of what could be estimated, the volume of output would usually defeat the purpose. A rather simple shorthand technique for printing any generating set is demonstrated below.

Suppose

$$
\mathbf{X} = \begin{bmatrix} 1 & 1 & 0 & 0 \\ 1 & 1 & 0 & 0 \\ 1 & 0 & 1 & 0 \\ 1 & 0 & 1 & 0 \\ 1 & 0 & 0 & 1 \\ 1 & 0 & 0 & 1 \end{bmatrix} \quad \text{and} \quad \boldsymbol{\beta} = \begin{bmatrix} \mu \\ A1 \\ A2 \\ A3 \end{bmatrix}
$$

Although **X** is a generating set for **L**, so also is

$$
\mathbf{X^*} = \begin{bmatrix} 1 & 1 & 0 & 0 \\ 1 & 0 & 1 & 0 \\ 1 & 0 & 0 & 1 \end{bmatrix}
$$

X* is formed from **X** by deleting duplicate rows.

Since all **L**s must be linear functions of the rows of **X*** for **Lβ** to be estimable, an **L** for a single-degree-of-freedom estimate can be represented symbolically as

L1*(1 1 0 0) + L2*(1 0 1 0) + L3*(1 0 0 1)

or

L = (L1+L2+L3, L1, L2, L3)

For this example, **Lβ** is estimable if and only if the first element of **L** is equal to the sum of the other elements of **L**, or

Lβ = (L1+L2+L3)*μ + L1*A1 + L2*A2 + L3*A3

is estimable for any values of L1, L2, and L3.

If other generating sets for **L** are represented symbolically, the symbolic notation looks different. However, the inherent nature of the rules is the same. For example, if row operations are performed on **X*** to produce an identity matrix in the first 3×3 submatrix

$$\mathbf{X^{**}} = \begin{bmatrix} 1 & 0 & 0 & 1 \\ 0 & 1 & 0 & -1 \\ 0 & 0 & 1 & -1 \end{bmatrix}$$

then **X**** is also a generating set for **L**. An **L** generated from **X**** can be represented symbolically as

L = (L1, L2, L3, L1−L2−L3)

although, again, the first element of **L** is equal to the sum of the other elements.

With the thousands of generating sets available, the question arises as to which one is the best to represent **L** symbolically. Clearly, a generating set containing a minimum of rows (of full row rank) and a maximum of zero elements is desirable. Since the GLM procedure computes a generalized inverse (g2) of **X′X** such that (**X′X**)⁻**X′X** usually contains numerous zeros and such that the nonzero rows are linearly independent, GLM uses the nonzero rows of (**X′X**)⁻**X′X** to represent **L** symbolically.

If the generating set represented symbolically is of full row rank, the number of symbols (L1, L2, . . .) represents the maximum rank of any testable hypothesis (in other words, the maximum number of linearly independent rows for any **L** matrix that can be constructed). By letting each symbol in turn take on the value of 1 while the others are set to 0, the original generating set can be reconstructed.

Introduction to Reduction Notation

Reduction notation can be used to represent differences in Sums of Squares for two models. The notation R(μ, A, B, C) denotes the complete main effects model for effects A, B, and C. The notation

R(A | μ, B, C)

denotes the difference in SS for the complete main effects model containing A, B, and C and the reduced model containing only B and C. In other words, this notation represents the differences in Model SS produced by

```
proc glm;
   class a b c;
   model y=a b c;
```

and

```
proc glm;
   class b c;
   model y=b c;
```

As another example, consider a regression equation with four independent variables. The notation $R(\beta_3, \beta_4 \mid \beta_1, \beta_2)$ denotes the differences in Model SS for

$$y = \beta_0 + \beta_1 x_1 + \beta_2 x_2 + \beta_3 x_3 + \beta_4 x_4 + \varepsilon$$

and

$$y = \beta_0 + \beta_1 x_1 + \beta_2 x_2 + \varepsilon \quad .$$

With PROC REG, this is the difference in Model SS for the models produced by

```
model y=x1 x2 x3 x4;
```

and

```
model y=x1 x2;
```

A One-Way Classification Model

For the model

$$Y = \mu + A_i + \varepsilon \qquad i = 1, 2, 3$$

the general form of estimable functions **Lb** is (from the previous example)

$$\mathbf{L\beta} = L1*\mu + L2*A_1 + L3*A_2 + (L1-L2-L3)*A_3$$

Thus,

$$\mathbf{L} = (L1, L2, L3, L1-L2-L3) \quad .$$

Tests involving only the parameters A1, A2, and A3 must have an **L** of the form

$$\mathbf{L} = (0, L2, L3, -L2-L3) \quad .$$

Since the **L** above involves only two symbols, at most a two degrees-of-freedom hypothesis can be constructed. For example, let L2=1 and L3=0; then let L2=0 and L3=1:

$$\mathbf{L} = \begin{bmatrix} 0 & 1 & 0 & -1 \\ 0 & 0 & 1 & -1 \end{bmatrix}$$

The **L** above can be used to test the hypothesis that A1=A2=A3. For this example, any **L** with two linearly independent rows with column 1 equal to zero produces the same Sum of Squares. For example, a pooled linear quadratic

$$\mathbf{L} = \begin{bmatrix} 0 & 1 & 0 & -1 \\ 0 & 1 & -2 & 1 \end{bmatrix}$$

gives the same SS. In fact, for any **L** of full row rank and any nonsingular matrix **K** of conformable dimensions

$$\text{SS(H0: } \mathbf{L\beta} = 0) = \text{SS(H0: } \mathbf{KL\beta} = 0)$$

A Three-Factor Main Effects Model

Consider a three-factor main effects model involving the CLASS variables A, B, and C, as shown in **Table 9.1**.

Table 9.1 Three-Factor Main Effects Model

Obs	A	B	C
1	1	2	1
2	1	1	2
3	2	1	3
4	2	2	2
5	2	2	2

The general form of an estimable function is shown in **Table 9.2**.

Table 9.2 General Form of an Estimable Function for Three-Factor Main Effects Model

Parameter	Coefficient
μ (Intercept)	L1
A1	L2
A2	L1−L2
B1	L4
B2	L1−L4
C1	L6
C2	L1+L2−L4−2*L6
C3	−L2+L4+L6

Since only four symbols (L1, L2, L4, and L6) are involved, the maximum rank hypothesis possible has four degrees of freedom. If an **L** matrix with four linearly independent rows is formed, with each row being generated using the rules above, then

$$SS(H0: \mathbf{L}\boldsymbol{\beta} = 0) = R(\mu, A, B, C)$$

In a main effects model, the usual hypothesis desired for a main effect is the equality of all the parameters. In this example, it is not possible to test such a hypothesis because of confounding caused by inadequate design points. The best that can be done is to construct a maximum rank hypothesis (MRH) involving only the parameters of the main effect in question. This can be done using the general form of estimable functions. Note the following:

- To get an MRH involving only the parameters of A, the coefficients of **L** associated with μ, B1, B2, C1, C2, and C3 must be equated to zero. Starting at the top of the general form, let L1=0, then L4=0, then L6=0. If C2 and C3 are not to be involved, then L2 must also be zero. Thus, A1−A2 is not estimable; that is, the MRH involving only the A parameters has zero rank and $R(A \mid \mu, B, C) = 0$.
- To obtain the MRH involving only the B parameters, let L1=L2=L6=0. But then to remove C2 and C3 from the comparison, L4 must also be set to 0. Thus, B1−B2 is not estimable and $R(B \mid \mu, A, C) = 0$.
- To obtain the MRH involving only the C parameters, let L1=L2=L4=0. Thus, the MRH involving only C parameters is

$$C1 - 2*C2 + C3 = K \quad \text{(for any K)}$$

or any multiple of the left-hand side equal to K. Furthermore,

$$SS(H0: C1 = 2*C2 - C3 = 0) = R(C \mid \mu, A, B) \quad .$$

A Multiple Regression Model

Let

$$E(Y) = \beta0 + \beta1*X1 + \beta2*X2 + \beta3*X3$$

If the **X′X** matrix is of full rank, the general form of estimable functions is as shown in **Table 9.3**.

Table 9.3   General Form of Estimable Functions for a Multiple
Regression Model When X′X Matrix Is of Full Rank

Parameter	Coefficient
$\beta0$	L1
$\beta1$	L2
$\beta2$	L3
$\beta3$	L4

To test, for example, the hypothesis that $\beta2=0$, let $L1=L2=L4=0$ and let $L3=1$. Then SS($\mathbf{L\beta}=0$)=R($\beta2 \mid \beta0,\beta1,\beta3$). In the full-rank case, all parameters, as well as any linear combination of parameters, are estimable.

Suppose, however, that $X3=2*X1+3*X2$. The general form of estimable functions is shown in **Table 9.4**.

Table 9.4   General Form of Estimable Functions for a Multiple Regression Model When X'X Matrix Is Not of Full Rank

Parameter	Coefficient
$\beta0$	L1
$\beta1$	L2
$\beta2$	L3
$\beta3$	2*L2+3*L3

For this example, it is possible to test H0: $\beta0=0$. However, $\beta1$, $\beta2$, and $\beta3$ are not estimable; that is,

R($\beta1 \mid \beta0, \beta2, \beta3$) = 0
R($\beta2 \mid \beta0, \beta1, \beta3$) = 0
R($\beta3 \mid \beta0, \beta1, \beta2$) = 0 .

Note on Symbolic Notation

The preceding examples demonstrate the ability to manipulate the symbolic representation of a generating set. Note that any operations performed on the symbolic notation have corresponding row operations that are performed on the generating set itself.

ESTIMABLE FUNCTIONS

Type I SS and Estimable Functions

The Type I SS and the associated hypotheses they test are by-products of the modified sweep operator used to compute a g2 inverse of **X'X** and a solution to the normal equations. For the model E(Y)=X1*B1+X2*B2+X3*B3, the Type I SS for each effect correspond to

Effect	Type I SS
B1	R(B1)
B2	R(B2 | B1)
B3	R(B3 | B1, B2)

The Type I SS are model-order dependent; each effect is adjusted only for the preceding effects in the model.

There are numerous ways to obtain a Type I hypothesis matrix **L** for each effect. One way is to form the **X'X** matrix and then reduce **X'X** to an upper triangular matrix by row operations, skipping over any rows with a zero diagonal. The non-zero rows of the resulting matrix associated with X1 provide an **L** such that

$$SS(H0: \mathbf{L}\boldsymbol{\beta} = 0) = R(B1) \quad .$$

The nonzero rows of the resulting matrix associated with X2 provide an **L** such that

$$SS(H0: \mathbf{L}\boldsymbol{\beta} = 0) = R(B1 \mid B2) \quad .$$

The last set of nonzero rows (associated with X3) provide an **L** such that

$$SS(H0: \mathbf{L}\boldsymbol{\beta} = 0) = R(B3 \mid B1, B2) \quad .$$

Another more formalized representation of Type I generating sets for B1, B2, and B3, respectively, is

$$\mathbf{G1} = (\mathbf{X1'X1} \mid \mathbf{X1'X2} \mid \mathbf{X1'X3})$$
$$\mathbf{G2} = (0 \mid \mathbf{X2'M1X2} \mid \mathbf{X2'M1X3})$$
$$\mathbf{G3} = (0 \mid 0 \mid \mathbf{X3'M2X3})$$

where

$$\mathbf{M1} = \mathbf{I} - \mathbf{X1(X1'X1)}^{-}\mathbf{X1'}$$

and

$$\mathbf{M2} = \mathbf{M1} - \mathbf{M1X2(X2'M1X2)}^{-}\mathbf{X2'M1} \quad .$$

Using the Type I generating set **G2** (for example), if an **L** is formed from linear combinations of the rows of **G2** such that **L** is of full row rank and of the same row rank as **G2**, then $SS(H0: \mathbf{L}\boldsymbol{\beta}=0)=R(B2 \mid B1)$.

In the GLM procedure, the Type I estimable functions printed symbolically when the E1 option is requested are

$$\mathbf{G1^*} = \mathbf{(X1'X1)}^{-}\mathbf{G1}$$
$$\mathbf{G2^*} = \mathbf{(X2'M1X2)}^{-}\mathbf{G2}$$
$$\mathbf{G3^*} = \mathbf{(X3'M2X3)}^{-}\mathbf{G3} \quad .$$

As can be seen from the nature of the generating sets **G1**, **G2**, and **G3**, only the Type I estimable functions for B3 are guaranteed not to involve the B1 and B2 parameters. The Type I hypothesis for B2 can (and usually does) involve B3 parameters. The Type I hypothesis for B1 usually involves B2 and B3 parameters.

There are, however, a number of models for which the Type I hypotheses are considered appropriate. These are

- balanced *ANOVA* models specified in proper sequence (that is, interactions do not precede main effects in the MODEL statement and so forth)
- purely nested models (specified in the proper sequence)
- polynomial regression models (in the proper sequence).

Type II SS and Estimable Functions

For main effects models and regression models, the general form of estimable functions can be manipulated to provide tests of hypotheses involving only the parameters of the effect in question. The same result can also be obtained by entering each effect in turn as the last effect in the model and obtaining the Type I SS for that effect. Using a modified reversible sweep operator, it is possible to obtain the same results without actually rerunning the model.

Thus, the Type II SS correspond to the R notation in which each effect is adjusted for all other effects possible. For a regression model such as

$$E(Y) = X1*B1 + X2*B2 + X3*B3$$

the Type II SS correspond to

Effect	SS
B1	R(B1 | B2, B3)
B2	R(B2 | B1, B3)
B3	R(B3 | B1, B2)

For a main effects model (A, B, and C as classification variables), the Type II SS correspond to

Effect	SS
A	R(A | B, C)
B	R(B | A, C)
C	R(C | A, B)

From an earlier discussion, you know that the Type II SS provide (for regression and main effects models) an MRH for each effect that does not involve the parameters of the other effects.

For models involving interactions and nested effects, it is not possible to obtain a test of a hypothesis for a main effect free of parameters of higher-level effects with which the main effect is involved (unless a priori parametric restrictions are assumed).

It is reasonable to assume, then, that any test of a hypothesis concerning an effect should involve the parameters of that effect and only those other parameters with which that effect is involved.

Definition: Given an effect E1 and another effect E2, E1 is contained in E2 provided that

1. both effects involve the same continuous variables, if any
2. E2 has more CLASS variables than does E1, and if E1 has CLASS variables, they all appear in E2.

Note: the effect μ is contained in all pure CLASS effects, but it is not contained in any effect involving a continuous variable. No effect is contained by μ.

Type II, Type III, and Type IV estimable functions rely on this definition, and all have one thing in common: the estimable functions involving an effect E1 also involve the parameters of all effects that contain E1, and they do not involve the parameters of effects that do not contain E1 (other than E1).

Definition: The Type II estimable functions for an effect E1 have an **L** (before reduction to full row rank) of the following form:

1. All columns of **L** associated with effects not containing E1 (except E1) should be zero.

2. The submatrix of **L** associated with effect E1 should be
(**X1′MX1**)⁻(**X1′MX1**).
3. Each of the remaining submatrices of **L** associated with an effect E2 that
contains E1 should be (**X1′MX2**)⁻(**X1′MX2**).

where

X0 = the columns of **X** whose associated effects do not contain E1.
X1 = the columns of **X** associated with E1.
X2 = the columns of **X** associated with an E2 effect that contains E1.
M = **I**−**X0**(**X0′X0**)⁻**X0′**.

For the model Y=A B A*B, the Type II SS correspond to

$$R(A \mid \mu, B), \quad R(B \mid \mu, A), \quad R(A*B \mid \mu, A, B)$$

for effects A, B, and A*B, respectively. For the model Y=A B(A) C(A B), the Type
II SS correspond to

$$R(A \mid \mu), \quad R(B(A) \mid \mu, A), \quad R(C(A B) \mid \mu, A, B(A))$$

for effects A, B(A), and C(A B), respectively. For the model Y=X X*X, the
Type II SS correspond to

$$R(X \mid \mu, X*X) \text{ and } R(X*X \mid \mu, X)$$

for X and X*X, respectively.

Example of Type II Estimable Functions

For a 2×2 factorial with w observations per cell, the general form of estimable
functions is shown in **Table 9.5**. Any nonzero values for L2, L4, and L6 can be
used to construct **L** vectors for computing the Type II SS for A, B, and A*B, respectively.

Table 9.5 General Form of Estimable Functions for 2×2 Factorial

Effect	Coefficient
μ	L1
A1	L2
A2	L1−L2
B1	L4
B2	L1−L4
AB11	L6
AB12	L2−L6
AB21	L4−L6
AB22	L1−L2−L4+L6

For a balanced 2×2 factorial with the same number of observations in every cell, the Type II estimable functions are shown in **Table 9.6**.

Table 9.6 Type II Estimable Functions for Balanced 2×2 Factorial

Effect	Coefficients for Effect		
	A	B	A*B
μ	0	0	0
A1	L2	0	0
A2	−L2	0	0
B1	0	L4	0
B2	0	−L4	0
AB11	0.5*L2	0.5*L4	L6
AB12	0.5*L2	−0.5*L4	−L6
AB21	−0.5*L2	0.5*L4	−L6
AB22	−0.5*L2	−0.5*L4	L6

For an unbalanced 2×2 factorial (with two observations in every cell except the AB22 cell, which contains only one observation), the general form of estimable functions is the same as if it were balanced since the same effects are still estimable. However, the Type II estimable functions for A and B are not the same as they were for the balanced design. The Type II estimable functions for this unbalanced 2×2 factorial are shown in **Table 9.7**.

Table 9.7 Type II Estimable Functions for Unbalanced 2×2 Factorial

Effect	Coefficients for Effect		
	A	B	A*B
μ	0	0	0
A1	L2	0	0
A2	−L2	0	0
B1	0	L4	0
B2	0	−L4	0
AB11	0.6*L2	0.6*L4	L6
AB12	0.4*L2	−0.6*L4	−L6
AB21	−0.6*L2	0.4*L4	−L6
AB22	−0.4*L2	−0.4*L4	L6

By comparing the hypothesis being tested in the balanced case to the hypothesis being tested in the unbalanced case for effects A and B, you can note that the

Type II hypotheses for A and B are dependent on the cell frequencies in the design. For unbalanced designs in which the cell frequencies are not proportional to the background population, the Type II hypotheses for effects that are contained in other effects are of questionable merit.

However, if an effect is not contained in any other effect, the Type II hypothesis for that effect is an MRH that does not involve any parameters except those associated with the effect in question.

Thus, Type II SS are appropriate for

- any balanced model
- any main effects model
- any pure regression model
- an effect not contained in any other effect (regardless of the model).

In addition to the above, the Type II SS is generally accepted by most statisticians for purely nested models.

Type III SS and Estimable Functions

You have seen that when an effect is contained in another effect, the Type II hypotheses for that effect are dependent on the cell frequencies. The philosophy behind both the Type III and Type IV hypotheses is that the tests of hypotheses made for any given effect should be the same for all designs with the same general form of estimable functions.

To demonstrate this concept, recall the hypotheses being tested by the Type II SS in the balanced 2×2 factorial shown in **Table 9.7**. Those hypotheses are precisely the ones that the Type III and Type IV employ for all 2×2 factorials that have at least one observation per cell. The Type III and Type IV hypotheses for a design without missing cells usually differ from the hypothesis employed for the same design with missing cells since the general form of estimable functions usually differs.

Construction of Type III Hypotheses

Type III hypotheses are constructed by working directly with the general form of estimable functions. The following steps are used to construct a hypothesis for an effect E1:

1. For every effect in the model except E1 and those effects that contain E1, equate the coefficients in the general form of estimable functions to zero.

   Note: if E1 is not contained in any other effect, this step defines the Type III hypothesis (as well as the Type II and Type IV hypotheses). If E1 is contained in other effects, go on to step 2.

   See the section **Type II SS and Estimable Functions** earlier in this chapter for a definition of when effect E1 is contained in another effect.
2. If necessary, equate new symbols to compound expressions in the E1 block in order to obtain the simplest form for the E1 coefficients.
3. Equate all symbolic coefficients outside of the E1 block to a linear function of the symbols in the E1 block in order to make the E1 hypothesis orthogonal to hypotheses associated with effects that contain E1.

By once again observing the Type II hypotheses being tested in the balanced 2×2 factorial, it is possible to verify that the A and A*B hypotheses are orthogonal and also that the B and A*B hypotheses are orthogonal. This principle of orthogonality between an effect and any effect that contains it holds for all balanced designs.

Thus, construction of Type III hypotheses for any design is a logical extension of a process that is used for balanced designs.

The Type III hypotheses are precisely the hypotheses being tested by programs that reparameterize using the usual assumptions (for example, all parameters for an effect summing to zero). When no missing cells exist in a factorial model, Type III SS coincide with Yates' weighted squares-of-means technique. When cells are missing in factorial models, the Type III SS coincide with those produced by Harvey's fixed-effects linear models program (see the HARVEY procedure in the *SUGI Supplemental Library User's Guide, Version 5 Edition*).

The following steps illustrate the construction of Type III estimable functions for a 2×2 factorial with no missing cells.

To obtain the A*B interaction hypothesis, start with the general form and equate the coefficients for effects μ, A, and B to zero, as shown in **Table 9.8**.

Table 9.8 Type III Hypothesis for A*B Interaction

Effect	General Form	L1=L2=L4=0
μ	L1	0
A1	L2	0
A2	L1−L2	0
B1	L4	0
B2	L1−L4	0
AB11	L6	L6
AB12	L2−L6	−L6
AB21	L4−L6	−L6
AB22	L1−L2−L4+L6	L6

The last column in **Table 9.8** represents the form of the MRH for A*B.

To obtain the Type III hypothesis for A, first start with the general form and equate the coefficients for effects μ and B to zero (let L1=L4=0). Next let L6=K*L2, and find the value of K that makes the A hypothesis orthogonal to the A*B hypothesis. In this case, K=0.5. Each of these steps is shown in **Table 9.9**.

In **Table 9.9**, the fourth column (under L6=K*L2) represents the form of all estimable functions not involving μ, B1, or B2. The prime difference between the Type II and Type III hypotheses for A is the way K is determined. Type II chooses K as a function of the cell frequencies, whereas Type III chooses K such that the estimable functions for A are orthogonal to the estimable functions for A*B.

Table 9.9 Type III Hypothesis for A

Effect	General Form	L1=L4=0	L6=K*L2	K=0.5
μ	L1	0	0	0
A1	L2	L2	L2	L2
A2	L1−L2	−L2	−L2	−L2
B1	L4	0	0	0
B2	L1−L4	0	0	0
AB11	L6	L6	K*L2	0.5*L2
AB12	L2−L6	L2−L6	(1−K)*L2	0.5*L2
AB21	L4−L6	−L6	−K*L2	−0.5*L2
AB22	L1−L2−L4+L6	−L2+L6	(K−1)*L2	−0.5*L2

An example of Type III estimable functions in a 3×3 factorial with unequal cell frequencies and missing diagonals is given in **Table 9.10** (N1 through N6 represent the nonzero cell frequencies).

Table 9.10 A 3×3 Factorial Design with Unequal Cell
Frequencies and Missing Diagonals

For any nonzero values of N1 through N6, the Type III estimable functions for each effect are shown in **Table 9.11**.

Table 9.11 Type III Estimable Functions for 3×3 Factorial Design with Unequal Cell Frequencies and Missing Diagonals

Effect	A	B	A*B
μ	0	0	0
A1	L2	0	0
A2	L3	0	0
A3	−L2−L3	0	0
B1	0	L5	0
B2	0	L6	0
B3	0	−L5−L6	0
AB12	0.667*L2+0.333*L3	0.333*L5+0.667*L6	L8
AB13	0.333*L2−0.333*L3	−0.333*L5−0.667*L6	−L8
AB21	0.333*L2+0.667*L3	0.667*L5+0.333*L6	−L8
AB23	−0.333*L2+0.333*L3	−0.667*L5−0.333*L6	L8
AB31	−0.333*L2−0.667*L3	0.333*L5−0.333*L6	L8
AB32	−0.667*L2−0.333*L3	−0.333*L5+0.333*L6	−L8

Type IV Estimable Functions

By once again looking at the Type II hypotheses being tested in the balanced 2×2 factorial (see **Table 9.7**), you can see another characteristic of the hypotheses employed for balanced designs: the coefficients of lower-order effects are averaged across each higher-level effect involving the same subscripts. For example, in the A hypothesis, the coefficients of AB11 and AB12 are equal to one-half the coefficient of A1, and the coefficients of AB21 and AB22 are equal to one-half the coefficient of A2. With this in mind then, the basic concept used to construct Type IV hypotheses is that the coefficients of any effect, say E1, are distributed equitably across higher-level effects that contain E1. When missing cells occur, this same general philosophy is adhered to, but care must be taken in the way the distributive concept is applied.

Construction of Type IV hypotheses begins as does the construction of the Type III hypotheses. That is, for an effect E1, equate to zero all coefficients in the general form that do not belong to E1 or to any other effect containing E1. If E1 is not contained in any other effect, then the Type IV hypothesis (and Type II and III) has been found. If E1 is contained in other effects, then simplify, if necessary, the coefficients associated with E1 so that they are all free coefficients or functions of other free coefficients in the E1 block.

To illustrate the method of resolving the free coefficients outside of the E1 block, suppose that you are interested in the estimable functions for an effect A and that A is contained in AB, AC, and ABC. (In other words, the main effects in the model are A, B, and C.)

With missing cells, the coefficients of intermediate effects (here they are AB and AC) do not always have an equal distribution of the lower-order coefficients, so the coefficients of the highest-order effects are determined first (here it is ABC). Once the highest-order coefficients are determined, the coefficients of intermediate effects are automatically determined.

The following process is performed for each free coefficient of A in turn. The resulting symbolic vectors are then added together to give the Type IV estimable functions for A.

1. Select a free coefficient of A, and set all other free coefficients of A to zero.
2. If any of the levels of A have zero as a coefficient, equate all of the coefficients of higher-level effects involving that level of A to zero. This step alone usually resolves most of the free coefficients remaining.
3. Check to see if any higher-level coefficients are now zero when the coefficient of the associated level of A is not zero. If this situation occurs, the Type IV estimable functions for A are not unique.
4. For each level of A in turn, if the A coefficient for that level is nonzero, count the number of times that level occurs in the higher-level effect. Then equate each of the higher-level coefficients to the coefficient of that level of A divided by the count.

An example of a 3×3 factorial with four missing cells (N1 through N5 represent positive cell frequencies) is shown in **Table 9.12**.

Table 9.12 3×3 Factorial Design with Four Missing Cells

		B		
		1	2	3
	1	N1	N2	
A	2	N3	N4	
	3			N5

The Type IV estimable functions are shown in **Table 9.13**.

Table 9.13   Type IV Estimable Functions for 3×3 Factorial Design
with Four Missing Cells

Effect	A	B	A*B
μ	0	0	0
A1	−L3	0	0
A2	L3	0	0
A3	0	0	0
B1	0	L5	0
B2	0	−L5	0
B3	0	0	0
AB11	−0.5*L3	0.5*L5	L8
AB12	−0.5*L3	−0.5*L5	−L8
AB21	0.5*L3	0.5*L5	−L8
AB22	0.5*L3	−0.5*L5	L8
AB33	0	0	0

A Comparison of Type III and Type IV Hypotheses

For the vast majority of designs, Type III and Type IV hypotheses for a given effect
are the same. Specifically, they are the same for any effect E1 that is not contained
in other effects for any design (with or without missing cells). For factorial designs
with no missing cells, the Type III and Type IV hypotheses coincide for all effects.
When there are missing cells, the hypotheses can differ. By using the GLM procedure, you can study the differences in the hypotheses. Each user must decide
on the appropriateness of the hypotheses for a particular model.

The Type III hypotheses for three-factor and higher completely nested designs
with unequal Ns in the lowest level differ from the Type II hypotheses; however,
the Type IV hypotheses do correspond to the Type II hypotheses in this case.

When missing cells occur in a design, the Type IV hypotheses may not be
unique. If this occurs in PROC GLM, you are notified, and you may need to consider defining your own specific comparisons.

REFERENCES

Freund, R.J., Littell, R.C., and Spector, P.C. (1986), *SAS System for Linear Models,
1986 Edition*, Cary, NC: SAS Institute Inc.

Goodnight, J.H. (1978), *Tests of Hypotheses in Fixed Effects Linear Models*, SAS
Technical Report R-101, Cary, NC: SAS Institute Inc.

The ACECLUS
Procedure

ABSTRACT

The ACECLUS (Approximate Covariance Estimation for CLUStering) procedure obtains approximate estimates of the pooled within-cluster covariance matrix when the clusters can be assumed to be multivariate normal with equal covariance matrices. Neither cluster membership nor the number of clusters need be known. PROC ACECLUS is useful for preprocessing data to be subsequently clustered by the CLUSTER or the FASTCLUS procedure. ACECLUS can produce output data sets containing the approximate within-cluster covariance estimate, eigenvalues and eigenvectors from a canonical analysis, and canonical variable scores. The method is a variation on an algorithm developed by Art, Gnanadesikan, and Kettenring (1982).

INTRODUCTION

Many clustering methods perform well with spherical clusters but poorly with elongated elliptical clusters (Everitt 1980, 77-97). If the elliptical clusters have roughly the same orientation and eccentricity, you can apply a linear transformation to the data to yield a spherical within-cluster covariance matrix, that is, a covariance matrix proportional to the identity. Equivalently, the distance between observations can be measured in the metric of the inverse of the pooled within-cluster covariance matrix. The remedy is difficult to apply, however, because you need to know what the clusters are in order to compute the sample within-cluster covariance matrix. One approach is to estimate iteratively both cluster membership and within-cluster covariance (Wolfe 1970; Hartigan 1975). Another approach is provided by Art, Gnanadesikan, and Kettenring (1982), who are referred to as AGK in the rest of this chapter. They have devised an ingenious method for estimating the within-cluster covariance matrix without knowledge of the clusters. The method can be applied before any of the usual clustering techniques, including hierarchical clustering methods.

First, AGK obtain a decomposition of the total-sample sum-of-squares-and-cross-products (SSCP) matrix into within-cluster and between-cluster SSCP matrices computed from pairwise differences between observations, rather than differences between observations and means. Then, AGK show how the within-cluster SSCP matrix based on pairwise differences can be approximated without knowing the number or the membership of the clusters. The approximate within-cluster SSCP matrix can be used to compute distances for cluster analysis, or it can be used in a canonical analysis similar to canonical discriminant analysis (see the chapter on the CANDISC procedure). AGK demonstrate by Monte Carlo calculations that their method can produce better clusters than the Euclidean metric even when the approximation to the within-cluster SSCP matrix is poor or the within-cluster covariances are moderately heterogeneous.

The algorithm used by ACECLUS differs slightly from the AGK algorithm. The ACECLUS algorithm is described first; then differences between ACECLUS and the AGK method are summarized.

Background

It is well known from the literature on nonparametric statistics that variances and, hence, covariances can be computed from pairwise differences instead of deviations from means. (For example, Puri and Sen (1971, 51-52) show that the variance is a U statistic of degree 2.) Let $\mathbf{X}=(x_{ij})$ be the data matrix with n observations (rows) and v variables (columns), and let $\bar{x}_j$ be the mean of the jth variable. The sample covariance matrix $\mathbf{S}=(s_{jk})$ is usually defined as

$$s_{jk} = \Sigma_{i=1}^{n}(x_{ij} - \bar{x}_j)(x_{ik} - \bar{x}_k) / (n - 1) .$$

$\mathbf{S}$ can also be computed as

$$s_{jk} = \Sigma_{i=2}^{n}\Sigma_{h=1}^{i-1}(x_{ij} - x_{hj})(x_{ik} - x_{hk}) / (n(n - 1)) .$$

Let $\mathbf{W}=(w_{jk})$ be the pooled within-cluster covariance matrix, q be the number of clusters, n_c be the number of observations in the cth cluster, and

$$d''_{ic} = 1 \quad \text{if observation } i \text{ is in cluster } c$$
$$= 0 \quad \text{otherwise.}$$

$\mathbf{W}$ is normally defined as

$$w_{jk} = \Sigma_{c=1}^{q}\Sigma_{i=1}^{n}d''_{ic}(x_{ij} - \bar{x}_{cj})(x_{ik} - \bar{x}_{ck}) / (n - q)$$

where $\bar{x}_{cj}$ is the mean of the jth variable in cluster c. Let

$$d'_{ih} = 1/n_c \quad \text{if observations } i \text{ and } h \text{ are in cluster } c$$
$$= 0 \quad \text{otherwise.}$$

W can also be computed as

$$w_{jk} = \Sigma^n_{i=2}\Sigma^{i-1}_{h=1}d'_{ih}\,(x_{ij} - x_{hj})(x_{ik} - x_{hk})\,/\,(n - q) \quad .$$

If the clusters are not known, d'_{ih} cannot be determined. However, an approximation to **W** can be obtained by using instead

$$d_{ih} = 1 \quad \text{if } \Sigma^v_{j=1}\Sigma^v_{k=1}m_{jk}(x_{ij} - x_{hj})(x_{ik} - x_{hk}) \leq u^2$$
$$= 0 \quad \text{otherwise}$$

where u is an appropriately chosen value and $\mathbf{M}=(m_{jk})$ is an appropriate metric. Let $\mathbf{A}=(a_{jk})$ be defined as

$$a_{jk} = \Sigma^n_{i=2}\Sigma^{i-1}_{h=1}d_{ih}(x_{ij} - x_{hj})(x_{ik} - x_{hk})\,/\,2(\Sigma^n_{i=2}\Sigma^{i-1}_{h=1}d_{ih}) \quad .$$

A equals **W** if all of the following conditions hold:

- all within-cluster distances in the metric **M** are less than or equal to u
- all between-cluster distances in the metric **M** are greater than u
- all clusters have the same number of members n_c.

If the clusters are of unequal size, **A** gives more weight to large clusters than **W** does, but this discrepancy should be of little importance if the population within-cluster covariance matrices are equal. There may be large differences between **A** and **W** if the cutoff u does not discriminate between pairs in the same cluster and pairs in different clusters. Lack of discrimination may occur for one of the following reasons:

- the clusters are not well separated
- **M** or u is not chosen appropriately.

In the former case, little can be done to remedy the problem. The question remains of how to choose **M** and u. Consider **M** first. The best choice for **M** is $\mathbf{W}^{-1}$, but **W** is not known. The solution is to use an iterative algorithm:

1. Obtain an initial estimate of **A**, such as the identity or the total-sample covariance matrix.
2. Let **M** equal $\mathbf{A}^{-1}$.
3. Recompute **A** using the formula above.
4. Repeat steps 2 and 3 until the estimate stabilizes.

Convergence is assessed by comparing values of **A** on successive iterations. Let $\mathbf{A}_i$ be the value of **A** on the ith iteration, and $\mathbf{A}_0$ be the initial estimate of **A**. Let **Z** be a user-specified $v \times v$ matrix. The convergence measure is

$$e_i = \|\mathbf{Z}'(\mathbf{A}_i - \mathbf{A}_{i-1})\mathbf{Z}\|\,/\,v$$

where $\|\dots\|$ indicates the Euclidean norm, that is, the square root of the sum of the squares of the elements of the matrix. In ACECLUS, **Z** can be the identity or an inverse factor of **S** or diag(**S**). Iteration stops when e_i falls below a user-specified value.

The remaining question of how to choose u has no simple answer. In practice, you must try several different values. ACECLUS provides four different ways of specifying u:

1. You can specify a constant value for u. This method is useful if the initial estimate of **A** is quite good.
2. You can specify a threshold value $t > 0$ that is multiplied by the root-mean-square distance between observations in the current metric on each iteration to give u. Thus the value of u changes from iteration to iteration. This method is appropriate if the initial estimate of **A** is poor.
3. You can specify a value p, $0 < p < 1$, to be transformed into a distance u such that approximately a proportion p of the pairwise Mahalanobis distances between observations in a random sample from a multivariate normal distribution will be less than u in repeated sampling. The transformation can be computed only if the number of observations exceeds the number of variables, preferably by at least 10 percent. This method also requires a good initial estimate of **A**.
4. You can specify a value p, $0 < p < 1$, to be transformed as above into a value t that is then multiplied by $1/\sqrt{2v}$ times the root-mean-square distance between observations in the current metric on each iteration to yield u. The value of u changes from iteration to iteration. This method can be used with a poor initial estimate of **A**.

In most cases the analysis should begin with the fourth method using values of p between 0.5 and 0.01 and using the full covariance matrix as the initial estimate of **A**.

Proportions p are transformed to distances t using the formula

$$t^2 = 2v\{[F^{-1}_{v,n-v}(p)]^{(n-v)/(n-1)}\}$$

where $F^{-1}_{v,n-v}$ is the quantile (inverse cumulative distribution) function of an F random variable with v and $n-v$ degrees of freedom. The squared Mahalanobis distance between a single pair of observations sampled from a multivariate normal distribution is distributed as $2v$ times an F random variable with degrees of freedom as above. The distances between two pairs of observations are correlated if the pairs have an observation in common. The quantile function is raised to the power given in the above formula to compensate approximately for the correlations among distances between pairs of observations that share a member. Monte Carlo studies indicate that the approximation is acceptable if the number of observations exceeds the number of variables by at least 10 percent.

If **A** becomes singular, step 2 in the iterative algorithm cannot be performed because **A** cannot be inverted. In this case, let **Z** be the matrix defined above in discussing the convergence measure, and let $\mathbf{Z'AZ = R'\Lambda R}$ where $\mathbf{R'R = RR' = I}$ and $\Lambda = (\lambda_{jk})$ is diagonal. Let $\Lambda^* = (\lambda_{jk}^*)$ be a diagonal matrix where $\lambda_{jj}^* = \max(\lambda_{jj}, g \, \mathrm{trace}(\Lambda))$, and $0 < g < 1$ is a user-specified singularity criterion. Then **M** is computed as $\mathbf{ZR'(\Lambda^*)^{-1}RZ'}$.

ACECLUS differs from the AGK method in several respects. The AGK method

- uses the identity matrix as the initial estimate, whereas the ACECLUS procedure allows you to specify any symmetric matrix as the initial estimate and defaults to the total-sample covariance matrix. The ACECLUS default was chosen to yield invariance under nonsingular linear transformations of the data but may sometimes obscure clusters that would be apparent if the identity matrix were used.
- carries out all computations with SSCP matrices, whereas the ACECLUS procedure uses estimated covariance matrices because covariances are easier to interpret than crossproducts are.

- uses the m pairs with the smallest distances to form the new estimate at each iteration, where m is specified by the user, whereas the ACECLUS procedure uses all pairs closer than a given cutoff value. Kettenring (1984, pers. comm.) says that the m-closest-pairs method seems to give the user more direct control. ACECLUS uses a distance cutoff because it yields a slight decrease in computer time and because in some cases, such as widely separated spherical clusters, the results are less sensitive to the choice of distance cutoff than to the choice of m. Much research remains to be done on this issue.
- uses a different convergence measure. Let $\mathbf{A}_i$ be computed on each iteration using the m-closest-pairs method, and let $\mathbf{B}_i = \mathbf{A}_{i-1}^{-1}\mathbf{A}_i - \mathbf{I}$ where $\mathbf{I}$ is the identity matrix. The AGK convergence measure is equivalent to $\text{trace}(\mathbf{B}_i^2)$.

Analyses of Fisher's (1936) iris data, consisting of measurements of petal and sepal length and width for fifty specimens from each of three iris species, are summarized in **Table 10.1**. The number of misclassified observations out of 150 is given for four clustering methods:

- k-means as implemented in PROC FASTCLUS with MAXC=3, MAXITER=99, and CONV=0
- Ward's minimum variance method as implemented in PROC CLUSTER
- average linkage on Euclidean distances as implemented in PROC CLUSTER
- the centroid method as implemented in PROC CLUSTER.

Each hierarchical analysis was followed by PROC TREE with NCL=3 to determine cluster assignments at the three-cluster level. Clusters with twenty or fewer observations were discarded by using the DOCK=20 option. The observations in a discarded cluster were considered unclassified.

Each method was applied to

- the raw data
- the data standardized to unit variance by the STANDARD procedure
- two standardized principal components accounting for 95 percent of the standardized variance and having an identity total-sample covariance matrix, computed by PROC PRINCOMP with the STD option
- four standardized principal components having an identity total-sample covariance matrix, computed by PROC PRINCOMP with the STD option
- the data transformed by PROC ACECLUS using seven different settings of the PROPORTION= (P=) option
- four canonical variables having an identity pooled within-species covariance matrix, computed using the CANDISC procedure.

Theoretically, the best results should be obtained by using the canonical variables from PROC CANDISC. ACECLUS yielded results comparable to CANDISC for values of the PROPORTION= option ranging from 0.005 to 0.02. At PROPORTION=0.04, average linkage and the centroid method showed some deterioration, but k-means and Ward's method continued to produce excellent classifications. At larger values of the PROPORTION= option, all methods did poorly, although no worse than with four standardized principal components.

Table 10.1   Number of Misclassified and Unclassified Observations Using Fisher's (1936) Iris Data

	Clustering Method			
Data	k-means	Ward's	Average Linkage	Centroid
raw data	16*	16*	25+12**	14*
standardized data	25	26	33+4	33+4
two standardized principal components	29	31	30+9	27+32
four standardized principal components	39	27	32+7	45+11
transformed by ACECLUS P=0.32	39	10+9	7+25	
transformed by ACECLUS P=0.16	39	18+9	7+19	7+26
transformed by ACECLUS P=0.08	19	9	3+13	5+16
transformed by ACECLUS P=0.04	4	5	1+19	3+12
transformed by ACECLUS P=0.02	4	3	3	3
transformed by ACECLUS P=0.01	4	4	3	4
transformed by ACECLUS P=0.005	4	4	4	4
canonical variables	3	5	4	4+1

* A single number represents misclassified observations with no unclassified observations.
** Where two numbers are separated by a plus sign, the first is the number of misclassified observations; the second is the number of unclassified observations.

This example shows that

- ACECLUS can produce results as good as those from the optimal transformation
- ACECLUS can be useful even when the within-cluster covariance matrices are moderately heterogeneous

- the choice of the distance cutoff as specified by the PROPORTION= or the THRESHOLD= option is important, and several values should be tried
- commonly used transformations such as standardization and principal components can produce poor classifications.

Although experience with the AGK and ACECLUS methods is limited, the results so far suggest that these methods help considerably more often than they hinder the subsequent cluster analysis, especially with normal-mixture techniques such as *k*-means and Ward's minimum variance method.

SPECIFICATIONS

The following statements invoke the ACECLUS procedure:

PROC ACECLUS *options*;
    VAR *variables*;
    FREQ *variable*;
    WEIGHT *variable*;
    BY *variables*;

Usually, only the VAR statement is used in addition to the PROC ACECLUS statement. The BY, FREQ, VAR, and WEIGHT statements are described after the PROC ACECLUS statement.

PROC ACECLUS Statement

PROC ACECLUS *options*;

The options listed below can be used in the PROC ACECLUS statement. You must specify either the PROPORTION= or the THRESHOLD= option but not both.

Data Set Options

The following options pertain to data sets used or created by PROC ACECLUS:

DATA=*SASdataset*
    names the SAS data set to be analyzed. If the DATA= option is omitted, the most recently created SAS data set is used.

OUT=*SASdataset*
    names an output SAS data set that contains all the original data as well as the canonical variables having an identity estimated within-cluster covariance matrix. If you want to create a permanent SAS data set, you must specify a two-level name. See "SAS Files" in the *SAS Language Guide, Release 6.03 Edition* for information on permanent SAS data sets.

OUTSTAT=*SASdataset*
    names a TYPE=ACE output SAS data set that contains means, standard deviations, number of observations, covariances, estimated within-cluster covariances, eigenvalues, and canonical coefficients. If you want to create a permanent SAS data set, you must specify a two-level name. See "SAS Files" in the *SAS Language Guide* for information on permanent SAS data sets.

Iterative Process Options

The following option tells how to initialize the iterative algorithm and can also specify an input data set:

INITIAL=FULL | F
INITIAL=DIAGONAL | D
INITIAL=IDENTITY | I
INITIAL=INPUT=*SASdataset*

    specifies the matrix to use for the initial estimate of the within-cluster covariance matrix. INITIAL=FULL uses the total-sample covariance matrix as the initial estimate of the within-cluster covariance matrix. INITIAL=DIAGONAL uses the diagonal matrix of sample variances as the initial estimate of the within-cluster covariance matrix. INITIAL=IDENTITY uses the identity matrix as the initial estimate of the within-cluster covariance matrix. INITIAL=INPUT=*SASdataset* names a SAS data set from which to obtain the initial estimate of the within-cluster covariance matrix. The data set can be TYPE=CORR, COV, SSCP, or ACE, or it can be an ordinary SAS data set. (See Appendix 2, "Special SAS Data Sets," for descriptions of CORR, COV, and SSCP data sets. See **Output Data Sets** later in this chapter for a description of ACE data sets.) If the INITIAL= option is not specified, the default is the matrix specified by the METRIC= option. If neither the INITIAL= nor the METRIC= option is specified, INITIAL=FULL is used if there are enough observations to obtain a nonsingular total-sample covariance matrix; otherwise, INITIAL=DIAGONAL is used.

The following options control the iterative process. You must specify either the THRESHOLD= or the PROPORTION= option.

ABSOLUTE
    causes the THRESHOLD= value or the threshold computed from the PROPORTION= option to be treated absolutely rather than relative to the root-mean-square distance between observations. Use the ABSOLUTE option only when you are confident that the initial estimate of the within-cluster covariance matrix is close to the final estimate, such as when the INITIAL= option specifies a data set created by a previous execution of PROC ACECLUS using the OUTSTAT= option.

CONVERGE=*c*
    specifies the convergence criterion. The default is 0.001. Iteration stops when the convergence measure falls below the value specified by the CONVERGE= option or when the iteration limit as specified by the MAXITER= option is exceeded, whichever happens first.

MAXITER=*n*
    specifies the maximum number of iterations. The default is 10.

PROPORTION=*p*
PERCENT=*p*
P=*p*
    specifies the approximate proportion of pairs to be included in the estimation of the within-cluster covariance matrix. The value of p must be greater than zero. If the value of p is greater than or equal to one, it is interpreted as a percentage and divided by 100. PROPORTION=0.02 and PROPORTION=2 are equivalent. A threshold value is computed from the PROPORTION= value under the assumption that the observations are sampled from a multivariate normal distribution.

SINGULAR=g

SING=g

specifies a singularity criterion $0<g<1$ for the total-sample covariance matrix **S** and the approximate within-cluster covariance estimate **A**. The default is SINGULAR=1E−4.

THRESHOLD=t

T=t

specifies the threshold for including pairs of observations in the estimation of the within-cluster covariance matrix. A pair of observations is included if the Euclidean distance between them is less than or equal to t times the root-mean-square distance computed over all pairs of observations.

Canonical Analysis Options

N=n

specifies the number of canonical variables to be computed. The default is the number of variables analyzed. N=0 suppresses the canonical analysis.

PREFIX=$name$

specifies a prefix for naming the canonical variables. By default the names are CAN1, CAN2, . . . , CANn. If PREFIX=ABC is specified, the variables are named ABC1, ABC2, ABC3, and so on. The number of characters in the prefix plus the number of digits required to designate the variables should not exceed eight.

Printed Output Options

NOPRINT

suppresses the printout.

PP

requests a PP probability plot of distances between pairs of observations computed in the last iteration.

QQ

requests a QQ probability plot of a power transformation of the distances between pairs of observations computed in the last iteration. Warning: the QQ plot may require an enormous amount of computer time.

SHORT

omits all items from the standard printout except for the iteration history and the eigenvalue table.

Metric Option

The last option, METRIC=, is rather technical. It affects the computations in a variety of ways, but for well-conditioned data the effects are subtle. For most data sets, the METRIC= option is not needed.

METRIC=FULL | F

METRIC=DIAGONAL | D

METRIC=IDENTITY | I

specifies the metric in which the computations are performed, implies the default value for the INITIAL= option, and specifies the matrix **Z** used in the formula for the convergence measure e_i and for checking singularity of the **A** matrix. METRIC=FULL uses the total-sample covariance matrix **S** and sets $\mathbf{Z}=\mathbf{S}^{-1/2}$, where the superscript $-1/2$ indicates an inverse factor. METRIC=DIAGONAL uses the diagonal matrix of sample variances diag(**S**) and sets $\mathbf{Z}=\text{diag}(\mathbf{S})^{-1/2}$. METRIC=IDENTITY uses the identity matrix **I** and sets $\mathbf{Z}=\mathbf{I}$. If METRIC= is not specified, METRIC=FULL is used if there are enough observations to obtain a nonsingular total-sample covariance matrix; otherwise, METRIC=DIAGONAL is used.

BY Statement

BY *variables*;

A BY statement can be used with PROC ACECLUS to obtain separate analyses on observations in groups defined by the BY variables. When a BY statement appears, the procedure expects the input data set to be sorted in the order of the BY variables.

If your input data set is not sorted in ascending order, use the SORT procedure with a similar BY statement to sort the data, or, if appropriate, use the BY statement options NOTSORTED or DESCENDING. For more information, see the discussion of the BY statement in "SAS Statements Used in the PROC Step" in the *SAS Language Guide, Release 6.03 Edition*.

If you specify the INITIAL=INPUT= option and the INITIAL=INPUT= data set does not contain any of the BY variables, the entire INITIAL=INPUT= data set provides the initial value for **A** for each BY group in the DATA= data set.

If the INITIAL=INPUT= data set contains some but not all of the BY variables, or if some BY variables do not have the same type or length in the INITIAL=INPUT= data set as in the DATA= data set, then PROC ACECLUS prints an error message and stops.

If all the BY variables appear in the INITIAL=INPUT= data set with the same type and length as in the DATA= data set, then each BY group in the INITIAL=INPUT= data set provides the initial value for **A** for the corresponding BY group in the DATA= data set. The BY groups in the INITIAL=INPUT= data set must be in the same order as in the DATA= data set. If you specify NOTSORTED in the BY statement, identical BY groups must occur in the same order in both data sets. If you do not specify NOTSORTED, some BY groups can appear in one data set but not in the other.

FREQ Statement

FREQ *variable*;

If a variable in your data set represents the frequency of occurrence for the observation, include the name of that variable in a FREQ statement. The procedure then treats the data set as if each observation appears *n* times, where *n* is the value of the FREQ variable for the observation. If a value of the FREQ variable is not integral, it is truncated to the largest integer not exceeding the given value. Observations with FREQ values less than one are not included in the analysis. The total number of observations is considered equal to the sum of the FREQ variable.

VAR Statement

VAR *variables*;

The VAR statement lists the numeric variables to be analyzed. If the VAR statement is omitted, all numeric variables not specified in other statements are analyzed.

WEIGHT Statement

WEIGHT *variable*;

If you want to use relative weights for each observation in the input data set, place the weights in a variable in the data set and specify that variable name in a WEIGHT statement. This is often done when the variance associated with each observation is different and the values of the weight variable are proportional to the reciprocals of the variances. The values of the WEIGHT variable can be nonintegral and are not truncated. An observation is used in the analysis only if the value of the WEIGHT variable is greater than zero.

The WEIGHT and FREQ statements have a similar effect, except in calculating the divisor of the **A** matrix.

DETAILS

Missing Values

Observations with missing values are omitted from the analysis and are given missing values for canonical variable scores in the OUT= data set.

Output Data Sets

OUT= Data Set

The OUT= data set contains all the variables in the original data set plus new variables containing the canonical variable scores. The N= option determines the number of new variables. The names of the new variables are formed by concatenating the value given by the PREFIX= option (or the prefix CAN if PREFIX= is not specified) and the numbers 1, 2, 3, and so on.

The OUT= data set can be used as input to PROC CLUSTER or PROC FASTCLUS. The cluster analysis should be performed on the canonical variables, not on the original variables.

OUTSTAT= Data Set

The OUTSTAT= data set is a TYPE=ACE data set containing the following variables:

- the BY variables, if any
- the two new character variables, _TYPE_ and _NAME_
- the variables analyzed, that is, those in the VAR statement, or, if there is no VAR statement, all numeric variables not listed in any other statement.

Each observation in the new data set contains some type of statistic as indicated by the _TYPE_ variable. The values of the _TYPE_ variable are as follows:

TYPE	Contents
MEAN	mean of each variable.
STD	standard deviation of each variable.
N	number of observations on which the analysis is based. This value is the same for each variable.
SUMWGT	sum of the weights if a WEIGHT statement is used. This value is the same for each variable.

COV covariances between each variable and the variable named by the _NAME_ variable. The number of observations with _TYPE_=COV is equal to the number of variables being analyzed.

ACE estimated within-cluster covariances between each variable and the variable named by the _NAME_ variable. The number of observations with _TYPE_=ACE is equal to the number of variables being analyzed.

EIGENVAL eigenvalues of INV(ACE)*(COV−ACE). If the N= option requests fewer than the maximum number of canonical variables, only the specified number of eigenvalues are produced, with missing values filling out the observation.

SCORE eigenvectors. The _NAME_ variable contains the name of the corresponding canonical variable as constructed from the PREFIX= option. The number of observations with _TYPE_=SCORE equals the number of canonical variables computed.

The OUTSTAT= data set can be used

- to initialize another execution of PROC ACECLUS
- to compute canonical variable scores with the SCORE procedure
- as input to the FACTOR procedure, specifying METHOD=SCORE, to rotate the canonical variables.

Computational Resources

Let

n = number of observations
v = number of variables
i = number of iterations.

The time required by PROC ACECLUS is roughly proportional to

$$2nv^2 + 10v^3 + i(n^2v/2 + nv^2 + 5v^3) \ .$$

The array storage required is roughly $8(2n(v+1)+4v^2)$ bytes.

Printed Output

Unless the SHORT option is specified, the ACECLUS procedure prints the following items:

1. Means and Standard Deviations of the input variables
2. the **S** matrix, labeled COV: Total Sample Covariances
3. the name or value of the matrix used for the Initial Within-Cluster Covariance Estimate
4. the Threshold value if the PROPORTION= option is specified.

For each iteration, PROC ACECLUS prints

5. the Iteration number
6. RMS Distance, the root-mean-square distance between all pairs of observations

7. the Distance Cutoff (u) for including pairs of observations in the estimate of the within-cluster covariances, which equals the RMS distance times the threshold
8. the number of Pairs Within Cutoff
9. the Convergence Measure (e_i) as specified by the METRIC= option.

If the SHORT option is not specified, PROC ACECLUS also prints

10. the **A** matrix, labeled ACE: Approximate Covariance Estimate Within Clusters.

The ACECLUS procedure prints a table of eigenvalues from the canonical analysis containing the following items:

11. Eigenvalues of Inv(ACE)*(COV−ACE)
12. the Difference between successive eigenvalues
13. the Proportion of variance explained by each eigenvalue
14. the Cumulative proportion of variance explained.

If the SHORT option is not specified, PROC ACECLUS prints

15. the Eigenvectors or raw canonical coefficients.

EXAMPLE

Transformation and Cluster Analysis of Fisher Iris Data

The iris data published by Fisher (1936) have been widely used for examples in discriminant analysis and cluster analysis. The sepal length, sepal width, petal length, and petal width were measured in millimeters on fifty iris specimens from each of three species, *Iris setosa, I. versicolor,* and *I. virginica.* Mezzich and Solomon (1980) discuss a variety of cluster analyses of the iris data.

In this example PROC ACECLUS is used to transform the data, and the clustering is performed by PROC FASTCLUS. Compare this with the example in the documentation for PROC FASTCLUS. The following statements produce **Output 10.1** through **10.4**:

```
data iris;
    title 'Fisher (1936) Iris Data';
    input sepallen sepalwid petallen petalwid spec_no aa;
    if spec_no=1 then species='Setosa    ';
    else if spec_no=2 then species='Versicolor';
    else species='Virginica ';
    label sepallen='Sepal length in mm.'
          sepalwid='Sepal width  in mm.'
          petallen='Petal length in mm.'
          petalwid='Petal width  in mm.';
    cards;
50 33 14 02 1 64 28 56 22 3 65 28 46 15 2 67 31 56 24 3
63 28 51 15 3 46 34 14 03 1 69 31 51 23 3 62 22 45 15 2
59 32 48 18 2 46 36 10 02 1 61 30 46 14 2 60 27 51 16 2
65 30 52 20 3 56 25 39 11 2 65 30 55 18 3 58 27 51 19 3
68 32 59 23 3 51 33 17 05 1 57 28 45 13 2 62 34 54 23 3
77 38 67 22 3 63 33 47 16 2 67 33 57 25 3 76 30 66 21 3
49 25 45 17 3 55 35 13 02 1 67 30 52 23 3 70 32 47 14 2
64 32 45 15 2 61 28 40 13 2 48 31 16 02 1 59 30 51 18 3
55 24 38 11 2 63 25 50 19 3 64 32 53 23 3 52 34 14 02 1
49 36 14 01 1 54 30 45 15 2 79 38 64 20 3 44 32 13 02 1
```

```
67 33 57 21 3 50 35 16 06 1 58 26 40 12 2 44 30 13 02 1
77 28 67 20 3 63 27 49 18 3 47 32 16 02 1 55 26 44 12 2
50 23 33 10 2 72 32 60 18 3 48 30 14 03 1 51 38 16 02 1
61 30 49 18 3 48 34 19 02 1 50 30 16 02 1 50 32 12 02 1
61 26 56 14 3 64 28 56 21 3 43 30 11 01 1 58 40 12 02 1
51 38 19 04 1 67 31 44 14 2 62 28 48 18 3 49 30 14 02 1
51 35 14 02 1 56 30 45 15 2 58 27 41 10 2 50 34 16 04 1
46 32 14 02 1 60 29 45 15 2 57 26 35 10 2 57 44 15 04 1
50 36 14 02 1 77 30 61 23 3 63 34 56 24 3 58 27 51 19 3
57 29 42 13 2 72 30 58 16 3 54 34 15 04 1 52 41 15 01 1
71 30 59 21 3 64 31 55 18 3 60 30 48 18 3 63 29 56 18 3
49 24 33 10 2 56 27 42 13 2 57 30 42 12 2 55 42 14 02 1
49 31 15 02 1 77 26 69 23 3 60 22 50 15 3 54 39 17 04 1
66 29 46 13 2 52 27 39 14 2 60 34 45 16 2 50 34 15 02 1
44 29 14 02 1 50 20 35 10 2 55 24 37 10 2 58 27 39 12 2
47 32 13 02 1 46 31 15 02 1 69 32 57 23 3 62 29 43 13 2
74 28 61 19 3 59 30 42 15 2 51 34 15 02 1 50 35 13 03 1
56 28 49 20 3 60 22 40 10 2 73 29 63 18 3 67 25 58 18 3
49 31 15 01 1 67 31 47 15 2 63 23 44 13 2 54 37 15 02 1
56 30 41 13 2 63 25 49 15 2 61 28 47 12 2 64 29 43 13 2
51 25 30 11 2 57 28 41 13 2 65 30 58 22 3 69 31 54 21 3
54 39 13 04 1 51 35 14 03 1 72 36 61 25 3 65 32 51 20 3
61 29 47 14 2 56 29 36 13 2 69 31 49 15 2 64 27 53 19 3
68 30 55 21 3 55 25 40 13 2 48 34 16 02 1 48 30 14 01 1
45 23 13 03 1 57 25 50 20 3 57 38 17 03 1 51 38 15 03 1
55 23 40 13 2 66 30 44 14 2 68 28 48 14 2 54 34 17 02 1
51 37 15 04 1 52 35 15 02 1 58 28 51 24 3 67 30 50 17 2
63 33 60 25 3 53 37 15 02 1
;
proc aceclus data=iris out=ace p=.02;
   var sepallen sepalwid petallen petalwid;
proc plot;
   plot can2*can1=spec_no;
proc fastclus data=ace maxc=3 maxiter=10 conv=0 out=clus;
   var can:;
proc freq;
   tables cluster*species;
run;
```

Output 10.1   Using PROC ACECLUS to Transform Fisher's Iris Data

```
                          Fisher (1936) Iris Data                              1

                  Approximate Covariance Estimation for Cluster Analysis

                    150 Observations    Proportion = 0.02
                      4 Variables       Converge =  0.001
               ❶    Means and Standard Deviations

          Variable            Mean          Std Dev       Label

          SEPALLEN         58.433333        8.280661      Sepal length in mm.
          SEPALWID         30.573333        4.358663      Sepal width  in mm.
          PETALLEN         37.580000       17.652982      Petal length in mm.
          PETALWID         11.993333        7.622377      Petal width  in mm.

                    ❷    COV: Total Sample Covariances

                         SEPALLEN      SEPALWID      PETALLEN      PETALWID

          SEPALLEN       68.56935       -4.2434      127.4315      51.62707
          SEPALWID       -4.2434       18.99794      -32.9656     -12.1639
          PETALLEN      127.4315       -32.9656      311.6278      129.5609
          PETALWID       51.62707      -12.1639      129.5609      58.10063

      ❸   Initial Within-Cluster Covariance Estimate = Full Covariance Matrix

                       ❹    Threshold = 0.334211      ❽
                                     ❼           Pairs         ❾
               ❺           ❻  RMS    Distance     Within      Convergence
            Iteration      Distance   Cutoff      Cutoff       Measure

                  1         2.828     0.945         408        0.465775
                  2        11.905     3.979         559        0.013487
                  3        13.152     4.396         940        0.029499
                  4        13.439     4.491        1506        0.046846
                  5        13.271     4.435        2036        0.046859
                  6        12.591     4.208        2285        0.025027
                  7        12.199     4.077        2366        0.009559
                  8        12.121     4.051        2402        0.003895
                  9        12.064     4.032        2417        0.002051
                 10        12.047     4.026        2429        0.000971

          ❿    ACE: Approximate Covariance Estimate Within Clusters

                         SEPALLEN      SEPALWID      PETALLEN      PETALWID

          SEPALLEN       11.73343      5.475504       4.95389      2.029024
          SEPALWID        5.475504     6.919926       2.421779     1.741252
          PETALLEN        4.95389      2.421779       6.537464     2.353026
          PETALWID        2.029024     1.741252       2.353026     2.051667
```

```
                          Fisher (1936) Iris Data                              2
                ⓫    Eigenvalues of Inv(ACE)*(COV-ACE)

                  Eigenvalue  ⓬ Difference  ⓭ Proportion  ⓮ Cumulative

          CAN1      63.7716      61.1593      0.936720      0.93672
          CAN2       2.6123       1.5561      0.038372      0.97509
          CAN3       1.0562       0.4167      0.015515      0.99061
          CAN4       0.6395         .         0.009394      1.00000
                             ⓯
                          Eigenvectors

                  CAN1        CAN2        CAN3        CAN4

          SEPALLEN  -.012009    -.098074    -.059852     0.402352    Sepal length in mm.
          SEPALWID  -.211068    -.000072     0.402391    -.225993    Sepal width  in mm.
          PETALLEN   0.324705    -.328583     0.110383    -.321069    Petal length in mm.
          PETALWID   0.266239     0.870434    -.085215     0.320286    Petal width  in mm.
```

Output 10.2   Plot of Transformed Iris Data: PROC PLOT

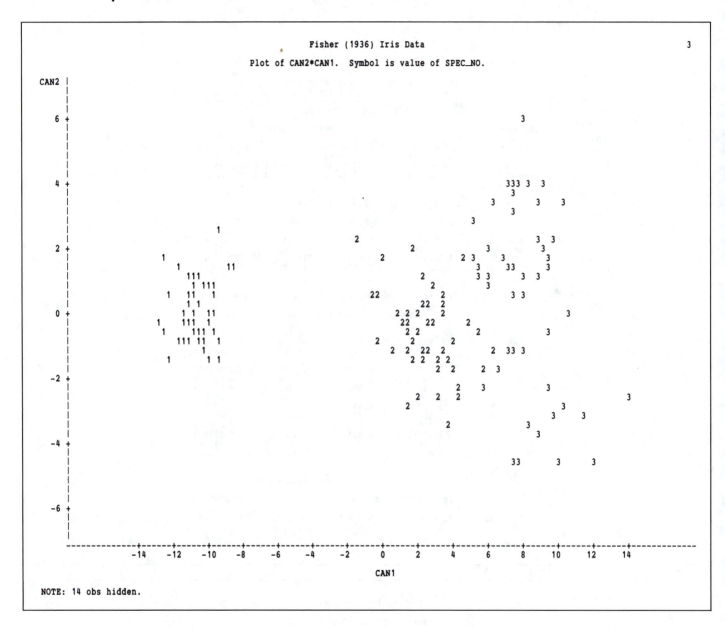

Output 10.3   Clustering of Transformed Iris Data: PROC FASTCLUS

```
                            Fisher (1936) Iris Data                              4

                             FASTCLUS Procedure

              Replace=FULL   Radius=0   Maxclusters=3   Maxiter=10   Converge=0


                                Initial Seeds

              Cluster       CAN1         CAN2         CAN3         CAN4
              ---------------------------------------------------------------
                 1        -12.9510      -0.2516       1.8471       2.7075
                 2         13.8749      -2.5641      -0.4212       1.9412
                 3         -0.3181       0.5975      -2.8784      -0.8496


                  Minimum Distance Between Seeds = 13.97481
```

```
                            Fisher (1936) Iris Data                              5

                  Iteration   Change in Cluster Seeds
                                    1           2           3
                  ---------------------------------------------
                      1     3.808506    5.853134    4.525106
                      2        0        0.695959    0.612287
                      3        0        0.213758    0.206935
                      4        0        0.20397     0.183291
                      5        0        0.067373    0.067414
                      6        0        0.070654    0.068153
                      7        0        0.06426     0.065474
                      8        0        0           0


                                Cluster Summary

                             RMS Std   Maximum Distance from   Nearest    Centroid
       Cluster   Frequency  Deviation   Seed to Observation    Cluster    Distance
       ----------------------------------------------------------------------------
          1         50       1.1016          5.2768              3        13.2845
          2         50       1.8880          6.8298              3         5.8580
          3         50       1.4138          5.3152              2         5.8580


                            Statistics for Variables

          Variable    Total STD    Within STD    R-Squared    RSQ/(1-RSQ)
          ------------------------------------------------------------------
          CAN1        8.048079      1.485370     0.966394      28.756658
          CAN2        1.900612      1.856463     0.058725       0.062389
          CAN3        1.433954      1.325184     0.157417       0.186826
          CAN4        1.280440      1.275497     0.021025       0.021477
          OVER-ALL    4.244987      1.502979     0.876324       7.085666

                         Pseudo F Statistic =    520.80
             Approximate Expected Over-All R-Squared =   0.80391
                      Cubic Clustering Criterion =      5.179
            WARNING: The two above values are invalid for correlated variables.


                                Cluster Means

              Cluster       CAN1         CAN2         CAN3         CAN4
              ---------------------------------------------------------------
                 1        -10.6752       0.0671       0.2707       0.1116
                 2          8.1299       0.5257       0.5184       0.1492
                 3          2.5453      -0.5927      -0.7891      -0.2608

                          Cluster Standard Deviations

              Cluster       CAN1         CAN2         CAN3         CAN4
              ---------------------------------------------------------------
                 1         0.95376       0.93194      1.39846      1.05822
                 2         1.79916       2.74387      1.27034      1.37052
                 3         1.57237       1.39357      1.30341      1.37205
```

Output 10.4   Crosstabulation of Cluster by Species for Fisher's Iris Data:
PROC FREQ

```
                          Fisher (1936) Iris Data                          6

                        TABLE OF CLUSTER BY SPECIES

            CLUSTER      SPECIES

            Frequency|
            Percent  |
            Row Pct  |
            Col Pct  |Setosa  |Versicol|Virginic|
                     |        |or      |a       |   Total
            ---------+--------+--------+--------+
                   1 |     50 |      0 |      0 |     50
                     |  33.33 |   0.00 |   0.00 |  33.33
                     | 100.00 |   0.00 |   0.00 |
                     | 100.00 |   0.00 |   0.00 |
            ---------+--------+--------+--------+
                   2 |      0 |      2 |     48 |     50
                     |   0.00 |   1.33 |  32.00 |  33.33
                     |   0.00 |   4.00 |  96.00 |
                     |   0.00 |   4.00 |  96.00 |
            ---------+--------+--------+--------+
                   3 |      0 |     48 |      2 |     50
                     |   0.00 |  32.00 |   1.33 |  33.33
                     |   0.00 |  96.00 |   4.00 |
                     |   0.00 |  96.00 |   4.00 |
            ---------+--------+--------+--------+
            Total          50       50       50      150
                        33.33    33.33    33.33   100.00
```

REFERENCES

Art, D., Gnanadesikan, R., and Kettenring, R. (1982), "Data-based Metrics for Cluster Analysis," *Utilitas Mathematica*, 21A, 75–99.

Everitt, B.S. (1980), *Cluster Analysis*, 2d Edition, London: Heineman Educational Books Ltd.

Fisher, R.A. (1936), "The Use of Multiple Measurements in Taxonomic Problems," *Annals of Eugenics*, 7, 179–188.

Hartigan, J.A. (1975), *Clustering Algorithms*, New York: John Wiley & Sons, Inc.

Mezzich, J.E and Solomon, H. (1980), *Taxonomy and Behavioral Science*, New York: Academic Press, Inc.

Puri, M.L. and Sen, P.K. (1971), *Nonparametric Methods in Multivariate Analysis*, New York: John Wiley & Sons, Inc.

Wolfe, J.H. (1970), "Pattern Clustering by Multivariate Mixture Analysis," *Multivariate Behavioral Research*, 5, 329–350.

Chapter 11
The ANOVA Procedure

ABSTRACT

The ANOVA procedure performs analysis of variance for balanced data from a wide variety of experimental designs.

INTRODUCTION

The ANOVA procedure is one of several procedures available in SAS/STAT software for *analysis of variance*, which is a technique for analyzing experimental data. A continuous response variable, known as a *dependent variable*, is measured under experimental conditions identified by classification variables, known as *independent variables*. The variation in the response is explained as being due to effects in the classification with random error accounting for the remaining variation. Fisher (1942) is the pioneering work.

The ANOVA procedure is designed to handle balanced data (that is, data with equal numbers of observations for every combination of the classification factors), whereas the GLM procedure can analyze both balanced and unbalanced data. Because ANOVA takes into account the special structure of a balanced design, it is faster and uses less storage than GLM for balanced data.

Use PROC ANOVA for the analysis of balanced data only, with the exceptions of Latin square designs, certain balanced incomplete blocks designs, completely nested (hierarchical) designs, and designs whose cell frequencies are proportional to each other and are also proportional to the background population. For further discussion, see Searle (1971, 138).

PROC ANOVA checks to see if your design is balanced. If it is not and your design is not one of the special cases described above, then your design is unbalanced and should be analyzed using PROC GLM. In either case, ANOVA prints a warning message to tell you the design is unbalanced, and the ANOVA analyses may not be valid. If you use ANOVA for analysis of unbalanced data, you must assume responsibility for the validity of the output.

Using PROC ANOVA Interactively

PROC ANOVA can be used interactively. After specifying a model with a MODEL statement and running ANOVA with a RUN statement, a variety of statements (such as MEANS, MANOVA, TEST, and REPEATED) can be executed without ANOVA recalculating the model sum of squares.

The **SPECIFICATIONS** section describes which statements may be used interactively. These interactive statements may be executed singly or in groups by following the single statement or group of statements with a RUN statement. Note that the MODEL statement cannot be repeated; ANOVA allows only one MODEL statement.

If you use ANOVA interactively, you can end the ANOVA procedure with a DATA step, another PROC step, an ENDSAS statement, or with a QUIT statement. The syntax of the QUIT statement is

```
quit;
```

When you are using ANOVA interactively, additional RUN statements do not end the procedure, but tell ANOVA to execute additional statements.

When a BY statement is used with PROC ANOVA, interactive processing is not possible; that is, once the first RUN statement is encountered, processing proceeds for each BY group in the data set, and no further statements are accepted by the procedure.

Specification of Effects

In SAS analysis-of-variance procedures, the variables that identify levels of the classifications are called *classification variables* and are declared in the CLASS statement. Classification variables can also be called *categorical*, *qualitative*, *discrete*, or *nominal variables*. The values of a class variable are called *levels*. Class variables can be either numeric or character. This is in contrast to the *response* (or *dependent*) *variables*, which are continuous. Response variables must be numeric.

The analysis-of-variance model specifies *effects*, which are combinations of classification variables used to explain the variability of the dependent variables in the following manner:

- Main effects are specified by writing the variables by themselves: A B C. Main effects used as independent variables test the hypothesis that the mean of the dependent variable is the same for each level of the factor in question, ignoring the other independent variables in the model.
- Crossed effects (interactions) are specified by joining the class variables with asterisks: A*B A*C A*B*C. Interaction terms in a model test the hypothesis that the effect of a factor does not depend on the levels of the other factors in the interaction.
- Nested effects are specified by following a main effect or crossed effect with a class variable or list of class variables enclosed in parentheses. The main effect or crossed effect is nested within the effects listed in parentheses: B(A) C*D(A B). Nested effects test hypotheses similar to interactions, but the levels of the nested variables are not the same for every combination within which they are nested.

The general form of an effect can be illustrated using the class variables A,B,C,D,E, and F:

   A*B*C(D E F)   .

The crossed list should come first, followed by the nested list in parentheses. Note that no asterisks appear within the nested list or immediately before the left parenthesis.

Main Effects Models

For a three-factor main effects model with A, B, and C as the factors and Y as the dependent variable, the necessary statements are

```
proc anova;
   class a b c;
   model y=a b c;
```

Models with Crossed Factors

To specify interactions in a factorial model, join effects with asterisks as described above. For example, these statements specify a complete factorial model, which includes all the interactions:

```
proc anova;
   class a b c;
   model y=a b c a*b a*c b*c a*b*c;
```

Bar Notation

You can shorten the specifications of a full factorial model by using bar notation. For example, the statements above can also be written

```
proc anova;
   class a b c;
   model y=a|b|c;
```

When the bar (|) is used, the expression on the right side of the equal sign is expanded from left to right using the equivalents of rules 2–4 given in Searle (1971, 390). In addition, you can specify the maximum number of variables involved in any effect that results from bar evaluation by specifying that maximum number, preceded by an @ sign, at the end of the bar effect. For example, the specification A | B | C@2 would result in only those effects which contain 2 or fewer variables; in this case A B A*B C A*C and B*C. Other examples of the bar notation are

A	C(B)	is equivalent to	A C(B) A*C(B)
A(B)	C(B)	is equivalent to	A(B) C(B) A*C(B)
A(B)	B(DE)	is equivalent to	A(B) B(D E)
A	B(A)	C	is equivalent to	A B(A) C A*C B*C(A)
A	B(A)	C@2	is equivalent to	A B(A) C A*C
A	B	C	D@2	is equivalent to	A B A*B C A*C B*C D A*D B*D C*D

Consult the description of the GLM procedure for further details on bar notation.

Nested Models

Write the effect that is nested within another effect first, followed by the other effect in parentheses. For example, if A and B are main effects and C is nested within A and B (that is, the levels of C that were observed were not the same for each combination of A and B), the statements for PROC ANOVA are

```
proc anova;
   class a b c;
   model y=a b c(a b);
```

The identity of a level is viewed within the context of the level of the containing effects. For example, if CITY is nested within STATE, then the identity of CITY is viewed within the context of STATE.

The distinguishing feature of a nested specification is that nested effects never appear as main effects. Another way of viewing nested effects is that they are effects that pool the main effect with the interaction of the nesting variable. See **Automatic Pooling** below.

Models Involving Nested, Crossed, and Main Effects

Asterisks and parentheses can be combined in the MODEL statement for models involving nested and crossed effects:

```
proc anova;
   class a b c;
   model y=a b(a) c(a) b*c(a);
```

Automatic Pooling

In line with the general philosophy of the GLM procedure, there is no difference between the statements

```
model y=a b(a);
```

and

```
model y=a a*b;
```

The effect B becomes a nested effect by virtue of the fact that it does not occur as a main effect. If B is not written as a main effect in addition to participating in A*B, then the sum of squares that would be associated with B is pooled into A*B.

This feature allows the automatic pooling of sums of squares. If an effect is omitted from the model, it is automatically pooled with all the higher-level effects containing the class variables in the omitted effect (or within-error). This feature is most useful in split-plot designs.

SPECIFICATIONS

These statements are available in PROC ANOVA:

PROC ANOVA *options*; }   required statement

CLASS *variables*; }   must precede the **MODEL** statement
                                                           and is a required statement

MODEL *dependents*=*effects* / *options*; }   required statement

ABSORB *variables*;   must appear before
BY *variables*;   the first **RUN** statement
FREQ *variable*;

MANOVA H=*effects* **E**=*effect*
    M=*equations* . . . **MNAMES**=*names*   can appear
      PREFIX=*name* / *options*;   anywhere after
MEANS *effects* / *options*;   the **MODEL** statement
REPEATED *factorname levels(levelvalues)*   and can be used
      transformation[, . . .] / *options*;   interactively
TEST H=*effects* **E**=*effect*;

The PROC ANOVA, CLASS, and MODEL statements are required and must precede the first RUN statement. The CLASS statement must precede the MODEL statement. If ABSORB, FREQ, or BY statements are used, they must precede the first RUN statement. MANOVA, MEANS, REPEATED, and TEST statements, if used, must follow the MODEL statement and can be specified in any order. These four statements can appear after the first RUN statement.

The statements used with the PROC ANOVA statement are the following (in alphabetical order):

ABSORB	absorbs classification effects in a model.
BY	processes BY groups.
CLASS	declares classification variables.
FREQ	specifies a frequency variable.
MANOVA	performs a multivariate analysis of variance.
MEANS	requests that means be printed and compared.
MODEL	defines the model to be fit.

REPEATED   performs multivariate and univariate repeated measures analysis of variance.

TEST   constructs tests using the sums of squares for effects and the error term you specify.

PROC ANOVA Statement

PROC ANOVA *options*;

The following options can be specified in the PROC ANOVA statement:

DATA=*SASdataset*
names the SAS data set to be analyzed by PROC ANOVA. If the DATA= option is omitted, ANOVA uses the most recently created SAS data set.

MANOVA
requests that PROC ANOVA use the multivariate mode of eliminating observations with missing values, that is, to eliminate an observation from the analysis if any of the dependent variables have missing values. This option is useful if you are using PROC ANOVA in interactive mode and will be performing a multivariate analysis.

MULTIPASS
requests that PROC ANOVA reread the input data set when necessary instead of writing the values of dependent variables to a utility file. This option decreases disk space usage. This option is only useful in rare situations and generally increases the execution time of the program.

OUTSTAT=*SASdataset*
names an output data set that will contain sums of squares, F statistics, and probability levels for each effect in the model. If the CANONICAL option of the MANOVA statement is used and there is no M= specification, the data set also contains results of the canonical analysis.

ABSORB Statement

ABSORB *variables*;

The technique of absorption, requested by the ABSORB statement, saves time and reduces storage requirements for certain types of models. The analysis of variance is adjusted for the absorbed effects. See the **Absorption** section in the chapter on the GLM procedure for more information.

Restrictions: when you use the ABSORB statement, the data set (or each BY group, if a BY statement appears) must be sorted by the variables in the ABSORB statement. Including an absorbed variable in the CLASS list or in the MODEL statement may produce erroneous sums of squares. The ABSORB statement, if used, must appear before the first RUN statement, or it is ignored.

BY Statement

BY *variables*;

A BY statement can be used with PROC ANOVA to obtain separate analyses on observations in groups defined by the BY variables. When a BY statement appears, the procedure expects the input data set to be sorted in order of the BY variables.

If your input data set is not sorted in ascending order, use the SORT procedure with a similar BY statement to sort the data, or, if appropriate, use the BY statement options NOTSORTED or DESCENDING. For more information, see the discussion of the BY statement in "SAS Statements Used in the PROC Step" in the *SAS Language Guide, Release 6.03 Edition.*

When both a BY and an ABSORB statement are used, observations must be sorted first by the variables in the BY statement and then by the variables in the ABSORB statement.

The BY statement, if used, must appear before the first RUN statement, or it is ignored. When you use a BY statement, the interactive features of PROC ANOVA are disabled.

CLASS Statement

CLASS *variables*;

Any variables used as classification variables in ANOVA must be declared first in the CLASS (or CLASSES) statement to identify the groups for the analysis. Typical classification variables are TRT, SEX, RACE, GROUP, and REP. They can be either numeric or character variables, but a character variable used in a CLASS statement cannot have a length greater than sixteen characters. The CLASS statement is required and must appear before the MODEL statement.

FREQ Statement

FREQ *variable*;

When a FREQ (or FREQUENCY) statement appears, each observation in the input data set is assumed to represent *n* observations in the experiment. For each observation, *n* is the value of the variable specified in the FREQ statement.

If the value of the FREQ variable is less than 1, the observation is not used in the analysis. If the value is not an integer, only the integer portion is used.

The analysis produced using a FREQ statement is identical to an analysis produced using a data set that contains *n* observations (where *n* is the value of the FREQ variable) in place of each observation of the input data set. Therefore, means and total degrees of freedom reflect the expanded number of observations.

If the FREQ statement is used, it must appear before the first RUN statement, or it is ignored.

MANOVA Statement

MANOVA H=*effects* E=*effect* M=*equation1,equation2, . . .*
         MNAMES=*list of names* PREFIX=*name* / *options*;

If the MODEL statement includes more than one dependent variable, additional multivariate statistics can be requested with the MANOVA statement.

When a MANOVA statement appears before the first RUN statement, ANOVA enters a multivariate mode with respect to the handling of missing values. Observations with missing independent or dependent variables are excluded from the analysis. If you have several dependent variables and want to use this mode of handling missing values, specify the MANOVA option in the PROC ANOVA statement.

The terms below are specified in the MANOVA statement:

H=*effects*   specifies effects in the preceding model to use as hypothesis matrices. For each **H** matrix (the SSCP matrix associated with that effect), the H= option prints the characteristic roots and vectors of $E^{-1}H$ (where **E** is the matrix associated with the error effect), Hotelling-Lawley trace, Pillai's trace, Wilks' criterion, and Roy's maximum root criterion with approximate *F* statistics. Use the keyword INTERCEPT to print tests for the intercept. To print tests for all effects listed in the MODEL statement, use the keyword _ALL_ in place of a list of effects. For background and further details, see the section **Multivariate Analysis of Variance** in the chapter on the GLM procedure.

E=*effect*   specifies the error effect. If E= is omitted, the error SSCP (residual) matrix from the analysis is used.

M=*equation1, equation2, . . .*
M= (*listofnumbers, . . .*)

specifies a transformation matrix for the dependent variables listed in the MODEL statement. The equations in the M= specification are of the form

$$\pm\ term\ [\pm term \ldots]$$

where *term* is either *dependentvariable* or *number*dependentvariable* and brackets indicate optional specifications. Alternatively, the transformation matrix can be input directly by entering the elements of the matrix with commas separating the rows and surrounding the entire specification with parentheses. When this alternate form of input is used, the number of elements in each row must equal the number of dependent variables. Although these combinations actually represent the columns of the **M** matrix, they are printed by rows. Examples of both types of equation specifications are shown after the options below.

When an M= specification is included, the analysis requested in the MANOVA statement is carried out for the variables defined by the equations in the specification, not the original dependent variables. Without an M= specification, the analysis is performed for the original dependent variables in the MODEL statement. Examples of the use of the M= specification are given below. For further information, see the section **Multivariate Analysis of Variance** in the chapter describing the GLM procedure.

If an M= specification is included without either the MNAMES= or PREFIX= options, the variables are labeled MVAR1, MVAR2, and so forth by default.

The following two terms allow you to specify labels for the transformed variables defined by the M= option:

MNAMES=*list of names*

provides names for the variables defined by the equations in the M= specification. Names in the list correspond to the M= equations.

PREFIX=*name*   is an alternative means of identifying the transformed variables defined by the M= specification. For example, if PREFIX=DIFF is specified, the transformed variables are labeled DIFF1, DIFF2, and so forth.

The options below can appear in the MANOVA statement after a slash (/):

CANONICAL

requests that a canonical analysis of the **H** and **E** matrices (transformed by the **M** matrix, if specified) be printed instead of the default printout of characteristic roots and vectors.

ORTH

requests that the transformation matrix in the M= specification of the MANOVA statement be orthonormalized by rows before the analysis.

PRINTE

requests printing of the **E** matrix. If the **E** matrix is the error SSCP (residual) matrix from the analysis, the partial correlations of the dependent variables given the independent variables are also printed.
For example, the statement

```
manova / printe;
```

prints the error SSCP matrix and the partial correlation matrix computed from the error SSCP matrix.

PRINTH

requests that the **H** matrix (the SSCP matrix) associated with each effect specified by the H= specification be printed.

SUMMARY

produces analysis-of-variance tables for each dependent variable. When no **M** matrix is specified, a table is printed for each original dependent variable from the MODEL statement; with an **M** matrix other than the identity, a table is printed for each transformed variable defined by the **M** matrix.

Here is an example:

```
proc anova;
   class a b;
   model y1-y5=a b(a);
   manova h=a e=b(a) / printh printe;
   manova h=b(a) / printe;
   manova h=a e=b(a) m=y1-y2,y2-y3,y3-y4,y4-y5
           prefix=diff;
   manova h=a e=b(a) m=(1 -1  0  0  0,
                        0  1 -1  0  0,
                        0  0  1 -1  0,
                        0  0  0  1 -1) prefix=diff;
```

The first MANOVA statement specifies A as the hypothesis effect and B(A) as the error effect. The PRINTH option requests that the **H** matrix associated with the A effect be printed, and the PRINTE option requests that the **E** matrix associated with the B(A) effect be printed.

The second MANOVA statement specifies B(A) as the hypothesis effect. Since no error effect is specified, PROC ANOVA uses the error SSCP matrix from the analysis as the **E** matrix. The PRINTE option requests that this **E** matrix be printed. Since the **E** matrix is the error SSCP matrix from the analysis, the partial correlation matrix computed from this matrix is also printed.

The third MANOVA statement requests the same analysis as the first MANOVA statement, but the analysis is carried out for variables transformed to be successive differences between the original dependent variables. The PREFIX=DIFF option specifies that the transformed variables be labeled as DIFF1, DIFF2, DIFF3, and DIFF4.

The fourth MANOVA statement has exactly the same effect as the third but uses the alternative form of specifying the M matrix.

As a second example of the use of the M= specification, consider the following:

```
proc anova;
   class group;
   model dose1-dose4=group;
   manova h=group m=-3*dose1-dose2+dose3+3*dose4,
                   dose1-dose2-dose3+dose4,
                   -dose1+3*dose2-3*dose3+dose4;
   mnames=linear quadrtic cubic / printe;
```

The M= specification gives a transformation of the dependent variables DOSE1 through DOSE4 into orthogonal polynomial components, and the MNAMES= option labels the transformed variables as LINEAR, QUADRTIC, and CUBIC, respectively. Since the PRINTE option is specified and the default residual matrix is used as an error term, the partial correlation matrix of the orthogonal polynomial components is also printed.

MEANS Statement

MEANS *effects / options;*

ANOVA can compute means of the dependent variables for any effect that appears on the right-hand side of the MODEL statement. You can use any number of MEANS statements, provided they appear after the MODEL statement. For example, if you specify

```
proc anova;
   class a b c;
   model y=a b c a*b;
   means a b c a*b;
```

means and standard deviations are printed for each level of the variables A, B, and C and for the combined levels of A and B. If you specify

```
proc anova;
   class a b;
   model y=a b a*b;
   means a*b;
```

means and standard deviations are printed for each of the combined levels of A and B.

The options below can appear in the MEANS statement after a slash (/). For a further discussion of these options, see **Comparisons of Means** in the chapter describing the GLM procedure.

Options to Select a Multiple Comparison Procedure

BON
   performs Bonferroni *t* tests of differences between means for all main effect means in the MEANS statement.

DUNCAN
   performs Duncan's multiple-range test on all main effect means given in the MEANS statement.

DUNNETT [(*formattedcontrolvalues*)]

performs Dunnett's two-tailed *t* test, testing if any treatments are significantly different from a single control for all main effects means in the MEANS statement.

To specify which level of the effect is the control, enclose its quoted formatted value in parentheses after the keyword. If more than one effect is specified in the MEANS statement, you can use a list of control values within the parentheses. By default, the first level of the effect is used as the control. For example,

```
means a / dunnett('CONTROL');
```

where CONTROL is the formatted control value of A. As another example,

```
means a b c / dunnett('CNTLA' 'CNTLB' 'CNTLC');
```

where CNTLA, CNTLB, and CNTLC are the formatted control values for A, B, and C, respectively.

DUNNETTL [(*formattedcontrolvalue*)]

performs Dunnett's one-tailed *t* test, testing if any treatment is significantly smaller than the control. Control level information is specified as described above for the DUNNETT option.

DUNNETTU [(*formattedcontrolvalue*)]

performs Dunnett's one-tailed *t* test, testing if any treatment is significantly larger than the control. Control level information is specified as described above for the DUNNETT option.

GABRIEL

performs Gabriel's multiple-comparison procedure on all main effect means in the MEANS statement.

REGWF

performs the Ryan-Einot-Gabriel-Welsch multiple *F* test on all main effect means in the MEANS statement.

REGWQ

performs the Ryan-Einot-Gabriel-Welsch multiple-range test on all main effect means in the MEANS statement.

SCHEFFE

performs Scheffe's multiple-comparison procedure on all main effect means in the MEANS statement.

SIDAK

performs pairwise *t* tests on differences between means with levels adjusted according to Sidak's inequality for all main effect means in the MEANS statement.

SMM
GT2

performs pairwise comparisons based on the studentized maximum modulus and Sidak's uncorrelated-*t* inequality, yielding Hochberg's GT2 method when sample sizes are unequal, for all main effect means in the MEANS statement.

SNK

performs the Student-Newman-Keuls multiple range test on all main effect means in the MEANS statement.

T

LSD

> performs pairwise *t* tests, equivalent to Fisher's least-significant-difference test in the case of equal cell sizes, for all main effect means in the MEANS statement.

TUKEY

> performs Tukey's studentized range test (HSD) on all main effect means in the MEANS statement.

WALLER

> requests that the Waller-Duncan *k*-ratio *t* test be performed on all main effect means in the MEANS statement. See the KRATIO= option below.

Options to Specify Details for Multiple Comparison Procedures

ALPHA=*p*

> gives the level of significance for comparisons among the means. The default ALPHA= value is 0.05. With the DUNCAN option, you may only specify values of 0.01, 0.05, or 0.1. For other options, you may use values between 0.0001 and 0.9999.

CLDIFF

> requests that the results of the BON, GABRIEL, SCHEFFE, SIDAK, SMM, GT2, T, LSD, and TUKEY options be presented as confidence intervals for all pairwise differences between means. CLDIFF is the default for unequal cell sizes unless DUNCAN, REGWF, REGWQ, SNK, or WALLER is specified.

CLM

> requests that the results of the BON, GABRIEL, SCHEFFE, SIDAK, SMM, T, and LSD options be presented as confidence intervals for the mean of each level of the variables specified in the MEANS statement.

E=*effect*

> specifies the error mean square to use in the multiple comparisons. If the E= option is omitted, PROC ANOVA uses the residual MS. The effect specified with the E= option must be a term in the model; otherwise, ANOVA uses the residual MS.

KRATIO=*value*

> gives the type1/type2 error seriousness ratio for the Waller-Duncan test. Reasonable values for KRATIO are 50, 100, 500, which roughly correspond for the two-level case to ALPHA levels of 0.1, 0.05, and 0.01. If the KRATIO= option is omitted, the procedure uses the default value of 100.

LINES

> requests that the results of the BON, DUNCAN, GABRIEL, REGWF, REGWQ, SCHEFFE, SIDAK, SMM, GT2, SNK, T, LSD, TUKEY, and WALLER options be presented by listing the means in descending order and indicating nonsignificant subsets by line segments beside the corresponding means. The LINES option is appropriate for equal cell sizes, for which it is the default. LINES is also the default if DUNCAN, REGWF, REGWQ, SNK, or WALLER is specified, or if there are only two cells of unequal size. If the cell sizes are unequal, the harmonic mean is used, which may lead to somewhat liberal tests if the cell sizes are highly disparate. The LINES option cannot be used in combination with the DUNNETT, DUNNETTL, or DUNNETTU options.

NOSORT
>   prevents the means from being sorted into descending order when
>   CLDIFF or CLM is specified.

MODEL Statement

>   MODEL *dependents*=*effects* / *options*;

The MODEL statement names the dependent variables and independent effects. The syntax of effects is described in **Specification of Effects** earlier in this chapter. If no effects are specified, ANOVA fits only the intercept, which tests the hypothesis that the mean of the dependent variable is zero.

The options listed below can be specified in the MODEL statement and must be separated from the list of independent effects by a slash (/):

INT
INTERCEPT
>   requests that ANOVA print the hypothesis tests associated with the
>   intercept as an effect in the model. PROC ANOVA always includes the
>   intercept in the model, but by default, it does not print associated tests
>   of hypotheses.

NOUNI
>   requests that ANOVA not print the univariate analyses that are produced
>   by default. Use NOUNI when you want only the multivariate statistics
>   produced by a MANOVA statement or when you are using the
>   REPEATED statement and are not interested in the original dependent
>   variables in the MODEL statement.

REPEATED Statement

>   REPEATED *factorname levels (levelvalues) transformation* [, . . .] / *options*;

When values of the dependent variables in the MODEL statement represent repeated measurements on the same experimental unit, the REPEATED statement allows you to test hypotheses about the measurement factors (often called *within-subject factors*), as well as the interactions of within-subject factors with independent variables in the MODEL statement (often called *between-subject factors*). The REPEATED statement provides both multivariate and univariate tests, as well as hypothesis tests for a variety of single-degree-of-freedom contrasts. When more than one within-subject factor is specified, *factornames* (and associated level and transformation information) must be separated by a comma in the REPEATED statement. There is no limit to the number of within-subject factors that can be specified. For more details, see **Repeated Measures Analysis of Variance** in the chapter on the GLM procedure.

When a REPEATED statement appears, the ANOVA procedure enters a multivariate mode of handling missing values. If any values for variables corresponding to each combination of the within-subject factors are missing, the observation is excluded from the analysis.

The terms below are specified in the REPEATED statement:

>   *factorname*   names a factor to be associated with the dependent
>   variables. The name should not be the same as any
>   variable name that already exists in the data set being
>   analyzed and should conform to the usual conventions
>   of SAS variable names.
>
>   *levels*   gives the number of levels associated with the factor
>   being defined. When there is only one within-subjects

factor, the number of levels is equal to the number of dependent variables. In this case, *levels* need not be specified. When more than one within-subject factor is defined, however, *levels* must be specified, and the product of the number of levels of all the factors must equal the number of dependent variables in the MODEL statement.

(levelvalues)   gives values that correspond to levels of a repeated-measures factor. These values are used to label output and as spacings for constructing orthogonal polynomial contrasts. The number of level values specified must correspond to the number of levels for that factor in the REPEATED statement. Note that the level values appear in parentheses.

The following *transformation* keywords define single-degree-of-freedom contrasts for factors specified in the REPEATED statement. Since the number of contrasts generated is always one less than the number of levels of the factor, the transformation you select gives you some control over which contrast is omitted from the analysis. If no transformation keyword is specified, the REPEATED statement uses the CONTRAST transformation.

CONTRAST [(*ordinalreferencelevel*)]

generates contrasts between levels of the factor and, optionally, a reference level that must appear in parentheses. The reference level corresponds to the ordinal value of the level rather than to the level value specified. Without a reference level, the last level is used by default. For example, to generate contrasts between the first level of a factor and the other levels, use

        contrast(1)

POLYNOMIAL   generates orthogonal polynomial contrasts. Level values, if provided, are used as spacings in the construction of the polynomials; otherwise, equal spacing is assumed.

HELMERT   generates contrasts between each level of the factor and the mean of subsequent levels.

MEAN [(*ordinalreferencelevel*)]

generates contrasts between levels of the factor and the mean of all other levels of the factor. Specifying a reference level eliminates the contrast between that level and the mean. Without a reference level, the contrast involving the last level is omitted. The reference level specification must appear in parentheses. See the CONTRAST transformation above for an example.

PROFILE   generates contrasts between adjacent levels of the factor.

The following options can appear in the REPEATED statement after a slash (/):

CANONICAL
    requests a canonical analysis of the **H** and **E** matrices corresponding to the transformed variables specified in the REPEATED statement.

NOM
    prints only the results of the univariate analyses.

NOU
> prints only the results of the multivariate analyses.

PRINTE
> prints the **E** matrix for each combination of within-subject factors, as well as partial correlation matrices for both the original dependent variables and the variables defined by the transformations specified in the REPEATED statement. In addition, the PRINTE option provides sphericity tests for each set of transformed variables. If the requested transformations are not orthogonal, the PRINTE option also provides a sphericity test for a set of orthogonal contrasts.

PRINTH
> prints the **H** (SSCP) matrix associated with each multivariate test.

PRINTM
> prints the transformation matrices that define the contrasts in the analysis. PROC ANOVA always prints the **M** matrix so that the transformed variables are defined by the rows, not the columns, of the **M** matrix on the printout. In other words, ANOVA actually prints **M'**.

PRINTRV
> prints the characteristic roots and vectors for each multivariate test.

SUMMARY
> produces analysis-of-variance tables for each contrast defined by the within-subjects factors. Along with tests for the effects of the independent variables specified in the MODEL statement, a term labeled MEAN tests the hypothesis that the overall mean of the contrast is zero.

When specifying more than one factor, list the dependent variables in the MODEL statement so that the within-subject factors defined in the REPEATED statement are nested. **The first factor defined in the REPEATED statement should be the one with values that change least frequently.** For example, assume three treatments are administered at each of four times, for a total of twelve dependent variables on each experimental unit. If the variables are listed in the MODEL statement as Y1−Y12, then the statement

```
repeated trt 3, time 4;
```

implies the following structure:

DEP VARIABLE	Y1	Y2	Y3	Y4	Y5	Y6	Y7	Y8	Y9	Y10	Y11	Y12
value of TRT	1	1	1	1	2	2	2	2	3	3	3	3
value of TIME	1	2	3	4	1	2	3	4	1	2	3	4

The REPEATED statement always produces a table like the one above.

TEST Statement

> TEST H=*effects* E=*effect;*

Although an *F* value is computed for all SS in the analysis using the residual MS as an error term, you can request additional *F* tests using other effects as error terms. You need this feature when a nonstandard error structure (as in a split plot) exists.

These terms are specified in the TEST statement:

> H=*effects*   specifies the effects in the preceding model to be used as hypothesis (numerator) effects.

E=*effect*   specifies one, and only one, effect to be used as the error (denominator) term. If you use a TEST statement, you must specify an error term with E=, for example,

```
proc anova;
   class a b c;
   model y=a|b(a)|c;
   test h=a e=b(a);
   test h=c a*c e=b*c(a);
```

DETAILS

Missing Values

The dependent variables are grouped based on the similarity of their patterns of missing values among the dependent variables. This feature is also used by GLM to treat missing values.

When a MANOVA or REPEATED statement appears before the first RUN statement, or when the MANOVA option of the PROC ANOVA statement is used, the ANOVA procedure enters a multivariate mode for handling missing values. If any values for dependent or independent variables are missing, the observation is excluded from the analysis.

Output Data Set

The OUTSTAT= option of the PROC ANOVA statement produces an output data set that contains

- the BY variables, if any.
- three new character variables, _TYPE_, _NAME_, and _SOURCE_. The _TYPE_ variable has the value ANOVA for observations corresponding to sums of squares, or CANCORR, STRUCTUR, or SCORE if a canonical analysis is performed through the MANOVA statement and no M= matrix is specified. For each observation in the data set, the _SOURCE_ variable contains the name of the model effect from which the corresponding statistics are generated. The _NAME_ variable contains the name of one of the dependent variables in the model, or in the case of canonical statistics, the name of one of the canonical variables (CAN1, CAN2, and so on).
- three new numeric variables, SS, F, and PROB, containing sums of squares, F values, and probabilities, respectively, for each model or contrast sum of squares generated in the analysis. For observations resulting from canonical analyses, these variables have missing values.

If there is more than one dependent variable, the data set also includes variables with the same name as the dependent variables. These represent the cross-products of the hypothesis matrices (for _TYPE_='ANOVA'), canonical correlations for each variable (for _TYPE_='CANCORR'), coefficients of the total structure matrix (for _TYPE_='STRUCTUR'), or raw canonical score coefficients (for _TYPE_='SCORE').

Use the output data set to perform special hypothesis tests (for example, with SAS/IML software), to reformat output, to produce canonical variates (through PROC SCORE), or to rotate structure matrices (through PROC FACTOR).

Computational Method

Let **X** represent the $n \times p$ design matrix. The columns of **X** contain only 0s and 1s. Let **Y** represent the $n \times 1$ vector of dependent variables.

In the GLM procedure, **X'X**, **X'Y**, and **Y'Y** are formed in main storage. However, in the ANOVA procedure, only the diagonals of **X'X** are computed, along with **X'Y** and **Y'Y**. Thus, ANOVA saves a considerable amount of storage as well as time.

The elements of **X'Y** are cell totals, and the diagonal elements of **X'X** are cell frequencies. Since ANOVA automatically pools omitted effects into the next higher-level effect containing the names of the omitted effect (or within-error), a slight modification to the rules given by Searle (1971, 389) is used.

1. The sum of squares for each effect is computed as if it were a main effect. In other words, for each effect, square each cell total and divide by its cell frequency. Add these quantities together, then subtract the correction factor for the mean (total squared over N).
2. For each effect involving two class names, subtract the SS for any main effect whose name is contained in the two-factor effect.
3. For each effect involving three class names, subtract the SS for all main effects and two-factor effects whose names are contained in the three-factor effect. If effects involving four or more class names are present, continue this process.

Printed Output

PROC ANOVA first prints a table that includes the following:

1. the name of each variable in the CLASS statement
2. the number of different values or Levels of the Class variables
3. the Values of the Class variables
4. the Number of observations in the data set and the number of observations excluded from the analysis because of missing values, if any.

PROC ANOVA then prints an analysis-of-variance table for each dependent variable in the MODEL statement. This table breaks down

5. the Total Sum of Squares for the dependent variable
6. into the portion attributed to the Model
7. and the portion attributed to Error.
8. The Mean Square term is
9. the Sum of Squares divided by
10. the degrees of freedom (DF).

The analysis-of-variance table also lists the following:

11. the Mean Square for Error (MSE), which is an estimate of σ^2, the variance of the true errors.
12. the F Value, which is the ratio produced by dividing the Mean Square for the Model by the Mean Square for Error. It tests how well the model as a whole (adjusted for the mean) accounts for the dependent variable's behavior. This F test is a test of the null hypothesis that all parameters except the intercept are zero.
13. the significance probability associated with the F statistic, labeled $Pr > F$.
14. R-Square, R^2, which measures how much variation in the dependent variable can be accounted for by the model. R^2, which can range from 0 to 1, is the ratio of the sum of squares for the model divided by the sum of squares for the corrected total. In general, the larger the R^2 value, the better the model fits the data.

15. C.V., the coefficient of variation, which is often used to describe the amount of variation in the population. The C.V. is 100 times the standard deviation of the dependent variable divided by the Mean. The coefficient of variation is often a preferred measure because it is unitless.
16. Root MSE, which estimates the standard deviation of the dependent variable. Root MSE is computed as the square root of Mean Square for Error, the mean square of the error term.
17. the Mean of the dependent variable.

For each effect (or source of variation) in the model, PROC ANOVA then prints the following:

18. DF, degrees of freedom
19. Anova SS, the sum of squares
20. the F Value for testing the hypothesis that the group means for that effect are equal
21. Pr > F, the significance probability value associated with the F Value.

When a TEST statement is used, ANOVA prints the results of the tests requested in the TEST statement. When a MANOVA statement is used and the model includes more than one dependent variable, ANOVA prints these additional statistics (not shown in example output):

22. the characteristic roots and vectors of $E^{-1}H$ for each H matrix (not shown)
23. the Hotelling-Lawley trace (not shown)
24. Pillai's trace (not shown)
25. Wilks' criterion (not shown)
26. Roy's maximum root criterion (not shown).

These MANOVA tests are discussed in Chapter 1, "Introduction to Regression Procedures."

EXAMPLES

Example 1: One-Way Layout with Means Comparisons

The following data are derived from an experiment by Erdman (1946) and analyzed in Chapters 7 and 8 of Steel and Torrie (1980). The measurements are the nitrogen content of red clover plants inoculated with cultures of *Rhizobium trifolii* strains of bacteria and a composite of five *Rhizobium meliloti* strains. Several different means comparisons methods are requested. The following statements produce **Output 11.1**:

```
data clover;
   input strain $ nitrogen @@;
   cards;
3DOK1   19.4   3DOK1   32.6   3DOK1   27.0   3DOK1   32.1   3DOK1   33.0
3DOK5   17.7   3DOK5   24.8   3DOK5   27.9   3DOK5   25.2   3DOK5   24.3
3DOK4   17.0   3DOK4   19.4   3DOK4    9.1   3DOK4   11.9   3DOK4   15.8
3DOK7   20.7   3DOK7   21.0   3DOK7   20.5   3DOK7   18.8   3DOK7   18.6
3DOK13  14.3   3DOK13  14.4   3DOK13  11.8   3DOK13  11.6   3DOK13  14.2
COMPOS  17.3   COMPOS  19.4   COMPOS  19.1   COMPOS  16.9   COMPOS  20.8
;
```

```
proc anova;
   class strain;
   model nitrogen=strain;
   means strain / duncan waller;
   means strain / lsd tukey cldiff;
run;
```

Output 11.1   One-Way Layout with Means Comparisons: PROC ANOVA

Analysis of Variance Procedure   1
Class Level Information

❶ Class   Levels **❷** **❸** Values

STRAIN   6   3DOK1 3DOK13 3DOK4 3DOK5 3DOK7 COMPOS

❹ Number of observations in data set = 30

Analysis of Variance Procedure   2

Dependent Variable: NITROGEN

Source	**❿** DF	**❾** Sum of Squares	**❽** Mean Square	**⓬** F Value	**⓭** Pr > F
Model	5	**❻** 847.04666667	169.40933333	14.37	0.0001
Error	24	**❼** 282.92800000	**⓫** 11.78866667		
Corrected Total	29	**❺** 1129.97466667			

⓮ R-Square	**⓯** C.V.	Root MSE	**⓱** NITROGEN Mean
0.749616	17.26515	3.43346278	19.88666667

Source	**⓲** DF	**⓳** Anova SS	Mean Square	**⓴** F Value	**㉑** Pr > F
STRAIN	5	847.04666667	169.40933333	14.37	0.0001

Analysis of Variance Procedure   3

Waller-Duncan K-ratio T test for variable: NITROGEN

NOTE: This test minimizes the Bayes risk under additive loss and certain other
      assumptions.

Kratio= 100 df= 24 MSE= 11.78867 F= 14.37053
         Critical Value of T= 1.91853
         Minimum Significant Difference= 4.1661

Means with the same letter are not significantly different.

Waller Grouping		Mean	N	STRAIN
	A	28.820	5	3DOK1
	B	23.980	5	3DOK5
C	B	19.920	5	3DOK7
C	D	18.700	5	COMPOS
E	D	14.640	5	3DOK4
E		13.260	5	3DOK13

```
                        Analysis of Variance Procedure                          4

                 Duncan's Multiple Range Test for variable: NITROGEN

       NOTE: This test controls the type I comparisonwise error rate, not the experimentwise
             error rate

                     Alpha= 0.05  df= 24  MSE= 11.78867

               Number of Means     2      3      4      5      6
               Critical Range   4.477  4.704  4.860  4.955  5.032

       Means with the same letter are not significantly different.

              Duncan Grouping          Mean     N  STRAIN

                            A         28.820     5  3DOK1

                            B         23.980     5  3DOK5
                            B
                       C    B         19.920     5  3DOK7
                       C
                       C    D         18.700     5  COMPOS
                            D
                       E    D         14.640     5  3DOK4
                       E
                       E              13.260     5  3DOK13
```

```
                        Analysis of Variance Procedure                          5

                        T tests (LSD) for variable: NITROGEN

       NOTE: This test controls the type I comparisonwise error rate not the experimentwise
             error rate.

               Alpha= 0.05  Confidence= 0.95  df= 24  MSE= 11.78867
                          Critical Value of T= 2.06390
                          Least Significant Difference= 4.4818

       Comparisons significant at the 0.05 level are indicated by '***'.

                                  Lower      Difference    Upper
                    STRAIN      Confidence    Between    Confidence
                  Comparison      Limit        Means       Limit

               3DOK1  - 3DOK5      0.358        4.840       9.322    ***
               3DOK1  - 3DOK7      4.418        8.900      13.382    ***
               3DOK1  - COMPOS     5.638       10.120      14.602    ***
               3DOK1  - 3DOK4      9.698       14.180      18.662    ***
               3DOK1  - 3DOK13    11.078       15.560      20.042    ***

               3DOK5  - 3DOK1     -9.322       -4.840      -0.358    ***
               3DOK5  - 3DOK7     -0.422        4.060       8.542
               3DOK5  - COMPOS     0.798        5.280       9.762    ***
               3DOK5  - 3DOK4      4.858        9.340      13.822    ***
               3DOK5  - 3DOK13     6.238       10.720      15.202    ***

               3DOK7  - 3DOK1    -13.382       -8.900      -4.418    ***
               3DOK7  - 3DOK5     -8.542       -4.060       0.422
               3DOK7  - COMPOS    -3.262        1.220       5.702
               3DOK7  - 3DOK4      0.798        5.280       9.762    ***
               3DOK7  - 3DOK13     2.178        6.660      11.142    ***

               COMPOS - 3DOK1    -14.602      -10.120      -5.638    ***
               COMPOS - 3DOK5     -9.762       -5.280      -0.798    ***
               COMPOS - 3DOK7     -5.702       -1.220       3.262
               COMPOS - 3DOK4     -0.422        4.060       8.542
               COMPOS - 3DOK13     0.958        5.440       9.922    ***

               3DOK4  - 3DOK1    -18.662      -14.180      -9.698    ***
               3DOK4  - 3DOK5    -13.822       -9.340      -4.858    ***
               3DOK4  - 3DOK7     -9.762       -5.280      -0.798    ***
               3DOK4  - COMPOS    -8.542       -4.060       0.422
               3DOK4  - 3DOK13    -3.102        1.380       5.862

               3DOK13 - 3DOK1    -20.042      -15.560     -11.078    ***
               3DOK13 - 3DOK5    -15.202      -10.720      -6.238    ***
               3DOK13 - 3DOK7    -11.142       -6.660      -2.178    ***
               3DOK13 - COMPOS    -9.922       -5.440      -0.958    ***
               3DOK13 - 3DOK4     -5.862       -1.380       3.102
```

```
                    Analysis of Variance Procedure                        6

         Tukey's Studentized Range (HSD) Test for variable: NITROGEN

        NOTE: This test controls the type I experimentwise error rate.

            Alpha= 0.05  Confidence= 0.95  df= 24  MSE= 11.78867
                 Critical Value of Studentized Range= 4.373
                    Minimum Significant Difference= 6.7142

     Comparisons significant at the 0.05 level are indicated by '***'.

                            Simultaneous           Simultaneous
                               Lower     Difference     Upper
                    STRAIN    Confidence   Between    Confidence
                  Comparison    Limit      Means        Limit

           3DOK1  - 3DOK5      -1.874      4.840       11.554
           3DOK1  - 3DOK7       2.186      8.900       15.614    ***
           3DOK1  - COMPOS      3.406     10.120       16.834    ***
           3DOK1  - 3DOK4       7.466     14.180       20.894    ***
           3DOK1  - 3DOK13      8.846     15.560       22.274    ***

           3DOK5  - 3DOK1     -11.554     -4.840        1.874
           3DOK5  - 3DOK7      -2.654      4.060       10.774
           3DOK5  - COMPOS     -1.434      5.280       11.994
           3DOK5  - 3DOK4       2.626      9.340       16.054    ***
           3DOK5  - 3DOK13      4.006     10.720       17.434    ***

           3DOK7  - 3DOK1     -15.614     -8.900       -2.186    ***
           3DOK7  - 3DOK5     -10.774     -4.060        2.654
           3DOK7  - COMPOS     -5.494      1.220        7.934
           3DOK7  - 3DOK4      -1.434      5.280       11.994
           3DOK7  - 3DOK13     -0.054      6.660       13.374

           COMPOS - 3DOK1     -16.834    -10.120       -3.406    ***
           COMPOS - 3DOK5     -11.994     -5.280        1.434
           COMPOS - 3DOK7      -7.934     -1.220        5.494
           COMPOS - 3DOK4      -2.654      4.060       10.774
           COMPOS - 3DOK13     -1.274      5.440       12.154

           3DOK4  - 3DOK1     -20.894    -14.180       -7.466    ***
           3DOK4  - 3DOK5     -16.054     -9.340       -2.626    ***
           3DOK4  - 3DOK7     -11.994     -5.280        1.434
           3DOK4  - COMPOS    -10.774     -4.060        2.654
           3DOK4  - 3DOK13     -5.334      1.380        8.094

           3DOK13 - 3DOK1     -22.274    -15.560       -8.846    ***
           3DOK13 - 3DOK5     -17.434    -10.720       -4.006    ***
           3DOK13 - 3DOK7     -13.374     -6.660        0.054
           3DOK13 - COMPOS    -12.154     -5.440        1.274
           3DOK13 - 3DOK4      -8.094     -1.380        5.334
```

The overall *F* test is significant, indicating that the model as a whole accounts for a significant portion of the variability in the dependent variable. The *F* test for STRAIN is also significant, indicating that the means for the different STRAINs are not all equal. Notice that these two *F* tests are identical; this occurs because STRAIN is the only term in the model.

The Waller-Duncan (WALLER) and Duncan (DUNCAN) multiple comparison tests give the same results. This does not always occur. From these two tests, you can conclude the following:

- The average nitrogen content for strain 3DOK1 is higher than the average for all other strains.
- The average nitrogen content for strain 3DOK5 is higher than the average for COMPOS, 3DOK4, and 3DOK13.
- The average nitrogen content for strain 3DOK7 is higher than the average for 3DOK4 and 3DOK13.
- The average nitrogen content for strain COMPOS is higher than the average for 3DOK13.
- Differences between all other averages are not significant.

The LSD tests give the same results as the previous two multiple comparison tests. Again, this is not always the case. For both the LSD and TUKEY tests, confidence intervals are given as a result of specifying the CLDIFF option. The TUKEY tests find fewer significant differences than the other three tests. This is not unexpected, as the TUKEY test controls the type 1 experimentwise error rate. For a complete discussion, see the section **Comparisons of Means** in the chapter on the GLM procedure.

Example 2: Randomized Complete Block

This example shows statements for the analysis of a randomized block. Because the data for the analysis are balanced, PROC ANOVA is used. The blocking variable, BLOCK, and the treatment variable, TRTMENT, appear in the CLASS statement, and the MODEL statement requests an analysis for each of the two dependent variables, YIELD and WORTH. The following statements produce **Output 11.2**:

```
title 'RANDOMIZED COMPLETE BLOCK';
data rcb;
   input block trtment $ yield worth;
   cards;
1 A 32.6 112
1 B 36.4 130
1 C 29.5 106
2 A 42.7 139
2 B 47.1 143
2 C 32.9 112
3 A 35.3 124
3 B 40.1 134
3 C 33.6 116
;
proc anova;
   class block trtment;
   model yield worth=block trtment;
run;
```

Output 11.2   Randomized Complete Block: PROC ANOVA

```
                        RANDOMIZED COMPLETE BLOCK                                1

                        Analysis of Variance Procedure
                          Class Level Information

                     Class     Levels     Values

                     BLOCK        3       1 2 3

                     TRTMENT      3       A B C

              Number of observations in data set = 9
```

```
                            RANDOMIZED COMPLETE BLOCK                              2
                           Analysis of Variance Procedure

Dependent Variable: YIELD

Source              DF        Sum of Squares        Mean Square      F Value        Pr > F

Model                4         225.27777778         56.31944444         8.94        0.0283

Error                4          25.19111111          6.29777778

Corrected Total      8         250.46888889

               R-Square             C.V.            Root MSE                 YIELD Mean

               0.899424          6.840047          2.50953736               36.68888889

Source              DF           Anova SS           Mean Square      F Value        Pr > F
BLOCK                2          98.17555556         49.08777778         7.79        0.0417
TRTMENT              2         127.10222222         63.55111111        10.09        0.0274
```

```
                            RANDOMIZED COMPLETE BLOCK                              3
                           Analysis of Variance Procedure

Dependent Variable: WORTH

Source              DF        Sum of Squares        Mean Square      F Value        Pr > F

Model                4        1247.33333333        311.83333333         8.28        0.0323

Error                4         150.66666667         37.66666667

Corrected Total      8        1398.00000000

               R-Square             C.V.            Root MSE                 WORTH Mean

               0.892227          4.949450          6.13731755              124.00000000

Source              DF           Anova SS           Mean Square      F Value        Pr > F
BLOCK                2         354.66666667        177.33333333         4.71        0.0889
TRTMENT              2         892.66666667        446.33333333        11.85        0.0209
```

For YIELD, both the BLOCK effect and the TRTMENT effects are significant. For this variable, blocking was useful, and there are significant differences between the three treatments.

For WORTH, the BLOCK effect is not significant at the 95% confidence level but is significant at the 90% confidence level. The usefulness of blocking should be determined by a significance level set before the analysis. However, since both variables are of interest, and BLOCK is significant for YIELD, blocking appears to be generally useful. For WORTH, there are significant differences between the three treatments.

Example 3: Split Plot

The statements below produce an analysis for a split-plot design. The CLASS statement includes the variables BLOCK, A, and B. The MODEL statement includes the independent effects BLOCK, A, BLOCK*A, B, and A*B. The TEST

statement asks for an *F* test using the BLOCK*A effect as the error term and the
A effect as the hypothesis effect. The following statements produce **Output 11.3**:

```
*-----------------Split Plot--------------------*
| B defines subplots within A*BLOCK whole plots.|
| The whole plot effects must be tested with a  |
| TEST statement against BLOCK*A. The subplot    |
| effects can be tested against the residual.    |
*-----------------------------------------------* ;

title 'SPLIT PLOT DESIGN';
data split;
   input block 1 a 2 b 3 response;
   cards;
142 40.0
141 39.5
112 37.9
111 35.4
121 36.7
122 38.2
132 36.4
131 34.8
221 42.7
222 41.6
212 40.3
211 41.6
241 44.5
242 47.6
231 43.6
232 42.8
;
proc anova;
   class block a b;
   model response=block a block*a b a*b;
   test h=a e=block*a;
run;
```

Output 11.3   Split Plot: PROC ANOVA

```
                        SPLIT PLOT DESIGN                          1

                     Analysis of Variance Procedure
                       Class Level Information

                     Class    Levels    Values

                     BLOCK       2      1 2

                     A           4      1 2 3 4

                     B           2      1 2


             Number of observations in data set = 16
```

```
                              SPLIT PLOT DESIGN                                    2
                          Analysis of Variance Procedure

Dependent Variable: RESPONSE

Source                DF        Sum of Squares      Mean Square      F Value      Pr > F

Model                 11         182.02000000      16.54727273        7.85        0.0306

Error                  4           8.43000000       2.10750000

Corrected Total       15         190.45000000

                R-Square                 C.V.            Root MSE          RESPONSE Mean

                0.955736             3.609007         1.45172311            40.22500000

Source                DF            Anova SS          Mean Square      F Value      Pr > F
BLOCK                  1         131.10250000      131.10250000       62.21        0.0014
A                      3          40.19000000       13.39666667        6.36        0.0530
BLOCK*A                3           6.92750000        2.30916667        1.10        0.4476
B                      1           2.25000000        2.25000000        1.07        0.3599
A*B                    3           1.55000000        0.51666667        0.25        0.8612

Tests of Hypotheses using the Anova MS for BLOCK*A as an error term

Source                DF            Anova SS          Mean Square      F Value      Pr > F

A                      3          40.19000000       13.39666667        5.80        0.0914
```

First, notice that the overall F test for the model is significant. The effect of BLOCK is significant. The effect of A is not significant: look at the F test produced by the TEST statement, not at the F test produced by default. Neither the B nor A*B effects are significant. The test for BLOCK*A is irrelevant, as this is simply the main-plot error.

Example 4: Latin Square Split Plot

The Latin square design below using data from Smith (1951) is used to evaluate 6 different sugar beet varieties arranged in a 6-row (REP) by 6-column (COL) square. Then the data are recollected for a second harvest. HARVEST then becomes a split plot on the original Latin square design for whole plots. The statements below produce **Output 11.4**:

```
data beets;
    do harvest=1 to 2;
        do rep=1 to 6;
            do col=1 to 6;
                input variety y @;
                output;
                end;
            end;
        end;
    cards;
    3 19.1 6 18.3 5 19.6 1 18.6 2 18.2 4 18.5
    6 18.1 2 19.5 4 17.6 3 18.7 1 18.7 5 19.9
    1 18.1 5 20.2 6 18.5 4 20.1 3 18.6 2 19.2
    2 19.1 3 18.8 1 18.7 5 20.2 4 18.6 6 18.5
    4 17.5 1 18.1 2 18.7 6 18.2 5 20.4 3 18.5
    5 17.7 4 17.8 3 17.4 2 17.0 6 17.6 1 17.6
    3 16.2 6 17.0 5 18.1 1 16.6 2 17.7 4 16.3
    6 16.0 2 15.3 4 16.0 3 17.1 1 16.5 5 17.6
    1 16.5 5 18.1 6 16.7 4 16.2 3 16.7 2 17.3
```

```
        2 17.5 3 16.0 1 16.4 5 18.0 4 16.6 6 16.1
        4 15.7 1 16.1 2 16.7 6 16.3 5 17.8 3 16.2
        5 18.3 4 16.6 3 16.4 2 17.6 6 17.1 1 16.5
        ;
    proc anova;
       class col rep variety harvest;
       model y=rep col variety rep*col*variety
              harvest harvest*rep
              harvest*variety;
       test h=rep col variety e=rep*col*variety;
       test h=harvest e=harvest*rep;
    run;
```

Output 11.4   Latin Square Split Plot: PROC ANOVA

```
                      Analysis of Variance Procedure                              1
                       Class Level Information

              Class     Levels     Values

              COL          6       1 2 3 4 5 6

              REP          6       1 2 3 4 5 6

              VARIETY      6       1 2 3 4 5 6

              HARVEST      2       1 2

           Number of observations in data set = 72
```

```
                      Analysis of Variance Procedure                              2
   Dependent Variable: Y

   Source            DF      Sum of Squares      Mean Square    F Value      Pr > F

   Model             46         98.91472222       2.15032005       7.22      0.0001

   Error             25          7.44847222       0.29793889

   Corrected Total   71        106.36319444

                 R-Square              C.V.           Root MSE            Y Mean

                 0.929971            3.085524        0.54583779        17.69027778

   Source            DF          Anova SS       Mean Square    F Value      Pr > F

   REP                5          4.32069444       0.86413889       2.90      0.0337
   COL                5          1.57402778       0.31480556       1.06      0.4075
   VARIETY            5         20.61902778       4.12380556      13.84      0.0001
   COL*REP*VARIETY   20          3.25444444       0.16272222       0.55      0.9144
   HARVEST            1         60.68347222      60.68347222     203.68      0.0001
   REP*HARVEST        5          7.71736111       1.54347222       5.18      0.0021
   VARIETY*HARVEST    5          0.74569444       0.14913889       0.50      0.7729

   Tests of Hypotheses using the Anova MS for COL*REP*VARIETY as an error term

   Source            DF          Anova SS       Mean Square    F Value      Pr > F

   REP                5          4.32069444       0.86413889       5.31      0.0029
   COL                5          1.57402778       0.31480556       1.93      0.1333
   VARIETY            5         20.61902778       4.12380556      25.34      0.0001

   Tests of Hypotheses using the Anova MS for REP*HARVEST as an error term

   Source            DF          Anova SS       Mean Square    F Value      Pr > F

   HARVEST            1         60.68347222      60.68347222      39.32      0.0015
```

First, note that the overall model is significant. The effects for REP and HARVEST are significant, while COL is not. The average Ys for the six different VARIETYs are significantly different. For these four tests, look at the output produced by the two TEST statements, not at the usual ANOVA output. The VARIETY*HARVEST interaction is not significant. All other effects in the default output should either be tested using the output from the TEST statements or are irrelevant as they are only error terms for portions of the model.

Example 5: Strip-Split Plot

In this example, the fertilizer treatments are laid out in vertical strips, which are then split into calcium-effect subplots. Soil type is stripped across the split-plot experiment, and the entire experiment is then replicated three times.

The input data are the 96 values of Y, arranged so that the calcium value (CA) changes most rapidly, then the fertilizer value (FERTIL), then the SOIL value, and finally, the REP value. Values are shown for CA (0 and 1); FERTIL (0, 1, 2, 3); SOIL (1, 2, 3); and REP (1, 2, 3, 4). The following example produces **Output 11.5**:

```
*------------Strip-Split Plot Design: Winter Barley--------------*
|                                                                |
| Fertilizer treatments are laid out in vertical strips which are|
| then split into calcium effect subplots. Soil type is then     |
| stripped across the split plot experiment. The whole experiment|
| is replicated three times.                                     |
|                                                                |
| Data from the notes of G. Cox and A. Rotti                     |
*----------------------------------------------------------------*;

   title 'STRIP-SPLIT PLOT';
   data barley;
      do rep=1 to 4;
         do soil=1 to 3;                  * 1=d 2=h 3=p;
            do fertil=0 to 3;
               do ca=0,1;
                  input y a;
                  output;
                  end;
               end;
            end;
         end;
      cards;
   4.91 4.63 4.76 5.04 5.38 6.21 5.60 5.08
   4.94 3.98 4.64 5.26 5.28 5.01 5.45 5.62
   5.20 4.45 5.05 5.03 5.01 4.63 5.80 5.90
   6.00 5.39 4.95 5.39 6.18 5.94 6.58 6.25
   5.86 5.41 5.54 5.41 5.28 6.67 6.65 5.94
   5.45 5.12 4.73 4.62 5.06 5.75 6.39 5.62
   4.96 5.63 5.47 5.31 6.18 6.31 5.95 6.14
   5.71 5.37 6.21 5.83 6.28 6.55 6.39 5.57
   4.60 4.90 4.88 4.73 5.89 6.20 5.68 5.72
   5.79 5.33 5.13 5.18 5.86 5.98 5.55 4.32
   5.61 5.15 4.82 5.06 5.67 5.54 5.19 4.46
   5.13 4.90 4.88 5.18 5.45 5.80 5.12 4.42
   ;
```

```
* Note that since the model is completely specified and several
* error terms are present, the TEST statement must be used to
* obtain the proper test statistics. The top portion of the output
* should be ignored since the residual error term is not
* meaningful here;

proc anova;
   class rep soil ca fertil;
   model y=rep
           fertil fertil*rep
           ca ca*fertil ca*rep(fertil)
           soil soil*rep
           soil*fertil soil*rep*fertil
           soil*ca soil*fertil*ca
           soil*ca*rep(fertil);
   test h=fertil         e=fertil*rep;
   test h=ca ca*fertil   e=ca*rep(fertil);
   test h=soil           e=soil*rep;
   test h=soil*fertil    e=soil*rep*fertil;
   test h=soil*ca
           soil*fertil*ca e=soil*ca*rep(fertil);
   means fertil ca soil ca*fertil;
run;
```

Output 11.5 Strip-Split Plot: PROC ANOVA

```
                            STRIP-SPLIT PLOT                                    1
                      Analysis of Variance Procedure
                         Class Level Information

                      Class    Levels    Values

                      REP         4      1 2 3 4

                      SOIL        3      1 2 3

                      CA          2      0 1

                      FERTIL      4      0 1 2 3

           Number of observations in data set = 96
```

```
                            STRIP-SPLIT PLOT                                    2
                      Analysis of Variance Procedure

Dependent Variable: Y

Source              DF      Sum of Squares      Mean Square      F Value      Pr > F

Model               95       31.89149583        0.33569996         .            .

Error                0            .                  .

Corrected Total     95       31.89149583

            R-Square              C.V.           Root MSE              Y Mean

            1.000000                0                0             5.42729167
```

(continued on next page)

(continued from previous page)

Source	DF	Anova SS	Mean Square	F Value	Pr > F
REP	3	6.27974583	2.09324861	.	.
FERTIL	3	7.22127083	2.40709028	.	.
REP*FERTIL	9	6.08211250	0.67579028	.	.
CA	1	0.27735000	0.27735000	.	.
CA*FERTIL	3	1.96395833	0.65465278	.	.
REP*CA(FERTIL)	12	1.76705833	0.14725486	.	.
SOIL	2	1.92658958	0.96329479	.	.
REP*SOIL	6	1.66761042	0.27793507	.	.
SOIL*FERTIL	6	0.68828542	0.11471424	.	.
REP*SOIL*FERTIL	18	1.58698125	0.08816563	.	.
SOIL*CA	2	0.04493125	0.02246562	.	.
SOIL*CA*FERTIL	6	0.18936042	0.03156007	.	.
REP*SOIL*CA(FERTIL)	24	2.19624167	0.09151007	.	.

Tests of Hypotheses using the Anova MS for REP*FERTIL as an error term

Source	DF	Anova SS	Mean Square	F Value	Pr > F
FERTIL	3	7.22127083	2.40709028	3.56	0.0604

Tests of Hypotheses using the Anova MS for REP*CA(FERTIL) as an error term

Source	DF	Anova SS	Mean Square	F Value	Pr > F
CA	1	0.27735000	0.27735000	1.88	0.1950
CA*FERTIL	3	1.96395833	0.65465278	4.45	0.0255

Tests of Hypotheses using the Anova MS for REP*SOIL as an error term

Source	DF	Anova SS	Mean Square	F Value	Pr > F
SOIL	2	1.92658958	0.96329479	3.47	0.0999

STRIP-SPLIT PLOT   3

Analysis of Variance Procedure

Dependent Variable: Y

Tests of Hypotheses using the Anova MS for REP*SOIL*FERTIL as an error term

Source	DF	Anova SS	Mean Square	F Value	Pr > F
SOIL*FERTIL	6	0.68828542	0.11471424	1.30	0.3063

Tests of Hypotheses using the Anova MS for REP*SOIL*CA(FERTIL) as an error term

Source	DF	Anova SS	Mean Square	F Value	Pr > F
SOIL*CA	2	0.04493125	0.02246562	0.25	0.7843
SOIL*CA*FERTIL	6	0.18936042	0.03156007	0.34	0.9059

STRIP-SPLIT PLOT   4

Analysis of Variance Procedure

Level of FERTIL	N	Mean	SD
0	24	5.18416667	0.48266395
1	24	5.12916667	0.38337082
2	24	5.75458333	0.53293265
3	24	5.64125000	0.63926801

Level of CA	N	Mean	SD
0	48	5.48104167	0.54186141
1	48	5.37354167	0.61565219

Level of SOIL	N	Mean	SD
1	32	5.54312500	0.55806369
2	32	5.51093750	0.62176315
3	32	5.22781250	0.51825224

(continued on next page)

(continued from previous page)

Level of CA	Level of FERTIL	N	Mean	SD
0	0	12	5.34666667	0.45029956
0	1	12	5.08833333	0.44986530
0	2	12	5.62666667	0.44707806
0	3	12	5.86250000	0.52886027
1	0	12	5.02166667	0.47615569
1	1	12	5.17000000	0.31826233
1	2	12	5.88250000	0.59856077
1	3	12	5.42000000	0.68409197

As the model is completely specified by the MODEL statement, the entire top portion of output should be ignored. Look at the output produced by the various TEST statements. The only significant effect is the CA*FERTIL interaction. The final portion of output shows the results of the MEANS statement. This portion shows means for various effects and combinations of effects, as requested. Because no multiple comparison procedures were requested, none are performed. You can examine the CA*FERTIL means to understand the interaction better.

REFERENCES

Erdman, L.W. (1946), "Studies to Determine if Antibiosis Occurs among Rhizobia," *Journal of the American Society of Agronomy*, 38, 251–258.

Fisher, R.A. (1942), *The Design of Experiments*, 3d Edition, Edinburgh: Oliver & Boyd.

Freund, R.J., Littell, R.C., and Spector, P.C. (1986), *SAS System for Linear Models, 1986 Edition*, Cary, NC: SAS Institute Inc.

Graybill, F.A. (1961), *An Introduction to Linear Statistical Models,* Vol. I, New York: McGraw-Hill Book Co.

Henderson, C.R. (1953), "Estimation of Variance and Covariance Components," *Biometrics*, 9, 226–252.

Remington, R.D. and Schork, M.A. (1970), *Statistics with Applications to the Biological and Health Sciences*, Englewood Cliffs, NJ: Prentice-Hall, Inc.

Scheffe, H. (1959), *The Analysis of Variance*, New York: John Wiley & Sons, Inc.

Searle, S.R. (1971), *Linear Models*, New York: John Wiley & Sons, Inc.

Smith, W.G. (1951), Dissertation Notes on Canadian Sugar Factories, Ltd., Alberta, Canada: Taber.

Snedecor, G.W. and Cochran, W.G. (1967), *Statistical Methods*, 6th Edition, Ames, IA: Iowa State University Press.

Steel, R.G.D. and Torrie, J.H. (1980), *Principles and Procedures of Statistics*, New York: McGraw-Hill Book Co.

Chapter 12

The CANCORR
Procedure

ABSTRACT

The CANCORR procedure performs canonical correlation, partial canonical correlation, and canonical redundancy analysis. The CANCORR procedure can create output data sets containing canonical coefficients and scores on canonical variables.

INTRODUCTION

Canonical correlation is a technique for analyzing the relationship between two sets of variables. Each set can contain several variables. Simple and multiple correlation are special cases of canonical correlation in which one or both sets contain a single variable.

The CANCORR procedure tests a series of hypotheses that each canonical correlation and all smaller canonical correlations are zero in the population.

CANCORR uses an F approximation (Rao 1973; Kshirsagar 1972) that gives better small sample results than the usual χ^2 approximation. At least one of the two sets of variables should have an approximate multivariate normal distribution in order for the probability levels to be valid.

Both standardized and unstandardized canonical coefficients are produced, as well as all correlations between canonical variables and the original variables. A canonical redundancy analysis (Stewart and Love 1968; Cooley and Lohnes 1971) can also be performed.

PROC CANCORR provides multiple regression analysis options to aid in interpreting the canonical correlation analysis. Then you can examine the linear regression of each variable on the opposite set of variables. CANCORR uses the least-squares criterion in linear regression analysis.

PROC CANCORR can produce a data set containing the scores on each canonical variable, and you can use the PRINT procedure to list these values. A plot of each canonical variable against its counterpart in the other group is often useful, and you can use PROC PLOT with the output data set to produce these plots.

A second output data set contains the canonical coefficients, which can be rotated by the FACTOR procedure.

Background

Canonical correlation was developed by Hotelling (1935, 1936). The application of canonical correlation is discussed by Cooley and Lohnes (1971), Tatsuoka (1971), and Mardia, Kent, and Bibby (1979). One of the best theoretical treatments is given by Kshirsagar (1972).

Given two sets of variables, the CANCORR procedure finds a linear combination from each set, called a canonical variable, such that the correlation between the two canonical variables is maximized. This correlation between the two canonical variables is the first canonical correlation. The coefficients of the linear combinations are canonical coefficients or canonical weights. It is customary to normalize the canonical coefficients so that each canonical variable has a variance of 1.

PROC CANCORR continues by finding a second set of canonical variables, uncorrelated with the first pair, that produces the second highest correlation coefficient. The process of constructing canonical variables continues until the number of pairs of canonical variables equals the number of variables in the smaller group.

Each canonical variable is uncorrelated with all the other canonical variables of either set except for the one corresponding canonical variable in the opposite set. The canonical coefficients are not generally orthogonal, however, so the canonical variables do not represent jointly perpendicular directions through the space of the original variables.

The first canonical correlation is at least as large as the multiple correlation between any variable and the opposite set of variables. It is possible for the first canonical correlation to be very high, even if all the multiple correlations are low. It is also possible for the first canonical correlation to be very large while all the multiple correlations for predicting one of the original variables from the opposite set of canonical variables are small. Canonical redundancy analysis (Stewart and Love 1968; Cooley and Lohnes 1971; van den Wollenberg 1977), available with the CANCORR procedure, examines how well the original variables can be predicted from the canonical variables.

PROC CANCORR can also perform partial canonical correlation, a multivariate generalization of ordinary partial correlation (Cooley and Lohnes 1971; Timm 1975). Most commonly used parametric statistical methods, ranging from t tests to multivariate analysis of covariance, are special cases of partial canonical correlation.

SPECIFICATIONS

You can use the following statements to invoke the CANCORR procedure:

PROC CANCORR *options*;
    VAR *variables*;
    WITH *variables*;
    PARTIAL *variables*;
    FREQ *variable*;
    WEIGHT *variable*;
    BY *variables*;

Usually, only the VAR and WITH statements are needed in addition to the PROC CANCORR statement. The WITH statement is required. The descriptions of the BY, FREQ, PARTIAL, VAR, WEIGHT, and WITH statements follow the description of the PROC CANCORR statement.

PROC CANCORR Statement

PROC CANCORR *options*;

The options available with the PROC CANCORR statement are discussed in the following sections:

- **Data Set Options**
- **Output Options**
- **Miscellaneous Options**
- **Regression Options**.

Data Set Options

DATA=*SASdataset*
    names the SAS data set to be analyzed by CANCORR. It can be an ordinary SAS data set or a TYPE=CORR or TYPE=COV data set. If the DATA= option is omitted, the most recently created SAS data set is used.

OUT=*SASdataset*
    names an output SAS data set to contain all the original data plus scores on the canonical variables. If you want to create a permanent SAS data set, you must specify a two-level name. The OUT= option cannot be used when the DATA= data set is TYPE=CORR or TYPE=COV. See "SAS Files" in the *SAS Language Guide, Release 6.03 Edition* for more information on permanent SAS data sets.

OUTSTAT=*SASdataset*
    produces a SAS data set containing various statistics including the canonical correlations and coefficients and the multiple regression statistics you request. If you want to create a permanent SAS data set, you must specify a two-level name. See "SAS Files" in the *SAS Language Guide* for more information on permanent SAS data sets.

Output Options

ALL
    prints all optional output.

CORR
C
    prints correlations among the original variables.

NCAN=*n*
    specifies the number of canonical variables for which full output is
    desired.

NOPRINT
    suppresses the printout.

REDUNDANCY
RED
    prints canonical redundancy statistics.

SHORT
    suppresses all default output except the tables of canonical correlations
    and multivariate statistics.

SIMPLE
S
    prints means and standard deviations.

VNAME='*label*'
VN='*label*'
    specifies a character constant up to forty characters long to refer to
    variables from the VAR statement on the printout. You should enclose
    the constant in single quotes. If you omit the VNAME= option, these
    variables are referred to as the VAR Variables.

VPREFIX=*name*
VP=*name*
    specifies a prefix for naming canonical variables from the VAR statement.
    By default, these canonical variables are given the names V1, V2, and so
    on. If you specify VPREFIX=ABC, the names are ABC1, ABC2, and so
    forth. The number of characters in the prefix plus the number of digits
    required to designate the variables should not exceed eight.

WNAME='*label*'
WN='*label*'
    specifies a character constant up to forty characters long to refer to
    variables from the WITH statement on the printout. You should enclose
    the constant in quotes. If you omit the WNAME= option, these
    variables are referred to as the WITH Variables.

WPREFIX=*name*
WP=*name*
    specifies a prefix for naming canonical variables from the WITH
    statement. By default, these canonical variables are given the names W1,
    W2, and so on. If you specify WPREFIX=XYZ, then the names are
    XYZ1, XYZ2, and so forth. The number of characters in the prefix plus
    the number of digits required to designate the variables should not
    exceed eight.

Miscellaneous Options

EDF=*errordf*
    specifies the error degrees of freedom from the regression analysis if the
    input observations are residuals from a regression. The effective number
    of observations is the EDF= value plus one. If you have 100
    observations, then specifying EDF=99 has the same effect as omitting
    the EDF= option.

NOINT
    indicates that the model should not contain the intercept.

RDF=*regressiondf*

specifies the regression degrees of freedom if the input observations are residuals from a regression analysis. The effective number of observations is the actual number minus the RDF= value. The degree of freedom for the intercept should not be included in the RDF= option.

SINGULAR=*p*
SING=*p*

specifies the singularity criterion, where $0<p<1$. If a variable in the VAR or WITH statement has an R^2 as large as $1-p$ when predicted from the variables listed before it in the statement, the variable is omitted from the canonical analysis and assigned canonical coefficients of zero. The default is SINGULAR=1E$-$8.

Regression Options

If you also specify the ALL option, all optional output associated with the multiple regression analyses is printed. Otherwise, you can request particular regression statistics by specifying the corresponding options.

B

requests raw regression coefficients.

CORRB

requests correlations among the regression coefficient estimates.

INT

requests that statistics for the intercept be included when B, SEB, T, and/or PROBT are specified.

PCORR

requests partial correlations between regressors and dependent variables, removing from each dependent variable and regressor the effects of all other regressors.

PROBT

requests probability levels for the *t* statistics.

SEB

requests standard errors of the regression coefficients.

SMC

requests squared multiple correlations and *F* tests.

SPCORR

requests semipartial correlations between regressors and dependent variables, removing from each regressor the effects of all other regressors.

SQPCORR

requests squared partial correlations between regressors and dependent variables, removing from each dependent variable and regressor the effects of all other regressors.

SQSPCORR

requests squared semipartial correlations between regressors and dependent variables, removing from each regressor the effects of all other regressors.

STB

requests standardized regression coefficients.

T

requests *t* statistics for the regression coefficients.

VDEP
WREG

 requests multiple regression analyses predicting the VAR variables from the WITH variables.

WDEP
VREG

 requests multiple regression analyses predicting the WITH variables from the VAR variables.

BY Statement

 BY *variables*;

You can use a BY statement with PROC CANCORR to obtain separate analyses on observations in groups defined by the BY variables. When a BY statement appears, the procedure expects the input data set to be sorted in order of the BY variables.

 If your input data set is not sorted in ascending order, use the SORT procedure with a similar BY statement to sort the data, or, if appropriate, use the BY statement options NOTSORTED or DESCENDING. For more information, see the discussion of the BY statement in "SAS Statements Used in the PROC Step" in the *SAS Language Guide*.

FREQ Statement

 FREQ *variable*;

If one variable in your input data set represents the frequency of occurrence for other values in the observation, specify the variable's name in a FREQ statement. CANCORR then treats the data set as if each observation appeared *n* times, where *n* is the value of the FREQ variable for the observation. If the value of the FREQ variable is less than one, the observation is not used in the analysis. Only the integer portion of the value is used. The total number of observations is considered equal to the sum of the FREQ variable when CANCORR calculates significance probabilities.

PARTIAL Statement

 PARTIAL *variables*;

The PARTIAL statement can be used to base the canonical analysis on partial correlations. The variables in the PARTIAL statement are partialled out of the VAR and WITH variables.

VAR Statement

 VAR *variables*;

The VAR statement lists the variables in the first of the two sets of variables to be analyzed. The variables must be numeric. If you omit the VAR statement, all numeric variables not mentioned in other statements make up the first set of variables.

WEIGHT Statement

> WEIGHT *variable*;

If you want to compute weighted product-moment correlation coefficients, give the name of the weighting variable in a WEIGHT statement. The WEIGHT and FREQ statements have a similar effect, except the WEIGHT statement does not alter the degrees of freedom or number of observations. An observation is used in the analysis only if the WEIGHT variable is greater than zero.

WITH Statement

> WITH *variables*;

The WITH statement lists the variables in the second set of variables to be analyzed. The variables must be numeric. The WITH statement is required.

DETAILS

Missing Values

If an observation has a missing value for any of the variables in the analysis, that observation is omitted from the analysis.

Output Data Sets

OUT= Data Set

The OUT= data set contains all the variables in the original data set plus new variables containing the canonical variable scores. The number of new variables is twice that specified by the NCAN= option. The names of the new variables are formed by concatenating the values given by the VPREFIX= and WPREFIX= options (the defaults are V and W) with the numbers 1, 2, 3, and so on. The new variables have mean 0 and variance equal to 1. An OUT= data set cannot be created if the DATA= data set is TYPE=CORR or TYPE=COV or if a PARTIAL statement is used.

OUTSTAT= Data Set

The OUTSTAT= data set is similar to the TYPE=CORR data set produced by the CORR procedure, but it contains several results in addition to those produced by CORR.

The new data set contains the following variables:

- the BY variables, if any
- two new character variables, _TYPE_ and _NAME_
- the variables analyzed (those in the VAR statement and the WITH statement).

Each observation in the new data set contains some type of statistic as indicated by the _TYPE_ variable. The values of the _TYPE_ variable are as follows:

TYPE	Contents
MEAN	means.
STD	standard deviations.
N	number of observations on which the analysis is based. This value is the same for each variable.

SUMWGT	sum of the weights if a WEIGHT statement is used. This value is the same for each variable.
CORR	correlations. The _NAME_ variable contains the name of the variable corresponding to each row of the correlation matrix.
CANCORR	canonical correlations.
SCORE	standardized canonical coefficients. The _NAME_ variable contains the name of the canonical variable.
RAWSCORE	raw canonical coefficients.
STRUCTUR	canonical structure.
RSQUARED	R^2s for the multiple regression analyses.
ADJRSQ	adjusted R^2s.
LCLRSQ	approximate 95% lower confidence limits for the R^2s.
UCLRSQ	approximate 95% upper confidence limits for the R^2s.
F	F statistics for the multiple regression analyses.
PROBF	probability levels for the F statistics.
CORRB	correlations among the regression coefficient estimates.
STB	standardized regression coefficients. The _NAME_ variable contains the name of the dependent variable.
B	raw regression coefficients.
SEB	standard errors of the regression coefficients.
T	t statistics for the regression coefficients.
PROBT	probability levels for the t statistics.
SPCORR	semipartial correlations between regressors and dependent variables.
SQSPCORR	squared semipartial correlations between regressors and dependent variables.
PCORR	partial correlations between regressors and dependent variables.
SQPCORR	squared partial correlations between regressors and dependent variables.

Computational Resources

Let

n = number of observations

v = number of VAR variables

w = number of WITH variables

p = max(v,w)

q = min(v,w) .

The time required to compute the correlation matrix is roughly proportional to

$$n(p + q)^2 .$$

The time required for the canonical analysis is roughly proportional to

$$p^3/6 + p^2q + 3pq^2/2 + 5q^3$$

but the coefficient for q^3 varies depending on the number of QR iterations in the singular value decomposition.

Printed Output

If SIMPLE is specified, PROC CANCORR prints

1. Means and Standard Deviations for each input variable.

If CORR is specified, PROC CANCORR prints

2. Correlations Among the input variables.

Unless NOPRINT is specified, PROC CANCORR prints a table of canonical correlations containing the following:

3. Canonical Correlations.
4. Adjusted Canonical Correlations (Lawley 1959), which are asymptotically less biased than the raw correlations and may be negative. The adjusted canonical correlations may not be computable and are printed as missing values if two canonical correlations are nearly equal or if some are close to zero. A missing value is also printed if an adjusted canonical correlation is larger than a previous adjusted canonical correlation.
5. Approx Standard Errors, which are the approximate standard errors of the canonical correlations.
6. Squared Canonical Correlations.
7. Eigenvalues of INV(E)*H, which are equal to CanRsq/(1−CanRsq), where CanRsq is the corresponding squared canonical correlation. Also printed for each eigenvalue is the Difference from the next eigenvalue, the Proportion of the sum of the eigenvalues, and the Cumulative proportion.
8. Likelihood Ratio for the hypothesis that the current canonical correlation and all smaller ones are 0 in the population. The likelihood ratio for all canonical correlations equals Wilks' lambda.
9. Approx F based on Rao's approximation to the distribution of the likelihood ratio (Rao 1973, 556; Kshirsagar 1972, 326).
10. Num DF and Den DF (numerator and denominator degrees of freedom) and Pr > F (probability level) associated with the F statistic.

Unless NOPRINT is specified, PROC CANCORR prints a table of multivariate statistics for the null hypothesis that all canonical correlations are zero in the population. These statistics are described in **Multivariate Tests** in Chapter 1, "Introduction to Regression Procedures." The statistics are as follows:

11. Wilks' Lambda
12. Pillai's Trace
13. Hotelling-Lawley Trace
14. Roy's Greatest Root.

For each of the statistics above, PROC CANCORR prints

15. an F approximation or upper bound
16. Num DF, the numerator degrees of freedom
17. Den DF, the denominator degrees of freedom
18. Pr > F, the probability level.

Unless SHORT or NOPRINT is specified, PROC CANCORR prints the following:

19. both Raw (unstandardized) and Standardized Canonical Coefficients normalized to give canonical variables with unit variance. Standardized coefficients can be used to compute canonical variable scores from the standardized (zero mean and unit variance) input variables. Raw coefficients can be used to compute canonical variable scores from the input variables without standardizing them.

20. all four Canonical Structure matrices, giving Correlations Between the canonical variables and the original variables.

If REDUNDANCY is specified, PROC CANCORR prints

21. the Canonical Redundancy Analysis (Stewart and Love 1968; Cooley and Lohnes 1971), including Raw (unstandardized) and Standardized Variance and Cumulative Proportion of the Variance of each set of variables Explained by Their Own Canonical Variables and Explained by The Opposite Canonical Variables

22. the Squared Multiple Correlations of each variable with the first m canonical variables of the opposite set, where m varies from 1 to the number of canonical correlations.

If VDEP is specified, PROC CANCORR performs multiple regression analyses predicting the VAR variables from the WITH variables. IF WDEP is specified, CANCORR performs multiple regression analyses predicting the WITH variables from the VAR variables. For each of these two analyses, CANCORR prints the following unless NOPRINT is specified:

23. if SMC is specified, Squared Multiple Correlations and F Tests (not shown). For each regression model, identified by its dependent variable name, CANCORR prints the R-Squared, Adjusted R-Squared (Wherry 1931), F Statistic, and Pr $>$ F. Also for each regression model, CANCORR prints an Approximate 95% Confidence Interval for the population R^2 (Helland 1987). These confidence limits are valid only when the regressors are random, and the regressors and dependent variables are approximately distributed according to a multivariate normal distribution.

    The average R^2s for the models considered, unweighted and weighted by variance, are also given.

24. if CORRB is specified, Correlations Among the Regression Coefficient Estimates (not shown).

25. if STB is specified, Standardized Regression Coefficients (not shown).

26. if B is specified, Raw Regression Coefficients (not shown).

27. if SEB is specified, Standard Errors of the Regression Coefficients (not shown).

28. if T is specified, T Statistics for the Regression Coefficients (not shown).

29. if PROBT is specified, Probability $>$ |T| for the Regression Coefficients (not shown).

30. if SPCORR is specified, Semipartial Correlations between regressors and dependent variables, Removing from Each Regressor the Effects of All Other Regressors (not shown).

31. if SQSPCORR is specified, Squared Semipartial Correlations between regressors and dependent variables, Removing from Each Regressor the Effects of All Other Regressors (not shown).

32. if PCORR is specified, Partial Correlations between regressors and dependent variables, Removing the Effects of All Other Regressors from Both Regressor and Criterion (not shown).
33. if SQPCORR is specified, Squared Partial Correlations between regressors and dependent variables, Removing the Effects of All Other Regressors from Both Regressor and Criterion (not shown).

EXAMPLE

Canonical Correlation Analysis of Fitness Club Data

Three physiological and three exercise variables were measured on twenty middle-aged men in a fitness club. The CANCORR procedure can be used to determine if the physiological variables are related in any way to the exercise variables. The following statements produce **Output 12.1**:

```
data fit;
    input weight waist pulse chins situps jumps;
    cards;
191  36  50   5  162   60
189  37  52   2  110   60
193  38  58  12  101  101
162  35  62  12  105   37
189  35  46  13  155   58
182  36  56   4  101   42
211  38  56   8  101   38
167  34  60   6  125   40
176  31  74  15  200   40
154  33  56  17  251  250
169  34  50  17  120   38
166  33  52  13  210  115
154  34  64  14  215  105
247  46  50   1   50   50
193  36  46   6   70   31
202  37  62  12  210  120
176  37  54   4   60   25
157  32  52  11  230   80
156  33  54  15  225   73
138  33  68   2  110   43
;
proc cancorr data=fit all
    vprefix=phys vname='Physiological Measurements'
    wprefix=exer wname='Exercises';
  var weight waist pulse;
  with chins situps jumps;
  title 'Middle-Aged Men in a Health Fitness Club';
  title2 'Data Courtesy of Dr. A. C. Linnerud, NC State Univ';
run;
```

Output 12.1   Fitness Club Data: PROC CANCORR

```
                        Middle-Aged Men in a Health Fitness Club                        1
                       Data Courtesy of Dr. A. C. Linnerud, NC State Univ
                         ❶ Means and Standard Deviations

   3 Physiological Measurements
   3 Exercises
  20 Observations

                            Variable        Mean            Std Dev

                            WEIGHT       178.600000        24.690505
                            WAIST         35.400000         3.201973
                            PULSE         56.100000         7.210373
                            CHINS          9.450000         5.286278
                            SITUPS       145.550000        62.566575
                            JUMPS         70.300000        51.277470
```

```
                        Middle-Aged Men in a Health Fitness Club                        2
                       Data Courtesy of Dr. A. C. Linnerud, NC State Univ
                        ❷ Correlations Among the Original Variables

              Correlations Among the Physiological Measurements

                             WEIGHT            WAIST            PULSE

              WEIGHT         1.0000           0.8702          -0.3658
              WAIST          0.8702           1.0000          -0.3529
              PULSE         -0.3658          -0.3529           1.0000


                        Correlations Among the Exercises

                              CHINS           SITUPS           JUMPS

              CHINS          1.0000           0.6957           0.4958
              SITUPS         0.6957           1.0000           0.6692
              JUMPS          0.4958           0.6692           1.0000


     Correlations Between the Physiological Measurements and the Exercises

                              CHINS           SITUPS           JUMPS

              WEIGHT         -0.3897          -0.4931          -0.2263
              WAIST          -0.5522          -0.6456          -0.1915
              PULSE           0.1506           0.2250           0.0349
```

```
                        Middle-Aged Men in a Health Fitness Club                        3
                       Data Courtesy of Dr. A. C. Linnerud, NC State Univ

                            Canonical Correlation Analysis

                                                             ❼
                                                       Eigenvalues of INV(E)*H
             ❸         ❹          ❺           ❻        = CanRsq/(1-CanRsq)
                      Adjusted    Approx     Squared
         Canonical   Canonical   Standard   Canonical
         Correlation Correlation  Error     Correlation  Eigenvalue  Difference  Proportion  Cumulative

      1   0.795608   0.754056   0.084197   0.632992     1.7247     1.6828     0.9734     0.9734
      2   0.200556  -.076399    0.220188   0.040223     0.0419     0.0366     0.0237     0.9970
      3   0.072570      .        0.228208   0.005266     0.0053        .       0.0030     1.0000

     Test of HO: The canonical correlations in the current row and all that follow are zero

                ❽  Likelihood    ❾          ❿
                      Ratio     Approx F   Num DF      Den DF      Pr > F

                 1  0.35039053   2.0482       9        34.22293    0.0635
                 2  0.95472266   0.1758       4        30          0.9491
                 3  0.99473355   0.0847       1        16          0.7748
```

(continued on next page)

(continued from previous page)

Multivariate Statistics and F Approximations

S=3   M=-0.5   **(15)** N=6

	Statistic	Value	**(15)** F	**(16)** Num DF	**(17)** Den DF	**(18)** Pr > F
(11)	Wilks' Lambda	0.35039053	2.0482	9	34.22293	0.0635
(12)	Pillai's Trace	0.67848151	1.5587	9	48	0.1551
(13)	Hotelling-Lawley Trace	1.77194146	2.4938	9	38	0.0238
(14)	Roy's Greatest Root	1.72473874	9.1986	3	16	0.0009

NOTE: F Statistic for Roy's Greatest Root is an upper bound.

Middle-Aged Men in a Health Fitness Club
Data Courtesy of Dr. A. C. Linnerud, NC State Univ

4

(19) Canonical Correlation Analysis

Raw Canonical Coefficients for the Physiological Measurements

	PHYS1	PHYS2	PHYS3
WEIGHT	-0.031404688	-0.076319506	-0.007735047
WAIST	0.4932416756	0.3687229894	0.1580336471
PULSE	-0.008199315	-0.032051994	0.1457322421

Raw Canonical Coefficients for the Exercises

	EXER1	EXER2	EXER3
CHINS	-0.066113986	-0.071041211	-0.245275347
SITUPS	-0.016846231	0.0019737454	0.0197676373
JUMPS	0.0139715689	0.0207141063	-0.008167472

Standardized Canonical Coefficients for the Physiological Measurements

	PHYS1	PHYS2	PHYS3
WEIGHT	-0.7754	-1.8844	-0.1910
WAIST	1.5793	1.1806	0.5060
PULSE	-0.0591	-0.2311	1.0508

Standardized Canonical Coefficients for the Exercises

	EXER1	EXER2	EXER3
CHINS	-0.3495	-0.3755	-1.2966
SITUPS	-1.0540	0.1235	1.2368
JUMPS	0.7164	1.0622	-0.4188

Middle-Aged Men in a Health Fitness Club
Data Courtesy of Dr. A. C. Linnerud, NC State Univ

5

(20) Canonical Structure

Correlations Between the Physiological Measurements and Their Canonical Variables

	PHYS1	PHYS2	PHYS3
WEIGHT	0.6206	-0.7724	-0.1350
WAIST	0.9254	-0.3777	-0.0310
PULSE	-0.3328	0.0415	0.9421

Correlations Between the Exercises and Their Canonical Variables

	EXER1	EXER2	EXER3
CHINS	-0.7276	0.2370	-0.6438
SITUPS	-0.8177	0.5730	0.0544
JUMPS	-0.1622	0.9586	-0.2339

(continued on next page)

(continued from previous page)

Correlations Between the Physiological Measurements and the Canonical Variables of the Exercises

	EXER1	EXER2	EXER3
WEIGHT	0.4938	-0.1549	-0.0098
WAIST	0.7363	-0.0757	-0.0022
PULSE	-0.2648	0.0083	0.0684

Correlations Between the Exercises and the Canonical Variables of the Physiological Measurements

	PHYS1	PHYS2	PHYS3
CHINS	-0.5789	0.0475	-0.0467
SITUPS	-0.6506	0.1149	0.0040
JUMPS	-0.1290	0.1923	-0.0170

Middle-Aged Men in a Health Fitness Club
Data Courtesy of Dr. A. C. Linnerud, NC State Univ

㉑ Canonical Redundancy Analysis

6

Raw Variance of the Physiological Measurements

Explained by

	Their Own Canonical Variables			The Opposite Canonical Variables	
	Proportion	Cumulative Proportion	Canonical R-Squared	Proportion	Cumulative Proportion
1	0.3712	0.3712	0.6330	0.2349	0.2349
2	0.5436	0.9148	0.0402	0.0219	0.2568
3	0.0852	1.0000	0.0053	0.0004	0.2573

Raw Variance of the Exercises

Explained by

	Their Own Canonical Variables			The Opposite Canonical Variables	
	Proportion	Cumulative Proportion	Canonical R-Squared	Proportion	Cumulative Proportion
1	0.4111	0.4111	0.6330	0.2602	0.2602
2	0.5635	0.9746	0.0402	0.0227	0.2829
3	0.0254	1.0000	0.0053	0.0001	0.2830

Standardized Variance of the Physiological Measurements

Explained by

	Their Own Canonical Variables			The Opposite Canonical Variables	
	Proportion	Cumulative Proportion	Canonical R-Squared	Proportion	Cumulative Proportion
1	0.4508	0.4508	0.6330	0.2854	0.2854
2	0.2470	0.6978	0.0402	0.0099	0.2953
3	0.3022	1.0000	0.0053	0.0016	0.2969

Middle-Aged Men in a Health Fitness Club
Data Courtesy of Dr. A. C. Linnerud, NC State Univ

7

Canonical Redundancy Analysis

Standardized Variance of the Exercises

Explained by

	Their Own Canonical Variables			The Opposite Canonical Variables	
	Proportion	Cumulative Proportion	Canonical R-Squared	Proportion	Cumulative Proportion
1	0.4081	0.4081	0.6330	0.2584	0.2584
2	0.4345	0.8426	0.0402	0.0175	0.2758
3	0.1574	1.0000	0.0053	0.0008	0.2767

㉒ Squared Multiple Correlations Between the Physiological Measurements and the First 'M' Canonical Variables of the Exercises

M	1	2	3
WEIGHT	0.2438	0.2678	0.2679
WAIST	0.5421	0.5478	0.5478
PULSE	0.0701	0.0702	0.0749

Squared Multiple Correlations Between the Exercises and the First 'M' Canonical Variables of the Physiological Measurements

M	1	2	3
CHINS	0.3351	0.3374	0.3396
SITUPS	0.4233	0.4365	0.4365
JUMPS	0.0167	0.0536	0.0539

Interpretation

The correlations between the physiological and exercise variables are moderate, the largest being −0.6456 between WAIST and SITUPS. There are larger within-set correlations: 0.8702 between WEIGHT and WAIST, 0.6957 between CHINS and SITUPS, and 0.6692 between SITUPS and JUMPS.

The first canonical correlation is 0.7956, which would appear to be substantially larger than any of the between-set correlations. The probability level for the null hypothesis that all the canonical correlations are 0 in the population is only 0.0635, so no firm conclusions can be drawn. The remaining canonical correlations are not worthy of consideration, as can be seen from the probability levels and especially from the negative adjusted canonical correlations.

Because the variables are not measured in the same units, the standardized coefficients rather than the raw coefficients should be interpreted. The correlations given in the canonical structure matrices should also be examined.

The first canonical variable for the physiological variables is a weighted difference of WAIST (1.5793) and WEIGHT (−0.7754), with more emphasis on WAIST. The coefficient for PULSE is near 0. The correlations between WAIST and WEIGHT and the first canonical variable are both positive, 0.9254 for WAIST and 0.6206 for WEIGHT. WEIGHT is therefore a suppressor variable, meaning that its coefficient and its correlation have opposite signs.

The first canonical variable for the exercise variables also shows a mixture of signs, subtracting SITUPS (−1.0540) and CHINS (−0.3495) from JUMPS (0.7164), with the most weight on SITUPS. All the correlations are negative, indicating that JUMPS is also a suppressor variable.

It may seem contradictory that a variable should have a coefficient of opposite sign from that of its correlation with the canonical variable. In order to understand how this can happen, consider a simplified situation: predicting SITUPS from WAIST and WEIGHT by multiple regression. In informal terms, it seems plausible that fat people should do fewer situps than skinny people. Assume that the men in the sample do not vary much in height, so there is a strong correlation between WAIST and WEIGHT (0.8702). Examine the relationships between fatness and the independent variables:

- People with large WAISTs tend to be fatter than people with small WAISTs. Hence, the correlation between WAIST and SITUPS should be negative.
- People with high WEIGHTs tend to be fatter than people with low WEIGHTs. Therefore, WEIGHT should correlate negatively with SITUPS.
- For a fixed value of WEIGHT, people with large WAISTs tend to be shorter and fatter. Thus, the multiple regression coefficient for WAIST should be negative.
- For a fixed value of WAIST, people with higher WEIGHTS tend to be taller and skinnier. The multiple regression coefficient for WEIGHT should therefore be positive, of opposite sign from the correlation between WEIGHT and SITUPS.

Therefore, the general interpretation of the first canonical correlation is that WEIGHT and JUMPS act as suppressor variables to enhance the correlation between WAIST and SITUPS. This canonical correlation may be strong enough to be of practical interest, but the sample size is not large enough to draw definite conclusions.

The canonical redundancy analysis shows that neither of the first pair of canonical variables is a good overall predictor of the opposite set of variables, the proportions of variance explained being 0.2854 and 0.2584. The second and third canonical variables add virtually nothing, with cumulative proportions for all three canonical variables being 0.2969 and 0.2767. The squared multiple correlations indicate that the first canonical variable of the physiological measurements has some predictive power for CHINS (0.3351) and SITUPS (0.4233) but almost none for JUMPS (0.0167). The first canonical variable of the exercises is a fairly good predictor of WAIST (0.5421), a poorer predictor of WEIGHT (0.2438), and nearly useless for predicting PULSE (0.0701).

REFERENCES

Cooley, W.W. and Lohnes, P.R. (1971), *Multivariate Data Analysis*, New York: John Wiley & Sons, Inc.

Fisher, R.A. (1938), *Statistical Methods for Research Workers*, 10th Edition, Edinburgh: Oliver & Boyd.

Hanson, R.J. and Norris, M.J. (1981), "Analysis of Measurements Based on the Singular Value Decomposition," *SIAM Journal of Scientific and Statistical Computing*, 2, 363–373.

Helland, I.S. (1987), "On the Interpretation and Use of R^2 in Regression Analysis," *Biometrics*, 43, 61–69.

Hotelling, H. (1935), "The Most Predictable Criterion," *Journal of Educational Psychology*, 26, 139–142.

Hotelling, H. (1936), "Relations Between Two Sets of Variables," *Biometrika*, 28, 321–377.

Kshirsagar, A.M. (1972), *Multivariate Analysis*, New York: Marcel Dekker, Inc.

Lawley, D.N. (1959), "Tests of Significance in Canonical Analysis," *Biometrika*, 46, 59–66.

Mardia, K.V., Kent, J.T., and Bibby, J.M. (1979), *Multivariate Analysis*, London: Academic Press, Inc.

Mulaik, S.A. (1972), *The Foundations of Factor Analysis*, New York: McGraw-Hill Book Co.

Rao, C.R. (1964), "The Use and Interpretation of Principal Component Analysis in Applied Research," *Sankhya A*, 26, 329–358.

Rao, C.R. (1973), *Linear Statistical Inference*, New York: John Wiley & Sons, Inc.

Stewart, D.K. and Love, W.A. (1968), "A General Canonical Correlation Index," *Psychological Bulletin*, 70, 160–163.

Tatsuoka, M.M. (1971), *Multivariate Analysis*, New York: John Wiley & Sons, Inc.

Timm, N.H. (1975), *Multivariate Analysis*, Monterey, CA: Brooks-Cole Publishing Co.

van den Wollenberg, A.L. (1977), "Redundancy Analysis—An Alternative to Canonical Correlation Analysis," *Psychometrika*, 42, 207–219.

Wherry, R.J. (1931), "A New Formula for Predicting the Shrinkage of the Coefficient of Multiple Correlation," *Annals of Mathematical Statistics*, 2, 440–457.

Chapter 13

The CANDISC
Procedure

ABSTRACT

The CANDISC procedure performs a canonical discriminant analysis, computes squared Mahalanobis distances, and does both univariate and multivariate one-way analyses of variance. Output data sets containing canonical coefficients and scores on the canonical variables can be created.

INTRODUCTION

Canonical discriminant analysis is a dimension-reduction technique related to principal component analysis and canonical correlation. Given a classification variable and several quantitative variables, the CANDISC procedure derives *canonical variables* (linear combinations of the quantitative variables) that summarize between-class variation in much the same way that principal components summarize total variation.

For each canonical correlation, CANDISC tests the hypothesis that it and all smaller canonical correlations are zero in the population. An F approximation (Rao 1973; Kshirsagar 1972) is used that gives better small-sample results than the usual chi-square approximation. The variables should have an approximate multivariate normal distribution within each class, with a common covariance matrix in order for the probability levels to be valid.

Both standardized and unstandardized canonical coefficients are printed, as well as the correlations between canonical variables and the original variables and the means of each class on the canonical variables.

The CANDISC procedure performs univariate and multivariate one-way analyses of variance and computes squared distances between class means based on the pooled within-class covariance matrix (Mahalanobis distances).

The procedure can produce an output data set containing the scores on each canonical variable. You can use the PRINT procedure to list these values and the PLOT procedure to plot pairs of canonical variables to aid visual interpretation of group differences. A second output data set contains canonical coefficients that can be rotated by the FACTOR procedure.

Background

Given two or more groups of observations with measurements on several quantitative variables, canonical discriminant analysis derives a linear combination of the variables that has the highest possible multiple correlation with the groups. This maximal multiple correlation is called the *first canonical correlation*. The coefficients of the linear combination are the *canonical coefficients* or *canonical weights*. The variable defined by the linear combination is the *first canonical variable* or *canonical component*. The second canonical correlation is obtained by finding the linear combination uncorrelated with the first canonical variable that has the highest possible multiple correlation with the groups. The process of extracting canonical variables can be repeated until the number of canonical variables equals the number of original variables or the number of classes minus one, whichever is smaller.

The first canonical correlation is at least as large as the multiple correlation between the groups and any of the original variables. If the original variables have high within-group correlations, the first canonical correlation can be large even if all the multiple correlations are small. In other words, the first canonical variable can show substantial differences among the classes, even if none of the original variables does.

It is customary to standardize the canonical coefficients so that the canonical variables have means equal to zero and pooled within-class variances equal to one. Canonical variables are sometimes called *discriminant functions*, but this usage is ambiguous because the DISCRIM procedure produces very different functions for classification that are also called discriminant functions.

Canonical discriminant analysis is equivalent to canonical correlation analysis between the quantitative variables and a set of dummy variables coded from the class variable. Canonical discriminant analysis is also equivalent to performing the following steps:

- Transform the variables so that the pooled within-class covariance matrix is an identity matrix.
- Compute class means on the transformed variables.
- Do a principal component analysis on the means, weighting each mean by the number of observations in the class. The eigenvalues are equal to

the ratio of between-class variation to within-class variation in the direction of each principal component.
- Back-transform the principal components into the space of the original variables, obtaining the canonical variables.

An interesting property of the canonical variables is that they are uncorrelated whether the correlation is calculated from the total sample or from the pooled within-class correlations. The canonical coefficients are not orthogonal, however, so the canonical variables do not represent perpendicular directions through the space of the original variables.

SPECIFICATIONS

The CANDISC procedure is invoked by the following statements:

PROC CANDISC *options*;
    VAR *variables*;
    CLASS *variable*;
    FREQ *variable*;
    WEIGHT *variable*;
    BY *variables*;

The CLASS statement is required. The BY, CLASS, FREQ, VAR, and WEIGHT statements are described after the PROC CANDISC statement.

PROC CANDISC Statement

PROC CANDISC *options*;

The options described in the following sections can appear in the PROC CANDISC statement.

Data Set Options

DATA=*SASdataset*
    names the data set to be analyzed. The data set can be an ordinary SAS data set or one of several specially structured data sets created by SAS statistical procedures. These specially structured data sets include TYPE=CORR, COV, CSSCP, and SSCP. If the DATA= option is omitted, the most recently created SAS data set is used.

OUT=*SASdataset*
    names an output SAS data set containing the original data and the canonical variable scores. To create a permanent SAS data set, specify a two-level name (see "SAS Files" in the *SAS Language Guide, Release 6.03 Edition* for more information on permanent SAS data sets).

OUTSTAT=*SASdataset*
    names a TYPE=CORR output SAS data set that contains various statistics including class means, standard deviations, correlations, canonical correlations, canonical structures, canonical coefficients, and means of canonical variables for each class. To create a permanent SAS data set, specify a two-level name (see "SAS Files" in the *SAS Language Guide* for more information on permanent SAS data sets).

Canonical Variables Options

NCAN=n

specifies the number of canonical variables to be computed. The value of n must be less than or equal to the number of variables. If you specify NCAN=0, the procedure prints the canonical correlations, but not the canonical coefficients, structures, or means. A negative value suppresses the canonical analysis entirely. Let v be the number of variables in the VAR statement and c be the number of classes. When the NCAN= option is not specified, only min(v, $c-1$) canonical variables are generated; when an OUT= output data set is also requested, v canonical variables will be generated, and the last $v-(c-1)$ canonical variables will have missing values.

PREFIX=name

specifies a prefix for naming the canonical variables. By default the names are CAN1, CAN2, . . . , CANn. If PREFIX=ABC is specified, the components are named ABC1, ABC2, ABC3, and so on. The number of characters in the prefix, plus the number of digits required to designate the canonical variables, should not exceed eight. The prefix is truncated if the combined length exceeds eight.

Singularity Option

SINGULAR=p

specifies the criterion for determining the singularity of the total-sample correlation matrix and the pooled within-class covariance matrix, where $0 < p < 1$. The default is SINGULAR=1E-8.

Let **T** be the total-sample correlation matrix. If the R^2 for predicting a quantitative variable in the VAR statement from the variables preceding it exceeds $1-p$, **T** is considered singular. If **T** is singular, the probability levels for the multivariate test statistics and canonical correlations are adjusted for the number of variables with R^2 exceeding $1-p$.

Let **S** be the pooled covariance matrix. If the partial R^2 for predicting a quantitative variable in the VAR statement from the variables preceding it, after controlling for the effect of the CLASS variable, exceeds $1-p$, **S** is considered singular.

If **S** is singular and the inverse of **S** (Squared Mahalanobis Distances) is required, a quasi-inverse will be used instead. Let v be the number of variables in the VAR statement and the nullity n be the number of variables among them, with partial R^2 exceeding $1-p$. CANDISC scales each variable to unit total-sample variance before calculating this quasi-inverse. The calculation is based on the spectral decomposition $S = \Gamma \Lambda \Gamma'$. Γ is a matrix of eigenvectors and Λ is a diagonal matrix of eigenvalues λ_j, $j=1, \ldots, v$. When the nullity n is less than v, set $\lambda_j^0 = \lambda_j$ for $j=1, \ldots, v-n$, and $\lambda_j^0 = p\bar{\lambda}$ for $j=v-n+1, \ldots, v$, where

$$\bar{\lambda} = \Sigma_{k=1}^{v-n} \lambda_k / (v - n) \quad .$$

When the nullity n is equal to v, set $\lambda_j^0 = p$, for $j=1, \ldots, v$. A quasi-inverse is then defined as $S^* = \Gamma \Lambda^* \Gamma'$, where Λ^* is a diagonal matrix of values $1/\lambda_j^0$, $j=1, \ldots, v$.

Printing Options

ANOVA
prints univariate statistics for testing the hypothesis that the class means are equal in the population for each variable.

BCORR
prints between-class correlations.

BCOV
prints between-class covariances. The between-class covariance matrix equals the between-class SSCP matrix divided by $n(c-1)/c$, where n is the number of observations and c is the number of classes. The between-class covariances should be interpreted in comparison with the total-sample and within-class covariances, not as formal estimates of population parameters.

BSSCP
prints the between-class SSCP matrix.

DISTANCE
prints squared Mahalanobis distances between class means.

PCORR
prints pooled within-class correlations (partial correlations based on the pooled within-class covariances).

PCOV
prints pooled within-class covariances.

PSSCP
prints the pooled within-class corrected SSCP matrix.

SIMPLE
prints simple descriptive statistics for the total sample and within each class.

STDMEAN
prints total-sample and pooled within-class standardized class means.

TCORR
prints total-sample correlations.

TCOV
prints total-sample covariances.

TSSCP
prints the total-sample corrected SSCP matrix.

WCORR
prints within-class correlations for each class level.

WCOV
prints within-class covariances for each class level.

WSSCP
prints the within-class corrected SSCP matrix for each class level.

ALL
activates all of the printing options above.

NOPRINT
suppresses the printout.

SHORT
suppresses the printing of canonical structures, canonical coefficients, and class means on canonical variables; only tables of canonical correlations and multivariate test statistics are printed.

BY Statement

BY *variables*;

A BY statement can be used with PROC CANDISC to obtain separate analyses on observations in groups defined by the BY variables. When a BY statement appears, the procedure expects the input data set to be sorted in order of the BY variables.

If your input data set is not sorted in ascending order, use the SORT procedure with a similar BY statement to sort the data, or, if appropriate, use the BY statement options NOTSORTED or DESCENDING. For more information, see the discussion of the BY statement in "SAS Statements Used in the PROC Step" in the *SAS Language Guide, Release 6.03 Edition*.

CLASS Statement

CLASS *variable*;

The values of the CLASS variable define the groups for analysis. Class levels are determined by the formatted values of the CLASS variable. The CLASS variable can be numeric or character. A CLASS statement is required.

FREQ Statement

FREQ *variable*;

If a variable in the data set represents the frequency of occurrence for the other values in the observation, include the variable's name in a FREQ statement. The procedure then treats the data set as if each observation appears n times, where n is the value of the FREQ variable for the observation. The total number of observations is considered to be equal to the sum of the FREQ variable when the procedure determines degrees of freedom for significance probabilities.

If the value of the FREQ variable is missing or less than one, the observation is not used in the analysis. If the value is not an integer, the value is truncated to an integer.

VAR Statement

VAR *variables*;

The VAR statement specifies the quantitative variables to be included in the analysis. If a VAR statement is not used, the analysis includes all numeric variables not listed in other statements.

WEIGHT Statement

WEIGHT *variable*;

To use relative weights for each observation in the input data set, place the weights in a variable in the data set and specify the name in a WEIGHT statement. This is often done when the variance associated with each observation is different and the values of the WEIGHT variable are proportional to the reciprocals of the variances. If the value of the WEIGHT variable is missing or less than zero, then a value of zero for the weight is assumed.

The WEIGHT and FREQ statements have a similar effect except that the WEIGHT statement does not alter the degrees of freedom.

DETAILS

Missing Values

If an observation has a missing value for any of the quantitative variables, it is omitted from the analysis. If an observation has a missing CLASS value but is otherwise complete, it is not used in computing the canonical correlations and coefficients; however, canonical variable scores are computed for that observation for the OUT= data set.

Input Data Set

The input DATA= data set can be an ordinary SAS data set or one of several specially structured data sets created by statistical procedures available with SAS/STAT software. The BY variable in these data sets becomes the CLASS variable in PROC CANDISC. These specially structured data sets include

- TYPE=CORR data sets created by PROC CORR using a BY statement
- TYPE=COV data sets created by PROC PRINCOMP using both the COV option and a BY statement
- TYPE=CSSCP data sets created by PROC CORR using the CSSCP option and a BY statement, where the OUT= data set is assigned TYPE=CSSCP with the TYPE= data set option
- TYPE=SSCP data sets created by PROC REG using both the OUTSSCP= option and a BY statement.

When the input data set is TYPE=CORR, TYPE=COV, or TYPE=CSSCP, CANDISC reads the number of observations for each class from the observations with _TYPE_='N' and the variable means in each class from the observations with _TYPE_='MEAN'. CANDISC then reads the within-class correlations from the observations with _TYPE_='CORR', the standard deviations from the observations with _TYPE_='STD' (data set TYPE=CORR), the within-class covariances from the observations with _TYPE_='COV' (data set TYPE=COV), or the within-class corrected sums of squares and crossproducts from the observations with _TYPE_='CSSCP' (data set TYPE=CSSCP).

When the data set does not include any observations with _TYPE_='CORR' (data set TYPE=CORR), _TYPE_='COV' (data set TYPE=COV), or _TYPE_='CSSCP' (data set TYPE=CSSCP) for each class, CANDISC reads the pooled within-class information from the data set. In this case, CANDISC reads the pooled within-class correlations from the observations with _TYPE_='PCORR', the pooled within-class standard deviations from the observations with _TYPE_='PSTD' (data set TYPE=CORR), the pooled within-class covariances from the observations with _TYPE_='PCOV' (data set TYPE=COV), or the pooled within-class corrected SSCP matrix from the observations with _TYPE_='PSSCP' (data set TYPE=CSSCP).

When the input data set is TYPE=SSCP, CANDISC reads the number of observations for each class from the observations with _TYPE_='N', the sum of weights of observations from the variable INTERCEP in observations with _TYPE_='SSCP' and _NAME_='INTERCEP', the variable sums from the variable=*variablenames* in observations with _TYPE_='SSCP' and _NAME_='INTERCEP', and the uncorrected sums of squares and crossproducts from the variable=*variablenames* in observations with _TYPE_='SSCP' and _NAME_=*variablenames*.

Output Data Sets

OUT= Data Set

The OUT= data set contains all the variables in the original data set plus new variables containing the canonical variable scores. The NCAN= option determines the number of new variables. The names of the new variables are formed as described in the PREFIX= option. The new variables have means equal to zero and pooled within-class variances equal to one. An OUT= data set cannot be created if the DATA= data set is not an ordinary SAS data set.

OUTSTAT= Data Set

The OUTSTAT= data set is similar to the TYPE=CORR data set produced by the CORR procedure but contains many results in addition to those produced by the CORR procedure.

The OUTSTAT= data set is TYPE=CORR and contains the following variables:

- the BY variables, if any
- the CLASS variable
- _TYPE_, a character variable of length 8 that identifies the type of statistic
- _NAME_, a character variable of length 8 that identifies the row of the matrix or the name of the canonical variable
- the quantitative variables, that is, those in the VAR statement, or, if there is no VAR statement, all numeric variables not listed in any other statement.

The observations, as identified by the variable _TYPE_, have the following _TYPE_ values:

TYPE	Contents
N	number of observations for both the total sample (CLASS variable missing) and within each class (CLASS variable present)
SUMWGT	sum of weights for both the total sample (CLASS variable missing) and within each class (CLASS variable present) if a WEIGHT statement is specified
MEAN	means for both the total sample (CLASS variable missing) and within each class (CLASS variable present)
STDMEAN	total-standardized class means
PSTDMEAN	pooled within-class standardized class means
STD	standard deviations for both the total sample (CLASS variable missing) and within each class (CLASS variable present)
PSTD	pooled within-class standard deviations
BSTD	between-class standard deviations
RSQUARED	univariate R^2s.

The following kinds of observations are identified by the combination of the variables _TYPE_ and _NAME_. When the _TYPE_ variable has one of the values below, the _NAME_ variable identifies the row of the matrix.

TYPE	Contents
CSSCP	corrected SSCP matrix for the total sample (CLASS variable missing) and within each class (CLASS variable present)
PSSCP	pooled within-class corrected SSCP matrix
BSSCP	between-class SSCP matrix
COV	covariance matrix for the total sample (CLASS variable missing) and within each class (CLASS variable present)
PCOV	pooled within-class covariance matrix
BCOV	between-class covariance matrix
CORR	correlation matrix for the total sample (CLASS variable missing) and within each class (CLASS variable present)
PCORR	pooled within-class correlation matrix
BCORR	between-class correlation matrix.

When the _TYPE_ variable has one of the following values, the _NAME_ variable identifies the canonical variable:

TYPE	Contents
CANCORR	canonical correlations
STRUCTUR	canonical structure
BSTRUCT	between canonical structure
PSTRUCT	pooled within canonical structure
SCORE	standardized canonical coefficients
RAWSCORE	raw canonical coefficients
CANMEAN	means of the canonical variables for each class.

Computational Resources

The amount of memory in bytes for temporary storage needed to process the data is roughly proportional to

$$c(4v^2 + 28v + 4l + 68) + 16v^2 + 96v + 4l$$

where

c = number of class levels
v = number of variables in the VAR list
l = length of the CLASS variable.

With the ANOVA option, the temporary storage must be increased by $16v$ bytes. The DISTANCE option requires an additional temporary storage of $4v^2 + 4v$ bytes.

Printed Output

The printed output from PROC CANDISC includes

1. Class Level Information, including the values of the classification variable, the Frequency and Weight of each value, and its Proportion in the total sample.

Optional output includes

2. Within-Class SSCP Matrices for each group (not shown)
3. Pooled Within-Class SSCP Matrix (not shown)
4. Between-Class SSCP Matrix (not shown)
5. Total-Sample SSCP Matrix (not shown)
6. Within-Class Covariance Matrices for each group (not shown)
7. Pooled Within-Class Covariance Matrix (not shown)
8. Between-Class Covariance Matrix (not shown), equal to the between-class SSCP matrix divided by $n(c-1)/c$, where n is the number of observations and c is the number of classes
9. Total-Sample Covariance Matrix (not shown)
10. Within-Class Correlation Coefficients and Prob $>$ |R| to test the hypothesis that the within-class population correlation coefficients are zero (not shown)
11. Pooled Within-Class Correlation Coefficients and Prob $>$ |R| to test the hypothesis that the partial population correlation coefficients are zero (not shown)
12. Between-Class Correlation Coefficients and Prob $>$ |R| to test the hypothesis that the between-class population correlation coefficients are zero (not shown)
13. Total-Sample Correlation Coefficients and Prob $>$ |R| to test the hypothesis that the total population correlation coefficients are zero (not shown)
14. Simple descriptive Statistics including N (the number of observations), Sum, Mean, Variance, and Standard Deviation for both the total sample and within each class (not shown)
15. Total-Sample Standardized Class Means (not shown), obtained by subtracting the grand mean from each class mean and dividing by the total sample standard deviation
16. Pooled Within-Class Standardized Class Means (not shown), obtained by subtracting the grand mean from each class mean and dividing by the pooled within-class standard deviation
17. Pairwise Squared Distances Between Groups
18. Univariate Test Statistics, including Total STD (total sample standard deviations), Pooled within STD (pooled within-class standard deviations), Between STD (between-class standard deviations), R-Squared (univariate R^2s), RSQ/(1−RSQ) ($R^2/(1-R^2)$), and F and Pr $>$ F (univariate F values and probability levels for one-way analyses of variance).

By default, the printout contains these statistics:

19. Multivariate Statistics and F Approximations including Wilks' Lambda, Pillai's Trace, Hotelling-Lawley Trace, and Roy's Greatest Root with F approximations, degrees of freedom (Num DF and Den DF), and probability values (Pr $>$ F). Each of these four multivariate statistics tests the hypothesis that the class means are equal in the population. See **Multivariate Tests** in Chapter 1, "Introduction to Regression Procedures," for more information.
20. Canonical Correlations.

21. Adjusted Canonical Correlations (Lawley 1959). These are asymptotically less biased than the raw correlations and can be negative. The adjusted canonical correlations may not be computable and are printed as missing values if two canonical correlations are nearly equal or if some are close to zero. A missing value is also printed if an adjusted canonical correlation is larger than a previous adjusted canonical correlation.

22. Approx Standard Error, approximate standard error of the canonical correlations.

23. Squared Canonical Correlations.

24. Eigenvalues of INV(E)*H. Each eigenvalue is equal to CanRsq/(1−CanRsq), where CanRsq is the corresponding squared canonical correlation and can be interpreted as the ratio of between-class variation to pooled within-class variation for the corresponding canonical variable. The table includes Eigenvalues, Differences between successive eigenvalues, the Proportion of the sum of the eigenvalues, and the Cumulative proportion.

25. Likelihood Ratio for the hypothesis that the current canonical correlation and all smaller ones are zero in the population. The likelihood ratio for all canonical correlations equals Wilks' lambda.

26. Approx F statistic based on Rao's approximation to the distribution of the likelihood ratio (Rao 1973, 556; Kshirsagar 1972, 326).

27. Num DF (numerator degrees of freedom), Den DF (denominator degrees of freedom), and Pr > F, the probability level associated with the F statistic.

The following statistics can be suppressed with the SHORT option:

28. Total Canonical Structure, giving total-sample correlations between the canonical variables and the original variables

29. Between Canonical Structure, giving between-class correlations between the canonical variables and the original variables

30. Pooled Within Canonical Structure, giving pooled within-class correlations between the canonical variables and the original variables

31. Standardized Canonical Coefficients, standardized to give canonical variables with zero mean and unit pooled within-class variance when applied to the standardized variables

32. Raw Canonical Coefficients, standardized to give canonical variables with zero mean and unit pooled within-class variance when applied to the raw variables

33. Class Means on Canonical Variables.

EXAMPLE

Analysis of Iris Data Using PROC CANDISC

The iris data published by Fisher (1936) have been widely used for examples in discriminant analysis and cluster analysis. The sepal length, sepal width, petal length, and petal width were measured in millimeters on fifty iris specimens from each of three species: *Iris setosa, I. versicolor,* and *I. virginica.* The following example is a canonical discriminant analysis that creates an output data set containing scores on the canonical variables and plots the canonical variables.

In the PROC CANDISC statement, the DISTANCE option prints squared Mahalanobis distances between class means. The ANOVA option requests CANDISC to test the hypothesis that the class means are equal using univariate statistics. The resulting R^2 values range from 0.400783 for SEPALWID to 0.941372 for

PETALLEN, and each variable is significant at the 0.0001 level. The multivariate test for differences between the classes is also significant at the 0.0001 level, which you would expect from the highly significant univariate test results.

The canonical coefficients for the first canonical variable, CAN1, show that the classes differ most widely on the linear combination -0.0829378*SEPALLEN -0.153447*SEPALWID$+0.220121$*PETALLEN$+0.281046$*PETALWID. The R^2 between CAN1 and the class variable, 0.969872, is much larger than the corresponding R^2 for CAN2, 0.222027. The plot of canonical variables also shows that CAN1 has most of the discriminatory power between the two canonical variables. The following statements produce **Output 13.1** and **13.2**:

```
proc format;
   value specname
      1='SETOSA    '
      2='VERSICOLOR'
      3='VIRGINICA ';
   value specchar
      1='S'
      2='O'
      3='V';
run;
data iris;
   title 'Fisher (1936) Iris Data';
   input sepallen sepalwid petallen petalwid species @@;
   format species specname.;
   label sepallen='Sepal Length in mm.'
         sepalwid='Sepal Width  in mm.'
         petallen='Petal Length in mm.'
         petalwid='Petal Width  in mm.';
   cards;
50 33 14 02 1 64 28 56 22 3 65 28 46 15 2 67 31 56 24 3
63 28 51 15 3 46 34 14 03 1 69 31 51 23 3 62 22 45 15 2
59 32 48 18 2 46 36 10 02 1 61 30 46 14 2 60 27 51 16 2
65 30 52 20 3 56 25 39 11 2 65 30 55 18 3 58 27 51 19 3
68 32 59 23 3 51 33 17 05 1 57 28 45 13 2 62 34 54 23 3
77 38 67 22 3 63 33 47 16 2 67 33 57 25 3 76 30 66 21 3
49 25 45 17 3 55 35 13 02 1 67 30 52 23 3 70 32 47 14 2
64 32 45 15 2 61 28 40 13 2 48 31 16 02 1 59 30 51 18 3
55 24 38 11 2 63 25 50 19 3 64 32 53 23 3 52 34 14 02 1
49 36 14 01 1 54 30 45 15 2 79 38 64 20 3 44 32 13 02 1
67 33 57 21 3 50 35 16 06 1 58 26 40 12 2 44 30 13 02 1
77 28 67 20 3 63 27 49 18 3 47 32 16 02 1 55 26 44 12 2
50 23 33 10 2 72 32 60 18 3 48 30 14 03 1 51 38 16 02 1
61 30 49 18 3 48 34 19 02 1 50 30 16 02 1 50 32 12 02 1
61 26 56 14 3 64 28 56 21 3 43 30 11 01 1 58 40 12 02 1
51 38 19 04 1 67 31 44 14 2 62 28 48 18 3 49 30 14 02 1
51 35 14 02 1 56 30 45 15 2 58 27 41 10 2 50 34 16 04 1
46 32 14 02 1 60 29 45 15 2 57 26 35 10 2 57 44 15 04 1
50 36 14 02 1 77 30 61 23 3 63 34 56 24 3 58 27 51 19 3
57 29 42 13 2 72 30 58 16 3 54 34 15 04 1 52 41 15 01 1
71 30 59 21 3 64 31 55 18 3 60 30 48 18 3 63 29 56 18 3
49 24 33 10 2 56 27 42 13 2 57 30 42 12 2 55 42 14 02 1
49 31 15 02 1 77 26 69 23 3 60 22 50 15 3 54 39 17 04 1
66 29 46 13 2 52 27 39 14 2 60 34 45 16 2 50 34 15 02 1
44 29 14 02 1 50 20 35 10 2 55 24 37 10 2 58 27 39 12 2
```

```
47 32 13 02 1 46 31 15 02 1 69 32 57 23 3 62 29 43 13 2
74 28 61 19 3 59 30 42 15 2 51 34 15 02 1 50 35 13 03 1
56 28 49 20 3 60 22 40 10 2 73 29 63 18 3 67 25 58 18 3
49 31 15 01 1 67 31 47 15 2 63 23 44 13 2 54 37 15 02 1
56 30 41 13 2 63 25 49 15 2 61 28 47 12 2 64 29 43 13 2
51 25 30 11 2 57 28 41 13 2 65 30 58 22 3 69 31 54 21 3
54 39 13 04 1 51 35 14 03 1 72 36 61 25 3 65 32 51 20 3
61 29 47 14 2 56 29 36 13 2 69 31 49 15 2 64 27 53 19 3
68 30 55 21 3 55 25 40 13 2 48 34 16 02 1 48 30 14 01 1
45 23 13 03 1 57 25 50 20 3 57 38 17 03 1 51 38 15 03 1
55 23 40 13 2 66 30 44 14 2 68 28 48 14 2 54 34 17 02 1
51 37 15 04 1 52 35 15 02 1 58 28 51 24 3 67 30 50 17 2
63 33 60 25 3 53 37 15 02 1
;
proc candisc data=iris out=outcan distance anova;
   class species;
   var sepallen sepalwid petallen petalwid;
run;
proc plot;
   plot can2*can1=species;
   format species specchar.;
   title2 'Plot of Canonical Variables';
run;
```

Output 13.1   Iris Data: PROC CANDISC

```
                         Fisher (1936) Iris Data                              1

                    CANONICAL DISCRIMINANT ANALYSIS

          150 Observations        149 DF Total
            4 Variables           147 DF Within Classes
            3 Classes               2 DF Between Classes

                 ❶ Class Level Information

              SPECIES    Frequency      Weight      Proportion

              SETOSA            50      50.0000        0.333333
              VERSICOLOR        50      50.0000        0.333333
              VIRGINICA         50      50.0000        0.333333
```

```
                         Fisher (1936) Iris Data                              2

    CANONICAL DISCRIMINANT ANALYSIS     PAIRWISE SQUARED DISTANCES BETWEEN GROUPS ⓱
               2                     -1
              D (i|j) = (X - X )' COV   (X - X )
                           i   j          i   j


                     Squared Distance to SPECIES
              From
            SPECIES      SETOSA     VERSICOLOR     VIRGINICA

            SETOSA            0       89.86419     179.38471
            VERSICOLOR  89.86419             0      17.20107
            VIRGINICA  179.38471      17.20107             0
```

```
                              Fisher (1936) Iris Data                              3

                         CANONICAL DISCRIMINANT ANALYSIS

                    ⓲  Univariate Test Statistics

                    F Statistics,    Num DF= 2  Den DF= 147

                                                      RSQ/
              Total      Pooled     Between                 
Variable       STD        STD        STD      R-Squared   (1-RSQ)        F        Pr > F   Label

SEPALLEN      8.2807     5.1479     7.9506    0.618706    1.6226      119.2645   0.0001   Sepal Length in mm.
SEPALWID      4.3587     3.3969     3.3682    0.400783    0.6688       49.1600   0.0001   Sepal Width  in mm.
PETALLEN     17.6530     4.3033    20.9070    0.941372   16.0566     1180.1612   0.0001   Petal Length in mm.
PETALWID      7.6224     2.0465     8.9673    0.928883   13.0613      960.0071   0.0001   Petal Width  in mm.

           Average R-Squared:  Unweighted = 0.7224358      Weighted by Variance = 0.8689444
                    ⓳  Multivariate Statistics and F Approximations

                         S=2    M=0.5    N=71

      Statistic                      Value         F      Num DF    Den DF   Pr > F

      Wilks' Lambda               0.02343863   199.1453      8       288     0.0001
      Pillai's Trace              1.19189883    53.4665      8       290     0.0001
      Hotelling-Lawley Trace     32.47732024   580.5321      8       286     0.0001
      Roy's Greatest Root        32.19192920  1166.957       4       145     0.0001

      NOTE: F Statistic for Roy's Greatest Root is an upper bound.
            NOTE: F Statistic for Wilks' Lambda is exact.
```

```
                              Fisher (1936) Iris Data                              4

                         CANONICAL DISCRIMINANT ANALYSIS
                                                          ⓴
                                                      Eigenvalues of INV(E)*H
              ㉑           ㉒          ㉓                = CanRsq/(1-CanRsq)
             Adjusted     Approx     Squared
  ⓴         Canonical    Standard   Canonical
 Canonical   Canonical     Error    Canonical
Correlation Correlation            Correlation  Eigenvalue  Difference  Proportion  Cumulative

1  0.984821  0.984508   0.002468   0.969872     32.1919     31.9065     0.9912     0.9912
2  0.471197  0.461445   0.063734   0.222027      0.2854        .        0.0088     1.0000

     Test of HO: The canonical correlations in the current row and all that follow are zero

              ㉕  Likelihood     ㉖              ㉗
                    Ratio      Approx F       Num DF    Den DF    Pr > F

              1   0.02343863   199.1453          8       288     0.0001
              2   0.77797337    13.7939          3       145     0.0001


                    ㉘  Total Canonical Structure

                              CAN1          CAN2

          SEPALLEN         0.791888      0.217593    Sepal Length in mm.
          SEPALWID        -0.530759      0.757989    Sepal Width  in mm.
          PETALLEN         0.984951      0.046037    Petal Length in mm.
          PETALWID         0.972812      0.222902    Petal Width  in mm.

                    ㉙  Between Canonical Structure

                              CAN1          CAN2

          SEPALLEN         0.991468      0.130348    Sepal Length in mm.
          SEPALWID        -0.825658      0.564171    Sepal Width  in mm.
          PETALLEN         0.999750      0.022358    Petal Length in mm.
          PETALWID         0.994044      0.108977    Petal Width  in mm.
```

(continued on next page)

(continued from previous page)

㉚ Pooled Within Canonical Structure

	CAN1	CAN2	
SEPALLEN	0.222596	0.310812	Sepal Length in mm.
SEPALWID	-0.119012	0.863681	Sepal Width in mm.
PETALLEN	0.706065	0.167701	Petal Length in mm.
PETALWID	0.633178	0.737242	Petal Width in mm.

㉛ Standardized Canonical Coefficients

	CAN1	CAN2	
SEPALLEN	-0.686779533	0.019958173	Sepal Length in mm.
SEPALWID	-0.668825075	0.943441829	Sepal Width in mm.
PETALLEN	3.885795047	-1.645118866	Petal Length in mm.
PETALWID	2.142238715	2.164135931	Petal Width in mm.

Fisher (1936) Iris Data   5

CANONICAL DISCRIMINANT ANALYSIS

㉜ Raw Canonical Coefficients

	CAN1	CAN2	
SEPALLEN	-.0829377642	0.0024102149	Sepal Length in mm.
SEPALWID	-.1534473068	0.2164521235	Sepal Width in mm.
PETALLEN	0.2201211656	-.0931921210	Petal Length in mm.
PETALWID	0.2810460309	0.2839187853	Petal Width in mm.

㉝ Class Means on Canonical Variables

SPECIES	CAN1	CAN2
SETOSA	-7.607599927	0.215133017
VERSICOLOR	1.825049490	-0.727899622
VIRGINICA	5.782550437	0.512766605

Output 13.2   Iris Data: PROC PLOT

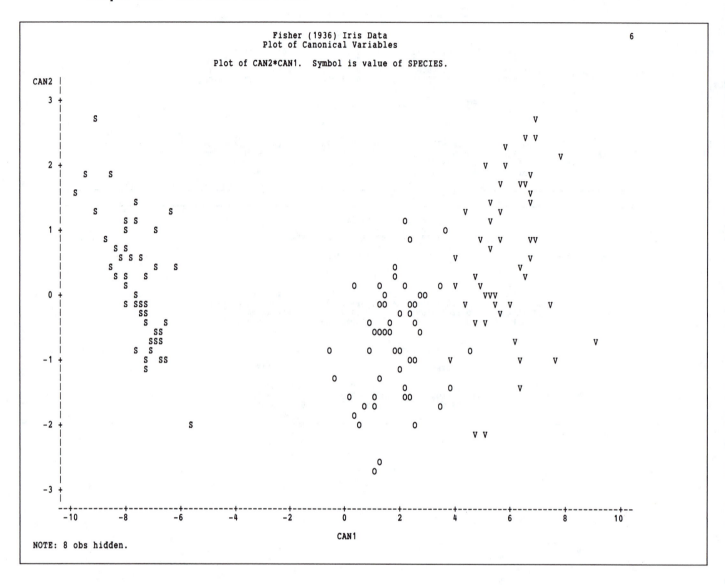

REFERENCES

Fisher, R.A. (1936), "The Use of Multiple Measurements in Taxonomic Problems," *Annals of Eugenics*, 7, 179–188.

Kshirsagar, A.M. (1972), *Multivariate Analysis*, New York: Marcel Dekker, Inc.

Lawley, D.N. (1959), "Tests of Significance in Canonical Analysis," *Biometrika*, 46, 59–66.

Rao, C.R. (1973), *Linear Statistical Inference*, New York: John Wiley & Sons, Inc.

Chapter 14

The CATMOD
Procedure

ABSTRACT

CATMOD is a procedure for CATegorical data MODeling. CATMOD analyzes data that can be represented by a contingency table. It fits linear models to functions of response frequencies and can be used for linear modeling, log-linear modeling, logistic regression, and repeated measurement analysis. CATMOD uses

- maximum-likelihood estimation of parameters for log-linear models and the analysis of generalized logits
- weighted-least-squares estimation of parameters for a wide range of general linear models.

INTRODUCTION

CATMOD provides a wide variety of categorical data analyses. Many of these are generalizations of continuous data analysis methods. For example, analysis of variance, in the traditional sense, refers to the analysis of means and the partitioning of variation among the means into various sources. Here, the term "analysis of variance" is used in a generalized sense to denote the analysis of response functions and the partitioning of variation among those functions into various sources. The response functions might be mean scores if the dependent variables are ordinally scaled. But they can also be marginal probabilities, cumulative logits, or other functions that incorporate the essential information from the dependent variables.

Types of Statistical Analyses

This section illustrates, by example, the wide variety of categorical data analyses that CATMOD provides. For each type of analysis, a brief description of the statistical problem and the SAS statements to provide the analysis are given.

Linear Model Analysis

Example: analyze the relationship between the dependent variables (R1, R2), and the independent variables (A, B). Analyze the marginal probabilities of the dependent variables, and use a main effects model.

```
proc catmod;
  weight wt;
  response marginals;
  model r1*r2=a b;
quit;
```

Log-Linear Model Analysis

Example: analyze the dependent variables (R1, R2, R3) with a log-linear model. Use maximum-likelihood analysis, and include the main effects and the R1*R2 interaction in the model. Obtain the predicted cell frequencies.

```
proc catmod;
  weight wt;
  model r1*r2*r3=_response_ / ml nogls pred=freq;
  loglin r1|r2 r3;
quit;
```

Logistic Regression

Example: analyze the relationship between the dependent variable (R) and the independent variables (X1, X2) with a logistic regression analysis. Use maximum-likelihood estimation.

```
proc catmod;
  weight wt;
  direct x1 x2;
  model r=x1 x2 / ml nogls;
quit;
```

Repeated Measures Analysis

Example: suppose the dependent variables (R1, R2, R3) represent the same type of measurement taken at three different times. Analyze the relationship among the dependent variables, the repeated measurement factor (TIME), and the independent variable (A).

```
proc catmod;
  weight wt;
  response marginals;
  model r1*r2*r3=_response_|a;
  repeated time 3 / _response_=time;
quit;
```

Analysis of Variance

Example: analyze the relationship between the dependent variable (R) and the independent variables (A, B). Analyze the mean of the dependent variable, and include all main effects and interactions in the model.

```
proc catmod;
  weight wt;
  response mean;
  model r=a|b;
quit;
```

Linear Regression

Example: analyze the relationship between the dependent variables (R1, R2) and the independent variables (X1, X2). Use a linear regression analysis, analyzing the marginal probabilities of the dependent variables.

```
proc catmod;
  weight wt;
  direct x1 x2;
  response marginals;
  model r1*r2=x1 x2;
quit;
```

Logistic Analysis of Ordinal Data

Example: analyze the relationship between the ordinally scaled dependent variable (R) and the independent variable (A). Use cumulative logits to take into account the ordinal nature of the dependent variable. Use weighted-least-squares estimation.

```
proc catmod;
  weight wt;
  response clogits;
  model r=_response_ a;
quit;
```

Sample Survey Analysis

Example: suppose the data set contains estimates of a vector of ten functions and its covariance matrix, estimated in such a way as to correspond to the sampling process that was used. Analyze the functions with respect to the independent variables (A, B). Use a main effects model.

```
proc catmod;
  response read b1-b10;
  model _f_=_response_;
  factors  a $ 2 , b $ 5  /  _response_=a b;
quit;
```

Parameter Estimation

Some of the parameters that can be estimated with the CATMOD procedure are as follows:

- covariance matrices
- cumulative or generalized logits
- marginal means or probabilities
- predicted cell frequencies or probabilities
- predicted response functions.

Hypothesis Testing

Some of the hypotheses that can be tested with the CATMOD procedure are as follows:

- independence
- goodness of fit
- linear hypotheses
- marginal homogeneity

- presence of intercepts and slopes
- presence of main effects and interactions.

Specification of Effects

The parameters of a linear model are generally divided into subsets that correspond to meaningful sources of variation in the response functions. These sources, called *effects*, can be specified in the MODEL, LOGLIN, FACTORS, REPEATED, and CONTRAST statements. Effects can be specified in any of the following ways:

- A main effect is a single class variable (that is, it induces classification levels): A   B   C.
- A crossed effect (or interaction) is two or more class variables joined by asterisks, for example, A   A*B   A*B*C.
- A nested effect is a main effect or an interaction, followed by a parenthetical field containing a main effect or an interaction. Multiple variables within the parentheses are assumed to form a crossed effect even when the asterisk is absent. Thus, the last two effects are identical: B(A)   C(A*B)   A*B(C*D)   A*B(C D).
- A nested-by-value effect is the same as a nested effect except that any variable in the parentheses can be followed by an equal sign and a value: B(A=1)   C(A B=1)   C*D(A=1 B=1).
- A direct effect is a variable specified in a DIRECT statement: X   Y.
- Direct effects can be crossed with other effects: X*Y   X*X*X   X*A*B(C D=1).

The variables for crossed and nested effects remain in the order in which they are first encountered. For example, in the model

```
model r=b  a  a*b  c(a b);
```

the effect A*B is reported as B*A since B appeared before A in the statement. Also, C(A B) is interpreted as C(A*B) and is therefore reported as C(B*A).

Bar Notation

You can shorten the specification of effects by using bar notation. For example, two methods of writing a full three-way factorial model are

```
proc catmod;
    model y=a  b  c  a*b  a*c  b*c  a*b*c;
```

and

```
proc catmod;
    model y=a|b|c;
```

When the bar (|) is used, the right- and left-hand sides become effects, and the cross of them becomes an effect. Multiple bars are permitted. The expressions are expanded from left to right, using rules 1 through 4 given in Searle (1971, 390):

- Multiple bars are evaluated left to right. For instance, A | B | C is {A | B} | C, which is {A B A*B} | C, which is A B A*B C A*C B*C A*B*C.
- Crossed and nested groups of variables are combined. For example, A(B) | C(D) generates A*C(B D), among other terms.
- Duplicate variables are removed. For example, A(C) | B(C) generates A*B(C), among other terms, and the extra C is removed.
- Effects are discarded if a variable occurs on both the crossed and nested sides of an effect. For instance, A(B) | B(D E) generates A*B(B D E), but this effect is eliminated immediately.

You can also specify the maximum number of variables involved in any effect that results from bar evaluation by specifying that maximum number, preceded by an @ sign, at the end of the bar effect. For example, the specification A | B | C @ 2 would result in only those effects which contain 2 or fewer variables; in this case A B A*B C A*C and B*C.

Other examples of the bar notation are

A | C(B)	is equivalent to	A C(B) A*C(B)
A(B) | C(B)	is equivalent to	A(B) C(B) A*C(B)
A(B) | B(D E)	is equivalent to	A(B) B(D E)
A | B(A) | C	is equivalent to	A B(A) C A*C B*C(A)
A | B(A) | C@2	is equivalent to	A B(A) C A*C
A | B | C | D@2	is equivalent to	A B A*B C A*C B*C D A*D B*D C*D

Background: The Underlying Model

CATMOD analyzes data that can be represented by a two-dimensional contingency table. The rows of the table correspond to populations (or samples) formed on the basis of one or more independent variables. The columns of the table correspond to observed responses formed on the basis of one or more dependent variables. The frequency in the (i,j)th cell is the number of subjects in the ith population that have the jth response. The frequencies in the table are assumed to follow a product multinomial distribution, corresponding to a sampling design in which a simple random sample is taken for each population. The contingency table can be represented as shown in **Table 14.1**.

Table 14.1   Contingency Table Representation

	Response			
Sample	1	2	...	r
1	n_{11}	n_{12}	...	n_{1r}	n_1
2	n_{21}	n_{22}	...	n_{2r}	n_2
...	...	...	...	...	...
s	n_{s1}	n_{s2}	...	n_{sr}	n_s

For each sample i, the probability of the jth response (π_{ij}) is estimated by the sample proportion, $p_{ij}=n_{ij}/n_i$. The vector (**p**) of all such proportions is then transformed into a vector of functions, denoted by **F**=**F(p)**. If π denotes the vector of true probabilities for the entire table, then the functions of the true probabilities, denoted by **F(π)**, are assumed to follow a linear model

$$\mathbf{E_A(F)} = \mathbf{F(\pi)} = \mathbf{X\beta}$$

where $\mathbf{E_A}$ denotes asymptotic expectation, **X** is the design matrix containing fixed constants, and β is a vector of parameters to be estimated.

CATMOD provides two estimation methods:

1. The maximum-likelihood method estimates the parameters of the linear model so as to maximize the value of the joint multinomial likelihood function of the responses. Maximum-likelihood estimation is available only for the standard log-linear response functions, which are used for logistic regression analysis and log-linear model analysis. For details of the theory, see Bishop, Fienberg, and Holland (1975).
2. The weighted-least-squares method minimizes the weighted residual sum of squares for the model. The weights are contained in the inverse covariance matrix of the functions **F(p)**. According to central limit theory, if the sample sizes are sufficiently large, the elements of **F** and **b** (the estimate of β) are approximately distributed as multivariate normal. This allows the computation of statistics for testing the goodness of fit of the model and the significance of other sources of variation. For details of the theory, see Grizzle, Starmer, and Koch (1969) or Koch et al. (1977, Appendix 1). Weighted-least-squares estimation is available for all types of response functions.

Following parameter estimation, hypotheses about linear combinations of the parameters can be tested. For that purpose, CATMOD computes generalized Wald (1943) statistics, which are approximately distributed as chi-square if the sample sizes are sufficiently large.

Linear Models Contrasted with Log-Linear Models

Linear model methods (as typified by the Grizzle, Starmer, Koch approach) make a very clear distinction between independent and dependent variables. The emphasis of these methods is estimation and hypothesis testing of the model parameters. Therefore, it is easy to test for differences among probabilities, perform repeated measurement analysis, and test for marginal homogeneity, but it is awkward to test independence and generalized independence. These methods are a natural extension of the usual *ANOVA* approach for continuous data.

In contrast, log-linear model methods (as typified by the Bishop, Fienberg, Holland approach) do not make an a priori distinction between independent and dependent variables, although model specifications that allow for the distinction can be made. The emphasis of these methods is on model building, goodness-of-fit tests, and estimation of cell frequencies or probabilities for the underlying contingency table. With these methods, it is easy to test independence and generalized independence, but it is awkward to test for differences among probabilities, do repeated measurement analysis, and test for marginal homogeneity.

Using CATMOD Interactively

CATMOD can be used interactively. After specifying a model with a MODEL statement and running CATMOD with a RUN statement, any statement can be executed without reinvoking CATMOD. The statements may be executed singly or in groups by following the single statement or group of statements with a RUN statement. Note that more than one MODEL statement can be used; this is an important difference from PROC GLM.

If you use CATMOD interactively, you can end the CATMOD procedure with a DATA step, another PROC step, an ENDSAS statement, or with a QUIT statement. The syntax of the QUIT statement is

```
quit;
```

When you are using CATMOD interactively, additional RUN statements do not end CATMOD, but tell the procedure to execute additional statements.

When the CATMOD procedure detects a BY statement, it disables interactive processing; that is, once the BY statement and the next RUN statement are encountered, processing proceeds for each BY group in the data set, and no additional statements are accepted by the procedure. For example, the statements

```
proc catmod;
    weight wt;
    response marginals;
    model r1*r2=a|b;
run;
    by sex;
run;
```

tell CATMOD to do three analyses: one for the entire data set, one for males, and one for females. Note that the BY statement may appear after the first RUN statement; this is an important difference from PROC GLM, which requires that the BY statement appear before the first RUN statement.

Acknowledgments

CATMOD is similar in capabilities to the GENCAT program by Landis, Stanish, Freeman, and Koch (1976) but has been adapted to match the design syntax of ANOVA and GLM in the SAS System. CATMOD replaced the FUNCAT procedure that appeared in earlier versions of the SAS System. The major enhancements contained in CATMOD are features that facilitate repeated measurement analysis and log-linear modeling. Moreover, there are numerous design features that make the CATMOD procedure more flexible and more informative.

SPECIFICATIONS

The following statements can be used with the CATMOD procedure:

PROC CATMOD *options*; }   required statement

DIRECT *variables*; }   must precede MODEL statement

MODEL *response_effect = design_effects / options*; } required statement

CONTRAST *'label' row_description,* }   cannot precede
   row_description, . . . ;   }   MODEL statement

BY *variables*;
FACTORS *factor_description, . . . / options*;
LOGLIN *effects*;
MODEL *response_effect = design_effects / options*;   can be used
POPULATION *variables*;   anywhere
REPEATED *factor_description, . . . / options*;
RESPONSE *function / options*;
WEIGHT *variable*;

All of the statements are interactive. The first RUN statement executes all of the previous statements. Any subsequent RUN statement executes only those statements that appear between the previous RUN statement and the current one.

If more than one CONTRAST statement appears between two RUN statements, all the CONTRAST statements are processed. If more than one RESPONSE statement appears between two RUN statements, then analyses associated with each RESPONSE statement are produced. For all other statements, there can be only one occurrence of the statement between any two RUN statements. For example, if there are two LOGLIN statements between two RUN statements, the first LOGLIN statement is ignored.

The PROC and MODEL statements are required. If used, the DIRECT statement must precede the MODEL statement. The CONTRAST statements, if any, must be preceded by the MODEL statement.

Of the LOGLIN, REPEATED, and FACTORS statements, only one can be specified between any two RUN statements since all of them specify the same information: how to partition the variation among the response functions within a population.

A QUIT statement executes any statements that have not been processed, and then signals CATMOD to terminate.

The purpose of each statement, other than the PROC statement, can be summarized as follows:

BY
determines groups in which data are to be processed separately.

CONTRAST
specifies a hypothesis to test.

DIRECT
specifies independent variables that are to be treated quantitatively (like continuous variables), rather than qualitatively (like class or discrete variables). These variables also help to determine the rows of the contingency table and distinguish response functions in one population from those in other populations.

FACTORS
specifies (1) the factors that distinguish response functions from others in the same population and (2) model effects, based on these factors, which help to determine the design matrix.

LOGLIN
specifies log-linear model effects.

MODEL
specifies (1) dependent variables, which determine the columns of the contingency table, (2) independent variables, which distinguish response functions in one population from those in other populations, and (3) model effects, which determine the design matrix and the way in which total variation among the response functions is partitioned.

POPULATION
specifies independent variables, which determine the rows of the contingency table and distinguish response functions in one population from those in other populations.

REPEATED
specifies (1) the repeated measurement factors that distinguish response functions from others in the same population and (2) model effects, based on these factors, which help to determine the design matrix.

RESPONSE
determines the response functions that are to be modeled.

WEIGHT
specifies a variable containing frequency counts.

PROC CATMOD Statement

PROC CATMOD *options*;

This statement invokes the procedure. Two options are available:

DATA=*SASdataset*
names the SAS data set containing the data to be analyzed. If the DATA=option is not given, CATMOD uses the most recently created SAS data set.

ORDER=DATA
specifies that variable levels are to be ordered according to the sequence in which they appear in the input stream. This, in turn, affects the ordering of the populations, the responses, and the parameters, as well as the definitions of the parameters. If ORDER=DATA is not specified, then the variable levels are ordered according to their internal sorting sequence (for example, numeric order or alphabetical order). See

the section **Ordering of Populations and Responses** later in this chapter for more information and examples.

BY Statement

> BY *variables*;

A BY statement can be used with PROC CATMOD to obtain separate analyses of groups determined by the BY variables. When a BY statement appears, the procedure expects the input data set to be sorted in order of the BY variables.

If your input data set is not sorted in ascending order, use the SORT procedure with a similar BY statement to sort the data, or, if appropriate, use the BY statement options NOTSORTED or DESCENDING. For more information, see the discussion of the BY statement in "SAS Statements Used in the PROC Step," in the *SAS Language Guide, Release 6.03 Edition*.

When a BY statement is used with PROC CATMOD, no further interactive processing is possible. In other words, once the BY statement appears, all statements up to the associated RUN statement are executed for each BY group in the data set. After the RUN statement, no further statements are accepted by the procedure.

CONTRAST Statement

> CONTRAST *'label' row_description, row_description, . . . ;*

where

> *row_description = @n effect values . . . @n effect values*

The CONTRAST statement constructs and tests linear functions of the parameters. Each *row_description* specifies one row of the matrix **C** that CATMOD uses to test the hypothesis **Cβ=0** . *Row_descriptions* are separated by a comma. The CONTRAST statements, if any, must be preceded by the MODEL statement. The following terms are specified in the CONTRAST statement:

'label'	specifies up to twenty-four characters of identifying information printed with the test. *'label'* is required.
@n	If the model type is not AVERAGED (refer to the AVERAGED option in the MODEL statement and in **Generation of the Design Matrix** in the **DETAILS** section of this chapter), then there is one set of parameters for each of the *q* response functions. The *@n* points to the parameters in the *n*th set. If *@n* is not given, *@1* is assumed. If the model type is AVERAGED, then the *@n* notation is invalid.
	The *@n* notation is seldom needed. It allows you to test the variation among response functions in the same population. However, it is usually easier to model and test such variation by using the _RESPONSE_ effect in the MODEL statement or by using the ALL_PARMS designation.
effect	is one of the effects listed in the MODEL statement. INTERCEPT can be specified for the intercept parameter. ALL_PARMS can be specified for the complete set of parameters.
values	are numbers that form the coefficients of the parameters associated with the given effect. If there are fewer values

than parameters for an effect, the remaining coefficients become zero.

Specifying Contrasts

CATMOD is parameterized differently than GLM, so you must be careful not to use the same contrasts that you would with GLM. Since CATMOD uses a full-rank parameterization, all estimable parameters are directly estimable without involving other parameters.

For example, suppose a class variable A has four levels. Then there are four parameters $(\alpha_1, \alpha_2, \alpha_3, \alpha_4)$, of which CATMOD uses only the first three. The fourth parameter is related to the others by the equation

$$\alpha_4 = -\alpha_1 - \alpha_2 - \alpha_3$$

To test the first versus the fourth level of A, you would test $\alpha_1 = \alpha_4$, which is

$$\alpha_1 = -\alpha_1 - \alpha_2 - \alpha_3$$

or, equivalently,

$$2\alpha_1 + \alpha_2 + \alpha_3 = 0 \quad .$$

Therefore, you would use the CONTRAST statement:

```
contrast '1 vs. 4'  a  2  1  1;
```

To contrast the third level with the average of the first two levels, you would test

$$(\alpha_1 + \alpha_2) / 2 = \alpha_3$$

or, equivalently,

$$\alpha_1 + \alpha_2 - 2\alpha_3 = 0$$

Therefore, you would use the CONTRAST statement:

```
contrast '1&2 vs. 3'  a  1  1  -2;
```

Other CONTRAST statements are constructed similarly, for example,

```
contrast '1 vs. 2     '  a  1  -1   0 ;
contrast '1&2 vs. 4   '  a  3   3   2 ;
contrast '1&2 vs. 3&4'   a  2   2   0 ;
contrast 'Main Effect'   a  1   0   0 ,
                         a  0   1   0 ,
                         a  0   0   1 ;
```

The actual form of the **C** matrix depends on the effects in the model. For example, if you specify

```
proc catmod;
   model y=a;
   contrast '1 vs. 4'  a  2  1  1;
```

then the **C** matrix is

$$\mathbf{C} = \begin{bmatrix} 0 & 2 & 1 & 1 \end{bmatrix}$$

since the first parameter corresponds to the intercept. But if there is a variable B with three levels and the MODEL statement is

```
model y=b a;
```

then the same CONTRAST statement induces the **C** matrix

$$\mathbf{C} = \begin{bmatrix} 0 & 0 & 0 & 2 & 1 & 1 \end{bmatrix}$$

since the first parameter corresponds to the intercept and the next two correspond to the B main effect.

The CONTRAST statement can also be used to test the joint effect of two or more effects in the MODEL statement. For example, the joint effect of A and B in the model given above has five degrees of freedom and is obtained by specifying:

```
contrast 'Joint Effect of A&B'    a 1 0 0 ,
                                  a 0 1 0 ,
                                  a 0 0 1 ,
                                  b 1 0   ,
                                  b 0 1   ;
```

The ordering of variable levels is determined by the ORDER= option in the PROC CATMOD statement. Whenever you specify a contrast that depends on the order of the variable levels, you should verify the order from the POPULATION PROFILES, the RESPONSE PROFILES, or the ONE-WAY table.

Using ALL_PARMS

The *effect* in the CONTRAST statement can be replaced by the keyword ALL_PARMS, which is then regarded as an effect with the same number of parameters as the number of columns in the design matrix. This is particularly useful when the design matrix is input directly, as in the following example:

```
model y=( 1 0 0 0 ,
          1 0 1 0 ,
          1 1 0 0 ,
          1 1 1 1 ) ;
contrast 'Main Effect of B' all_parms 0 1 0 0 ;
contrast 'Main Effect of C' all_parms 0 0 1 0 ;
contrast 'B*C Interaction ' all_parms 0 0 0 1 ;
```

DIRECT Statement

DIRECT *variables*;

The DIRECT statement lists numeric variables to be treated in a quantitative, rather than qualitative, way. The DIRECT statement is useful for logistic regression, which is described in the **DETAILS** section. If used, the DIRECT statement must precede the MODEL statement. For example, if the variable X has five levels, and you specify

```
proc catmod;
   direct x;
   model y=x;
```

then the main effect X induces only one column in the design matrix, rather than four. The values inserted into the design matrix are the actual values of X.

FACTORS Statement

FACTORS *factor_description, . . . / options;*

where

   factor_description = factor_name $ levels

and *factor_descriptions* are separated from each other by a comma.

The FACTORS statement identifies factors that distinguish response functions from others in the same population. It also specifies how those factors are incorporated into the model. It can be used whenever there is more than one response function per population and the keyword _RESPONSE_ is used in the MODEL statement. The name, type, and number of levels of each factor, and the identification of each level can be specified.

factor_name   gives the name of a factor that corresponds to two or more response functions. *Factor_name* should conform to naming conventions of SAS variables, and it should not be the same as the name of a variable that already exists in the data set being analyzed.

$ indicates that the factor is character-valued. If the $ is omitted, then the factor is assumed to be numeric. The type of the factor is relevant only when the PROFILE option is used or when the _RESPONSE_= option specifies nested-with-value effects.

levels   specifies the number of levels of the corresponding factor. If there is only one such factor, and the number is omitted, then CATMOD assumes that the number of levels is equal to the number of response functions per population (*q*). Unless the PROFILE option is specified, the number *q* must either be equal to, or be a multiple of, the product of the number of levels of all the factors.

The three options below can be specified in the FACTORS statement after the slash (/):

PROFILE=*(matrix)*
   specifies the values assumed by the factors for each response function. There should be one column for each factor, and the values in a given column (character or numeric) should match the type of the corresponding factor. Character values are restricted to 16 characters or less. If there are *q* response functions per population, then the matrix must have *i* rows, where *q* must either be equal to, or be a multiple of, *i*. Adjacent rows of the matrix should be separated by a comma.

   The values in the PROFILE matrix are useful for specifying models in those situations where the study design is not a full factorial with respect to the factors. They can also be used to specify nested-with-value effects in the _RESPONSE_= option. If character values are specified in both places (the PROFILE= option and the _RESPONSE_= option), then the values must match with respect to whether or not they are enclosed in quotes (that is, enclosed in quotes in both places or in neither place).

RESPONSE=*effects*
   specifies design effects. The variables named in the effects must be *factor_names* that appear in the FACTORS statement. If the _RESPONSE_= option is omitted, then CATMOD builds a full factorial _RESPONSE_ effect with respect to the factors.

TITLE=*'title'*
> causes the *title* to be printed at the top of certain pages of output that correspond to this FACTORS statement.

The format of the FACTORS statement is identical to that of the REPEATED statement. In fact, repeated measurement factors are simply special cases of factors in which some of the response functions correspond to multiple dependent variables that are measurements on the same experimental (or sampling) units.

The FACTORS statement cannot be specified for an analysis that also contains the REPEATED or LOGLIN statement since all of them specify the same information: how to partition the variation among the response functions within a population.

The FACTORS statement is perhaps most useful when the response functions and their covariance matrix are read directly from the input data set. In this case, CATMOD reads the response functions as though they were from one population (this poses no problem in the multiple-population case because the appropriately constructed covariance matrix is also read directly). Thus, the FACTORS statement can be used to partition the variation among the response functions into appropriate sources, even when the functions actually represent separate populations.

As an example of how the FACTORS statement is useful, consider the case where the response functions and their covariance matrix are read directly from the input data set. The TYPE=EST data set might be created in the following manner:

```
data direct(type=est);
   input b1-b4 _type_ $ _name_ $8.;
   cards;
0.590463   0.384720   0.273269   0.136458   parms    .
0.001690   0.000911   0.000474   0.000432   cov      b1
0.000911   0.001823   0.000031   0.000102   cov      b2
0.000474   0.000031   0.001056   0.000477   cov      b3
0.000432   0.000102   0.000477   0.000396   cov      b4
;
```

Suppose the response functions correspond to four populations that represent the cross-classification of age (2 groups) by sex. Then the FACTORS statement can be used to identify these two factors and to name the effects in the model. The CATMOD statements required to fit a main effects model to these data are

```
proc catmod data=direct;
  response read b1-b4;
  model _f_=_response_;
  factors age 2, sex 2 / _response_=age sex;
```

If you wanted to specify some nested-with-value effects, you could change the FACTORS statement to

```
factors age $ 2, sex $ 2 /
   _response_=age sex(age='under 30') sex(age='30 & over')
   profile=( 'under 30'    male    ,
             'under 30'    female  ,
             '30 & over'   male    ,
             '30 & over'   female );
```

If, by design or chance, the study contained no male subjects under 30 years of age, then there would be only three response functions, and a main-effects model could be specified as

```
proc catmod data=direct;
  response read b2-b4;
  model _f_=_response_;
  factors age $ 2, sex $ 2 /  _response_ = age sex
    profile=( 'under 30'   female ,
              '30 & over'   male   ,
              '30 & over'   female );
```

When two or more factors are specified and the PROFILE= option is omitted, CATMOD presumes that the response functions are ordered so that the levels of the rightmost factor change most rapidly. For the first example above, the order implied by the FACTORS statement is

Response Function	Dependent Variable	AGE	SEX
1	B1	1	1
2	B2	1	2
3	B3	2	1
4	B4	2	2

For additional examples of how the FACTORS statement can be used, see the section on the REPEATED statement later in this chapter. All of the examples in that section are applicable, with REPEATED replaced by FACTORS.

LOGLIN Statement

LOGLIN *effects / option;*

The LOGLIN statement is used to define log-linear model effects. It can be used whenever the response functions are the standard ones (generalized logits).

When the LOGLIN statement is used, the keyword _RESPONSE_ should be specified in the MODEL statement. For further information on log-linear model analysis, see **Log-Linear Model Analysis** in the **DETAILS** section of this chapter.

effects   specifies design effects that contain dependent variables in the MODEL statement.

The option below can be specified in the LOGLIN statement after the slash (/).

TITLE=*'title'*
    causes the *title* to be printed at the top of certain pages of output that correspond to this LOGLIN statement.

The LOGLIN statement cannot be specified for an analysis that also contains the REPEATED or FACTORS statement since all of them specify the same information: how to partition the variation among the response functions within a population.

As an example of how the LOGLIN statement is used,

```
proc catmod;
   model a*b*c=_response_;
   loglin  a|b|c @ 2;
```

yields a log-linear model analysis that contains all main effects and two-variable interactions. For more examples of log-linear model analysis, see **Log-Linear Model Analysis** in the **DETAILS** section of this chapter.

MODEL Statement

MODEL *response_effect=design_effects / options;*

CATMOD requires a MODEL statement.

response_effect   indicates the dependent variables that determine the response categories (the columns of the underlying contingency table). *Response_effect* is either a single variable or a crossed effect having two or more variables joined by asterisks. The dependent variable _f_ indicates that the response functions and their estimated covariance matrix will be read directly into CATMOD.

design_effects   specify potential sources of variation (such as main effects and interactions) to be included in the model. Thus, they determine the number of model parameters, as well as the interpretation of such parameters. In addition, if there is no POPULATION statement, any variables contained in the specification of *design_effects* are used by CATMOD to determine the populations (the rows of the underlying contingency table).

     Design_effects can be any of those described in the section **Specification of Effects**, or they can be defined by specifying the actual design matrix, enclosed in parentheses. Also, the keyword _RESPONSE_ can be used in place of a variable name in the specification of *design_effects*, except that an effect cannot be nested within _RESPONSE_. For more information on the _RESPONSE_ effect, see the sections **Log-Linear Model Analysis** and **Repeated Measures Analysis** later in this chapter.

Some examples of MODEL statements are

`model r=a b;`	main effects only
`model r=a b a*b;`	main effects with interaction
`model r=a b(a);`	nested effect
`model r=a|b;`	complete factorial
`model r=a b(a=1) b(a=2);`	nested-by-value effects
`model r*s=_response_;`	log-linear model
`model r*s=a _response_(a);`	nested repeated measurement factor
`model _f_=_response_;`	direct input of the response functions

The relationship between these specifications and the structure of the design matrix **X** is described in **Generation of the Design Matrix** in the **DETAILS** section of this chapter.

The options below can be specified in the MODEL statement after a slash (/).

Options to Request Additional Computation and Printing

CORRB
> prints the estimated correlation matrix of the parameter estimates.

COV
> prints S_i, the covariance matrix of the response functions for each population.

COVB
> prints the estimated covariance matrix of the parameter estimates.

FREQ
> prints the two-way frequency table for the cross-classification of populations by responses.

ML
> requests maximum-likelihood estimates. This option is available only when generalized logits are used.

ONEWAY
> produces a one-way table of frequencies for each variable used in the analysis. This table is useful in determining the order of the observed levels for each variable.

PREDICT
PRED=FREQ
PRED=PROB
> prints the observed and predicted values of the response functions for each population, together with their standard errors and the residuals (observed−predicted). In addition, if the response functions are the standard ones (generalized logits), then PRED=FREQ specifies the computation and printing of predicted cell frequencies, while PRED=PROB (or just PREDICT) specifies the computation and printing of predicted cell probabilities.

PROB
> prints the two-way table of probability estimates for the cross-classification of populations by responses. These estimates sum to one across the response categories for each population.

TITLE='title'
> causes the title to be printed at the top of certain pages of output that correspond to this MODEL statement.

XPX
> prints $X'S^{-1}X$, the crossproducts matrix for the normal equations.

Options to Suppress Computation and Printing

NODESIGN
> suppresses printing of the design matrix **X**.

NOGLS
> suppresses the computation of the generalized (weighted) least-squares estimates. This is useful when only the maximum-likelihood estimates are needed. In that case, you must specify the ML option, and the ML parameter estimates start out at zero in the iterative estimation procedure. This option is particularly useful for logistic regression and for

log-linear models in which random zeros have been replaced by some very small frequency (such as $1E-10$).

NOINT

suppresses the intercept term in the model.

NOITER

suppresses printing of parameter estimates and other information at each iteration of a maximum-likelihood analysis.

NOPARM

suppresses printing of the estimated parameters and the statistics for testing that each parameter is zero.

NOPROFILE

suppresses printing of the population profiles and the response profiles.

NORESPONSE

suppresses printing of the _RESPONSE_ matrix for log-linear models. For further information, see the log-linear modeling section in **Generation of the Design Matrix** later in this chapter.

Options to Specify Details of Computation and Printing

ADDCELL=*number*

specifies that *number* be added to the frequency count in each cell, where *number* is any positive number. This option has no effect on maximum-likelihood analysis; it is only used for weighted-least-squares analysis.

AVERAGED

specifies that dependent variable effects can be modeled and that independent variable main effects are averaged across the response functions in a population. For further information on the effect of using (or not using) the AVERAGED option, see **Generation of the Design Matrix**. Direct input of the design matrix or specification of _RESPONSE_ in the MODEL statement automatically induces an AVERAGED model type.

EPSILON=*number*

specifies the convergence criterion for the maximum-likelihood estimation of the parameters. The iterative estimation process stops when the proportional change in the log likelihood is less than EPSILON, or after MAXITER iterations, whichever comes first. If the EPSILON= option is omitted, then EPSILON=$1E-8$.

MAXITER=*number*

specifies the maximum number of iterations to be used for the maximum-likelihood estimation of the parameters. If the MAXITER= option is omitted, then MAXITER=20.

Specifying the Design Matrix Directly

If you specify the design matrix directly, adjacent rows of the matrix must be separated by a comma, and the matrix must have $q*s$ rows, where s is the number of populations, and q is the number of response functions per population. The first q rows correspond to the response functions for the first population, the second set of q rows corresponds to the functions for the second population, and so forth. An example of a MODEL statement using direct specification of the design matrix is

```
model r=( 1 0 ,
          1 1 ,
          1 2 ,
          1 3 );
```

When you input the design matrix directly, you also have the option of specifying that any subsets of the parameters be tested for equality to zero. Indicate each subset by specifying the appropriate column numbers of the design matrix, followed by an equal sign and a label (24 characters or less, in single quotes) that describes the subset. Adjacent subsets are separated by a comma, and the entire specification is enclosed in parentheses and placed after the design matrix. An example of a MODEL statement using this option is

```
model r=( 1  1  0  0 ,
          1  1  0  1 ,
          1  1  0  2 ,
          1  0  1  0 ,
          1  0  1  1 ,
          1  0  1  2 ,
          1 -1 -1  0 ,
          1 -1 -1  1 ,
          1 -1 -1  2 ) ( 1='Intercept',
                         2 3='Group main effect',
                           4='Linear effect of time' );
```

If you input the design matrix directly, but do not specify any subsets of the parameters to be tested, then CATMOD tests the effect of MODEL | MEAN, which represents the significance of the model beyond what is explained by an overall mean. For the previous example, the MODEL | MEAN effect would be the same as that obtained by specifying

```
(2 3 4='model|mean')
```

at the end of the MODEL statement.

POPULATION Statement

POPULATION *variables*;

The POPULATION statement specifies that populations are to be formed on the basis of cross-classifications of the specified variables. If you do not specify the POPULATION statement, then populations are formed on the basis of cross-classifications of the independent variables in the MODEL statement. The POPULATION statement has two major uses:

1. When you enter the design matrix directly, there are no independent variables in the MODEL statement; therefore, the POPULATION statement is the only way of inducing more than one population.
2. When you fit a reduced model, the POPULATION statement may be necessary if you want to induce the same number of populations as there were for the saturated model.

To illustrate the first use, suppose you specify the following statements:

```
data one;
   input a $ b $ wt @@;
   cards;
yes yes 23   yes no 31   no yes 47   no no 50
;
```

```
proc catmod;
   weight wt;
   population b;
   model a=( 1 0 ,
             1 1 );
```

Since the dependent variable A has two levels, there is one response function per population. Since the variable B has two levels, there are two populations. Thus, the MODEL statement is valid since the number of rows in the design matrix (2) is the same as the total number of response functions. If the POPULATION statement had been omitted, there would have been only one population and one response function, and the MODEL statement would have been invalid.

To illustrate the second use, suppose you specify

```
data two;
   input a $ b $ y wt @@;
   cards;
yes  yes  1  23        yes  yes  2  63
yes  no   1  31        yes  no   2  70
no   yes  1  47        no   yes  2  80
no   no   1  50        no   no   2  84
;
proc catmod;
   weight wt;
   model y=a b a*b;
```

These statements induce four populations and produce the following design matrix and analysis-of-variance table.

$$\mathbf{X} = \begin{bmatrix} 1 & 1 & 1 & 1 \\ 1 & 1 & -1 & -1 \\ 1 & -1 & 1 & -1 \\ 1 & -1 & -1 & 1 \end{bmatrix}$$

Source	DF	Chi-Square	Prob
INTERCEPT	1	48.10	0.0001
A	1	3.47	0.0625
B	1	0.25	0.6186
A*B	1	0.19	0.6638
RESIDUAL	0	0.00	1.0000

Since the B and A*B effects are nonsignificant ($p>0.10$), you may want to fit the reduced model that contains only the A effect. If your new statements are

```
proc catmod;
   weight wt;
   model y=a;
```

then only two populations are induced, and the design matrix and the analysis-of-variance table are as follows:

$$\mathbf{X} = \begin{bmatrix} 1 & 1 \\ 1 & -1 \end{bmatrix}$$

Source	DF	Chi-Square	Prob
INTERCEPT	1	47.94	0.0001
A	1	3.33	0.0678
RESIDUAL	0	0.00	1.0000

However, if the new statements are

```
proc catmod;
   weight wt;
   population a b;
   model y=a;
```

then four populations are induced, and the design matrix and the analysis-of-variance table are as follows:

$$
X = \begin{bmatrix} 1 & 1 \\ 1 & 1 \\ 1 & -1 \\ 1 & -1 \end{bmatrix}
$$

Source	DF	Chi-Square	Prob
INTERCEPT	1	47.76	0.0001
A	1	3.30	0.0694
RESIDUAL	2	0.35	0.8374

The advantage of the latter analysis is that it retains four populations for the reduced model, thereby creating a built-in goodness-of-fit test: the residual chi-square. Such a test is important because the cumulative (or joint) effect of deleting two or more effects from the model may be significant, even if the individual effects are not.

The resulting differences between the two analyses are due to the fact that the latter analysis uses pure weighted-least-squares estimates with respect to the four populations that were actually sampled. The former analysis pools populations and therefore uses parameter estimates that can be regarded as weighted-least-squares estimates of maximum-likelihood-predicted cell frequencies. In any case, the estimation methods are asymptotically equivalent; therefore, the results are very similar. If the ML option had been specified in the MODEL statement, then the parameter estimates would have been identical for the two analyses.

REPEATED Statement

REPEATED *factor_description*, . . . / *options*;

where

factor_description = *factor_name* $ *levels*

and *factor_descriptions* are separated from each other by a comma.

The REPEATED statement is used to incorporate repeated measurement factors into the model. It can be used whenever there is more than one dependent variable and the keyword _RESPONSE_ is used in the MODEL statement. If the dependent variables correspond to one or more repeated measurement factors, you can use the REPEATED statement to define _RESPONSE_ in terms of those factors. You can specify the name, type, and number of levels of each factor, as well as the identification of each level.

The REPEATED statement cannot be specified for an analysis that also contains the FACTORS or LOGLIN statement since all of them specify the same information: how to partition the variation among the response functions within a population.

factor_name   gives the name of a repeated measurement factor that corresponds to two or more response functions. *Factor_name* should conform to naming conventions of SAS variables, and it should not be the same as the name of a variable that already exists in the data set being analyzed.

$ indicates that the factor is character-valued. If the $ is omitted, then the factor is assumed to be numeric. The type of the factor is relevant only when the PROFILE option is used or when the _RESPONSE_= option specifies nested-with-value effects.

levels   specifies the number of levels of the corresponding repeated measurement factor. If there is only one such factor and the number is omitted, then CATMOD assumes that the number of levels is equal to the number of response functions per population (q) . Unless the PROFILE option is specified, the number q must either be equal to, or be a multiple of, the product of the number of levels of all the factors.

The three options below can be specified in the REPEATED statement after the slash (/):

PROFILE=(*matrix*);
   specifies the values assumed by the factors for each response function. There should be one column for each factor, and the values in a given column (character or numeric) should match the type of the corresponding factor. Character values are restricted to 16 characters or less. If there are q response functions per population, then the matrix must have i rows, where q must either be equal to, or be a multiple of, i. Adjacent rows of the matrix should be separated by a comma.

   The values in the PROFILE matrix are useful for specifying models in those situations where the study design is not a full factorial with respect to the factors. They can also be used to specify nested-with-value effects in the _RESPONSE_= option. If character values are specified in both the PROFILE= option and the _RESPONSE_= option, then the values must match with respect to whether or not they are enclosed in quotes (that is, enclosed in quotes in both places or in neither place).

RESPONSE=*effects*
   specifies design effects. The variables named in the effects must be *factor_names* that appear in the REPEATED statement. If the _RESPONSE_= option is omitted, then CATMOD builds a full factorial _RESPONSE_ effect with respect to the repeated measurement factors.

TITLE='*title*'
   causes the *title* to be printed at the top of certain pages of output that correspond to this REPEATED statement.

For further information and numerous examples of the REPEATED statement, see the section **Repeated Measures Analysis** later in this chapter.

RESPONSE Statement

RESPONSE *function* / *options*;

The RESPONSE statement specifies functions of the response probabilities. It is these response functions that are modeled as linear combinations of the parameters. If no RESPONSE statement is specified, CATMOD uses the default standard response functions (generalized logits, which are explained in detail below). More than one RESPONSE statement can be specified, in which case each RESPONSE statement produces a separate analysis. If the computed response functions for any population are linearly dependent (yielding a singular covariance matrix), then CATMOD prints an error message and stops processing. See **Cautions** in the **DETAILS** section for methods of dealing with this. *Function* specification is one of the following:

CLOGIT
CLOGITS
specifies that the response functions are cumulative logits of the marginal probabilities for each of the dependent variables. For each dependent variable, the response functions are a set of linearly independent cumulative logits, obtained by taking the logarithms of the ratios of two probabilities. The denominator of the kth ratio is the cumulative probability, c_k, corresponding to the kth level of the variable, and the numerator is $1-c_k$ (Agresti 1984, 113-114). If a dependent variable has two levels, then CATMOD computes its cumulative logit as the negative of its generalized logit. Cumulative logits should be used only when the dependent variables are ordinally scaled.

JOINT
specifies that the response functions are the joint response probabilities. A linearly independent set is created by deleting the last response probability.

LOGIT
LOGITS
specifies that the response functions are generalized logits of the marginal probabilities for each of the dependent variables. For each dependent variable, the response functions are a set of linearly independent generalized logits, obtained by taking the logarithms of the ratios of two probabilities. The denominator of each ratio is the marginal probability corresponding to the last observed level of the variable, and the numerators are the marginal probabilities corresponding to each of the other levels. If there is one dependent variable, then specifying LOGIT is equivalent to using the standard response functions.

MARGINAL
MARGINALS
specifies that the response functions are marginal probabilities for each of the dependent variables in the MODEL statement. For each dependent variable, the response functions are a set of linearly independent marginals, obtained by deleting the marginal probability corresponding to the last level.

MEAN
MEANS
specifies that the response functions are the means of the dependent variables in the MODEL statement. This specification requires that all of the dependent variables be numeric.

READ *variables*
specifies that the response functions and their covariance matrix are to be read directly from the input data set with one response function for each variable named.

transformation   specifies response functions that can be expressed by using successive applications of the four operations matrix literal **LOG**, **EXP**, or **+** matrix literal. The operations are described in detail below.

The three options below can be specified in the RESPONSE statement after a slash (/):

OUT=*SASdataset*
    produces a SAS data set that contains, for each population, the observed and predicted values of the response functions, their standard errors, and the residuals. Moreover, if the standard response functions are used, the data set also includes observed and predicted values of the cell frequencies or the cell probabilities. For further information, see **Output Data Sets** later in this chapter.

OUTEST=*SASdataset*
    produces a SAS data set that contains the estimated parameter vector and its estimated covariance matrix. For further information, see **Output Data Sets** later in this chapter.

    If you want an output data set to be a permanent SAS data set, you must specify a two-level name. See "SAS Files" in the *SAS Language Guide* for more information on permanent SAS data sets.

TITLE=*'title'*
    causes the *title* to be printed at the top of certain pages of output that correspond to this RESPONSE statement.

Example response statements are shown below:

Example	Result
`response marginals;`	marginals for each dependent variable
`response means;`	the mean of each dependent variable
`response logits;`	generalized logits of the marginal probabilities
`response clogits;`	cumulative logits of the marginal probabilities
`response joint;`	the joint probabilities
`response 1 -1 log;`	the logit
`response / out=pred1;`	generalized logits and an output data set
`response 1 2 3;`	the mean score, with scores of 1, 2, and 3 corresponding to the three response levels
`response read b1-b4;`	four response functions and their covariance matrix, read directly from the input data set

Using a Transformation to Specify Response Functions

Transformation, if specified, is applied to the vector that contains the sample proportions in each population. *Transformation* can be any combination of the following four operations:

Operation	Specification
linear combination	matrix literal
logarithm	**LOG**
exponential	**EXP**
adding constant	**+** matrix literal

The **LOG** of a vector transforms each element of the vector into its natural logarithm; the **EXP** of a vector transforms each element into its exponential function (antilogarithm). If more than one operation is specified, then CATMOD applies the operations consecutively from right to left. If two matrix literals appear next to each other, they should be separated by an asterisk, in which case CATMOD multiplies the two matrices.

A matrix literal is a series of numbers with each row of the matrix separated from the next by a comma, for example,

```
response 1 0 0 , 0 1 0;
```

specifies a linear response function for data that have $r=3$ response categories. The matrix literal specifies a 2×3 matrix, which is applied to each population as follows:

$$\begin{bmatrix} F1 \\ F2 \end{bmatrix} = \begin{bmatrix} 1 & 0 & 0 \\ 0 & 1 & 0 \end{bmatrix} * \begin{bmatrix} P1 \\ P2 \\ P3 \end{bmatrix}$$

where P1, P2, and P3 are sample proportions for the three response categories in a population, and F1 and F2 are the two response functions computed for that population. This response function, therefore, sets F1=P1 and F2=P2 in each population.

As another example of the linear response function, suppose you have two dependent variables corresponding to two observers who evaluate the same subjects. If the observers grade on the same three-point scale, and if all nine possible responses are observed, then the following RESPONSE statement would compute the probability that the observers agree on their assessments:

```
response    1 0 0    0 1 0    0 0 1;
```

Another way of writing this response function is

$$F = P11 + P22 + P33 = \begin{bmatrix} 1\ 0\ 0 & 0\ 1\ 0 & 0\ 0\ 1 \end{bmatrix} * \begin{bmatrix} P11 \\ P12 \\ P13 \\ P21 \\ P22 \\ P23 \\ P31 \\ P32 \\ P33 \end{bmatrix}$$

where Pij denotes the probability that a subject gets a grade of i from the first observer and j from the second observer.

If the function is a compound function, requiring more than one operation to specify it, then the operations should be listed in order so that the first operation to be applied is on the right, and the last operation to be applied is on the left. For example, if there are two response levels, the response function

```
response 1 -1 log;
```

is equivalent to the matrix expression:

$$F = \begin{bmatrix} 1 & -1 \end{bmatrix} * \begin{bmatrix} \log(P1) \\ \log(P2) \end{bmatrix}$$

As a programming statement, this would appear as

```
f1=log(p1)-log(p2);
```

which is the logit function

```
f1=log(p1 / (1-p1));
```

since P2=1−P1 when there are only two response levels.

Another example of a compound response function is

```
response 1 -1 exp 1 0 0 1 , 0 1 1 0 log;
```

which is equivalent to the matrix expression

F = A * EXP (B * LOG (P));

where **P** is the vector of sample proportions for some population,

$$\mathbf{A} = \begin{bmatrix} 1 & -1 \end{bmatrix} \quad \text{and} \quad \mathbf{B} = \begin{bmatrix} 1 & 0 & 0 & 1 \\ 0 & 1 & 1 & 0 \end{bmatrix} \quad .$$

If the four responses are based on two dependent variables, each with the same two levels, then the function can also be written as

```
f=p11*p22-p12*p21;
```

which is the crossproduct ratio for a 2×2 table.

The Standard Response Functions

If no RESPONSE statement is specified, CATMOD computes the standard response functions, which contrast the log of each response probability with the log of the probability for the last response category. If there are r response categories, then there are $r-1$ standard response functions. For example, if there are four response categories, using no RESPONSE statement is equivalent to specifying

```
response  1 0 0 -1,
          0 1 0 -1,
          0 0 1 -1  log;
```

This results in three response functions:

$$\mathbf{F} = \begin{bmatrix} F1 \\ F2 \\ F3 \end{bmatrix} = \begin{bmatrix} \log(P1/P4) \\ \log(P2/P4) \\ \log(P3/P4) \end{bmatrix} \quad .$$

If there were only two response levels, the resulting response function would be a logit. Thus, the standard response functions are called generalized logits. They are useful in dealing with the log-linear model:

$$\pi = \mathbf{EXP} (\mathbf{X\beta}) \quad .$$

If **C** denotes the matrix in the RESPONSE statement given above, then because of the restriction that the probabilities sum to 1, it follows that an equivalent model is

$$\mathbf{C\ LOG} (\pi) = (\mathbf{CX})\beta$$

But **C LOG** (**P**) is simply the vector of standard response functions. Thus, the equation means that fitting a log-linear model on the cell probabilities is equivalent to fitting a linear model on the generalized logits.

WEIGHT Statement

WEIGHT *variable*;

A WEIGHT statement can be used to refer to a variable containing the cell frequencies, which need not be integers. The WEIGHT statement lets you use summary data sets containing a count variable. See **Input Data Set** in the **DETAILS** section for further information concerning the WEIGHT statement.

DETAILS

Missing Values

Observations with missing values for any variable listed in the MODEL, POPULATION, or WEIGHT statements are omitted from the analysis.

Input Data Set

Data to be analyzed by CATMOD must be in a SAS data set containing either

- raw data values (variable values for every subject)
- frequency counts and the corresponding variable values
- response function values and their covariance matrix.

If a WEIGHT statement is used, then CATMOD uses the values of the WEIGHT variable as the frequency counts. If the READ function is specified in the RESPONSE statement, then CATMOD expects the input data set to contain the values of response functions and their covariance matrix. Otherwise, CATMOD assumes the SAS data set contains raw data values.

Raw Data Values

If raw data are used, CATMOD first counts the number of observations having each combination of values for all variables used in the MODEL and POPULATION statements. For example, suppose the variables A and B each take on the values 1 and 2, and their frequencies can be represented as follows:

	A=1	A=2
B=1	2	1
B=2	3	0

The SAS data set containing the raw data might be as follows:

data set RAW:	OBS	A	B
	1	1	1
	2	1	1
	3	1	2
	4	1	2
	5	1	2
	6	2	1

and the statements for CATMOD would be

```
proc catmod data=raw;
   model a=b;
```

Frequency Counts

If your data set contains frequency counts, then use the WEIGHT statement in CATMOD to specify the variable containing the frequencies. For example, you could create the following data set:

data set SUMMARY:	OBS	A	B	COUNT
	1	1	1	2
	2	1	2	3
	3	2	1	1

in which case the corresponding CATMOD statements would be

```
proc catmod data=summary;
   weight count;
   model a=b;
```

The data set SUMMARY can be created directly, or it can be created from data set RAW by using PROC FREQ:

```
proc freq data=raw;
   tables a*b / out=summary;
```

Response Functions

If you want to read in the response functions and their covariance matrix, rather than have CATMOD compute them, create a TYPE=EST data set. In addition to having one variable name for each function, the data set should have two additional variables: _TYPE_ and _NAME_. The variable _TYPE_ should have the value 'PARMS' when the observation contains the response functions; it should have the value 'COV' when the observation contains elements of the covariance matrix of the response functions. The variable _NAME_ (length 8) is used only when _TYPE_ = 'COV', in which case it should contain the name of the variable that has its covariance elements stored in that observation. In the following data set, for example, the covariance between the second and fourth response functions is 0.000102.

```
data direct(type=est);
   input b1-b4 _type_ $ _name_ $8.;
   cards;
0.590463   0.384720   0.273269   0.136458   PARMS   .
0.001690   0.000911   0.000474   0.000432   COV     B1
0.000911   0.001823   0.000031   0.000102   COV     B2
0.000474   0.000031   0.001056   0.000477   COV     B3
0.000432   0.000102   0.000477   0.000396   COV     B4
;
```

In order to tell CATMOD that the input data set contains the values of response functions and their covariance matrix,

- specify the READ function in the RESPONSE statement, and
- specify _f_ as the dependent variable in the MODEL statement.

For example, suppose the response functions correspond to four populations that represent the cross-classification of two age groups by two race groups. Then the FACTORS statement can be used to identify these two factors and to name the effects in the model. The CATMOD statements required to fit a main-effects model to these data are

```
proc catmod data=direct;
   response read b1-b4;
   model _f_=_response_;
   factors age 2, race 2 / _response_=age race;
```

Ordering of Populations and Responses

Suppose you specify the following statements:

```
data one;
   input a $ b $ wt @@;
   cards;
yes yes 23    yes no 31    no yes 47    no no 50
;
proc catmod;
   weight wt;
   model a=b;
```

Then the ordering of populations and responses corresponds to the alphabetical order of the levels of the character variables

POPULATION PROFILES			RESPONSE PROFILES	
Sample	B		Response	A
1	no		1	no
2	yes		2	yes

and the parameter for the main effect of B corresponds to the first level of B, which is NO. However, if you specify the ORDER=DATA option

```
proc catmod order=data;
```

then the ordering of populations and responses is

POPULATION PROFILES			RESPONSE PROFILES	
Sample	B		Response	A
1	yes		1	yes
2	no		2	no

and the parameter for the main effect of B corresponds to the first level of B, which is YES. Thus, you can use the ORDER=DATA option to ensure that populations and responses are ordered in a specific way. But since this also affects the definitions and the ordering of the parameters, you must exercise caution when using the _RESPONSE_ effect, the CONTRAST statement, or direct input of the design matrix. See the **Cautions** section for additional examples.

An alternative method of ensuring that populations and responses are ordered in a specific way is to replace any character variables by numeric variables and to assign formatted values such as "yes" and "no" to the numeric levels.

Output Data Sets

OUT= Data Set

This output data set contains, for each population, observed and predicted values of the response functions, their standard errors, and the residuals. In addition, if the standard response functions are used, the data set includes observed and predicted values for the cell frequencies or the cell probabilities, together with their standard errors and residuals. For the standard response functions, there are $s*(2q+1)$ observations in the data set for each BY group, where s is the number of populations, and q is the number of response functions per population. Otherwise, there are $s*q$ observations in the data set for each BY group. The new data set contains the BY variables (if any) and the following new variables:

SAMPLE	specifies the population number.
TYPE	specifies a character variable with three possible values. When _TYPE_='FUNCTION', the observed and predicted values are values of the response functions. When _TYPE_='PROB', they are values of the cell probabilities. When _TYPE_='FREQ', they are values of the cell frequencies.
NUMBER	specifies the sequence number of the response function or the cell probability or the cell frequency.
OBS	specifies the observed value.
SEOBS	specifies the standard error of the observed value.
PRED	specifies the predicted value.
SEPRED	specifies the standard error of the predicted value.
RESID	specifies the residual (observed−predicted).

OUTEST= Data Set

This output data set, which contains the estimated parameter vector and its estimated covariance matrix, has TYPE=EST. For each BY group, there are $p+1$

observations in the data set, where p is the number of estimated parameters. The data set contains the following variables:

- the BY variables, if any.
- the new character variable _TYPE_, with two possible values. When _TYPE_='PARMS', the variables B1, B2, and so on, contain parameter estimates; when _TYPE_='COV', they contain covariance estimates.
- the new character variable _NAME_. When _TYPE_='PARMS', _NAME_ is blank, but when _TYPE_='COV', _NAME_ has one of the values B1, B2, and so on, corresponding to the parameter names.
- one variable for each estimated parameter: B1, B2, and so on.

See Appendix 2, "Special SAS Data Sets," for more information on special SAS data sets.

Logistic Regression

Logistic regression refers to an analysis in which the response functions are the logits of the dependent variable. Generally, the independent variables are treated quantitatively (like continuous variables), rather than qualitatively (like class variables, in which case the analysis is sometimes called a logistic analysis).

CATMOD can compute two different types of logits automatically (plus other types, by using more complicated RESPONSE statements):

- Generalized logits are used for nominally scaled dependent variables. Maximum-likelihood estimation is available for the analysis of these logits.
- Cumulative logits are used for ordinally scaled dependent variables. If the dependent variable has two response levels, you can use maximum-likelihood estimation. Otherwise, only weighted-least-squares estimation is available for the analysis of these logits.

If the dependent variable has only two responses, then the cumulative logit is the negative of the generalized logit, as computed by CATMOD.

If you want CATMOD to treat the independent variables as quantitative variables, specify them in a DIRECT statement, as well as in the MODEL statement.

Generalized Logits

Use the ML and NOGLS options to request maximum-likelihood analysis and to suppress the generalized-least-squares analysis. Generalized logits are computed by default when there is no RESPONSE statement.

```
proc catmod;
   direct x1 x2 x3;
   model r=x1 x2 x3 / ml nogls;
```

When the dependent variable has two responses, the parameter estimates from CATMOD are the same as those from a logistic regression program such as LOGIST except that the signs are reversed. This is because CATMOD normalizes with respect to the minimum value of the dependent variable, while LOGIST normalizes with respect to the maximum value. The chi-square statistics and the predicted values are, of course, identical. Use cumulative logits if you want the parameters to be identical to those of LOGIST. (The LOGIST procedure is described in the *SUGI Supplemental Library User's Guide, Version 5 Edition* and in SAS Technical Report P-175, *Changes and Enhancements to the SAS System, Release 5.18, under OS and CMS.*)

Cumulative Logits

If your dependent variable is ordinally scaled, you can specify the analysis of cumulative logits that take into account the ordinal nature of the dependent variable:

```
proc catmod;
    response clogits;
    direct x1 x2 x3;
    model r=x1 x2 x3;
```

In the special case where the dependent variable has two response levels, you can use maximum-likelihood estimation for the analysis of the cumulative logits:

```
proc catmod;
    response clogits;
    direct x1 x2 x3;
    model r=x1 x2 x3 / ml nogls;
```

Logistic Analysis

If some of the independent variables are class variables, they are specified in the MODEL statement but not in the DIRECT statement:

```
proc catmod;
    direct x;
    model r=x a|b / ml nogls;
```

Continuous Variables

If the independent variables are actually continuous variables, then each observation represents a separate sample. At this extreme of sparseness, the weighted-least-squares method is inappropriate since there are too many zero frequencies. Therefore, the maximum-likelihood method should be used. CATMOD was not designed optimally for continuous variables and therefore may be less efficient than a program designed specifically to handle continuous data.

Log-Linear Model Analysis

When the response functions are the standard ones (generalized logits), then inclusion of the keyword _RESPONSE_ in every effect on the right-hand side of the MODEL statement induces a log-linear model. The keyword _RESPONSE_ simply tells CATMOD that you want to model the variation among the dependent variables. You then specify the actual model in the LOGLIN statement.

One word of caution about log-linear model analyses is that sampling zeros in the input data set should be replaced by some positive number close to zero (such as $1E-20$) by adding one line to the DATA step, and that such data containing sampling zeros should be analyzed with maximum-likelihood estimation. See the **Cautions** section and **Example 5** for further information and an illustration.

One Population

The usual log-linear model analysis has one population, which means that all of the variables are dependent variables. For example, the statements

```
proc catmod;
    weight wt;
    model r1*r2=_response_ / ml nogls;
    loglin  r1|r2;
```

yield a maximum-likelihood analysis of a saturated log-linear model for the dependent variables R1 and R2.

If you want to fit a reduced model with respect to the dependent variables (for example, a model of independence or conditional independence), specify the reduced model in the LOGLIN statement. For example, the statements

```
proc catmod;
   weight wt;
   model r1*r2=_response_ / ml nogls pred;
   loglin  r1 r2;
```

yield a main-effects log-linear model analysis of the factors R1 and R2. The output includes Wald statistics for the individual effects R1 and R2, as well as predicted cell probabilities. Moreover, the goodness-of-fit statistic is the likelihood ratio test for the hypothesis of independence between R1 and R2.

Multiple Populations

You can do log-linear model analysis with multiple populations by using a POPULATION statement or by including effects on the right-hand side of the MODEL statement that contain independent variables. Each effect must include the _RESPONSE_ keyword.

For example, suppose the dependent variables R1 and R2 are dichotomous, and the independent variable GROUP has three levels. Then

```
proc catmod;
   weight wt;
   model r1*r2=_response_  group*_response_ / ml nogls;
   loglin r1|r2;
```

specifies a saturated model (3 df for _RESPONSE_ and 6 df for the interaction between _RESPONSE_ and GROUP). From another point of view, _RESPONSE_*GROUP can be regarded as a main effect for GROUP with respect to the 3 response functions, while _RESPONSE_ can be regarded as an intercept effect with respect to the functions. In other words, these statements give essentially the same results as the logistic analysis:

```
proc catmod;
   weight wt;
   model r1*r2=group / ml nogls;
```

The ability to model the interaction between the independent and the dependent variables becomes particularly useful when a reduced model is specified for the dependent variables. For example,

```
proc catmod;
   weight wt;
   model r1*r2=_response_  group*_response_ / ml nogls;
   loglin  r1 r2;
```

specifies a model with 2 df for _RESPONSE_ (1 for R1 and 1 for R2) and 4 df for the interaction of _RESPONSE_*GROUP. The likelihood-ratio goodness-of-fit statistic (3 df) tests the hypothesis that R1 and R2 are independent in each of the 3 groups.

Repeated Measures Analysis

If there are multiple dependent variables and the variables represent repeated measurements of the same observational unit, then the variation among the dependent variables can be attributed to one or more repeated measurement factors. When the response functions are not the standard ones (generalized logits), the factors can be included in the model by specifying the keyword _RESPONSE_ on the right-hand side of the MODEL statement. A REPEATED statement is then used to identify the factors.

One Population

Consider an experiment in which each subject is measured at three times, and the response functions are marginal probabilities for each of the dependent variables. If the dependent variables each had k levels, then CATMOD would compute $k-1$ response functions for each time. Differences among the response functions with respect to these times could be attributed to the repeated measurement factor TIME. To incorporate the TIME variation into the model, specify

```
proc catmod;
   response marginals;
   model t1*t2*t3=_response_;
   repeated time 3 / _response_=time;
```

These statements would induce a TIME effect that would have $2*(k-1)$ degrees of freedom since there are $k-1$ response functions at each time point.

Now suppose that at each time point, each subject has X-rays taken, and the X-rays are read by two different radiologists. This would create six dependent variables that represent the 3×2 cross-classification of the repeated measurement factors TIME and READER. A saturated model with respect to these factors could be obtained by specifying

```
proc catmod;
   response marginals;
   model r11*r12*r21*r22*r31*r32=_response_;
   repeated time 3, reader 2 / _response_=time reader time*reader;
```

If you want to fit a main effects model with respect to TIME and READER, then change the REPEATED statement to

```
   repeated time 3, reader 2 / _response_=time reader;
```

If you want to fit a main effects model for TIME, but only for one of the readers, the REPEATED statement might look like

```
   repeated time 3, reader 2 / _response_=time(reader=SMITH)
                      profile =( '1'   SMITH ,
                                 '1'   JONES ,
                                 '2'   SMITH ,
                                 '2'   JONES ,
                                 '3'   SMITH ,
                                 '3'   JONES );
```

If JONES had been unavailable for a reading at time 3, then there would only be $5*(k-1)$ response functions, even though CATMOD would be expecting some multiple of 6 ($=3*2$). In that case, the PROFILE option would be necessary to indicate which repeated measurement profiles were actually represented:

```
   repeated time 3, reader 2 / _response_=time(reader=SMITH)
                      profile =( '1'   SMITH ,
                                 '1'   JONES ,
                                 '2'   SMITH ,
                                 '2'   JONES ,
                                 '3'   SMITH );
```

When two or more repeated measurement factors are specified, CATMOD presumes that the response functions are ordered so that the levels of the right-most factor change most rapidly. If the RESPONSE statement specifies MEANS or MARGINALS, then the dependent variables should be specified in the same order. For this example, the order implied by the REPEATED statement is

Response Function	Dependent Variable	TIME	READER
1	R11	1	1
2	R12	1	2
3	R21	2	1
4	R22	2	2
5	R31	3	1
6	R32	3	2

where R_{ij} corresponds to Time i and Reader j. Thus, the order of dependent variables in the MODEL statement must agree with the order implied by the REPEATED statement.

Multiple Populations

When there are variables specified in the POPULATION statement or on the right-hand side of the MODEL statement, these variables induce multiple populations. CATMOD can then model these independent variables, the repeated measurement factors, and interactions between the two.

For example, suppose that there are five groups of subjects, that each subject in the study is measured at three different times, and that the dichotomous dependent variables are labeled T1, T2, and T3. Then the statements

```
proc catmod;
   weight wt;
   population group;
   response marginals;
   model t1*t2*t3=_response_;
   repeated time / _response_=time;
```

induce the computation of three response functions for each population. CATMOD then regards _RESPONSE_ as a variable with three levels corresponding to the three response functions in each population and forms an effect with 2 df. The MODEL statement tells CATMOD to fit the main effect of TIME.

In general, the MODEL statement tells CATMOD how to integrate the independent variables and the repeated measurement factors into the model. For example, the following MODEL statements result in the indicated analyses:

`model t1*t2*t3=group / averaged;`	specifies the GROUP main effect (with 4 df).
`model t1*t2*t3=_response_;`	specifies the TIME main effect (with 2 df).
`model t1*t2*t3=_response_*group;`	specifies the interaction between TIME and GROUP (with 8 df).
`model t1*t2*t3=_response_|group;`	specifies both main effects, and the interaction between TIME and GROUP (with 14 df).
`model t1*t2*t3=_response_(group);`	specifies a TIME main effect within each GROUP (with 10 df).

But

`model t1*t2*t3=group(_response_);`	is invalid.

Generation of the Design Matrix

Each row of the design matrix (corresponding to a population) is generated by a unique combination of independent variable values. The columns of the design matrix are produced from the effect specifications in the MODEL, LOGLIN, FACTORS, and REPEATED statements. For details on effect specifications, see **Specification of Effects** earlier in this chapter. This section is divided into three parts:

- one response function per population
- two or more response functions per population (excluding log-linear models)
- log-linear models.

One Response Function Per Population

Intercept   When there is one response function per population, all design matrices start with a column of 1s for the intercept unless the NOINT option is specified or the design matrix is input directly.

Main effects   If a class variable A has k levels, then its main effect has $k-1$ degrees of freedom, and the design matrix has $k-1$ columns that correspond to the first $k-1$ levels of A. The ith column contains a 1 in the ith row, a -1 in the last row, and zeros everywhere else. If α_i denotes the parameter that corresponds to the ith level of variable A, then the $k-1$ columns yield estimates of the independent parameters, $\alpha_1, \alpha_2, \ldots, \alpha_{k-1}$. The last parameter is not needed because CATMOD constrains the k parameters to sum to zero. In other words, CATMOD uses a full-rank center-point parameterization to build design matrices. Here are two examples:

Data Levels	Design Columns
A	A

A		
1	1	0
2	0	1
3	−1	−1

B	B

B	
1	1
2	−1

Crossed effects (interactions)   Crossed effects (such as A*B) are formed by the horizontal direct products of main effects. For example,

Data Levels		Design Matrix Columns				
A	B	A		B	A*B	
1	1	1	0	1	1	0
1	2	1	0	−1	−1	0
2	1	0	1	1	0	1
2	2	0	1	−1	0	−1
3	1	−1	−1	1	−1	−1
3	2	−1	−1	−1	1	1

The number of degrees of freedom for a crossed effect (that is, the number of design matrix columns) is equal to the product of the numbers of degrees of freedom for the separate effects.

Nested effects   The effect A(B) is read "A within B" and is like specifying an A main effect for every value of B. If n_a and n_b are the number of levels in A and B, respectively, then the number of columns for A(B) is $(n_a-1)n_b$ if every combination of levels exists in the data. For example,

Data Levels		Design Matrix Columns			
B	A	A(B)			
1	1	1	0	0	0
1	2	0	1	0	0
1	3	−1	−1	0	0
2	1	0	0	1	0
2	2	0	0	0	1
2	3	0	0	−1	−1

CATMOD actually allocates a column for all possible combinations of values even though some combinations may not be present in the data.

Nested-by-value effects   Instead of nesting an effect within all values of the main effect, you can nest an effect within specified values of the nested variable (A(B=1), for example). The four degrees of freedom for the A(B) effect shown above can also be obtained by specifying the two separate nested effects with values:

Data Levels		Design Matrix Columns			
B	A	A(B=1)		A(B=2)	
1	1	1	0	0	0
1	2	0	1	0	0
1	3	−1	−1	0	0
2	1	0	0	1	0
2	2	0	0	0	1
2	3	0	0	−1	−1

Each effect has n_a-1 degrees of freedom, assuming a complete combination. Thus, for the example, each effect has two degrees of freedom.

Direct effects   To request that the actual values of a variable be inserted into the design matrix, declare the variable in a DIRECT statement, and specify the effect by the variable name. For example, specifying the effects X1 and X2 in both the MODEL and DIRECT statements results in

Data Levels		Design Columns	
X1	X2	X1	X2
1	1	1	1
2	4	2	4
3	9	3	9

Unless there is a POPULATION statement that excludes the direct variables, those variables help induce the classification for the sample populations to be defined. In general, the variables should not be continuous in the sense that every subject has a different value because this would induce a separate population for each subject (note, however, that such a strategy is used purposely for logistic regression).

If there is a POPULATION statement that omits mention of the direct variables, then the values of the direct variables must be identical for all subjects in a given population since there can only be one independent variable profile for each population.

Two or More Response Functions Per Population

When there is more than one response function per population, the structure of the design matrix depends on whether or not the model type is AVERAGED (refer to the AVERAGED option in the MODEL statement). The model type is AVERAGED if independent variable effects are averaged over the multiple responses within a population, rather than being nested in them.

The following subsections illustrate the effect of specifying (or not specifying) an AVERAGED model type. This section does not apply to log-linear models. See **Log-Linear Model Design Matrices** later in this chapter for log-linear model design matrix generation.

Model type not AVERAGED   Suppose the variable A has two levels, and you specify

```
proc catmod;
   model y=a;
```

If the variable Y has two levels, then there is only one response function per population, and the design matrix is

Sample	Design Matrix INTERCEPT	A
1	1	1
2	1	−1

But if the variable Y has three levels, then there are two response functions per population, and the design matrix above is assumed to hold for each of the two response functions. The response functions are always ordered so that the multiple response functions within a population are grouped together. For this example, the design matrix would be

Sample	Response Function Number	Design Matrix INTERCEPT		A	
1	1	1	0	1	0
1	2	0	1	0	1
2	1	1	0	−1	0
2	2	0	1	0	−1

Since the same submatrix applies to each of the multiple response functions, CATMOD prints only the submatrix (that is, the one it would print if there were only one response function per population), rather than the entire design matrix.

Model type AVERAGED   When the model type is AVERAGED (for example, when the AVERAGED option is specified in the MODEL statement), CATMOD does not assume that the same submatrix applies to each of the q response functions per population. Rather, it averages any independent variable effects across the functions, and it allows you to study variation among the q functions. The first column of the design matrix is always a column of 1s corresponding to the intercept, unless the NOINT option is specified in the MODEL statement or the design matrix is input directly. Also, since the design matrix does not have any special submatrix structure, CATMOD prints the entire matrix.

For example, suppose the dependent variable Y has three levels, the independent variable A has two levels, and you specify

```
proc catmod;
   response 1 0 0 , 0 1 0;
   model y=a / averaged;
```

Then there are two response functions per population, and the response functions are always ordered so that the multiple response functions within a population are grouped together. For this example, the design matrix would be

Sample	Response Function Number	Design Matrix INTERCEPT	A
1	1	1	1
1	2	1	1
2	1	1	−1
2	2	1	−1

Note that the model now has only two degrees of freedom. The remaining two degrees of freedom in the residual correspond to variation among the three levels of the dependent variable. Generally, that variation tends to be statistically significant and therefore should not be left out of the model. You can include it in the model by including the two effects, _RESPONSE_ and _RESPONSE_*A, but if the study is not a repeated measurement study, those sources of variation tend to be uninteresting. Thus, the usual solution for this type of study (one dependent variable) is to exclude the AVERAGED option from the MODEL statement.

An AVERAGED model type is automatically induced whenever the _RESPONSE_ keyword is used in the MODEL statement. The _RESPONSE_ effect models variation among the q response functions per population. If there is no REPEATED, FACTORS, or LOGLIN statement, then CATMOD builds a main effect with $q-1$ degrees of freedom. For example, three response functions would induce the following design columns:

Response Function Number	Design Columns _RESPONSE_	
1	1	0
2	0	1
3	−1	−1

If there is more than one population, then the _RESPONSE_ effect is averaged over the populations. Also, the _RESPONSE_ effect can be crossed with any other effect, or it can be nested within an effect.

If there is a REPEATED statement that contains only one repeated measurement factor, then CATMOD builds the design columns for _RESPONSE_ in the same way, except that the printed output labels the main effect with the factor name, rather than with the word _RESPONSE_. For example, suppose an independent variable A has two levels, and the input statements are

```
proc catmod;
   response marginals;
   model time1*time2=a _response_ a*_response_;
   repeated time 2 / _response_=time;
```

If TIME1 and TIME2 each have two levels (so that they each have one independent marginal probability), then the RESPONSE statement causes CATMOD to compute two response functions per population. Thus, the design matrix would be

Sample	Response Function Number	Design Matrix INTERCEPT	A	TIME	A*TIME
1	1	1	1	1	1
1	2	1	1	−1	−1
2	1	1	−1	1	−1
2	2	1	−1	−1	1

However, if TIME1 and TIME2 each have three levels (so that they each have two independent marginal probabilities), then the RESPONSE statement causes CATMOD to compute four response functions per population. In that case, since TIME has two levels, CATMOD groups the functions into sets of 2(=4/2) and constructs the above submatrix for each function in the set. This results in the following design matrix, which is obtained from the previous one by multiplying each element by an identity matrix of order two:

Sample	Response Function	INTERCEPT		A		TIME		A*TIME	
1	P(TIME1=1)	1	0	1	0	1	0	1	0
1	P(TIME1=2)	0	1	0	1	0	1	0	1
1	P(TIME2=1)	1	0	1	0	−1	0	−1	0
1	P(TIME2=2)	0	1	0	1	0	−1	0	−1
2	P(TIME1=1)	1	0	−1	0	1	0	−1	0
2	P(TIME1=2)	0	1	0	−1	0	1	0	−1
2	P(TIME2=1)	1	0	−1	0	−1	0	1	0
2	P(TIME2=2)	0	1	0	−1	0	−1	0	1

If there is a REPEATED statement that contains two or more repeated measurement factors, then CATMOD builds the design columns for _RESPONSE_ according to the definition of _RESPONSE_ in the REPEATED statement. For example, suppose you specify

```
proc catmod;
   response marginals;
   model r11*r12*r21*r22=_response_;
   repeated time 2, place 2 / _response_=time place;
```

If each of the dependent variables had two levels, then CATMOD would build four response functions. The _RESPONSE_ effect would generate a main effects model with respect to TIME and PLACE:

Response Function Number	Variable	TIME	PLACE	Design Matrix INTERCEPT	_RESPONSE_	
1	R11	1	1	1	1	1
2	R12	1	2	1	1	−1
3	R21	2	1	1	−1	1
4	R22	2	2	1	−1	−1

Log-Linear Model Design Matrices

When the response functions are the standard ones (generalized logits), then inclusion of the keyword _RESPONSE_ in every design effect induces a log-linear model. The design matrix for a log-linear model looks different from a standard design matrix because the standard one is transformed by the same linear transformation that converts the r response probabilities to $r-1$ generalized logits. For example, suppose the dependent variables X and Y each have two levels, and you specify a saturated log-linear model analysis:

```
proc catmod;
   model x*y=_response_;
   loglin  x y x*y;
```

Then the cross-classification of X and Y yields four response probabilities, P11, P12, P21, and P22, which are then reduced to three generalized logit response functions, $F1=\log(P11/P22)$, $F2=\log(P12/P22)$, and $F3=\log(P21/P22)$.

Since the saturated log-linear model implies that

$$
\begin{bmatrix} \log P11 \\ \log P12 \\ \log P21 \\ \log P22 \end{bmatrix} = \begin{bmatrix} 1 & 1 & 1 & 1 \\ 1 & 1 & -1 & -1 \\ 1 & -1 & 1 & -1 \\ 1 & -1 & -1 & 1 \end{bmatrix} \gamma - \lambda \begin{bmatrix} 1 \\ 1 \\ 1 \\ 1 \end{bmatrix}
$$

$$
= \begin{bmatrix} 1 & 1 & 1 \\ 1 & -1 & -1 \\ -1 & 1 & -1 \\ -1 & -1 & 1 \end{bmatrix} \beta - \delta \begin{bmatrix} 1 \\ 1 \\ 1 \\ 1 \end{bmatrix}
$$

where γ and β are parameter vectors, and λ and δ are normalizing constants required by the restriction that the probabilities sum to 1, it follows that the MODEL statement yields

$$
\begin{bmatrix} F1 \\ F2 \\ F3 \end{bmatrix} = \begin{bmatrix} 1 & 0 & 0 & -1 \\ 0 & 1 & 0 & -1 \\ 0 & 0 & 1 & -1 \end{bmatrix} \begin{bmatrix} \log P11 \\ \log P12 \\ \log P21 \\ \log P22 \end{bmatrix}
$$

$$
= \begin{bmatrix} 1 & 0 & 0 & -1 \\ 0 & 1 & 0 & -1 \\ 0 & 0 & 1 & -1 \end{bmatrix} \begin{bmatrix} 1 & 1 & 1 \\ 1 & -1 & -1 \\ -1 & 1 & -1 \\ -1 & -1 & 1 \end{bmatrix} \beta
$$

$$
= \begin{bmatrix} 2 & 2 & 0 \\ 2 & 0 & -2 \\ 0 & 2 & -2 \end{bmatrix} \beta
$$

Thus, the design matrix is

Sample	Response Function Number	Design Matrix		
		X	Y	X*Y
1	1	2	2	0
1	2	2	0	-2
1	3	0	2	-2

Design matrices for reduced models are constructed similarly. For example, suppose you request a main effects log-linear model analysis of the factors X and Y:

```
proc catmod;
   model x*y=_response_;
   loglin  x y;
```

Since the main-effects log-linear model implies that

$$
\begin{bmatrix} \log P11 \\ \log P12 \\ \log P21 \\ \log P22 \end{bmatrix}
=
\begin{bmatrix} 1 & 1 & 1 \\ 1 & 1 & -1 \\ 1 & -1 & 1 \\ 1 & -1 & -1 \end{bmatrix} \gamma
-
\lambda \begin{bmatrix} 1 \\ 1 \\ 1 \\ 1 \end{bmatrix}
$$

$$
=
\begin{bmatrix} 1 & 1 \\ 1 & -1 \\ -1 & 1 \\ -1 & -1 \end{bmatrix} \beta
-
\delta \begin{bmatrix} 1 \\ 1 \\ 1 \\ 1 \end{bmatrix}
$$

it follows that the MODEL statement yields

$$
\begin{bmatrix} F1 \\ F2 \\ F3 \end{bmatrix}
=
\begin{bmatrix} 1 & 0 & 0 & -1 \\ 0 & 1 & 0 & -1 \\ 0 & 0 & 1 & -1 \end{bmatrix}
\begin{bmatrix} \log P11 \\ \log P12 \\ \log P21 \\ \log P22 \end{bmatrix}
$$

$$
=
\begin{bmatrix} 1 & 0 & 0 & -1 \\ 0 & 1 & 0 & -1 \\ 0 & 0 & 1 & -1 \end{bmatrix}
\begin{bmatrix} 1 & 1 \\ 1 & -1 \\ -1 & 1 \\ -1 & -1 \end{bmatrix} \beta
$$

$$
=
\begin{bmatrix} 2 & 2 \\ 2 & 0 \\ 0 & 2 \end{bmatrix} \beta
$$

Therefore, the corresponding design matrix is

Sample	Response Function Number	Design Matrix X	Y
1	1	2	2
1	2	2	0
1	3	0	2

Since it is difficult to tell from the final design matrix whether CATMOD used the parameterization that you intended, CATMOD prints the untransformed _RESPONSE_ matrix for log-linear models. For example, the main effects model in the last example would induce the printing of the following matrix:

RESPONSE MATRIX

	1	2
1	1	1
2	1	−1
3	−1	1
4	−1	−1

The printing of this matrix can be suppressed with the NORESPONSE option in the MODEL statement.

Cautions

Effective Sample Size

Since the method depends on asymptotic approximations, you need to be careful that the sample sizes are sufficiently large to support the asymptotic normal distributions of the response functions. A general guideline is that you would like to have an effective sample size of at least 25 to 30 for each response function that is being analyzed. For example, if you have one dependent variable and $r=4$ response levels, and you use the standard response functions to compute three generalized logits for each population, then you would like the sample size of each population to be at least 75. Moreover, the subjects should be dispersed throughout the table so that less than 20% of the response functions have an effective sample size less than 5. For example, if each population had less than 5 subjects in the first response category, then it would be wiser to pool this category with another, rather than to assume the asymptotic normality of the first response function. Or, if the dependent variable is ordinally scaled, an alternative is to request the mean score response function, rather than three generalized logits.

If there is more than one dependent variable, and you specify RESPONSE MEANS, then the effective sample size for each response function is the same as the actual sample size. Thus, a sample size of 30 could be sufficient to support four response functions, provided that the functions were the means of four dependent variables.

A Singular Covariance Matrix

If there is a singular (noninvertible) covariance matrix for the response functions in any population, then CATMOD prints an error message and stops processing. You have several options available to correct this situation:

- You can reduce the number of response functions according to how many can be supported by the populations with the smallest sample sizes.
- If there are three or more levels for any independent variable, you can pool the levels into a fewer number of categories, thereby reducing the number of populations. However, your interpretation of results must be done more cautiously since such pooling implies a different sampling scheme and masks any differences that existed among the pooled categories.
- If there are two or more independent variables, you can delete at least one of them from the model. However, this is just another form of pooling, and therefore, the same cautions that apply to the previous option also apply here.
- If there is one independent variable, then in some situations, you might simply eliminate the populations that are causing the covariance matrices to be singular.
- You can use the ADDCELL option in the MODEL statement to add a small amount (say, 0.5) to every cell frequency, but this can seriously bias the results if the cell frequencies are small.

Zero Frequencies

If you use the standard response functions and there are zero frequencies, you should use maximum-likelihood estimation rather than weighted least squares to analyze the data. For weighted-least-squares analysis, CATMOD always computes the observed response functions. If CATMOD needs to take the logarithm of a zero proportion, it prints a warning and then proceeds to take the log of a small value ($0.5/n_i$ for the probability) in order to continue. This can produce invalid results if the cells contain too few observations. The ML analysis, on the other hand, does not require computation of the observed response functions and therefore yields valid results for the parameter estimates and all of the predicted values.

For any log-linear model analysis, it is important to remember that CATMOD creates response profiles only for those profiles that are actually observed. Thus, for any log-linear model analysis with one population (the usual case), there are no zeros in the contingency table, which means that CATMOD treats all zero frequencies as structural zeros. If there is more than one population, then a zero can appear in the body of the contingency table, in which case the zero is treated as a sampling zero. If you want zero frequencies to be interpreted as sampling zeros, simply insert a one-line statement into the data step that changes each zero to a very small number (such as $1E-20$). See Bishop, Fienberg, and Holland (1975) for a discussion of the issues and **Example 5** for an illustration of a log-linear model analysis of data that contain both structural and random zeros.

If weighted-least-squares analysis is used for a contingency table that contains zero cell frequencies, then avoid using the LOG transformation as the first transformation on the observed proportions. In general, it may be better to change the response functions or to pool some of the response categories than to settle for the 0.5 correction or to use the ADDCELL option.

Testing the Wrong Hypothesis

If you use the keyword _RESPONSE_ in the MODEL statement, and you specify MARGINALS, LOGITS or CLOGITS in your RESPONSE statement, you may receive the following warning message printed by CATMOD:

```
Warning: The _RESPONSE_ effect may be testing the wrong
         hypothesis since the marginal levels of the
         dependent variables do not coincide. Consult the
         response profiles and the CATMOD documentation.
```

The following examples illustrate situations in which the _RESPONSE_ effect tests the wrong hypothesis.

Example 1: Zeros in the marginal frequencies   Suppose you specify the following statements:

```
data a1;
   input time1 time2 aa;
   cards;
1 2    2 3    1 3
;
proc catmod;
   response marginals;
   model time1*time2=_response_;
   repeated time 2 / _response_=time;
```

One marginal probability is computed for each dependent variable, resulting in two response functions. The model is a saturated one: one degree of freedom for the intercept, and one for the main effect of TIME. Except for the warning message, CATMOD produces an analysis with no apparent errors, but the RESPONSE PROFILES printed by CATMOD are

RESPONSE PROFILES

Response	TIME1	TIME2
1	1	2
2	1	3
3	2	3

Since RESPONSE MARGINALS yields marginal probabilities for every level but the last, the two response functions being analyzed are Prob(TIME1=1) and Prob(TIME2=2). Thus, the TIME effect is testing the hypothesis that Prob(TIME1=1)=Prob(TIME2=2). What it *should* be testing is the hypothesis

Prob(TIME1=1) = Prob(TIME2=1)
Prob(TIME1=2) = Prob(TIME2=2)
Prob(TIME1=3) = Prob(TIME2=3)

but there are not enough data to support the test (assuming that none of the probabilities are structural zeros by the design of the study).

Example 2: The ORDER=DATA option   Suppose you specify

```
data a1;
   input time1 time2 @@;
   cards;
2 1    2 2    1 1    1 2    2 1
;
proc catmod order=data;
   response marginals;
   model time1*time2=_response_;
   repeated time 2 / _response_=time;
```

As in the first example, one marginal probability is computed for each dependent variable, resulting in two response functions. The model is also the same: one degree of freedom for the intercept and one for the main effect of TIME. CATMOD issues the warning message and prints the following RESPONSE PROFILES:

RESPONSE PROFILES

Response	TIME1	TIME2
1	2	1
2	2	2
3	1	1
4	1	2

Although the marginal levels are the same for the two dependent variables, they are not in the same order because the ORDER=DATA option specified that they be ordered according to their appearance in the input stream. Since RESPONSE MARGINALS yields marginal probabilities for every level except the last, the two response functions being analyzed are Prob(TIME1=2) and Prob(TIME2=1). Thus, the TIME effect is testing the hypothesis that Prob(TIME1=2)=Prob(TIME2=1). What it *should* be testing is the hypothesis

Prob(TIME1=1) = Prob(TIME2=1)
Prob(TIME1=2) = Prob(TIME2=2)

Whenever the above warning message appears, look at the RESPONSE PROFILES or the ONE-WAY table to determine what hypothesis is actually being tested. For the latter example, a correct analysis can be obtained by deleting the ORDER=DATA option or by reordering the data so that the (1,1) observation is first.

Computational Method

The notation used in CATMOD differs slightly from that used in other literature. A summary of the basic dimensions and the notation for a contingency table is given below. See **Computational Formulas** for a complete description.

Summary of Basic Dimensions

s = number of populations or samples (= number of rows in the underlying contingency table)

r = number of response categories (= number of columns in the underlying contingency table)

q = number of response functions computed for each population

d = number of parameters.

Notation

A column vector of 1s is denoted by $\mathbf{j}$. A square matrix of 1s is denoted by $\mathbf{J}$. Σ_k is the sum over all the possible values of k. $\mathbf{DIAG}_n(\mathbf{p})$ is the diagonal matrix formed from the first n elements of the vector $\mathbf{p}$. The inverse is $\mathbf{DIAG}_n^{-1}(\mathbf{p})$. $\mathbf{DIAG}(\mathbf{A}_1, \mathbf{A}_2, \ldots \mathbf{A}_k)$ denotes a block diagonal matrix with the $\mathbf{A}$ matrices on the main diagonal. Input data can be represented by a contingency table, as shown in **Table 14.2**:

Table 14.2   Input Data Represented by a Contingency Table

Population	Response 1	2	...	r	
1	n_{11}	n_{12}	...	n_{1r}	n_1
2	n_{21}	n_{22}	...	n_{2r}	n_2
...	...	...	...	...	...
s	n_{s1}	n_{s2}	...	n_{sr}	n_s

Let n_i denote the row sum $\Sigma_j n_{ij}$.

Computational Formulas

The following calculations are shown for each population and then for all populations combined:

			Dimension

Probability Estimates

jth response $p_{ij} = n_{ij} / n_i$ 1×1

ith population $\mathbf{p}_i = \begin{bmatrix} p_{i1} \\ p_{i2} \\ \dots \\ p_{ir} \end{bmatrix}$ $r \times 1$

all populations $\mathbf{p} = \begin{bmatrix} \mathbf{p}_1 \\ \mathbf{p}_2 \\ \dots \\ \mathbf{p}_s \end{bmatrix}$ $sr \times 1$

Variance of Probability Estimates

ith population $\mathbf{V}_i = \left(\mathbf{DIAG}\,(\mathbf{p}_i) - \mathbf{p}_i\,\mathbf{p}_i' \right) / n_i$ $r \times r$

all populations $\mathbf{V} = \mathbf{DIAG}\,(\mathbf{V}_1, \mathbf{V}_2, \dots, \mathbf{V}_s)$ $sr \times sr$

Response Functions

ith population $\mathbf{F}_i = \mathbf{F}\,(\mathbf{p}_i)$ $q \times 1$

all populations $\mathbf{F} = \begin{bmatrix} \mathbf{F}_1 \\ \mathbf{F}_2 \\ \dots \\ \mathbf{F}_s \end{bmatrix}$ $sq \times 1$

Dimension

Derivative of Function with Respect to Probability Estimates

ith population	$\mathbf{H}_i = \partial \mathbf{F}(\mathbf{p}_i) / \partial \mathbf{p}_i$	$q \times r$
all populations	$\mathbf{H} = \mathbf{DIAG}(\mathbf{H}_1, \mathbf{H}_2, \ldots, \mathbf{H}_s)$	$sq \times sr$

Variance of Functions

ith population	$\mathbf{S}_i = \mathbf{H}_i \mathbf{V}_i \mathbf{H}_i'$	$q \times q$
all populations	$\mathbf{S} = \mathbf{DIAG}(\mathbf{S}_1, \mathbf{S}_2, \ldots, \mathbf{S}_s)$	$sq \times sq$

Inverse Variance of Functions

ith population	$\mathbf{S}^i = (\mathbf{S}_i)^{-1}$	$q \times q$
all populations	$\mathbf{S}^{-1} = \mathbf{DIAG}(\mathbf{S}^1, \mathbf{S}^2, \ldots, \mathbf{S}^s)$	$sq \times sq$

Derivative Table for Compound Functions: Y = F(G(p))

In the following section, let $\mathbf{G}(\mathbf{p})$ be a vector of functions of $\mathbf{p}$, and let $\mathbf{D}$ denote $\partial \mathbf{G}/\partial \mathbf{p}$, the first derivative matrix of $\mathbf{G}$ with respect to $\mathbf{p}$:

Function	$\mathbf{Y} = \mathbf{F}(\mathbf{G})$	Derivative($\partial \mathbf{Y}/\partial \mathbf{p}$)
Multiply matrix	$\mathbf{Y} = \mathbf{A}^*\mathbf{G}$	$\mathbf{A}^*\mathbf{D}$
Logarithm	$\mathbf{Y} = \mathbf{LOG}(\mathbf{G})$	$\mathbf{DIAG}^{-1}(\mathbf{G})^*\mathbf{D}$
Exponential	$\mathbf{Y} = \mathbf{EXP}(\mathbf{G})$	$\mathbf{DIAG}(\mathbf{Y})^*\mathbf{D}$
Add constant	$\mathbf{Y} = \mathbf{G}+\mathbf{A}$	$\mathbf{D}$

Default Response Functions: Generalized Logits

In this section, subscripts i for the population are suppressed.

$$f_j = \log(p_j/p_r) \quad \text{for } j = 1, \ldots, r-1$$

$$\text{for each population } i = 1, \ldots, s$$

1. Inverse of response functions for a population

$$p_j = \exp(f_j)/(1 + \Sigma_k \exp(f_k)) \quad \text{for } j = 1, \ldots, r-1$$

$$p_r = 1/(1 + \Sigma_k \exp(f_k))$$

2. Form of F and derivative for a population

$$\mathbf{F} = \mathbf{K} \text{ LOG } (\mathbf{p}) = (\mathbf{I}_{r-1}, -\mathbf{j}) \text{LOG } (\mathbf{p})$$

$$\mathbf{H} = \partial \mathbf{F}/\partial \mathbf{p} = (\mathbf{DIAG}_{r-1}^{-1}(\mathbf{p}), (-1/p_r) \mathbf{j})$$

3. Covariance results for a population

$$\mathbf{S} = \mathbf{H V H'} = \left(\mathbf{DIAG}_{r-1}^{-1}(\mathbf{p}) + (1/p_r)\mathbf{J}_{r-1}\right)/n$$

where **V**, **H**, and **J** are as defined above.

$$\mathbf{S}^{-1} = n \, (\mathbf{DIAG}_{r-1} \, (\mathbf{p}) - \mathbf{qq'}) \quad \text{where } \mathbf{q} = \mathbf{DIAG}_{r-1} \, (\mathbf{p}) \, \mathbf{j}$$

$$\mathbf{S}^{-1}\mathbf{F} = n \, \mathbf{DIAG}_{r-1} \, (\mathbf{p}) \, \mathbf{F} - (n \, \Sigma_j \, p_j \, f_j) \mathbf{q}$$

$$\mathbf{F'S}^{-1}\mathbf{F} = n \, \Sigma_j \, p_j \, f_j^2 - n \, (\Sigma_j \, p_j \, f_j)^2$$

The following calculations are shown for each population and then for all populations combined:

Dimension

Design Matrix

*i*th population	$\mathbf{X}_i$	$q \times d$
all populations	$\mathbf{X} = \begin{bmatrix} \mathbf{X}_1 \\ \mathbf{X}_2 \\ \ldots \\ \mathbf{X}_s \end{bmatrix}$	$sq \times d$

Crossproduct of Design Matrix

*i*th population	$\mathbf{C}_i = \mathbf{X}_i' \mathbf{S}^i \mathbf{X}_i$	$d \times d$
all populations	$\mathbf{C} = \mathbf{X'S}^{-1}\mathbf{X} = \Sigma_i \, \mathbf{C}_i$	$d \times d$

Crossproduct of Design Matrix with Function

$$\mathbf{R} = \mathbf{X'S}^{-1}\mathbf{F} = \Sigma_i \, \mathbf{X}_i' \mathbf{S}^i \, \mathbf{F}_i \qquad d \times 1$$

Weighted-Least-Squares Estimates

$$\mathbf{b} = \mathbf{C}^{-1}\mathbf{R} = (\mathbf{X'S}^{-1}\mathbf{X})^{-1}(\mathbf{X'S}^{-1}\mathbf{F}) \qquad d \times 1$$

Covariance of Weighted-Least-Squares Estimates

$$\mathbf{COV} \, (\mathbf{b}) = \mathbf{C}^{-1} \qquad d \times d$$

Predicted Response Functions

$$\hat{F} = Xb \qquad\qquad sq \times 1$$

Residual Chi-Square

$$RSS = F'S^{-1}F - \hat{F}'S^{-1}\hat{F} \qquad\qquad 1 \times 1$$

Chi-Square for H_0: $L\beta = 0$

$$Q = (Lb)'(LC^{-1}L')^{-1}(Lb) \qquad\qquad 1 \times 1$$

Maximum-Likelihood Method

Let C be the Hessian matrix and G be the gradient of the log-likelihood function (both functions of π and the parameters β). Let p_i^* denote the vector containing the first $r - 1$ sample proportions from population i, and let π_i^* denote the corresponding vector of probability estimates from the current iteration. Starting with the least-squares estimates b_0 of β, the probabilities $\pi(b)$ are computed, and b is calculated iteratively by the Newton-Raphson method until it converges. λ is a step-halving factor that equals one at the start of each iteration. For any iteration in which the likelihood decreases, CATMOD uses a series of subiterations in which λ is iteratively divided by two. The subiterations continue until the likelihood is greater than that of the previous iteration. If the likelihood has not reached that point after ten subiterations, then convergence is assumed, and a warning message is printed.

Sometimes, infinite parameters may be present in the model, either because of the presence of one or more zero frequencies or because of a poorly specified model with collinearity among the estimates. If an estimate is tending toward infinity, then CATMOD flags the parameter as infinite and holds the estimate fixed in subsequent iterations. CATMOD regards a parameter to be infinite when two conditions hold:

1. the absolute value of its estimate exceeds five divided by the range of the corresponding variable
2. the standard error of its estimate is at least three times greater than the estimate itself.

The estimator of the asymptotic covariance matrix of the maximum-likelihood predicted probabilities is given by Imrey, Koch, and Stokes (1981, eq. 2.18).

The following equations summarize the method:

$$b_{k+1} = b_k - \lambda C^{-1}G$$

where

$$C = X'S\pi^{-1}X$$

$$\mathbf{N} = \begin{bmatrix} n_1(\mathbf{p}_1^* - \boldsymbol{\pi}_1^*) \\ \cdot \\ \cdot \\ \cdot \\ n_s(\mathbf{p}_s^* - \boldsymbol{\pi}_s^*) \end{bmatrix}$$

$$\mathbf{G} = \mathbf{X}'\mathbf{N} \quad .$$

Printed Output

CATMOD prints the following information in a header section:

1. the Response effect
2. the Weight Variable, if one is specified
3. the Data Set name
4. the number of Response Levels (R)
5. the number of samples or Populations (S)
6. the Total Frequency (N), which is the total sample size
7. the number of Observations (Obs) from the data set (the number of data records).

Except for the analysis-of-variance table, all of the following items can be printed or suppressed, depending on your specification of statements and options:

8. The ONEWAY option induces printing of the ONE-WAY FREQUENCIES for each variable used in the analysis.
9. The populations (or samples) are defined in a section labeled POPULATION PROFILES. The Sample Size and the values of the defining variables are printed for each Sample. Printing is suppressed if the NOPROFILE option is specified.
10. The observed responses are defined in a section labeled RESPONSE PROFILES. The values of the defining variables are printed for each Response, unless the NOPROFILE option is specified.
11. If the FREQ option is specified, then the RESPONSE FREQUENCIES are printed for each population.
12. If the PROB option is specified, then the RESPONSE PROBABILITIES are printed for each population.
13. If the COV option is specified, the COVARIANCE MATRIX of the response functions is printed for each Sample (not shown).
14. The Response Functions are printed next to the DESIGN MATRIX, unless the COV option is specified, in which case they are printed next to the COVARIANCE MATRIX of the functions.
15. The DESIGN MATRIX is printed for weighted-least-squares analyses unless the NODESIGN option is specified. If the model type is AVERAGED, then the design matrix is printed with *q*s* rows, assuming *q* response functions for each of *s* populations. Otherwise, the design matrix is printed with only *s* rows since the model is the same for each of the *q* response functions.
16. The X'*INV(S)*X MATRIX is printed for weighted-least-squares analyses if the XPX option is specified (not shown).
17. The ANALYSIS OF VARIANCE TABLE for the weighted-least-squares analysis gives the results of significance tests for each of the *design_effects* in the right-hand side of the MODEL statement. If

RESPONSE is a *design_effect* and is defined explicitly in the LOGLIN, FACTORS, or REPEATED statement, then the table contains test statistics for the individual effects constituting the _RESPONSE_ effect. If the design matrix is input directly, then the content of the printed output depends on whether you specify any subsets of the parameters to be tested. If you specify one or more subsets, then the table contains one test for each subset. Otherwise, the table contains one test for the effect MODEL | MEAN. In every case, the table also contains the RESIDUAL goodness-of-fit test. Printed for each test of significance are the Source of variation, the number of degrees of freedom (DF), the Chi-Square value (which is a Wald statistic), and the significance probability (Prob).

18. The ANALYSIS OF WEIGHTED-LEAST-SQUARES ESTIMATES table gives the Effect in the model for which parameters are formed, the Parameter number, the least-squares Estimate, the estimated Standard Error of the parameter estimate, the Chi-Square value (a Wald statistic) for testing that the parameter is zero, and the significance probability (Prob) of the test (not shown).

19. The COVARIANCE MATRIX OF THE PARAMETER ESTIMATES for the weighted-least-squares analysis gives the estimated covariance matrix of the least-squares estimates of the parameters, provided the COVB option is specified.

20. The CORRELATION MATRIX OF THE PARAMETER ESTIMATES for the weighted-least-squares analysis gives the estimated correlation matrix of the least-squares estimates of the parameters, provided that the CORRB option is specified.

21. The MAXIMUM LIKELIHOOD ANALYSIS is printed when the ML option is specified for the standard response functions (generalized logits). It gives the Iteration number, the number of step-halving Sub-Iterations, -2 Log Likelihood for that iteration, the Convergence Criterion, and the Parameter Estimates for each iteration.

22. The MAXIMUM LIKELIHOOD ANALYSIS OF VARIANCE TABLE, printed when the ML option is specified for the standard response functions, is similar to the table produced for the least-squares analysis. The Chi-Square test for each effect is a Wald test based on the information matrix from the likelihood calculations. The LIKELIHOOD RATIO statistic compares the specified model with the unrestricted model and is an appropriate goodness-of-fit test for the model.

23. The ANALYSIS OF MAXIMUM LIKELIHOOD ESTIMATES, printed when the ML option is specified for the standard response functions, is similar to the one produced for the least-squares analysis. The table includes the maximum-likelihood estimates, the estimated Standard Errors based on the information matrix, and the Wald Statistics (Chi-Square) based on the estimated standard errors.

24. The COVARIANCE MATRIX OF THE MAXIMUM LIKELIHOOD ESTIMATES gives the estimated covariance matrix of the maximum-likelihood estimates of the parameters, provided that the COVB and ML options are specified for the standard response functions.

25. The CORRELATION MATRIX OF THE MAXIMUM LIKELIHOOD ESTIMATES gives the estimated correlation matrix of the maximum-likelihood estimates of the parameters, provided that the CORRB and ML options are specified for the standard response functions.

26. For each source of variation specified in a CONTRAST statement, the ANALYSIS OF CONTRASTS gives the label for the source, the number of degrees of freedom (DF), the Chi-Square value (which is a Wald statistic), and the significance probability (Prob).

27. Specification of the PREDICT option in the MODEL statement has the following effect. Printed for each response function within each population are the Observed and Predicted Function values, their Standard Errors, and the Residual (Observed−Predicted). If the line size is large enough, the printed output also includes the values of the variables that define the populations. If the response functions are the default ones (generalized logits), additional information printed for each response within each population includes the Observed and Predicted cell probabilities, their Standard Errors, and the Residual. The first cell probability is labeled P1, the second P2, and so forth. However, specifying PRED=FREQ in the MODEL statement results in printing of the predicted cell frequencies, rather than the predicted cell probabilities. The first cell frequency is labeled F1, the second F2, and so forth.

28. When there are multiple RESPONSE statements, the output for each statement starts on a new page. For each RESPONSE statement, the corresponding title, if specified, is printed at the top of each page (not shown).

29. If the ADDCELL= option is specified in the MODEL statement, and if there is a weighted least squares analysis specified, the adjusted sample size for each population (with number added to each cell) is labeled ADJ. SAMPLE SIZE. Similarly, the adjusted frequencies and probabilities are labeled ADJUSTED RESPONSE FREQUENCIES and ADJUSTED RESPONSE PROBABILITIES, respectively (not shown).

30. If _RESPONSE_ is defined explicitly in the LOGLIN, FACTORS, or REPEATED statement, then the definition is printed as a NOTE whenever _RESPONSE_ appears in the printed output.

EXAMPLES

The examples in this section illustrate the following ten types of analysis:

1. Linear response function, $r=2$ responses
2. Mean score response function, $r=3$ responses
3. Logistic regression, standard response function
4. Log-linear model, three dependent variables
5. Log-linear model, structural zeros and random zeros
6. Repeated measures, two levels of response, three populations
7. Repeated measures, four levels of response, one population
8. Repeated measures, logistic analysis of growth curve
9. Repeated measures, two repeated measurement factors
10. Direct input of response functions and covariance matrix.

Example 1: Linear Response Function, r=2 Responses

The choice of detergent brand is related to three other categorical variables. The linear response function yields one probability, Pr (brand preference=M), as the response function to be analyzed. The first model is a saturated one, containing all of the main effects and interactions. The second is a reduced model containing only the main effects. The following statements produce **Output 14.1**:

```
*---------------------CATMOD EXAMPLE 1-----------------------------*
|                                                                 |
|                    Detergent Preference Study                   |
|                    --------------------------                   |
| The data are from a consumer blind trial of detergent preference. |
| The variables measured in the study were                        |
|     softness=softness of laundry water (soft, med, hard)        |
|     prev=previous user of brand m? (yes, no)                    |
|     temp=temperature of laundry water (high, low)               |
|     brand=brand preferred (m, x).                               |
|                                                                 |
| From: Ries and Smith (1963).                                    |
|       See also Cox (1970, 38).                                  |
|                                                                 |
| Illustrate: linear response function, r=2 responses             |
|                                                                 |
*-----------------------------------------------------------------*;


title 'DETERGENT PREFERENCE STUDY';
data deterg;
   input softness $ brand $ prev $ temp $ count @@;
   cards;
soft x yes high 19 soft x yes low 57 soft x no high 29 soft x no low 63
soft m yes high 29 soft m yes low 49 soft m no high 27 soft m no low 53
med  x yes high 23 med  x yes low 47 med  x no high 33 med  x no low 66
med  m yes high 47 med  m yes low 55 med  m no high 23 med  m no low 50
hard x yes high 24 hard x yes low 37 hard x no high 42 hard x no low 68
hard m yes high 43 hard m yes low 52 hard m no high 30 hard m no low 42
;
proc catmod;
   response 1 0;
   weight count;
   model brand=softness|prev|temp / freq prob nodesign;
   title2 'SATURATED MODEL';
run;

   model brand=softness prev temp / noprofile;
   title2 'MAIN EFFECTS MODEL';
run;
quit;
```

Output 14.1   Detergent Preference Study: Linear Model Analysis

```
                      DETERGENT PREFERENCE STUDY                        1
                           SATURATED MODEL

                          CATMOD PROCEDURE

❷❶ Response: BRAND                   ❹ Response Levels (R)=    2
❷ Weight Variable: COUNT          ❺❻ Populations      (S)=   12
❸ Data Set: DETERG                   Total Frequency  (N)= 1008
                                  ❼ Observations    (Obs)=   24


                    ❾ POPULATION PROFILES

                                         Sample
        Sample  SOFTNESS  PREV  TEMP      Size
        ----------------------------------------
           1    hard      no    high       72
           2    hard      no    low       110
           3    hard      yes   high       67
           4    hard      yes   low        89
           5    med       no    high       56
           6    med       no    low       116
           7    med       yes   high       70
           8    med       yes   low       102
           9    soft      no    high       56
          10    soft      no    low       116
          11    soft      yes   high       48
          12    soft      yes   low       106


                 ❿ RESPONSE PROFILES

                 Response  BRAND
                 ---------------
                    1       m
                    2       x


                ⓫ RESPONSE FREQUENCIES

                       Response Number
               Sample      1       2
               ------------------------
                  1       30      42
                  2       42      68
                  3       43      24
                  4       52      37
                  5       23      33
                  6       50      66
                  7       47      23
                  8       55      47
                  9       27      29
                 10       53      63
                 11       29      19
                 12       49      57
```

DETERGENT PREFERENCE STUDY
SATURATED MODEL   2

⑫ RESPONSE PROBABILITIES

	Response Number	
Sample	1	2
1	0.41667	0.58333
2	0.38182	0.61818
3	0.64179	0.35821
4	0.58427	0.41573
5	0.41071	0.58929
6	0.43103	0.56897
7	0.67143	0.32857
8	0.53922	0.46078
9	0.48214	0.51786
10	0.4569	0.5431
11	0.60417	0.39583
12	0.46226	0.53774

⑰ ANALYSIS OF VARIANCE TABLE

Source	DF	Chi-Square	Prob
INTERCEPT	1	983.13	0.0000
SOFTNESS	2	0.09	0.9575
PREV	1	22.68	0.0000
SOFTNESS*PREV	2	3.85	0.1457
TEMP	1	3.67	0.0555
SOFTNESS*TEMP	2	0.23	0.8914
PREV*TEMP	1	2.26	0.1324
SOFTNESS*PREV*TEMP	2	0.76	0.6850
RESIDUAL	0	.	.

⑱ ANALYSIS OF WEIGHTED-LEAST-SQUARES ESTIMATES

Effect	Parameter	Estimate	Standard Error	Chi-Square	Prob
INTERCEPT	1	0.5069	0.0162	983.13	0.0000
SOFTNESS	2	-0.00073	0.0225	0.00	0.9740
	3	0.00623	0.0226	0.08	0.7830
PREV	4	-0.0770	0.0162	22.68	0.0000
SOFTNESS*PREV	5	-0.0299	0.0225	1.77	0.1831
	6	-0.0152	0.0226	0.45	0.5007
TEMP	7	0.0310	0.0162	3.67	0.0555
SOFTNESS*TEMP	8	-0.00786	0.0225	0.12	0.7265
	9	-0.00298	0.0226	0.02	0.8953
PREV*TEMP	10	-0.0243	0.0162	2.26	0.1324
SOFTNESS*PREV*TEMP	11	0.0187	0.0225	0.69	0.4064
	12	-0.0138	0.0226	0.37	0.5415

```
                        DETERGENT PREFERENCE STUDY                              3
                          MAIN-EFFECTS MODEL

                           CATMOD PROCEDURE

Response: BRAND                 Response Levels (R)=    2
Weight Variable: COUNT          Populations     (S)=   12
Data Set: DETERG                Total Frequency (N)= 1008
                                Observations   (Obs)=   24
```

| | ⑭ Response | | ⑮ DESIGN MATRIX | | | |
Sample	Function	1	2	3	4	5
1	0.41667	1	1	0	1	1
2	0.38182	1	1	0	1	-1
3	0.64179	1	1	0	-1	1
4	0.58427	1	1	0	-1	-1
5	0.41071	1	0	1	1	1
6	0.43103	1	0	1	1	-1
7	0.67143	1	0	1	-1	1
8	0.53922	1	0	1	-1	-1
9	0.48214	1	-1	-1	1	1
10	0.45690	1	-1	-1	1	-1
11	0.60417	1	-1	-1	-1	1
12	0.46226	1	-1	-1	-1	-1

```
                     ANALYSIS OF VARIANCE TABLE
```

Source	DF	Chi-Square	Prob
INTERCEPT	1	1004.93	0.0000
SOFTNESS	2	0.24	0.8859
PREV	1	20.96	0.0000
TEMP	1	3.95	0.0468
RESIDUAL	7	8.26	0.3100

```
            ANALYSIS OF WEIGHTED-LEAST-SQUARES ESTIMATES
```

Effect	Parameter	Estimate	Standard Error	Chi-Square	Prob
INTERCEPT	1	0.5080	0.0160	1004.93	0.0000
SOFTNESS	2	-0.00256	0.0218	0.01	0.9066
	3	0.0104	0.0218	0.23	0.6342
PREV	4	-0.0711	0.0155	20.96	0.0000
TEMP	5	0.0319	0.0161	3.95	0.0468

The first analysis-of-variance table shows that all of the interactions are nonsignificant. Therefore, a main effects model was fitted. The second analysis-of-variance table shows that previous use of Brand M, together with the temperature of the laundry water, are significant factors in preferring Brand M laundry detergent. The table also shows that the additive model fits since the goodness-of-fit statistic (the residual chi-square) is nonsignificant.

The negative coefficient for PREV in the last table of estimates indicates that the first level of PREV (which, from the table of population profiles, is NO) has a smaller probability of preferring Brand M than the second level of PREV. In other words, previous users of Brand M are much more likely to prefer it than those who had never used it before.

Similarly, the positive coefficient for TEMP in the last table of estimates indicates that the first level of TEMP (which, from the table of population profiles, is HIGH) has a larger probability of preferring Brand M than the second level of TEMP. In other words, those who do their laundry in hot water are more likely to prefer Brand M than those who do their laundry in cold water.

Example 2: Mean Score Response Function, r = 3 Responses

The response variable is ordinally scaled with three levels, so assignment of scores is appropriate (0=none, 0.5=slight, 1=moderate). For these scores, the response function yields the mean score. The ORDER= option is used so that the levels of the response variable remain in the correct order. A main effects model is fitted. The following statements produce **Output 14.2**:

```
*-------------------CATMOD EXAMPLE 2---------------------------------*
|                                                                    |
|                    Dumping Syndrome Data                           |
|                    --------------------                            |
|  Four surgical operations for duodenal ulcers were compared in a   |
|  clinical trial at four hospitals. The response was the severity   |
|  of an undesirable complication called dumping syndrome. The       |
|  operations were                                                   |
|      a. drainage and vagotomy                                      |
|      b. 25% resection and vagotomy                                 |
|      c. 50% resection and vagotomy                                 |
|      d. 75% resection                                              |
|                                                                    |
|  From: Grizzle, Starmer, and Koch (1969, 489-504).                 |
|                                                                    |
|  Illustrate: mean score response function, r=3 responses           |
|                                                                    |
*--------------------------------------------------------------------*;


title 'DUMPING SYNDROME DATA';
data operate;
   input hospital trt $ severity $ wt aa;
   cards;
1 a none 23     1 a slight  7     1 a moderate 2
1 b none 23     1 b slight 10     1 b moderate 5
1 c none 20     1 c slight 13     1 c moderate 5
1 d none 24     1 d slight 10     1 d moderate 6
2 a none 18     2 a slight  6     2 a moderate 1
2 b none 18     2 b slight  6     2 b moderate 2
2 c none 13     2 c slight 13     2 c moderate 2
2 d none  9     2 d slight 15     2 d moderate 2
3 a none  8     3 a slight  6     3 a moderate 3
3 b none 12     3 b slight  4     3 b moderate 4
3 c none 11     3 c slight  6     3 c moderate 2
3 d none  7     3 d slight  7     3 d moderate 4
4 a none 12     4 a slight  9     4 a moderate 1
4 b none 15     4 b slight  3     4 b moderate 2
4 c none 14     4 c slight  8     4 c moderate 3
4 d none 13     4 d slight  6     4 d moderate 4
;
proc catmod order=data;
   weight wt;
   response 0  0.5  1;
   model severity=trt hospital / freq oneway;
   title2 'MAIN EFFECTS MODEL';
quit;
```

Output 14.2   Surgical Data: Analysis of Mean Scores

```
                        DUMPING SYNDROME DATA                              1
                        MAIN-EFFECTS MODEL

                          CATMOD PROCEDURE

Response: SEVERITY            Response Levels (R)=    3
Weight Variable: WT          Populations     (S)=   16
Data Set: OPERATE            Total Frequency (N)=  417
                             Observations  (Obs)=   48


              ⑧  ONE-WAY FREQUENCIES

              Variable    Value   Frequency
              ---------------------------------
              SEVERITY     none       240
                          slight      129
                         moderate      48

              TRT            a          96
                            b         104
                            c         110
                            d         107

              HOSPITAL       1         148
                            2         105
                            3          74
                            4          90


                      POPULATION PROFILES
                                        Sample
              Sample  TRT  HOSPITAL      Size
              -------------------------------
                 1     a      1           32
                 2     a      2           25
                 3     a      3           17
                 4     a      4           22
                 5     b      1           38
                 6     b      2           26
                 7     b      3           20
                 8     b      4           20
                 9     c      1           38
                10     c      2           28
                11     c      3           19
                12     c      4           25
                13     d      1           40
                14     d      2           26
                15     d      3           18
                16     d      4           23
```

```
                        DUMPING SYNDROME DATA                              2
                        MAIN-EFFECTS MODEL

                        RESPONSE PROFILES

              Response  SEVERITY
              ------------------
                 1       none
                 2       slight
                 3       moderate


                    RESPONSE FREQUENCIES

                       Response Number
              Sample     1      2      3
              --------------------------------
                 1      23      7      2
                 2      18      6      1
                 3       8      6      3
                 4      12      9      1
                 5      23     10      5
                 6      18      6      2
```

(continued on next page)

(continued from previous page)

```
 7     12      4      4
 8     15      3      2
 9     20     13      5
10     13     13      2
11     11      6      2
12     14      8      3
13     24     10      6
14      9     15      2
15      7      7      4
16     13      6      4
```

DUMPING SYNDROME DATA   3
MAIN-EFFECTS MODEL

Sample	Response Function	1	2	DESIGN MATRIX 3	4	5	6	7
1	0.17188	1	1	0	0	1	0	0
2	0.16000	1	1	0	0	0	1	0
3	0.35294	1	1	0	0	0	0	1
4	0.25000	1	1	0	0	-1	-1	-1
5	0.26316	1	0	1	0	1	0	0
6	0.19231	1	0	1	0	0	1	0
7	0.30000	1	0	1	0	0	0	1
8	0.17500	1	0	1	0	-1	-1	-1
9	0.30263	1	0	0	1	1	0	0
10	0.30357	1	0	0	1	0	1	0
11	0.26316	1	0	0	1	0	0	1
12	0.28000	1	0	0	1	-1	-1	-1
13	0.27500	1	-1	-1	-1	1	0	0
14	0.36538	1	-1	-1	-1	0	1	0
15	0.41667	1	-1	-1	-1	0	0	1
16	0.30435	1	-1	-1	-1	-1	-1	-1

ANALYSIS OF VARIANCE TABLE

Source	DF	Chi-Square	Prob
INTERCEPT	1	248.77	0.0000
TRT	3	8.90	0.0307
HOSPITAL	3	2.33	0.5065
RESIDUAL	9	6.33	0.7069

ANALYSIS OF WEIGHTED-LEAST-SQUARES ESTIMATES

Effect	Parameter	Estimate	Standard Error	Chi-Square	Prob
INTERCEPT	1	0.2724	0.0173	248.77	0.0000
TRT	2	-0.0552	0.0270	4.17	0.0411
	3	-0.0365	0.0289	1.59	0.2073
	4	0.0248	0.0280	0.78	0.3757
HOSPITAL	5	-0.0204	0.0264	0.60	0.4388
	6	-0.0178	0.0268	0.44	0.5055
	7	0.0531	0.0352	2.28	0.1312

The one-way frequencies table and the response profiles verify that the response levels are in the correct order (none, slight, moderate) so that the response scores get applied appropriately (0, 0.5, 1.0). If the ORDER=DATA option had not been used, the levels would have been in a different order.

The analysis-of-variance table shows that the additive model fits, that the treatment effect is significant, and that the hospital effect is not significant. The coefficients of TRT in the table of estimates show that the first two treatments (with negative coefficients) have lower mean scores than the last two treatments (the fourth coefficient, not shown, must be positive since the four must sum to zero). In other words, the less severe treatments (the first two) cause significantly less severe dumping syndrome complications.

Example 3: Logistic Regression, Standard Response Function

For logistic regression, *design_effects* are declared in a DIRECT statement, and the NOGLS and ML options are specified. The following statements produce **Output 14.3**:

```
*-----------------CATMOD EXAMPLE 3-----------------------*
|                                                         |
|          Maximum Likelihood Logistic Regression         |
|          ---------------------------------------        |
|   Ingots prepared with different heating and soaking times are |
|   tested for readiness to roll.                         |
|                                                         |
|   From: Cox (1970, 67-68).                              |
|                                                         |
|   Illustrate: logistic regression, standard response function |
|                                                         |
*---------------------------------------------------------*;
```

```
title 'MAXIMUM-LIKELIHOOD LOGISTIC REGRESSION';
data ingots;
   input heat soak nready ntotal @@;
   count=nready;
   y=1;
   output;
   count=ntotal-nready;
   y=0;
   output;
   drop nready ntotal;
   cards;
 7  1.0  0  10    7  1.7  0  17    7  2.2  0   7    7  2.8  0  12
 7  4.0  0   9   14  1.0  0  31   14  1.7  0  43   14  2.2  2  33
14  2.8  0  31   14  4.0  0  19   27  1.0  1  56   27  1.7  4  44
27  2.2  0  21   27  2.8  1  22   27  4.0  1  16   51  1.0  3  13
51  1.7  0   1   51  2.2  0   1   51  4.0  0   1
;
proc catmod;
   weight count;
   direct heat soak;
   model y=heat soak / freq ml nogls covb corrb;
quit;
```

Output 14.1   Maximum-Likelihood Logistic Regression

```
                MAXIMUM LIKELIHOOD LOGISTIC REGRESSION                           1

                           CATMOD PROCEDURE

Response: Y                        Response Levels (R)=     2
Weight Variable: COUNT             Populations     (S)=    19
Data Set: INGOTS                   Total Frequency (N)=   387
                                   Observations  (Obs)=    25




                        POPULATION PROFILES
                                        Sample
                  Sample  HEAT  SOAK     Size
                  ----------------------------
                     1      7     1       10
                     2      7    1.7      17
                     3      7    2.2       7
                     4      7    2.8      12
                     5      7     4        9
                     6     14     1       31
                     7     14    1.7      43
                     8     14    2.2      33
                     9     14    2.8      31
                    10     14     4       19
                    11     27     1       56
                    12     27    1.7      44
                    13     27    2.2      21
                    14     27    2.8      22
                    15     27     4       16
                    16     51     1       13
                    17     51    1.7       1
                    18     51    2.2       1
                    19     51     4        1




                        RESPONSE PROFILES

                       Response   Y
                       -----------
                          1       0
                          2       1
```

```
                MAXIMUM LIKELIHOOD LOGISTIC REGRESSION                           2

                         RESPONSE FREQUENCIES

                              Response Number
                    Sample       1        2
                    ----------------------------
                       1        10        0
                       2        17        0
                       3         7        0
                       4        12        0
                       5         9        0
                       6        31        0
                       7        43        0
                       8        31        2
                       9        31        0
                      10        19        0
                      11        55        1
                      12        40        4
                      13        21        0
                      14        21        1
                      15        15        1
                      16        10        3
                      17         1        0
                      18         1        0
                      19         1        0
```

(continued on next page)

(continued from previous page)

㉑ MAXIMUM LIKELIHOOD ANALYSIS

Iteration	Sub Iteration	-2 Log Likelihood	Convergence Criterion	Parameter Estimates 1	2	3
0	0	536.49592	1.0000	0	0	0
1	0	152.58961	0.7156	2.1594	-0.0139	-0.003733
2	0	106.76066	0.3003	3.5334	-0.0363	-0.0120
3	0	96.692171	0.0943	4.7489	-0.0640	-0.0299
4	0	95.383825	0.0135	5.4138	-0.0790	-0.0498
5	0	95.345659	0.000400	5.5539	-0.0819	-0.0564
6	0	95.345613	4.8289E-7	5.5592	-0.0820	-0.0568
7	0	95.345613	7.731E-13	5.5592	-0.0820	-0.0568

㉒ MAXIMUM LIKELIHOOD ANALYSIS OF VARIANCE TABLE

Source	DF	Chi-Square	Prob
INTERCEPT	1	24.65	0.0000
HEAT	1	11.95	0.0005
SOAK	1	0.03	0.8639
LIKELIHOOD RATIO	16	13.75	0.6171

MAXIMUM LIKELIHOOD LOGISTIC REGRESSION   3

㉓ ANALYSIS OF MAXIMUM LIKELIHOOD ESTIMATES

Effect	Parameter	Estimate	Standard Error	Chi-Square	Prob
INTERCEPT	1	5.5592	1.1197	24.65	0.0000
HEAT	2	-0.0820	0.0237	11.95	0.0005
SOAK	3	-0.0568	0.3312	0.03	0.8639

㉔ COVARIANCE MATRIX OF THE MAXIMUM LIKELIHOOD ESTIMATES

	1	2	3
1	1.2537133	-0.0215664	-0.2817648
2	-0.0215664	0.0005633	0.0026243
3	-0.2817648	0.0026243	0.1097020

㉕ CORRELATION MATRIX OF THE MAXIMUM LIKELIHOOD ESTIMATES

	1	2	3
1	1.0000000	-0.8115214	-0.7597670
2	-0.8115214	1.0000000	0.3338261
3	-0.7597670	0.3338261	1.0000000

The analysis-of-variance table shows that the model fits since the likelihood-ratio goodness-of-fit test is nonsignificant. It also shows that the length of heating time is a significant factor with respect to readiness, but that length of soaking time is not.

From the table of maximum-likelihood estimates, the fitted model is

$$E(\text{the logit}) = 5.559 - 0.082(\text{HEAT}) - 0.057(\text{SOAK}) \quad .$$

Predicted values of the logits, as well as the probabilities of readiness, could be obtained by specifying the PRED option in the MODEL statement. In addition, since soaking time is nonsignificant, you could go on to fit another model that deleted the variable SOAK.

Example 4: Log-Linear Model, Three Dependent Variables

This analysis reproduces the predicted cell frequencies for Bartlett's data using a log-linear model of no three-variable interaction (Bishop, Fienberg, and Holland 1975, 89). As in their text, the variable levels are simply labeled 1 and 2. The following statements produce **Output 14.4**:

```
*-------------------CATMOD EXAMPLE 4------------------------------------*
|                                                                       |
|                          Bartlett's Data                              |
|                          ---------------                              |
| Cuttings of two different lengths were planted at one of two time     |
| points, and their survival status was recorded. The variables are     |
|    v1=survival status (dead or alive)                                 |
|    v2=time of planting (spring or at_once)                            |
|    v3=length of cutting (long or short).                              |
|                                                                       |
| From: Bishop, Fienberg, and Holland (1975, 89)                        |
|                                                                       |
| Illustrate: log-linear model, three dependent variables               |
|                                                                       |
*----------------------------------------------------------------------*;

title 'BARTLETT''S DATA';
data b;
   input v3 v2 v1 wt @@;
   cards;
1 1 1 156     1 1 2 84     1 2 1 84     1 2 2 156
2 1 1 107     2 1 2 133    2 2 1 31     2 2 2 209
;
proc catmod;
   weight wt;
   model v3*v2*v1=_response_ / nogls noparm noresponse pred=freq ml;
   loglin v3|v2|v1 @ 2;
   title2 'MODEL WITH NO 3-VARIABLE INTERACTION';
quit;
```

Output 14.4   Analysis of Bartlett's Data: Log-Linear Model

```
                              BARTLETT'S DATA                                    1
                        MODEL WITH NO 3-VARIABLE INTERACTION
                              CATMOD PROCEDURE

          Response: V3*V2*V1              Response Levels (R)=      8
          Weight Variable: WT            Populations       (S)=      1
          Data Set: B                    Total Frequency (N)=     960
                                         Observations  (Obs)=       8


                                   Sample
                          Sample    Size
                          ------------------
                            1        960


                           RESPONSE PROFILES

                     Response  V3  V2  V1
                     --------------------
                         1      1   1   1
                         2      1   1   2
                         3      1   2   1
                         4      1   2   2
                         5      2   1   1
                         6      2   1   2
                         7      2   2   1
                         8      2   2   2


                       MAXIMUM LIKELIHOOD ANALYSIS

                                              Parameter Estimates
              Sub      -2 Log    Convergence
  Iteration Iteration Likelihood  Criterion      1         2         3         4         5         6
  -----------------------------------------------------------------------------------------------------
      0        0      3992.5278    1.0000        0         0         0         0         0         0
      1        0      3812.5059    0.0451    1.11E-17  2.961E-17 -2.22E-17  -0.2125    0.2125    0.3083
      2        0      3800.2168    0.003223   0.0494    0.0752   -0.0752    -0.2486    0.2486    0.3502
      3        0      3800.12      0.0000255  0.0555    0.0809   -0.0809    -0.2543    0.2543    0.3568
      4        0      3800.12      3.6909E-9  0.0556    0.0810   -0.0810    -0.2544    0.2544    0.3569
```

```
                              BARTLETT'S DATA                                    2
                        MODEL WITH NO 3-VARIABLE INTERACTION

                  MAXIMUM LIKELIHOOD ANALYSIS OF VARIANCE TABLE

              Source            DF   Chi-Square    Prob
              -------------------------------------------------
              V3                 1      2.64      0.1041
              V2                 1      5.25      0.0220
              V3*V2              1      5.25      0.0220
              V1                 1     48.94      0.0000
              V3*V1              1     48.94      0.0000
              V2*V1              1     95.01      0.0000

              LIKELIHOOD RATIO   1      2.29      0.1299
```

```
                              BARTLETT'S DATA                                    3
                      MODEL WITH NO 3-VARIABLE INTERACTION
  27  MAXIMUM LIKELIHOOD PREDICTED VALUES FOR RESPONSE FUNCTIONS AND FREQUENCIES

                           -------Observed-------   -------Predicted------
                  Function              Standard                Standard
  Sample  V3 V2 V1 Number  Function      Error      Function     Error     Residual
  ----------------------------------------------------------------------------------
    1                 1   -0.2924782  0.10580617  -0.2356473  0.09848616  -0.056831
                      2   -0.9115175  0.12918766  -0.9494184  0.1299476   0.03790099
                      3   -0.9115175  0.12918766  -0.9494184  0.1299476   0.03790099
                      4   -0.2924782  0.10580617  -0.2356473  0.09848616  -0.056831
                      5   -0.6695054  0.11887171  -0.6936188  0.12017169  0.02411336
                      6   -0.4519851  0.11092108  -0.3896985  0.1022668   -0.0622866
                      7   -1.908347   0.19246494  -1.7314626  0.14296911  -0.1768845

           1  1  1   F1      156     11.4302231   161.096138  11.0737946  -5.0961381
           1  1  2   F2       84      8.75499857   78.9038609  7.8086133   5.09613909
           1  2  1   F3       84      8.75499857   78.9038609  7.8086133   5.09613909
           1  2  2   F4      156     11.4302231   161.096138  11.0737946  -5.0961381
           2  1  1   F5      107      9.75058759  101.903861   8.9243041   5.09613941
           2  1  2   F6      133     10.7039226   138.096139  10.3343404  -5.0961386
           2  2  1   F7       31      5.47713048   36.0961431  4.82631486  -5.0961431
           2  2  2   F8      209     12.7866711   203.90386   12.2128493   5.09614031
```

The analysis-of-variance table shows that the model fits since the likelihood-ratio test for the three-variable interaction is nonsignificant. All of the two-variable interactions, however, are significant, showing that there is mutual dependence among all three variables.

The upper section of the predicted-value table gives observed and predicted values for the generalized logits. The lower section of the table gives observed and predicted cell frequencies, their standard errors, and residuals.

Example 5: Log-Linear Model, Structural Zeros and Random Zeros

This example illustrates a log-linear model of independence, using data that contain structural zero frequencies, as well as random (sampling) zero frequencies. The structural zeros are automatically deleted by CATMOD. The sampling zeros should be replaced in the DATA step by some positive number close to zero (such as 1E—20). Also, the row for Monkey T is deleted since it contains all zeros; therefore, the cell frequencies predicted by a model of independence are also zero. The following statements produce **Output 14.5**:

```
*--------------------CATMOD EXAMPLE 5------------------------------------*
|                                                                        |
|                    Behavior of Squirrel Monkeys                        |
|                    ---------------------------                         |
|  In a population of 6 squirrel monkeys, the joint distribution of      |
|  genital display with respect to (active role, passive role) was       |
|  observed. Since a monkey cannot have both the active and passive      |
|  roles in the same interaction, the diagonal cells of the table        |
|  are structural zeros.                                                 |
|                                                                        |
|  From: Fienberg (1980, Table 8-2)                                      |
|                                                                        |
|  Illustrate: log-linear model, structural zeros and random zeros       |
|                                                                        |
*------------------------------------------------------------------------*;

title 'BEHAVIOR OF SQUIRREL MONKEYS';
data display;
   input active $ passive $ wt @@;
   if active ne 't';
   if active ne passive then if wt=0 then wt=1e-20;
   cards;
r r 0     r s 1     r t 5     r u 8     r v 9     r w 0
s r 29    s s 0     s t 14    s u 46    s v 4     s w 0
t r 0     t s 0     t t 0     t u 0     t v 0     t w 0
u r 2     u s 3     u t 1     u u 0     u v 38    u w 2
v r 0     v s 0     v t 0     v u 0     v v 0     v w 1
w r 9     w s 25    w t 4     w u 6     w v 13    w w 0
;
proc catmod;
   weight wt;
   model active*passive=_response_
       / ml nogls freq pred=freq noparm noresponse;
   loglin active passive;
   title2 'TEST QUASI-INDEPENDENCE FOR THE INCOMPLETE TABLE';
quit;
```

Output 14.5 Log-Linear Model Analysis with Zero Frequencies

```
                         BEHAVIOR OF SQUIRREL MONKEYS                              1
                  TEST QUASI-INDEPENDENCE FOR THE INCOMPLETE TABLE

                              CATMOD PROCEDURE

        Response: ACTIVE*PASSIVE          Response Levels (R)=    25
        Weight Variable: WT               Populations      (S)=     1
        Data Set: DISPLAY                 Total Frequency (N)=    220
                                          Observations  (Obs)=     25


                                     Sample
                         Sample       Size
                         ----------------------
                            1          220



                          RESPONSE PROFILES

                     Response  ACTIVE  PASSIVE
                     -------------------------
                         1       r        s
                         2       r        t
                         3       r        u
                         4       r        v
                         5       r        w
                         6       s        r
                         7       s        t
                         8       s        u
                         9       s        v
                        10       s        w
                        11       u        r
                        12       u        s
                        13       u        t
                        14       u        v
                        15       u        w
                        16       v        r
                        17       v        s
                        18       v        t
                        19       v        u
                        20       v        w
                        21       w        r
                        22       w        s
                        23       w        t
                        24       w        u
                        25       w        v



                          RESPONSE FREQUENCIES

                                Response Number
Sample       1        2        3        4        5        6        7        8        9
---------------------------------------------------------------------------------------
   1         1        5        8        9      1E-20       29       14       46       4
```

```
                         BEHAVIOR OF SQUIRREL MONKEYS                              2
                  TEST QUASI-INDEPENDENCE FOR THE INCOMPLETE TABLE
                          RESPONSE FREQUENCIES

                                Response Number
Sample      10       11       12       13       14       15       16       17       18
---------------------------------------------------------------------------------------
   1       1E-20      2        3        1        38       2      1E-20    1E-20    1E-20


                          RESPONSE FREQUENCIES

                                Response Number
        Sample      19       20       21       22       23       24       25
        ---------------------------------------------------------------------
           1       1E-20      1        9        25       4        6        13
```

(continued on next page)

(continued from previous page)

MAXIMUM LIKELIHOOD ANALYSIS

Iteration	Sub Iteration	-2 Log Likelihood	Convergence Criterion	Parameter Estimates 1	2	3
0	0	1416.3054	1.0000	0	0	0
1	0	1238.2417	0.1257	-0.4976	1.1112	0.1722
2	0	1205.1264	0.0267	-0.3420	1.0962	0.5612
3	0	1199.5068	0.004663	-0.1570	1.2687	0.7058
4	0	1198.6271	0.000733	-0.0466	1.3791	0.8170
5	0	1198.5611	0.0000551	-0.002748	1.4230	0.8609
6	0	1198.5603	6.5351E-7	0.002760	1.4285	0.8664
7	0	1198.5603	1.217E-10	0.002837	1.4285	0.8665

Iteration	Parameter Estimates 4	5	6	7	8	9
0	0	0	0	0	0	0
1	-0.8804	-0.006978	0.0827	-0.4735	0.7287	0.5791
2	-1.7549	0.2233	0.3899	-0.4086	0.7875	0.5728
3	-2.3992	0.3034	0.4360	-0.3162	0.8812	0.6703
4	-2.8422	0.3309	0.4625	-0.2890	0.9085	0.6968
5	-3.0176	0.3334	0.4649	-0.2866	0.9110	0.6992
6	-3.0396	0.3334	0.4649	-0.2865	0.9110	0.6992
7	-3.0399	0.3334	0.4649	-0.2865	0.9110	0.6992

BEHAVIOR OF SQUIRREL MONKEYS   3
TEST QUASI-INDEPENDENCE FOR THE INCOMPLETE TABLE

MAXIMUM LIKELIHOOD ANALYSIS OF VARIANCE TABLE

Source	DF	Chi-Square	Prob
ACTIVE	4	56.58	0.0000
PASSIVE	5	47.94	0.0000
LIKELIHOOD RATIO	15	135.17	0.0000

BEHAVIOR OF SQUIRREL MONKEYS   4
TEST QUASI-INDEPENDENCE FOR THE INCOMPLETE TABLE

MAXIMUM LIKELIHOOD PREDICTED VALUES FOR RESPONSE FUNCTIONS AND FREQUENCIES

Sample	ACTIVE	PASSIVE	Function Number	Observed Function	Observed Standard Error	Predicted Function	Predicted Standard Error	Residual
1			1	-2.5649494	1.03774904	-0.973554	0.33901898	-1.5913953
			2	-0.9555114	0.52623481	-1.7250404	0.34543788	0.76952896
			3	-0.4855078	0.44935852	-0.5275144	0.30925387	0.0420066
			4	-0.3677248	0.43362909	-0.7392682	0.24900568	0.37154345
			5	-48.616651	1E10	-3.560517	0.63410407	-45.056134
			6	0.80234647	0.33377513	0.32058886	0.2662902	0.48175761
			7	0.07410797	0.38516444	-0.2993416	0.29563358	0.37344956
			8	1.26369204	0.31410541	0.89818441	0.25085737	0.36550763
			9	-1.178655	0.57177187	0.6864306	0.17339604	-1.8650856
			10	-48.616651	1E10	-2.1348182	0.60807083	-46.481833
			11	-1.8718022	0.75955453	-0.2414953	0.28721789	-1.6303069
			12	-1.4663371	0.64051262	-0.1099394	0.30356781	-1.3563977
			13	-2.5649494	1.03774904	-0.8614257	0.31479379	-1.7035236
			14	1.0726368	0.32130806	0.12434644	0.20434511	0.94829036
			15	-1.8718022	0.75955453	-2.6969023	0.61743258	0.82510014
			16	-48.616651	1E10	-4.1478747	1.02450813	-44.468777
			17	-48.616651	1E10	-4.0163187	1.03006239	-44.600332
			18	-48.616651	1E10	-4.7678051	1.03245707	-43.848846
			19	-48.616651	1E10	-3.5702791	1.02079389	-45.046372
			20	-2.5649494	1.03774904	-6.6032817	1.16128927	4.03833233
			21	-0.3677248	0.43362909	-0.3658417	0.20295917	-0.001883
			22	0.65392647	0.34194017	-0.2342858	0.23279368	0.88821229
			23	-1.178655	0.57177187	-0.9857722	0.23940797	-0.1928828
			24	-0.7731899	0.49354812	0.21175381	0.18500696	-0.9849437

(continued on next page)

(continued from previous page)

r	s	F1	1	0.99772468	5.25950838	1.36156002	-4.2595084
r	t	F2	5	2.21051208	2.48072585	0.6910659	2.51927415
r	u	F3	8	2.77652497	8.21594841	1.85514611	-0.2159484
r	v	F4	9	2.93799561	6.64804868	1.50931986	2.35195132
r	w	F5	1E-20	1E-10	0.39576868	0.2402678	-0.3957687
s	r	F6	29	5.01769596	19.1859928	3.14791495	9.81400723
s	t	F7	14	3.62064786	10.321716	2.16959874	3.67828404
s	u	F8	46	6.03173426	34.1846262	4.42870591	11.8153738
s	v	F9	4	1.98173478	27.6609647	3.72278813	-23.660965
s	w	F10	1E-20	1E-10	1.64670026	0.95271227	-1.6467003
u	r	F11	2	1.40777064	10.936396	2.12321968	-8.936396
u	s	F12	3	1.72020083	12.4740717	2.55433555	-9.4740717
u	t	F13	1	0.99772468	5.8835826	1.3806555	-4.8835826
u	v	F14	38	5.60681404	15.7672979	2.68469221	22.2327021
u	w	F15	2	1.40777064	0.93865177	0.55164479	1.06134823
v	r	F16	1E-20	1E-10	0.21996583	0.22177911	-0.2199658
v	s	F17	1E-20	1E-10	0.2508934	0.25370612	-0.2508934
v	t	F18	1E-20	1E-10	0.11833763	0.12031391	-0.1183376
v	u	F19	1E-20	1E-10	0.39192393	0.39325479	-0.3919239
v	w	F20	1	0.99772468	0.01887928	0.02172759	0.98112072
w	r	F21	9	2.93799561	9.6576454	1.80865595	-0.6576454
w	s	F22	25	4.70734436	11.0155266	2.27501884	13.9844734
w	t	F23	4	1.98173478	5.19563797	1.18445235	-1.195638
w	u	F24	6	2.41585671	17.2075014	2.77209793	-11.207501
w	v	F25	13	3.49740163	13.9236886	2.24158038	-0.9236886

The analysis-of-variance table shows that the model of independence does not fit since the likelihood-ratio test for the interaction is significant. In other words, active and passive behaviors of the squirrel monkeys are dependent behavior roles.

The lower section of the predicted-value table gives predicted cell frequencies, but since the model does not fit, these should be ignored.

Example 6: Repeated Measures, 2 Response Levels, 3 Populations

The analysis of the marginal probabilities is directed at assessing the main effects of the repeated measurement factor (TRIAL) and the independent variable (GROUP), as well as their interaction. Since the interaction is significant, a reduced model is fitted in which the only trial effect is that within group 3. The residual goodness-of-fit statistic tests the joint effect of TRIAL(GROUP=1) and TRIAL(GROUP=2). Although the contingency table is incomplete (only thirteen of the sixteen possible responses are observed), this poses no problem in the

computation of the marginal probabilities. The following statements produce
Output 14.6:

```
*-------------------------CATMOD EXAMPLE 6-------------------------*
|                                                                 |
|                  Multi-Population Repeated Measures             |
|                  -----------------------------------            |
|  Subjects from 3 groups have their response (0 or 1) recorded at |
|  each of four trials.                                           |
|                                                                 |
|  From: Guthrie (1981).                                         |
|                                                                 |
|  Illustrate: repeated measures, 2 levels of response, 3 populations |
|                                                                 |
*-----------------------------------------------------------------*;

title 'MULTI-POPULATION REPEATED MEASURES';
data group;
   input a b c d group wt @@;
   cards;
1 1 1 1 2 2     0 0 0 0 2 2     0 0 1 0 1 2     0 0 1 0 2 2
0 0 0 1 1 4     0 0 0 1 2 1     0 0 0 1 3 3     1 0 0 1 2 1
0 0 1 1 1 1     0 0 1 1 2 2     0 0 1 1 3 5     0 1 0 0 1 4
0 1 0 0 2 1     0 1 0 1 2 1     0 1 0 1 3 2     0 1 1 0 3 1
1 0 0 0 1 3     1 0 0 0 2 1     0 1 1 1 2 1     0 1 1 1 3 2
1 0 1 0 1 1     1 0 1 1 2 1     1 0 1 1 3 2
;
proc catmod;
   weight wt;
   response marginals;
   model a*b*c*d=group _response_ group*_response_ / freq nodesign;
   repeated trial 4;
   title2 'SATURATED MODEL';
run;

   model a*b*c*d=group _response_(group=3) / noprofile noparm;
   title2 'TRIAL NESTED WITHIN GROUP 3';
run;
quit;
```

Output 14.6 Analysis of Multiple-Population Repeated Measures

```
                    MULTI-POPULATION REPEATED MEASURES                    1
                            SATURATED MODEL

                          CATMOD PROCEDURE

Response: A*B*C*D              Response Levels (R)=   13
Weight Variable: WT            Populations    (S)=    3
Data Set: GROUP                Total Frequency (N)=   45
                               Observations  (Obs)=   23


                       POPULATION PROFILES
                                     Sample
                   Sample  GROUP      Size
                   -------------------------
                     1       1         15
                     2       2         15
                     3       3         15



                       RESPONSE PROFILES

                   Response  A  B  C  D
                   --------------------
                      1      0  0  0  0
                      2      0  0  0  1
                      3      0  0  1  0
                      4      0  0  1  1
                      5      0  1  0  0
                      6      0  1  0  1
                      7      0  1  1  0
                      8      0  1  1  1
                      9      1  0  0  0
                     10      1  0  0  1
                     11      1  0  1  0
                     12      1  0  1  1
                     13      1  1  1  1



                      RESPONSE FREQUENCIES

                              Response Number
Sample      1        2        3        4        5        6        7
------------------------------------------------------------------------
  1         0        4        2        1        4        0        0
  2         2        1        2        2        1        1        0
  3         0        3        0        5        0        2        1
```

```
                    MULTI-POPULATION REPEATED MEASURES                    2
                            SATURATED MODEL

                      RESPONSE FREQUENCIES

                              Response Number
Sample      8        9       10       11       12       13
------------------------------------------------------------------
  1         0        3        0        1        0        0
  2         1        1        1        0        1        2
  3         2        0        0        0        2        0


                    ANALYSIS OF VARIANCE TABLE

          Source              DF   Chi-Square    Prob
          ------------------------------------------------
          INTERCEPT            1      354.88     0.0000
          GROUP               2       24.79     0.0000
          TRIAL               3       21.45     0.0001
          GROUP*_RESPONSE_    6       18.71     0.0047

          RESIDUAL            0        .          .

    ㉚  NOTE: _RESPONSE_ = TRIAL
```

(continued on next page)

(continued from previous page)

```
                 ANALYSIS OF WEIGHTED-LEAST-SQUARES ESTIMATES

                                           Standard    Chi-
        Effect            Parameter  Estimate  Error    Square   Prob
        -----------------------------------------------------------------
        INTERCEPT              1      0.5833   0.0310   354.88   0.0000
        GROUP                 2      0.1333   0.0335    15.88   0.0001
                              3     -0.0333   0.0551     0.37   0.5450
        TRIAL                 4      0.1722   0.0557     9.57   0.0020
                              5      0.1056   0.0647     2.66   0.1028
                              6     -0.0722   0.0577     1.57   0.2107
        GROUP*_RESPONSE_      7     -0.1556   0.0852     3.33   0.0679
                              8     -0.0889   0.0953     0.87   0.3511
                              9      0.0889   0.0822     1.17   0.2793
                             10     -0.0556   0.0800     0.48   0.4877
                             11      0.0111   0.0866     0.02   0.8979
                             12     -0.0111   0.0824     0.02   0.8927

        NOTE: _RESPONSE_ = TRIAL
```

```
                 MULTI-POPULATION REPEATED MEASURES                        3
                    TRIAL NESTED WITHIN GROUP 3

                         CATMOD PROCEDURE

        Response: A*B*C*D            Response Levels (R)=    13
        Weight Variable: WT         Populations     (S)=     3
        Data Set: GROUP             Total Frequency (N)=    45
                                    Observations  (Obs)=    23


                Function  Response              DESIGN MATRIX
        Sample   Number   Function    1    2    3    4    5    6
        -----------------------------------------------------------------
           1        1     0.73333     1    1    0    0    0    0
                    2     0.73333     1    1    0    0    0    0
                    3     0.73333     1    1    0    0    0    0
                    4     0.66667     1    1    0    0    0    0

           2        1     0.66667     1    0    1    0    0    0
                    2     0.66667     1    0    1    0    0    0
                    3     0.46667     1    0    1    0    0    0
                    4     0.40000     1    0    1    0    0    0

           3        1     0.86667     1   -1   -1    1    0    0
                    2     0.66667     1   -1   -1    0    1    0
                    3     0.33333     1   -1   -1    0    0    1
                    4     0.06667     1   -1   -1   -1   -1   -1

                    ANALYSIS OF VARIANCE TABLE

        Source               DF   Chi-Square    Prob
        -----------------------------------------------------
        INTERCEPT             1      386.94     0.0000
        GROUP                2       25.42     0.0000
        _RESPONSE_(GROUP=3)  3       75.07     0.0000

        RESIDUAL             6        5.09     0.5319

        NOTE: _RESPONSE_ = TRIAL
```

The first analysis-of-variance table shows that there is a significant interaction between the independent variable GROUP and the repeated measurement factor TRIAL. Thus, an intermediate model (not shown) was fitted in which the effects TRIAL and GROUP*TRIAL were replaced by TRIAL(GROUP=1), TRIAL(GROUP=2), and TRIAL(GROUP=3). Of these three effects, only the last was significant, so it was retained in the final model.

The last analysis-of-variance table shows that the final model fits, that there is a significant GROUP effect, and that there is a significant TRIAL effect in group 3.

Example 7: Repeated Measures, 4 Response Levels, 1 Population

This example illustrates a repeated measurement analysis in which there are more than two levels of response. Since there are four levels, the RESPONSE statement induces the computation of three marginal probabilities for each dependent variable, resulting in six response functions for analysis. Since the model contains a repeated measurement factor (SIDE) with two levels (RIGHT, LEFT), CATMOD groups the functions into sets of three (=6/2). Therefore, the SIDE effect has three degrees of freedom (one for each marginal probability), and it is the appropriate test of marginal homogeneity. The following statements produce **Output 14.7**:

```
*----------------------------CATMOD EXAMPLE 7----------------------------*
|                                                                        |
|                    Testing Vision: Right Eye vs. Left                  |
|                    ---------------------------------                   |
|   7477 women aged 30-39 were tested for vision in both right and       |
|   left eyes. Marginal homogeneity is tested by the main effect of      |
|   the repeated measurement factor, SIDE.                               |
|                                                                        |
|   From: Grizzle, Starmer and Koch (1969, 493).                         |
|                                                                        |
|   Illustrate: repeated measures, 4 levels of response, 1 population    |
|                                                                        |
*------------------------------------------------------------------------*;

title 'VISION SYMMETRY';
data vision;
   input right left count @@;
   cards;
1 1 1520    1 2  266    1 3  124    1 4  66
2 1  234    2 2 1512    2 3  432    2 4  78
3 1  117    3 2  362    3 3 1772    3 4 205
4 1   36    4 2   82    4 3  179    4 4 492
;
proc catmod;
   weight count;
   response marginals;
   model right*left=_response_ / freq;
   repeated side 2;
   title2 'TEST OF MARGINAL HOMOGENEITY';
quit;
```

Output 14.7   Vision Study: Analysis of Marginal Homogeneity

```
                        VISION SYMMETRY                                1
                   TEST OF MARGINAL HOMOGENEITY

                        CATMOD PROCEDURE

   Response: RIGHT*LEFT            Response Levels (R)=    16
   Weight Variable: COUNT          Populations     (S)=     1
   Data Set: VISION                Total Frequency (N)=  7477
                                   Observations  (Obs)=    16


                              Sample
                   Sample      Size
                   ----------------
                      1        7477



                        RESPONSE PROFILES

                   Response  RIGHT  LEFT
                   ---------------------
                        1      1     1
                        2      1     2
                        3      1     3
                        4      1     4
                        5      2     1
                        6      2     2
                        7      2     3
                        8      2     4
                        9      3     1
                       10      3     2
                       11      3     3
                       12      3     4
                       13      4     1
                       14      4     2
                       15      4     3
                       16      4     4



                     RESPONSE FREQUENCIES

                               Response Number
    Sample    1      2      3      4      5      6      7      8
    ----------------------------------------------------------------
      1     1520    266    124     66    234   1512    432     78



                     RESPONSE FREQUENCIES

                               Response Number
    Sample    9     10     11     12     13     14     15     16
    ----------------------------------------------------------------
      1      117    362   1772    205     36     82    179    492
```

```
                        VISION SYMMETRY                                2
                   TEST OF MARGINAL HOMOGENEITY

             Function  Response          DESIGN MATRIX
    Sample   Number    Function    1    2    3    4    5    6
    ----------------------------------------------------------------
      1        1       0.26428     1    0    0    1    0    0
               2       0.30173     0    1    0    0    1    0
               3       0.32847     0    0    1    0    0    1
               4       0.25505     1    0    0   -1    0    0
               5       0.29718     0    1    0    0   -1    0
               6       0.33529     0    0    1    0    0   -1
```

(continued on next page)

(continued from previous page)

```
                        ANALYSIS OF VARIANCE TABLE

            Source                DF    Chi-Square    Prob
            ------------------------------------------------
            INTERCEPT              3      78744.17    0.0000
            SIDE                   3         11.98    0.0075

            RESIDUAL               0           .         .


                ANALYSIS OF WEIGHTED-LEAST-SQUARES ESTIMATES
                                        Standard    Chi-
            Effect      Parameter  Estimate  Error  Square   Prob
            ------------------------------------------------------------
            INTERCEPT        1      0.2597   0.00468  3073.03  0.0000
                             2      0.2995   0.00464  4160.17  0.0000
                             3      0.3319   0.00483  4725.25  0.0000
            SIDE             4      0.00461  0.00194     5.65  0.0174
                             5      0.00227  0.00255     0.80  0.3726
                             6     -0.00341  0.00252     1.83  0.1757
```

The analysis-of-variance table shows that the SIDE effect is significant, so there is not marginal homogeneity between left-eye vision and right-eye vision. In other words, the distribution of the quality of right-eye vision differs significantly from the quality of left-eye vision in the same subjects.

Example 8: Repeated Measures, Logistic Analysis of Growth Curve

The data are from a longitudinal study in which patients from four populations (2 diagnoses × 2 treatments) were measured at three times to assess their response (N=Normal or A=Abnormal) to treatment. The analysis is directed at assessing the effect of the repeated measurement factor, TIME, as well as the independent variables, DIAG and TRTMENT. The RESPONSE statement is used to compute the logits of the marginal probabilities. The times used in the design matrix (0, 1, 2) correspond to the logarithms (base 2) of the actual times (1, 2, 4). The following statements produce **Output 14.8**:

```
*---------------------------CATMOD EXAMPLE 8---------------------------*
|                                                                     |
|                    Growth Curve Analysis                            |
|                    ---------------------                            |
|   Subjects from 2 diagnostic groups (mild or severe) are given one  |
|   of 2 treatments (std or new), and their response to treatment     |
|   (n=normal or a=abnormal) is recorded at each of 3 times           |
|   (weeks 1, 2, and 4).                                              |
|                                                                     |
|   From: Koch et al.(1977).                                          |
|                                                                     |
|   Illustrate: repeated measures, logistic analysis of growth curve  |
|                                                                     |
*--------------------------------------------------------------------*;

title 'GROWTH CURVE ANALYSIS';
data growth2;
    input diag $ trt $ week1 $ week2 $ week4 $ count @@;
```

```
       cards;
mild std n n n 16      severe std n n n  2
mild std n n a 13      severe std n n a  2
mild std n a n  9      severe std n a n  8
mild std n a a  3      severe std n a a  9
mild std a n n 14      severe std a n n  9
mild std a n a  4      severe std a n a 15
mild std a a n 15      severe std a a n 27
mild std a a a  6      severe std a a a 28
mild new n n n 31      severe new n n n  7
mild new n n a  0      severe new n n a  2
mild new n a n  6      severe new n a n  5
mild new n a a  0      severe new n a a  2
mild new a n n 22      severe new a n n 31
mild new a n a  2      severe new a n a  5
mild new a a n  9      severe new a a n 32
mild new a a a  0      severe new a a a  6
;
proc catmod order=data;
   title2 'REDUCED LOGISTIC MODEL';
   weight count;
   population diag trt;
   response logit;
   model week1*week2*week4=(1 0 0 0 ,
                            1 0 1 0 ,
                            1 0 2 0 ,
                            1 0 0 0 ,
                            1 0 0 1 ,
                            1 0 0 2 ,
                            0 1 0 0 ,
                            0 1 1 0 ,
                            0 1 2 0 ,
                            0 1 0 0 ,
                            0 1 0 1 ,
                            0 1 0 2 )(1='Mild diagnosis, week 1',
                                      2='Severe diagnosis, week 1',
                                      3='Time effect for std trt',
                                      4='Time effect for new trt')
                                      / freq;
   contrast 'Diagnosis effect, week 1' all_parms 1 -1  0  0;
   contrast 'Equal time effects' all_parms 0  0  1 -1;
quit;
```

Output 14.8 Logistic Analysis of Growth Curve

```
                         GROWTH CURVE ANALYSIS                           1
                         REDUCED LOGISTIC MODEL

                            CATMOD PROCEDURE

    Response: WEEK1*WEEK2*WEEK4        Response Levels (R)=      8
    Weight Variable: COUNT             Populations      (S)=      4
    Data Set: GROWTH2                  Total Frequency  (N)=    340
                                       Observations   (Obs)=     29


                          POPULATION PROFILES
                                              Sample
                 Sample   DIAG    TRT          Size
                 ----------------------------------
                    1     mild    std           80
                    2     mild    new           70
                    3     severe  std          100
                    4     severe  new           90


                          RESPONSE PROFILES

                 Response  WEEK1   WEEK2   WEEK4
                 ----------------------------------
                    1        n       n       n
                    2        n       n       a
                    3        n       a       n
                    4        n       a       a
                    5        a       n       n
                    6        a       n       a
                    7        a       a       n
                    8        a       a       a


                          RESPONSE FREQUENCIES

                                    Response Number
        Sample    1      2      3      4      5      6      7      8
        ------------------------------------------------------------------
          1      16     13      9      3     14      4     15      6
          2      31      0      6      0     22      2      9      0
          3       2      2      8      9      9     15     27     28
          4       7      2      5      2     31      5     32      6
```

```
                         GROWTH CURVE ANALYSIS                           2
                         REDUCED LOGISTIC MODEL

                 Function  Response        DESIGN MATRIX
        Sample    Number   Function      1      2      3      4
        ------------------------------------------------------------------
          1         1      0.05001       1      0      0      0
                    2      0.35364       1      0      1      0
                    3      0.73089       1      0      2      0

          2         1      0.11441       1      0      0      0
                    2      1.29928       1      0      0      1
                    3      3.52636       1      0      0      2

          3         1     -1.32493       0      1      0      0
                    2     -0.94446       0      1      1      0
                    3     -0.16034       0      1      2      0

          4         1     -1.53148       0      1      0      0
                    2      0             0      1      0      1
                    3      1.60944       0      1      0      2
```

(continued on next page)

(continued from previous page)

```
                    ANALYSIS OF VARIANCE TABLE

         Source                  DF    Chi-Square    Prob
         -------------------------------------------------------
         Mild diagnosis, week 1   1        0.28      0.5955
         Severe diagnosis, week 1 1      100.48      0.0000
         Time effect for std trt  1       26.35      0.0000
         Time effect for new trt  1      125.09      0.0000

         RESIDUAL                 8        4.20      0.8387


             ANALYSIS OF WEIGHTED-LEAST-SQUARES ESTIMATES

                                     Standard    Chi-
     Effect         Parameter  Estimate  Error   Square    Prob
     ----------------------------------------------------------------
     MODEL              1      -0.0716  0.1348     0.28    0.5955
                        2      -1.3529  0.1350   100.48    0.0000
                        3       0.4944  0.0963    26.35    0.0000
                        4       1.4552  0.1301   125.09    0.0000


              26  ANALYSIS OF CONTRASTS

     Contrast                     DF    Chi-Square    Prob
     -------------------------------------------------------
     Diagnosis effect, week 1      1       77.02      0.0000
     Equal time effects            1       59.12      0.0000
```

The analysis-of-variance table shows that the data can be adequately modeled by two parameters that represent diagnosis effects at week 1 and two log-linear time effects (one for each treatment). Both of the time effects are significant.

The analysis of contrasts shows that the diagnosis effect at week 1 is highly significant. Since the estimate of the logit for the severe diagnosis effect (parameter 2) is more negative than it is for the mild diagnosis effect (parameter 1), there is a smaller predicted probability of the first response (normal) for the severe diagnosis group. In other words, those subjects with a severe diagnosis have a significantly higher probability of abnormal response at week 1 than those subjects with a mild diagnosis.

The analysis of contrasts also shows that the time effect for the standard treatment is significantly different than the one for the new treatment. The table of parameter estimates shows that the time effect for the new treatment (parameter 4) is stronger than it is for the standard treatment (parameter 3).

Example 9: Repeated Measures, Two Repeated Measurement Factors

This example illustrates a repeated measurement analysis in which there are two repeated measurement factors. For the first two models, the response functions are marginal probabilities, and the repeated measurement factors are TIME and TRTMENT. The first model is a saturated one, containing effects for TIME, TRTMENT, and TIME*TRTMENT. The second fits a main effect model with respect to TRTMENT.

The third CATMOD procedure illustrates a RESPONSE statement that, at each time, computes the sensitivity and specificity of the test diagnostic procedure with respect to the standard procedure. Since these are measures of the relative accuracy of the two diagnostic procedures, the repeated measurement factors in this case are labeled TIME and ACCURACY. Only fifteen of the sixteen possible responses are observed, so additional care must be taken in formulating the RESPONSE statement for computation of sensitivity and specificity. The following statements produce **Output 14.9**:

```
*-------------------------CATMOD EXAMPLE 9-------------------------*
|                                                                 |
|                Diagnostic Procedure Comparison                  |
|                ------------------------------                   |
| Two diagnostic procedures (standard and test) are done on each  |
| subject, and the results of both are evaluated at each of two   |
| times as being positive or negative.                            |
|                                                                 |
| From: MacMillan et al.(1981).                                   |
|                                                                 |
|                                                                 |
| Illustrate: repeated measures, 2 repeated measurement factors   |
|                                                                 |
*-----------------------------------------------------------------*;
```

```
title 'DIAGNOSTIC PROCEDURE COMPARISON';
data a;
   input std1 $ test1 $ std2 $ test2 $ wt ∂∂;
   cards;
neg neg neg neg 509    neg neg neg pos  4    neg neg pos neg  17
neg neg pos pos   3    neg pos neg neg 13    neg pos neg pos   8
neg pos pos pos   8    pos neg neg neg 14    pos neg neg pos   1
pos neg pos neg  17    pos neg pos pos  9    pos pos neg neg   7
pos pos neg pos   4    pos pos pos neg  9    pos pos pos pos 170
;

proc catmod;
   title2 'MARGINAL SYMMETRY, SATURATED MODEL';
   weight wt;
   response marginals;
   model std1*test1*std2*test2=_response_ / freq noparm;
   repeated time 2, trtment 2 / _response_=time trtment time*trtment;
run;

   title2 'MARGINAL SYMMETRY, REDUCED MODEL';
   model std1*test1*std2*test2=_response_ / noprofile corrb;
   repeated time 2, trtment 2 / _response_=trtment;
run;

   title2 'SENSITIVITY AND SPECIFICITY ANALYSIS, MAIN EFFECTS MODEL';
   model std1*test1*std2*test2=_response_ / covb noprofile;
   repeated time 2, accuracy 2 / _response_=time accuracy;
   response exp  1 -1  0  0  0  0  0  0 ,
                 0  0  1 -1  0  0  0  0 ,
                 0  0  0  0  1 -1  0  0 ,
                 0  0  0  0  0  0  1 -1

             log 0 0 0 0   0 0 0   0 0 0 0   1 1 1 1 ,
                 0 0 0 0   0 0 0   1 1 1 1   1 1 1 1 ,
                 1 1 1 1   0 0 0   0 0 0 0   0 0 0 0 ,
                 1 1 1 1   1 1 1   0 0 0 0   0 0 0 0 ,
                 0 0 0 1   0 0 1   0 0 0 1   0 0 0 1 ,
                 0 0 1 1   0 0 1   0 0 1 1   0 0 1 1 ,
                 1 0 0 0   1 0 0   1 0 0 0   1 0 0 0 ,
                 1 1 0 0   1 1 0   1 1 0 0   1 1 0 0 ;
   run;
quit;
```

Output 14.9   Diagnosis Data: Two Repeated Measurement Factors

```
                         DIAGNOSTIC PROCEDURE COMPARISON                        1
                         MARGINAL SYMMETRY, SATURATED MODEL

                               CATMOD PROCEDURE

         Response: STD1*TEST1*STD2*TEST2    Response Levels (R)=    15
         Weight Variable: WT                Populations      (S)=     1
         Data Set: A                        Total Frequency (N)=    793
                                            Observations   (Obs)=    15


                                         Sample
                               Sample     Size
                               ----------------
                                  1        793



                              RESPONSE PROFILES

                        Response  STD1  TEST1  STD2  TEST2
                        -----------------------------------
                            1     neg    neg   neg    neg
                            2     neg    neg   neg    pos
                            3     neg    neg   pos    neg
                            4     neg    neg   pos    pos
                            5     neg    pos   neg    neg
                            6     neg    pos   neg    pos
                            7     neg    pos   pos    pos
                            8     pos    neg   neg    neg
                            9     pos    neg   neg    pos
                           10     pos    neg   pos    neg
                           11     pos    neg   pos    pos
                           12     pos    pos   neg    neg
                           13     pos    pos   neg    pos
                           14     pos    pos   pos    neg
                           15     pos    pos   pos    pos



                             RESPONSE FREQUENCIES

                                     Response Number
        Sample      1       2       3       4       5       6       7       8
        --------------------------------------------------------------------
           1       509      4      17       3      13       8       8      14



                             RESPONSE FREQUENCIES

                                     Response Number
        Sample      9      10      11      12      13      14      15
        --------------------------------------------------------------------
           1        1      17       9       7       4       9     170
```

```
                    DIAGNOSTIC PROCEDURE COMPARISON                              2
                    MARGINAL SYMMETRY, SATURATED MODEL

              Function   Response         DESIGN MATRIX
      Sample   Number    Function    1       2       3       4
      -----------------------------------------------------------
         1        1       0.70870    1       1       1       1
                  2       0.72383    1       1      -1      -1
                  3       0.70618    1      -1       1      -1
                  4       0.73897    1      -1      -1       1


                    ANALYSIS OF VARIANCE TABLE

      Source             DF    Chi-Square    Prob
      ------------------------------------------------
      INTERCEPT           1      2385.34     0.0000
      TIME                1         0.85     0.3570
      TRTMENT             1         8.20     0.0042
      TIME*TRTMENT        1         2.40     0.1215

      RESIDUAL            0          .          .
```

```
                    DIAGNOSTIC PROCEDURE COMPARISON                              3
                    MARGINAL SYMMETRY, REDUCED MODEL

                         CATMOD PROCEDURE

Response: STD1*TEST1*STD2*TEST2      Response Levels (R)=    15
Weight Variable: WT                  Populations      (S)=     1
Data Set: A                          Total Frequency (N)=    793
                                     Observations  (Obs)=     15


                                       DESIGN
                   Function   Response  MATRIX
          Sample    Number    Function    1       2
          ------------------------------------------------
             1         1       0.70870    1       1
                       2       0.72383    1      -1
                       3       0.70618    1       1
                       4       0.73897    1      -1


                    ANALYSIS OF VARIANCE TABLE

      Source             DF    Chi-Square    Prob
      ------------------------------------------------
      INTERCEPT           1      2386.97     0.0000
      TRTMENT             1         9.55     0.0020

      RESIDUAL            2         3.51     0.1731


              ANALYSIS OF WEIGHTED-LEAST-SQUARES ESTIMATES

                                        Standard   Chi-
      Effect        Parameter  Estimate   Error   Square   Prob
      --------------------------------------------------------------
      INTERCEPT         1       0.7196   0.0147  2386.97  0.0000
      TRTMENT           2      -0.0128   0.00416    9.55  0.0020
```

20 CORRELATION MATRIX OF THE PARAMETER ESTIMATES

```
                          1              2
          ------------------------------------------
            1       1.0000000      0.0419376
            2       0.0419376      1.0000000
```

```
                  DIAGNOSTIC PROCEDURE COMPARISON                        4
            SENSITIVITY AND SPECIFICITY ANALYSIS, MAIN-EFFECTS MODEL

                          CATMOD PROCEDURE

Response: STD1*TEST1*STD2*TEST2      Response Levels (R)=   15
Weight Variable: WT                  Populations     (S)=    1
Data Set: A                          Total Frequency (N)=  793
                                     Observations  (Obs)=   15


              Function   Response    DESIGN MATRIX
      Sample   Number    Function     1      2      3
      -------------------------------------------------
         1        1      0.82251      1      1      1
                  2      0.94840      1      1     -1
                  3      0.81545      1     -1      1
                  4      0.96964      1     -1     -1

                 ANALYSIS OF VARIANCE TABLE

         Source            DF   Chi-Square    Prob
         ---------------------------------------------
         INTERCEPT          1    6448.79     0.0000
         TIME               1       4.10     0.0428
         ACCURACY           1      38.81     0.0000

         RESIDUAL           1       1.00     0.3178


            ANALYSIS OF WEIGHTED-LEAST-SQUARES ESTIMATES

                                       Standard   Chi-
    Effect        Parameter  Estimate    Error    Square    Prob
    -----------------------------------------------------------------
    INTERCEPT         1       0.8892    0.0111   6448.79   0.0000
    _RESPONSE_        2      -0.00932   0.00460      4.10   0.0428
                      3      -0.0702    0.0113      38.81   0.0000

    NOTE: _RESPONSE_ = TIME ACCURACY
```

⑲ COVARIANCE MATRIX OF THE PARAMETER ESTIMATES

```
                    1              2              3
      -----------------------------------------------------
      1      0.00012260     2.292E-06      0.00010137
      2      2.292E-06      0.00002116    -5.873E-06
      3      0.00010137    -5.873E-06      0.00012697
```

The first analysis-of-variance table shows that there is no significant effect of TIME, either by itself or in its interaction with TRTMENT. Thus, the second model includes only the TRTMENT effect.

The analysis-of-variance table for the reduced model shows that the model fits and that the treatment effect is significant. The negative parameter estimate for TRTMENT in the table of estimates shows that the first level of treatment (STD) has a smaller probability of the first response level (neg) than the second level of treatment (TEST). In other words, the standard diagnostic procedure gives a significantly higher probability of a positive response than the test diagnostic procedure.

For the sensitivity and specificity analysis, the four response functions printed next to the design matrix represent the following:

1. sensitivity, time 1
2. specificity, time 1
3. sensitivity, time 2
4. specificity, time 2.

The sensitivities and specificities are for the test diagnostic procedure relative to the standard procedure.

The analysis-of-variance table shows that an additive model fits, that there is a significant effect of time, and that the sensitivity is significantly different from the specificity.

The table of estimates shows that the predicted sensitivities and specificities are lower for time 1 (since parameter 2 is negative). It also shows that the sensitivity is significantly less than the specificity.

Example 10: Direct Input of Response Functions and Covariance Matrix

This example illustrates the ability of CATMOD to operate on a vector of functions and the corresponding covariance matrix, which already exist. The estimates under investigation are composite indices summarizing the responses to eighteen psychological questions pertaining to general well-being. These estimates were computed for domains corresponding to an age by sex cross-classification. The covariance matrix was calculated via the method of balanced repeated replications. The analysis is directed at obtaining a description of the variation among these domain estimates. The following statements produce **Output 14.10**:

```
*------------------------CATMOD EXAMPLE 10--------------------------*
|                                                                   |
|                   Health Survey Data Analysis                     |
|                   ---------------------------                     |
|  Variational models are fit to health survey data. Estimates      |
|  of a well-being index have been computed for domains corresponding |
|  to an age by sex cross-classification.                           |
|                                                                   |
|  From: Koch and Stokes (1979).                                    |
|                                                                   |
|                                                                   |
|  Illustrate: directly input response functions, FACTOR statement, |
|              interactivity, title in MODEL statement.             |
*-------------------------------------------------------------------*;

data fbeing(type=est);
   input #1  b1-b5  _type_ $  _name_ $8. #2 b6-b10;
   cards;
   7.93726   7.92509   7.82815   7.73696   8.16791   parms     .
   7.24978   7.18991   7.35960   7.31937   7.55184
   0.00739   0.00019   0.00146  -0.00082   0.00076   cov       b1
   0.00189   0.00118   0.00140  -0.00140   0.00039
   0.00019   0.01172   0.00183   0.00029   0.00083   cov       b2
  -0.00123  -0.00629  -0.00088  -0.00232   0.00034
   0.00146   0.00183   0.01050  -0.00173   0.00011   cov       b3
   0.00434  -0.00059  -0.00055   0.00023  -0.00013
  -0.00082   0.00029  -0.00173   0.01335   0.00140   cov       b4
   0.00158   0.00212   0.00211   0.00066   0.00240
   0.00076   0.00083   0.00011   0.00140   0.01430   cov       b5
  -0.00050  -0.00098   0.00239  -0.00010   0.00213
   0.00189  -0.00123   0.00434   0.00158  -0.00050   cov       b6
   0.01110   0.00101   0.00177  -0.00018  -0.00082
   0.00118  -0.00629  -0.00059   0.00212  -0.00098   cov       b7
   0.00101   0.02342   0.00144   0.00369   0.25300
   0.00140  -0.00088  -0.00055   0.00211   0.00239   cov       b8
```

```
      0.00177    0.00144    0.01060    0.00157    0.00226
     -0.00140   -0.00232    0.00023    0.00066   -0.00010    cov      b9
     -0.00018    0.00369    0.00157    0.02298    0.00918
      0.00039    0.00034   -0.00013    0.00240    0.00213    cov      b10
     -0.00082    0.00253    0.00226    0.00918    0.01921
    ;
proc catmod data=fbeing;
    title 'COMPLEX SAMPLE SURVEY ANALYSIS';
    response read b1-b10;
    factors sex $ 2, age $  5 /  _response_=sex age
      profile=(male      '25-34' ,
               male      '35-44' ,
               male      '45-54' ,
               male      '55-64' ,
               male      '65-74' ,
               female    '25-34' ,
               female    '35-44' ,
               female    '45-54' ,
               female    '55-64' ,
               female    '65-74' );
    model _f_=_response_ / title='Main Effects for Sex and Age';
run;

    contrast 'No Age Effect for Age<65' all_parms 0 0 1 0 0 -1 ,
                                        all_parms 0 0 0 1 0 -1 ,
                                        all_parms 0 0 0 0 1 -1 ;
run;

    model _f_=(1  1  1,
               1  1  1,
               1  1  1,
               1  1  1,
               1  1 -1,
               1 -1  1,
               1 -1  1,
               1 -1  1,
               1 -1  1,
               1 -1 -1)
                        ( 1='Intercept' ,
                          2='Sex'        ,
                          3='Age (25-64 vs. 65-74)' )
               / title='Binary Age Effect (25-64 vs. 65-74)' ;
run;
quit;
```

Output 14.10   Health Survey Data: Using Direct Input

```
                        COMPLEX SAMPLE SURVEY ANALYSIS                        1

                         Main Effects for Sex and Age

                              CATMOD PROCEDURE

               Response Functions Directly Input from Data Set FBEING

            Function   Response              DESIGN MATRIX
   Sample    Number    Function    1     2     3     4     5     6
   ------------------------------------------------------------------------
      1         1       7.93726     1     1     1     0     0     0
                2       7.92509     1     1     0     1     0     0
                3       7.82815     1     1     0     0     1     0
                4       7.73696     1     1     0     0     0     1
                5       8.16791     1     1    -1    -1    -1    -1
                6       7.24978     1    -1     1     0     0     0
                7       7.18991     1    -1     0     1     0     0
                8       7.35960     1    -1     0     0     1     0
                9       7.31937     1    -1     0     0     0     1
               10       7.55184     1    -1    -1    -1    -1    -1


                         ANALYSIS OF VARIANCE TABLE

            Source              DF    Chi-Square     Prob
            --------------------------------------------------
            INTERCEPT            1     28089.07     0.0000
            SEX                  1        65.84     0.0000
            AGE                  4         9.21     0.0561

            RESIDUAL             4         2.92     0.5713


                  ANALYSIS OF WEIGHTED-LEAST-SQUARES ESTIMATES

                                        Standard    Chi-
           Effect        Parameter  Estimate  Error  Square    Prob
           ----------------------------------------------------------
           INTERCEPT         1       7.6319   0.0455 28089.07  0.0000
           _RESPONSE_        2       0.2900   0.0357    65.84  0.0000
                             3      -0.00780  0.0645     0.01  0.9037
                             4      -0.0465   0.0636     0.54  0.4642
                             5      -0.0343   0.0557     0.38  0.5387
                             6      -0.1098   0.0764     2.07  0.1506

           NOTE: _RESPONSE_ = SEX AGE
```

```
                        COMPLEX SAMPLE SURVEY ANALYSIS                        2

                         Main Effects for Sex and Age

                            ANALYSIS OF CONTRASTS

          Contrast              DF   Chi-Square    Prob
          ------------------------------------------------
          No Age Effect for Age<65   3     0.72    0.8678
```

```
                    COMPLEX SAMPLE SURVEY ANALYSIS                          3

                     Binary Age Effect (25-64 vs. 65-74)

                             CATMOD PROCEDURE

         Response Functions Directly Input from Data Set FBEING

                 Function   Response     DESIGN MATRIX
        Sample    Number    Function     1       2      3
        ---------------------------------------------------------
           1         1       7.93726     1       1      1
                     2       7.92509     1       1      1
                     3       7.82815     1       1      1
                     4       7.73696     1       1      1
                     5       8.16791     1       1     -1
                     6       7.24978     1      -1      1
                     7       7.18991     1      -1      1
                     8       7.35960     1      -1      1
                     9       7.31937     1      -1      1
                    10       7.55184     1      -1     -1


                      ANALYSIS OF VARIANCE TABLE

        Source                     DF    Chi-Square     Prob
        ---------------------------------------------------------
        Intercept                   1      19087.16    0.0000
        Sex                         1         72.64    0.0000
        Age (25-64 vs. 65-74)       1          8.49    0.0036

        RESIDUAL                    7          3.64    0.8198


             ANALYSIS OF WEIGHTED-LEAST-SQUARES ESTIMATES

                                         Standard   Chi-
        Effect        Parameter Estimate   Error   Square    Prob
        ---------------------------------------------------------------
        MODEL             1       7.7183   0.0559 19087.16  0.0000
                          2       0.2800   0.0329    72.64  0.0000
                          3      -0.1304   0.0448     8.49  0.0036
```

The first analysis-of-variance table shows that the additive model fits and that there is a significant effect of both sex and age. The analysis of the contrast shows that there is no significant difference among the four age groups that are under age 65. Thus, the second model contains a binary age effect (less than 65 versus 65 and over).

The second analysis-of-variance table shows that the model fits (note that the goodness-of-fit statistic is the sum of the previous one plus the chi-square for the contrast matrix). The age and sex effects are significant. Since the second parameter in the table of estimates is positive, males (the first level for the sex variable) have a higher predicted index of well-being than females. Since the third parameter estimate is negative, those younger than age 65 (the first level of age) have a lower predicted index of well-being than those 65 and older.

REFERENCES

Agresti, A. (1984), *Analysis of Ordinal Categorical Data*, New York: John Wiley & Sons, Inc.

Bishop, Y.M.M., Fienberg, S.E., and Holland, P.W. (1975), *Discrete Multivariate Analysis: Theory and Practice*, Cambridge, MA: The MIT Press.

Cox, D.R. (1970), *The Analysis of Binary Data*, New York: Halsted Press.

Fienberg, S.E. (1980), *The Analysis of Cross-Classified Categorical Data*, 2d Edition, Cambridge, MA: The MIT Press.

Forthofer, R.N. and Koch, G.G. (1973), "An Analysis of Compounded Functions of Categorical Data," *Biometrics*, 29, 143–157.

Forthofer, R.N. and Lehnen R.G. (1981), *Public Program Analysis: A New Categorical Data Approach*, Belmont, CA: Wadsworth.

Guthrie, D. (1981), "Analysis of Dichotomous Variables in Repeated Measures Experiments," *Psychological Bulletin*, 90, 189–195.

Grizzle, J.E., Starmer, C.F., and Koch, G.G. (1969), "Analysis of Categorical Data by Linear Models," *Biometrics*, 25, 489–504.

Imrey, P.B., Koch. G.G., and Stokes, M.E. (1981). "Categorical Data Analysis: Some Reflections on the Log Linear Model and Logistic Regression. Part I: Historical and Methodological Overview," *International Statistical Review*, 49, 265–283.

Koch, G.G., Landis, J.R., Freeman, J.L., Freeman, D.H., and Lehnen, R.G. (1977), "A General Methodology for the Analysis of Experiments with Repeated Measurement of Categorical Data," *Biometrics*, 33, 133–158.

Koch, G.G. and Stokes, M.E. (1979), "Annotated Computer Applications of Weighted Least Squares Methods for Illustrative Analyses of Examples Involving Health Survey Data." Technical Report prepared for the U.S. National Center for Health Statistics.

Landis, J.R., Stanish, W.M., Freeman, J.L. and Koch, G.G. (1976), "A Computer Program for the Generalized Chi-Square Analysis of Categorical Data Using Weighted Least Squares, (GENCAT)," *Computer Programs in Biomedicine*, 6, 196–231.

MacMillan, J., Becker, C., Koch, G.G., Stokes, M., and Vandiviere, H.M. (1981), "An Application of Weighted Least Squares Methods to the Analysis of Measurement Process Components of Variability in an Observational Study," *American Statistical Association Proceedings of Survey Research Methods*, 680–685.

Ries, P.N. and Smith, H. (1963), "The Use of Chi-Square for Preference Testing in Multidimensional Problems," *Chemical Engineering Progress*, 59, 39–43.

Searle, S.R. (1971), *Linear Models*, New York: John Wiley & Sons, Inc.

Wald, A. (1943), "Tests of Statistical Hypotheses Concerning General Parameters When the Number of Observations Is Large," *Transactions of the American Mathematical Society*, 54, 426–482.

Chapter 15

The CLUSTER
Procedure

ABSTRACT

The CLUSTER procedure hierarchically clusters the observations in a SAS data set using one of eleven methods. The data can be numeric coordinates or distances. CLUSTER creates an output data set from which the TREE procedure can draw a tree diagram or output clusters at a specified level of the tree.

INTRODUCTION

The CLUSTER procedure finds hierarchical clusters of the observations in a SAS data set. The data can be coordinates or distances. If the data are coordinates, CLUSTER computes (possibly squared) Euclidean distances. The clustering methods available are average linkage, the centroid method, complete linkage, density linkage (including Wong's hybrid and kth-nearest-neighbor methods), maximum-likelihood for mixtures of spherical multivariate normal distributions with equal variances but possibly unequal mixing proportions, the flexible-beta method, McQuitty's similarity analysis, the median method, single linkage, two-stage density linkage, and Ward's minimum-variance method.

All methods are based on the usual agglomerative hierarchical clustering procedure. Each observation begins in a cluster by itself. The two closest clusters are merged to form a new cluster that replaces the two old clusters. Merging of the two closest clusters is repeated until only one cluster is left. The various clustering methods differ in how the distance between two clusters is computed. Each method is described in **Clustering Methods** later in this chapter.

CLUSTER prints a history of the clustering process, giving statistics useful for estimating the number of clusters in the population from which the data were sampled. CLUSTER also creates an output data set that can be used by the TREE procedure to draw a tree diagram of the cluster hierarchy or to output a partition at any desired level.

Before you perform a cluster analysis on coordinate data, it is necessary to consider scaling or transforming the variables since variables with large variances tend to have more effect on the resulting clusters than those with small variances. The ACECLUS procedure is useful for performing linear transformations of the variables. Also, the PRINCOMP procedure with the STD option may be considered, although in some cases it tends to obscure clusters or magnify the effect of error in the data when all components are retained. The STD option in CLUSTER provides the easiest way to make a pretense of addressing this issue while avoiding any serious thought. Outliers should be removed before using PRINCOMP or before using CLUSTER with the STD option unless the TRIM= option is also used.

Nonlinear transformations of the variables may change the number of population clusters and should therefore be approached with caution. For most applications, the variables should be transformed so that equal differences are of equal practical importance. An interval scale of measurement is required. Ordinal or ranked data are generally not appropriate.

Agglomerative hierarchical clustering is discussed in all standard references on cluster analysis, for example, Anderberg (1973), Sneath and Sokal (1973), Hartigan (1975), Everitt (1980), and Spath (1980). An especially good introduction is given by Massart and Kaufman (1983). Anyone considering doing a hierarchical cluster analysis should study the Monte Carlo results of Milligan (1980), Milligan and Cooper (1985), and Cooper and Milligan (1984). Other essential, though more advanced, references on hierarchical clustering include Hartigan (1977, 60-68; 1981), Wong (1982), Wong and Schaack (1982), and Wong and Lane (1983). See Blashfield and Aldenderfer (1978) for a discussion of the confusing terminology in hierarchical cluster analysis. See Milligan and Cooper (1987) for a Monte Carlo study on various methods of variable standardization.

SPECIFICATIONS

Use the following statements to invoke the CLUSTER procedure:

PROC CLUSTER *options*;
    VAR *variables*;
    ID *variable*;
    COPY *variables*;
    FREQ *variable*;
    RMSSTD *variable*;
    BY *variables*;

Usually only the VAR statement and possibly the ID and COPY statements are needed in addition to the PROC CLUSTER statement. The descriptions of the BY, COPY, FREQ, ID, RMSSTD, and VAR statements follow the description of the PROC CLUSTER statement.

PROC CLUSTER Statement

PROC CLUSTER *options*;

The METHOD= option must be specified. In addition, the options described in the next seven sections can appear in the PROC CLUSTER statement.

Data Set Options

DATA=*SASdataset*
    names the input data set containing observations to be clustered. If the DATA= option is omitted, the most recently created SAS data set is used. If the data set is TYPE=DISTANCE, the data are interpreted as a distance matrix; the number of variables must equal the number of observations in the data set or in each BY group. The distances are assumed to be Euclidean, but the procedure accepts other types of distances or dissimilarities. If the data set is not TYPE=DISTANCE, the data are interpreted as coordinates in a Euclidean space, and Euclidean distances are computed.

    All methods produce the same results when used with coordinate data as when used with Euclidean distances computed from the coordinates. However, the DIM= option must be used with distance data if METHOD=TWOSTAGE or METHOD=DENSITY is specified or if the TRIM= option is used.

    Certain methods that are most naturally defined in terms of coordinates require *squared* Euclidean distances to be used in the combinatorial distance formulas (Lance and Williams 1967). For this reason, distance data are automatically squared when used with METHOD=AVERAGE, CENTROID, MEDIAN, or WARD. If you want the combinatorial formulas to be applied to the (unsquared) distances with these methods, use the NOSQUARE option.

OUTTREE=*SASdataset*
    names an output data set that can be used by the TREE procedure to draw a tree diagram. The data set must be given a two-level name if it is

to be saved. See "SAS Files" in the *SAS Language Guide, Release 6.03 Edition* for a discussion of permanent data sets. If the OUTTREE= option is omitted, the data set is named using the DATA*n* convention and is not permanently saved. If you do not want to create an output data set, use OUTTREE=_NULL_.

Options to Select the Type of Cluster Analysis

METHOD=*name*

M=*name*

specifies what clustering method to use. The METHOD= option is required. Any one of the eleven methods listed below can be specified for *name*:

AVERAGE AVE	requests average linkage (group average, unweighted pair-group meth od using arithmetic averages, UPGMA). Distance data are squared unless you specify the NOSQUARE option.
CENTROID CEN	requests the centroid method (unweighted pair-group method using centroids, UPGMC, centroid sorting, weighted-group method). Distance data are squared unless you specify the NOSQUARE option.
COMPLETE COM	requests complete linkage (furthest neighbor, maximum method, diame ter method, rank order typal analysis). To reduce distortion of clusters by outliers, the TRIM= option is recommended.
DENSITY DEN	requests density linkage, a class of clustering methods using nonparametric probability density estimation. You must also specify one of the K=, R=, or HYBRID options to indicate the type of density estimation to be used. See also the MODE= and DIM= options. The NONORM option has no effect with this method.
EML	requests maximum-likelihood hierarchical clustering for mixtures of spherical multivariate normal distributions with equal variances but possibly unequal mixing proportions. Use METHOD=EML only with coordinate data. See the PENALTY= option. The NONORM option has no effect with this method. The EML method is much slower than the other methods in the CLUSTER procedure.
FLEXIBLE FLE	requests the Lance-Williams flexible-beta method. See the BETA= option.
MCQUITTY MCQ	requests McQuitty's similarity analysis (weighted average linkage, weighted pair-group method using arithmetic averages, WPGMA).
MEDIAN MED	requests Gower's median method (weighted pair-group method using centroids, WPGMC). Distance data are squared unless the NOSQUARE option is specified.

SINGLE   requests single linkage (nearest neighbor, minimum
SIN   method, connectedness method, elementary linkage
          analysis, or dendritic method). To reduce chaining, you
          should use the TRIM= option with METHOD=SINGLE.

TWOSTAGE requests two-stage density linkage. You must also specify
TWO   one of the K=, R=, or HYBRID options to indicate the
          type of density estimation to be used. See also the
          MODE= and DIM= options. The NONORM option has
          no effect with this method.

WARD   requests Ward's minimum-variance method (error sum of
WAR   squares, trace W). Distance data are squared unless you
          specify the NOSQUARE option. To reduce distortion by
          outliers, the TRIM= option is recommended. See the
          NONORM option.

Options to Specify Details for Clustering Methods

BETA=n

specifies the beta parameter for METHOD=FLEXIBLE. The value should
be less than 1, usually between 0 and -1. The default is BETA=-0.25.
Milligan (1987) suggests a somewhat smaller value, perhaps -0.5, for
data with many outliers.

MODE=n

specifies that when two clusters are joined, each must have at least n
members for either cluster to be designated a modal cluster. If
MODE=1 is specified, each cluster must also have a maximum density
greater than the fusion density for either cluster to be designated a
modal cluster. Use the MODE= option only with METHOD=DENSITY
or TWOSTAGE. With METHOD=TWOSTAGE, the MODE= option
affects the number of modal clusters formed. With METHOD=DENSITY,
MODE= does not affect the clustering process but does determine the
number of modal clusters reported on the printout and identified by the
MODE variable in the output data set. If you specify the K= option,
the default value of MODE= is the same as the value of K= because
the use of kth-nearest-neighbor density estimation limits the resolution
that can be obtained for clusters with fewer than k members. If the K=
option is not specified, the default is MODE=2. If MODE=0 is
specified, the default value is used instead of 0. If a FREQ statement is
used or the _FREQ_ variable exists in the input data set, the MODE=
value is compared to the number of observations in each cluster, not to
the sum of the frequencies.

PENALTY=p

specifies the penalty coefficient used with METHOD=EML. See
Clustering Methods later in this chapter. The default is PENALTY=2.

Options to Control Data Processing before Clustering

NOEIGEN

suppresses computation of eigenvalues for the cubic clustering criterion.
Specifying NOEIGEN saves time if the number of variables is large but
should be used only if the variables are nearly uncorrelated or if you are
not interested in the cubic clustering criterion. If you specify NOEIGEN

and the variables are highly correlated, the cubic clustering criterion may be very liberal. NOEIGEN applies only to coordinate data.

NONORM

prevents the distances from being normalized to unit mean or unit root mean square with most methods. With METHOD=WARD, NONORM prevents the between-cluster sum of squares from being normalized by the total sum of squares to yield a squared semipartial correlation. The NONORM option has no effect on the clustering criteria for METHOD=DENSITY, EML, or TWOSTAGE.

NOSQUARE

prevents input distances from being squared with METHOD=AVERAGE, CENTROID, MEDIAN, or WARD.

STANDARD
STD

standardizes the variables to mean 0 and standard deviation 1. The STANDARD option applies only to coordinate data.

TRIM=p

requests that points with low estimated probability densities be omitted from the analysis. If $p<1$, then p is the proportion of observations omitted. If $p\geq1$, then p is interpreted as a percentage. The specification TRIM=10, trimming 10 percent of the points, is a reasonable value for many data sets. Densities are estimated by the kth-nearest-neighbor or uniform-kernel methods. You must use either the K= or R= option when specifying the TRIM= option. (See also the DIM= option, below.) Trimmed points are indicated by a negative value of _FREQ_ in the OUTTREE= data set.

If the STANDARD option is specified in combination with the TRIM= option, the variables are standardized both before and after trimming.

The TRIM= option is useful for removing outliers and reducing chaining. Trimming is highly recommended with METHOD=WARD or METHOD=COMPLETE because clusters from these methods can be severely distorted by outliers. Trimming is also valuable with METHOD=SINGLE since single linkage is the method most susceptible to chaining. Most other methods also benefit from trimming. However, trimming is unnecessary with METHOD=TWOSTAGE or DENSITY when kth-nearest-neighbor density estimation is used.

Use of TRIM= may spuriously inflate the cubic clustering criterion and the pseudo F and t^2 statistics. Trimming only outliers improves the accuracy of the statistics, but trimming saddle regions between clusters yields excessively large values.

Options to Control Density Estimation

DIM=n

specifies the dimensionality to be used when computing density estimates with the TRIM= option, METHOD=DENSITY, or METHOD=TWOSTAGE. The default is the number of variables if the data are coordinates; the default is 1 if the data are distances.

If you request an analysis that requires density estimation (the TRIM= option, METHOD=DENSITY, or METHOD=TWOSTAGE), you must specify one and only one of the following three options:

HYBRID

requests Wong's (1982) hybrid clustering method in which density estimates are computed from a preliminary cluster analysis using the *k*-means method. The DATA= data set must contain means, frequencies, and root-mean-square standard deviations of the preliminary clusters (see the FREQ and RMSSTD statements). The MEAN= data set produced by the FASTCLUS procedure is suitable for input to the CLUSTER procedure for hybrid clustering. You must specify either METHOD=DENSITY or METHOD=TWOSTAGE with the HYBRID option. HYBRID cannot be used with the TRIM= option.

K=*n*

specifies the number of neighbors to use for *k*th-nearest-neighbor density estimation (Silverman 1986, 19–21, 96–99). The number of neighbors must be at least two but less than the number of observations. See the MODE= option.

R=*n*

specifies the radius of the sphere of support for uniform-kernel density estimation (Silverman 1986, 11–13, 75–94).

Options to Control Printing of the Cluster History

CCC

prints the cubic clustering criterion and approximate expected R^2 under the uniform null hypothesis (Sarle 1983). The statistics associated with the RSQUARE option, R^2 and semipartial R^2, are also printed. The CCC option applies only to coordinate data.

NOID

suppresses printing the ID values of the clusters joined at each generation of the cluster history.

NOTIE

prevents CLUSTER from checking for ties for minimum distance between clusters at each generation of the cluster history. If your data are measured with sufficient precision that ties are unlikely, then you can specify NOTIE to slightly reduce the time and space required by the procedure. See **Ties** later in this chapter.

PRINT=*n*

P=*n*

specifies the number of generations of the cluster history to print. The default is to print all generations. PRINT=0 suppresses the cluster history.

PSEUDO

prints pseudo F and t^2 statistics. This option is effective only when the data are coordinates or METHOD=AVERAGE, CENTROID, or WARD. See **Miscellaneous Formulas** later in this chapter.

RMSSTD

prints the root-mean-square standard deviation of each cluster. This option is effective only when the data are coordinates or METHOD=AVERAGE, CENTROID, or WARD. See **Miscellaneous Formulas** later in this chapter.

RSQUARE

RSQ

prints R^2 and semipartial R^2. This option is effective only when the data are coordinates or METHOD=AVERAGE or CENTROID. The R^2 and semipartial R^2 statistics are always printed with METHOD=WARD. See **Miscellaneous Formulas** later in this chapter.

Other Printing Options

NOPRINT
   suppresses the printout.

SIMPLE
S
   prints means, standard deviations, skewness, kurtosis, and a coefficient
   of bimodality. The SIMPLE option applies only to coordinate data.

BY Statement

   BY *variables*;

A BY statement can be used with PROC CLUSTER to obtain separate analyses
on observations in groups defined by the BY variables. When a BY statement
appears, the procedure expects the input data set to be sorted in order of the
BY variables.

   If your input data set is not sorted in ascending order, use the SORT procedure
with a similar BY statement to sort the data, or, if appropriate, use the BY statement options NOTSORTED or DESCENDING. For more information, see the discussion of the BY statement in "SAS Statements Used in the PROC Step" in the
SAS Language Guide.

COPY Statement

   COPY *variables*;

The variables in the COPY statement are copied from the input data set to the
OUTTREE= data set. Observations in the OUTTREE= data set that represent
clusters of more than one observation from the input data set have missing values
for the COPY variables.

FREQ Statement

   FREQ *variable*;

If one variable in the input data set represents the frequency of occurrence for
other values in the observation, specify the variable's name in a FREQ statement.
CLUSTER then treats the data set as if each observation appeared *n* times, where
n is the value of the FREQ variable for the observation. Nonintegral values of the
FREQ variable are truncated to the largest integer less than the FREQ value.

   If the FREQ statement is omitted but the DATA= data set contains a variable
called _FREQ_, then frequencies are obtained from the _FREQ_ variable. If neither a FREQ statement nor a _FREQ_ variable is present, each observation is
assumed to have a frequency of one.

   If each observation in the DATA= data set represents a cluster (for example,
clusters formed by PROC FASTCLUS), the variable specified in the FREQ statement should give the number of original observations in each cluster.

   A FREQ statement or _FREQ_ variable is required when the HYBRID option
is used.

   With most clustering methods, the same clusters are obtained from a data set
with a FREQ variable as from a similar data set without a FREQ variable, if each
observation is repeated as many times as the value of the FREQ variable in the
first data set. The DENSITY and TWOSTAGE methods are exceptions, however,
because two identical observations can be absorbed one at a time by a cluster
with a higher density. If you are using a FREQ statement with either the DENSITY
or TWOSTAGE methods, see the MODE=option.

ID Statement

ID *variable*;

The values of the ID variable identify observations in the printed cluster history and in the OUTTREE= data set. If the ID statement is omitted, each observation is denoted by OB*n*, where *n* is the observation number.

RMSSTD Statement

RMSSTD *variable*;

If the coordinates in the DATA= data set represent cluster means (for example, formed by the FASTCLUS procedure), you can obtain accurate statistics in the cluster histories for METHOD=AVERAGE, CENTROID, or WARD if the data set contains

- a variable giving the number of original observations in each cluster (see the discussion of the FREQ statement earlier in this chapter)
- a variable giving the root-mean-square standard deviation of each cluster.

Specify the name of the variable containing root-mean-square standard deviations in the RMSSTD statement. If the RMSSTD statement is used, the FREQ statement must also be specified.

If the RMSSTD statement is omitted but the DATA= data set contains a variable called _RMSSTD_, then root-mean-square standard deviations are obtained from the _RMSSTD_ variable.

An RMSSTD statement or _RMSSTD_ variable is required when the HYBRID option is used.

A data set created by FASTCLUS using the MEAN= option contains _FREQ_ and _RMSSTD_ variables, so you do not have to use FREQ and RMSSTD statements when using such a data set as input to the CLUSTER procedure.

VAR Statement

VAR *variables*;

The VAR statement lists numeric variables to be used in the cluster analysis. If the VAR statement is omitted, all numeric variables not listed in other statements are used.

DETAILS

Clustering Methods

The following notation is used, with lowercase symbols generally pertaining to observations, uppercase symbols to clusters:

n number of observations

v number of variables if data are coordinates

G number of clusters at any given level of the hierarchy

x_i or $\mathbf{x}_i$ *i*th observation (row vector if coordinate data)

C_K *K*th cluster, subset of $\{1, 2, \ldots, n\}$

N_K number of observations in C_K

$\bar{\mathbf{x}}$ sample mean vector

$\bar{\mathbf{x}}_K$ mean vector for cluster C_K

$\|\mathbf{x}\|$ Euclidean length of the vector $\mathbf{x}$, that is, the square root of the sum of the squares of the elements of $\mathbf{x}$

T $\Sigma_{i=1}^{n} \|\mathbf{x}_i - \bar{\mathbf{x}}\|^2$

W_K $\Sigma_{i \epsilon C_k} \|\mathbf{x}_i - \bar{\mathbf{x}}_K\|^2$

P_G ΣW_J, where summation is over the G clusters at the Gth level of the hierarchy.

B_{KL} $W_M - W_K - W_L$ if $C_M = C_K \cup C_L$

$d(\mathbf{x},\mathbf{y})$ any distance or dissimilarity measure between observations or vectors $\mathbf{x}$ and $\mathbf{y}$

D_{KL} any distance or dissimilarity measure between clusters C_K and C_L.

The distance between two clusters can be defined either directly or combinatorially (Lance and Williams 1967), that is, by an equation for updating a distance matrix when two clusters are joined. In all combinatorial formulas below, it is assumed that clusters C_K and C_L are merged to form C_M, and the formula gives the distance between the new cluster C_M and any other cluster C_J.

For an introduction to most of the methods used in the CLUSTER procedure, see Massart and Kaufman (1983).

Average Linkage

The distance between two clusters is defined by

$$D_{KL} = \Sigma_{i \epsilon C_K} \Sigma_{j \epsilon C_L} d(x_i, x_j) / (N_K N_L) \quad .$$

If $d(\mathbf{x},\mathbf{y}) = \|\mathbf{x} - \mathbf{y}\|^2$ then

$$D_{KL} = \|\bar{\mathbf{x}}_K - \bar{\mathbf{x}}_L\|^2 + W_K/N_K + W_L/N_L \quad .$$

The combinatorial formula is

$$D_{JM} = (N_K D_{JK} + N_L D_{JL}) / N_M \quad .$$

In average linkage the distance between two clusters is the average distance between pairs of observations, one in each cluster. Average linkage tends to join clusters with small variances and is slightly biased toward producing clusters with the same variance.

Average linkage was originated by Sokal and Michener (1958).

Centroid Method

The distance between two clusters is defined by

$$D_{KL} = \|\bar{\mathbf{x}}_K - \bar{\mathbf{x}}_L\|^2 \quad .$$

If $d(\mathbf{x},\mathbf{y}) = \|\mathbf{x} - \mathbf{y}\|^2$ then the combinatorial formula is

$$D_{JM} = (N_K D_{JK} + N_L D_{JL}) / N_M - N_K N_L D_{KL} / N_M^2 \quad .$$

In the centroid method the distance between two clusters is defined as the (squared) Euclidean distance between their centroids or means. The centroid method is more robust to outliers than most other hierarchical methods but in other respects may not perform as well as Ward's method or average linkage (Milligan 1980).

The centroid method was originated by Sokal and Michener (1958).

Complete Linkage

The distance between two clusters is defined by

$$D_{KL} = \max_{i \in C_K} \max_{j \in C_L} d(x_i, x_j) \quad .$$

The combinatorial formula is

$$D_{JM} = \max (D_{JK}, D_{JL}) \quad .$$

In complete linkage the distance between two clusters is the maximum distance between an observation in one cluster and an observation in the other cluster. Complete linkage is strongly biased toward producing clusters with roughly equal diameters and can be severely distorted by moderate outliers (Milligan 1980).

Complete linkage was originated by Sorensen (1948).

Density Linkage

The phrase *density linkage* is used here to refer to a class of clustering methods using nonparametric probability density estimates (for example, Hartigan 1975, 205–212; Wong 1982; Wong and Lane 1983). Density linkage consists of two steps:

1. A new dissimilarity measure, d^*, based on density estimates and adjacencies is computed. If x_i and x_j are adjacent (the definition of *adjacency* depends on the method of density estimation), then $d^*(x_i, x_j)$ is the reciprocal of an estimate of the density midway between x_i and x_j; otherwise, $d^*(x_i, x_j)$ is infinite.
2. A single linkage cluster analysis is performed using d^*.

The CLUSTER procedure supports three types of density linkage: the *k*th-nearest-neighbor method, the uniform kernel method, and Wong's hybrid method.

The *k*th-nearest-neighbor method (Wong and Lane 1983) uses *k*th-nearest neighbor density estimates. Let $r_k(x)$ be the distance from point x to the *k*th-nearest observation, where k is the value specified for the K= option. Consider a closed sphere centered at x with radius $r_k(x)$. The estimated density at x, $f(x)$, is the proportion of observations within the sphere divided by the volume of the sphere. The new dissimilarity measure is computed as

$$d^*(x_i, x_j) = (1/2)(1/f(x_i) + 1/f(x_j)) \quad \text{if } d(x_i, x_j) \le \max (r_k(x_i), r_k(x_j))$$

$$= \infty \quad \text{otherwise.}$$

Wong and Lane (1983) show that *k*th-nearest-neighbor density linkage is strongly set consistent for high-density (density-contour) clusters if k is chosen such that $k/n \to 0$ and $k/\ln(n) \to \infty$ as $n \to \infty$. Wong and Schaack (1982) discuss methods for estimating the number of population clusters using *k*th-nearest-neighbor clustering.

The uniform-kernel method uses uniform-kernel density estimates. Let r be the value specified for the R= option. Consider a closed sphere centered at point x with radius r. The estimated density at x, $f(x)$, is the proportion of observations within the sphere divided by the volume of the sphere. The new dissimilarity measure is computed as

$$d^*(x_i, x_j) = (1/2)(1/f(x_i) + 1/f(x_j)) \quad \text{if } d(x_i, x_j) \le r$$

$$= \infty \quad \text{otherwise.}$$

Wong's (1982) hybrid clustering method uses density estimates based on a preliminary cluster analysis by the k-means method. The preliminary clustering can be done by the FASTCLUS procedure, using the MEAN= option to create a data set containing cluster means, frequencies, and root-mean-square standard deviations. This data set is used as input to the CLUSTER procedure, and the HYBRID option is specified with METHOD=DENSITY to request the hybrid analysis. The hybrid method is appropriate for very large data sets but should not be used with small data sets, say fewer than 100 observations in the original data. In the following discussion, the term *cluster* refers to a *preliminary cluster*, that is, an observation in the DATA= data set.

For cluster C_K, N_K and W_K are obtained from the input data set, as are the cluster means or the distances between the cluster means. Clusters C_K and C_L are considered adjacent if the midpoint between $\bar{x}_K$ and $\bar{x}_L$ is closer to either $\bar{x}_K$ or $\bar{x}_L$ than to any other cluster mean or, equivalently, if $d^2(\bar{x}_K, \bar{x}_L) < d^2(\bar{x}_K, \bar{x}_M) + d^2(\bar{x}_L, \bar{x}_M)$ for all other clusters C_M, $M \ne K$ or L. The new dissimilarity measure is computed as

$$d^*(\bar{x}_K, \bar{x}_L) = \frac{(W_K + W_L + (N_K + N_L)d^2(\bar{x}_K, \bar{x}_L)/4)^{v/2}}{(N_K + N_L)^{1+v/2}} \quad \text{if } C_K \text{ and } C_L \text{ are adjacent}$$

$$= \infty \quad \text{otherwise .}$$

The values of the K= and R= options are called *smoothing parameters*. Small values of K= or R= produce jagged density estimates and, as a consequence, many modes. Large values of K= or R= produce smoother density estimates and fewer modes. In the hybrid method, the smoothing parameter is the number of clusters in the preliminary cluster analysis. The number of modes in the final analysis tends to increase as the number of clusters in the preliminary analysis increases. Wong (1982) suggests using $n^{0.3}$ preliminary clusters, where n is the number of observations in the original data set. There is no general rule-of-thumb for selecting K= or R= values. For all types of density linkage, you should repeat the analysis with several different values of the smoothing parameter (Wong and Schaack 1982).

Since infinite d^* values occur in density linkage, the final number of clusters may exceed one when there are wide gaps between the clusters or when the smoothing parameter results in little smoothing.

Density linkage applies no constraints to the shapes of the clusters and, unlike most other hierarchical clustering methods, is capable of recovering clusters with elongated or irregular shapes. Since density linkage employs less prior knowledge about the shape of the clusters than do methods restricted to compact clusters, density linkage is less effective at recovering compact clusters from small samples than are methods that always recover compact clusters, regardless of the data.

EML

The distance between two clusters is given by

$$D_{KL} = nv \ln(1 + B_{KL}/P_G) - 2(N_M \ln(N_M) - N_K \ln(N_K) - N_L \ln(N_L)) \quad .$$

EML joins clusters to maximize the likelihood at each level of the hierarchy under the following assumptions:

- multivariate normal mixture
- equal spherical covariance matrices
- unequal sampling probabilities.

EML is similar to Ward's minimum-variance method but removes the bias toward equal-sized clusters. Practical experience has indicated that EML is somewhat biased toward unequal-sized clusters. The PENALTY= option can be used to adjust the degree of bias. If PENALTY=p is specified, the formula is modified to

$$D_{KL} = nv \ln (1 + B_{KL}/P_G) - p(N_M \ln (N_M) - N_K \ln (N_K) - N_L \ln (N_L)) \quad .$$

The EML method was derived by W.S. Sarle of SAS Institute Inc. from the maximum-likelihood formula obtained by Symons (1981, 37, eq. 8) for disjoint clustering. There are currently no other published references on the EML method.

Flexible-Beta Method

The combinatorial formula is

$$D_{JM} = (D_{JK} + D_{JL})(1-b)/2 + D_{KL}b$$

where b is the value of the BETA= option, or -0.25 by default. The flexible-beta method was developed by Lance and Williams (1967) .

McQuitty's Similarity Analysis

The combinatorial formula is

$$D_{JM} = (D_{JK} + D_{JL})/2 \quad .$$

The method was independently developed by Sokal and Michener (1958) and McQuitty (1966).

Median Method

If $d(\mathbf{x},\mathbf{y}) = \| \mathbf{x} - \mathbf{y} \|^2$, then the combinatorial formula is

$$D_{JM} = (D_{JK} + D_{JL})/2 - D_{KL}/4 \quad .$$

The median method was developed by Gower (1967).

Single Linkage

The distance between two clusters is defined by

$$D_{KL} = \min_{i \,\epsilon C_K} \min_{j \,\epsilon C_L} d(x_i, x_j) \quad .$$

The combinatorial formula is

$$D_{JM} = \min (D_{JK}, D_{JL}) \quad .$$

In single linkage the distance between two clusters is the minimum distance between an observation in one cluster and an observation in the other cluster.

Single linkage has many desirable theoretical properties (Jardine and Sibson 1971; Fisher and Van Ness 1971; Hartigan 1981) but has fared poorly in Monte Carlo studies (for example, Milligan 1980). By imposing no constraints on the shape of clusters, single linkage sacrifices performance in the recovery of compact clusters in return for the ability to detect elongated and irregular clusters. You must also recognize that single linkage tends to chop off the tails of distributions before separating the main clusters (Hartigan 1981). The notorious chaining tendency of single linkage can be alleviated by the TRIM= option (Wishart 1969, 296–298).

Density linkage and two-stage density linkage retain most of the virtues of single linkage while performing better with compact clusters and possessing better asymptotic properties (Wong and Lane 1983).

Single linkage was originated by Florek et al. (1951a, 1951b) and later reinvented by McQuitty (1957) and Sneath (1957).

Two-Stage Density Linkage

If you specify METHOD=DENSITY, the modal clusters often merge before all the points in the tails have clustered. METHOD=TWOSTAGE is a modification of density linkage that ensures that all points are assigned to modal clusters before the modal clusters are allowed to join. The CLUSTER procedure supports the same three varieties of two-stage density linkage as of ordinary density linkage: kth-nearest neighbor, uniform kernel, and hybrid.

In the first stage, disjoint modal clusters are formed. The algorithm is the same as the single linkage algorithm ordinarily used with density linkage, with one exception: two clusters are joined only if at least one of the two clusters has fewer members than the number specified by the MODE= option. At the end of the first stage, each point belongs to one modal cluster.

In the second stage, the modal clusters are hierarchically joined by single linkage. The final number of clusters may exceed one when there are wide gaps between the clusters or when the smoothing parameter is small.

Each stage forms a tree that can be printed by the TREE procedure. By default, the TREE procedure prints the tree from the first stage. To obtain the tree for the second stage, use the option HEIGHT=MODE in the PROC TREE statement. You can also produce a single tree diagram containing both stages, with the number of clusters as the height axis, by using HEIGHT=N in the PROC TREE statement. To produce an output data set from TREE containing the modal clusters, use _HEIGHT_ for the HEIGHT variable (the default) and specify LEVEL=0.

Two-stage density linkage was developed by W.S. Sarle of SAS Institute Inc. There are currently no other published references on two-stage density linkage.

Ward's Minimum-Variance Method

The distance between two clusters is defined by

$$D_{KL} = B_{KL} = \|\bar{\mathbf{x}}_K - \bar{\mathbf{x}}_L\|^2 / (1/N_K + 1/N_L) \quad .$$

If $d(\mathbf{x},\mathbf{y}) = \|\mathbf{x}-\mathbf{y}\|^2/2$ then the combinatorial formula is

$$D_{JM} = ((N_J + N_K)D_{JK} + (N_J + N_L)D_{JL} - N_J D_{KL}) / (N_J + N_M) \quad .$$

In Ward's minimum-variance method, the distance between two clusters is the *ANOVA* sum of squares between the two clusters added up over all the variables. At each generation, the within-cluster sum of squares is minimized over all partitions obtainable by merging two clusters from the previous generation. The sums of squares are easier to interpret when they are divided by the total sum of squares to give proportions of variance.

Ward's method joins clusters to maximize the likelihood at each level of the hierarchy under the following assumptions:

- multivariate normal mixture
- equal spherical covariance matrices
- equal sampling probabilities.

Ward's method tends to join clusters with a small number of observations and is strongly biased toward producing clusters with roughly the same number of observations. It is also very sensitive to outliers (Milligan 1980).

Ward (1963) describes a class of hierarchical clustering methods including the minimum variance method.

Miscellaneous Formulas

The root-mean-square standard deviation of a cluster C_K is

$$\text{RMSSTD} = \sqrt{W_K / (v(N_K - 1))} \ .$$

The R^2 statistic for a given level of the hierarchy is

$$R^2 = 1 - (P_G/T) \ .$$

The squared semipartial correlation for joining clusters C_K and C_L is

$$\text{semipartial } R^2 = B_{KL} / T \ .$$

Formulas for the cubic-clustering criterion and approximate expected R^2 are given in Sarle (1983).

The pseudo F statistic for a given level is

$$\text{pseudo } F = ((T - P_G) / (G - 1)) / (P_G/(n - G)) \ .$$

The pseudo t^2 statistic for joining C_K and C_L is

$$\text{pseudo } t^2 = B_{KL} / ((W_K + W_L) / (N_K + N_L - 2)) \ .$$

The pseudo F and t^2 statistics may be useful indicators of the number of clusters but are *not* distributed as F and t^2 random variables. If the data were independently sampled from a multivariate normal distribution with a scalar covariance matrix and if the clustering method allocated observations to clusters randomly (which no clustering method actually does), then the pseudo F statistic would be distributed as an F random variable with $v(G-1)$ and $v(n-G)$ degrees of freedom. Under the same assumptions, the pseudo t^2 statistic would be distributed as an F random variable with v and $v(N_K+N_L-2)$ degrees of freedom. The pseudo t^2 statistic differs computationally from Hotelling's T^2 in that the latter uses a general symmetric covariance matrix instead of a scalar covariance matrix. The pseudo F statistic was suggested by Calinski and Harabasz (1974). The pseudo t^2 statistic is related to the $J_e(2)/J_e(1)$ statistic of Duda and Hart (1973) by

$$J_e(2)/J_e(1) = (W_K + W_L) / W_M = 1 / (1 + ((t^2 / (N_K + N_L - 2))) \ .$$

See Milligan and Cooper (1983) and Cooper and Milligan (1984) regarding the performance of the above statistics in estimating the number of population clusters. Conservative tests for the number of clusters using the pseudo F and t^2 statistics can be obtained by the Bonferroni approach (Hawkins, Muller, and ten Krooden 1982, 337–340).

Ultrametrics

A dissimilarity measure d(x,y) is called an *ultrametric* if it satisfies the following conditions:

- d(x,x) = 0 for all x
- d(x,y) $\geq$ 0 for all x,y
- d(x,y) = d(y,x) for all x,y
- d(x,y) $\leq$ max(d(x,z), d(y,z)) for all x, y, and z.

Any hierarchical clustering method induces a dissimilarity measure on the observations, say $h(x_i,x_j)$. Let C_M be the cluster with the fewest members that contains both x_i and x_j. Assume C_M was formed by joining C_K and C_L. Then define $h(x_i,x_j)=D_{KL}$.

If the fusion of C_K and C_L reduced the number of clusters from g to $g-1$, then define $D_{(g)}=D_{KL}$. Johnson (1967) shows that if

$$0 \leq D_{(n)} \leq D_{(n-1)} \leq \ldots \leq D_{(2)}$$

then $h(.\,,.)$ is an ultrametric. A method that always satisfies the above condition is said to be a *monotonic* or *ultrametric clustering method*. All methods implemented in CLUSTER except CENTROID, EML, and MEDIAN are ultrametric (Milligan 1979; Batagelj 1981).

Algorithms

Anderberg (1973) describes three algorithms for implementing agglomerative hierarchical clustering: stored data, stored distance, and sorted distance. The algorithms used by CLUSTER for each method are indicated in **Table 15.1**. For METHOD=AVERAGE, CENTROID, or WARD, either the stored data or the stored distance algorithm can be used. For these methods, if the data are distances or the NOSQUARE option is specified, the stored distance algorithm is used; otherwise, the stored data algorithm is used.

Computational Resources

CLUSTER stores the data (including the COPY and ID variables) in memory or, if necessary, on disk. If eigenvalues are computed, the covariance matrix is stored in memory. If the stored distance or sorted distance algorithm is used, the distances are stored in memory or, if necessary, on disk.

With coordinate data, the increase in CPU time is roughly proportional to the number of variables. The VAR statement should list the variables in order of decreasing variance for greatest efficiency.

For both coordinate and distance data, the dominant factor determining CPU time is the number of observations. For density methods with coordinate data, the asymptotic time requirements are somewhere between $n\ln(n)$ and n^2, depending on how the smoothing parameter increases. For other methods except EML, time is roughly proportional to n^2. For the EML method, time is roughly proportional to n^3.

Table 15.1   Three Algorithms for Implementing Agglomerative Hierarchical
Clustering

Method	Algorithm		
	Stored Data	Stored Distance	Sorted Distance
AVERAGE	x	x	
CENTROID	x	x	
COMPLETE		x	
DENSITY			x
EML	x		
FLEXIBLE		x	
MCQUITTY		x	
MEDIAN		x	
SINGLE		x	
TWOSTAGE			x
WARD	x	x	

Missing Values

If the data are coordinates, observations with missing values are excluded from the analysis. If the data are distances, missing values are not allowed in the lower triangle of the distance matrix. The upper triangle is ignored.

Ties

At each level of the clustering algorithm, CLUSTER must identify the pair of clusters with the minimum distance. Sometimes, usually when the data are discrete, there may be two or more pairs with the same minimum distance. In such cases the tie must be broken in some arbitrary way. If there are ties, then the results of the cluster analysis depend on the order of the observations in the data set. The presence of ties is reported in the SAS log and in the column of the cluster history labeled Tie unless the NOTIE option is specifed or METHOD=DENSITY or TWOSTAGE is used.

CLUSTER breaks ties as follows. Each cluster is identified by the smallest observation number among its members. For each pair of clusters, there is a smaller identification number and a larger identification number. If two or more pairs of clusters are tied for minimum distance between clusters, the pair that has the minimum larger identification number is merged. If there is a tie for minimum larger identification number, the pair that has the minimum smaller identification number is merged. This method for breaking ties is different from that used in previous versions. The change in the algorithm may produce changes in the resulting clusters.

A tie means that the level in the cluster history at which the tie occurred and possibly some of the subsequent levels are not uniquely determined. Ties that occur early in the cluster history usually have little effect on the later stages. Ties that occur in the middle part of the cluster history are cause for further investigation. Ties late in the cluster history indicate important indeterminacies.

The importance of ties can be assessed by repeating the cluster analysis for several different random permutations of the observations. The discrepancies at a given level can be examined by crosstabulating the clusters obtained at that level for all of the permutations. See **Example 4** for details.

Output Data Set

The OUTTREE= data set contains one observation for each observation in the input data set, plus one observation for each cluster of two or more observations, that is, one observation for each node of the cluster tree. The total number of output observations is usually $2n-1$, where n is the number of input observations. The density methods may produce fewer output observations when the number of clusters cannot be reduced to one.

The label of the OUTTREE= data set identifies the type of cluster analysis performed and is automatically printed when the TREE procedure is invoked.

The variables in the OUTTREE= data set are as follows:

- the BY variables, if any.
- _NAME_, a character variable giving the name of the node. If the node is a cluster, the name is CLn, where n is the number of the cluster. If the node is an observation, the name is OBn, where n is the observation number. If the node is an observation and the ID statement is used, the name is the formatted value of the ID variable.
- _PARENT_, a character variable giving the value of _NAME_ of the parent of the node.
- _NCL_, the number of clusters.
- _FREQ_, the number of observations in the current cluster.
- _HEIGHT_, the distance or similarity between the last clusters joined, as defined in **Clustering Methods** earlier in this chapter. _HEIGHT_ is used by the TREE procedure as the default height axis. The label of the _HEIGHT_ variable identifies the between-cluster distance measure. For METHOD=TWOSTAGE, _HEIGHT_ contains the densities at which clusters joined in the first stage; for clusters formed in the second stage, _HEIGHT_ is a very small negative number.
- the ID variable, if any.
- the COPY variables, if any.

If the input data set contains coordinates and METHOD=AVERAGE, CENTROID, or WARD, then the following variables appear in the output data set:

- _DIST_, the Euclidean distance between the means of the last clusters joined
- _AVLINK_, the average distance between the last clusters joined.

If the input data set contains coordinates or METHOD=AVERAGE, CENTROID, or WARD, then the following variables appear in the output data set:

- _RMSSTD_, the root-mean-square standard deviation of the current cluster
- _SPRSQ_, the semipartial squared multiple correlation or the decrease in the proportion of variance accounted for due to joining two clusters to form the current cluster
- _RSQ_, the squared multiple correlation
- _PSF_, the pseudo F statistic
- _PST2_, the pseudo t^2 statistic.

If METHOD=EML is used, then the following variable appears in the output data set:

- _LNLR_, the log-likelihood ratio.

If the input data set contains coordinates, the following variables appear in the output data set:

- the variables containing the coordinates used in the cluster analysis. For output observations that correspond to input observations, the values of the coordinates are the same in both data sets except for some slight numeric error possibly introduced by standardizing and unstandardizing if the STANDARD option is used. For output observations that correspond to clusters of more than one input observation, the values of the coordinates are the cluster means.
- _ERSQ_, the approximate expected value of R^2 under the uniform null hypothesis.
- _RATIO_, equal to $(1-\_ERSQ\_)/(1-\_RSQ\_)$.
- _LOGR_, natural logarithm of _RATIO_.
- _CCC_, the cubic clustering criterion.

The variables _ERSQ_, _RATIO_, _LOGR_, and _CCC_ have missing values when the number of clusters is greater than one-fifth the number of observations.
If nonparametric density estimates are requested, the output data set contains

- _DENS_, the maximum density in the current cluster.

If METHOD=TWOSTAGE or METHOD=DENSITY is used, the following variable appears in the output data set:

- _MODE_, pertaining to the modal clusters. With METHOD=DENSITY, _MODE_ indicates the number of modal clusters contained by the current cluster. With METHOD=TWOSTAGE, _MODE_ gives the maximum density in each modal cluster and the fusion density, d^*, for clusters containing two or more modal clusters; for clusters containing no modal clusters, _MODE_ is missing.

Printed Output

If you specify the SIMPLE option and the data are coordinates, CLUSTER prints simple descriptive statistics for each variable:

1. the Mean (not shown).
2. the standard deviation, Std Dev (not shown).
3. the Skewness (not shown).
4. the Kurtosis (not shown).
5. a coefficient of Bimodality (not shown)

$$b = (m_3^2 + 1) / (m_4 + 3*((n - 1)**2) / (n - 2)*(n - 3)) \quad .$$

where m_3 is skewness and m_4 is kurtosis. Values of b greater than 0.555 (the value for a uniform population) may indicate bimodal or multimodal marginal distributions. The maximum of 1.0 is obtained for a population with only two distinct values. Very heavy-tailed distributions have small values of b regardless of the number of modes.

If the data are coordinates and NOEIGEN is not specified, CLUSTER prints

6. the Eigenvalues of the Correlation or Covariance Matrix
7. the Difference between successive eigenvalues

8. the Proportion of variance explained by each eigenvalue
9. the Cumulative proportion of variance explained.

If the data are coordinates, CLUSTER prints

10. the Root-Mean-Square Total-Sample Standard Deviation of the variables.

If the distances are normalized, CLUSTER prints either

11. the Root-Mean-Square Distance Between Observations

or

12. the Mean Distance Between Observations

depending on whether squared or unsquared distances are used.

For the generations in the clustering process specified by the PRINT= option, CLUSTER prints

13. the Number of Clusters or NCL.
14. the names of the Clusters Joined. The observations are identified by the formatted value of the ID variable if any, otherwise by OBn, where n is the observation number. Clusters of two or more observations are identified as CLn, where n is the number of clusters existing after the cluster in question is formed.
15. the number of observations in the new cluster, Frequency of New Cluster or FREQ.

If you specify the RMSSTD option and if the data are coordinates or you specify METHOD=AVERAGE, CENTROID, or WARD, the CLUSTER procedure prints

16. the root-mean-square standard deviation of the new cluster, RMS Std of New Cluster or RMS Std (not shown).

The procedure prints the following items if you specify METHOD=WARD. It also prints them if you specify RSQUARE and either the data are coordinates or you specify METHOD=AVERAGE or CENTROID:

17. the decrease in the proportion of variance accounted for resulting from joining the two clusters, Semipartial R-Squared or SPRSQ. This equals the between-cluster sum of squares divided by the corrected total sum of squares.
18. the squared multiple correlation, R-Squared or RSQ. R^2 is the proportion of variance accounted for by the clusters.

If you specify the CCC option and the data are coordinates, the procedure prints the following:

19. Approximate Expected R-Squared or ERSQ, the approximate expected value of R^2 under the uniform null hypothesis.
20. the Cubic Clustering Criterion or CCC. The cubic clustering criterion and approximate expected R^2 are given missing values when the number of clusters is greater than one-fifth the number of observations.

If you specify the PSEUDO option and if the data are coordinates or METHOD=AVERAGE, CENTROID, or WARD, then the following are printed:

21. Pseudo F or PSF, the pseudo F statistic measuring the separation among all the clusters at the current level
22. Pseudo t**2 or PST2, the pseudo t^2 statistic measuring the separation between the two clusters most recently joined.

If you specify the NOSQUARE option along with METHOD=AVERAGE, CLUSTER prints

23. (Normalized) Average Distance or (Norm) Aver Dist, the average distance between pairs of objects in the two clusters joined with one object from each cluster (not shown).

If you specify METHOD=AVERAGE but do not specify the NOSQUARE option, CLUSTER prints

24. (Normalized) RMS Distance or (Norm) RMS Dist, the root-mean-square distance between pairs of objects in the two clusters joined with one object from each cluster.

If you specify METHOD=CENTROID, CLUSTER prints

25. (Normalized) Centroid Distance or (Norm) Cent Dist, the distance between the two cluster centroids.

If METHOD=COMPLETE, CLUSTER prints

26. (Normalized) Maximum Distance or (Norm) Max Dist, the maximum distance between the two clusters.

If METHOD=DENSITY or METHOD=TWOSTAGE, CLUSTER prints

27. Fusion Density or Fusion Dens, the value of d^* as defined in **Clustering Methods** earlier in this chapter.
28. the Maximum Density in Each Cluster joined, including the Lesser or Min, and the Greater or Max, of the two maximum density values.

If METHOD=EML, CLUSTER prints

29. Log Likelihood Ratio or LNLR
30. Log Likelihood or LNLIKE.

If METHOD=FLEXIBLE, CLUSTER prints

31. (Normalized) Flexible Distance or (Norm) Flex Dist, the distance between the two clusters based on the Lance-Williams flexible formula.

If METHOD=MEDIAN, CLUSTER prints

32. (Normalized) Median Distance or (Norm) Med Dist, the distance between the two clusters based on the median method.

If METHOD=MCQUITTY, CLUSTER prints

33. (Normalized) McQuitty's Similarity or (Norm) MCQ, the distance between the two clusters based on McQuitty's similarity method.

If METHOD=SINGLE, CLUSTER prints

34. (Normalized) Minimum Distance or (Norm) Min Dist, the minimum distance between the two clusters.

If you specify the NONORM option along with METHOD=WARD, CLUSTER prints

35. Between_Cluster Sum of Squares or BSS, the *ANOVA* sum of squares between the two clusters joined (not shown).

If neither NOTIE nor METHOD=TWOSTAGE or DENSITY is specified, CLUSTER prints

36. Tie, where a T in the column indicates a tie for minimum distance and a blank indicates the absence of a tie.

After the cluster history, if METHOD=TWOSTAGE or DENSITY, CLUSTER prints

37. the number of modal clusters.

EXAMPLES

Example 1: Cluster Analysis of Flying Mileages between Ten American Cities

This first example clusters ten American cities based on the flying mileages between them. Six clustering methods are shown with corresponding tree diagrams produced by the TREE procedure. The EML method cannot be used because it requires coordinate data. The other omitted methods produce the same clusters, although not the same distances between clusters, as one of the illustrated methods: complete linkage and the flexible-beta method yield the same clusters as Ward's method, McQuitty's similarity analysis produces the same clusters as average linkage, and the median method corresponds to the centroid method.

All of the methods suggest a division of the cities into two clusters along the east-west dimension. There is disagreement, however, about which cluster Denver should belong to. Some of the methods indicate a possible third cluster containing Denver and Houston. The following statements produce **Output 15.1**:

```
title 'CLUSTER ANALYSIS OF FLYING MILEAGES BETWEEN 10 AMERICAN CITIES';

data mileages(type=distance);
   input (atlanta chicago denver houston losangel
          miami newyork sanfran seattle washdc) (5.)
          @55 city $15.;
   cards;
    0                                                    ATLANTA
   587    0                                              CHICAGO
  1212  920    0                                         DENVER
   701  940  879    0                                    HOUSTON
  1936 1745  831 1374    0                               LOS ANGELES
   604 1188 1726  968 2339    0                          MIAMI
   748  713 1631 1420 2451 1092    0                     NEW YORK
  2139 1858  949 1645  347 2594 2571    0               SAN FRANCISCO
  2182 1737 1021 1891  959 2734 2408  678    0          SEATTLE
   543  597 1494 1220 2300  923  205 2442 2329    0     WASHINGTON D.C.
  ;
```

```
proc cluster data=mileages method=average pseudo;
   id city;
proc tree horizontal spaces=2;
   id city;

proc cluster data=mileages method=centroid pseudo;
   id city;
proc tree horizontal spaces=2;
   id city;

proc cluster data=mileages method=density k=3;
   id city;
proc tree horizontal spaces=2;
   id city;

proc cluster data=mileages method=single;
   id city;
proc tree horizontal spaces=2;
   id city;

proc cluster data=mileages method=twostage k=3;
   id city;
proc tree horizontal spaces=2;
   id city;

proc cluster data=mileages method=ward pseudo;
   id city;
proc tree horizontal spaces=2;
   id city;
run;
```

Output 15.1   Six Different Clustering Methods: PROC CLUSTER and PROC TREE

```
                    CLUSTER ANALYSIS OF FLYING MILEAGES BETWEEN 10 AMERICAN CITIES              1

                              Average Linkage Cluster Analysis

                    Root-Mean-Square Distance Between Observations   = 1580.242
```

⑬ Number of Clusters	⑭ Clusters Joined		⑮ Frequency of New Cluster	㉑ Pseudo F	㉒ Pseudo t**2	㉔ Normalized RMS Distance	㊱ Tie
9	NEW YORK	WASHINGTON D.C.	2	66.72	.	0.129727	
8	LOS ANGELES	SAN FRANCISCO	2	39.25	.	0.219587	
7	ATLANTA	CHICAGO	2	21.66	.	0.371462	
6	CL7	CL9	4	14.52	3.45	0.414859	
5	CL8	SEATTLE	3	12.44	7.30	0.525534	
4	DENVER	HOUSTON	2	13.91	.	0.556244	
3	CL6	MIAMI	5	15.49	3.75	0.618457	
2	CL3	CL4	7	16.02	5.32	0.800540	
1	CL2	CL5	10	.	16.02	1.296665	

```
                    CLUSTER ANALYSIS OF FLYING MILEAGES BETWEEN 10 AMERICAN CITIES              2

                              Average Linkage Cluster Analysis

                              Average Distance between Clusters

                1.3    1.2    1.1    1    0.9    0.8    0.7    0.6    0.5    0.4    0.3    0.2    0.1    0
                +------+------+------+------+------+------+------+------+------+------+------+------+------+
      ATLANTA   XXXXXXXXXXXXXXXXXXXXXXXXXXXXXXXXXXXXXXXXXXXXXXXXXXXXXXX...........................
                XXXXXXXXXXXXXXXXXXXXXXXXXXXXXXXXXXXXXXXXXXXXXXXXXXXXXX
                XXXXXXXXXXXXXXXXXXXXXXXXXXXXXXXXXXXXXXXXXXXXXXXXXXXXXX
      CHICAGO   XXXXXXXXXXXXXXXXXXXXXXXXXXXXXXXXXXXXXXXXXXXXXXXXXXXX...........................
                XXXXXXXXXXXXXXXXXXXXXXXXXXXXXXXXXXXXXXXXXXXXXXXXXXXX
                XXXXXXXXXXXXXXXXXXXXXXXXXXXXXXXXXXXXXXXXXXXXXXXXXXXX
     NEW YORK   XXXXXXXXXXXXXXXXXXXXXXXXXXXXXXXXXXXXXXXXXXXXXXXXXXXXXXXXXXXXXXXXXXXX...
                XXXXXXXXXXXXXXXXXXXXXXXXXXXXXXXXXXXXXXXXXXXXXXXXXXXXXXXXXXXXXXXXXXXX
                XXXXXXXXXXXXXXXXXXXXXXXXXXXXXXXXXXXXXXXXXXXXXXXXXXXXXXXXXXXXXXXXXXXX
WASHINGTON D.C. XXXXXXXXXXXXXXXXXXXXXXXXXXXXXXXXXXXXXXXXXXXXXXXXXXXXXXXXXXXX........
                XXXXXXXXXXXXXXXXXXXXXXXXXXXXXXXXXXXXXXXXXXXXXX
C               XXXXXXXXXXXXXXXXXXXXXXXXXXXXXXXXXXXXXXXXXXXXXX
I     MIAMI     XXXXXXXXXXXXXXXXXXXXXXXXXXXXXXXXXXXXXXX................................
T               XXXXXXXXXXXXXXXXXXXXXXXXXXXXXXXXXXXXX
Y               XXXXXXXXXXXXXXXXXXXXXXXXXXXXXXXXXXXXX
     DENVER     XXXXXXXXXXXXXXXXXXXXXXXXXXXXXXXXXXXXXXXXXX.....................................
                XXXXXXXXXXXXXXXXXXXXXXXXXXXXXXXXXXXXXXXXXX
                XXXXXXXXXXXXXXXXXXXXXXXXXXXXXXXXXXXXXXXXXX
     HOUSTON    XXXXXXXXXXXXXXXXXXXXXXXXXXXXXXXXXXXXXXXXXX.....................................
                X
                X
   LOS ANGELES  XXXXXXXXXXXXXXXXXXXXXXXXXXXXXXXXXXXXXXXXXXXXXXXXXXXXXXXXXXXXXXX.............
                XXXXXXXXXXXXXXXXXXXXXXXXXXXXXXXXXXXXXXXXXXXXXXXXXXXXXXXXXXXXX
                XXXXXXXXXXXXXXXXXXXXXXXXXXXXXXXXXXXXXXXXXXXXXXXXXXXXXXXXXXXXX
  SAN FRANCISCO  XXXXXXXXXXXXXXXXXXXXXXXXXXXXXXXXXXXXXXXXXXXXXXXXXXXXXXXXXXXXXXXXX.............
                XXXXXXXXXXXXXXXXXXXXXXXXXXXXXXXXXXXXXXXXXXXXXXXXXXXXXXXXX
                XXXXXXXXXXXXXXXXXXXXXXXXXXXXXXXXXXXXXXXXXXXXXXXXXXXXXXXXX
     SEATTLE    XXXXXXXXXXXXXXXXXXXXXXXXXXXXXXXXXXXXXXXXXXXXXXXXXXXXX.........................
```

CLUSTER ANALYSIS OF FLYING MILEAGES BETWEEN 10 AMERICAN CITIES   3

Centroid Hierarchical Cluster Analysis

⑪ Root-Mean-Square Distance Between Observations = 1580.242   ㉕

Number of Clusters	Clusters Joined		Frequency of New Cluster	Pseudo F	Pseudo t**2	Normalized Centroid Distance	Tie
9	NEW YORK	WASHINGTON D.C.	2	66.72	.	0.129727	
8	LOS ANGELES	SAN FRANCISCO	2	39.25	.	0.219587	
7	ATLANTA	CHICAGO	2	21.66	.	0.371462	
6	CL7	CL9	4	14.52	3.45	0.365246	
5	CL8	SEATTLE	3	12.44	7.30	0.513937	
4	DENVER	CL5	4	12.41	2.13	0.533679	
3	CL6	MIAMI	5	14.23	3.75	0.574270	
2	CL3	HOUSTON	6	22.06	2.61	0.609053	
1	CL2	CL4	10	.	22.06	1.173036	

CLUSTER ANALYSIS OF FLYING MILEAGES BETWEEN 10 AMERICAN CITIES   4

Centroid Hierarchical Cluster Analysis

Distance between Cluster Centroids

```
                CLUSTER ANALYSIS OF FLYING MILEAGES BETWEEN 10 AMERICAN CITIES                    5

                        Density Linkage Cluster Analysis

                                    K = 3

                                                                    ㉘
                                                              Maximum Density
                                                               in Each Cluster
       Number                                      ㉗
         of                            Frequency   Fusion
      Clusters   Clusters Joined       of New      Density     Lesser    Greater
                                       Cluster

           9     ATLANTA        WASHINGTON D.C.        2      0.000265   0.000256   0.000276
           8     CL9            CHICAGO                3      0.000263   0.000251   0.000276
           7     CL8            NEW YORK               4      0.000239    0.00021   0.000276
           6     CL7            HOUSTON                5      0.000205   0.000171   0.000276
           5     CL6            MIAMI                  6      0.000205   0.000163   0.000276
           4     LOS ANGELES    SAN FRANCISCO          2      0.000199   0.000181   0.000221
           3     CL4            SEATTLE                3      0.000183   0.000156   0.000221
           2     DENVER         CL3                    4      0.000175   0.000171   0.000221
           1     CL5            CL2                   10      0.000171   0.000221   0.000276  *

                    * indicates fusion of two modal clusters
               ㊲ 2 modal clusters have been formed.
```

```
                CLUSTER ANALYSIS OF FLYING MILEAGES BETWEEN 10 AMERICAN CITIES                    6

                        Density Linkage Cluster Analysis

                                Cluster Fusion Density

          0.00016        0.00018        0.0002        0.00022       0.00024        0.00026       0.00028
          +--------------+--------------+--------------+--------------+--------------+--------------+
   ATLANTA             XXXXXXXXXXXXXXXXXXXXXXXXXXXXXXXXXXXXXXXXXXXXXXXXXXXXXXXXXXXXXXX
                       XXXXXXXXXXXXXXXXXXXXXXXXXXXXXXXXXXXXXXXXXXXXXXXXXXXXXXXXXXXXXXX
                       XXXXXXXXXXXXXXXXXXXXXXXXXXXXXXXXXXXXXXXXXXXXXXXXXXXXXXXXXXXXXXX
WASHINGTON D.C.        XXXXXXXXXXXXXXXXXXXXXXXXXXXXXXXXXXXXXXXXXXXXXXXXXXXXXXXXXXXXXXX
                       XXXXXXXXXXXXXXXXXXXXXXXXXXXXXXXXXXXXXXXXXXXXXXXXXXXXXXXXXXXXXXX
                       XXXXXXXXXXXXXXXXXXXXXXXXXXXXXXXXXXXXXXXXXXXXXXXXXXXXXXXXXXXXXXX
   CHICAGO             XXXXXXXXXXXXXXXXXXXXXXXXXXXXXXXXXXXXXXXXXXXXXXXXXXXXXXXXXXXXXXX.
                       XXXXXXXXXXXXXXXXXXXXXXXXXXXXXXXXXXXXXXXXXXXXXXXXXXXX
                       XXXXXXXXXXXXXXXXXXXXXXXXXXXXXXXXXXXXXXXXXXXXXXXXXXXX
  NEW YORK             XXXXXXXXXXXXXXXXXXXXXXXXXXXXXXXXXXXXXXXXXXXXXX.................
                       XXXXXXXXXXXXXXXXXXXXXXXXXXXXX
C                      XXXXXXXXXXXXXXXXXXXXXXXXXXXXX
I  HOUSTON             XXXXXXXXXXXXXXXXXXXXXXXXXXXXX...............................
T                      XXXXXXXXXXXXXXXXXXXXXXXXXXXXX
Y  MIAMI               XXXXXXXXXXXXXXXXXXXXXXXXXXXXX...............................
                       X
                       X
  DENVER               XXXX.........................................................
                       XXXX
                       XXXX
LOS ANGELES            XXXXXXXXXXXXXXXXXXXXXXXX.....................................
                       XXXXXXXXXXXXXXXXXXXXXXXX
                       XXXXXXXXXXXXXXXXXXXXXXXX
SAN FRANCISCO          XXXXXXXXXXXXXXXXXXXXXXXX.....................................
                       XXXXXXXXXXX
                       XXXXXXXXXXX
   SEATTLE             XXXXXXXXXXX.................................................
```

CLUSTER ANALYSIS OF FLYING MILEAGES BETWEEN 10 AMERICAN CITIES   7

Single Linkage Cluster Analysis

⑫ Mean Distance Between Observations   = 1417.133

Number of Clusters	Clusters Joined		Frequency of New Cluster	㉞ Normalized Minimum Distance	Tie
9	NEW YORK	WASHINGTON D.C.	2	0.144658	
8	LOS ANGELES	SAN FRANCISCO	2	0.244861	
7	ATLANTA	CL9	3	0.383168	
6	CL7	CHICAGO	4	0.414216	
5	CL6	MIAMI	5	0.426213	
4	CL8	SEATTLE	3	0.478431	
3	CL5	HOUSTON	6	0.494661	
2	DENVER	CL4	4	0.586395	
1	CL3	CL2	10	0.620266	

CLUSTER ANALYSIS OF FLYING MILEAGES BETWEEN 10 AMERICAN CITIES   8

Single Linkage Cluster Analysis

Minimum Distance between Clusters

```
              0.65  0.6  0.55  0.5  0.45  0.4  0.35  0.3  0.25  0.2  0.15  0.1  0.05   0
              +-----+-----+-----+-----+-----+-----+-----+-----+-----+-----+-----+-----+-----+
   ATLANTA    XXXXXXXXXXXXXXXXXXXXXXXXXXXXXXXXXX.......................................................
              XXXXXXXXXXXXXXXXXXXXXXXXXXXXXXXXXX
              XXXXXXXXXXXXXXXXXXXXXXXXXXXXXXXXXX
  NEW YORK    XXXXXXXXXXXXXXXXXXXXXXXXXXXXXXXXXXXXXXXXXXXXXXXXXXXXXXXXXXXX...................
              XXXXXXXXXXXXXXXXXXXXXXXXXXXXXXXXXXXXXXXXXXXXXXXXXXXXXXXXXXXX
              XXXXXXXXXXXXXXXXXXXXXXXXXXXXXXXXXXXXXXXXXXXXXXXXXXXXXXXXXXXX
WASHINGTON D.C. XXXXXXXXXXXXXXXXXXXXXXXXXXXXXXXXXXXXXXXXXXXXXXXXXXXXXXXXXXXX...................
              XXXXXXXXXXXXXXXXXXXXXXXXXXXXXXX
              XXXXXXXXXXXXXXXXXXXXXXXXXXXXXXX
   CHICAGO    XXXXXXXXXXXXXXXXXXXXXXXXXXXXXXX........................................................
              XXXXXXXXXXXXXXXXXXXXXXXXXXXXXX
              XXXXXXXXXXXXXXXXXXXXXXXXXXXXXX
     MIAMI    XXXXXXXXXXXXXXXXXXXXXXXXXXXXXX........................................................
C             XXXXXXXXXXXXXXXXXX
I             XXXXXXXXXXXXXXXXXX
T             XXXXXXXXXXXXXXXXXX
Y  HOUSTON    XXXXXXXXXXXXXXXXXX........................................................................
              X
              X
    DENVER    XXXXXX.................................................................................
              XXXXX
              XXXXX
 LOS ANGELES  XXXXXXXXXXXXXXXXXXXXXXXXXXXXXXXXXXXXXXXXXXXXX.................................
              XXXXXXXXXXXXXXXXXXXXXXXXXXXXXXXXXXXXXXXXXXXXX
              XXXXXXXXXXXXXXXXXXXXXXXXXXXXXXXXXXXXXXXXXXXXX
SAN FRANCISCO XXXXXXXXXXXXXXXXXXXXXXXXXXXXXXXXXXXXXXXXXXXXX...............................
              XXXXXXXXXXXXXXXXXXXX
              XXXXXXXXXXXXXXXXXXXX
   SEATTLE    XXXXXXXXXXXXXXXXXXXX....................................................................
```

CLUSTER ANALYSIS OF FLYING MILEAGES BETWEEN 10 AMERICAN CITIES   9

Two-Stage Density Linkage Clustering

K = 3

Number of Clusters	Clusters Joined		Frequency of New Cluster	Fusion Density	Maximum Density in Each Cluster	
					Lesser	Greater
9	ATLANTA	WASHINGTON D.C.	2	0.000265	0.000256	0.000276
8	CL9	CHICAGO	3	0.000263	0.000251	0.000276
7	CL8	NEW YORK	4	0.000239	0.00021	0.000276
6	CL7	HOUSTON	5	0.000205	0.000171	0.000276
5	CL6	MIAMI	6	0.000205	0.000163	0.000276
4	LOS ANGELES	SAN FRANCISCO	2	0.000199	0.000181	0.000221
3	CL4	SEATTLE	3	0.000183	0.000156	0.000221
2	DENVER	CL3	4	0.000175	0.000171	0.000221

2 modal clusters have been formed.

Number of Clusters	Clusters Joined		Frequency of New Cluster	Fusion Density	Maximum Density in Each Cluster	
					Lesser	Greater
1	CL5	CL2	10	0.000171	0.000221	0.000276

CLUSTER ANALYSIS OF FLYING MILEAGES BETWEEN 10 AMERICAN CITIES   10

Two-Stage Density Linkage Clustering

Cluster Fusion Density

```
                0       0.00005      0.0001      0.00015       0.0002      0.00025      0.0003
                +---------------+---------------+---------------+---------------+---------------+---------------+
       ATLANTA  XXXXXXXXXXXXXXXXXXXXXXXXXXXXXXXXXXXXXXXXXXXXXXXXXXXXXXXXXXXXXXXXXXXXXXXXXXXXXXXX
                XXXXXXXXXXXXXXXXXXXXXXXXXXXXXXXXXXXXXXXXXXXXXXXXXXXXXXXXXXXXXXXXXXXXXXXXXXXXXXXX
                XXXXXXXXXXXXXXXXXXXXXXXXXXXXXXXXXXXXXXXXXXXXXXXXXXXXXXXXXXXXXXXXXXXXXXXXXXXXXXXX
WASHINGTON D.C. XXXXXXXXXXXXXXXXXXXXXXXXXXXXXXXXXXXXXXXXXXXXXXXXXXXXXXXXXXXXXXXXXXXXXXXXXXXXXXX
                XXXXXXXXXXXXXXXXXXXXXXXXXXXXXXXXXXXXXXXXXXXXXXXXXXXXXXXXXXXXXXXXXXXXXXXXXXXXXXX
       CHICAGO  XXXXXXXXXXXXXXXXXXXXXXXXXXXXXXXXXXXXXXXXXXXXXXXXXXXXXXXXXXXXXXXXXXXXXXXXXXXXXX.
                XXXXXXXXXXXXXXXXXXXXXXXXXXXXXXXXXXXXXXXXXXXXXXXXXXXXXXXXXXXXXXXXXXXXXXXXXX
                XXXXXXXXXXXXXXXXXXXXXXXXXXXXXXXXXXXXXXXXXXXXXXXXXXXXXXXXXXXXXXXXXXXXXXXXXX
      NEW YORK  XXXXXXXXXXXXXXXXXXXXXXXXXXXXXXXXXXXXXXXXXXXXXXXXXXXXXXXXXXXXXXXXXXXXX........
                XXXXXXXXXXXXXXXXXXXXXXXXXXXXXXXXXXXXXXXXXXXXXXXXXXXXXXXXXXXXXXXXXXX
   C            XXXXXXXXXXXXXXXXXXXXXXXXXXXXXXXXXXXXXXXXXXXXXXXXXXXXXXXXXXXXXXXXXXX
   I   HOUSTON  XXXXXXXXXXXXXXXXXXXXXXXXXXXXXXXXXXXXXXXXXXXXXXXXXXXXXXXXXXXXXXXXXXX...................
   T            XXXXXXXXXXXXXXXXXXXXXXXXXXXXXXXXXXXXXXXXXXXXXXXXXXXXXXXXXXXXXXXXXXX
   Y    MIAMI   XXXXXXXXXXXXXXXXXXXXXXXXXXXXXXXXXXXXXXXXXXXXXXXXXXXXXXXXXXXXXXXXXXX...................
                X
                X
        DENVER  XXXXXXXXXXXXXXXXXXXXXXXXXXXXXXXXXXXXXXXXXXXXXXXXXXXXXX.......................
                XXXXXXXXXXXXXXXXXXXXXXXXXXXXXXXXXXXXXXXXXXXXXXXXXXXXXX
   LOS ANGELES  XXXXXXXXXXXXXXXXXXXXXXXXXXXXXXXXXXXXXXXXXXXXXXXXXXXXXXXX..................
                XXXXXXXXXXXXXXXXXXXXXXXXXXXXXXXXXXXXXXXXXXXXXXXXXXXXXXXX
 SAN FRANCISCO  XXXXXXXXXXXXXXXXXXXXXXXXXXXXXXXXXXXXXXXXXXXXXXXXXXXXXXXX..................
                XXXXXXXXXXXXXXXXXXXXXXXXXXXXXXXXXXXXXXXXXXXXXXXXXXXXXXXXXX
                XXXXXXXXXXXXXXXXXXXXXXXXXXXXXXXXXXXXXXXXXXXXXXXXXXXXXXXXXX
       SEATTLE  XXXXXXXXXXXXXXXXXXXXXXXXXXXXXXXXXXXXXXXXXXXXXXXXXXXXXXXXXX.......................
```

CLUSTER ANALYSIS OF FLYING MILEAGES BETWEEN 10 AMERICAN CITIES   11

Ward's Minimum Variance Cluster Analysis

Root-Mean-Square Distance Between Observations   = 1580.242

Number of Clusters	Clusters Joined		Frequency of New Cluster	❶❼ Semipartial R-Squared	❶❽ R-Squared	Pseudo F	Pseudo t**2	Tie
9	NEW YORK	WASHINGTON D.C.	2	0.001870	0.998130	66.72	.	
8	LOS ANGELES	SAN FRANCISCO	2	0.005358	0.992773	39.25	.	
7	ATLANTA	CHICAGO	2	0.015332	0.977441	21.66	.	
6	CL7	CL9	4	0.029646	0.947795	14.52	3.45	
5	DENVER	HOUSTON	2	0.034379	0.913417	13.19	.	
4	CL8	SEATTLE	3	0.039131	0.874286	13.91	7.30	
3	CL6	MIAMI	5	0.058629	0.815658	15.49	3.75	
2	CL3	CL5	7	0.148757	0.666901	16.02	5.32	
1	CL2	CL4	10	0.666901	0.000000	.	16.02	

CLUSTER ANALYSIS OF FLYING MILEAGES BETWEEN 10 AMERICAN CITIES   12

Ward's Minimum Variance Cluster Analysis

Semi-Partial R-Squared

```
            0.7  0.65   0.6  0.55   0.5  0.45   0.4  0.35   0.3  0.25   0.2  0.15   0.1  0.05    0
            +-----+-----+-----+-----+-----+-----+-----+-----+-----+-----+-----+-----+-----+-----+
   ATLANTA  XXXXXXXXXXXXXXXXXXXXXXXXXXXXXXXXXXXXXXXXXXXXXXXXXXXXXXXXXXXXXXXXXXXXXXXXXXXXXXXXXX..
            XXXXXXXXXXXXXXXXXXXXXXXXXXXXXXXXXXXXXXXXXXXXXXXXXXXXXXXXXXXXXXXXXXXXXXXXXXXXXXXX
            XXXXXXXXXXXXXXXXXXXXXXXXXXXXXXXXXXXXXXXXXXXXXXXXXXXXXXXXXXXXXXXXXXXXXXXXXXXXXXXX
   CHICAGO  XXXXXXXXXXXXXXXXXXXXXXXXXXXXXXXXXXXXXXXXXXXXXXXXXXXXXXXXXXXXXXXXXXXXXXXXXXXXXXXXXX..
            XXXXXXXXXXXXXXXXXXXXXXXXXXXXXXXXXXXXXXXXXXXXXXXXXXXXXXXXXXXXXXXXXXXXXXXXXXXXXXXXXX
            XXXXXXXXXXXXXXXXXXXXXXXXXXXXXXXXXXXXXXXXXXXXXXXXXXXXXXXXXXXXXXXXXXXXXXXXXXXXXXXXXX
  NEW YORK  XXXXXXXXXXXXXXXXXXXXXXXXXXXXXXXXXXXXXXXXXXXXXXXXXXXXXXXXXXXXXXXXXXXXXXXXXXXXXXXXXXXX
            XXXXXXXXXXXXXXXXXXXXXXXXXXXXXXXXXXXXXXXXXXXXXXXXXXXXXXXXXXXXXXXXXXXXXXXXXXXXXXXXXXXX
            XXXXXXXXXXXXXXXXXXXXXXXXXXXXXXXXXXXXXXXXXXXXXXXXXXXXXXXXXXXXXXXXXXXXXXXXXXXXXXXXXXXX
WASHINGTON D.C. XXXXXXXXXXXXXXXXXXXXXXXXXXXXXXXXXXXXXXXXXXXXXXXXXXXXXXXXXXXXXXXXXXXXXXXXXXXXXXXX
            XXXXXXXXXXXXXXXXXXXXXXXXXXXXXXXXXXXXXXXXXXXXXXXXXXXXXXXXXXXXXXXXXXXXXXXXXXXXXXX
C           XXXXXXXXXXXXXXXXXXXXXXXXXXXXXXXXXXXXXXXXXXXXXXXXXXXXXXXXXXXXXXXXXXXXXXXXX
I     MIAMI XXXXXXXXXXXXXXXXXXXXXXXXXXXXXXXXXXXXXXXXXXXXXXXXXXXXXXXXXXXXXXXXXXXXXXXXXXX.......
T           XXXXXXXXXXXXXXXXXXXXXXXXXXXXXXXXXXXXXXXXXXXXXXXXXXXXXXXXXXXXXXXXXX
Y    DENVER XXXXXXXXXXXXXXXXXXXXXXXXXXXXXXXXXXXXXXXXXXXXXXXXXXXXXXXXXXXXXXXXXXXXXXXXXXX.....
            XXXXXXXXXXXXXXXXXXXXXXXXXXXXXXXXXXXXXXXXXXXXXXXXXXXXXXXXXXXXXXXXXXXXXXXXXXX
            XXXXXXXXXXXXXXXXXXXXXXXXXXXXXXXXXXXXXXXXXXXXXXXXXXXXXXXXXXXXXXXXXXXXXXXXXXX
   HOUSTON  XXXXXXXXXXXXXXXXXXXXXXXXXXXXXXXXXXXXXXXXXXXXXXXXXXXXXXXXXXXXXXXXXXXXXXXXXXX.....
            X
            X
LOS ANGELES XXXXXXXXXXXXXXXXXXXXXXXXXXXXXXXXXXXXXXXXXXXXXXXXXXXXXXXXXXXXXXXXXXXXXXXXXXXXXXXXX.
            XXXXXXXXXXXXXXXXXXXXXXXXXXXXXXXXXXXXXXXXXXXXXXXXXXXXXXXXXXXXXXXXXXXXXXXXXXXXXXXXX
            XXXXXXXXXXXXXXXXXXXXXXXXXXXXXXXXXXXXXXXXXXXXXXXXXXXXXXXXXXXXXXXXXXXXXXXXXXXXXXXX
SAN FRANCISCO XXXXXXXXXXXXXXXXXXXXXXXXXXXXXXXXXXXXXXXXXXXXXXXXXXXXXXXXXXXXXXXXXXXXXXXXXXXXXX
            XXXXXXXXXXXXXXXXXXXXXXXXXXXXXXXXXXXXXXXXXXXXXXXXXXXXXXXXXXXXXXXXXXXXXXXXXXXXXXX
            XXXXXXXXXXXXXXXXXXXXXXXXXXXXXXXXXXXXXXXXXXXXXXXXXXXXXXXXXXXXXXXXXXXXXXXXXXXXXXX
   SEATTLE  XXXXXXXXXXXXXXXXXXXXXXXXXXXXXXXXXXXXXXXXXXXXXXXXXXXXXXXXXXXXXXXXXXXXXXXXXXXXXXX.....
```

Example 2: Crude Birth and Death Rates in 1976

The data for the next example are crude birth and death rates per 100,000 population in 1976 for seventy-four countries. Twelve cluster analyses are performed with ten methods. Scatter plots showing cluster membership at selected levels are produced instead of tree diagrams. The following statements produce **Output 15.2**:

```
title 'CRUDE BIRTH AND DEATH RATES IN 1976';
data vital;
   input country & $20. birth death @@;
   cards;
AFGHANISTAN          52 30   ALGERIA             50 16
ANGOLA               47 23   ARGENTINA           22 10
AUSTRALIA            16 8    AUSTRIA             12 13
BANGLADESH           47 19   BELGIUM             12 12
BRAZIL               36 10   BULGARIA            17 10
BURMA                38 15   CAMEROON            42 22
CANADA               16 7    CHILE               22 7
CHINA                31 11   TAIWAN              26 5
COLOMBIA             34 10   CUBA                20 6
CZECHOSLOVAKIA       19 11   ECUADOR             42 11
EGYPT                39 13   ETHIOPIA            48 23
FRANCE               14 11   GERMAN DEM REP      12 14
GERMANY, FED REP OF  10 12   GHANA               46 14
GREECE               16 9    GUATEMALA           40 14
HUNGARY              18 12   INDIA               36 15
INDONESIA            38 16   IRAN                42 12
IRAQ                 48 14   ITALY               14 10
IVORY COAST          48 23   JAPAN               16 6
KENYA                50 14   KOREA, DEM PEO REP  43 12
KOREA, REPUBLIC OF   26 6    MADAGASCAR          47 22
MALAYSIA             30 6    MEXICO              40 7
MOROCCO              47 16   MOZAMBIQUE          45 18
NEPAL                46 20   NETHERLANDS         13 8
NIGERIA              49 22   PAKISTAN            44 14
PERU                 40 13   PHILIPPINES         34 10
POLAND               20 9    PORTUGAL            19 10
RHODESIA             48 14   ROMANIA             19 10
SAUDI ARABIA         49 19   SOUTH AFRICA        36 12
SPAIN                18 8    SRI LANKA           26 9
SUDAN                49 17   SWEDEN              12 11
SWITZERLAND          12 9    SYRIA               47 14
TANZANIA             47 17   THAILAND            34 10
TURKEY               34 12   USSR                18 9
UGANDA               48 17   UNITED KINGDOM      12 12
UNITED STATES        15 9    UPPER VOLTA         50 28
VENEZUELA            36 6    VIETNAM             42 17
YUGOSLAVIA           18 8    ZAIRE               45 18
;
proc plot;
   plot death*birth / hpos=86 vpos=26;
run;
```

Output 15.2   Plot of Raw Data for 1976 Birth and Death Rates: PROC PLOT

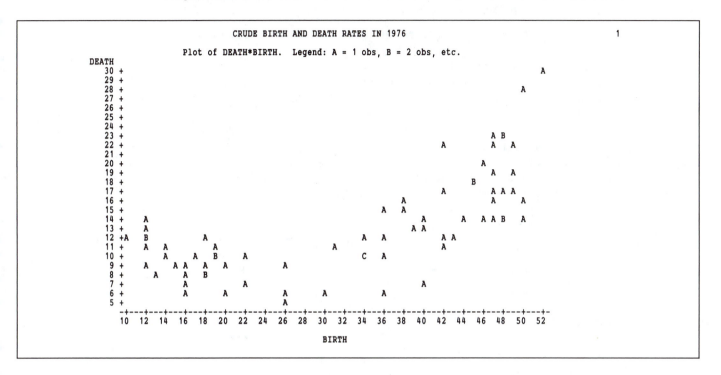

Each cluster analysis is performed by a macro called ANALYZE. The macro takes two arguments. The first, &METHOD, specifies the value of the METHOD= option to be used in the PROC CLUSTER statement. The second, &NCL, must be specified as a list of integers, separated by blanks, indicating the number of clusters desired in each scatter plot. For example, the first invocation of ANALYZE specifies the AVERAGE method and requests plots of 2, 3, 4, and 8 clusters. When two-stage density linkage is used, the K= and R= options are specified as part of the first argument.

The ANALYZE macro first invokes the CLUSTER procedure with METHOD=&METHOD, where &METHOD represents the value of the first argument to ANALYZE. A %DO loop follows that processes &NCL, the list of numbers of clusters to plot. The macro variable &K is a counter that indexes the numbers within &NCL. The %SCAN function picks out the &Kth number in &NCL, which is then assigned to the macro variable &N. When &K exceeds the number of numbers in &NCL, %SCAN returns a null string. Thus, the %DO loop executes while &N is not equal to a null string. In the %WHILE condition, a null string is indicated by the absence of any nonblank characters between the comparison operator ^= and the right parenthesis that terminates the condition.

Within the %DO loop, the TREE procedure creates an output data set containing &N clusters. The PLOT procedure then produces a scatter plot in which each observation is identified by the number of the cluster to which it belongs. The TITLE2 statement uses double quotes so that &N and &METHOD can be used within the title. At the end of the loop, &K is incremented by 1, and the next

number is extracted from &NCL by %SCAN. The following statements produce
Output 15.3 through **Output 15.12**:

```
title 'CLUSTER ANALYSIS OF BIRTH AND DEATH RATES IN 74 COUNTRIES';

%macro analyze(method,ncl);
proc cluster data=vital out=tree method=&method p=15 ccc pseudo;
   var birth death;
   title2;
%let k=1;
%let n=%scan(&ncl,&k);
%do %while(&n^=);
   proc tree data=tree noprint out=out ncl=&n;
      copy birth death;
   proc plot;
      plot death*birth=cluster / hpos=86 vpos=26;
      title2 "Plot of &n Clusters from METHOD=&METHOD";
   run;
   %let k=%eval(&k+1);
   %let n=%scan(&ncl,&k);
   %end;
%mend;

%analyze(average,2 3 4 8)
%analyze(centroid,)
%analyze(complete,3 8)
%analyze(eml,3 8)
%analyze(flexible,4)
%analyze(mcquitty,9)
%analyze(median,)
%analyze(single,3 6)
%analyze(two k=6,3)
%analyze(two k=10,2)
%analyze(two r=5,3)
%analyze(ward,8)
```

Some results differ from those in previous releases of SAS software because
of numerous ties. For average linkage, the CCC has peaks at 2, 4, 8, and 12 clusters, but the 4-cluster peak is lower than the 2-cluster peak. The pseudo F statistic
has peaks at 3, 8, and 12 clusters. The pseudo t^2 statistic drops sharply at 2 clusters, continues to fall as far as 4 clusters, and has a particularly low value at 8 and
12 clusters. However, there are not enough data to seriously consider as many
as 12 clusters. Scatter plots are given for 2, 3, 4, and 8 clusters. The results are
shown in **Output 15.3**.

Output 15.3   Birth and Death Rates: PROC CLUSTER with
METHOD=AVERAGE and PROC PLOT

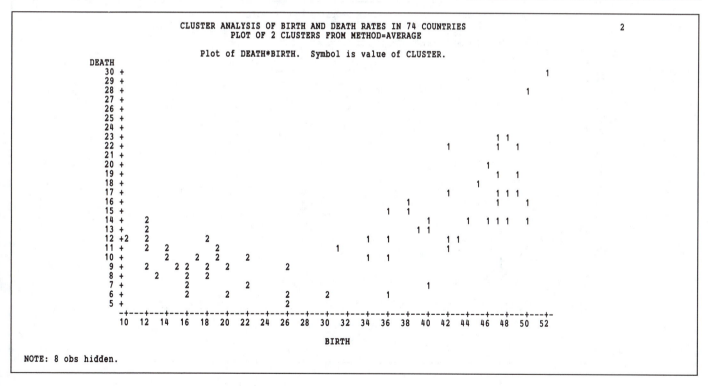

```
            CLUSTER ANALYSIS OF BIRTH AND DEATH RATES IN 74 COUNTRIES                    1

                          Average Linkage Cluster Analysis

                          Eigenvalues of the Covariance Matrix

                ❻ Eigenvalue  ❼ Difference  ❽ Proportion  ❾ Cumulative

              1      205.619       191.684      0.936528      0.93653
              2       13.936          .         0.063472      1.00000

        ❿ Root-Mean-Square Total-Sample Standard Deviation = 10.47748
          Root-Mean-Square Distance Between Observations   = 20.95496
```

Number of Clusters	Clusters Joined		Frequency of New Cluster	Semipartial R-Squared	R-Squared	⓳ Approximate Expected R-squared	⓴ Cubic Clustering Criterion	Pseudo F	Pseudo t**2	Normalized RMS Distance	Tie
15	CL18	CL34	11	0.001432	0.985902	.	.	294.71	6.77	0.204640	
14	CL20	OB41	4	0.000770	0.985132	0.977256	3.7546	305.81	2.85	0.209829	
13	CL24	CL23	15	0.003145	0.981987	0.974631	3.0341	277.12	13.93	0.214107	
12	CL22	OB72	7	0.001035	0.980951	0.971547	3.5689	290.26	4.41	0.226362	
11	CL12	CL26	11	0.003198	0.977754	0.967879	3.2820	276.89	10.75	0.248295	
10	CL15	CL19	21	0.006561	0.971192	0.963450	2.1384	239.73	20.72	0.258033	
9	CL41	OB12	6	0.001768	0.969424	0.958006	2.8703	257.61	28.33	0.281516	
8	CL17	CL16	9	0.003168	0.966257	0.951163	3.3731	269.99	11.54	0.302086	
7	CL13	CL9	21	0.009841	0.956416	0.942319	2.5856	245.04	23.09	0.332988	
6	CL10	CL32	27	0.012461	0.943955	0.930469	2.0198	229.06	23.74	0.350163	
5	CL8	CL11	20	0.013927	0.930028	0.913803	1.9963	229.28	22.86	0.377926	
4	CL27	CL7	23	0.014885	0.915144	0.888695	2.6853	251.64	17.18	0.577278	
3	CL6	CL14	31	0.028481	0.886662	0.842018	2.4796	277.72	30.71	0.587309	
2	CL4	CL5	43	0.096203	0.790460	0.709627	2.9901	271.61	68.05	0.652804	
1	CL2	CL3	74	0.790460	0.000000	0.000000	0.0000	.	271.61	1.340796	

```
            CLUSTER ANALYSIS OF BIRTH AND DEATH RATES IN 74 COUNTRIES                    2
                      PLOT OF 2 CLUSTERS FROM METHOD=AVERAGE

                 Plot of DEATH*BIRTH.  Symbol is value of CLUSTER.

DEATH
  30 +                                                               1
  29 +
  28 +                                                          1
  27 +
  26 +
  25 +
  24 +
  23 +                                                    1 1
  22 +                                           1      1   1
  21 +
  20 +                                              1
  19 +                                                 1   1
  18 +                                            1
  17 +                                         1     1 1 1
  16 +                                  1                      1
  15 +                              1  1
  14 +     2                                    1    1 1 1 1   1
  13 +     2                                 1 1
  12 +2    2        2                 1   1          1 1
  11 +     2   2      2         1                   1
  10 +       2   2  2  2     2            1   1
   9 +   2   2 2  2  2    2          2
   8 +    2     2   2  2
   7 +         2        2
   6 +         2     2          2      2
   5 +                   2
     -+---+---+---+---+---+---+---+---+---+---+---+---+---+---+---+---+---+---+---+---+---+-
      10  12  14  16  18  20  22  24  26  28  30  32  34  36  38  40  42  44  46  48  50  52
                                     BIRTH
```

NOTE: 8 obs hidden.

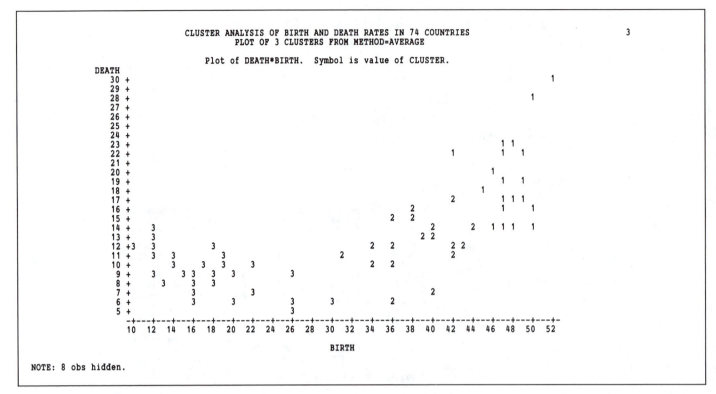

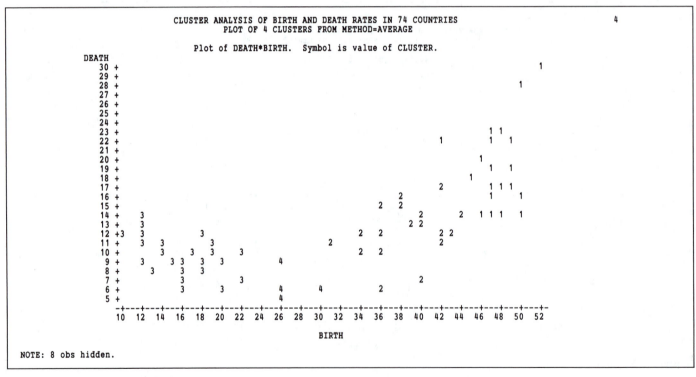

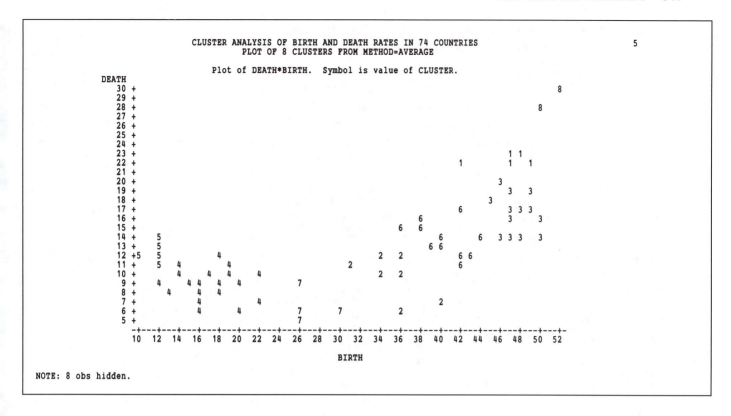

CLUSTER ANALYSIS OF BIRTH AND DEATH RATES IN 74 COUNTRIES   5
PLOT OF 8 CLUSTERS FROM METHOD=AVERAGE

Plot of DEATH*BIRTH. Symbol is value of CLUSTER.

NOTE: 8 obs hidden.

For the centroid method, the CCC has a sharp peak at 2 clusters and higher but less sharp peaks at 8 and 12 clusters. The pseudo F statistic also has peaks at 2, 8, and 12 clusters. The pseudo t^2 statistic plummets dramatically at 2 clusters and drops at 12 clusters, but provides no corroboration for 8 clusters. Both the 2- and 8-cluster partitions are the same as for average linkage. The results are shown in **Output 15.4**.

Output 15.4   Birth and Death Rates: PROC CLUSTER with
METHOD=CENTROID

```
                    CLUSTER ANALYSIS OF BIRTH AND DEATH RATES IN 74 COUNTRIES                           6

                             Centroid Hierarchical Cluster Analysis

                                Eigenvalues of the Covariance Matrix

                         Eigenvalue      Difference      Proportion      Cumulative

                    1      205.619        191.684         0.936528        0.93653
                    2       13.936           .            0.063472        1.00000

                Root-Mean-Square Total-Sample Standard Deviation = 10.47748
                Root-Mean-Square Distance Between Observations   = 20.95496
```

Number of Clusters	Clusters Joined		Frequency of New Cluster	Semipartial R-Squared	R-Squared	Approximate Expected R-squared	Cubic Clustering Criterion	Pseudo F	Pseudo t**2	Normalized Centroid Distance	Tie
15	CL19	CL30	11	0.001432	0.983287	.	.	247.94	6.77	0.178734	
14	CL18	OB41	4	0.000770	0.982517	0.977256	2.3236	259.38	2.85	0.193519	
13	OB42	OB71	2	0.000530	0.981987	0.974631	3.0341	277.12	.	0.196760	
12	CL20	OB72	7	0.001035	0.980951	0.971547	3.5689	290.26	4.41	0.209980	
11	CL15	CL21	21	0.006561	0.974390	0.967879	2.0239	239.70	20.72	0.213826	
10	CL12	CL24	11	0.003198	0.971192	0.963450	2.1384	239.73	10.75	0.214137	
9	CL17	CL13	9	0.003168	0.968024	0.958006	2.4654	245.98	11.54	0.272630	
8	CL41	OB12	6	0.001768	0.966257	0.951163	3.3731	269.99	28.33	0.278261	
7	CL16	CL8	21	0.009841	0.956416	0.942319	2.5856	245.04	23.09	0.289501	
6	CL11	CL35	27	0.012461	0.943955	0.930469	2.0198	229.06	23.74	0.312187	
5	CL9	CL10	20	0.013927	0.930028	0.913803	1.9963	229.28	22.86	0.320457	
4	CL7	CL5	41	0.080198	0.849830	0.888695	-2.9642	132.05	73.03	0.534560	
3	CL6	CL14	31	0.028481	0.821349	0.842018	-0.9180	163.21	30.71	0.546254	
2	CL25	CL4	43	0.030889	0.790460	0.709627	2.9901	271.61	10.27	0.768912	
1	CL2	CL3	74	0.790460	0.000000	0.000000	0.0000	.	271.61	1.265573	

Complete linkage shows CCC peaks at 4 and 8 clusters. The pseudo F statistic peaks at 3 and 8 clusters. The further increase of the CCC and pseudo F statistic at 11 clusters and beyond does not appear to represent real clusters. The pseudo t^2 statistic indicates 3 or 4 clusters, but does not support 8 clusters. The 4-cluster partition is the same as for average linkage except for a single point, Vietnam. The 3- and 8-cluster partitions are plotted. The results are shown in **Output 15.5**.

Output 15.5   Birth and Death Rates: PROC CLUSTER with
METHOD=COMPLETE and PROC PLOT

CLUSTER ANALYSIS OF BIRTH AND DEATH RATES IN 74 COUNTRIES   7

Complete Linkage Cluster Analysis

Eigenvalues of the Covariance Matrix

	Eigenvalue	Difference	Proportion	Cumulative
1	205.619	191.684	0.936528	0.93653
2	13.936	.	0.063472	1.00000

Root-Mean-Square Total-Sample Standard Deviation = 10.47748
Mean Distance Between Observations   = 17.59606

Number of Clusters	Clusters Joined		Frequency of New Cluster	Semipartial R-Squared	R-Squared	Approximate Expected R-squared	Cubic Clustering Criterion	Pseudo F	Pseudo t**2	Normalized Maximum Distance 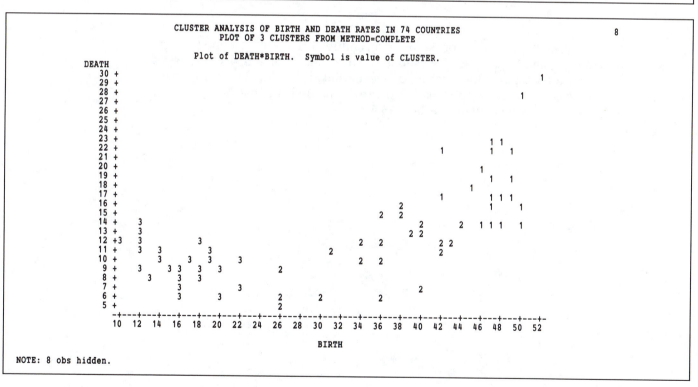 ㉖	Tie
15	CL30	OB15	7	0.000725	0.987450	.	.	331.58	5.45	0.289782	
14	CL31	CL27	10	0.001529	0.985921	0.977256	4.2362	323.21	11.40	0.345689	
13	CL24	CL38	13	0.001903	0.984019	0.974631	4.0945	312.99	13.82	0.359430	
12	CL35	CL21	14	0.004579	0.979439	0.971547	2.8894	268.49	25.24	0.401855	
11	CL20	CL13	17	0.002793	0.976646	0.967879	2.8480	263.47	9.76	0.413735	
10	CL19	CL26	10	0.003355	0.973292	0.963450	2.8183	259.14	16.33	0.458185	
9	CL12	CL16	16	0.003051	0.970241	0.958006	3.1151	264.90	5.67	0.488878	
8	CL15	CL22	9	0.003168	0.967073	0.951163	3.5965	276.92	11.54	0.559719	
7	CL18	CL9	22	0.008092	0.958981	0.942319	3.1453	261.07	13.96	0.642968	
6	CL11	CL14	27	0.015896	0.943085	0.930469	1.8755	225.35	41.03	0.738802	
5	CL8	CL10	19	0.012086	0.930999	0.913803	2.1300	232.75	20.37	0.758219	
4	CL29	CL7	24	0.015289	0.915711	0.888695	2.7517	253.49	16.87	0.971127	
3	CL5	CL17	23	0.029421	0.886290	0.842018	2.4551	276.70	26.31	1.143700	
2	CL6	CL3	50	0.306979	0.579311	0.709627	-3.3977	99.15	187.74	1.935590	
1	CL4	CL2	74	0.579311	0.000000	0.000000	0.0000	.	99.15	2.596867	

CLUSTER ANALYSIS OF BIRTH AND DEATH RATES IN 74 COUNTRIES   8
PLOT OF 3 CLUSTERS FROM METHOD=COMPLETE

Plot of DEATH*BIRTH.   Symbol is value of CLUSTER.

```
DEATH
  30 +                                                                    1
  29 +
  28 +                                                           1
  27 +
  26 +
  25 +
  24 +
  23 +                                                     1 1
  22 +                                         1         1   1
  21 +                                                   1
  20 +                                             1
  19 +                                                   1   1
  18 +                                           1
  17 +                                     1         1 1 1
  16 +                           2   2                1     1
  15 +                         2   2                            1
  14 +     3                             2       2   1 1 1   1
  13 +     3                                   2 2
  12 +3    3           3                       2 2
  11 +     3   3     3     3         2     2         2 2
  10 +       3     3 3 3   3             2   2         2
   9 +     3   3 3 3 3                 2
   8 +       3     3 3                                2
   7 +             3     3
   6 +             3     3         2     2       2
   5 +                           2
     -+---+---+---+---+---+---+---+---+---+---+---+---+---+---+---+---+---+---+---+---+---+-
      10  12  14  16  18  20  22  24  26  28  30  32  34  36  38  40  42  44  46  48  50  52
                                        BIRTH
```

NOTE: 8 obs hidden.

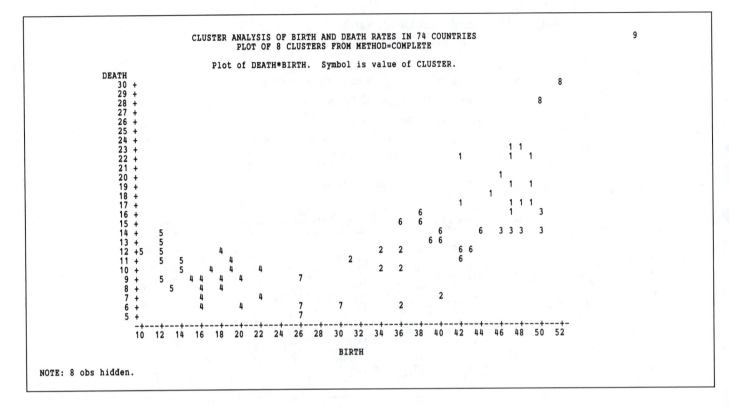

Plot of DEATH*BIRTH. Symbol is value of CLUSTER.

NOTE: 8 obs hidden.

The EML method has CCC peaks at 2, 4, 8, and 12 clusters and pseudo F statistic peaks at 3, 8, and 12 clusters. The pseudo t^2 statistic indicates 2, 3, 4, or 8 clusters. The 2-cluster partition is the same as for average linkage, while the 4-cluster partition is the same as for complete linkage. The 3- and 8-cluster partitions are plotted. The results are shown in **Output 15.6**.

Output 15.6 Birth and Death Rates: PROC CLUSTER with METHOD=EML
and PROC PLOT

CLUSTER ANALYSIS OF BIRTH AND DEATH RATES IN 74 COUNTRIES   10

Equal Variance Maximum Likelihood Method

Eigenvalues of the Covariance Matrix

	Eigenvalue	Difference	Proportion	Cumulative
1	205.619	191.684	0.936528	0.93653
2	13.936	.	0.063472	1.00000

Root-Mean-Square Total-Sample Standard Deviation = 10.47748
Root-Mean-Square Distance Between Observations = 20.95496

⑬ NCL	Clusters	Joined	⑮ FREQ	SPRSQ	RSQ	ERSQ	CCC	Pseudo F	Pseudo t**2	㉙ LNLR	㉚ LNLIKE	Tie
15	CL23	OB41	4	0.000770	0.986196	.	.	301.1	2.8	3.9907	-430.2	
14	CL32	OB72	5	0.000855	0.985341	0.977256	3.8798	310.2	7.5	3.8881	-434.1	
13	CL22	CL38	11	0.001432	0.983909	0.974631	4.0342	310.8	6.8	3.3656	-437.5	
12	CL14	OB12	6	0.001142	0.982767	0.971547	4.4601	321.4	3.8	4.7394	-442.2	
11	CL19	CL24	10	0.003355	0.979413	0.967879	3.9745	299.7	16.3	12.8644	-455.1	
10	CL42	CL12	11	0.004058	0.975354	0.963450	3.5404	281.4	14.1	11.4711	-466.5	
9	CL13	CL20	21	0.006561	0.968793	0.958006	2.6855	252.2	20.7	5.8705	-472.4	
8	CL18	CL17	9	0.003168	0.965625	0.951163	3.2040	264.9	11.5	4.7735	-477.2	
7	CL16	CL10	22	0.010079	0.955546	0.942319	2.4033	240.0	21.0	7.5572	-484.7	
6	CL9	CL34	27	0.012461	0.943085	0.930469	1.8755	225.4	23.7	7.9665	-492.7	
5	CL8	CL11	19	0.012086	0.930999	0.913803	2.1300	232.7	20.4	2.2130	-494.9	
4	CL28	CL7	24	0.015289	0.915711	0.888695	2.7517	253.5	16.9	15.8522	-510.8	
3	CL6	CL15	31	0.028481	0.887229	0.842018	2.5170	279.3	30.7	19.2411	-530.0	
2	CL4	CL5	43	0.096770	0.790460	0.709627	2.9901	271.6	69.1	32.6669	-562.7	
1	CL2	CL3	74	0.790460	0.000000	0.000000	0.0000	.	271.6	130.7	-693.4	

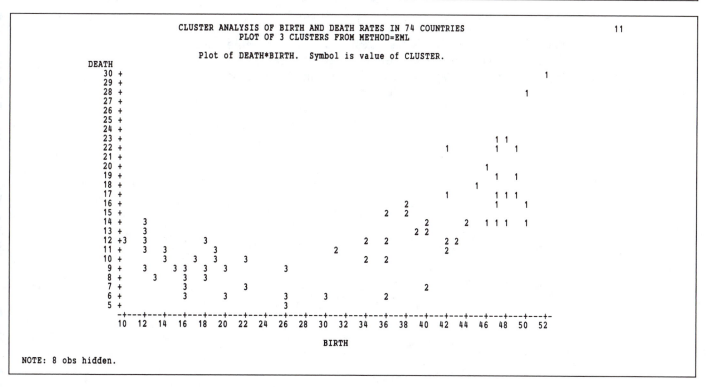

CLUSTER ANALYSIS OF BIRTH AND DEATH RATES IN 74 COUNTRIES   11
PLOT OF 3 CLUSTERS FROM METHOD=EML

Plot of DEATH*BIRTH. Symbol is value of CLUSTER.

NOTE: 8 obs hidden.

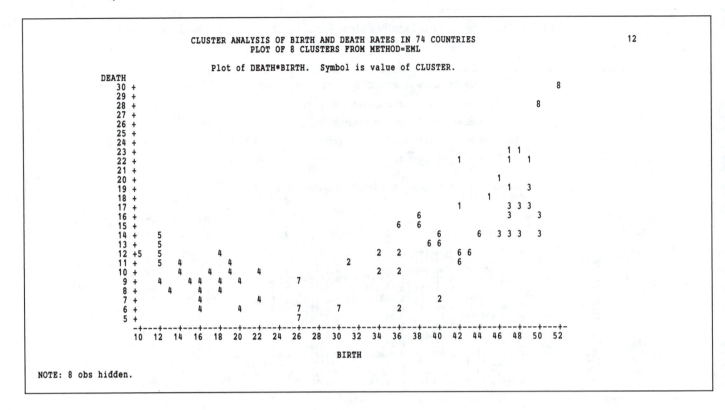

```
                CLUSTER ANALYSIS OF BIRTH AND DEATH RATES IN 74 COUNTRIES                    12
                           PLOT OF 8 CLUSTERS FROM METHOD=EML

                     Plot of DEATH*BIRTH.   Symbol is value of CLUSTER.

   DEATH
     30 +                                                                          8
     29 +
     28 +                                                                  8
     27 +
     26 +
     25 +
     24 +
     23 +                                                          1 1
     22 +                                              1           1   1
     21 +
     20 +                                                      1
     19 +                                                      1   3
     18 +                                                  1
     17 +                                          1           3 3 3
     16 +                              6                       3       3
     15 +                          6 6
     14 +     5                              6         6   3 3 3   3
     13 +     5                          6 6
     12 +5    5           4                           6 6
     11 +     5       4   4                 2       6
     10 +       4   4 4 4   4     4           2 2
      9 +   4     4 4   4   4       7
      8 +     4       4 4
      7 +         4       4                     2
      6 +         4       4     7     7       2
      5 +                     7
        -+---+---+---+---+---+---+---+---+---+---+---+---+---+---+---+---+---+---+---+---+---+-
        10  12  14  16  18  20  22  24  26  28  30  32  34  36  38  40  42  44  46  48  50  52

                                              BIRTH

NOTE: 8 obs hidden.
```

For the flexible-beta method, the CCC suggests 4 or 8 clusters while the pseudo F statistic indicates 3 or 8 or more. The pseudo t^2 statistic supports 3 or 4 clusters. The 3-cluster partition is the same as for complete linkage. The 4-cluster partition is plotted. The results are shown in **Output 15.7**.

Output 15.7   Birth and Death Rates: PROC CLUSTER with
METHOD=FLEXIBLE and PROC PLOT

CLUSTER ANALYSIS OF BIRTH AND DEATH RATES IN 74 COUNTRIES   13

Flexible-Beta Cluster Analysis

Eigenvalues of the Covariance Matrix   **31**

	Eigenvalue	Difference	Proportion	Cumulative
1	205.619	191.684	0.936528	0.93653
2	13.936	.	0.063472	1.00000

Beta = -0.25

Root-Mean-Square Total-Sample Standard Deviation = 10.47748
Mean Distance Between Observations   = 17.59606

Number of Clusters	Clusters Joined		Frequency of New Cluster	Semipartial R-Squared	R-Squared	Approximate Expected R-squared	Cubic Clustering Criterion	Pseudo F	Pseudo t**2	Normalized Flexible Distance	Tie
15	OB12	CL25	4	0.001066	0.987402	.	.	330.31	5.12	0.343431	
14	CL24	CL37	8	0.001586	0.985816	0.977256	4.1707	320.79	8.80	0.352825	
13	CL31	CL28	10	0.001577	0.984239	0.974631	4.2175	317.44	12.32	0.399275	
12	CL19	CL20	13	0.002574	0.981664	0.971547	3.9082	301.76	12.35	0.464427	
11	CL14	CL21	17	0.003071	0.978593	0.967879	3.6257	288.00	11.48	0.564675	
10	CL16	CL27	10	0.003355	0.975239	0.963450	3.4983	280.07	16.33	0.566741	
9	CL18	CL23	9	0.003168	0.972071	0.958006	3.6893	282.79	11.54	0.622744	
8	CL38	CL15	9	0.004619	0.967452	0.951163	3.7022	280.25	18.67	0.691317	
7	CL9	CL17	13	0.012914	0.954538	0.942319	2.1964	234.46	22.20	0.921506	
6	CL12	CL8	22	0.008471	0.946067	0.930469	2.3796	238.56	15.10	0.922004	
5	CL11	CL13	27	0.015896	0.930171	0.913803	2.0158	229.78	41.03	1.257746	
4	CL33	CL6	24	0.015289	0.914883	0.888695	2.6549	250.80	16.87	1.513395	
3	CL7	CL10	23	0.028593	0.886290	0.842018	2.4551	276.70	24.70	1.803143	
2	CL4	CL3	47	0.146462	0.739828	0.709627	1.0065	204.74	74.79	3.877577	
1	CL2	CL5	74	0.739828	0.000000	0.000000	0.0000	.	204.74	10.17657	

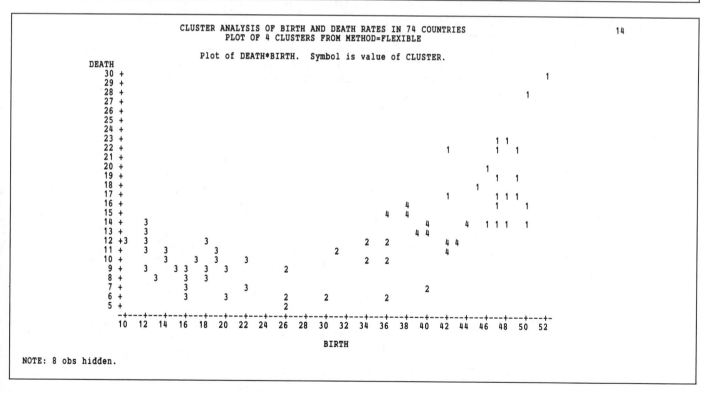

For McQuitty's similarity analysis and the median method, the statistics indicate 9 clusters. The 9-cluster partition is plotted. The results are shown in **Output 15.8** and **Output 15.9**.

Output 15.8   Birth and Death Rates: PROC CLUSTER with METHOD=MCQUITTY and PROC PLOT

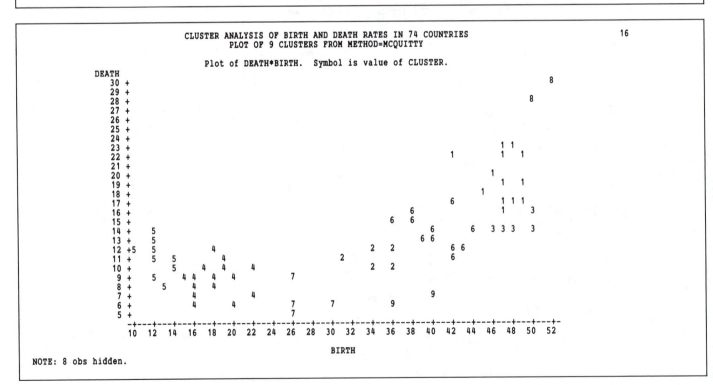

```
                   CLUSTER ANALYSIS OF BIRTH AND DEATH RATES IN 74 COUNTRIES                        15

                            McQuitty's Similarity Analysis

                          Eigenvalues of the Covariance Matrix

                     Eigenvalue     Difference     Proportion     Cumulative

                 1      205.619      191.684        0.936528       0.93653
                 2       13.936         .           0.063472       1.00000

              Root-Mean-Square Total-Sample Standard Deviation = 10.47748
              Mean Distance Between Observations                = 17.59606                       ㉝
```

Number of Clusters	Clusters Joined		Frequency of New Cluster	Semipartial R-Squared	R-Squared	Approximate Expected R-squared	Cubic Clustering Criterion	Pseudo F	Pseudo t**2	Normalized McQuitty's Similarity Tie
15	CL31	OB15	7	0.000725	0.985723	.	.	290.96	5.45	0.234748
14	CL27	OB72	5	0.001154	0.984568	0.977256	3.4259	294.47	7.40	0.253041
13	CL40	CL22	14	0.004579	0.979989	0.974631	2.1022	248.94	25.24	0.253803
12	CL20	OB41	4	0.000770	0.979220	0.971547	2.7949	265.60	2.85	0.257488
11	CL21	CL14	11	0.003079	0.976141	0.967879	2.6565	257.75	9.91	0.286648
10	CL17	CL24	17	0.002948	0.973193	0.963450	2.7852	258.16	10.69	0.297551
9	CL13	OB12	15	0.001970	0.971223	0.958006	3.4186	274.21	3.79	0.356484
8	CL15	CL12	11	0.010924	0.960299	0.951163	1.8897	228.06	36.40	0.406224
7	CL10	CL18	27	0.015896	0.944403	0.942319	0.3396	189.68	41.03	0.432286
6	CL23	CL9	21	0.008204	0.936199	0.930469	0.8056	199.56	16.01	0.467426
5	CL6	CL11	32	0.030191	0.906008	0.913803	-0.8287	166.28	38.03	0.484724
4	CL8	CL16	13	0.005158	0.900850	0.888695	1.1445	212.00	4.01	0.490149
3	CL5	CL4	45	0.124390	0.776460	0.842018	-2.5916	123.31	72.95	0.782193
2	CL25	CL3	47	0.036632	0.739828	0.709627	1.0065	204.74	8.33	1.213211
1	CL2	CL7	74	0.739828	0.000000	0.000000	0.0000	.	204.74	1.858258

```
               CLUSTER ANALYSIS OF BIRTH AND DEATH RATES IN 74 COUNTRIES                  16
                        PLOT OF 9 CLUSTERS FROM METHOD=MCQUITTY

                   Plot of DEATH*BIRTH.  Symbol is value of CLUSTER.

  DEATH
     30 +                                                                       8
     29 +
     28 +                                                                  8
     27 +
     26 +
     25 +
     24 +
     23 +                                                              1 1
     22 +                                            1              1    1
     21 +
     20 +                                                    1
     19 +                                                 1    1
     18 +                                            1
     17 +                                    6                   1 1 1
     16 +                             6                                  1   3
     15 +                        6  6                         6  3 3 3   3
     14 +    5                              6               6
     13 +    5                                            6 6
     12 +5   5              4              2    2        6 6
     11 +    5       5         4        2         2      6
     10 +    5  5      4    4   4                2   2
      9 +    5     4  4   4    4         7
      8 +      5      4   4
      7 +              4       4                         9
      6 +             4     4         7     7       9
      5 +                            7
        -+---+---+---+---+---+---+---+---+---+---+---+---+---+---+---+---+---+---+---+---+---+-
         10  12  14  16  18  20  22  24  26  28  30  32  34  36  38  40  42  44  46  48  50  52

                                           BIRTH

NOTE: 8 obs hidden.
```

Output 15.9 Birth and Death Rates: PROC CLUSTER with
METHOD=MEDIAN

CLUSTER ANALYSIS OF BIRTH AND DEATH RATES IN 74 COUNTRIES   17

Median Hierarchical Cluster Analysis

Eigenvalues of the Covariance Matrix

	Eigenvalue	Difference	Proportion	Cumulative
1	205.619	191.684	0.936528	0.93653
2	13.936	.	0.063472	1.00000

Root-Mean-Square Total-Sample Standard Deviation = 10.47748
Root-Mean-Square Distance Between Observations   = 20.95496

Number of Clusters	Clusters Joined		Frequency of New Cluster	Semipartial R-Squared	R-Squared	Approximate Expected R-squared	Cubic Clustering Criterion	Pseudo F	Pseudo t**2	Normalized Median Distance ㉜	Tie
15	CL36	OB15	7	0.000725	0.983306	.	.	248.22	5.45	0.190886	
14	CL40	CL24	14	0.004579	0.978726	0.977256	0.5902	212.34	25.24	0.194624	
13	OB42	OB71	2	0.000530	0.978196	0.974631	1.3417	228.05	.	0.196760	
12	CL18	OB41	4	0.000770	0.977426	0.971547	2.0587	244.05	2.85	0.199989	
11	CL25	OB72	5	0.001154	0.976272	0.967879	2.7059	259.21	7.40	0.205690	
10	CL20	CL11	11	0.003079	0.973193	0.963450	2.7852	258.16	9.91	0.204585	
9	CL14	OB12	15	0.001970	0.971223	0.958006	3.4186	274.21	3.79	0.279258	
8	CL15	CL12	11	0.010924	0.960299	0.951163	1.8897	228.06	36.40	0.317053	
7	CL22	CL9	21	0.008204	0.952095	0.942319	1.7134	221.93	16.01	0.365785	
6	CL7	CL10	32	0.030191	0.921904	0.930469	-1.0882	160.54	38.03	0.332639	
5	CL16	CL19	27	0.015896	0.906008	0.913803	-0.8287	166.28	41.03	0.370001	
4	CL8	CL13	13	0.005158	0.900850	0.888695	1.1445	212.00	4.01	0.374537	
3	CL6	CL4	45	0.124390	0.776460	0.842018	-2.5916	123.31	72.95	0.605848	
2	CL23	CL3	47	0.036632	0.739828	0.709627	1.0065	204.74	8.33	0.997064	
1	CL2	CL5	74	0.739828	0.000000	0.000000	0.0000	.	204.74	1.489842	

The CCC and pseudo *F* statistics are not appropriate for use with single linkage because of the method's tendency to chop off tails of distributions. The pseudo t^2 statistic can be used by looking for *large* values and taking the number of clusters to be one greater than the level at which the large pseudo t^2 value is printed. For these data there are large values at levels 2, 5, and 11, suggesting 3, 6, or 12 clusters. The 3-cluster partition is the same as the 2-cluster partition from average linkage except that two outliers, Afghanistan and Upper Volta, have been separated. The results are shown in **Output 15.10**.

Output 15.10   Birth and Death Rates: PROC CLUSTER with
METHOD=SINGLE and PROC PLOT

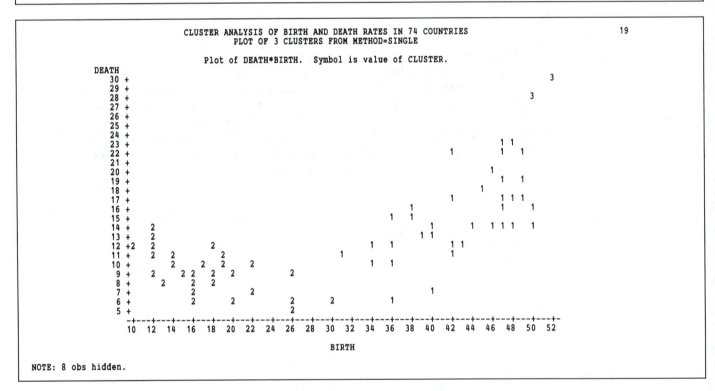

```
                    CLUSTER ANALYSIS OF BIRTH AND DEATH RATES IN 74 COUNTRIES                        18

                              Single Linkage Cluster Analysis

                             Eigenvalues of the Covariance Matrix

                       Eigenvalue      Difference      Proportion      Cumulative

                    1    205.619        191.684         0.936528        0.93653
                    2     13.936           .            0.063472        1.00000

              Root-Mean-Square Total-Sample Standard Deviation = 10.47748
              Mean Distance Between Observations                =  17.59606

                                                                                      Normalized
 Number                   Frequency                    Approximate      Cubic
   of                      of New     Semipartial       Expected     Clustering   Pseudo   Pseudo    Minimum
Clusters Clusters Joined   Cluster    R-Squared  R-Squared R-squared  Criterion      F      t**2    Distance  Tie

   15   CL17    CL16         28       0.022820   0.927695      .           .        54.07   21.25   0.127078   T
   14   CL15    CL66         30       0.000302   0.927393   0.977256   -10.2521     58.95    0.17   0.127078
   13   CL19    CL18         27       0.004721   0.922673   0.974631    -9.8756     60.65    5.66   0.160742   T
   12   OB1     OB70          2       0.000250   0.922423   0.971547    -8.9215     67.02     .     0.160742
   11   CL14    CL21         36       0.044574   0.877849   0.967879   -11.9349     45.28   29.31   0.170493   T
   10   CL55    OB58          3       0.000510   0.877340   0.963450   -10.8777     50.86   16.33   0.170493
    9   CL11    OB15         37       0.010520   0.866819   0.958006   -10.4401     52.88    3.82   0.179715   T
    8   CL9     OB72         38       0.000219   0.866601   0.951163    -9.1678     61.25    0.07   0.179715
    7   CL10    OB41          4       0.000770   0.865831   0.942319    -7.7885     72.06    2.85   0.227324   T
    6   CL8     OB71         39       0.008405   0.857426   0.930469    -6.7265     81.79    2.91   0.227324
    5   CL13    CL7          31       0.028481   0.828945   0.913803    -6.5605     83.59   30.71   0.234320   T
    4   CL6     OB42         40       0.004579   0.824366   0.888695    -4.5146    109.52    1.51   0.234320
    3   CL4     OB12         41       0.003017   0.821349   0.842018    -0.9180    163.21    0.98   0.254155
    2   CL3     CL5          72       0.744191   0.077158   0.709627   -10.5974      6.02  292.00   0.289782
    1   CL12    CL2          74       0.077158   0.000000   0.000000     0.0000      .       6.02   0.306044
```

```
                    CLUSTER ANALYSIS OF BIRTH AND DEATH RATES IN 74 COUNTRIES                        19
                             PLOT OF 3 CLUSTERS FROM METHOD=SINGLE

                         Plot of DEATH*BIRTH.  Symbol is value of CLUSTER.

   DEATH
     30 +                                                                         3
     29 +
     28 +                                                                  3
     27 +
     26 +
     25 +
     24 +
     23 +                                                      1 1
     22 +                                    1              1    1
     21 +
     20 +                                                 1
     19 +                                              1    1
     18 +                                        1
     17 +                                    1         1 1 1
     16 +                              1              1    1
     15 +                            1 1
     14 +   2                     1        1  1 1 1    1
     13 +   2                            1 1
     12 + 2  2            2                1 1
     11 +   2  2        2       1     1  1    1
     10 +   2  2  2  2  2      2           1  1
      9 +   2   2 2  2  2  2          2
      8 +    2    2  2
      7 +        2      2
      6 +        2     2       2    2      1
      5 +              2
        -+---+---+---+---+---+---+---+---+---+---+---+---+---+---+---+---+---+---+---+---+---+---+-
         10  12  14  16  18  20  22  24  26  28  30  32  34  36  38  40  42  44  46  48  50  52
                                                  BIRTH

NOTE: 8 obs hidden.
```

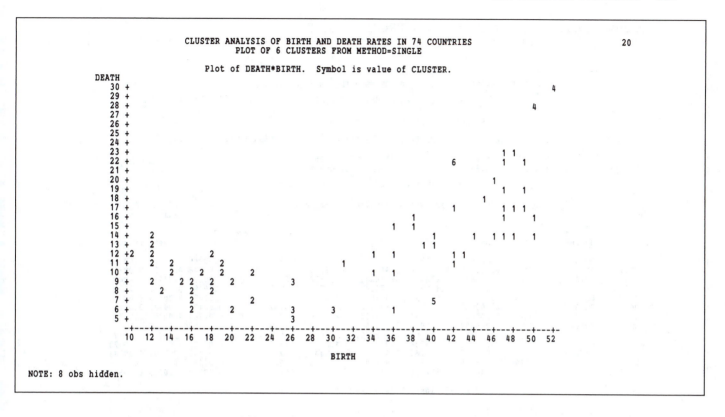

CLUSTER ANALYSIS OF BIRTH AND DEATH RATES IN 74 COUNTRIES
PLOT OF 6 CLUSTERS FROM METHOD=SINGLE

Plot of DEATH*BIRTH. Symbol is value of CLUSTER.

NOTE: 8 obs hidden.

For kth-nearest-neighbor density linkage, the number of modes as a function of k is as follows (not all of these analyses are shown):

k	modes
3	12
4	7
5	5
6–7	3
8–26	2
28+	1

Thus, there is strong evidence of 2 modes and a slight indication of the possibility of 3 modes. Scatter plots are given for 2 clusters with K=10, and 3 clusters with K=6. Uniform-kernel density linkage gives similar results except that Afghanistan and Upper Volta are considered a separate mode. The 3-cluster scatter plot with R=5 is shown. The results are shown in **Output 15.11.**

Output 15.11   Birth and Death Rates: PROC CLUSTER with
METHOD=TWOSTAGE and PROC PLOT

```
                CLUSTER ANALYSIS OF BIRTH AND DEATH RATES IN 74 COUNTRIES                    21

                          Two-Stage Density Linkage Clustering

                          Eigenvalues of the Covariance Matrix

                     Eigenvalue      Difference      Proportion      Cumulative

              1        205.619        191.684         0.936528        0.93653
              2         13.936            .            0.063472       1.00000

                                      K = 6

             Root-Mean-Square Total-Sample Standard Deviation = 10.47748
```

											Maximum Density in Each Cluster	
NCL	Clusters	Joined	FREQ	SPRSQ	RSQ	ERSQ	CCC	Pseudo F	Pseudo t**2	Fusion Density	Lesser	Greater
15	CL16	OB30	13	0.000693	0.944943	.	.	72.3	0.9	0.00246	0.00199	0.00323
14	CL15	OB31	14	0.000919	0.944024	0.977256	-7.9545	77.8	1.2	0.00246	0.00199	0.00323
13	CL17	OB72	23	0.001620	0.942404	0.974631	-7.2652	83.2	1.7	0.00206	0.00152	0.00688
12	CL14	OB15	15	0.002461	0.939943	0.971547	-6.6447	88.2	3.1	0.00188	0.00132	0.00323
11	CL12	OB71	16	0.002348	0.937595	0.967879	-5.9341	94.7	2.6	0.00184	0.00129	0.00323
10	OB12	CL13	24	0.002668	0.934927	0.963450	-5.1825	102.2	2.7	0.00172	0.00103	0.00688
9	CL11	OB41	17	0.004802	0.930125	0.958006	-4.6058	108.2	4.7	0.00161	0.00108	0.00323
8	CL19	OB58	28	0.006043	0.924081	0.951163	-4.0250	114.8	6.1	0.00147	0.00103	0.0129
7	CL8	OB39	29	0.006401	0.917681	0.942319	-3.2815	124.5	5.5	0.00123	0.00081	0.0129
6	CL9	OB42	18	0.001943	0.915738	0.930469	-1.8000	147.8	1.6	0.00123	0.00076	0.00323
5	CL10	OB70	25	0.006977	0.908761	0.913803	-0.5442	171.8	6.6	0.00112	0.0007	0.00688
4	CL7	OB16	30	0.006459	0.902302	0.888695	1.2906	215.5	4.8	0.00103	0.0007	0.0129
3	OB1	CL5	26	0.010040	0.892262	0.842018	2.8579	294.0	7.7	0.00062	0.00035	0.00688

```
                        3 modal clusters have been formed.
```

											Maximum Density in Each Cluster	
NCL	Clusters	Joined	FREQ	SPRSQ	RSQ	ERSQ	CCC	Pseudo F	Pseudo t**2	Fusion Density	Lesser	Greater
2	CL6	CL3	44	0.107277	0.784986	0.709627	2.7537	262.9	71.2	0.00291	0.00323	0.00688
1	CL4	CL2	74	0.784986	0.000000	0.000000	0.0000	.	262.9	0.00105	0.00688	0.0129

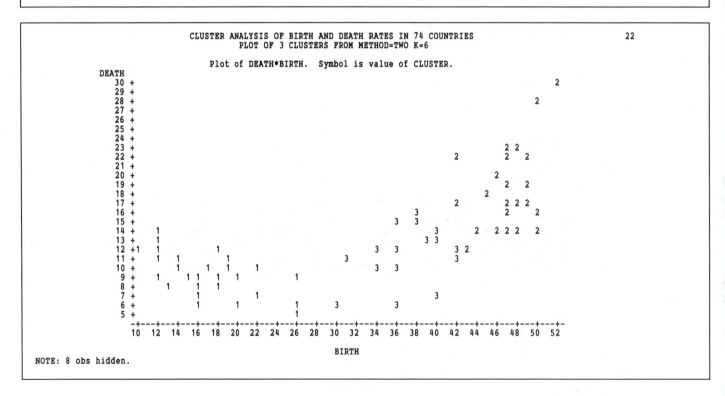

```
                CLUSTER ANALYSIS OF BIRTH AND DEATH RATES IN 74 COUNTRIES                    22
                          PLOT OF 3 CLUSTERS FROM METHOD=TWO K=6

                    Plot of DEATH*BIRTH.  Symbol is value of CLUSTER.
```

NOTE: 8 obs hidden.

CLUSTER ANALYSIS OF BIRTH AND DEATH RATES IN 74 COUNTRIES   23

Two-Stage Density Linkage Clustering

Eigenvalues of the Covariance Matrix

	Eigenvalue	Difference	Proportion	Cumulative
1	205.619	191.684	0.936528	0.93653
2	13.936	.	0.063472	1.00000

K = 10

Root-Mean-Square Total-Sample Standard Deviation = 10.47748

										Maximum Density in Each Cluster	
NCL	Clusters	Joined	FREQ	SPRSQ	RSQ	ERSQ	CCC	Pseudo F	Pseudo t**2	Fusion Density	Lesser	Greater
15	OB20	CL16	34	0.002092	0.901873	.	.	38.7	0.9	0.00185	0.00134	0.00602
14	OB31	CL15	35	0.002382	0.899491	0.977256	-13.1243	41.3	1.1	0.00179	0.00134	0.00602
13	OB17	CL14	36	0.008524	0.890967	0.974631	-12.9201	41.5	3.9	0.00176	0.00134	0.00602
12	CL13	OB50	37	0.008063	0.882904	0.971547	-12.5836	42.5	3.4	0.00176	0.00134	0.00602
11	CL12	OB64	38	0.007639	0.875266	0.967879	-12.1219	44.2	3.0	0.00176	0.00134	0.00602
10	CL18	OB58	28	0.006043	0.869222	0.963450	-11.4533	47.3	6.1	0.00158	0.00095	0.00946
9	OB42	CL11	39	0.005298	0.863924	0.958006	-10.6346	51.6	2.0	0.00158	0.00115	0.00602
8	OB15	CL9	40	0.010301	0.853623	0.951163	-10.0148	55.0	3.7	0.00148	0.00105	0.00602
7	CL8	OB71	41	0.008277	0.845347	0.942319	-9.0994	61.0	2.8	0.00128	0.00086	0.00602
6	CL10	OB39	29	0.006401	0.838946	0.930469	-7.8682	70.8	5.5	0.00126	0.00073	0.00946
5	OB41	CL7	42	0.014995	0.823950	0.913803	-6.8360	80.7	4.9	0.00123	0.00091	0.00602
4	CL6	OB16	30	0.006459	0.817492	0.888695	-4.8945	104.5	4.8	0.00121	0.00065	0.00946
3	CL5	OB70	43	0.013868	0.803623	0.842018	-1.6243	145.3	4.1	0.00087	0.00048	0.00602
2	OB1	CL3	44	0.018638	0.784986	0.709627	2.7537	262.9	5.2	0.00056	0.00029	0.00602

2 modal clusters have been formed.

										Maximum Density in Each Cluster	
NCL	Clusters	Joined	FREQ	SPRSQ	RSQ	ERSQ	CCC	Pseudo F	Pseudo t**2	Fusion Density	Lesser	Greater
1	CL4	CL2	74	0.784986	0.000000	0.000000	0.0000	.	262.9	0.001	0.00602	0.00946

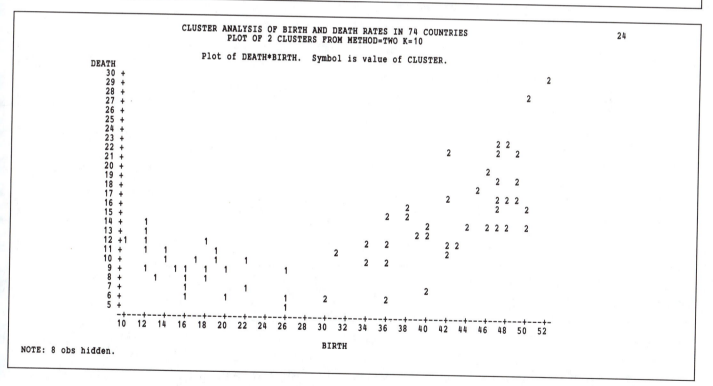

CLUSTER ANALYSIS OF BIRTH AND DEATH RATES IN 74 COUNTRIES   24
PLOT OF 2 CLUSTERS FROM METHOD=TWO K=10

Plot of DEATH*BIRTH. Symbol is value of CLUSTER.

NOTE: 8 obs hidden.

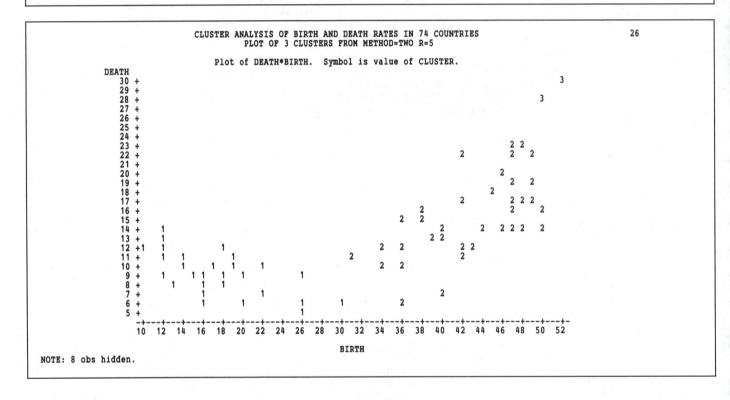

CLUSTER ANALYSIS OF BIRTH AND DEATH RATES IN 74 COUNTRIES   25

Two-Stage Density Linkage Clustering

Eigenvalues of the Covariance Matrix

	Eigenvalue	Difference	Proportion	Cumulative
1	205.619	191.684	0.936528	0.93653
2	13.936	.	0.063472	1.00000

R = 5

Root-Mean-Square Total-Sample Standard Deviation = 10.47748

										Pseudo	Pseudo	Fusion	Maximum Density in Each Cluster	
NCL	Clusters	Joined	FREQ	SPRSQ	RSQ	ERSQ	CCC			Pseudo F	Pseudo t**2	Fusion Density	Lesser	Greater
15	CL16	OB31	34	0.002429	0.901910	.	.			38.7	1.1	0.00175	0.00138	0.0031
14	OB17	CL15	35	0.008466	0.893444	0.977256	-13.6403			38.7	3.9	0.00165	0.00138	0.0031
13	CL14	OB50	36	0.007995	0.885449	0.974631	-13.3576			39.3	3.4	0.00165	0.00138	0.0031
12	CL13	OB64	37	0.007563	0.877886	0.971547	-12.9568			40.5	3.0	0.00165	0.00138	0.0031
11	OB12	CL12	38	0.002620	0.875266	0.967879	-12.1219			44.2	1.0	0.00153	0.00103	0.0031
10	CL28	OB58	28	0.006043	0.869222	0.963450	-11.4533			47.3	6.1	0.00141	0.00103	0.00379
9	CL11	OB71	39	0.008994	0.860229	0.958006	-10.8770			50.0	3.4	0.00134	0.00103	0.0031
8	CL10	OB39	29	0.006401	0.853828	0.951163	-10.0020			55.1	5.5	0.00124	0.00086	0.00379
7	OB16	CL8	30	0.006459	0.847369	0.942319	-8.9780			62.0	4.8	0.00124	0.00086	0.00379
6	OB15	CL9	40	0.010135	0.837234	0.930469	-7.9673			70.0	3.6	0.00111	0.00086	0.0031
5	CL6	OB42	41	0.004747	0.832487	0.913803	-6.3602			85.7	1.6	0.00101	0.00069	0.0031
4	CL7	OB41	31	0.010889	0.821598	0.888695	-4.6693			107.5	7.1	0.00083	0.00069	0.00379
3	OB1	OB70	2	0.000250	0.821349	0.842018	-0.9180			163.2	.	0.00034	0.00034	0.00034

3 modal clusters have been formed.

CLUSTER ANALYSIS OF BIRTH AND DEATH RATES IN 74 COUNTRIES   26
PLOT OF 3 CLUSTERS FROM METHOD=TWO R=5

Plot of DEATH*BIRTH. Symbol is value of CLUSTER.

```
DEATH
  30 +                                                              3
  29 +
  28 +                                                         3
  27 +
  26 +
  25 +
  24 +
  23 +                                               2 2
  22 +                                     2         2   2
  21 +
  20 +                                           2
  19 +                                         2    2   2
  18 +                                       2
  17 +                                 2          2 2 2
  16 +                                           2       2
  15 +                           2   2
  14 +   1                               2      2  2 2 2   2
  13 +   1                             2 2
  12 +1  1           1              2   2      2 2
  11 +   1   1      1        2       2          2
  10 +   1   1   1  1   1                2   2
   9 + 1   1 1 1   1       1
   8 +   1   1 1
   7 +       1               2
   6 +       1       1     1       2
   5 +               1
     +--+---+---+---+---+---+---+---+---+---+---+---+---+---+---+---+---+---+---+---+---+-
       10  12  14  16  18  20  22  24  26  28  30  32  34  36  38  40  42  44  46  48  50  52
                                          BIRTH
```

NOTE: 8 obs hidden.

For Ward's method, the CCC indicates 2, 4, 8, or 12 clusters while the pseudo *F* statistic suggests 3, 8, or 12 clusters. The 2-cluster partition is the same as for average linkage, while the 3-cluster partition differs only for Vietnam. The 4-cluster partition is the same as for complete linkage. The 8-cluster partition is plotted. The results are shown in **Output 15.12**.

Output 15.12   Birth and Death Rates: PROC CLUSTER with
METHOD=WARD and PROC PLOT

```
                    CLUSTER ANALYSIS OF BIRTH AND DEATH RATES IN 74 COUNTRIES                    27

                          Ward's Minimum Variance Cluster Analysis

                              Eigenvalues of the Covariance Matrix

                        Eigenvalue      Difference      Proportion      Cumulative

                  1       205.619        191.684         0.936528        0.93653
                  2        13.936           .            0.063472        1.00000

                 Root-Mean-Square Total-Sample Standard Deviation = 10.47748
                 Root-Mean-Square Distance Between Observations    = 20.95496
```

Number of Clusters	Clusters Joined		Frequency of New Cluster	Semipartial R-Squared	R-Squared	Approximate Expected R-squared	Cubic Clustering Criterion	Pseudo F	Pseudo t**2	Tie
15	OB12	CL26	4	0.001066	0.987234	.	.	325.90	5.12	
14	CL39	CL32	8	0.001274	0.985960	0.977256	4.2607	324.12	13.13	
13	CL31	CL27	10	0.001577	0.984383	0.974631	4.2987	320.41	12.32	
12	CL24	CL38	8	0.001586	0.982797	0.971547	4.4752	322.00	8.80	
11	CL12	CL21	17	0.003071	0.979726	0.967879	4.1113	304.44	11.48	
10	CL19	CL22	9	0.003168	0.976558	0.963450	3.9902	296.24	11.54	
9	CL17	CL28	10	0.003355	0.973203	0.958006	4.0637	295.08	16.33	
8	CL14	CL15	12	0.003978	0.969226	0.951163	4.2134	296.95	11.92	
7	CL33	CL8	14	0.010141	0.959085	0.942319	3.1686	261.76	16.09	
6	CL10	CL9	19	0.012086	0.946998	0.930469	2.5428	243.00	20.37	
5	CL7	CL16	24	0.015392	0.931606	0.913803	2.2146	234.97	17.07	
4	CL11	CL13	27	0.015896	0.915711	0.888695	2.7517	253.49	41.03	
3	CL4	CL18	31	0.028481	0.887229	0.842018	2.5170	279.30	30.71	
2	CL5	CL6	43	0.096770	0.790460	0.709627	2.9901	271.61	69.12	
1	CL2	CL3	74	0.790460	0.000000	0.000000	0.0000	.	271.61	

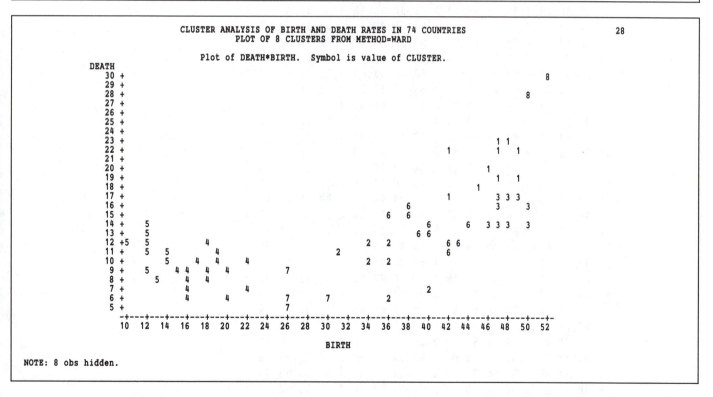

```
                    CLUSTER ANALYSIS OF BIRTH AND DEATH RATES IN 74 COUNTRIES                    28
                              PLOT OF 8 CLUSTERS FROM METHOD=WARD

                         Plot of DEATH*BIRTH.   Symbol is value of CLUSTER.
     DEATH
       30 +                                                                      8
       29 +
       28 +                                                                 8
       27 +
       26 +
       25 +
       24 +
       23 +                                                           1 1
       22 +                                                     1     1 1
       21 +
       20 +                                                   1
       19 +                                                     1   1
       18 +                                               1
       17 +                                             1   3 3 3
       16 +                                6                3       3
       15 +                             6  6
       14 +    5                                       6   3 3 3   3
       13 +    5                                    6 6
       12 +5   5          4                   2  2        6 6
       11 +    5       5                   2               6
       10 +     5     4   4  4   4                2  2
        9 +   5   4  4  4   4              7
        8 +  5        4  4
        7 +          4         4                       2
        6 +          4     4       7    7         2
        5 +                   7
           --+---+---+---+---+---+---+---+---+---+---+---+---+---+---+---+---+---+---+---+---+---+-
            10  12  14  16  18  20  22  24  26  28  30  32  34  36  38  40  42  44  46  48  50  52
                                               BIRTH
  NOTE: 8 obs hidden.
```

In summary, most of the clustering methods indicate 2, 3, 4, or 8 clusters. Most methods agree at the 2-cluster level, but at the other levels, there is considerable disagreement about the composition of the clusters. The presence of numerous ties also complicates the analysis; see **Example 4**.

Example 3: Cluster Analysis of Fisher Iris Data

The iris data published by Fisher (1936) have been widely used for examples in discriminant analysis and cluster analysis. The sepal length, sepal width, petal length, and petal width were measured in millimeters on fifty iris specimens from each of three species, *Iris setosa, I. versicolor,* and *I. virginica.* Mezzich and Solomon (1980) discuss a variety of cluster analyses of the iris data.

This example analyzes the iris data by Ward's method and two-stage density linkage and then illustrates how the FASTCLUS procedure can be used in combination with CLUSTER to analyze large data sets.

```
title 'CLUSTER ANALYSIS OF FISHER (1936) IRIS DATA';
data iris;
   input sepallen sepalwid petallen petalwid spec_no @@;
   if spec_no=1 then species='SETOSA    ';
   if spec_no=2 then species='VERSICOLOR';
   if spec_no=3 then species='VIRGINICA ';
   label sepallen='SEPAL LENGTH IN MM.'
         sepalwid='SEPAL WIDTH  IN MM.'
         petallen='PETAL LENGTH IN MM.'
         petalwid='PETAL WIDTH  IN MM.';
   cards;
50 33 14 02 1 64 28 56 22 3 65 28 46 15 2 67 31 56 24 3
63 28 51 15 3 46 34 14 03 1 69 31 51 23 3 62 22 45 15 2
59 32 48 18 2 46 36 10 02 1 61 30 46 14 2 60 27 51 16 2
65 30 52 20 3 56 25 39 11 2 65 30 55 18 3 58 27 51 19 3
68 32 59 23 3 51 33 17 05 1 57 28 45 13 2 62 34 54 23 3
77 38 67 22 3 63 33 47 16 2 67 33 57 25 3 76 30 66 21 3
49 25 45 17 3 55 35 13 02 1 67 30 52 23 3 70 32 47 14 2
64 32 45 15 2 61 28 40 13 2 48 31 16 02 1 59 30 51 18 3
55 24 38 11 2 63 25 50 19 3 64 32 53 23 3 52 34 14 02 1
49 36 14 01 1 54 30 45 15 2 79 38 64 20 3 44 32 13 02 1
67 33 57 21 3 50 35 16 06 1 58 26 40 12 2 44 30 13 02 1
77 28 67 20 3 63 27 49 18 3 47 32 16 02 1 55 26 44 12 2
50 23 33 10 2 72 32 60 18 3 48 30 14 03 1 51 38 16 02 1
61 30 49 18 3 48 34 19 02 1 50 30 16 02 1 50 32 12 02 1
61 26 56 14 3 64 28 56 21 3 43 30 11 01 1 58 40 12 02 1
51 38 19 04 1 67 31 44 14 2 62 28 48 18 3 49 30 14 02 1
51 35 14 02 1 56 30 45 15 2 58 27 41 10 2 50 34 16 04 1
46 32 14 02 1 60 29 45 15 2 57 26 35 10 2 57 44 15 04 1
50 36 14 02 1 77 30 61 23 3 63 34 56 24 3 58 27 51 19 3
57 29 42 13 2 72 30 58 16 3 54 34 15 04 1 52 41 15 01 1
71 30 59 21 3 64 31 55 18 3 60 30 48 18 3 63 29 56 18 3
49 24 33 10 2 56 27 42 13 2 57 30 42 12 2 55 42 14 02 1
49 31 15 02 1 77 26 69 23 3 60 22 50 15 3 54 39 17 04 1
66 29 46 13 2 52 27 39 14 2 60 34 45 16 2 50 34 15 02 1
44 29 14 02 1 50 20 35 10 2 55 24 37 10 2 58 27 39 12 2
47 32 13 02 1 46 31 15 02 1 69 32 57 23 3 62 29 43 13 2
74 28 61 19 3 59 30 42 15 2 51 34 15 02 1 50 35 13 03 1
56 28 49 20 3 60 22 40 10 2 73 29 63 18 3 67 25 58 18 3
49 31 15 01 1 67 31 47 15 2 63 23 44 13 2 54 37 15 02 1
56 30 41 13 2 63 25 49 15 2 61 28 47 12 2 64 29 43 13 2
51 25 30 11 2 57 28 41 13 2 65 30 58 22 3 69 31 54 21 3
54 39 13 04 1 51 35 14 03 1 72 36 61 25 3 65 32 51 20 3
61 29 47 14 2 56 29 36 13 2 69 31 49 15 2 64 27 53 19 3
68 30 55 21 3 55 25 40 13 2 48 34 16 02 1 48 30 14 01 1
```

```
45 23 13 03 1 57 25 50 20 3 57 38 17 03 1 51 38 15 03 1
55 23 40 13 2 66 30 44 14 2 68 28 48 14 2 54 34 17 02 1
51 37 15 04 1 52 35 15 02 1 58 28 51 24 3 67 30 50 17 2
63 33 60 25 3 53 37 15 02 1
;
```

The following macro, SHOW, is used in the subsequent analyses to display cluster results. It invokes the FREQ procedure to crosstabulate clusters and species. The CANDISC procedure computes canonical variables for discriminating among the clusters, and the first two canonical variables are plotted to show cluster membership. See the chapter "The CANDISC Procedure" for a canonical discriminant analysis of the iris species.

```
%macro show;
proc freq;
    tables cluster*species;
proc candisc noprint out=can;
    class cluster;
    var petal: sepal:;
proc plot;
    plot can2*can1=cluster / vpos=26;
run;
%mend;
```

The first analysis clusters the iris data by Ward's method and plots the CCC and pseudo F and t^2 statistics. The CCC has a local peak at 3 clusters but a higher peak at 5 clusters. The pseudo F statistic indicates 3 clusters, while the pseudo t^2 statistic suggests 3 or 6 clusters. For large numbers of clusters, Version 6 of the SAS System produces somewhat different results than previous versions of CLUSTER. This is due to changes in the treatment of ties. Results are identical for 5 or fewer clusters.

The TREE procedure creates an output data set containing the 3-cluster partition for use by the SHOW macro. The FREQ procedure reveals 16 misclassifications. The results are shown in **Output 15.13**.

```
title2 'BY WARD''S METHOD';
proc cluster data=iris method=ward print=15 ccc pseudo;
    var petal: sepal:;
    copy species;
proc plot;
    plot _ccc_*_ncl_ / vpos=26
        haxis=1 to 30 by 1;
    plot _psf_*_ncl_='F'  _pst2_*_ncl_='T' / vpos=26
        overlay haxis=1 to 30 by 1 vaxis=0 to 600 by 100;
proc tree noprint ncl=3 out=out;
    copy petal: sepal: species;
%show
```

Output 15.13   Cluster Analysis of Fisher Iris Data: PROC CLUSTER with
METHOD=WARD

```
                    CLUSTER ANALYSIS OF FISHER (1936) IRIS DATA                          1
                                 BY WARD'S METHOD

                         Ward's Minimum Variance Cluster Analysis

                            Eigenvalues of the Covariance Matrix

                    Eigenvalue     Difference     Proportion     Cumulative

                1     422.824        398.557        0.924619       0.92462
                2      24.267         16.446        0.053066       0.97769
                3       7.821          5.437        0.017103       0.99479
                4       2.384            .          0.005212       1.00000

              Root-Mean-Square Total-Sample Standard Deviation = 10.69224
              Root-Mean-Square Distance Between Observations   = 30.24221

                              Frequency                        Approximate    Cubic
 Number                        of New     Semipartial           Expected    Clustering   Pseudo    Pseudo
   of                           New       R-Squared   R-Squared R-squared    Criterion      F       t**2     Tie
Clusters   Clusters Joined     Cluster

   15      CL24     CL28          15      0.001641    0.971069   0.957871     5.9289     323.67     9.83
   14      CL21     CL53           7      0.001873    0.969196   0.955418     5.8500     329.15     5.09
   13      CL18     CL48          15      0.002271    0.966925   0.952670     5.6903     333.76     8.92
   12      CL16     CL23          24      0.002274    0.964651   0.949541     4.6323     342.36     9.63
   11      CL14     CL43          12      0.002500    0.962151   0.945886     4.6746     353.35     5.77
   10      CL26     CL20          22      0.002694    0.959457   0.941547     4.8105     368.12    12.87
    9      CL27     CL17          31      0.003060    0.956397   0.936296     5.0184     386.59    17.78
    8      CL35     CL15          23      0.003095    0.953302   0.929791     5.4430     414.11    13.81
    7      CL10     CL47          26      0.005811    0.947491   0.921496     5.4262     430.06    19.07
    6      CL8      CL13          38      0.006042    0.941449   0.910514     5.8061     463.08    16.26
    5      CL9      CL19          50      0.010532    0.930917   0.895232     5.8170     488.48    43.19
    4      CL12     CL11          36      0.017245    0.913673   0.872331     3.9867     515.08    41.00
    3      CL6      CL7           64      0.030051    0.883621   0.826664     4.3292     558.06    57.25
    2      CL4      CL3          100      0.111026    0.772595   0.696871     3.8329     502.82   115.57
    1      CL5      CL2          150      0.772595    0.000000   0.000000     0.0000        .      502.82
```

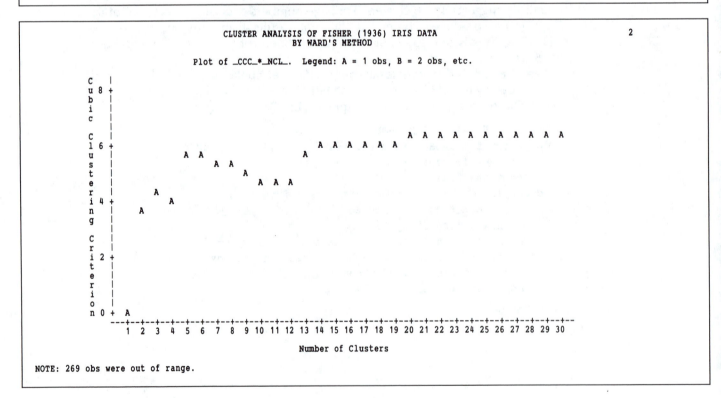

```
                    CLUSTER ANALYSIS OF FISHER (1936) IRIS DATA                          2
                                 BY WARD'S METHOD

                 Plot of _CCC_*_NCL_.  Legend: A = 1 obs, B = 2 obs, etc.
```

NOTE: 269 obs were out of range.

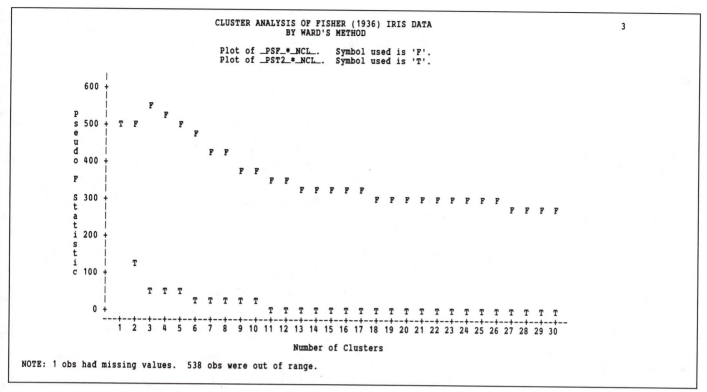

```
                    CLUSTER ANALYSIS OF FISHER (1936) IRIS DATA                    3
                              BY WARD'S METHOD

                    Plot of _PSF_*_NCL_.   Symbol used is 'F'.
                    Plot of _PST2_*_NCL_.  Symbol used is 'T'.

        |
   600 +
        |
P       |
s   500 +    T  F        F
e       |            F
u       |                F
d   400 +
o       |                   F  F
F       |                       F  F
S   300 +                              F  F  F  F  F         F  F  F  F  F  F  F  F
t       |                                                                           F  F  F  F
a       |
t   200 +
i       |
s       |    T
t   100 +
i       |
c       |       T  T  T
     0 +                 T  T  T  T  T        T  T  T  T  T  T  T  T  T  T  T  T  T  T  T  T  T  T  T  T
        ---+--+--+--+--+--+--+--+--+--+--+--+--+--+--+--+--+--+--+--+--+--+--+--+--+--+--+--+--+--
           1  2  3  4  5  6  7  8  9 10 11 12 13 14 15 16 17 18 19 20 21 22 23 24 25 26 27 28 29 30

                                    Number of Clusters
```

NOTE: 1 obs had missing values. 538 obs were out of range.

```
                    CLUSTER ANALYSIS OF FISHER (1936) IRIS DATA                    4
                              BY WARD'S METHOD

                         TABLE OF CLUSTER BY SPECIES

        CLUSTER        SPECIES

        Frequency|
        Percent  |
        Row Pct  |
        Col Pct  |SETOSA  |VERSICOL|VIRGINIC|
                 |        |OR      |A       |  Total
        ---------+--------+--------+--------+
             1   |      0 |     49 |     15 |     64
                 |   0.00 |  32.67 |  10.00 |  42.67
                 |   0.00 |  76.56 |  23.44 |
                 |   0.00 |  98.00 |  30.00 |
        ---------+--------+--------+--------+
             2   |      0 |      1 |     35 |     36
                 |   0.00 |   0.67 |  23.33 |  24.00
                 |   0.00 |   2.78 |  97.22 |
                 |   0.00 |   2.00 |  70.00 |
        ---------+--------+--------+--------+
             3   |     50 |      0 |      0 |     50
                 |  33.33 |   0.00 |   0.00 |  33.33
                 | 100.00 |   0.00 |   0.00 |
                 | 100.00 |   0.00 |   0.00 |
        ---------+--------+--------+--------+
        Total          50       50       50      150
                    33.33    33.33    33.33   100.00
```

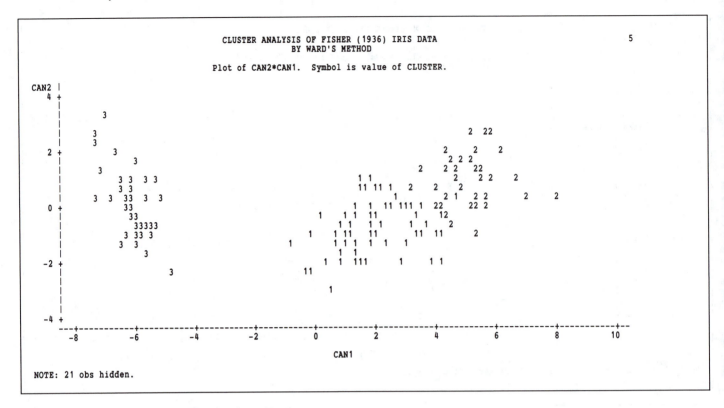

CLUSTER ANALYSIS OF FISHER (1936) IRIS DATA
BY WARD'S METHOD

Plot of CAN2*CAN1. Symbol is value of CLUSTER.

NOTE: 21 obs hidden.

The second analysis uses two-stage density linkage. The raw data suggest 2 or 6 modes instead of 3:

k	modes
3	12
4–6	6
7	4
8	3
9–50	2
51+	1

However, the ACECLUS procedure can be used to reveal 3 modes. This analysis uses K=8 to produce 3 clusters for comparison with other analyses. There are only 6 misclassifications. The results are shown in **Output 15.14**.

```
title2 'By Two-Stage Density Linkage';
proc cluster data=iris method=twostage k=8 print=15 ccc pseudo;
   var petal: sepal:;
   copy species;
proc tree noprint ncl=3 out=out;
   copy petal: sepal: species;
%show
```

Output 15.14   Cluster Analysis of Fisher Iris Data: PROC CLUSTER with METHOD=TWOSTAGE

```
                    CLUSTER ANALYSIS OF FISHER (1936) IRIS DATA                          1
                          BY TWO-STAGE DENSITY LINKAGE

                       Two-Stage Density Linkage Clustering

                     Eigenvalues of the Covariance Matrix

              Eigenvalue      Difference      Proportion      Cumulative

           1   422.824         398.557         0.924619        0.92462
           2    24.267          16.446         0.053066        0.97769
           3     7.821           5.437         0.017103        0.99479
           4     2.384            .            0.005212        1.00000

                                   K = 8

          Root-Mean-Square Total-Sample Standard Deviation = 10.69224
```

									Pseudo	Pseudo	Fusion	Maximum Density in Each Cluster	
NCL	Clusters	Joined	FREQ	SPRSQ	RSQ	ERSQ	CCC		F	t**2	Density	Lesser	Greater
15	CL17	OB127	44	0.002545	0.915526	0.957871	-10.9751		104.5	3.4	4.69E-6	2.48E-6	4.22E-5
14	CL16	OB137	50	0.002333	0.913193	0.955418	-10.5442		110.1	5.6	4.37E-6	2.21E-6	0.0012
13	CL15	OB74	45	0.002947	0.910246	0.952670	-10.1612		115.8	3.7	4.27E-6	2.56E-6	4.22E-5
12	OB49	CL28	46	0.003575	0.906672	0.949541	-8.0044		121.9	5.2	3.87E-6	2.08E-6	0.0001
11	OB85	CL12	47	0.003581	0.903091	0.945886	-7.6193		129.5	4.8	3.87E-6	2.08E-6	0.0001
10	CL11	OB98	48	0.003340	0.899751	0.941547	-7.0928		139.6	4.1	3.46E-6	1.78E-6	0.0001
9	CL13	OB24	46	0.003686	0.896065	0.936296	-6.4798		152.0	4.4	3.36E-6	2.41E-6	4.22E-5
8	OB25	CL10	49	0.001922	0.894143	0.929791	-5.4810		171.3	2.2	3.24E-6	1.65E-6	0.0001
7	CL8	OB121	50	0.003517	0.890626	0.921496	-4.4745		194.1	4.0	3.11E-6	1.65E-6	0.0001
6	CL9	OB45	47	0.004195	0.886431	0.910514	-3.2622		224.8	4.6	1.7E-6	9.99E-7	4.22E-5
5	CL6	OB39	48	0.004889	0.881541	0.895232	-1.7155		269.8	5.0	1.29E-6	7.26E-7	4.22E-5
4	CL5	OB21	49	0.004949	0.876592	0.872331	0.3459		345.7	4.7	1.16E-6	6.49E-7	4.22E-5
3	CL4	OB90	50	0.004736	0.871857	0.826664	3.2827		500.1	4.1	8.59E-7	4.44E-7	4.22E-5

```
                     3 modal clusters have been formed.
```

									Pseudo	Pseudo	Fusion	Maximum Density in Each Cluster	
NCL	Clusters	Joined	FREQ	SPRSQ	RSQ	ERSQ	CCC		F	t**2	Density	Lesser	Greater
2	CL3	CL7	100	0.099262	0.772595	0.696871	3.8329		502.8	91.9	3.16E-5	4.22E-5	0.0001

```
                    CLUSTER ANALYSIS OF FISHER (1936) IRIS DATA                          2
                          BY TWO-STAGE DENSITY LINKAGE

                         TABLE OF CLUSTER BY SPECIES

              CLUSTER       SPECIES

              Frequency|
              Percent  |
              Row Pct  |
              Col Pct  |SETOSA  |VERSICOL|VIRGINIC|
                       |        |OR      |A       |   Total
              ---------+--------+--------+--------+
                     1 |     50 |      0 |      0 |     50
                       |  33.33 |   0.00 |   0.00 |  33.33
                       | 100.00 |   0.00 |   0.00 |
                       | 100.00 |   0.00 |   0.00 |
              ---------+--------+--------+--------+
                     2 |      0 |     47 |      3 |     50
                       |   0.00 |  31.33 |   2.00 |  33.33
                       |   0.00 |  94.00 |   6.00 |
                       |   0.00 |  94.00 |   6.00 |
              ---------+--------+--------+--------+
                     3 |      0 |      3 |     47 |     50
                       |   0.00 |   2.00 |  31.33 |  33.33
                       |   0.00 |   6.00 |  94.00 |
                       |   0.00 |   6.00 |  94.00 |
              ---------+--------+--------+--------+
              Total          50       50       50      150
                           33.33    33.33    33.33   100.00
```

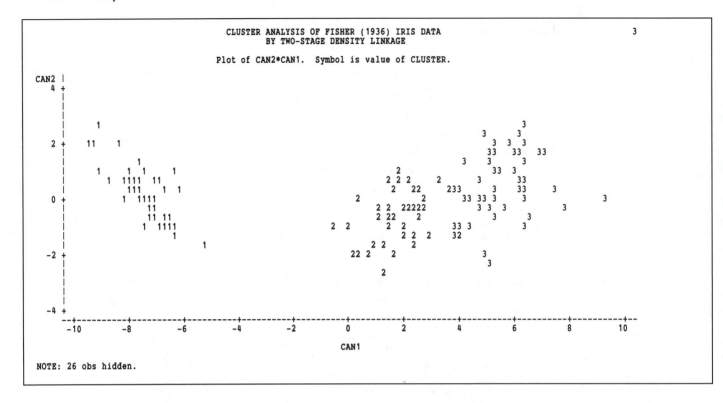

```
                     CLUSTER ANALYSIS OF FISHER (1936) IRIS DATA                              3
                          BY TWO-STAGE DENSITY LINKAGE

                     Plot of CAN2*CAN1.  Symbol is value of CLUSTER.
```

NOTE: 26 obs hidden.

The CLUSTER procedure is not practical for very large data sets because with most methods the CPU time varies as the square or cube of the number of observations. The FASTCLUS procedure requires time proportional to the number of observations and can therefore be used with much larger data sets than CLUSTER. If you want to hierarchically cluster a very large data set, you can use FASTCLUS for a preliminary cluster analysis producing a large number of clusters and then use CLUSTER to hierarchically cluster the preliminary clusters.

FASTCLUS automatically creates variables _FREQ_ and _RMSSTD_ in the MEAN= output data set. These variables are then automatically used by CLUSTER in the computation of various statistics.

The iris data are used to illustrate the process of clustering clusters. In the preliminary analysis, FASTCLUS produces ten clusters, which are then crosstabulated with species. The data set containing the preliminary clusters is sorted in preparation for later merges. The results are shown in **Output 15.15**.

```
title2 'Preliminary Analysis by FASTCLUS';
proc fastclus data=iris summary maxc=10 maxiter=99 converge=0
             mean=mean out=prelim cluster=preclus;
   var petal: sepal:;
proc freq;
   tables preclus*species;
proc sort data=prelim;
   by preclus;
run;
```

Output 15.15 Preliminary Analysis of Fisher Iris Data: PROC FASTCLUS

```
                CLUSTER ANALYSIS OF FISHER (1936) IRIS DATA                    1
                     PRELIMINARY ANALYSIS BY FASTCLUS

                          FASTCLUS Procedure

      Replace=FULL  Radius=0  Maxclusters=10   Maxiter=99  Converge=0


                             Cluster Summary

                      RMS Std   Maximum Distance from   Nearest   Centroid
    Cluster  Frequency Deviation    Seed to Observation   Cluster   Distance
    -----------------------------------------------------------------------
       1         9      2.7067          8.2027               5       8.7362
       2        19      2.2001          7.7340               4       6.2243
       3        18      2.1496          6.2173               8       7.5049
       4         4      2.5249          5.3268               2       6.2243
       5         3      2.7234          5.8214               1       8.7362
       6         7      2.2939          5.1508               2       9.3318
       7        17      2.0274          6.9576              10       7.9503
       8        18      2.2628          7.1135               3       7.5049
       9        22      2.2666          7.5029               8       9.0090
      10        33      2.0594         10.0033               7       7.9503

                        Pseudo F Statistic =   370.58
                 Observed Over-All R-Squared =  0.95971
      Approximate Expected Over-All R-Squared =  0.82928
                   Cubic Clustering Criterion =   27.077
       WARNING: The two above values are invalid for correlated variables.
```

```
                CLUSTER ANALYSIS OF FISHER (1936) IRIS DATA                    2
                     PRELIMINARY ANALYSIS BY FASTCLUS

                       TABLE OF PRECLUS BY SPECIES

        PRECLUS     SPECIES

        Frequency|
        Percent  |
        Row Pct  |
        Col Pct  |SETOSA  |VERSICOL|VIRGINIC|
                 |        |OR      |A       |   Total
        ---------+--------+--------+--------+
              1  |     0  |     0  |     9  |      9
                 |  0.00  |  0.00  |  6.00  |   6.00
                 |  0.00  |  0.00  |100.00  |
                 |  0.00  |  0.00  | 18.00  |
        ---------+--------+--------+--------+
              2  |     0  |    19  |     0  |     19
                 |  0.00  | 12.67  |  0.00  |  12.67
                 |  0.00  |100.00  |  0.00  |
                 |  0.00  | 38.00  |  0.00  |
        ---------+--------+--------+--------+
              3  |     0  |    18  |     0  |     18
                 |  0.00  | 12.00  |  0.00  |  12.00
                 |  0.00  |100.00  |  0.00  |
                 |  0.00  | 36.00  |  0.00  |
        ---------+--------+--------+--------+
              4  |     0  |     3  |     1  |      4
                 |  0.00  |  2.00  |  0.67  |   2.67
                 |  0.00  | 75.00  | 25.00  |
                 |  0.00  |  6.00  |  2.00  |
        ---------+--------+--------+--------+
              5  |     0  |     0  |     3  |      3
                 |  0.00  |  0.00  |  2.00  |   2.00
                 |  0.00  |  0.00  |100.00  |
                 |  0.00  |  0.00  |  6.00  |
        ---------+--------+--------+--------+
        Total         50       50       50      150
                    33.33    33.33    33.33   100.00
        (Continued)
```

```
                CLUSTER ANALYSIS OF FISHER (1936) IRIS DATA              3
                     PRELIMINARY ANALYSIS BY FASTCLUS

                       TABLE OF PRECLUS BY SPECIES

        PRECLUS      SPECIES

        Frequency|
        Percent  |
        Row Pct  |
        Col Pct  |SETOSA  |VERSICOL|VIRGINIC|
                 |        |OR      |A       |     Total
        ---------+--------+--------+--------+
              6  |     0  |     7  |     0  |      7
                 |  0.00  |  4.67  |  0.00  |   4.67
                 |  0.00  |100.00  |  0.00  |
                 |  0.00  | 14.00  |  0.00  |
        ---------+--------+--------+--------+
              7  |    17  |     0  |     0  |     17
                 | 11.33  |  0.00  |  0.00  |  11.33
                 |100.00  |  0.00  |  0.00  |
                 | 34.00  |  0.00  |  0.00  |
        ---------+--------+--------+--------+
              8  |     0  |     3  |    15  |     18
                 |  0.00  |  2.00  | 10.00  |  12.00
                 |  0.00  | 16.67  | 83.33  |
                 |  0.00  |  6.00  | 30.00  |
        ---------+--------+--------+--------+
              9  |     0  |     0  |    22  |     22
                 |  0.00  |  0.00  | 14.67  |  14.67
                 |  0.00  |  0.00  |100.00  |
                 |  0.00  |  0.00  | 44.00  |
        ---------+--------+--------+--------+
             10  |    33  |     0  |     0  |     33
                 | 22.00  |  0.00  |  0.00  |  22.00
                 |100.00  |  0.00  |  0.00  |
                 | 66.00  |  0.00  |  0.00  |
        ---------+--------+--------+--------+
        Total         50       50       50      150
                   33.33    33.33    33.33   100.00
```

The following macro, CLUS, clusters the preliminary clusters. There is one argument to choose the METHOD= specification to be used by CLUSTER. The TREE procedure creates an output data set containing the 3-cluster partition, which is sorted and merged with the OUT= data set from FASTCLUS to determine to which cluster each of the original 150 observations belongs. The SHOW macro is then used to display the results. The results are shown in **Output 15.16** and **Output 15.17**.

```
%macro clus(method);
proc cluster data=mean method=&method ccc pseudo;
   var petal: sepal:;
   copy preclus;
proc tree noprint ncl=3 out=out;
   copy petal: sepal: preclus;
proc sort data=out;
   by preclus;
data clus;
   merge prelim out;
   by preclus;
run;
%show
%mend;
```

The CLUS macro is now invoked using Ward's method, which produces sixteen misclassifications, and Wong's hybrid method, which produces twenty-two mis-classifications.

```
title2 'Clustering Clusters by Ward''s Method';
%clus(ward);
title2 'Clustering Clusters by Wong''s Hybrid Method';
%clus(twostage hybrid);
```

Output 15.16   Clustering Clusters: PROC CLUSTER with Ward's Method

```
                        CLUSTER ANALYSIS OF FISHER (1936) IRIS DATA                          1
                           CLUSTERING CLUSTERS BY WARD'S METHOD

                           Ward's Minimum Variance Cluster Analysis

                              Eigenvalues of the Covariance Matrix

                    Eigenvalue      Difference      Proportion      Cumulative

              1      416.976         398.666         0.950106        0.95011
              2       18.310          14.953         0.041720        0.99183
              3        3.357           3.127         0.007649        0.99948
              4        0.230             .           0.000524        1.00000

            Root-Mean-Square Total-Sample Standard Deviation = 10.69224
            Root-Mean-Square Distance Between Observations    = 30.24221
```

Number of Clusters	Clusters Joined		Frequency of New Cluster	Semipartial R-Squared	R-Squared	Approximate Expected R-squared	Cubic Clustering Criterion	Pseudo F	Pseudo t**2	Tie
9	OB2	OB4	23	0.001879	0.957836	0.932483	6.2627	400.38	6.33	
8	OB1	OB5	12	0.002520	0.955315	0.926089	6.7495	433.69	5.85	
7	CL9	OB6	30	0.006945	0.948370	0.917957	6.2778	437.79	19.51	
6	OB3	OB8	36	0.007440	0.940930	0.907217	6.2076	458.76	26.02	
5	OB7	OB10	50	0.010408	0.930522	0.892304	6.1465	485.50	42.24	
4	CL8	OB9	34	0.016180	0.914342	0.869844	4.2772	519.48	39.33	
3	CL7	CL6	66	0.031800	0.882542	0.824273	4.3930	552.26	59.72	
2	CL4	CL3	100	0.109947	0.772595	0.694823	3.9366	502.82	113.15	
1	CL2	CL5	150	0.772595	0.000000	0.000000	0.0000	.	502.82	

```
                        CLUSTER ANALYSIS OF FISHER (1936) IRIS DATA                          2
                           CLUSTERING CLUSTERS BY WARD'S METHOD

                             TABLE OF CLUSTER BY SPECIES

                   CLUSTER     SPECIES

                   Frequency|
                   Percent  |
                   Row Pct  |
                   Col Pct  |SETOSA  |VERSICOL|VIRGINIC|
                            |        |OR      |A       |  Total
                   ---------+--------+--------+--------+
                         1  |     0  |    50  |    16  |    66
                            |  0.00  | 33.33  | 10.67  | 44.00
                            |  0.00  | 75.76  | 24.24  |
                            |  0.00  |100.00  | 32.00  |
                   ---------+--------+--------+--------+
                         2  |     0  |     0  |    34  |    34
                            |  0.00  |  0.00  | 22.67  | 22.67
                            |  0.00  |  0.00  |100.00  |
                            |  0.00  |  0.00  | 68.00  |
                   ---------+--------+--------+--------+
                         3  |    50  |     0  |     0  |    50
                            | 33.33  |  0.00  |  0.00  | 33.33
                            |100.00  |  0.00  |  0.00  |
                            |100.00  |  0.00  |  0.00  |
                   ---------+--------+--------+--------+
                   Total         50       50       50      150
                              33.33    33.33    33.33   100.00
```

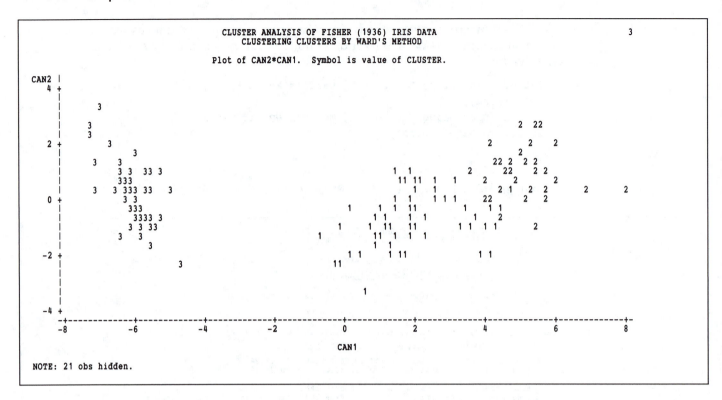

```
        CLUSTER ANALYSIS OF FISHER (1936) IRIS DATA                    3
          CLUSTERING CLUSTERS BY WARD'S METHOD

        Plot of CAN2*CAN1.  Symbol is value of CLUSTER.

CAN2 |
   4 +
     |
     |        3
     |
     |      3
     |      3
   2 +         3
     |            3
     |     3    3
     |       3 3  33 3
     |        333
   0 +     3   3 333 33    3
     |        3 3
     |         333
     |        3333 3
     |       3  3 33
     |        3   3
  -2 +         3
     |            3
     |
     |
  -4 +
     +--+---------+---------+---------+---------+---------+---------+--+
       -8        -6        -4        -2        0         2         4   6        8

                            CAN1

NOTE: 21 obs hidden.
```

Output 15.17 Clustering Clusters: PROC CLUSTER with Wong's Hybrid Method

```
        CLUSTER ANALYSIS OF FISHER (1936) IRIS DATA                    4
       CLUSTERING CLUSTERS BY WONG'S HYBRID METHOD

            Two-Stage Density Linkage Clustering

            Eigenvalues of the Covariance Matrix

        Eigenvalue   Difference   Proportion   Cumulative

   1      416.976      398.666     0.950106     0.95011
   2       18.310       14.953     0.041720     0.99183
   3        3.357        3.127     0.007649     0.99948
   4        0.230          .       0.000524     1.00000

                    Hybrid Method

Root-Mean-Square Total-Sample Standard Deviation = 10.47465
```

								Pseudo	Pseudo	Fusion	Maximum Density in Each Cluster	
NCL	Clusters	Joined	FREQ	SPRSQ	RSQ	ERSQ	CCC	F	t**2	Density	Lesser	Greater
9	OB7	OB10	50	0.010845	0.947178	0.953499	-1.6507	316.0	42.2	0.0491	0.0710	0.122
8	OB3	OB8	36	0.007752	0.939426	0.947813	-1.9439	314.6	26.0	0.0341	0.0481	0.0591
7	OB2	OB4	23	0.001958	0.937469	0.940518	-0.6583	357.3	6.3	0.0290	0.0109	0.0565
6	CL8	OB9	58	0.020261	0.917208	0.930812	-2.3928	319.1	46.3	0.0253	0.0572	0.0591
5	CL7	OB6	30	0.007237	0.909971	0.917243	-1.1426	366.4	19.5	0.0162	0.0215	0.0565
4	OB1	CL6	67	0.030471	0.879500	0.895458	-1.4027	355.2	41.0	0.0103	0.0133	0.0591
3	OB5	CL4	70	0.014418	0.865082	0.848940	1.1895	471.3	12.3	0.00632	0.00767	0.0591

```
            3 modal clusters have been formed.
```

								Pseudo	Pseudo	Fusion	Maximum Density in Each Cluster	
NCL	Clusters	Joined	FREQ	SPRSQ	RSQ	ERSQ	CCC	F	t**2	Density	Lesser	Greater
2	CL5	CL3	100	0.102032	0.763049	0.715981	2.3391	476.6	89.5	0.0238	0.0565	0.0591
1	CL2	CL9	150	0.805026	0.000000	0.000000	0.0000	.	502.8	0.00163	0.0591	0.122

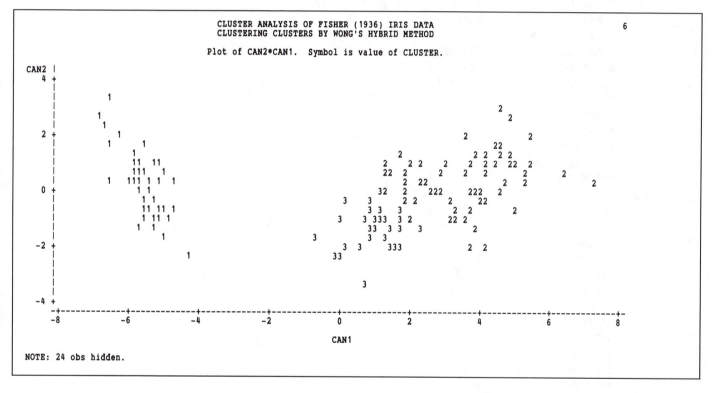

```
                CLUSTER ANALYSIS OF FISHER (1936) IRIS DATA                    5
               CLUSTERING CLUSTERS BY WONG'S HYBRID METHOD

                      TABLE OF CLUSTER BY SPECIES

         CLUSTER      SPECIES

         Frequency|
         Percent  |
         Row Pct  |
         Col Pct  |SETOSA  |VERSICOL|VIRGINIC|
                  |        |OR      |A       |  Total
         ---------+--------+--------+--------+
               1  |     50 |      0 |      0 |     50
                  |  33.33 |   0.00 |   0.00 |  33.33
                  | 100.00 |   0.00 |   0.00 |
                  | 100.00 |   0.00 |   0.00 |
         ---------+--------+--------+--------+
               2  |      0 |     21 |     49 |     70
                  |   0.00 |  14.00 |  32.67 |  46.67
                  |   0.00 |  30.00 |  70.00 |
                  |   0.00 |  42.00 |  98.00 |
         ---------+--------+--------+--------+
               3  |      0 |     29 |      1 |     30
                  |   0.00 |  19.33 |   0.67 |  20.00
                  |   0.00 |  96.67 |   3.33 |
                  |   0.00 |  58.00 |   2.00 |
         ---------+--------+--------+--------+
         Total         50       50       50      150
                     33.33    33.33    33.33   100.00
```

```
                CLUSTER ANALYSIS OF FISHER (1936) IRIS DATA                    6
               CLUSTERING CLUSTERS BY WONG'S HYBRID METHOD

              Plot of CAN2*CAN1.  Symbol is value of CLUSTER.

CAN2 |
   4 +
     |
     |       1
     |     1                                                  2
     |     1  1                                                 2
   2 +       1                                        2              2
     |      1   1                                   22
     |        1                                 2  2  22
     |      11  11                            2  2 2 22  2
     |       111   1                        2  2   2 2    22  2
     |     1  111 1  1  1                  2  22  2   2 2    2 2     2      2
   0 +       1 1                          32  2   222   222   2
     |        1 1                     3   3     2  2      2  22
     |       11 11  1                 3 3   3       2  2
     |        1 111 1              3   3 333  3 2   22 2
     |         1  1                 33  3 3   3            2
  -2 +           1                 3   3  3              2  2
     |         1                   3  3   333
     |                            33
     |
     |                            3
  -4 +
     +--------+--------+--------+--------+--------+--------+--------+--------+--
    -8       -6       -4       -2        0        2        4        6        8
                                       CAN1

NOTE: 24 obs hidden.
```

Example 4: Evaluating the Effects of Ties

If at some level of the cluster history there is a tie for minimum distance between clusters, then one or more levels of the sample cluster tree are not uniquely determined. This example shows how the degree of indeterminacy can be assessed.

Mammals have four kinds of teeth: incisors, canines, premolars, and molars. The data set below gives the number of teeth of each kind on one side of the top and bottom jaws for thirty-two mammals.

```
title 'HIERARCHICAL CLUSTER ANALYSIS OF MAMMALS'' TEETH DATA';
title2 'Evaluating the Effects of Ties';

data teeth;
   input mammal $ 1-16
         @21 (v1-v8) (1.);
   label v1='Top incisors'
         v2='Bottom incisors'
         v3='Top canines'
         v4='Bottom canines'
         v5='Top premolars'
         v6='Bottom premolars'
         v7='Top molars'
         v8='Bottom molars';
   cards;
BROWN BAT        23113333
MOLE             32103333
SILVER HAIR BAT  23112333
PIGMY BAT        23112233
HOUSE BAT        23111233
RED BAT          13112233
PIKA             21002233
RABBIT           21003233
BEAVER           11002133
GROUNDHOG        11002133
GRAY SQUIRREL    11001133
HOUSE MOUSE      11000033
PORCUPINE        11001133
WOLF             33114423
BEAR             33114423
RACCOON          33114432
MARTEN           33114412
WEASEL           33113312
WOLVERINE        33114412
BADGER           33113312
RIVER OTTER      33114312
SEA OTTER        32113312
JAGUAR           33113211
COUGAR           33113211
FUR SEAL         32114411
SEA LION         32114411
GREY SEAL        32113322
ELEPHANT SEAL    21114411
REINDEER         04103333
ELK              04103333
DEER             04003333
MOOSE            04003333
;
```

Since all eight variables are measured in the same units, it is not strictly necessary to rescale the data. However, the canines have much less variance than the other kinds of teeth and will therefore have little effect on the analysis if the variables are not standardized. The analysis is run with and without standardization to allow comparison of the results. The results are shown in **Output 15.18** and **Output 15.19**.

```
proc cluster data=teeth method=average nonorm outtree=_null_;
   var v1-v8;
   id mammal;
   title3 'Raw Data';
run;
proc cluster data=teeth std method=average nonorm outtree=_null_;
   var v1-v8;
   id mammal;
   title3 'Standardized Data';
run;
```

Output 15.18 Average Linkage Analysis of Mammals' Teeth Data: PROC CLUSTER with Raw Data

```
            HIERARCHICAL CLUSTER ANALYSIS OF MAMMALS' TEETH DATA                   1
                      Evaluating the Effects of Ties
                               Raw Data

                     Average Linkage Cluster Analysis

                     Eigenvalues of the Covariance Matrix

             Eigenvalue      Difference      Proportion      Cumulative

        1      3.76799         2.33557        0.584039        0.58404
        2      1.43242         0.91782        0.222025        0.80606
        3      0.51460         0.08415        0.079763        0.88583
        4      0.43045         0.30021        0.066720        0.95255
        5      0.13024         0.03815        0.020187        0.97274
        6      0.09209         0.04217        0.014274        0.98701
        7      0.04992         0.01604        0.007738        0.99475
        8      0.03389           .           0.005253        1.00000

        Root-Mean-Square Total-Sample Standard Deviation = 0.898027

   Number                                       Frequency
     of                                          of New        RMS
  Clusters   Clusters Joined                     Cluster     Distance     Tie

     31      BEAVER             GROUNDHOG            2       0.000000       T
     30      GRAY SQUIRREL      PORCUPINE           2       0.000000       T
     29      WOLF               BEAR                2       0.000000       T
     28      MARTEN             WOLVERINE           2       0.000000       T
     27      WEASEL             BADGER              2       0.000000       T
     26      JAGUAR             COUGAR              2       0.000000       T
     25      FUR SEAL           SEA LION            2       0.000000       T
     24      REINDEER           ELK                 2       0.000000       T
     23      DEER               MOOSE               2       0.000000
     22      BROWN BAT          SILVER HAIR BAT     2       1.000000       T
     21      PIGMY BAT          HOUSE BAT           2       1.000000       T
     20      PIKA               RABBIT              2       1.000000       T
     19      CL31               CL30                4       1.000000       T
     18      CL28               RIVER OTTER         3       1.000000       T
     17      CL27               SEA OTTER           3       1.000000       T
     16      CL24               CL23                4       1.000000
     15      CL21               RED BAT             3       1.224745
     14      CL17               GREY SEAL           4       1.290994
     13      CL29               RACCOON             3       1.414214       T
     12      CL25               ELEPHANT SEAL       3       1.414214
     11      CL18               CL14                7       1.554563
     10      CL22               CL15                5       1.581139
      9      CL20               CL19                6       1.870829       T
      8      CL11               CL26                9       1.927248
```

(continued on next page)

(continued from previous page)

7	CL8	CL12	12	2.227771
6	MOLE	CL13	4	2.236068
5	CL9	HOUSE MOUSE	7	2.483277
4	CL6	CL7	16	2.565801
3	CL10	CL16	9	2.810694
2	CL3	CL5	16	3.705423
1	CL2	CL4	32	4.293891

Output 15.19   Average Linkage Analysis of Mammals' Teeth Data: PROC CLUSTER with Standardized Data

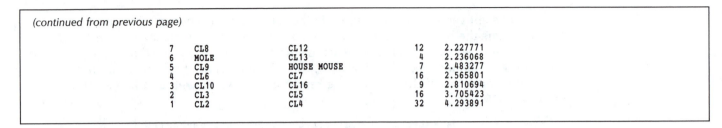

```
                HIERARCHICAL CLUSTER ANALYSIS OF MAMMALS' TEETH DATA                    2
                          Evaluating the Effects of Ties
                                Standardized Data

                          Average Linkage Cluster Analysis

                      Eigenvalues of the Correlation Matrix

                    Eigenvalue    Difference    Proportion    Cumulative

           1         4.74154       3.27459       0.592692      0.59269
           2         1.46695       0.70824       0.183369      0.77606
           3         0.75871       0.25146       0.094839      0.87090
           4         0.50725       0.30265       0.063406      0.93431
           5         0.20460       0.05926       0.025575      0.95988
           6         0.14534       0.03450       0.018168      0.97805
           7         0.11084       0.04607       0.013855      0.99190
           8         0.06477         .           0.008096      1.00000

           The data have been standardized to mean 0 and variance 1
           Root-Mean-Square Total-Sample Standard Deviation =         1
```

Number of Clusters	Clusters Joined		Frequency of New Cluster	RMS Distance	Tie
31	BEAVER	GROUNDHOG	2	0.000000	T
30	GRAY SQUIRREL	PORCUPINE	2	0.000000	T
29	WOLF	BEAR	2	0.000000	T
28	MARTEN	WOLVERINE	2	0.000000	T
27	WEASEL	BADGER	2	0.000000	T
26	JAGUAR	COUGAR	2	0.000000	T
25	FUR SEAL	SEA LION	2	0.000000	T
24	REINDEER	ELK	2	0.000000	T
23	DEER	MOOSE	2	0.000000	
22	PIGMY BAT	RED BAT	2	0.915722	
21	CL28	RIVER OTTER	3	0.916885	
20	CL31	CL30	4	0.942809	T
19	BROWN BAT	SILVER HAIR BAT	2	0.942809	T
18	PIKA	RABBIT	2	0.942809	
17	CL27	SEA OTTER	3	0.984732	
16	CL22	HOUSE BAT	3	1.143749	
15	CL21	CL17	6	1.331380	
14	CL25	ELEPHANT SEAL	3	1.344709	
13	CL19	CL16	5	1.468751	
12	CL15	GREY SEAL	7	1.631351	
11	CL29	RACCOON	3	1.691987	
10	CL18	CL20	6	1.735672	
9	CL12	CL26	9	2.028486	
8	CL24	CL23	4	2.189126	
7	CL9	CL14	12	2.267363	
6	CL10	HOUSE MOUSE	7	2.316955	
5	CL11	CL7	15	2.648426	
4	CL13	MOLE	6	2.862439	
3	CL4	CL8	10	3.519403	
2	CL3	CL6	17	4.126486	
1	CL2	CL5	32	4.775261	

There are ties at 16 levels for the raw data but at only 10 levels for the standardized data. There are more ties for the raw data because the increments between successive values are the same for all of the raw variables but different for the standardized variables.

One way to assess the importance of the ties in the analysis is to repeat the analysis on several random permutations of the observations and then to see to what extent the results are consistent at the interesting levels of the cluster history. Three macros are presented to facilitate this process.

```
*------------------------------------------------------------------+
|                                                                  |
| The macro CLUSPERM randomly permutes observations and does a     |
| cluster analysis for each permutation. The arguments are as      |
| follows:                                                         |
|                                                                  |
|    data    data set name                                         |
|    var     list of variables to cluster                          |
|    id      id variable for proc cluster                          |
|    method  clustering method (and possibly other options)        |
|    nperm   number of random permutations.                        |
|                                                                  |
+------------------------------------------------------------------;


%macro CLUSPERM(data,var,id,method,nperm);

*------CREATE TEMPORARY DATA SET WITH RANDOM NUMBERS------;
data _temp_;
   set &data;
   array _random_ _ran_1-_ran_&nperm;
   do over _random_;
      _random_=ranuni(835297461);
      end;
run;

*------PERMUTE AND CLUSTER THE DATA------;
%do n=1 %to &nperm;
   proc sort data=_temp_(keep=_ran_&n &var &id) out=_perm_;
      by _ran_&n;
   proc cluster method=&method noprint outtree=_tree_&n;
      var &var;
      id &id;
   run;
   %end;

%mend;


*------------------------------------------------------------------+
|                                                                  |
| The macro PLOTPERM plots various cluster statistics against the  |
| number of clusters for each permutation. The arguments are as    |
| follows:                                                         |
|                                                                  |
|    stats   names of variables from tree data set                 |
|    nclus   maximum number of clusters to be plotted              |
|    nperm   number of random permutations.                        |
|                                                                  |
+------------------------------------------------------------------;


%macro PLOTPERM(stat,nclus,nperm);
```

```
*------CONCATENATE TREE DATA SETS FOR 20 OR FEWER CLUSTERS------;
data _plot_;
    set %do n=1 %to &nperm; _tree_&n(in=_in_&n) %end; ;
    if _ncl_ <= &nclus;
    %do n=1 %to &nperm;
        if _in_&n then _perm_=&n;
        %end;
    label _perm_='permutation number';
    keep _ncl_ &stat _perm_;
run;

*------PLOT THE REQUESTED STATISTICS BY NUMBER OF CLUSTERS------;
proc plot;
    plot (&stat)*_ncl_=_perm_ / vpos=26;
run;

%mend;
```

```
*-----------------------------------------------------------------+
|                                                                 |
| The macro TREEPERM generates cluster-membership variables for a |
| specified number of clusters for each permutation. PROC PRINT lists |
| the objects in each cluster-combination, and PROC TABULATE gives |
| the frequencies and means. The arguments are as follows:        |
|                                                                 |
|    var     list of variables to cluster (no "-" or ":" allowed) |
|    id      id variable for proc cluster                         |
|    meanfmt format for printing means in PROC TABULATE           |
|    nclus   number of clusters desired                           |
|    nperm   number of random permutations.                       |
|                                                                 |
+-----------------------------------------------------------------;

%macro TREEPERM(var,id,meanfmt,nclus,nperm);

*------CREATE DATA SETS GIVING CLUSTER MEMBERSHIP------;
%do n=1 %to &nperm;
    proc tree data=_tree_&n noprint n=&nclus
                out=_out_&n(drop=clusname rename=(cluster=_clus_&n));
        copy &var;
        id &id;
    proc sort;
        by &id &var;
    run;
    %end;

*------MERGE THE CLUSTER VARIABLES------;
data _merge_;
    merge %do n=1 %to &nperm; _out_&n %end; ;
    by &id &var;
    length all_clus $ %eval(3 * &nperm);
    %do n=1 %to &nperm;
        substr( all_clus, %eval(1+(&n-1)*3), 3) =
            put( _clus_&n, 3.);
        %end;
run;
```

```
*------PRINT AND TABULATE CLUSTER COMBINATIONS------;
proc sort;
   by _clus_:;
proc print;
   var &var;
   id &id;
   by all_clus notsorted;
proc tabulate order=data formchar='              ';
   class all_clus;
   var &var;
   table all_clus, n='FREQ'*f=5. mean*f=&meanfmt*(&var) /
      rts=%eval(&nperm*3+1);
run;
```

```
%mend;
```

To use the above macros, it is first convenient to define a macro, VLIST, listing the teeth variables, since the forms V1–V8 or V: cannot be used with TABULATE in the TREEPERM macro:

```
*------TABULATE does not accept hyphens or colons in VAR lists------;
%let vlist=v1 v2 v3 v4 v5 v6 v7 v8;
```

CLUSPERM is then called to analyze ten random permutations. PLOTPERM plots the pseudo F and t^2 statistics and the cubic clustering criterion. Since the data are discrete, the pseudo F statistic and the cubic clustering criterion can be expected to increase as the number of clusters increases, so local maxima or large jumps in these statistics are more relevant than the global maximum in determining the number of clusters. For the raw data, only the pseudo t^2 statistic indicates the possible presence of clusters, with the 4-cluster level being suggested. Hence TREEPERM is used to analyze the results at the 4-cluster level:

```
title3 'Raw Data';

*------CLUSTER RAW DATA WITH AVERAGE LINKAGE------;
%clusperm( teeth, &vlist, mammal, average, 10);

*------PLOT STATISTICS FOR THE LAST 20 LEVELS------;
%plotperm( _psf_ _pst2_ _ccc_, 20, 10);

*------ANALYZE THE 4-CLUSTER LEVEL------;
%treeperm( &vlist, mammal, 9.1, 4, 10);
```

The results are shown in **Output 15.20**.

Output 15.20   Analysis of Ten Random Permutations of Raw Mammals'
Teeth Data: Indeterminacy at the 4-Cluster Level

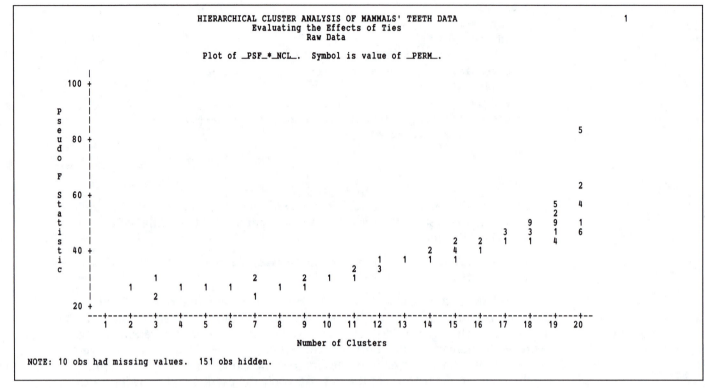

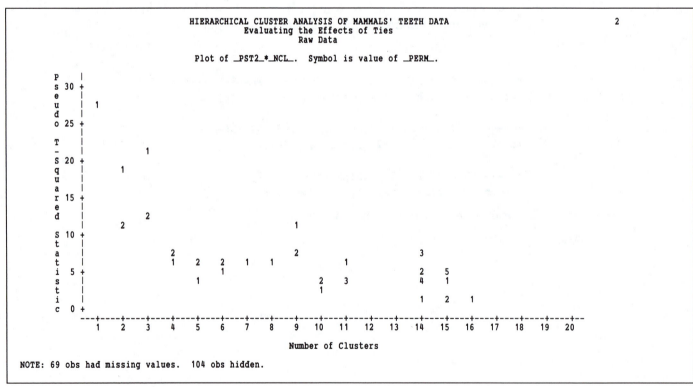

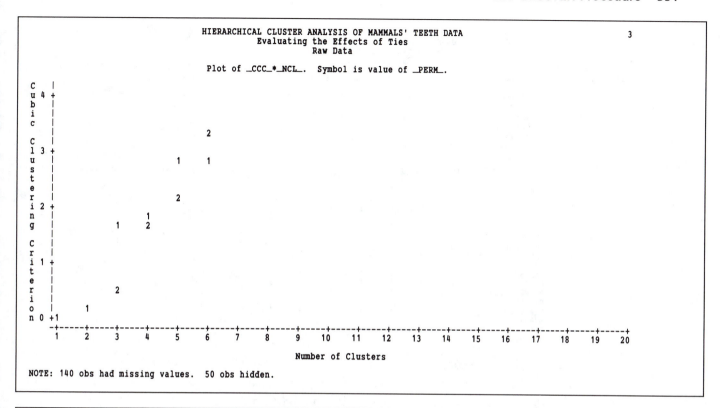

HIERARCHICAL CLUSTER ANALYSIS OF MAMMALS' TEETH DATA
Evaluating the Effects of Ties
Raw Data

Plot of _CCC_*_NCL_. Symbol is value of _PERM_.

```
C     |
u  4  +
b     |
i     |
c     |
      |
C     |                          2
l  3  +
u     |                   1      1
s     |
t     |
e     |                   2
r  2  +
i     |             1
n     |         1   2
g     |
C     |
r  1  +
i     |
t     |
e     |         2
r     |
i     |     1
o     |
n  0  +1
      -+----+----+----+----+----+----+----+----+----+----+----+----+----+----+----+----+----+----+----+----+
       1    2    3    4    5    6    7    8    9   10   11   12   13   14   15   16   17   18   19   20
```

Number of Clusters

NOTE: 140 obs had missing values. 50 obs hidden.

HIERARCHICAL CLUSTER ANALYSIS OF MAMMALS' TEETH DATA
Evaluating the Effects of Ties
Raw Data

MEAN

			FREQ	Top incisors	Bottom incisors	Top canines	Bottom canines	Top premolars	Bottom premolars	Top molars	Bottom molars
ALL_CLUS											
1 3 1 1 1 3 3 3 2 3			4	0.0	4.0	0.5	0.0	3.0	3.0	3.0	3.0
2 2 2 2 2 2 1 2 1 1			15	2.9	2.6	1.0	1.0	3.6	3.4	1.3	1.8
2 4 2 2 4 2 1 2 1 1			1	3.0	2.0	1.0	0.0	3.0	3.0	3.0	3.0
3 1 3 3 3 1 2 1 3 2			5	1.0	1.0	0.0	0.0	1.2	0.8	3.0	3.0
3 4 3 3 4 1 2 1 3 2			2	2.0	1.0	0.0	0.0	2.5	2.0	3.0	3.0
4 4 4 4 4 4 4 4 4 4			5	1.8	3.0	1.0	1.0	2.0	2.4	3.0	3.0

```
                HIERARCHICAL CLUSTER ANALYSIS OF MAMMALS' TEETH DATA                    5
                            Evaluating the Effects of Ties
                                    Raw Data
------------------------------- ALL_CLUS=' 1  3  1  1  1  3  3  3  2  3' ------------------------------

            MAMMAL    V1    V2    V3    V4    V5    V6    V7    V8

            DEER       0     4     0     0     3     3     3     3
            ELK        0     4     1     0     3     3     3     3
            MOOSE      0     4     0     0     3     3     3     3
            REINDEER   0     4     1     0     3     3     3     3


------------------------------- ALL_CLUS=' 2  2  2  2  2  2  1  2  1  1' ------------------------------

            MAMMAL    V1    V2    V3    V4    V5    V6    V7    V8

            BADGER         3     3     1     1     3     3     1     2
            BEAR           3     3     1     1     4     4     2     3
            COUGAR         3     3     1     1     3     2     1     1
            ELEPHANT SEAL  2     1     1     1     4     4     1     1
            FUR SEAL       3     2     1     1     4     4     1     1
            GREY SEAL      3     2     1     1     3     3     2     2
            JAGUAR         3     3     1     1     3     2     1     1
            MARTEN         3     3     1     1     4     4     1     2
            RACCOON        3     3     1     1     4     4     3     2
            RIVER OTTER    3     3     1     1     4     3     1     2
            SEA LION       3     2     1     1     4     4     1     1
            SEA OTTER      3     2     1     1     3     3     1     2
            WEASEL         3     3     1     1     3     3     1     2
            WOLF           3     3     1     1     4     4     2     3
            WOLVERINE      3     3     1     1     4     4     1     2


------------------------------- ALL_CLUS=' 2  4  2  2  4  2  1  2  1  1' ------------------------------

            MAMMAL    V1    V2    V3    V4    V5    V6    V7    V8

            MOLE       3     2     1     0     3     3     3     3


------------------------------- ALL_CLUS=' 3  1  3  3  3  1  2  1  3  2' ------------------------------

            MAMMAL    V1    V2    V3    V4    V5    V6    V7    V8

            BEAVER        1     1     0     0     2     1     3     3
            GRAY SQUIRREL 1     1     0     0     1     1     3     3
            GROUNDHOG     1     1     0     0     2     1     3     3
            HOUSE MOUSE   1     1     0     0     0     0     3     3
            PORCUPINE     1     1     0     0     1     1     3     3


------------------------------- ALL_CLUS=' 3  4  3  3  4  1  2  1  3  2' ------------------------------

            MAMMAL    V1    V2    V3    V4    V5    V6    V7    V8

            PIKA       2     1     0     0     2     2     3     3
            RABBIT     2     1     0     0     3     2     3     3
```

```
                HIERARCHICAL CLUSTER ANALYSIS OF MAMMALS' TEETH DATA                    6
                            Evaluating the Effects of Ties
                                    Raw Data
------------------------------- ALL_CLUS=' 4  4  4  4  4  4  4  4  4' ------------------------------

            MAMMAL    V1    V2    V3    V4    V5    V6    V7    V8

            BROWN BAT       2     3     1     1     3     3     3     3
            HOUSE BAT       2     3     1     1     1     2     3     3
            PIGMY BAT       2     3     1     1     2     2     3     3
            RED BAT         1     3     1     1     2     2     3     3
            SILVER HAIR BAT 2     3     1     1     2     3     3     3
```

From the TABULATE and PRINT output it can be seen that two types of clustering were obtained. In one case the mole is grouped with the carnivores, while the pika and rabbit are grouped with the rodents. In the other case both the mole and the lagomorphs are grouped with the bats.

Next, the analysis is repeated with the standardized data. The pseudo F and t^2 statistics indicate 3 or 4 clusters, while the cubic clustering criterion shows a sharp rise up to 4 clusters and then levels off up to 6 clusters. So TREEPERM is used again at the 4-cluster level. In this case there is no indeterminacy, as the same four clusters are obtained with every permutation, although in different orders. It must be emphasized, however, that lack of indeterminacy in no way indicates validity. The results are shown in **Output 15.21**.

```
title3 'Standardized Data';

*------CLUSTER STANDARDIZED DATA WITH AVERAGE LINKAGE------;
%clusperm( teeth, &vlist, mammal, average std, 10);

*------PLOT STATISTICS FOR THE LAST 20 LEVELS------;
%plotperm( _psf_ _pst2_ _ccc_, 20, 10);

*------ANALYZE THE 4-CLUSTER LEVEL------;
%treeperm( &vlist, mammal, 9.1, 4, 10);
```

Output 15.21   Analysis of Ten Random Permutations of Standardized Mammals' Teeth Data: No Indeterminacy at the 4-Cluster Level

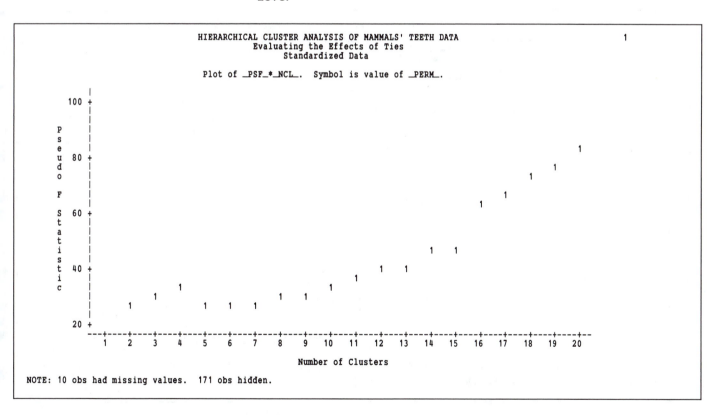

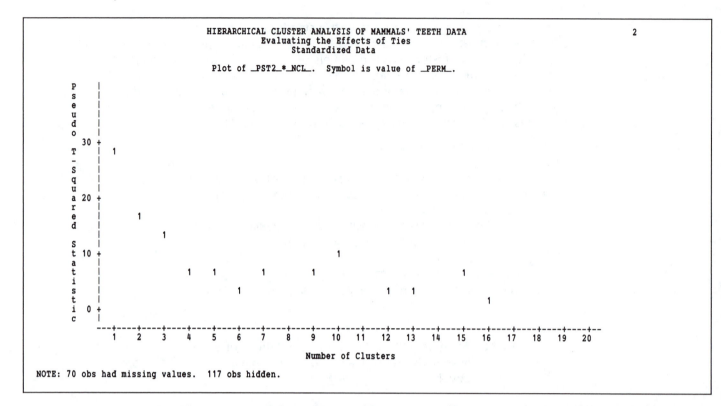

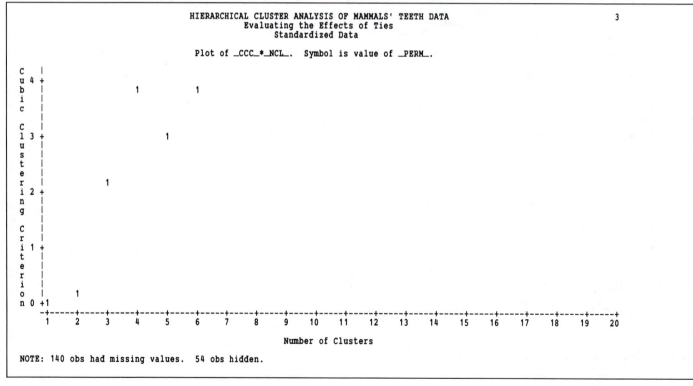

HIERARCHICAL CLUSTER ANALYSIS OF MAMMALS' TEETH DATA
Evaluating the Effects of Ties
Standardized Data

4

MEAN

ALL_CLUS								FREQ	Top incisors	Bottom incisors	Top canines	Bottom canines	Top premolars	Bottom premolars	Top molars	Bottom molars
1 3 1 1 1 3 3 3 2 3								4	0.0	4.0	0.5	0.0	3.0	3.0	3.0	3.0
2 2 2 2 2 2 1 2 1 1								15	2.9	2.6	1.0	1.0	3.6	3.4	1.3	1.8
3 1 3 3 3 1 2 1 3 2								7	1.3	1.0	0.0	0.0	1.6	1.1	3.0	3.0
4 4 4 4 4 4 4 4 4 4								6	2.0	2.8	1.0	0.8	2.2	2.5	3.0	3.0

HIERARCHICAL CLUSTER ANALYSIS OF MAMMALS' TEETH DATA
Evaluating the Effects of Ties
Standardized Data

5

------------------------------------- ALL_CLUS=' 1 3 1 1 1 3 3 3 2 3' -------------------------------------

MAMMAL	V1	V2	V3	V4	V5	V6	V7	V8
DEER	0	4	0	0	3	3	3	3
ELK	0	4	1	0	3	3	3	3
MOOSE	0	4	0	0	3	3	3	3
REINDEER	0	4	1	0	3	3	3	3

------------------------------------- ALL_CLUS=' 2 2 2 2 2 2 1 2 1 1' -------------------------------------

MAMMAL	V1	V2	V3	V4	V5	V6	V7	V8
BADGER	3	3	1	1	3	3	1	2
BEAR	3	3	1	1	4	4	2	3
COUGAR	3	3	1	1	3	2	1	1
ELEPHANT SEAL	2	1	1	1	4	4	1	1
FUR SEAL	3	2	1	1	4	4	1	1
GREY SEAL	3	2	1	1	3	3	2	2
JAGUAR	3	3	1	1	3	2	1	1
MARTEN	3	3	1	1	4	4	1	2
RACCOON	3	3	1	1	4	4	3	2
RIVER OTTER	3	3	1	1	4	3	1	2
SEA LION	3	2	1	1	4	4	1	1
SEA OTTER	3	2	1	1	3	3	1	2
WEASEL	3	3	1	1	3	3	1	2
WOLF	3	3	1	1	4	4	2	3
WOLVERINE	3	3	1	1	4	4	1	2

------------------------------------- ALL_CLUS=' 3 1 3 3 3 1 2 1 3 2' -------------------------------------

MAMMAL	V1	V2	V3	V4	V5	V6	V7	V8
BEAVER	1	1	0	0	2	1	3	3
GRAY SQUIRREL	1	1	0	0	1	1	3	3
GROUNDHOG	1	1	0	0	2	1	3	3
HOUSE MOUSE	1	1	0	0	0	0	3	3
PIKA	2	1	0	0	2	2	3	3
PORCUPINE	1	1	0	0	1	1	3	3
RABBIT	2	1	0	0	3	2	3	3

------------------------------------- ALL_CLUS=' 4 4 4 4 4 4 4 4 4 4' -------------------------------------

MAMMAL	V1	V2	V3	V4	V5	V6	V7	V8
BROWN BAT	2	3	1	1	3	3	3	3
HOUSE BAT	2	3	1	1	1	2	3	3
MOLE	3	2	1	0	3	3	3	3
PIGMY BAT	2	3	1	1	2	2	3	3
RED BAT	1	3	1	1	2	2	3	3
SILVER HAIR BAT	2	3	1	1	2	3	3	3

REFERENCES

Anderberg, M.R. (1973), *Cluster Analysis for Applications*, New York: Academic Press, Inc.

Batagelj, V. (1981), "Note on Ultrametric Hierarchical Clustering Algorithms," *Psychometrika*, 46, 351–352.

Blashfield, R.K. and Aldenderfer, M.S. (1978), "The Literature on Cluster Analysis," *Multivariate Behavioral Research*, 13, 271–295.

Calinski, T. and Harabasz, J. (1974), "A Dendrite Method for Cluster Analysis," *Communications in Statistics*, 3, 1–27.

Cooper, M.C. and Milligan, G.W. (1984), "The Effect of Error on Determining the Number of Clusters," *College of Administrative Science Working Paper Series 84–2*, Columbus, OH: The Ohio State University.

Duda, R.O. and Hart, P.E. (1973), *Pattern Classification and Scene Analysis*, New York: John Wiley & Sons, Inc.

Everitt, B.S. (1980), *Cluster Analysis*, 2d Edition, London: Heineman Educational Books Ltd.

Fisher, L. and Van Ness, J.W. (1971), "Admissible Clustering Procedures," *Biometrika*, 58, 91–104.

Fisher, R.A. (1936), "The Use of Multiple Measurements in Taxonomic Problems," *Annals of Eugenics*, 7, 179–188.

Florek, K., Lukaszewicz, J., Perkal, J., and Zubrzycki, S. (1951a), "Sur la Liaison et la Division des Points d'un Ensemble Fini," *Colloquium Mathematicae*, 2, 282–285.

Florek, K., Lukaszewicz, J., Perkal, J., and Zubrzycki, S. (1951b), "Taksonomia Wroclawska," *Przeglad Antropol.*, 17, 193–211.

Gower, J.C. (1967), "A Comparison of Some Methods of Cluster Analysis," *Biometrics*, 23, 623–637.

Hartigan, J.A. (1975), *Clustering Algorithms*, New York: John Wiley & Sons, Inc.

Hartigan, J.A. (1977), "Distribution Problems in Clustering," in *Classification and Clustering*, ed. J. Van Ryzin, New York: Academic Press, Inc.

Hartigan, J.A. (1981), "Consistency of Single Linkage for High-density Clusters," *Journal of the American Statistical Association*, 76, 388–394.

Hawkins, D.M., Muller, M.W., and ten Krooden, J.A. (1982), "Cluster Analysis," in *Topics in Applied Multivariate Analysis*, ed. D.M. Hawkins, Cambridge: Cambridge University Press.

Jardine, N. and Sibson, R. (1971), *Mathematical Taxonomy*, New York: John Wiley & Sons, Inc.

Johnson, S.C. (1967), "Hierarchical Clustering Schemes," *Psychometrika*, 32, 241–254.

Lance, G.N. and Williams, W.T. (1967), "A General Theory of Classificatory Sorting Strategies. I. Hierarchical Systems," *Computer Journal*, 9, 373–380.

Massart, D.L. and Kaufman, L. (1983), *The Interpretation of Analytical Chemical Data by the Use of Cluster Analysis*, New York: John Wiley & Sons, Inc.

McQuitty, L.L. (1957), "Elementary Linkage Analysis for Isolating Orthogonal and Oblique Types and Typal Relevancies," *Educational and Psychological Measurement*, 17, 207–229.

McQuitty, L.L. (1966), "Similarity Analysis by Reciprocal Pairs for Discrete and Continuous Data," *Educational and Psychological Measurement*, 26, 825–831.

Mezzich, J.E and Solomon, H. (1980), *Taxonomy and Behavioral Science*, New York: Academic Press, Inc.

Milligan, G.W. (1979), "Ultrametric Hierarchical Clustering Algorithms," *Psychometrika*, 44, 343–346.

Milligan, G.W. (1980), "An Examination of the Effect of Six Types of Error Perturbation on Fifteen Clustering Algorithms," *Psychometrika*, 45, 325–342.

Milligan, G.W. (1987), "A Study of the Beta-Flexible Clustering Method," *College of Administrative Science Working Paper Series*, 87–61 Columbus, OH: The Ohio State University

Milligan, G.W. and Cooper, M.C. (1985), "An Examination of Procedures for Determining the Number of Clusters in a Data Set," *Psychometrika*, 50, 159–179.

Milligan, G.W. and Cooper, M.C. (1987), "A Study of Variable Standardization," *College of Administrative Science Working Paper Series*, 87–63, Columbus, OH: The Ohio State University.

Sarle, W.S. (1983), *Cubic Clustering Criterion*, SAS Technical Report A-108, Cary, NC: SAS Institute Inc.

Silverman, B.W. (1986), *Density Estimation*, New York: Chapman and Hall.

Sneath, P.H.A. (1957), "The Application of Computers to Taxonomy," *Journal of General Microbiology*, 17, 201–226.

Sneath, P.H.A. and Sokal, R.R. (1973), *Numerical Taxonomy*, San Francisco: Freeman.

Sokal, R.R. and Michener, C.D. (1958), "A Statistical Method for Evaluating Systematic Relationships," *University of Kansas Science Bulletin*, 38, 1409–1438.

Sorensen, T. (1948), "A Method of Establishing Groups of Equal Amplitude in Plant Sociology Based on Similarity of Species Content and Its Application to Analyses of the Vegetation on Danish Commons," *Biologiske Skrifter*, 5, 1–34.

Spath, H. (1980), *Cluster Analysis Algorithms*, Chichester, England: Ellis Horwood.

Symons, M.J. (1981), "Clustering Criteria and Multivariate Normal Mixtures," *Biometrics*, 37, 35–43.

Ward, J.H. (1963), "Hierarchical Grouping to Optimize an Objective Function," *Journal of the American Statistical Association*, 58, 236–244.

Wishart, D. (1969), "Mode Analysis: A Generalisation of Nearest Neighbour Which Reduces Chaining Effects," in *Numerical Taxonomy*, ed. A.J. Cole, London: Academic Press.

Wong, M.A. (1982), "A Hybrid Clustering Method for Identifying High-Density Clusters," *Journal of the American Statistical Association*, 77, 841–847.

Wong, M.A. and Lane, T. (1983), "A *k*th Nearest Neighbor Clustering Procedure," *Journal of the Royal Statistical Society*, Series B, 45, 362–368.

Wong, M.A. and Schaack, C. (1982), "Using the *k*th Nearest Neighbor Clustering Procedure to Determine the Number of Subpopulations," *American Statistical Association 1982 Proceedings of the Statistical Computing Section*, 40–48.

ABSTRACT

The DISCRIM procedure computes various discriminant functions for classifying observations into two or more groups on the basis of one or more quantitative variables. When the distribution within each group is assumed to be multivariate normal, a parametric method based on multivariate normal distribution theory is used to derive a linear or quadratic discriminant function. Otherwise, a nonparametric method that does not make any assumptions about the distributions can be used.

INTRODUCTION

For a set of observations containing one or more quantitative variables and a classification variable defining groups of observations, PROC DISCRIM develops a discriminant criterion to classify each observation into one of the groups. The derived discriminant criterion from this data set can be applied to a second data set during the same execution of DISCRIM. The data set that DISCRIM uses to derive the discriminant criterion is called the *training* or *calibration data set*.

When the distribution within each group is assumed to be multivariate normal, a parametric method can be used to develop a discriminant function. The discriminant function, also known as a *classification criterion*, is determined by a measure of generalized squared distance (Rao 1973). The classification criterion can be based on either the individual within-group covariance matrices (yielding a quadratic function) or the pooled covariance matrix (yielding a linear function); it also takes into account the prior probabilities of the groups. The calibration information can be stored in a special SAS data set and applied to other data sets.

When no assumptions can be made about the distribution within each group, or when the distribution is assumed to be different from multivariate normal distribution, nonparametric methods can be used to estimate the group-specific densities. These methods include the *kernel method* and *k-nearest-neighbor methods* (Rosenblatt 1956; Parzen 1962). The kernel method uses uniform, normal, Epanechnikov, biweight, or triweight kernels in the density estimation.

Either Mahalanobis distance or Euclidean distance can be used to determine proximity. Mahalanobis distance can be based on either the full covariance matrix or the diagonal matrix of variances. With a *k*-nearest-neighbor method, the pooled covariance matrix is used to calculate the Mahalanobis distances. With a kernel method, either the individual within-group covariance matrices or the pooled covariance matrix can be used to calculate the Mahalanobis distances. With the estimated group-specific densities and their associated prior probabilities, the posterior probability estimates of group membership for each class can be evaluated.

Canonical discriminant analysis is a dimension-reduction technique related to principal component analysis and canonical correlation. Given a classification variable and several quantitative variables, DISCRIM derives *canonical variables* (linear combinations of the quantitative variables) that summarize between-class variation in much the same way that principal components summarize total variation. (See "The CANDISC Procedure" for more information on canonical discriminant analysis.)

The DISCRIM procedure can produce an output data set containing various statistics such as means, standard deviations, and correlations. If a parametric method is used, the discriminant function is also stored in the data set to classify future observations. When canonical discriminant analysis is performed, the output data set includes canonical coefficients that can be rotated by the FACTOR procedure. DISCRIM can also produce a second type of output data set containing the classification results for each observation. When canonical discriminant analysis is performed, this output data set also includes canonical variable scores for each observation. A third type of output data set containing the group-specific density estimates at each observation can also be produced in the procedure.

DISCRIM evaluates the performance of a discriminant criterion by estimating *error rates* (probabilities of misclassification) in the classification of future observations. These error-rate estimates include error-count estimates and posterior probability error-rate estimates. When the input data set is an ordinary SAS data set, the error rate can also be estimated by crossvalidation.

Do not confuse discriminant analysis with *cluster analysis*. All varieties of discriminant analysis require prior knowledge of the classes, usually in the form of a sample from each class. In cluster analysis the data do not include information on class membership; the purpose is to construct a classification. See Chapter 5, "Introduction to Discriminant Procedures," for a discussion of discriminant analysis and the SAS/STAT procedures available.

Background

The notation below is used to describe the classification methods:

$\mathbf{x}$ a *p*-dimensional vector containing the quantitative variables of an observation

$\mathbf{S}$ the pooled covariance matrix

t a subscript to distinguish the groups

n_t the number of training set observations in group t.

$\mathbf{m}_t$ the *p*-dimensional vector containing variable means in group t

$\mathbf{S}_t$ the covariance matrix within group t

$|\mathbf{S}_t|$ the determinant of $\mathbf{S}_t$

q_t the prior probability of membership in group t

$p(t \mid \mathbf{x})$ the posterior probability of an observation $\mathbf{x}$ belonging to group t.

Bayes' Theorem

Assuming that the prior probabilities of group membership are known and the group-specific densities at $\mathbf{x}$ can be estimated, DISCRIM computes $p(t \mid \mathbf{x})$, the probability of $\mathbf{x}$ belonging to group t, by applying Bayes' theorem:

$$p(t \mid \mathbf{x}) = q_t f_t(\mathbf{x}) / f(\mathbf{x})$$

where $f_t(\mathbf{x})$ is the group-specific density estimate at $\mathbf{x}$ from group t, and $f(\mathbf{x}) = \Sigma_t q_t f_t(\mathbf{x})$ is the estimated unconditional density at $\mathbf{x}$.

DISCRIM partitions a p-dimensional vector space into regions R_t, where the region R_t is the subspace containing all p-dimensional vectors $\mathbf{y}$ such that $p(t \mid \mathbf{y})$ is the largest among all groups. An observation is classified as coming from group t if it lies in region R_t.

Parametric Methods

Assuming that each group has a multivariate normal distribution, DISCRIM develops a discriminant function or classification criterion using a measure of generalized squared distance. The classification criterion is based on either the individual within-group covariance matrices or on the pooled covariance matrix; it also takes into account the prior probabilities of the classes. Each observation is placed in the class from which it has the smallest generalized squared distance. DISCRIM also computes the posterior probability of an observation belonging to each class.

The squared distance from $\mathbf{x}$ to group t is

$$d_t^2(\mathbf{x}) = (\mathbf{x} - \mathbf{m}_t)' \mathbf{V}_t^{-1} (\mathbf{x} - \mathbf{m}_t)$$

where $\mathbf{V}_t = \mathbf{S}_t$ if the within-group covariance matrices are used, or $\mathbf{V}_t = \mathbf{S}$ if the pooled covariance matrix is used.

The group-specific density estimate at $\mathbf{x}$ from group t is then given by

$$f_t(\mathbf{x}) = (2\pi)^{-p/2} |\mathbf{V}_t|^{-1/2} \exp\left(-0.5 d_t^2(\mathbf{x})\right) \quad .$$

Using Bayes' theorem, the posterior probability of $\mathbf{x}$ belonging to group t is

$$p(t \mid \mathbf{x}) = \frac{q_t \, f_t(\mathbf{x})}{\Sigma_u \, q_u \, f_u(\mathbf{x})} \quad .$$

The generalized squared distance from $\mathbf{x}$ to group t is defined as

$$D_t^2(\mathbf{x}) = d_t^2(\mathbf{x}) + g_1(t) + g_2(t)$$

where

$g_1(t) = \log_e |\mathbf{S}_t|$ if the within-group covariance matrices are used, or

$g_1(t) = 0$ if the pooled covariance matrix is used; and

$g_2(t) = -2 \log_e(q_t)$ if the prior probabilities are not all equal, or

$g_2(t) = 0$ if the prior probabilities are all equal.

The posterior probability of x belonging to group t is then equal to

$$p(t \mid \mathbf{x}) = \frac{\exp\left(-0.5 \; D_t^2(\mathbf{x})\right)}{\Sigma_u \exp\left(-0.5 \; D_u^2(\mathbf{x})\right)} \quad .$$

An observation is classified into group u if setting $t=u$ produces the largest value of $p(t \mid \mathbf{x})$ or the smallest value of $D_t^2(\mathbf{x})$. If this largest posterior probability is less than the threshold specified, $\mathbf{x}$ is classified into group OTHER.

Nonparametric Methods

Nonparametric discriminant methods are based on nonparametric estimates of group-specific probability densities. Either a kernel method or the k-nearest-neighbor method can be used to generate a nonparametric density estimate in each group and to produce a classification criterion. The kernel method uses uniform, normal, Epanechnikov, biweight, or triweight kernels in the density estimation.

Either Mahalanobis distance or Euclidean distance can be used to determine proximity. When the k-nearest-neighbor method is used, the Mahalanobis distances are based on the pooled covariance matrix. When a kernel method is used, the Mahalanobis distances are based on either the individual within-group covariance matrices or the pooled covariance matrix. Either the full covariance matrix or the diagonal matrix of variances can be used to calculate the Mahalanobis distances.

The squared distance between two observation vectors, $\mathbf{x}$ and $\mathbf{y}$, in group t is given by

$$d_t^2(\mathbf{x},\mathbf{y}) = (\mathbf{x} - \mathbf{y})' \mathbf{V}_t^{-1}(\mathbf{x} - \mathbf{y})$$

where $\mathbf{V}_t$ has one of the following forms:

$\mathbf{V}_t = \mathbf{S}$ the pooled covariance matrix

$\mathbf{V}_t = \text{diag}(\mathbf{S})$ the diagonal matrix of the pooled covariance matrix

$\mathbf{V}_t = \mathbf{S}_t$ the covariance matrix within group t

$\mathbf{V}_t = \text{diag}(\mathbf{S}_t)$ the diagonal matrix of the covariance matrix within group t

$\mathbf{V}_t = \mathbf{I}$ the identity matrix.

The classification of an observation vector $\mathbf{x}$ is based on the estimated group-specific densities from the training set. From these estimated densities, the posterior probabilities of group membership at $\mathbf{x}$ are evaluated. An observation $\mathbf{x}$ is classified into group u if setting $t=u$ produces the largest value of $p(t \mid \mathbf{x})$. If there is a tie for the largest probability or this largest probability is less than the threshold specified, $\mathbf{x}$ is classified into group OTHER.

The kernel method uses a fixed radius, r, and a specified kernel, K_t, to estimate the group t density at each observation vector $\mathbf{x}$. Let $\mathbf{z}$ be a p-dimensional vector. Then the volume of a p-dimensional unit sphere bounded by $\mathbf{z}'\mathbf{z} = 1$ is

$$v_0 = \frac{\pi^{p/2}}{\Gamma(p/2 + 1)}$$

where Γ represents the gamma function (see the *SAS Language Guide, Release 6.03 Edition*).

Thus, in group t, the volume of a p-dimensional ellipsoid bounded by $\{z \mid z'V_t^{-1}z = r^2\}$ is

$$v_r(t) = r^p \mid V_t \mid^{1/2} v_0 \quad .$$

The kernel method uses one of the following densities as the kernel density in group t.

Uniform Kernel

$$K_t(z) = \frac{1}{v_r(t)} \quad \text{if } z'V_t^{-1}z \leq r^2$$
$$= 0 \quad \text{elsewhere.}$$

Normal Kernel   (with mean zero, variance $r^2 V_t$)

$$K_t(z) = \frac{1}{c_0(t)} \exp\left(-0.5 z'V_t^{-1}z / r^2\right)$$

where $c_0(t) = (2\pi)^{p/2} r^p \mid V_t \mid^{1/2}$.

Epanechnikov Kernel

$$K_t(z) = c_1(t) (1 - z'V_t^{-1}z / r^2) \quad \text{if } z'V_t^{-1}z \leq r^2$$
$$= 0 \quad \text{elsewhere}$$

where $c_1(t) = (1 + p/2)/v_r(t)$.

Biweight Kernel

$$K_t(z) = c_2(t) (1 - z'V_t^{-1}z / r^2)^2 \quad \text{if } z'V_t^{-1}z \leq r^2$$
$$= 0 \quad \text{elsewhere}$$

where $c_2(t) = (1 + p/4) c_1(t)$.

Triweight Kernel

$$K_t(z) = c_3(t) (1 - z'V_t^{-1}z / r^2)^3 \quad \text{if } z'V_t^{-1}z \leq r^2$$
$$= 0 \quad \text{elsewhere}$$

where $c_3(t) = (1 + p/6) c_2(t)$.

The group t density at x is estimated by

$$f_t(x) = \frac{1}{n_t} \Sigma_y K_t(x - y)$$

where the summation is over all observations y in group t, and K_t is the specified kernel function. The posterior probability of membership in group t is then given by

$$p(t \mid x) = \frac{q_t f_t(x)}{f(x)}$$

where $f(\mathbf{x}) = \Sigma_u q_u f_u(\mathbf{x})$ is the estimated unconditional density. If $f(\mathbf{x})$ is zero, the observation $\mathbf{x}$ is classified into group OTHER.

The uniform-kernel method treats $K_t(\mathbf{z})$ as a multivariate uniform function with density uniformly distributed over $\mathbf{z}'\mathbf{V}_t^{-1}\mathbf{z} \le r^2$. Let k_t be the number of training set observations $\mathbf{y}$ from group t within the closed ellipsoid centered at $\mathbf{x}$ specified by $d_t^2(\mathbf{x},\mathbf{y}) \le r^2$. Then the group t density at $\mathbf{x}$ is estimated by

$$f_t(\mathbf{x}) = \frac{k_t}{n_t \, v_r(t)} \; .$$

When the pooled within-group covariance matrix is used in calculating the squared distance, $v_r(t)$ is a constant, independent of group membership. The posterior probability of $\mathbf{x}$ belonging to group t is then given by

$$p(t \mid \mathbf{x}) = \frac{q_t k_t / n_t}{\Sigma_u \, q_u k_u / n_u} \; .$$

If the closed ellipsoid centered at $\mathbf{x}$ does not include any training set observations, $f(\mathbf{x})$ is zero and $\mathbf{x}$ is classified into group OTHER. When the prior probabilities are equal, $p(t \mid \mathbf{x})$ is proportional to k_t/n_t, $\mathbf{x}$ is classified into the group that has the highest proportion of observations being in the closed ellipsoid. When the prior probabilities are proportional to the group sizes, $p(t \mid \mathbf{x}) = k_t/\Sigma_u k_u$, $\mathbf{x}$ is classified into the group that has the largest number of observations being enclosed in the closed ellipsoid.

The nearest-neighbor method fixes the number, k, of training set points for each observation $\mathbf{x}$. The method finds the radius $r_k(\mathbf{x})$, which is the distance from $\mathbf{x}$ to the kth nearest training set point in the metric $\mathbf{V}_t^{-1}$. Consider a closed ellipsoid centered at $\mathbf{x}$ bounded by $\{\mathbf{z} \mid (\mathbf{z}-\mathbf{x})'\mathbf{V}_t^{-1}(\mathbf{z}-\mathbf{x}) = r_k^2(\mathbf{x})\}$; the nearest-neighbor method is equivalent to the uniform-kernel method with a location-dependent radius $r_k(\mathbf{x})$.

Using the k-nearest-neighbor rule, the k smallest distances are saved. Of these k distances, let k_t represent the number of distances that are associated with group t. Then, as in the uniform-kernel method, the estimated group t density at $\mathbf{x}$ is

$$f_t(\mathbf{x}) = \frac{k_t}{n_t \, v_k(\mathbf{x})}$$

where $v_k(\mathbf{x})$ is the volume of the ellipsoid bounded by $\{\mathbf{z} \mid (\mathbf{z}-\mathbf{x})'\mathbf{V}_t^{-1}(\mathbf{z}-\mathbf{x}) = r_k^2(\mathbf{x})\}$. Since the pooled within-group covariance matrix is used to calculate the distances used in the nearest-neighbor method, the volume $v_k(\mathbf{x})$ is a constant independent of group membership. When $k=1$ is used in the nearest-neighbor rule, $\mathbf{x}$ is classified into the group associated with the $\mathbf{y}$ point that yields the smallest squared distance $d_t^2(\mathbf{x},\mathbf{y})$.

With a specified squared distance formula (METRIC=, POOL=), the values of r and k determine the degree of irregularity in the estimation of the density function, and are called smoothing parameters. Small values of r or k produce jagged density estimates and large values of r or k produce smoother density estimates. Various methods for choosing the smoothing parameters have been suggested, and there is as yet no simple solution to this problem.

For a fixed kernel shape, one way to choose the smoothing parameter r is to plot estimated densities with different values of r and to choose the estimate that is most in accordance with the prior information about the density. For many applications this approach is satisfactory.

Another way of selecting the smoothing parameter r is to choose a value that optimizes a given criterion. Different groups may have different sets of optimal values. Assume that the unknown density has bounded and continuous second derivatives, and the kernel is a symmetric probability density function. One criterion is to minimize an approximate mean integrated square error of the estimated density (Rosenblatt 1956). The resulting optimal value of r depends on the density function and the kernel. A reasonable choice for the smoothing parameter r is to optimize the criterion with the assumption that group t has a normal distribution with covariance matrix $\mathbf{V}_t$. Then, in group t, the resulting optimal value for r is given by

$$\left(\frac{A(K_t)}{n_t}\right)^{1/(p+4)}$$

where the optimal constant $A(K_t)$ depends on the kernel K_t (Epanechnikov 1969). For some useful kernels, the constants $A(K_t)$ are given by

$$A(K_t) = \frac{2^{p+1}(p+2)\ \Gamma(p/2)}{p}$$

with a uniform kernel,

$$A(K_t) = \frac{4}{2p+1}$$

with a normal kernel, and

$$A(K_t) = \frac{2^{p+2}p^2(p+2)\ (p+4)\ \Gamma(p/2)}{2p+1}$$

with an Epanechnikov kernel.

The selections of $A(K_t)$ above are derived under the assumption that the data in each group are from a multivariate normal distribution with covariance matrix $\mathbf{V}_t$. However, when the Euclidean distances are used in calculating the squared distance ($\mathbf{V}_t = \mathbf{I}$), the smoothing constant should be multiplied by s, where s is an estimate of standard errors for all variables. A reasonable choice for s is $s = (\Sigma s_{jj}\ /p)^{1/2}$, where s_{jj} are group t marginal variances.

DISCRIM uses only a single smoothing parameter for all groups. However, with the selection of the matrix to be used in the distance formula (using the METRIC= or POOL= options), individual groups and variables can have different scalings. When $\mathbf{V}_t$, the matrix used in calculating the squared distances, is an identity matrix, the kernel estimate on each data point is scaled equally for all variables in all groups. When $\mathbf{V}_t$ is the diagonal matrix of a covariance matrix, each variable in group t is scaled separately by its variance in the kernel estimation, where the variance can be the pooled variance ($\mathbf{V}_t = \mathbf{S}$) or an individual within-group variance ($\mathbf{V}_t = \mathbf{S}_t$). When $\mathbf{V}_t$ is a full covariance matrix the variables in group t are scaled simultaneously by $\mathbf{V}_t$ in the kernel estimation.

In nearest-neighbor methods, the choice of k is usually relatively uncritical (Hand 1982). However, nearest-neighbor methods are best used in applications where the choice of k is not critical (Silverman 1986, 98–99). A practical approach is to try several different values of the smoothing parameters within the context of the particular application and to choose the one which gives the most satisfactory results.

Classification Error-Rate Estimates

A classification criterion can be evaluated by its performance in the classification of future observations. DISCRIM uses two types of error rate estimates to evaluate the derived classification criterion based on parameters estimated by the training sample:

- error-count estimates
- posterior probability error-rate estimates.

The error-count estimate is calculated by applying the classification criterion derived from the training sample to a test set and then counting the number of misclassified observations. The group-specific error-count estimate is the proportion of misclassified observations in the group. When the test set is independent of the training sample, the estimate is unbiased. However, it can have a large variance, especially if the test set is small.

When the input data set is an ordinary SAS data set and no independent test sets are available, the same data set can be used both to define and to evaluate the classification criterion. The resulting error-count estimate has an optimistic bias and is called an apparent error rate. To reduce the bias, the data can be split into two sets, one set for deriving the discriminant function and the other set for estimating the error rate. Such a split-sample method has the unfortunate effect of reducing the effective sample size.

Another way to reduce bias is crossvalidation (Lachenbruch and Mickey 1968). Crossvalidation treats $n-1$ out of n training observations as a training set. It determines the discriminant functions based on these $n-1$ observations and then applies them to classify the one observation left out. This is done for each of the n training observations. The misclassification rate for each group is the proportion of sample observations in that group that are misclassified. This method achieves a nearly unbiased estimate but with a relatively large variance.

To reduce the variance in an error-count estimate, smoothed error-rate estimates are suggested (Glick 1978). Instead of summing terms that are either zero or one as in the error-count estimator, the smoothed estimator uses a continuum of values between zero and one in the terms that are summed. The resulting estimator has a smaller variance than the error-count estimate.

The posterior probability error-rate estimates (see **DETAILS**) are smoothed error rate estimates. The posterior probability estimates for each group are based on the posterior probabilities of the observations classified into that same group. The posterior probability estimates provide good estimates of the error rate when the posterior probabilities are accurate. When a parametric classification criterion (linear or quadratic discriminant function) is derived from a non-normal population, the resulting posterior probability error-rate estimators may not be appropriate.

The overall error-rate is estimated through a weighted average of the individual group-specific error-rate estimates, where the prior probabilities are used as the weights.

To reduce both the bias and the variance of the estimator, Hora and Wilcox (1982) compute the posterior probability estimates based on crossvalidation. The resulting estimates are intended to have both low variance from using the posterior probability estimate, and low bias from crossvalidation. They use Monte Carlo studies on two-group multivariate normal distributions to compare the crossvalidation posterior probability estimates with three other estimators: the apparent error rate, crossvalidation estimator, and posterior probability estimator. They conclude that the crossvalidation posterior probability estimator has a lower mean squared error in their simulations.

SPECIFICATIONS

The following statements are used with the DISCRIM procedure:

PROC DISCRIM *options;*
    CLASS *variable;*
    VAR *variables;*
    PRIORS *probabilities;*
    FREQ *variable;*
    WEIGHT *variable;*
    ID *variable;*
    TESTCLASS *variable;*
    TESTFREQ *variable;*
    TESTID *variable;*
    BY *variables;*

The CLASS statement is required. The following sections describe the PROC DISCRIM statement and then discuss the other statements (in alphabetical order).

PROC DISCRIM Statement

    PROC DISCRIM *options;*

These options can appear in the PROC DISCRIM statement.

Input Data Set Options

    DATA=*SASdataset*
        names the data set to be analyzed. The data set can be an ordinary
        SAS data set or one of several specially structured data sets created by
        SAS/STAT procedures. These specially structured data sets include
        TYPE=CORR, TYPE=COV, TYPE=CSSCP, TYPE=SSCP, TYPE=LINEAR,
        TYPE=QUAD, and TYPE=MIXED. The input data set must be an
        ordinary SAS data set if METHOD=NPAR is used. If the DATA= option
        is omitted, the most recently created SAS data set is used.

    TESTDATA=*SASdataset*
        names an ordinary SAS data set whose observations are to be classified.
        The quantitative variable names in this data set must match those in the
        DATA= data set.

When the TESTDATA= option is specified, TESTCLASS, TESTFREQ, and TESTID statements can also be used.

Output Data Set Options

Six output options can be used to create output data sets from DISCRIM. Use a two-level name to create a permanent data set (see "SAS Files" in the *SAS Language Guide* for more information on permanent SAS data sets).

When the input data set is an ordinary SAS data set or TYPE=CORR, TYPE=COV, TYPE=CSSCP, or TYPE=SSCP, the following option can be used to generate discriminant statistics.

    OUTSTAT=*SASdataset*
        names an output SAS data set containing various statistics such as
        means, standard deviations, and correlations. When the CANONICAL
        option is specified, canonical correlations, canonical structures, canonical
        coefficients, and means of canonical variables for each class are included
        in the data set. If METHOD=NORMAL is used, the output data set also

includes coefficients of the discriminant functions, and the output data set is TYPE=LINEAR (POOL=YES), TYPE=QUAD (POOL=NO), or TYPE=MIXED (POOL=TEST). If METHOD=NPAR is used, this output data set is TYPE=CORR.

When the input data set is an ordinary SAS data set, the following three options can be used to generate classification results and group-specific density estimates:

OUT=*SASdataset*
names an output SAS data set containing all the data from the DATA= data set, plus the posterior probabilities and the class into which each observation is classified by resubstitution. When the CANONICAL option is specified, the data set also contains new variables with canonical variable scores.

OUTCROSS=*SASdataset*
names an output SAS data set containing all the data from the DATA= data set, plus the posterior probabilities and the class into which each observation is classified by crossvalidation. When the CANONICAL option is specified, the data set also contains new variables with canonical variable scores.

OUTD=*SASdataset*
names an output SAS data set containing all the data from the DATA= data set, plus the group-specific density estimates for each observation.

When the TESTDATA= option is used, the following two options can be used to generate classification results and group-specific density estimates for observations in the test data set:

TESTOUT=*SASdataset*
names an output SAS data set containing all the data from the TESTDATA= data set, plus the posterior probabilities and the class into which each observation is classified. When the CANONICAL option is specified, the data set also contains new variables with canonical variable scores.

TESTOUTD=*SASdataset*
names an output SAS data set containing all the data from the TESTDATA= data set, plus the group-specific density estimates for each observation.

Options to Select the Type of Discriminant Analysis

METHOD=NORMAL
METHOD=NPAR
determines the method to use in deriving the classification criterion. When METHOD=NORMAL is specified, a parametric method based on a multivariate normal distribution within each class is used to derive a linear or quadratic discriminant function. When METHOD= NPAR is specified, a nonparametric method is used. METHOD=NORMAL is the default.

POOL=YES
POOL=NO
POOL=TEST
determines whether the pooled or within-group covariance matrix is the basis of the measure of the squared distance. POOL=YES uses the pooled covariance matrix in calculating the (generalized) squared

distances. POOL=NO uses the individual within-group covariance matrices in calculating the distances. POOL=YES is the default.

When METHOD=NORMAL is used, POOL=TEST requests Bartlett's modification of the likelihood ratio test (Morrison 1976; Anderson 1984) of the homogeneity of the within-group covariance matrices. The test is unbiased (Perlman 1980). However, it is not robust to non-normality. If the test statistic is significant at the level specified by the SLPOOL= option (below), the within-group covariance matrices are used. Otherwise, the pooled covariance matrix is used. The discriminant function coefficients are printed only when the pooled covariance matrix is used.

SLPOOL=p

specifies the significance level for the test of homogeneity. The SLPOOL= option is used only when POOL=TEST is also specified. If POOL=TEST appears but SLPOOL= is not specified, 0.10 is used as the significance level for the test.

Options Concerning the Use of a Nonparametric Method (METHOD=NPAR)

Choose either the K= or R= option. Do not specify both.

K=k

specifies a k value for the k-nearest-neighbor rule. An observation $\mathbf{x}$ is classified into a group based on the information from the k nearest neighbors of $\mathbf{x}$.

R=r

specifies a radius r value for kernel density estimation. With uniform, Epanechnikov, biweight, or triweight kernels, an observation $\mathbf{x}$ is classified into a group based on the information from observations $\mathbf{y}$ in the training set within the radius r of $\mathbf{x}$, that is, the group t observations $\mathbf{y}$ with squared distance $d_t^2(\mathbf{x},\mathbf{y}) \leq r^2$. When a normal kernel is used, the classification of an observation $\mathbf{x}$ is based on the information of the estimated group-specific densities from all observations in the training set. $r^2 \mathbf{V}_t$ is used as the group t covariance matrix in the normal-kernel density, where $\mathbf{V}_t$ is the matrix used in calculating the squared distances.

KERNEL=UNI | UNIFORM
KERNEL=NOR | NORMAL
KERNEL=EPA | EPANECHNIKOV
KERNEL=BIW | BIWEIGHT
KERNEL=TRI | TRIWEIGHT

specifies a kernel density to estimate the group-specific densities. You can use the KERNEL= option only when the R= option is specified. KERNEL=UNIFORM is the default.

METRIC=FULL
METRIC=DIAGONAL
METRIC=IDENTITY

specifies the metric in which the computations of squared distances are performed. METRIC=FULL uses either the pooled covariance matrix (POOL=YES) or individual within-group covariance matrices (POOL=NO) to compute the squared distances. METRIC=DIAGONAL uses either the diagonal matrix of the pooled covariance matrix (POOL=YES) or diagonal matrices of individual within-group covariance matrices (POOL=NO) to compute the squared distances. METRIC=IDENTITY uses Euclidean distance. METRIC=FULL is the default. When METHOD=NORMAL is specified, METRIC=FULL is used.

Option Concerning the Classification Rule

THRESHOLD=p

specifies the minimum acceptable posterior probability for classification, where $0 < p < 1$. If the largest posterior probability of group membership is less than the THRESHOLD value, the observation is classified into group OTHER. The default is THRESHOLD=0 (technically outside your stated range of values).

Option for Determining Singularity

SINGULAR=p

specifies the criterion for determining the singularity of a matrix, where $0 < p < 1$. The default is SINGULAR=1E−8.

Let **T** be the total-sample correlation matrix. If the R^2 for predicting a quantitative variable in the VAR statement from the variables preceding it exceeds $1 - p$, **T** is considered singular. If **T** is singular, the probability levels for the multivariate test statistics and canonical correlations are adjusted for the number of variables with R^2 exceeding $1 - p$.

Let S_t be the group t covariance matrix and **S** be the pooled covariance matrix. In group t, if the R^2 for predicting a quantitative variable in the VAR statement from the variables preceding it exceeds $1 - p$, S_t is considered singular. Similarly, if the partial R^2 for predicting a quantitative variable in the VAR statement from the variables preceding it, after controlling for the effect of the CLASS variable, exceeds $1 - p$, **S** is considered singular.

Let **V** be a singular covariance matrix. **V** can be either a within-group covariance matrix or the pooled covariance matrix. Let v be the number of variables in the VAR statement and the nullity n be the number of variables among them, with (partial) R^2 exceeding $1 - p$. If the determinant of **V** (Testing of Homogeneity of Within Covariance Matrices) or the inverse of **V** (Squared Distances and Generalized Squared Distances) is required, a quasi-determinant or quasi-inverse will be used instead. DISCRIM scales each variable to unit total-sample variance before calculating this quasi-determinant or quasi-inverse. The calculation is based on the spectral decomposition $\mathbf{V} = \mathbf{\Gamma} \mathbf{\Lambda} \mathbf{\Gamma}'$. $\mathbf{\Gamma}$ is a matrix of eigenvectors, and $\mathbf{\Lambda}$ is a diagonal matrix of eigenvalues λ_j, $j = 1, \ldots, v$. When the nullity n is less than v, set $\lambda_j^0 = \lambda_j$ for $j = 1, \ldots, v - n$, and $\lambda_j^0 = p\bar{\lambda}$ for $j = v - n + 1, \ldots, v$, where $\bar{\lambda} = \Sigma_{k=1}^{v-n} \lambda_k / (v - n)$. When the nullity n is equal to v, set $\lambda_j^0 = p$, for $j = 1, \ldots, v$. A quasi-determinant is then defined as the product of λ_j^0, $j = 1, \ldots, v$. Similarly, a quasi-inverse of a singular V is defined as $\mathbf{V}^* = \mathbf{\Gamma} \mathbf{\Lambda}^* \mathbf{\Gamma}'$, where $\mathbf{\Lambda}^*$ is a diagonal matrix of values $1/\lambda_j^0$, $j = 1, \ldots, v$.

Options Concerning Canonical Discriminant Analysis

CANONICAL
CAN

requests canonical discriminant analysis.

CANPREFIX=name

specifies a prefix for naming the canonical variables. By default the names are CAN1, CAN2, . . . , CANn. If CANPREFIX=ABC is specified,

the components are named ABC1, ABC2, ABC3, and so on. The number
of characters in the prefix, plus the number of digits required to
designate the canonical variables, should not exceed eight. The prefix
will be truncated if the combined length exceeds eight.

NCAN=n

specifies the number of canonical variables to be computed. The value
of n must be less than or equal to the number of variables. If the
NCAN=0 option is specified, the procedure prints the canonical
correlations but not the canonical coefficients, structures, or means. Let
v be the number of variables in the VAR statement and c be the number
of classes. When the NCAN= option is not specified, only min(v, $c-1$)
canonical variables are generated; when an output data set (OUT=,
OUTCROSS=, TESTOUT=) is also requested, v canonical variables are
generated. In this case, the last $v-(c-1)$ canonical variables have
missing values.

The CANONICAL option is activated when either the NCAN= or the
CANPREFIX= option is specified. A discriminant criterion is always derived in
PROC DISCRIM. If you want canonical discriminant analysis without the use of
discriminant criterion, PROC CANDISC should be used.

Options for Resubstitution Classification

When the input data set is an ordinary SAS data set, the following options can
be used:

LIST

prints the resubstitution classification results for each observation.

LISTERR

prints the resubstitution classification results for misclassified
observations only.

NOCLASSIFY

suppresses the resubstitution classification of the input DATA= data set.

Options for Crossvalidation Classification

The CROSSVALIDATE option is set when the CROSSLIST, CROSSLISTERR, or
OUTCROSS= option is specified.

CROSSLIST

prints the cross-validation classification results for each observation.

CROSSLISTERR

prints the cross-validation classification results for misclassified
observations only.

CROSSVALIDATE

requests the cross-validation classification of the input DATA= data set.
When a parametric method is used, DISCRIM classifies each observation
in the DATA= data set using a discriminant function computed from the
other observations in the DATA= data set, excluding the observation
being classified. When a nonparametric method is used, the pooled
covariance matrix (within-class covariance matrices) used to compute
the distances is based on all observations in the data set and does not
exclude the observation being classified. However, the observation
being classified is excluded from the nonparametric density estimation (if
the R= option is specified) or the k nearest neighbors (if the K= option
is specified) of that observation.

Options for Test Data Classification

TESTLIST
lists classification results for all observations in the TESTDATA=data set.

TESTLISTERR
lists only misclassified observations in the TESTDATA=data set but only if a TESTCLASS statement is also used.

Option for Error-Rate Estimation

POSTERR
prints the posterior probability error-rate estimates of the classification criterion based on the classification results.

Options to Control Printing

The following options control the printing of correlations:

BCORR
prints between-class correlations.

PCORR
prints pooled within-class correlations.

TCORR
prints total-sample correlations.

WCORR
prints within-class correlations for each class level.

The following options control the printing of covariances:

BCOV
prints between-class covariances. The between-class covariance matrix equals the between-class SSCP matrix divided by $n(c-1)/c$, where n is the number of observations and c is the number of classes. The between-class covariances should be interpreted in comparison with the total-sample and within-class covariances, not as formal estimates of population parameters.

PCOV
prints pooled within-class covariances.

TCOV
prints total-sample covariances.

WCOV
prints within-class covariances for each class level.

The following options control the printing of the SSCP matrix:

BSSCP
prints the between-class SSCP matrix.

PSSCP
prints the pooled within-class corrected SSCP matrix.

TSSCP
prints the total-sample corrected SSCP matrix.

WSSCP
prints the within-class corrected SSCP matrix for each class level.

Additional options to control printing are as follows:

ALL
> activates all options in this section. When the derived classification criterion is used to classify observations, the ALL option also activates the POSTERR option.

ANOVA
> prints univariate statistics for testing the hypothesis that the class means are equal in the population for each variable.

DISTANCE
> prints squared distances between class means. The squared distances are based on the specification of the POOL= and METRIC= options.

MANOVA
> prints multivariate statistics for testing the hypothesis that the class means are equal in the population.

SIMPLE
> prints simple descriptive statistics for the total sample and within each class.

STDMEAN
> prints total-sample and pooled within-class standardized class means.

Options to Suppress Printing

NOPRINT
> suppresses the printout.

SHORT
> suppresses the printing of certain items in the default printout. If METHOD=NORMAL is used, DISCRIM suppresses the printing of determinants and generalized squared distances between-class means and discriminant function coefficients. When the CANONICAL option is specified, DISCRIM suppresses the printing of canonical structures, canonical coefficients, and class means on canonical variables; only tables of canonical correlations are printed.

BY Statement

> BY *variables*;

A BY statement can be used with PROC DISCRIM to obtain separate analyses on observations in groups defined by the BY variables. When a BY statement appears, the procedure expects the DATA= data set to be sorted in order of the BY variables.

If your DATA= data set is not sorted in ascending order, use the SORT procedure with a similar BY statement to sort the data, or, if appropriate, use the BY statement options NOTSORTED or DESCENDING. For more information, see the discussion of the BY statement in "SAS Statements Used in the PROC Step" in the *SAS Language Guide*.

If the TESTDATA= option is specified and the TESTDATA=data set does not contain any of the BY variables, then the entire TESTDATA= data set is classified according to the discriminant functions computed in each BY group in the DATA= data set.

If the TESTDATA= data set contains some but not all of the BY variables, or if some BY variables do not have the same type or length in the TESTDATA= data set as in the DATA= data set, then DISCRIM prints an error message and stops.

If all BY variables appear in the TESTDATA= data set with the same type and length as in the DATA= data set, then each BY group in the TESTDATA= data set is classified by the discriminant function from the corresponding BY group in the DATA= data set. The BY groups in the TESTDATA= data set must be in the same order as in the DATA= data set. If NOTSORTED is specified in the BY statement, there must be exactly the same BY groups in the same order in both data sets. If NOTSORTED is not specified, some BY groups may appear in one data set but not in the other. If some BY groups appear in the TESTDATA= data set but not in the DATA= data set, and an output test data set is requested using the TESTOUT= or TESTOUTD= option, these BY groups will not be included in the output data set.

CLASS Statement

CLASS *variable*;

The values of the classification variable define the groups for analysis. Class levels are determined by the formatted values of the CLASS variable. The specified variable can be numeric or character. A CLASS statement is required.

FREQ Statement

FREQ *variable*;

If a variable in the data set represents the frequency of occurrence for the other values in the observation, include the variable's name in a FREQ statement. The procedure then treats the data set as if each observation appears *n* times, where *n* is the value of the FREQ variable for the observation. The total number of observations is considered to be equal to the sum of the FREQ variable when the procedure determines degrees of freedom for significance probabilities.

If the value of the FREQ variable is missing or less than one, the observation is not used in the analysis. If the value is not an integer, the value is truncated to an integer.

ID Statement

ID *variable*;

The ID statement is effective only when LIST or LISTERR appears in the PROC DISCRIM statement. When DISCRIM prints the classification results, the ID variable is printed for each observation, rather than the observation number.

PRIORS Statement

PRIORS EQUAL;
PRIORS PROPORTIONAL | PROP;
PRIORS *probabilities*;

To set the prior probabilities equal, use

```
priors equal;
```

To set the prior probabilities proportional to the sample sizes, use

```
priors proportional;
```

For other than equal or proportional priors, give the prior probability wanted for each level of the classification variable. Each class level can be written as either a SAS name or a quoted string, and it must be followed by an equal sign and a numeric constant between zero and one. For example, to define prior probabilities for each level of GRADE, where GRADE's values are A, B, C, and D, the PRIORS statement can be

```
priors a=.1  b=.3  c=.5  d=.1;
```

If GRADE is numeric, with formatted values of '1', '2', and '3', the PRIORS statement can be

```
priors '1'=.3  '2'=.6  '3'=.1;
```

The specified class levels must exactly match the formatted values of the CLASS variable. For example, if a CLASS variable C has the format 4.2 and a value 5, the PRIORS statement must specify '5.00', not '5.0' or '5'. If the prior probabilities do not sum to one, these probabilities are scaled proportionally to have the sum equal to one. PRIORS EQUAL is the default.

TESTCLASS Statement

TESTCLASS *variable*;

The TESTCLASS statement names the variable in the TESTDATA=data set to determine whether an observation in the TESTDATA=data set is misclassified. The TESTCLASS variable should have the same type (character or numeric) and length as the variable given in the CLASS statement. DISCRIM considers an observation misclassified when the formatted value of the TESTCLASS variable does not match the group into which the TESTDATA= observation is classified. When the TESTCLASS statement is missing and TESTDATA=data set contains the variable given in the CLASS statement, the CLASS variable is used as the TESTCLASS variable.

TESTFREQ Statement

TESTFREQ *variable*;

If a variable in the TESTDATA=data set represents the frequency of occurrence for the other values in the observation, include the variable's name in a TESTFREQ statement. The procedure then treats the data set as if each observation appears *n* times, where *n* is the value of the TESTFREQ variable for the observation.

If the value of the TESTFREQ variable is missing or less than one, the observation is not used in the analysis. If the value is not an integer, the value is truncated to an integer.

TESTID Statement

TESTID *variable*;

The TESTID statement is effective only when TESTLIST or TESTLISTERR appears in the PROC DISCRIM statement. When DISCRIM prints the classification results for the TESTDATA=data set, the TESTID variable is printed for each observation, rather than the observation number. The variable given in the TESTID statement must be in the TESTDATA=data set.

VAR Statement

VAR *variables*;

The VAR statement specifies the quantitative variables to be included in the analysis. The default is all numeric variables not listed in other statements.

WEIGHT Statement

WEIGHT *variable*;

To use relative weights for each observation in the input data set, place the weights in a variable in the data set and specify the name in a WEIGHT statement. This is often done when the variance associated with each observation is different and the values of the weight variable are proportional to the reciprocals of the variances. If the value of the WEIGHT variable is missing or less than zero, then a value of zero for the weight is used.

The WEIGHT and FREQ statements have a similar effect except that the WEIGHT statement does not alter the degrees of freedom.

DETAILS

Missing Values

Observations with missing values for variables in the analysis are excluded from the development of the classification criterion. When the values of the classification variable are missing, the observation is excluded from the development of the classification criterion, but if no other variables in the analysis have missing values for that observation, the observation is classified and printed with the classification results.

Computational Resources

In the following discussion, let

n = number of observations in the training data set
v = number of variables
c = number of class levels
k = number of canonical variables
l = length of the CLASS variable.

Memory Requirements

The amount of temporary storage required depends on the discriminant method used and the options specified. The amount of temporary storage in bytes needed to process the data is

$$c(8v^2 + 32v + 3l + 128) + 16v^2 + 96v + 4l \ .$$

A parametric method (METHOD=NORMAL) requires an additional temporary memory of $24v^2+88v$ bytes. When CROSSVALIDATE is specified, this temporary storage must be increased by $8v^2+40v$ bytes. When a nonparametric method (METHOD=NPAR) is used, an additional temporary storage of $20v^2+84v$ bytes is needed if METRIC=FULL is used to evaluate the distances.

With the MANOVA option, the temporary storage must be increased by $16v^2+88v$ bytes. The CANONICAL option requires a temporary storage of $4v^2+92v+8k(v+c)$ bytes. The POSTERR option requires a temporary storage of $8c^2+64c+96$ bytes. Additional temporary storage is also required for classification summary and for each output data set.

For example, in the PROC statement

```
proc discrim manova;
   class gp;
   var x1 x2 x3;
```

If the CLASS variable GP has a length of eight and the input data set contains two class levels, the procedure requires a temporary storage of 1992 bytes. This includes 1104 bytes for data processing, 480 bytes for using a parametric method, and 408 bytes for specifying the MANOVA option.

Time Requirements

The following factors determine the time requirements of discriminant analysis.

1. The time needed for reading the data and computing covariance matrices is proportional to nv^2. DISCRIM must also look up each class level in the list. The time for this is proportional to $\log(c)$; this is faster if the data are sorted by the CLASS variable. The time for this step is proportional to a value ranging from n to $n \log(c)$.
2. The time for inverting a covariance matrix is proportional to v^3.
3. With a parametric method, the time required to classify each observation is proportional to cv for a linear discriminant function and is proportional to cv^2 for a quadratic discriminant function. When the CROSSVALIDATE option is specified, the discriminant function is updated for each observation in the classification. A substantial amount of time is required.
4. With a nonparametric method, the data are stored in a tree structure (Friedman, Bentley, and Finkel 1977). The time required to organize the observations into the tree structure is proportional to $nv \log(n)$. The time for performing each tree search is proportional to $\log(n)$. When the normal KERNEL= option is specified, all observations in the training sample contribute to the density estimation. More computer time is needed.
5. The time required for the canonical discriminant analysis is proportional to v^3.

Each of the above factors has a different constant of proportionality.

Posterior Probability Error-Rate Estimates

The posterior probability error-rate estimates (Fukunaga and Kessell 1973; Glick 1978; Hora and Wilcox 1982) for each group are based on the posterior probabilities of the observations classified into that same group.

The notation below is used to describe the posterior probability error rates:

$\mathbf{x}$ a vector containing the variables of an observation

t a subscript to distinguish the groups

f_t the probability density function in group t

q_t the prior probability for group t

$p(t \mid \mathbf{x})$ the posterior probability of $\mathbf{x}$ for group t

e_t the classification error rate for group t.

A sample of observations with classification results can be used to estimate the posterior error rates. The notation below is used to describe the sample:

S the set of observations in the (training) sample

n the number of observations of S

n_t the number of observations of S in group t

R_t the set of observations such that the posterior probability belonging to group t is the largest

R_{ut} the set of observations from group u such that the posterior probability belonging to group t is the largest.

The classification error rate for group t is defined as

$$e_t = 1 - \int_{R_t} f_t(\mathbf{x}) \, d\mathbf{x}$$

The posterior probability of $\mathbf{x}$ for group t can be written as

$$p(t \mid \mathbf{x}) = \frac{q_t \, f_t(\mathbf{x})}{f(\mathbf{x})}$$

where $f(\mathbf{x}) = \Sigma_u q_u f_u(\mathbf{x})$ is the unconditional density of $\mathbf{x}$.

Thus, by replacing $f_t(\mathbf{x})$ with $p(t \mid \mathbf{x}) \, f(\mathbf{x})/q_t$, the error rate is

$$e_t = 1 - \frac{1}{q_t} \int_{R_t} p(t \mid \mathbf{x}) \, f(\mathbf{x}) \, d\mathbf{x} \quad .$$

An estimator of e_t, unstratified over the groups from which the observations come, is then given by

$$\hat{e}_t \text{ (unstratified)} = 1 - \frac{1}{nq_t} \Sigma_{R_t} p(t \mid \mathbf{x})$$

where $p(t \mid \mathbf{x})$ is estimated from the classification criterion, and the summation is over all sample observations of S classified into group t. The true group membership of each observation is not required in the estimation.

Further, replacing $f(\mathbf{x})$ with $\Sigma_u q_u f_u(\mathbf{x})$, the error rate can be written as

$$e_t = 1 - \frac{1}{q_t} \Sigma_u \, q_u \int_{R_{ut}} p(t \mid \mathbf{x}) \, f_u(\mathbf{x}) \, d\mathbf{x}$$

and an estimator stratified over the group from which the observations come is given by

$$\hat{e}_t \text{ (stratified)} = 1 - \frac{1}{q_t} \Sigma_u \, q_u \frac{1}{n_u} (\Sigma_{R_{ut}} p(t \mid \mathbf{x})) \quad .$$

The inner summation is over all sample observations of S coming from group u and classified into group t. The stratified estimate uses only the observations with known group membership. When the prior probabilities of the group membership are proportional to the group sizes, the stratified estimate is the same as the unstratified estimator.

The estimated group-specific error rates can be less than zero, usually due to a large discrepancy between prior probabilities of group membership and group sizes. To have a reliable estimate for group-specific error rate estimates, the group sizes should be at least approximately proportional to the prior probabilities of group membership.

A total error rate is defined as a weighted average of the individual group error rates

$$e = \Sigma_t \, q_t \, e_t$$

and can be estimated from

$$\hat{e} \text{ (unstratified)} = \Sigma_t q_t \hat{e}_t \text{ (unstratified)}$$

or

$$\hat{e} \text{ (stratified)} = \Sigma_t q_t \hat{e}_t \text{ (stratified)} \quad .$$

The total unstratified error rate estimate can also be written as

$$\hat{e} \text{ (unstratified)} = 1 - \frac{1}{n} \Sigma_t \Sigma_{R_t} p(t \mid \mathbf{x})$$

which is one minus the average value of the maximum posterior probabilities for each observation in the sample. The prior probabilities of group membership do not appear explicitly in this overall estimate.

Saving and Using Calibration Information

When METHOD=NORMAL is used to derive a linear or quadratic discriminant function, the calibration information developed by DISCRIM can be saved in a SAS data set by using the OUTSTAT= option in the procedure. DISCRIM then creates a specially structured SAS data set of TYPE=LINEAR, TYPE=QUAD, or TYPE=MIXED that contains the calibration information.

To use this calibration information to classify observations in another data set,

* give the name of the calibration data set after the DATA= option in the PROC DISCRIM statement, and
* give the name of the data set to be classified after the TESTDATA= option in the PROC DISCRIM statement.

Here is an example:

```
data original;
   input position x1 x2;
   cards;
data lines
;
proc discrim outstat=info;
   class position;
data check;
   input position x1 x2;
   cards;
second set of data lines
;
proc discrim data=info testdata=check testlist;
   class position;
```

The first DATA step creates the SAS data set ORIGINAL, which DISCRIM uses to develop a classification criterion. Specifying OUTSTAT=INFO in the PROC DISCRIM statement causes DISCRIM to store the calibration information in a new data set called INFO. The next DATA step creates the data set CHECK. The second PROC DISCRIM statement specifies DATA=INFO and TESTDATA=CHECK so that the classification criterion developed earlier is applied to the CHECK data set.

Input Data Sets

DATA= Data Set

When METHOD=NPAR is used, an ordinary SAS data set is required as the input DATA=data set. When METHOD=NORMAL is used, the DATA=data set can be an ordinary SAS data set or one of several specially structured data sets created by SAS/STAT procedures. These specially structured data sets include

- TYPE=CORR data sets created by PROC CORR using a BY statement
- TYPE=COV data sets created by PROC PRINCOMP using both the COV option and a BY statement
- TYPE=CSSCP data sets created by PROC CORR using the CSSCP option and a BY statement, where the OUT=data set is assigned TYPE=CSSCP with the TYPE= data set option
- TYPE=SSCP data sets created by PROC REG using both the OUTSSCP= option and a BY statement
- TYPE=LINEAR, TYPE=QUAD, and TYPE=MIXED data sets produced by previous runs of DISCRIM using both METHOD=NORMAL and OUTSTAT= options.

When the input data set is TYPE=CORR, TYPE=COV, TYPE=CSSCP, or TYPE=SSCP, the BY variable in these data sets becomes the CLASS variable in DISCRIM.

When the input data set is TYPE=CORR, TYPE=COV, or TYPE=CSSCP, DISCRIM reads the number of observations for each class from the observations with _TYPE_='N', and the variable means in each class from the observations with _TYPE_='MEAN'. DISCRIM then reads the within-class correlations from the observations with _TYPE_='CORR' and the standard deviations from the observations with _TYPE_='STD' (data set TYPE=CORR), the within-class covariances from the observations with _TYPE_='COV' (data set TYPE=COV), or the within-class corrected sums of squares and crossproducts from the observations with _TYPE_='CSSCP' (data set TYPE=CSSCP).

When POOL=YES is used and the data set does not include any observations with _TYPE_ ='CSSCP' (data set TYPE=CSSCP), _TYPE_='COV' (data set TYPE=COV), _TYPE_='CORR' (data set TYPE=CORR) for each class, DISCRIM reads the pooled within-class information from the data set. In this case, DISCRIM reads the pooled within-class covariances from the observations with _TYPE_='PCOV' (data set TYPE=COV), or the pooled within-class correlations from the observations with _TYPE_='PCORR' and the pooled within-class standard deviations from the observations with _TYPE_='PSTD' (data set TYPE=CORR) or the pooled within-class corrected SSCP matrix from the observations with _TYPE_='PSSCP' (data set TYPE=CSSCP).

When the input data set is TYPE=SSCP, DISCRIM reads the number of observations for each class from the observations with _TYPE_='N', the sum of weights of observations for each class from the variable INTERCEP in observations with _TYPE_='SSCP' and _NAME_='INTERCEP', the variable sums from the variable=*variablenames* in observations with _TYPE_='SSCP' and _NAME_='INTERCEP', and the uncorrected sums of squares and crossproducts from the variable=*variablenames* in observations with _TYPE_='SSCP' and _NAME_='*variablenames*'.

When the input data set is TYPE=LINEAR, TYPE=QUAD, or TYPE=MIXED, DISCRIM reads the prior probabilities for each class from the observations with variable _TYPE_='PRIOR'.

When the input data set is TYPE=LINEAR, DISCRIM reads the coefficients of the linear discriminant functions from the observations with variable _TYPE_='LINEAR' (see below).

When the input data set is TYPE=QUAD, DISCRIM reads the coefficients of the quadratic discriminant functions from the observations with variable _TYPE_='QUAD' (see below).

When the input data set is TYPE=MIXED, DISCRIM reads the coefficients of the linear discriminant functions from the observations with variable _TYPE_='LINEAR'. If there are no observations with _TYPE_='LINEAR', DISCRIM then reads the coefficients of the quadratic discriminant functions from the observations with variable _TYPE_='QUAD'.

TESTDATA= Data Set

The TESTDATA= data set is an ordinary SAS data set whose observations are to be classified. The quantitative variable names in this data set must match those in the DATA=data set. The TESTCLASS statement can be used to specify the variable containing group membership information of the TESTDATA= data set observations. When the TESTCLASS statement is missing and the TESTDATA= data set contains the variable given in the CLASS statement, this variable is used as the TESTCLASS variable. The TESTCLASS variable should have the same type (character or numeric) and length as the variable given in the CLASS statement. DISCRIM considers an observation misclassified when the value of the TESTCLASS variable's does not match the group into which the TESTDATA= observation is classified.

Output Data Sets

When an output data set includes variables containing the posterior probabilities of group membership (OUT=, OUTCROSS=, or TESTOUT= data sets) or group-specific density estimates (OUTD= or TESTOUTD= data sets), the names of these variables are constructed from the formatted 8-character value of the class levels converted to SAS names. That is , if the formatted value looks like a numeric constant, DISCRIM changes the characters '+', '−', and '.' to 'P', 'N', and 'D', respectively. If the first character is numeric, an underscore is prefixed to the value, truncating the last character of an 8-character value. Any remaining invalid characters are replaced by underscores.

OUT= Data Set

The OUT= data set contains all the variables in the DATA= data set, plus new variables containing the posterior probabilities and the resubstitution classification results. The names of the new variables containing the posterior probabilities are constructed from the formatted values of the class levels converted to SAS names. A new variable, _INTO_, with the same attributes as the CLASS variable, gives the class to which each observation is assigned. If an observation is classified into group OTHER, the variable _INTO_ has a missing value. When the CANONICAL option is specified, the data set also contains new variables with canonical variable scores. The NCAN= option determines the number of canonical variables. The names of the canonical variables are constructed as described in the CANPREFIX= option. The canonical variables have means equal to zero and pooled within-class variances equal to one.

OUTD= Data Set

The OUTD= data set contains all the variables in the DATA= data set, plus new variables containing the group-specific density estimates. The names of the new variables containing the density estimates are constructed from the formatted values of the class levels.

OUTCROSS= Data Set

The OUTCROSS= data set contains all the variables in the DATA= data set, plus new variables containing the posterior probabilities and the classification results of crossvalidation. The names of the new variables containing the posterior probabilities are constructed from the formatted values of the class levels. A new variable, _INTO_, with the same attributes as the CLASS variable, gives the class to which each observation is assigned. When an observation is classified into group OTHER, the variable _INTO_ will have a missing value. When the CANONICAL option is specified, the data set also contains new variables with canonical variable scores. The NCAN= option determines the number of new variables. The names of the new variables are constructed as described in the CANPREFIX= option. The new variables have mean zero and pooled within-class variance equal to one.

An OUT=, OUTD=, or OUTCROSS= data set cannot be created if the DATA= data set is not an ordinary SAS data set.

TESTOUT= Data Set

The TESTOUT= data set contains all the variables in the TESTDATA= data set, plus new variables containing the posterior probabilities and the classification results. The names of the new variables containing the posterior probabilities are formed from the formatted values of the class levels. A new variable, _INTO_, with the same attributes as the CLASS variable, gives the class to which each observation is assigned. If an observation is classified into group OTHER, the variable _INTO_ has a missing value. When the CANONICAL option is specified, the data set also contains new variables with canonical variable scores. The NCAN= option determines the number of new variables. The names of the new variables are formed as described in the CANPREFIX= option.

TESTOUTD= Data Set

The TESTOUTD= data set contains all the variables in the TESTDATA= data set, plus new variables containing the group-specific density estimates. The names of the new variables containing the density estimates are formed from the formatted values of the class levels.

OUTSTAT= Data Set

The OUTSTAT= data set is similar to the TYPE=CORR data set produced by the CORR procedure. The data set contains various statistics such as means, standard deviations, and correlations. When the CANONICAL option is specified, canonical correlations, canonical structures, canonical coefficients, and means of canonical variables for each class are included in the data set. If METHOD=NORMAL is used, the output data set also includes coefficients of the discriminant functions, and the data set is TYPE=LINEAR (POOL=YES), TYPE=QUAD (POOL=NO), or TYPE=MIXED (POOL=TEST). If METHOD=NPAR is used, this output data set is TYPE=CORR.

The OUTSTAT= data set contains the following variables:

- the BY variables, if any
- the CLASS variable
- _TYPE_, a character variable of length 8 that identifies the type of statistic
- _NAME_, a character variable of length 8 that identifies the row of the matrix, the name of the canonical variable, or the type of the discriminant function coefficients

- the quantitative variables, that is, those in the VAR statement, or, if there is no VAR statement, all numeric variables not listed in any other statement.

The observations, as identified by the variable _TYPE_, have the following _TYPE_ values:

TYPE	Contents
N	number of observations for both the total sample (CLASS variable missing) and within each class (CLASS variable present)
SUMWGT	sum of weights for both the total sample (CLASS variable missing) and within each class (CLASS variable present), if a WEIGHT statement is specified
MEAN	means for both the total sample (CLASS variable missing) and within each class (CLASS variable present)
PRIOR	prior probability for each class
STDMEAN	total-standardized class means
PSTDMEAN	pooled within-class standardized class means
STD	standard deviations for both the total sample (CLASS variable missing) and within each class (CLASS variable present)
PSTD	pooled within-class standard deviations
BSTD	between-class standard deviations
RSQUARED	univariate R^2s
DETERM	determinant or quasi-determinant of the within-class covariance matrix either pooled (CLASS variable missing) or not pooled (CLASS variable present).

The following kinds of observations are identified by the combination of the variables _TYPE_ and _NAME_. When the _TYPE_ variable has one of the values below, the _NAME_ variable identifies the row of the matrix.

TYPE	Contents
CSSCP	corrected SSCP matrix for both the total sample (CLASS variable missing) and within each class (CLASS variable present)
PSSCP	pooled within-class corrected SSCP matrix
BSSCP	between-class SSCP matrix
COV	covariance matrix for both the total sample (CLASS variable missing) and within each class (CLASS variable present)
PCOV	pooled within-class covariance matrix
BCOV	between-class covariance matrix
CORR	correlation matrix for both the total sample (CLASS variable missing) and within each class (CLASS variable present)
PCORR	pooled within-class correlation matrix
BCORR	between-class correlation matrix.

When canonical discriminant analysis is requested, the _TYPE_ variable can have one of the values below. The _NAME_ variable identifies a canonical variable.

TYPE	Contents
CANCORR	canonical correlations
STRUCTUR	canonical structure
BSTRUCT	between canonical structure
PSTRUCT	pooled within-class canonical structure
SCORE	standardized canonical coefficients
RAWSCORE	raw canonical coefficients
CANMEAN	means of the canonical variables for each class.

When METHOD=NORMAL is used, the _TYPE_ variable can have one of the variables below. The _NAME_ variable identifies different types of coefficients in the discriminant function. The values of the _TYPE_ variable are as follows:

TYPE	Contents
LINEAR	coefficients of the linear discriminant functions
QUAD	coefficients of the quadratic discriminant functions.

The values of the _NAME_ variable are as follows:

NAME	Contents
variable names	quadratic coefficients of the quadratic discriminant functions (a symmetric matrix for each class)
LINEAR	linear coefficients of the discriminant functions
CONST	constant coefficients of the discriminant functions.

Printed Output

The printed output from PROC DISCRIM includes the following:

1. Class Level Information, including the values of the classification variable, Output SAS Name constructed from each class value (if there is an output data set containing the posterior probabilities or the density estimates), the Frequency and Weight of each value, its Proportion in the total sample, and the Prior Probability for each class level.

Optional output includes the following:

2. Within-Class SSCP Matrices for each group (not shown).
3. Pooled Within-Class SSCP Matrix (not shown).
4. Between-Class SSCP Matrix (not shown).
5. Total-Sample SSCP Matrix (not shown).
6. Within-Class Covariance Matrices, S_t, for each group.
7. Pooled Within-Class Covariance Matrix, **S**.
8. Between-Class Covariance Matrix (not shown), equal to the between-class SSCP matrix divided by $n(c-1)/c$, where n is the number of observations and c is the number of classes.
9. Total-Sample Covariance Matrix (not shown).
10. Within-Class Correlation Coefficients and Prob $> |R|$ to test the hypothesis that the within-class population correlation coefficients are zero (not shown).

11. Pooled Within-Class Correlation Coefficients and Prob > |R| to test the hypothesis that the partial population correlation coefficients are zero (not shown).

12. Between-Class Correlation Coefficients and Prob > |R| to test the hypothesis that the between-class population correlation coefficients are zero (not shown).

13. Total-Sample Correlation Coefficients and Prob > |R| to test the hypothesis that the total population correlation coefficients are zero (not shown).

14. Simple descriptive Statistics including N (the number of observations), Sum, Mean, Variance, and Standard Deviation for both the total sample and within each class (not shown).

15. Total-Sample Standardized Class Means, obtained by subtracting the grand mean from each class mean and dividing by the total sample standard deviation (not shown).

16. Pooled Within-Class Standardized Class Means, obtained by subtracting the grand mean from each class mean and dividing by the pooled within-class standard deviation (not shown).

17. Pairwise Squared Distances Between Groups.

18. Univariate Test Statistics, including Total STD (total-sample standard deviations), Pooled STD (pooled within-class standard deviations), Between STD (between-class standard deviations), R-Squared (univariate R^2s), RSQ/(1−RSQ) ($R^2/(1−R^2)$), and F and Prob > F (univariate F values and probability levels for one-way analyses of variance).

19. Multivariate Statistics and F Approximations including Wilks' Lambda, Pillai's Trace, Hotelling-Lawley Trace, and Roy's Greatest Root with F approximations, degrees of freedom (Num DF and Den DF), and probability values (Pr > F). Each of these four multivariate statistics tests the hypothesis that the class means are equal in the population. See **Multivariate Tests** in Chapter 1, "Introduction to Regression Procedures," for more information.

If METHOD=NORMAL is used, the following three statistics are printed:

20. Covariance Matrix Information including Covariance Matrix Rank and Natural Log of Determinant of the Covariance Matrix for each group (POOL=TEST, POOL=NO) and for the pooled within-group (POOL=TEST, POOL=YES).

21. Optionally, Test of Homogeneity of Within Covariance Matrices (the results of a chi-square test of homogeneity of the within-group covariance matrices) (Morrison 1976; Kendall, Stuart, and Ord 1983; Anderson 1984).

22. Pairwise Generalized Squared Distances Between Groups.

If the CANONICAL option is specified, the printout contains these statistics:

23. Canonical Correlations (not shown).

24. Adjusted Canonical Correlations (Lawley 1959) (not shown). These are asymptotically less biased than the raw correlations and can be negative. The adjusted canonical correlations may not be computable and are printed as missing values if two canonical correlations are nearly equal or if some are close to zero. A missing value is also printed if an adjusted canonical correlation is larger than a previous adjusted canonical correlation.

25. Approx Standard Error, approximate standard error of the canonical correlations (not shown).

26. Squared Canonical Correlations (not shown).

27. Eigenvalues of INV(E)*H (not shown). Each eigenvalue is equal to CANRSQ/(1−CANRSQ), where CANRSQ is the corresponding squared canonical correlation, and can be interpreted as the ratio of between-class variation to within-class variation for the corresponding canonical variable. The table includes Eigenvalues, Differences between successive eigenvalues, the Proportion of the sum of the eigenvalues, and the Cumulative proportion.

28. Likelihood Ratio for the hypothesis that the current canonical correlation and all smaller ones are zero in the population (not shown). The likelihood ratio for all canonical correlations equals Wilks' lambda.

29. Approx F statistic based on Rao's approximation to the distribution of the likelihood ratio (Rao 1973, 556; Kshirsagar 1972, 326) (not shown).

30. Num DF (numerator degrees of freedom), Den DF (denominator degrees of freedom), and Pr > F, the probability level associated with the F statistic (not shown).

The following statistic concerns the classification criterion:

31. the Linear Discriminant Function, but only if METHOD=NORMAL and the pooled covariance matrix is used to calculate the (generalized) squared distances.

When the input DATA= data set is an ordinary SAS data set, the printout includes the following:

32. Optionally, the Resubstitution Results including Obs, the observation number (if an ID statement is included, the values of the ID variable are printed instead of the observation number), the actual group for the observation, the group into which the developed criterion would classify it, and the Posterior Probability of its Membership in each group.

33. Resubstitution Summary, a summary of the performance of the classification criterion based on resubstitution classification results.

34. Error Count Estimate of the resubstitution classification results.

35. Optionally, Posterior Probability Error Rate Estimates of the resubstitution classification results.

If the CROSSVALIDATE option is specified, the printout contains these statistics:

36. Optionally, the Cross-validation Results including Obs, the observation number (if an ID statement is included, the values of the ID variable are printed instead of the observation number), the actual group for the observation, the group into which the developed criterion would classify it, and the Posterior Probability of its Membership in each group.

37. Cross-Validation Summary, a summary of the performance of the classification criterion based on cross-validation classification results.

38. Error Count Estimate of the cross-validation classification results.

39. Optionally, Posterior Probability Error Rate Estimates of the cross-validation classification results.

If the TESTDATA= option is specified, the printout contains these statistics:

40. Optionally, the Classification Results including Obs, the observation number (if a TESTID statement is included, the values of the ID variable are printed instead of the observation number), the actual group for the observation (if a TESTCLASS statement is included), the group into which the developed criterion would classify it, and the Posterior Probability of its Membership in each group.

41. Classification Summary, a summary of the performance of the classification criterion.
42. Error Count Estimate of the test data classification results.
43. Optionally, Posterior Probability Error Rate Estimates of the test data classification results (not shown).

EXAMPLES

The iris data published by Fisher (1936) have been widely used for examples in discriminant analysis and cluster analysis. The sepal length, sepal width, petal length, and petal width were measured in millimeters on fifty iris specimens from each of three species, *Iris setosa, I. versicolor,* and *I. virginica.* The iris data are used in **Example 1** through **Example 4. Example 5** and **Example 6** use remote-sensing data on crops. In this data set, the observations are grouped into five crops: clover, corn, cotton, soybeans, and sugar beets. Four measures called X1 through X4 make up the descriptive variables.

Example 1: Univariate Density Estimates and Posterior Probabilities

In this example, several discriminant analyses are run with a single quantitative variable, petal width, so that density estimates and posterior probabilities can be plotted easily. The example produces **Output 16.1** through **Output 16.5**. PROC CHART is used to display the sample distribution of petal width in the three species. Note the overlapping between species *I. versicolor* and *I. virginica* that the bar chart shows. These statements produce **Output 16.1**:

```
proc format;
    value specname
        1='SETOSA    '
        2='VERSICOLOR'
        3='VIRGINICA ';
    value specchar
        1='S'
        2='O'
        3='V';
run;
data iris;
    title 'Discriminant Analysis of Fisher (1936) Iris Data';
    input sepallen sepalwid petallen petalwid species @@;
    format species specname.;
    label sepallen='Sepal Length in mm.'
          sepalwid='Sepal Width  in mm.'
          petallen='Petal Length in mm.'
          petalwid='Petal Width  in mm.';
    cards;
50 33 14 02 1 64 28 56 22 3 65 28 46 15 2 67 31 56 24 3
63 28 51 15 3 46 34 14 03 1 69 31 51 23 3 62 22 45 15 2
59 32 48 18 2 46 36 10 02 1 61 30 46 14 2 60 27 51 16 2
65 30 52 20 3 56 25 39 11 2 65 30 55 18 3 58 27 51 19 3
68 32 59 23 3 51 33 17 05 1 57 28 45 13 2 62 34 54 23 3
77 38 67 22 3 63 33 47 16 2 67 33 57 25 3 76 30 66 21 3
49 25 45 17 3 55 35 13 02 1 67 30 52 23 3 70 32 47 14 2
64 32 45 15 2 61 28 40 13 2 48 31 16 02 1 59 30 51 18 3
55 24 38 11 2 63 25 50 19 3 64 32 53 23 3 52 34 14 02 1
```

```
49 36 14 01 1 54 30 45 15 2 79 38 64 20 3 44 32 13 02 1
67 33 57 21 3 50 35 16 06 1 58 26 40 12 2 44 30 13 02 1
77 28 67 20 3 63 27 49 18 3 47 32 16 02 1 55 26 44 12 2
50 23 33 10 2 72 32 60 18 3 48 30 14 03 1 51 38 16 02 1
61 30 49 18 3 48 34 19 02 1 50 30 16 02 1 50 32 12 02 1
61 26 56 14 3 64 28 56 21 3 43 30 11 01 1 58 40 12 02 1
51 38 19 04 1 67 31 44 14 2 62 28 48 18 3 49 30 14 02 1
51 35 14 02 1 56 30 45 15 2 58 27 41 10 2 50 34 16 04 1
46 32 14 02 1 60 29 45 15 2 57 26 35 10 2 57 44 15 04 1
50 36 14 02 1 77 30 61 23 3 63 34 56 24 3 58 27 51 19 3
57 29 42 13 2 72 30 58 16 3 54 34 15 04 1 52 41 15 01 1
71 30 59 21 3 64 31 55 18 3 60 30 48 18 3 63 29 56 18 3
49 24 33 10 2 56 27 42 13 2 57 30 42 12 2 55 42 14 02 1
49 31 15 02 1 77 26 69 23 3 60 22 50 15 3 54 39 17 04 1
66 29 46 13 2 52 27 39 14 2 60 34 45 16 2 50 34 15 02 1
44 29 14 02 1 50 20 35 10 2 55 24 37 10 2 58 27 39 12 2
47 32 13 02 1 46 31 15 02 1 69 32 57 23 3 62 29 43 13 2
74 28 61 19 3 59 30 42 15 2 51 34 15 02 1 50 35 13 03 1
56 28 49 20 3 60 22 40 10 2 73 29 63 18 3 67 25 58 18 3
49 31 15 01 1 67 31 47 15 2 63 23 44 13 2 54 37 15 02 1
56 30 41 13 2 63 25 49 15 2 61 28 47 12 2 64 29 43 13 2
51 25 30 11 2 57 28 41 13 2 65 30 58 22 3 69 31 54 21 3
54 39 13 04 1 51 35 14 03 1 72 36 61 25 3 65 32 51 20 3
61 29 47 14 2 56 29 36 13 2 69 31 49 15 2 64 27 53 19 3
68 30 55 21 3 55 25 40 13 2 48 34 16 02 1 48 30 14 01 1
45 23 13 03 1 57 25 50 20 3 57 38 17 03 1 51 38 15 03 1
55 23 40 13 2 66 30 44 14 2 68 28 48 14 2 54 34 17 02 1
51 37 15 04 1 52 35 15 02 1 58 28 51 24 3 67 30 50 17 2
63 33 60 25 3 53 37 15 02 1
;
proc chart data=iris;
   vbar petalwid / subgroup=species midpoints=0 to 30;
   format species specchar.;
run;
```

Output 16.1 Sample Distribution of Petal Width in Three Species

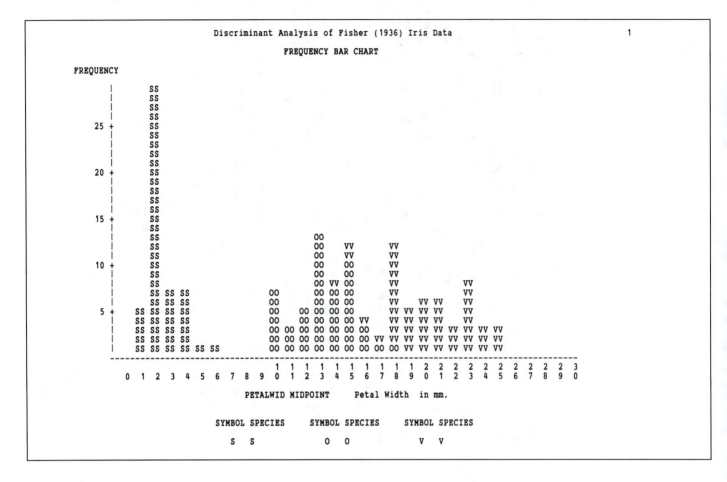

In order to plot the density estimates and posterior probabilities, a data set called PLOTDATA is created containing equally spaced values from −5 to 30, covering the range of petal width with a little to spare on each end. The PLOTDATA data set is used with the TESTDATA= option in PROC DISCRIM.

```
data plotdata;
   do petalwid=-5 to 30 by .5;
      output;
      end;
run;
```

The same plots are produced after each discriminant analysis, so a macro can be used to reduce the amount of typing required. The macro PLOT uses two data sets. The data set PLOTD, containing density estimates, is created by the TESTOUTD= option in DISCRIM. The data set PLOTP, containing posterior probabilities, is created by the TESTOUT= option. For each data set, the macro PLOT removes uninteresting values (near zero) and does an overlay plot showing all three species on a single plot. These statements create the macro PLOT:

```
%macro plot;
   data plotd;
      set plotd;
      if setosa<.002 then setosa=.;
```

```
      if versicol<.002 then versicol=.;
      if virginic<.002 then virginic=.;
   run;

   proc plot data=plotd;
      plot setosa*petalwid='S'
           versicol*petalwid='O'
           virginic*petalwid='V'
           / overlay vpos=27 vaxis=0 to .6 by .1;
      title3 'Plot of Estimated Densities';
   run;

   data plotp;
      set plotp;
      if setosa<.01 then setosa=.;
      if versicol<.01 then versicol=.;
      if virginic<.01 then virginic=.;
   run;

   proc plot data=plotp;
      plot setosa*petalwid='S'
           versicol*petalwid='O'
           virginic*petalwid='V'
           / overlay vpos=18 vaxis=0 to 1 by .2;
      title3 'Plot of Posterior Probabilities';
   run;
   %mend;
```

The first analysis uses normal-theory methods (METHOD=NORMAL) assuming equal variances (POOL=YES) in the three classes. The NOCLASSIFY option suppresses the resubstitution classification results of the input data set observations. The CROSSLISTERR option lists the observations that are misclassified under crossvalidation and prints crossvalidation error-rate estimates. The following statements produce **Output 16.2**:

```
proc discrim data=iris testdata=plotdata testout=plotp testoutd=plotd
          method=normal pool=yes short noclassify crosslisterr;
   class species;
   var petalwid;
   title2 'Using Normal Density Estimates with Equal Variance';
run;

%plot
```

Output 16.2 Normal Density Estimates with Equal Variance

```
                    Discriminant Analysis of Fisher (1936) Iris Data             1
                    Using Normal Density Estimates with Equal Variance

                              DISCRIMINANT ANALYSIS

                150 Observations      149 DF Total
                  1 Variables         147 DF Within Classes
                  3 Classes             2 DF Between Classes
                               ❶
                          Class Level Information

                        Output                                         Prior
          SPECIES       SAS Name    Frequency      Weight   Proportion  Probability

          SETOSA        SETOSA           50     50.0000     0.333333    0.333333
          VERSICOLOR    VERSICOL         50     50.0000     0.333333    0.333333
          VIRGINICA     VIRGINIC         50     50.0000     0.333333    0.333333
```

```
                    Discriminant Analysis of Fisher (1936) Iris Data             2
                    Using Normal Density Estimates with Equal Variance

     DISCRIMINANT ANALYSIS     CLASSIFICATION RESULTS FOR CALIBRATION DATA: WORK.IRIS

            ㊱ Cross-validation Results using Linear Discriminant Function

  Generalized Squared Distance Function:        Posterior Probability of Membership in each SPECIES:
```

$$D_j^2(X) = (X-\bar{X}_{(X)j})' COV_{(X)}^{-1} (X-\bar{X}_{(X)j}) \qquad Pr(j|X) = exp(-.5\, D_j^2(X))\ /\ SUM_k\ exp(-.5\, D_k^2(X))$$

```
                                           Posterior Probability of Membership in SPECIES:
               From          Classified
     Obs      SPECIES       into SPECIES      SETOSA      VERSICOLOR      VIRGINICA

       5    VIRGINICA      VERSICOLOR *      0.0000        0.9610         0.0390
       9    VERSICOLOR     VIRGINICA  *      0.0000        0.0952         0.9048
      57    VIRGINICA      VERSICOLOR *      0.0000        0.9940         0.0060
      78    VIRGINICA      VERSICOLOR *      0.0000        0.8009         0.1991
      91    VIRGINICA      VERSICOLOR *      0.0000        0.9610         0.0390
     148    VERSICOLOR     VIRGINICA  *      0.0000        0.3828         0.6172

                        * Misclassified observation
```

```
                    Discriminant Analysis of Fisher (1936) Iris Data             3
                    Using Normal Density Estimates with Equal Variance

     DISCRIMINANT ANALYSIS     CLASSIFICATION SUMMARY FOR CALIBRATION DATA: WORK.IRIS

            ㊲ Cross-validation Summary using Linear Discriminant Function

  Generalized Squared Distance Function:        Posterior Probability of Membership in each SPECIES:
```

$$D_j^2(X) = (X-\bar{X}_{(X)j})' COV_{(X)}^{-1} (X-\bar{X}_{(X)j}) \qquad Pr(j|X) = exp(-.5\, D_j^2(X))\ /\ SUM_k\ exp(-.5\, D_k^2(X))$$

```
                  Number of Observations and Percents Classified into SPECIES:

     From SPECIES      SETOSA      VERSICOLOR      VIRGINICA        Total

       SETOSA            50             0              0             50
                       100.00          0.00           0.00         100.00

       VERSICOLOR         0            48              2             50
                         0.00         96.00           4.00         100.00

       VIRGINICA          0             4             46             50
                         0.00          8.00          92.00         100.00

       Total             50            52             48            150
       Percent         33.33         34.67          32.00         100.00

       Priors         0.3333        0.3333         0.3333
```

(continued on next page)

(continued from previous page)

38 Error Count Estimates for SPECIES:

	SETOSA	VERSICOLOR	VIRGINICA	Total
Rate	0.0000	0.0400	0.0800	0.0400
Priors	0.3333	0.3333	0.3333	

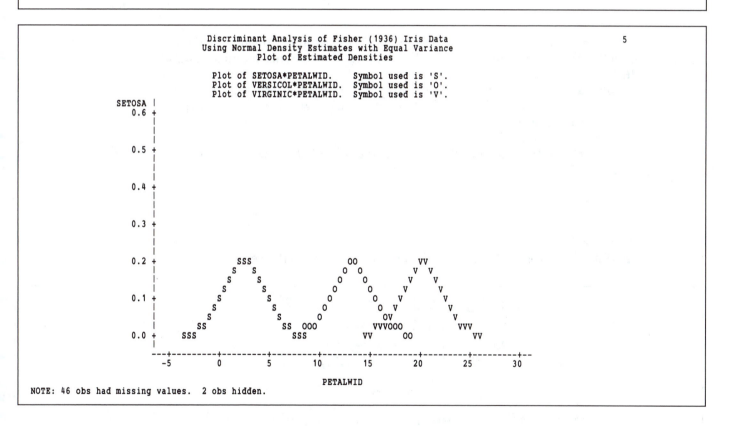

Discriminant Analysis of Fisher (1936) Iris Data
Using Normal Density Estimates with Equal Variance   4

DISCRIMINANT ANALYSIS   CLASSIFICATION SUMMARY FOR TEST DATA: WORK.PLOTDATA

Classification Summary using Linear Discriminant Function

Generalized Squared Distance Function: Posterior Probability of Membership in each SPECIES:

$$D^2_j(X) = (X - \bar{X}_j)' \, COV^{-1} \, (X - \bar{X}_j)$$

$$Pr(j|X) = \exp(-.5 \, D^2_j(X)) \,/\, \underset{k}{SUM} \exp(-.5 \, D^2_k(X))$$

Number of Observations and Percents Classified into SPECIES:

	SETOSA	VERSICOLOR	VIRGINICA	Total
Total	26	18	27	71
Percent	36.62	25.35	38.03	100.00
Priors	0.3333	0.3333	0.3333	

Discriminant Analysis of Fisher (1936) Iris Data
Using Normal Density Estimates with Equal Variance   5
Plot of Estimated Densities

Plot of SETOSA*PETALWID.   Symbol used is 'S'.
Plot of VERSICOL*PETALWID. Symbol used is 'O'.
Plot of VIRGINIC*PETALWID. Symbol used is 'V'.

NOTE: 46 obs had missing values. 2 obs hidden.

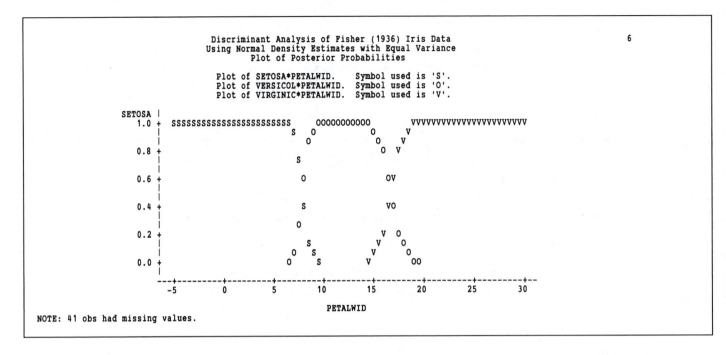

```
                Discriminant Analysis of Fisher (1936) Iris Data                    6
                Using Normal Density Estimates with Equal Variance
                       Plot of Posterior Probabilities

            Plot of SETOSA*PETALWID.   Symbol used is 'S'.
            Plot of VERSICOL*PETALWID.  Symbol used is 'O'.
            Plot of VIRGINIC*PETALWID.  Symbol used is 'V'.

SETOSA |
   1.0 + SSSSSSSSSSSSSSSSSSSSSSSSS     OOOOOOOOOOO      VVVVVVVVVVVVVVVVVVVVVVVVVVV
       |                        S  O           O   V
       |                           O          O   V
   0.8 +                                          O V
       |                        S                O V
   0.6 +                          O              OV
       |
   0.4 +                        S               VO
       |                        O
   0.2 +                                     V  O
       |                         S           V   O
       |                       O  S          V    O
   0.0 +                         O    S      V      OO
       |
       ---+---------+---------+---------+---------+---------+---------+---------+--
         -5        0         5        10        15        20        25        30

                                    PETALWID
NOTE: 41 obs had missing values.
```

The next analysis uses normal-theory methods assuming unequal variances (POOL=NO) in the three classes. The following statements produce **Output 16.3**:

```
proc discrim data=iris testdata=plotdata testout=plotp testoutd=plotd
          method=normal pool=no short noclassify crosslisterr;
   class species;
   var petalwid;
   title2 'Using Normal Density Estimates with Unequal Variance';
run;


%plot
```

Output 16.3   Normal Density Estimates with Unequal Variance

```
                Discriminant Analysis of Fisher (1936) Iris Data                    1
                Using Normal Density Estimates with Unequal Variance

                            DISCRIMINANT ANALYSIS

              150 Observations      149 DF Total
                1 Variables         147 DF Within Classes
                3 Classes             2 DF Between Classes


                           Class Level Information

                      Output                                   Prior
        SPECIES       SAS Name    Frequency    Weight   Proportion   Probability

        SETOSA        SETOSA           50     50.0000    0.333333     0.333333
        VERSICOLOR    VERSICOL         50     50.0000    0.333333     0.333333
        VIRGINICA     VIRGINIC         50     50.0000    0.333333     0.333333
```

Discriminant Analysis of Fisher (1936) Iris Data
Using Normal Density Estimates with Unequal Variance   2

DISCRIMINANT ANALYSIS   CLASSIFICATION RESULTS FOR CALIBRATION DATA: WORK.IRIS

Cross-validation Results using Quadratic Discriminant Function

Generalized Squared Distance Function: Posterior Probability of Membership in each SPECIES:

$$D^2_j(X) = (X-\bar{X}_{(X)j})' \, COV^{-1}_{(X)j} \, (X-\bar{X}_{(X)j}) + \ln |COV_{(X)j}|$$ $$Pr(j|X) = \exp(-.5 \, D^2_j(X)) \, / \, \underset{k}{SUM} \, \exp(-.5 \, D^2_k(X))$$

Posterior Probability of Membership in SPECIES:

Obs	From SPECIES	Classified into SPECIES	SETOSA	VERSICOLOR	VIRGINICA
5	VIRGINICA	VERSICOLOR *	0.0000	0.8740	0.1260
9	VERSICOLOR	VIRGINICA *	0.0000	0.0686	0.9314
42	SETOSA	VERSICOLOR *	0.4923	0.5073	0.0004
57	VIRGINICA	VERSICOLOR *	0.0000	0.9602	0.0398
78	VIRGINICA	VERSICOLOR *	0.0000	0.6558	0.3442
91	VIRGINICA	VERSICOLOR *	0.0000	0.8740	0.1260
148	VERSICOLOR	VIRGINICA *	0.0000	0.2871	0.7129

* Misclassified observation

Discriminant Analysis of Fisher (1936) Iris Data
Using Normal Density Estimates with Unequal Variance   3

DISCRIMINANT ANALYSIS   CLASSIFICATION SUMMARY FOR CALIBRATION DATA: WORK.IRIS

Cross-validation Summary using Quadratic Discriminant Function

Generalized Squared Distance Function: Posterior Probability of Membership in each SPECIES:

$$D^2_j(X) = (X-\bar{X}_{(X)j})' \, COV^{-1}_{(X)j} \, (X-\bar{X}_{(X)j}) + \ln |COV_{(X)j}|$$ $$Pr(j|X) = \exp(-.5 \, D^2_j(X)) \, / \, \underset{k}{SUM} \, \exp(-.5 \, D^2_k(X))$$

Number of Observations and Percents Classified into SPECIES:

From SPECIES	SETOSA	VERSICOLOR	VIRGINICA	Total
SETOSA	49 98.00	1 2.00	0 0.00	50 100.00
VERSICOLOR	0 0.00	48 96.00	2 4.00	50 100.00
VIRGINICA	0 0.00	4 8.00	46 92.00	50 100.00
Total Percent	49 32.67	53 35.33	48 32.00	150 100.00
Priors	0.3333	0.3333	0.3333	

Error Count Estimates for SPECIES:

	SETOSA	VERSICOLOR	VIRGINICA	Total
Rate	0.0200	0.0400	0.0800	0.0467
Priors	0.3333	0.3333	0.3333	

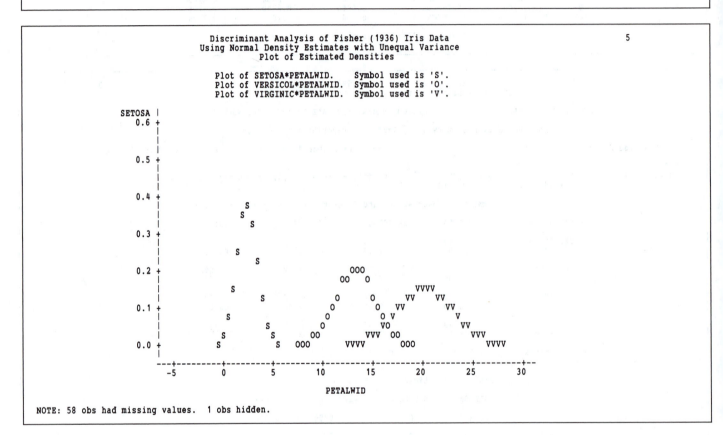

```
                    Discriminant Analysis of Fisher (1936) Iris Data                    4
                  Using Normal Density Estimates with Unequal Variance

         DISCRIMINANT ANALYSIS      CLASSIFICATION SUMMARY FOR TEST DATA: WORK.PLOTDATA

              Classification Summary using Quadratic Discriminant Function

   Generalized Squared Distance Function:        Posterior Probability of Membership in each SPECIES:

   2           _        -1     _                                 2                    2
   D (X) = (X-X )' COV   (X-X ) + ln |COV |      Pr(j|X) = exp(-.5 D (X)) / SUM exp(-.5 D (X))
   j          j    j       j         j                             j     k           k

                    Number of Observations and Percents Classified into SPECIES:

                         SETOSA     VERSICOLOR     VIRGINICA        Total
              Total          23             20            28           71
            Percent       32.39          28.17         39.44       100.00

            Priors       0.3333         0.3333        0.3333
```

```
                    Discriminant Analysis of Fisher (1936) Iris Data                    5
                  Using Normal Density Estimates with Unequal Variance
                             Plot of Estimated Densities

              Plot of SETOSA*PETALWID.     Symbol used is 'S'.
              Plot of VERSICOL*PETALWID.   Symbol used is 'O'.
              Plot of VIRGINIC*PETALWID.   Symbol used is 'V'.


   SETOSA |
      0.6 +
          |
          |
          |
      0.5 +
          |
          |
          |                      S
      0.4 +                     S
          |                      S
          |
          |                        S
      0.3 +
          |                   S
          |                     S
          |                                      000
      0.2 +                                    00  0
          |                                                       VVVV
          |                 S                                   VV    VV
          |                   S        0          0          VV        VV
      0.1 +               S            0       0   0  VV            VV
          |                                 0     0   V              V
          |             S          0                 VO                VV
          |           S        S     00              00               VVV
      0.0 +         S        S     000    VVVV     000              VVVV
          |
          ---+---------+---------+---------+---------+---------+---------+---------+--
            -5         0         5        10        15        20        25        30
                                          PETALWID
```

NOTE: 58 obs had missing values.   1 obs hidden.

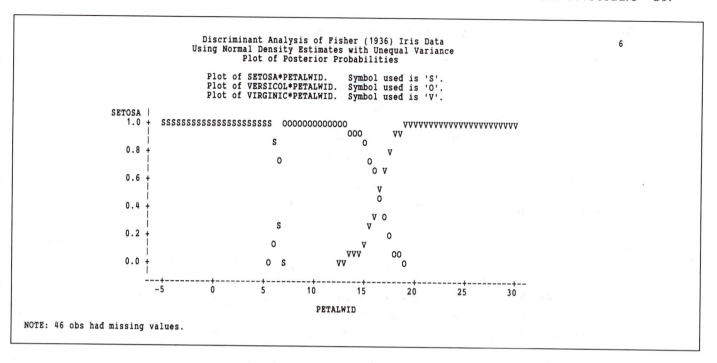

NOTE: 46 obs had missing values.

Two more analyses are run with nonparametric methods (METHOD=NPAR), specifically kernel density estimates with normal kernels (KERNEL=NORMAL). The first of these uses equal bandwidths (smoothing parameters) (POOL=YES) in each class. The use of equal bandwidths does not constrain the density estimates to be of equal variance. The following statements produce **Output 16.4**:

```
proc discrim data=iris testdata=plotdata testout=plotp testoutd=plotd
             method=npar kernel=normal r=.4 pool=yes
             short noclassify crosslisterr;
   class species;
   var petalwid;
   title2 'Using Kernel Density Estimates with Equal Bandwidth';
run;

%plot
```

Output 16.4   Kernel Density Estimates with Equal Bandwidth

```
                   Discriminant Analysis of Fisher (1936) Iris Data              1
                   Using Kernel Density Estimates with Equal Bandwidth

                            DISCRIMINANT ANALYSIS

              150 Observations          149 DF Total
                1 Variables             147 DF Within Classes
                3 Classes                 2 DF Between Classes

                          Class Level Information

                    Output                                        Prior
       SPECIES      SAS Name    Frequency       Weight  Proportion  Probability

    SETOSA          SETOSA          50       50.0000    0.333333    0.333333
    VERSICOLOR      VERSICOL        50       50.0000    0.333333    0.333333
    VIRGINICA       VIRGINIC        50       50.0000    0.333333    0.333333
```

```
                   Discriminant Analysis of Fisher (1936) Iris Data              2
                   Using Kernel Density Estimates with Equal Bandwidth

    DISCRIMINANT ANALYSIS    CLASSIFICATION RESULTS FOR CALIBRATION DATA: WORK.IRIS

              Cross-validation Results using Normal Kernel Density

    Squared Distance Function:         Posterior Probability of Membership in each SPECIES:
```

$$D^2(X,Y) = (X-Y)' COV^{-1} (X-Y) \qquad F(X|j) = n_j^{-1} \ \underset{i}{SUM} \ exp(-.5 \ D^2(X,Y_{ji}) / R^2)$$

$$Pr(j|X) = PRIOR_j \ F(X|j) \ / \ \underset{k}{SUM} \ PRIOR_k \ F(X|k)$$

```
                                     Posterior Probability of Membership in SPECIES:
         Obs      From         Classified
                SPECIES       into SPECIES     SETOSA    VERSICOLOR    VIRGINICA

           5   VIRGINICA      VERSICOLOR *    0.0000      0.8848       0.1152
           9   VERSICOLOR     VIRGINICA  *    0.0000      0.0430       0.9570
          57   VIRGINICA      VERSICOLOR *    0.0000      0.9482       0.0518
          78   VIRGINICA      VERSICOLOR *    0.0000      0.8093       0.1907
          91   VIRGINICA      VERSICOLOR *    0.0000      0.8848       0.1152
         148   VERSICOLOR     VIRGINICA  *    0.0000      0.2548       0.7452

                       * Misclassified observation
```

```
                   Discriminant Analysis of Fisher (1936) Iris Data              3
                   Using Kernel Density Estimates with Equal Bandwidth

    DISCRIMINANT ANALYSIS    CLASSIFICATION SUMMARY FOR CALIBRATION DATA: WORK.IRIS

              Cross-validation Summary using Normal Kernel Density

    Squared Distance Function:         Posterior Probability of Membership in each SPECIES:
```

$$D^2(X,Y) = (X-Y)' COV^{-1} (X-Y) \qquad F(X|j) = n_j^{-1} \ \underset{i}{SUM} \ exp(-.5 \ D^2(X,Y_{ji}) / R^2)$$

$$Pr(j|X) = PRIOR_j \ F(X|j) \ / \ \underset{k}{SUM} \ PRIOR_k \ F(X|k)$$

```
             Number of Observations and Percents Classified into SPECIES:

    From SPECIES      SETOSA    VERSICOLOR    VIRGINICA       Total

      SETOSA             50          0            0            50
                     100.00       0.00         0.00        100.00

      VERSICOLOR          0         48            2            50
                       0.00      96.00         4.00        100.00
```

(continued on next page)

(continued from previous page)

	SETOSA	VERSICOLOR	VIRGINICA	Total
VIRGINICA	0 0.00	4 8.00	46 92.00	50 100.00
Total Percent	50 33.33	52 34.67	48 32.00	150 100.00
Priors	0.3333	0.3333	0.3333	

Error Count Estimates for SPECIES:

	SETOSA	VERSICOLOR	VIRGINICA	Total
Rate	0.0000	0.0400	0.0800	0.0400
Priors	0.3333	0.3333	0.3333	

Discriminant Analysis of Fisher (1936) Iris Data
Using Kernel Density Estimates with Equal Bandwidth   4

DISCRIMINANT ANALYSIS   CLASSIFICATION SUMMARY FOR TEST DATA: WORK.PLOTDATA

Classification Summary using Normal Kernel Density

Squared Distance Function: Posterior Probability of Membership in each SPECIES:

$$D^2(X,Y) = (X-Y)' COV^{-1} (X-Y)$$

$$F(X|j) = n_j^{-1} \sum_i exp(-.5\, D^2(X,Y_{ji}) / R^2)$$

$$Pr(j|X) = PRIOR_j\, F(X|j) / \sum_k PRIOR_k\, F(X|k)$$

Number of Observations and Percents Classified into SPECIES:

	SETOSA	VERSICOLOR	VIRGINICA	Total
Total Percent	26 36.62	18 25.35	27 38.03	71 100.00
Priors	0.3333	0.3333	0.3333	

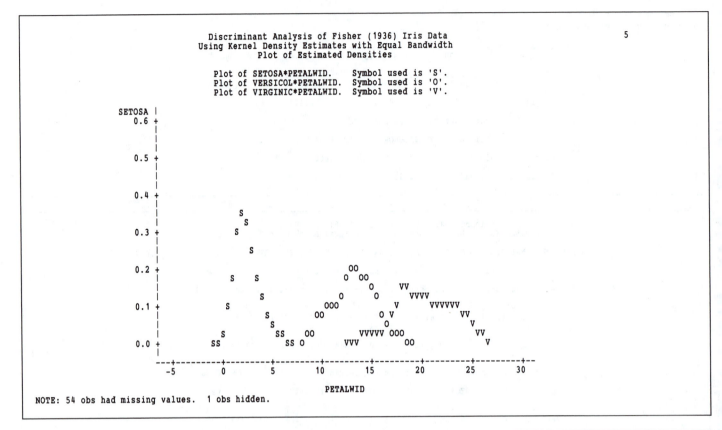

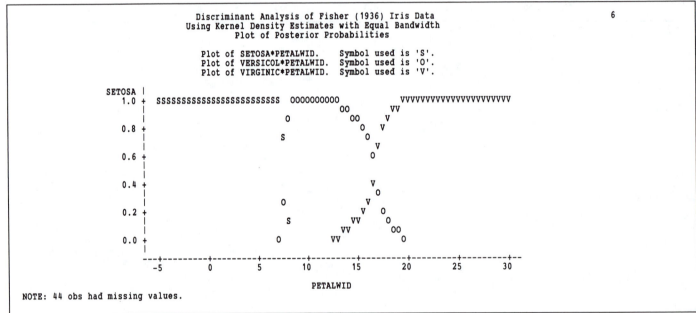

Another nonparametric analysis is run with unequal bandwidths (POOL=NO). These statements produce **Output 16.5**:

```
proc discrim data=iris testdata=plotdata testout=plotp testoutd=plotd
             method=npar kernel=normal r=.4 pool=no
             short noclassify crosslisterr;
   class species;
   var petalwid;
   title2 'Using Kernel Density Estimates with Unequal Bandwidth';
run;


%plot
```

Output 16.5   Kernel Density Estimates with Unequal Bandwidth

```
                    Discriminant Analysis of Fisher (1936) Iris Data                    1
                   Using Kernel Density Estimates with Unequal Bandwidth

                             DISCRIMINANT ANALYSIS

                  150 Observations      149 DF Total
                    1 Variables         147 DF Within Classes
                    3 Classes             2 DF Between Classes


                         Class Level Information

                     Output                                      Prior
        SPECIES      SAS Name    Frequency    Weight    Proportion    Probability

        SETOSA       SETOSA          50      50.0000     0.333333      0.333333
        VERSICOLOR   VERSICOL        50      50.0000     0.333333      0.333333
        VIRGINICA    VIRGINIC        50      50.0000     0.333333      0.333333
```

```
                    Discriminant Analysis of Fisher (1936) Iris Data                    2
                   Using Kernel Density Estimates with Unequal Bandwidth

     DISCRIMINANT ANALYSIS      CLASSIFICATION RESULTS FOR CALIBRATION DATA: WORK.IRIS

               Cross-validation Results using Normal Kernel Density

Squared Distance Function:          Posterior Probability of Membership in each SPECIES:
```

$$D^2_j(X,Y) = (X-Y)' \, COV^{-1}_j \, (X-Y)$$

$$F(X|j) = n^{-1}_j \sum_i \exp(-.5 \, D^2(X,Y_{ji}) / R^2_{ji})$$

$$Pr(j|X) = PRIOR_j \, F(X|j) \, / \, \sum_k PRIOR_k \, F(X|k)$$

```
                                        Posterior Probability of Membership in SPECIES:
            From        Classified
Obs         SPECIES     into SPECIES    SETOSA      VERSICOLOR    VIRGINICA

  5         VIRGINICA   VERSICOLOR *    0.0000      0.8827        0.1173
  9         VERSICOLOR  VIRGINICA  *    0.0000      0.0466        0.9534
 57         VIRGINICA   VERSICOLOR *    0.0000      0.9406        0.0594
 78         VIRGINICA   VERSICOLOR *    0.0000      0.7234        0.2766
 91         VIRGINICA   VERSICOLOR *    0.0000      0.8827        0.1173
148         VERSICOLOR  VIRGINICA  *    0.0000      0.2275        0.7725

                     * Misclassified observation
```

Discriminant Analysis of Fisher (1936) Iris Data
Using Kernel Density Estimates with Unequal Bandwidth   3

DISCRIMINANT ANALYSIS   CLASSIFICATION SUMMARY FOR CALIBRATION DATA: WORK.IRIS

Cross-validation Summary using Normal Kernel Density

Squared Distance Function: Posterior Probability of Membership in each SPECIES:

$$D^2_j(X,Y) = (X-Y)' \, COV^{-1}_j \, (X-Y) \qquad F(X|j) = n^{-1}_j \, \underset{i}{SUM} \, \exp(-.5 \, D^2_j(X,Y_{ji}) / R^2)$$

$$Pr(j|X) = PRIOR_j \, F(X|j) / \underset{k}{SUM} \, PRIOR_k \, F(X|k)$$

Number of Observations and Percents Classified into SPECIES:

From SPECIES	SETOSA	VERSICOLOR	VIRGINICA	Total
SETOSA	50	0	0	50
	100.00	0.00	0.00	100.00
VERSICOLOR	0	48	2	50
	0.00	96.00	4.00	100.00
VIRGINICA	0	4	46	50
	0.00	8.00	92.00	100.00
Total	50	52	48	150
Percent	33.33	34.67	32.00	100.00
Priors	0.3333	0.3333	0.3333	

Error Count Estimates for SPECIES:

	SETOSA	VERSICOLOR	VIRGINICA	Total
Rate	0.0000	0.0400	0.0800	0.0400
Priors	0.3333	0.3333	0.3333	

Discriminant Analysis of Fisher (1936) Iris Data
Using Kernel Density Estimates with Unequal Bandwidth   4

DISCRIMINANT ANALYSIS   CLASSIFICATION SUMMARY FOR TEST DATA: WORK.PLOTDATA

Classification Summary using Normal Kernel Density

Squared Distance Function: Posterior Probability of Membership in each SPECIES:

$$D^2_j(X,Y) = (X-Y)' \, COV^{-1}_j \, (X-Y) \qquad F(X|j) = n^{-1}_j \, \underset{i}{SUM} \, \exp(-.5 \, D^2_j(X,Y_{ji}) / R^2)$$

$$Pr(j|X) = PRIOR_j \, F(X|j) / \underset{k}{SUM} \, PRIOR_k \, F(X|k)$$

Number of Observations and Percents Classified into SPECIES:

	SETOSA	VERSICOLOR	VIRGINICA	Total
Total	25	18	28	71
Percent	35.21	25.35	39.44	100.00
Priors	0.3333	0.3333	0.3333	

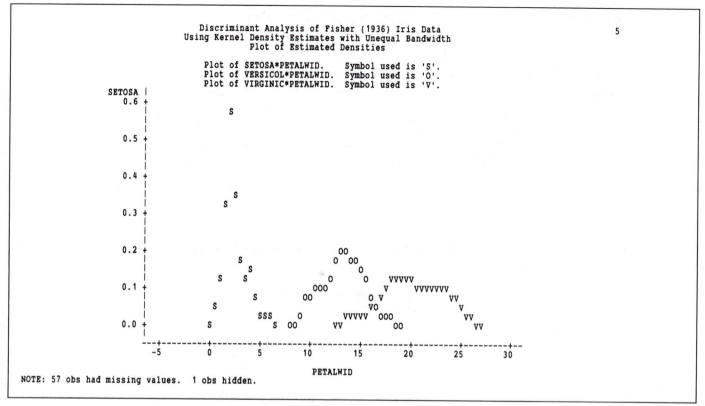

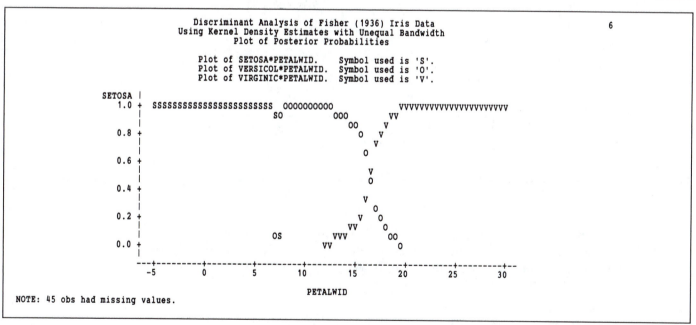

Example 2: Bivariate Density Estimates and Posterior Probabilities

In this example, four more discriminant analyses of iris data are run with two quantitative variables, petal width and petal length. The example produces **Output 16.6** through **Output 16.10**. A scatter plot shows the joint sample distribution.

```
proc plot data=iris;
   plot petalwid*petallen=species
         / vpos=17 vaxis=-4 to 28 by 2 hpos=76 haxis=0 to 75 by 5;
   format species specchar.;
   title2;
run;
```

Output 16.6 Joint Sample Distribution of Petal Width and Petal Length in Three Species

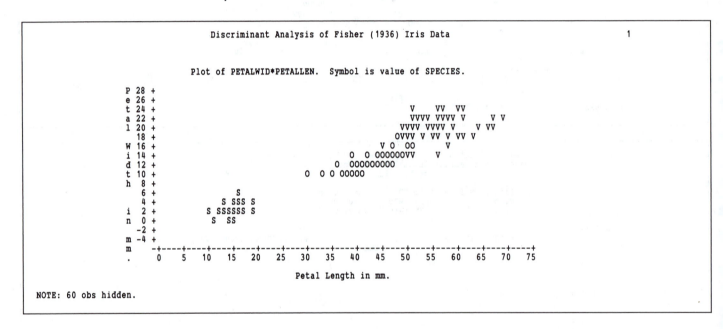

Another data set is created for plotting, containing a grid of points suitable for contour plots. The large number of points in the grid makes the following analyses very time-consuming. If you attempt to duplicate these examples, begin with a much smaller number of points in the grid.

```
data plotdata;
   do petalwid=-4 to 28 by 2;
      do petallen=0 to 75;
         output;
         end;
      end;
run;
```

A macro CONTOUR is defined to make contour plots of density estimates and posterior probabilities. Classification results are also plotted on the same grid.

```
%macro contour;
   proc plot data=plotd;
      plot petalwid*petallen=setosa
           petalwid*petallen=versicol
           petalwid*petallen=virginic
           / contour=6 vpos=17 hpos=76 haxis=0 to 75 by 5;
      title3 'Plot of Estimated Densities';
   run;

   proc plot data=plotp;
      plot petalwid*petallen=setosa
           petalwid*petallen=versicol
           petalwid*petallen=virginic
           / contour=6 vpos=17 hpos=76 haxis=0 to 75 by 5;
      title3 'Plot of Posterior Probabilities';
   run;

   proc plot data=plotp;
      plot petalwid*petallen=_into_
           / vpos=17 hpos=76 haxis=0 to 75 by 5;
      format _into_ specchar.;
      title3 'Plot of Classification Results';
   run;
   %mend;
```

A normal-theory analysis (METHOD=NORMAL) assuming equal covariance matrices (POOL=YES) illustrates the linearity of the classification boundaries. These statements produce **Output 16.7**:

```
proc discrim data=iris testdata=plotdata testout=plotp testoutd=plotd
             method=normal pool=yes short noclassify crosslisterr;
   class species;
   var petal:;
   title2 'Using Normal Density Estimates with Equal Variance';
run;

%contour
```

Output 16.7   Normal Density Estimates with Equal Variance

```
                 Discriminant Analysis of Fisher (1936) Iris Data                    1
                 Using Normal Density Estimates with Equal Variance

                            DISCRIMINANT ANALYSIS

                150 Observations      149 DF Total
                  2 Variables         147 DF Within Classes
                  3 Classes             2 DF Between Classes


                           Class Level Information

                      Output                                    Prior
          SPECIES      SAS Name    Frequency    Weight    Proportion   Probability

          SETOSA       SETOSA         50       50.0000    0.333333     0.333333
          VERSICOLOR   VERSICOL       50       50.0000    0.333333     0.333333
          VIRGINICA    VIRGINIC       50       50.0000    0.333333     0.333333
```

```
                 Discriminant Analysis of Fisher (1936) Iris Data                    2
                 Using Normal Density Estimates with Equal Variance

     DISCRIMINANT ANALYSIS     CLASSIFICATION RESULTS FOR CALIBRATION DATA: WORK.IRIS

              Cross-validation Results using Linear Discriminant Function

   Generalized Squared Distance Function:     Posterior Probability of Membership in each SPECIES:

   2              _        -1    _                             2              2
   D (X) = (X-X    )' COV    (X-X  )       Pr(j|X) = exp(-.5 D (X)) / SUM exp(-.5 D (X))
    j        (X)j   (X)    (X)j                            j       k        k

                                           Posterior Probability of Membership in SPECIES:
              Obs      From      Classified
                      SPECIES    into SPECIES    SETOSA    VERSICOLOR    VIRGINICA

               5     VIRGINICA   VERSICOLOR *    0.0000      0.8453       0.1547
               9     VERSICOLOR  VIRGINICA  *    0.0000      0.2130       0.7870
              25     VIRGINICA   VERSICOLOR *    0.0000      0.8322       0.1678
              57     VIRGINICA   VERSICOLOR *    0.0000      0.8057       0.1943
              91     VIRGINICA   VERSICOLOR *    0.0000      0.8903       0.1097
             148     VERSICOLOR  VIRGINICA  *    0.0000      0.3118       0.6882

                         * Misclassified observation
```

```
                 Discriminant Analysis of Fisher (1936) Iris Data                    3
                 Using Normal Density Estimates with Equal Variance

     DISCRIMINANT ANALYSIS     CLASSIFICATION SUMMARY FOR CALIBRATION DATA: WORK.IRIS

              Cross-validation Summary using Linear Discriminant Function

   Generalized Squared Distance Function:     Posterior Probability of Membership in each SPECIES:

   2              _        -1    _                             2              2
   D (X) = (X-X    )' COV    (X-X  )       Pr(j|X) = exp(-.5 D (X)) / SUM exp(-.5 D (X))
    j        (X)j   (X)    (X)j                            j       k        k

                  Number of Observations and Percents Classified into SPECIES:

          From SPECIES      SETOSA    VERSICOLOR    VIRGINICA      Total

            SETOSA             50          0            0           50
                            100.00       0.00         0.00        100.00

            VERSICOLOR          0         48            2           50
                              0.00      96.00         4.00        100.00

            VIRGINICA           0          4           46           50
                              0.00       8.00        92.00        100.00

               Total           50         52           48          150
               Percent       33.33      34.67        32.00        100.00

               Priors       0.3333     0.3333       0.3333
```

(continued on next page)

(continued from previous page)

```
                    Error Count Estimates for SPECIES:

                  SETOSA      VERSICOLOR    VIRGINICA       Total

           Rate   0.0000        0.0400        0.0800       0.0400

           Priors 0.3333        0.3333        0.3333
```

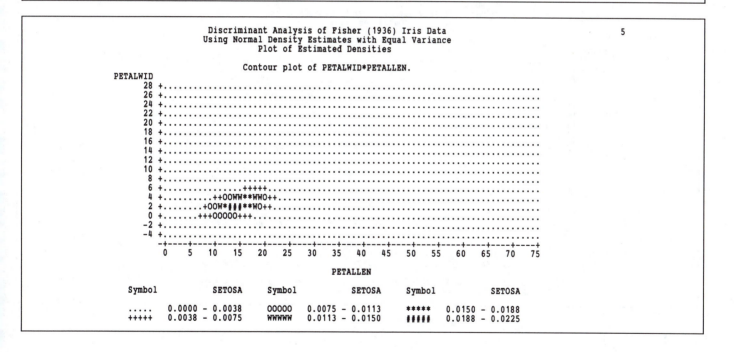

```
                Discriminant Analysis of Fisher (1936) Iris Data                    4
                Using Normal Density Estimates with Equal Variance

     DISCRIMINANT ANALYSIS    CLASSIFICATION SUMMARY FOR TEST DATA: WORK.PLOTDATA

                Classification Summary using Linear Discriminant Function

Generalized Squared Distance Function:        Posterior Probability of Membership in each SPECIES:

 2        _        -1  _                                        2               2
D (X) = (X-X )' COV   (X-X )          Pr(j|X) = exp(-.5 D (X)) / SUM exp(-.5 D (X))
 j          j           j                                 j       k           k

                Number of Observations and Percents Classified into SPECIES:

                  SETOSA      VERSICOLOR    VIRGINICA       Total
           Total    415          543          334          1292
           Percent 32.12        42.03        25.85        100.00

           Priors 0.3333        0.3333        0.3333
```

```
                Discriminant Analysis of Fisher (1936) Iris Data                    5
                Using Normal Density Estimates with Equal Variance
                           Plot of Estimated Densities

                      Contour plot of PETALWID*PETALLEN.
   PETALWID
      28 +..............................................................
      26 +..............................................................
      24 +..............................................................
      22 +..............................................................
      20 +..............................................................
      18 +..............................................................
      16 +..............................................................
      14 +..............................................................
      12 +..............................................................
      10 +..............................................................
       8 +..............................................................
       6 +..................+++++........................................
       4 +.........++OOWW**WWO++.........................................
       2 +........+OOW*###**WO++.........................................
       0 +.......+++OOOOO+++.............................................
      -2 +..............................................................
      -4 +..............................................................
         -+----+----+----+----+----+----+----+----+----+----+----+----+----+----+----+
          0    5   10   15   20   25   30   35   40   45   50   55   60   65   70   75

                                     PETALLEN

      Symbol         SETOSA   Symbol           SETOSA   Symbol          SETOSA

      .....   0.0000 - 0.0038  00000   0.0075 - 0.0113  *****   0.0150 - 0.0188
      +++++   0.0038 - 0.0075  WWWWW   0.0113 - 0.0150  #####   0.0188 - 0.0225
```

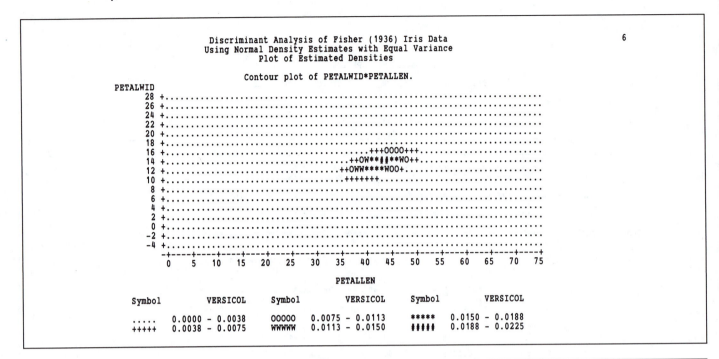

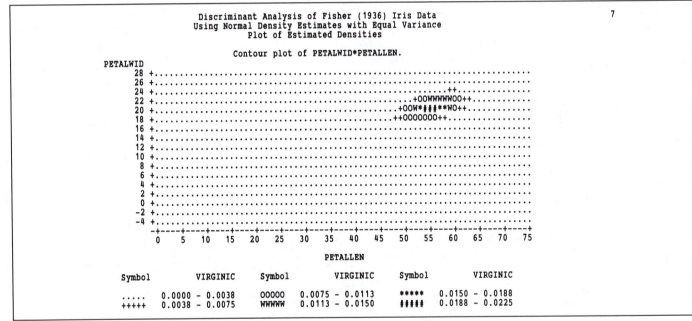

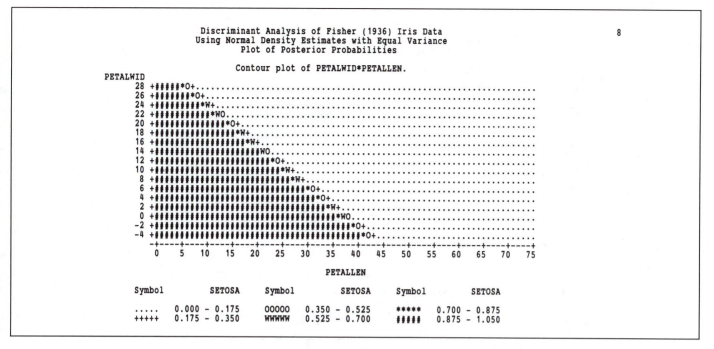

Discriminant Analysis of Fisher (1936) Iris Data
Using Normal Density Estimates with Equal Variance
Plot of Posterior Probabilities

Contour plot of PETALWID*PETALLEN.

Symbol	SETOSA	Symbol	SETOSA	Symbol	SETOSA
.....	0.000 - 0.175	OOOOO	0.350 - 0.525	*****	0.700 - 0.875
+++++	0.175 - 0.350	WWWWW	0.525 - 0.700	#####	0.875 - 1.050

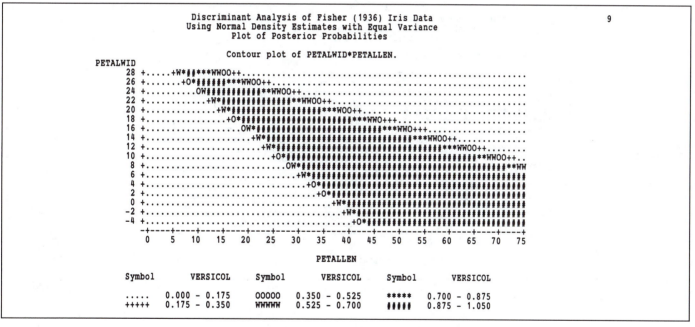

Discriminant Analysis of Fisher (1936) Iris Data
Using Normal Density Estimates with Equal Variance
Plot of Posterior Probabilities

Contour plot of PETALWID*PETALLEN.

Symbol	VERSICOL	Symbol	VERSICOL	Symbol	VERSICOL
.....	0.000 - 0.175	OOOOO	0.350 - 0.525	*****	0.700 - 0.875
+++++	0.175 - 0.350	WWWWW	0.525 - 0.700	#####	0.875 - 1.050

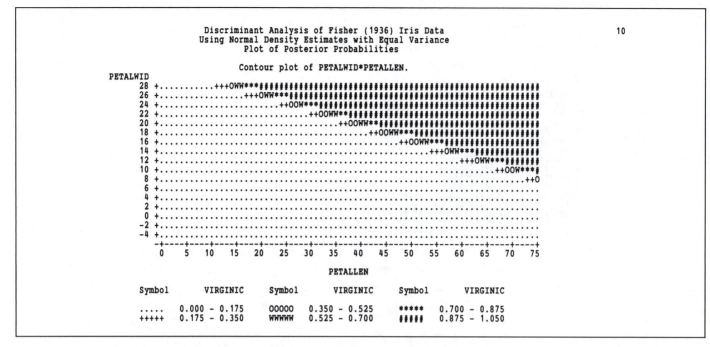

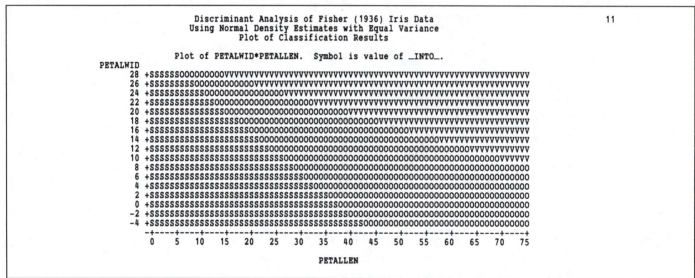

A normal-theory analysis assuming unequal covariance matrices (POOL=NO) illustrates quadratic classification boundaries. These statements produce **Output 16.8**:

```
proc discrim data=iris testdata=plotdata testout=plotp testoutd=plotd
        method=normal pool=no short noclassify crosslisterr;
    class species;
    var petal:;
    title2 'Using Normal Density Estimates with Unequal Variance';
run;

%contour
```

Output 16.8 Normal Density Estimates with Unequal Variance

```
                        Discriminant Analysis of Fisher (1936) Iris Data            1
                        Using Normal Density Estimates with Unequal Variance

                                DISCRIMINANT ANALYSIS

                    150 Observations        149 DF Total
                      2 Variables           147 DF Within Classes
                      3 Classes               2 DF Between Classes


                           Class Level Information

                    Output                                           Prior
         SPECIES     SAS Name    Frequency      Weight    Proportion  Probability

         SETOSA      SETOSA           50       50.0000     0.333333    0.333333
         VERSICOLOR  VERSICOL         50       50.0000     0.333333    0.333333
         VIRGINICA   VIRGINIC         50       50.0000     0.333333    0.333333
```

```
                        Discriminant Analysis of Fisher (1936) Iris Data            2
                        Using Normal Density Estimates with Unequal Variance

       DISCRIMINANT ANALYSIS     CLASSIFICATION RESULTS FOR CALIBRATION DATA: WORK.IRIS

              Cross-validation Results using Quadratic Discriminant Function
```

Generalized Squared Distance Function:

Posterior Probability of Membership in each SPECIES:

$$D_j^2(X) = (X - \bar{X}_{(X)j})' COV_{(X)j}^{-1} (X - \bar{X}_{(X)j}) + \ln |COV_{(X)j}|$$

$$Pr(j|X) = \exp(-.5\, D_j^2(X)) / \underset{k}{SUM} \exp(-.5\, D_k^2(X))$$

```
                                            Posterior Probability of Membership in SPECIES:
              Obs        From       Classified
                        SPECIES     into SPECIES    SETOSA    VERSICOLOR    VIRGINICA

               5     VIRGINICA     VERSICOLOR *     0.0000      0.7288        0.2712
               9     VERSICOLOR    VIRGINICA  *     0.0000      0.0903        0.9097
              25     VIRGINICA     VERSICOLOR *     0.0000      0.5196        0.4804
              91     VIRGINICA     VERSICOLOR *     0.0000      0.8335        0.1665
             148     VERSICOLOR    VIRGINICA  *     0.0000      0.4675        0.5325

                     * Misclassified observation
```

```
                        Discriminant Analysis of Fisher (1936) Iris Data            3
                        Using Normal Density Estimates with Unequal Variance

       DISCRIMINANT ANALYSIS     CLASSIFICATION SUMMARY FOR CALIBRATION DATA: WORK.IRIS

              Cross-validation Summary using Quadratic Discriminant Function
```

Generalized Squared Distance Function:

Posterior Probability of Membership in each SPECIES:

$$D_j^2(X) = (X - \bar{X}_{(X)j})' COV_{(X)j}^{-1} (X - \bar{X}_{(X)j}) + \ln |COV_{(X)j}|$$

$$Pr(j|X) = \exp(-.5\, D_j^2(X)) / \underset{k}{SUM} \exp(-.5\, D_k^2(X))$$

```
              Number of Observations and Percents Classified into SPECIES:

         From SPECIES      SETOSA    VERSICOLOR    VIRGINICA      Total

           SETOSA            50           0            0            50
                          100.00        0.00         0.00        100.00

           VERSICOLOR         0          48            2            50
                            0.00       96.00         4.00        100.00

           VIRGINICA          0           3           47            50
                            0.00        6.00        94.00        100.00

              Total          50          51           49           150
              Percent      33.33       34.00        32.67        100.00

              Priors      0.3333      0.3333       0.3333
```

(continued on next page)

(continued from previous page)

                    Error Count Estimates for SPECIES:

                    SETOSA   VERSICOLOR   VIRGINICA   Total

        Rate   0.0000   0.0400   0.0600   0.0333

        Priors   0.3333   0.3333   0.3333

                    Discriminant Analysis of Fisher (1936) Iris Data   4
                    Using Normal Density Estimates with Unequal Variance

    DISCRIMINANT ANALYSIS   CLASSIFICATION SUMMARY FOR TEST DATA: WORK.PLOTDATA

            Classification Summary using Quadratic Discriminant Function

Generalized Squared Distance Function: Posterior Probability of Membership in each SPECIES:

$$D_j^2(X) = (X-\bar{X}_j)' \, COV_j^{-1} \, (X-\bar{X}_j) + \ln |COV_j|$$

$$Pr(j|X) = \exp(-.5\, D_j^2(X)) \,/\, \mathrm{SUM}_k \exp(-.5\, D_k^2(X))$$

            Number of Observations and Percents Classified into SPECIES:

                    SETOSA   VERSICOLOR   VIRGINICA   Total

        Total   163   167   962   1292
        Percent   12.62   12.93   74.46   100.00

        Priors   0.3333   0.3333   0.3333

                    Discriminant Analysis of Fisher (1936) Iris Data   5
                    Using Normal Density Estimates with Unequal Variance
                            Plot of Estimated Densities

                    Contour plot of PETALWID*PETALLEN.

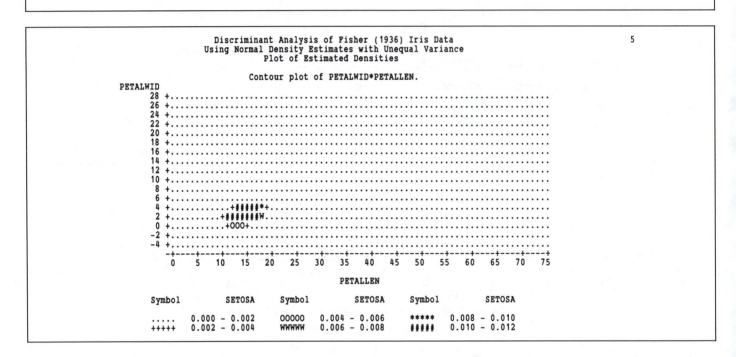

```
PETALWID
   28 +..........................................................................
   26 +..........................................................................
   24 +..........................................................................
   22 +..........................................................................
   20 +..........................................................................
   18 +..........................................................................
   16 +..........................................................................
   14 +..........................................................................
   12 +..........................................................................
   10 +..........................................................................
    8 +..........................................................................
    6 +..........................................................................
    4 +...........+#####*+.......................................................
    2 +..........+#######W.......................................................
    0 +..........+OOO+...........................................................
   -2 +..........................................................................
   -4 +..........................................................................
      -+----+----+----+----+----+----+----+----+----+----+----+----+----+----+----+
       0    5   10   15   20   25   30   35   40   45   50   55   60   65   70   75
                                    PETALLEN
```

Symbol   SETOSA   Symbol   SETOSA   Symbol   SETOSA

.....   0.000 - 0.002   OOOOO   0.004 - 0.006   *****   0.008 - 0.010
+++++   0.002 - 0.004   WWWWW   0.006 - 0.008   #####   0.010 - 0.012

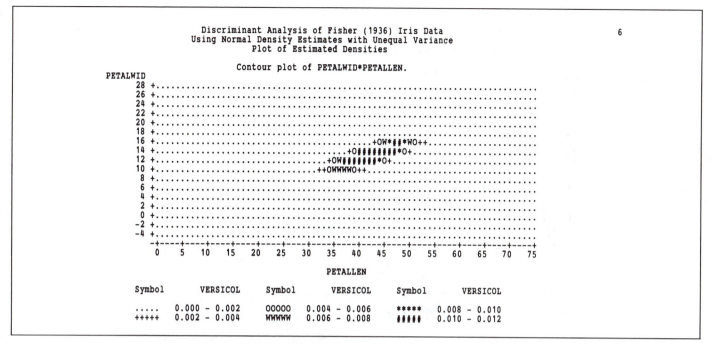

```
                  Discriminant Analysis of Fisher (1936) Iris Data              6
                 Using Normal Density Estimates with Unequal Variance
                            Plot of Estimated Densities

                       Contour plot of PETALWID*PETALLEN.
   PETALWID
      28 +..................................................................
      26 +..................................................................
      24 +..................................................................
      22 +..................................................................
      20 +..................................................................
      18 +..................................................................
      16 +......................................+OW*##*WO++.................
      14 +.....................................+O#########*O+...............
      12 +.....................................+OW#######*O+................
      10 +....................................++OWWWWO++...................
       8 +..................................................................
       6 +..................................................................
       4 +..................................................................
       2 +..................................................................
       0 +..................................................................
      -2 +..................................................................
      -4 +..................................................................
        -+----+----+----+----+----+----+----+----+----+----+----+----+----+----+
         0    5   10   15   20   25   30   35   40   45   50   55   60   65   70   75

                                  PETALLEN

         Symbol      VERSICOL      Symbol      VERSICOL      Symbol      VERSICOL

         .....   0.000 - 0.002     OOOOO   0.004 - 0.006     *****   0.008 - 0.010
         +++++   0.002 - 0.004     WWWWW   0.006 - 0.008     #####   0.010 - 0.012
```

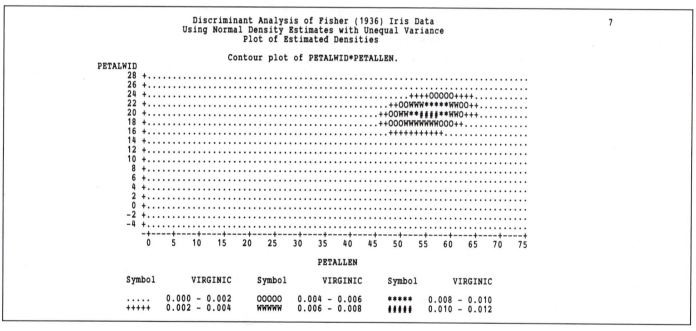

```
                  Discriminant Analysis of Fisher (1936) Iris Data              7
                 Using Normal Density Estimates with Unequal Variance
                            Plot of Estimated Densities

                       Contour plot of PETALWID*PETALLEN.
   PETALWID
      28 +..................................................................
      26 +..................................................................
      24 +.................................................++++OOOOO++++.........
      22 +..............................................++OOWWW*****WWOO++........
      20 +.............................................++OOWW**#####**WWO+++.......
      18 +............................................++OOOWWWWWWWOOO++...........
      16 +.............................................+++++++++++..............
      14 +..................................................................
      12 +..................................................................
      10 +..................................................................
       8 +..................................................................
       6 +..................................................................
       4 +..................................................................
       2 +..................................................................
       0 +..................................................................
      -2 +..................................................................
      -4 +..................................................................
        -+----+----+----+----+----+----+----+----+----+----+----+----+----+----+
         0    5   10   15   20   25   30   35   40   45   50   55   60   65   70   75

                                  PETALLEN

         Symbol      VIRGINIC      Symbol      VIRGINIC      Symbol      VIRGINIC

         .....   0.000 - 0.002     OOOOO   0.004 - 0.006     *****   0.008 - 0.010
         +++++   0.002 - 0.004     WWWWW   0.006 - 0.008     #####   0.010 - 0.012
```

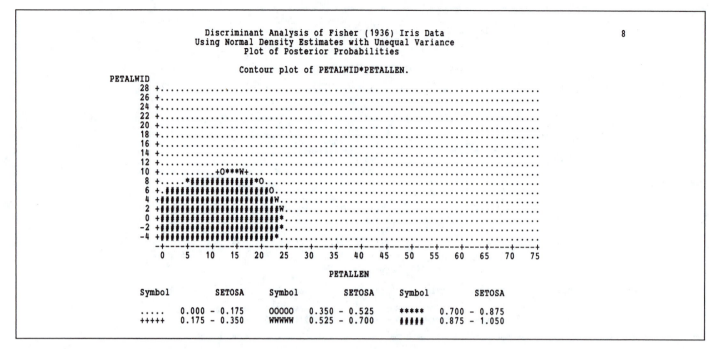

Discriminant Analysis of Fisher (1936) Iris Data
Using Normal Density Estimates with Unequal Variance
Plot of Posterior Probabilities   8

Contour plot of PETALWID*PETALLEN.

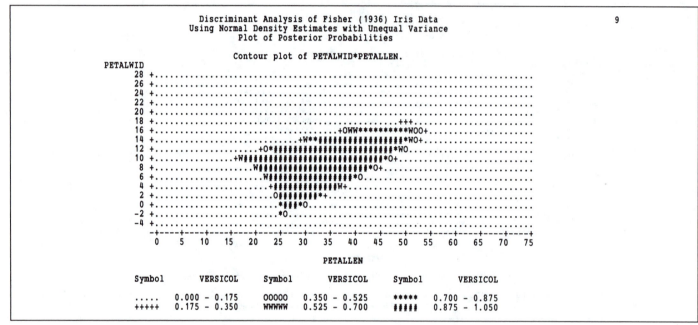

Discriminant Analysis of Fisher (1936) Iris Data
Using Normal Density Estimates with Unequal Variance
Plot of Posterior Probabilities   9

Contour plot of PETALWID*PETALLEN.

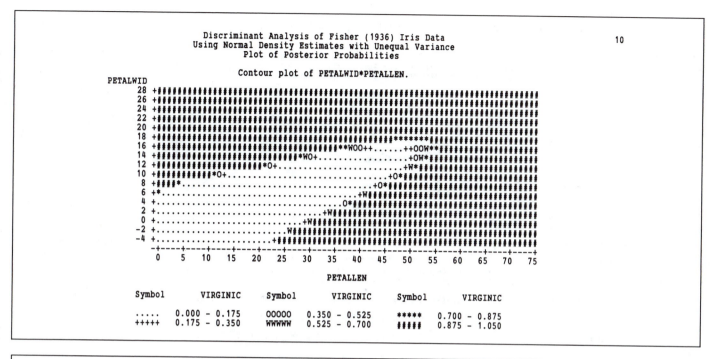

```
                     Discriminant Analysis of Fisher (1936) Iris Data                    10
                     Using Normal Density Estimates with Unequal Variance
                                Plot of Posterior Probabilities

                        Contour plot of PETALWID*PETALLEN.
       PETALWID
        28 +###########################################################################
        26 +###########################################################################
        24 +###########################################################################
        22 +###########################################################################
        20 +###########################################################################
        18 +###########################################################################
        16 +#####################################**WOO++......++OOW**###################
        14 +###########################################*WO+................+OW*#########
        12 +##########################################*O+..................+W*#########
        10 +#############*O+..............................+O*#########################
         8 +####*...........................................+O*#######################
         6 +*...........................................O*W#########################
         4 +...............................................O*#######################
         2 +...........................................+W#########################
         0 +...........................................+W#########################
        -2 +..................................W#######################################
        -4 +..........................+#############################################
           +----+----+----+----+----+----+----+----+----+----+----+----+----+----+----+
           0    5   10   15   20   25   30   35   40   45   50   55   60   65   70   75

                                        PETALLEN


     Symbol      VIRGINIC      Symbol      VIRGINIC      Symbol      VIRGINIC

     .....     0.000 - 0.175    OOOOO    0.350 - 0.525   *****    0.700 - 0.875
     +++++     0.175 - 0.350    WWWWW    0.525 - 0.700   #####    0.875 - 1.050
```

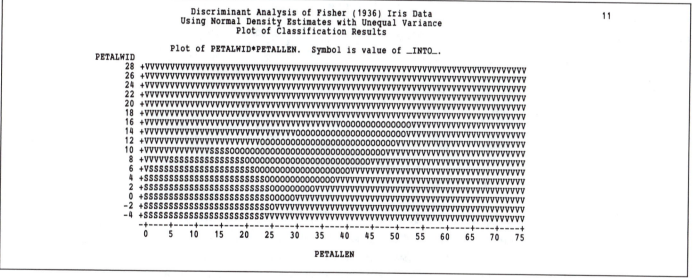

```
                     Discriminant Analysis of Fisher (1936) Iris Data                    11
                     Using Normal Density Estimates with Unequal Variance
                                Plot of Classification Results

                 Plot of PETALWID*PETALLEN.   Symbol is value of _INTO_.
       PETALWID
        28 +VVVVVVVVVVVVVVVVVVVVVVVVVVVVVVVVVVVVVVVVVVVVVVVVVVVVVVVVVVVVVVVVVVVVVVVVVV
        26 +VVVVVVVVVVVVVVVVVVVVVVVVVVVVVVVVVVVVVVVVVVVVVVVVVVVVVVVVVVVVVVVVVVVVVVVVVV
        24 +VVVVVVVVVVVVVVVVVVVVVVVVVVVVVVVVVVVVVVVVVVVVVVVVVVVVVVVVVVVVVVVVVVVVVVVVVV
        22 +VVVVVVVVVVVVVVVVVVVVVVVVVVVVVVVVVVVVVVVVVVVVVVVVVVVVVVVVVVVVVVVVVVVVVVVVVV
        20 +VVVVVVVVVVVVVVVVVVVVVVVVVVVVVVVVVVVVVVVVVVVVVVVVVVVVVVVVVVVVVVVVVVVVVVVVVV
        18 +VVVVVVVVVVVVVVVVVVVVVVVVVVVVVVVVVVVVVVVVVVVVVVVVVVVVVVVVVVVVVVVVVVVVVVVVVV
        16 +VVVVVVVVVVVVVVVVVVVVVVVVVVVVVVVVVVVVVVVVVVVVVOOOOOOOOOOOOOOOVVVVVVVVVVVVVVVVVVVV
        14 +VVVVVVVVVVVVVVVVVVVVVVVVVVVVVVVVOOOOOOOOOOOOOOOOOOOOVVVVVVVVVVVVVVVVVVVVVVV
        12 +VVVVVVVVVVVVVVVVVVVVVVVVVOOOOOOOOOOOOOOOOOOOOOVVVVVVVVVVVVVVVVVVVVVVVVVVVV
        10 +VVVVVVVVVVVVVSSSSOOOOOOOOOOOOOOOOOOOOOOVVVVVVVVVVVVVVVVVVVVVVVVVVVVVVVVVVV
         8 +VVVVVSSSSSSSSSSSSSSSSSOOOOOOOOOOOOOOOOOVVVVVVVVVVVVVVVVVVVVVVVVVVVVVVVVVVV
         6 +VSSSSSSSSSSSSSSSSSSSSOOOOOOOOOOOOOOOVVVVVVVVVVVVVVVVVVVVVVVVVVVVVVVVVVVVVV
         4 +SSSSSSSSSSSSSSSSSSSSSSSSOOOOOOOOOOOOOVVVVVVVVVVVVVVVVVVVVVVVVVVVVVVVVVVVVV
         2 +SSSSSSSSSSSSSSSSSSSSSSSOOOOOOOOOVVVVVVVVVVVVVVVVVVVVVVVVVVVVVVVVVVVVVVVVVV
         0 +SSSSSSSSSSSSSSSSSSSSSSSOOOOOOVVVVVVVVVVVVVVVVVVVVVVVVVVVVVVVVVVVVVVVVVVVVV
        -2 +SSSSSSSSSSSSSSSSSSSSSSSSSOVVVVVVVVVVVVVVVVVVVVVVVVVVVVVVVVVVVVVVVVVVVVVVVV
        -4 +SSSSSSSSSSSSSSSSSSSSSSSSSVVVVVVVVVVVVVVVVVVVVVVVVVVVVVVVVVVVVVVVVVVVVVVVVV
           +----+----+----+----+----+----+----+----+----+----+----+----+----+----+----+
           0    5   10   15   20   25   30   35   40   45   50   55   60   65   70   75
                                        PETALLEN
```

A nonparametric analysis (METHOD=NPAR) follows, using normal kernels (KERNEL=NORMAL) and equal bandwidths (POOL=YES) in each class. These statements produce **Output 16.9**:

```
proc discrim data=iris testdata=plotdata testout=plotp testoutd=plotd
        method=npar kernel=normal r=.5 pool=yes
        short noclassify crosslisterr;
   class species;
   var petal:;
   title2 'Using Kernel Density Estimates with Equal Bandwidth';
run;


%contour
```

Output 16.9 Kernel Density Estimates with Equal Bandwidth

```
                    Discriminant Analysis of Fisher (1936) Iris Data                    1
                    Using Kernel Density Estimates with Equal Bandwidth

                              DISCRIMINANT ANALYSIS

              150 Observations        149 DF Total
                2 Variables           147 DF Within Classes
                3 Classes               2 DF Between Classes


                            Class Level Information

                         Output                                         Prior
         SPECIES         SAS Name   Frequency      Weight    Proportion  Probability

         SETOSA          SETOSA           50      50.0000     0.333333   0.333333
         VERSICOLOR      VERSICOL         50      50.0000     0.333333   0.333333
         VIRGINICA       VIRGINIC         50      50.0000     0.333333   0.333333
```

```
                    Discriminant Analysis of Fisher (1936) Iris Data                    2
                    Using Kernel Density Estimates with Equal Bandwidth

   DISCRIMINANT ANALYSIS     CLASSIFICATION RESULTS FOR CALIBRATION DATA: WORK.IRIS

              Cross-validation Results using Normal Kernel Density

Squared Distance Function:          Posterior Probability of Membership in each SPECIES:
```
$$D^2(X,Y) = (X-Y)'\ COV^{-1}\ (X-Y) \qquad F(X|j) = n_j^{-1} \underset{i}{SUM}\ exp(\ -.5\ D^2(X,Y_{ji})\ /\ R^2\ )$$

$$Pr(j|X) = PRIOR_j\ F(X|j)\ /\ \underset{k}{SUM}\ PRIOR_k\ F(X|k)$$

```
                                       Posterior Probability of Membership in SPECIES:
         Obs      From          Classified
                 SPECIES        into SPECIES      SETOSA     VERSICOLOR    VIRGINICA

           5     VIRGINICA      VERSICOLOR *      0.0000       0.7512       0.2488
           9     VERSICOLOR     VIRGINICA  *      0.0000       0.0785       0.9215
          25     VIRGINICA      VERSICOLOR *      0.0000       0.5912       0.4088
          91     VIRGINICA      VERSICOLOR *      0.0000       0.8385       0.1615
         148     VERSICOLOR     VIRGINICA  *      0.0000       0.4074       0.5926

                           * Misclassified observation
```

```
                    Discriminant Analysis of Fisher (1936) Iris Data                    3
                    Using Kernel Density Estimates with Equal Bandwidth

   DISCRIMINANT ANALYSIS     CLASSIFICATION SUMMARY FOR CALIBRATION DATA: WORK.IRIS

              Cross-validation Summary using Normal Kernel Density

Squared Distance Function:          Posterior Probability of Membership in each SPECIES:
```
$$D^2(X,Y) = (X-Y)'\ COV^{-1}\ (X-Y) \qquad F(X|j) = n_j^{-1} \underset{i}{SUM}\ exp(\ -.5\ D^2(X,Y_{ji})\ /\ R^2\ )$$

$$Pr(j|X) = PRIOR_j\ F(X|j)\ /\ \underset{k}{SUM}\ PRIOR_k\ F(X|k)$$

```
              Number of Observations and Percents Classified into SPECIES:

     From SPECIES       SETOSA     VERSICOLOR    VIRGINICA       Total

         SETOSA             50            0            0            50
                        100.00         0.00         0.00        100.00

         VERSICOLOR          0           48            2            50
                          0.00        96.00         4.00        100.00

         VIRGINICA           0            3           47            50
                          0.00         6.00        94.00        100.00
```

(continued on next page)

(continued from previous page)

Total	50	51	49	150
Percent	33.33	34.00	32.67	100.00
Priors	0.3333	0.3333	0.3333	

Error Count Estimates for SPECIES:

	SETOSA	VERSICOLOR	VIRGINICA	Total
Rate	0.0000	0.0400	0.0600	0.0333
Priors	0.3333	0.3333	0.3333	

Discriminant Analysis of Fisher (1936) Iris Data
Using Kernel Density Estimates with Equal Bandwidth   4

DISCRIMINANT ANALYSIS   CLASSIFICATION SUMMARY FOR TEST DATA: WORK.PLOTDATA

Classification Summary using Normal Kernel Density

Squared Distance Function: Posterior Probability of Membership in each SPECIES:

$$D^2(X,Y) = (X-Y)' COV^{-1} (X-Y)$$

$$F(X|j) = n_j^{-1} \, \underset{i}{SUM} \, \exp(-.5 \, D^2(X,Y_{ji}) \, / \, R^2)$$

$$Pr(j|X) = PRIOR_j \, F(X|j) \, / \, \underset{k}{SUM} \, PRIOR_k \, F(X|k)$$

Number of Observations and Percents Classified into SPECIES:

	SETOSA	VERSICOLOR	VIRGINICA	Total
Total	365	313	614	1292
Percent	28.25	24.23	47.52	100.00
Priors	0.3333	0.3333	0.3333	

Discriminant Analysis of Fisher (1936) Iris Data
Using Kernel Density Estimates with Equal Bandwidth
Plot of Estimated Densities   5

Contour plot of PETALWID*PETALLEN.

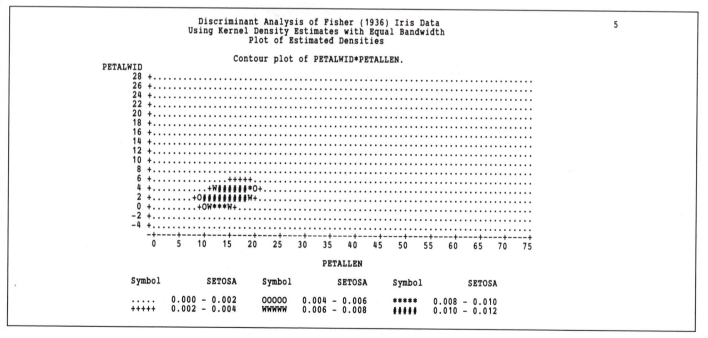

Symbol	SETOSA	Symbol	SETOSA	Symbol	SETOSA
.....	0.000 - 0.002	00000	0.004 - 0.006	*****	0.008 - 0.010
+++++	0.002 - 0.004	WWWWW	0.006 - 0.008	#####	0.010 - 0.012

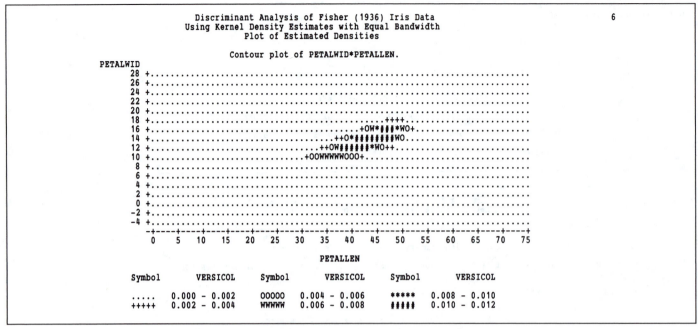

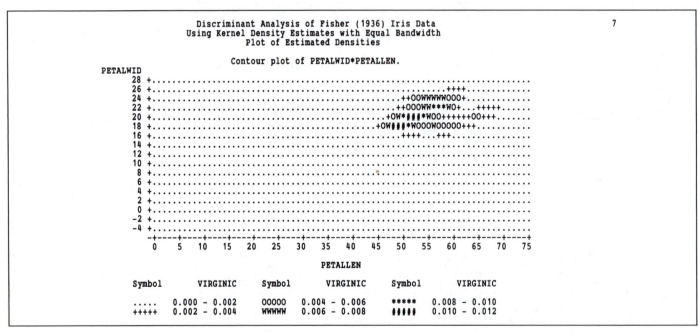

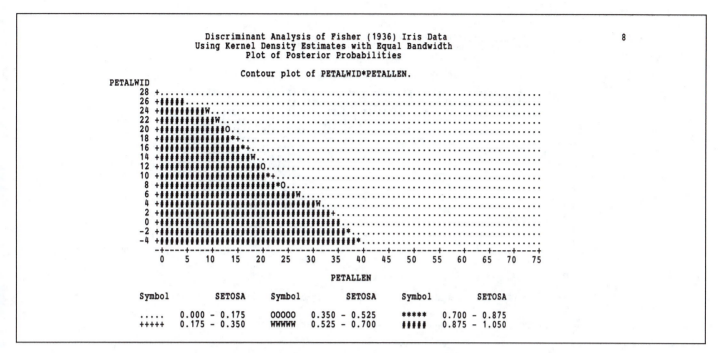

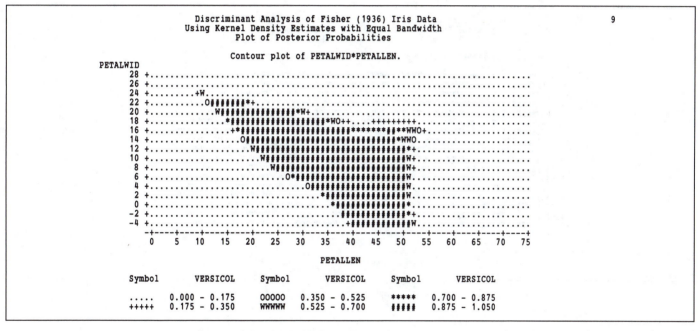

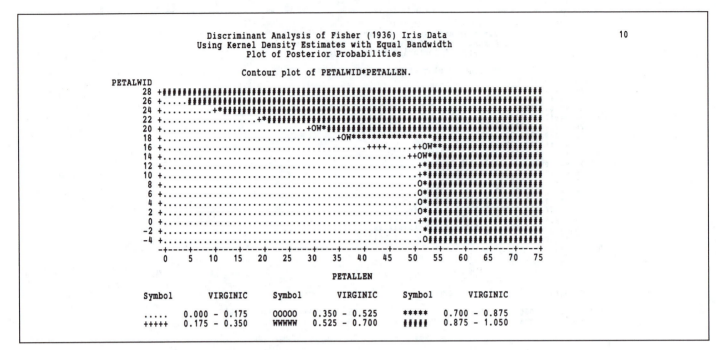

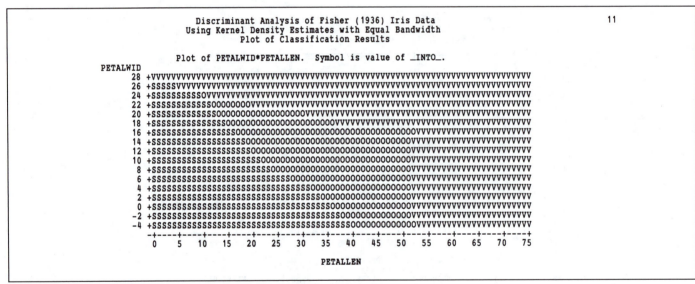

Another nonparametric analysis is run with unequal bandwidths (POOL=NO). These statements produce **Output 16.10**:

```
proc discrim data=iris testdata=plotdata testout=plotp testoutd=plotd
          method=npar kernel=normal r=.5 pool=no
          short noclassify crosslisterr;
     class species;
     var petal:;
     title2 'Using Kernel Density Estimates with Unequal Bandwidth';
run;


%contour
```

Output 16.10   Kernel Density Estimates with Unequal Bandwidth

```
                    Discriminant Analysis of Fisher (1936) Iris Data                    1
                  Using Kernel Density Estimates with Unequal Bandwidth

                               DISCRIMINANT ANALYSIS

                 150 Observations        149 DF Total
                   2 Variables           147 DF Within Classes
                   3 Classes               2 DF Between Classes


                            Class Level Information

                    Output                                          Prior
         SPECIES     SAS Name    Frequency      Weight    Proportion   Probability

         SETOSA      SETOSA           50     50.0000      0.333333     0.333333
         VERSICOLOR  VERSICOL         50     50.0000      0.333333     0.333333
         VIRGINICA   VIRGINIC         50     50.0000      0.333333     0.333333
```

```
                    Discriminant Analysis of Fisher (1936) Iris Data                    2
                  Using Kernel Density Estimates with Unequal Bandwidth

     DISCRIMINANT ANALYSIS       CLASSIFICATION RESULTS FOR CALIBRATION DATA: WORK.IRIS

               Cross-validation Results using Normal Kernel Density
```

Squared Distance Function: Posterior Probability of Membership in each SPECIES:

$$D^2_j(X,Y) = (X-Y)' COV^{-1}_j (X-Y) \qquad F(X|j) = n^{-1}_j \sum_i exp(-.5\ D^2(X,Y_{ji})\ /\ R^2)$$

$$Pr(j|X) = PRIOR_j\ F(X|j)\ /\ \sum_k PRIOR_k\ F(X|k)$$

```
                                      Posterior Probability of Membership in SPECIES:
        Obs       From       Classified
                SPECIES     into SPECIES    SETOSA    VERSICOLOR    VIRGINICA

          5    VIRGINICA    VERSICOLOR *    0.0000     0.7860       0.2140
          9    VERSICOLOR   VIRGINICA  *    0.0000     0.0506       0.9494
         91    VIRGINICA    VERSICOLOR *    0.0000     0.8824       0.1176
        148    VERSICOLOR   VIRGINICA  *    0.0000     0.3726       0.6274

                        * Misclassified observation
```

```
                    Discriminant Analysis of Fisher (1936) Iris Data                    3
                  Using Kernel Density Estimates with Unequal Bandwidth

     DISCRIMINANT ANALYSIS       CLASSIFICATION SUMMARY FOR CALIBRATION DATA: WORK.IRIS

               Cross-validation Summary using Normal Kernel Density
```

Squared Distance Function: Posterior Probability of Membership in each SPECIES:

$$D^2_j(X,Y) = (X-Y)' COV^{-1}_j (X-Y) \qquad F(X|j) = n^{-1}_j \sum_i exp(-.5\ D^2(X,Y_{ji})\ /\ R^2)$$

$$Pr(j|X) = PRIOR_j\ F(X|j)\ /\ \sum_k PRIOR_k\ F(X|k)$$

```
              Number of Observations and Percents Classified into SPECIES:

       From SPECIES      SETOSA     VERSICOLOR    VIRGINICA      Total

         SETOSA            50           0            0            50
                        100.00        0.00         0.00        100.00

         VERSICOLOR         0          48            2            50
                          0.00       96.00         4.00        100.00

         VIRGINICA          0           2           48            50
                          0.00        4.00        96.00        100.00
```

(continued on next page)

(continued from previous page)

	SETOSA	VERSICOLOR	VIRGINICA	Total
Total	50	50	50	150
Percent	33.33	33.33	33.33	100.00
Priors	0.3333	0.3333	0.3333	

Error Count Estimates for SPECIES:

	SETOSA	VERSICOLOR	VIRGINICA	Total
Rate	0.0000	0.0400	0.0400	0.0267
Priors	0.3333	0.3333	0.3333	

Discriminant Analysis of Fisher (1936) Iris Data
Using Kernel Density Estimates with Unequal Bandwidth   4

DISCRIMINANT ANALYSIS   CLASSIFICATION SUMMARY FOR TEST DATA: WORK.PLOTDATA

Classification Summary using Normal Kernel Density

Squared Distance Function: Posterior Probability of Membership in each SPECIES:

$$D^2(X,Y) = (X-Y)' \, COV_j^{-1} \, (X-Y)$$

$$F(X|j) = n_j \; \underset{i}{SUM} \; \exp(-.5 \; D^2(X,Y_{ji}) \, / \, R^2)$$

$$Pr(j|X) = PRIOR_j \; F(X|j) \, / \, \underset{k}{SUM} \; PRIOR_k \; F(X|k)$$

Number of Observations and Percents Classified into SPECIES:

	SETOSA	VERSICOLOR	VIRGINICA	Total
Total	165	180	947	1292
Percent	12.77	13.93	73.30	100.00
Priors	0.3333	0.3333	0.3333	

Discriminant Analysis of Fisher (1936) Iris Data   5
Using Kernel Density Estimates with Unequal Bandwidth
Plot of Estimated Densities

Contour plot of PETALWID*PETALLEN.

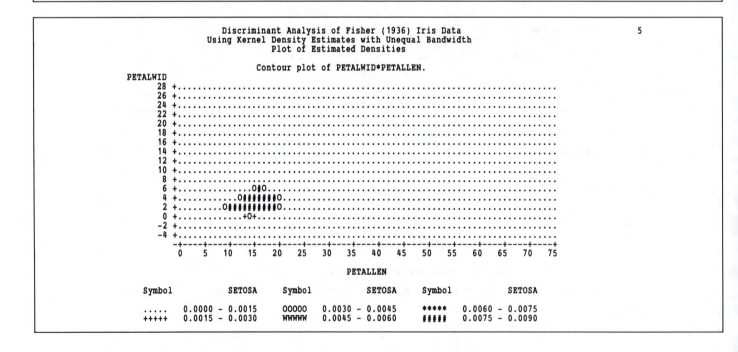

Symbol	SETOSA	Symbol	SETOSA	Symbol	SETOSA
.....	0.0000 - 0.0015	00000	0.0030 - 0.0045	*****	0.0060 - 0.0075
+++++	0.0015 - 0.0030	WWWWW	0.0045 - 0.0060	#####	0.0075 - 0.0090

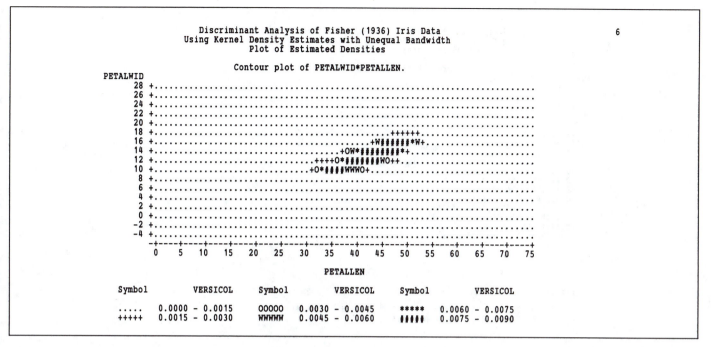

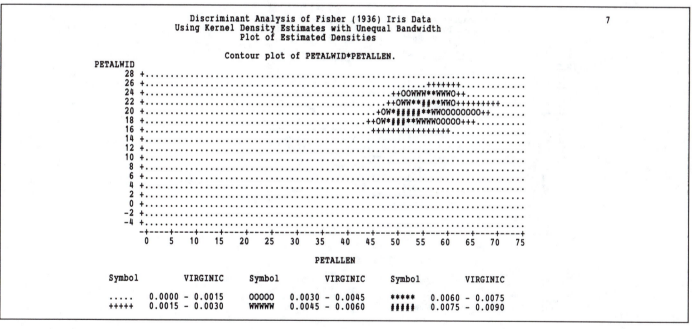

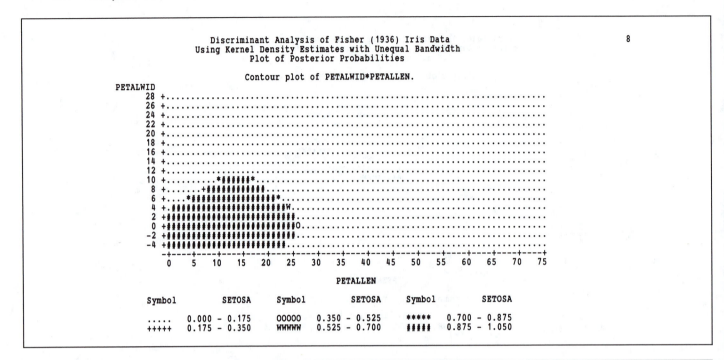

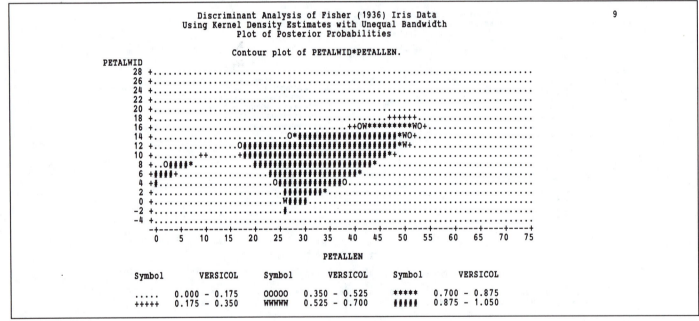

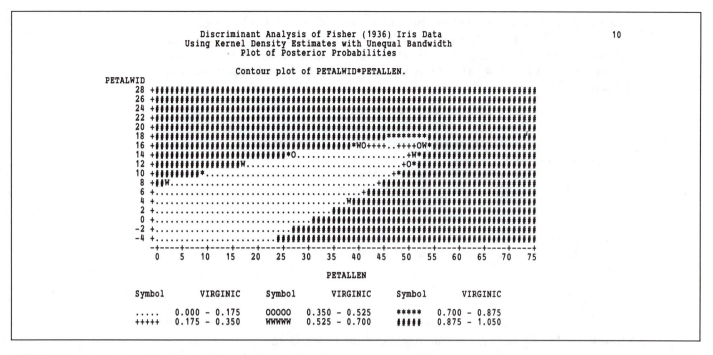

Discriminant Analysis of Fisher (1936) Iris Data
Using Kernel Density Estimates with Unequal Bandwidth
Plot of Posterior Probabilities

Contour plot of PETALWID*PETALLEN.

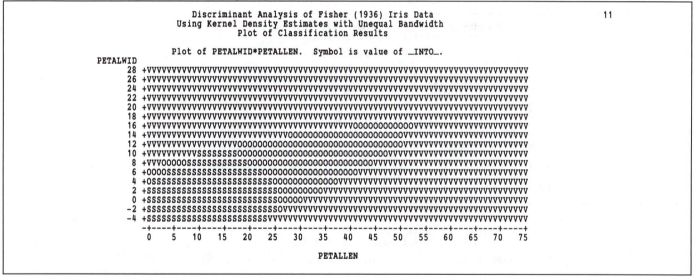

Discriminant Analysis of Fisher (1936) Iris Data
Using Kernel Density Estimates with Unequal Bandwidth
Plot of Classification Results

Plot of PETALWID*PETALLEN.   Symbol is value of _INTO_.

Example 3: Normal-Theory Discriminant Analysis of Iris Data

In this example, DISCRIM uses normal-theory methods to classify the iris data used in **Example 1**. POOL=TEST tests the homogeneity of the within-group covariance matrices. Since the resulting test statistic is significant at the 0.10 level, the within-group covariance matrices are used to derive the quadratic discriminant criterion. The WCOV and PCOV options print the within-group covariance matrices and the pooled covariance matrix. The DISTANCE option prints squared distances between classes. The ANOVA and MANOVA options test the hypothesis that the class means are equal, using univariate statistics and multivariate statistics. All statistics are significant at the 0.0001 level. The LISTERR option lists the misclassified observations under resubstitution. The CROSSLISTERR option lists the observations that are misclassified under crossvalidation and prints crossvalidation error-rate estimates. The resubstitution error count estimate, 0.02, is not larger than the crossvalidate error count estimate, 0.0267, as would be expected. The OUTSTAT= option generates a TYPE=MIXED (POOL=TEST) output data set containing various statistics such as means, covariances, and coefficients of the discriminant function. The following statements produce **Output 16.11** and **Output 16.12**:

```
proc discrim data=iris outstat=irisstat
             wcov pcov method=normal pool=test
             distance anova manova listerr crosslisterr;
   class species;
   var sepallen sepalwid petallen petalwid;
   title2 'Using Quadratic Discriminant Function';
run;

proc print data=irisstat;
   title2 'Output Discriminant Statistics';
run;
```

Output 16.11   Quadratic Discriminant Analysis of Iris Data

```
                  Discriminant Analysis of Fisher (1936) Iris Data                     1
                        Using Quadratic Discriminant Function

                             DISCRIMINANT ANALYSIS

                  150 Observations          149 DF Total
                    4 Variables             147 DF Within Classes
                    3 Classes                 2 DF Between Classes


                          Class Level Information

                                                                Prior
            SPECIES       Frequency        Weight     Proportion    Probability

            SETOSA             50        50.0000       0.333333      0.333333
            VERSICOLOR         50        50.0000       0.333333      0.333333
            VIRGINICA          50        50.0000       0.333333      0.333333
```

```
                  Discriminant Analysis of Fisher (1936) Iris Data                     2
                        Using Quadratic Discriminant Function

            DISCRIMINANT ANALYSIS          WITHIN-CLASS COVARIANCE MATRICES ❻

                      SPECIES = SETOSA      DF = 49

    Variable        SEPALLEN        SEPALWID        PETALLEN        PETALWID

    SEPALLEN      12.42489796      9.92163265      1.63551020      1.03306122    Sepal Length in mm.
    SEPALWID       9.92163265     14.36897959      1.16979592      0.92979592    Sepal Width  in mm.
    PETALLEN       1.63551020      1.16979592      3.01591837      0.60693878    Petal Length in mm.
    PETALWID       1.03306122      0.92979592      0.60693878      1.11061224    Petal Width  in mm.

    -------------------------------------------------------------------------------------------

                      SPECIES = VERSICOLOR    DF = 49

    Variable        SEPALLEN        SEPALWID        PETALLEN        PETALWID

    SEPALLEN      26.64326531      8.51836735     18.28979592      5.57795918    Sepal Length in mm.
    SEPALWID       8.51836735      9.84693878      8.26530612      4.12040816    Sepal Width  in mm.
    PETALLEN      18.28979592      8.26530612     22.08163265      7.31020408    Petal Length in mm.
    PETALWID       5.57795918      4.12040816      7.31020408      3.91061224    Petal Width  in mm.

    -------------------------------------------------------------------------------------------
```

(continued on next page)

(continued from previous page)

```
                    SPECIES = VIRGINICA    DF = 49

   Variable      SEPALLEN        SEPALWID        PETALLEN        PETALWID

   SEPALLEN    40.43428571      9.37632653     30.32897959      4.90938776     Sepal Length in mm.
   SEPALWID     9.37632653     10.40040816      7.13795918      4.76285714     Sepal Width  in mm.
   PETALLEN    30.32897959      7.13795918     30.45877551      4.88244898     Petal Length in mm.
   PETALWID     4.90938776      4.76285714      4.88244898      7.54326531     Petal Width  in mm.
```

```
                   Discriminant Analysis of Fisher (1936) Iris Data                    3
                       Using Quadratic Discriminant Function

                              DISCRIMINANT ANALYSIS

          ❼  Pooled Within-Class Covariance Matrix    DF = 147

   Variable      SEPALLEN        SEPALWID        PETALLEN        PETALWID

   SEPALLEN    26.50081633      9.27210884     16.75142857      3.84013605     Sepal Length in mm.
   SEPALWID     9.27210884     11.53877551      5.52435374      3.27102041     Sepal Width  in mm.
   PETALLEN    16.75142857      5.52435374     18.51877551      4.26653061     Petal Length in mm.
   PETALWID     3.84013605      3.27102041      4.26653061      4.18816327     Petal Width  in mm.
```

```
                   Discriminant Analysis of Fisher (1936) Iris Data                    4
                       Using Quadratic Discriminant Function

    DISCRIMINANT ANALYSIS     WITHIN COVARIANCE MATRIX INFORMATION  ⑳

                        Covariance      Natural Log of Determinant
              SPECIES   Matrix Rank     of the Covariance Matrix

              SETOSA          4                  5.35332
              VERSICOLOR      4                  7.54636
              VIRGINICA       4                  9.49362
                Pooled        4                  8.46214
```

```
                   Discriminant Analysis of Fisher (1936) Iris Data                    5
                       Using Quadratic Discriminant Function

    DISCRIMINANT ANALYSIS     TEST OF HOMOGENEITY OF WITHIN COVARIANCE MATRICES  ㉑

        Notation: K   = Number of Groups

                  P   = Number of Variables

                  N   = Total Number of Observations - Number of Groups

                  N(i) = Number of Observations in the i'th Group - 1
```

$$
V = \frac{\prod |\text{Within SS Matrix}(i)|^{N(i)/2}}{|\text{Pooled SS Matrix}|^{N/2}}
$$

$$
RHO = 1.0 - \left[SUM \frac{1}{N(i)} - \frac{1}{N} \right] \frac{2P^2 + 3P - 1}{6(P+1)(K-1)}
$$

$$
DF = .5(K-1)P(P+1)
$$

(continued on next page)

(continued from previous page)

Under null hypothesis: $-2\ \mathrm{RHO}\ \ln \left[\ \dfrac{N^{PN/2}\ V}{\prod\limits_i N(i)^{PN(i)/2}}\ \right]$ is distributed approximately as chi-square(DF)

Test Chi-Square Value =   140.943050 with   20 DF   Prob > Chi-Sq = 0.0001

Since the chi-square value is significant at the 0.1000 level,
the within covariance matrices will be used in the discriminant function.
Reference: Morrison, D.F.   Multivariate Statistical Methods p252.

Discriminant Analysis of Fisher (1936) Iris Data
Using Quadratic Discriminant Function   6

DISCRIMINANT ANALYSIS   PAIRWISE SQUARED DISTANCES BETWEEN GROUPS **17**

$$D^2(i|j) = (\bar{X}_i - \bar{X}_j)' \, \mathrm{COV}_j^{-1} \, (\bar{X}_i - \bar{X}_j)$$

Squared Distance to SPECIES

From SPECIES	SETOSA	VERSICOLOR	VIRGINICA
SETOSA	0	103.19382	168.76759
VERSICOLOR	323.06203	0	13.83875
VIRGINICA	706.08494	17.86670	0

Discriminant Analysis of Fisher (1936) Iris Data
Using Quadratic Discriminant Function   7

DISCRIMINANT ANALYSIS   PAIRWISE GENERALIZED SQUARED DISTANCES BETWEEN GROUPS **22**

$$D^2(i|j) = (\bar{X}_i - \bar{X}_j)' \, \mathrm{COV}_j^{-1} \, (\bar{X}_i - \bar{X}_j) + \ln |\mathrm{COV}_j|$$

Generalized Squared Distance to SPECIES

From SPECIES	SETOSA	VERSICOLOR	VIRGINICA
SETOSA	5.35332	110.74017	178.26121
VERSICOLOR	328.41535	7.54636	23.33238
VIRGINICA	711.43826	25.41306	9.49362

Discriminant Analysis of Fisher (1936) Iris Data
Using Quadratic Discriminant Function   8

DISCRIMINANT ANALYSIS

18 Univariate Test Statistics

F Statistics,   Num DF= 2   Den DF= 147

Variable	Total STD	Pooled STD	Between STD	R-Squared	RSQ/ (1-RSQ)	F	Pr > F	Label
SEPALLEN	8.2807	5.1479	7.9506	0.618706	1.6226	119.2645	0.0001	Sepal Length in mm.
SEPALWID	4.3587	3.3969	3.3682	0.400783	0.6688	49.1600	0.0001	Sepal Width in mm.
PETALLEN	17.6530	4.3033	20.9070	0.941372	16.0566	1180.1612	0.0001	Petal Length in mm.
PETALWID	7.6224	2.0465	8.9673	0.928883	13.0613	960.0071	0.0001	Petal Width in mm.

Average R-Squared: Unweighted = 0.7224358   Weighted by Variance = 0.8689444

(continued on next page)

(continued from previous page)

⑲ Multivariate Statistics and F Approximations

S=2   M=0.5   N=71

Statistic	Value	F	Num DF	Den DF	Pr > F
Wilks' Lambda	0.02343863	199.1453	8	288	0.0001
Pillai's Trace	1.19189883	53.4665	8	290	0.0001
Hotelling-Lawley Trace	32.47732024	580.5321	8	286	0.0001
Roy's Greatest Root	32.19192920	1166.957	4	145	0.0001

NOTE: F Statistic for Roy's Greatest Root is an upper bound.
NOTE: F Statistic for Wilks' Lambda is exact.

Discriminant Analysis of Fisher (1936) Iris Data
Using Quadratic Discriminant Function   9

DISCRIMINANT ANALYSIS   CLASSIFICATION RESULTS FOR CALIBRATION DATA: WORK.IRIS

㉜ Resubstitution Results using Quadratic Discriminant Function

Generalized Squared Distance Function: Posterior Probability of Membership in each SPECIES:

$$D_j^2(X) = (X - \bar{X}_j)' \, COV_j^{-1} \, (X - \bar{X}_j) + \ln |COV_j|$$

$$Pr(j|X) = \exp(-.5 \, D_j^2(X)) \, / \, SUM_k \exp(-.5 \, D_k^2(X))$$

Posterior Probability of Membership in SPECIES:

Obs	From SPECIES	Classified into SPECIES	SETOSA	VERSICOLOR	VIRGINICA
5	VIRGINICA	VERSICOLOR *	0.0000	0.6050	0.3950
9	VERSICOLOR	VIRGINICA *	0.0000	0.3359	0.6641
12	VERSICOLOR	VIRGINICA *	0.0000	0.1543	0.8457

* Misclassified observation

Discriminant Analysis of Fisher (1936) Iris Data
Using Quadratic Discriminant Function   10

DISCRIMINANT ANALYSIS   CLASSIFICATION SUMMARY FOR CALIBRATION DATA: WORK.IRIS

㉝ Resubstitution Summary using Quadratic Discriminant Function

Generalized Squared Distance Function: Posterior Probability of Membership in each SPECIES:

$$D_j^2(X) = (X - \bar{X}_j)' \, COV_j^{-1} \, (X - \bar{X}_j) + \ln |COV_j|$$

$$Pr(j|X) = \exp(-.5 \, D_j^2(X)) \, / \, SUM_k \exp(-.5 \, D_k^2(X))$$

Number of Observations and Percents Classified into SPECIES:

From SPECIES	SETOSA	VERSICOLOR	VIRGINICA	Total
SETOSA	50 100.00	0 0.00	0 0.00	50 100.00
VERSICOLOR	0 0.00	48 96.00	2 4.00	50 100.00
VIRGINICA	0 0.00	1 2.00	49 98.00	50 100.00
Total Percent	50 33.33	49 32.67	51 34.00	150 100.00
Priors	0.3333	0.3333	0.3333	

㉞ Error Count Estimates for SPECIES:

	SETOSA	VERSICOLOR	VIRGINICA	Total
Rate	0.0000	0.0400	0.0200	0.0200
Priors	0.3333	0.3333	0.3333	

Discriminant Analysis of Fisher (1936) Iris Data
Using Quadratic Discriminant Function

DISCRIMINANT ANALYSIS   CLASSIFICATION RESULTS FOR CALIBRATION DATA: WORK.IRIS

Cross-validation Results using Quadratic Discriminant Function

Generalized Squared Distance Function: Posterior Probability of Membership in each SPECIES:

$$D_j^2(X) = (X-\bar{X}_{(X)j})'\,COV_{(X)j}^{-1}\,(X-\bar{X}_{(X)j}) + \ln |COV_{(X)j}|$$ $$Pr(j|X) = \exp(-.5\,D_j^2(X))\,/\,\underset{k}{SUM}\,\exp(-.5\,D_k^2(X))$$

Posterior Probability of Membership in SPECIES:

Obs	From SPECIES	Classified into SPECIES	SETOSA	VERSICOLOR	VIRGINICA
5	VIRGINICA	VERSICOLOR *	0.0000	0.6632	0.3368
8	VERSICOLOR	VIRGINICA *	0.0000	0.3134	0.6866
9	VERSICOLOR	VIRGINICA *	0.0000	0.1616	0.8384
12	VERSICOLOR	VIRGINICA *	0.0000	0.0713	0.9287

* Misclassified observation

Discriminant Analysis of Fisher (1936) Iris Data
Using Quadratic Discriminant Function

DISCRIMINANT ANALYSIS   CLASSIFICATION SUMMARY FOR CALIBRATION DATA: WORK.IRIS

Cross-validation Summary using Quadratic Discriminant Function

Generalized Squared Distance Function: Posterior Probability of Membership in each SPECIES:

$$D_j^2(X) = (X-\bar{X}_{(X)j})'\,COV_{(X)j}^{-1}\,(X-\bar{X}_{(X)j}) + \ln |COV_{(X)j}|$$ $$Pr(j|X) = \exp(-.5\,D_j^2(X))\,/\,\underset{k}{SUM}\,\exp(-.5\,D_k^2(X))$$

Number of Observations and Percents Classified into SPECIES:

From SPECIES	SETOSA	VERSICOLOR	VIRGINICA	Total
SETOSA	50	0	0	50
	100.00	0.00	0.00	100.00
VERSICOLOR	0	47	3	50
	0.00	94.00	6.00	100.00
VIRGINICA	0	1	49	50
	0.00	2.00	98.00	100.00
Total	50	48	52	150
Percent	33.33	32.00	34.67	100.00
Priors	0.3333	0.3333	0.3333	

Error Count Estimates for SPECIES:

	SETOSA	VERSICOLOR	VIRGINICA	Total
Rate	0.0000	0.0600	0.0200	0.0267
Priors	0.3333	0.3333	0.3333	

Output 16.12   Output Statistics from Iris Data

```
                 Discriminant Analysis of Fisher (1936) Iris Data                    1
                        Output Discriminant Statistics
```

OBS	SPECIES	_TYPE_	_NAME_	SEPALLEN	SEPALWID	PETALLEN	PETALWID
1	.	N		150.00	150.00	150.00	150.00
2	SETOSA	N		50.00	50.00	50.00	50.00
3	VERSICOLOR	N		50.00	50.00	50.00	50.00
4	VIRGINICA	N		50.00	50.00	50.00	50.00
5	.	MEAN		58.43	30.57	37.58	11.99
6	SETOSA	MEAN		50.06	34.28	14.62	2.46
7	VERSICOLOR	MEAN		59.36	27.70	42.60	13.26
8	VIRGINICA	MEAN		65.88	29.74	55.52	20.26
9	SETOSA	PRIOR		0.33	0.33	0.33	0.33
10	VERSICOLOR	PRIOR		0.33	0.33	0.33	0.33
11	VIRGINICA	PRIOR		0.33	0.33	0.33	0.33
12	SETOSA	CSSCP	SEPALLEN	608.82	486.16	80.14	50.62
13	SETOSA	CSSCP	SEPALWID	486.16	704.08	57.32	45.56
14	SETOSA	CSSCP	PETALLEN	80.14	57.32	147.78	29.74
15	SETOSA	CSSCP	PETALWID	50.62	45.56	29.74	54.42
16	VERSICOLOR	CSSCP	SEPALLEN	1305.52	417.40	896.20	273.32
17	VERSICOLOR	CSSCP	SEPALWID	417.40	482.50	405.00	201.90
18	VERSICOLOR	CSSCP	PETALLEN	896.20	405.00	1082.00	358.20
19	VERSICOLOR	CSSCP	PETALWID	273.32	201.90	358.20	191.62
20	VIRGINICA	CSSCP	SEPALLEN	1981.28	459.44	1486.12	240.56
21	VIRGINICA	CSSCP	SEPALWID	459.44	509.62	349.76	233.38
22	VIRGINICA	CSSCP	PETALLEN	1486.12	349.76	1492.48	239.24
23	VIRGINICA	CSSCP	PETALWID	240.56	233.38	239.24	369.62
24	.	PSSCP	SEPALLEN	3895.62	1363.00	2462.46	564.50
25	.	PSSCP	SEPALWID	1363.00	1696.20	812.08	480.84
26	.	PSSCP	PETALLEN	2462.46	812.08	2722.26	627.18
27	.	PSSCP	PETALWID	564.50	480.84	627.18	615.66
28	.	BSSCP	SEPALLEN	6321.21	-1995.27	16524.84	7127.93
29	.	BSSCP	SEPALWID	-1995.27	1134.49	-5723.96	-2293.27
30	.	BSSCP	PETALLEN	16524.84	-5723.96	43710.28	18677.40
31	.	BSSCP	PETALWID	7127.93	-2293.27	18677.40	8041.33
32	.	CSSCP	SEPALLEN	10216.83	-632.27	18987.30	7692.43
33	.	CSSCP	SEPALWID	-632.27	2830.69	-4911.88	-1812.43
34	.	CSSCP	PETALLEN	18987.30	-4911.88	46432.54	19304.58
35	.	CSSCP	PETALWID	7692.43	-1812.43	19304.58	8656.99
36	.	RSQUARED		0.62	0.40	0.94	0.93
37	SETOSA	COV	SEPALLEN	12.42	9.92	1.64	1.03
38	SETOSA	COV	SEPALWID	9.92	14.37	1.17	0.93
39	SETOSA	COV	PETALLEN	1.64	1.17	3.02	0.61
40	SETOSA	COV	PETALWID	1.03	0.93	0.61	1.11
41	VERSICOLOR	COV	SEPALLEN	26.64	8.52	18.29	5.58
42	VERSICOLOR	COV	SEPALWID	8.52	9.85	8.27	4.12
43	VERSICOLOR	COV	PETALLEN	18.29	8.27	22.08	7.31
44	VERSICOLOR	COV	PETALWID	5.58	4.12	7.31	3.91
45	VIRGINICA	COV	SEPALLEN	40.43	9.38	30.33	4.91
46	VIRGINICA	COV	SEPALWID	9.38	10.40	7.14	4.76
47	VIRGINICA	COV	PETALLEN	30.33	7.14	30.46	4.88
48	VIRGINICA	COV	PETALWID	4.91	4.76	4.88	7.54
49	.	PCOV	SEPALLEN	26.50	9.27	16.75	3.84
50	.	PCOV	SEPALWID	9.27	11.54	5.52	3.27
51	.	PCOV	PETALLEN	16.75	5.52	18.52	4.27
52	.	PCOV	PETALWID	3.84	3.27	4.27	4.19
53	.	BCOV	SEPALLEN	63.21	-19.95	165.25	71.28
54	.	BCOV	SEPALWID	-19.95	11.34	-57.24	-22.93
55	.	BCOV	PETALLEN	165.25	-57.24	437.10	186.77

```
                 Discriminant Analysis of Fisher (1936) Iris Data                    2
                        Output Discriminant Statistics
```

OBS	SPECIES	_TYPE_	_NAME_	SEPALLEN	SEPALWID	PETALLEN	PETALWID
56	.	BCOV	PETALWID	71.28	-22.93	186.77	80.41
57	.	COV	SEPALLEN	68.57	-4.24	127.43	51.63
58	.	COV	SEPALWID	-4.24	19.00	-32.97	-12.16
59	.	COV	PETALLEN	127.43	-32.97	311.63	129.56
60	.	COV	PETALWID	51.63	-12.16	129.56	58.10
61	SETOSA	STD		3.52	3.79	1.74	1.05
62	VERSICOLOR	STD		5.16	3.14	4.70	1.98
63	VIRGINICA	STD		6.36	3.22	5.52	2.75
64	.	PSTD		5.15	3.40	4.30	2.05
65	.	BSTD		7.95	3.37	20.91	8.97
66	.	STD		8.28	4.36	17.65	7.62
67	SETOSA	CORR	SEPALLEN	1.00	0.74	0.27	0.28
68	SETOSA	CORR	SEPALWID	0.74	1.00	0.18	0.23
69	SETOSA	CORR	PETALLEN	0.27	0.18	1.00	0.33

(continued on next page)

(continued from previous page)

				SEPALLEN	SEPALWID	PETALLEN	PETALWID
70	SETOSA	CORR	PETALWID	0.28	0.23	0.33	1.00
71	VERSICOLOR	CORR	SEPALLEN	1.00	0.53	0.75	0.55
72	VERSICOLOR	CORR	SEPALWID	0.53	1.00	0.56	0.66
73	VERSICOLOR	CORR	PETALLEN	0.75	0.56	1.00	0.79
74	VERSICOLOR	CORR	PETALWID	0.55	0.66	0.79	1.00
75	VIRGINICA	CORR	SEPALLEN	1.00	0.46	0.86	0.28
76	VIRGINICA	CORR	SEPALWID	0.46	1.00	0.40	0.54
77	VIRGINICA	CORR	PETALLEN	0.86	0.40	1.00	0.32
78	VIRGINICA	CORR	PETALWID	0.28	0.54	0.32	1.00
79	.	PCORR	SEPALLEN	1.00	0.53	0.76	0.36
80	.	PCORR	SEPALWID	0.53	1.00	0.38	0.47
81	.	PCORR	PETALLEN	0.76	0.38	1.00	0.48
82	.	PCORR	PETALWID	0.36	0.47	0.48	1.00
83	.	BCORR	SEPALLEN	1.00	-0.75	0.99	1.00
84	.	BCORR	SEPALWID	-0.75	1.00	-0.81	-0.76
85	.	BCORR	PETALLEN	0.99	-0.81	1.00	1.00
86	.	BCORR	PETALWID	1.00	-0.76	1.00	1.00
87	.	CORR	SEPALLEN	1.00	-0.12	0.87	0.82
88	.	CORR	SEPALWID	-0.12	1.00	-0.43	-0.37
89	.	CORR	PETALLEN	0.87	-0.43	1.00	0.96
90	.	CORR	PETALWID	0.82	-0.37	0.96	1.00
91	SETOSA	STDMEAN		-1.01	0.85	-1.30	-1.25
92	VERSICOLOR	STDMEAN		0.11	-0.66	0.28	0.17
93	VIRGINICA	STDMEAN		0.90	-0.19	1.02	1.08
94	SETOSA	PSTDMEAN		-1.63	1.09	-5.34	-4.66
95	VERSICOLOR	PSTDMEAN		0.18	-0.85	1.17	0.62
96	VIRGINICA	PSTDMEAN		1.45	-0.25	4.17	4.04
97	.	DETERM		4732.18	4732.18	4732.18	4732.18
98	SETOSA	DETERM		211.31	211.31	211.31	211.31
99	VERSICOLOR	DETERM		1893.83	1893.83	1893.83	1893.83
100	VIRGINICA	DETERM		13274.79	13274.79	13274.79	13274.79
101	SETOSA	QUAD	SEPALLEN	-0.09	0.06	0.02	0.02
102	SETOSA	QUAD	SEPALWID	0.06	-0.08	-0.01	0.01
103	SETOSA	QUAD	PETALLEN	0.02	-0.01	-0.19	0.09
104	SETOSA	QUAD	PETALWID	0.02	0.01	0.09	-0.53
105	SETOSA	QUAD	_LINEAR_	4.46	-0.76	3.36	-3.13
106	SETOSA	QUAD	_CONST_	-121.83	-121.83	-121.83	-121.83
107	VERSICOLOR	QUAD	SEPALLEN	-0.05	0.02	0.04	-0.03
108	VERSICOLOR	QUAD	SEPALWID	0.02	-0.10	-0.01	0.10
109	VERSICOLOR	QUAD	PETALLEN	0.04	-0.01	-0.10	0.13
110	VERSICOLOR	QUAD	PETALWID	-0.03	0.10	0.13	-0.44

Discriminant Analysis of Fisher (1936) Iris Data   3
Output Discriminant Statistics

OBS	SPECIES	_TYPE_	_NAME_	SEPALLEN	SEPALWID	PETALLEN	PETALWID
111	VERSICOLOR	QUAD	_LINEAR_	1.8013	1.5961	0.3269	-1.4713
112	VERSICOLOR	QUAD	_CONST_	-76.5490	-76.5490	-76.5490	-76.5490
113	VIRGINICA	QUAD	SEPALLEN	-0.0527	0.0174	0.0498	-0.0089
114	VIRGINICA	QUAD	SEPALWID	0.0174	-0.0794	-0.0055	0.0424
115	VIRGINICA	QUAD	PETALLEN	0.0498	-0.0055	-0.0670	0.0145
116	VIRGINICA	QUAD	PETALWID	-0.0089	0.0424	0.0145	-0.0966
117	VIRGINICA	QUAD	_LINEAR_	0.7372	1.3245	0.6234	0.9662
118	VIRGINICA	QUAD	_CONST_	-75.8208	-75.8208	-75.8208	-75.8208

Example 4: Epanechnikov-Kernel Discriminant Analysis of Iris Data

In this example, DISCRIM uses a nonparametric method (METHOD=NPAR) to classify the same iris data of **Example 1**. A kernel method with density estimates from Epanechnikov kernels (R=, KERNEL=EPA) is used. DISCRIM uses equal bandwidths (smoothing parameters) (POOL=YES) in each class. The use of equal bandwidths does not constrain the density estimates to be of equal variance. Note that the smoothing parameter R=1.8 is obtained by assuming that each group has a multivariate normal distribution with a sample size of fifty and by minimizing an approximate mean integrated square error of the estimated density. The LISTERR option lists the observations that are misclassified under resubstitution. The CROSSLISTERR option lists the observations that are misclassified under crossvalidation and prints crossvalidation error-rate estimates. Note that under crossvalidation, six observations with missing posterior probabilities are classified into group OTHER. For each of these six observations, the corresponding ellipsoid does not contain any training set observations other than itself. The group-specific estimated densities are zero for these observations. The POSTERR option prints the posterior error-rate estimates of the classification results. The OUTD= option generates an output data set containing the group-specific density estimates for each observation in the input data set. The first thirty observations in the output data set are printed. The following statements produce **Output 16.13** and **Output 16.14**:

```
proc discrim data=iris outd=outd
              method=npar kernel=epa pool=yes r=1.8
              listerr crosslisterr posterr;
   class species;
   var sepallen sepalwid petallen petalwid;
   title2 'Using Epanechnikov-Kernel Discriminant Analysis';
run;

proc print data=outd(obs=30);
   title2 'Output Density Estimates of Iris Data';
run;
```

Output 16.13   Epanechnikov-Kernel Discriminant Analysis

```
                    Discriminant Analysis of Fisher (1936) Iris Data                    1
                    Using Epanechnikov-Kernel Discriminant Analysis

                            DISCRIMINANT ANALYSIS

               150 Observations        149 DF Total
                 4 Variables           147 DF Within Classes
                 3 Classes               2 DF Between Classes

                          Class Level Information

                     Output                                         Prior
         SPECIES      SAS Name     Frequency      Weight    Proportion    Probability

         SETOSA       SETOSA            50       50.0000     0.333333      0.333333
         VERSICOLOR   VERSICOL          50       50.0000     0.333333      0.333333
         VIRGINICA    VIRGINIC          50       50.0000     0.333333      0.333333
```

```
                    Discriminant Analysis of Fisher (1936) Iris Data                    2
                    Using Epanechnikov-Kernel Discriminant Analysis

  DISCRIMINANT ANALYSIS      CLASSIFICATION RESULTS FOR CALIBRATION DATA: WORK.IRIS

           Resubstitution Results using Epanechnikov Kernel Density

 Squared Distance Function:         Posterior Probability of Membership in each SPECIES:

 2              -1                      -1          2          2
D (X,Y) = (X-Y)' COV  (X-Y)      F(X|j) = n  SUM ( 1.0 - D (X,Y ) / R  )
                                          j  i              ji

                                 Pr(j|X) = PRIOR  F(X|j) / SUM PRIOR  F(X|k)
                                                j         k       k

                                        Posterior Probability of Membership in SPECIES:
           From          Classified
   Obs     SPECIES       into SPECIES     SETOSA     VERSICOLOR    VIRGINICA

     5     VIRGINICA     VERSICOLOR *     0.0000       0.5931        0.4069
     9     VERSICOLOR    VIRGINICA  *     0.0000       0.4492        0.5508
    12     VERSICOLOR    VIRGINICA  *     0.0000       0.2807        0.7193

                        * Misclassified observation
```

Discriminant Analysis of Fisher (1936) Iris Data
Using Epanechnikov-Kernel Discriminant Analysis

3

DISCRIMINANT ANALYSIS   CLASSIFICATION SUMMARY FOR CALIBRATION DATA: WORK.IRIS

Resubstitution Summary using Epanechnikov Kernel Density

Squared Distance Function: Posterior Probability of Membership in each SPECIES:

$$D^2(X,Y) = (X-Y)' \, COV^{-1} \, (X-Y)$$

$$F(X|j) = n_j^{-1} \, \underset{i}{SUM} \, (\, 1.0 - D^2(X,Y_{ji}) \, / \, R^2 \,)$$

$$Pr(j|X) = PRIOR_j \, F(X|j) \, / \, \underset{k}{SUM} \, PRIOR_k \, F(X|k)$$

Number of Observations and Percents Classified into SPECIES:

From SPECIES	SETOSA	VERSICOLOR	VIRGINICA	Total
SETOSA	50 100.00	0 0.00	0 0.00	50 100.00
VERSICOLOR	0 0.00	48 96.00	2 4.00	50 100.00
VIRGINICA	0 0.00	1 2.00	49 98.00	50 100.00
Total Percent	50 33.33	49 32.67	51 34.00	150 100.00
Priors	0.3333	0.3333	0.3333	

Error Count Estimates for SPECIES:

	SETOSA	VERSICOLOR	VIRGINICA	Total
Rate	0.0000	0.0400	0.0200	0.0200
Priors	0.3333	0.3333	0.3333	

Discriminant Analysis of Fisher (1936) Iris Data
Using Epanechnikov-Kernel Discriminant Analysis

4

DISCRIMINANT ANALYSIS   CLASSIFICATION RESULTS FOR CALIBRATION DATA: WORK.IRIS

Resubstitution Results using Epanechnikov Kernel Density

Squared Distance Function: Posterior Probability of Membership in each SPECIES:

$$D^2(X,Y) = (X-Y)' \, COV^{-1} \, (X-Y)$$

$$F(X|j) = n_j^{-1} \, \underset{i}{SUM} \, (\, 1.0 - D^2(X,Y_{ji}) \, / \, R^2 \,)$$

$$Pr(j|X) = PRIOR_j \, F(X|j) \, / \, \underset{k}{SUM} \, PRIOR_k \, F(X|k)$$

Number of Observations and Average Posterior Probabilities
Classified into SPECIES:

From SPECIES	SETOSA	VERSICOLOR	VIRGINICA
SETOSA	50 1.0000	0 .	0 .
VERSICOLOR	0 .	48 0.9832	2 0.6351
VIRGINICA	0 .	1 0.5931	49 0.9723
Total	50 1.0000	49 0.9753	51 0.9591
Priors	0.3333	0.3333	0.3333

(continued on next page)

(continued from previous page)

㉟ Posterior Probability Error Rate Estimates for SPECIES:

Estimate	SETOSA	VERSICOLOR	VIRGINICA	Total
Stratified	0.0000	0.0442	0.0218	0.0220
Unstratified	0.0000	0.0442	0.0218	0.0220
Priors	0.3333	0.3333	0.3333	

Discriminant Analysis of Fisher (1936) Iris Data
Using Epanechnikov-Kernel Discriminant Analysis   5

DISCRIMINANT ANALYSIS   CLASSIFICATION RESULTS FOR CALIBRATION DATA: WORK.IRIS

Cross-validation Results using Epanechnikov Kernel Density

Squared Distance Function: Posterior Probability of Membership in each SPECIES:

$$D^2(X,Y) = (X-Y)' COV^{-1} (X-Y) \qquad F(X|j) = n_j^{-1} \, \underset{i}{SUM} \, (1.0 - D^2(X,Y_{ji}) / R^2)$$

$$Pr(j|X) = PRIOR_j \, F(X|j) / \underset{k}{SUM} \, PRIOR_k \, F(X|k)$$

Posterior Probability of Membership in SPECIES:

Obs	From SPECIES	Classified into SPECIES	SETOSA	VERSICOLOR	VIRGINICA
5	VIRGINICA	VERSICOLOR *	0.0000	0.8692	0.1308
9	VERSICOLOR	VIRGINICA *	0.0000	0.2241	0.7759
12	VERSICOLOR	VIRGINICA *	0.0000	0.0000	1.0000
25	VIRGINICA	OTHER ∂	.	.	.
57	VIRGINICA	OTHER ∂	.	.	.
74	VIRGINICA	OTHER ∂	.	.	.
90	VIRGINICA	OTHER ∂	.	.	.
91	VIRGINICA	VERSICOLOR *	0.0000	1.0000	0.0000
118	VERSICOLOR	VIRGINICA *	0.0000	0.2082	0.7918
137	SETOSA	OTHER ∂	.	.	.
147	VIRGINICA	OTHER ∂	.	.	.

* Misclassified observation   ∂ Threshold probability not met

---

Discriminant Analysis of Fisher (1936) Iris Data
Using Epanechnikov-Kernel Discriminant Analysis   6

DISCRIMINANT ANALYSIS   CLASSIFICATION SUMMARY FOR CALIBRATION DATA: WORK.IRIS

Cross-validation Summary using Epanechnikov Kernel Density

Squared Distance Function: Posterior Probability of Membership in each SPECIES:

$$D^2(X,Y) = (X-Y)' COV^{-1} (X-Y) \qquad F(X|j) = n_j^{-1} \, \underset{i}{SUM} \, (1.0 - D^2(X,Y_{ji}) / R^2)$$

$$Pr(j|X) = PRIOR_j \, F(X|j) / \underset{k}{SUM} \, PRIOR_k \, F(X|k)$$

Number of Observations and Percents Classified into SPECIES:

From SPECIES	SETOSA	VERSICOLOR	VIRGINICA	OTHER	Total
SETOSA	49 98.00	0 0.00	0 0.00	1 2.00	50 100.00
VERSICOLOR	0 0.00	47 94.00	3 6.00	0 0.00	50 100.00
VIRGINICA	0 0.00	2 4.00	43 86.00	5 10.00	50 100.00
Total Percent	49 32.67	49 32.67	46 30.67	6 4.00	150 100.00
Priors	0.3333	0.3333	0.3333		

(continued on next page)

(continued from previous page)

```
          Error Count Estimates for SPECIES:

                SETOSA    VERSICOLOR    VIRGINICA      Total

        Rate    0.0200      0.0600        0.1400      0.0733

        Priors  0.3333      0.3333        0.3333
```

DISCRIMINANT ANALYSIS   CLASSIFICATION RESULTS FOR CALIBRATION DATA: WORK.IRIS

Cross-validation Results using Epanechnikov Kernel Density

Squared Distance Function: Posterior Probability of Membership in each SPECIES:

$$D^2(X,Y) = (X-Y)' \, COV^{-1} \, (X-Y) \qquad F(X|j) = n_j^{-1} \sum_i \left(1.0 - D^2(X,Y_{ji}) / R^2 \right)$$

$$Pr(j|X) = PRIOR_j \, F(X|j) \; / \; \sum_k PRIOR_k \, F(X|k)$$

Number of Observations and Average Posterior Probabilities
Classified into SPECIES:

From SPECIES	SETOSA	VERSICOLOR	VIRGINICA
SETOSA	49	0	0
	1.0000	.	.
VERSICOLOR	0	47	3
	.	0.9892	0.8559
VIRGINICA	0	2	43
	.	0.9346	0.9687
Total	49	49	46
	1.0000	0.9870	0.9613
Priors	0.3333	0.3333	0.3333

㊴ Posterior Probability Error Rate Estimates for SPECIES:

Estimate	SETOSA	VERSICOLOR	VIRGINICA	Total
Stratified	0.0200	0.0327	0.1156	0.0561
Unstratified	0.0200	0.0327	0.1156	0.0561
Priors	0.3333	0.3333	0.3333	

Output 16.14 Output Density Estimates of Iris Data

```
                  Discriminant Analysis of Fisher (1936) Iris Data                    1
                     Output Density Estimates of Iris Data

 OBS   SEPALLEN   SEPALWID   PETALLEN   PETALWID    SPECIES       SETOSA     VERSICOL     VIRGINIC

  1       50         33         14          2       SETOSA      .00033094   .00000000   .00000000
  2       64         28         56         22       VIRGINICA   .00000000   .00000000   .00007734
  3       65         28         46         15       VERSICOLOR  .00000000   .00010644   .00000000
  4       67         31         56         24       VIRGINICA   .00000000   .00000000   .00007418
  5       63         28         51         15       VIRGINICA   .00000000   .00003143   .00002157
  6       46         34         14          3       SETOSA      .00020058   .00000000   .00000000
  7       69         31         51         23       VIRGINICA   .00000000   .00000000   .00002944
  8       62         22         45         15       VERSICOLOR  .00000000   .00002457   .00000000
  9       59         32         48         18       VERSICOLOR  .00000000   .00002607   .00003197
 10       46         36         10          2       SETOSA      .00009332   .00000000   .00000000
 11       61         30         46         14       VERSICOLOR  .00000000   .00015189   .00000245
 12       60         27         51         16       VERSICOLOR  .00000000   .00001684   .00004315
 13       65         30         52         20       VIRGINICA   .00000000   .00000000   .00011153
 14       56         25         39         11       VERSICOLOR  .00000000   .00014709   .00000000
 15       65         30         55         18       VIRGINICA   .00000000   .00000930   .00006972
 16       58         27         51         19       VIRGINICA   .00000000   .00000000   .00007420
 17       68         32         59         23       VIRGINICA   .00000000   .00000000   .00009697
 18       51         33         17          5       SETOSA      .00008239   .00000000   .00000000
 19       57         28         45         13       VERSICOLOR  .00000000   .00012167   .00000173
 20       62         34         54         23       VIRGINICA   .00000000   .00000000   .00003769
 21       77         38         67         22       VIRGINICA   .00000000   .00000000   .00001823
 22       63         33         47         16       VERSICOLOR  .00000000   .00008116   .00000000
 23       67         33         57         25       VIRGINICA   .00000000   .00000000   .00006645
 24       76         30         66         21       VIRGINICA   .00000000   .00000000   .00003831
 25       49         25         45         17       VIRGINICA   .00000000   .00000000   .00001684
 26       55         35         13          2       SETOSA      .00007211   .00000000   .00000000
 27       67         30         52         23       VIRGINICA   .00000000   .00000000   .00004068
 28       70         32         47         14       VERSICOLOR  .00000000   .00009615   .00000000
 29       64         32         45         15       VERSICOLOR  .00000000   .00012807   .00000000
 30       61         28         40         13       VERSICOLOR  .00000000   .00012241   .00000000
```

Example 5: Linear Discriminant Analysis of Remote-Sensing Data on Crops

In this example, remote-sensing data described at the beginning of the section are used. In the first PROC DISCRIM statement, DISCRIM uses normal-theory methods (METHOD=NORMAL) assuming equal variances (POOL=YES) in five crops. The PRIORS statement, PRIORS PROP, sets the prior probabilities proportional to the sample sizes. The LIST option lists the resubstitution classification results for each observation. The CROSSVALIDATE option prints crossvalidation error-rate estimates. The OUTSTAT= option stores the calibration information in a new data set to classify future observations. The second DISCRIM statement uses this calibration information to classify a test data set. The TESTLIST option lists the classification results for each observation in the test data set. Note that the values of the identification variable, XVALUES, are obtained by rereading the X1 through X4 fields in the data lines as a single character variable. The following statements produce **Output 16.15** through **Output 16.17**:

```
data crops;
   title 'Discriminant Analysis of Remote Sensing Data on Five Crops';
   input crop $ 1-10 x1-x4 xvalues $ 11-21;
   cards;
CORN      16 27 31 33
CORN      15 23 30 30
CORN      16 27 27 26
CORN      18 20 25 23
CORN      15 15 31 32
CORN      15 32 32 15
CORN      12 15 16 73
SOYBEANS  20 23 23 25
```

```
SOYBEANS    24 24 25 32
SOYBEANS    21 25 23 24
SOYBEANS    27 45 24 12
SOYBEANS    12 13 15 42
SOYBEANS    22 32 31 43
COTTON      31 32 33 34
COTTON      29 24 26 28
COTTON      34 32 28 45
COTTON      26 25 23 24
COTTON      53 48 75 26
COTTON      34 35 25 78
SUGARBEETS22 23 25 42
SUGARBEETS25 25 24 26
SUGARBEETS34 25 16 52
SUGARBEETS54 23 21 54
SUGARBEETS25 43 32 15
SUGARBEETS26 54  2 54
CLOVER      12 45 32 54
CLOVER      24 58 25 34
CLOVER      87 54 61 21
CLOVER      51 31 31 16
CLOVER      96 48 54 62
CLOVER      31 31 11 11
CLOVER      56 13 13 71
CLOVER      32 13 27 32
CLOVER      36 26 54 32
CLOVER      53 08 06 54
CLOVER      32 32 62 16
;
proc discrim data=crops outstat=cropstat
             method=normal pool=yes
             list crossvalidate;
   class crop;
   priors prop;
   id xvalues;
   var x1-x4;
   title2 'Using Linear Discriminant Function';
run;

data test;
   input crop $ 1-10 x1-x4 xvalues $ 11-21;
   cards;
CORN       16 27 31 33
SOYBEANS   21 25 23 24
COTTON     29 24 26 28
SUGARBEETS54 23 21 54
CLOVER     32 32 62 16
;
proc discrim data=cropstat testdata=test testout=tout
             testlist;
   class crop;
   testid xvalues;
   var x1-x4;
   title2 'Classification of Test Data';
run;
```

```
proc print data=tout;
    title2 'Output Classification Results of Test Data';
run;
```

Output 16.15   Linear Discriminant Function on Crop Data

```
                 Discriminant Analysis of Remote Sensing Data on Five Crops                    1
                         Using Linear Discriminant Function

                              DISCRIMINANT ANALYSIS

             36 Observations        35 DF Total
              4 Variables           31 DF Within Classes
              5 Classes              4 DF Between Classes


                            Class Level Information

                                                            Prior
           CROP         Frequency      Weight    Proportion    Probability

           CLOVER            11      11.0000      0.305556      0.305556
           CORN               7       7.0000      0.194444      0.194444
           COTTON             6       6.0000      0.166667      0.166667
           SOYBEANS           6       6.0000      0.166667      0.166667
           SUGARBEETS         6       6.0000      0.166667      0.166667
```

```
                 Discriminant Analysis of Remote Sensing Data on Five Crops                    2
                         Using Linear Discriminant Function

      DISCRIMINANT ANALYSIS        POOLED COVARIANCE MATRIX INFORMATION

            Covariance            Natural Log of Determinant
           Matrix Rank           of the Covariance Matrix

                4                         21.3018939
```

```
                 Discriminant Analysis of Remote Sensing Data on Five Crops                    3
                         Using Linear Discriminant Function

    DISCRIMINANT ANALYSIS     PAIRWISE GENERALIZED SQUARED DISTANCES BETWEEN GROUPS
```

$$D^2(i|j) = (\bar{X}_i - \bar{X}_j)'\,COV^{-1}\,(\bar{X}_i - \bar{X}_j) - 2 \ln PRIOR_j$$

```
                       Generalized Squared Distance to CROP

    From CROP      CLOVER        CORN       COTTON      SOYBEANS    SUGARBEETS

    CLOVER        2.37125     7.52830      4.44969     6.16665      5.07262
    CORN          6.62433     3.27522      5.46798     4.31383      6.47395
    COTTON        3.23741     5.15968      3.58352     5.01819      4.87908
    SOYBEANS      4.95438     4.00552      5.01819     3.58352      4.65998
    SUGARBEETS    3.86034     6.16564      4.87908     4.65998      3.58352
```

```
         Discriminant Analysis of Remote Sensing Data on Five Crops              4
                    Using Linear Discriminant Function

              DISCRIMINANT ANALYSIS     LINEAR DISCRIMINANT FUNCTION  ③①

                         -1 _                                        -1 _
     Constant = -.5 X' COV   X  + ln PRIOR    Coefficient Vector = COV   X
              j        j    j                                            j

                                     CROP

                 CLOVER        CORN       COTTON     SOYBEANS    SUGARBEETS

     CONSTANT   -10.98457   -7.72070   -11.46537    -7.28260    -9.80179
     X1           0.08907   -0.04180     0.02462    0.0000369    0.04245
     X2           0.17379    0.11970     0.17596     0.15896     0.20988
     X3           0.11899    0.16511     0.15880     0.10622     0.06540
     X4           0.15637    0.16768     0.18362     0.14133     0.16408
```

```
         Discriminant Analysis of Remote Sensing Data on Five Crops              5
                    Using Linear Discriminant Function

     DISCRIMINANT ANALYSIS    CLASSIFICATION RESULTS FOR CALIBRATION DATA: WORK.CROPS

          Resubstitution Results using Linear Discriminant Function

  Generalized Squared Distance Function:      Posterior Probability of Membership in each CROP:

   2              -1 _                                    2              2
  D (X) = (X-X )' COV  (X-X ) - 2 ln PRIOR   Pr(j|X) = exp(-.5 D (X)) / SUM exp(-.5 D (X))
   j        j        j           j                            j      k          k
```

Posterior Probability of Membership in CROP:

XVALUES	From CROP	Classified into CROP		CLOVER	CORN	COTTON	SOYBEANS	SUGARBEETS
16 27 31 33	CORN	CORN		0.0894	0.4054	0.1763	0.2392	0.0897
15 23 30 30	CORN	CORN		0.0769	0.4558	0.1421	0.2530	0.0722
16 27 27 26	CORN	CORN		0.0982	0.3422	0.1365	0.3073	0.1157
18 20 25 23	CORN	CORN		0.1052	0.3634	0.1078	0.3281	0.0955
15 15 31 32	CORN	CORN		0.0588	0.5754	0.1173	0.2087	0.0398
15 32 32 15	CORN	SOYBEANS	*	0.0972	0.3278	0.1318	0.3420	0.1011
12 15 16 73	CORN	CORN		0.0454	0.5238	0.1849	0.1376	0.1083
20 23 23 25	SOYBEANS	SOYBEANS		0.1330	0.2804	0.1176	0.3305	0.1385
24 24 25 32	SOYBEANS	SOYBEANS		0.1768	0.2483	0.1586	0.2660	0.1502
21 25 23 24	SOYBEANS	SOYBEANS		0.1481	0.2431	0.1200	0.3318	0.1570
27 45 24 12	SOYBEANS	SUGARBEETS	*	0.2357	0.0547	0.1016	0.2721	0.3359
12 13 15 42	SOYBEANS	CORN	*	0.0549	0.4749	0.0920	0.2768	0.1013
22 32 31 43	SOYBEANS	COTTON	*	0.1474	0.2606	0.2624	0.1848	0.1448
31 32 33 34	COTTON	CLOVER	*	0.2815	0.1518	0.2377	0.1767	0.1523
29 24 26 28	COTTON	SOYBEANS	*	0.2521	0.1842	0.1529	0.2549	0.1559
34 32 28 45	COTTON	CLOVER	*	0.3125	0.1023	0.2404	0.1357	0.2091
26 25 23 24	COTTON	SOYBEANS	*	0.2121	0.1809	0.1245	0.3045	0.1780
53 48 75 26	COTTON	CLOVER	*	0.4837	0.0391	0.4384	0.0223	0.0166
34 35 25 78	COTTON	COTTON		0.2256	0.0794	0.3810	0.0592	0.2548
22 23 25 42	SUGARBEETS	CORN	*	0.1421	0.3066	0.1901	0.2231	0.1381
25 25 24 26	SUGARBEETS	SOYBEANS	*	0.1969	0.2050	0.1354	0.2960	0.1667
34 25 16 52	SUGARBEETS	SUGARBEETS		0.2928	0.0871	0.1665	0.1479	0.3056
54 23 21 54	SUGARBEETS	CLOVER	*	0.6215	0.0194	0.1250	0.0496	0.1845
25 43 32 15	SUGARBEETS	SOYBEANS	*	0.2258	0.1135	0.1646	0.2770	0.2191
26 54 2 54	SUGARBEETS	SUGARBEETS		0.0850	0.0081	0.0521	0.0661	0.7887
12 45 32 54	CLOVER	COTTON	*	0.0693	0.2663	0.3394	0.1460	0.1789
24 58 25 34	CLOVER	SUGARBEETS	*	0.1647	0.0376	0.1680	0.1452	0.4845
87 54 61 21	CLOVER	CLOVER		0.9328	0.0003	0.0478	0.0025	0.0165
51 31 31 16	CLOVER	CLOVER		0.6642	0.0205	0.0872	0.0959	0.1322
96 48 54 62	CLOVER	CLOVER		0.9215	0.0002	0.0604	0.0007	0.0173
31 31 11 11	CLOVER	SUGARBEETS	*	0.2525	0.0402	0.0473	0.3012	0.3588
56 13 13 71	CLOVER	CLOVER		0.6132	0.0212	0.1226	0.0408	0.2023
32 13 27 32	CLOVER	CLOVER		0.2669	0.2616	0.1512	0.2260	0.0943
36 26 54 32	CLOVER	COTTON	*	0.2650	0.2645	0.3495	0.0918	0.0292
53 08 06 54	CLOVER	CLOVER		0.5914	0.0237	0.0676	0.0781	0.2392
32 32 62 16	CLOVER	COTTON	*	0.2163	0.3180	0.3327	0.1125	0.0206

```
                         * Misclassified observation
```

Discriminant Analysis of Remote Sensing Data on Five Crops   6
Using Linear Discriminant Function

DISCRIMINANT ANALYSIS   CLASSIFICATION SUMMARY FOR CALIBRATION DATA: WORK.CROPS

Resubstitution Summary using Linear Discriminant Function

Generalized Squared Distance Function: Posterior Probability of Membership in each CROP:

$$D^2_j(X) = (X-\bar{X}_j)' COV^{-1} (X-\bar{X}_j) - 2 \ln PRIOR_j \qquad Pr(j|X) = \exp(-.5 D^2_j(X)) / SUM_k \exp(-.5 D^2_k(X))$$

Number of Observations and Percents Classified into CROP:

From CROP	CLOVER	CORN	COTTON	SOYBEANS	SUGARBEETS	Total
CLOVER	6 54.55	0 0.00	3 27.27	0 0.00	2 18.18	11 100.00
CORN	0 0.00	6 85.71	0 0.00	1 14.29	0 0.00	7 100.00
COTTON	3 50.00	0 0.00	1 16.67	2 33.33	0 0.00	6 100.00
SOYBEANS	0 0.00	1 16.67	1 16.67	3 50.00	1 16.67	6 100.00
SUGARBEETS	1 16.67	1 16.67	0 0.00	2 33.33	2 33.33	6 100.00
Total Percent	10 27.78	8 22.22	5 13.89	8 22.22	5 13.89	36 100.00
Priors	0.3056	0.1944	0.1667	0.1667	0.1667	

㉞ Error Count Estimates for CROP:

	CLOVER	CORN	COTTON	SOYBEANS	SUGARBEETS	Total
Rate	0.4545	0.1429	0.8333	0.5000	0.6667	0.5000
Priors	0.3056	0.1944	0.1667	0.1667	0.1667	

Discriminant Analysis of Remote Sensing Data on Five Crops   7
Using Linear Discriminant Function

DISCRIMINANT ANALYSIS   CLASSIFICATION SUMMARY FOR CALIBRATION DATA: WORK.CROPS

Cross-validation Summary using Linear Discriminant Function

Generalized Squared Distance Function: Posterior Probability of Membership in each CROP:

$$D^2_j(X) = (X-\bar{X}_{(X)j})' COV^{-1}_{(X)} (X-\bar{X}_{(X)j}) - 2 \ln PRIOR_j \qquad Pr(j|X) = \exp(-.5 D^2_j(X)) / SUM_k \exp(-.5 D^2_k(X))$$

Number of Observations and Percents Classified into CROP:

From CROP	CLOVER	CORN	COTTON	SOYBEANS	SUGARBEETS	Total
CLOVER	4 36.36	3 27.27	1 9.09	0 0.00	3 27.27	11 100.00
CORN	0 0.00	4 57.14	1 14.29	2 28.57	0 0.00	7 100.00
COTTON	3 50.00	0 0.00	0 0.00	2 33.33	1 16.67	6 100.00
SOYBEANS	0 0.00	1 16.67	1 16.67	3 50.00	1 16.67	6 100.00
SUGARBEETS	2 33.33	1 16.67	0 0.00	2 33.33	1 16.67	6 100.00
Total Percent	9 25.00	9 25.00	3 8.33	9 25.00	6 16.67	36 100.00
Priors	0.3056	0.1944	0.1667	0.1667	0.1667	

(continued on next page)

(continued from previous page)

```
              Error Count Estimates for CROP:

                  CLOVER      CORN     COTTON    SOYBEANS    SUGARBEETS     Total

        Rate      0.6364     0.4286    1.0000     0.5000       0.8333      0.6667

        Priors    0.3056     0.1944    0.1667     0.1667       0.1667
```

Output 16.16 Classification of Test Data

```
                    Discriminant Analysis of Remote Sensing Data on Five Crops                    1
                                  Classification of Test Data

         DISCRIMINANT ANALYSIS      CLASSIFICATION RESULTS FOR TEST DATA: WORK.TEST

            ㊿  Classification Results using Linear Discriminant Function

      Generalized Squared Distance Function:      Posterior Probability of Membership in each CROP:

         2       _      -1  _                                       2              2
        D (X) = (X-X )' COV  (X-X )         Pr(j|X) = exp(-.5 D (X)) / SUM exp(-.5 D (X))
         j          j          j                               j     k          k

                                    Posterior Probability of Membership in CROP:

       XVALUES        From         Classified
                      CROP         into CROP        CLOVER      CORN     COTTON    SOYBEANS    SUGARBEETS

       16 27 31 33    CORN         CORN             0.0894     0.4054    0.1763    0.2392      0.0897
       21 25 23 24    SOYBEANS     SOYBEANS         0.1481     0.2431    0.1200    0.3318      0.1570
       29 24 26 28    COTTON       SOYBEANS   *     0.2521     0.1842    0.1529    0.2549      0.1559
       54 23 21 54    SUGARBEETS   CLOVER     *     0.6215     0.0194    0.1250    0.0496      0.1845
       32 32 62 16    CLOVER       COTTON     *     0.2163     0.3180    0.3327    0.1125      0.0206

                            * Misclassified observation
```

```
                    Discriminant Analysis of Remote Sensing Data on Five Crops                    2
                                  Classification of Test Data

         DISCRIMINANT ANALYSIS      CLASSIFICATION SUMMARY FOR TEST DATA: WORK.TEST

            ㊶  Classification Summary using Linear Discriminant Function

      Generalized Squared Distance Function:      Posterior Probability of Membership in each CROP:

         2       _      -1  _                                       2              2
        D (X) = (X-X )' COV  (X-X )         Pr(j|X) = exp(-.5 D (X)) / SUM exp(-.5 D (X))
         j          j          j                               j     k          k

                       Number of Observations and Percents Classified into CROP:

       From CROP       CLOVER      CORN      COTTON    SOYBEANS    SUGARBEETS      Total

        CLOVER             0          0          1          0           0            1
                        0.00       0.00     100.00       0.00        0.00       100.00

        CORN               0          1          0          0           0            1
                        0.00     100.00       0.00       0.00        0.00       100.00

        COTTON             0          0          0          1           0            1
                        0.00       0.00       0.00     100.00        0.00       100.00

        SOYBEANS           0          0          0          1           0            1
                        0.00       0.00       0.00     100.00        0.00       100.00

        SUGARBEETS         1          0          0          0           0            1
                      100.00       0.00       0.00       0.00        0.00       100.00

        Total              1          1          1          2           0            5
        Percent        20.00      20.00      20.00      40.00        0.00       100.00

        Priors        0.3056     0.1944     0.1667     0.1667       0.1667
```

(continued on next page)

(continued from previous page)

42 Error Count Estimates for CROP:

	CLOVER	CORN	COTTON	SOYBEANS	SUGARBEETS	Total
Rate	1.0000	0.0000	1.0000	0.0000	1.0000	0.6389
Priors	0.3056	0.1944	0.1667	0.1667	0.1667	

Output 16.17   Output Classification Results of Test Data

```
                   Discriminant Analysis of Remote Sensing Data on Five Crops                    3
                         Output Classification Results of Test Data

OBS  CROP        X1  X2  X3  X4    XVALUES      CLOVER    CORN     COTTON   SOYBEANS  SUGARBEE  _INTO_

 1   CORN        16  27  31  33  16 27 31 33   0.08935  0.40543  0.17632  0.23918   0.08972   CORN
 2   SOYBEANS    21  25  23  24  21 25 23 24   0.14811  0.24308  0.11999  0.33184   0.15698   SOYBEANS
 3   COTTON      29  24  26  28  29 24 26 28   0.25213  0.18420  0.15294  0.25486   0.15588   SOYBEANS
 4   SUGARBEETS  54  23  21  54  54 23 21 54   0.62150  0.01937  0.12498  0.04962   0.18452   CLOVER
 5   CLOVER      32  32  62  16  32 32 62 16   0.21633  0.31799  0.33266  0.11246   0.02056   COTTON
```

Example 6: Quadratic Discriminant Analysis of Remote-Sensing Data on Crops

In this example, DISCRIM uses normal-theory methods (METHOD=NORMAL) assuming unequal variances (POOL=NO) for the remote-sensing data of **Example 5**. The PRIORS statement, PRIORS PROP, sets the prior probabilities proportional to the sample sizes. The CROSSVALIDATE option prints crossvalidation error-rate estimates. Note that the total error count estimate by crossvalidation (0.5556) is much larger than the total error count estimate by resubstitution (0.1111). The following statements produce **Output 16.18**:

```
proc discrim data=crops
             method=normal pool=no
             crossvalidate;
   class crop;
   priors prop;
   id xvalues;
   var x1-x4;
   title2 'Using Quadratic Discriminant Function';
run;
```

Output 16.18   Quadratic Discriminant Function on Crop Data

```
                Discriminant Analysis of Remote Sensing Data on Five Crops          1
                       Using Quadratic Discriminant Function

                            DISCRIMINANT ANALYSIS

                36 Observations      35 DF Total
                 4 Variables         31 DF Within Classes
                 5 Classes            4 DF Between Classes


                          Class Level Information

                                                            Prior
        CROP          Frequency      Weight    Proportion  Probability

        CLOVER           11         11.0000     0.305556    0.305556
        CORN              7          7.0000     0.194444    0.194444
        COTTON            6          6.0000     0.166667    0.166667
        SOYBEANS          6          6.0000     0.166667    0.166667
        SUGARBEETS        6          6.0000     0.166667    0.166667
```

```
                Discriminant Analysis of Remote Sensing Data on Five Crops          2
                       Using Quadratic Discriminant Function

        DISCRIMINANT ANALYSIS      WITHIN COVARIANCE MATRIX INFORMATION

                             Covariance    Natural Log of Determinant
            CROP            Matrix Rank    of the Covariance Matrix

            CLOVER               4                23.64618
            CORN                 4                11.13472
            COTTON               4                13.23569
            SOYBEANS             4                12.45263
            SUGARBEETS           4                17.76293
```

```
                Discriminant Analysis of Remote Sensing Data on Five Crops          3
                       Using Quadratic Discriminant Function

        DISCRIMINANT ANALYSIS    PAIRWISE GENERALIZED SQUARED DISTANCES BETWEEN GROUPS
```

$$D^2(i|j) = (\bar{X}_i - \bar{X}_j)' \, COV_j^{-1} \, (\bar{X}_i - \bar{X}_j) + \ln |COV_j| - 2 \ln PRIOR_j$$

```
                        Generalized Squared Distance to CROP

    From CROP       CLOVER        CORN       COTTON     SOYBEANS    SUGARBEETS

    CLOVER         26.01743       1320     104.18297   194.10546    31.40816
    CORN           27.73809     14.40994  150.50763    38.36252    25.55421
    COTTON         26.38544    588.86232   16.81921    52.03266    37.15560
    SOYBEANS       27.07134     46.42131   41.01631    16.03615    23.15920
    SUGARBEETS     26.80188    332.11563   43.98280   107.95676    21.34645
```

Discriminant Analysis of Remote Sensing Data on Five Crops   4
Using Quadratic Discriminant Function

DISCRIMINANT ANALYSIS   CLASSIFICATION SUMMARY FOR CALIBRATION DATA: WORK.CROPS

Resubstitution Summary using Quadratic Discriminant Function

Generalized Squared Distance Function: Posterior Probability of Membership in each CROP:

$$D^2_j(X) = (X-\bar{X}_j)' COV^{-1}_j (X-\bar{X}_j) + \ln |COV_j| - 2 \ln PRIOR_j \qquad Pr(j|X) = \exp(-.5 D^2_j(X)) / \underset{k}{SUM} \exp(-.5 D^2_k(X))$$

Number of Observations and Percents Classified into CROP:

From CROP	CLOVER	CORN	COTTON	SOYBEANS	SUGARBEETS	Total
CLOVER	9	0	0	0	2	11
	81.82	0.00	0.00	0.00	18.18	100.00
CORN	0	7	0	0	0	7
	0.00	100.00	0.00	0.00	0.00	100.00
COTTON	0	0	6	0	0	6
	0.00	0.00	100.00	0.00	0.00	100.00
SOYBEANS	0	0	0	6	0	6
	0.00	0.00	0.00	100.00	0.00	100.00
SUGARBEETS	0	0	1	1	4	6
	0.00	0.00	16.67	16.67	66.67	100.00
Total	9	7	7	7	6	36
Percent	25.00	19.44	19.44	19.44	16.67	100.00
Priors	0.3056	0.1944	0.1667	0.1667	0.1667	

Error Count Estimates for CROP:

	CLOVER	CORN	COTTON	SOYBEANS	SUGARBEETS	Total
Rate	0.1818	0.0000	0.0000	0.0000	0.3333	0.1111
Priors	0.3056	0.1944	0.1667	0.1667	0.1667	

Discriminant Analysis of Remote Sensing Data on Five Crops   5
Using Quadratic Discriminant Function

DISCRIMINANT ANALYSIS   CLASSIFICATION SUMMARY FOR CALIBRATION DATA: WORK.CROPS

Cross-validation Summary using Quadratic Discriminant Function

Generalized Squared Distance Function: Posterior Probability of Membership in each CROP:

$$D^2_j(X) = (X-\bar{X}_{(X)j})' COV^{-1}_{(X)j} (X-\bar{X}_{(X)j}) + \ln |COV_{(X)j}| - 2 \ln PRIOR_j \qquad Pr(j|X) = \exp(-.5 D^2_j(X)) / \underset{k}{SUM} \exp(-.5 D^2_k(X))$$

Number of Observations and Percents Classified into CROP:

From CROP	CLOVER	CORN	COTTON	SOYBEANS	SUGARBEETS	Total
CLOVER	9	0	0	0	2	11
	81.82	0.00	0.00	0.00	18.18	100.00
CORN	3	2	0	0	2	7
	42.86	28.57	0.00	0.00	28.57	100.00
COTTON	3	0	2	0	1	6
	50.00	0.00	33.33	0.00	16.67	100.00
SOYBEANS	3	0	0	2	1	6
	50.00	0.00	0.00	33.33	16.67	100.00
SUGARBEETS	3	0	1	1	1	6
	50.00	0.00	16.67	16.67	16.67	100.00
Total	21	2	3	3	7	36
Percent	58.33	5.56	8.33	8.33	19.44	100.00
Priors	0.3056	0.1944	0.1667	0.1667	0.1667	

(continued on next page)

(continued from previous page)

Error Count Estimates for CROP:

	CLOVER	CORN	COTTON	SOYBEANS	SUGARBEETS	Total
Rate	0.1818	0.7143	0.6667	0.6667	0.8333	0.5556
Priors	0.3056	0.1944	0.1667	0.1667	0.1667	

REFERENCES

Anderson, T.W. (1984), *An Introduction to Multivariate Statistical Analysis*, 2d Edition, New York: John Wiley & Sons, Inc.

Cover, T.M. and Hart, P.E. (1967), "Nearest Neighbor Pattern Classification," *IEEE Transactions on Information Theory*, IT-13, 21–27.

Epanechnikov, V.A. (1969), "Nonparametric Estimation of a Multivariate Probability Density," *Theory of Probability and its Applications*, 14, 153–158.

Fisher, R.A. (1936), "The Use of Multiple Measurements in Taxonomic Problems," *Annals of Eugenics*, 7, 179–188.

Fix, E. and Hodges, J.L., Jr. (1959), "Discriminatory Analysis: Nonparametric Discrimination: Consistency Properties," *Report No. 4, Project No. 21-49-004, School of Aviation Medicine*, Randolph Air Force Base, TX.

Friedman, J.H., Bentley, J.L., and Finkel, R.A. (1977), "An Algorithm for Finding Best Matches in Logarithmic Expected Time," *ACM Transactions on Mathematical Software*, 3, 209–226.

Fukunaga, K. and Kessel, D.L. (1973), "Nonparametric Bayes Error Estimation Using Unclassified Samples," *IEEE Transactions on Information Theory*, 19, 434–440.

Glick, N. (1978), "Additive Estimators for Probabilities of Correct Classification," *Pattern Recognition*, 10, 211–222.

Hand, D.J. (1981), *Discrimination and Classification*, New York: John Wiley & Sons, Inc.

Hand, D.J. (1982), *Kernel Discriminant Analysis*, New York: Research Studies Press.

Hand, D.J. (1986), "Recent Advances in Error Rate Estimation," *Pattern Recognition Letters*, 4, 335–346.

Hora, S.C. and Wilcox, J.B. (1982), "Estimation of Error Rates in Several-Population Discriminant Analysis," *Journal of Marketing Research*, XIX, 57–61.

Kendall, M.G., Stuart, A., and Ord, J.K. (1983), *The Advanced Theory of Statistics*, Vol. 3, 4th Edition, New York: Macmillan Publishing Co., Inc.

Kshirsagar, A.M. (1972), *Multivariate Analysis*, New York: Marcel Dekker.

Lawley, D.N. (1959), "Tests of Significance in Canonical Analysis," *Biometrika*, 46, 59–66.

Lachenbruch, P.A. and Mickey, M.A. (1968), "Estimation of Error Rates in Discriminant Analysis," *Technometrics*, 10, 1–10.

Morrison, D.F. (1976), *Multivariate Statistical Methods*, New York: McGraw-Hill.

Parzen, E. (1962), "On Estimation of a Probability Density Function and Mode," *Annals of Mathematical Statistics*, 33, 1065–1076.

Perlman, M.D. (1980), "Unbiasedness of the Likelihood Ratio Tests for Equality of Several Covariance Matrices and Equality of Several Multivariate Normal Populations," *Annals of Statistics*, 8, 247–263.

Rao, C. R. (1973), *Linear Statistical Inference and Its Applications*, 2d Edition, New York: John Wiley & Sons, Inc.

Rosenblatt, M. (1956), "Remarks on Some Nonparametric Estimates of a Density Function," *Annals of Mathematical Statistics*, 27, 832–837.

Silverman, B. W. (1986), *Density Estimation for Statistics and Data Analysis*, New York: Chapman and Hall.

Snapinn, S.M. and Knoke, J.D. (1985), "An Evaluation of Smoothed Classification Error-Rate Estimators," *Technometrics*, 27, 199–206.

Chapter 17

The FACTOR
Procedure

ABSTRACT

The FACTOR procedure performs several types of common factor and component analysis. Both orthogonal and oblique rotations are available. You can compute scoring coefficients by the regression method, and you can write estimated factor scores to an output data set. All major statistics computed by PROC FACTOR can also be saved in an output data set.

INTRODUCTION

The FACTOR procedure performs a variety of common factor and component analyses and rotations. Input can be multivariate data, a correlation matrix, a covariance matrix, a factor pattern, or a matrix of scoring coefficients. Either the correlation or covariance matrix can be factored. Most results can be saved in an output data set.

PROC FACTOR can process output from other procedures. For example, the canonical coefficients from multivariate analyses in the GLM procedure can be rotated with FACTOR.

The methods for factor extraction are principal component analysis, principal factor analysis, iterated principal factor analysis, unweighted least-squares factor analysis, maximum-likelihood (canonical) factor analysis, alpha factor analysis, image component analysis, and Harris component analysis. A variety of methods for prior communality estimation are also available.

The methods for rotation are varimax, quartimax, equamax, orthomax with user-specified gamma, promax with user-specified exponent, Harris-Kaiser case II with user-specified exponent, and oblique Procrustean with a user-specified target pattern.

Output includes means, standard deviations, correlations, Kaiser's measure of sampling adequacy, eigenvalues, a scree plot, eigenvectors, prior and final communality estimates, the unrotated factor pattern, residual and partial correlations, the rotated primary factor pattern, the primary factor structure, interfactor correlations, the reference structure, reference axis correlations, the variance explained by each factor both ignoring and eliminating other factors, plots of both rotated and unrotated factors, squared multiple correlation of each factor with the variables, and scoring coefficients.

Any topics that are not given explicit references are discussed in Mulaik (1972) or Harman (1976).

Background

See the chapter on the PRINCOMP procedure for a discussion of principal component analysis.

Common factor analysis was invented by Spearman (1904). Gould (1981) gives an interesting nontechnical history of factor analysis. Kim and Mueller (1978) provide a very elementary discussion of the common factor model. Gorsuch (1974) contains a broad survey of factor analysis, and Gorsuch (1974) and Cattell (1978) are useful as guides to practical research methodology. Harman (1976) gives a lucid discussion of many of the more technical aspects of factor analysis, especially oblique rotation. Morrison (1976) and Mardia, Kent, and Bibby (1979) provide excellent statistical treatments of common factor analysis. Mulaik (1972) is the most thorough and authoritative general reference on factor analysis and is highly recommended to anyone comfortable with matrix algebra.

A frequent source of confusion in the field of factor analysis is the term *factor*. It sometimes refers to a hypothetical, unobservable variable, as in the phrase *common factor*. In this sense, *factor analysis* must be distinguished from component analysis since a component is an observable linear combination. *Factor* is also used in the sense of *matrix factor*, in that one matrix is a factor of a second matrix if the first matrix multiplied by its transpose equals the second matrix. In this sense, *factor analysis* refers to all methods of data analysis using matrix factors, including component analysis and common factor analysis.

A *common factor* is an unobservable, hypothetical variable that contributes to the variance of at least two of the observed variables. The unqualified term "factor" often refers to a common factor. A *unique factor* is an unobservable, hypothetical variable that contributes to the variance of only one of the observed variables. The model for common factor analysis posits one unique factor for each observed variable.

The equation for the common factor model is

$$y_{ij} = x_{i1}b_{1j} + x_{i2}b_{2j} + \ldots + x_{iq}b_{qj} + e_{ij}$$

where

y_{ij} is the value of the ith observation on the jth variable

x_{ik} is the value of the ith observation on the kth common factor

b_{kj} is the regression coefficient of the kth common factor for predicting the jth variable

e_{ij} is the value of the ith observation on the jth unique factor

q is the number of common factors

and it is assumed for convenience that all variables have a mean of 0. In matrix terms, these equations reduce to

$$\mathbf{Y} = \mathbf{XB} + \mathbf{E} \quad .$$

In the preceding equation $\mathbf{X}$ is the matrix of factor scores, and $\mathbf{B}'$ is the factor pattern.

There are two critical assumptions:

- The unique factors are uncorrelated with each other.
- The unique factors are uncorrelated with the common factors.

In principal component analysis, the residuals are generally correlated with each other. In common factor analysis, the unique factors play the role of residuals and are defined to be uncorrelated both with each other and with the common factors. Each common factor is assumed to contribute to at least two variables; otherwise, it would be a unique factor.

When the factors are initially extracted, it is also assumed for convenience that the common factors are uncorrelated with each other and have unit variance. In this case, the common factor model implies that the covariance s_{jk} between the jth and kth variables, $j \neq k$, is given by

$$s_{jk} = b_{1j}b_{1k} + b_{2j}b_{2k} + \ldots + b_{qj}b_{qk}$$

or

$$\mathbf{S} = \mathbf{B}'\mathbf{B} + \mathbf{U}^2$$

where $\mathbf{S}$ is the covariance matrix of the observed variables, and $\mathbf{U}^2$ is the diagonal covariance matrix of the unique factors.

If the original variables were standardized to unit variance, the formula above would yield correlations instead of covariances. It is in this sense that common factors explain the correlations among the observed variables. The difference between the correlation predicted by the common factor model and the actual correlation is the *residual correlation*. A good way to assess the goodness-of-fit of the common factor model is to examine the residual correlations.

The common factor model implies that the partial correlations among the variables, removing the effects of the common factors, must all be 0. When the common factors are removed, only unique factors, which are by definition uncorrelated, remain.

The assumptions of common factor analysis imply that the common factors are, in general, not linear combinations of the observed variables. In fact, even if the data contain measurements on the entire population of observations, you cannot compute the scores of the observations on the common factors. Although the common factor scores cannot be computed directly, they can be estimated in a variety of ways.

The problem of factor score indeterminacy has led several factor analysts to propose methods yielding components that can be considered approximations to common factors. Since these components are defined as linear combinations, they are computable. The methods include Harris component analysis and image component analysis. The advantage of producing determinate component scores is offset by the fact that, even if the data fit the common factor model perfectly, component methods do not generally recover the correct factor solution. You should not use any type of component analysis if you really want a common factor analysis (Dziuban and Harris 1973; Lee and Comrey 1979).

After the factors have been estimated, it is necessary to interpret them. Interpretation usually means assigning to each common factor a name that reflects the importance of the factor in predicting each of the observed variables, that is, the coefficients in the pattern matrix corresponding to the factor. Factor interpretation is a subjective process. It can sometimes be made less subjective by *rotating* the common factors, that is, by applying a nonsingular linear transformation. A rotated pattern matrix in which all the coefficients are close to 0 or ±1 is easier to interpret than a pattern with many intermediate elements. Therefore, most rotation methods attempt to optimize a function of the pattern matrix that measures, in some sense, how close the elements are to 0 or ±1.

After the initial factor extraction, the common factors are uncorrelated with each other. If the factors are rotated by an *orthogonal transformation*, the rotated factors are also uncorrelated. If the factors are rotated by an *oblique transformation*, the rotated factors become correlated. Oblique rotations often produce more useful patterns than do orthogonal rotations. However, a consequence of correlated factors is that there is no single unambiguous measure of the importance of a factor in explaining a variable. Thus, for oblique rotations, the pattern matrix does not provide all the necessary information for interpreting the factors; you must also examine the *factor structure* and the *reference structure*.

Rotating a set of factors does not change the statistical explanatory power of the factors. You cannot say that any rotation is better than any other rotation from a statistical point of view; all rotations are equally good statistically. Therefore, the choice among different rotations must be based on nonstatistical grounds. For most applications, the preferred rotation is that which is most easily interpretable.

If two rotations give rise to different interpretations, those two interpretations must not be regarded as conflicting. Rather, they are two different ways of looking at the same thing, two different points of view in the common-factor space. Any conclusion that depends on one and only one rotation being correct is invalid.

Outline of Use

Principal Component Analysis

The most important type of analysis performed by the FACTOR procedure is principal component analysis. The statement

```
proc factor;
```

results in a principal component analysis. The output includes all the eigenvalues and the pattern matrix for eigenvalues greater than one.

Most applications require additional output. For example, you may want to compute principal component scores for use in subsequent analyses or obtain a graphical aid to help decide how many components to keep. You should save the results of the analysis in a permanent SAS data library by using the OUTSTAT= option. (See the *SAS Language Guide, Release 6.03 Edition* for more information on permanent SAS data libraries and librefs.) Assuming your SAS data library has the libref SAVE and the data are in a SAS data set called RAW, you could do a principal component analysis as follows:

```
proc factor data=raw method=principal scree mineigen=0 score
     outstat=save.fact_all;
```

The SCREE option produces a plot of the eigenvalues that is helpful in deciding how many components to use. The MINEIGEN=0 option causes all components with variance greater than zero to be retained. The SCORE option requests that scoring coefficients be computed. The OUTSTAT= option saves the results in a specially structured SAS data set. The name of the data set, in this case FACT_ALL, is arbitrary. To compute principal component scores, use the SCORE procedure:

```
proc score data=raw score=save.fact_all out=save.scores;
```

The SCORE procedure uses the data and the scoring coefficients that were saved in SAVE.FACT_ALL to compute principal component scores. The component scores are placed in variables named FACTOR1, FACTOR2, . . . , FACTORn, and saved in the data set SAVE.SCORES. If you know ahead of time how many principal components you want to use, you can obtain the scores directly from FACTOR by specifying the NFACTORS= and OUT= options. To get scores from three principal components, specify

```
proc factor data=raw method=principal nfactors=3 out=save.scores;
```

To plot the scores for the first three components use the PLOT procedure:

```
proc plot;
   plot factor2*factor1 factor3*factor1 factor3*factor2;
```

Principal Factor Analysis

The simplest and computationally most efficient method of common factor analysis is principal factor analysis, which is obtained the same way as principal component analysis except for the use of the PRIORS= option. The usual form of the initial analysis is

```
proc factor data=raw method=principal scree mineigen=0 priors=smc
     outstat=save.fact_all;
```

The squared multiple correlations (SMC) of each variable with all the other variables are used as the prior communality estimates. If your correlation matrix is singular, you should specify PRIORS=MAX instead of PRIORS=SMC. The SCREE and MINEIGEN= options serve the same purpose as in the principal component analysis above. Saving the results with the OUTSTAT= option allows you to examine the eigenvalues and scree plot before deciding how many factors to rotate and to try several different rotations without re-extracting the factors. The OUTSTAT= data set is automatically marked TYPE=FACTOR, so the FACTOR procedure realizes that it contains statistics from a previous analysis instead of data.

After looking at the eigenvalues to estimate the number of factors, you can try some rotations. Two and three factors can be rotated with the following statements:

```
proc factor data=save.fact_all method=principal n=2 rotate=promax
     round reorder score outstat=save.fact_2;
proc factor data=save.fact_all method=principal n=3 rotate=promax
     round reorder score outstat=save.fact_3;
```

The output data set from the previous run is used as input for these analyses. The options N=2 and N=3 specify the number of factors to be rotated. The specification ROTATE=PROMAX requests a promax rotation, which has the advantage of providing both orthogonal and oblique rotations with only one invocation of PROC FACTOR. The ROUND option causes the various factor matrices to be printed in an easily interpretable format, and the REORDER option causes the variables to be reordered on the printout so that variables associated with the same factor appear next to each other.

You can now compute and plot factor scores for the two-factor promax-rotated solution as follows:

```
proc score data=raw score=save.fact_2 out=save.scores;
proc plot;
   plot factor2*factor1;
```

Maximum-Likelihood Factor Analysis

Although principal factor analysis is perhaps the most commonly used method of common factor analysis, most statisticians prefer maximum-likelihood (ML) factor analysis (Lawley and Maxwell 1971). ML estimation has desirable asymptotic properties (Bickel and Doksum 1977) and gives better estimates than principal factor analysis in large samples. You can test hypotheses about the number of common factors using the ML method.

The ML solution is equivalent to Rao's (1955) canonical factor solution and Howe's solution maximizing the determinant of the partial correlation matrix (Morrison 1976). Thus, as a descriptive method, ML factor analysis does not require a multivariate normal distribution. The validity of the χ^2 test for the number of factors does require approximate normality plus additional regularity conditions that are usually satisfied in practice (Geweke and Singleton 1980).

The ML method is more computationally demanding than principal factor analysis for two reasons. First, the communalities are estimated iteratively, and each iteration takes about as much computer time as principal factor analysis. The number of iterations typically ranges from about five to twenty. Second, if you want to extract different numbers of factors, as is often the case, you must run the FACTOR procedure once for each number of factors. Therefore, an ML analysis can take 100 times as long as a principal factor analysis.

You can use principal factor analysis to get a rough idea of the number of factors before doing an ML analysis. If you think that there are between one and three factors, you can use the following statements for the ML analysis:

```
proc factor data=raw method=ml n=1
     outstat=save.fact1;
proc factor data=raw method=ml n=2 rotate=promax
     outstat=save.fact2;
proc factor data=raw method=ml n=3 rotate=promax
     outstat=save.fact3;
```

The output data sets can be used for trying different rotations, computing scoring coefficients, or restarting the procedure in case it does not converge within the allotted number of iterations.

The ML method cannot be used with a singular correlation matrix and is especially prone to Heywood cases. (See **Heywood Cases and Other Anomalies** in the **DETAILS** section of this chapter for a discussion of Heywood cases.) If you have problems with ML, the best alternative is METHOD=ULS for unweighted least-squares factor analysis.

SPECIFICATIONS

The FACTOR procedure is invoked by the following statements:

> **PROC FACTOR** *options*;
> **VAR** *variables*;
> **PRIORS** *communalities*;
> **PARTIAL** *variables*;
> **FREQ** *variable*;
> **WEIGHT** *variable*;
> **BY** *variables*;

Usually only the VAR statement is needed in addition to the PROC FACTOR statement. The descriptions of the BY, FREQ, PARTIAL, PRIORS, VAR, and WEIGHT statements follow the description of the PROC FACTOR statement.

PROC FACTOR Statement

> PROC FACTOR *options*;

The options available with the PROC FACTOR statement are discussed in the following sections:

- **Data Set Options**
- **Factor Extraction Options**
- **Rotation Options**
- **Output Options**
- **Miscellaneous Options**.

Data Set Options

DATA=*SASdataset*
  names the input data set, which can be an ordinary SAS data set or a specially structured SAS data set as described in **Input Data Set** later in this chapter. If the DATA= option is omitted, the most recently created SAS data set is used.

OUT=*SASdataset*
  creates a data set containing all the data from the DATA= data set plus variables called FACTOR1, FACTOR2, and so on, containing estimated factor scores. The DATA= data set must contain multivariate data, not correlations or covariances. The NFACTORS= option must also be specified to determine the number of factor score variables. If you want to create a permanent SAS data set, you must specify a two-level name. See "SAS Files" in the *SAS Language Guide* for more information on permanent data sets.

OUTSTAT=*SASdataset*
  names an output data set containing most of the results of the analysis. The output data set is described in detail in **Output Data Sets** later in this chapter. If you want to create a permanent SAS data set, you must

specify a two-level name. See "SAS Files" in the *SAS Language Guide* for more information on permanent data sets.

TARGET=*SASdataset*

names a data set containing the target pattern for Procrustes rotation (see the ROTATE= option below). The TARGET= data set must contain variables with the same names as those being factored. Each observation in the TARGET= data set becomes one column of the target factor pattern. Missing values are treated as zeros. _NAME_ and _TYPE_ variables are not required and are ignored if present.

Factor Extraction Options

METHOD=*name*

M=*name*

specifies the method for extracting factors. The default is METHOD=PRINCIPAL unless the DATA= data set is TYPE=FACTOR, in which case the default is METHOD=PATTERN. Valid values for *METHOD*=*name* are as follows:

METHOD=ALPHA | A

produces alpha factor analysis.

METHOD=HARRIS | H

yields Harris component analysis of $S^{-1}RS^{-1}$ (Harris 1962), a noniterative approximation to canonical component analysis. This method is equivalent to METHOD=IMAGE in base SAS software Release 79.5 and requires a nonsingular correlation matrix.

METHOD=IMAGE | I

yields principal component analysis of the image covariance matrix, not Kaiser's (1963, 1970) or Kaiser and Rice's (1974) image analysis. A nonsingular correlation matrix is required.

METHOD=ML | M

performs maximum-likelihood factor analysis with an algorithm due, except for minor details, to Fuller (1981, pers. comm.). METHOD=ML requires a nonsingular correlation matrix.

METHOD=PATTERN

reads a factor pattern from a TYPE=FACTOR, CORR, or COV data set. If you create a TYPE=FACTOR data set in a DATA step, only observations containing the factor pattern (_TYPE_='PATTERN') and, if the factors are correlated, the interfactor correlations (_TYPE_='FCORR') are required.

METHOD=PRINCIPAL | PRIN | P

yields principal component analysis if no PRIORS option or statement is used or if PRIORS=ONE is specified; if a PRIORS statement or a PRIORS= value other than PRIORS=ONE is specified, a principal factor analysis is performed.

METHOD=PRINIT

yields iterated principal factor analysis.

METHOD=SCORE
> reads scoring coefficients (_TYPE_='SCORE') from a TYPE=FACTOR, CORR, or COV data set. The data set must also contain either a correlation or a covariance matrix.

METHOD=ULS | U
> produces unweighted least squares factor analysis.

PRIORS=*name*
specifies a method for computing prior communality estimates. You can specify numeric values for the prior communality estimates by using the PRIORS statement. Valid values for PRIORS=*name* are as follows:

PRIORS=ASMC | A
> sets the prior communality estimates proportional to the squared multiple correlations but adjusted so that their sum is equal to that of the maximum absolute correlations (Cureton 1968).

PRIORS=INPUT | I
> reads the prior communality estimates from the first observation with either _TYPE_='PRIORS' or _TYPE_='COMMUNAL' in the DATA= data set (which must be TYPE=FACTOR).

PRIORS=MAX | M
> sets the prior communality estimate for each variable to its maximum absolute correlation with any other variable.

PRIORS=ONE | O
> sets all prior communalities to 1.0.

PRIORS=RANDOM | R
> sets the prior communality estimates to pseudo-random numbers uniformly distributed between 0 and 1.

PRIORS=SMC | S
> sets the prior communality estimate for each variable to its squared multiple correlation with all other variables.

The default prior communality estimates are as follows:

METHOD=	PRIORS=
PRINCIPAL	ONE
PRINIT	ONE
ALPHA	SMC
ULS	SMC
ML	SMC
HARRIS	(not applicable)
IMAGE	(not applicable)
PATTERN	(not applicable)
SCORE	(not applicable)

CONVERGE=c

CONV=c

specifies the convergence criterion for METHOD=PRINIT, ULS, ALPHA, or ML. Iteration stops when the maximum change in the communalities is less than the CONVERGE= value. The default value is 0.001.

COVARIANCE

COV

requests factoring of the covariance matrix instead of the correlation matrix. The COV option can be used only with METHOD=PRINCIPAL, PRINIT, ULS, or IMAGE.

MAXITER=n

specifies the maximum number of iterations with METHOD=PRINIT, ULS, ALPHA, or ML. The default is 30.

RANDOM=n

specifies a positive integer as a starting value for the pseudo-random number generator for use with PRIORS=RANDOM. If you do not specify the RANDOM= option, the time of day is used to initialize the pseudo-random number sequence.

WEIGHT

requests that a weighted correlation or covariance matrix be factored. The WEIGHT option can be used only with METHOD=PRINCIPAL, PRINIT, ULS, or IMAGE. The input data set must be TYPE=CORR, COV, or FACTOR, and the variable weights are obtained from an observation with _TYPE_='WEIGHT'.

The following options jointly control the number of factors extracted. If two or more of the NFACTORS=, MINEIGEN=, and PROPORTION= options are specified, the number of factors retained is the minimum number satisfying any of the criteria.

MINEIGEN=n

MIN=n

specifies the smallest eigenvalue for which a factor is retained. The MINEIGEN= option cannot be used with METHOD=PATTERN or METHOD=SCORE. The default is 0 unless neither the NFACTORS= nor the PROPORTION= option is specified and one of the following conditions holds:

- If METHOD=ALPHA or METHOD=HARRIS, then MINEIGEN=1.
- If METHOD=IMAGE, then

$$\text{MINEIGEN} = \frac{\text{total image variance}}{\text{number of variables}} \quad .$$

- For any other METHOD= option, if prior communality estimates of 1.0 are used, then

$$\text{MINEIGEN} = \frac{\text{total weighted variance}}{\text{number of variables}} \quad .$$

When an unweighted correlation matrix is factored, this value is 1.

NFACTORS=*n*
NFACT=*n*
N=*n*

specifies the maximum number of factors to be extracted and determines the amount of core storage to be allocated for factor matrices. The default is the number of variables. Specifying a number that is small relative to the number of variables can substantially decrease the amount of memory required to run PROC FACTOR, especially with oblique rotations. If NFACTORS=0 is specified, eigenvalues are computed, but no factors are extracted. If NFACTORS=−1 is specified, neither eigenvalues nor factors are computed. You can use the NFACTORS= option with METHOD=PATTERN or METHOD=SCORE to specify a smaller number of factors than are present in the data set.

PROPORTION=*n*
PERCENT=*n*
P=*n*

specifies the proportion of common variance to be accounted for by the retained factors using the prior communality estimates. If the value is greater than one, it is interpreted as a percentage and divided by 100. PROPORTION=0.75 and PERCENT=75 are equivalent. The default is 1.0 or 100%. You cannot specify the PROPORTION= option with METHOD=PATTERN or METHOD=SCORE.

By default, METHOD=PRINIT, ULS, ALPHA, and ML stop iterating and set the number of factors to 0 if an estimated communality exceeds 1. The following options allow processing to continue:

HEYWOOD
HEY

sets to 1 any communality greater than 1, allowing iterations to proceed.

ULTRAHEYWOOD
ULTRA

allows communalities to exceed 1. The ULTRAHEYWOOD option can cause convergence problems because communalities can become extremely large, and ill-conditioned Hessians may occur.

Rotation Options

ROTATE=*name*
R=*name*

gives the rotation method. The default is ROTATE=NONE. Valid values for ROTATE=*name* are as follows:

ROTATE=EQUAMAX | E

specifies equamax rotation.

ROTATE=HK

specifies Harris-Kaiser case II orthoblique rotation. You can use the HKPOWER= option to set the power of the square roots of the eigenvalues by which the eigenvectors are scaled.

ROTATE=NONE | N

specifies that no rotation be performed.

ROTATE=ORTHOMAX

specifies general orthomax rotation with the weight specified by the GAMMA= option.

ROTATE=PROCRUSTES

>specifies oblique Procrustes rotation with target pattern given by the TARGET= data set. The unrestricted least squares method is used with factors scaled to unit length after rotation.

ROTATE=PROMAX | P

>specifies promax rotation. The PREROTATE= and POWER= options can be used with ROTATE=PROMAX.

ROTATE=QUARTIMAX | Q

>specifies quartimax rotation.

ROTATE=VARIMAX | V

>specifies varimax rotation.

GAMMA=*n*

specifies the orthomax weight. You can use this option only with ROTATE=ORTHOMAX or PREROTATE=ORTHOMAX.

HKPOWER=*n*

HKP=*n*

specifies the power of the square roots of the eigenvalues used to rescale the eigenvectors for Harris-Kaiser (ROTATE=HK) rotation. Values between 0.0 and 1.0 are reasonable. The default value is 0.0, yielding the independent cluster solution. A value of 1.0 is equivalent to a varimax rotation. You can also specify the HKPOWER= option with ROTATE=QUARTIMAX, VARIMAX, EQUAMAX, or ORTHOMAX, in which case the Harris-Kaiser rotation uses the specified orthogonal rotation method.

NORM=*name*

specifies the method for normalizing the rows of the factor pattern for rotation. If you specify NORM=KAISER, Kaiser's normalization is used. If you specify NORM=WEIGHT, the rows are weighted by the Cureton-Mulaik technique (Cureton and Mulaik 1975). If you specify NORM=COV, the rows of the pattern matrix are rescaled to represent covariances instead of correlations. If you specify NORM=NONE or NORM=RAW, normalization is not performed. The default is NORM=KAISER.

POWER=*n*

specifies the power to be used in computing the target pattern for ROTATE=PROMAX. The default value is 3.

PREROTATE=*name*

PRE=*name*

specifies the prerotation method for ROTATE=PROMAX. Any rotation method other than PROMAX or PROCRUSTES can be used. The default is VARIMAX. If a previously rotated pattern is read using METHOD=PATTERN, PREROTATE=NONE should be specified.

Output Options

ALL

prints all optional output except plots. When the input data set is TYPE=CORR, COV, or FACTOR, simple statistics, correlations, and MSA are not printed.

CORR

C

prints the correlation matrix.

EIGENVECTORS

EV

prints the eigenvectors.

FLAG=n

causes absolute values larger than n to be flagged by an asterisk when the FLAG= option is used with the ROUND option. The default value is the root mean square of all the values in the matrix being printed.

FUZZ=n

causes correlations and factor loadings with absolute values less than the specified number to print as missing values. For partial correlations, the FUZZ= value is divided by 2. For residual correlations, the FUZZ= value is divided by 4. The exact values in any matrix can be obtained from the output data set.

MSA

prints the partial correlations between each pair of variables controlling for all other variables (the negative anti-image correlations) and Kaiser's measure of sampling adequacy (Kaiser 1970; Kaiser and Rice 1974; Cerny and Kaiser 1977).

NPLOT=n

specifies the number of factors to be plotted. The default is all the factors. The smallest allowable value is 2. If you specify NPLOT=n, all pairs of the first n factors are plotted, giving a total of $n(n-1)/2$ plots.

PLOT

plots the factor pattern after rotation.

PREPLOT

plots the factor pattern before rotation.

PRINT

prints input factor pattern or scoring coefficients and related statistics. In oblique cases, the reference and factor structures are computed and printed. The PRINT option is effective only with METHOD=PATTERN or METHOD=SCORE.

REORDER

RE

causes the rows (variables) of various factor matrices to be reordered on the printout. Variables with their highest absolute loading (reference structure loading for oblique rotations) on the first factor are printed first, from largest to smallest loading, followed by variables with their highest absolute loading on the second factor, and so on. The order of the variables in the output data set is not affected. The factors are not reordered.

RESIDUALS

RES

prints the residual correlation matrix and the associated partial correlation matrix.

ROUND

   prints correlation and loading matrices with entries multiplied by 100
   and rounded to the nearest integer. The exact values can be obtained
   from the output data set. (See also the FLAG= option.)

SCORE

   prints the factor scoring coefficients. The squared multiple correlation of
   each factor with the variables is also printed except in the case of
   unrotated principal components.

SCREE

   prints a scree plot of the eigenvalues (Cattell 1966, 1978; Cattell and
   Vogelman 1977; Horn and Engstrom 1979).

SIMPLE
S

   prints means and standard deviations.

Miscellaneous Options

NOCORR

   prevents the correlation matrix from being transferred to the
   OUTSTAT= data set when METHOD=PATTERN is specified. The
   NOCORR option greatly reduces memory requirements when there are
   many variables but few factors.

NOINT

   requests that no intercept be used; covariances or correlations are not
   corrected for the mean.

SINGULAR=p
SING=p

   specifies the singularity criterion, where $0 < p < 1$. The default value is
   $1E-8$.

VARDEF=$divisor$

   specifies the divisor to be used in the calculation of variances and
   covariances. Possible values for $divisor$ are N, DF, WEIGHT or WGT, and
   WDF. VARDEF=N requests that the number of observations (n) be used
   as the divisor. VARDEF=DF requests that the error degrees of freedom,
   $n-i$ (before partialling) or $n-p-i$ (after partialling), be used, where p is
   the number of degrees of freedom of the variables in the PARTIAL
   statement, and i is 0 if the NOINT option is specified, 1 otherwise.
   VARDEF=WEIGHT or WGT requests that the sum of the weights (w) be
   used. VARDEF=WDF requests that $w-i$ (before partialling) or $w-p-i$
   (after partialling) be used. The default value is DF.

BY Statement

   BY $variables$;

You can use a BY statement with PROC FACTOR to obtain separate analyses on
observations in groups defined by the BY variables. When a BY statement
appears, the procedure expects the DATA= data set to be sorted in order of the
BY variables.

   If your DATA= data set is not sorted in ascending order, use the SORT procedure with a similar BY statement to sort the data, or, if appropriate, use the BY
statement options NOTSORTED or DESCENDING. For more information, see the
discussion of the BY statement in "SAS Statements Used in the PROC Step" in
the *SAS Language Guide*.

If you specify the TARGET= option and the TARGET= data set does not contain any of the BY variables, then the entire TARGET= data set is used as a Procrustean target for each BY group in the DATA= data set.

If the TARGET= data set contains some but not all of the BY variables, or if some BY variables do not have the same type or length in the TARGET= data set as in the DATA= data set, then FACTOR prints an error message and stops.

If all the BY variables appear in the TARGET= data set with the same type and length as in the DATA= data set, then each BY group in the TARGET= data set is used as a Procrustean target for the corresponding BY group in the DATA= data set. The BY groups in the TARGET= data set must be in the same order as in the DATA= data set. If you specify NOTSORTED in the BY statement, there must be identical BY groups in the same order in both data sets. If you do not specify NOTSORTED, some BY groups can appear in one data set but not in the other.

FREQ Statement

FREQ *variable*;

If a variable in your data set represents the frequency of occurrence for the other values in the observation, include the variable's name in a FREQ statement. The procedure then treats the data set as if each observation appears *n* times, where *n* is the value of the FREQ variable for the observation. The total number of observations is considered equal to the sum of the FREQ variable when the procedure computes significance probabilities.

The WEIGHT and FREQ statements have a similar effect, except in determining the number of observations.

PARTIAL Statement

PARTIAL *variables*;

If you want the analysis to be based on a partial correlation or covariance matrix, use the PARTIAL statement to list the variables to be partialled out.

PRIORS Statement

PRIORS *communalities*;

The PRIORS statement specifies numeric values between 0.0 and 1.0 for the prior communality estimates for each variable. The first numeric value corresponds to the first variable in the VAR statement, the second value to the second variable, and so on. The number of numeric values must equal the number of variables, for example,

```
proc factor;
   var    x  y  z;
   priors .7 .8 .9;
```

You can specify various methods for computing prior communality estimates with the PRIORS= option of the PROC FACTOR statement. Refer to that option for a description of the default prior communality estimates.

VAR Statement

VAR *variables*;

The VAR statement lists the numeric variables to be analyzed. If the VAR statement is omitted, all numeric variables not given in other statements are analyzed.

WEIGHT Statement

WEIGHT *variable*;

If you want to use relative weights for each observation in the input data set, specify a variable containing weights in a WEIGHT statement. This is often done when the variance associated with each observation is different and the values of the weight variable are proportional to the reciprocals of the variances.

DETAILS

Input Data Set

The FACTOR procedure can read an ordinary SAS data set containing raw data or a special TYPE=CORR, TYPE=COV, or TYPE=FACTOR data set containing previously computed statistics. A TYPE=CORR data set can be created by the CORR procedure or various other procedures such as the PRINCOMP procedure. It contains means, standard deviations, the sample size, the correlation matrix, and possibly other statistics if it was created by some procedure other than CORR. A TYPE=COV data set is similar to a TYPE=CORR data set but contains a covariance matrix. A TYPE=FACTOR data set can be created by the FACTOR procedure and is described in **Output Data Sets**.

If your data set has many observations and you plan to run FACTOR several times, you can save computer time by first creating a TYPE=CORR data set and using it as input to FACTOR:

```
proc corr    data=raw out=correl;    * create TYPE=CORR data set;
proc factor data=correl method=ml; * maximum likelihood;
proc factor data=correl;              * principal components;
```

The data set created by the CORR procedure is automatically given the TYPE=CORR attribute, so you do not have to specify TYPE=CORR. However, if you use a DATA step with a SET statement to modify the correlation data set, you must use the TYPE=CORR attribute in the new data set. You can use a VAR statement with FACTOR when reading a TYPE=CORR data set to select a subset of the variables or change the order of the variables.

Problems can arise from using the CORR procedure when there are missing data. By default, PROC CORR computes each correlation from all observations that have values present for the pair of variables involved (pairwise deletion). The resulting correlation matrix may have negative eigenvalues. If you specify the NOMISS option with the CORR procedure, observations with any missing values are completely omitted from the calculations (listwise deletion), and there is no possibility of negative eigenvalues.

FACTOR can also create a TYPE=FACTOR data set, which includes all the information in a TYPE=CORR data set, and use it for repeated analyses. For a TYPE=FACTOR data set, the default value of the METHOD= option is PATTERN. The following statements give the same FACTOR results as the previous example:

```
proc factor data=raw method=ml outstat=fact; * maximum likelihood;
proc factor data=fact method=prin;            * principal components;
```

You can use a TYPE=FACTOR data set to try several different rotation methods on the same data without repeatedly extracting the factors. In the following example, the second and third PROC FACTOR statements use the data set FACT created by the first PROC FACTOR statement:

```
proc factor data=raw outstat=fact; * principal components;
proc factor rotate=varimax;         * varimax rotation;
proc factor rotate=quartimax;       * quartimax rotation;
```

You can create a TYPE=CORR or TYPE=FACTOR data set in a DATA step. Be sure to specify the TYPE= option in parentheses after the data set name in the DATA statement and include the _TYPE_ and _NAME_ variables. In a TYPE=CORR data set, only the correlation matrix (_TYPE_='CORR') is necessary. It can contain missing values as long as every pair of variables has at least one nonmissing value:

```
data correl(type=corr);
   _type_='CORR';
   input _name_ $ x y z;
   cards;
x   1.0  .   .
y    .7 1.0  .
z    .5  .4 1.0
;
proc factor;
```

You can create a TYPE=FACTOR data set containing only a factor pattern (_TYPE_='PATTERN') and use the FACTOR procedure to rotate it:

```
data pat(type=factor);
   _type_='PATTERN';
   input _name_ $ x y z;
   cards;
factor1 .5  .7  .3
factor2 .8  .2  .8
;
proc factor rotate=promax prerotate=none;
```

If the input factors are oblique, you must also include the interfactor correlation matrix with _TYPE_='FCORR':

```
data pat(type=factor);
   _type_='FCORR';
   input _type_ $ _name_ $ x y z;
   cards;
pattern factor1  .5   .7   .3
pattern factor2  .8   .2   .8
fcorr   factor1 1.0   .2   .
fcorr   factor2  .2  1.0   .
;
proc factor rotate=promax prerotate=none;
```

Some procedures, such as PRINCOMP and CANDISC, produce TYPE=CORR data sets containing scoring coefficients (_TYPE_='SCORE'). These coefficients can be input to PROC FACTOR and rotated by using the METHOD=SCORE option. The input data set must contain the correlation matrix as well as the scoring coefficients:

```
proc princomp data=raw n=2 outstat=prin;
proc factor data=prin method=score rotate=varimax;
```

Output Data Sets

The OUT= data set contains all the data in the DATA= data set plus new variables called FACTOR1, FACTOR2, and so on, containing estimated factor scores. If more than 99 factors are requested, the new variable names are FACT1, FACT2, and so on. Each estimated factor score is computed as a linear combination of the standardized values of the variables that were factored. The coefficients are printed if the SCORE option is specified and are labeled Standardized Scoring Coefficients.

The OUTSTAT= data set is similar to the TYPE=CORR data set produced by the CORR procedure but is TYPE=FACTOR and contains many results in addition to those produced by PROC CORR.

The output data set contains the following variables:

- the BY variables, if any
- two new character variables, _TYPE_ and _NAME_
- the variables analyzed, that is, those in the VAR statement, or, if there is no VAR statement, all numeric variables not listed in any other statement.

Each observation in the output data set contains some type of statistic as indicated by the _TYPE_ variable. The _NAME_ variable is blank except where otherwise indicated. The values of the _TYPE_ variable are as follows:

TYPE	Contents
MEAN	means.
STD	standard deviations.
N	sample size.
CORR	correlations. The _NAME_ variable contains the name of the variable corresponding to each row of the correlation matrix.
IMAGE	image coefficients. The _NAME_ variable contains the name of the variable corresponding to each row of the image coefficient matrix.
IMAGECOV	image covariance matrix. The _NAME_ variable contains the name of the variable corresponding to each row of the image covariance matrix.
COMMUNAL	final communality estimates.
PRIORS	prior communality estimates, or estimates from the last iteration for iterative methods.
WEIGHT	variable weights.
EIGENVAL	eigenvalues.
UNROTATE	unrotated factor pattern. The _NAME_ variable contains the name of the factor.
RESIDUAL	residual correlations. The _NAME_ variable contains the name of the variable corresponding to each row of the residual correlation matrix.
TRANSFOR	transformation matrix from rotation. The _NAME_ variable contains the name of the factor.
FCORR	interfactor correlations. The _NAME_ variable contains the name of the factor.
PATTERN	factor pattern. The _NAME_ variable contains the name of the factor.

RCORR   reference axis correlations. The _NAME_ variable
contains the name of the factor.

REFERENC   reference structure. The _NAME_ variable contains the
name of the factor.

STRUCTUR   factor structure. The _NAME_ variable contains the
name of the factor.

SCORE   scoring coefficients. The _NAME_ variable contains the
name of the factor.

Missing Values

If the DATA= data set contains data (rather than a matrix or factor pattern), then observations with missing values for any variables in the analysis are omitted from the computations. If a correlation or covariance matrix is read, it can contain missing values as long as every pair of variables has at least one nonmissing entry. Missing values in a pattern or scoring coefficient matrix are treated as zeros.

Cautions

- The amount of time that FACTOR takes is roughly proportional to the cube of the number of variables. Factoring 100 variables therefore takes about 1000 times as long as factoring 10 variables. Iterative methods (PRINIT, ALPHA, ULS, ML) can also take 100 times as long as non-iterative methods (PRINCIPAL, IMAGE, HARRIS).
- No computer program is capable of reliably determining the optimal number of factors since the decision is ultimately subjective. You should not blindly accept the number of factors obtained by default; instead, use your own judgment to make a decision.
- Singular correlation matrices cause problems with PRIORS=SMC and METHOD=ML. Singularities can result from using a variable that is the sum of other variables, coding too many dummy variables from a classification variable, or having more variables than observations.
- If you use the CORR procedure to compute the correlation matrix and there are missing data and the NOMISS option is not specified, then the correlation matrix can have negative eigenvalues.
- If a TYPE=CORR or TYPE=FACTOR data set is copied or modified using a DATA step, the new data set does not automatically have the same TYPE as the old data set. You must specify the TYPE= data set option in the DATA statement. If you try to analyze a data set that has lost its TYPE=CORR attribute, FACTOR prints a warning message saying that the data set contains _NAME_ and _TYPE_ variables but analyzes the data set as an ordinary SAS data set.
- For a TYPE=FACTOR data set, the default is METHOD=PATTERN, not METHOD=PRIN.
- In base SAS software Release 82, the OUT= option was an undocumented alias for the OUTSTAT= option. Now, OUT= and OUTSTAT= are separate options.

Factor Scores

The FACTOR procedure can compute estimated factor scores directly if you specify the NFACTORS= and OUT= options, or indirectly using the SCORE procedure. The latter method is preferable if you use the FACTOR procedure interactively to determine the number of factors, the rotation method, or various other aspects of the analysis. To compute factor scores for each observation using the SCORE procedure,

- use the SCORE option in the PROC FACTOR statement
- create a TYPE=FACTOR output data set with the OUTSTAT= option
- use the SCORE procedure with both the raw data and the TYPE=FACTOR data set
- do not use the TYPE= option in the PROC SCORE statement.

For example, the following statements could be used:

```
proc factor data=raw score outstat=fact;
proc score  data=raw score=fact out=scores;
```

or

```
proc corr   data=raw out=correl;
proc factor data=correl score outstat=fact;
proc score  data=raw score=fact out=scores;
```

A component analysis (principal, image, or Harris) produces scores with mean zero and variance one. If you have done a common factor analysis, the true factor scores have mean zero and variance one, but the computed factor scores are only estimates of the true factor scores. These estimates have mean zero but variance equal to the squared multiple correlation of the factor with the variables. The estimated factor scores may have small nonzero correlations even if the true factors are uncorrelated.

Variable Weights and Variance Explained

A principal component analysis of a correlation matrix treats all variables as equally important. A principal component analysis of a covariance matrix gives more weight to variables with larger variances. A principal component analysis of a covariance matrix is equivalent to an analysis of a weighted correlation matrix, where the weight of each variable is equal to its variance. Variables with large weights tend to have larger loadings on the first component and smaller residual correlations than variables with small weights.

You may want to give weights to variables using values other than their variances. Mulaik (1972) explains how to obtain a maximally reliable component by means of a weighted principal component analysis. With the FACTOR procedure, you can indirectly give arbitrary weights to the variables by using the COV option and rescaling the variables to have variance equal to the desired weight, or you can give arbitrary weights directly by using the WEIGHT option and including the weights in a TYPE=CORR data set.

Arbitrary variable weights can be used with METHOD=PRINCIPAL, PRINIT, ULS, or IMAGE. Alpha and ML factor analyses compute variable weights based on the communalities (Harman 1976, 217-218). For alpha factor analysis, the weight of a variable is the reciprocal of its communality. In ML factor analysis, the weight is the reciprocal of the uniqueness. Harris component analysis uses weights equal to the reciprocal of one minus the squared multiple correlation of each variable with the other variables.

For uncorrelated factors, the variance explained by a factor can be computed with or without taking the weights into account. The usual method for computing variance accounted for by a factor is to take the sum of squares of the corresponding column of the factor pattern, yielding an unweighted result. If the square of each loading is multiplied by the weight of the variable before the sum is taken, the result is the weighted variance explained, which is equal to the corresponding eigenvalue except in image analysis. Whether the weighted or unweighted result is more important depends on the purpose of the analysis.

In the case of correlated factors, the variance explained by a factor can be computed with or without taking the other factors into account. If you want to ignore the other factors, the variance explained is given by the weighted or unweighted sum of squares of the appropriate column of the factor structure since the factor structure contains simple correlations. If you want to subtract the variance explained by the other factors from the amount explained by the factor in question (the Type II variance explained), you can take the weighted or unweighted sum of squares of the appropriate column of the reference structure because the reference structure contains semipartial correlations. There are other ways of measuring the variance explained. For example, given a prior ordering of the factors, by eliminating from each factor the variance explained by previous factors you could compute a Type I variance explained. Harman (1976, 268-270) gives another method, which is based on direct and joint contributions.

Heywood Cases and Other Anomalies

Since communalities are squared correlations, you would expect them always to lie between 0 and 1. It is a mathematical peculiarity of the common factor model, however, that final communality estimates may exceed 1. If a communality equals 1, the situation is referred to as a Heywood case, and if a communality exceeds 1, it is an ultra-Heywood case. An ultra-Heywood case implies that some unique factor has negative variance, a clear indication that something is wrong. Possible causes include

- bad prior communality estimates
- too many common factors
- too few common factors
- not enough data to provide stable estimates
- the common factor model is not an appropriate model for the data.

An ultra-Heywood case renders a factor solution invalid. Factor analysts disagree about whether or not a factor solution with a Heywood case can be considered legitimate.

Theoretically, the communality of a variable should not exceed its reliability. Violation of this condition is called a quasi-Heywood case and should be regarded with the same suspicion as an ultra-Heywood case.

Elements of the factor structure and reference structure matrices can exceed 1 only in the presence of an ultra-Heywood case. On the other hand, an element of the factor pattern may exceed 1 in an oblique rotation.

The maximum-likelihood method is especially susceptible to quasi- or ultra-Heywood cases. During the iteration process, a variable with high communality is given a high weight; this tends to increase its communality, which increases its weight, and so on.

It is often stated that the squared multiple correlation of a variable with the other variables is a lower bound to its communality. This is true if the common factor model fits the data perfectly but is not generally the case with real data. A final communality estimate that is less than the squared multiple correlation can therefore indicate poor fit, possibly due to not enough factors. It is by no means as serious a problem as an ultra-Heywood case. Factor methods using the Newton-Raphson method can actually produce communalities less than 0, a result even more disastrous than an ultra-Heywood case.

The squared multiple correlation of a factor with the variables may exceed 1, even in the absence of ultra-Heywood cases. This situation is also cause for alarm. Alpha factor analysis seems to be especially prone to this problem, but it does not occur with maximum likelihood. If a squared multiple correlation is negative, too many factors have been retained.

With data that do not fit the common factor model perfectly, you can expect some of the eigenvalues to be negative. If an iterative factor method converges properly, the sum of the eigenvalues corresponding to rejected factors should be 0; hence, some eigenvalues are positive and some negative. If a principal factor analysis fails to yield any negative eigenvalues, the prior communality estimates are probably too large. Negative eigenvalues cause the cumulative proportion of variance explained to exceed 1 for a sufficiently large number of factors. The cumulative proportion of variance explained by the retained factors should be approximately 1 for principal factor analysis and should converge to 1 for iterative methods. Occasionally, a single factor can explain more than 100 percent of the common variance in a principal factor analysis, indicating that the prior communality estimates are too low.

If a squared canonical correlation or a coefficient alpha is negative, too many factors have been retained.

Principal component analysis, unlike common factor analysis, has none of the above problems if the covariance or correlation matrix is computed correctly from a data set with no missing values. Various methods for missing value correlation or severe rounding of the correlations can produce negative eigenvalues in principal components.

Computational Resources

Let

n = number of observations
v = number of variables
f = number of factors
i = number of iterations during factor extraction
r = number of iterations during factor rotation.

The time required to compute . . .	is roughly proportional to
an overall factor analysis	iv^3
the correlation matrix	nv^2
PRIORS=SMC or ASMC	v^3
PRIORS=MAX	v^2
eigenvalues	v^3
final eigenvectors	fv^2
ROTATE=VARIMAX, QUARTIMAX, EQUAMAX, ORTHOMAX, PROMAX, or HK	rvf^2
ROTATE=PROCRUSTES	vf^2

Each iteration in METHOD=PRINIT or ALPHA requires computation of eigenvalues and f eigenvectors.

Each iteration in METHOD=ML or ULS requires computation of eigenvalues and $v-f$ eigenvectors.

Printed Output

PROC FACTOR output includes

1. Mean and Std Dev (standard deviation) of each variable and the number of observations if SIMPLE is specified.
2. Correlations if CORR is specified.
3. Inverse Correlation Matrix if ALL is specified (not shown).
4. Partial Correlations Controlling all other Variables (negative anti-image correlations) if MSA is specified. If the data are appropriate for the common factor model, the partial correlations should be small.
5. Kaiser's Measure of Sampling Adequacy (Kaiser 1970; Kaiser and Rice 1974; Cerny and Kaiser 1977) if MSA is specified, both overall and for each variable. The MSA is a summary of how small the partial correlations are relative to the ordinary correlations. Values greater than 0.8 can be considered good. Values less than 0.5 require remedial action, either by deleting the offending variables or including other variables related to the offenders.
6. Prior Communality Estimates, unless 1.0s are used or METHOD=IMAGE, HARRIS, PATTERN, or SCORE.
7. Squared Multiple Correlations of each variable with all the other variables if METHOD=IMAGE or HARRIS (not shown).
8. Image Coefficients if METHOD=IMAGE (not shown).
9. Image Covariance Matrix if METHOD=IMAGE (not shown).
10. Preliminary Eigenvalues based on the prior communalities if METHOD=PRINIT, ALPHA, ML, or ULS, including the Total and the Average of the eigenvalues, the Difference between successive eigenvalues, the Proportion of variation represented, and the Cumulative proportion of variation.
11. the number of factors that will be retained unless METHOD=PATTERN or SCORE.
12. a Scree Plot of Eigenvalues if the SCREE option is specified. The preliminary eigenvalues are used if METHOD=PRINIT, ALPHA, ML, or ULS.
13. the iteration history if METHOD=PRINIT, ALPHA, ML, or ULS, containing the iteration number (Iter); the Criterion being optimized (Joreskog 1977); the Ridge value for the iteration if METHOD=ML or ULS; the maximum Change in any communality estimate; and the Communalities.
14. Significance tests if METHOD=ML, including Chi-square, df, and Prob>chi**2 for H0: No common factors and H0: factors retained are sufficient to explain the correlations. The variables should have an approximate multivariate normal distribution for the probability levels to be valid. Lawley and Maxwell (1971) suggest that the number of observations should exceed the number of variables by fifty or more, although Geweke and Singleton (1980) claim that as few as ten observations are adequate with five variables and one common factor. Certain regularity conditions must also be satisfied for the χ^2 test to be valid (Geweke and Singleton 1980), but in practice these conditions usually are satisfied. The notation Prob>chi**2 means "the probability under the null hypothesis of obtaining a greater χ^2 statistic than that observed."
15. Akaike's Information Criterion if METHOD=ML. Akaike's information criterion (AIC) (Akaike 1973, 1974) is a general criterion for estimating the best number of parameters to include in a model when maximum-likelihood estimation is used. The number of factors that yields the

smallest value of AIC is considered best. AIC, like the chi-square test, tends to include factors that are statistically significant but inconsequential for practical purposes.

16. Schwarz's Bayesian Criterion if METHOD=ML. Schwarz's Bayesian criterion (SBC) (Schwarz 1978) is another criterion, similar to AIC, for determining the best number of parameters. The number of factors that yields the smallest value of SBC is considered best. SBC seems to be less inclined to include trivial factors than either AIC or the chi-square test.

17. Tucker and Lewis's Reliability Coefficient if METHOD=ML (Tucker and Lewis 1973).

18. Squared Canonical Correlations if METHOD=ML. These are the same as the squared multiple correlations for predicting each factor from the variables.

19. Coefficient Alpha for Each Factor if METHOD=ALPHA (not shown).

20. Eigenvectors if EIGENVECTORS or ALL is specified, unless METHOD=PATTERN or SCORE (not shown).

21. Eigenvalues of the (Weighted) (Reduced) (Image) Correlation or Covariance Matrix, unless METHOD=PATTERN or SCORE. Included are the Total and the Average of the eigenvalues, the Difference between successive eigenvalues, the Proportion of variation represented, and the Cumulative proportion of variation.

22. the Factor Pattern, which is equal to both the matrix of standardized regression coefficients for predicting variables from common factors and the matrix of correlations between variables and common factors since the extracted factors are uncorrelated.

23. Variance explained by each factor, both Weighted and Unweighted if variable weights are used.

24. Final Communality Estimates, including the Total communality; or Final Communality Estimates and Variable Weights, including the Total communality, both Weighted and Unweighted, if variable weights are used. Final communality estimates are the squared multiple correlations for predicting the variables from the estimated factors and can be obtained by taking the sum of squares of each row of the factor pattern, or a weighted sum of squares if variable weights are used.

25. Residual Correlations With Uniqueness on the Diagonal if RESIDUAL or ALL is specified.

26. Root Mean Square Off-diagonal Residuals, both Over-all and for each variable, if RESIDUAL or ALL is specified.

27. Partial Correlations Controlling Factors if RESIDUAL or ALL is specified.

28. Root Mean Square Off-diagonal Partials, both Over-all and for each variable, if RESIDUAL or ALL is specified.

29. a Plot of Factor Pattern for unrotated factors if PREPLOT is specified; the number of plots is determined by the NPLOT= option.

30. Variable Weights for Rotation if NORM=WEIGHT is specified.

31. Factor Weights for Rotation if HKPOWER= is specified (not shown).

32. Orthogonal Transformation Matrix if an orthogonal rotation is requested.

33. Rotated Factor Pattern if an orthogonal rotation is requested.

34. Variance explained by each factor after rotation. If an orthogonal rotation is requested and if variable weights are used, both weighted and unweighted values are given.

35. Target Matrix for Procrustean Transformation if ROTATE=PROCRUSTES or PROMAX.

36. the Procrustean Transformation Matrix if ROTATE=PROCRUSTES or PROMAX.

37. the Normalized Oblique Transformation Matrix if an oblique rotation is requested, which for ROTATE=PROMAX is the product of the prerotation and the Procrustean rotation.

38. Inter-factor Correlations if an oblique rotation is requested.

39. Rotated Factor Pattern (Std Reg Coefs) if an oblique rotation is requested, giving standardized regression coefficients for predicting the variables from the factors.

40. Reference Axis Correlations if an oblique rotation is requested. These are the partial correlations between the primary factors when all factors other than the two being correlated are partialled out.

41. the Reference Structure (Semipartial Correlations) if an oblique rotation is requested. The reference structure is the matrix of semipartial correlations (Kerlinger and Pedhazur 1973) between variables and common factors, removing from each common factor the effects of other common factors. If the common factors are uncorrelated, the reference structure is equal to the factor pattern.

42. Variance explained by each factor eliminating the effects of all other factors if an oblique rotation is requested. Both Weighted and Unweighted values are given if variable weights are used. These variances are equal to the (weighted) sum of the squared elements of the reference structure corresponding to each factor.

43. Factor Structure (Correlations) if an oblique rotation is requested. The (primary) factor structure is the matrix of correlations between variables and common factors. If the common factors are uncorrelated, the factor structure is equal to the factor pattern.

44. Variance explained by each factor ignoring the effects of all other factors if an oblique rotation is requested. Both Weighted and Unweighted values are given if variable weights are used. These variances are equal to the (weighted) sum of the squared elements of the factor structure corresponding to each factor.

45. Final Communality Estimates for the rotated factors if the ROTATE= option is specified. The estimates should equal the unrotated communalities.

46. Squared Multiple Correlations of the Variables With Each Factor if SCORE or ALL is specified, except for unrotated principal components (not shown).

47. Standardized Scoring Coefficients if SCORE or ALL is specified (not shown).

48. Plots of the Factor Pattern for rotated factors if PLOT is specified and an orthogonal rotation is requested. The number of plots is determined by the NPLOT= option.

49. Plots of the Reference Structure for rotated factors if PLOT is specified and an oblique rotation is requested. The number of plots is determined by the NPLOT= option. Included are the Reference Axis Correlation and the Angle between the reference axes for each pair of factors plotted.

If ROTATE=PROMAX is used, the output includes results for both the prerotation and the Procrustean rotation.

EXAMPLES

Example 1: Principal Component Analysis

The data in the example below are five socioeconomic variables for twelve census tracts in the Los Angeles Standard Metropolitan Statistical Area as given by Harman (1976). The five variables represent total population, median school years, total employment, miscellaneous professional services, and median house value.

The first analysis is a principal component analysis. Simple descriptive statistics and correlations are also printed. This example produces **Output 17.1:**

```
data socecon;
   title 'Five Socioeconomic Variables';
   title2 'See Page 14 of Harman: Modern Factor Analysis, 3rd Ed';
   input pop school employ services house;
   cards;
5700     12.8     2500     270     25000
1000     10.9     600      10      10000
3400     8.8      1000     10      9000
3800     13.6     1700     140     25000
4000     12.8     1600     140     25000
8200     8.3      2600     60      12000
1200     11.4     400      10      16000
9100     11.5     3300     60      14000
9900     12.5     3400     180     18000
9600     13.7     3600     390     25000
9600     9.6      3300     80      12000
9400     11.4     4000     100     13000
;
proc factor data=socecon simple corr;
   title3 'Principal Component Analysis';
run;
```

There are two large eigenvalues, 2.873314 and 1.796660, which together account for 93.4 percent of the standardized variance. Thus, the first two principal components provide an adequate summary of the data for most purposes. Three components, explaining 97.7 percent of the variation, should be sufficient for almost any application. FACTOR retains two components on the basis of the eigenvalues-greater-than-one rule since the third eigenvalue is only 0.214837.

The first component has large positive loadings for all five variables. The correlation with SERVICES (0.93239) is especially high. The second component is a contrast of POP (0.80642) and EMPLOY (0.72605) against SCHOOL (-0.54476) and HOUSE (-0.55818), with a very small loading on SERVICES (-0.10431).

The final communality estimates show that all the variables are well accounted for by two components, with final communality estimates ranging from 0.880236 for SERVICES to 0.987826 for POP.

Output 17.1 Principal Component Analysis: PROC FACTOR

```
                          Five Socioeconomic Variables                          1
                  See Page 14 of Harman: Modern Factor Analysis, 3rd Ed
                            Principal Component Analysis

                    Means and Standard Deviations from 12 observations

                         POP       SCHOOL      EMPLOY     SERVICES      HOUSE
   ❶  Mean       6241.66667  11.4416667  2333.33333  120.833333      17000
      Std Dev    3439.99427  1.78654483  1241.21153  114.927513  6367.53128
                            ❷  Correlations

                         POP      SCHOOL     EMPLOY    SERVICES     HOUSE
      POP          1.00000     0.00975    0.97245    0.43887    0.02241
      SCHOOL       0.00975     1.00000    0.15428    0.69141    0.86307
      EMPLOY       0.97245     0.15428    1.00000    0.51472    0.12193
      SERVICES     0.43887     0.69141    0.51472    1.00000    0.77765
      HOUSE        0.02241     0.86307    0.12193    0.77765    1.00000
```

```
                          Five Socioeconomic Variables                          2
                  See Page 14 of Harman: Modern Factor Analysis, 3rd Ed
                            Principal Component Analysis

Initial Factor Method: Principal Components
                    ❻  Prior Communality Estimates: ONE

            Eigenvalues of the Correlation Matrix: Total = 5  Average = 1

                         1          2          3          4          5
   ㉑ Eigenvalue   2.873314   1.796660   0.214837   0.099934   0.015255
      Difference   1.076654   1.581823   0.114903   0.084679
      Proportion     0.5747     0.3593     0.0430     0.0200     0.0031
      Cumulative     0.5747     0.9340     0.9770     0.9969     1.0000

   ⓫  2 factors will be retained by the MINEIGEN criterion.
                         ㉒  Factor Pattern

                              FACTOR1    FACTOR2

              POP          0.58096    0.80642
              SCHOOL       0.76704   -0.54476
              EMPLOY       0.67243    0.72605
              SERVICES     0.93239   -0.10431
              HOUSE        0.79116   -0.55818

                  Variance explained by each factor

                         FACTOR1    FACTOR2
                 ㉓     2.873314   1.796660

   ㉔  Final Communality Estimates: Total = 4.669974

             POP      SCHOOL     EMPLOY    SERVICES     HOUSE
         0.987826   0.885106   0.979306   0.880236   0.937500
```

Example 2: Principal Factor Analysis

The next example is a principal factor analysis using squared multiple correlations for the prior communality estimates (PRIORS=SMC). Kaiser's measure of sampling adequacy (MSA) is requested. A scree plot of the eigenvalues is printed. The RESIDUAL correlations and partial correlations are computed. The PREPLOT option plots the unrotated factor pattern.

Specifying ROTATE=PROMAX produces an orthogonal varimax prerotation followed by an oblique rotation. The REORDER option reorders the variables according to their largest factor loadings. The SCORE option requests scoring coefficients. The PLOT procedure produces a plot of the reference structure.

An OUTSTAT= data set is created by PROC FACTOR and printed, as shown in **Output 17.2**.

---

476   Chapter 17

```
proc factor data=socecon priors=smc msa scree residual preplot
   rotate=promax reorder plot
   outstat=fact_all;
   title3 'Principal Factor Analysis with Promax Rotation';
proc print;
   title3 'Factor Output Data Set';
run;
```

Output 17.2   Principal Factor Analysis: PROC FACTOR and PROC PRINT

```
                         Five Socioeconomic Variables                              1
                See Page 14 of Harman: Modern Factor Analysis, 3rd Ed
                      Principal Factor Analysis with Promax Rotation

Initial Factor Method: Principal Factors

          ❹ Partial Correlations Controlling all other Variables

                        POP      SCHOOL    EMPLOY   SERVICES    HOUSE

          POP         1.00000   -0.54465   0.97083   0.09612    0.15871
          SCHOOL     -0.54465    1.00000   0.54373   0.04996    0.64717
          EMPLOY      0.97083    0.54373   1.00000   0.06689   -0.25572
          SERVICES    0.09612    0.04996   0.06689   1.00000    0.59415
          HOUSE       0.15871    0.64717  -0.25572   0.59415    1.00000


          ❺ Kaiser's Measure of Sampling Adequacy: Over-all MSA = 0.57536759

                    POP      SCHOOL    EMPLOY   SERVICES    HOUSE
                  0.472079  0.551588  0.488511  0.806644  0.612814


                     Prior Communality Estimates: SMC

                    POP      SCHOOL    EMPLOY   SERVICES    HOUSE
                  0.968592  0.822285  0.969181  0.785724  0.847019

Eigenvalues of the Reduced Correlation Matrix:   Total = 4.39280116   Average = 0.87856023

                         1          2          3          4          5
          Eigenvalue  2.734301   1.716069   0.039563  -0.024523  -0.072608
          Difference  1.018232   1.676506   0.064086   0.048084
          Proportion    0.6225     0.3907     0.0090    -0.0056    -0.0165
          Cumulative    0.6225     1.0131     1.0221     1.0165     1.0000

             2 factors will be retained by the PROPORTION criterion.
```

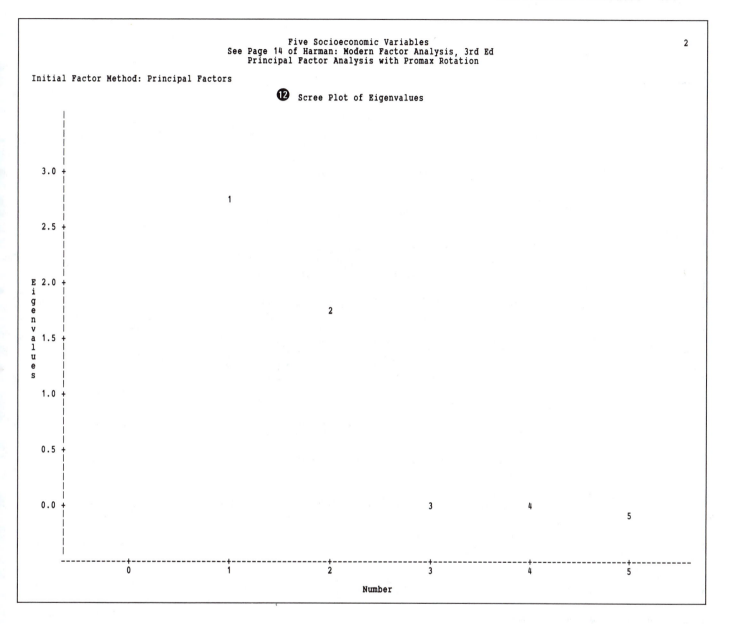

Initial Factor Method: Principal Factors

⓬ Scree Plot of Eigenvalues

Initial Factor Method: Principal Factors

Factor Pattern

	FACTOR1	FACTOR2
SERVICES	0.87899	-0.15847
HOUSE	0.74215	-0.57806
EMPLOY	0.71447	0.67936
SCHOOL	0.71370	-0.55515
POP	0.62533	0.76621

Variance explained by each factor

FACTOR1	FACTOR2
2.734301	1.716069

Final Communality Estimates: Total = 4.450370

POP	SCHOOL	EMPLOY	SERVICES	HOUSE
0.978113	0.817564	0.971999	0.797743	0.884950

25 Residual Correlations With Uniqueness on the Diagonal

	POP	SCHOOL	EMPLOY	SERVICES	HOUSE
POP	0.02189	-0.01118	0.00514	0.01063	0.00124
SCHOOL	-0.01118	0.18244	0.02151	-0.02390	0.01248
EMPLOY	0.00514	0.02151	0.02800	-0.00565	-0.01561
SERVICES	0.01063	-0.02390	-0.00565	0.20226	0.03370
HOUSE	0.00124	0.01248	-0.01561	0.03370	0.11505

26 Root Mean Square Off-diagonal Residuals: Over-all = 0.01693282

POP	SCHOOL	EMPLOY	SERVICES	HOUSE
0.008153	0.018130	0.013828	0.021517	0.019602

27 Partial Correlations Controlling Factors

	POP	SCHOOL	EMPLOY	SERVICES	HOUSE
POP	1.00000	-0.17693	0.20752	0.15975	0.02471
SCHOOL	-0.17693	1.00000	0.30097	-0.12443	0.08614
EMPLOY	0.20752	0.30097	1.00000	-0.07504	-0.27509
SERVICES	0.15975	-0.12443	-0.07504	1.00000	0.22093
HOUSE	0.02471	0.08614	-0.27509	0.22093	1.00000

Initial Factor Method: Principal Factors

28 Root Mean Square Off-diagonal Partials: Over-all = 0.18550132

POP	SCHOOL	EMPLOY	SERVICES	HOUSE
0.158508	0.190259	0.231818	0.154470	0.182015

Five Socioeconomic Variables
See Page 14 of Harman: Modern Factor Analysis, 3rd Ed
Principal Factor Analysis with Promax Rotation

5

Initial Factor Method: Principal Factors

29 Plot of Factor Pattern for FACTOR1 and FACTOR2

```
                              FACTOR1
                                1
                         D     .9
                               .8
              E                .7                C
              B                                    A
                               .6
                               .5
                               .4
                               .3
                               .2
                               .1                      F
 -1 -.9-.8-.7-.6-.5-.4-.3-.2-.1  0 .1 .2 .3 .4 .5 .6 .7 .8 .9 1.0 A
                                                           C
                              -.1                          T
                              -.2                          O
                                                           R
                              -.3                          2
                              -.4
                              -.5
                              -.6
                              -.7
                              -.8
                              -.9
                              -1

   POP    =A    SCHOOL  =B    EMPLOY  =C    SERVICES=D    HOUSE   =E
```

Five Socioeconomic Variables
See Page 14 of Harman: Modern Factor Analysis, 3rd Ed
Principal Factor Analysis with Promax Rotation

6

Prerotation Method: Varimax

32 Orthogonal Transformation Matrix

	1	2
1	0.78895	0.61446
2	-0.61446	0.78895

33 Rotated Factor Pattern

	FACTOR1	FACTOR2
HOUSE	0.94072	-0.00004
SCHOOL	0.90419	0.00055
SERVICES	0.79085	0.41509
POP	0.02255	0.98874
EMPLOY	0.14625	0.97499

(continued on next page)

(continued from previous page)

㉞ Variance explained by each factor

```
        FACTOR1    FACTOR2
        2.349857   2.100513
```

Final Communality Estimates: Total = 4.450370

```
     POP      SCHOOL   EMPLOY   SERVICES   HOUSE
  0.978113  0.817564  0.971999  0.797743  0.884950
```

                    Five Socioeconomic Variables   7
      See Page 14 of Harman: Modern Factor Analysis, 3rd Ed
              Principal Factor Analysis with Promax Rotation

Prerotation Method: Varimax

㊽ Plot of Factor Pattern for FACTOR1 and FACTOR2

```
                            FACTOR1
                              1
                              E
                             .B
                             .8              D
                             .7
                             .6
                             .5
                             .4
                             .3
                             .2
                             .1                         C   F
                                                            A
                                                            C
  -1 -.9-.8-.7-.6-.5-.4-.3-.2-.1  0 .1 .2 .3 .4 .5 .6 .7 .8 .9 A.0T
                            -.1                              O
                                                            R
                            -.2                             2
                            -.3
                            -.4
                            -.5
                            -.6
                            -.7
                            -.8
                            -.9
                             -1
        POP     =A    SCHOOL  =B    EMPLOY  =C    SERVICES=D    HOUSE   =E
```

Rotation Method: Promax

㉟ Target Matrix for Procrustean Transformation

	FACTOR1	FACTOR2
HOUSE	1.00000	-0.00000
SCHOOL	1.00000	0.00000
SERVICES	0.69421	0.10045
POP	0.00001	1.00000
EMPLOY	0.00326	0.96793

㊱ Procrustean Transformation Matrix

	1	2
1	1.04117	-0.09865
2	-0.10572	0.96303

㊲ Normalized Oblique Transformation Matrix

	1	2
1	0.73803	0.54202
2	-0.70555	0.86528

㊳ Inter-factor Correlations

	FACTOR1	FACTOR2
FACTOR1	1.00000	0.20188
FACTOR2	0.20188	1.00000

㊴ Rotated Factor Pattern (Std Reg Coefs)

	FACTOR1	FACTOR2
HOUSE	0.95558	-0.09792
SCHOOL	0.91842	-0.09352
SERVICES	0.76053	0.33932
POP	-0.07908	1.00192
EMPLOY	0.04799	0.97509

㊵ Reference Axis Correlations

	FACTOR1	FACTOR2
FACTOR1	1.00000	-0.20188
FACTOR2	-0.20188	1.00000

Rotation Method: Promax

㊶ Reference Structure (Semipartial Correlations)

	FACTOR1	FACTOR2
HOUSE	0.93591	-0.09590
SCHOOL	0.89951	-0.09160
SERVICES	0.74487	0.33233
POP	-0.07745	0.98129
EMPLOY	0.04700	0.95501

㊷ Variance explained by each factor eliminating other factors

FACTOR1	FACTOR2
2.248089	2.003020

(continued on next page)

(continued from previous page)

43 Factor Structure (Correlations)

	FACTOR1	FACTOR2
HOUSE	0.93582	0.09500
SCHOOL	0.89954	0.09189
SERVICES	0.82903	0.49286
POP	0.12319	0.98596
EMPLOY	0.24484	0.98478

44 Variance explained by each factor ignoring other factors

FACTOR1	FACTOR2
2.447349	2.202280

45 Final Communality Estimates: Total = 4.450370

POP	SCHOOL	EMPLOY	SERVICES	HOUSE
0.978113	0.817564	0.971999	0.797743	0.884950

Five Socioeconomic Variables
See Page 14 of Harman: Modern Factor Analysis, 3rd Ed
Principal Factor Analysis with Promax Rotation

10

Rotation Method: Promax

49 Plot of Reference Structure for FACTOR1 and FACTOR2
Reference Axis Correlation = -0.2019 Angle = 101.6471

```
                              FACTOR1
                                 1
                              E
                              B .9
                                .8
                                .7        D
                                .6
                                .5
                                .4
                                .3
                                .2
                                .1                            F
                                                             A
                                                          C  C
-1 -.9-.8-.7-.6-.5-.4-.3-.2-.1  0 .1 .2 .3 .4 .5 .6 .7 .8 .9 1.0 T
                                                             O
                               -.1                        A  R
                                                             2
                               -.2
                               -.3
                               -.4
                               -.5
                               -.6
                               -.7
                               -.8
                               -.9
                               -1
        POP   =A   SCHOOL  =B   EMPLOY  =C   SERVICES=D   HOUSE  =E
```

```
                         Five Socioeconomic Variables
                  See Page 14 of Harman: Modern Factor Analysis, 3rd Ed
                              Factor Output Data Set

  OBS    _TYPE_     _NAME_       POP      SCHOOL    EMPLOY   SERVICES     HOUSE

    1    MEAN                  6241.67   11.4417   2333.33   120.833   17000.00
    2    STD                   3439.99    1.7865   1241.21   114.928    6367.53
    3    N                       12.00   12.0000     12.00    12.000      12.00
    4    CORR      POP            1.00    0.0098      0.97     0.439       0.02
    5    CORR      SCHOOL         0.01    1.0000      0.15     0.691       0.86
    6    CORR      EMPLOY         0.97    0.1543      1.00     0.515       0.12
    7    CORR      SERVICES       0.44    0.6914      0.51     1.000       0.78
    8    CORR      HOUSE          0.02    0.8631      0.12     0.778       1.00
    9    COMMUNAL                 0.98    0.8176      0.97     0.798       0.88
   10    PRIORS                   0.97    0.8223      0.97     0.786       0.85
   11    EIGENVAL                 2.73    1.7161      0.04    -0.025      -0.07
   12    UNROTATE  FACTOR1        0.63    0.7137      0.71     0.879       0.74
   13    UNROTATE  FACTOR2        0.77   -0.5552      0.68    -0.158      -0.58
   14    RESIDUAL  POP            0.02   -0.0112      0.01     0.011       0.00
   15    RESIDUAL  SCHOOL        -0.01    0.1824      0.02    -0.024       0.01
   16    RESIDUAL  EMPLOY         0.01    0.0215      0.03    -0.006      -0.02
   17    RESIDUAL  SERVICES       0.01   -0.0239     -0.01     0.202       0.03
   18    RESIDUAL  HOUSE          0.00    0.0125     -0.02     0.034       0.12
   19    PRETRANS  FACTOR1        0.79   -0.6145        .        .          .
   20    PRETRANS  FACTOR2        0.61    0.7889        .        .          .
   21    PREROTAT  FACTOR1        0.02    0.9042      0.15     0.791       0.94
   22    PREROTAT  FACTOR2        0.99    0.0006      0.97     0.415      -0.00
   23    TRANSFOR  FACTOR1        0.74   -0.7055        .        .          .
   24    TRANSFOR  FACTOR2        0.54    0.8653        .        .          .
   25    FCORR     FACTOR1        1.00    0.2019        .        .          .
   26    FCORR     FACTOR2        0.20    1.0000        .        .          .
   27    PATTERN   FACTOR1       -0.08    0.9184      0.05     0.761       0.96
   28    PATTERN   FACTOR2        1.00   -0.0935      0.98     0.339      -0.10
   29    RCORR     FACTOR1        1.00   -0.2019        .        .          .
   30    RCORR     FACTOR2       -0.20    1.0000        .        .          .
   31    REFERENC  FACTOR1       -0.08    0.8995      0.05     0.745       0.94
   32    REFERENC  FACTOR2        0.98   -0.0916      0.96     0.332      -0.10
   33    STRUCTUR  FACTOR1        0.12    0.8995      0.24     0.829       0.94
   34    STRUCTUR  FACTOR2        0.99    0.0919      0.98     0.493       0.09
```

If the data are appropriate for the common factor model, the partial correlations controlling the other variables should be small compared to the original correlations. The partial correlation between SCHOOL and HOUSE, for example, is 0.65, slightly less than the original correlation of 0.86. The partial correlation between POP and SCHOOL is −0.54, which is much larger in absolute value than the original correlation and an indication of trouble. Kaiser's MSA is a summary, for each variable and for all variables together, of how much smaller the partial correlations are than the original correlations. Values of 0.8 or 0.9 are considered good, while MSAs below 0.5 are unacceptable. POP, SCHOOL, and EMPLOY have very poor MSAs. Only SERVICES has a good MSA. The overall MSA of 0.58 is sufficiently poor that additional variables should be included in the analysis to define the common factors better. A commonly used rule-of-thumb is that there should be at least three variables per factor. You can see below that there seem to be two common factors in these data, so more variables are needed for a reliable analysis.

The SMCs are all fairly large; hence, the factor loadings do not differ greatly from the principal component analysis.

The eigenvalues show clearly that two common factors are present. There are two large positive eigenvalues that together account for 101.31% of the common variance, which is as close to 100% as you are ever likely to get without iterating. The scree plot shows a sharp bend at the third eigenvalue, reinforcing the above conclusion.

The principal factor pattern is similar to the principal component pattern. For example, SERVICES has the largest loading on the first factor, POP the smallest. POP and EMPLOY have large positive loadings on the second factor, HOUSE and SCHOOL have large negative loadings.

The final communality estimates are all fairly close to the priors, only HOUSE having increased appreciably from 0.847019 to 0.884950. Nearly 100% of the common variance is accounted for. The residual correlations are low, the largest being 0.03. The partial correlations are not quite as impressive since the uniqueness values are also rather small. These results indicate that the SMCs are good but not quite optimal communality estimates.

The plot of the unrotated factor pattern shows two tight clusters of variables, HOUSE and SCHOOL at the negative end of FACTOR2, EMPLOY and POP at the positive end. SERVICES is in between but closer to HOUSE and SCHOOL. A good rotation would put the reference axes through the two clusters.

The varimax rotation puts one axis through HOUSE and SCHOOL but misses POP and EMPLOY slightly. The promax rotation places an axis through POP and EMPLOY but misses HOUSE and SCHOOL. Since an independent-cluster solution would be possible if it were not for SERVICES, a Harris-Kaiser rotation weighted by the Cureton-Mulaik technique should be used.

The output data set shown in **Output 17.2** can be used for Harris-Kaiser rotation by deleting observations with _TYPE_='PATTERN' and _TYPE_='FCORR', which are for the promax-rotated factors, and changing _TYPE_='UNROTATE' to 'PATTERN'. The following statements produce **Output 17.3**:

```
data fact2(type=factor);
   set;
   if _type_='PATTERN'|_type_='FCORR' then delete;
   if _type_='UNROTATE' then _type_='PATTERN';
proc factor rotate=hk norm=weight reorder plot;
   title3 'Harris-Kaiser Rotation with Cureton-Mulaik Weights';
run;
```

The variable SERVICES receives a small weight, and the axes are placed as desired.

Output 17.3   Harris-Kaiser Rotation: PROC FACTOR

```
                          Five Socioeconomic Variables                          1
                  See Page 14 of Harman: Modern Factor Analysis, 3rd Ed
                    Harris-Kaiser Rotation with Cureton-Mulaik Weights

Rotation Method: Harris-Kaiser

                        ㉚  Variable Weights for Rotation

                   POP     SCHOOL    EMPLOY   SERVICES    HOUSE
                0.959827  0.939454  0.997464  0.121948  0.940073


                        Oblique Transformation Matrix

                                    1         2

                         1       0.73537   0.61899
                         2      -0.68283   0.78987

                        Inter-factor Correlations

                                 FACTOR1   FACTOR2

                      FACTOR1    1.00000   0.08358
                      FACTOR2    0.08358   1.00000
```

(continued on next page)

(continued from previous page)

```
                      Rotated Factor Pattern (Std Reg Coefs)

                                   FACTOR1   FACTOR2

                      HOUSE        0.94048   0.00279
                      SCHOOL       0.90391   0.00327
                      SERVICES     0.75459   0.41892
                      POP         -0.06335   0.99227
                      EMPLOY       0.06152   0.97885

                        Reference Axis Correlations

                                   FACTOR1   FACTOR2

                      FACTOR1      1.00000  -0.08358
                      FACTOR2     -0.08358   1.00000

                 Reference Structure (Semipartial Correlations)

                                   FACTOR1   FACTOR2

                      HOUSE        0.93719   0.00278
                      SCHOOL       0.90075   0.00326
                      SERVICES     0.75195   0.41745
                      POP         -0.06312   0.98880
                      EMPLOY       0.06130   0.97543

          Variance explained by each factor eliminating other factors

                             FACTOR1   FACTOR2
                             2.262854  2.103473
```

```
                           Five Socioeconomic Variables                      2
                 See Page 14 of Harman: Modern Factor Analysis, 3rd Ed
                    Harris-Kaiser Rotation with Cureton-Mulaik Weights

Rotation Method: Harris-Kaiser

                          Factor Structure (Correlations)

                                   FACTOR1   FACTOR2

                      HOUSE        0.94071   0.08139
                      SCHOOL       0.90419   0.07882
                      SERVICES     0.78960   0.48198
                      POP          0.01958   0.98698
                      EMPLOY       0.14332   0.98399

              Variance explained by each factor ignoring other factors

                             FACTOR1   FACTOR2
                             2.346896  2.187516


              Final Communality Estimates: Total = 4.450370

               POP     SCHOOL    EMPLOY  SERVICES    HOUSE
            0.978113  0.817564  0.971999  0.797743  0.884950
```

```
                              Five Socioeconomic Variables                              3
                     See Page 14 of Harman: Modern Factor Analysis, 3rd Ed
                          Harris-Kaiser Rotation with Cureton-Mulaik Weights

Rotation Method: Harris-Kaiser


                              Plot of Reference Structure for FACTOR1 and FACTOR2
                         Reference Axis Correlation = -0.0836  Angle = 94.7941

                                         FACTOR1
                                            1
                                            E
                                           .B

                                           .8            D
                                           .7

                                           .6

                                           .5

                                           .4

                                           .3

                                           .2
                                                                            F
                                           .1                               A
                                                                          C C
       -1 -.9-.8-.7-.6-.5-.4-.3-.2-.1  0 .1 .2 .3 .4 .5 .6 .7 .8 .9 1.0T
                                                                          A O
                                          -.1                               R
                                                                            2
                                          -.2

                                          -.3

                                          -.4

                                          -.5

                                          -.6

                                          -.7

                                          -.8

                                          -.9

                                          -1


              POP    =A     SCHOOL =B    EMPLOY =C    SERVICES=D    HOUSE  =E
```

Example 3: Maximum-Likelihood Factor Analysis

This example uses maximum-likelihood factor analyses for one, two, and three factors. It is already apparent from the principal factor analysis that the best number of common factors is almost certainly two. The one- and three-factor ML solutions reinforce this conclusion and illustrate some of the numerical problems that can occur. The following statements produce **Output 17.4**:

```
proc factor data=socecon method=ml heywood n=1;
   title3 'Maximum-Likelihood Factor Analysis with One Factor';
proc factor data=socecon method=ml heywood n=2;
   title3 'Maximum-Likelihood Factor Analysis with Two Factors';
proc factor data=socecon method=ml heywood n=3;
   title3 'Maximum-Likelihood Factor Analysis with Three Factors';
run;
```

Output 17.4   Maximum-Likelihood Factor Analysis: PROC FACTOR

```
                         Five Socioeconomic Variables                              1
                  See Page 14 of Harman: Modern Factor Analysis, 3rd Ed
                    Maximum-Likelihood Factor Analysis with One Factor

Initial Factor Method: Maximum Likelihood

                       Prior Communality Estimates: SMC

                     POP      SCHOOL    EMPLOY   SERVICES    HOUSE
                  0.968592   0.822285  0.969181  0.785724  0.847019

            Preliminary Eigenvalues:  Total = 76.1165859  Average = 15.2233172

                            1         2         3         4         5
     ⑩  Eigenvalue   63.701009  13.054719  0.327639 -0.347281 -0.619501
        Difference   50.646289  12.727080  0.674920  0.272220
        Proportion      0.8369     0.1715    0.0043   -0.0046   -0.0081
        Cumulative      0.8369     1.0084    1.0127    1.0081    1.0000

                  1 factors will be retained by the NFACTOR criterion.

        Iter  Criterion  Ridge   Change   Communalities
     ⑬   1    6.54292    0.000   0.10330   0.93828 0.72227 1.00000 0.71940 0.74371
         2    3.12327    0.000   0.72885   0.94566 0.02380 1.00000 0.26493 0.01487

                          Unable to improve criteria.
                        Try a different 'PRIORS' statement.

     ⑭  Significance tests based on 12 observations:

            Test of H0: No common factors.
                vs HA: At least one common factor.

            Chi-square = 54.252   df = 10   Prob>chi**2 = 0.0000

            Test of H0: 1 Factors are sufficient.
                vs HA: More factors are needed.

            Chi-square = 24.466   df = 5   Prob>chi**2 = 0.0002

     ⑮  Akaike's Information Criterion = 57.479238669
     ⑯  Schwarz's Bayesian Criterion = 31.164152583
     ⑰  Tucker and Lewis's Reliability Coefficient = 0.120231384

                    ⑱  Squared Canonical Correlations

                               FACTOR1
                              1.000000

    Eigenvalues of the Weighted Reduced Correlation Matrix:  Total = 0  Average = 0

                        1         2         3         4         5
        Eigenvalue      .     1.927160 -0.228313 -0.792956 -0.905891
        Difference      .     2.155473  0.564643  0.112935
```

```
                         Five Socioeconomic Variables                              2
                  See Page 14 of Harman: Modern Factor Analysis, 3rd Ed
                    Maximum-Likelihood Factor Analysis with One Factor

Initial Factor Method: Maximum Likelihood

                               Factor Pattern

                                 FACTOR1

                       POP        0.97245
                       SCHOOL     0.15428
                       EMPLOY     1.00000
                       SERVICES   0.51472
                       HOUSE      0.12193

                     Variance explained by each factor

                                 FACTOR1
                     Weighted    17.801063
                     Unweighted   2.249260
```

(continued on next page)

(continued from previous page)

```
                    Final Communality Estimates and Variable Weights
              Total Communality: Weighted = 17.801063   Unweighted = 2.249260

                          POP      SCHOOL    EMPLOY   SERVICES   HOUSE
           Communality  0.945656  0.023803  1.000000  0.264935  0.014866
           Weight      18.401165  1.024384     .      1.360424  1.015090
```

```
                                                                                     3
                            Five Socioeconomic Variables
                     See Page 14 of Harman: Modern Factor Analysis, 3rd Ed
                      Maximum-Likelihood Factor Analysis with Two Factors

Initial Factor Method: Maximum Likelihood

                          Prior Communality Estimates: SMC

                     POP      SCHOOL    EMPLOY   SERVICES   HOUSE
                  0.968592  0.822285  0.969181  0.785724  0.847019

          Preliminary Eigenvalues:  Total = 76.1165859   Average = 15.2233172

                           1          2          3          4          5
          Eigenvalue  63.701009 13.054719  0.327639 -0.347281 -0.619501
          Difference  50.646289 12.727080  0.674920  0.272220
          Proportion   0.8369     0.1715     0.0043    -0.0046    -0.0081
          Cumulative   0.8369     1.0084     1.0127     1.0081     1.0000

            2 factors will be retained by the NFACTOR criterion.

     Iter Criterion   Ridge   Change   Communalities
      1    0.34312    0.000   0.04710   1.00000 0.80672 0.95058 0.79348 0.89412
      2    0.30722    0.000   0.03068   1.00000 0.80821 0.96023 0.81048 0.92480
      3    0.30679    0.000   0.00629   1.00000 0.81149 0.95948 0.81677 0.92023
      4    0.30674    0.000   0.00218   1.00000 0.80985 0.95963 0.81498 0.92241
      5    0.30673    0.000   0.00071   1.00000 0.81019 0.95955 0.81569 0.92187

                        Convergence criteria satisfied.

              Significance tests based on 12 observations:

                 Test of H0: No common factors.
                    vs HA: At least one common factor.

                 Chi-square = 54.252   df = 10   Prob>chi**2 = 0.0000

                 Test of H0: 2 Factors are sufficient.
                    vs HA: More factors are needed.

                 Chi-square = 2.198   df = 1   Prob>chi**2 = 0.1382

              Akaike's Information Criterion = 31.68078504
              Schwarz's Bayesian Criterion = 19.234739068
              Tucker and Lewis's Reliability Coefficient = 0.7292200071

                        Squared Canonical Correlations

                          FACTOR1    FACTOR2
                          1.000000   0.951889

     Eigenvalues of the Weighted Reduced Correlation Matrix:  Total = 19.7853157   Average = 4.94632893

                           1          2          3          4          5
          Eigenvalue      .      19.785314  0.543185 -0.039771 -0.503412
          Difference      .      19.242129  0.582956  0.463641
          Proportion      .       1.0000     0.0275    -0.0020    -0.0254
          Cumulative      .       1.0000     1.0275     1.0254     1.0000
```

```
                          Five Socioeconomic Variables                          4
                   See Page 14 of Harman: Modern Factor Analysis, 3rd Ed
                   Maximum-Likelihood Factor Analysis with Two Factors

Initial Factor Method: Maximum Likelihood

                                 Factor Pattern

                                FACTOR1    FACTOR2

                    POP         1.00000    0.00000
                    SCHOOL      0.00975    0.90003
                    EMPLOY      0.97245    0.11797
                    SERVICES    0.43887    0.78930
                    HOUSE       0.02241    0.95989

                          Variance explained by each factor

                                    FACTOR1    FACTOR2
                    Weighted      24.432971  19.785314
                    Unweighted     2.138861   2.368353

                   Final Communality Estimates and Variable Weights
              Total Communality: Weighted = 44.218285   Unweighted = 4.507214

                         POP     SCHOOL    EMPLOY   SERVICES     HOUSE
        Communality  1.000000  0.810145  0.959571  0.815603   0.921894
        Weight          .       5.268294 24.724667 5.425646  12.799679
```

```
                          Five Socioeconomic Variables                          5
                   See Page 14 of Harman: Modern Factor Analysis, 3rd Ed
                   Maximum-Likelihood Factor Analysis with Three Factors

Initial Factor Method: Maximum Likelihood

                       Prior Communality Estimates: SMC

                      POP     SCHOOL    EMPLOY   SERVICES    HOUSE
                   0.968592  0.822285  0.969181  0.785724  0.847019

              Preliminary Eigenvalues:  Total = 76.1165859   Average = 15.2233172

                              1          2          3          4          5
        Eigenvalue      63.701009  13.054719   0.327639  -0.347281  -0.619501
        Difference      50.646289  12.727080   0.674920   0.272220
        Proportion        0.8369     0.1715     0.0043    -0.0046    -0.0081
        Cumulative        0.8369     1.0084     1.0127     1.0081     1.0000

                     3 factors will be retained by the NFACTOR criterion.
        WARNING: Too many factors for a unique solution.

        Iter Criterion   Ridge    Change   Communalities
          1    0.17980   0.031    0.05014   0.96081 0.84184 1.00000 0.80175 0.89716
          2    0.00164   0.031    0.06784   0.98081 0.88713 1.00000 0.79559 0.96500
          3 4.13501E-6   0.031    0.00939   0.98195 0.88603 1.00000 0.80498 0.96751
          4 2.53532E-8   0.031    0.00063   0.98202 0.88585 1.00000 0.80561 0.96735

                          Converged, but not to a proper optimum.
                          Try a different 'PRIORS' statement.

                    Significance tests based on 12 observations:

                    Test of H0: No common factors.
                         vs HA: At least one common factor.

                    Chi-square = 54.252   df = 10   Prob>chi**2 = 0.0000

                    Test of H0: 3 Factors are sufficient.
                         vs HA: More factors are needed.

                    Chi-square = 0.000   df = -2   Prob>chi**2 =  .

                    Akaike's Information Criterion = 34.000000304
                    Schwarz's Bayesian Criterion = 21.121706675
                    Tucker and Lewis's Reliability Coefficient = 0

                         Squared Canonical Correlations

                        FACTOR1    FACTOR2    FACTOR3
                       1.000000   0.975189   0.689446

        Eigenvalues of the Weighted Reduced Correlation Matrix:  Total = 41.5254193  Average = 10.3813548
```

(continued on next page)

(continued from previous page)

		1	2	3	4	5
Eigenvalue	.		39.305483	2.220057	0.000087	-0.000207
Difference	.		37.085426	2.219969	0.000295	
Proportion	.		0.9465	0.0535	0.0000	-0.0000
Cumulative	.		0.9465	1.0000	1.0000	1.0000

```
                              Five Socioeconomic Variables                        6
                    See Page 14 of Harman: Modern Factor Analysis, 3rd Ed
                    Maximum-Likelihood Factor Analysis with Three Factors

Initial Factor Method: Maximum Likelihood

                                   Factor Pattern

                          FACTOR1     FACTOR2     FACTOR3

              POP         0.97245    -0.11233    -0.15409
              SCHOOL      0.15428     0.89108     0.26083
              EMPLOY      1.00000    -0.00000     0.00000
              SERVICES    0.51472     0.72416    -0.12766
              HOUSE       0.12193     0.97227    -0.08473

                         Variance explained by each factor

                          FACTOR1     FACTOR2     FACTOR3
           Weighted     54.611524   39.305483    2.220057
           Unweighted    2.249260    2.276344    0.115254

                 Final Communality Estimates and Variable Weights
           Total Communality: Weighted = 96.137063   Unweighted = 4.640858

                      POP       SCHOOL     EMPLOY    SERVICES     HOUSE
           Communality  0.982017  0.885852  1.000000   0.805643   0.967347
           Weight      55.606690  8.760719     .       5.144426  30.625108
```

With one factor, the solution on the second iteration is so close to the optimum that FACTOR cannot find a better solution even though the convergence criterion has not been met, hence you receive this message:

    Unable to improve criteria.

When this message appears, you should try rerunning FACTOR with different prior communality estimates to make sure that the solution is correct. In this case, other prior estimates lead to the same solution or possibly to worse local optima, as indicated by Criterion or Chi-square values.

The variable EMPLOY has a communality of 1.0 and, therefore, an infinite weight that is printed below the final communality estimate as a missing value (.). The first eigenvalue is also infinite. Infinite values are ignored in computing the total of the eigenvalues and the total final communality.

The two-factor analysis converges without incident. This time, however, the POP variable is a Heywood case.

The three-factor analysis generates this message:

    WARNING: Too many factors for a unique solution.

The number of parameters in the model exceeds the number of elements in the correlation matrix from which they can be estimated, so an infinite number of different perfect solutions can be obtained. The Criterion approaches zero ($2.53532E-08$) at an improper optimum, as indicated by this message:

    Converged, but not to a proper optimum.

The degrees of freedom for the chi-square test are -2, so a probability level cannot be computed for three factors. Note also that the variable EMPLOY is a Heywood case again.

The probability levels for the chi-square test are 0.0001 for the hypothesis of no common factors, 0.0002 for one common factor, and 0.1382 for two common factors. Therefore the two-factor model seems to be an adequate representation. Akaike's information criterion and Schwarz's Bayesian criterion attain their minimum values at two common factors, so there is little doubt that two factors are appropriate for these data.

REFERENCES

Akaike, H. (1973), "Information Theory and the Extension of the Maximum Likelihood Principle," in *2nd International Symposium on Information Theory*, eds. V.N. Petrov and F. Csaki, Budapest: Akailseoniai-Kiudo, 267–281.

Akaike, H. (1974), "A New Look at the Statistical Identification Model," *IEEE Transactions on Automatic Control*, 19, 716–723.

Bickel, P.J. and Doksum, K.A. (1977), *Mathematical Statistics*, San Francisco: Holden-Day.

Cattell, R.B. (1966), "The Scree Test for the Number of Factors," *Multivariate Behavioral Research*, 1, 245–276.

Cattell, R.B. (1978), *The Scientific Use of Factor Analysis*, New York: Plenum.

Cattell, R.B. and Vogelman, S. (1977), "A Comprehensive Trial of the Scree and KG Criteria for Determining the Number of Factors," *Multivariate Behavioral Research*, 12, 289–325.

Cerny, B.A. and Kaiser, H.F. (1977), "A Study of a Measure of Sampling Adequacy for Factor-Analytic Correlation Matrices," *Multivariate Behavioral Research*, 12, 43–47.

Cureton, E.E. (1968), *A Factor Analysis of Project TALENT Tests and Four Other Test Batteries*, (Interim Report 4 to the U.S. Office of Education, Cooperative Research Project No. 3051.) Palo Alto: Project TALENT Office, American Institutes for Research and University of Pittsburgh.

Cureton, E.E. and Mulaik, S.A. (1975), "The Weighted Varimax Rotation and the Promax Rotation," *Psychometrika*, 40, 183–195.

Dziuban, C.D. and Harris, C.W. (1973), "On the Extraction of Components and the Applicability of the Factor Model," *American Educational Research Journal*, 10, 93–99.

Geweke, J.F. and Singleton, K.J. (1980), "Interpreting the Likelihood Ratio Statistic in Factor Models When Sample Size Is Small," *Journal of the American Statistical Association*, 75, 133–137.

Gorsuch, R.L. (1974), *Factor Analysis*, Philadelphia: W.B. Saunders Co.

Gould, S.J. (1981), *The Mismeasure of Man*, New York: W.W. Norton & Co., Inc.

Harman, H.H. (1976), *Modern Factor Analysis*, 3d Edition, Chicago: University of Chicago Press.

Harris, C.W. (1962), "Some Rao-Guttman Relationships," *Psychometrika*, 27, 247–263.

Horn, J.L. and Engstrom, R. (1979), "Cattell's Scree Test in Relation to Bartlett's Chi-Square Test and Other Observations on the Number of Factors Problem," *Multivariate Behavioral Research*, 14, 283–300.

Joreskog, K.G. (1962), "On the Statistical Treatment of Residuals in Factor Analysis," *Psychometrika*, 27, 335–354.

Joreskog, K.G. (1977), "Factor Analysis by Least-Squares and Maximum Likelihood Methods," in *Statistical Methods for Digital Computers*, eds. K. Enslein, A. Ralston, and H.S. Wilf, New York: John Wiley & Sons, Inc.

Kaiser, H.F. (1963), "Image Analysis," in *Problems in Measuring Change*, ed. C.W. Harris, Madison, WI: University of Wisconsin Press.

Kaiser, H.F. (1970), "A Second Generation Little Jiffy," *Psychometrika*, 35, 401–415.

Kaiser, H.F. and Cerny, B.A. (1979), "Factor Analysis of the Image Correlation Matrix," *Educational and Psychological Measurement*, 39, 711–714.

Kaiser, H.F. and Rice, J. (1974), "Little Jiffy, Mark IV," *Educational and Psychological Measurement*, 34, 111–117.

Kerlinger, F.N. and Pedhazur, E.J. (1973), *Multiple Regression in Behavioral Research*, New York: Holt, Rinehart & Winston, Inc.

Kim, J.O. and Mueller, C.W. (1978), *Introduction to Factor Analysis: What It Is and How To Do It*, Sage University Paper Series on Quantitative Applications in the Social Sciences, series no. 07–013, Beverly Hills: Sage Publications.

Lawley, D.N. and Maxwell, A.E. (1971), *Factor Analysis as a Statistical Method*, New York: Macmillan Publishing Co., Inc.

Lee, H.B. and Comrey, A.L. (1979), "Distortions in a Commonly Used Factor Analytic Procedure," *Multivariate Behavioral Research*, 14, 301–321.

Mardia, K.V., Kent, J.T., and Bibby, J.M. (1979), *Multivariate Analysis*, London: Academic Press.

McDonald, R.P. (1975), "A Note on Rippe's Test of Significance in Common Factor Analysis," *Psychometrika*, 40, 117–119.

Morrison, D.F. (1976), *Multivariate Statistical Methods*, 2d Edition, New York: McGraw-Hill Book Co.

Mulaik, S.A. (1972), *The Foundations of Factor Analysis*, New York: McGraw-Hill Book Co.

Rao, C.R. (1955), "Estimation and Tests of Significance in Factor Analysis," *Psychometrika*, 20, 93–111.

Schwarz, G. (1978), "Estimating the Dimension of a Model," *Annals of Statistics*, 6, 461–464.

Spearman, C. (1904), "General Intelligence Objectively Determined and Measured," *American Journal of Psychology*, 15, 201–293.

Tucker, L.R. and Lewis, C. (1973), "A Reliability Coefficient for Maximum Likelihood Factor Analysis," *Psychometrika*, 38, 1–10.

Chapter 18
The FASTCLUS
Procedure

ABSTRACT

The FASTCLUS procedure is designed for disjoint clustering of very large data sets and can find good clusters with only two or three passes over the data. You specify the maximum number of clusters and, optionally, the minimum radius of the clusters. The procedure can produce an output data set containing a cluster membership variable as well as an output data set containing cluster means.

INTRODUCTION

PROC FASTCLUS performs a disjoint cluster analysis on the basis of Euclidean distances computed from one or more quantitative variables. The observations are divided into clusters such that every observation belongs to one and only one cluster (the clusters do not form a tree structure as they do in the CLUSTER procedure). If you want separate analyses for different numbers of clusters, you must run PROC FASTCLUS once for each analysis.

The FASTCLUS procedure is intended for use with large data sets, from approximately 100 to 100,000 observations. With small data sets, the results may be highly sensitive to the order of the observations in the data set.

PROC FASTCLUS prints brief summaries of the clusters it finds. For more extensive examination of the clusters, you can request an output data set containing a cluster membership variable.

Background

The FASTCLUS procedure combines an effective method for finding initial clusters with a standard iterative algorithm for minimizing the sum of squared distances from the cluster means. The result is an efficient procedure for disjoint clustering of large data sets. PROC FASTCLUS was directly inspired by Hartigan's *leader algorithm* (1975) and MacQueen's *k-means algorithm* (1967).

PROC FASTCLUS uses a method that Anderberg (1973) calls *nearest centroid sorting*. A set of points called *cluster seeds* is selected as a first guess of the means of the clusters. Each observation is assigned to the nearest seed to form temporary clusters. The seeds are then replaced by the means of the temporary clusters, and the process is repeated until no further changes occur in the clusters. Similar techniques are described in most references on clustering (Anderberg 1973; Hartigan 1975; Everitt 1980; Spath 1980).

The FASTCLUS procedure differs from other nearest centroid sorting methods in the way the initial cluster seeds are selected. The initialization method of PROC FASTCLUS guarantees that if there exist clusters such that all distances between observations in the same cluster are less than all distances between observations in different clusters, and if you tell PROC FASTCLUS the correct number of clusters to find, then it always finds such a clustering without iterating. Even with clusters that are not as well separated, FASTCLUS usually finds initial seeds that are sufficiently good so that few iterations are required. The importance of initial seed selection is demonstrated by Milligan (1980).

The initialization method used by the FASTCLUS procedure makes it sensitive to outliers. PROC FASTCLUS can be an effective procedure for detecting outliers because outliers often appear as clusters with only one member.

The clustering is done on the basis of Euclidean distances computed from one or more numeric variables. If there are missing values, PROC FASTCLUS computes an adjusted distance using the nonmissing values. Observations that are very close to each other are usually assigned to the same cluster, while observations that are far apart are in different clusters.

The FASTCLUS procedure operates in four steps:

1. Observations called *cluster seeds* are selected.
2. Optionally, temporary clusters are formed by assigning each observation to the cluster with the nearest seed. Each time an observation is assigned, the cluster seed is updated as the current mean of the cluster (DRIFT option).
3. Optionally, clusters are formed by assigning each observation to the nearest seed. After all observations are assigned, the cluster seeds are replaced by the cluster means. This step can be repeated until the changes in the cluster seeds become small or zero (MAXITER=$n \geq 1$).
4. Final clusters are formed by assigning each observation to the nearest seed.

The initial cluster seeds must be observations with no missing values. You can specify the maximum number of seeds (and hence clusters) using the

MAXCLUSTERS= option. You can also specify a minimum distance by which the seeds must be separated using the RADIUS= option.

PROC FASTCLUS always selects the first complete (no missing values) observation as the first seed. The next complete observation that is separated from the first seed by at least the distance specified in the RADIUS= option becomes the second seed. Later observations are selected as new seeds if they are separated from all previous seeds by at least the radius, as long as the maximum number of seeds is not exceeded.

If an observation is complete but fails to qualify as a new seed, PROC FASTCLUS considers using it to replace one of the old seeds. Two tests are made to see if the observation can qualify as a new seed.

First, an old seed is replaced if the distance between the observation and the closest seed is greater than the minimum distance between seeds. The seed that is replaced is selected from the two seeds that are closest to each other. The seed that is replaced is the one of these two that is least distant to the closest of the remaining seeds when the other seed is replaced by the current observation.

If the observation fails the first test for seed replacement, a second test is made. The observation replaces the nearest seed if the smallest distance from the observation to all seeds other than the nearest one is greater than the shortest distance from the nearest seed to all other seeds. If this test is failed, PROC FASTCLUS goes on to the next observation.

You can use the REPLACE= option to limit seed replacement. You can omit the second test for seed replacement (REPLACE=PART), causing PROC FASTCLUS to run faster, but the seeds selected may not be as widely separated as those obtained by the default method. You can also suppress seed replacement entirely by specifying REPLACE=NONE. In this case PROC FASTCLUS runs much faster, but you must choose a good value for the RADIUS= option in order to get good clusters. This method is similar to Hartigan's leader algorithm (1975, 74–78) and the *simple cluster-seeking algorithm* described by Tou and Gonzalez (1974, 90–92).

SPECIFICATIONS

You can use the following statements to invoke the FASTCLUS procedure:

> **PROC FASTCLUS** *options*;
>   **VAR** *variables*;
>   **ID** *variable*;
>   **FREQ** *variable*;
>   **WEIGHT** *variable*;
>   **BY** *variables*;

Usually only the VAR statement is used in addition to the PROC FASTCLUS statement. The BY, FREQ, ID, VAR, and WEIGHT statements are described after the PROC FASTCLUS statement.

PROC FASTCLUS Statement

> PROC FASTCLUS *options*;

Data Set Options

> DATA=*SASdataset*
>   names the input data set containing observations to be clustered. If the DATA= option is omitted, the most recently created SAS data set is used.

SEED=*SASdataset*
:   names an input data set from which initial cluster seeds are to be
    selected. If the SEED= option is not specified, initial seeds are selected
    from the DATA= data set.

MEAN=*SASdataset*
:   names an output data set to contain the cluster means and other
    statistics for each cluster. If you want to create a permanent SAS data
    set, you must specify a two-level name. See "SAS Files" in the *SAS
    Language Guide, Release 6.03 Edition* for more information on permanent
    data sets.

OUT=*SASdataset*
:   names an output data set to contain all the original data, plus the new
    variables CLUSTER and DISTANCE. See "SAS Files" in the *SAS Language
    Guide* for more information on permanent data sets.

CLUSTER=*name*
:   specifies a name for the variable in the MEAN= and OUT= data sets
    that indicates cluster membership. The default name for this variable is
    CLUSTER.

Options for Initial Cluster Seed Selection

The following options control initial cluster seed selection. You must specify
either the RADIUS= or the MAXCLUSTERS= option.

MAXCLUSTERS=*n*
MAXC=*n*
:   specifies the maximum number of clusters allowed. If the
    MAXCLUSTERS= option is omitted, a value of 100 is assumed.

RADIUS=*t*
:   establishes the minimum distance criterion for selecting new seeds. No
    observation is considered as a new seed unless its minimum distance to
    previous seeds exceeds the value given by the RADIUS= option. The
    default value is 0. If REPLACE=RANDOM is specified, the RADIUS=
    option is ignored.

RANDOM=*n*
:   specifies a positive integer as starting value for the pseudo-random
    number generator for use with REPLACE=RANDOM. If the RANDOM=
    option is not specified, the time of day is used to initialize the pseudo-
    random number sequence.

REPLACE=FULL | PART | NONE | RANDOM
:   specifies how seed replacement is performed. REPLACE=FULL requests
    default seed replacement as described above. REPLACE=PART requests
    seed replacement only when the distance between the observation and
    the closest seed is greater than the minimum distance between seeds.
    REPLACE=NONE suppresses seed replacement. REPLACE=RANDOM
    selects a simple pseudo-random sample of complete observations as
    initial cluster seeds.

Options for Final Cluster Seed Computation

The following options for the FASTCLUS statement control computation of final cluster seeds:

CONVERGE=c
CONV=c

> specifies the convergence criterion. Iterations terminate when the maximum distance by which any seed has changed is less than or equal to the minimum distance between initial seeds times the CONVERGE= value. The default is 0.02. Use the CONVERGE= option only if you have specified a MAXITER= value greater than 1.

DELETE=n

> deletes cluster seeds to which n or fewer observations have been assigned. Deletion occurs after processing for the DRIFT option is completed and after each iteration specified by the MAXITER= option. Cluster seeds are not deleted after the final assignment of observations to clusters, so in rare cases a final cluster may not have more than n members. The DELETE= option is ineffective if you specify MAXITER=0 and do not specify DRIFT. By default, no cluster seeds are deleted.

DRIFT

> executes the second of the four steps described in the **Background** section earlier in this chapter. After initial seed selection, each observation is assigned to the cluster with the nearest seed. After an observation is processed, the seed of the cluster to which it was assigned is recalculated as the mean of the observations currently assigned to the cluster. Thus, the cluster seeds drift about rather than remaining fixed for the duration of the pass.

MAXITER=n

> specifies the maximum number of iterations for recomputing cluster seeds. When the value of MAXITER= is greater than 0, PROC FASTCLUS executes the third of the four steps described in the **Background** section earlier in this chapter. In each iteration, each observation is assigned to the nearest seed, and the seeds are recomputed as the means of the clusters. The default value of the MAXITER= option is 1.

STRICT
STRICT=s

> prevents an observation from being assigned to a cluster if its distance to the nearest cluster seed exceeds the value of the STRICT= option. If STRICT is used without a numeric value, the RADIUS= option must be specified and its value is used instead. In the OUT= data set, observations that are not assigned due to the STRICT option are given a negative cluster number, the absolute value of which indicates the cluster with the nearest seed.

Miscellaneous Options

DISTANCE

> requests that distances between the cluster means be printed.

IMPUTE

> requests imputation of missing values in the OUT= data set. If an observation has a missing value for a variable used in the cluster analysis, the missing value is replaced by the corresponding value in the

cluster seed to which the observation is assigned. If the observation is not assigned to a cluster, missing values are not replaced.

LIST
lists all observations, giving the value of the ID variable (if any), the number of the cluster to which the observation is assigned, and the distance between the observation and the final cluster seed.

NOMISS
excludes observations with missing values from the analysis. However, if the IMPUTE option is also specified, observations with missing values are included in the final cluster assignments.

NOPRINT
suppresses all printed output.

SHORT
suppresses printing of the initial cluster seeds, cluster means, and standard deviations.

SUMMARY
suppresses printing of the initial cluster seeds, statistics for variables, cluster means, and standard deviations.

VARDEF=*divisor*
specifies the divisor to be used in the calculation of variances and covariances. Possible values for *divisor* are N, DF, WEIGHT or WGT, and WDF. VARDEF=N requests that the number of observations (n) be used as the divisor. VARDEF=DF requests that the error degrees of freedom, $n-c$, be used, where c is the number of clusters. VARDEF=WEIGHT or WGT requests that the sum of the weights (w) be used. VARDEF=WDF requests that the sum of the weights minus the number of clusters, $w-c$, be used. The default value is DF.

BY Statement

BY *variables*;

A BY statement can be used with PROC FASTCLUS to obtain separate analyses on observations in groups defined by the BY variables. When a BY statement appears, the procedure expects the DATA= data set to be sorted in order of the BY variables.

If your DATA= data set is not sorted in ascending order, use the SORT procedure with a similar BY statement to sort the data, or, if appropriate, use the BY statement options NOTSORTED or DESCENDING. For more information, see the discussion of the BY statement in "SAS Statements Used in the PROC Step" in the *SAS Language Guide*.

If the SEED= option is specified and the SEED= data set does not contain any of the BY variables, then the entire SEED= data set is used to obtain initial cluster seeds for each BY group in the DATA= data set.

If the SEED= data set contains some but not all of the BY variables, or if some BY variables do not have the same type or length in the SEED= data set as in the DATA= data set, then PROC FASTCLUS prints an error message and stops.

If all the BY variables appear in the SEED= data set with the same type and length as in the DATA= data set, then each BY group in the SEED= data set is used to obtain initial cluster seeds for the corresponding BY group in the DATA= data set. The BY groups in the SEED= data set must be in the same order as in the DATA= data set. If NOTSORTED is specified in the BY statement, there must be exactly the same BY groups in the same order in both data sets. If

NOTSORTED is not specified, some BY groups can appear in one data set but not in the other.

FREQ Statement

> FREQ *variable*;

If a variable in your data set represents the frequency of occurrence for the observation, include the name of that variable in a FREQ statement. The procedure then treats the data set as if each observation appears *n* times, where *n* is the value of the FREQ variable. If the value of the FREQ variable is less than 1, the observation is not used in the analysis. Only the integer portion of the value is used. The total number of observations is considered equal to the sum of the FREQ variable when PROC FASTCLUS calculates significance probabilities.

ID Statement

> ID *variable*;

The ID variable, which can be character or numeric, identifies observations on the printout when the LIST option is specified.

VAR Statement

> VAR *variables*;

The VAR statement lists the numeric variables to be used in the cluster analysis. If the VAR statement is omitted, all numeric variables not listed in other statements are used.

WEIGHT Statement

> WEIGHT *variable*;

The values of the WEIGHT variable are used to compute weighted cluster means. The WEIGHT and FREQ statements have a similar effect, except the WEIGHT statement does not alter the degrees of freedom or the number of observations. The WEIGHT variable can take nonintegral values. An observation is used in the analysis only if the value of the WEIGHT variable is greater than zero.

DETAILS

Missing Values

Observations with all missing values are excluded from the analysis. If you specify NOMISS, observations with any missing values are excluded. Observations with missing values cannot be cluster seeds.

The distance between an observation with missing values and a cluster seed is obtained by computing the squared distance based on the nonmissing values, multiplying by the ratio of the number of variables to the number of nonmissing values, and taking the square root:

$$\sqrt{(n/m) \, \Sigma \, (x_i - s_i)^2}$$

where

n = number of variables
m = number of variables with nonmissing values
x_i = value of the ith variable for the observation
s_i = value of the ith variable for the seed

and the summation is taken over variables with nonmissing values.

Output Data Sets

OUT= Data Set

The OUT= data set contains

- the original variables.
- a new variable taking values from 1 to the value specified in the MAXCLUSTERS= option, indicating the cluster to which each observation has been assigned. The variable name is specified by the CLUSTER= option; the default name is CLUSTER.
- a new variable DISTANCE giving the distance from the observation to its cluster seed.

If the IMPUTE option is used, the OUT= data set also contains

- a new variable _IMPUTE_ giving the number of imputed values in each observation.

MEAN= Data Set

The MEAN= data set contains one observation for each cluster. The variables are as follows:

- the BY variables, if any.
- a new variable giving the cluster number. The variable name is specified by the CLUSTER= option. The default name is CLUSTER.
- either the FREQ variable or a new variable called _FREQ_ giving the number of observations in the cluster.
- the WEIGHT variable, if any.
- a new variable _RMSSTD_ giving the root-mean-square standard deviation for the cluster.
- a new variable _RADIUS_ giving the maximum distance between any observation in the cluster and the cluster seed.
- a new variable _GAP_ containing the distance between the current cluster mean and the nearest other cluster mean.
- a new variable _NEAR_ specifying the cluster number of the nearest cluster.
- the VAR variables giving the cluster means.

Computational Resources

Let

n = number of observations
v = number of variables
c = number of clusters
p = number of passes over the data set.

The overall time required by PROC FASTCLUS is roughly proportional to *nvcp* if c is small with respect to n.

Initial seed selection requires one pass over the data set. If the observations are in random order, the time required is roughly proportional to

$$nvc + vc^2$$

unless you specify REPLACE=NONE. In that case, a complete pass may not be necessary, and the time is roughly proportional to mvc, where $c \leq m \leq n$.

The DRIFT option, each iteration, and the final assignment of cluster seeds each require one pass, with time for each pass roughly proportional to nvc.

For greatest efficiency, you should list the variables in the VAR statement in order of decreasing variance.

Usage Notes

Before using PROC FASTCLUS, decide whether your variables should be standardized in some way. If all variables are measured in the same units, standardization may not be necessary. Otherwise, some form of standardization is strongly recommended. The STANDARD procedure can standardize all variables to mean zero and variance one. The FACTOR or PRINCOMP procedures can compute standardized principal component scores. The ACECLUS procedure can transform the variables according to an estimated within-cluster covariance matrix.

The easiest way to use PROC FASTCLUS is to specify the MAXCLUSTERS= and LIST options. It is usually desirable to try several values of the MAXCLUSTERS= option.

PROC FASTCLUS produces relatively little printed output. In most cases you should create an output data set and use other procedures such as PRINT, PLOT, CHART, MEANS, DISCRIM, or CANDISC to study the clusters. Macros are useful for running PROC FASTCLUS repeatedly with other procedures.

A simple application of FASTCLUS with two variables may proceed as follows:

```
proc standard mean=0 std=1 out=stan;
   var v1 v2;
proc fastclus data=stan out=clust maxclusters=2;
   var v1 v2;
proc plot;
   plot v2*v1=cluster;
proc fastclus data=stan out=clust maxclusters=3;
   var v1 v2;
proc plot;
   plot v2*v1=cluster;
```

If you have more than two variables, you can use the CANDISC procedure to compute canonical variables for plotting the clusters, for example,

```
proc standard mean=0 std=1 out=stan;
   var v1-v10;
proc fastclus data=stan out=clust maxclusters=3;
   var v1-v10;
proc candisc out=can;
   var v1-v10;
   class cluster;
proc plot;
   plot can2*can1=cluster;
```

If the data set is not too large, it may also be helpful to use

```
proc sort;
   by cluster distance;
proc print;
   by cluster;
```

to list the clusters. By examining the values of DISTANCE, you can determine if any observations are unusually far from their cluster seeds.

It is often advisable, especially if the data set is large or contains outliers, to make a preliminary FASTCLUS run with a large number of clusters, perhaps 20 to 100. Use MAXITER=0 and MEAN=*SASdataset*. You can save time on subsequent runs by selecting cluster seeds from this output data set using the SEED= option.

You should check the preliminary clusters for outliers, which often appear as clusters with only one member. Use a DATA step to delete outliers from the data set created by the MEAN= option before using it as a SEED= data set in later runs. If there are severe outliers, the subsequent FASTCLUS runs should use the STRICT option to prevent the outliers from distorting the clusters.

The MEAN= data set can be used with the PLOT procedure to plot _GAP_ by _FREQ_. An overlay of _RADIUS_ by _FREQ_ provides a baseline against which to compare the values of _GAP_. Outliers appear in the upper-left area of the plot, with large values of _GAP_ and small _FREQ_ values. Good clusters appear in the upper-right area, with large values of both _GAP_ and _FREQ_. Good potential cluster seeds appear in the lower right, as well as in the upper right, since large _FREQ_ values indicate high-density regions. Small _FREQ_ values in the left part of the plot indicate poor cluster seeds because the points are in low-density regions. It often helps to remove all clusters with small frequencies even though the clusters may not be remote enough to be considered outliers. Removing points in low-density regions improves cluster separation and provides visually sharper cluster outlines in scatter plots.

Printed Output

Unless the SHORT or SUMMARY options are specified, PROC FASTCLUS prints

1. Initial Seeds, cluster seeds selected after one pass through the data
2. Change in Cluster Seeds for each iteration if MAXITER=$n>1$ is specified.

PROC FASTCLUS prints a Cluster Summary, giving the following for each cluster:

3. Cluster number
4. Frequency, the number of observations in the cluster
5. Weight, the sum of the weights of the observations in the cluster, if a WEIGHT statement is specified (not shown)
6. RMS Std Deviation, the root mean square across variables of the cluster standard deviations, which is equal to the root-mean-square distance between observations in the cluster
7. Maximum Distance from Seed to Observation, the maximum distance from the cluster seed to any observation in the cluster
8. Nearest Cluster, the number of the cluster with mean closest to the mean of the current cluster
9. Centroid Distance, the distance between the centroids (means) of the current cluster and the nearest other cluster.

A table of statistics for each variable is printed unless the SUMMARY option is specified. The table contains

10. Total STD, the total standard deviation
11. Within STD, the pooled within-cluster standard deviation
12. R-Squared, the R^2 for predicting the variable from the cluster
13. RSQ/(1−RSQ), the ratio of between-cluster variance to within-cluster variance ($R^2/(1−R^2)$)
14. OVER-ALL, all of the above quantities pooled across variables.

PROC FASTCLUS also prints

15. Pseudo F Statistic, $(R^2/(c−1)) /(1−R^2/(n−c))$, where R^2 is the observed overall R^2, c is the number of clusters, and n is the number of observations. The pseudo F statistic was suggested by Calinski and Harabasz (1974). See Milligan and Cooper (1983) and Cooper and Milligan (1984) regarding the use of the pseudo F statistic in estimating the number of clusters.

If the SUMMARY option is specified, PROC FASTCLUS prints

16. Observed Over-All R-Squared.

PROC FASTCLUS also prints

17. Approximate Expected Over-All R-Squared, the approximate expected value of the overall R^2 under the uniform null hypothesis assuming that the variables are uncorrelated. The value is missing if the number of clusters is greater than one-fifth the number of observations.
18. Cubic Clustering Criterion, computed under the assumption that the variables are uncorrelated. The value is missing if the number of clusters is greater than one-fifth the number of observations.

    If you are interested in the approximate expected R^2 or the cubic clustering criterion but your variables are correlated, you should cluster principal component scores from PROC PRINCOMP. Both of these statistics are described by Sarle (1983). The performance of the cubic clustering criterion in estimating the number of clusters is examined by Milligan and Cooper (1983) and Cooper and Milligan (1984).

Unless the SHORT or SUMMARY option is specified, PROC FASTCLUS prints

19. Cluster Means for each variable
20. Cluster Standard Deviations for each variable.

If the DISTANCE option is specified, PROC FASTCLUS prints

21. Distances Between Cluster Means (not shown).

EXAMPLES

Example 1: Fisher's Iris Data

The iris data published by Fisher (1936) have been widely used for examples in discriminant analysis and cluster analysis. The sepal length, sepal width, petal length, and petal width were measured in millimeters on fifty iris specimens from each of three species, *Iris setosa, I. versicolor,* and *I. virginica.* Mezzich and Solomon (1980) discuss a variety of cluster analyses of the iris data.

In this example the FASTCLUS procedure is used to find two and, then, three clusters. An output data set is created, and PROC FREQ is invoked to compare the clusters with the species classification. See **Output 18.1** and **Output 18.2** for these results. For three clusters, the CANDISC procedure is used to compute canonical variables for plotting the clusters. See **Output 18.3** for the results.

```
data iris;
   title 'Fisher (1936) Iris Data';
   input sepallen sepalwid petallen petalwid spec_no @@;
   if spec_no=1 then species='Setosa     ';
   else if spec_no=2 then species='Versicolor';
   else species='Virginica ';
   label sepallen='Sepal length in mm.'
         sepalwid='Sepal width  in mm.'
         petallen='Petal length in mm.'
         petalwid='Petal width  in mm.';
   cards;
50 33 14 02 1 64 28 56 22 3 65 28 46 15 2
67 31 56 24 3 63 28 51 15 3 46 34 14 03 1
69 31 51 23 3 62 22 45 15 2 59 32 48 18 2
46 36 10 02 1 61 30 46 14 2 60 27 51 16 2
65 30 52 20 3 56 25 39 11 2 65 30 55 18 3
58 27 51 19 3 68 32 59 23 3 51 33 17 05 1
57 28 45 13 2 62 34 54 23 3 77 38 67 22 3
63 33 47 16 2 67 33 57 25 3 76 30 66 21 3
49 25 45 17 3 55 35 13 02 1 67 30 52 23 3
70 32 47 14 2 64 32 45 15 2 61 28 40 13 2
48 31 16 02 1 59 30 51 18 3 55 24 38 11 2
63 25 50 19 3 64 32 53 23 3 52 34 14 02 1
49 36 14 01 1 54 30 45 15 2 79 38 64 20 3
44 32 13 02 1 67 33 57 21 3 50 35 16 06 1
58 26 40 12 2 44 30 13 02 1 77 28 67 20 3
63 27 49 18 3 47 32 16 02 1 55 26 44 12 2
50 23 33 10 2 72 32 60 18 3 48 30 14 03 1
51 38 16 02 1 61 30 49 18 3 48 34 19 02 1
50 30 16 02 1 50 32 12 02 1 61 26 56 14 3
64 28 56 21 3 43 30 11 01 1 58 40 12 02 1
51 38 19 04 1 67 31 44 14 2 62 28 48 18 3
49 30 14 02 1 51 35 14 02 1 56 30 45 15 2
58 27 41 10 2 50 34 16 04 1 46 32 14 02 1
60 29 45 15 2 57 26 35 10 2 57 44 15 04 1
50 36 14 02 1 77 30 61 23 3 63 34 56 24 3
58 27 51 19 3 57 29 42 13 2 72 30 58 16 3
54 34 15 04 1 52 41 15 01 1 71 30 59 21 3
64 31 55 18 3 60 30 48 18 3 63 29 56 18 3
49 24 33 10 2 56 27 42 13 2 57 30 42 12 2
55 42 14 02 1 49 31 15 02 1 77 26 69 23 3
60 22 50 15 3 54 39 17 04 1 66 29 46 13 2
52 27 39 14 2 60 34 45 16 2 50 34 15 02 1
44 29 14 02 1 50 20 35 10 2 55 24 37 10 2
58 27 39 12 2 47 32 13 02 1 46 31 15 02 1
69 32 57 23 3 62 29 43 13 2 74 28 61 19 3
59 30 42 15 2 51 34 15 02 1 50 35 13 03 1
56 28 49 20 3 60 22 40 10 2 73 29 63 18 3
67 25 58 18 3 49 31 15 01 1 67 31 47 15 2
63 23 44 13 2 54 37 15 02 1 56 30 41 13 2
63 25 49 15 2 61 28 47 12 2 64 29 43 13 2
```

```
51 25 30 11 2 57 28 41 13 2 65 30 58 22 3
69 31 54 21 3 54 39 13 04 1 51 35 14 03 1
72 36 61 25 3 65 32 51 20 3 61 29 47 14 2
56 29 36 13 2 69 31 49 15 2 64 27 53 19 3
68 30 55 21 3 55 25 40 13 2 48 34 16 02 1
48 30 14 01 1 45 23 13 03 1 57 25 50 20 3
57 38 17 03 1 51 38 15 03 1 55 23 40 13 2
66 30 44 14 2 68 28 48 14 2 54 34 17 02 1
51 37 15 04 1 52 35 15 02 1 58 28 51 24 3
67 30 50 17 2 63 33 60 25 3 53 37 15 02 1
;

proc fastclus data=iris maxc=2 maxiter=10 out=clus;
   var sepallen sepalwid petallen petalwid;
proc freq;
   tables cluster*species;
run;

proc fastclus data=iris maxc=3 maxiter=10 out=clus;
   var sepallen sepalwid petallen petalwid;
proc freq;
   tables cluster*species;
run;

proc candisc anova out=can;
   class cluster;
   var sepallen sepalwid petallen petalwid;
   title2 'Canonical Discriminant Analysis of Iris Clusters';
proc plot;
   plot can2*can1=cluster;
   title2 'Plot of Canonical Variables Identified by Cluster';
run;
```

Output 18.1   Fisher's Iris Data: PROC FASTCLUS with MAXC=2 and PROC FREQ

```
                        Fisher (1936) Iris Data                           1

                          FASTCLUS Procedure

         Replace=FULL  Radius=0  Maxclusters=2   Maxiter=10  Converge=0.02

                          ❶ Initial Seeds

         Cluster    SEPALLEN      SEPALWID      PETALLEN      PETALWID
         ---------------------------------------------------------------
            1        43.0000       30.0000       11.0000        1.0000
            2        77.0000       26.0000       69.0000       23.0000

               Minimum Distance Between Seeds = 70.85196
```

Fisher (1936) Iris Data   2

Iteration   Change in Cluster Seeds ②
                              1   2
----
         1   13.49301   22.41357
         2   4.22265   1.869944
         3   1.235213   0.542766

Cluster Summary

③ Cluster	④ Frequency	⑥ RMS Std Deviation	⑦ Maximum Distance from Seed to Observation	⑧ Nearest Cluster	⑨ Centroid Distance
1	53	3.7050	21.1621	2	39.2879
2	97	5.6779	24.6430	1	39.2879

Statistics for Variables

Variable	⑩ Total STD	⑪ Within STD	⑫ R-Squared	⑬ RSQ/(1-RSQ)
SEPALLEN	8.280661	5.493128	0.562896	1.287784
SEPALWID	4.358663	3.703931	0.282710	0.394137
PETALLEN	17.652982	6.803310	0.852470	5.778291
PETALWID	7.622377	3.572004	0.781868	3.584390
⑭ OVER-ALL	10.692237	5.072913	0.776410	3.472463

Pseudo F Statistic =   513.92 ⑮
Approximate Expected Over-All R-Squared =   0.51539 ⑰
Cubic Clustering Criterion =   14.806 ⑱
WARNING: The two above values are invalid for correlated variables.

⑲ Cluster Means

Cluster	SEPALLEN	SEPALWID	PETALLEN	PETALWID
1	50.0566	33.6981	15.6038	2.9057
2	63.0103	28.8660	49.5876	16.9588

⑳ Cluster Standard Deviations

Cluster	SEPALLEN	SEPALWID	PETALLEN	PETALWID
1	3.42735	4.39661	4.40428	2.10553
2	6.33689	3.26799	7.80058	4.15561

Fisher (1936) Iris Data   3

TABLE OF CLUSTER BY SPECIES

CLUSTER   SPECIES

Frequency / Percent / Row Pct / Col Pct	Setosa	Versicolor	Virginica	Total
1	50	3	0	53
	33.33	2.00	0.00	35.33
	94.34	5.66	0.00	
	100.00	6.00	0.00	
2	0	47	50	97
	0.00	31.33	33.33	64.67
	0.00	48.45	51.55	
	0.00	94.00	100.00	
Total	50	50	50	150
	33.33	33.33	33.33	100.00

Output 18.2 Fisher's Iris Data: PROC FASTCLUS with MAXC=3 and PROC
FREQ

```
                          Fisher (1936) Iris Data                           4

                            FASTCLUS Procedure

            Replace=FULL  Radius=0  Maxclusters=3   Maxiter=10  Converge=0.02


                              Initial Seeds

            Cluster     SEPALLEN     SEPALWID      PETALLEN      PETALWID
            ---------------------------------------------------------------
               1        58.0000      40.0000       12.0000        2.0000
               2        77.0000      38.0000       67.0000       22.0000
               3        49.0000      25.0000       45.0000       17.0000


              Minimum Distance Between Seeds = 38.23611
```

```
                          Fisher (1936) Iris Data                           5

               Iteration   Change in Cluster Seeds
                                      1          2          3
               ----------------------------------------------------
                   1      10.14091   12.25656   11.41484
                   2            0    1.753477   1.212276
                   3            0    0.69766    0.473303


                            Cluster Summary

                            RMS Std    Maximum Distance from    Nearest    Centroid
   Cluster    Frequency    Deviation    Seed to Observation     Cluster    Distance
   ----------------------------------------------------------------------------------
      1          50         2.7803          12.4803                3       33.5693
      2          38         4.0168          14.9736                3       17.9718
      3          62         4.0398          16.9272                2       17.9718


                         Statistics for Variables

        Variable     Total STD     Within STD     R-Squared     RSQ/(1-RSQ)
        -----------------------------------------------------------------------
        SEPALLEN      8.280661      4.394883       0.722096       2.598359
        SEPALWID      4.358663      3.248163       0.452102       0.825156
        PETALLEN     17.652982      4.214314       0.943773      16.784895
        PETALWID      7.622377      2.452436       0.897872       8.791618
        OVER-ALL     10.692237      3.661982       0.884275       7.641194

                        Pseudo F Statistic =    561.63
             Approximate Expected Over-All R-Squared =   0.62728
                        Cubic Clustering Criterion =    25.021
             WARNING: The two above values are invalid for correlated variables.


                              Cluster Means

            Cluster     SEPALLEN     SEPALWID      PETALLEN      PETALWID
            ---------------------------------------------------------------
               1        50.0600      34.2800       14.6200        2.4600
               2        68.5000      30.7368       57.4211       20.7105
               3        59.0161      27.4839       43.9355       14.3387


                        Cluster Standard Deviations

            Cluster     SEPALLEN     SEPALWID      PETALLEN      PETALWID
            ---------------------------------------------------------------
               1         3.52490      3.79064       1.73664       1.05386
               2         4.94155      2.90092       4.88590       2.79872
               3         4.66410      2.96284       5.08895       2.97500
```

```
                          Fisher (1936) Iris Data                              6
                        TABLE OF CLUSTER BY SPECIES

         CLUSTER    SPECIES

         Frequency|
         Percent  |
         Row Pct  |
         Col Pct  |Setosa  |Versicol|Virginic|
                  |        |or      |la      |  Total
         ---------+--------+--------+--------+
               1  |     50 |      0 |      0 |     50
                  |  33.33 |   0.00 |   0.00 |  33.33
                  | 100.00 |   0.00 |   0.00 |
                  | 100.00 |   0.00 |   0.00 |
         ---------+--------+--------+--------+
               2  |      0 |      2 |     36 |     38
                  |   0.00 |   1.33 |  24.00 |  25.33
                  |   0.00 |   5.26 |  94.74 |
                  |   0.00 |   4.00 |  72.00 |
         ---------+--------+--------+--------+
               3  |      0 |     48 |     14 |     62
                  |   0.00 |  32.00 |   9.33 |  41.33
                  |   0.00 |  77.42 |  22.58 |
                  |   0.00 |  96.00 |  28.00 |
         ---------+--------+--------+--------+
         Total          50       50       50      150
                     33.33    33.33    33.33   100.00
```

Output 18.3   Fisher's Iris Data: PROC CANDISC and PROC PLOT

```
                          Fisher (1936) Iris Data                              7
                Canonical Discriminant Analysis of Iris Clusters

                        CANONICAL DISCRIMINANT ANALYSIS

         150 Observations          149 DF Total
           4 Variables             147 DF Within Classes
           3 Classes                 2 DF Between Classes


                          Class Level Information

           CLUSTER      Frequency         Weight      Proportion

                 1             50        50.0000        0.333333
                 2             38        38.0000        0.253333
                 3             62        62.0000        0.413333
```

```
                          Fisher (1936) Iris Data                              8
                Canonical Discriminant Analysis of Iris Clusters

                        CANONICAL DISCRIMINANT ANALYSIS

                          Univariate Test Statistics

                   F Statistics,    Num DF= 2   Den DF= 147

              Total      Pooled    Between              RSQ/
Variable       STD         STD        STD    R-Squared  (1-RSQ)        F      Pr > F   Label

SEPALLEN     8.2807      4.3949     8.5893    0.722096   2.5984   190.9794    0.0001   Sepal length in mm.
SEPALWID     4.3587      3.2482     3.5774    0.452102   0.8252    60.6490    0.0001   Sepal width  in mm.
PETALLEN    17.6530      4.2143    20.9336    0.943773  16.7849  1233.6898    0.0001   Petal length in mm.
PETALWID     7.6224      2.4524     8.8164    0.897872   8.7916   646.1839    0.0001   Petal width  in mm.

             Average R-Squared:  Unweighted = 0.7539604        Weighted by Variance = 0.8842753
```

(continued on next page)

(continued from previous page)

Multivariate Statistics and F Approximations

S=2   M=0.5   N=71

Statistic	Value	F	Num DF	Den DF	Pr > F
Wilks' Lambda	0.03222337	164.5474	8	288	0.0001
Pillai's Trace	1.25669612	61.2875	8	290	0.0001
Hotelling-Lawley Trace	21.06722883	376.5767	8	286	0.0001
Roy's Greatest Root	20.63266809	747.9342	4	145	0.0001

NOTE: F Statistic for Roy's Greatest Root is an upper bound.
NOTE: F Statistic for Wilks' Lambda is exact.

Fisher (1936) Iris Data
Canonical Discriminant Analysis of Iris Clusters   9

CANONICAL DISCRIMINANT ANALYSIS

	Canonical Correlation	Adjusted Canonical Correlation	Approx Standard Error	Squared Canonical Correlation	Eigenvalue	Difference	Proportion	Cumulative
					Eigenvalues of INV(E)*H = CanRsq/(1-CanRsq)			
1	0.976613	0.976123	0.003787	0.953774	20.6327	20.1981	0.9794	0.9794
2	0.550384	0.543354	0.057107	0.302923	0.4346	.	0.0206	1.0000

Test of HO: The canonical correlations in the current row and all that follow are zero

	Likelihood Ratio	Approx F	Num DF	Den DF	Pr > F
1	0.03222337	164.5474	8	288	0.0001
2	0.69707749	21.0038	3	145	0.0001

Total Canonical Structure

	CAN1	CAN2	
SEPALLEN	0.831965	0.452137	Sepal length in mm.
SEPALWID	-0.515082	0.810630	Sepal width in mm.
PETALLEN	0.993520	0.087514	Petal length in mm.
PETALWID	0.966325	0.154745	Petal width in mm.

Between Canonical Structure

	CAN1	CAN2	
SEPALLEN	0.956160	0.292846	Sepal length in mm.
SEPALWID	-0.748136	0.663545	Sepal width in mm.
PETALLEN	0.998770	0.049580	Petal length in mm.
PETALWID	0.995952	0.089883	Petal width in mm.

Pooled Within Canonical Structure

	CAN1	CAN2	
SEPALLEN	0.339314	0.716082	Sepal length in mm.
SEPALWID	-0.149614	0.914351	Sepal width in mm.
PETALLEN	0.900839	0.308136	Petal length in mm.
PETALWID	0.650123	0.404282	Petal width in mm.

Standardized Canonical Coefficients

	CAN1	CAN2	
SEPALLEN	0.047747341	1.021487262	Sepal length in mm.
SEPALWID	-0.577569244	0.864455153	Sepal width in mm.
PETALLEN	3.341309573	-1.283043758	Petal length in mm.
PETALWID	0.996451144	0.900476563	Petal width in mm.

Fisher (1936) Iris Data
Canonical Discriminant Analysis of Iris Clusters   10

CANONICAL DISCRIMINANT ANALYSIS

Raw Canonical Coefficients

	CAN1	CAN2	
SEPALLEN	0.0057661265	0.1233581748	Sepal length in mm.
SEPALWID	-.1325106494	0.1983303556	Sepal width in mm.
PETALLEN	0.1892773419	-.0726814163	Petal length in mm.
PETALWID	0.1307270927	0.1181359305	Petal width in mm.

Class Means on Canonical Variables

CLUSTER	CAN1	CAN2
1	-6.131527227	0.244761516
2	4.931414018	0.861972277
3	1.922300462	-0.725693908

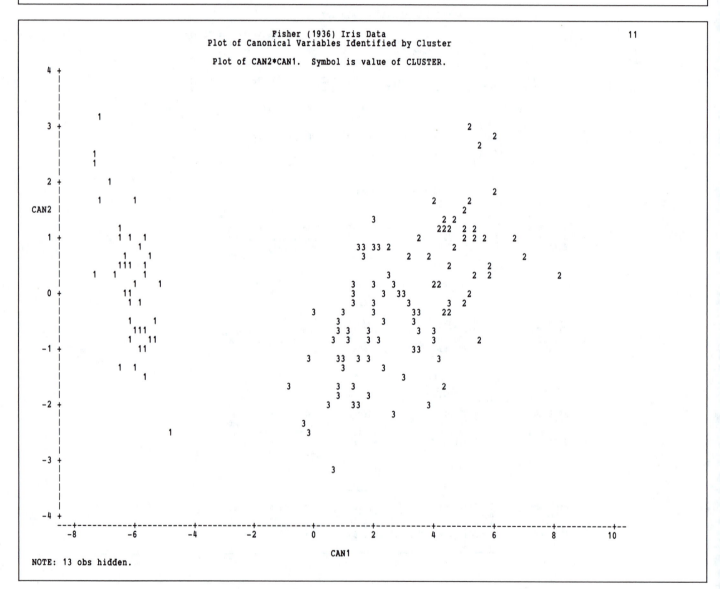

Fisher (1936) Iris Data
Plot of Canonical Variables Identified by Cluster   11

Plot of CAN2*CAN1. Symbol is value of CLUSTER.

NOTE: 13 obs hidden.

Example 2: Outliers

The second example involves data artificially generated to contain two clusters
and several severe outliers. A preliminary analysis specifies twenty clusters and
outputs a MEAN= data set to be used for a diagnostic plot. The exact number
of initial clusters is not important; similar results could be obtained with ten or
fifty initial clusters. Examination of the plot suggests that clusters with more than
five (again, the exact number is not important) observations may yield good seeds
for the main analysis. A DATA step deletes clusters with five or fewer observations, and the remaining cluster means provide seeds for the next FASTCLUS
analysis. Two clusters are requested, and the STRICT= option is specified to prevent outliers from distorting the results. The STRICT= value is chosen to be close
to the _GAP_ and _RADIUS_ values of the larger clusters in the diagnostic plot;
the exact value is not critical. A final FASTCLUS run assigns the outliers to clusters.
The results are shown in **Output 18.4** through **Output 18.6**.

```
*------------------------------------------------------------------+
|        Create artificial data set with two clusters              |
|        and some outliers.                                        |
+------------------------------------------------------------------;

   title 'Using FASTCLUS to Analyze Data with Outliers';
   data x;
      drop n;
      do n=1 to 100;
         x=rannor(12345)+2;
         y=rannor(12345);
         output;
         end;
      do n=1 to 100;
         x=rannor(12345)-2;
         y=rannor(12345);
         output;
         end;
      do n=1 to 10;
         x=10*rannor(12345);
         y=10*rannor(12345);
         output;
         end;
   run;


*------------------------------------------------------------------+
|        Run FASTCLUS with many clusters and MEAN= output data set  |
|        for diagnostic plot.                                      |
+------------------------------------------------------------------;

   title2 'Preliminary FASTCLUS Analysis with 20 Clusters';
   proc fastclus data=x mean=mean1 maxc=20 maxiter=0 summary;
      var x y;
   proc plot data=mean1;
      plot _gap_*_freq_='G' _radius_*_freq_='R' / overlay;
   run;
```

```
*----------------------------------------------------------------+
|        Remove low-frequency clusters.                          |
+----------------------------------------------------------------;

data seed;
   set mean1;
   if _freq_>5;
run;
```

Output 18.4   Preliminary Analysis of Data with Outliers: PROC FASTCLUS
and PROC PLOT

```
                 Using FASTCLUS to Analyze Data with Outliers                1
                 Preliminary FASTCLUS Analysis with 20 Clusters

                            FASTCLUS Procedure

                 Replace=FULL   Radius=0   Maxclusters=20    Maxiter=0


                              Cluster Summary

                      RMS Std    Maximum Distance from    Nearest    Centroid
   Cluster  Frequency Deviation   Seed to Observation     Cluster    Distance
   ----------------------------------------------------------------------------
      1          8     0.4753          1.1924                19       1.7205
      2          1       .                  0                6        6.2847
      3         44     0.6252          1.6774                5        1.4386
      4          1       .                  0                20       5.2130
      5         38     0.5603          1.4528                3        1.4386
      6          2     0.0542          0.1085                2        6.2847
      7          1       .                  0                14       2.5094
      8          2     0.6480          1.2961                1        1.8450
      9          1       .                  0                7        9.4534
     10          1       .                  0                18       4.2514
     11          1       .                  0                16       4.7582
     12         20     0.5911          1.6291                16       1.5601
     13          5     0.6682          1.4244                3        1.9553
     14          1       .                  0                7        2.5094
     15          5     0.4074          1.2678                3        1.7609
     16         22     0.4168          1.5139                19       1.4936
     17          8     0.4031          1.4794                5        1.5564
     18          1       .                  0                10       4.2514
     19         45     0.6475          1.6285                16       1.4936
     20          3     0.5719          1.3642                15       1.8999
                        Pseudo F Statistic =     207.58
                 Observed Over-All R-Squared =   0.95404  ⓰
     Approximate Expected Over-All R-Squared =   0.96103
                 Cubic Clustering Criterion =    -2.503
         WARNING: The two above values are invalid for correlated variables.
```

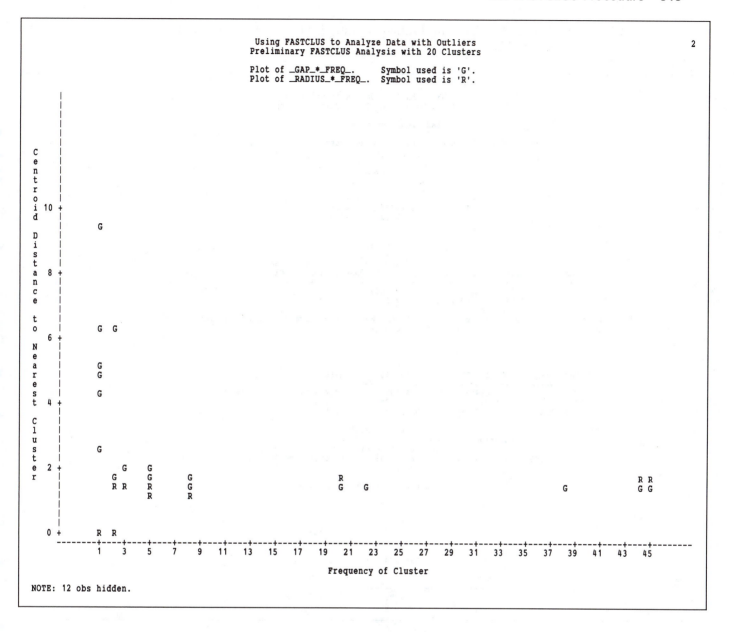

Using FASTCLUS to Analyze Data with Outliers
Preliminary FASTCLUS Analysis with 20 Clusters

Plot of _GAP_*_FREQ_.   Symbol used is 'G'.
Plot of _RADIUS_*_FREQ_. Symbol used is 'R'.

NOTE: 12 obs hidden.

```
*-------------------------------------------------------------------+
|      Run FASTCLUS again, selecting seeds from the                 |
|      high-frequency clusters in the previous analysis.            |
|      STRICT= prevents outliers from distorting the results.       |
+-------------------------------------------------------------------;

title2 'FASTCLUS Analysis Using STRICT= to Omit Outliers';
proc fastclus data=x seed=seed
    maxc=2 strict=3.0 out=out mean=mean2;
  var x y;
proc plot data=out;
  plot y*x=cluster;
run;
```

Output 18.5   Cluster Analysis with Outliers Omitted: PROC FASTCLUS and
PROC PLOT

```
                  Using FASTCLUS to Analyze Data with Outliers                    1
                  FASTCLUS Analysis Using STRICT= to Omit Outliers

                              FASTCLUS Procedure

            Replace=FULL  Radius=0  Strict=3  Maxclusters=2   Maxiter=1


                                Initial Seeds

                    Cluster          X             Y
                    -------------------------------------
                       1          2.79417      -0.06597
                       2         -2.02730      -2.05121


                               Cluster Summary

                          RMS Std   Maximum Distance from   Nearest   Centroid
          Cluster  Frequency  Deviation  Seed to Observation   Cluster   Distance
          ---------------------------------------------------------------------
             1        99       0.9501          2.9589            2        3.7666
             2        99       0.9290          2.8011            1        3.7666

      12 Observation(s) were not assigned to a cluster because the minimum distance to a cluster seed
                              exceeded the STRICT= value.


                            Statistics for Variables

          Variable     Total STD    Within STD    R-Squared    RSQ/(1-RSQ)
          ---------------------------------------------------------------------
          X            2.068537      0.870977      0.823609      4.669219
          Y            1.021128      1.003520      0.039093      0.040683
          OVER-ALL     1.631188      0.939589      0.669891      2.029303

                        Pseudo F Statistic =    397.74
               Approximate Expected Over-All R-Squared =  0.60615
                        Cubic Clustering Criterion =    3.197
              WARNING: The two above values are invalid for correlated variables.


                               Cluster Means

                    Cluster          X             Y
                    -------------------------------------
                       1          1.82511       0.14121
                       2         -1.91991      -0.26156


                          Cluster Standard Deviations

                    Cluster          X             Y
                    -------------------------------------
                       1          0.88955       1.00697
                       2          0.85200       1.00006
```

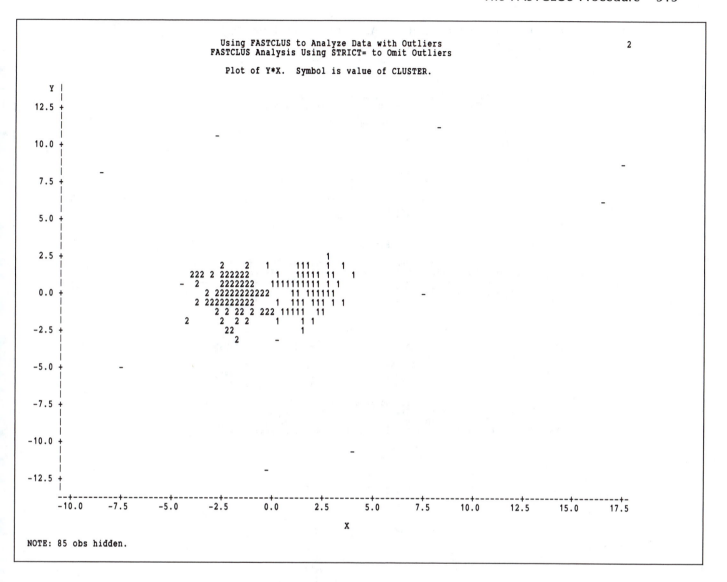

Using FASTCLUS to Analyze Data with Outliers
FASTCLUS Analysis Using STRICT= to Omit Outliers

Plot of Y*X.   Symbol is value of CLUSTER.

NOTE: 85 obs hidden.

```
*--------------------------------------------------------------------+
|        Run FASTCLUS one more time with zero iterations             |
|        to assign outliers and tails to clusters.                   |
+--------------------------------------------------------------------;


    title2 'Final FASTCLUS Analysis Assigning Outliers to Clusters';
    proc fastclus data=x seed=mean2 maxc=2 maxiter=0 out=out;
       var x y;
    proc plot data=out;
       plot y*x=cluster;
    run;
```

Output 18.6   Final Analysis with Outliers Assigned to Clusters: PROC
FASTCLUS and PROC PLOT

```
                      Using FASTCLUS to Analyze Data with Outliers
                   Final FASTCLUS Analysis Assigning Outliers to Clusters

                                 FASTCLUS Procedure

                  Replace=FULL   Radius=0   Maxclusters=2   Maxiter=0


                                   Initial Seeds

                          Cluster          X             Y
                          --------------------------------------
                             1          1.82511       0.14121
                             2         -1.91991      -0.26156


                                  Cluster Summary

                            RMS Std    Maximum Distance from   Nearest   Centroid
         Cluster   Frequency  Deviation   Seed to Observation   Cluster   Distance
         --------------------------------------------------------------------------
            1        103       2.2569        17.9426               2       4.3753
            2        107       1.8371        11.7362               1       4.3753


                               Statistics for Variables

          Variable    Total STD    Within STD    R-Squared    RSQ/(1-RSQ)
          --------------------------------------------------------------------
          X           2.927212     1.955291      0.555950      1.252000
          Y           2.152484     2.147544      0.009347      0.009435
          OVER-ALL    2.569218     2.053669      0.364119      0.572621

                            Pseudo F Statistic =    119.11
                  Approximate Expected Over-All R-Squared =  0.49090
                           Cubic Clustering Criterion =   -5.338
                WARNING: The two above values are invalid for correlated variables.


                                   Cluster Means

                          Cluster          X             Y
                          --------------------------------------
                             1          2.28002       0.26394
                             2         -2.07555      -0.15135


                             Cluster Standard Deviations

                          Cluster          X             Y
                          --------------------------------------
                             1          2.41226       2.08992
                             2          1.37936       2.20157
```

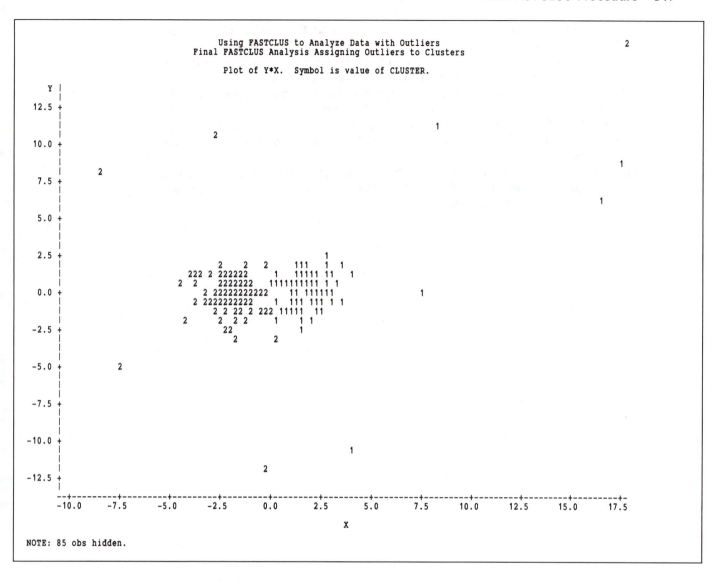

NOTE: 85 obs hidden.

REFERENCES

Anderberg, M.R. (1973), *Cluster Analysis for Applications*, New York: Academic Press, Inc.

Calinski, T. and Harabasz, J. (1974), "A Dendrite Method for Cluster Analysis," *Communications in Statistics*, 3, 1–27.

Cooper, M.C. and Milligan, G.W. (1984), "The Effect of Error on Determining the Number of Clusters," *College of Administrative Science Working Paper Series 84-2*, Columbus, OH: Ohio State University.

Everitt, B.S. (1980), *Cluster Analysis*, Second Edition, London: Heineman Educational Books Ltd.

Fisher, R.A. (1936), "The Use of Multiple Measurements in Taxonomic Problems," *Annals of Eugenics*, 7, 179–188.

Hartigan, J.A. (1975), *Clustering Algorithms*, New York: John Wiley & Sons, Inc.

MacQueen, J.B. (1967), "Some Methods for Classification and Analysis of Multivariate Observations," *Proceedings of the Fifth Berkeley Symposium on Mathematical Statistics and Probability*, 1, 281–297.

Mezzich, J.E and Solomon, H. (1980), *Taxonomy and Behavioral Science*, New York: Academic Press, Inc.

Milligan, G.W. (1980), "An Examination of the Effect of Six Types of Error Perturbation on Fifteen Clustering Algorithms," *Psychometrika*, 45, 325–342.

Milligan, G.W. and Cooper, M.C. (1983), "An Examination of Procedures for Determining the Number of Clusters in a Data Set," *College of Administrative Science Working Paper Series 83–51*, Columbus, OH: Ohio State University.

Sarle, W.S. (1983), "The Cubic Clustering Criterion," SAS Technical Report A-108, Cary, NC: SAS Institute Inc.

Spath, H. (1980), *Cluster Analysis Algorithms*, Chichester, England: Ellis Horwood.

Tou, J.T. and Gonzalez, R.C. (1974), *Pattern Recognition Principles*, Reading, MA: The Addison-Wesley Publishing Co.

ABSTRACT

The FREQ procedure produces one-way to *n*-way frequency and crosstabulation tables. For two-way tables, PROC FREQ computes tests and measures of association. For *n*-way tables, PROC FREQ does stratified analysis, computing statistics within, as well as across, strata. Frequencies can also be output to a SAS data set.

INTRODUCTION

Frequency tables show the distribution of variable values. For example, if a variable A has six possible values, a frequency table for A shows how many observations in the data set have the first value of A, how many have the second value, and so on.

Crosstabulation tables show combined frequency distributions for two or more variables. For example, a crosstabulation table for the variables SEX and EMPLOY shows the number of working females, the number of nonworking females, the number of working males, and the number of nonworking males.

One-Way Frequency Tables

If you want a one-way frequency table for a variable, simply name the variable in a TABLES statement. For example, the statements

```
proc freq;
   tables a;
```

produce a one-way frequency table giving the values of A and the frequency of each value.

Two-Way Crosstabulation Tables

If you want a crosstabulation table for two variables, give their names separated by an asterisk. Values of the first variable form the rows of the table, and values of the second variable form the columns. For example, the statements

```
proc freq;
   tables a*b;
```

produce a crosstabulation table with values of A down the side and values of B across the top.

For some pairs of variables, you may want information about the existence or the strength of any association between the variables or both. With respect to the existence of an association, PROC FREQ computes statistics that test the null hypothesis of no association. With respect to the strength of an association, PROC FREQ computes measures of association that tend to be close to zero when there is no association and close to the maximum (or minimum) value when there is perfect association. You can request the computation and printing of these statistics by specifying one or more options in the TABLES statement. For information on specific statistics computed by PROC FREQ, see **Tests and Measures of Association** later in this chapter.

In choosing measures of association to use in analyzing a two-way table, you should consider the study design (which indicates whether the row and column variables are dependent or independent), the measurement scale of the variables (nominal, ordinal, or interval), the type of association that each measure is designed to detect, and any assumptions required for valid interpretation of a measure. You should exercise care in selecting measures that are appropriate for your data. For more information to guide you in choosing measures of association for a specific set of data, see Hayes (1963) and Garson (1971). For an advanced treatment, refer to Goodman and Kruskal (1979) or Bishop, Fienberg, and Holland (1975, Chapter 11).

Similar comments apply to the choice and interpretation of the test statistics. For example, the Mantel-Haenszel chi-square statistic requires an ordinal scale for both variables and is designed to detect a linear association. The Pearson chi-square, on the other hand, is appropriate for all variables and can detect any kind of association, but it is less powerful for detecting a linear association because its power is dispersed over a greater number of degrees of freedom (except for 2×2 tables).

N-Way Crosstabulation Tables

If you want a three-way (or *n*-way) crosstabulation table, give the three (or *n*) variable names separated by asterisks in the TABLES statement. Values of the last variable form the columns of a contingency table; values of the next-to-last variable form the rows. Each level (or combination of levels) of the other variables form one stratum, and a separate contingency table is produced for each stratum. For example, the statements

```
proc freq;
    tables a*b*c*d / cmh;
```

produce *k* tables, where *k* is the number of different combinations of values for the variables A and B. Each table has the values of C down the side and the values of D across the top.

The CMH option in the TABLES statement gives a stratified statistical analysis of the relationship between C and D, after controlling for A and B. The stratified analysis provides a convenient way to adjust for the possible confounding effects of A and B without being forced to estimate parameters for them. The analysis produces Cochran-Mantel-Haenszel statistics, and for 2×2 tables, it includes estimation of the common relative risk (case-control and cohort studies) and Breslow's test for homogeneity of the odds ratios. See the **Summary Statistics** section for details of the stratified analysis.

Note: multi-way tables can generate a great deal of printed output. For example, if the variables A, B, C, D, and E each have ten levels, five-way tables of A*B*C*D*E could generate 4000 or more pages of output.

PROC FREQ Contrasted with Other SAS Procedures

Many other SAS procedures can collect frequency counts. PROC FREQ is distinguished by its ability to compute chi-square tests and measures of association for two-way and *n*-way tables. Other procedures to consider for counting are the following: PROC TABULATE for more general table layouts, PROC SUMMARY for output data sets, and PROC CHART for bar charts and other graphical representations. The FREQ option in PROC UNIVARIATE provides one-way frequency tables. PROC CATMOD can be used for general linear model analysis of categorical data.

SPECIFICATIONS

The statements available in PROC FREQ are

PROC FREQ *options*;
   TABLES *requests* / *options*;
   WEIGHT *variable*;
   BY *variables*;

Usually, only the TABLES statement is needed in addition to the PROC FREQ statement. The BY, TABLES, and WEIGHT statements are described after the PROC FREQ statement.

PROC FREQ Statement

   PROC FREQ *options*;

You can use the following options in the PROC FREQ statement:

DATA=*SASdataset*
   specifies the data set to be used by PROC FREQ. If the DATA= option is omitted, FREQ uses the most recently created data set.

FORMCHAR(1,2,7)='*string*'
   defines the characters to be used for constructing the outlines and dividers for the cells of contingency tables. The string should be three characters long. The characters are used to denote (1) vertical divider, (2) horizontal divider, and (3) vertical-horizontal intersection. Any character or hexadecimal string can be used to customize table appearance. Specifying FORMCHAR(1,2,7)='   ' (3 blanks) produces tables with no outlines or dividers. If you do not specify the FORMCHAR option, FREQ uses the default FORMCHAR(1,2,7)='| − +'. See the CALENDAR and TABULATE procedures in the *SAS Procedures Guide, Release 6.03 Edition* for further information.

ORDER=FREQ
ORDER=DATA
ORDER=INTERNAL
ORDER=FORMATTED
   specifies the order in which the variable levels are to be reported. If ORDER=FREQ, levels are ordered by descending frequency count so that the levels with the largest frequencies come first. If ORDER=DATA, levels are put in the order in which they first occur in the input data, provided they have nonzero weights. If ORDER=INTERNAL, then the levels are ordered by the internal value. If ORDER=FORMATTED, levels are ordered by the external formatted value. If you omit the ORDER= option PROC FREQ orders by the internal value. The ORDER= option does not apply to missing values, which are always ordered first.

PAGE
  request that FREQ print only one table per page. Otherwise, FREQ prints multiple tables per page as space permits.

BY Statement

  BY *variables*;

A BY statement can be used with PROC FREQ to obtain separate analyses for the groups defined by the BY variables. When a BY statement appears, the procedure expects the input data set to be sorted in order of the BY variables.

  If your input data set is not sorted in ascending order, use the SORT procedure with a similar BY statement to sort the data, or, if appropriate, use the BY statement options NOTSORTED or DESCENDING. For more information, see the discussion of the BY statement in "SAS Statements Used in the PROC Step" in the *SAS Language Guide, Release 6.03 Edition*.

TABLES Statement

  TABLES *requests / options*;

For each frequency or crosstabulation table that you want, put a table request in the TABLES statement.

  requests   are composed of one or more variable names joined by asterisks. A one-way frequency is generated by a single name. Two-way crosstabulations are generated by two variables joined with an asterisk. Any number of variables can be joined for a multi-way table. A grouping syntax is also available to make the specifications of many tables easier. Several variables can be put in parentheses and joined to other effects.

For example,

`tables a*(b c);`	is equivalent to	`tables a*b a*c;`
`tables (a b)*(c d);`	is equivalent to	`tables a*c b*c a*d b*d;`
`tables (a b c)*d;`	is equivalent to	`tables a*d b*d c*d;`
`tables a--c;`	is equivalent to	`tables a b c;`
`tables (a--c)*d;`	is equivalent to	`tables a*d b*d c*d;`

  Any number of requests can be given in one TABLES statement, and any number of TABLES statements can be included in one execution of PROC FREQ. If there is no TABLES statement, FREQ does one-way frequencies for all of the variables in the data set.

  If you request a one-way frequency table for a variable and do not specify any options, FREQ produces frequencies, cumulative frequencies, percentages of the total frequency, and cumulative percentages for each level of the variable.

  If you request a two-way or *n*-way crosstabulation table and do not specify any options, FREQ produces crosstabulation tables that include cell frequencies, cell percentages of the total frequency, cell percentages of row frequencies, and cell percentages of column frequencies. Missing levels of each variable are excluded from the table, but the total frequency of missing subjects is printed below each table.

The options below can be used in the TABLES statement after a slash (/).

General Options

LIST

prints two-way to *n*-way tables in a list format rather than as crosstabulation tables. The LIST option cannot be used when statistical tests or measures of association are requested. Expected cell frequencies are not printed when LIST is specified, even if the EXPECTED option is specified.

MISSING

requests that FREQ interpret missing values as nonmissing and include them in calculations of percentages and other statistics.

OUT=*SASdataset*

sets up an output SAS data set containing variable values and frequency counts. If more than one table request appears in the TABLES statement, the contents of the data set correspond to the last table request in the TABLES statement. For details on the output data set created by PROC FREQ, see **Output Data Set** later in this chapter. If you want to create a permanent SAS data set, you must specify a two-level name. See "SAS Files" in the *SAS Language Guide* for more information on permanent SAS data sets.

Options to Request Statistical Analysis

ALL

requests all of the tests and measures given by the CHISQ, MEASURES, and CMH options. The number of CMH statistics computed can be controlled by CMH1 and CMH2.

CHISQ

requests a chi-square (χ^2) test of homogeneity or independence for each stratum, together with measures of association based on chi-square. The tests include Pearson chi-square, likelihood ratio chi-square, and Mantel-Haenszel chi-square. The measures include the phi coefficient, the contingency coefficient, and Cramer's V. For 2×2 tables, Fisher's Exact Test is also included. The formulas for these tests and measures are given in the **DETAILS** section.

CMH

requests Cochran-Mantel-Haenszel statistics, which test for association between the row variable and the column variable after adjusting for all other variables in the TABLES statement. In addition, for 2×2 tables, FREQ gives the estimate of the common relative risk for both case-control and cohort studies and the corresponding confidence intervals. Breslow's test for homogeneity of the odds ratios is also given for the 2×2 case. The formulas for these statistics are given in the **DETAILS** section.

CMH1

requests the same summary information as the CMH option, except that the only Cochran-Mantel-Haenszel statistic requested is the first one, which is the correlation statistic with one degree of freedom. Except for 2×2 tables, this request requires less memory than the CMH option, which can require an enormous amount for large tables.

CMH2

requests the same summary information as the CMH option, except that the only Cochran-Mantel-Haenszel statistics requested are the first two, which are the correlation and the mean score (*ANOVA*) statistics. Except for tables with two columns, this request requires less memory than the CMH option, which can require an enormous amount for large tables.

EXACT

requests Fisher's exact test for tables that are larger than 2×2. The computational algorithm is the network algorithm given by Mehta and Patel (1983). Although the computational algorithm is faster than previous algorithms by orders of magnitude, the computational time can still be prohibitive, depending on the size of the table and the sample size. The test is generally not practical (in terms of CPU time and memory usage) when

$$\frac{n}{(r-1)(c-1)} > 5$$

where n is the sample size of the table, r is the number of rows, and c is the number of columns. The practicality increases as the sample size per degree of freedom decreases toward zero. This option is not turned on when the ALL option is specified.

MEASURES

requests a basic set of measures of association and their asymptotic standard errors (ASE). The measures include Pearson and Spearman correlation coefficients, gamma, Kendall's tau-b, Stuart's tau-c, Somers' D, lambda (symmetric and asymmetric), uncertainty coefficients (symmetric and asymmetric), and for 2×2 tables, odds ratios, risk ratios, and the corresponding confidence intervals. The formulas for these measures are given in the **DETAILS** section.

Options to Specify Details of Statistical Analysis

ALPHA=p

specifies that confidence intervals are to be $100(1-p)$ percent confidence intervals, where $0.0001 < p < 0.9999$. If no ALPHA level is specified, FREQ uses ALPHA=0.05. If the specified ALPHA is between 0 and 1 but is outside the limits, the closest limit is used. For example, if you specify ALPHA=0.000001, an ALPHA of 0.0001 is used. If the specified ALPHA is less than 0 or greater than 1, FREQ prints an error message.

SCORES=RANK
SCORES=TABLE
SCORES=RIDIT
SCORES=MODRIDIT

specifies the type of row and column scores to be used by the Cochran-Mantel-Haenszel statistics and by the Pearson correlation. For numeric variables, TABLE scores are the values of the row headings and the column headings. For character variables, TABLE scores are defined by the row numbers and column numbers. The other scores, defined in the **Summary Statistics** section, yield nonparametric analyses. If no scores are specified, FREQ uses TABLE scores.

Options to Request Additional Table Information

CELLCHI2
> requests that FREQ print each cell's contribution to the total χ^2 statistic. This is computed as $(frequency - expected)^2/expected$.

CUMCOL
> requests that cumulative column percentages be printed in the cells.

DEVIATION
> requests that, for each cell, FREQ print the deviation of the cell frequency from the expected value.

EXPECTED
> requests that the expected cell frequencies under the hypothesis of independence (or homogeneity) be printed. If both the EXPECTED and LIST options are requested, expected cell frequencies are not printed.

MISSPRINT
> asks FREQ to print missing value frequencies for two-way to *n*-way tables, even though the frequencies are not used in the calculation of statistics.

SPARSE
> causes the procedure to write out or print information about all possible combinations of levels of the variables in the table request, even when some combinations of levels do not occur in the data. This option affects printouts under the LIST option and output data sets.

Options to Suppress Printing

NOCOL
> suppresses printing of the column percentages in cells of a crosstabulation.

NOCUM
> suppresses printing of the cumulative frequencies and cumulative percentages for one-way frequencies and for frequencies in list format.

NOFREQ
> suppresses printing of the cell frequencies for a crosstabulation. This also suppresses frequencies for row totals.

NOPERCENT
> suppresses printing of cell percentages for a crosstabulation. This also suppresses printing of percentages for row totals and column totals in a crosstabulation. For one-way frequencies and frequencies in list format, the NOPERCENT option supresses printing of percentages and cumulative percentages.

NOPRINT
> suppresses printing of the tables, but allows printing of the statistics specified by the CHISQ, MEASURES, CMH, EXACT, and ALL options.

NOROW
> suppresses printing of the row percentages in cells of a crosstabulation.

WEIGHT Statement

WEIGHT *variable*;

Normally, each observation contributes a value of one to the frequency counts. (In other words, each observation represents one subject.) However, when a WEIGHT statement appears, each observation contributes the weighting variable's value for that observation. (For example, a weight of three means that the observation represents three subjects.)

If the value of the weight variable is missing or zero, the corresponding observation is ignored. If the value of the weight variable is negative, the frequencies (as measured by the weighted values) are printed, but the computation and printing of percentages and other statistics are suppressed. If an output data set is created, the variable PERCENT is created and assigned a value of missing for each observation.

FREQ uses double precision floating-point arithmetic to accumulate the counts or weights. Values are summed and then printed with decimal places, if appropriate.

Only one WEIGHT statement can be used, and that statement applies to counts collected for all tables.

For example, suppose a data set contains variables RACE, SEX, and HRSWORK. The statements

```
proc freq;
   tables race*sex;
```

produce a table showing how many nonwhite females, nonwhite males, white females, and white males are present. The statements

```
proc freq;
   tables race*sex;
   weight hrswork;
```

produce a table showing the number of hours worked by nonwhite females, by nonwhite males, and so on.

DETAILS

Missing Values

Missing value frequencies do not appear in contingency tables or frequency tables, but the total frequency of missing subjects is given below each table. In all cases, the statistics do not include missing values.

Missing value frequencies can be printed by specifying the MISSPRINT option in the TABLES statement; they can be included in the computation of statistics by specifying the MISSING option.

Limitations

Any number of TABLES statements can be included after the PROC FREQ statement. Since FREQ builds all the tables requested in all TABLES statements in one pass of the data, there is essentially no loss of efficiency when you use multiple TABLES statements.

A TABLES statement can contain any number of table requests, and each request can include any number of variables. The maximum number of levels allowed for any one variable is 32,767. If you have a variable with more than 32,767 levels, use PROC SUMMARY and PROC PRINT, or reduce the number of levels by using the FORMAT statement.

FREQ stores each combination of values in memory. When FREQ is compiling and developing multi-way tables or when some variables have many levels, you may run out of main storage. If increasing the region size is impractical, use PROC SORT to sort the data set by one or more of the variables and then use PROC FREQ with a BY statement that includes the sorted variables.

The FREQ procedure handles both internal and formatted values up to length 16 on both the printout and the output data set. Longer data values are truncated to sixteen characters, and a warning message is printed on the SAS log.

Frequency values with more than seven significant digits may be printed in scientific notation (E format), in which case only the first few significant digits of the mantissa are printed. If you need more significant digits than FREQ prints, you can specify an output data set with the OUT= option. Then use

```
proc print data=freqdata;
   format count best32.;
```

where FREQDATA is the OUT= data set produced by PROC FREQ.

The variable COUNT, containing the frequency values, is then printed with additional significant digits. For more information on formats, see "SAS Informats and Formats" and "SAS Statements Used in the PROC Step" in the *SAS Language Guide*.

Output Data Set

The new data set produced by PROC FREQ contains one observation for each combination of the variable values in the table request. Each observation contains these variables plus two new variables, COUNT and PERCENT, which give the frequency and cell percentage, respectively, for the combination of variable values.

For example, consider the statements

```
proc freq;
   tables a a*b / out=d;
```

The output data set D corresponds to the rightmost table request, A*B. If A has two values (1 and 2) and B has three values (1, 2, and 3), the output data set D can have up to six observations, one for each combination of the A and B values. In observation 1, A=1 and B=1; in observation 2, A=1 and B=2; and so on. The data set also contains the variables COUNT and PERCENT. COUNT's value in each observation is the number of subjects that have the given combination of A and B values; PERCENT's value is the percent of the total number of subjects having that A and B combination.

When FREQ collects different class values into the same formatted level, it saves the smallest internal value to output in the output data set.

Computational Resources

For each variable, PROC FREQ stores all of the levels in memory, requiring 56 bytes for each level. If FREQ runs out of memory, it stops collecting levels on the variable with the most levels and returns the memory so that counting can continue. The procedure then builds the tables that do not contain the disabled variables.

For two-way and *n*-way tables, FREQ uses a utility file to store frequencies when the number of nonzero cells exceeds 63. Nevertheless, for any single contingency table requested, FREQ builds the entire table in memory, regardless of whether the cells of the table have zero frequencies or not. Thus, if variables A, B, and C each have 10 levels, then a table request for A*B*C requires 1000 cells*8 bytes per cell = 8000 bytes, even though there may be only 10 observations.

Grouping with Formats

When you use PROC FREQ, remember that FREQ groups the variables according to their formatted values. If you assign a format to a variable with a FORMAT statement, the variable's values are formatted for printing before FREQ divides the observations into groups for the frequency counts.

For example, say a variable X has the values 1.3, 1.7, and 2.0, among others. Each of these values appears as a level in the frequency table. If you want each value rounded to a single digit, you include the statement

```
format x 1.;
```

after the PROC FREQ statement. The frequency table levels are then 1 and 2.

Formatted character variables are treated in the same way: the formatted values are used to divide the observations into groups. For character variables, formatted or not, only the first sixteen characters are used to determine the groups.

If you use formats to put missing and nonmissing values into one group, PROC FREQ treats that entire group of formatted values as missing.

You can also use the FORMAT statement to assign formats created by PROC FORMAT to variables. Formats created by PROC FORMAT can serve two purposes: they can define the levels, and they can label the levels. You can use the same data with different formats to collect counts on different partitions of the class values.

In frequency tables, values of both character and numeric variables appear in ascending order by the original (unformatted) values unless you specify otherwise with the ORDER= option.

Tests and Measures of Association

Definitions and Notation

Suppose a two-way table represents the crosstabulation of variables X and Y. Let the rows of the table be labeled by the values X_i, $i=1, 2, \ldots, R$, and the columns by Y_j, $j=1, 2, \ldots, C$. Let ln denote natural logarithm (base e), let the cell frequency in the ith row and the jth column be denoted n_{ij}, and define the following:

$$n_{\bullet j} = \Sigma_i\, n_{ij} \text{ (column totals)}$$

$$n_{i\bullet} = \Sigma_j\, n_{ij} \text{ (row totals)}$$

$$n = \Sigma_i\Sigma_j\, n_{ij} \text{ (overall total)}$$

$$A_{ij} = \Sigma_{k>i}\Sigma_{l>j}\, n_{kl} + \Sigma_{k<i}\Sigma_{l<j}\, n_{kl}$$

$$D_{ij} = \Sigma_{k>i}\Sigma_{l<j}\, n_{kl} + \Sigma_{k<i}\Sigma_{l>j}\, n_{kl}$$

$$P = \Sigma_i\Sigma_j\, n_{ij}A_{ij} \text{ (twice the number of concordances)}$$

$$Q = \Sigma_i\Sigma_j\, n_{ij}\, D_{ij} \text{ (twice the number of discordances)}.$$

Statistics Produced for Each Two-Way Table

All of the test statistics in this section test the null hypothesis of no association between the row variable and the column variable. When n is large, the chi-square statistics are distributed approximately as χ^2 when the null hypothesis is true. Throughout this section, let *var* denote the asymptotic variance of the most recently defined estimator. Its square root, the asymptotic standard error (ASE), is included in the printed output.

The following subsections give the formulas that PROC FREQ uses to compute statistics for two-way tables. For further information on the formulas and on the applicability and interpretation of each statistic, consult the cited references or those listed in the **INTRODUCTION**.

Chi-square (Q_P)   The Pearson chi-square statistic involves the differences between the observed and expected frequencies. The alternative hypothesis for this statistic is one of general association. The chi-square distribution has $(R-1)(C-1)$ degrees of freedom (df) and is determined as

$$Q_P = \Sigma_i \Sigma_j (n_{ij} - m_{ij})^2 / m_{ij}$$

where

$$m_{ij} = n_{i\bullet}n_{\bullet j} / n \quad .$$

Reference: Fienberg (1977, 9).

Continuity-adjusted chi-square (Q_C)   The adjusted chi-square statistic for 2×2 tables is similar to the Pearson chi-square, except that it is adjusted for the continuity of the χ^2 distribution. It has $(R-1)(C-1)$ df and is determined as

$$Q_C = \Sigma_i \Sigma_j [\max(0, |n_{ij} - m_{ij}| - 0.5)]^2 / m_{ij} \quad .$$

Reference: Fienberg (1977, 21).

Likelihood ratio chi-square (G^2)   The likelihood ratio chi-square statistic involves the ratios between the observed and expected frequencies. The alternative hypothesis for this statistic is one of general association. The χ^2 distribution has $(R-1)(C-1)$ df and is determined as

$$G^2 = 2 \Sigma_i \Sigma_j n_{ij} \ln(n_{ij} / m_{ij}) \quad .$$

Reference: Fienberg (1977, 36).

Mantel-Haenszel chi-square (Q_{MH})   The Mantel-Haenszel chi-square statistic tests the alternative hypothesis that there is a linear association between the row variable and the column variable. The χ^2 distribution has 1 df and is determined as

$$Q_{MH} = (n - 1)r^2$$

where r^2 is the Pearson correlation between the row variable and the column variable. Both the MH statistic and the Pearson correlation use the scores specified with the SCORES option.

References: Mantel and Haenszel (1959); Landis, Heyman, and Koch (1978).

Fisher's exact test   For 2×2 tables, Fisher's exact test yields the probability of observing a table that gives at least as much evidence of association as the one actually observed, given that the null hypothesis is true. With row and column margins considered fixed, the hypergeometric probability, p, of every possible table is computed, and the p value is defined as

$$PROB = \Sigma_A p \quad .$$

For two-tailed tests, A is the set of tables with p less than or equal to the probability of the observed table. For left-tailed (right-tailed) tests, A is the set of tables where the frequency in the (1,1) cell is less than (greater than) or equal to that of the observed table.

For general $r \times c$ tables, the two-tailed p value is defined the same way as it is for 2×2 tables. The computational algorithm is the network algorithm given by Mehta and Patel (1983).

Reference: Kendall and Stuart (1979, 580-585).

Phi coefficient (φ)   The phi coefficient is derived from the chi-square statistic. Range: $-1 \leq \varphi \leq 1$, though the attainable upper bound may be less than 1, depending on the marginal distributions. The phi coefficient is determined as

$$\varphi = (n_{11}n_{22} - n_{12}n_{21}) / \sqrt{n_{1\bullet}n_{2\bullet}n_{\bullet 1}n_{\bullet 2}} \quad \text{for } 2 \times 2 \text{ tables,}$$

$$\varphi = \sqrt{Q_P / n} \quad \text{otherwise.}$$

Reference: Fleiss (1981, 59–60).

Contingency coefficient (P)   The contingency coefficient is also derived from chi-square. Range: $0 \leq P \leq 1$, though the attainable upper bound may be less than 1, depending on the marginal distributions. The contingency coefficient is

$$P = \sqrt{Q_P / (Q_P + n)} \quad .$$

Reference: Kendall and Stuart (1979, 587-588).

Cramer's V   A third measure of association derived from chi-square is Cramer's V, designed so that the attainable upper bound is always 1. Range: $-1 \leq V \leq 1$. For 2×2 tables, $V = \varphi$; otherwise,

$$V = \sqrt{(Q_P / n) / \min(R - 1, C - 1)} \quad .$$

Reference: Kendall and Stuart (1979, 588).

Gamma (γ)   The estimator of gamma is based only on the number of concordant and discordant pairs of observations. It ignores tied pairs (that is, pairs of observations that have equal values of X or equal values of Y). If the two variables are independent, then the estimator of gamma tends to be close to zero. Gamma is appropriate only when both variables lie on an ordinal scale. Range: $-1 \leq \gamma \leq 1$. Gamma is estimated by

$$G = (P - Q) / (P + Q)$$

with

$$var = 16 \, \Sigma n_{ij} (QA_{ij} - PD_{ij})^2 / (P + Q)^4 \quad .$$

References: Goodman and Kruskal (1963; 1972).

Kendall's tau-b (τ_b)   Kendall's tau-b is similar to gamma except that tau-b uses a correction for ties. Tau-b is appropriate only when both variables lie on an ordinal scale. Range: $-1 \leq \tau_b \leq 1$. It is estimated by

$$t_b = (P - Q) / w = (P - Q) / \sqrt{w_r w_c}$$

with

$$var = [\Sigma_i \Sigma_j \, n_{ij} (2w d_{ij} + t_b v_{ij})^2 - n^3 t_b^2 (w_r + w_c)^2] / w^4$$

where

$$w_r = n^2 - \Sigma_i n_{i\bullet}^2$$

$$w_c = n^2 - \Sigma_j n_{\bullet j}^2$$

$$d_{ij} = A_{ij} - D_{ij}$$

$$v_{ij} = n_{i\bullet}w_c + n_{\bullet j}w_r \quad .$$

Reference: Goodman and Kruskal (1972).

Stuart's tau-c (τ_c)   Stuart's tau-c makes an adjustment for table size in addition to a correction for ties. Tau-c is appropriate only when both variables lie on an ordinal scale. Range: $-1 \leq \tau_c \leq 1$. It is estimated by

$$t_c = (P-Q) / [n^2(m-1)/m]$$

with

$$var = 4m^2[\Sigma_i\Sigma_j n_{ij}d_{ij}^2 - (P-Q)^2/n] / (m-1)^2 n^4$$

where

$$m = \min(R,C)$$

$$d_{ij} = A_{ij} - D_{ij} \quad .$$

Reference: Brown and Benedetti (1976).

Somers' D (C | R)   Somers' D is an asymmetric modification of tau-b. C | R denotes that the row variable X is regarded as an independent variable, while the column variable Y is regarded as dependent. Somers' D differs from tau-b in that it uses a correction only for pairs that are tied on the independent variable. Somers' D is appropriate only when both variables lie on an ordinal scale. Range: $-1 \leq D \leq 1$. Formulas for Somers' D(R | C) are obtained by interchanging the indices.

$$D(C | R) = (P - Q) / w_r$$

with

$$var = 4\Sigma_i\Sigma_j n_{ij}[w_r d_{ij} - (P - Q)(n - n_{i\bullet})]^2 / w_r^4$$

where

$$w_r = n^2 - \Sigma_i n_{i\bullet}^2$$

$$d_{ij} = A_{ij} - D_{ij} \quad .$$

References: Somers (1962); Goodman and Kruskal (1972).

Pearson correlation coefficient (r) The Pearson correlation coefficient is computed by using the scores specified in the SCORES option. It is appropriate only when both variables lie on an ordinal scale. Range: $-1 \leq r \leq 1$. The Pearson correlation coefficient is computed as

$$r = v / w = ss_{rc} / \sqrt{ss_r ss_c}$$

with

$$var = \Sigma_i \Sigma_j \, n_{ij} [w(r_i - \bar{r})(c_j - \bar{c}) - b_{ij} v / 2w]^2 / w^4$$

where the r_i are the row scores, the c_j are the column scores, and

$$\bar{r} = \Sigma_i \Sigma_j \, n_{ij} r_i / n$$

$$\bar{c} = \Sigma_i \Sigma_j \, n_{ij} c_j / n$$

$$ss_r = \Sigma_i \Sigma_j \, n_{ij} (r_i - \bar{r})^2$$

$$ss_c = \Sigma_i \Sigma_j \, n_{ij} (c_j - \bar{c})^2$$

$$ss_{rc} = \Sigma_i \Sigma_j \, n_{ij} (r_i - \bar{r})(c_j - \bar{c})$$

$$b_{ij} = (r_i - \bar{r})^2 ss_c + (c_j - \bar{c})^2 ss_r \quad .$$

References: Snedecor and Cochran (1980, 175); Brown and Benedetti (1976).

Spearman rank correlation coefficient (r_s) The Spearman correlation coefficient is computed by using rank scores $r1_i$ and $c1_j$, defined in the **Summary Statistics** section later in this chapter. The formulas are those given for the Pearson correlation coefficient, with $r_i = r1_i$ and $c_j = c1_j$. It is appropriate only when both variables lie on an ordinal scale. Range: $-1 \leq r_s \leq 1$.

References: Snedecor and Cochran (1980, 192); Brown and Benedetti (1976).

Lambda asymmetric C | R Asymmetric Lambda, ($\lambda[C \mid R]$), is interpreted as the probable improvement in predicting the column variable Y given that one has knowledge of the row variable X. Range: $0 \leq \lambda[C \mid R] \leq 1$. It is computed as

$$\lambda[C \mid R] = (\Sigma_i \, r_i - r) / (n - r)$$

with

$$var = (n - \Sigma_i \, r_i)[\Sigma_i \, r_i + r - 2\Sigma_i \, (r_i \mid l_i = l)] / (n - r)^3$$

where

$$r_i = \max_j (n_{ij})$$

$$r = \max_j (n_{\bullet j}) \quad .$$

Also,

let l_i be the unique value of j such that $r_i = n_{ij}$, and

let l be the unique value of j such that $r = n_{\bullet j}$.

Because of the uniqueness assumptions, ties in the frequencies or in the marginal totals must be broken in an arbitrary but consistent manner. In case of ties, l is defined here as the smallest value of j such that $r = n_{\bullet j}$. For a given i, if there is at least one value j such that $n_{ij} = r_i = c_j$, then l_i is defined here to be the smallest such value of j. Otherwise, if $n_{il} = r_i$, then l_i is defined to be equal to l. If neither condition is true, then l_i is taken to be the smallest value of j such that $n_{ij} = r_i$. The formulas for lambda asymmetric R | C can be obtained by interchanging the indices.

Reference: Goodman and Kruskal (1963).

Lambda symmetric (λ)   The two asymmetric lambdas are averaged to obtain the nondirectional lambda. Range: $0 \leq \lambda \leq 1$. Lambda symmetric is defined as

$$\lambda = (\Sigma_i r_i + \Sigma_j c_j - r - c) / (2n - r - c) = (w - v) / w$$

with

$$var = \{wvy - 2w^2[1 - \Sigma_i\Sigma_j (n_{ij} | j = l_i, i = k_j)] - 2v^2(1 - n_{kl})\} / w^4$$

where

$$w = 2n - r - c$$

$$v = 2n - \Sigma_i r_i - \Sigma_j c_j$$

$$x = \Sigma_i [r_i | l_i = l] + \Sigma_j [c_j | k_j = k] + r_k + c_l$$

$$y = 8n - w - v - 2x \quad .$$

Reference: Goodman and Kruskal (1963).

Uncertainty coefficient C | R   The uncertainty coefficient, U[C | R], is the proportional reduction in the uncertainty (entropy) of the column variable Y that results from knowing the value of the row variable X. Range: $0 \leq U[C | R] \leq 1$. The formulas for U[R | C] can be obtained by interchanging the indices.

$$U[C | R] = [H(X) + H(Y) - H(XY)] / H(Y) = v / w$$

with

$$var = \Sigma_i\Sigma_j n_{ij}\{H(Y) \ln(n_{ij} / n_{i\bullet}) + [H(X) - H(XY)]\ln(n_{\bullet j} / n)\}^2 / n^2 w^4$$

where

$$H(X) = -\Sigma_i (n_{i\bullet} / n) \ln (n_{i\bullet} / n)$$

$$H(Y) = -\Sigma_j (n_{\bullet j} / n) \ln (n_{\bullet j} / n)$$

$$H(XY) = -\Sigma_i\Sigma_j (n_{ij} / n) \ln (n_{ij} / n) \quad .$$

References: Theil (1972, 115-120); Goodman and Kruskal (1972).

Uncertainty coefficient (U)   The uncertainty coefficient, U, is the symmetric version of the two asymmetric coefficients. Range: $0 \leq U \leq 1$. It is defined as

$$U = 2[H(X) + H(Y) - H(XY)] / [H(X) + H(Y)]$$

with

$$var = 4\ \Sigma_i \Sigma_j\ n_{ij}\ \{H(XY)\ \ln\ (n_{i\bullet}n_{\bullet j}\ /\ n^2)$$

$$-[H(X) + H(Y)]\ \ln\ (n_{ij}\ /\ n)\}^2\ /\ n^2[H(X) + H(Y)]^4\ .$$

Reference: Goodman and Kruskal (1972).

Relative risk estimates   For two dichotomous variables, disease (D) and exposure (E) to a risk factor, the relative risk of disease is defined as

$$RR = Prob\ (D = yes\ |\ E = yes)\ /\ Prob\ (D = yes\ |\ E = no)\ .$$

Relative risk estimates are computed only for 2×2 tables, in which case the table is presumed to be set up with E as the row variable and D as the column variable. Throughout this section, z is the $100(1-\alpha/2)$ percent point of the Normal $(0,1)$ distribution. The estimation of the relative risk depends on the study design:

1. Case-control studies It is assumed that the (E=yes, D=yes) cell is on the main diagonal. The estimate of the relative risk is the odds ratio,

$$OR\ = n_{11}n_{22}\ /\ n_{12}n_{21}\ .$$

The $100(1-\alpha)$ percent confidence interval for OR is obtained as

$$\left(OR\ \exp\left[-z\ \sqrt{v}\right],\ OR\ \exp\left[z\sqrt{v}\right]\right)$$

where

$$v = var\ (\ln\ OR) = \frac{1}{n_{11}} + \frac{1}{n_{12}} + \frac{1}{n_{21}} + \frac{1}{n_{22}}\ .$$

If any of the four cell frequencies are zero, the estimates are not computed.

2. Cohort studies It is assumed that (E=yes) is the first row of the contingency table. If (D=yes) is the first column, then use the estimates labeled COL1 RISK. Otherwise, use the estimates labeled COL2 RISK. Define

$$p_1 = n_{11}\ /\ n_{1\bullet}$$

$$p_2 = n_{21}\ /\ n_{2\bullet}\ .$$

The COL1 relative risk is estimated by

$$RR = p_1\ /\ p_2$$

and the corresponding $100(1-\alpha)$ percent confidence interval is

$$\left(\mathrm{RR}\ \exp\left[-z\sqrt{v}\right],\ \mathrm{RR}\ \exp\left[z\sqrt{v}\right]\right)$$

where

$$v = \mathrm{var}\,(\ln\ \mathrm{RR}) = (1-p_1)\,/\,n_{11} + (1-p_2)\,/\,n_{21}\quad.$$

If either n_{11} or n_{21} is zero, the estimates are not computed. The COL2 relative risk estimates are computed similarly.

Reference: Kleinbaum, Kupper, and Morgenstern (1982, 299).

Summary Statistics

Suppose there are q strata, indexed by $h=1, 2, \ldots, q$, and within each stratum is a contingency table with X as the row variable and Y as the column variable. For table h, let the cell frequency in the ith row and jth column be denoted by n_{hij}, with corresponding marginal totals denoted by $n_{hi\bullet}$ and $n_{h\bullet j}$ and with overall total N_h. The CMH summary statistics use row and column scores, for which there are several choices.

For numeric variables, TABLE scores are the values of the row headings and column headings; for character variables, they are defined as the row numbers and column numbers. TABLE scores are the same for each of the q tables and are used by PROC FREQ if no choice of scores is specified with the SCORES option.

RANK scores, which can be used to obtain nonparametric analyses, are defined by

$$\text{Row scores:}\quad r1_{hi} = \Sigma_{k<i}\,n_{hk\bullet} + (n_{hi\bullet} + 1)\,/\,2 \qquad i = 1, 2, \ldots, R$$

$$\text{Col scores:}\quad c1_{hj} = \Sigma_{l<j}\,n_{h\bullet l} + (n_{h\bullet j} + 1)\,/\,2 \qquad j = 1, 2, \ldots, C\quad.$$

RIDIT scores (Bross 1958; Mack and Skillings 1980) also yield nonparametric analyses, but they are standardized by the stratum sample size. RIDIT scores are derived from RANK scores as

$$r2_{hi} = r1_{hi}\,/\,N_h$$

$$c2_{hj} = c1_{hj}\,/\,N_h\quad.$$

Modified ridit (MODRIDIT) scores (van Elteren 1960, Lehmann 1975), which also yield nonparametric analyses, represent the expected values of the within-stratum order statistics for the uniform distribution on (0,1). Modified ridit scores are derived from rank scores as

$$r3_{hi} = r1_{hi}\,/\,(N_h + 1)$$

$$c3_{hj} = c1_{hj}\,/\,(N_h + 1)\quad.$$

Since the formulas for the CMH statistics are more easily defined in terms of matrices, the following notation is used. Vectors are presumed to be column vectors unless they are transposed ($'$):

$$\mathbf{n}_{hi}' = (n_{hi1}, n_{hi2}, \ldots, n_{hiC})$$
$$(1 \times C)$$

$$\mathbf{n}_h' = (\mathbf{n}_{h1}', \mathbf{n}_{h2}', \ldots, \mathbf{n}_{hR}')$$
$$(1 \times RC)$$

$$P_{hi\bullet} = n_{hi\bullet} / N_h$$

$$P_{h\bullet j} = n_{h\bullet j} / N_h$$

$$\mathbf{P}_{h^{\star}\bullet}' = (P_{h1\bullet}, P_{h2\bullet}, \ldots, P_{hR\bullet})$$

$$\mathbf{P}_{h\bullet^{\star}}' = (P_{h\bullet 1}, P_{h\bullet 2}, \ldots, P_{h\bullet C}) \quad .$$

Cochran-Mantel-Haenszel (CMH) Statistics

Assume that the strata are independent and that the marginal totals of each stratum are fixed. The null hypothesis, H_0, is that there is no association between X and Y in any of the strata. The corresponding model is the multiple hypergeometric, which implies that under H_0, the expected value and covariance matrix of the frequencies are, respectively,

$$\mathbf{m}_h = \mathbf{E}[\mathbf{n}_h \mid H_0] = N_h (\mathbf{P}_{h\bullet^{\star}} \otimes \mathbf{P}_{h^{\star}\bullet})$$

and

$$\mathbf{Var}\,[\mathbf{n}_h \mid H_0] = c[(\mathbf{D}_{Ph\bullet^{\star}} - \mathbf{P}_{h\bullet^{\star}}\mathbf{P}_{h\bullet^{\star}}') \otimes (\mathbf{D}_{Ph^{\star}\bullet} - \mathbf{P}_{h^{\star}\bullet}\mathbf{P}_{h^{\star}\bullet}')]$$

where

$$c = N_h^2 / (N_h - 1)$$

and where $\otimes$ denotes Kronecker product multiplication and $\mathbf{D}_a$ is a diagonal matrix with elements of $\mathbf{a}$ on the main diagonal.

The generalized CMH statistic (Landis, Heyman, and Koch 1978) is defined as

$$Q_{CMH} = \mathbf{G}'\mathbf{V}_{\mathbf{G}}^{-1}\mathbf{G}$$

where

$$\mathbf{G} = \Sigma_h \mathbf{B}_h (\mathbf{n}_h - \mathbf{m}_h)$$

$$\mathbf{V}_{\mathbf{G}} = \Sigma_h \mathbf{B}_h [\mathbf{Var}(\mathbf{n}_h \mid H_0)]\mathbf{B}_h'$$

and where

$$\mathbf{B}_h = \mathbf{C}_h \otimes \mathbf{R}_h$$

is a matrix of fixed constants based on column scores $\mathbf{C}_h$ and row scores $\mathbf{R}_h$. When the null hypothesis is true, the CMH statistic is approximately distributed as chi-square with degrees of freedom equal to the rank of $\mathbf{B}_h$.

A word of caution is necessary. CMH statistics have low power for detecting an association in which the patterns of association for some of the strata are in the opposite direction of the patterns displayed by other strata. Thus, a nonsignificant CMH statistic suggests either that there is no association or that no pattern of association had enough strength or consistency to dominate any other pattern. FREQ computes the following types of CMH statistics:

The correlation statistic (df = 1)   The correlation statistic, with one degree of freedom, was popularized by Mantel and Haenszel (1959) and Mantel (1963) and is therefore known as the Mantel-Haenszel statistic.

The alternative hypothesis in this case is that there is a linear association between X and Y in at least one stratum. If either X or Y does not lie on an ordinal (or interval) scale, then this statistic is meaningless.

The matrix C_h has dimension $1 \times C$, and the scores, one for each column, are specified in the SCORES option. Similarly, the matrix R_h has dimension $1 \times R$, and these scores, one for each row, are also controlled by the SCORES option.

When there is only one stratum, this CMH statistic reduces to $(N-1)r^2$, where r is the correlation coefficient between X and Y. When nonparametric (RANK or RIDIT) scores are specified, then the statistic reduces to $(N-1)r_s^2$, where r_s is the Spearman rank correlation coefficient between X and Y. When there is more than one stratum, then the CMH statistic becomes a stratum-adjusted correlation statistic.

The ANOVA statistic (df = R − 1)   This statistic can be used only when the column variable Y lies on an ordinal (or interval) scale so that the mean score of Y is a meaningful notion. In that case, the mean score is computed for each row of the table, and the alternative hypothesis is that, for at least one stratum, the mean scores of the R rows are unequal. In other words, the statistic is sensitive to location differences among the R distributions of Y.

The matrix C_h has dimension $1 \times C$, and the scores, one for each column, are specified in the SCORES option. The matrix R_h has dimension $(R-1) \times R$ and is created internally by FREQ as

$$R_h = [I_{R-1}, -J_{R-1}]$$

where I_{R-1} is an identity matrix of rank R−1, and J_{R-1} is an $(R-1) \times 1$ vector of ones. This matrix has the effect of forming R−1 independent contrasts of the R mean scores.

When there is only one stratum, this CMH statistic is essentially an analysis-of-variance (ANOVA) statistic in the sense that it is a function of the variance ratio F statistic that would be obtained from a one-way ANOVA on the dependent variable Y. If nonparametric scores are specified in this case, then the ANOVA statistic is a Kruskal-Wallis test.

If there is more than one stratum, then the CMH statistic corresponds to a stratum-adjusted ANOVA or Kruskal-Wallis test. In the special case where there is one subject per row and one subject per column in the contingency table of each stratum, this CMH statistic is identical to Friedman's chi-square.

The general association statistic (df = (R − 1)(C − 1))   This statistic is always interpretable because it does not require an ordinal scale for either X or Y. The alternative hypothesis is that, for at least one stratum, there is some kind of association between X and Y.

The matrix R_h is the same as the one used for the ANOVA statistic. The matrix C_h is defined similarly as

$$C_h = [I_{C-1}, -J_{C-1}] .$$

Both score matrices are generated internally by FREQ.

When there is only one stratum, then the general association CMH statistic reduces to $[(N-1)/N]Q_P$, where Q_P is the Pearson chi-square statistic. When there is more than one stratum, then the CMH statistic becomes a stratum-adjusted Pearson chi-square statistic. Note that a similar adjustment can be made by summing the Pearson chi-squares across the strata. However, the latter statistic requires a large sample size in each stratum to support the resulting chi-square distribution with $q(R-1)(C-1)$ df. The CMH statistic requires only a large overall sample size since it has only $(R-1)(C-1)$ df.

References: Cochran (1954); Mantel and Haenszel (1959); Mantel (1963); Birch (1965); Landis, Heyman, and Koch (1978).

Adjusted Relative Risk Estimates

The notation and definitions from **Relative risk estimates** are also used in this section. If you would like RR estimates of E, which are adjusted for confounding variables A and B, specify

```
proc freq;
   tables a*b*e*d / all;
```

As before, E must be the row variable, D must be the column variable, and RR estimates are computed only when E and D each have two levels. Throughout this section, z is the $100(1-\alpha/2)$ percent point of the Normal (0,1) distribution, and Q is the general association CMH statistic. (Note that the value of the general association statistic is independent of the scores that are specified.) Tables with a zero row or column are not included in any of the summary relative risk computations. The estimation procedure depends on the study design.

Case-control studies   It is assumed that the (E=yes, D=yes) cell is on the main diagonal of the matrix in each stratum. Two sets of estimators are given for case-control studies:

1. Mantel-Haenszel estimate and test-based confidence interval The adjusted odds ratio estimator is given by

$$OR_{MH} = [\Sigma_h\, n_{h11}n_{h22} \,/\, N_h] \,/\, [\Sigma_h\, n_{h12}n_{h21} \,/\, N_h]$$

and is always computed unless the denominator is zero. The corresponding $100(1-\alpha)\%$ test-based confidence interval is given by

$$\left(OR_{MH}^{1-z/\sqrt{Q}}\, ,\, OR_{MH}^{1+z/\sqrt{Q}}\right)$$

if $OR_{MH}>1$. Otherwise, the lower and upper limits are reversed. The confidence interval is computed unless Q=0 or OR_{MH} is undefined.

2. Logit estimator with precision-based confidence interval This odds ratio estimator (Woolf 1955) is given by

$$OR_L = \exp\left[(\Sigma_h\, w_h \ln OR_h) \,/\, \Sigma\, w_h\right]$$

and the corresponding $100(1-\alpha)$ percent confidence interval is

$$\left(OR_L \exp\left[-z / \sqrt{\Sigma_h w_h} \right], \ OR_L \exp\left[z / \sqrt{\Sigma_h w_h} \right] \right)$$

where OR_h is the odds ratio for stratum h, and

$$w_h = 1 / var (ln \ OR_h) \quad.$$

If any cell frequency in a stratum h is zero, then $1/2$ is added to each cell of the stratum before OR_h and w_h are computed (Haldane 1955), and a warning is printed.

Cohort studies   It is assumed that (E=yes) is the first row of the contingency tables. If (D=yes) is the first column, then use the estimates labeled COL1 RISK. Otherwise, use the estimates labeled COL2 RISK. The COL1 estimators are given in this section; the COL2 estimators have corresponding definitions. Two sets of estimators are given for cohort studies:

1. Mantel-Haenszel estimate and test-based confidence interval The adjusted relative risk estimator is given by

$$RR_{MH} = [\Sigma_h \ n_{h11} n_{h2\bullet} / N_h] / [\Sigma_h \ n_{h21} n_{h1\bullet} / N_h]$$

and is always computed unless the denominator is zero. The corresponding $100(1-\alpha)\%$ test-based confidence interval is given by

$$\left(RR_{MH}^{1-z/\sqrt{Q}}, \ RR_{MH}^{1+z/\sqrt{Q}} \right)$$

if $RR_{MH} > 1$. Otherwise, the lower and upper limits are reversed. The confidence interval is computed unless $Q=0$ or RR_{MH} is undefined.

2. Logit estimator with precision-based confidence interval This relative risk estimator is given by

$$RR_L = \exp \left[(\Sigma_h \ w_h \ ln \ RR_h) / \Sigma \ w_h \right]$$

and the corresponding $100(1-\alpha)$ percent confidence interval is

$$\left(RR_L \exp\left[-z / \sqrt{\Sigma_h w_h} \right], \ RR_L \exp\left[z / \sqrt{\Sigma_h w_h} \right] \right)$$

where RR_h is the relative risk estimator for stratum h, and

$$w_h = 1 / var (ln RR_h) \quad.$$

If n_{h11} or n_{h21} is zero, then $1/2$ is added to each cell of the stratum before RR_h and w_h are computed, and a warning is printed.

Reference: Kleinbaum, Kupper, and Morgenstern (1982, Sections 17.4, 17.5).

Breslow-Day Test for Homogeneity of the Odds Ratios

This statistic tests the hypothesis that the odds ratios from the q strata are all equal. When the hypothesis is true, the statistic is distributed approximately as chi-square with $q-1$ degrees of freedom. The statistic is defined as

$$Q_{BD} = \Sigma_h \left[n_{h11} - \text{Exp} \left(n_{h11} \mid OR_{MH} \right) \right]^2 / \text{Var} \left(n_{h11} \mid OR_{MH} \right)$$

where Exp and Var denote expected value and variance, respectively. If $OR_{MH}=0$ or if it is undefined, then FREQ does not compute the statistic, and a warning message is printed. The summation does not include any tables with a zero row or column.

A note of caution is appropriate here. Unlike the Cochran-Mantel-Haenszel statistics, the Breslow-Day test requires a large sample size within each stratum, and this limits its usefulness. In addition, the validity of the CMH tests does not depend on any assumption of homogeneity of the odds ratios, and therefore, the Breslow-Day test should never be used as such an indicator of validity.

Reference: Breslow and Day (1980, 142).

Sample Size Summary

The total sample size and the frequency of missing subjects are printed. The effective sample size is the frequency of nonmissing subjects.

Printed Output

For a one-way table showing the frequency distribution of a single variable, PROC FREQ prints these items:

1. the name of the variable and its values (not shown)
2. Frequency counts (not shown), giving the number of subjects that have each value
3. Cumulative Frequency counts (not shown), giving the sum of the frequency counts of that value and all other values listed above it in the table (the total number of nonmissing subjects is the last cumulative frequency)
4. percentages, labeled Percent (not shown), giving the percent of the total number of subjects represented by that value
5. Cumulative Percent values (not shown), giving the percent of the total number of subjects represented by that value and all others previously listed in the table.

Two-way tables can be printed either as crosstabulation tables (the default) or as lists (when the LIST option is specified). Each cell of a crosstabulation table may contain items 6 through 12:

6. Frequency counts, giving the number of subjects that have the indicated values of the two variables.
7. Percent, the percentage of the total frequency count represented by that cell.
8. Row Pct, or the row percentage, the percent of the total frequency count for that row represented by the cell.
9. Col Pct, or column percent, the percent of the total frequency count for that column represented by the cell.
10. if the EXPECTED option is specified, the expected cell frequency under the hypothesis of independence (not shown).

11. if the DEVIATION option is specified, the deviation of the cell frequency from the expected value (not shown).

12. if the CELLCHI2 option is specified, the cell's contribution to the total chi-square statistic (not shown).

13. If the CHISQ option is specified, the following statistics are printed for the two-way table in each stratum: Pearson Chi-Square, Likelihood Ratio Chi-Square, Continuity-Adjusted Chi-Square, Mantel-Haenszel Chi-Square, Fisher's Exact Test (for 2×2 tables), the Phi Coefficient, the Contingency Coefficient, Cramer's V, the Sample Size, and the Frequency Missing. For each test statistic, its degrees of freedom (DF) and its significance probability (Prob) are also printed.

14. If the EXACT option is specified, the two-tailed p value from Fisher's exact test is printed, regardless of the size of the table. In addition, all of the statistics requested by the CHISQ option are also printed.

15. If the MEASURES option is specified, the following statistics and their asymptotic standard errors (ASE) are printed for the two-way table in each stratum: Gamma, Kendall's Tau-b, Stuart's Tau-c, Somers' D, Pearson Correlation, Spearman Correlation, Lambda Asymmetric, Lambda Symmetric, and the Uncertainty Coefficient (Symmetric and Asymmetric). Also printed are Sample Size, Frequency Missing, and (for 2×2 tables) Estimates of the Relative Risk for Case-Control and Cohort studies, together with their Confidence Bounds.

16. If the CMH option is specified, the following statistics are printed: Total Sample Size, Total Frequency Missing, and three Cochran-Mantel-Haenszel summary statistics (the correlation statistic, the *ANOVA* statistic, and the general association statistic), with corresponding degrees of freedom (DF) and significance probabilities (Prob). For 2×2 tables, the additional statistics printed are stratum-adjusted estimates (both Mantel-Haenszel and logit estimates) of the common relative risk for case-control and cohort studies, together with their confidence intervals, and the Breslow-Day test for homogeneity of the odds ratios.

17. If the ALL option is specified, all of the statistics requested by the CHISQ, MEASURES, and CMH options are printed (not shown).

18. If two contingency tables can fit on a page, one table above the other, then the tables are printed in that manner. Similarly, a table and its corresponding statistics are printed on the same page, provided that they fit (not shown).

EXAMPLES

Example 1: Fisher's Exact Test for 3×6 Table

When the sample size is small relative to the size of a contingency table, chi-square may not be a valid test. In that case, Fisher's exact test is a more appropriate test of no association. In the following table, the sample size is 9, and the number of degrees of freedom for the chi-square statistic is 10. Since the sample size per degree of freedom is much less than 5, Fisher's exact test is likely to be quite feasible in this situation. The test is requested by the EXACT option in the TABLES statement. The output shows that the chi-square statistic and Fisher's

exact test yield somewhat different results. The following statements produce
Output 19.1:

```
data;
   do a=1 to 3;
      do b=1 to 6;
         input wt @@;
         output;
         end;
      end;
   cards;
2 0 0 0 0 0
0 1 2 0 0 0
0 0 0 1 2 1
;
proc freq;
   weight wt;
   tables a*b / exact;
   title 'Fisher''s Exact Test for 3 by 6 Table';
run;
```

Output 19.1   Fisher's Exact Test for 3×6 Table: PROC FREQ

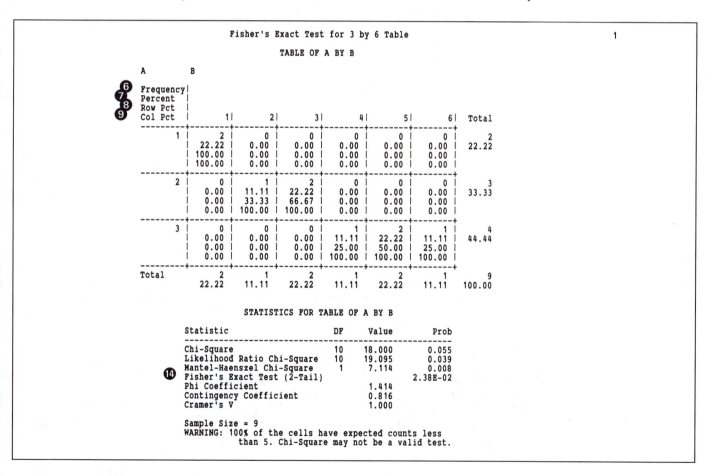

```
              Fisher's Exact Test for 3 by 6 Table                          1
                        TABLE OF A BY B

A        B
  Frequency|
  Percent  |
  Row Pct  |
  Col Pct  |     1|     2|     3|     4|     5|     6| Total
  ---------+------+------+------+------+------+------+
        1  |    2 |    0 |    0 |    0 |    0 |    0 |     2
           |22.22 | 0.00 | 0.00 | 0.00 | 0.00 | 0.00 | 22.22
           |100.00| 0.00 | 0.00 | 0.00 | 0.00 | 0.00 |
           |100.00| 0.00 | 0.00 | 0.00 | 0.00 | 0.00 |
  ---------+------+------+------+------+------+------+
        2  |    0 |    1 |    2 |    0 |    0 |    0 |     3
           | 0.00 |11.11 |22.22 | 0.00 | 0.00 | 0.00 | 33.33
           | 0.00 |33.33 |66.67 | 0.00 | 0.00 | 0.00 |
           | 0.00 |100.00|100.00| 0.00 | 0.00 | 0.00 |
  ---------+------+------+------+------+------+------+
        3  |    0 |    0 |    0 |    1 |    2 |    1 |     4
           | 0.00 | 0.00 | 0.00 |11.11 |22.22 |11.11 | 44.44
           | 0.00 | 0.00 | 0.00 |25.00 |50.00 |25.00 |
           | 0.00 | 0.00 | 0.00 |100.00|100.00|100.00|
  ---------+------+------+------+------+------+------+
  Total         2      1      2      1      2      1       9
            22.22  11.11  22.22  11.11  22.22  11.11  100.00


              STATISTICS FOR TABLE OF A BY B

  Statistic                       DF      Value      Prob
  --------------------------------------------------------
  Chi-Square                      10     18.000     0.055
  Likelihood Ratio Chi-Square     10     19.095     0.039
  Mantel-Haenszel Chi-Square       1      7.114     0.008
  Fisher's Exact Test (2-Tail)                      2.38E-02
  Phi Coefficient                         1.414
  Contingency Coefficient                 0.816
  Cramer's V                              1.000

  Sample Size = 9
  WARNING: 100% of the cells have expected counts less
           than 5. Chi-Square may not be a valid test.
```

Example 2: Analysis of 2×2 Table

The following example illustrates the analysis of a single 2×2 table. Fisher's exact test includes left- and right-tailed *p* values, as well as the two-tailed *p* value. The results indicate substantial evidence of a moderately strong negative association. The following statements produce **Output 19.2**:

```
data;
   do a=1 to 2;
      do b=1 to 2;
         input wt @@;
         output;
         end;
      end;
   cards;
3  11  6  2
;
proc freq;
   weight wt;
   tables a*b / chisq measures;
   title 'Analysis of 2 by 2 Table';
run;
```

Output 19.2   Analysis of 2×2 Table: PROC FREQ

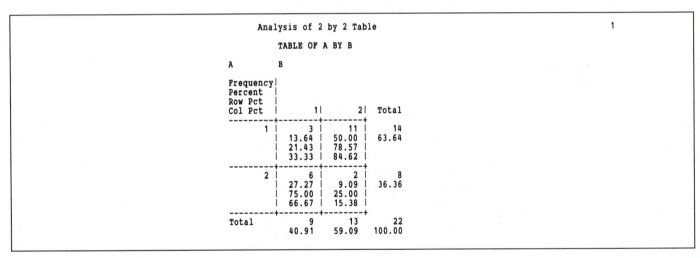

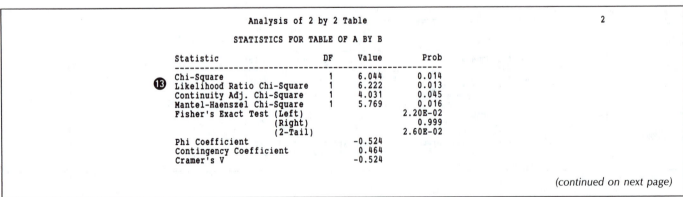

(continued on next page)

(continued from previous page)

⑮

```
Statistic                               Value      ASE
--------------------------------------------------------
Gamma                                  -0.833     0.160
Kendall's Tau-b                        -0.524     0.185
Stuart's Tau-c                         -0.496     0.184

Somers' D C|R                          -0.536     0.188
Somers' D R|C                          -0.513     0.186

Pearson Correlation                    -0.524     0.185
Spearman Correlation                   -0.524     0.185

Lambda Asymmetric C|R                   0.444     0.234
Lambda Asymmetric R|C                   0.375     0.296
Lambda Symmetric                        0.412     0.251

Uncertainty Coefficient C|R             0.209     0.156
Uncertainty Coefficient R|C             0.216     0.159
Uncertainty Coefficient Symmetric       0.212     0.157


            Estimates of the Relative Risk (Row1/Row2)

                                              95%
    Type of Study           Value      Confidence Bounds
    ----------------------------------------------------
    Case-Control            0.091      0.012      0.704
    Cohort (Col1 Risk)      0.286      0.097      0.841
    Cohort (Col2 Risk)      3.143      0.918     10.763


    Sample Size = 22
    WARNING:  50% of the cells have expected counts less
              than 5. Chi-Square may not be a valid test.
```

Example 3: Evans County Study

Data for the following example are from the Evans County cohort study of coronary heart disease. Data for the variable CAT, however, are hypothetical. The data are given in Table 17.7 and used in Examples 17.2 and 17.9 of Kleinbaum, Kupper, and Morgenstern (1982).

The purpose of the analysis is to evaluate the association between serum catecholamine (CAT) and coronary heart disease (CHD) after controlling for AGE and electrocardiogram abnormality (ECG). The summary statistics show that the association is significant ($p=0.04$) and that subjects with high serum catecholamine are about 1.7 times more likely to develop coronary heart disease than those subjects with low serum catecholamine. The NOPRINT option suppresses printing of the contingency tables. The CHISQ and MEASURES options are excluded in order to suppress the computation and printing of statistics on the individual tables. The following statements produce **Output 19.3**:

```
data chd;
   input age $ ecg $ chd $ cat $ wt;
   cards;
<55  0  yes  yes    1
<55  0  yes   no   17
<55  0   no  yes    7
<55  0   no   no  257
<55  1  yes  yes    3
<55  1  yes   no    7
<55  1   no  yes   14
<55  1   no   no   52
55+  0  yes  yes    9
55+  0  yes   no   15
```

```
55+  0    no   yes    30
55+  0    no   no    107
55+  1   yes   yes    14
55+  1   yes   no      5
55+  1    no   yes    44
55+  1    no   no     27
;
proc freq order=data;
   weight wt;
   tables age*ecg*cat*chd / noprint cmh;
   title 'Example 17.9 from Kleinbaum, et al. , p. 353';
run;
```

Output 19.3   Evans County Study of Heart Disease: PROC FREQ

```
            Example 17.9 from Kleinbaum, et al., p. 353                    1

                   SUMMARY STATISTICS FOR CAT BY CHD
                     CONTROLLING FOR AGE AND ECG


            Cochran-Mantel-Haenszel Statistics (Based on Table Scores)
⑯  Statistic   Alternative Hypothesis      DF      Value      Prob
   --------------------------------------------------------------------
       1        Nonzero Correlation         1      4.153      0.042
       2        Row Mean Scores Differ      1      4.153      0.042
       3        General Association         1      4.153      0.042


              Estimates of the Common Relative Risk (Row1/Row2)
                                                      95%
          Type of Study   Method        Value   Confidence Bounds
          --------------------------------------------------------
          Case-Control    Mantel-Haenszel   1.891    1.025    3.490
            (Odds Ratio)  Logit             1.906    1.030    3.526

          Cohort          Mantel-Haenszel   1.696    1.020    2.818
            (Col1 Risk)   Logit             1.712    1.032    2.840

          Cohort          Mantel-Haenszel   0.900    0.814    0.996
            (Col2 Risk)   Logit             0.904    0.811    1.008

          The confidence bounds for the M-H estimates are test-based.


             Breslow-Day Test for Homogeneity of the Odds Ratios

          Chi-Square =   0.164        DF =   3        Prob = 0.983


          Total Sample Size = 609
```

Example 4: Friedman's Chi-Square

Eight subjects were asked to display certain emotions while under hypnosis (Lehmann 1975, 264). The null hypothesis is that hypnosis has the same effect on skin potential for each of the following four emotions: fear, happiness (joy), depression (sadness), and calmness. Skin potential was measured in millivolts, and the four measurements were then ranked within each subject. Since there are no tied ranks within a subject, the analysis of variance CMH statistic is

Friedman's chi-square (Q=6.45, $p=0.09$). The NOPRINT option is used to suppress printing of the contingency tables. These statements produce **Output 19.4**:

```
data hypnosis;
   input subject emotion $ ranking aa;
   cards;
1 fear 4    1 joy 3    1 sadness 1    1 calmness 2
2 fear 4    2 joy 2    2 sadness 3    2 calmness 1
3 fear 3    3 joy 2    3 sadness 4    3 calmness 1
4 fear 4    4 joy 1    4 sadness 2    4 calmness 3
5 fear 1    5 joy 4    5 sadness 3    5 calmness 2
6 fear 4    6 joy 3    6 sadness 2    6 calmness 1
7 fear 4    7 joy 1    7 sadness 2    7 calmness 3
8 fear 3    8 joy 4    8 sadness 2    8 calmness 1
;
proc freq;
   tables subject*emotion*ranking / noprint cmh;
   title 'Friedman''s Chi-Square';
run;
```

Output 19.4 Friedman's Chi-Square: PROC FREQ

```
                        Friedman's Chi-Square                              1

                 SUMMARY STATISTICS FOR EMOTION BY RANKING
                         CONTROLLING FOR SUBJECT

         Cochran-Mantel-Haenszel Statistics (Based on Table Scores)

         Statistic   Alternative Hypothesis    DF    Value    Prob
         ----------------------------------------------------------
             1       Nonzero Correlation        1    0.240    0.624
             2       Row Mean Scores Differ     3    6.450    0.092
             3       General Association        9   10.500    0.312


         Total Sample Size = 32
```

REFERENCES

Birch, M.W. (1965), "The Detection of Partial Association, II: The General Case," *Journal of the Royal Statistical Society, B,* 27, 111–124.

Bishop, Y., Fienberg, S.E., and Holland, P.W. (1975), *Discrete Multivariate Analysis: Theory and Practice,* Cambridge, MA: MIT Press.

Blalock, H.M., Jr. (1960), *Social Statistics,* New York: McGraw-Hill Book Co.

Breslow, N.E. and Day, N.E. (1980), *Statistical Methods in Cancer Research, Volume 1: The Analysis of Case-Control Studies,* Lyon: International Agency for Research on Cancer.

Bross, I.D.J. (1958), "How to Use Ridit Analysis," *Biometrics* , 14, 18–38.

Brown, M.B. and Benedetti, J.K. (1976), "Asymptotic Standard Errors and Their Sampling Behavior for Measures of Association and Correlation in the Two-way Contingency Table," Technical Report No. 23, Health Sciences Computing Facility, University of California, Los Angeles.

Cochran, W.G. (1954), "Some Methods for Strengthening the Common χ^2 Tests," *Biometrics,* 10, 417–451.

Fienberg, S.E. (1977), *The Analysis of Cross-Classified Data*, Cambridge, MA: MIT Press.

Fleiss, J.L. (1981), *Statistical Methods for Rates and Proportions*, 2d Edition, New York: John Wiley & Sons, Inc.

Garson, G.D. (1971), *Handbook of Political Science Methods*, Boston, MA: Holbrook Press, Inc.

Goodman, L.A. and Kruskal, W.H. (1954, 1959, 1963, 1972), "Measures of Association for Cross-Classification I, II, III, and IV," *Journal of the American Statistical Association*, 49, 732–764; 54, 123–163; 58, 310–364; 67, 415–421.

Goodman, L.A. and Kruskal, W.H. (1979), *Measures of Association for Cross Classification*, New York: Springer-Verlag (reprint of JASA articles above).

Haldane, J.B.S. (1955), "The Estimation and Significance of the Logarithm of a Ratio of Frequencies," *Annals of Human Genetics*, 20, 309–314.

Hayes, W.L. (1963), *Psychological Statistics*, New York: Holt, Rinehart and Winston, Inc.

Kendall, M. and Stuart, A. (1979), *The Advanced Theory of Statistics, Volume 2*, New York: Macmillan Publishing Company, Inc.

Kleinbaum, D.G., Kupper, L.L., and Morgenstern, H. (1982) *Epidemiologic Research: Principles and Quantitative Methods*, Belmont, CA: Wadsworth, Inc.

Landis, R.J., Heyman, E.R., and Koch, G.G. (1978), "Average Partial Association in Three-way Contingency Tables: A Review and Discussion of Alternative Tests," *International Statistical Review*, 46, 237–254.

Lehmann, E.L. (1975), *Nonparametrics: Statistical Methods Based on Ranks*, San Francisco: Holden-Day.

Mack, G.A. and Skillings, J.H. (1980), "A Friedman-Type Rank Test for Main Effects in a Two-Factor ANOVA," *Journal of the American Statistical Association*, 75, 947–951.

Mantel, N. (1963), "Chi-square Tests with One Degree of Freedom: Extensions of the Mantel-Haenszel Procedure," *Journal of the American Statistical Association*, 58, 690–700.

Mantel, N. and Haenszel, W. (1959), "Statistical Aspects of the Analysis of Data from Retrospective Studies of Disease," *Journal of the National Cancer Institute*, 22, 719–748.

Mehta, C.R. and Patel, N.R. (1983), "A Network Algorithm for Performing Fisher's Exact Test in $r \times c$ Contingency Tables," *Journal of the American Statistical Association, 78*, 427–434.

Snedecor, G.W. and Cochran, W.G. (1980), *Statistical Methods*, 7th Edition, Ames, IA: Iowa State University Press.

Somers, R.H. (1962), "A New Asymmetric Measure of Association for Ordinal Variables," *American Sociological Review*, 27, 799–811.

Theil, H. (1972), *Statistical Decomposition Analysis*, Amsterdam: North-Holland Publishing Company.

van Elteren, P.H. (1960), "On the Combination of Independent Two-Sample Tests of Wilcoxon," *Bulletin of the International Statistical Institute*, 37, 351–361.

Woolf, B. (1955), "On Estimating the Relationship between Blood Group and Disease," *Annals of Human Genetics*, 19, 251–253.

ABSTRACT

The GLM procedure uses the method of least squares to fit general linear models. Among the statistical methods available in PROC GLM are regression, analysis of variance, analysis of covariance, multivariate analysis of variance, and partial correlation.

INTRODUCTION

PROC GLM analyzes data within the framework of **G**eneral **L**inear **M**odels, hence the name GLM. GLM handles classification variables, which have discrete levels, as well as continuous variables, which measure quantities. Thus GLM can be used for many different analyses including

- simple regression
- multiple regression
- analysis of variance (*ANOVA*), especially for unbalanced data
- analysis of covariance
- response-surface models
- weighted regression
- polynomial regression
- partial correlation
- multivariate analysis of variance (*MANOVA*)
- repeated measures analysis of variance.

PROC GLM Features

The following list summarizes the features in PROC GLM:

- When more than one dependent variable is specified, GLM automatically groups together those variables that have the same pattern of missing values within the data set or within a BY group. This ensures that the analysis for each dependent variable brings into use all possible observations.
- GLM can be used interactively. After specifying and running a model, a variety of statements can be executed without GLM recomputing the model parameters or sums of squares.
- GLM allows you to specify any degree of interaction (crossed effects) and nested effects. It also provides for polynomial, continuous-by-class, and continuous-nesting-class effects.
- Through the concept of estimability, GLM can provide tests of hypotheses for the effects of a linear model regardless of the number of missing cells or the extent of confounding. GLM prints the Sum of Squares (SS) associated with each hypothesis tested and, upon request, the form of the estimable functions employed in the test. GLM can produce the general form of all estimable functions.
- The MANOVA statement allows you to specify both the hypothesis effects and the error effect to use for a multivariate analysis of variance.
- GLM can create an output data set containing a wide variety of diagnostic measures and all of the original variables. In addition, GLM can create an output data set containing sums of squares and crossproducts and results of canonical analyses performed using the MANOVA statement.

- The REPEATED statement allows you to specify effects in the model that represent repeated measurements on the same experimental unit, and it provides both univariate and multivariate tests of hypotheses.
- The RANDOM statement allows you to specify random effects in the model; expected mean squares are printed for each Type I, Type II, Type III, Type IV, and contrast mean square used in the analysis. Upon request, *F* tests using appropriate mean squares or linear combinations of mean squares as error terms are performed.
- The ESTIMATE statement allows you to specify an **L** vector for estimating a linear function of the parameters **Lβ**.
- The CONTRAST statement allows you to specify a contrast vector or matrix for testing the hypothesis that **Lβ**=0. When specified, the CONTRASTs are also incorporated into analyses using the MANOVA and REPEATED statements.

PROC GLM Contrasted with Other SAS Procedures

As described above, GLM can be used for many different analyses and has many special features not available in other SAS procedures. However, for some types of analyses, other procedures are available. As discussed in **PROC GLM for Multiple Regression** and **PROC GLM for Unbalanced ANOVA** later in this chapter, sometimes these other procedures are more efficient than GLM. The following procedures perform some of the same analyses as GLM:

ANOVA
: performs analysis of variance for balanced designs. ANOVA is generally more efficient than GLM for these models.

NESTED
: performs analysis of variance and estimates variance components for nested random models. NESTED is generally more efficient than GLM for these models.

NPAR1WAY
: performs nonparametric one-way analysis of rank scores. This can also be done using PROC RANK and PROC GLM.

REG
: performs general-purpose regression. REG allows several MODEL statements and gives additional regression diagnostics, especially for detection of collinearity.

RSREG
: builds quadratic response-surface regression models and performs canonical and ridge analysis. RSREG is generally recommended for data from a response surface experiment.

TTEST
: compares the means of two groups of observations. Also, tests for equality of variances for the two groups. TTEST is usually more efficient than GLM for this type of data.

VARCOMP
: estimates variance components for a general linear model.

Using PROC GLM Interactively

GLM can be used interactively. After you specify a model with a MODEL statement and run GLM with a RUN statement, a variety of statements can be executed without reinvoking GLM.

The **SPECIFICATIONS** section describes which statements can be used interactively. These interactive statements can be executed singly or in groups by following the single statement or group of statements with a RUN statement. Note that the MODEL statement cannot be repeated; PROC GLM allows only one MODEL statement.

If you use GLM interactively, you can end the GLM procedure with a DATA step, another PROC step, an ENDSAS statement, or with a QUIT statement. The syntax of the QUIT statement is

```
quit;
```

When you are using GLM interactively, additional RUN statements do not end the procedure but tell GLM to execute additional statements.

When a BY statement is used with PROC GLM, interactive processing is not possible; that is, once the first RUN statement is encountered, processing proceeds for each BY group in the data set, and no further statements are accepted by the procedure.

Specification of Effects

Each term in a model, called an *effect*, is a variable or combination of variables. Effects are specified with a special notation using variable names and operators. There are two kinds of variables: *classification* (or *class*) *variables* and *continuous variables*. There are two primary operators: *crossing* and *nesting*. A third operator, the *bar operator*, is used to simplify effect specification.

In an analysis-of-variance model, independent variables must be variables that identify classification levels. In the SAS System these are called *class variables* and are declared in the CLASS statement. (They may also be called *categorical*, *qualitative*, *discrete*, or *nominal variables*.) Class variables may be either *numeric* or *character*. The values of a class variable are called *levels*. For example, the class variable SEX has the levels "male" and "female."

In a model, an independent variable that is not declared in the CLASS statement is assumed to be continuous. Continuous variables, which must be numeric, are used for response variables and covariates. For example, the heights and weights of subjects are continuous variables.

Types of Effects

There are seven different types of effects used in GLM. In the following list assume that A, B, C, D, and E are class variables and X1, X2, and Y are continuous variables:

- Regressor effects are specified by writing continuous variables by themselves: X1   X2.
- Polynomial effects are specified by joining two or more continuous variables with asterisks: X1*X1   X1*X2.
- Main effects are specified by writing class variables by themselves: A   B   C.
- Crossed effects (interactions) are specified by joining class variables with asterisks: A*B   B*C   A*B*C.
- Nested effects are specified by following a main effect or crossed effect with a class variable or list of class variables enclosed in parentheses. The main effect or crossed effect is nested within the effects listed in parentheses:

    B(A)   C(B A)   D*E(C B A)   .

    Note: B(A) is read "B nested within A."
- Continuous-by-class effects are written by joining continuous variables and class variables with asterisks: X1*A.

- Continuous-nesting-class effects consist of continuous variables followed by a list of class variables enclosed in parentheses: X1(A)   X1*X2(A B).

One example of the general form of an effect involving several variables is

X1*X2*A*B*C(D E)   .

This example contains crossed continuous terms by crossed classification terms nested within multiple class variables. The continuous list comes first, followed by the crossed list, followed by the nested list in parentheses. Note that no asterisks appear within the nested list or immediately before the left parenthesis. For details on how the design matrix and parameters are defined with respect to the effects specified in this section, see **Parameterization of GLM Models** in the **DETAILS** section later in this chapter.

The MODEL statement and several other statements use these effects. Some examples of MODEL statements using various kinds of effects are shown below. A, B, and C represent class variables; and Y1, Y2, X1, and X2 represent continuous variables.

Specification	Kind of Model
`model y=x1;`	simple regression
`model y=x1 x2;`	multiple regression
`model y=x1 x1*x1;`	polynomial regression
`model y1 y2=x1 x2;`	multivariate regression
`model y=a;`	one-way *ANOVA*
`model y=a b c;`	main effects model
`model y=a b a*b;`	factorial model (with interaction)
`model y=a b(a) c(b a);`	nested model
`model y1 y2=a b;`	multivariate analysis of variance (*MANOVA*)
`model y=a x1;`	analysis-of-covariance model
`model y=a x1(a);`	separate-slopes model
`model y=a x1 x1*a;`	homogeneity-of-slopes model

The Bar Operator

You can shorten the specification of a factorial model using the bar operator. For example, two ways of writing a full three-way factorial are

```
proc glm;
   class a b c;
   model y=a b c a*b a*c b*c a*b*c;
```

and

```
proc glm;
   class a b c;
   model y=a|b|c;
```

When the bar (|) is used, the right- and left-hand sides become effects, and the cross of them becomes an effect. Multiple bars are permitted. The expressions are expanded from left to right, using rules 2–4 given in Searle (1971, 390):

- Multiple bars are evaluated left to right. For instance, A | B | C is {A | B } | C, which is {A B A*B } | C, which is

    A B A*B C A*C B*C A*B*C .

- Crossed and nested groups of variables are combined. For example, A(B) | C(D) generates A*C(B D), among other terms.
- Duplicate variables are removed. For example, A(C) | B(C) generates A*B(C), among other terms, and the extra C is removed.
- Effects are discarded if a variable occurs on both the crossed and nested sides of an effect. For instance, A(B) | B(D E) generates A*B(B D E), but this effect is eliminated immediately.

You can also specify the maximum number of variables involved in any effect that results from bar evaluation by specifying that maximum number, preceded by an @ sign, at the end of the bar effect. For example, the specification A | B | C@2 would result in only those effects that contain 2 or fewer variables: in this case A B A*B C A*C and B*C.

Other examples of the bar notation are

A	C(B)	is equivalent to	A C(B) A*C(B)
A(B)	C(B)	is equivalent to	A(B) C(B) A*C(B)
A(B)	B(D E)	is equivalent to	A(B) B(D E)
A	B(A)	C	is equivalent to	A B(A) C A*C B*C(A)
A	B(A)	C@2	is equivalent to	A B(A) C A*C
A	B	C	D@2	is equivalent to	A B A*B C A*C B*C
			D A*D B*D C*D

PROC GLM for Multiple Regression

In multiple regression, the values of a dependent variable (also called a response variable) are described or predicted in terms of one or more independent or explanatory variables. The statements

```
proc glm;
   model dependent=independents;
```

can be used to describe a multiple regression model in GLM. The REG procedure provides additional statistics for multiple regression and is often more efficient than GLM for these models.

PROC GLM for Unbalanced *ANOVA*

The ANOVA procedure should be used whenever possible for analysis of variance because ANOVA processes data more efficiently than GLM. However, GLM should be used in most unbalanced situations, that is, models where there are unequal numbers of observations for the different combinations of CLASS variables specified in the MODEL statement.

Here is an example of a 2×2 factorial model. The data are shown in a table and then read into a SAS data set:

		A	
		1	2
B	1	12 14	20 18
	2	11 9	17

```
data exp;
   input a $ b $ y aa;
   cards;
A1 B1 12 A1 B1 14 A1 B2 11 A1 B2 9
A2 B1 20 A2 B1 18 A2 B2 17
;
```

Note that there is only one value for the second levels of A and B. Since one cell contains a different number of values from the other cells in the table, this is an unbalanced design and GLM should be used. The statements needed for this two-way factorial model are

```
proc glm;
   class a b;
   model y=a b a*b;
```

The results from PROC GLM are shown in **Output 20.1**.

Output 20.1   Two-Way Factorial: GLM Procedure

```
                    General Linear Models Procedure                    1
                       Class Level Information

              Class    Levels    Values

               A          2      A1 A2

               B          2      B1 B2

          Number of observations in data set = 7
```

```
                                                                                 2
                        General Linear Models Procedure
Dependent Variable: Y
Source              DF         Sum of Squares      Mean Square    F Value     Pr > F
Model                3           91.71428571      30.57142857      15.29     0.0253
Error                3            6.00000000       2.00000000
Corrected Total      6           97.71428571
              R-Square              C.V.              Root MSE              Y Mean
              0.938596           9.801480           1.41421356           14.42857143
Source              DF             Type I SS        Mean Square    F Value     Pr > F
A                    1           80.04761905      80.04761905      40.02     0.0080
B                    1           11.26666667      11.26666667       5.63     0.0982
A*B                  1            0.40000000       0.40000000       0.20     0.6850
Source              DF            Type III SS       Mean Square    F Value     Pr > F
A                    1           67.60000000      67.60000000      33.80     0.0101
B                    1           10.00000000      10.00000000       5.00     0.1114
A*B                  1            0.40000000       0.40000000       0.20     0.6850
```

Four types of estimable functions of parameters are available for testing hypotheses in GLM. For data with no missing cells, the Type III and Type IV estimable functions are the same and test the same hypotheses that would be tested if the data were balanced.

The Type III results on this printout indicate a significant A effect but no significant B effect or A*B interaction.

SPECIFICATIONS

Although there are numerous statements and options available in GLM, many applications use only a few of them. Often you can find the features you need by looking at an example or by quickly scanning through this section. The statements available in GLM are

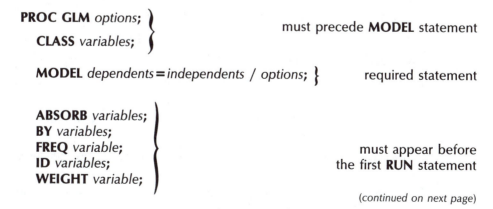

PROC GLM *options;*   must precede **MODEL** statement
    CLASS *variables;*

    MODEL *dependents = independents / options;*   required statement

    ABSORB *variables;*
BY *variables;*
FREQ *variable;*   must appear before
ID *variables;*   the first **RUN** statement
WEIGHT *variable;*

(continued on next page)

(continued from previous page)

> **CONTRAST** *'label'* *effect values* . . . / *options*;
> **ESTIMATE** *'label'* *effect values* . . . / *options*;
> **LSMEANS** *effects* / *options*;
> **MANOVA H=***effects* **E=***effect*
>   **M=***equations* . . . **MNAMES=***names*
>   **PREFIX=** *name* / *options*;
> **MEANS** *effects* / *options*;
> **OUTPUT OUT=***SASdataset keywords=names* . . . ;
> **RANDOM** *effects* / *options*;
> **REPEATED** *factorname levels(levelvalues)*
>   *transformation*[, . . .] / *options*;
> **TEST H=***effects* **E=***effect* / *options*;

can appear anywhere after the **MODEL** statement and can be used interactively

The PROC GLM and MODEL statements are required. If classification effects are used, the class variables must be declared in a CLASS statement, and the CLASS statement must appear before the MODEL statement. In addition, if you use a CONTRAST (or TEST) statement in combination with a MANOVA, RANDOM, or REPEATED statement, the CONTRAST (or TEST) statement must be entered first in order for the CONTRAST to be included in the MANOVA, RANDOM, or REPEATED analysis.

The statements used with PROC GLM in addition to the PROC statement are as follows (in alphabetical order):

ABSORB	absorbs classification effects in a model.
BY	processes BY groups.
CLASS	declares classification variables.
CONTRAST	constructs and tests linear functions of the parameters.
ESTIMATE	also constructs and tests linear functions of the parameters.
FREQ	specifies a frequency variable.
ID	identifies observations on printed output.
LSMEANS	computes least-squares (marginal) means.
MANOVA	performs a multivariate analysis of variance.
MEANS	requests that means be printed and compared.
MODEL	defines the model to be fit.
OUTPUT	requests an output data set containing diagnostics for each observation.
RANDOM	declares certain effects to be random and computes expected mean squares.
REPEATED	performs multivariate and univariate repeated measures analysis of variance.
TEST	constructs tests using the sums of squares for effects and the error term you specify.
WEIGHT	specifies a variable for weighting observations.

PROC GLM Statement

> PROC GLM *options*;

Six options can be used in the PROC GLM statement:

DATA=*SASdataset*
:   names the SAS data set to be used by GLM. If the DATA= option is omitted, GLM uses the most recently created SAS data set.

MANOVA
:   requests that PROC GLM use the multivariate mode of eliminating observations with missing values, that is, to eliminate an observation from the analysis if any of the dependent variables have missing values. This option is useful if you are using PROC GLM in interactive mode and will be performing a multivariate analysis.

MULTIPASS
:   requests that PROC GLM reread the input data set when necessary, instead of writing the necessary values of dependent variables to a utility file. This option decreases disk space usage at the expense of increased execution times, and is only useful in rare situations.

NOPRINT
:   suppresses the normal printout of results. When the NOPRINT option is used, no printed output is produced. This option is generally useful only when one or more output data sets are being produced by PROC GLM.

ORDER=FREQ
ORDER=DATA
ORDER=INTERNAL
ORDER=FORMATTED
:   specifies the order in which you want the levels of the classification variables (specified in the CLASS statement) to be sorted. This ordering determines which parameters in the model correspond to each level in the data, so the ORDER= option may be useful when you are using CONTRAST or ESTIMATE statements. If you specify ORDER=FREQ, levels are sorted by descending frequency count so that levels with the most observations come first. If you specify ORDER=DATA, levels are sorted in the order in which they first occur in the input data. If you specify ORDER=INTERNAL, then the levels are sorted by the internal value. If you specify ORDER=FORMATTED, levels are ordered by the external formatted value. If you omit the ORDER= option, PROC GLM orders by the formatted value.

OUTSTAT=*SASdataset*
:   names an output data set that will contain sums of squares, *F* statistics, and probability levels for each effect in the model, as well as for each CONTRAST statement used. If the CANONICAL option of the MANOVA statement is used and there is no M= specification, the data set also contains results of the canonical analysis. See **Output Data Sets** in the **DETAILS** section later in this chapter for more information.

ABSORB Statement

> ABSORB *variables*;

Absorption is a computational technique that provides a large reduction in time and memory requirements for certain types of models.

For a main effect variable that does not participate in interactions, you can absorb the effect by naming it in an ABSORB statement. This means that the effect can be adjusted out before the construction and solution of the rest of the model. This is particularly useful when the effect has a large number of levels.

Several variables can be specified, in which case each one is assumed to be nested in the preceding variable in the ABSORB statement.

Restrictions: when the ABSORB statement is used, the data set (or each BY group) must be sorted by the variables in the ABSORB statement. GLM cannot produce predicted values or create an output data set of diagnostic values if ABSORB is used. If the ABSORB statement is used, it must appear before the first RUN statement or it is ignored.

See **Absorption** in the **DETAILS** section later in this chapter for more information.

BY Statement

BY *variables*;

A BY statement can be used with PROC GLM to obtain separate analyses on observations in groups defined by the BY variables. When a BY statement appears, the procedure expects the input data set to be sorted in order of the BY variables.

If your input data set is not sorted in ascending order, use the SORT procedure with a similar BY statement to sort the data, or, if appropriate, use the BY statement options NOTSORTED or DESCENDING. For more information, see the discussion of the BY statement in "SAS Statements Used in the PROC Step" in the *SAS Language Guide, Release 6.03 Edition.*

When a BY statement is used with PROC GLM, interactive processing is not possible; that is, once the first RUN statement is encountered, processing proceeds for each BY group in the data set, and no further statements are accepted by the procedure. If the BY statement appears after the first RUN statement, it is ignored.

When both a BY and an ABSORB statement are used, observations must be sorted first by the variables in the BY statement, and then by the variables in the ABSORB statement.

CLASS Statement

CLASS *variables*;

The CLASS (or CLASSES) statement names the classification variables to be used in the analysis. Typical class variables are TRTMENT, SEX, RACE, GROUP, and REP. If the CLASS statement is used, it must appear before the MODEL statement.

Classification variables can be either character or numeric. Only the first sixteen characters of a character variable are used.

Class levels are determined from the formatted values of the CLASS variables. Thus, you can use formats to group values into levels. See the discussion of the FORMAT procedure, the FORMAT statement, and "SAS Informats and Formats" in the *SAS Language Guide*.

CONTRAST Statement

CONTRAST *'label' effect values . . . / options*;

The CONTRAST statement provides a mechanism for obtaining custom hypothesis tests. This is achieved by specifying an **L** vector or matrix for testing the univariate hypothesis **Lβ**=0 or the multivariate hypothesis **LβM**=0. Thus, to use this feature you must be familiar with the details of the model parameterization that PROC GLM uses. (See **Parameterization of GLM Models** in the **DETAILS** section for more information.)

There is no limit to the number of CONTRAST statements, but they must come after the MODEL statement.

If you use a CONTRAST statement and a MANOVA or REPEATED statement, appropriate tests for contrasts are carried out as part of the MANOVA or REPEATED analysis. If you use a CONTRAST statement and a RANDOM statement, the expected mean square of the contrast is printed. In these cases, you must enter the CONTRAST statement before the MANOVA, REPEATED, or RANDOM statement.

In the CONTRAST statement,

> *label* is twenty characters and is used on the printout to identify the contrast. The label must be enclosed in single quotes. A label must be supplied for every contrast specified.

> *effect* is the name of an effect that appears in the MODEL statement; the keyword INTERCEPT may be used as an effect when an intercept is fitted in the model. You do not need to include all effects that are in the MODEL statement.

> *values* are constants that are elements of the **L** vector associated with the effect.

These options are available in the CONTRAST statement and are specified after a slash (/):

E

requests that the entire **L** vector be printed.

E=*effect*

specifies an effect in the model to use as an error term. If none is specified, the error MS is used. If you specify an effect, it is used as the denominator in *F* tests in univariate analysis. If you specify an effect, and a MANOVA or REPEATED statement is also present, the effect is used as the basis of the **E** matrix.

ETYPE=*n*

specifies the type (1, 2, 3, or 4) of the E= effect. If E= is specified and ETYPE= is not, the highest type computed in the analysis is used.

SINGULAR=*number*

tunes the estimability checking. If ABS(**L**−**LH**)>C*SINGULAR for any row in the contrast, then the **L** is declared nonestimable. **H** is the $(\mathbf{X'X})^{-}\mathbf{X'X}$ matrix, and C is ABS(**L**) except for rows where **L** is zero, and then it is 1. The default is 1E−4.

As stated above, the CONTRAST statement allows you to perform custom hypothesis tests. If the hypothesis is testable in the univariate case, SS(H_0: **Lβ**=0) is computed as

$$(\mathbf{Lb})'(\mathbf{L(X'X)}^{-}\mathbf{L'})^{-1}(\mathbf{Lb})$$

where $\mathbf{b}=(\mathbf{X'X})^{-}\mathbf{X'y}$. This is the SS printed on the analysis-of-variance table.

For multivariate testable hypotheses, the usual multivariate tests are performed using

$$\mathbf{H} = \mathbf{M'(Lb)'(L(X'X)}^{-}\mathbf{L'})^{-1}(\mathbf{Lb})\mathbf{M} \quad .$$

The **L** matrix should be of full row rank. However, if it is not, the degrees of freedom associated with the hypotheses are reduced to the row rank of **L**. The

SS computed in this situation are equivalent to the SS computed using an **L** matrix with any row deleted that is a linear combination of previous rows.

Multiple-degree-of-freedom hypotheses can be specified by separating the rows of the **L** matrix with commas, as shown below. For example, for the model

```
model y=a b;
```

with A at 5 levels and B at 2 levels, the parameter vector is

$$(\mu \quad \alpha_1 \ \alpha_2 \ \alpha_3 \ \alpha_4 \ \alpha_5 \ \beta_1 \ \beta_2) \quad .$$

To test the hypothesis that the pooled A linear and A quadratic effect is zero, you can use the following **L** matrix:

$$L = \begin{bmatrix} 0 & -2 & -1 & 0 & 1 & 2 & 0 & 0 \\ 0 & 2 & -1 & -2 & -1 & 2 & 0 & 0 \end{bmatrix}$$

The corresponding CONTRAST statement is

```
contrast 'A LINEAR & QUADRATIC'
         a -2 -1  0  1 2,
         a  2 -1 -2 -1 2;
```

If the first level of A is a control level and you want a test of control versus others, you can use this statement:

```
contrast 'CONTROL VS OTHERS'  a -1 .25 .25 .25 .25;
```

See the discussion of the ESTIMATE statement below and **Specification of ESTIMATE Expressions** later in this chapter for rules on specification, construction, distribution, and estimability in the CONTRAST statement.

ESTIMATE Statement

ESTIMATE *'label' effect values . . . / options;*

The ESTIMATE statement can be used to estimate linear functions of the parameters by multiplying the vector **L** by the parameter estimate vector **b** resulting in **Lb**. All of the elements of the **L** vector may be given, or if only certain portions of the **L** vector are given, the remaining elements are constructed by GLM from the context (in a manner similar to rule 4 discussed in the section **Least-Squares Means**).

The linear function is checked for estimability. The estimate **Lb**, where $b=(X'X)^-X'y$, is printed along with its associated standard error, $\sqrt{L(X'X)^-L's^2}$, and t test.

There is no limit to the number of ESTIMATE statements, but they must come after the MODEL statement. In a given ESTIMATE statement, you do not need to include all effects in the MODEL statement.

In the ESTIMATE statement,

> *label*   is twenty characters or less and is used on the printout to identify the estimate. The label must be enclosed in single quotes. A label must be supplied for every estimate specified.

    effect   is the name of an effect that appears in the MODEL statement; the keyword INTERCEPT may be used as an effect when an intercept is fitted in the model.

    values are constants that are the elements of the **L** vector associated with the preceding effect. For example, with no options,

```
estimate 'A1 VS A2' A  1  -1;
```

forms an estimate that is the difference between the parameters estimated for the first and second levels of the CLASS variable A.

The options below can appear in the ESTIMATE statement after a slash (/):

DIVISOR=*number*

specifies a value by which to divide all coefficients so that fractional coefficients can be entered as integer numerators. For example,

```
estimate '1 / 3(A1+A2) - 2 / 3A3' a 1 1 -2 / divisor=3;
```

instead of

```
estimate '1 / 3(A1+A2) - 2 / 3A3' A .33333 .33333 -.66667;
```

E

requests that the entire **L** vector be printed.

SINGULAR=*number*

tunes the estimability checking. If $ABS(\mathbf{L}-\mathbf{LH})>C*SINGULAR$, then the **L** is declared nonestimable. **H** is the $(\mathbf{X'X})^{-}\mathbf{X'X}$ matrix, and C is $ABS(\mathbf{L})$ except for rows where **L** is zero, and then it is 1. The default is $1E-4$.

See also **Specification of ESTIMATE Expressions** later in this chapter.

FREQ Statement

    FREQ *variable*;

When a FREQ statement appears, each observation in the input data set is assumed to represent *n* observations in the experiment. For each observation, *n* is the value of the variable specified in the FREQ statement.

If the value of the FREQ statement variable is missing or is less than 1, the observation is not used in the analysis. If the value is not an integer, only the integer portion is used.

The analysis produced using a FREQ statement is identical to an analysis produced using a data set that contains *n* observations in place of each observation of the input data set, where *n* is the value of the variable specified in the FREQ statement. Therefore, means and total degrees of freedom reflect the expanded number of observations.

If the FREQ statement is used, it must appear before the first RUN statement or it is ignored.

ID Statement

    ID *variables*;

When predicted values are requested as a MODEL statement option, values of the variables given in the ID statement are printed beside each observed, predicted, and residual value for identification. Although there are no restrictions on the length of ID variables, GLM may truncate the number of values printed in order to print on one line. GLM prints a maximum of five ID variables.

If the ID statement is used, it must appear before the first RUN statement or it is ignored.

LSMEANS Statement

LSMEANS *effects* / *options*;

Least-squares means are computed for each effect listed in the LSMEANS statement.

Least-squares estimates of marginal means (LSMs) are to unbalanced designs as class and subclass arithmetic means are to balanced designs. LSMs are simply estimators of the class or subclass marginal means that would be expected had the design been balanced. For further information, see **Least-Squares Means** in the **DETAILS** section.

Least-squares means can be computed for any effect involving class variables as long as the effect is in the model. Any number of LSMEANS statements can be used. They must be given after the MODEL statement.

Here is an example:

```
proc glm;
   class a b;
   model y=a b a*b;
   lsmeans a b a*b;
```

Least-squares means are printed for each level of the A, B, and A*B effects.

The options below can appear in the LSMEANS statement after a slash (/):

COV
   requests that covariances be included in the output data set specified in the OUT= option of the LSMEANS statement. If no OUT= option is specified in the LSMEANS statement, the COV option has no effect. When you specify the COV option, you can specify only one effect in the LSMEANS statement.

E
   prints the estimable functions used to compute the LSM.

E=*effect*
   specifies an effect in the model to use as an error term. The mean square for the specified effect is used when standard errors (with the STDERR option) and probabilities (with the STDERR, PDIFF, or TDIFF options) are calculated. If neither STDERR nor PDIFF nor TDIFF is specified, the E= option is ignored. If STDERR, PDIFF, or TDIFF is specified and E= is not, the error MS is used for calculating standard errors and probabilities.

ETYPE=*n*
   specifies the type (1, 2, 3, or 4) of the E= effect. If E= is specified and ETYPE= is not, the highest type computed in the analysis is used.

NOPRINT
   requests that the normal printed output from the LSMEANS statement be suppressed. This option is useful when an output data set is requested using the OUT= option of the LSMEANS statement.

OUT=*SASdataset*
   specifies the name of an output data set to contain the values, standard errors, and, optionally, the covariances (see the COV option above) of the least-squares means. For more information, see **Output Data Sets** in the **DETAILS** section.

PDIFF

> requests that all possible probability values for the hypotheses
> H_0: LSM(i)=LSM(j) be printed.

SINGULAR=*number*

> tunes the estimability checking. If ABS(**L**−**LH**)>C*SINGULAR for any
> row, then the **L** is declared nonestimable. **H** is the $(\mathbf{X'X})^-\mathbf{X'X}$ matrix, and
> C is ABS(**L**) except for rows where **L** is zero, and then it is 1. The default
> is 1E−4.

STDERR

> prints the standard error of the LSM and the probability level for the
> hypothesis H_0: LSM=0.

TDIFF

> requests that the *t* values for the hypotheses H_0: LSM(i)=LSM(j) be
> printed along with the corresponding probabilities.

For further information on the output data set created by the LSMEANS statement, see **Output Data Sets**.

MANOVA Statement

> MANOVA H=*effects* E=*effect* M=*equation1,equation2,* . . .
> MNAMES=*names* PREFIX=*name* / *options*;

If the MODEL statement includes more than one dependent variable, additional
multivariate statistics can be requested with the MANOVA statement.

When a MANOVA statement appears before the first RUN statement, GLM
enters a multivariate mode with respect to the handling of missing values; observations with missing independent or dependent variables are excluded from the
analysis. If you want to use this mode of handling missing values and do not need
any multivariate analyses, specify the MANOVA option in the PROC GLM statement.

If you use a CONTRAST statement with a MANOVA statement, the CONTRAST
statement must appear before the MANOVA statement.

The terms below are specified in the MANOVA statement:

H=*effects*   specifies effects in the preceding model to use as
hypothesis matrices. For each **H** matrix (the SSCP matrix
associated with that effect), the H= specification prints
the characteristic roots and vectors of $\mathbf{E}^{-1}\mathbf{H}$ (where **E** is
the matrix associated with the error effect), Hotelling-
Lawley trace, Pillai's trace, Wilks' criterion, and Roy's
maximum root criterion with approximate *F* statistic. Use
the keyword INTERCEPT to print tests for the intercept.
To print tests for all effects listed in the MODEL
statement, use the keyword _ALL_ in place of a list of
effects. For background and further details, see
Multivariate Analysis of Variance in the **DETAILS** section.

E=*effect*   specifies the error effect. If you omit the E=
specification, the error SSCP (residual) matrix from the
analysis is used.

M=equation1,equation2, . . .
M= (listofnumbers, . . .)

specifies a transformation matrix for the dependent variables listed in the MODEL statement. The equations in the M= specification are of the form

$$\pm term \; [\pm term \ldots]$$

where *term* is either *dependentvariable* or *number*dependentvariable* and brackets indicate optional specifications. Alternatively, the transformation matrix can be input directly by entering the elements of the matrix with commas separating the rows, and parentheses surrounding the matrix. When this alternate form of input is used, the number of elements in each row must equal the number of dependent variables. Although these combinations actually represent the columns of the **M** matrix, they are printed by rows.

When you include an M= specification, the analysis requested in the MANOVA statement is carried out for the variables defined by the equations in the specification, not the original dependent variables. If M= is omitted, the analysis is performed for the original dependent variables in the MODEL statement.

If an M= specification is included without either the MNAMES= or PREFIX= option, the variables are labeled MVAR1, MVAR2, and so forth by default. Examples of the use of the M= specification are given below. For further information, see **Multivariate Analysis of Variance**.

The following two terms allow you to specify labels for the transformed variables defined by the M= specification:

MNAMES=*names*   provides names for the variables defined by the equations in the M= specification. Names in the list correspond to the M= equations or the rows of the M matrix (as it is entered).

PREFIX=*name*   is an alternative means of identifying the transformed variables defined by the M= specification. For example, if you specify PREFIX=DIFF, the transformed variables are labeled DIFF1, DIFF2, and so forth.

The options below can appear in the MANOVA statement after a slash (/):

CANONICAL
requests that a canonical analysis of the **H** and **E** matrices (transformed by the **M** matrix, if specified) be printed instead of the default printout of characteristic roots and vectors.

ETYPE=*n*
specifies the type (1, 2, 3, or 4) of the **E** matrix. You need this option if you use the E= specification (rather than residual error) and you want to specify the type of SS used for the effect. If an ETYPE= value of *n* is given, the corresponding test must have been performed in the MODEL statement, either by options SS*n*, E*n*, or the default Type I and Type III.

If no ETYPE= option appears in the MANOVA statement, the ETYPE= value defaults to the highest type (largest *n*) used in the analysis.

HTYPE=*n*

specifies the type (1, 2, 3, or 4) of the **H** matrix. See ETYPE= above for more details.

ORTH

requests that the transformation matrix in the M= specification of the MANOVA statement be orthonormalized by rows before the analysis.

PRINTE

requests printing of the **E** matrix. If the **E** matrix is the error SSCP (residual) matrix from the analysis, the partial correlations of the dependent variables given the independent variables are also printed.
   For example, the statement

```
manova / printe;
```

prints the error SSCP matrix and the partial correlation matrix computed from the error SSCP matrix.

PRINTH

requests that the **H** matrix (the SSCP matrix) associated with each effect specified by the H= specification be printed.

SUMMARY

produces analysis-of-variance tables for each dependent variable. When no **M** matrix is specified, a table is printed for each original dependent variable from the MODEL statement; with an **M** matrix other than the identity, a table is printed for each transformed variable defined by the **M** matrix.

Here is an example:

```
proc glm;
   class a b;
   model y1-y5=a b(a);
   manova h=a e=b(a) / printh printe htype=1 etype=1;
   manova h=b(a) / printe;
   manova h=a e=b(a) m=y1-y2,y2-y3,y3-y4,y4-y5
         prefix=diff;
   manova h=a e=b(a) m=(1 -1  0  0  0,
                        0  1 -1  0  0,
                        0  0  1 -1  0,
                        0  0  0  1 -1) prefix=diff;
```

Since this MODEL statement requests no options for type of sums of squares, GLM uses Type I and Type III. The first MANOVA statement specifies A as the hypothesis effect and B(A) as the error effect. The PRINTH option requests that the **H** matrix associated with the A effect be printed, and the PRINTE option requests that the **E** matrix associated with the B(A) effect be printed. The HTYPE=1 option specifies that the **H** matrix be Type I; the ETYPE=1 option specifies that the **E** matrix be Type I.

The second MANOVA statement specifies B(A) as the hypothesis effect. Since no error effect is specified, GLM uses the error SSCP matrix from the analysis as the **E** matrix. The PRINTE option requests that this **E** matrix be printed. Since the **E** matrix is the error SSCP matrix from the analysis, the partial correlation matrix computed from this matrix is also printed.

The third MANOVA statement requests the same analysis as the first MANOVA statement, but the analysis is carried out for variables transformed to be successive differences between the original dependent variables. The PREFIX=DIFF option specifies that the transformed variables be labeled DIFF1, DIFF2, DIFF3, and DIFF4. Finally, the fourth MANOVA statement has the identical effect as the third, but it uses an alternative form of the M= specification.

As a second example of the use of the M= specification, consider the following:

```
proc glm;
   class group;
   model dose1-dose4=group;
   manova h=group m=-3*dose1-dose2+dose3+3*dose4,
               dose1-dose2-dose3+dose4,
               -dose1+3*dose2-3*dose3+dose4
         mnames=linear quadrtic cubic / printe;
```

The M= specification gives a transformation of the dependent variables DOSE1 through DOSE4 into orthogonal polynomial components, and the MNAMES= option labels the transformed variables LINEAR, QUADRTIC, and CUBIC, respectively. Since the PRINTE option is specified and the default residual matrix is used as an error term, the partial correlation matrix of the orthogonal polynomial components is also printed.

MEANS Statement

MEANS *effects* / *options*;

For any effect that appears on the right-hand side of the model and that does not contain any continuous variables, GLM can compute means of all continuous variables in the model. You can use any number of MEANS statements, provided they appear after the MODEL statement. See **Comparisons of Means** in the **DETAILS** section for more information about multiple comparison methods. For example, suppose A and B each have two levels. Then,

```
proc glm;
   class a b;
   model y=a b a*b;
   means a*b;
```

Means and standard deviations are printed for each of the four combinations of levels for A*B. For the model

```
model y=a x a*x;
```

where X is a continuous variable, the effects X and A*X cannot be used in the MEANS statement.

The options below can appear in the MEANS statement after a slash (/):

Options to Request Printouts

DEPONLY
  indicates that only the dependent variable means are to be printed. By default, GLM prints means for all continuous variables, including independent variables.

Options to Select a Multiple Comparison Procedure

BON
  performs Bonferroni *t* tests of differences between means for all main effect means in the MEANS statement.

DUNCAN
:   performs Duncan's multiple-range test on all main effect means given in the MEANS statement.

DUNNETT [(*formattedcontrolvalues*)]
:   performs Dunnett's two-tailed *t* test, testing if any treatments are significantly different from a single control for all main effects means in the MEANS statement.

    To specify which level of the effect is the control, enclose its quoted formatted value in parentheses after the keyword. If more than one effect is specified in the MEANS statement, you can use a list of control values within the parentheses. By default, the first level of the effect is used as the control. For example,

    ```
    means a / dunnett('CONTROL');
    ```

    where CONTROL is the formatted control value of A. As another example,

    ```
    means a b c / dunnett('CNTLA' 'CNTLB' 'CNTLC');
    ```

    where CNTLA, CNTLB, and CNTLC are the formatted control values for A, B, and C, respectively.

DUNNETTL [(*formattedcontrolvalue*)]
:   performs Dunnett's one-tailed *t* test, testing if any treatment is significantly smaller than the control. Control level information is specified as described above for the DUNNETT option.

DUNNETTU [(*formattedcontrolvalue*)]
:   performs Dunnett's one-tailed *t* test, testing if any treatment is significantly larger than the control. Control level information is specified as described above for the DUNNETT option.

GABRIEL
:   performs Gabriel's multiple-comparison procedure on all main effect means in the MEANS statement.

REGWF
:   performs the Ryan-Einot-Gabriel-Welsch multiple *F* test on all main effect means in the MEANS statement.

REGWQ
:   performs the Ryan-Einot-Gabriel-Welsch multiple-range test on all main effect means in the MEANS statement.

SCHEFFE
:   performs Scheffe's multiple-comparison procedure on all main effect means in the MEANS statement.

SIDAK
:   performs pairwise *t* tests on differences between means with levels adjusted according to Sidak's inequality for all main effect means in the MEANS statement.

SMM
GT2
:   performs pairwise comparisons based on the studentized maximum modulus and Sidak's uncorrelated-*t* inequality, yielding Hochberg's GT2 method when sample sizes are unequal, for all main effect means in the MEANS statement.

SNK
:   performs the Student-Newman-Keuls multiple range test on all main effect means in the MEANS statement.

T

LSD

performs pairwise *t* tests, equivalent to Fisher's least-significant-difference test in the case of equal cell sizes, for all main effect means in the MEANS statement.

TUKEY

performs Tukey's studentized range test (HSD) on all main effect means in the MEANS statement.

WALLER

requests that the Waller-Duncan *k*-ratio *t* test be performed on all main effect means in the MEANS statement. See the KRATIO= and HTYPE= options below.

Options to Specify Details for Multiple Comparison Procedures

ALPHA=*p*

gives the level of significance for comparisons among the means. The default ALPHA= value is 0.05. With the DUNCAN option, you may only specify values of 0.01, 0.05, or 0.1. For other options, you may use values between 0.0001 and 0.9999.

CLDIFF

requests that the results of the BON, GABRIEL, SCHEFFE, SIDAK, SMM, GT2, T, LSD, and TUKEY options be presented as confidence intervals for all pairwise differences between means. CLDIFF is the default for unequal cell sizes unless DUNCAN, REGWF, REGWQ, SNK, or WALLER is specified.

CLM

requests that the results of the BON, GABRIEL, SCHEFFE, SIDAK, SMM, T, and LSD options be presented as confidence intervals for the mean of each level of the variables specified in the MEANS statement.

E=*effect*

specifies the error mean square to use in the multiple comparisons. If the E= option is omitted, GLM uses the residual Mean Square (MS). The effect specified with the E= option must be a term in the model; otherwise, the procedure uses the residual MS.

ETYPE=*n*

specifies the type of mean square for the error effect. When E=*effect* is specified, you may need to indicate which type (1, 2, 3, or 4) of MS is to be used. The *n* value must be one of the types specified or implied by the MODEL statement. The default MS type is the highest type used in the analysis.

HTYPE=*n*

gives the MS type for the hypothesis MS. The HTYPE= option is needed only when the WALLER option is specified. The default HTYPE= value is the highest type used in the model.

KRATIO=*value*

gives the type1/type2 error seriousness ratio for the Waller-Duncan test. Reasonable values for KRATIO are 50, 100, 500, which roughly correspond for the two-level case to ALPHA levels of 0.1, 0.05, and 0.01. If the KRATIO= option is omitted, the procedure uses the default value of 100.

LINES
   requests that the results of the BON, DUNCAN, GABRIEL, REGWF, REGWQ, SCHEFFE, SIDAK, SMM, GT2, SNK, T, LSD, TUKEY, and WALLER options be presented by listing the means in descending order and indicating nonsignificant subsets by line segments beside the corresponding means. The LINES option is appropriate for equal cell sizes, for which it is the default. LINES is also the default if DUNCAN, REGWF, REGWQ, SNK, or WALLER is specified, or if there are only two cells of unequal size. If the cell sizes are unequal, the harmonic mean is used, which may lead to somewhat liberal tests if the cell sizes are highly disparate. The LINES option cannot be used in combination with the DUNNETT, DUNNETTL, or DUNNETTU options.

NOSORT
   prevents the means from being sorted into descending order when CLDIFF or CLM is specified.

MODEL Statement

   MODEL *dependents=independents / options*;

The MODEL statement names the dependent variables and independent effects. The syntax of effects is described in the introductory section **Specification of Effects**. If no independent effects are specified, only an intercept term is fit.
   These options can be specified in the MODEL statement after a slash (/):

Options for the Intercept

INTERCEPT
INT
   requests that GLM print the hypothesis tests associated with the intercept as an effect in the model. By default, the intercept is included in the model, but no tests of hypotheses associated with it are printed. When the INT option is specified, these tests are printed.

NOINT
   requests that the intercept parameter not be included in the model.

Options to Request Printouts

NOUNI
   requests that no univariate statistics be printed. You typically use the NOUNI option with a multivariate or repeated measures analysis of variance when you do not need the standard univariate output printed. Note that the NOUNI option in a MODEL statement does not affect the univariate output produced by the REPEATED statement.

SOLUTION
   requests that GLM print a solution to the normal equations (parameter estimates). GLM always prints a solution when no CLASS statement appears.

TOLERANCE
   requests that the tolerances used in the SWEEP routine be printed. The tolerances are of the form C/USS or C/CSS, as described in the discussion of SINGULAR (under **Tuning Options** later in this section). The tolerance value for the intercept is not divided by its uncorrected SS.

Options to Control Standard Hypothesis Tests

E

requests that the general form of all estimable functions be printed.

E1

requests that the Type I estimable functions for each effect in the model be printed.

E2

requests that the Type II estimable functions for each effect in the model be printed.

E3

requests that the Type III estimable functions for each effect in the model be printed.

E4

requests that the Type IV estimable functions for each effect in the model be printed.

SS1

requests that the Sum of Squares (SS) associated with Type I estimable functions for each effect be printed.

SS2

requests that the SS associated with Type II estimable functions for each effect be printed.

SS3

requests that the SS associated with Type III estimable functions for each effect be printed.

SS4

requests that the SS associated with Type IV estimable functions for each effect be printed.

Note: if E1, E2, E3, or E4 is specified, GLM prints the corresponding SS for each effect. By default, the procedure prints the Type I and Type III SS for each effect.

Options for Predicted and Residual Values

ALPHA=p

specifies the alpha level for confidence intervals. The only acceptable values for ALPHA are 0.01, 0.05, and 0.10. If no ALPHA level is given, GLM uses 0.05.

CLI

prints confidence limits for individual predicted values for each observation. CLI should not be used with CLM; it is ignored if CLM is also specified.

CLM

prints confidence limits for a mean predicted value for each observation.

P

prints observed, predicted, and residual values for each observation that does not contain missing values for independent variables. The Durbin-Watson statistic is also printed when P is specified. The PRESS statistic is also printed if either CLM or CLI is specified.

Options to Print Intermediate Calculations

XPX

prints the **X'X** crossproducts matrix.

INVERSE

I

prints the inverse or the generalized inverse of the **X'X** matrix.

Tuning Options

SINGULAR=*value*

tunes the sensitivity of the regression routine to linear dependencies in the design. If a diagonal pivot element is less than C*SINGULAR as GLM sweeps the **X'X** matrix, the associated design column is declared to be linearly dependent with previous columns, and the associated parameter is zeroed.

The C value adjusts the check to the relative scale of the variable. C is equal to the corrected SS for the variable, unless the corrected SS is 0, in which case C is 1. If NOINT is specified but the ABSORB option is not, GLM uses the uncorrected SS instead.

Note: the default value of SINGULAR, $1E-7$, may be too small, but this value is necessary in order to handle the high-degree polynomials used in the literature to compare regression routines.

ZETA=*value*

tunes the sensitivity of the check for estimability for Type III and Type IV functions. Any element in the estimable function basis with an absolute value less than ZETA is set to zero. The default value for ZETA is $1E-8$, which suffices for all *ANOVA*-type models.

Note: although it is possible to generate data for which this absolute check can be defeated, the check suffices in most practical examples. Additional research needs to be performed to make this check relative rather than absolute.

OUTPUT Statement

OUTPUT OUT=*SASdataset*
     PREDICTED | P=*names*
     RESIDUAL | R=*names*
     L95M=*names*
     U95M=*names*
     L95=*names*
     U95=*names*
     STDP=*names*
     STDR=*names*
     STDI=*names*
     STUDENT=*names*
     COOKD=*names*
     H=*names*
     PRESS=*names*
     RSTUDENT=*names*
     DFFITS=*names*
     COVRATIO=*names*;

The OUTPUT statement creates a new SAS data set. All the variables in the original data set are included in the new data set, along with variables named in the

OUTPUT statement. These new variables contain the values of a variety of diagnostic measures that are calculated for each observation in the data set. If you want to create a permanent SAS data set, you must specify a two-level name (see "SAS Files" in the *SAS Language Guide* for more information on permanent SAS data sets).

The option below is given in the OUTPUT statement:

OUT=*SASdataset*
   gives the name of the new data set. If the OUT= option is omitted, the new data set is named using the DATA*n* convention.

These values can be calculated and output to the new data set:

PREDICTED | P=*names*
   predicted values.

RESIDUAL | R=*names*
   residuals, calculated as ACTUAL minus PREDICTED.

L95M=*names*
   lower bound of a 95% confidence interval for the expected value (mean) of the dependent variable.

U95M=*names*
   upper bound of a 95% confidence interval for the expected value (mean) of the dependent variable.

L95=*names*
   lower bound of a 95% confidence interval for an individual prediction. This includes the variance of the error, as well as the variance of the parameter estimates.

U95=*names*
   upper bound of a 95% confidence interval for an individual prediction.

STDP=*names*
   standard error of the mean predicted value.

STDR=*names*
   standard error of the residual.

STDI=*names*
   standard error of the individual predicted value.

STUDENT=*names*
   studentized residuals, the residual divided by its standard error.

COOKD=*names*
   Cook's D influence statistic.

H=*names*
   leverage, $x_i(\mathbf{X'X})^{-1}x_i'$.

PRESS=*names*
   residual for the *i*th observation that results from dropping the *i*th observation from the parameter estimates. This is the residual divided by $(1-h)$ where h is the leverage above.

RSTUDENT=*names*
   a studentized residual with the current observation deleted.

DFFITS=*names*
   standard influence of observation on predicted value.

COVRATIO=*names*
   standard influence of observation on covariance of betas.

(See **Influence Diagnostics** in the **DETAILS** section of "The REG Procedure" and Chapter 1, "Introduction to Regression Procedures," for details on the calculation of these statistics.)

For example, the statements

```
proc glm;
   class a b;
   model y=a b a*b;
   output out=new p=yhat r=resid stdr=eresid;
```

create an output data set named NEW. In addition to all the variables from the original data set, NEW contains the variable YHAT, whose values are predicted values of the dependent variable Y. NEW also contains the variable RESID, whose values are the residual values of Y, and the variable ERESID, whose values are the standard errors of the residuals.

Here is another example:

```
proc glm;
   by group;
   class a;
   model y1-y5=a x(a);
   output out=pout predicted=py1-py5;
```

Data set POUT contains five new variables, PY1 through PY5. PY1's values are the predicted values of Y1; PY2's values are the predicted values of Y2; and so on.

For more information on the data set produced by the OUTPUT statement, see **Output Data Sets** in the **DETAILS** section.

RANDOM Statement

RANDOM *effects* / *options*;

The RANDOM statement specifies which effects in the model are random. When you use a RANDOM statement, GLM always prints the expected value of each Type III, Type IV, or contrast MS used in the analysis. Since the estimable function basis is not automatically calculated for Type I and Type II sums of squares, the E1 (for Type I) or E2 (for Type II) option must be specified in the MODEL statement in order for the RANDOM statement to produce expected mean squares for Type I or Type II sums of squares. Note that PROC GLM only uses the information pertaining to expected mean squares when you specify the TEST option of the RANDOM statement (see below). Since other features in GLM assume that all effects are fixed, all other tests and all estimability checks are based on a fixed effects model, even when you use a RANDOM statement.

You can use as many RANDOM statements as you want, provided that they appear after the MODEL statement. If you use a CONTRAST statement with a RANDOM statement, you must enter the CONTRAST statement before the RANDOM statement.

The list of effects in the RANDOM statement should contain one or more of the pure classification effects (main effects, crossed effects, or nested effects) specified in the MODEL statement. The levels of each effect specified are assumed to be normally and independently distributed with common variance. Levels in different effects are assumed to be independent.

The options below can appear in the RANDOM statement after a slash (/):

Q

requests a complete printout of all quadratic forms in the fixed effects that appear in the expected mean squares.

TEST

> requests that hypothesis tests for each effect specified in the model be carried out, using appropriate error terms as determined by the expected mean squares.

Note that GLM does not automatically declare interactions to be random when the effects in the interaction are declared random. For example,

```
random a b;
```

does not produce the same expected mean squares or tests as

```
random a b a*b;
```

To ensure correct tests, all random interactions and random main effects need to be listed in the RANDOM statement.

See **Expected Mean Squares for Random Effects** later in this chapter for more information on the calculation of expected mean squares and the tests that are produced by the TEST option. See Chapter 2, "Introduction to Analysis-of-Variance Procedures," and "The VARCOMP Procedure" for more information on random effects.

REPEATED Statement

> REPEATED *factorname levels* (*levelvalues*) *transformation* [, . . .] / *options*;

When values of the dependent variables in the MODEL statement represent repeated measurements on the same experimental unit, the REPEATED statement allows you to test hypotheses about the measurement factors (often called *within-subject factors*) as well as the interactions of within-subject factors with independent variables in the MODEL statement (often called *between-subject factors*). The REPEATED statement provides multivariate and univariate tests as well as hypothesis tests for a variety of single-degree-of-freedom contrasts. When more than one within-subject factor is specified, the *factornames* (and associated level and transformation information) must be separated by a comma in the REPEATED statement. (An example is given later in this section.) There is no limit to the number of within-subject factors that can be specified.

When a REPEATED statement appears, the GLM procedure enters a multivariate mode of handling missing values. If any values for variables corresponding to each combination of the within-subject factors are missing, the observation is excluded from the analysis.

If you use a CONTRAST (or TEST) statement with a REPEATED statement, you must enter it before the REPEATED statement.

The terms below are specified in the REPEATED statement:

factorname   names a factor to be associated with the dependent variables. The name should not be the same as any variable name that already exists in the data set being analyzed and should conform to the usual conventions of SAS variable names.

levels   gives the number of levels associated with the factor being defined. When there is only one within-subject factor, the number of levels is equal to the number of dependent variables. In this case, *levels* need not be specified. When more than one within-subject factor is defined, however, *levels* must be specified, and the product of the levels of all the factors must equal the number of dependent variables in the MODEL statement.

(*levelvalues*)   gives values that correspond to levels of a repeated-measures factor. These values are used to label output and as spacings for constructing orthogonal polynomial contrasts. The number of level values specified must correspond to the number of levels for that factor in the REPEATED statement. Note that the level values appear in parentheses.

The following *transformation* keywords define single-degree-of-freedom contrasts for factors specified in the REPEATED statement. Since the number of contrasts generated is always one less than the number of levels of the factor, you have some control over which contrast is omitted from the analysis by which transformation you select. If no transformation keyword is specified, REPEATED uses the CONTRAST transformation.

CONTRAST [(*ordinalreferencelevel*)]

generates contrasts between levels of the factor and, optionally, a reference level that must appear in parentheses. The reference level corresponds to the ordinal value of the level rather than the level value specified. Without a reference level, the last level is used by default. Reference level specification must appear in parentheses. For example, to generate contrasts between the first level of a factor and the other levels, use

```
contrast(1)
```

POLYNOMIAL   generates orthogonal polynomial contrasts. Level values, if provided, are used as spacings in the construction of the polynomials; otherwise, equal spacing is assumed.

HELMERT   generates contrasts between each level of the factor and the mean of subsequent levels.

MEAN [(*ordinalreferencelevel*)]

generates contrasts between levels of the factor and the mean of all other levels of the factor. Specifying a reference level eliminates the contrast between that level and the mean. Without a reference level, the contrast involving the last level is omitted. Reference level specification must appear in parentheses. See the CONTRAST transformation above for an example.

PROFILE   generates contrasts between adjacent levels of the factor.

The following options can appear in the REPEATED statement after a slash (/):

CANONICAL
   requests a canonical analysis of the **H** and **E** matrices corresponding to the transformed variables specified in the REPEATED statement.

HTYPE=*n*
   specifies the type of the **H** matrix used in the multivariate tests and the type of sums of squares used in the univariate tests. See the HTYPE= option in the specifications for the MANOVA statement for further details.

NOM
   prints only the results of the univariate analyses.

NOU
>   prints only the results of the multivariate analyses.

PRINTE
>   prints the **E** matrix for each combination of within-subject factors, as well as partial correlation matrices for both the original dependent variables and the variables defined by the transformations specified in the REPEATED statement. In addition, the PRINTE option provides sphericity tests for each set of transformed variables. If the requested transformations are not orthogonal, the PRINTE option also provides a sphericity test for a set of orthogonal contrasts.

PRINTH
>   prints the **H** (SSCP) matrix associated with each multivariate test.

PRINTM
>   prints the transformation matrices that define the contrasts in the analysis. GLM always prints the **M** matrix so that the transformed variables are defined by the rows, not the columns, of the **M** matrix on the printout. In other words, GLM actually prints **M**′.

PRINTRV
>   prints the characteristic roots and vectors for each multivariate test.

SUMMARY
>   produces analysis-of-variance tables for each contrast defined by the within-subject factors. Along with tests for the effects of the independent variables specified in the MODEL statement, a term labeled MEAN tests the hypothesis that the overall mean of the contrast is zero.

When specifying more than one factor, list the dependent variables in the MODEL statement so that the within-subject factors defined in the REPEATED statement are nested; that is, the first factor defined in the REPEATED statement should be the one with values that change least frequently. For example, assume three treatments are administered at each of four times, for a total of twelve dependent variables on each experimental unit. If the variables are listed in the MODEL statement as Y1 through Y12, then the statement

```
repeated trt 3, time 4;
```

implies the following structure:

DEP VARIABLE	Y1	Y2	Y3	Y4	Y5	Y6	Y7	Y8	Y9	Y10	Y11	Y12
value of TRT	1	1	1	1	2	2	2	2	3	3	3	3
value of TIME	1	2	3	4	1	2	3	4	1	2	3	4

The REPEATED statement always produces a table like the one above.
  See **Repeated Measures Analysis of Variance** in the **DETAILS** section for more information.

TEST Statement

>   TEST H=*effects* E=*effect* / *options*;

Although an *F* value is computed for all SS in the analysis using the residual MS as an error term, you may request additional *F* tests using other effects as error terms. You need a TEST statement when a nonstandard error structure (as in a split-plot) exists. However, in most unbalanced models with nonstandard error structures, most MSs are not independent and do not have equal expectations under the null hypothesis.

GLM does not check any of the assumptions underlying the *F* statistic. **When you specify a TEST statement, you assume sole responsibility for the validity of the *F* statistic produced.** To help validate a test, you can use the RANDOM statement and inspect the expected mean squares, or you can use the TEST option of the RANDOM statement.

You may use as many TEST statements as you want, provided they appear after the MODEL statement. If you use a TEST statement, E= is required.

These terms are specified in the TEST statement:

> H=*effects*   specifies which effects in the preceding model are to be used as hypothesis (numerator) effects.
>
> E=*effect*   specifies one, and only one, effect to use as the error (denominator) term. The E= specification is required.

By default, the SS type for all hypothesis SS and error SS is the highest type computed in the model. If the hypothesis type or error type is to be another type that was computed in the model, you should specify one or both of these options after a slash (/):

ETYPE=*n*

> specifies the type of SS to use for the error term. The type must be a type computed in the model ($n=1$, 2, 3, or 4).

HTYPE=*n*

> specifies the type of SS to use for the hypothesis. The type must be a type computed in the model ($n=1$, 2, 3, or 4).

This example illustrates the TEST statement with a split-plot model:

```
proc glm;
   class a b c;
   model y=a  b(a) c a*c b*c(a);
   test h=a e=b(a)/ htype=1 etype=1;
   test h=c a*c e=b*c(a) / htype=1 etype=1;
```

WEIGHT Statement

WEIGHT *variable*;

When a WEIGHT statement is used, a weighted residual sum of squares

$$\Sigma_i w_i(y_i - \hat{y}_i)^2$$

is minimized, where w_i is the value of the variable specified in the WEIGHT statement, y_i is the observed value of the response variable, and $\hat{y}_i$ is the predicted value of the response variable.

The observation is used in the analysis only if the value of the WEIGHT statement variable is greater than zero.

The WEIGHT statement has no effect on degrees of freedom or number of observations, but is used by the MEANS statement when calculating means and performing multiple range tests. The normal equations used when a WEIGHT statement is present are

$$\boldsymbol{\beta} = (\mathbf{X'WX})^{-}\mathbf{X'WY}$$

where **W** is a diagonal matrix consisting of the values of the variable specified in the WEIGHT statement.

If the weights for the observations are proportional to the reciprocals of the error variances, then the weighted least-squares estimates are BLUE (best linear unbiased estimators).

If the WEIGHT statement is used, it must appear before the first RUN statement or it is ignored.

DETAILS

Parameterization of GLM Models

GLM constructs a linear model according to the specifications in the MODEL statement. Each effect generates one or more columns in a design matrix X. This section shows precisely how X is built.

Intercept

All models automatically include a column of 1s to estimate an intercept parameter μ. You can use the NOINT option to suppress the intercept.

Regression Effects

Regression effects (covariates) have the values of the variables copied into the design matrix directly. Polynomial terms are multiplied out and then installed in X.

Main Effects

If a class variable has m levels, GLM generates m columns in the design matrix for its main effect. Each column is an indicator variable for a given level. The order of the columns is the sort order of the values of their levels and can be controlled with the ORDER= option of the PROC GLM statement. For example,

data			A		B		
A	B	μ	A1	A2	B1	B2	B3
1	1	1	1	0	1	0	0
1	2	1	1	0	0	1	0
1	3	1	1	0	0	0	1
2	1	1	0	1	1	0	0
2	2	1	0	1	0	1	0
2	3	1	0	1	0	0	1

There are more columns for these effects than there are degrees of freedom for them; in other words, GLM is using an over-parameterized model.

Crossed Effects

First, GLM reorders the terms to correspond to the order of the variables in the CLASS statement; thus, B*A becomes A*B if A precedes B in the CLASS statement. Then GLM generates columns for all combinations of levels that occur in the data. The order of the columns is such that the rightmost variables in the cross index faster than the leftmost variables. Empty columns (that would contain all zeros) are not generated.

data			A		B			A*B					
A	B	μ	A1	A2	B1	B2	B3	A1B1	A1B2	A1B3	A2B1	A2B2	A2B3
1	1	1	1	0	1	0	0	1	0	0	0	0	0
1	2	1	1	0	0	1	0	0	1	0	0	0	0
1	3	1	1	0	0	0	1	0	0	1	0	0	0
2	1	1	0	1	1	0	0	0	0	0	1	0	0
2	2	1	0	1	0	1	0	0	0	0	0	1	0
2	3	1	0	1	0	0	1	0	0	0	0	0	1

In the above matrix, main-effects columns are not linearly independent of crossed-effect columns; in fact, the column space for the crossed effects contains the space of the main effect.

Nested Effects

Nested effects are generated in the same manner as crossed effects. Hence the design columns generated by the following statements are the same (but the ordering of the columns is different):

```
model y=a b(a);        (B nested within A)
```

and

```
model=a a*b;           (omitted main effect for B).
```

The nesting operator in GLM is more a notational convenience than an operation distinct from crossing. Nested effects are characterized by the property that the nested variables never appear as main effects. The order of the variables within nesting parentheses is made to correspond to the order of these variables in the CLASS statement. The order of the columns is such that variables outside the parentheses index faster than those inside the parentheses, and the rightmost nested variables index faster than the leftmost variables.

data			A		B(A)					
A	B	μ	A1	A2	B1A1	B2A1	B3A1	B1A2	B2A2	B3A2
1	1	1	1	0	1	0	0	0	0	0
1	2	1	1	0	0	1	0	0	0	0
1	3	1	1	0	0	0	1	0	0	0
2	1	1	0	1	0	0	0	1	0	0
2	2	1	0	1	0	0	0	0	1	0
2	3	1	0	1	0	0	0	0	0	1

Continuous-Nesting-Class Effects

When a continuous variable nests with a class variable, the design columns are constructed by multiplying the continuous values into the design columns for the class effect.

data			A		X(A)	
X	A	μ	A1	A2	X(A1)	X(A2)
21	1	1	1	0	21	0
24	1	1	1	0	24	0
22	1	1	1	0	22	0
28	2	1	0	1	0	28
19	2	1	0	1	0	19
23	2	1	0	1	0	23

This model estimates a separate slope for **X** within each level of A.

Continuous-by-Class Effects

Continuous-by-class effects generate the same design columns as continuous-nesting-class effects. The two models are made different by the presence of the continuous variable as a regressor by itself, as well as a contributor to a compound effect.

data			X	A		X*A	
X	A	μ	X	A1	A2	X*A1	X*A2
21	1	1	21	1	0	21	0
24	1	1	24	1	0	24	0
22	1	1	22	1	0	22	0
28	2	1	28	0	1	0	28
19	2	1	19	0	1	0	19
23	2	1	23	0	1	0	23

Continuous-by-class effects are used to test the homogeneity of slopes. If the continuous-by-class effect is nonsignificant, the effect can be removed so that the response with respect to **X** is the same for all levels of the class variables.

General Effects

An example that combines all the effects is

    X1*X2*A*B*C(D E)   .

The continuous list comes first, followed by the crossed list, followed by the nested list in parentheses.

The sequencing of parameters is not important to learn unless you contemplate using the CONTRAST or ESTIMATE statements to compute some function of the parameter estimates.

Effects may be retitled by GLM to correspond to ordering rules. For example, B*A(E D) may be retitled A*B(D E) to satisfy the following:

- Class variables that occur outside parentheses (crossed effects) are sorted in the order they appear in the CLASS statement.
- Variables within parentheses (nested effects) are sorted in the order they appear in a CLASS statement.

The sequencing of the parameters generated by an effect can be described by which variables have their levels indexed faster:

- Variables in the crossed part index faster than variables in the nested list.
- Within a crossed or nested list, variables to the right index faster than variables to the left.

For example, suppose a model includes four effects—A, B, C, and D—each having two levels, 1 and 2. If the CLASS statement is

```
class a b c d;
```

then the order of the parameters for the effect B*A(C D), which is retitled A*B(C D), is

$$A_1B_1C_1D_1 \rightarrow A_1B_2C_1D_1 \rightarrow A_2B_1C_1D_1 \rightarrow A_2B_2C_1D_1 \rightarrow A_1B_1C_1D_2 \rightarrow$$

$$A_1B_2C_1D_2 \rightarrow A_2B_1C_1D_2 \rightarrow A_2B_2C_1D_2 \rightarrow A_1B_1C_2D_1 \rightarrow A_1B_2C_2D_1 \rightarrow$$

$$A_2B_1C_1D_2 \rightarrow A_2B_2C_2D_1 \rightarrow A_1B_1C_2D_2 \rightarrow A_1B_2C_2D_2 \rightarrow A_2B_1C_2D_2 \rightarrow$$

$$A_2B_2C_2D_2 \quad .$$

Note that first the crossed effects B and A are sorted in the order that they appear in the CLASS statement so that A precedes B in the parameter list. Then, for each combination of the nested effects in turn, combinations of A and B appear. B moves fastest because it is rightmost in the cross list. Then A moves next fastest. D moves next fastest. C is the slowest since it is leftmost in the nested list.

When numeric levels are used, levels are sorted by their character format, which may not correspond to their numeric sort sequence. Therefore, it is advisable to include a format for numeric levels or to use the ORDER=INTERNAL option in the PROC GLM statement to ensure that levels are sorted by their internal values.

Degrees of Freedom

For models with class variables, there are more design columns constructed than there are degrees of freedom for the effect. Thus, there are linear dependencies among the columns. In this event, the parameters are not estimable; there is an infinite number of least-squares solutions. GLM uses a generalized (g2) inverse to obtain values for the estimates. The solution values are not printed unless the SOLUTION option is specified. The solution has the characteristic that estimates are zero whenever the design column for that parameter is a linear combination of previous columns. (Strictly termed, the solution values should not be called estimates.) With this full parameterization, hypothesis tests are constructed to test linear functions of the parameters that are estimable.

Other procedures (such as PROC CATMOD) reparameterize models to full rank using certain restrictions on the parameters. GLM does not reparameterize, making the hypotheses that are commonly tested more understandable. See Goodnight (1978) for additional reasons for not reparameterizing.

GLM does not actually construct the design matrix **X**; rather, the procedure constructs directly the crossproduct matrix **X′X**, which is made up of counts, sums, and crossproducts.

Hypothesis Testing in GLM

See Chapter 9, "The Four Types of Estimable Functions," for a complete discussion of the four standard types of hypothesis tests.

Example

To illustrate the four types of tests and the principles upon which they are based, consider a two-way design with interaction based on these data:

		B	
		1	2
A	1	23.5 23.7	28.7
	2	8.9	5.6 8.9
	3	10.3 12.5	13.6 14.6

Invoke GLM and ask for all the estimable functions options to examine what GLM can test. The code below is followed by the summary *ANOVA* table from the printout. See **Output 20.2**.

```
data example;
   input a b y aa;
   cards;
1 1 23.5  1 1 23.7  1 2 28.7  2 1  8.9  2 2  5.6
2 2  8.9  3 1 10.3  3 1 12.5  3 2 13.6  3 2 14.6
;
proc glm;
   class a b;
   model y=a b a*b / e e1 e2 e3 e4;
run;
```

Output 20.2   Summary *ANOVA* Table: PROC GLM

```
                        General Linear Models Procedure
Dependent Variable: Y

Source              DF      Sum of Squares        Mean Square      F Value      Pr > F

Model                5       520.47600000       104.09520000        49.66       0.0011

Error                4         8.38500000         2.09625000

Corrected Total      9       528.86100000

            R-Square              C.V.             Root MSE                   Y Mean

            0.984145          9.633022          1.44784322               15.03000000
```

The following sections show the general form of estimable functions and discuss the four standard tests, their properties, and abbreviated printouts for the two-way crossed example.

Estimability

Output 20.3 is the general form of estimable functions for the example. In order to be testable, a hypothesis must be able to fit within the framework printed here.

Output 20.3   General Form of Estimable Functions: PROC GLM

```
                        General Linear Models Procedure
                        General Form of Estimable Functions

Effect          Coefficients

INTERCEPT       L1

A        1      L2
         2      L3
         3      L1-L2-L3

B        1      L5
         2      L1-L5

A*B      1 1    L7
         1 2    L2-L7
         2 1    L9
         2 2    L3-L9
         3 1    L5-L7-L9
         3 2    L1-L2-L3-L5+L7+L9
```

If a hypothesis is estimable, the Ls in the above scheme can be set to values that match the hypothesis. All the standard tests in GLM can be shown in the format above, with some of the Ls zeroed and some set to functions of other Ls.

The following sections show how many of the hypotheses can be tested by comparing the model sum-of-squares regression from one model to a submodel. The notation used is

$$SS(\textit{Beffects} \mid \textit{Aeffects}) = SS(\textit{Beffects,Aeffects}) - SS(\textit{Aeffects})$$

where SS(*Aeffects*) denotes the regression model sum of squares for the model consisting of *Aeffects*. This notation is equivalent to the reduction notation defined by Searle (1971) and summarized in Chapter 9, "The Four Types of Estimable Functions."

Type I Tests

Type I sums of squares, also called *sequential sums of squares*, are the incremental improvement in error SS as each effect is added to the model. They can be computed by fitting the model in steps and recording the difference in SSE at each step.

Source	Type I SS
A	$SS(A \mid \mu)$
B	$SS(B \mid \mu, A)$
A*B	$SS(A*B \mid \mu, A, B)$

Type I SS are printed by default because they are easy to obtain and can be used in various hand calculations to produce SS values for a series of different models.

The Type I hypotheses have these properties:

- Type I SS for all effects add up to the model SS. None of the other SS types have this property, except in special cases.
- Type I hypotheses can be derived from rows of the Forward-Dolittle transformation of **X'X** (a transformation that reduces **X'X** to an upper triangular matrix by row operations).
- Type I SS are statistically independent from each other if the residual errors are independent and identically normally distributed.
- Type I hypotheses depend on the order in which effects are specified in the MODEL.
- Type I hypotheses are uncontaminated by effects preceding the effect being tested; however, the hypotheses usually involve parameters for effects following the tested effect in the model. For example, in the model

      y=a b;

  the Type I hypothesis for B does not involve A parameters, but the Type I hypothesis for A does involve B parameters.
- Type I hypotheses are functions of the cell counts for unbalanced data; the hypotheses are not usually the same hypotheses that are tested if the data are balanced.
- Type I SS are useful for polynomial models where you want to know the contribution of a term as though it had been made orthogonal to preceding effects. Thus, Type I SS correspond to tests of the orthogonalized polynomials.

The Type I estimable functions and associated tests for the example are shown in **Output 20.4**.

Output 20.4   Type I Estimable Functions and Associated Tests: PROC GLM

```
                              General Linear Models Procedure

Type I Estimable Functions for: A      Functions for: B             Functions for: A*B

Effect          Coefficients           Effect        Coefficients    Effect        Coefficients

INTERCEPT       0                      INTERCEPT      0              INTERCEPT      0

A       1       L2                     A       1      0             A       1      0
        2       L3                             2      0                     2      0
        3       -L2-L3                         3      0                     3      0

B       1       0.1667*L2-0.1667*L3    B       1      L5            B       1      0
        2       -0.1667*L2+0.1667*L3           2      -L5                   2      0

A*B   1 1       0.6667*L2              A*B   1 1      0.2857*L5     A*B   1 1      L7
      1 2       0.3333*L2                    1 2      -0.2857*L5          1 2      -L7
      2 1       0.3333*L3                    2 1      0.2857*L5          2 1      L9
      2 2       0.6667*L3                    2 2      -0.2857*L5          2 2      -L9
      3 1       -0.5*L2-0.5*L3               3 1      0.4286*L5          3 1      -L7-L9
      3 2       -0.5*L2-0.5*L3               3 2      -0.4286*L5         3 2      L7+L9


   Source               DF          Type I SS          Mean Square        F Value      Pr > F
   A                    2          494.03100000        247.01550000         117.84      0.0003
   B                    1           10.71428571         10.71428571           5.11      0.0866
   A*B                  2           15.73071429          7.86535714           3.75      0.1209
```

Type II Tests

The Type II tests can also be calculated by comparing the error SS for subset models. The Type II SS are the reduction in error SS due to adding the term after all other terms have been added to the model except terms that contain the effect being tested. An effect is contained in another effect if it can be derived by deleting terms in the effect. For example, A and B are both contained in A*B. For this model

Source	Type II SS
A	SS(A | μ,B)
B	SS(B | μ,A)
A*B	SS(A*B | μ,A,B)

Type II SS have these properties:

- Type II SS do not necessarily add to the model SS.
- The hypothesis for an effect does not involve parameters of other effects except for containing effects (which it must involve to be estimable).
- Type II SS are invariant to the ordering of effects in the model.
- For unbalanced designs, Type II hypotheses for effects that are contained in other effects are not usually the same hypotheses that are tested if the data are balanced. The hypotheses are generally functions of the cell counts.

The Type II estimable functions and associated tests for the example are shown in **Output 20.5**.

Output 20.5   Type II Estimable Functions and Associated Tests: PROC GLM

```
                              General Linear Models Procedure

Type II Estimable Functions for: A      Functions for: B            Functions for: A*B

Effect        Coefficients              Effect       Coefficients    Effect       Coefficients

INTERCEPT     0                         INTERCEPT    0               INTERCEPT    0

A      1      L2                        A      1     0               A      1     0
       2      L3                               2     0                      2     0
       3      -L2-L3                            3     0                      3     0

B      1      0                         B      1     L5              B      1     0
       2      0                                2     -L5                     2     0

A*B   1 1     0.619*L2+0.0476*L3        A*B   1 1    0.2857*L5       A*B   1 1    L7
      1 2     0.381*L2-0.0476*L3              1 2    -0.2857*L5            1 2    -L7
      2 1     -0.0476*L2+0.381*L3             2 1    0.2857*L5             2 1    L9
      2 2     0.0476*L2+0.619*L3              2 2    -0.2857*L5            2 2    -L9
      3 1     -0.5714*L2-0.4286*L3           3 1    0.4286*L5             3 1    -L7-L9
      3 2     -0.4286*L2-0.5714*L3           3 2    -0.4286*L5            3 2    L7+L9


      Source            DF          Type II SS         Mean Square        F Value      Pr > F

      A                 2          499.12028571       249.56014286        119.05       0.0003
      B                 1           10.71428571        10.71428571          5.11       0.0866
      A*B               2           15.73071429         7.86535714          3.75       0.1209
```

Type III and Type IV Tests

Type III and Type IV SS, sometimes referred to as *partial sums of squares*, are considered by many to be the most desirable. These SS cannot in general be computed by comparing model SS from several models using GLM's parameterization. (However, they can sometimes be computed by reduction for methods that reparameterize to full rank.) In GLM they are computed by constructing an estimated hypothesis matrix **L** and then computing the SS associated with the hypothesis **Lβ**=0. As long as there are no missing cells in the design, Type III and Type IV SS are the same.

These are properties of Type III and Type IV SS:

- The hypothesis for an effect does not involve parameters of other effects except for containing effects (which it must involve to be estimable).
- The hypotheses to be tested are invariant to the ordering of effects in the model.
- The hypotheses are the same hypotheses that are tested if there are no missing cells. They are not functions of cell counts.
- The SS do not normally add up to the model SS.

The SS are constructed from the general form of estimable functions. Type III and Type IV tests are different only if the design has missing cells. In this case, the Type III tests have an orthogonality property, while the Type IV tests have a balancing property. These properties are discussed in Chapter 9, "The Four Types of Estimable Functions." For this example, Type IV tests are identical to the Type III tests that are shown in **Output 20.6**.

Output 20.6   Type III Estimable Functions and Associated Tests: PROC GLM

```
                              General Linear Models Procedure
Type III Estimable Functions for: A      Functions for: B              Functions for: A*B

Effect          Coefficients            Effect        Coefficients      Effect        Coefficients

INTERCEPT       0                       INTERCEPT     0                 INTERCEPT     0

A        1      L2                      A      1      0                 A      1      0
         2      L3                             2      0                        2      0
         3      -L2-L3                         3      0                        3      0

B        1      0                       B      1      L5                B      1      0
         2      0                              2      -L5                      2      0

A*B     1 1     0.5*L2                  A*B   1 1     0.3333*L5         A*B   1 1     L7
        1 2     0.5*L2                        1 2     -0.3333*L5              1 2     -L7
        2 1     0.5*L3                        2 1     0.3333*L5               2 1     L9
        2 2     0.5*L3                        2 2     -0.3333*L5              2 2     -L9
        3 1     -0.5*L2-0.5*L3                3 1     0.3333*L5               3 1     -L7-L9
        3 2     -0.5*L2-0.5*L3                3 2     -0.3333*L5              3 2     L7+L9


  Source           DF          Type III SS              Mean Square           F Value       Pr > F
  A                2           479.10785714             239.55392857          114.28        0.0003
  B                1             9.45562500               9.45562500            4.51        0.1009
  A*B              2            15.73071429               7.86535714            3.75        0.1209
```

Absorption

Absorption is a computational technique used to reduce computing resource needs in certain cases. The classic use of absorption occurs when a blocking factor with a large number of levels is a term in the model.

For example, the statements

```
proc glm;
    absorb herd;
    class a b;
    model y=a b a*b;
```

are equivalent to

```
proc glm;
    class herd a b;
    model y=herd a b a*b;
```

with the exception that the Type II, Type III, or Type IV SS for HERD are not computed when HERD is absorbed.

Several effects may be absorbed at one time. For example, these statements

```
proc glm;
    absorb herd cow;
    class a b;
    model y=a b a*b;
```

are equivalent to

```
proc glm;
    class herd cow a b;
    model y=herd cow(herd) a b a*b;
```

When you use absorption, the size of the **X′X** matrix is a function only of the effects in the MODEL statement. The effects being absorbed do not contribute to the size of the **X′X** matrix.

For the example above, A and B could be absorbed:

```
proc glm;
    absorb a b;
    class herd cow;
    model y=herd cow(herd);
```

Although the sources of variation in the results are listed as

```
a b(a) herd cow(herd)
```

all types of estimable functions for HERD and COW(HERD) are free of A, B, and A*B parameters.

To illustrate the savings in computing using the ABSORB statement, GLM was run on generated data with 1147 degrees of freedom in the model with these statements:

```
data a;
    length herd cow trtment 4;
    do herd=1 to 40;
        n=1+ranuni(1234567)*60;
        do cow=1 to n;
            do trtment=1 to 3;
                do rep=1 to 2;
                    y=herd / 5+cow / 10+trtment+rannor(1234567);
                    output;
                    end;
                end;
            end;
        end;
    drop n;
proc glm;
    class herd cow trtment;
    model y=herd cow(herd) trtment;
run;
```

This analysis would have required over 6 megabytes of memory for the **X'X** matrix had GLM solved it directly. However, in the statements below, GLM only needs a 4×4 matrix for the intercept and treatment because the other effects are absorbed.

```
proc glm;
    absorb herd cow;
    class trtment;
    model y=trtment;
```

These statements produce the printout shown in **Output 20.7**.

Output 20.7   Absorption Technique: PROC GLM

```
                    General Linear Models Procedure                        1
                      Class Level Information

                   Class    Levels    Values

                   TRTMENT     3      1 2 3


             Number of observations in data set = 6876
```

```
                    General Linear Models Procedure                        2
Dependent Variable: Y

Source              DF        Sum of Squares      Mean Square    F Value    Pr > F

Model              1147      52049.89684152       45.37916028     44.17     0.0

Error              5728       5884.55787531        1.02733203

Corrected Total    6875      57934.45471683

                R-Square           C.V.          Root MSE              Y Mean

                0.898427        12.48196        1.01357389          8.12031348


Source              DF         Type I SS          Mean Square    F Value    Pr > F

HERD                 39     36230.70919768       928.99254353     904.28     0.0
COW(HERD)          1106     11375.42905347        10.28519806      10.01     0.0
TRTMENT               2      4443.75859037      2221.87929518    2162.77     0.0

Source              DF        Type III SS         Mean Square    F Value    Pr > F

TRTMENT               2      4443.75859037      2221.87929518    2162.77     0.0
```

Specification of ESTIMATE Expressions

For this example of the regression model

```
    model y=x1 x2 x3;
```

the associated parameters are β_0, β_1, β_2, and β_3 (where β_0 represents the intercept). To estimate $3\beta_1 + 2\beta_2$, you need the following **L** vector:

$$\mathbf{L} = (0\ 3\ 2\ 0)\ \ .$$

The corresponding ESTIMATE statement is

```
    estimate '3B1+2B2'  x1 3  x2 2;
```

To estimate $\beta_0 + \beta_1 - 2\beta_3$ you need this **L** vector:

$$\mathbf{L} = (1\ 1\ 0\ -2)\ \ .$$

The corresponding ESTIMATE statement is

```
    estimate 'B0+B1-2B3' intercept 1 x1 1 x3 -2;
```

Now consider models involving class variables such as

```
model y=a b a*b;
```

with the associated parameters:

$$(\mu \ \alpha_1 \ \alpha_2 \ \alpha_3 \ \beta_1 \ \beta_2 \ \alpha\beta_{11} \ \alpha\beta_{12} \ \alpha\beta_{21} \ \alpha\beta_{22} \ \alpha\beta_{31} \ \alpha\beta_{32}) \ .$$

To estimate the least-squares mean for α_1, you need the following **L** vector:

$$\mathbf{L} = (1 \ | \ 1 \ 0 \ 0 \ | \ 0.5 \ 0.5 \ | \ 0.5 \ 0.5 \ 0 \ 0 \ 0 \ 0)$$

and you could use this ESTIMATE statement:

```
estimate 'LSM(A1)' intercept 1 a 1 b 0.5 0.5 a*b 0.5 0.5;
```

Note in the above statement that only one element of **L** is specified following the A effect, even though A has three levels. Whenever the list of constants following an effect name is shorter than the effect's number of levels, zeros are used as the remaining constants. In the event that the list of constants is longer than the number of levels for the effect, the extra constants are ignored, and a warning message is printed.

To estimate the A linear effect in the model above, assuming equally spaced levels for A, the following **L** can be used:

$$\mathbf{L} = (0 \ | \ -1 \ 0 \ 1 \ | \ 0 \ 0 \ | \ -0.5 \ -0.5 \ 0 \ 0 \ 0.5 \ 0.5) \ .$$

The ESTIMATE statement for the above **L** is written as

```
estimate 'A LINEAR' a -1 0 1;
```

If the elements of **L** are not specified for an effect that contains a specified effect, then the elements of the specified effect are equitably distributed over the levels of the higher-order effect. In addition, if the intercept is specified in an ESTIMATE or CONTRAST statement, it is distributed over all classification effects that are not contained by any other specified effect. The distribution of lower-order coefficients to higher-order effect coefficients follows the same general rules as in the LSMEANS statement and is similar to that used to construct Type IV **L**s. In the previous example, the -1 associated with α_1 is divided by the number of $\alpha\beta_{1j}$ parameters; then each $\alpha\beta_{1j}$ coefficient is set to -1/number of $\alpha\beta_{1j}$. The 1 associated with α_3 is distributed among the $\alpha\beta_{3j}$ parameters in a similar fashion. In the event that an unspecified effect contains several specified effects, only that specified effect with the most factors in common with the unspecified effect is used for distribution of coefficients to the higher-order effect.

Note: numerous syntactical expressions for the ESTIMATE statement were considered, including many that involved specifying the effect and level information associated with each coefficient. For models involving higher-level effects, the requirement of specifying level information would lead to very bulky specifications. Consequently, the simpler form of the ESTIMATE statement described above was implemented. The syntax of this ESTIMATE statement puts a burden on you to know a priori the order of the parameter list associated with each effect. You can use the ORDER= option of the PROC GLM statement to ensure that the levels of the classification effects are sorted appropriately. When you first begin to use this statement, use the E option to make sure that the actual **L** constructed is the one you envisioned.

A Note on Estimability

Each **L** is checked for estimability using the relationship: **L**=**LH** where **H**= (**X′X**)⁻**X′X**. The **L** vector is declared nonestimable, if for any i

$$\text{ABS}(\mathbf{L}_i - (\mathbf{LH})_i) > \begin{cases} 1\text{E}-4 & \text{if } \mathbf{L}_i = 0 \text{ or} \\ 1\text{E}-4^*\text{ABS}(\mathbf{L}_i) & \text{otherwise.} \end{cases}$$

Continued fractions (like 1/3) should be specified to at least six decimal places, or the DIVISOR parameter should be used.

Comparisons of Means

When comparing more than two means, an *ANOVA F* test tells you if the means are significantly different from each other, but it does not tell you which means differ from which other means. Multiple comparison methods (also called *mean separation tests*) give you more detailed information about the differences among the means. A variety of multiple comparison methods are available with the MEANS statement in the ANOVA and GLM procedures.

By *multiple comparisons* we mean more than one comparison among three or more means. There is a serious lack of standardized terminology in the literature on comparison of means. Einot and Gabriel (1975), for example, use the term *multiple comparison procedure* to mean what we define below as a *step-down multiple-stage test*. Some methods for multiple comparisons have not yet been given names, such as those referred to below as REGWQ and REGWF. When reading the literature, you may need to determine what methods are being discussed based on the formulas and references given.

When you interpret multiple comparisons, remember that failure to reject the hypothesis that two or more means are equal should not lead you to conclude that the population means are in fact equal. Failure to reject the null hypothesis implies only that the difference between population means, if any, is not large enough to be detected with the given sample size. A related point is that nonsignificance is nontransitive: given three sample means, the largest and smallest may be significantly different from each other, while neither is significantly different from the middle one. Nontransitive results of this type occur frequently in multiple comparisons.

Multiple comparisons can also lead to counter-intuitive results when the cell sizes are unequal. Consider four cells labeled A, B, C, and D, with sample means in the order A>B>C>D. If A and D each have two observations, and B and C each have 10,000 observations, then the difference between B and C may be significant, while the difference between A and D is not.

Confidence intervals may be more useful than significance tests in multiple comparisons. Confidence intervals show the degree of uncertainty in each comparison in an easily interpretable way; they make it easier to assess the practical significance of a difference, as well as the statistical significance; and they are less likely to lead nonstatisticians to the invalid conclusion that nonsignificantly different sample means imply equal population means.

Pairwise Comparisons

The simplest approach to multiple comparisons is to do a t test on every pair of means (the T option in the MEANS statement). For the ith and jth means you can reject the null hypothesis that the population means are equal if

$$|\bar{y}_i - \bar{y}_j| \, / \, s \sqrt{1/n_i + 1/n_j} \geq t(\alpha;v)$$

where $\bar{y}_i$ and $\bar{y}_j$ are the means, n_i and n_j are the number of observations in the two cells, s is the root mean square error based on v degrees of freedom, α is the significance level, and $t(\alpha;v)$ is the two-tailed critical value from a Student's t distribution. If the cell sizes are all equal to, say, n, the above formula can be rearranged to give

$$|\bar{y}_i - \bar{y}_j| \geq t(\alpha;v)\, s \sqrt{2/n}$$

the value of the right-hand side being Fisher's least significant difference (LSD).

There is a problem with repeated t tests, however. Suppose there are ten means and each t test is performed at the 0.05 level. There are $10(10-1)/2 = 45$ pairs of means to compare, each with a 0.05 probability of a type 1 error (a false rejection of the null hypothesis). The chance of making at least one type 1 error is much higher than 0.05. It is difficult to calculate the exact probability, but you can derive a pessimistic approximation by assuming the comparisons are independent, giving an upper bound to the probability of making at least one type 1 error (the experimentwise error rate) of

$$1 - (1 - 0.05)^{45} = 0.90 \quad .$$

The actual probability is somewhat less than 0.90, but as the number of means increases, the chance of making at least one type 1 error approaches 1.

If you decide to control the individual type 1 error rates for each comparison, you are controlling the comparisonwise error rate. On the other hand, if you want to control the overall type 1 error rate for all the comparisons, you are controlling the experimentwise error rate. It is up to you to decide whether to control the comparisonwise error rate or the experimentwise error rate, but there are many situations in which the experimentwise error rate should be held to a small value. Statistical methods for making two or more inferences while controlling the probability of making at least one type 1 error are called *simultaneous inference methods* (Miller 1981), although Einot and Gabriel (1975) use the term *simultaneous test procedure* in a much more restrictive sense.

It has been suggested that the experimentwise error rate can be held to the α level by performing the overall *ANOVA F* test at the α level and making further comparisons only if the F test is significant, as in Fisher's protected LSD. This assertion is false if there are more than three means (Einot and Gabriel 1975). Consider again the situation with ten means. Suppose that one population mean differs from the others by a sufficiently large amount that the power (probability of correctly rejecting the null hypothesis) of the F test is near 1 but that all the other population means are equal to each other. There will be $9(9-1)/2 = 36$ t tests of true null hypotheses, with an upper limit of 0.84 on the probability of at least one type 1 error. Thus, you must distinguish between the experimentwise error rate under the complete null hypothesis, in which all population means are equal, and the experimentwise error rate under a partial null hypothesis, in which some means are equal but others differ. The following abbreviations are used in the discussion below:

CER   comparisonwise error rate

EERC   experimentwise error rate under the complete null hypothesis

EERP   experimentwise error rate under a partial null hypothesis

MEER   maximum experimentwise error rate under any complete or partial null hypothesis.

A preliminary F test controls the EERC but not the EERP or the MEER.

The MEER can be controlled at the α level by setting the CER to a sufficiently small value. The Bonferroni inequality (Miller 1981) has been widely used for this purpose. If

$$CER = \alpha/c$$

where c is the total number of comparisons, then the MEER is less than α. Bonferroni t tests (the BON option) with MEER $< \alpha$ declare two means to be significantly different if

$$|\bar{y}_i - \bar{y}_j| \ / \ s\sqrt{1/n_i + 1/n_j} \geq t(\varepsilon;\nu)$$

where $\varepsilon = \alpha/(k(k-1)/2)$ for comparison of k means. If the cell sizes are equal, the test simplifies to

$$|\bar{y}_i - \bar{y}_j| \geq t(\varepsilon;\nu)\, s\sqrt{2/n}\quad.$$

Sidak (1967) has provided a tighter bound, showing that

$$CER = 1 - (1 - \alpha)^{1/c}$$

also ensures MEER $\leq \alpha$ for any set of c comparisons. A Sidak t test (Games 1977), provided by the SIDAK option, is thus given by

$$|\bar{y}_i - \bar{y}_j| \ / \ s\sqrt{1/n_i + 1/n_j} \geq t(\varepsilon;\nu)$$

where $\varepsilon = 1-(1-\alpha)^{1/(k(k-1)/2)}$ for comparison of k means. If the sample sizes are equal, the test simplifies to

$$|\bar{y}_i - \bar{y}_j| \geq t(\varepsilon;\nu)\, s\sqrt{2/n}\quad.$$

You can use the Bonferroni additive inequality and the Sidak multiplicative inequality to control the MEER for any set of contrasts or other hypothesis tests, not just pairwise comparisons. The Bonferroni inequality can provide simultaneous inferences in any statistical application requiring tests of more than one hypothesis. Other methods discussed below for pairwise comparisons can also be adapted for general contrasts (Miller 1981).

Scheffe (1953, 1959) proposed another method to control the MEER for any set of contrasts or other linear hypotheses in the analysis of linear models, including pairwise comparisons, obtained with the SCHEFFE option. Two means are declared significantly different if

$$|\bar{y}_i - \bar{y}_j|/s\sqrt{1/n_i + 1/n_j} \geq \sqrt{(k-1)F(\alpha;k-1,\nu)}$$

or, for equal cell sizes,

$$|\bar{y}_i - \bar{y}_j| \geq s\sqrt{(k-1)F(\alpha;k-1,\nu)(2/n)}$$

where $F(\alpha;k-1,\nu)$ is the α-level critical value of an F distribution with $k-1$ numerator degrees of freedom and ν denominator degrees of freedom.

Scheffe's test is compatible with the overall *ANOVA* F test in that Scheffe's method never declares a contrast significant if the overall F test is nonsignificant. Most other multiple comparison methods can find significant contrasts when the overall F is nonsignificant and therefore suffer a loss of power when used with a preliminary F test.

Scheffe's method may be more powerful than the Bonferroni or Sidak methods if the number of comparisons is large relative to the number of means. For pairwise comparisons, Sidak t tests are generally more powerful.

Tukey (1952, 1953) proposed a test designed specifically for pairwise comparisons based on the studentized range, sometimes called the "honestly significant difference test," that controls the MEER when the sample sizes are equal. Tukey (1953) and Kramer (1956) independently proposed a modification for unequal cell sizes. The Tukey or Tukey-Kramer method is provided by the TUKEY option. There is not yet a general proof that the Tukey-Kramer procedure controls the MEER, but the method has fared extremely well in Monte Carlo studies (Dunnett 1980). The Tukey-Kramer method is more powerful than the Bonferroni, Sidak, or Scheffe methods for pairwise comparisons. Two means are considered significantly different by the Tukey-Kramer criterion if

$$| \bar{y}_i - \bar{y}_j | / s \sqrt{(1/n_i + 1/n_j)/2} \geq q(\alpha;k,\nu)$$

where $q(\alpha;k,\nu)$ is the α-level critical value of a studentized range distribution of k independent normal random variables with ν degrees of freedom. For equal cell sizes, Tukey's method rejects the null hypothesis of equal population means if

$$| \bar{y}_i - \bar{y}_j | \geq q(\alpha;k,\nu) \, s / \sqrt{n} \quad .$$

Hochberg (1974) devised a method (the GT2 or SMM option) similar to Tukey's, but it uses the studentized maximum modulus instead of the studentized range and employs Sidak's (1967) uncorrelated-t inequality. It was proved to hold the MEER at a level not exceeding α with unequal sample sizes. It is generally less powerful than the Tukey-Kramer method and always less powerful than Tukey's test for equal cell sizes. Two means are declared significantly different if

$$| \bar{y}_i - \bar{y}_j | / s \sqrt{1/n_i + 1/n_j} \geq m(\alpha;c,\nu)$$

where $m(\alpha;c,\nu)$ is the α-level critical value of the studentized maximum modulus distribution of c independent normal random variables with ν degrees of freedom and $c = k(k-1)/2$. For equal cell sizes, the test simplifies to

$$| \bar{y}_i - \bar{y}_j | \geq m(\alpha;c,\nu) \, s \sqrt{2/n} \quad .$$

Gabriel (1978) proposed another method (the GABRIEL option) based on the studentized maximum modulus for unequal cell sizes that rejects if

$$| \bar{y}_i - \bar{y}_j | / s \left(1/\sqrt{2n_i} + 1/\sqrt{2n_j} \right) \geq m(\alpha;k,\nu) \quad .$$

For equal cell sizes, Gabriel's test is equivalent to Hochberg's GT2 method. For unequal cell sizes, Gabriel's method is more powerful than GT2 but may become liberal with highly disparate cell sizes (see also Dunnett 1980). Gabriel's test is the only method for unequal sample sizes that lends itself to a convenient graphical representation. Assuming $\bar{y}_i > \bar{y}_j$, the above inequality can be rewritten as

$$\bar{y}_i - m(\alpha;k,\nu) \, s / \sqrt{2n_i} \geq \bar{y}_j + m(\alpha;k,\nu) \, s / \sqrt{2n_j} \quad .$$

The expression on the left does not depend on j, nor does the expression on the right depend on i. Hence you can form what Gabriel calls an (l,u)-interval around each sample mean and declare two means to be significantly different if their (l,u)-intervals do not overlap.

Comparing All Treatments to a Control

One special case of means comparison is that in which the only comparisons that need to be tested are between a set of new treatments and a single control. In this case, you can achieve better power by using a method that is restricted to test only comparisons to the single control mean. Dunnett (1955) proposed a test for this situation which declares a mean significantly different from the control if

$$| \bar{y}_i - \bar{y}_0 | \geq d(\alpha;k,v,\rho)\, s \sqrt{ 1/n_i + 1/n_0 }$$

where $\bar{y}_0$ is the control mean, and $d(\alpha;k,v,\rho)$ is the critical value of the "many-one t statistic" (Miller 1981; Krishnaiah and Armitage 1966) for k means to be compared to a control, with v degrees of freedom and correlation ρ. The correlation term arises because each of the treatment means is being compared to the same control. When the number of observations for the control is different from that of the treatments, but all the treatments have the same number of observations, then the correlation between the comparisons is $n_t/(n_0+n_t)$, where n_0 is the sample size of the control, and n_t is the sample size of each of the treatments. For example, in the case where all sample sizes (both control and treatment) are equal, the correlation between any two comparisons of treatments to control is $1/2$. If the treatments do not have the same number of observations, then the correlation is calculated using the harmonic mean of the sample sizes of the treatments as their "common" sample size. Dunnett's test holds the MEER to a level not exceeding the stated α.

Multiple-Stage Tests

You can use all of the methods discussed so far to obtain simultaneous confidence intervals (Miller 1981). By sacrificing the facility for simultaneous estimation, it is possible to obtain simultaneous tests with greater power using multiple-stage tests (MSTs). MSTs come in both step-up and step-down varieties (Welsch 1977). The step-down methods, which have been more widely used, are available in SAS/STAT software.

Step-down MSTs first test the homogeneity of all of the means at a level γ_k. If the test results in a rejection, then each subset of $k-1$ means is tested at level γ_{k-1}; otherwise, the procedure stops. In general, if the hypothesis of homogeneity of a set of p means is rejected at the γ_p level, then each subset of $p-1$ means is tested at the γ_{p-1} level; otherwise, the set of p means is considered not to differ significantly and none of its subsets are tested. The many varieties of MSTs that have been proposed differ in the levels γ_p and the statistics on which the subset tests are based. Clearly, the EERC of a step-down MST is not greater than γ_k, and the CER is not greater than γ_2, but the MEER is a complicated function of γ_p, $p=2, \ldots , k$.

MSTs can be used with unequal cell sizes, but the resulting operating characteristics are undesirable, so only the balanced case is considered here. With equal sample sizes, the means can be arranged in ascending or descending order, and only contiguous subsets need be tested. It is common practice to report the results of an MST by writing the means in such an order and drawing lines parallel to the list of means spanning the homogeneous subsets. This form of presentation is also convenient for pairwise comparisons with equal cell sizes.

The best known MSTs are the Duncan (the DUNCAN option) and Student-Newman-Keuls (the SNK option) methods (Miller 1981). Both use the studentized range statistic and, hence, are called *multiple range tests*. Duncan's method is often called the "new" multiple range test despite the fact that it is one of the oldest MSTs in current use. The Duncan and SNK methods differ in the γ_p values used. For Duncan's method they are

$$\gamma_p = 1 - (1 - \alpha)^{p-1}$$

whereas the SNK method uses

$$\gamma_p = \alpha \quad .$$

Duncan's method controls the CER at the α level. Its operating characteristics appear similar to those of Fisher's unprotected LSD or repeated t tests at level α (Petrinovich and Hardyck 1969). Since repeated t tests are easier to compute, easier to explain, and applicable to unequal sample sizes, Duncan's method is not recommended. Several published studies (for example, Carmer and Swanson 1973) have claimed that Duncan's method is superior to Tukey's because of greater power without considering that the greater power of Duncan's method is due to its higher type 1 error rate (Einot and Gabriel 1975).

The SNK method holds the EERC to the α level but does not control the EERP (Einot and Gabriel 1975). Consider ten population means that occur in five pairs such that means within a pair are equal, but there are large differences between pairs. Making the usual sampling assumptions and also assuming that the sample sizes are very large, all subset homogeneity hypotheses for three or more means are rejected. The SNK method then comes down to five independent tests, one for each pair, each at the α level. Letting α be 0.05, the probability of at least one false rejection is

$$1 - (1 - 0.05)^5 = 0.23 \quad .$$

As the number of means increases, the MEER approaches 1. Therefore, the SNK method cannot be recommended.

A variety of MSTs that control the MEER have been proposed, but these methods are not as well known as those of Duncan and SNK. An approach developed by Ryan (1959, 1960), Einot and Gabriel (1975), and Welsch (1977) sets

$$\gamma_p = 1 - (1 - \alpha)^{p/k} \quad \text{for } p < k - 1$$

$$= \alpha \quad \text{for } p \geq k - 1 \quad .$$

You can use either range or F statistics, leading to what we call the REGWQ and REGWF methods, respectively, after the authors' initials. Assuming the sample means have been arranged in descending order from $\bar{y}_1$ through $\bar{y}_k$, the homogeneity of means $\bar{y}_i, \ldots, \bar{y}_j$, $i<j$, is rejected by REGWQ if

$$\bar{y}_i - \bar{y}_j \geq q(\gamma_p; p, v)s / \sqrt{n}$$

or by REGWF if

$$n(\Sigma \bar{y}_u^2 - (\Sigma \bar{y}_u)^2 / k) / (p - 1)s^2 \geq F(\gamma_p; p - 1, v)$$

where $p=j-i+1$ and the summations are over $u = i, \ldots, j$ (Einot and Gabriel 1975).

REGWQ and REGWF appear to be the most powerful step-down MSTs in the current literature (for example, Ramsey 1978). REGWF has the advantage of being compatible with the overall *ANOVA F* test in that REGWF rejects the complete null hypothesis if and only if the overall *F* test does so since the latter is identical to the first step in REGWF. Use of a preliminary *F* test decreases the power of all the other multiple comparison methods discussed above except for Scheffe's test.

Other multiple comparison methods proposed by Peritz (Marcus, Peritz, and Gabriel 1976; Begun and Gabriel 1981) and Welsch (1977) are still more powerful than the REGW procedures. These methods have not yet been implemented in SAS/STAT software.

Bayesian Approach

Waller and Duncan (1969) and Duncan (1975) take an approach to multiple comparisons that differs from all the methods discussed above in minimizing the Bayes risk under additive loss rather than controlling type 1 error rates. For each pair of population means μ_i and μ_j, null (H_0^{ij}) and alternative (H_a^{ij}) hypotheses are defined:

$$H_0^{ij}: \mu_i - \mu_j \leq 0$$

$$H_a^{ij}: \mu_i - \mu_j > 0 \quad .$$

For any *i,j* pair, let d_0 indicate a decision in favor of H_0^{ij} and d_a indicate a decision in favor of H_a^{ij}, and let $\delta = \mu_i - \mu_j$. The loss function for the decision on the *i,j* pair is

$$\begin{aligned} L(d_0 \mid \delta) &= 0 \quad \text{if } \delta \leq 0 \\ &= \delta \quad \text{if } \delta > 0 \end{aligned}$$

$$\begin{aligned} L(d_a \mid \delta) &= -k\delta \quad \text{if } \delta \leq 0 \\ &= 0 \quad \text{if } \delta > 0 \end{aligned}$$

where *k* represents a constant that you specify rather than the number of means. The loss for the joint decision involving all pairs of means is the sum of the losses for each individual decision. The population means are assumed to have a normal prior distribution with unknown variance, the logarithm of the variance of the means having a uniform prior distribution. For the *i,j* pair, the null hypothesis is rejected if

$$\bar{y}_i - \bar{y}_j \geq t_B s \sqrt{2/n}$$

where t_B is the Bayesian *t* value (Waller and Kemp 1975) depending on *k*, the *F* statistic for the one-way *ANOVA*, and the degrees of freedom for *F*. The value of t_B is a decreasing function of *F*, so the Waller-Duncan test becomes more liberal as *F* increases.

Recommendations

In summary, if you want to control the CER, the recommended methods are repeated *t* tests or Fisher's unprotected LSD (the T or LSD option). If you want to control the MEER, do not need confidence intervals, and have equal cell sizes, then the REGWF and REGWQ methods are recommended. If you want to control the MEER and need confidence intervals or have unequal cell sizes, then the Tukey or Tukey-Kramer methods (the TUKEY option) are recommended. If you agree with the Bayesian approach and Waller and Duncan's assumptions, you should use the Waller-Duncan test (the WALLER option).

Least-Squares Means

Simply put, least-squares means, or *population marginal means*, are the expected value of class or subclass means that you would expect for a balanced design involving the class variable with all covariates at their mean value. This informal concept is explained further in Searle, Speed, and Milliken (1980).

To construct a least-squares mean (LSM) for a given level of a given effect, construct a set of Xs according to the following rules and use them in the linear model with the parameter estimates to yield the value of the LSM:

1. Hold all covariates (continuous variables) to their mean value.
2. Consider effects contained by the given effect. Give the Xs for levels associated with the given level a value of 1. Make the other Xs equal to 0. (See Chapter 9, "The Four Types of Estimable Functions," for a definition of containing.)
3. Consider the given effect. Make the X associated with the given level equal to 1. Set the Xs for the other levels to 0.
4. Consider the effects that contain the given effect. If these effects are not nested within the given effect, then for the columns associated with the given level, use $1/k$, where k is the number of such columns. If these effects are nested within the given effect, then for the columns associated with the given level, use $1/k_1 k_2$, where k_1 is the number of nested levels within this combination of nested effects, and k_2 is the number of such combinations. For the other columns use 0.
5. Consider the other effects not yet considered. If there are no nested factors, then use $1/j$, where j is the number of levels in the effect. If there are nested factors, use $1/j_1 j_2$, where j_1 is the number of nested levels within a given combination of nested effects, and j_2 is the number of such combinations.

The consequence of these rules is that the sum of the Xs within any classification effect is 1. This set of Xs forms a linear combination of the parameters that is checked for estimability before it is evaluated.

For example, consider the model:

```
proc glm;
   class a b c;
   model y=a b a*b c x;
   lsmeans a b a*b c;
```

Assume A has 3 levels, B has 2, and C has 2, and assume that every combination of levels of A and B exists in the data. Assume also that X is a continuous variable with an average of 12.5. Then the least-squares means are computed by the following linear combinations of the parameter estimates:

		A			B		A*B						C		X
	μ	1	2	3	1	2	11	21	31	12	22	32	1	2	X
LSM( )	1	1/3	1/3	1/3	1/2	1/2	1/6	1/6	1/6	1/6	1/6	1/6	1/2	1/2	12.5
LSM(A1)	1	1	0	0	1/2	1/2	1/2	0	0	1/2	0	0	1/2	1/2	12.5
LSM(A2)	1	0	1	0	1/2	1/2	0	1/2	0	0	1/2	0	1/2	1/2	12.5
LSM(A3)	1	0	0	1	1/2	1/2	0	0	1/2	0	0	1/2	1/2	1/2	12.5
LSM(B1)	1	1/3	1/3	1/3	1	0	1/3	1/3	1/3	0	0	0	1/2	1/2	12.5
LSM(B2)	1	1/3	1/3	1/3	0	1	0	0	0	1/3	1/3	1/3	1/2	1/2	12.5
LSM(AB11)	1	1	0	0	1	0	1	0	0	0	0	0	1/2	1/2	12.5
LSM(AB12)	1	1	0	0	0	1	0	0	0	1	0	0	1/2	1/2	12.5
LSM(AB21)	1	0	1	0	1	0	0	1	0	0	0	0	1/2	1/2	12.5
LSM(AB22)	1	0	1	0	0	1	0	0	0	0	1	0	1/2	1/2	12.5
LSM(AB31)	1	0	0	1	1	0	0	0	1	0	0	0	1/2	1/2	12.5
LSM(AB32)	1	0	0	1	0	1	0	0	0	0	0	1	1/2	1/2	12.5
LSM(C1)	1	1/3	1/3	1/3	1/2	1/2	1/6	1/6	1/6	1/6	1/6	1/6	1	0	12.5
LSM(C2)	1	1/3	1/3	1/3	1/2	1/2	1/6	1/6	1/6	1/6	1/6	1/6	0	1	12.5

Multivariate Analysis of Variance

If you fit several dependent variables to the same effects, you may want to make tests jointly involving parameters of several dependent variables. Suppose you have p dependent variables, k parameters for each dependent variable, and n observations. The models can be collected into one equation:

$$\mathbf{Y} = \mathbf{X\beta} + \mathbf{\varepsilon}$$

where $\mathbf{Y}$ is $n \times p$, $\mathbf{X}$ is $n \times k$, $\mathbf{\beta}$ is $k \times p$, and $\mathbf{\varepsilon}$ is $n \times p$. Each of the p models can be estimated and tested separately. However, you may also want to consider the joint distribution, and test the p models simultaneously.

For multivariate tests, you need to make some assumptions about the errors. With p dependent variables, there are $n \times p$ errors that are independent across observations but not across dependent variables. Assume

$$\text{vec}(\mathbf{\varepsilon}) \sim N(\mathbf{0}, \mathbf{I}_n \otimes \mathbf{\Sigma})$$

where $\text{vec}(\mathbf{\varepsilon})$ strings $\mathbf{\varepsilon}$ out by rows, $\otimes$ denotes Kronecker product multiplication, and $\mathbf{\Sigma}$ is $p \times p$. $\mathbf{\Sigma}$ can be estimated by

$$\mathbf{S} = (\mathbf{e'e}) / (n - r) = (\mathbf{Y} - \mathbf{Xb})'(\mathbf{Y} - \mathbf{Xb}) / (n - r)$$

where $\mathbf{b} = (\mathbf{X'X})^-\mathbf{X'Y}$, r is the rank of the $\mathbf{X}$ matrix, and $\mathbf{e}$ is the vector of residuals.

If $\mathbf{S}$ is scaled to unit diagonals, the values in $\mathbf{S}$ are called *partial correlations of the Ys adjusting for the Xs*. This matrix can be printed by GLM if PRINTE is specified as a MANOVA option.

The multivariate general linear hypothesis is written:

$$\mathbf{L\beta M} = 0 \quad .$$

You can form hypotheses for linear combinations across columns, as well as across rows of $\boldsymbol{\beta}$.

The MANOVA statement of the GLM procedure tests special cases where **L** is for Type I, Type II, Type III, or Type IV tests, and **M** is the $p \times p$ identity matrix. These tests are joint tests that the Type I, Type II, Type III, or Type IV hypothesis holds for all dependent variables in the model and are often sufficient to test all hypotheses of interest.

When these special cases are not appropriate, you can specify your own **L** and **M** matrices by using the CONTRAST statement (which is used by MANOVA whenever it is present) and the M= specification of the MANOVA statement, respectively. Another alternative is to use a REPEATED statement, which automatically generates a variety of **M** matrices useful in repeated measures analysis of variance. See the section on the REPEATED statement and **Repeated Measures Analysis of Variance** later in this chapter for more information.

One useful way to think of a MANOVA analysis with an **M** matrix other than the identity is as an analysis of a set of transformed variables defined by the columns of the **M** matrix. You should note, however, that GLM always prints the **M** matrix so that the transformed variables are defined by the rows, not the columns, of the **M** matrix on the printout.

All multivariate tests carried out by GLM first construct the matrices **H** and **E** that correspond to the numerator and denominator of a univariate F test.

$$\mathbf{H} = \mathbf{M'(Lb)'(L(X'X)^- L')^{-1}(Lb)M}$$

$$\mathbf{E} = \mathbf{M'(Y'Y - b'(X'X)b)M} \quad .$$

The diagonal elements of **H** and **E** correspond to the hypothesis and error SS for univariate tests. When the **M** matrix is the identity matrix (the default), these tests are for the original dependent variables on the left-hand side of the MODEL statement. When an **M** matrix other than the identity is specified, the tests are for transformed variables defined by the columns of the **M** matrix. (The **M** matrix is always printed when the M= option is specified in the MANOVA statement.) These tests can be studied by requesting the SUMMARY option, which produces univariate analyses for each original or transformed variable.

Four test statistics, all functions of the eigenvalues of $\mathbf{E}^{-1}\mathbf{H}$ (or $\mathbf{(E+H)}^{-1}\mathbf{H}$), are constructed:

- Wilks' lambda=det(**E**)/det(**H**+**E**)
- Pillai's trace=trace(**H**(**H**+ **E**)$^{-1}$)
- Hotelling-Lawley trace=trace(**E**$^{-1}$**H**)
- Roy's maximum root=λ, largest eigenvalue of **E**$^{-1}$**H**.

All four are reported with F approximations. For further details on these four statistics, see **Multivariate Tests** in Chapter 1, "Introduction to Regression Procedures."

Repeated Measures Analysis of Variance

When several measurements are taken on the same experimental unit (person, plant, machine, and so on), the measurements tend to be correlated with each other. When the measurements represent qualitatively different things, such as weight, length, and width, this correlation is taken into account by use of multivariate methods, such as multivariate analysis of variance. When the measurements can be thought of as responses to levels of an experimental factor of interest, such as time, treatment, or dose, the correlation can be taken into account by performing a repeated measures analysis of variance.

PROC GLM provides both univariate and multivariate tests for repeated measures. For an overall reference on univariate repeated measures, see Winer (1971). The multivariate approach is covered in Cole and Grizzle (1966). For a discussion of the relative merits of the two approaches, see LaTour and Miniard (1983).

Organization of Data for Repeated Measures Analysis

In order to deal efficiently with the correlation of repeated measures, GLM uses the multivariate method of specifying the model, even if only a univariate analysis is desired. In some cases, data may already be entered in the univariate mode, that is, each repeated measure listed as a separate observation along with a variable that represents the experimental unit (subject) on which measurement was taken. Consider the following data set OLD:

SUBJ	GROUP	TIME	Y
1	1	1	15
1	1	2	19
1	1	3	25
2	1	1	21
2	1	2	18
2	1	3	17
1	2	1	14
1	2	2	12
1	2	3	16
2	2	1	11
2	2	2	20
2	2	3	21
.			
.			
.			
10	3	1	14
10	3	2	18
10	3	3	16

Notice how there are three observations for each subject, corresponding to measurements taken at time 1, 2, and 3. These data could be analyzed using the following statements:

```
proc glm data=old;
   classes group subj time;
   model y=group subj(group) time group*time;
   test h=group e=subj(group);
```

However, a more complete and efficient repeated measures analysis could be performed using data set NEW:

GROUP	Y1	Y2	Y3
1	15	19	25
1	21	18	17
2	14	12	16
2	11	20	21
.			
.			
.			
3	14	18	16

In NEW, the three measurements for a subject are all in one observation. For example, 15, 19, and 25 are the measurements for subject 1 for time 1, 2, and

3. For these data, the statements for a repeated measures analysis (assuming default options) would be

```
proc glm data=new;
   class group;
   model y1-y3=group / nouni;
   repeated time;
```

To convert the univariate form of repeated measures data to the multivariate form, you can use a program like the following:

```
proc sort data=old;
   by group subj;
data new(keep=y1-y3 group);
   array yy{3} y1-y3;
   do time=1 to 3;
      set old;
      by group subj;
      yy{time}=y;
      if last.subj then return;
      end;
```

Alternatively, you could use PROC TRANSPOSE to achieve the same results with a program like this one:

```
proc sort data=old;
   by group subj;
proc transpose out=new(rename=(_1=y1 _2=y2 _3=y3));
   by group subj;
   id time;
```

See the *SAS Language Guide* for more information on rearrangement of data sets.

Hypothesis Testing in Repeated Measures Analysis

In repeated measures analysis of variance, the effects of interest are

- between-subject effects (such as GROUP in the previous example)
- within-subject effects (such as TIME in the previous example)
- interactions between the two types of effects (such as GROUP*TIME in the previous example).

Repeated measures analyses are distinguished from other multivariate analyses because of interest in testing hypotheses about the within-subject effects and the within-subject-by-between-subject interactions.

For tests that involve only between-subjects effects, both the multivariate and univariate approaches give rise to the same tests. These tests are provided for all effects in the MODEL statement, as well as for any CONTRASTs specified. The *ANOVA* table for these tests is labeled "Tests of Hypotheses for Between Subjects Effects" on the GLM printout. These tests are constructed by first adding together the dependent variables in the model. Then an analysis of variance is performed on the sum divided by the square root of the number of dependent variables. For example, the statements

```
model y1-y3=group;
repeated time;
```

give a one-way analysis of variance using $Y1+Y2+Y3/\sqrt{3}$ as the dependent variable for performing tests of hypothesis on the between-subject effect

GROUP. Tests for between-subject effects are tests of the hypothesis **LβM** = 0, where **M** is simply a vector of 1s.

For within-subject effects and for within-subject-by-between-subject interaction effects, the univariate and multivariate approaches yield different tests. These tests are provided for the within-subject effects, and the interactions between these effects and the other effects in the MODEL statement, as well as for any CONTRASTs specified. The univariate tests are labeled "Univariate Tests of Hypotheses for Within Subject Effects" on the GLM printout. Results for multivariate tests are labeled "Repeated Measures Analysis of Variance" on the GLM printout.

The multivariate tests provided for within-subjects effects and interactions involving these effects are Wilks' Lambda, Pillai's Trace, Hotelling-Lawley Trace, and Roy's maximum root. For further details on these four statistics, see **Multivariate Tests** in Chapter 1, "Introduction to Regression Procedures." As an example, the statements

```
model y1-y3=group;
repeated time;
```

produce multivariate tests for the within-subject effect TIME and the interaction GROUP*TIME.

The multivariate tests for within-subject effects are produced by testing the hypothesis **LβM** = 0, where the **L** matrix is the usual matrix corresponding to Type I, Type II, Type III, or Type IV hypotheses tests, and the **M** matrix is one of several matrices that you can specify in the REPEATED statement. The only assumption required for valid tests is that the dependent variables in the model have a multivariate normal distribution with a common covariance matrix across the between-subject effects.

The univariate tests for within-subject effects and interactions involving these effects require some assumptions for the probabilities provided by the ordinary F tests to be correct. Specifically, these tests require certain patterns of covariance matrices, known as Type H covariances (Huynh and Feldt 1970). Data with these patterns in the covariance matrices are said to satisfy the Huynh-Feldt condition. You can test this assumption (and the Huynh-Feldt condition) by applying a sphericity test (Anderson 1958) to any set of variables defined by an orthogonal contrast transformation. Such a set of variables is known as a set of orthogonal components. When you use the PRINTE option of the REPEATED statement, this sphericity test is applied both to the transformed variables defined by the REPEATED statement and to a set of orthogonal components if the specified transformation was not orthogonal. It is the test applied to the orthogonal components that is important in determining if your data have Type H covariance structure. When there are only two levels of the within-subject effect, there is only one transformed variable, and a sphericity test cannot be applied, nor is one needed. The sphericity test is labeled "Test for Sphericity" on the GLM printout.

If your data satisfy the assumptions above, use the usual F tests to test univariate hypotheses for the within-subject effects and associated interactions.

If your data do not satisfy the assumption of Type H covariance, an adjustment to numerator and denominator degrees of freedom can be used. Two such adjustments, based on a degrees of freedom adjustment factor known as ε (epsilon) (Box 1954), are provided in PROC GLM. Both adjustments estimate ε and then multiply the numerator and denominator degrees of freedom by this estimate before determining significance levels for the F tests. Significance levels associated with the adjusted tests are labeled "Adj Pr > F" on the GLM printout. The first adjustment, initially proposed for use in data analysis by Greenhouse and Geisser (1959), is labeled "Greenhouse-Geisser Epsilon" and represents the maximum-likelihood estimate of Box's ε factor. Significance levels associated with adjusted *F* tests are labeled "G-G" on the printout. Huynh and Feldt (1976) have shown that the G-G estimate tends to be biased downward (that is, too conservative), especially for small samples, and have proposed an alternative estimator that is constructed using unbiased estimators of the numerator and denominator of Box's ε. Huynh and Feldt's estimator is labeled "Huynh-Feldt Epsilon" on the GLM printout, and the significance levels associated with adjusted *F* tests are labeled "H-F." Although ε must be in the range of 0 to 1, the H-F estimator can be outside this range. When the H-F estimator is greater than 1, a value of 1 is used in all calculations for probabilities, and the H-F probabilities are not adjusted. In summary, if your data do not meet the assumptions, use adjusted *F* tests. However, in cases where the sphericity test is dramatically rejected ($p \leq 0.0001$), all these univariate tests should be interpreted cautiously.

The univariate sums of squares for hypotheses involving within-subject effects can be easily calculated from the **H** and **E** matrices corresponding to the multivariate tests described in **Multivariate Analysis of Variance** earlier in this chapter. If the **M** matrix is orthogonal, the univariate sums of squares is calculated as the trace (sum of diagonal elements) of the appropriate **H** matrix; if it is not orthogonal, GLM calculates the trace of the **H** matrix that would result from an orthogonal **M** matrix transformation. The appropriate error term for the univariate *F* tests is constructed in a similar way from the error SSCP matrix and is labeled Error(*factorname*), where *factorname* indicates the **M** matrix that was used in the transformation.

When the design specifies more than one repeated measures factor, GLM computes the **M** matrix for a given effect as the direct (Kronecker) product of the **M** matrices defined by the REPEATED statement if the factor is involved in the effect or a vector of 1s if the factor is not involved. The test for the main effect of a repeated-measures factor is constructed using an **L** matrix that corresponds to a test that the mean of the observation is zero. Thus, the main effect test for repeated measures is a test that the means of the variables defined by the **M** matrix are all equal to zero, while interactions involving repeated-measures effects are tests that the between-subjects factors involved in the interaction have no effect on the means of the transformed variables defined by the **M** matrix. In addition, you can specify other **L** matrices to test hypotheses of interest by using the CONTRAST statement, which is used by REPEATED whenever it is present. To see which combinations of the original variables the transformed variables represent, you can specify the PRINTM option in the REPEATED statement. This option prints **M**', which is labeled as M in the GLM printout. The tests produced are the same for any choice of transformation (**M**) matrix specified in the REPEATED statement; however, depending on the nature of the repeated measurements being studied, a particular choice of transformation matrix, coupled with the CANONICAL or SUMMARY options, can provide additional insight into the data being studied.

Transformations Used in Repeated Measures Analysis of Variance

As mentioned in the specifications of the REPEATED statement, several different **M** matrices can be generated automatically, based on the transformation that you specify in the REPEATED statement. Remember that both the univariate and multivariate tests that GLM performs are unaffected by the choice of transformation; the choice of transformation is only important when you are trying to study the nature of a repeated measures effect, particularly with the CANONICAL and SUMMARY options. If one of these matrices does not meet your needs for a particular analysis, you may want to use the M= option of the MANOVA statement to perform the tests of interest.

The following sections describe the transformations available in the REPEATED statement, provide an example of the **M** matrix that is produced, and give guidelines for the use of the transformation. As in the GLM printout, the printed matrix is labeled M. This is the **M′** matrix.

CONTRAST transformation   This is the default used by the REPEATED statement. It is useful when one level of the repeated measures effect can be thought of as a control level against which the others are compared. For example, if five drugs are administered to each of several animals and the first drug is a control or placebo, the statements

```
proc glm;
   model d1-d5= / nouni;
   repeated drug 5 contrast(1) / summary;
```

produce the following **M** matrix:

$$
M = \begin{bmatrix}
-1 & 1 & 0 & 0 & 0 \\
-1 & 0 & 1 & 0 & 0 \\
-1 & 0 & 0 & 1 & 0 \\
-1 & 0 & 0 & 0 & 1
\end{bmatrix}
$$

When you examine the analysis of variance tables produced by the SUMMARY option, you can tell which of the drugs differed significantly from the placebo.

POLYNOMIAL transformation   This transformation is useful when the levels of the repeated measure represent quantitative values of a treatment, such as dose or time. If the levels are unequally spaced, *level values* can be specified in parentheses after the number of levels in the REPEATED statement. For example, if five levels of a drug corresponding to 1, 2, 5, 10 and 20 milligrams are administered to different treatment groups, represented by GROUP, the statements

```
proc glm;
   class group;
   model r1-r5=group / nouni;
   repeated dose 5 (1 2 5 10 20) polynomial / summary;
```

produce the following **M** matrix:

$$
M = \begin{bmatrix}
-0.4250 & -0.3606 & -0.1674 & 0.1545 & 0.7984 \\
0.4349 & 0.2073 & -0.3252 & -0.7116 & 0.3946 \\
-0.4331 & 0.1366 & 0.7253 & -0.5108 & 0.0821 \\
0.4926 & -0.7800 & 0.3743 & -0.0936 & 0.0066
\end{bmatrix}
$$

The SUMMARY option in this example provides univariate *ANOVAs* for the variables defined by the rows of the above **M** matrix. In this case, they represent the linear, quadratic, cubic, and quartic trends for dose and are labeled DOSE.1, DOSE.2, DOSE.3, and DOSE.4, respectively.

HELMERT transformation   Since the Helmert transformation compares a level of a repeated measure to the mean of subsequent levels, it is useful when interest lies in the point at which responses cease to change. For example, if four levels of a repeated measures factor represent responses to treatments administered over time to males and females, the statements

```
proc glm;
   class sex;
   model resp1-resp4=sex / nouni;
   repeated trtmnt 4 helmert / canon;
```

produce the following **M** matrix:

$$
\mathbf{M} = \begin{bmatrix}
1 & -0.33333 & -0.33333 & -0.33333 \\
0 & 1 & -0.50000 & -0.50000 \\
0 & 0 & 1 & -1
\end{bmatrix}
$$

To determine the point at which the treatment effect reaches a plateau, you can examine the canonical coefficients based on the **H** and **E** matrices corresponding to the main effect of TRTMNT and conclude that the plateau was reached when these coefficients became small.

MEAN transformation   This transformation can be useful in the same types of situations that the CONTRAST transformation is useful. For the statements in the CONTRAST section above, if you substitute

```
repeated drug 5 mean;
```

for the REPEATED statement in that example, the following **M** matrix is produced:

$$
\mathbf{M} = \begin{bmatrix}
1 & -0.25 & -0.25 & -0.25 & -0.25 \\
-0.25 & 1 & -0.25 & -0.25 & -0.25 \\
-0.25 & -0.25 & 1 & -0.25 & -0.25 \\
-0.25 & -0.25 & -0.25 & 1 & -0.25
\end{bmatrix}
$$

As with the CONTRAST transformation, if you want to omit a level other than the last, you can specify it in parentheses after the keyword MEAN in the REPEATED statement.

PROFILE transformation   When a repeated measure represents a series of factors administered over time, but a polynomial response is unreasonable, a profile transformation may prove useful. As an example, consider a training program in which four different methods are employed to teach students at several different schools. The repeated measure is the score on tests administered after each of the methods is completed. The statements

```
proc glm;
   class school;
   model t1-t4=school / nouni;
   repeated method 4 profile / summary nom;
```

produce the following **M** matrix:

$$
\mathbf{M} = \begin{bmatrix} 1 & -1 & 0 & 0 \\ 0 & 1 & -1 & 0 \\ 0 & 0 & 1 & -1 \end{bmatrix}
$$

To determine the point at which an improvement in test scores takes place, the analyses of variance for the transformed variables representing the differences between adjacent tests can be examined. These analyses are requested by the SUMMARY option in the REPEATED statement, and the variables are labeled METHOD.1, METHOD.2, and METHOD.3.

Expected Mean Squares for Random Effects

The RANDOM statement in GLM declares one or more effects in the model to be random rather than fixed. By default, GLM prints the coefficients of the expected mean squares for all terms in the model. In addition, when the TEST option in the RANDOM statement is specified, it determines what tests are appropriate, and provides F ratios and probabilities for these tests.

The expected mean squares are computed as follows. Consider the model

$$
Y = X_0\beta_0 + X_1\beta_1 + \ldots + X_k\beta_k + \varepsilon
$$

where β_0 represents the fixed effects, and β_1, β_2, $\ldots$, ε represent the random effects. Random effects are assumed to be normally and independently distributed. For any **L** in the row space of

$$
\mathbf{X} = (X_0 \mid X_1 \mid X_2 \mid \ldots \mid X_k)
$$

then

$$
E(SS_L) = \beta_0'\mathbf{C}_0'\mathbf{C}_0\beta_0 + SSQ(\mathbf{C}_1)\sigma_1^2 + SSQ(\mathbf{C}_2)\sigma_2^2 + \ldots + SSQ(\mathbf{C}_k)\sigma_k^2 + rank(\mathbf{L})\sigma_\varepsilon^2
$$

where **C** is of the same dimensions as **L** and partitioned as the **X** matrix. In other words,

$$
\mathbf{C} = (\mathbf{C}_0 \mid \mathbf{C}_1 \mid \ldots \mid \mathbf{C}_k)
$$

Furthermore, **C**=**ML**, where **M** is the inverse of the lower triangular Cholesky decomposition matrix of **L(X'X)⁻L'**. SSQ(**A**) is defined as tr(**A'A**).

For the model in this MODEL statement

```
model y=a b(a) c a*c;
```

with B(A) declared as random, the expected mean square of each effect is printed as

Var(Error) + *constant**Var(B(A)) + Q(A,C,A*C)   .

If any fixed effects appear in the expected mean square of an effect, the letter Q followed by the list of fixed effects in the expected value is printed. The actual numeric values of the quadratic form (**Q** matrix) can be printed using the Q option.

To determine appropriate means squares for testing the effects in the model, the TEST option in the RANDOM statement performs the following:

1. First, it forms a matrix of coefficients of the expected mean squares of those effects which were declared to be random.
2. Next, for each effect in the model, it determines the combination of these expected mean squares which will produce an expectation that includes all the terms in the expected mean square of the effect of interest except the one corresponding to the effect of interest. For example, if the expected mean square of an effect A*B is

$$Var(Error) + 3*Var(A) + Var(A*B)$$

   GLM determines the combination of other expected mean squares in the model that will have expectation

$$Var(Error) + 3*Var(A)   .$$

3. If the above criterion is met by the expected mean square of a single effect in the model (as is often the case in balanced designs), the *F* test is formed directly. In this case, the mean square of the effect of interest is used as the numerator, the mean square of the single effect whose expected mean square satisfies the criterion is used as the denominator, and the degrees of freedom for the test are simply the usual model degrees of freedom.
4. When more than one mean square must be combined to achieve the appropriate expectation, an approximation is employed to determine the appropriate degrees of freedom (Satterthwaite 1946). When effects other than the effect of interest are listed after the Q in the printout, tests of hypotheses involving the effect of interest are not valid unless all other fixed effects involved in it are assumed to be zero. When tests such as these are performed by using the TEST option in the RANDOM statement, a note is printed reminding you that further assumptions are necessary for the validity of these tests. Remember that although the tests are not valid unless these assumptions are made, this does not provide a basis for these assumptions to be true. The particulars of a given experiment must be examined to determine if the assumption is reasonable.

See Goodnight and Speed (1978) and Milliken and Johnson (1984, Chapters 22 and 23) for further theoretical discussion.

Missing Values

For an analysis involving one dependent variable, GLM uses an observation if values are present for that dependent variable and all the variables used in independent effects.

For an analysis involving multiple dependent variables without the MANOVA or REPEATED statement, or without the MANOVA option in the PROC GLM statement, a missing value in one dependent variable does not eliminate the observation from the analysis of other nonmissing dependent variables. For an analysis with the MANOVA or REPEATED statement, or with the MANOVA option in the PROC GLM statement, GLM requires values for all dependent variables to be present for an observation.

During processing, GLM groups the dependent variables on their missing values across observations so that sums and crossproducts can be collected in the most efficient manner.

Computational Resources

Memory

For large problems, most of the memory resources are required for holding the **X′X** matrix of the sums and crossproducts. The section on **Parameterization of GLM Models** earlier in this chapter describes how columns of the **X** matrix are allocated for various types of effects. For each level that occurs in the data for a combination of class variables in a given effect, a row and column for **X′X** is needed.

An example illustrates the calculation. Suppose A has 20 levels, B has 4, and C has 3. Then consider the model

```
proc glm;
  class a b c;
  model y1 y2 y3=a b a*b c a*c b*c a*b*c x1 x2;
```

The **X′X** matrix (bordered by **X′Y** and **Y′Y**) can have as many as 425 rows and columns:

1	for the intercept term
20	for A
4	for B
80	for A*B
3	for C
60	for A*C
12	for B*C
240	for A*B*C
2	for X1 and X2 (continuous variables)
3	for Y1, Y2, and Y3 (dependent variables).

The matrix has 425 rows and columns only if all combinations of levels occurred for each effect in the model. For m rows and columns, $8*m^2$ bytes are needed for crossproducts. In this case, $8*425^2$ is 1,445,000 bytes. To convert to K units, divide by 1024 to get 1411K.

The required memory grows as the square of the number of columns of **X** and **X′X**; most is for the A*B*C interaction. Without A*B*C, you have 185 columns and need 268K for **X′X**. Without either A*B*C or A*B, you need 86K. If A is recoded to have ten levels, then the full model has only 220 columns and requires 378K.

The second time that a large amount of memory is needed is when Type III, Type IV, or contrast sums of squares are being calculated. This memory requirement is a function of the number of degrees of freedom of the model being analyzed and the maximum degrees of freedom for any single source. Let RANK equal the sum of the model degrees of freedom, MAXDF be the maximum number of degrees of freedom for any single source, and NY be the number of dependent variables in the model. Then the memory requirement in bytes is

$$8 * \frac{\text{RANK*(RANK + 1)}}{2} + \text{NY*RANK} + \frac{\text{MAXDF*(MAXDF + 1)}}{2} + \text{NY*MAXDF} \quad .$$

Unfortunately, these quantities are not available when the **X′X** matrix is being constructed, so GLM may occasionally request additional memory even after you have increased the memory allocation available to the program.

If you have a large model that will exceed the memory capacity of your computer, these are your options:

- cut out terms, especially high-level interactions
- cut down the number of levels for variables with many levels
- use the ABSORB statement for parts of the model that are large
- use the REPEATED statement for repeated measures variables
- use PROC ANOVA or PROC REG rather than PROC GLM, if your design allows.

CPU time

For large problems, two operations consume a lot of CPU time: the collection of sums and crossproducts and the solution of the normal equations.

The time required for collecting sums and crossproducts is difficult to calculate because it is a complicated function of the model. For a model with m columns and n rows (observations) in $\mathbf{X}$, the worst case occurs if all columns are continuous variables, involving $n*m^2/2$ multiplications and additions. If the columns are levels of a classification, then only m sums may be needed, but a significant amount of time may be spent in look-up operations. Solving the normal equations requires time for approximately $m^3/2$ multiplications and additions.

Suppose you know that Type IV sums of squares will be appropriate for the model you are analyzing (for example, if your design has no missing cells). You can specify the SS4 option in your MODEL statement, which saves CPU time by requesting the Type IV sums of squares instead of the more computationally burdensome Type III sums of squares. This proves especially useful if you have a factor in your model that has many levels and is involved in several interactions.

Computational Method

Let $\mathbf{X}$ represent the $n \times p$ design matrix. (When effects containing only class variables are involved, the columns of $\mathbf{X}$ corresponding to these effects contain only 0s and 1s. No reparameterization is made.) Let $\mathbf{Y}$ represent the $n \times 1$ vector of dependent variables.

The normal equations $\mathbf{X'X\beta} = \mathbf{X'Y}$ are solved using a modified sweep routine that produces a generalized (g2) inverse $(\mathbf{X'X})^-$ and a solution $\mathbf{b} = (\mathbf{X'X})^-\mathbf{X'y}$ (Pringle and Raynor 1971).

For each effect in the model, a matrix $\mathbf{L}$ is computed such that the rows of $\mathbf{L}$ are estimable. Tests of the hypothesis $\mathbf{L\beta} = 0$ are then made by first computing

$$SS(\mathbf{L\beta} = 0) = (\mathbf{Lb})'(\mathbf{L}(\mathbf{X'X})^-\mathbf{L'})^{-1}(\mathbf{Lb})$$

then computing the associated F value using the mean squared error.

Output Data Sets

Data Set Produced by the OUTPUT Statement

The OUTPUT statement produces an output data set that contains the following:

- all original data from the SAS data set input to GLM
- the new variables corresponding to the diagnostic measures requested in the OUTPUT statement (PREDICTED=variables, RESIDUAL=variables, and so on).

With multiple dependent variables, a name can be specified for any of the diagnostic measures for each of the dependent variables in the order in which they occur in the MODEL statement.

For example, suppose the input data set A contains the variables Y1, Y2, Y3, X1, and X2. Then you can code

```
proc glm data=a;
   model y1 y2 y3=x1;
   output p=y1hat y2hat y3hat r=y1resid l95m=y1lcl u95m=y1ucl;
```

The output data set contains Y1, Y2, Y3, X1, X2, Y1HAT, Y2HAT, Y3HAT, Y1RESID, Y1LCL, and Y1UCL. X2 is output even though it was not used by GLM. Although predicted values are generated for all three dependent variables, residuals are output for only the first dependent variable.

When any independent variable in the analysis is missing for an observation, then all new variables that correspond to diagnostic measures are missing for the observation in the output data set.

When a dependent variable in the analysis is missing for an observation, then some new variables that correspond to diagnostic measures are missing for the observation in the output data set, and some are still available. Specifically, in this case, the new variables that correspond to COOKD, COVRATIO, DFFITS, PRESS, R, RSTUDENT, STDR, and STUDENT are missing in the output data set. The variables corresponding to H, L95, L95M, P, STDI, STDP, U95, and U95M are not missing in this case.

Data Set Produced by the OUTSTAT= Option in the PROC GLM Statement

The OUTSTAT= option in the PROC GLM statement produces an output data set that contains

- the BY variables, if any.
- three new character variables: _TYPE_, _NAME_, and _SOURCE_. The _TYPE_ variable may take the values 'SS1', 'SS2', 'SS3', 'SS4', or 'CONTRAST', corresponding to the various types of sums of squares generated, or the values 'CANCORR', 'STRUCTUR', or 'SCORE', if a canonical analysis is performed through the MANOVA statement and no M= matrix is specified. For each observation in the data set, the _SOURCE_ variable contains the name of the model effect or contrast label from which the corresponding statistics are generated. The _NAME_ variable contains the name of one of the dependent variables in the model, or in the case of canonical statistics, the name of one of the canonical variables (CAN1, CAN2, and so forth).
- four new numeric variables: SS, DF, F, and PROB, containing sums of squares, degrees of freedom, F values, and probabilities, respectively, for each model or contrast sum of squares generated in the analysis. For observations resulting from canonical analyses, these variables have missing values.
- if there is more than one dependent variable, then variables with the same names as the dependent variables represent
  - for _TYPE_='SS1', 'SS2', 'SS3', 'SS4', or 'CONTRAST', the crossproducts of the hypothesis matrices
  - for _TYPE_='CANCORR', canonical correlations for each variable
  - for _TYPE_='STRUCTUR', coefficients of the total structure matrix
  - for _TYPE_='SCORE', raw canonical score coefficients.

The output data set can be used to perform special hypothesis tests (for example, with PROC IML in SAS/IML software), to reformat output, to produce canonical variates (through PROC SCORE), or to rotate structure matrices (through PROC FACTOR).

Data Set Produced by the OUT= Option in the LSMEANS Statement

The OUT= option in the LSMEANS statement produces an output data set that contains

- the unformatted values of each classification variable specified in any effect in the LSMEANS statement.
- a new variable, LSMEAN, which contains the least square mean for the specified levels of the classification variables.
- a new variable, STDERR, which contains the standard error of the least square mean.

The covariances among the least square means are also output when the COV option is specified along with the OUT= option. In this case, only one effect may be specified in the LSMEANS statement, and the following variables are included in the output data set:

- new variables, COV1, COV2, . . . , COVn, where n is the number of levels of the effect specified in the LSMEANS statement. These variables contain the covariances of each least squares mean with each other least squares mean.
- a new variable, NUMBER, which provides an index for each observation to identify the covariances which correspond to that observation. The covariances for the observation with NUMBER equal to n can be found in the variable COVn.

Printed Output

The GLM procedure produces the following printed output by default:

1. The overall analysis-of-variance table breaks down the Total Sum of Squares for the dependent variable
2. into the portion attributed to the Model
3. and the portion attributed to Error.
4. The Mean Square term is the
5. Sum of Squares divided by the
6. degrees of freedom (DF).
7. The Mean Square for Error is an estimate of σ^2, the variance of the true errors.
8. The F Value is the ratio produced by dividing the Mean Square for the Model by the Mean Square for Error. It tests how well the model as a whole (adjusted for the mean) accounts for the dependent variable's behavior. An F test is a joint test to determine that all parameters except the intercept are zero.
9. A small significance probability, Pr > F, indicates that some linear function of the parameters is significantly different from zero.
10. R-Square, R^2, measures how much variation in the dependent variable can be accounted for by the model. R^2, which can range from 0 to 1, is the ratio of the sum of squares for the model divided by the sum of squares for the corrected total. In general, the larger the value of R^2, the better the model's fit.
11. C.V., the coefficient of variation, which describes the amount of variation in the population, is 100 times the standard deviation estimate of the dependent variable, Root MSE, divided by the Mean. The coefficient of variation is often a preferred measure because it is unitless.
12. Root MSE estimates the standard deviation of the dependent variable (or equivalently, the error term) and equals the square root of the Mean Square for Error.
13. Mean is the sample mean of the dependent variable.

These tests are used primarily in analysis-of-variance applications:

14. The Type I SS measures incremental sums of squares for the model as each variable is added.
15. The Type III SS is the sum of squares that results when that variable is added last to the model.
16. The F Value and Pr > F values for Type III tests, where each effect is adjusted for every other effect.

These items are used primarily in regression applications:

17. The Estimates for the model Parameters (the intercept and the coefficients).
18. T for H_0: Parameter=0 is the Student's t value for testing the null hypothesis that the parameter (if it is estimable) equals zero.
19. The significance level, Pr > |T|, is the probability of getting a larger value of t if the parameter is truly equal to zero. A very small value for this probability leads to the conclusion that the independent variable contributes significantly to the model.
20. The Std Error of Estimate is the standard error of the estimate of the true value of the parameter.

Other portions of output are discussed in the examples below.

EXAMPLES

Example 1: Balanced Data from Randomized Complete Block with Means Comparisons and Contrasts

Since these data are balanced, you can obtain the same answer more efficiently using the ANOVA procedure; however, GLM presents the results in a slightly different way. Notice that since the data are balanced, the Type I and Type III SS are the same and equal the ANOVA SS.

First, the standard analysis is shown followed by an analysis that uses the SOLUTION option and includes MEANS and CONTRAST statements. The ORDER=DATA option in the second PROC GLM statement is used so that the ordering of coefficients in the CONTRAST statement can correspond to the ordering in the input data. The SOLUTION option requests a printout of the parameter estimates, which are only printed by default if there are no CLASS variables. A MEANS statement is used to request a printout of the means with two multiple comparison procedures requested. In experiments with well-understood treatment levels, CONTRAST statements are preferable to a blanket means comparison method. The following statements produce **Output 20.8** and **Output 20.9**:

```
*---------------SNAPDRAGON EXPERIMENT---------------*
| As reported by Stenstrom, 1940, an experiment was |
| undertaken to investigate how snapdragons grew in |
| various soils. Each soil type was used in three   |
| blocks.                                           |
*---------------------------------------------------*;

data plants;
   input type $ a;
   do block=1 to 3;
      input stemleng a;
      output;
      end;
   cards;
```

```
CLARION  32.7 32.3 31.5
CLINTON  32.1 29.7 29.1
KNOX     35.7 35.9 33.1
O'NEILL  36.0 34.2 31.2
COMPOST  31.8 28.0 29.2
WABASH   38.2 37.8 31.9
WEBSTER  32.5 31.1 29.7
;
proc glm;
   class type block;
   model stemleng=type block;
proc glm order=data;
   class type block;
   model stemleng=type block / solution;

   *-type-order--------------------clrn-cltn-knox-onel-cpst-wbsh-wstr;
   contrast 'COMPOST VS OTHERS' type -1  -1  -1  -1   6  -1  -1;
   contrast 'RIVER SOILS VS.NON' type -1 -1  -1  -1   0   5  -1,
                                 type -1   4  -1  -1   0   0  -1;
   contrast 'GLACIAL VS DRIFT'  type -1   0   1   1   0   0  -1;
   contrast 'CLARION VS WEBSTER' type -1  0   0   0   0   0   1;
   contrast 'KNOX VS ONEILL'    type  0   0   1  -1   0   0   0;
run;
   means type / waller regwq;
run:
```

Output 20.8 Standard Analysis for Randomized Complete Block: PROC GLM

```
                        General Linear Models Procedure                        1
                           Class Level Information

             Class    Levels   Values

             TYPE       7     CLARION CLINTON COMPOST KNOX O'NEILL WABASH WEBSTER

             BLOCK      3     1 2 3


             Number of observations in data set = 21
```

```
                        General Linear Models Procedure                        2

Dependent Variable: STEMLENG
Source          ❻ DF      ❺ Sum of Squares    ❹ Mean Square   ❽ F Value   ❾ Pr > F

Model            8        ❷ 142.18857143        17.77357143      10.80      0.0002

Error            12       ❸ 19.74285714       ❼ 1.64523810

Corrected Total  20       ❶ 161.93142857

        ❿ R-Square          ⓫ C.V.            ⓬ Root MSE           ⓭ STEMLENG Mean
          0.878079            3.939745           1.28266835            32.55714286
```

(continued on next page)

(continued from previous page)

Source	DF	⑭ Type I SS	Mean Square	F Value	Pr > F
TYPE	6	103.15142857	17.19190476	10.45	0.0004
BLOCK	2	39.03714286	19.51857143	11.86	0.0014

Source	DF	⑮ Type III SS	Mean Square	⑯ F Value	⑯ Pr > F
TYPE	6	103.15142857	17.19190476	10.45	0.0004
BLOCK	2	39.03714286	19.51857143	11.86	0.0014

This analysis shows that the stem length is significantly different for the different soil types. In addition, there are significant differences in stem length between the three blocks in the experiment.

Output 20.9 Randomized Complete Block with Means Comparisons and Contrasts: PROC GLM

```
                    General Linear Models Procedure                          3
                       Class Level Information

              Class    Levels   Values

              TYPE        7     CLARION CLINTON KNOX O'NEILL COMPOST WABASH WEBSTER

              BLOCK       3     1 2 3


                  Number of observations in data set = 21
```

```
                    General Linear Models Procedure                          4
```

Dependent Variable: STEMLENG

Source	DF	Sum of Squares	Mean Square	F Value	Pr > F
Model	8	142.18857143	17.77357143	10.80	0.0002
Error	12	19.74285714	1.64523810		
Corrected Total	20	161.93142857			

	R-Square	C.V.	Root MSE	STEMLENG Mean
	0.878079	3.939745	1.28266835	32.55714286

Source	DF	Type I SS	Mean Square	F Value	Pr > F
TYPE	6	103.15142857	17.19190476	10.45	0.0004
BLOCK	2	39.03714286	19.51857143	11.86	0.0014

Source	DF	Type III SS	Mean Square	F Value	Pr > F
TYPE	6	103.15142857	17.19190476	10.45	0.0004
BLOCK	2	39.03714286	19.51857143	11.86	0.0014

Ⓐ
Contrast	DF	Contrast SS	Mean Square	F Value	Pr > F
COMPOST VS OTHERS	1	29.24198413	29.24198413	17.77	0.0012
RIVER SOILS VS.NON	2	48.24694444	24.12347222	14.66	0.0006
GLACIAL VS DRIFT	1	22.14083333	22.14083333	13.46	0.0032
CLARION VS WEBSTER	1	1.70666667	1.70666667	1.04	0.3285
KNOX VS ONEILL	1	1.81500000	1.81500000	1.10	0.3143

(continued on next page)

(continued from previous page)

⑧ Parameter		⑰ Estimate	⑱ T for H0: Parameter=0	⑲ Pr > |T|	⑳ Std Error of Estimate
INTERCEPT		29.35714286 B	34.96	0.0001	0.83970354
TYPE	CLARION	1.06666667 B	1.02	0.3285	1.04729432
	CLINTON	-0.80000000 B	-0.76	0.4597	1.04729432
	KNOX	3.80000000 B	3.63	0.0035	1.04729432
	O'NEILL	2.70000000 B	2.58	0.0242	1.04729432
	COMPOST	-1.43333333 B	-1.37	0.1962	1.04729432
	WABASH	4.86666667 B	4.65	0.0006	1.04729432
	WEBSTER	0.00000000 B	.	.	.
BLOCK	1	3.32857143 B	4.85	0.0004	0.68561507
	2	1.90000000 B	2.77	0.0169	0.68561507
	3	0.00000000 B	.	.	.

NOTE: The X'X matrix has been found to be singular and a generalized inverse was used to solve the normal equations. Estimates followed by the letter 'B' are biased, and are not unique estimators of the parameters.

Ⓒ General Linear Models Procedure   5

Waller-Duncan K-ratio T test for variable: STEMLENG

NOTE: This test minimizes the Bayes risk under additive loss and certain other assumptions.

Kratio= 100 df= 12 MSE= 1.645238 F= 10.44949
Critical Value of T= 2.12034
Minimum Significant Difference= 2.2206

Means with the same letter are not significantly different.

Waller Grouping		Mean	N	TYPE
	A	35.967	3	WABASH
	A			
	A	34.900	3	KNOX
	A			
B	A	33.800	3	O'NEILL
B				
B	C	32.167	3	CLARION
	C			
D	C	31.100	3	WEBSTER
D	C			
D	C	30.300	3	CLINTON
D				
D		29.667	3	COMPOST

General Linear Models Procedure   6

Ryan-Einot-Gabriel-Welsch Multiple Range Test for variable: STEMLENG

NOTE: This test controls the type I experimentwise error rate.

Alpha= 0.05 df= 12 MSE= 1.645238

Number of Means	2	3	4	5	6	7
Critical Range	2.9876505	3.2838353	3.4396291	3.5402498	3.5178074	3.6653904

Means with the same letter are not significantly different.

REGWQ Grouping			Mean	N	TYPE
	A		35.967	3	WABASH
	A				
B	A		34.900	3	KNOX
B	A				
B	A	C	33.800	3	O'NEILL
B		C			
B	D	C	32.167	3	CLARION
	D	C			
	D	C	31.100	3	WEBSTER
	D				
	D		30.300	3	CLINTON
	D				
	D		29.667	3	COMPOST

The circled letters on the printout correspond to the descriptions below:

A. The section of output labeled Contrast shows the result of the CONTRAST statements. The contrast label, the degrees of freedom for the contrast, the Contrast SS, Mean Square, F Value, and Pr > F are shown for each contrast requested. In this example, the contrasts show
- the stem length of plants grown in compost soil is significantly different from the stem length of plants grown in other soils
- the stem length of plants grown in river soils is significantly different from the stem length of those grown in non-river soils
- the stem length of plants grown in glacial soils (CLARION and WEBSTER) is significantly different from the stem length of those grown in drift soils (KNOX and O'NEILL).
- stem lengths for CLARION and WEBSTER are not significantly different
- stem lengths for KNOX and O'NEILL are not significantly different.

B. The section of output labeled Parameter gives estimates for the parameters and results of *t* tests about the parameters. The B following the parameter estimates means the estimates are biased and do not represent a unique solution to the normal equations.

C. The final two pages of output give results of the Waller-Duncan and REGWQ multiple comparison procedures. For each test, notes and information pertinent to the test are given on the printout. The TYPE means are arranged from highest to lowest. Means with the same letter are not significantly different.

Example 2: Regression with Mileage Data

A car is tested for gas mileage at various speeds to determine at what speed the car achieves the greatest gas mileage. A quadratic response surface is fit to the experimental data. The following statements produce **Output 20.10** and **Output 20.11**:

```
*-----------GASOLINE MILEAGE EXPERIMENT------------;

data mileage;
   input mph mpg @@;
   cards;
20 15.4 30 20.2 40 25.7 50 26.2 50 26.6 50 27.4 55   . 60 24.8
;
proc glm;
   model mpg=mph mph*mph / p clm;
   output out=pp p=mpgpred r=resid;
proc plot data=pp;
   plot mpg*mph='A' mpgpred*mph='P' / overlay;
run;
```

Output 20.10   Regression: PROC GLM

```
                        General Linear Models Procedure                         1

                    Number of observations in data set = 8

   NOTE: Due to missing values, only 7 observations can be used in this analysis.
```

```
                        General Linear Models Procedure                         2

Dependent Variable: MPG

Source              DF      Sum of Squares      Mean Square     F Value     Pr > F

Model                2        111.80861827      55.90430913       77.96     0.0006

Error                4          2.86852459       0.71713115

Corrected Total      6        114.67714286

             R-Square             C.V.          Root MSE              MPG Mean

             0.974986          3.564553        0.84683596            23.75714286

Source              DF           Type I SS      Mean Square     F Value     Pr > F

MPH                  1         85.64464286      85.64464286      119.43     0.0004
MPH*MPH              1         26.16397541      26.16397541       36.48     0.0038

Source              DF         Type III SS      Mean Square     F Value     Pr > F

MPH                  1         41.01171219      41.01171219       57.19     0.0016
MPH*MPH              1         26.16397541      26.16397541       36.48     0.0038

                                            T for H0:       Pr > |T|    Std Error of
Parameter               Estimate          Parameter=0                     Estimate

INTERCEPT            -5.985245902            -1.88          0.1334       3.18522249
MPH                   1.305245902             7.56          0.0016       0.17259876
MPH*MPH              -0.013098361            -6.04          0.0038       0.00216852

Observation      Observed        Predicted       Residual      Lower 95% CL    Upper 95% CL
                  Value           Value                          for Mean        for Mean

     1          15.40000000     14.88032787     0.51967213     12.69704271     17.06361303
     2          20.20000000     21.38360656    -1.18360656     20.01729041     22.74992270
     3          25.70000000     25.26721311     0.43278689     23.87461925     26.65980698
     4          26.20000000     26.53114754    -0.33114754     25.44574892     27.61654616
     5          26.60000000     26.53114754     0.06885246     25.44574892     27.61654616
     6          27.40000000     26.53114754     0.86885246     25.44574892     27.61654616
     7   *                      26.18073770          .         24.88681059     27.47466482
     8          24.80000000     25.17540984    -0.37540984     23.05957840     27.29124127

* Observation was not used in this analysis

         Sum of Residuals                         -0.00000000
         Sum of Squared Residuals                  2.86852459
         Sum of Squared Residuals - Error SS      -0.00000000
         Press Statistic                          23.18107335
         First Order Autocorrelation              -0.54376613
         Durbin-Watson D                           2.94425592
```

This output shows that both the linear and quadratic terms in the regression model are significant. The model fits well, with an R^2 of 0.97. The estimated equation is

$$MPG = -5.9852 + 1.3052*MPH - 0.0131*MPH*MPH \quad .$$

The section labeled Observation shows the results of requesting the P and CLM options. For each observation, the observed, predicted, and residual values are shown. In addition, the 95% confidence limits for a mean predicted value are shown for each observation. Note that the observation with a missing value for MPH was not used in the analysis, but predicted and confidence limit values are shown.

The final portion of output gives some additional information on the residuals. The Press statistic gives the sum of squares of predicted residual errors, as described in Chapter 1, "Introduction to Regression Procedures." The First Order Autocorrelation and the Durbin-Watson D statistic, which tests for the presence of first-order autocorrelation, are also given. **Output 20.11** shows the actual and predicted values for the data.

Output 20.11 Plot of Mileage Data

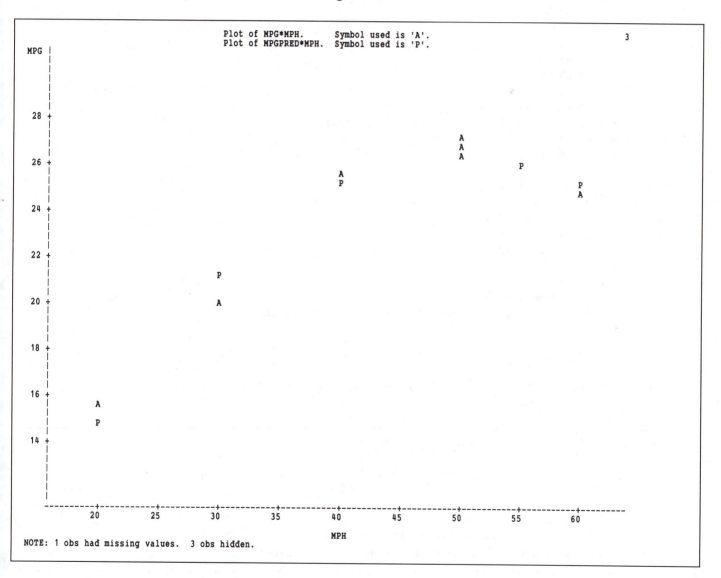

Example 3: Unbalanced *ANOVA* for Two-Way Design with Interaction

This example uses data from Kutner (1974) to illustrate a two-way analysis of variance. The original data source is Afifi and Azen (1972). These statements produce **Output 20.12**:

```
*-------------------------------------------------------------------*
| A two-way analysis-of-variance example using the data from        |
| Kutner (1974, p. 98). Original data source: Afifi and             |
| Azen (1972, p. 166).                                              |
*-------------------------------------------------------------------- *;


data a;
   input drug disease @;
   do i=1 to 6;
      input y @;
      output;
      end;
   cards;
1 1 42 44 36 13 19 22
1 2 33  . 26  . 33 21
1 3 31 -3  . 25 25 24
2 1 28  . 23 34 42 13      *Kutner's 24 changed to 34;
2 2  . 34 33 31  . 36
2 3  3 26 28 32  4 16
3 1  .  .  1 29  . 19
3 2  . 11  9  7  1 -6
3 3 21  1  .  9  3  .
4 1 24  .  9 22 -2 15
4 2 27 12 12 -5 16 15
4 3 22  7 25  5 12  .
;
proc glm;
   class drug disease;
   model y=drug disease drug*disease / ss1 ss2 ss3 ss4;
run;
```

Output 20.12   Unbalanced *ANOVA* for Two-Way Design with Interaction: PROC GLM

```
                         General Linear Models Procedure                              1
                            Class Level Information

                      Class     Levels    Values

                      DRUG         4      1 2 3 4

                      DISEASE      3      1 2 3


                    Number of observations in data set = 72

      NOTE: Due to missing values, only 58 observations can be used in this analysis.
```

```
                              General Linear Models Procedure                           2

Dependent Variable: Y

Source                  DF         Sum of Squares       Mean Square      F Value       Pr > F

Model                   11         4259.33850575       387.21259143        3.51         0.0013

Error                   46         5080.81666667       110.45253623

Corrected Total         57         9340.15517241

                     R-Square                C.V.              Root MSE                 Y Mean

                     0.456024             55.66750            10.50964016            18.87931034

Source                  DF            Type I SS          Mean Square      F Value       Pr > F

DRUG                     3         3133.23850575      1044.41283525        9.46         0.0001
DISEASE                  2          418.83374069       209.41687035        1.90         0.1617
DRUG*DISEASE             6          707.26625931       117.87770988        1.07         0.3958

Source                  DF           Type II SS          Mean Square      F Value       Pr > F

DRUG                     3         3063.43286350      1021.14428783        9.25         0.0001
DISEASE                  2          418.83374069       209.41687035        1.90         0.1617
DRUG*DISEASE             6          707.26625931       117.87770988        1.07         0.3958

Source                  DF          Type III SS          Mean Square      F Value       Pr > F

DRUG                     3         2997.47186048       999.15728683        9.05         0.0001
DISEASE                  2          415.87304632       207.93652316        1.88         0.1637
DRUG*DISEASE             6          707.26625931       117.87770988        1.07         0.3958

Source                  DF          Type IV SS           Mean Square      F Value       Pr > F

DRUG                     3         2997.47186048       999.15728683        9.05         0.0001
DISEASE                  2          415.87304632       207.93652316        1.88         0.1637
DRUG*DISEASE             6          707.26625931       117.87770988        1.07         0.3958
```

This analysis shows a significant difference among the four drugs. The DISEASE effect and the DRUG*DISEASE interaction are not significant.

Example 4: Analysis of Covariance

Analysis of covariance combines some of the features of regression and analysis of variance. Typically, a continuous variable (the covariate) is introduced into the model of an analysis-of-variance experiment.

Data in the following example were selected from a larger experiment on the use of drugs in the treatment of leprosy (Snedecor and Cochran 1967, 422).

Variables in the study are

DRUG two antibiotics (A and D) and a control (F)

X a pre-treatment score of leprosy bacilli

Y a post-treatment score of leprosy bacilli.

Ten patients were selected for each treatment (DRUG), and six sites on each patient were measured for leprosy bacilli.

The covariate (a pre-treatment score) is included in the model for increased precision in determining the effect of drug treatments on the post-treatment count of bacilli.

The code for creating the data set and invoking GLM is shown below; it produces **Output 20.13**.

```
* From Snedecor and Cochran (1967, p.422).

data drugtest;
   input drug $ x y @@;
   cards;
A 11  6  A  8  0  A  5  2  A 14  8  A 19 11
A  6  4  A 10 13  A  6  1  A 11  8  A  3  0
D  6  0  D  6  2  D  7  3  D  8  1  D 18 18
D  8  4  D 19 14  D  8  9  D  5  1  D 15  9
F 16 13  F 13 10  F 11 18  F  9  5  F 21 23
F 16 12  F 12  5  F 12 16  F  7  1  F 12 20
;
proc glm;
   class drug;
   model y=drug x / solution;
   lsmeans drug / stderr pdiff;
run;
```

Output 20.13   Analysis of Covariance: PROC GLM

```
                        General Linear Models Procedure                        1
                          Class Level Information

                      Class     Levels    Values

                      DRUG         3       A D F


             Number of observations in data set = 30
```

```
                        General Linear Models Procedure                        2
Dependent Variable: Y

Source            DF       Sum of Squares      Mean Square    F Value    Pr > F

Model              3         871.49740304      290.49913435     18.10    0.0001

Error             26         417.20259696       16.04625373

Corrected Total   29        1288.70000000

             R-Square             C.V.          Root MSE             Y Mean

             0.676261          50.70604        4.00577754         7.90000000


Source            DF            Type I SS      Mean Square    F Value    Pr > F

DRUG               2       Ⓐ 293.60000000      146.80000000      9.15    0.0010
X                  1          577.89740304      577.89740304     36.01    0.0001

Source            DF          Type III SS      Mean Square    F Value    Pr > F

DRUG               2       Ⓑ  68.55371060       34.27685530      2.14    0.1384
X                  1          577.89740304      577.89740304     36.01    0.0001
```

(continued on next page)

(continued from previous page)

Parameter		Estimate	T for H0: Parameter=0	Pr > |T|	Std Error of Estimate
INTERCEPT		-0.434671164 B	-0.18	0.8617	2.47135356
DRUG	A	-3.446138280 B	-1.83	0.0793	1.88678065
	D	-3.337166948 B	-1.80	0.0835	1.85386642
	F	0.000000000 B	.	.	.
X		0.987183811	6.00	0.0001	0.16449757

NOTE: The X'X matrix has been found to be singular and a generalized inverse was used to solve the normal equations. Estimates followed by the letter 'B' are biased, and are not unique estimators of the parameters.

```
                        General Linear Models Procedure                        3
                             Least Squares Means
                    C            D                E
       DRUG         Y         Std Err    Pr > |T|   Pr > |T| H0: LSMEAN(i)=LSMEAN(j)
                  LSMEAN       LSMEAN    H0:LSMEAN=0  i/j    1        2        3

        A        6.7149635   1.2884943    0.0001      1     .      0.9521   0.0793
        D        6.8239348   1.2724690    0.0001      2   0.9521     .      0.0835
        F       10.1611017   1.3159234    0.0001      3   0.0793   0.0835     .
```

NOTE: To ensure overall protection level, only probabilities associated with pre-planned comparisons should be used.

The circled letters on the printout correspond to the descriptions that follow:

A. The Type I SS for DRUG gives the between-drug sums of squares that would be obtained for the analysis-of-variance model Y=DRUG.

B. Type III SS for DRUG gives the DRUG SS adjusted for the covariate.

C. The LSMEANS printed are the same as adjusted means (means adjusted for the covariate).

D. The STDERR option in the LSMEANS statement causes the standard error of the least-squares means and the probability of getting a larger t value under the hypothesis H_0: LSM=0 to be printed.

E. Specifying the PDIFF option causes all probability values for the hypothesis H_0: LSM(I)=LSM(J) to be printed.

Example 5: Three-Way Analysis of Variance with Contrasts

This example uses data from Cochran and Cox (1957, 176) to illustrate a three-way factorial design with replication and two uses of the CONTRAST statement. The object of the study is to determine the effects of electric current on denervated muscle.

The variables are

REP	the replicate number, 1 or 2
TIME	the length of time the current was applied to the muscle, ranging from 1 to 4
CURRENT	the level of electric current applied, ranging from 1 to 4
NUMBER	the number of treatments per day, ranging from 1 to 3
Y	the weight of the denervated muscle.

The code below produces **Output 20.14**:

```
data one;
   do rep=1 to 2;
      do time=1 to 4;
         do current=1 to 4;
            do number=1 to 3;
               input y @@;
               output;
               end;
            end;
         end;
      end;
   cards;
72 74 69 61 61 65 62 65 70 85 76 61
67 52 62 60 55 59 64 65 64 67 72 60
57 66 72 72 43 43 63 66 72 56 75 92
57 56 78 60 63 58 61 79 68 73 86 71
46 74 58 60 64 52 71 64 71 53 65 66
44 58 54 57 55 51 62 61 79 60 78 82
53 50 61 56 57 56 56 56 71 56 58 69
46 55 64 56 55 57 64 66 62 59 58 88
;
proc glm;
   class rep current time number;
   model y=rep current|time|number;
   contrast 'TIME IN CURRENT 3'
      time 1 0 0 -1 current*time 0 0 0 0 0 0 0 0 1 0 0 -1,
      time 0 1 0 -1 current*time 0 0 0 0 0 0 0 0 0 1 0 -1,
      time 0 0 1 -1 current*time 0 0 0 0 0 0 0 0 0 0 1 -1;
   contrast 'CURR 1 VS. CURR 2' current 1 -1;
run;
```

The first CONTRAST statement examines the effects of TIME within level 3 of CURRENT. Note that since there are three degrees of freedom, it is necessary to specify three rows in the CONTRAST statement, separated by commas. Since the parameterization that PROC GLM uses is determined in part by the ordering of the variables in the CLASS statement, CURRENT was specified before TIME so that the TIME parameters would be nested within the CURRENT*TIME parameters; thus, the CURRENT*TIME parameters in each row are simply the TIME parameters of that row within the appropriate level of CURRENT.

The second CONTRAST statement isolates a single degree of freedom effect corresponding to the difference between the first two levels of CURRENT. You can use such a contrast in a large experiment where certain preplanned comparisons are important, but you want to take advantage of the additional error degrees of freedom available when all levels of the factors are considered.

Output 20.14 Three-Way Analysis of Variance with Contrasts: PROC GLM

```
                     General Linear Models Procedure                        1
                        Class Level Information

                      Class    Levels    Values

                      REP         2      1 2

                      CURRENT     4      1 2 3 4

                      TIME        4      1 2 3 4

                      NUMBER      3      1 2 3


             Number of observations in data set = 96
```

```
                     General Linear Models Procedure                        2

Dependent Variable: Y

Source                 DF      Sum of Squares     Mean Square    F Value    Pr > F

Model                  48      5782.91666667    120.47743056       1.77    0.0261

Error                  47      3199.48958333     68.07424645

Corrected Total        95      8982.40625000

          R-Square              C.V.            Root MSE                Y Mean

          0.643805            13.05105          8.25071188           63.21875000


Source                 DF          Type I SS      Mean Square    F Value    Pr > F

REP                     1       605.01041667     605.01041667       8.89    0.0045
CURRENT                 3      2145.44791667     715.14930556      10.51    0.0001
TIME                    3       223.11458333      74.37152778       1.09    0.3616
CURRENT*TIME            9       298.67708333      33.18634259       0.49    0.8756
NUMBER                  2       447.43750000     223.71875000       3.29    0.0461
CURRENT*NUMBER          6       644.39583333     107.39930556       1.58    0.1747
TIME*NUMBER             6       367.97916667      61.32986111       0.90    0.5023
CURRENT*TIME*NUMBER    18      1050.85416667      58.38078704       0.86    0.6276

Source                 DF        Type III SS      Mean Square    F Value    Pr > F

REP                     1       605.01041667     605.01041667       8.89    0.0045
CURRENT                 3      2145.44791667     715.14930556      10.51    0.0001
TIME                    3       223.11458333      74.37152778       1.09    0.3616
CURRENT*TIME            9       298.67708333      33.18634259       0.49    0.8756
NUMBER                  2       447.43750000     223.71875000       3.29    0.0461
CURRENT*NUMBER          6       644.39583333     107.39930556       1.58    0.1747
TIME*NUMBER             6       367.97916667      61.32986111       0.90    0.5023
CURRENT*TIME*NUMBER    18      1050.85416667      58.38078704       0.86    0.6276

Contrast               DF        Contrast SS      Mean Square    F Value    Pr > F

TIME IN CURRENT 3       3        34.83333333      11.61111111       0.17    0.9157
CURR 1 VS. CURR 2       1        99.18750000      99.18750000       1.46    0.2334
```

The output above shows significant main effects for REP, CURRENT, and NUMBER. None of the interactions are significant, nor are the contrasts significant.

Example 6: Multivariate Analysis of Variance

Using data from A. Anderson, Oregon State University, this example illustrates
a multivariate analysis of variance. See **Output 20.15**.

```
*---------MULTIVARIATE ANALYSIS OF VARIANCE-------*
| Data from A. Anderson, Oregon State University. |
| Four different response variables are measured. |
| The hypothesis to be tested is that sex does    |
| not affect any of the four responses.           |
*-------------------------------------------------*;

data skull;
   input sex $ length basilar zygomat postorb @@;
   cards;
M 6460 4962 3286 1100 M 6252 4773 3239 1061 M 5772 4480 3200 1097
M 6264 4806 3179 1054 M 6622 5113 3365 1071 M 6656 5100 3326 1012
M 6441 4918 3153 1061 M 6281 4821 3133 1071 M 6606 5060 3227 1064
M 6573 4977 3392 1110 M 6563 5025 3234 1090 M 6552 5086 3292 1010
M 6535 4939 3261 1065 M 6573 4962 3320 1091 M 6537 4990 3309 1059
M 6302 4761 3204 1135 M 6449 4921 3256 1068 M 6481 4887 3233 1124
M 6368 4824 3258 1130 M 6372 4844 3306 1137 M 6592 5007 3284 1148
M 6229 4746 3257 1153 M 6391 4834 3244 1169 M 6560 4981 3341 1038
M 6787 5181 3334 1104 M 6384 4834 3195 1064 M 6282 4757 3180 1179
M 6340 4791 3300 1110 M 6394 4879 3272 1241 M 6153 4557 3214 1039
M 6348 4886 3160  991 M 6534 4990 3310 1028 M 6509 4951 3282 1104
F 6287 4845 3218  996 F 6583 4992 3300 1107 F 6518 5023 3246 1035
F 6432 4790 3249 1117 F 6450 4888 3259 1060 F 6379 4844 3266 1115
F 6424 4855 3322 1065 F 6615 5088 3280 1179 F 6760 5206 3337 1219
F 6521 5011 3208  989 F 6416 4889 3200 1001 F 6511 4910 3230 1100
F 6540 4997 3320 1078 F 6780 5259 3358 1174 F 6336 4781 3165 1126
F 6472 4954 3125 1178 F 6476 4896 3148 1066 F 6276 4709 3150 1134
F 6693 5177 3236 1131 F 6328 4792 3214 1018 F 6661 5104 3395 1141
F 6266 4721 3257 1031 F 6660 5146 3374 1069 F 6624 5032 3384 1154
F 6331 4819 3278 1008 F 6298 4683 3270 1150
;
proc glm;
   class sex;
   model length basilar zygomat postorb=sex;
   manova h=sex / printe printh;
   title 'MULTIVARIATE ANALYSIS OF VARIANCE';
run;
```

Output 20.15   Multivariate Analysis of Variance: PROC GLM

```
                    MULTIVARIATE ANALYSIS OF VARIANCE                          1

                     General Linear Models Procedure
                         Class Level Information

                     Class    Levels   Values

                     SEX         2     F M

            Number of observations in data set = 59
```

MULTIVARIATE ANALYSIS OF VARIANCE   2

General Linear Models Procedure

Dependent Variable: LENGTH

Source	DF	Sum of Squares	Mean Square	F Value	Pr > F
Model	1	47060.93163060	47060.93163060	1.59	0.2119
Error	57	1683039.20396262	29527.00357829		
Corrected Total	58	1730100.13559322			

R-Square	C.V.	Root MSE	LENGTH Mean
0.027201	2.662355	171.83423285	6454.22033898

Source	DF	Type I SS	Mean Square	F Value	Pr > F
SEX	1	47060.93163052	47060.93163052	1.59	0.2119

Source	DF	Type III SS	Mean Square	F Value	Pr > F
SEX	1	47060.93163052	47060.93163052	1.59	0.2119

MULTIVARIATE ANALYSIS OF VARIANCE   3

General Linear Models Procedure

Dependent Variable: BASILAR

Source	DF	Sum of Squares	Mean Square	F Value	Pr > F
Model	1	23985.10578408	23985.10578408	1.02	0.3174
Error	57	1343555.19930067	23571.14384738		
Corrected Total	58	1367540.30508475			

R-Square	C.V.	Root MSE	BASILAR Mean
0.017539	3.122939	153.52896745	4916.16949153

Source	DF	Type I SS	Mean Square	F Value	Pr > F
SEX	1	23985.10578405	23985.10578405	1.02	0.3174

Source	DF	Type III SS	Mean Square	F Value	Pr > F
SEX	1	23985.10578405	23985.10578405	1.02	0.3174

MULTIVARIATE ANALYSIS OF VARIANCE   4

General Linear Models Procedure

Dependent Variable: ZYGOMAT

Source	DF	Sum of Squares	Mean Square	F Value	Pr > F
Model	1	66.95272805	66.95272805	0.01	0.9045
Error	57	262647.62354313	4607.85304462		
Corrected Total	58	262714.57627119			

R-Square	C.V.	Root MSE	ZYGOMAT Mean
0.000255	2.082299	67.88116856	3259.91525424

Source	DF	Type I SS	Mean Square	F Value	Pr > F
SEX	1	66.95272806	66.95272806	0.01	0.9045

Source	DF	Type III SS	Mean Square	F Value	Pr > F
SEX	1	66.95272806	66.95272806	0.01	0.9045

MULTIVARIATE ANALYSIS OF VARIANCE   5

General Linear Models Procedure

Dependent Variable: POSTORB

Source	DF	Sum of Squares	Mean Square	F Value	Pr > F
Model	1	192.91266644	192.91266644	0.06	0.8132
Error	57	195162.71445221	3423.90727109		
Corrected Total	58	195355.62711864			

R-Square	C.V.	Root MSE	POSTORB Mean
0.000987	5.359188	58.51416300	1091.84745763

Source	DF	Type I SS	Mean Square	F Value	Pr > F
SEX	1	192.91266643	192.91266643	0.06	0.8132

Source	DF	Type III SS	Mean Square	F Value	Pr > F
SEX	1	192.91266643	192.91266643	0.06	0.8132

Ⓐ   E = Error SS&CP Matrix

	LENGTH	BASILAR	ZYGOMAT	POSTORB
LENGTH	1683039.204	1430839.7517	386107.03613	74382.903263
BASILAR	1430839.7517	1343555.1993	324249.61888	38106.472028
ZYGOMAT	386107.03613	324249.61888	262647.62354	33070.588578
POSTORB	74382.903263	38106.472028	33070.588578	195162.71445

MULTIVARIATE ANALYSIS OF VARIANCE   6

Ⓑ   General Linear Models Procedure
Multivariate Analysis of Variance

Partial Correlation Coefficients from the Error SS&CP Matrix / Prob > |r|

DF = 56	LENGTH	BASILAR	ZYGOMAT	POSTORB
LENGTH	1.000000 0.0	0.951516 0.0001	0.580729 0.0001	0.129786 0.3315
BASILAR	0.951516 0.0001	1.000000 0.0	0.545840 0.0001	0.074417 0.5788
ZYGOMAT	0.580729 0.0001	0.545840 0.0001	1.000000 0.0	0.146069 0.2739
POSTORB	0.129786 0.3315	0.074417 0.5788	0.146069 0.2739	1.000000 0.0

MULTIVARIATE ANALYSIS OF VARIANCE   7

General Linear Models Procedure
Multivariate Analysis of Variance

Ⓒ   H = Type III SS&CP Matrix for SEX

	LENGTH	BASILAR	ZYGOMAT	POSTORB
LENGTH	47060.931631	33597.044862	1775.0655644	3013.0797874
BASILAR	33597.044862	23985.105784	1267.2285765	2151.0533958
ZYGOMAT	1775.0655644	1267.2285765	66.952728063	113.64871005
POSTORB	3013.0797874	2151.0533958	113.64871005	192.91266643

(continued on next page)

(continued from previous page)

D Characteristic Roots and Vectors of: E Inverse * H, where
H = Type III SS&CP Matrix for SEX   E = Error SS&CP Matrix

Characteristic Root	Percent	Characteristic Vector V'EV=1			
		LENGTH	BASILAR	ZYGOMAT	POSTORB
0.0452508453	100.00	-0.00181900	0.00111840	0.00115382	-0.00005517
0.0000000000	0.00	0.00000988	-0.00013768	0.00206573	0.00016394
0.0000000000	0.00	-0.00072073	0.00082270	-0.00035855	0.00229481
0.0000000000	0.00	-0.00173862	0.00247593	-0.00025123	-0.00030423

E Manova Test Criteria and Exact F Statistics for the Hypothesis of no Overall SEX Effect
H = Type III SS&CP Matrix for SEX   E = Error SS&CP Matrix

S=1   M=1   N=26

Statistic	Value	F	Num DF	Den DF	Pr > F
Wilks' Lambda	0.95670815	0.6109	4	54	0.6566
Pillai's Trace	0.04329185	0.6109	4	54	0.6566
Hotelling-Lawley Trace	0.04525085	0.6109	4	54	0.6566
Roy's Greatest Root	0.04525085	0.6109	4	54	0.6566

The output above first gives the univariate analyses for each of the dependent variables. These analyses can be supressed using the NOUNI option in the MODEL statement. These analyses show SEX is not significant for any single variable.

The circled letters on the printout correspond to the descriptions below:

A. This portion of output is the result of the PRINTE option in the MANOVA statement. This portion shows elements of the error matrix, also called the Error Sums of Squares and Crossproducts matrix. The diagonal elements of this matrix are the error sums of squares from the corresponding univariate analyses.

B. This portion is also produced as a result of the PRINTE option, and shows the partial correlation matrix associated with the E matrix. In this example, it appears that LENGTH and BASILAR are highly correlated ($r=0.95$). Also, it appears that POSTORB is not correlated with LENGTH, BASILAR, and ZYGOMAT ($r=0.13$, 0.07, and 0.15, respectively).

C. The PRINTH option produces the SSCP matrix for SEX (the H=specification in the MANOVA statement). Since the Type III SS are the highest level SS produced by GLM by default, and since the HTYPE= option is not used, the SSCP matrix for SEX gives the type III **H** matrix. The diagonal elements of this matrix are the model sums of squares from the corresponding univariate analyses.

D. The characteristic roots and vectors of $E^{-1}H$ are shown. Note that the Type III **H** matrix is used.

E. The Manova Test Criteria are printed as a result of the MANOVA statement. This section shows four test statistics and their associated probabilities. In this example, all four tests give the same result, although this is not always the case. Notice how the probability levels for the multivariate tests differ from the univariate levels. This section of output identifies the **H** and **E** matrices used in the statistical tests.

Example 7: Repeated Measures Analysis of Variance

This example uses data from Cole and Grizzle (1966) to illustrate a commonly occurring repeated measures *ANOVA* design. Sixteen dogs were randomly assigned to four groups. (One animal is removed from the analysis due to a missing value for one dependent variable.) Dogs in each group received either morphine or trimethaphan (variable DRUG) and had either depleted or intact histamine levels (variable DEPL) before receiving the drugs. The dependent variable is the blood concentration of histamine at 0, 1, 3, and 5 minutes after injection of the drug. Logarithms were applied to these concentrations to minimize correlation between the mean and the variance of the data.

These SAS statements perform both univariate and multivariate repeated measures analyses and produce **Output 20.16**:

```
data dogs;
   input drug $ depl $ hist0 hist1 hist3 hist5;
   lhist0=log(hist0); lhist1=log(hist1);
   lhist3=log(hist3); lhist5=log(hist5);
   cards;
MORPHINE N   .04   .20   .10   .08
MORPHINE N   .02   .06   .02   .02
MORPHINE N   .07  1.40   .48   .24
MORPHINE N   .17   .57   .35   .24
MORPHINE Y   .10   .09   .13   .14
MORPHINE Y   .12   .11   .10   .
MORPHINE Y   .07   .07   .06   .07
MORPHINE Y   .05   .07   .06   .07
TRIMETH  N   .03   .62   .31   .22
TRIMETH  N   .03  1.05   .73   .60
TRIMETH  N   .07   .83  1.07   .80
TRIMETH  N   .09  3.13  2.06  1.23
TRIMETH  Y   .10   .09   .09   .08
TRIMETH  Y   .08   .09   .09   .10
TRIMETH  Y   .13   .10   .12   .12
TRIMETH  Y   .06   .05   .05   .05
;
proc glm;
   class drug depl;
   model lhist0--lhist5=drug depl drug*depl / nouni;
   repeated time 4 (0 1 3 5) polynomial / short summary;
run;
```

The NOUNI option in the MODEL statement suppresses the individual *ANOVAs* for the original dependent variables. These analyses are usually of no interest in a repeated measures analysis. The POLYNOMIAL option in the REPEATED statement indicates that the transformation used to implement the repeated measures analysis is an orthogonal polynomial transformation, and the SUMMARY option requests that the univariate analyses for the orthogonal polynomial contrast variables be printed. The parenthetical numbers (0 1 3 5) determine the spacing of the orthogonal polynomials used in the analysis.

Output 20.16   Repeated Measures Analysis of Variance: PROC GLM

```
                    General Linear Models Procedure                          1
                       Class Level Information

             Class     Levels    Values

             DRUG         2      MORPHINE TRIMETH

             DEPL         2      N Y


             Number of observations in data set = 16

NOTE: Observations with missing values will not be included in this analysis.  Thus, only 15 observations can
      be used in this analysis.
```

```
                    General Linear Models Procedure                          2
                    Repeated Measures Analysis of Variance
                     Repeated Measures Level Information
(A)  Dependent Variable    LHIST0    LHIST1    LHIST3    LHIST5

         Level of TIME        0         1         3         5


(B)  Manova Test Criteria and Exact F Statistics for the Hypothesis of no TIME Effect
         H = Type III SS&CP Matrix for TIME    E = Error SS&CP Matrix

                       S=1    M=0.5    N=3.5

     Statistic               Value          F       Num DF    Den DF    Pr > F

     Wilks' Lambda           0.11097706   24.0326       3         9     0.0001
     Pillai's Trace          0.88902294   24.0326       3         9     0.0001
     Hotelling-Lawley Trace  8.01087137   24.0326       3         9     0.0001
     Roy's Greatest Root     8.01087137   24.0326       3         9     0.0001


     Manova Test Criteria and Exact F Statistics for the Hypothesis of no TIME*DRUG Effect
         H = Type III SS&CP Matrix for TIME*DRUG    E = Error SS&CP Matrix

                       S=1    M=0.5    N=3.5

     Statistic               Value          F       Num DF    Den DF    Pr > F

     Wilks' Lambda           0.34155984    5.7832       3         9     0.0175
     Pillai's Trace          0.65844016    5.7832       3         9     0.0175
     Hotelling-Lawley Trace  1.92774470    5.7832       3         9     0.0175
     Roy's Greatest Root     1.92774470    5.7832       3         9     0.0175


     Manova Test Criteria and Exact F Statistics for the Hypothesis of no TIME*DEPL Effect
         H = Type III SS&CP Matrix for TIME*DEPL    E = Error SS&CP Matrix

                       S=1    M=0.5    N=3.5

     Statistic               Value          F       Num DF    Den DF    Pr > F

     Wilks' Lambda           0.12339988   21.3112       3         9     0.0002
     Pillai's Trace          0.87660012   21.3112       3         9     0.0002
     Hotelling-Lawley Trace  7.10373567   21.3112       3         9     0.0002
     Roy's Greatest Root     7.10373567   21.3112       3         9     0.0002
```

B   General Linear Models Procedure   3
                      Repeated Measures Analysis of Variance

      Manova Test Criteria and Exact F Statistics for the Hypothesis of no TIME*DRUG*DEPL Effect
            H = Type III SS&CP Matrix for TIME*DRUG*DEPL   E = Error SS&CP Matrix

                              S=1   M=0.5   N=3.5

      Statistic   Value   F   Num DF   Den DF   Pr > F

         Wilks' Lambda   0.19383010   12.4775   3   9   0.0015
         Pillai's Trace   0.80616990   12.4775   3   9   0.0015
         Hotelling-Lawley Trace 4.15915732   12.4775   3   9   0.0015
         Roy's Greatest Root   4.15915732   12.4775   3   9   0.0015

C   General Linear Models Procedure   4
                      Repeated Measures Analysis of Variance
                    Tests of Hypotheses for Between Subjects Effects

      Source   DF   Type III SS   Mean Square   F Value   Pr > F

      DRUG   1   5.99336243   5.99336243   2.71   0.1281
      DEPL   1   15.44840703   15.44840703   6.98   0.0229
      DRUG*DEPL   1   4.69087508   4.69087508   2.12   0.1734

      Error   11   24.34683348   2.21334850

D   General Linear Models Procedure   5
                      Repeated Measures Analysis of Variance
                 Univariate Tests of Hypotheses for Within Subject Effects

                                                                          Adj Pr > F
      Source   DF   Type III SS   Mean Square   F Value   Pr > F   G - G   H - F

      TIME   3   12.05898677   4.01966226   53.44   0.0001   0.0001   0.0001
      TIME*DRUG   3   1.84429514   0.61476505   8.17   0.0003   0.0039   0.0008
      TIME*DEPL   3   12.08978557   4.02992852   53.57   0.0001   0.0001   0.0001
      TIME*DRUG*DEPL   3   2.93077939   0.97692646   12.99   0.0001   0.0005   0.0001

      Error(TIME)   33   2.48238887   0.07522391

                           Greenhouse-Geisser Epsilon = 0.5694
                             Huynh-Feldt Epsilon = 0.8475

E   General Linear Models Procedure   6
                      Repeated Measures Analysis of Variance
                     Analysis of Variance of Contrast Variables

          TIME.N represents the nth degree polynomial contrast for TIME

      Contrast Variable: TIME.1

      Source   DF   Type III SS   Mean Square   F Value   Pr > F

      MEAN   1   2.00963483   2.00963483   34.99   0.0001
      DRUG   1   1.18069076   1.18069076   20.56   0.0009
      DEPL   1   1.36172504   1.36172504   23.71   0.0005
      DRUG*DEPL   1   2.04346848   2.04346848   35.58   0.0001

      Error   11   0.63171161   0.05742833

      Contrast Variable: TIME.2

      Source   DF   Type III SS   Mean Square   F Value   Pr > F

      MEAN   1   5.40988418   5.40988418   57.15   0.0001
      DRUG   1   0.59173192   0.59173192   6.25   0.0295
      DEPL   1   5.94945506   5.94945506   62.86   0.0001
      DRUG*DEPL   1   0.67031587   0.67031587   7.08   0.0221

      Error   11   1.04118707   0.09465337

```
Contrast Variable: TIME.3  Ⓔ

Source        DF          Type III SS         Mean Square        F Value        Pr > F

MEAN          1           4.63946776          4.63946776         63.04          0.0001
DRUG          1           0.07187246          0.07187246          0.98          0.3443
DEPL          1           4.77860547          4.77860547         64.94          0.0001
DRUG*DEPL     1           0.21699504          0.21699504          2.95          0.1139

Error         11          0.80949018          0.07359002
```

The circled letters on the output correspond to the descriptions below:

A. This portion of output gives information on the repeated measures effect. In this example, the within-subject (within-DOG) effect is TIME, which has the levels 0, 1, 3, and 5.

B. This section of output gives multivariate analyses for within-subject effects and related interactions. For the example, the TIME effect is significant. In addition, the TIME*DRUG*DEPL interaction is significant. This means the effect of TIME on the blood concentration of histamine is different for the four DRUG*DEPL combinations studied.

C. This section gives tests of hypotheses for between-subject (between-DOG) effects. This section tests the hypotheses that the different DRUGs, DEPLs and their interaction have no effects on the dependent variables, while ignoring the within-DOG effects. From this analysis, there is a significant between-DOG effect for DEPL. The interaction and the main effect for DRUG are not significant.

D. This section gives univariate analyses for within-subject (within-DOG) effects and related interactions. For the example, the results are the same as for the multivariate analyses. This is not always the case. In addition, before the univariate analyses are used to make conclusions about the data, the result of the sphericity test should be examined. This test is given by the PRINTE option in the REPEATED statement and is not shown here. If the sphericity test is rejected, use the adjusted G-G or H-F probabilities. See **Repeated Measures Analysis of Variance** earlier in this chapter for more information.

E. This section of output is produced by the SUMMARY option in the REPEATED statement. If the POLYNOMIAL option had not been used, a similar section would have been printed using the default CONTRAST transformation.

This section shows the linear, quadratic, and cubic trends for TIME, labeled as TIME.1, TIME.2, and TIME.3, respectively. In each case, the Source labeled MEAN gives a test for the respective trend.

Example 8: Mixed Model Analysis of Variance Using the RANDOM Statement

Milliken and Johnson (1984) present an example of an unbalanced mixed model. Three machines, which were considered as a fixed effect, and six employees, which were considered a random effect, were studied. Each employee operated each machine for either one, two or three different times. The dependent variable was an overall rating, which took into account the number and quality of components produced.

The following statements form the data set and perform a mixed model analysis of variance by requesting the TEST option in the RANDOM statement. Note that the MACHINE*PERSON interaction is declared as a random effect; in general, when an interaction involves a random effect, it too should be declared as random. The results of the analysis are shown in **Output 20.17**.

```
data machine;
   input machine person rating @@;
   cards;
1 1 52.0    1 2 51.8    1 2 52.8    1 3 60.0    1 4 51.1    1 4 52.3
1 5 50.9    1 5 51.8    1 5 51.4    1 6 46.4    1 6 44.8    1 6 49.2
2 1 64.0    2 2 59.7    2 2 60.0    2 2 59.0    2 3 68.6    2 3 65.8
2 4 63.2    2 4 62.8    2 4 62.2    2 5 64.8    2 5 65.0    2 6 43.7
2 6 44.2    2 6 43.0    3 1 67.5    3 1 67.2    3 1 66.9    3 2 61.5
3 2 61.7    3 2 62.3    3 3 70.8    3 3 70.6    3 3 71.0    3 4 64.1
3 4 66.2    3 4 64.0    3 5 72.1    3 5 72.0    3 5 71.1    3 6 62.0
3 6 61.4    3 6 60.5
;
proc glm;
   class machine person;
   model rating = machine person machine*person;
   random person machine*person / test;
run;
```

The TEST option in the RANDOM statement requests that GLM determine the appropriate F tests based on PERSON and MACHINE*PERSON being treated as random effects. As you can see in the output, this requires that a linear combination of mean squares be constructed to test both the MACHINE and PERSON hypotheses; thus, F tests using Satterthwaite approximations are used.

Output 20.17   Mixed Model Analysis of Variance: PROC GLM

```
                        General Linear Models Procedure                        1
                          Class Level Information

                  Class    Levels    Values

                  MACHINE     3      1 2 3

                  PERSON      6      1 2 3 4 5 6


              Number of observations in data set = 44
```

```
                        General Linear Models Procedure                        2

Dependent Variable: RATING

Source              DF        Sum of Squares        Mean Square      F Value     Pr > F

Model               17        3061.74333333         180.10254902      206.41     0.0001

Error               26          22.68666667           0.87256410

Corrected Total     43        3084.43000000

          R-Square              C.V.              Root MSE            RATING Mean

          0.992645            1.560754            0.93411140          59.85000000
```

(continued on next page)

(continued from previous page)

Source	DF	Type I SS	Mean Square	F Value	Pr > F
MACHINE	2	1648.66472222	824.33236111	944.72	0.0001
PERSON	5	1008.76358308	201.75271662	231.22	0.0001
MACHINE*PERSON	10	404.31502803	40.43150280	46.34	0.0001

Source	DF	Type III SS	Mean Square	F Value	Pr > F
MACHINE	2	1238.19762557	619.09881279	709.52	0.0001
PERSON	5	1011.05383401	202.21076680	231.74	0.0001
MACHINE*PERSON	10	404.31502803	40.43150280	46.34	0.0001

General Linear Models Procedure   3

Source	Type III Expected Mean Square
MACHINE	Var(Error) + 2.137 Var(MACHINE*PERSON) + Q(MACHINE)
PERSON	Var(Error) + 2.2408 Var(MACHINE*PERSON) + 6.7224 Var(PERSON)
MACHINE*PERSON	Var(Error) + 2.3162 Var(MACHINE*PERSON)

General Linear Models Procedure   4
Tests of Hypotheses for Mixed Model Analysis of Variance

Dependent Variable: RATING

Source: MACHINE
Error: 0.9226*MS(MACHINE*PERSON) + 0.0774*MS(Error)

DF	Type III MS	Denominator DF	Denominator MS	F Value	Pr > F
2	619.09881279	10.04	37.370383818	16.567	0.0007

Source: PERSON
Error: 0.9674*MS(MACHINE*PERSON) + 0.0326*MS(Error)

DF	Type III MS	Denominator DF	Denominator MS	F Value	Pr > F
5	202.2107668	10.01	39.143708026	5.166	0.0133

Source: MACHINE*PERSON
Error: MS(Error)

DF	Type III MS	Denominator DF	Denominator MS	F Value	Pr > F
10	40.431502803	26	0.8725641026	46.336	0.0001

REFERENCES

Afifi, A.A. and Azen, S.P. (1972), *Statistical Analysis: A Computer-Oriented Approach*, New York: Academic Press, Inc.

Anderson, T.W. (1958), *An Introduction to Multivariate Statistical Analysis*, New York: John Wiley & Sons, Inc.

Begun, J.M. and Gabriel, K.R. (1981), "Closure of the Newman-Keuls Multiple Comparisons Procedure," *Journal of the American Statistical Association*, 76, 374.

Belsley, D.A., Kuh, E., and Welsch, R.E. (1980), *Regression Diagnostics*, New York: John Wiley & Sons, Inc.

Box, G.E.P. (1954), "Some Theorems on Quadratic Forms Applied in the Study of Analysis of Variance Problems. II, Effects of Inequality of Variance and of Correlation Between Errors in the Two-Way Classification," *Annals of Mathematical Statistics*, 25, 484–498.

Carmer, S.G. and Swanson, M.R. (1973), "Evaluation of Ten Pairwise Multiple Comparison Procedures by Monte-Carlo Methods," *Journal of the American Statistical Association*, 68, 66–74.

Cochran, W.G. and Cox, G.M. (1957), *Experimental Designs*, 2d edition. New York: John Wiley & Sons, Inc.

Cole, J.W.L. and Grizzle, J.E. (1966), "Applications of Multivariate Analysis of Variance to Repeated Measures Experiments," *Biometrics*, 22, 810–828.

Draper, N.R. and Smith, H. (1966), *Applied Regression Analysis*, New York: John Wiley & Sons, Inc.

Duncan, D.B. (1975), "*t*-Tests and Intervals for Comparisons Suggested by the Data," *Biometrics*, 31, 339–359.

Dunnett, C.W. (1955), "A Multiple Comparisons Procedure for Comparing Several Treatments with a Control," *Journal of the American Statistical Association*, 50, 1096–1121.

Dunnett, C.W. (1980), "Pairwise Multiple Comparisons in the Homogeneous Variance, Unequal Sample Size Case," *Journal of the American Statistical Association*, 75, 789–795.

Einot, I. and Gabriel, K.R. (1975), "A Study of the Powers of Several Methods of Multiple Comparisons," *Journal of the American Statistical Association*, 70, 351.

Freund, R.J., Littell, R.C., and Spector, P.C. (1986), *SAS System for Linear Models, 1986 Edition*, Cary, NC: SAS Institute Inc.

Gabriel, K.R. (1978), "A Simple Method of Multiple Comparisons of Means," *Journal of the American Statistical Association*, 73, 364.

Games, P.A. (1977), "An Improved *t* Table for Simultaneous Control on *g* Contrasts," *Journal of the American Statistical Association*, 72, 531–534.

Goodnight, J.H. (1976), "The New General Linear Models Procedure," *Proceedings of the First International SAS Users' Conference*, Cary, NC: SAS Institute Inc.

Goodnight, J.H. (1978), *Tests of the Hypotheses in Fixed-Effects Linear Models*, SAS Technical Report R-101, Cary, NC: SAS Institute Inc.

Goodnight, J.H. (1979), "A Tutorial on the Sweep Operator," *American Statistician*, 33, 149–158. (Also available as *The Sweep Operator: Its Importance in Statistical Computing*, SAS Technical Report R-106.)

Goodnight, J.H. and Harvey, W.R. (1978), *Least-Squares Means in the Fixed-Effects General Linear Models*, SAS Technical Report R-103, Cary, NC: SAS Institute Inc.

Goodnight, J.H. and Speed, F.M. (1978), *Computing Expected Mean Squares*, SAS Technical Report R-102, Cary, NC: SAS Institute Inc.

Graybill, F.A. (1961), *An Introduction to Linear Statistical Models, Volume I*, New York: McGraw-Hill Book Co.

Greenhouse, S.W. and Geisser, S. (1959), "On Methods in the Analysis of Profile Data," *Psychometrika*, 32, 95–112.

Harvey, W.R. (1975), *Least-squares Analysis of Data with Unequal Subclass Numbers*, USDA Report ARS H-4.

Heck, D.L. (1960), "Charts of Some Upper Percentage Points of the Distribution of the Largest Characteristic Root," *Annals of Mathematical Statistics*, 31, 625–642.

Hochberg, Y. (1974), "Some Conservative Generalizations of the T-Method in Simultaneous Inference," *Journal of Multivariate Analysis*, 4, 224–234.

Hocking, R.R. (1976), "The Analysis and Selection of Variables in a Linear Regression," *Biometrics*, 32, 1–50.

Huynh, H. and Feldt, L. S. (1970), "Conditions under Which Mean Square Ratios in Repeated Measurements Designs Have Exact F-Distributions," *Journal of the American Statistical Association*, 65, 1582–1589.

Huynh, H. and Feldt, L.S. (1976), "Estimation of the Box Correction for Degrees of Freedom from Sample Data in the Randomized Block and Split Plot Designs," *Journal of Educational Statistics*, 1, 69-82.

Kennedy, W.J., Jr. and Gentle, J.E. (1980), *Statistical Computing*, New York: Marcel Dekker, Inc.

Kramer, C.Y. (1956), "Extension of Multiple Range Tests to Group Means with Unequal Numbers of Replications," *Biometrics*, 12, 307–310.

Krishnaiah, P.R. and Armitage, J.V. (1966), "Tables for Multivariate *t* Distribution," *Sankhya, Series B*, 31–56.

Kutner, M.H. (1974), "Hypothesis Testing in Linear Models (Eisenhart Model)," *American Statistician*, 28, 98–100.

LaTour, S.A. and Miniard, P.W. (1983), "The Misuse of Repeated Measures Analysis in Marketing Research," *Journal of Marketing Research*, XX, 45–57.

Marcus, R., Peritz, E., and Gabriel, K.R. (1976), "On Closed Testing Procedures with Special Reference to Ordered Analysis of Variance," *Biometrika*, 63, 655–660.

Miller, R.G., Jr. (1981), *Simultaneous Statistical Inference*, New York: Springer-Verlag.

Milliken, G.A. and Johnson, D.E. (1984), *Analysis of Messy Data, Volume I: Designed Experiments*, Belmont, CA: Lifetime Learning Publications.

Morrison, D.F. (1976), *Multivariate Statistical Methods*, 2d Edition, New York: McGraw-Hill Book Co.

Petrinovich, L.F. and Hardyck, C.D. (1969), "Error Rates for Multiple Comparison Methods: Some Evidence Concerning the Frequency of Erroneous Conclusions," *Psychological Bulletin*, 71, 43–54.

Pillai, K.C.S. (1960), *Statistical Tables for Tests of Multivariate Hypotheses*, Manila: The Statistical Center, University of the Philippines.

Pringle, R.M. and Raynor, A.A. (1971), *Generalized Inverse Matrices with Applications to Statistics*, New York: Hafner Publishing Co.

Ramsey, P.H. (1978), "Power Differences Between Pairwise Multiple Comparisons," *Journal of the American Statistical Association*, 73, 363.

Rao, C.R. (1965), *Linear Statistical Inference and Its Applications*, New York: John Wiley & Sons, Inc.

Ryan, T.A. (1959), "Multiple Comparisons in Psychological Research," *Psychological Bulletin*, 56, 26–47.

Ryan, T.A. (1960), "Significance Tests for Multiple Comparison of Proportions, Variances, and Other Statistics," *Psychological Bulletin*, 57, 318–328.

Satterthwaite, F. E. (1946), "An Approximate Distribution of Estimates of Variance Components," *Biometrics Bulletin*, 2, 110–114.

Schatzoff, M. (1966), "Exact Distributions of Wilks' Likelihood Ratio Criterion," *Biometrika*, 53, 347–358.

Scheffe, H. (1953), "A Method for Judging All Contrasts in the Analysis of Variance," *Biometrika*, 40, 87–104.

Scheffe, H. (1959), *The Analysis of Variance*, New York: John Wiley & Sons, Inc.

Searle, S.R. (1971), *Linear Models*, New York: John Wiley & Sons, Inc.

Searle, S.R., Speed, F.M., and Milliken, G.A. (1980), "Populations Marginal Means in the Linear Model: An Alternative to Least Squares Means," *The American Statistician*, 34, 216–221.

Sidak, Z. (1967), "Rectangular Confidence Regions for the Means of Multivariate Normal Distributions," *Journal of the American Statistical Association*, 62, 626–633.

Snedecor, G.W. and Cochran, W.G. (1967), *Statistical Methods*, Ames, IA: Iowa State University Press.

Steel, R.G.D. and Torrie, J.H. (1960), *Principles and Procedures of Statistics*, New York: McGraw-Hill Book Co.

Tukey, J.W. (1952), "Allowances for Various Types of Error Rates," Unpublished IMS address, Chicago, IL.

Tukey, J.W. (1953), "The Problem of Multiple Comparisons," Unpublished manuscript.

Waller, R.A. and Duncan, D.B. (1969), "A Bayes Rule for the Symmetric Multiple Comparison Problem," *Journal of the American Statistical Association*, 64, 1484–1499, and (1972) "Corrigenda," 67, 253–255.

Waller, R.A. and Kemp, K.E. (1976), "Computations of Bayesian t-Values for Multiple Comparisons," *Journal of Statistical Computation and Simulation*, 75, 169–172.

Welsch, R.E. (1977), "Stepwise Multiple Comparison Procedures," *Journal of the American Statistical Association*, 72, 359.

Winer, B. J. (1971), *Statistical Principles in Experimental Design*, 2d Edition, New York: McGraw-Hill Book Co.

Chapter 21

The LIFEREG
Procedure

ABSTRACT

The LIFEREG procedure fits parametric models to failure-time data that may be right-, left-, or interval-censored. The models for the response variable consist of a linear effect composed of the covariables together with a random disturbance term. The distribution of the random disturbance can be taken from a class of distributions that includes the extreme value, normal, logistic, and, by using a log transformation, the exponential, Weibull, log-normal, log-logistic, and gamma distributions.

More explicitly the model assumed for the response **y** is

$$\mathbf{y} = \mathbf{X}\boldsymbol{\beta} + \sigma\boldsymbol{\varepsilon}$$

where **y** is the vector of response values, often the log of the failure times, **X** is a matrix of covariates or independent variables, **β** is a vector of unknown regression parameters, σ is an unknown scale parameter, and **ε** is a vector of errors assumed to come from a known distribution such as the standard normal distribution. In general, the distribution may depend on additional shape parameters. These models are equivalent to accelerated failure-time models when the log of the response is the quantity being modeled. The effect of the covariates in an accelerated failure time model then is to change the scale, and not the location, of a baseline distribution of failure times.

The parameters are estimated by maximum likelihood using a Newton-Raphson algorithm. The estimates of the standard errors of the parameter estimates are computed from the inverse of the observed information matrix.

INTRODUCTION

The accelerated failure time model assumes that the effect of independent variables on an event-time distribution is multiplicative on the event time. Usually, the scale function is $\exp(\mathbf{x}'\boldsymbol{\beta})$, where **x** is the vector of covariate values and **β** is a vector of unknown parameters. Thus, if T_0 is an event time sampled from the baseline distribution corresponding to values of zero for the covariates, then the accelerated failure time model specifies that if the vector of covariates had been **x**, the event time would have been $T = \exp(\mathbf{x}'\boldsymbol{\beta})T_0$. If $y = \log(T)$ and $y_0 = \log(T_0)$, then

$$y = \mathbf{x}'\boldsymbol{\beta} + y_0 \quad .$$

This is a linear model with y_0 playing the role of the error term.

In terms of survival or exceedance probabilities this model is

$$\text{Prob}\,(T > t \,|\, \mathbf{x}) = \text{Prob}\,(T_0 > \exp(-\mathbf{x}'\boldsymbol{\beta})t)$$

where the probability on the left-hand side of the equal sign is evaluated given the value **x** for the covariates, and the right-hand side is computed using the baseline probability distribution but at a scaled value of the argument. The right-hand side of the equation represents the value of the baseline Survival Distribution Function evaluated at $\exp(-\mathbf{x}'\boldsymbol{\beta})t$.

Usually, an intercept parameter and a scale parameter are allowed in the model above. In terms of the original untransformed event times, the effects of the intercept term and the scale term are to scale the event time and power the event time, respectively. That is, if

$$\log(T) = \mu + \sigma\log(T_0) \quad \text{then } T = \exp(\mu)T_0^{\sigma} \quad .$$

Although it is possible to fit these models to the original response variable using the NOLOG option, it is more common to model the log of the response variable. Because of this log transformation, zero values for the observed failure times are not allowed unless the NOLOG option is specified. Similarly, small values for the observed failure times lead to large negative values for the transformed response. The parameter estimates for the normal distribution are sensitive to large negative values, and care must be taken that the fitted model is not unduly influenced by them. Likewise, values that are extremely large even after the log transformation will have a strong influence in fitting the extreme value (Weibull) and normal distributions. You should examine the residuals and check the effects of removing observations with large residuals or extreme values of covariates on the model parameters.

The standard errors of the parameter estimates are computed from large sample normal approximations using the observed information matrix. In small samples, these approximations may be poor. See Lawless (1982) for additional discussion and references. Better confidence intervals can sometimes be constructed by transforming the parameters. For example, it is often the case that large sample theory is more accurate for $\log(\sigma)$ than σ. Therefore it may be more accurate to construct confidence intervals for $\log(\sigma)$ and transform these into confidence intervals for σ. The parameter estimates and their estimated covariance matrix are available in an output SAS data set and can be used to construct additional tests or confidence intervals for the parameters. Alternatively, tests of parameters can be based on log-likelihood ratios. See Cox and Oakes (1984) for a discussion of the merits of some possible test methods including score, Wald, and likelihood ratio tests. It is believed that log-likelihood ratio tests are generally more reliable in small samples than tests based on the information matrix.

The log-likelihood function is computed using the log of the failure time as a response. This log likelihood differs from the log likelihood obtained using the failure time as the response by an additive term of $\Sigma \log(t_i)$, where the sum is over the noncensored failure times. This term does not depend on the unknown parameters and does not affect parameter or standard error estimates. However, many published values of log likelihoods use the failure time as the basic response variable and hence differ by the above additive term from the value computed by the LIFEREG procedure.

The classic Tobit model (Tobin 1958) also fits into this class of models but with data usually censored on the left. The data considered by Tobin in his original paper came from a survey of consumers where the response variable was the ratio of expenditures on durable goods to the total disposable income. The two independent variables were the age of the head of household and the ratio of liquid assets to total disposable income. Because many observations in this data set had a value of zero for the response variable, the model fit by Tobin was

$$\mathbf{y} = \max(\mathbf{x}'\beta + \varepsilon, 0)$$

which is a regression model with left-censoring.

SPECIFICATIONS

The following statements can be used with PROC LIFEREG:

PROC LIFEREG *options*;
*label:***MODEL** *response=variables / options*;
  CLASS *variables*;
  WEIGHT *variable*;
  OUTPUT OUT=*SASdataset options*;
  BY *variables*;

The PROC LIFEREG statement invokes the procedure. The MODEL statement is required and specifies what variables are to be used in the regression part of the model as well as what distribution is to be used for the error or random component of the model. Only main effects can be specified in the MODEL statements. More complicated specifications of categorical effects, such as those allowed in the GLM procedure, are not supported in the LIFEREG procedure. Initial values can be specified in the MODEL statement. If no initial values are specified, the starting estimates are obtained by ordinary least squares. The CLASS statement specifies which independent variables are to be treated as categorical. The WEIGHT statement is used to specify a variable whose values are used to weight the observations. Observations with zero or negative weights are not used to fit the model. The OUTPUT statement is used to request an output data set containing predicted values and residuals. The following sections describe the PROC LIFEREG statement and then discuss the other statements (in alphabetical order).

PROC LIFEREG Statement

PROC LIFEREG *options*;

The options that can appear in the PROC LIFEREG statement are listed below:

DATA=*SASdataset*
>   specifies the input SAS data set. If the DATA= option is omitted, the most recently created SAS data set is used.

COVOUT
>   requests that the OUTEST= SAS data set contain the estimated covariance matrix as well as the parameter estimates.

NOPRINT
>   requests that the procedure not produce any printed results.

ORDER=FREQ
ORDER=DATA
ORDER=INTERNAL
ORDER=FORMATTED
>   specifies the order in which you want the levels of the classification variables (specified in the CLASS statement) to be sorted. This ordering determines which parameters in the model correspond to each level in the data. If you specify ORDER=FREQ, levels are sorted by descending frequency count so that levels with the most observations come first. If you specify ORDER=DATA, levels are sorted in the order in which they first occur in the input data. If you specify ORDER=INTERNAL, then the levels are sorted by the internal value. If you specify ORDER=FORMATTED, levels are ordered by the external formatted value. If you omit the ORDER= option, PROC LIFEREG orders by the formatted internal value.

OUTEST=*SASdataset*
>   requests that a SAS data set be created containing the parameter estimates, the maximized log likelihood and, optionally, the estimated covariance matrix. See **OUTEST= Output Data Set** in the **DETAILS** section for a detailed description of the contents of the OUTEST= data set. This data set is not created if class variables are used.

BY Statement

BY *variables*;

A BY statement can be used with PROC LIFEREG to obtain separate analyses on observations in groups defined by the BY variables. When a BY statement appears, the procedure expects the input data set to be sorted in order of the BY variables.

If your input data set is not sorted in ascending order, use the SORT procedure with a similar BY statement to sort the data, or, if appropriate, use the BY statement options NOTSORTED or DESCENDING. For more information, see the discussion of the BY statement in "SAS Statements Used in the PROC Step" in the *SAS Language Guide, Release 6.03 Edition*.

CLASS Statement

CLASS *variables*;

Any variables that are to be treated as classification variables instead of quantitative numeric variables must be listed in the CLASS statement. If a variable listed in the CLASS statement is also used as an independent variable in a MODEL statement, then indicator variables are generated for the levels assumed by the CLASS variable. Using a CLASS statement precludes the ability to output parameter estimates to a SAS data set.

MODEL Statement

label: MODEL *variable* [* *censor*(*number list*)]=*variables* / *options*;
label: MODEL (*lower,upper*)=*variables* / *options*;
label: MODEL *events* / *trials*=*variables* / *options*;

Multiple MODEL statements can be used with one invocation of the LIFEREG procedure. The optional *label* is used to label the model estimates in the output SAS data set and in the printed output. The response can be specified in one of the ways listed above.

The first MODEL syntax allows for a response that may be right-censored. The first *variable* is the response variable, possibly right-censored. If the response can be right-censored, then a second variable, labeled *censor* above, must appear after the response variable, together with a list of parenthesized values that are separated by commas or blanks to indicate censoring. That is, if the *censor* variable takes on a value given in the list that follows, the response is a right-censored value; otherwise, it is an observed value.

The second MODEL syntax specifies two variables, *lower* and *upper*, that contain values of the endpoints of the censoring interval. If the two values are the same and not missing, it is assumed that there is no censoring and the actual response value was observed. If the lower value is missing, then the upper value is used as a left-censored value. If the upper value is missing, then the lower value is taken as a right-censored value. If both values are present and the lower value is less than the upper value, it is assumed that the values specify a censoring interval. If the lower value is greater than the upper value or both values are missing, then the observation is not used in the analysis although predicted values can still be obtained if none of the covariates is missing.

The third MODEL syntax specifies two variables that contain count data for a binary response. The value of the first variable, *events*, is the number of successes. The value of the second variable, *trials*, is the number of tries. The values of both *events* and (*trials—events*) must be nonnegative, and *trials* must be positive for the response to be valid. The values of the two variables do not need to be integers and are not modified to be integers.

The variables following the equal sign are the covariates in the model. No higher order effects, such as interactions, are allowed in the covariables list; only variable names are allowed to appear in this list. However, a class variable can be used as a main effect, and indicator variables will be generated for the class levels.

Examples of three valid MODEL statements are

```
a:model time*flag(1,3)=temp trtment;
b:model (start,finish)=;
c:model r / n=dose      ;
```

Model statement A indicates that the response is contained in a variable named TIME and that if the variable FLAG takes on the values 1 or 3 the observation is right-censored. The independent variables are TEMP and TRTMENT, either of which could be a class variable. Model statement B indicates that the response is known to be in the interval between the values of the variables START and FINISH and that there are no covariates except for a default intercept term. Model statement C indicates a binary response with the variable R containing the number of responses and the variable N containing the number of trials.

The following options can appear in the MODEL statement:

Model Specification Options

DISTRIBUTION | DIST | D=*distributiontype*
> specifies the distribution type assumed for the failure time. Valid values for *distributiontype* are as follows:

> WEIBULL   specifies the Weibull distribution, which is the default.

> EXPONENTIAL
> > specifies the exponential distribution, which is treated as a Weibull distribution with the scale parameter restricted to the value 1.

> LNORMAL   specifies the log-normal distribution.

> LLOGISTIC   specifies the log-logistic distribution.

> GAMMA   specifies a gamma distribution.

> NORMAL   specifies a normal distribution, which is equivalent to the log-normal distribution with the NOLOG option specified.

> LOGISTIC   specifies a logistic distribution, which is equivalent to the log-logistic distribution with the NOLOG option specified.

NOLOG
> requests that no log transformation of the response variable be performed. The default is to model the log of the indicated response variable.

The following two options concern the intercept term:

INTERCPT=*value*
> requests that the intercept term be initialized at the number specified by *value*.

NOINT
> requests that the intercept term be held fixed. If no initial intercept value is given, the intercept is set at the value zero. Because of the usual log transformation of the response, the intercept parameter is usually a scale parameter for the untransformed response.

The following option sets initial values for the regression parameters:

INITIAL=*values*

sets initial values for the regression parameters. This option can be helpful in the case of convergence difficulty. The values listed are used to initialize the regression coefficients for the covariates specified in the MODEL statement. The intercept parameter is initialized with the INTERCPT= option and is not included here. The values are assigned to the variables in the MODEL statement in the same order as they are listed in the MODEL statement. Note that a class variable requires $k-1$ values when the class variable takes on k different levels. The order of the class levels is determined by the ORDER= option. If there is no intercept term, the first class variable requires k initial values. If a BY statement is used, all class variables must take on the same number of levels in each BY group or no meaningful initial values can be specified.

The following four options concern parameter specification:

SCALE=*value*

requests that the scale parameter be initialized at this value. Note that the exponential model is the same as a Weibull model with the scale parameter fixed at the value 1.

NOSCALE

requests that the scale parameter be held fixed. If no value is specified with the SCALE= option, the scale parameter is fixed at the value 1. Note that if the log transformation has been applied to the response, the effect of the scale parameter is a power transformation of the original response.

SHAPE1=*value*

requests that the first shape parameter be initialized to this value. If the specified distribution does not depend on this parameter, then this option has no effect. See **Distributions Allowed** in the **DETAILS** section of this chapter for descriptions of the parameterizations of the distributions.

NOSHAPE1

requests that the first shape parameter be held fixed. If no value is specified with the SHAPE1= option, this parameter is fixed at a value that depends on the DISTRIBUTION type.

Model Fitting Options

CONVERGE=*value*

gives the convergence criterion. The iterations are considered to have converged when the maximum change in the parameter estimates between Newton-Raphson steps is less than the value specified. The change is a relative change if the parameter is greater than 0.01 in absolute value; otherwise, it is an absolute change. The default is 0.001.

MAXIT=*number*

gives the maximum allowed iterations that will be attempted during the model estimation. The default is 50.

SINGULAR=*value*

gives the tolerance for testing singularity of the information matrix and the crossproducts matrix for the initial least-squares estimates. Roughly, the test requires that a pivot be at least this number times the original diagonal value. The default is 1E−12.

Printing Options

CORRB
> requests that the estimated correlation matrix of the parameter estimates be printed.

COVB
> requests that the inverse observed information matrix be printed as an estimate of the covariance matrix of the parameters.

ITPRINT
> requests that the iteration history and the final evaluation of the gradient and the second derivative matrix (Hessian) be printed.

OUTPUT Statement

OUTPUT OUT=*SASdataset keyword=name* . . . ;

The OUTPUT statement requests that fitted values and estimated quantiles be written to a SAS data set. Each OUTPUT statement applies to the preceding MODEL statement. See **Example 1** and **Example 2** for an illustration of the OUTPUT statement.

The following options can be specified in the OUTPUT statement:

CENSORED=*name*
> specifies the name of an indicator variable that is created to signal censoring. The variable takes on the value 1 if the observation was censored; otherwise, it is 0.

CDF=*name*
> specifies the name of a variable to contain the estimates of the cumulative distribution function evaluated at the observed response. See **Predicted Values** later in this chapter for more information.

CONTROL=*variable*
> specifies a variable in the input data set to control the estimation of quantiles. See **Example 1** for an illustration. If *variable* has the value of 1, estimates for all the values listed in the QUANTILE= list are computed for that observation in the input data set; otherwise, no estimates are computed. If no CONTROL= variable is specified, all quantiles are estimated for all observations. If the response variable in the MODEL statement is binomial, then this option is not used.

OUT=*SASdataset*
> names the output SAS data set. If you want to create a permanent SAS data set, you must specify a two-level name (see "SAS Files" in the *SAS Language Guide, Release 6.03 Edition* for more information on permanent data sets). If the OUT= option is omitted, the SAS System names the new data set using the DATA*n* naming convention.

PREDICTED=*name*
P=*name*
> specifies the name of the variable to contain the quantile estimates or the estimated probabilities, $1-F(-\mathbf{x}'\mathbf{b})$, if the response variable in the corresponding MODEL statement is binomial.

QUANTILES=*values*
QUANTILE=*values*
Q=*values*
> specifies a list of values separated by blanks for which quantiles are to be calculated. The values must be between 0 and 1, noninclusive. For

each value, a corresponding quantile is estimated. The default is Q=0.5. This option is not used if the response variable in the corresponding MODEL statement is binomial.

The following variable is always added to the OUTPUT data set if the response is not binomial:

> _PROB_ a numeric variable giving the probability value for the quantile estimates. These are the values taken from the QUANTILES= list above and are given as values between 0 and 1 and not as values between 0 and 100.

STD _ERR=*name*
STD=*name*

specifies the name of a variable to contain the estimates of the standard errors of the estimated quantiles or $x'\beta$. If the response used in the MODEL statement is a binomial response, then these are the standard errors of $x'\beta$. Otherwise, they are the standard errors of the quantile estimates. These estimates can be used to compute confidence intervals for the quantiles. However, if the model is fit to the log of the event time, better confidence intervals can usually be computed by transforming the confidence intervals for the log response. See **Example 1** for such a transformation.

XBETA=*name*

specifies the name of a variable to contain the computed value of $x'b$, where x is the covariate vector and b is the vector of parameter estimates.

In addition to the above optional variables, all other variables in the input data set are added to the OUTPUT data set.

WEIGHT Statement

WEIGHT *variable*;

If you want to use weights for each observation in the input data set, place the weights in a variable in the data set and specify the name in a WEIGHT statement. The values of the WEIGHT variable can be nonintegral and are not truncated. Observations with nonpositive or missing values for the weight variable do not contribute to the analysis.

DETAILS

Missing Values

Any observation with missing values for the dependent variable is not used in the model estimation unless it is one and only one of the values in an interval specification. Also, if one of the independent variables or the censoring variable is missing, the observation is not used. For any observation to be used in the estimation of a model, only the variables needed in that model have to be nonmissing. Predicted values are computed for all observations with no missing independent variable values. If the censoring variable is missing, the CENSORED= variable in the OUT= SAS data set is also missing.

Main Effects

Unlike the GLM procedure, only main effect terms are allowed in the model specification. For numeric variables, this is a linear term equal to the value of the variable unless the variable appears in the CLASS statement. For variables listed in the CLASS statement, PROC LIFEREG creates indicator variables (variables taking the values zero or one) for every level of the variable except the last level. The levels are ordered according to the ORDER= option. If there is no intercept term, the first class variable has indicator variables created for all levels including the last level.

Computational Method

An initial ordinary least-squares calculation ignoring the censoring information is performed to compute the starting values for the parameter estimates and also to estimate the rank of the design matrix X. The INITIAL= parameter can be used to override these starting values. Columns of X that are judged linearly dependent on other columns have the corresponding parameters set to zero. The test for linear dependence is controlled by the SINGULAR= option in the MODEL statement. The variables are included in the model in the order listed in the MODEL statement except that the non-class variables are included in the model before any class variables.

The log-likelihood function is maximized by means of a ridge-stabilized Newton-Raphson algorithm.

A composite chi-square test statistic is computed for each class variable, testing whether there is any effect from any of the levels of the variable. This statistic is computed as a quadratic form in the appropriate parameter estimates using the corresponding submatrix of the asymptotic covariance matrix estimate. The asymptotic covariance matrix is computed as the inverse of the observed information matrix. Note that if the NOINT option is specified and class variables are used, the first class variable contains a contribution from an intercept term.

Model Specifications

Suppose there are n observations from the model $y = X\beta + \sigma\varepsilon$, where X is an $n \times k$ matrix of covariate values, y is a vector of responses, and ε is a vector of errors with survival distribution function S, cumulative distribution function F, and probability density function f. That is, $S(t) = PROB\ (\varepsilon_i > t)$, $F(t) = PROB(\varepsilon_i \leq t)$, and $f(t) = dF(t)/dt$, where ε_i is a component of the error vector. Then if all the responses are observed, the log-likelihood, L, can be written as

$$L = \Sigma \log (f(w_i) / \sigma) \quad \text{where } w_i = (y_i - x_i'\beta) / \sigma \ .$$

If some of the responses are left-, right-, or interval-censored, the log-likelihood can be written as

$$L = \Sigma \log (f(w_i) / \sigma) + \Sigma \log (S(w_i)) + \Sigma \log (F(w_i)) + \Sigma \log (F(w_i) - F(v_i))$$

with the first sum over uncensored observations, the second sum over right-censored observations, the third sum over left-censored observations, the last sum over interval-censored observations, and $v_i = (z_i - x_i'\beta)/\sigma$, where z_i is the lower end of a censoring interval.

If the response is specified in the binomial format, *events / trials*, then the log-likelihood function is

$$L = \Sigma r_i \log (P_i) + (n_i - r_i)\log (1 - P_i)$$

where r_i is the number of events and n_i is the number of trials for the ith observation. In this case, $P_i = 1 - F(-x_i'\beta)$. For the symmetric distributions, logistic and normal, this is the same as $F(\mathbf{x}'\boldsymbol{\beta})$. Additional information on censored and limited dependent variable models can be found in Kalbfleisch and Prentice (1980) and Maddala (1983).

The covariance matrix of the final parameter estimates is computed as the inverse of the negative of the second derivative matrix at the final parameter estimates. The negative of the second derivative matrix is denoted $\mathbf{I}$ and called the observed information matrix. If $\mathbf{I}$ is not positive definite, a positive definite submatrix of $\mathbf{I}$ is inverted, and the remaining rows and columns of the inverse are set to zero. If some of the parameters, such as the scale and intercept, are restricted, the corresponding elements of the estimated covariance matrix are set to zero.

For restrictions placed on the intercept, scale, and shape parameters, one-degree-of-freedom Lagrange Multiplier test statistics are computed. These statistics are computed as

$$\chi^2 = g^2/V$$

where g is the derivative of the log likelihood with respect to the restricted parameter at the restricted maximum and

$$V = \mathbf{I}_{11} - \mathbf{I}_{12}\,\mathbf{I}_{22}^{-1}\,\mathbf{I}_{21}$$

where the 1 subscripts refer to the restricted parameter and the 2 subscripts refer to the unrestricted parameters. The information matrix is evaluated at the restricted maximum. These statistics are asymptotically distributed as chi squares with one degree of freedom under the null hypothesis that the restrictions are valid, provided that some regularity conditions are satisfied. See Rao (1973, 418) for a more complete discussion. It is possible for these statistics to be missing if the observed information matrix is not positive definite. Higher degree-of-freedom tests for multiple restrictions are not currently computed.

In the **Example 2**, a Weibull model and an exponential model are both fit to the same data. The exponential distribution is equivalent to a Weibull distribution with the scale parameter constrained to one. A Lagrange multiplier test statistic is computed to test this constraint. Notice that this test statistic is comparable to the Wald test statistic for testing that the scale is one. The Wald statistic is the result of squaring the difference of the estimate of the scale parameter from one and dividing this by the square of its estimated standard error.

Distributions Allowed

The baseline distributions allowed are listed below. For each distribution, the baseline survival distribution function (S) and the probability density function (f) are listed for the additive random disturbance. Also the corresponding survival distribution function (G) and its density function (g) are given for the exponentially transformed random disturbance. The chosen baseline functions define the meaning of the intercept, scale, and shape parameters. Only the gamma distribution has a free shape parameter in the parameterizations given below. Notice that some of the distributions do not have mean zero and that σ is not in general the standard deviation of the baseline distribution. Additionally, it is worth mentioning that for the Weibull distribution, the accelerated failure time model is also a proportional-hazards model, but that the parameterization for the covariates differs by a multiple of the scale parameter from the parameterization commonly used for the proportional hazards model.

Exponential

$$S(w) = \exp(-\exp(w - \mu))$$
$$f(w) = \exp(w - \mu)\exp(-\exp(w - \mu))$$

$$G(t) = \exp(-\alpha t)$$
$$g(t) = \alpha\exp(-\alpha t)$$

where $\exp(-\mu) = \alpha$.

Weibull

$$S(w) = \exp(-\exp((w - \mu)/\sigma))$$
$$f(w) = \exp((w - \mu)/\sigma)\exp(-\exp((w - \mu)/\sigma))/\sigma$$

$$G(t) = \exp(-\alpha t^{\gamma})$$
$$g(t) = \gamma\alpha t^{\gamma - 1}\exp(-\alpha t^{\gamma})$$

where $\sigma = 1/\gamma$ and $\alpha = \exp(-\mu/\sigma)$.

Log-normal

$$S(w) = 1 - \Phi((w - \mu)/\sigma)$$
$$f(w) = \exp(-(w - \mu)^2/2\sigma^2)/(\sqrt{2\pi}\,\sigma)$$

$$G(t) = 1 - \Phi((\log(t) - \mu)/\sigma)$$
$$g(t) = \exp(-(\log(t) - \mu)^2/2\sigma^2)/(\sqrt{2\pi}\,\sigma t)$$

where Φ is the cumulative distribution function for the normal distribution.

Log-logistic

$$S(w) = 1/(1 + \exp((w - \mu)/\sigma))$$
$$f(w) = \exp((w - \mu)/\sigma)/(1 + \exp((w - \mu)/\sigma))^2\sigma$$

$$G(t) = 1/(1 + \alpha t^{\gamma})$$
$$g(t) = \alpha\gamma t^{\gamma - 1}/(1 + \alpha t^{\gamma})^2$$

where $\gamma = 1/\sigma$ and $\alpha = \exp(-\mu/\sigma)$.

Gamma

(with $\mu = 0$, $\sigma = 1$)

$$S(w) = \Gamma(1/\delta^2, \exp(\delta w)/\delta^2)/\Gamma(1/\delta^2) \quad \text{if } \delta > 0$$
$$S(w) = 1 - \Gamma(1/\delta^2, \exp(\delta w)/\delta^2)/\Gamma(1/\delta^2) \quad \text{if } \delta < 0$$
$$f(w) = |\delta|(\exp(\delta w)/\delta^2)^{(1/\delta^2)}\exp(-\exp(\delta w)/\delta^2)/\Gamma(1/\delta^2)$$

$$G(t) = \Gamma(1/\delta^2, t^{\delta}/\delta^2)/\Gamma(1/\delta^2) \quad \text{if } \delta > 0$$
$$G(t) = 1 - \Gamma(1/\delta^2, t^{\delta}/\delta^2)/\Gamma(1/\delta^2) \quad \text{if } \delta < 0$$
$$g(t) = |\delta|(t^{\delta}/\delta^2)^{(1/\delta^2)}\exp(-t^{\delta}/\delta^2)/(t\Gamma(1/\delta^2))$$

where $\Gamma(z)$ denotes the complete gamma function, $\Gamma(a,z)$ denotes the incomplete gamma function, and δ is a free shape parameter. The δ parameter is referred to as SHAPE1 by the program.

Again note that the expected value of the baseline log response is, in general, not zero and that the distributions are not symmetric in all cases. Thus for a given set of covariates, $\mathbf{x}$, the expected value of the log response is not always $\mathbf{x}'\boldsymbol{\beta}$.

Some relations among the distributions are as follows:

- The gamma with SHAPE1=1 is a Weibull distribution.
- The gamma with SHAPE1=0 is a log-normal distribution.
- The Weibull with SCALE=1 is an exponential distribution.

Predicted Values

For a given set of covariates, $\mathbf{x}$, the pth quantile of the log response, y_p, is given by

$$y_p = \mathbf{x}'\boldsymbol{\beta} + \sigma w_p$$

where w_p is the pth quantile of the baseline distribution. The estimated quantile is computed by replacing the unknown parameters with their estimates, including any shape parameters on which the baseline distribution might depend. The estimated quantile of the original response is obtained by taking the exponential of the estimated log quantile unless the NOLOG option was specified in the preceding MODEL statement. The standard errors of the quantile estimates are computed using the estimated covariance matrix of the parameter estimates and a Taylor series expansion of the quantile estimate. The standard error is computed as

$$STD = \sqrt{\mathbf{z}'\mathbf{V}\mathbf{z}}$$

where $\mathbf{V}$ is the estimated covariance matrix of the parameter vector $(\boldsymbol{\beta}',\sigma,\delta)'$, and $\mathbf{z}$ is the vector

$$\mathbf{z} = \begin{bmatrix} \mathbf{x} \\ \hat{w}_p \\ \hat{\sigma}\partial w_p / \partial\delta \end{bmatrix}$$

where δ is the vector of the shape parameters. Unless the NOLOG option is specified, this standard error estimate is converted into a standard error estimate for $\exp(y_p)$ as $\exp(\hat{y}_p)$ STD. It may be more desirable to compute confidence limits for the log response and convert them back to the original response variable than to use the standard error estimates for $\exp(y_p)$ directly. See **Example 1** for a 90% confidence interval of the response constructed by exponentiating a confidence interval for the log response.

The variable, CDF, is computed as

$$CDF_i = F((y_i - \mathbf{x}'_i\mathbf{b}) / \hat{\sigma})$$

where F is the baseline cumulative distribution function.

OUTEST= Output Data Set

The OUTEST= data set contains parameter estimates and the log likelihood for the specified models. A set of observations is created for each MODEL statement specified. You can use a label in the MODEL statement to distinguish between the estimates for different MODEL statements. If the COVOUT option is specified, the OUTEST= data set also contains the estimated covariance matrix of the parameter estimates.

The OUTEST= data set is not created if there are any CLASS variables in any models. If created, this data set contains each variable used as a dependent or independent variable in any MODEL statement. One observation consists of parameter values for the model with the dependent variable having the value −1. If the COVOUT option is specified, there are additional observations containing the rows of the estimated covariance matrix. For these observations the dependent variable contains the parameter estimate for the corresponding row variable. The variables listed below are also added to the data set:

_MODEL _	a character variable of length 8 containing the label of the MODEL statement if present or blank otherwise
_NAME _	a character variable of length 8 containing the name of the dependent variable for the parameter estimates observations or the name of the row for the covariance matrix estimates
_TYPE _	a character variable of length 8 containing the type of the observation, either PARMS for parameter estimates or COV for covariance estimates
DIST	a character variable of length 8 containing the name of the distribution modeled
_LNLIKE _	a numeric variable containing the last computed value of the log likelihood
INTERCEP	a numeric variable containing the intercept parameter estimates and covariances
_SCALE _	a numeric variable containing the scale parameter estimates and covariances
_SHAPE1 _	a numeric variable containing the first shape parameter estimates and covariances if the specified distribution has additional shape parameters.

Any BY variables specified are also added to the OUTEST= data set.

Computational Resources

Let p be the number of parameters estimated in the model. Then the minimum working space (in bytes) needed is

$$16p^2 + 100p \quad .$$

However, if sufficient space is available, the input data set is also kept in memory; otherwise, the input data set is reread for each evaluation of the likelihood function and its derivatives, with the resulting execution time of the procedure substantially increased.

Let n be the number of observations used in the model estimation. Then each evaluation of the likelihood function and its first and second derivatives requires $O(np^2)$ multiplications and additions and n individual function evaluations for the log density or log distribution function and n evaluations of the first and second derivatives of the function. The calculation of each updating step from the gradient and Hessian requires $O(p^3)$ multiplications and additions.

Printed Output

For each model PROC LIFEREG prints

1. the name of the Data Set
2. the name of the Dependent Variable
3. the name of the Censoring Variable
4. the Censoring Value(s) that indicate a censored observation
5. the number of Noncensored and Censored Values
6. the final estimate of the maximized Loglikelihood
7. the iteration history and the Last Evaluation of the Gradient and Hessian if the ITPRINT option was specified (not shown).

For each independent variable in the model the LIFEREG procedure prints

8. the name of the Variable
9. the degrees of freedom (DF) associated with the variable in the model
10. the Estimate of the parameter
11. the standard error (Std Err) estimate from the observed information matrix
12. an approximate ChiSquare statistic for testing that the parameter is zero (the class variables also have an overall chi-square test statistic computed that precedes the individual level parameters)
13. the probability of a larger chi-square value (Pr>Chi)
14. the Label of the variable or, if the variable is a class level, the Value of the class variable.

If there were constrained parameters in the model, such as the scale or intercept, then LIFEREG prints

15. a Lagrange Multiplier test for the constraint.

EXAMPLES

Example 1: Motorette Failure

This example fits a Weibull model and a log normal model to the example given in Kalbfleisch and Prentice (1980, 5). An output data set called MODEL is specified to contain the parameter estimates. By default, the natural log of the variable TIME is used internally by the procedure as the response. After this log transformation, the Weibull model is fit using the extreme value baseline distribution and the log-normal is fit using the normal baseline distribution. Since the extreme value and normal distributions do not contain any shape parameters, the variable SHAPE1 is missing in the OUTPUT data set. An additional output data set is requested that contains the predicted quantiles and their standard errors for values of the covariate corresponding to TEMP=130 and 150. This is done with the CONTROL variable, which is set to 1 for only two observations. Using the standard error estimates obtained from the output data set, approximate 90% confidence limits are then created in a subsequent DATA step for the log response. These confidence limits are then converted back to the original scale by the exponential function. The following statements produce **Output 21.1**:

```
Title 'Motorette Failures With Operating Temperature as a Covariate';
data;
    input time censor temp aa;
    if _N_=1 then do;
        temp=130;
        time=.;
```

```
        control=1;
        z=1000 / (273.2+temp);
        output;
        temp=150;
        time=.;
        control=1;
        z=1000 / (273.2+TEMP);
        output;
        end;
    if temp>150;
    control=0;
    z=1000 / (273.2+temp);
    output;
    cards;
8064 0 150 8064 0 150 8064 0 150 8064 0 150 8064 0 150
8064 0 150 8064 0 150 8064 0 150 8064 0 150 8064 0 150
1764 1 170 2772 1 170 3444 1 170 3542 1 170 3780 1 170
4860 1 170 5196 1 170 5448 0 170 5448 0 170 5448 0 170
 408 1 190  408 1 190 1344 1 190 1344 1 190 1440 1 190
1680 0 190 1680 0 190 1680 0 190 1680 0 190 1680 0 190
 408 1 220  408 1 220  504 1 220  504 1 220  504 1 220
 528 0 220  528 0 220  528 0 220  528 0 220  528 0 220
;

proc lifereg outest=models covout;
A:model time*censor(0)=z;
B:model time*censor(0)=z / dist=lnormal;
    output out=out quantiles=.1 .5 .9 std=std p=predtime
           control=control;

proc print data=models;
    id _model_;
    title 'fitted models';

data;        /* 90% confidence interval for the response */
    set out;
    ltime=log(predtime);
    stde =std / predtime;
    upper=exp(ltime+1.64*stde);
    lower=exp(ltime-1.64*stde);

proc print;
    id temp;
    title 'quantile estimates and confidence limits';
run;
```

Output 21.1   Motorette Failure: PROC LIFEREG

```
                Motorette Failures With Operating Temperature as a Covariate                    1
                              L I F E R E G   P R O C E D U R E

 ❶  Data Set          =WORK.DATA1
 ❷  Dependent Variable=Log(TIME)
 ❸  Censoring Variable=CENSOR
 ❹  Censoring Value(s)=     0
    Noncensored Values=    17  Right Censored Values=      13 ❺
    Left Censored Values=  0  Interval Censored Values=    0
    Observations with Missing Values=   2
 ❻  Log Likelihood for WEIBULL -22.95148315

        ❾      ❿       ⓫       ⓬       ⓭      ⓮
 ❽  Variable DF   Estimate  Std Err ChiSquare Pr>Chi Label/Value

    INTERCPT  1 -11.89122 1.965507  36.6019  0.0001 Intercept
    Z         1 9.03834032 0.905993  99.52392 0.0001
    SCALE     1 0.36128138 0.079501            Extreme value scale parameter
```

```
                Motorette Failures With Operating Temperature as a Covariate                    2
                              L I F E R E G   P R O C E D U R E

    Data Set          =WORK.DATA1
    Dependent Variable=Log(TIME)
    Censoring Variable=CENSOR
    Censoring Value(s)=     0
    Noncensored Values=    17  Right Censored Values=      13
    Left Censored Values=  0  Interval Censored Values=    0
    Observations with Missing Values=   2
    Log Likelihood for LNORMAL -24.47381031


    Variable DF   Estimate  Std Err ChiSquare Pr>Chi Label/Value

    INTERCPT  1 -10.470563  2.77192  14.26851 0.0002 Intercept
    Z         1  8.3220835 1.284124  42.00011 0.0001
    SCALE     1  0.6040344 0.110729            Normal scale parameter
```

```
                                         fitted models                                          3

 _MODEL_   _NAME_     _TYPE_   _DIST_    _LNLIKE_   INTERCEP      TIME        Z       _SCALE_   _SHAPE1_

    A      TIME       PARMS    WEIBULL  -22.9515   -11.8912   -1.0000    9.03834    0.36128      .
    A      INTERCPT   COV      WEIBULL  -22.9515     3.8632  -11.8912   -1.77878    0.03448      .
    A      Z          COV      WEIBULL  -22.9515    -1.7788    9.0383    0.82082   -0.01488      .
    A      SCALE      COV      WEIBULL  -22.9515     0.0345    0.3613   -0.01488    0.00632      .
    B      TIME       PARMS    LNORMAL  -24.4738   -10.4706   -1.0000    8.32208    0.60403      .
    B      INTERCPT   COV      LNORMAL  -24.4738     7.6835  -10.4706   -3.55566    0.03267      .
    B      Z          COV      LNORMAL  -24.4738    -3.5557    8.3221    1.64897   -0.01285      .
    B      SCALE      COV      LNORMAL  -24.4738     0.0327    0.6040   -0.01285    0.01226      .
```

```
                              quantile estimates and confidence limits                          4

 TEMP  TIME  CENSOR  CONTROL      Z     _PROB_   PREDTIME     STD      LTIME    STDE     UPPER      LOWER

 130    .      0        1    2.48016    0.1     12033.19   5482.34    9.3954  0.45560  25402.68   5700.09
 130    .      0        1    2.48016    0.5     26095.68  11359.45   10.1695  0.43530  53285.36  12779.95
 130    .      0        1    2.48016    0.9     56592.19  26036.90   10.9436  0.46008 120349.65  26611.42
 150    .      0        1    2.36295    0.1      4536.88   1443.07    8.4200  0.31808   7643.71   2692.83
 150    .      0        1    2.36295    0.5      9838.86   2901.15    9.1941  0.29487  15957.38   6066.36
 150    .      0        1    2.36295    0.9     21336.97   7172.34    9.9682  0.33615  37029.72  12294.62
```

Example 2: VA Lung Cancer Data

This example uses data presented in Kalbfeisch and Prentice (1980, Appendix 1). The response is the survival time in days of a group of lung cancer patients. The covariates are type of cancer cell (CELL), type of therapy (THERAPY), prior therapy (PRIOR), age in years (AGE), time in months from diagnosis to entry into the trial (DIAGTIME), and a measure of the overall status of the patient at entry into the trial (KPS). The first three variables are taken to be class variables although only CELL has more than two levels. The censored values are given as negative, and a censoring indicator (CENSOR) is created. Before beginning any modeling, you should do preliminary investigations of the data with graphic and other descriptive methods. However, this chapter concentrates only on the use of the LIFEREG procedure, and the following does not constitute a complete analysis of the data.

Models are fit to the survival time using the Weibull, log-normal, and log-logistic baseline distributions. The exponential distribution is also fit. The Lagrange multiplier test arising from this model tests whether the exponential model is adequate relative to the Weibull model. An output data set containing predicted values from the Weibull model is also created. The OUTPUT statement must immediately follow the desired MODEL statement.

The following statements produce **Output 21.2**:

```
title 'VA Lung Cancer Data from Appendix I of K&P';
data valung;
   drop check x4 m;
   retain therapy cell;
   infile cards column=column;
   length prior  $ 3 check  $ 1;
   label t        ='Failure or Censoring Time'
         kps      ='Karnofsky Performance Status'
         diagtime ='Months Till Randomization'
         age      ='Age in Years'
         prior    ='Prior Treatment?'
         cell     ='Cell Type'
         therapy  ='Type of Treatment';
   m=column;
   input check $ @@;
   if m>column then m=1;
   if check='s' or check='t' then input @m therapy $ cell $;
      else input @m t kps diagtime age x4 @@;
   if t>.;
      censor=(t<0); t=abs(t);
   if x4=10 then prior='yes';
            else prior='no';
   cards;
standard squamous
   72 60   7 69  0    411 70   5 64 10    228 60   3 38  0
  126 60   9 63 10    118 70  11 65 10     10 20   5 49  0
   82 40  10 69 10    110 80  29 68  0    314 50  18 43  0
 -100 70   6 70  0     42 60   4 81  0      8 40  58 63 10
  144 30   4 63  0    -25 80   9 52 10     11 70  11 48 10
standard small
   30 60   3 61  0    384 60   9 42  0      4 40   2 35  0
   54 80   4 63 10     13 60   4 56  0   -123 40   3 55  0
  -97 60   5 67  0    153 60  14 63 10     59 30   2 65  0
  117 80   3 46  0     16 30   4 53 10    151 50  12 69  0
   22 60   4 68  0     56 80  12 43 10     21 40   2 55 10
   18 20  15 42  0    139 80   2 64  0     20 30   5 65  0
   31 75   3 65  0     52 70   2 55  0    287 60  25 66 10
```

```
    18 30   4 60   0     51 60   1 67   0    122 80  28 53   0
    27 60   8 62   0     54 70   1 67   0      7 50   7 72   0
    63 50  11 48   0    392 40   4 68   0     10 40  23 67  10
standard adeno
     8 20  19 61  10     92 70  10 60   0     35 40   6 62   0
   117 80   2 38   0    132 80   5 50   0     12 50   4 63  10
   162 80   5 64   0      3 30   3 43   0     95 80   4 34   0
standard large
   177 50  16 66  10    162 80   5 62   0    216 50  15 52   0
   553 70   2 47   0    278 60  12 63   0     12 40  12 68  10
   260 80   5 45   0    200 80  12 41  10    156 70   2 66   0
  -182 90   2 62   0    143 90   8 60   0    105 80  11 66   0
   103 80   5 38   0    250 70   8 53  10    100 60  13 37  10
test squamous
   999 90  12 54  10    112 80   6 60   0    -87 80   3 48   0
  -231 50   8 52  10    242 50   1 70   0    991 70   7 50  10
   111 70   3 62   0      1 20  21 65  10    587 60   3 58   0
   389 90   2 62   0     33 30   6 64   0     25 20  36 63   0
   357 70  13 58   0    467 90   2 64   0    201 80  28 52  10
     1 50   7 35   0     30 70  11 63   0     44 60  13 70  10
   283 90   2 51   0     15 50  13 40  10
test small
    25 30   2 69   0   -103 70  22 36  10     21 20   4 71   0
    13 30   2 62   0     87 60   2 60   0      2 40  36 44  10
    20 30   9 54  10      7 20  11 66   0     24 60   8 49   0
    99 70   3 72   0      8 80   2 68   0     99 85   4 62   0
    61 70   2 71   0     25 70   2 70   0     95 70   1 61   0
    80 50  17 71   0     51 30  87 59  10     29 40   8 67   0
test adeno
    24 40   2 60   0     18 40   5 69  10    -83 99   3 57   0
    31 80   3 39   0     51 60   5 62   0     90 60  22 50  10
    52 60   3 43   0     73 60   3 70   0      8 50   5 66   0
    36 70   8 61   0     48 10   4 81   0      7 40   4 58   0
   140 70   3 63   0    186 90   3 60   0     84 80   4 62  10
    19 50  10 42   0     45 40   3 69   0     80 40   4 63   0
test large
    52 60   4 45   0    164 70  15 68  10     19 30   4 39  10
    53 60  12 66   0     15 30   5 63   0     43 60  11 49  10
   340 80  10 64  10    133 75   1 65   0    111 60   5 64   0
   231 70  18 67  10    378 80   4 65   0     49 30   3 37   0
;

proc lifereg;
   class prior therapy cell;
   model t*censor(1)=kps age diagtime prior cell therapy /
                 dist=weibull;
   output out=out cdf=f p=pred censored=flag;
   model t*censor(1)=kps age diagtime prior cell therapy /
                 dist=exponential;
   model T*censor(1)=kps age diagtime prior cell therapy /
                 dist=lnormal;
   model T*censor(1)=kps age diagtime prior cell therapy /
                 dist=llogistic;
proc print;
run;
```

Output 21.2   VA Lung Cancer Data: PROC LIFEREG

```
                    VA Lung Cancer Data from Appendix I of K&P                      1

                         L I F E R E G   P R O C E D U R E
                              Class Level Information

               Class     Levels    Values

               PRIOR       2       no yes

               CELL        4       adeno large small squamous

               THERAPY     2       standard test

                     Number of observations used = 137
```

```
                    VA Lung Cancer Data from Appendix I of K&P                      2

                         L I F E R E G   P R O C E D U R E

Data Set        =WORK.VALUNG
Dependent Variable=Log(T)      Failure or Censoring Time
Censoring Variable=CENSOR
Censoring Value(s)=     1
Noncensored Values=   128  Right Censored Values=       9
Left Censored Values=   0  Interval Censored Values=    0
Loglikelihood for WEIBULL -196.1386213


        Variable  DF   Estimate  Std Err  ChiSquare  Pr>Chi Label/Value
        INTERCPT   1  2.98959331 0.709345   17.7627   0.0001 Intercept
        KPS        1  0.0300683  0.004828   38.78887  0.0001 Karnofsky Performance Status
        AGE        1  0.00609918 0.008553    0.508475 0.4758 Age in Years
        DIAGTIME   1 -0.0004688  0.008361    0.003144 0.9553 Months Till Randomization

        PRIOR      1                         0.042763 0.8362 Prior Treatment?
                   1  0.04389765 0.212279    0.042763 0.8362 no
                   0  0          0           .        .      yes


        CELL       3                        22.02965  0.0001 Cell Type
                   1 -1.1327251  0.257598   19.3359   0.0001 adeno
                   1 -0.3976808  0.254749    2.436927 0.1185 large
                   1 -0.8261846  0.246312   11.2508   0.0008 small
                   0  0          0           .        .      squamous


        THERAPY    1                         1.495897 0.2213 Type of Treatment
                   1  0.22852267 0.186844    1.495897 0.2213 standard
                   0  0          0           .        .      test

        SCALE      1  0.92811527 0.061545                    Extreme value scale parameter
```

```
              VA Lung Cancer Data from Appendix I of K&P                    3

                   L I F E R E G   P R O C E D U R E
                     Class Level Information

            Class     Levels    Values

            PRIOR       2       no yes

            CELL        4       adeno large small squamous

            THERAPY     2       standard test

                 Number of observations used = 137
```

```
              VA Lung Cancer Data from Appendix I of K&P                    4

                   L I F E R E G   P R O C E D U R E

Data Set        =WORK.VALUNG
Dependent Variable=Log(T)      Failure or Censoring Time
Censoring Variable=CENSOR
Censoring Value(s)=      1
Noncensored Values=  128  Right Censored Values=       9
Left Censored Values=   0  Interval Censored Values=   0
Loglikelihood for EXPONENT -196.7463712


      Variable  DF   Estimate   Std Err  ChiSquare  Pr>Chi  Label/Value
      INTERCPT   1  2.91956377  0.752159  15.06666   0.0001  Intercept
      KPS        1  0.03062403  0.005108  35.94996   0.0001  Karnofsky Performance Status
      AGE        1  0.00610766  0.009161   0.444531   0.5049  Age in Years
      DIAGTIME   1  -0.000297   0.00897    0.001097   0.9736  Months Till Randomization

      PRIOR      1                         0.04757   0.8273  Prior Treatment?
                 1  0.04948164  0.226871   0.04757   0.8273  no
                 0      0          0        .         .      yes


      CELL       3                        18.82178   0.0003  Cell Type
                 1  -1.1131212  0.275825  16.28611   0.0001  adeno
                 1  -0.3772199  0.272626   1.9145    0.1665  large
                 1  -0.8202447  0.262111   9.79305   0.0018  small
                 0      0          0        .         .      squamous


      THERAPY    1                         1.221858  0.2690  Type of Treatment
                 1  0.21956531  0.198634   1.221858  0.2690  standard
                 0      0          0        .         .      test

   ⓯ SCALE       0      1          0                         Extreme value scale parameter
        Lagrange Multiplier ChiSquare for Scale 1.3771706423 Pr>Chi is 0.2406.
```

```
                    VA Lung Cancer Data from Appendix I of K&P                    5
                          L I F E R E G   P R O C E D U R E
                            Class Level Information

                    Class    Levels    Values

                    PRIOR       2      no yes

                    CELL        4      adeno large small squamous

                    THERAPY     2      standard test

                    Number of observations used = 137
```

```
                    VA Lung Cancer Data from Appendix I of K&P                    6

                          L I F E R E G   P R O C E D U R E

Data Set        =WORK.VALUNG
Dependent Variable=Log(T)    Failure or Censoring Time
Censoring Variable=CENSOR
Censoring Value(s)=      1
Noncensored Values=    128   Right Censored Values=       9
Left Censored Values=    0   Interval Censored Values=    0
Loglikelihood for NORMAL -195.2222289


     Variable  DF    Estimate  Std Err  ChiSquare  Pr>Chi  Label/Value
     INTERCPT   1   1.3969047  0.687131  4.132892   0.0421  Intercept
     KPS        1   0.03729538 0.004842  59.33226   0.0001  Karnofsky Performance Status
     AGE        1   0.01278756 0.008899  2.064662   0.1507  Age in Years
     DIAGTIME   1  -0.0012385  0.009704  0.016288   0.8984  Months Till Randomization

     PRIOR      1                        0.221982   0.6375  Prior Treatment?
                1   0.10667088 0.226406  0.221982   0.6375  no
                0       0         0          .       .      yes


     CELL       3                        12.55481   0.0057  Cell Type
                1  -0.6542245  0.283856  5.312008   0.0212  adeno
                1   0.11875999 0.280177  0.17967    0.6717  large
                1  -0.6065537  0.249295  5.919868   0.0150  small
                0       0         0          .       .      squamous


     THERAPY    1                        0.792061   0.3735  Type of Treatment
                1   0.16910486 0.19001   0.792061   0.3735  standard
                0       0         0          .       .      test

     SCALE      1   1.05982287 0.066337                     Normal scale parameter
```

```
                VA Lung Cancer Data from Appendix I of K&P                      7

                      L I F E R E G   P R O C E D U R E
                         Class Level Information

                   Class     Levels    Values

                   PRIOR       2       no yes

                   CELL        4       adeno large small squamous

                   THERAPY     2       standard test

                   Number of observations used = 137
```

```
                VA Lung Cancer Data from Appendix I of K&P                      8

                      L I F E R E G   P R O C E D U R E

        Data Set       =WORK.VALUNG
        Dependent Variable=Log(T)     Failure or Censoring Time
        Censoring Variable=CENSOR
        Censoring Value(s)=       1
        Noncensored Values=   128  Right Censored Values=       9
        Left Censored Values=   0  Interval Censored Values=    0
        Loglikelihood for LOGISTIC -192.5298424


           Variable  DF   Estimate   Std Err  ChiSquare  Pr>Chi  Label/Value
           INTERCPT   1   1.833792  0.697812  6.905944  0.0086  Intercept
           KPS        1  0.03606026 0.004484  64.67655  0.0001  Karnofsky Performance Status
           AGE        1   0.008546  0.008921  0.917646  0.3381  Age in Years
           DIAGTIME   1  0.00210661 0.010269   0.04208  0.8375  Months Till Randomization

           PRIOR      1                        0.233315  0.6291  Prior Treatment?
                      1  0.10200928 0.211187  0.233315  0.6291  no
                      0      0         0         .        .     yes


           CELL       3                        16.09257  0.0011  Cell Type
                      1 -0.7425488  0.272132   7.445421  0.0064  adeno
                      1  0.01662671 0.26956    0.003805  0.9508  large
                      1 -0.7079773  0.249254   8.067793  0.0045  small
                      0      0         0         .        .     squamous


           THERAPY    1                        0.24333   0.6218  Type of Treatment
                      1  0.08846214 0.179333   0.24333   0.6218  standard
                      0      0         0         .        .     test

           SCALE      1  0.57900028 0.042955                    Logistic scale parameter
```

```
                VA LUNG CANCER DATA FROM APPENDIX I of K&P                      9

OBS  THERAPY    CELL      PRIOR    T   KPS  DIAGTIME  AGE  CENSOR  _PROB_   PRED      F     FLAG

  1  STANDARD  SQUAMOUS   NO      72   60      7       69    0     0.5    171.316  0.23845   0
  2  STANDARD  SQUAMOUS   YES    411   70      5       64    0     0.5    215.021  0.75169   0
  3  STANDARD  SQUAMOUS   NO     228   60      3       38    0     0.5    142.068  0.68460   0
  4  STANDARD  SQUAMOUS   YES    126   60      9       63    0     0.5    157.918  0.41927   0
  5  STANDARD  SQUAMOUS   YES    118   70     11       65    0     0.5    215.729  0.30360   0
  6  STANDARD  SQUAMOUS   NO      10   20      5       49    0     0.5     45.592  0.12644   0
  7  STANDARD  SQUAMOUS   YES     82   40     10       69    0     0.5     89.733  0.46688   0
  8  STANDARD  SQUAMOUS   NO     110   80     29       68    0     0.5    307.496  0.20466   0
  9  STANDARD  SQUAMOUS   NO     314   50     18       43    0     0.5    107.672  0.88877   0
 10  STANDARD  SQUAMOUS   NO     100   70      6       70    1     0.5    232.935  0.24324   1
 11  STANDARD  SQUAMOUS   NO      42   60      4       81    0     0.5    184.584  0.13119   0
 12  STANDARD  SQUAMOUS   YES      8   40     58       63    0     0.5     84.584  0.05315   0
 13  STANDARD  SQUAMOUS   NO     144   30      4       63    0     0.5     67.106  0.79362   0
 14  STANDARD  SQUAMOUS   YES     25   80      9       52    1     0.5    269.442  0.05209   1
 15  STANDARD  SQUAMOUS   YES     11   70     11       48    0     0.5    194.481  0.03090   0
 16  STANDARD  SMALL      NO      30   60      3       61    0     0.5     71.551  0.23792   0
 17  STANDARD  SMALL      NO     384   60      9       42    0     0.5     63.542  0.99189   0
 18  STANDARD  SMALL      NO       4   40      2       35    0     0.5     33.479  0.06784   0
 19  STANDARD  SMALL      YES     54   80      4       63    0     0.5    126.419  0.24210   0
 20  STANDARD  SMALL      NO      13   60      4       56    0     0.5     69.369  0.10783   0
 21  STANDARD  SMALL      NO     123   40      3       55    1     0.5     37.805  0.91550   1
 22  STANDARD  SMALL      NO      97   60      5       67    1     0.5     74.148  0.60380   1
 23  STANDARD  SMALL      YES    153   60     14       63    0     0.5     68.962  0.80519   0
 24  STANDARD  SMALL      NO      59   30      2       65    0     0.5     29.762  0.76517   0
 25  STANDARD  SMALL      NO     117   80      3       46    0     0.5    119.138  0.49326   0
```

(continued on next page)

(continued from previous page)

26	STANDARD	SMALL	YES	16	30	4	53	0	0.5	26.448	0.33190	0
27	STANDARD	SMALL	NO	151	50	12	69	0	0.5	55.384	0.87029	0
28	STANDARD	SMALL	NO	22	60	4	68	0	0.5	74.637	0.16962	0
29	STANDARD	SMALL	YES	56	80	12	43	0	0.5	111.483	0.28115	0
30	STANDARD	SMALL	YES	21	40	2	55	0	0.5	36.198	0.31990	0
31	STANDARD	SMALL	NO	18	20	15	42	0	0.5	19.033	0.47937	0
32	STANDARD	SMALL	NO	139	80	2	64	0	0.5	133.025	0.51652	0
33	STANDARD	SMALL	NO	20	30	5	65	0	0.5	29.720	0.36388	0
34	STANDARD	SMALL	NO	31	75	3	65	0	0.5	115.103	0.15519	0
35	STANDARD	SMALL	NO	52	70	2	55	0	0.5	93.220	0.30896	0
36	STANDARD	SMALL	YES	287	60	25	66	0	0.5	69.874	0.95826	0
37	STANDARD	SMALL	NO	18	30	4	60	0	0.5	28.841	0.34104	0
38	STANDARD	SMALL	NO	51	60	1	67	0	0.5	74.287	0.37010	0
39	STANDARD	SMALL	NO	122	80	28	53	0	0.5	122.886	0.49730	0
40	STANDARD	SMALL	NO	27	60	8	62	0	0.5	71.820	0.21460	0
41	STANDARD	SMALL	NO	54	70	1	67	0	0.5	100.346	0.29920	0
42	STANDARD	SMALL	NO	7	50	7	72	0	0.5	56.539	0.07040	0
43	STANDARD	SMALL	NO	63	50	11	48	0	0.5	48.749	0.59898	0
44	STANDARD	SMALL	NO	392	40	4	68	0	0.5	40.905	0.99963	0
45	STANDARD	SMALL	YES	10	40	23	67	0	0.5	38.566	0.14947	0
46	STANDARD	ADENO	YES	8	20	19	61	0	0.5	15.025	0.29635	0
47	STANDARD	ADENO	NO	92	70	10	60	0	0.5	70.469	0.60300	0
48	STANDARD	ADENO	NO	35	40	6	62	0	0.5	28.997	0.57213	0
49	STANDARD	ADENO	NO	117	80	2	38	0	0.5	83.548	0.63077	0
50	STANDARD	ADENO	NO	132	80	5	50	0	0.5	89.766	0.65012	0
51	STANDARD	ADENO	YES	12	50	4	63	0	0.5	37.751	0.18259	0
52	STANDARD	ADENO	NO	162	80	5	64	0	0.5	97.767	0.69710	0
53	STANDARD	ADENO	NO	3	30	3	43	0	0.5	19.145	0.08980	0
54	STANDARD	ADENO	NO	95	80	4	34	0	0.5	81.458	0.55872	0
55	STANDARD	LARGE	YES	177	50	16	66	0	0.5	79.737	0.80537	0
56	STANDARD	LARGE	NO	162	80	5	62	0	0.5	201.429	0.42198	0

VA LUNG CANCER DATA FROM APPENDIX I of K&P   10

OBS	THERAPY	CELL	PRIOR	T	KPS	DIAGTIME	AGE	CENSOR	_PROB_	PRED	F	FLAG
57	STANDARD	LARGE	NO	216	50	15	52	0	0.5	76.532	0.87997	0
58	STANDARD	LARGE	NO	553	70	2	47	0	0.5	136.275	0.95650	0
59	STANDARD	LARGE	NO	278	60	12	63	0	0.5	110.707	0.84576	0
60	STANDARD	LARGE	YES	12	40	12	68	0	0.5	59.867	0.11545	0
61	STANDARD	LARGE	NO	260	80	5	45	0	0.5	181.590	0.63956	0
62	STANDARD	LARGE	YES	200	80	12	41	0	0.5	169.047	0.56431	0
63	STANDARD	LARGE	NO	156	70	2	66	0	0.5	153.018	0.50723	0
64	STANDARD	LARGE	NO	182	90	2	62	1	0.5	272.469	0.36158	1
65	STANDARD	LARGE	NO	143	90	8	60	0	0.5	268.410	0.29651	0
66	STANDARD	LARGE	NO	105	80	11	66	0	0.5	205.824	0.28512	0
67	STANDARD	LARGE	NO	103	80	5	38	0	0.5	174.000	0.32563	0
68	STANDARD	LARGE	YES	250	70	8	53	0	0.5	134.903	0.74008	0
69	STANDARD	LARGE	YES	100	60	13	37	0	0.5	90.373	0.53839	0
70	TEST	SQUAMOUS	YES	999	90	12	54	0	0.5	292.746	0.92582	0
71	TEST	SQUAMOUS	NO	112	80	6	60	0	0.5	235.551	0.26739	0
72	TEST	SQUAMOUS	NO	87	80	3	48	1	0.5	219.235	0.22591	1
73	TEST	SQUAMOUS	YES	231	50	8	52	1	0.5	87.030	0.86252	1
74	TEST	SQUAMOUS	NO	242	50	1	70	0	0.5	101.821	0.82824	0
75	TEST	SQUAMOUS	YES	991	70	7	50	0	0.5	156.943	0.99358	0
76	TEST	SQUAMOUS	NO	111	70	3	62	0	0.5	176.770	0.34285	0
77	TEST	SQUAMOUS	YES	1	20	21	65	0	0.5	37.993	0.01367	0
78	TEST	SQUAMOUS	NO	587	60	3	58	0	0.5	127.711	0.97228	0
79	TEST	SQUAMOUS	NO	389	90	2	62	0	0.5	322.687	0.57163	0
80	TEST	SQUAMOUS	NO	33	30	6	64	0	0.5	53.673	0.33662	0
81	TEST	SQUAMOUS	NO	25	20	36	63	0	0.5	38.942	0.34948	0
82	TEST	SQUAMOUS	NO	357	70	13	58	0	0.5	171.703	0.78243	0
83	TEST	SQUAMOUS	NO	467	90	2	64	0	0.5	326.648	0.63897	0
84	TEST	SQUAMOUS	YES	201	80	28	52	0	0.5	212.496	0.47943	0
85	TEST	SQUAMOUS	NO	1	50	7	35	0	0.5	82.017	0.00599	0
86	TEST	SQUAMOUS	NO	30	70	11	63	0	0.5	177.186	0.09722	0
87	TEST	SQUAMOUS	YES	44	60	13	70	0	0.5	130.892	0.19276	0
88	TEST	SQUAMOUS	NO	283	90	2	51	0	0.5	301.748	0.47631	0
89	TEST	SQUAMOUS	YES	15	50	13	40	0	0.5	80.698	0.10694	0
90	TEST	SMALL	NO	25	30	2	69	0	0.5	24.266	0.51117	0
91	TEST	SMALL	YES	103	70	22	36	1	0.5	62.632	0.69415	1
92	TEST	SMALL	NO	21	20	4	71	0	0.5	18.168	0.55524	0
93	TEST	SMALL	NO	13	30	2	62	0	0.5	23.252	0.30959	0
94	TEST	SMALL	NO	87	60	2	60	0	0.5	56.614	0.66754	0
95	TEST	SMALL	YES	2	40	36	44	0	0.5	26.508	0.04191	0
96	TEST	SMALL	YES	20	30	9	54	0	0.5	21.124	0.47977	0
97	TEST	SMALL	NO	7	20	11	66	0	0.5	17.565	0.22682	0
98	TEST	SMALL	NO	24	60	8	49	0	0.5	52.791	0.25655	0
99	TEST	SMALL	NO	99	70	3	72	0	0.5	82.241	0.57107	0
100	TEST	SMALL	NO	8	80	2	68	0	0.5	108.463	0.04092	0
101	TEST	SMALL	NO	99	85	4	62	0	0.5	121.416	0.42668	0
102	TEST	SMALL	NO	61	70	2	71	0	0.5	81.779	0.39675	0
103	TEST	SMALL	NO	25	70	2	70	0	0.5	81.282	0.17682	0

(continued on next page)

(continued from previous page)

104	TEST	SMALL	NO	95	70	1	61	0	0.5	76.977	0.58084	0
105	TEST	SMALL	NO	80	50	17	71	0	0.5	44.506	0.72851	0
106	TEST	SMALL	YES	51	30	87	59	0	0.5	20.997	0.83527	0
107	TEST	SMALL	NO	29	40	8	67	0	0.5	32.290	0.46063	0
108	TEST	ADENO	NO	24	40	2	60	0	0.5	22.836	0.51871	0
109	TEST	ADENO	YES	18	40	5	69	0	0.5	23.056	0.41190	0
110	TEST	ADENO	NO	83	99	3	57	1	0.5	132.107	0.34301	1
111	TEST	ADENO	NO	31	80	3	39	0	0.5	66.855	0.26128	0
112	TEST	ADENO	NO	51	60	5	62	0	0.5	42.119	0.57337	0

VA LUNG CANCER DATA FROM APPENDIX I of K&P   11

OBS	THERAPY	CELL	PRIOR	T	KPS	DIAGTIME	AGE	CENSOR	_PROB_	PRED	F	FLAG
113	TEST	ADENO	YES	90	60	22	50	0	0.5	37.168	0.83427	0
114	TEST	ADENO	NO	52	60	3	43	0	0.5	37.546	0.62638	0
115	TEST	ADENO	NO	73	60	3	70	0	0.5	44.267	0.69524	0
116	TEST	ADENO	NO	8	50	5	66	0	0.5	31.951	0.14436	0
117	TEST	ADENO	NO	36	70	8	61	0	0.5	56.468	0.34738	0
118	TEST	ADENO	NO	48	10	4	81	0	0.5	10.522	0.97146	0
119	TEST	ADENO	NO	7	40	4	58	0	0.5	22.538	0.17851	0
120	TEST	ADENO	NO	140	70	3	63	0	0.5	57.296	0.83717	0
121	TEST	ADENO	NO	186	90	3	60	0	0.5	102.647	0.73158	0
122	TEST	ADENO	YES	84	80	4	62	0	0.5	73.585	0.55041	0
123	TEST	ADENO	NO	19	50	10	42	0	0.5	27.536	0.37169	0
124	TEST	ADENO	NO	45	40	3	69	0	0.5	24.113	0.74272	0
125	TEST	ADENO	NO	80	40	4	63	0	0.5	23.236	0.92765	0
126	TEST	LARGE	NO	52	60	4	45	0	0.5	79.228	0.35618	0
127	TEST	LARGE	YES	164	70	15	68	0	0.5	117.242	0.63032	0
128	TEST	LARGE	YES	19	30	4	39	0	0.5	29.660	0.34882	0
129	TEST	LARGE	NO	53	60	12	66	0	0.5	89.717	0.32505	0
130	TEST	LARGE	NO	15	30	5	63	0	0.5	35.859	0.23740	0
131	TEST	LARGE	YES	43	60	11	49	0	0.5	77.443	0.30769	0
132	TEST	LARGE	YES	340	80	10	64	0	0.5	154.914	0.80147	0
133	TEST	LARGE	NO	133	75	1	65	0	0.5	140.716	0.47914	0
134	TEST	LARGE	NO	111	60	5	64	0	0.5	88.921	0.58532	0
135	TEST	LARGE	YES	231	70	18	67	0	0.5	116.365	0.76567	0
136	TEST	LARGE	NO	378	80	4	65	0	0.5	163.315	0.81951	0
137	TEST	LARGE	NO	49	30	3	37	0	0.5	30.629	0.68336	0

Example 3: Tobit Analysis

The data set below mimics the data used by Tobin and includes twenty observations with a response variable DURABLE, which is left-censored at zero, and two independent variables, AGE and LIQUTY.

The following statements produce **Output 21.3**:

```
title 'Estimation of Tobit Model for Durable Goods Expenditures';
data;
    input durable age liquty ǝǝ;
    if durable=0 then lower=.;
    else lower=durable;
    label durable='Durable Goods Purchase'
          age     ='Age in Years'
          liquty ='Liquidity Ratio Times 1000';
    cards;
0.0 57.7 236    0.0 59.8 216   10.4 46.8 207    0.0 39.9 219
0.7 50.9 283    0.0 44.3 284    0.0 58.0 249    0.0 33.4 240
0.0 48.5 207    3.7 45.1 221    0.0 58.9 246    3.5 48.1 266
0.0 41.7 220    0.0 51.7 275    0.0 40.0 277    6.1 46.1 214
0.0 47.7 238    3.0 50.0 269    1.5 34.1 231    0.0 53.1 251
;
proc lifereg;
    model (lower, durable)=age liquty / d=normal;
run;
```

Output 21.3   Tobit Analysis

```
              Estimation of Tobit Model for Durable Goods Expenditures                    1
                          L I F E R E G   P R O C E D U R E
      Data Set        =WORK.DATA7
      Dependent Variable=LOWER
      Dependent Variable=DURABLE     Durable Goods Purchase
      Noncensored Values=     7  Right Censored Values=       0
      Left Censored Values=  13  Interval Censored Values=    0
      Loglikelihood for NORMAL -28.92596097


         Variable  DF   Estimate  Std Err  ChiSquare  Pr>Chi Label/Value
         INTERCPT   1 15.2771204  16.03272  0.907964   0.3407 Intercept
         AGE        1 -0.1340075  0.218931  0.374664   0.5405 Age in Years
         LIQUTY     1 -0.0451356  0.058269  0.600026   0.4386 Liquidity Ratio Times 1000
         SCALE      1  5.56934983 1.728144                    Normal scale parameter
```

REFERENCES

Cox, D.R. (1972), "Regression Models and Life Tables (with discussion)," *Journal of the Royal Statistical Society*, Series B, 34, 187–220.

Cox, D.R. and Oakes, D. (1984), *Analysis of Survival Data*, London: Chapman and Hall.

Elandt-Johnson, R.C. and Johnson, N.L. (1980), *Survival Models and Data Analysis*, New York: John Wiley & Sons, Inc.

Gross, A.J. and Clark, V.A. (1975), *Survival Distributions: Reliability Applications in the Biomedical Sciences*, New York: John Wiley & Sons, Inc.

Kalbfleisch, J.D. and Prentice, R.L. (1980), *The Statistical Analysis of Failure Time Data*, New York: John Wiley & Sons, Inc.

Lawless, J.E. (1982), *Statistical Models and Methods for Lifetime Data*, New York: John Wiley & Sons, Inc.

Lee, E.T. (1980), *Statistical Methods for Survival Data Analysis*, Belmont, CA: Lifetime Learning Publications.

Maddala, G.S. (1983) *Limited-Dependent and Qualitative Variables in Econometrics*, New York: Cambridge University Press.

Rao, C.R. (1973), *Linear Statistical Inference and Its Applications*, New York: John Wiley & Sons, Inc.

Tobin, J. (1958), "Estimation of Relationships for Limited Dependent Variables," *Econometrica*, 26, 24–36.

Chapter 22
The NESTED Procedure

ABSTRACT

The NESTED procedure performs random effects analysis of variance and covariance for data from an experiment with a nested (hierarchical) structure.[1]

INTRODUCTION

A random effects model for data from a completely nested design with two factors has the following form:

$$y_{ijr} = \mu + \alpha_i + \beta_{ij} + \varepsilon_{ijr}$$

where

y_{ijr} is the value of the dependent variable observed at the rth replication with the first factor at its ith level and the second factor at its jth level.

μ is the overall (fixed) mean of the sampling population.

$\alpha_i, \beta_{ij}, \varepsilon_{ijr}$ are mutually uncorrelated random effects with zero means and respective variances σ_1^2, σ_2^2, and σ_ε^2 (the variance components).

This model is appropriate for an experiment with a multi-stage nested sampling design. An example of this is given in the **EXAMPLE** section, where four turnip plants were randomly chosen (the first factor), then three leaves were randomly chosen from each plant (the second factor nested within the first), and then two samples were taken from each leaf (the different replications at fixed levels of the two factors).

The NESTED procedure performs a computationally efficient analysis of variance and analysis of covariance for such data, estimating the different components of variance and also testing for their significance if the design is balanced (see **Unbalanced Data** later in this chapter). Although the ANOVA, GLM, and VARCOMP procedures provide similar analyses, PROC NESTED is both easier to use and more efficient for this special type of design. This is especially true when the design involves a large number of factors, levels, or observations. For example, to specify a four-factor completely nested design in GLM, ANOVA, or VARCOMP, you use the form

```
class a b c d;
model y=a b(a) c(a b) d(a b c);
```

However, to specify the same design in NESTED, you simply use the form

```
class a b c d;
var y;
```

In addition, the ANOVA and GLM procedures require TEST statements to perform appropriate tests, and the VARCOMP procedure requires the tests be performed by hand. PROC NESTED, however, makes one assumption about the input data that the other procedures do not. **The data set that PROC NESTED uses must first be sorted by the classification or CLASS variables defining the effects.** But as the data are usually stored in this order, this assumption is not often an inconvenient constraint.

SPECIFICATIONS

The NESTED procedure is specified by the following statements:

> **PROC NESTED** *options*;
> **CLASS** *variables*;
> **VAR** *variables*;
> **BY** *variables*;

The PROC NESTED and CLASS statements are required. The BY, CLASS, and VAR statements are described after the PROC NESTED statement.

PROC NESTED Statement

PROC NESTED *options*;

The following options can appear in the PROC NESTED statement:

AOV
:   prints only the analysis of variance statistics when there is more than one dependent variable. The analysis of covariance statistics are suppressed.

DATA=*SASdataset*
:   names the SAS data set to be used by PROC NESTED. If the DATA= option is omitted, the most recently created SAS data set is used.

BY Statement

> BY *variables*;

A BY statement can be used with PROC NESTED to obtain separate analyses of observations in groups defined by the BY variables. The input data set must be sorted in order of the BY variables.

Note that your data must be sorted first by the BY variables and then by the CLASS variables. If your data set is not sorted in ascending order, use the SORT procedure with a similar BY statement to sort the data, or, if appropriate, use the BY statement options NOTSORTED or DESCENDING. For more information, see the discussion of the BY statement in "SAS Statements Used in the PROC Step" in the *SAS Language Guide, Release 6.03 Edition*.

CLASS Statement

> CLASS *variables*;

A CLASS statement specifying the classification variables for the analysis must be included. **The data set must be sorted by the classification variables in the order that they are given in the CLASS statement.** Use PROC SORT to sort the data if they are not already sorted.

Values of a variable in the CLASS statement denote the levels of an effect. The name of that variable is also the name of the corresponding effect. The second effect is assumed to be nested within the first effect, the third effect is assumed to be nested within the second effect, and so on.

VAR Statement

> VAR *variables*;

The VAR statement lists the dependent variables for the analysis. The dependent variables must be numeric variables. If the VAR statement is omitted, NESTED performs an analysis of variance for all numeric variables in the data set, except those already specified in the CLASS statement.

DETAILS

Missing Values

An observation with missing values for any of the variables used by NESTED is omitted from the analysis. Blank values of character CLASS variables are treated as missing values.

Unbalanced Data

A completely nested design is defined to be unbalanced if the groups corresponding to the levels of some classification variable are not all of the same size. NESTED can compute unbiased estimates for the variance components in an unbalanced design, but because the sums of squares on which these estimates are based no longer have χ^2 distributions under a Gaussian model for the data, F tests for the significance of the variance components cannot be computed. NESTED checks to see that the design is balanced. If it is not, a warning is output to that effect, and the columns corresponding to the F tests in the analysis of variance are left blank.

General Random Effects Model

A random effects model for data from a completely nested design with n factors has the general form

$$y_{i_1 i_2 \ldots i_n r} = \mu + \alpha_{i_1} + \beta_{i_1 i_2} + \ldots + \varepsilon_{i_1 i_2 \ldots i_n r}$$

where

$y_{i_1 i_2 \ldots i_n r}$ is the value of the dependent variable observed at the rth replication with factor j at level i_j, for $j = 1, \ldots, n$.

μ is the overall (fixed) mean of the sampled population.

$\alpha_{i_1}, \beta_{i_1 i_2}, \ldots, \varepsilon_{i_1 i_2 \ldots i_n r}$
   are mutually uncorrelated random effects with zero means and respective variances $\sigma_1^2, \sigma_2^2, \ldots, \sigma_\varepsilon^2$.

Analysis of Covariance

When more than one dependent variable is specified, NESTED prints a descriptive analysis of the covariance between each pair of dependent variables in addition to a separate analysis of variance for each variable. The analysis of covariance is computed under the basic random effects model for each pair of dependent variables:

$$y_{i_1 i_2 \ldots i_n r} = \mu + \alpha_{i_1} + \beta_{i_1 i_2} + \ldots + \varepsilon_{i_1 i_2 \ldots i_n r}$$

$$y'_{i_1 i_2 \ldots i_n r} = \mu' + \alpha'_{i_1} + \beta'_{i_1 i_2} + \ldots + \varepsilon'_{i_1 i_2 \ldots i_n r}$$

where the notation is the same as that used in the general random effects model above. There is an additional assumption that all the random effects in the two models are mutually uncorrelated except for corresponding effects, for which

$$\text{Corr}\,(\alpha_{i_1}, \alpha'_{i_1}) = \rho_1$$

$$\text{Corr}\,(\beta_{i_1 i_2}, \beta'_{i_1 i_2}) = \rho_2$$

$$\vdots$$

$$\text{Corr}\,(\varepsilon_{i_1 i_2 \ldots i_n r}, \varepsilon'_{i_1 i_2 \ldots i_n r}) = \rho_\varepsilon \quad .$$

Error Terms in *F* Tests

Random effects ANOVAs are distinguished from fixed effects ANOVAs by which error mean squares are used as the denominator for F tests. Under a fixed effects model, there is only one true error term in the model, and the corresponding mean square is used as the denominator for all tests. This is how the usual analysis is computed in PROC ANOVA, for example. However, in a random effects model for a nested experiment, mean squares are compared sequentially. The correct denominator in the test for the first factor is the mean square due to the second factor; the correct denominator in the test for the second factor is the mean square due to the third; and so on. Only the mean square due to the last factor, the one at the bottom of the nesting order, should be compared to the error mean square.

Computational Method

The building blocks of the NESTED analysis are the sums of squares for the dependent variables for each classification variable within the factors that precede it in the model, corrected for the factors that follow it. For example, for a two-factor nested design, NESTED computes the following sums of squares:

Total SS	$\Sigma_{ijr}(y_{ijr}-y_{\bullet\bullet\bullet})^2$
SS for Factor 1	$\Sigma_i \ n_{i\bullet}(y_{i\bullet\bullet}/n_{i\bullet}-y_{\bullet\bullet\bullet}/n_{\bullet\bullet})^2$
SS for Factor 2	
within Factor 1	$\Sigma_{ij} \ n_{ij}(y_{ij\bullet}/n_{ij}-y_{i\bullet\bullet}/n_{i\bullet})^2$
Error SS	$\Sigma_{ijr}(y_{ijr}-y_{ij\bullet}/n_{ij})^2$

where y_{ijr} is the rth replication, n_{ij} is the number of replications at level i of the first factor and level j of the second, and a dot as a subscript indicates summation over the corresponding index. If there is more than one dependent variable, NESTED also computes the corresponding sums of crossproducts for each pair. The expected value of the sum of squares for a given classification factor is a linear combination of the variance components corresponding to this factor and to the factors that are nested within it, and for each factor, the coefficients of this linear combination are computed. (The efficiency of NESTED is partly due to the fact that these various sums can be accumulated with just one pass through the data, assuming that the data have been sorted by the classification variables.) Finally, estimates of the variance components are derived as the solution to the set of linear equations that arise from equating the mean squares to their expected values.

Printed Output

PROC NESTED prints the following items for each dependent variable:

1. Coefficients of Expected Mean Squares, the coefficients of the $n+1$ variance components making up the expected mean square. Denoting the element in the ith row and jth column of this matrix by C_{ij}, the expected value of the mean square due to the ith classification factor is

$$C_{i1}\sigma_1^2 + \ldots + C_{in}\sigma_n^2 + C_{i,n+1}\sigma_\varepsilon^2 \quad .$$

C_{ij} is always zero for $i>j$, and if the design is balanced, C_{ij} is equal to the common size of all classification groups of the jth factor for $i\leq j$. Finally, the mean square for error is always an unbiased estimate of σ_ε^2. In other words, $C_{n+1,n+1}=1$.

For every dependent variable, NESTED prints an analysis of variance table. Each table contains the following:

2. each Variance Source in the model (the different components of variance) and the total variance.
3. Degrees of Freedom for the corresponding sum of squares.
4. Sum of Squares for each classification factor. The sum of squares for a given classification factor is the sum of squares in the dependent variable within the factors that precede it in the model, corrected for the factors that follow it. (See **Computational Method** above.)
5. F Value for a factor, which is the ratio of its mean square to the appropriate error mean square. To test whether the associated variance

component is greater than zero under a Gaussian model for the data, the significance levels are in the column headed Pr > F.

6. the appropriate Error Term for an F test, which is the mean square due to the next classification factor in the nesting order. (See **Error Terms in F Tests** earlier in this chapter.)

7. Mean Square due to a factor, which is the corresponding sum of squares divided by the degrees of freedom.

8. estimates of the Variance Components. These are computed by equating the mean squares to their expected values and solving for the variance terms. (See **Computational Method** earlier in this chapter.)

9. Percent of Total, the proportion of variance due to each source. For the ith factor, the value is

$$100 \times \frac{\text{source variance component}}{\text{total variance component}}$$

10. Mean, the overall average of the dependent variable. This gives an unbiased estimate of the mean of the population. Its variance is estimated by a certain linear combination of the estimated variance components, which is identical to the mean square due to the first factor in the model divided by the total number of observations when the design is balanced.

If there is more than one dependent variable, then NESTED prints an analysis of covariance table for each pair of dependent variables (unless the AOV option is specified in the PROC NESTED statement). For each source of variation, this table includes the following:

11. Degrees of Freedom (not shown)
12. Sum of Products (not shown)
13. Mean Products (not shown)
14. Covariance Component, the estimate of the covariance component (not shown).

Items in the analysis of covariance table are computed analogously to their counterparts in the analysis of variance table. The analysis of covariance table also includes the following:

15. Variance Component Correlation for a given factor (not shown). This is an estimate of the correlation between corresponding effects due to this factor. This correlation is the ratio of the covariance component for this factor to the square root of the product of the variance components for the factor for the two different dependent variables. (See **Analysis of Covariance** earlier in this chapter.)

16. Mean Square Correlation for a given classification factor (not shown). This is the ratio of the Mean Products for this factor to the square root of the product of the Mean Squares for the factor for the two different dependent variables.

EXAMPLE

Variability of Calcium Concentration in Turnip Greens

In the following example from Snedecor and Cochran (1967), an experiment is conducted to determine the variability of calcium concentration in turnip greens. Four plants are selected at random; then three leaves are randomly selected from each plant. Two 100-mg samples are taken from each leaf. The amount of calcium is determined by microchemical methods.

Because the data are read in sorted order, it is not necessary to use PROC SORT on the class variables. LEAF is nested in PLANT; SAMPLE is nested in LEAF and is left for the residual term. All the effects are random effects. The following statements read the data and invoke PROC NESTED. These statements produce **Output 22.1**:

```
title 'CALCIUM CONCENTRATION IN TURNIP LEAVES -- NESTED RANDOM MODEL';
title2 'Snedecor and Cochran, STATISTICAL METHODS, 1967, p. 286';
data turnip;
   do plant=1 to 4;
      do leaf=1 to 3;
         do sample=1 to 2;
            input calcium @@;
            output;
            end;
         end;
      end;
   cards;
3.28 3.09 3.52 3.48 2.88 2.80
2.46 2.44 1.87 1.92 2.19 2.19
2.77 2.66 3.74 3.44 2.55 2.55
3.78 3.87 4.07 4.12 3.31 3.31
;
proc nested;
   classes plant leaf;
   var calcium;
run;
```

Output 22.1   Analysis of Calcium Concentration in Turnip Greens Using PROC NESTED

```
        CALCIUM CONCENTRATION IN TURNIP LEAVES -- NESTED RANDOM MODEL              1
           Snedecor and Cochran, STATISTICAL METHODS, 1967, p. 286
           ❶  Coefficients of Expected Mean Squares

              Source      PLANT        LEAF        ERROR

              PLANT         6           2            1
              LEAF          0           2            1
              ERROR         0           0            1
```

```
        CALCIUM CONCENTRATION IN TURNIP LEAVES -- NESTED RANDOM MODEL              2
           Snedecor and Cochran, STATISTICAL METHODS, 1967, p. 286

        Nested Random Effects Analysis of Variance for Variable CALCIUM
```

❷ Variance Source	❸ Degrees of Freedom	❹ Sum of Squares	❺ F Value	❺ Pr > F	❻ Error Term	❼ Mean Square	❽ Variance Component	❾ Percent of Total
TOTAL	23	10.270396				0.446539	0.532938	100.0000
PLANT	3	7.560346	7.66517	0.009725	LEAF	2.520115	0.365223	68.5302
LEAF	8	2.630200	49.4089	0.000000	ERROR	0.328775	0.161060	30.2212
ERROR	12	0.079850				0.006654	0.006654	1.2486

```
              ❿  Mean                          3.01208333
                 Standard error of mean        0.32404445
```

REFERENCES

Snedecor, G.W. and Cochran, W.G. (1967), *Statistical Methods*, 6th Edition, Ames, IA: Iowa State University Press.

Steel, R.G.D. and Torrie, J.H. (1980), *Principles and Procedures of Statistics*, New York: McGraw-Hill Book Co.

NOTE

1. PROC NESTED is modeled after the General Purpose Nested Analysis of Variance program of the Dairy Cattle Research Branch of the United States Department of Agriculture. That program was originally written by M.R. Swanson, Statistical Reporting Service, United States Department of Agriculture.

Chapter 23

The NLIN Procedure

ABSTRACT

The NLIN (NonLINear regression) procedure produces least-squares or weighted least-squares estimates of the parameters of a nonlinear model.

INTRODUCTION

PROC NLIN fits nonlinear regression models by least squares. Nonlinear models are more difficult to specify and estimate than linear models. Instead of simply listing regressor variables, you must write the regression expression, declare parameter names, guess starting values for them, and possibly specify derivatives of the model with respect to the parameters. Some models are difficult to fit, and there is no guarantee that the procedure will be able to fit the model successfully.

The NLIN procedure first examines the starting value specifications of the parameters. If a grid of values is specified, NLIN evaluates the residual sum of squares at each combination of values to determine the best set of values to start the iterative algorithm. Then NLIN uses one of these five iterative methods:

- steepest-descent or gradient method
- Newton method
- modified Gauss-Newton method
- Marquardt method
- multivariate secant or false position (DUD) method.

The Gauss-Newton and Marquardt iterative methods regress the residuals onto the partial derivatives of the model with respect to the parameters until the estimates converge. The Newton iterative method regresses the residuals onto a function of the first and second derivatives of the model with respect to the parameters until the estimates converge.

For each nonlinear model to be analyzed, you must specify the following:

- the names and starting values of the parameters to be estimated
- the model (using a single dependent variable)
- partial derivatives of the model with respect to each parameter (except for the DUD method)
- the second derivatives of the model with respect to each parameter (only for the Newton method).

You can also

- confine the estimation procedure to a certain range of values of the parameters by imposing bounds on the estimates
- specify convergence criteria in terms of SSE, the parameter estimates, or both
- produce new SAS data sets containing predicted values, residuals, parameter estimates and SSE at each iteration, the covariance matrix of parameter estimates, and other statistics
- define your own objective function to be minimized.

The NLIN procedure can be used for segmented models (see **Example 4**) or robust regression (see **Example 5**). It can also be used to compute maximum-likelihood estimates for certain models (see Jennrich and Moore 1975; Charnes, Frome, and Yu 1976).

SPECIFICATIONS

You can use the following statements to invoke PROC NLIN:

PROC NLIN *options;*
   MODEL *dependent = expression;*   } required statements
   PARAMETERS | PARMS *parameter = values . . . ;*

   other program statements
   BOUNDS *expressions . . . ;*
   BY *variables;*
   DER.parameter[.parameter] = expression;   } optional statements
   ID *variables;*
   OUTPUT OUT = *SASdataset keyword = names;*

A vertical bar (|) denotes a choice between two specifications. The *other program statements* are valid SAS expressions that usually appear in the DATA step. NLIN allows you to create new variables within the procedure and use them in the nonlinear analysis. NLIN automatically creates several variables that are also available for use in the analysis. See **Special Variables** in the **DETAILS** section for more information. The PROC NLIN, PARMS, and MODEL statements are required. The statements used in NLIN in addition to the PROC statement are the following (in alphabetical order):

BOUNDS	restrains the parameter estimates within specified bounds
BY	specifies variables to define subgroups for the analysis
DER	specifies the first and second partial derivatives
ID	specifies additional variables to add to the output data set
MODEL	defines the relationship between the dependent and independent variables
OUTPUT	creates an output data set containing statistics for each observation
PARMS	identifies parameters to be estimated and the starting values for each parameter

other program statements
          execute assignment statements, ARRAY statements, DO loops, program control statements, and create new variables.

PROC NLIN Statement

   PROC NLIN *options;*

The options below can appear in the PROC NLIN statement:

Data Set Options

DATA = *SASdataset*
   names the SAS data set containing the data to be analyzed by PROC NLIN. If the DATA = option is omitted, the most recently created SAS data set is used.

OUTEST = *SASdataset*
   names the SAS data set to contain the parameter estimates produced at each iteration by PROC NLIN. See **Output Data Sets** later in this chapter

for details. If you want to create a permanent SAS data set, you must specify a two-level name. See "SAS Files" in the *SAS Language Guide, Release 6.03 Edition* for more information on permanent SAS data sets.

Grid Search Option

BEST=*n*
requests that PROC NLIN print the residual sums of squares only for the best *n* combinations of possible starting values from the grid. When the BEST= option is not specified, NLIN prints the residual sum of squares for every combination of possible parameter starting values.

Option to Choose an Iteration Method

METHOD=GAUSS
METHOD=MARQUARDT
METHOD=NEWTON
METHOD=GRADIENT
METHOD=DUD
specifies the iterative method NLIN uses. If the METHOD= option is not specified and DER statements are present, METHOD=GAUSS is used. If the METHOD= option is not specified and DER statements are not present, METHOD=DUD is used. See **Computational Methods** in the **DETAILS** section for details.

Options to Control Step Size

NOHALVE
turns off the step-size search during iteration. This option is used with some types of weighted regression problems and is available only when SMETHOD=HALVE. See **Example 5** for an illustration.

RHO=*value*
specifies a value to use in controlling the step-size search. The default value for RHO is 0.1 except when METHOD=MARQUARDT, where it is 10. See **Computational Methods** for more details.

SMETHOD=HALVE
SMETHOD=GOLDEN
SMETHOD=ARMGOLD
SMETHOD=CUBIC
specifies the step-size search method NLIN uses. SMETHOD=HALVE is the default. See **Computational Methods** for details.

STEP=*i*
places a limit on the number of step-halvings. The default value of *i* is 20. The value of *i* must be a positive integer. The value specified in the STEP= option also becomes the initial value of the _HALVE_ special variable. Assigning _HALVE_ a value in a program statement overrides this initial value.

TAU=*value*
specifies a value to use in controlling the step-size search. The default value for TAU is 1 except when METHOD=MARQUARDT, where it is 0.01. See **Computational Methods** for more details.

Options to Specify Details of Iteration

G4

specifies that a g4 or Moore-Penrose inverse be used in parameter estimation.

G4SINGULAR

specifies that a g4 or Moore-Penrose inverse be used in parameter estimation if the Jacobian is (or becomes) of less than full rank.

SAVE

specifies that, when the iteration limit is exceeded, the parameter estimates from the final iteration are output to the OUTEST= data set. These parameter estimates are located in the observation with _NAME_=FINAL. If the SAVE option is not specified, the parameter estimates from the final iteration are not output to the data set.

SIGSQ=*value*

specifies a value to replace the mean square error for computing the standard errors of the estimates. The SIGSQ= option is used with maximum-likelihood estimation.

Tuning Options

CONVERGEOBJ=c
CONVERGE=c

specifies that the change in SSE is to be used as the convergence criterion. The iterations are said to have converged for CONVERGEOBJ=c if

$$(SSE^{i-1} - SSE^i) / (SSE^i + 10^{-6}) < c$$

where SSE^i is the SSE for the ith iteration. The default value of c is 10^{-8} The constant c should be a small positive number. See **Computational Methods** for more details.

CONVERGEPARM=c

specifies that the maximum change among parameter estimates be used as the convergence criterion. The iterations are said to have converged for CONVERGEPARM=c if

$$\max_j (| \beta_j^{i-1} - \beta_j^i |) / (| \beta_j^{i-1} |) < c$$

where β_j^i is the value of the jth parameter at the ith iteration.

The default convergence criterion for NLIN is SSE. If you specify CONVERGEOBJ=c, the specified c is used instead of the default of 10^{-8}. If you specify CONVERGEPARM=c, the maximum change in parameters is used as the convergence criterion (instead of SSE). If you specify both the CONVERGEOBJ= and CONVERGEPARM= options, NLIN continues to iterate until the decrease in SSE is sufficiently small (as determined by CONVERGEOBJ) and the maximum change among the parameters is sufficiently small (as determined by CONVERGEPARM).

Other tuning options are

EFORMAT

requests that NLIN print all numeric values in scientific E-notation. This is useful if your parameters have very different scales.

MAXITER=*i*

places a limit on the number of iterations NLIN performs before it gives up trying to converge. The *i* value must be a positive integer. The default is 50.

BOUNDS Statement

BOUNDS *expressions* . . . ;

The BOUNDS statement restrains the parameter estimates within specified bounds. In each BOUNDS statement, you can specify a series of bounds separated by commas. Each bound contains an *expression* consisting of a *parameter name*, an *inequality comparison operator*, and a *value*. In a single-bounded expression, these three elements follow one another in the order described. The following are examples of valid single-bounded expressions:

```
bounds a<=20;
bounds c>30;
```

Double-bounded expressions are also permitted. In these expressions, a *value* is followed by an *inequality comparison operator*, a *parameter name*, another *inequality comparison operator*, and a final *value*, for example,

```
bounds 0<=B<=10;
bounds 15<x1<=30;
```

If you need to restrict an expression involving several parameters, for example, A+B<1, you can reparameterize the model so that the expression becomes a parameter.

For more information on valid expressions, see "SAS Expressions" in the *SAS Language Guide*.

If the iteration procedure sticks at the boundary of a constrained parameter, the computational method sets that parameter at its boundary and then searches the subspace produced by the remaining parameters. If the procedure cannot perform another step in the iteration using only the remaining parameters, the procedure stops. If the procedure can perform another step in the iteration using only the remaining parameters, the procedure performs the step and then uses the entire space (defined by all parameters) to try to perform the next step in the iteration.

BY Statement

BY *variables*;

A BY statement can be used with PROC NLIN to obtain separate analyses on observations in groups defined by the BY variables. When a BY statement appears, the procedure expects the input data set to be sorted in order of the BY variables.

If your input data set is not sorted in ascending order, use the SORT procedure with a similar BY statement to sort the data, or, if appropriate, use the BY statement options NOTSORTED or DESCENDING. For more information, see the discussion of the BY statement in "SAS Statements Used in the PROC Step" in the *SAS Language Guide*.

DER Statements

> DER.*parameter*=*expression*;
> DER.*parameter*.*parameter*=*expression*;

The DER statement specifies first or second partial derivatives. Use the first form shown above to specify first partial derivatives, and use the second form to specify second partial derivatives.

For most of the computational methods, you must specify the first partial derivative for each parameter to be estimated. For the NEWTON method, you must specify each of the first and the second derivatives. The expression can be an algebraic representation of the partial derivative of the expression in the MODEL statement with respect to the parameter or parameters that appear in the left-hand side of the DER statement. Numerical derivatives can also be used. The expression in the DER statement must conform to the rules for a valid SAS expression and can include any quantities that the MODEL statement expression contains.

The set of statements below specifies that a model

$$Y = \beta_0(1 - e^{-\beta_1 x})$$

be fitted by the modified Gauss-Newton method, where observed values of the dependent and independent variables are contained in the SAS variables Y and X, respectively.

```
proc nlin;
   parms b0=0 to 10
         b1=.01 to .09 by .005;
   model y=b0*(1-exp(-b1*x));
   der.b0=1-exp(-b1*x);
   der.b1=b0*x*exp(-b1*x);
```

Replacing the last three statements above with the statements

```
temp=exp(-b1*x);
model y=b0*(1-temp);
der.b0=1-temp;
der.b1=b0*x*temp;
```

saves computer time, since the expression EXP(−B1*X) is evaluated only once per program execution rather than three times, as in the earlier example. Note the program statement

```
temp=exp(-b1*x);
```

in the example above. Program statements are discussed in **Other Program Statements with PROC NLIN** later in this chapter.

If necessary, numerical rather than analytical derivatives can be used (see **Example 3** later in this chapter).

To fit the model using the NEWTON method, use the following statements:

```
proc nlin method=newton;
   parms b0=0 to 10
         b1=.01 to .09 by .005;
   temp=exp(-b1*x);
   model y=b0*(1-temp);
   der.b0=1-temp;
   der.b1=b0*x*temp;
   der.b0.b0=0;
   der.b0.b1=x*temp;
   der.b1.b1=-der.b1*x;
```

Note that you do not need to specify both DER.B0.B1 and DER.B1.B0. If you do specify both, the procedure interprets this as a duplicate specification and uses whichever derivative was specified last.

ID Statement

ID *variables*;

The ID statement specifies additional variables to place in the output data set created by the OUTPUT statement. Any variable on the left-hand side of any assignment statement is eligible. Also, the special variables created by the procedure can be specified. Variables in the input data set do not need to be specified in the ID statement since they are automatically included in the output data set.

MODEL Statement

MODEL *dependent=expression*;

The MODEL statement defines the prediction equation by declaring the dependent variable and defining an expression that evaluates predicted values. The expression can be any valid SAS expression yielding a numeric result. The expression can include parameter names, variables in the data set, and variables created by program statements in the NLIN procedure. Any operators or functions that can be used in a DATA step can also be used in the MODEL statement.

A statement such as

```
model y=expression;
```

is translated into the form

```
model.y=expression;
```

using the compound variable name MODEL.Y to hold the predicted value. You can use this assignment as an alternative to the MODEL statement. Either a MODEL statement or an assignment to a compound variable such as MODEL.Y must appear.

OUTPUT Statement

```
OUTPUT OUT=SASdataset
    PREDICTED | P=name
    RESIDUAL | R=name
    L95M=name
    U95M=name
    L95=name
    U95=name
    STDI=name
    STDP=name
    STDR=name
    STUDENT=name
    PARMS=names
    SSE | ESS=name
    H=name
    WEIGHT=name;
```

The OUTPUT statement specifies an output data set to contain statistics calculated for each observation. For each statistic, specify the keyword, an equal sign, and a variable name for the statistic in the output data set. All of the names appearing in the OUTPUT statement must be valid SAS names, and none of the new variable names may match a variable already existing in the data set to which NLIN is applied.

If an observation includes a missing value for one of the independent variables, both the predicted value and the residual value are missing for that observation. If the iterations fail to converge, all the values of all the variables named in the OUTPUT statement are missing values.

The option below is given in the OUTPUT statement:

OUT=*SASdataset*

names the SAS data set to be created by PROC NLIN when an OUTPUT statement is included. The new data set includes all the variables in the data set to which NLIN is applied. Also included are any ID variables specified in the ID statement, plus new variables whose names are specified in the OUTPUT statement. If you want to create a permanent SAS data set, you must specify a two-level name. See "SAS Files" in the *SAS Language Guide* for more information on permanent SAS data sets.

The values below can be calculated and output to the new data set. However, with METHOD=DUD, the following statistics are not available: H, L95, L95M, STDP, STDR, STUDENT, U95, and U95M. These statistics are all calculated using the leverage, H, as defined below. For METHOD=DUD, the Jacobian is not available since no derivatives are specified with this method.

PREDICTED=*name*
P=*name*

names a variable in the output data set to contain the predicted values of the dependent variable.

RESIDUAL=*name*
R=*name*

names a variable in the output data set to contain the residuals (actual values minus predicted values).

L95M=*name*

names a variable to contain the lower bound of an approximate 95% confidence interval for the expected value (mean). See also U95M= below.

U95M=*name*

names a variable to contain the upper bound of an approximate 95% confidence interval for the expected value (mean). See also L95M= above.

L95=*name*

names a variable to contain the lower bound of an approximate 95% confidence interval for an individual prediction. This includes the variance of the error as well as the variance of the parameter estimates. See also U95= below.

U95=*name*

names a variable to contain the upper bound of an approximate 95% confidence interval for an individual prediction. See also L95= above.

STDI=*name*

names a variable to contain the standard error of the individual predicted value.

STDP=*name*

names a variable to contain the standard error of the mean predicted value.

STDR=*name*
names a variable to contain the standard error of the residual.

STUDENT=*name*
names a variable to contain the studentized residuals, which are residuals divided by their standard errors.

PARMS=*names*
names variables in the output data set to contain parameter estimates. These can be the same variable names as listed in the PARAMETERS statement; however, you can choose new names for the parameters identified in the sequence from the PARAMETERS statement. Note that for each of these new variables, the values are the same for every observation in the new data set.

SSE=*name*
ESS=*name*
names a variable to include in the new data set. The values for the variable are the residual sums of squares finally determined by the procedure. The values of the variable are the same for every observation in the new data set.

H=*name*
names a variable to contain the leverage, $x_i(\mathbf{X'X})^{-1}x_i'$, where $\mathbf{X}=\partial\mathbf{F}/\partial\boldsymbol{\beta}$ and x_i is the *i*th row of $\mathbf{X}$. If the _WEIGHT_ special variable is specified, the leverage is $w_i x_i(\mathbf{X'WX})^{-1}x_i'$.

WEIGHT=*name*
names a variable in the output data set that contains the _WEIGHT_ special variable.

PARAMETERS Statement

PARAMETERS *parameter*=*values* . . . ;
PARMS *parameter*=*values* . . . ;

A PARAMETERS (or PARMS) statement must follow the PROC NLIN statement. Several parameter names and values can appear. The parameter names must all be valid SAS names and must not duplicate the names of any variables in the data set to which the NLIN procedure is applied. Only one PARMS statement is allowed.

In each *parameter*=*values* specification, the parameter name identifies a parameter to be estimated, both in subsequent procedure statements and in NLIN's printed output. *Values* specify the possible starting values of the parameter.

Usually, only one value is specified for each parameter. If you specify several values for each parameter, NLIN evaluates the model at each point on the grid. The value specifications can take any of several forms:

m	a single value
*m*1, *m*2, . . . , *mn*	several values
m TO *n*	a sequence where *m* equals the starting value, *n* equals the ending value, and the increment equals 1.
m TO *n* BY *i*	a sequence where *m* equals the starting value, *n* equals the ending value, and the increment is *i*.
*m*1, *m*2 TO *m*3	mixed values and sequences.

This PARMS statement names five parameters and sets their possible starting values as shown:

```
parms  b0=0
       b1=4 to 8
       b2=0 to .6 by .2
       b3=1, 10, 100
       b4=0, .5, 1 to 4;
```

Possible starting values				
B0	B1	B2	B3	B4
0	4	0	1	0
	5	0.2	10	0.5
	6	0.4	100	1
	7	0.6		2
	8			3
				4

Residual sums of squares are calculated for each of the 1*5*4*3*6=360 combinations of possible starting values. (This can take a long time.)

See **Special Variables** in the **DETAILS** section for information on programming parameter starting values.

Other Program Statements with PROC NLIN

PROC NLIN is different from other SAS procedures in that many of the statements normally used only in a DATA step can also be used in NLIN. Several SAS program statements can be used after the PROC NLIN statement. These statements can appear anywhere in PROC NLIN, but new variables must be created before they appear in other statements. For example, the following statements are valid since they create the variable TEMP before they use it in the MODEL statement:

```
proc nlin;
   parms b0=0 to 2 by 0.5 b1=0.01 to 0.09 by 0.01;
   temp=exp(-b1*x);
   model y=b0*(1-temp);
```

The following statements are not valid:

```
proc nlin;
   parms b0=0 to 2 by 0.5 b1=0.01 to 0.09 by 0.01;
   model y=b0*(1-temp);
   temp=exp(-b1*x);
```

PROC NLIN can process assignment statements, explicitly or implicitly subscripted ARRAY statements, explicitly or implicitly subscripted array references, IF statements, SAS functions, and program control statements. You can use program statements to create new SAS variables for the duration of the procedure. These variables are not permanently included in the data set to which NLIN is applied. Program statements can include variables in the DATA= data set, parameter names, variables created by preceding program statements within NLIN, and special variables used by NLIN.

All of the following SAS program statements can be used in PROC NLIN:

- ARRAY
- assignment
- CALL
- DO
- iterative DO
- DO UNTIL
- DO WHILE
- END
- FILE
- GO TO
- IF-THEN/ELSE
- LINK-RETURN
- PUT (defaults to the log)
- RETAIN
- RETURN
- SELECT
- sum.

The statements described above can use the special variables created by NLIN. Consult **Special Variables** for more information on special variables.

DETAILS

Missing Values

If the value of any one of the SAS variables involved in the model is missing from an observation, that observation is omitted from the analysis. If only the value of the dependent variable is missing, that observation has a predicted value calculated for it when you use an OUTPUT statement and specify the PREDICTED= option.

If an observation includes a missing value for one of the independent variables, both the predicted value and the residual value are missing for that observation. If the iterations fail to converge, all the values of all the variables named in the OUTPUT statement are missing values.

Special Variables

Several special variables are created automatically and can be used in PROC NLIN program statements.

Special Variables Whose Values are Set by PROC NLIN

The values of the six special variables below are set by NLIN and should not be reset to a different value by programming statements:

ERROR   is set to 1 if a numerical error or invalid argument to a function occurs during the current execution of the program. It is reset to 0 before each new execution.

ITER   represents the current iteration number. The variable _ITER_ is set to −1 during the grid search phase. For METHOD=DUD, _ITER_ is set to very large negative numbers during the initialization phase.

MODEL   is set to 1 for passes through the data when only the predicted values are needed, not the derivatives. It is 0 when both predicted values and derivatives are needed. If your derivative calculations consume a lot of time, you can save resources by coding

```
if _model_ then return;
```

after your MODEL statement but before your derivative calculations.

_N_   indicates the number of times the NLIN step has been executed. It is never reset for successive passes through the data set.

OBS   indicates the observation number in the data set for the current program execution. It is reset to 1 to start each pass through the data set (unlike _N_).

SSE   has the error sum of squares of the last iteration. During the grid search phase, _SSE_ is set to 0. For iteration 0, _SSE_ is set to the SSE associated with the point chosen from the grid search.

Special Variables Used to Determine Convergence Criteria

The two special variables _HALVE_ and _LOSS_ can be used to determine convergence criteria:

HALVE   is a special variable that is checked to control step-halving during execution. The value of _HALVE_ is the maximum number of step-halvings that are done during an iteration before a nonconvergence message is printed and execution terminates. The value of _HALVE_ overrides the value of the STEP= option in the PROC NLIN statement.

LOSS   is used to determine the criterion function for convergence and step-shortening. PROC NLIN looks for the variable _LOSS_ in the program statements and, if it is defined, uses the (weighted) sum of this value instead of residual sum of squares to determine the criterion function for convergence and step-shortening. This feature is useful in certain types of maximum-likelihood estimation where the residual sum of squares is not the basic criterion.

Weighted Regression with the _WEIGHT_ Special Variable

To get weighted least-squares estimates of parameters, the _WEIGHT_ variable can be given a value in an assignment statement:

```
_weight_=expression;
```

When this statement is included, the expression on the right-hand side of the assignment statement is evaluated for each observation in the data set to be analyzed. The values obtained are taken as inverse elements of the diagonal variance-covariance matrix of the dependent variable.

When a variable name is given after the equal sign, the values of the variable are taken as the inverse elements of the variance-covariance matrix. The larger the _WEIGHT_ value, the more importance the observation is given.

If the _WEIGHT_= statement is not used, the default value of 1 is used, and regular least-squares estimates are obtained.

Example: Using Special Variables to Specify Starting Values

For the derivative methods (GAUSS, MARQUARDT, and GRADIENT), the parameter values in the procedure are updated after the first observation of iteration 0. If you want to supply starting parameter values in your program (rather than using the values in the PARMS statement), follow this example:

```
proc nlin;
   parms b0=1 b1=1;
   if _iter_=0 then if _obs_=1 then do;
      b0=b0start;
      b1=b1start;
      end;
   model y=expression;
   der.b0=expression;
   der.b1=expression;
```

where B0START and B1START are in the input data set or calculated with program statements.

Troubleshooting

This section describes a number of problems that can occur in your analysis with PROC NLIN.

Excessive Time

If you specify a grid of starting values that contains many points, the analysis may take excessive time since the procedure must go through the entire data set for each point on the grid.

The analysis may also take excessive time if your problem takes many iterations to converge since each iteration requires as much time as a linear regression with predicted values and residuals calculated.

Dependencies

The matrix of partial derivatives may be singular, possibly indicating an over-parameterized model. For example, if B0 starts at zero in the following model, the derivatives for B1 are all zero for the first iteration.

```
parms b0=0 b1=.022;
model pop=b0*exp(b1*(year-1790));
der.b0=exp(b1*(year-1790));
der.b1=(year-1790)*b0*exp(b1*(year-1790));
```

The first iteration changes a subset of the parameters; then the procedure can make progress in succeeding iterations. This singularity problem is local. The next example shows a global problem.

You may have a term B2 in the exponent that is nonidentifiable since it trades roles with B0.

```
parms b0=3.9 b1=.022 b2=0;
model pop=b0*exp(b1*(year-1790)+b2);
der.b0=exp(b1*(year-1790)+b2);
der.b1=(year-1790)*b0*exp(b1*(year-1790)+b2);
der.b2=b0*exp(b1*(year-1790)+b2);
```

Unable to Improve

The method may lead to steps that do not improve the estimates even after a series of step-halvings. If this happens, the procedure issues a message stating that it was unable to make further progress, but it then prints the warning message

```
PROC NLIN failed to converge
```

and prints out the results. This often means that you have not converged at all. You should check the derivatives very closely and check the sum-of-squares error surface before proceeding. If NLIN has not converged, try a different set of starting values, a different METHOD= specification, the G4 option, or a different model.

Divergence

The iterative process may diverge, resulting in overflows in computations. It is also possible that parameters will enter a space where arguments to such functions as LOG and SQRT become illegal. For example, consider the following model:

```
parms b=0;
model y=x / b;
```

Suppose that Y happens to be all zero and X is nonzero. There is no least-squares estimate for B since the SSE declines as B approaches infinity or minus infinity. The same model could be parameterized with no problem into Y=A*X.

If you actually run the model, the procedure claims to converge after awhile since, by default, it measures convergence with respect to changes in the sum-of-squares error rather than to the parameter estimates. If you have divergence problems, try reparameterizing, selecting different starting values, or including a BOUNDS statement.

Local Minimum

The program may converge nicely to a local rather than a global minimum. For example, consider the following model:

```
parms a=1 b=-1;
model y=(1-a*x)*(1-b*x);
der.a=-x*(1-b*x);
der.b=-x*(1-a*x);
```

Once a solution is found, an equivalent solution with the same SSE is to switch the values between A and B.

Discontinuities

The computational methods assume that the model is a continuous and smooth function of the parameters. If this is not true, the method does not work. For example, the following models do not work:

```
model y=a+int(b*x);
```

```
model y=a+b*x+4*(z>c);
```

Responding to Trouble

NLIN does not necessarily produce a good solution the first time. Much depends on specifying good initial values for the parameters. You can specify a grid of values in the PARMS statement to search for good starting values. While most practical models should give you no trouble, other models may require switching to a different iteration method or an inverse computation method. METHOD=MARQUARDT sometimes works when the default method (Gauss-Newton) does not work.

Computational Methods

For the system of equations represented by the nonlinear model

$$\mathbf{Y} = \mathbf{F}(\beta_0, \beta_1, \ldots, \beta_r, \mathbf{X}_1, \mathbf{X}_2, \ldots, \mathbf{X}_n) + \varepsilon = \mathbf{F}(\beta) + \varepsilon$$

where $\mathbf{X}$ is a matrix of the independent variables, β is a vector of the parameters, ε is the error vector, and $\mathbf{F}$ is a function of the independent variables and the parameters; there are two approaches to solving for the minimum. The first method is to minimize

$$L(\beta) = 0.5 \ (\mathbf{e}'\mathbf{e}) \quad \text{where } \mathbf{e} = \mathbf{Y} - \mathbf{F}(\beta) \quad .$$

The second method is to solve the nonlinear "normal" equations

$$\mathbf{X}'\mathbf{F}(\beta) = \mathbf{X}'\mathbf{e}$$

where

$$\mathbf{X} = \partial \mathbf{F} / \partial \beta \quad .$$

In the nonlinear situation, both $\mathbf{X}$ and $\mathbf{F}(\beta)$ are functions of β and a closed-form solution generally does not exist. Thus NLIN uses an iterative process: a starting value for β is chosen and continually improved until the error sum of squares $\varepsilon'\varepsilon$ (SSE) is minimized.

The iterative techniques NLIN uses are similar to a series of linear regressions involving the matrix $\mathbf{X}$ evaluated for the current values of β and $\mathbf{e}=\mathbf{Y}-\mathbf{F}(\beta)$, the residuals evaluated for the current values of β.

The iterative process begins at some point β_0. Then $\mathbf{X}$ and $\mathbf{Y}$ are used to compute a Δ such that

$$\text{SSE}(\beta_0 + k\Delta) < \text{SSE}(\beta_0) \quad .$$

The four methods differ in how Δ is computed to change the vector of parameters.

Steepest descent	$\Delta = \mathbf{X}'\mathbf{e}$
Gauss-Newton	$\Delta = (\mathbf{X}'\mathbf{X})^{-}\mathbf{X}'\mathbf{e}$
Newton	$\Delta = (\mathbf{G}^{-})\mathbf{X}'\mathbf{e}$
Marquardt	$\Delta = (\mathbf{X}'\mathbf{X} + \lambda\text{diag}\,(\mathbf{X}'\mathbf{X})^{-}\mathbf{X}'\mathbf{e}$

The default method used to compute $(\mathbf{X}'\mathbf{X})^{-}$ is the sweep operator producing a g2 inverse. In some cases it would be preferable to use a g4 or Moore-Penrose inverse. If the G4 option is specified in the PROC NLIN statement, a g4 inverse is used to calculate Δ on each iteration. If the G4SINGULAR option is specified, a g4 inverse is used to calculate Δ when $\mathbf{X}'\mathbf{X}$ is singular.

Steepest Descent (Gradient)

The steepest descent method is based on the gradient of $\varepsilon'\varepsilon$:

$$0.5 \, \partial\varepsilon'\varepsilon \, / \, \partial\beta = -\mathbf{XY} + \mathbf{XF}(\beta) = -\mathbf{X'e} \quad .$$

The quantity $-\mathbf{X'e}$ is the gradient along which $\varepsilon'\varepsilon$ increases. Thus $\Delta = \mathbf{X'e}$ is the direction of steepest descent.

Using the method of steepest descent, let

$$\beta_{i+1} = \beta_i + k\Delta$$

where the scalar k is chosen such that

$$\mathrm{SSE}(\beta_i + k\Delta) < \mathrm{SSE}(\beta_i) \quad .$$

Note: the steepest descent method may converge very slowly and is therefore not generally recommended. It is sometimes useful when the initial values are poor.

Newton

The Newton method uses the second derivatives and solves the equation

$$\Delta = \mathbf{G}^-\mathbf{X'e}$$

where

$$\mathbf{G} = (\mathbf{X'X}) + \Sigma H(\beta)\mathbf{e}$$

and $H(\beta)$ is the hessian of $\mathbf{e}$:

$$H_{ij}(\beta) = \partial^2 \mathbf{e} \, / \, \partial\beta_i\partial\beta_j \quad .$$

Gauss-Newton

The Gauss-Newton method uses the Taylor series

$$\mathbf{F}(\beta) = \mathbf{F}(\beta_0) + \mathbf{X}(\beta - \beta_0) + \ldots$$

where $\mathbf{X} = \partial\mathbf{F}/\partial\beta$ is evaluated at $\beta = \beta_0$.

Substituting the first two terms of this series into the normal equations

$$\mathbf{X'F}(\beta) = \mathbf{X'Y}$$

$$\mathbf{X'}(\mathbf{F}(\beta_0) + \mathbf{X}(\beta - \beta_0)) = \mathbf{X'Y}$$

$$\mathbf{X'F}(\beta_0)'\mathbf{X}(\beta - \beta_0)'\mathbf{Y}$$

$$(\mathbf{X'X})(\beta - \beta_0) = \mathbf{X'Y} - \mathbf{X'F}(\beta_0)$$

$$(\mathbf{X'X})\Delta = \mathbf{X'e}$$

and therefore

$$\Delta = (\mathbf{X'X})^-\mathbf{X'e} \quad .$$

Caution: if $X'X$ is singular or becomes singular, NLIN computes Δ using a generalized inverse for the iterations after singularity occurs. If $X'X$ is still singular for the last iteration, the solution should be examined.

Marquardt

The Marquardt updating formula is as follows:

$$\Delta = (X'X + \lambda \text{diag}(X'X))^{-1} X'e \ .$$

The Marquardt method is a compromise between Gauss-Newton and steepest descent (Marquardt 1963). As $\lambda \to 0$, the direction approaches Gauss-Newton. As $\lambda \to \infty$, the direction approaches steepest descent.

Marquardt's studies indicate that the average angle between Gauss-Newton and steepest descent directions is about $90°$. A choice of λ between 0 and infinity produces a compromise direction.

By default, PROC NLIN chooses $\lambda = 10^{-3}$ to start and computes a Δ. If $SSE(\beta_0 + \Delta) < SSE(\beta_0)$, then $\lambda = \lambda / 10$ for the next iteration. Each time $SSE(\beta_0 + \Delta) > SSE(\beta_0)$, then $\lambda = \lambda * 10$.

If G4 is specified in the PROC NLIN statement, λ is determined using the eigenvalues of $(X'X)$. If the smallest eigenvalue is less than 0.00001, λ is the absolute value of the smallest eigenvalue plus 0.00001. Otherwise, λ is zero. This method tries to pick the smallest value of λ such that $(X'X + \lambda \text{diag}(X'X))$ is positive definite. If TAU or RHO is specified, a step-size search is conducted.

If TAU or RHO is specifed but G4 is not, NLIN chooses $\lambda = TAU$ to start and computes a Δ. If $SSE(\beta_0 + \Delta) < SSE(\beta_0)$, then $\lambda = \lambda / RHO$ for the next iteration. Each time $SSE(\beta + \Delta) > SSE(\beta_0)$, then $\lambda = \lambda * RHO$. In the Marquardt method, the default value for TAU is 0.01 and for RHO is 10.

Note: if the SSE decreases on each iteration, then $\lambda \to 0$, and you are essentially using Gauss-Newton. If SSE does not improve, then λ is increased until you are moving in the steepest descent direction.

Marquardt's method is equivalent to performing a series of ridge regressions and is useful when the parameter estimates are highly correlated or the objective function is not well approximated by a quadratic.

Secant Method (DUD)

The multivariate secant method is like Gauss-Newton, except that the derivatives are estimated from the history of iterations rather than supplied analytically. The method is also called the *method of false position* or the DUD method for Doesn't Use Derivatives (Ralston and Jennrich 1978). If only one parameter is being estimated, the derivative for iteration $i+1$ can be estimated from the previous two iterations:

$$der_{i+1} = (\hat{Y}_i - \hat{Y}_{i-1}) / (b_i - b_{i-1}) \ .$$

When k parameters are to be estimated, the method uses the last $k+1$ iterations to estimate the derivatives.

Step-Size Search

The default method of finding the step size k is step-halving using SMETHOD = HALVE. If $SSE(\beta_0 + \Delta) > SSE(\beta_0)$, compute $SSE(\beta_0 + 0.5\Delta)$, $SSE(\beta_0 + 0.25\Delta)$, . . . , until a smaller SSE is found.

If SMETHOD=GOLDEN is specified, the step size k is determined by a golden section search. The parameter TAU determines the length of the initial interval to be searched, with the interval having length TAU or 2*TAU, depending on $SSE(\beta_0 + \Delta)$. The RHO parameter specifies how fine the search is to be. The SSE at each endpoint of the interval is evaluated, and a new subinterval is chosen. The size of the interval is reduced until its length is less than RHO. One pass through the data is required each time the interval is reduced. Hence, if RHO is very small relative to TAU, a large amount of time can be spent determining a step size. For more information on the GOLDEN search, see Kennedy and Gentle (1980).

If SMETHOD=ARMGOLD is specified, the step size is determined by the Goldstein-Armijo method. This method attempts to avoid premature termination caused by small step sizes. The step size used is the first term of the sequence $k=1, 0.5, 0.25, \ldots$, that satisfies the following equation:

$$SSE(\beta^i + k\Delta) \le SSE(\beta^i) - \tau k X'e\Delta \qquad \tau \in (0, 0.5).$$

where τ is the default value of 0.5 or the specified TAU value. However, if you specify TAU>0.5, the default value of 0.5 is used instead.

If SMETHOD=CUBIC is specified, NLIN performs a cubic interpolation to estimate the step size. If the estimated step size does not result in a decrease in SSE, step-halving is used.

Output Data Sets

The data set produced by the OUTEST= option in the PROC NLIN statement contains the parameter estimates on each iteration including the grid search. The variable _ITER_ contains the iteration number. The variable _TYPE_ denotes whether the observation contains iteration parameter estimates ('ITER'), final parameter estimates ('FINAL'), or covariance estimates ('COVB'). For the DUD method, _TYPE_ is set to 'DUD' for iterations with _ITER_ set to a large negative number. The variable _NAME_ contains the parameter name for covariances, and the variable _SSE_ contains the objective function value for the parameter estimates.

The data set produced by the OUTPUT statement contains statistics calculated for each observation. In addition, the data set contains all the variables in the input data set and any ID variables that are specified in the ID statement.

Printed Output

In addition to the output data sets, NLIN also produces the items below:

1. the estimates of the parameters and the residual Sums of Squares determined in each iteration
2. a list of the residual Sums of Squares associated with all or some of the combinations of possible starting values of parameters

If the convergence criterion is met, NLIN prints

3. an analysis-of-variance table including as sources of variation Regression, Residual, Uncorrected Total, and Corrected Total
4. Parameter Estimates
5. an asymptotically valid standard error of the estimate, Asymptotic Std. Error
6. an Asymptotic 95% Confidence Interval for the estimate of the parameter
7. an Asymptotic Correlation Matrix of the parameters.

EXAMPLES

Example 1: Negative Exponential Growth Curve

This example demonstrates typical NLIN specifications for Marquardt's method and a grid of starting values. The predicted values and residuals are output for plotting. The following statements produce **Output 23.1**:

```
title 'NEGATIVE EXPONENTIAL: Y=B0*(1-EXP(-B1*X))';
data a;
   input x y aa;
   cards;
020 0.57 030 0.72 040 0.81 050 0.87 060 0.91 070 0.94
080 0.95 090 0.97 100 0.98 110 0.99 120 1.00 130 0.99
140 0.99 150 1.00 160 1.00 170 0.99 180 1.00 190 1.00
200 0.99 210 1.00
;
proc nlin best=10 method=marquardt;
   parms b0=0 to 2 by .5  b1=.01 to .09 by .01;
   model y=b0*(1-exp(-b1*x));
   der.b0=1-exp(-b1*x);
   der.b1=b0*x*exp(-b1*x);
   output out=b p=yhat r=yresid;
proc plot data=b;
   plot y*x='a' yhat*x='p' / overlay vpos=25;
   plot yresid*x / vref=0 vpos=25;
run;
```

Output 23.1 Negative Exponential Growth Function: PROC NLIN METHOD=MARQUARDT and PROC PLOT

```
                          NEGATIVE EXPONENTIAL: Y=B0*(1-EXP(-B1*X))                                    1

              Non-Linear Least Squares Grid Search     Dependent Variable Y   ❷
                                  B0               B1 Sum of Squares
                            1.000000         0.040000       0.001404
                            1.000000         0.050000       0.016811
                            1.000000         0.060000       0.055155
                            1.000000         0.030000       0.066571
                            1.000000         0.070000       0.097284
                            1.000000         0.080000       0.136536
                            1.000000         0.090000       0.170839
                            1.000000         0.020000       0.419285
                            1.500000         0.010000       0.975724
                            1.000000         0.010000       2.165290


              Non-Linear Least Squares Iterative Phase   Dependent Variable Y      Method: Marquardt
                            Iter        B0               B1 Sum of Squares
              ❶               0    1.000000         0.040000       0.001404
                              1    0.996139         0.041857       0.000580
                              2    0.996192         0.041952       0.000577
                              3    0.996189         0.041954       0.000577
                              4    0.996189         0.041954       0.000577

NOTE: Convergence criterion met.
```

(continued on next page)

(continued from previous page)

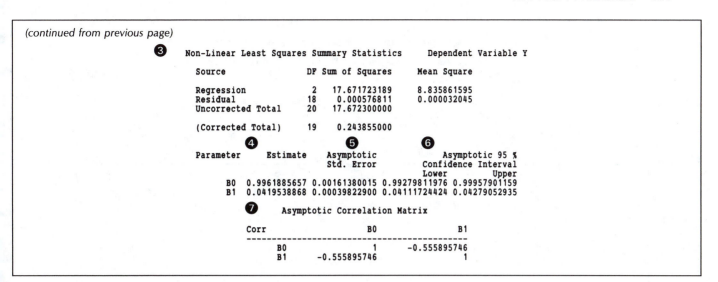

❸ Non-Linear Least Squares Summary Statistics   Dependent Variable Y

Source	DF	Sum of Squares	Mean Square
Regression	2	17.671723189	8.835861595
Residual	18	0.000576811	0.000032045
Uncorrected Total	20	17.672300000	
(Corrected Total)	19	0.243855000	

Parameter	**❹** Estimate	**❺** Asymptotic Std. Error	**❻** Asymptotic 95 % Confidence Interval Lower	Upper
B0	0.9961885657	0.00161380015	0.99279811976	0.99957901159
B1	0.0419538868	0.00039822900	0.04111724424	0.04279052935

❼   Asymptotic Correlation Matrix

Corr	B0	B1
B0	1	-0.555895746
B1	-0.555895746	1

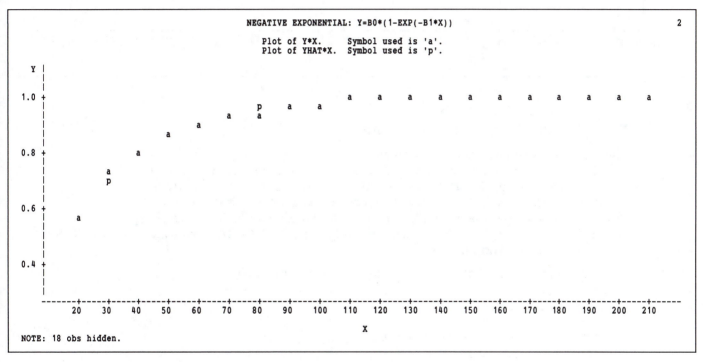

NEGATIVE EXPONENTIAL: Y=B0*(1-EXP(-B1*X))   2

Plot of Y*X.   Symbol used is 'a'.
Plot of YHAT*X.   Symbol used is 'p'.

NOTE: 18 obs hidden.

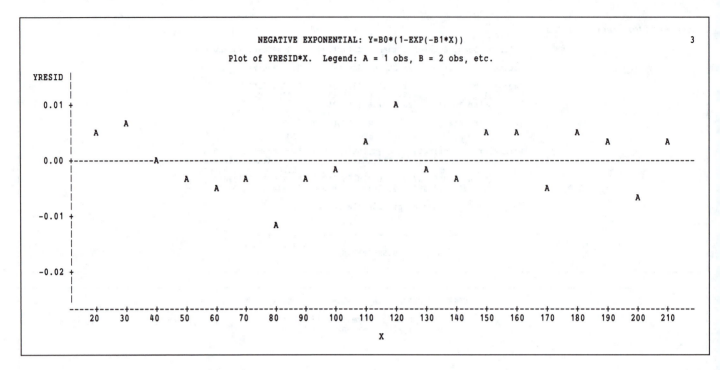

Example 2: CES Production Function

The CES production function in economics models the quantity produced as a function of inputs such as capital, K, and labor, L. Arrow, Chenery, Minhas, and Solow developed the CES production function and named it for its property of constant elasticity of substitution. A is the efficiency parameter, D is the distribution or factor share parameter, and R is the substitution parameter. This example was described by Lutkepohl in the work by Judge et al. (1980). The following statements produce **Output 23.2**:

```
title 'CES MODEL: LOGQ = B0 + A*LOG(D*L**R+(1-D)*K**R)';
data ces;
   input l k logq @@;
   cards;
.228 .802 -1.359  .258 .249 -1.695
.821 .771   .193  .767 .511  -.649
.495 .758  -.165  .487 .425  -.270
.678 .452  -.473  .748 .817   .031
.727 .845  -.563  .695 .958  -.125
.458 .084 -2.218  .981 .021 -3.633
.002 .295 -5.586  .429 .277  -.773
.231 .546 -1.315  .664 .129 -1.678
.631 .017 -3.879  .059 .906 -2.301
.811 .223 -1.377  .758 .145 -2.270
.050 .161 -2.539  .823 .006 -5.150
.483 .836  -.324  .682 .521  -.253
.116 .930 -1.530  .440 .495  -.614
.456 .185 -1.151  .342 .092 -2.089
.358 .485  -.951  .162 .934 -1.275
;
```

```
proc nlin data=ces;
    parms b0=1 a=-1 d=.5 r=-1;
    lr=l**r;
    kr=k**r;
    z=d*lr+(1-d)*kr;
    model logq=b0+a*log(z);
    der.b0=1;
    der.a =log(z);
    der.d =(a/z)*(lr-kr);
    der.r =(a/z)*(d*log(l)*lr+(1-d)*log(k)*kr);
run;
```

Output 23.2   CES Production Function: PROC NLIN

```
                    CES MODEL: LOGQ = B0 + A*LOG(D*L**R+(1-D)*K**R)                              1

          Non-Linear Least Squares Iterative Phase     Dependent Variable LOGQ     Method: Gauss-Newton
        Iter        B0              A                D              R Sum of Squares
          0     1.000000       -1.000000         0.500000      -1.000000    37.096512
          1     0.533488       -0.481091         0.450601      -1.499936    35.486564
          2     0.320516       -0.307656         0.383160      -2.309682    22.690597
          3     0.124790       -0.287428         0.301408      -3.418181     1.845468
          4     0.124044       -0.307921         0.317150      -3.204351     1.833362
          5     0.122933       -0.355632         0.349730      -2.800352     1.820337
          6     0.125085       -0.324295         0.330214      -3.089113     1.774004
          7     0.124011       -0.342505         0.340530      -2.951604     1.762108
          8     0.124713       -0.332754         0.334596      -3.038983     1.761177
          9     0.124346       -0.338244         0.337849      -2.993735     1.761057
         10     0.124563       -0.335197         0.336024      -3.020171     1.761043
         11     0.124446       -0.336890         0.337035      -3.005870     1.761040
         12     0.124512       -0.335947         0.336471      -3.013966     1.761040
         13     0.124476       -0.336471         0.336785      -3.009505     1.761039
         14     0.124496       -0.336179         0.336610      -3.012002     1.761039
         15     0.124485       -0.336341         0.336707      -3.010617     1.761039
NOTE: Convergence criterion met.

          Non-Linear Least Squares Summary Statistics     Dependent Variable LOGQ

              Source          DF Sum of Squares   Mean Square

              Regression       4   130.00369371    32.50092343
              Residual        26     1.76103929     0.06773228
              Uncorrected Total 30  131.76473300

              (Corrected Total) 29    61.28965430


          Parameter    Estimate     Asymptotic              Asymptotic 95 %
                                     Std. Error          Confidence Interval
                                                         Lower          Upper
              B0    0.124485105   0.0783429642  -0.0365498914   0.2855201005
              A    -0.336341238   0.2721800618  -0.8958109440   0.2231284680
              D     0.336707458   0.1360850556   0.0569828319   0.6164320846
              R    -3.010617415   2.3229032585  -7.7853756933   1.7641408635


                         Asymptotic Correlation Matrix

        Corr            B0              A                D              R
        -------------------------------------------------------------------------
          B0            1       0.2964899511   -0.176549933   -0.32669583
          A     0.2964899511          1        -0.783557332   -0.999129892
          D    -0.176549933   -0.783557332          1         0.7833628736
          R    -0.32669583    -0.999129892    0.7833628736          1
```

Example 3: Probit Model with Numerical Derivatives

This example fits the population of the United States across time to the inverse of the cumulative normal distribution function. Numerical derivatives are coded since the analytic derivatives are messy.

The C parameter is the upper population limit. The A and B parameters scale time. The following statements produce **Output 23.3**:

```
title 'U.S. POPULATION GROWTH';
title2 'PROBIT MODEL WITH NUMERICAL DERIVATIVES';
data uspop;
    input pop :6.3 @@;
    retain year 1780;
    year=year+10;
    yearsq=year*year;
    cards;
3929 5308 7239 9638 12866 17069 23191 31443 39818 50155
62947 75994 91972 105710 122775 131669 151325 179323 203211
;
proc nlin data=uspop;
    parms a=-2.4 b=.012 c=400;
    delta=.0001;
    x=year-1790;
    pophat=c*probnorm(a+b*x);
    model pop=pophat;
    der.a=(pophat-c*probnorm((a-delta)+b*x)) / delta;
    der.b=(pophat-c*probnorm(a+(b-delta)*x)) / delta;
    der.c=pophat / c;
    output out=p p=predict;
proc plot data=p;
    plot pop*year predict*year='p' / overlay vpos=30;
run;
```

Output 23.3   Probit Model with Numerical Derivatives: PROC NLIN

```
                              U.S. POPULATION GROWTH                                    1
                         PROBIT MODEL WITH NUMERICAL DERIVATIVES

   Non-Linear Least Squares Iterative Phase     Dependent Variable POP      Method: Gauss-Newton
           Iter          A              B              C Sum of Squares
            0       -2.400000       0.012000      400.000000      7174.590805
            1       -2.271908       0.012623      399.066499       209.327927
            2       -2.302425       0.012661      404.804742       177.392064
            3       -2.302788       0.012628      407.072751       177.370044
            4       -2.302819       0.012629      407.079801       177.369804
            5       -2.302818       0.012629      407.082668       177.369803
NOTE: Convergence criterion met.

           Non-Linear Least Squares Summary Statistics     Dependent Variable POP

           Source             DF Sum of Squares     Mean Square

           Regression          3  164227.89925     54742.63308
           Residual           16     177.36980        11.08561
           Uncorrected Total  19  164405.26906

           (Corrected Total)  18   71922.76175


           Parameter   Estimate    Asymptotic            Asymptotic 95 %
                                    Std. Error         Confidence Interval
                                                      Lower           Upper
               A      -2.3028183   0.032832711    -2.37242015    -2.23321637
               B       0.0126285   0.000956986     0.01059980     0.01465722
               C     407.0826677  61.784898470   276.10518493   538.06015048
```

(continued on next page)

(continued from previous page)

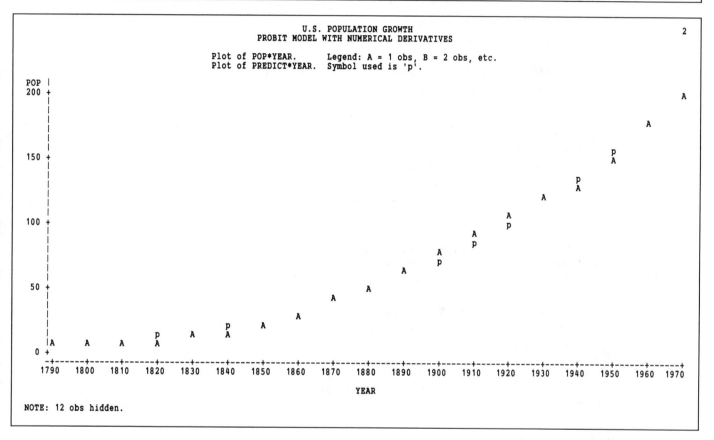

```
                          Asymptotic Correlation Matrix

      Corr                    A                B                C
      --------------------------------------------------------------------
           A            1         -0.007910181      -0.219797799
           B    -0.007910181            1           -0.972273297
           C    -0.219797799     -0.972273297             1
```

```
                          U.S. POPULATION GROWTH                              2
                    PROBIT MODEL WITH NUMERICAL DERIVATIVES

          Plot of POP*YEAR.      Legend: A = 1 obs, B = 2 obs, etc.
          Plot of PREDICT*YEAR.  Symbol used is 'p'.

  POP |
  200 +                                                                   A
      |
      |
      |                                                              A
      |
  150 +                                                         p
      |                                                         A
      |                                                    p
      |                                               A    A
      |                                          A    p
  100 +                                     A    p
      |                                A    p
      |                           A    p
      |                      A    p
      |                 A
   50 +            A
      |       A
      |  A
      |A    A    A    p    A    p
      |              A         A
    0 +A    A    A    A    A    A
      -+----+----+----+----+----+----+----+----+----+----+----+----+----+----+----+----+----+----+----+
      1790 1800 1810 1820 1830 1840 1850 1860 1870 1880 1890 1900 1910 1920 1930 1940 1950 1960 1970

                                         YEAR

  NOTE: 12 obs hidden.
```

Example 4: Segmented Model

From theoretical considerations you can hypothesize that

$$y = a + bx + cx^2 \quad \text{if } x < x_0$$

$$y = p \quad \text{if } x > x_0 \ .$$

That is, for values of x less than x_0, the equation relating y and x is quadratic (a parabola), and for values of x greater than x_0, the equation is constant (a horizontal line). PROC NLIN can fit such a segmented model even when the joint point, x_0, is unknown.

The curve must be continuous (the two sections must meet at x_0), and the curve must be smooth (the first derivatives with respect to x are the same at x_0).

These conditions imply that

$$x_0 = -b / 2c$$

$$p = a - b^2 / 4c \ .$$

The segmented equation includes only three parameters; however, the equation is nonlinear with respect to these parameters.

You can write program statements with PROC NLIN to conditionally execute different sections of code for the two parts of the model, depending on whether x is less than x_0.

A PUT statement is used to print the constrained parameters every time the program is executed for the first observation (where $x=1$). The following statements produce **Output 23.4**:

```
*---------FITTING A SEGMENTED MODEL USING NLIN-----*
|    |                                             |
|  Y | QUADRATIC          PLATEAU                   |
|    | Y=A+B*X+C*X*X      Y=P                       |
|    |                    ...................... |
|    |              .     :                        |
|    |            .       :                        |
|    |          .         :                        |
|    |         .          :                        |
|    |        .           :                        |
|    +-------------------------------------------X |
|                    X0                            |
|                                                  |
| CONTINUITY RESTRICTION: P=A+B*X0+C*X0**2         |
| SMOOTHNESS RESTRICTION: 0=B+2*C*X0 SO X0=-B/(2*C)|
*-------------------------------------------------*;

title 'QUADRATIC MODEL WITH PLATEAU';
data a;
   input y x @@;
   cards;
.46 1  .47  2 .57 3 .61  4 .62  5 .68  6 .69  7
.78 8  .70  9 .74 10 .77 11 .78 12 .74 13 .80 13
.80 15 .78 16
;
proc nlin;
   parms a=.45 b=.05 c=-.0025;
   file print;
   x0=-.5*b / c;                * ESTIMATE JOIN POINT;
   db=-.5 / c;                  * DERIV OF X0 WRT B;
   dc=.5*b / c**2;              * DERIV OF X0 WRT C;
   if x<x0 then do;             * QUADRATIC PART OF MODEL;
      model y=a+b*x+c*x*x;
      der.a=1;
      der.b=x;
      der.c=x*x;
      end;
   else do;                     * PLATEAU PART OF MODEL;
      model y=a+b*x0+c*x0*x0;
      der.a=1;
      der.b=x0+b*db+        2*c*x0*db;
      der.c=    b*dc+x0*x0+2*c*x0*dc;
      end;
```

```
        if _obs_=1 & _model_=1 then do; * PRINT OUT IF 1ST OBS;
           plateau=a+b*x0+c*x0*x0;
           put x0=plateau=;
           end;
        output out=b predicted=yp;
     proc plot;
        plot y*x yp*x='*' / overlay vpos=35;
     run;
```

Output 23.4   Segmented Model: PROC NLIN and PROC PLOT

```
                               QUADRATIC MODEL WITH PLATEAU                                        1
X0=10 PLATEAU=0.7

             Non-Linear Least Squares Iterative Phase    Dependent Variable Y    Method: Gauss-Newton
                Iter          A             B              C Sum of Squares
                   0       0.450000      0.050000      -0.002500       0.056231
X0=13.165937363 PLATEAU=0.793662174
                   1       0.388118      0.061605      -0.002340       0.011764
X0=12.822300972 PLATEAU=0.7780505759
                   2       0.393040      0.060053      -0.002342       0.010068
X0=12.755624517 PLATEAU=0.7775530672
                   3       0.392216      0.060418      -0.002368       0.010066
X0=12.74846438 PLATEAU=0.7775025883
                   4       0.392126      0.060459      -0.002371       0.010066
X0=12.74774162 PLATEAU=0.7774978936
                   5       0.392116      0.060463      -0.002372       0.010066
X0=12.747669162 PLATEAU=0.7774974276
                   6       0.392115      0.060463      -0.002372       0.010066
NOTE: Convergence criterion met.

                   Non-Linear Least Squares Summary Statistics      Dependent Variable Y

                   Source             DF Sum of Squares    Mean Square

                   Regression          3  7.7256340095    2.5752113365
                   Residual           13  0.0100659905    0.0007743070
                   Uncorrected Total  16  7.7357000000

                   (Corrected Total)  15  0.1869437500


                   Parameter    Estimate      Asymptotic              Asymptotic 95 %
                                             Std. Error          Confidence Interval
                                                                 Lower           Upper
                          A  0.3921153660  0.02667414696  0.33448940946  0.44974132253
                          B  0.0604631414  0.00842304248  0.04226627534  0.07866000749
                          C  -.0023715371  0.00055131779  -.00356258609  -.00118048817


                            Asymptotic Correlation Matrix

                   Corr            A              B              C
                   -------------------------------------------------------------
                          A         1        -0.90202496    0.8124326974
                          B   -0.90202496          1       -0.978795219
                          C   0.8124326974   -0.978795219         1
```

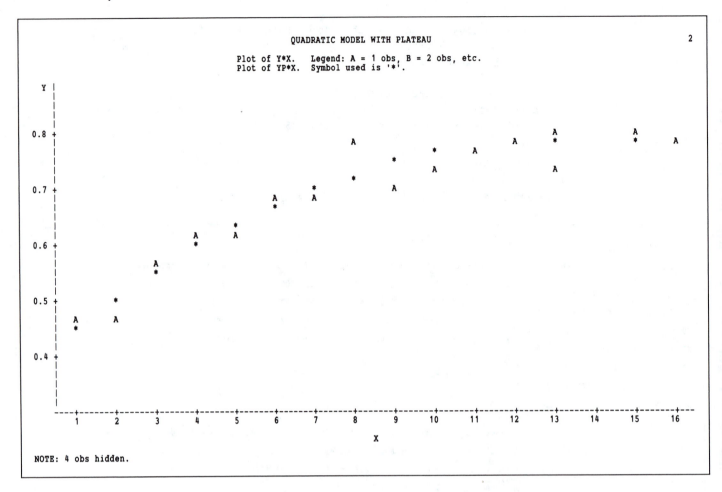

Example 5: Iteratively Reweighted Least Squares

The NLIN procedure is suited to methods that make the weight a function of the parameters in each iteration since the _WEIGHT_ variable can be computed with program statements. The NOHALVE option is used because the SSE definition is modified at each iteration and the step-shortening criteria is thus circumvented.

Iteratively reweighted least squares (IRLS) can produce estimates for many of the robust regression criteria suggested in the literature. These methods act like automatic outlier rejectors since large residual values lead to very small weights. Holland and Welsch (1977) outline several of these robust methods. For example, the biweight criterion suggested by Beaton and Tukey (1974) tries to minimize

$$S_{biweight} = \Sigma \, \rho(r)$$

where

$$\rho(r) = (B^2 / 2)(1 - (1 - (r / B)^2)^2) \quad \text{if } |r| \leq B$$

or

$$\rho(r) = (B^2 / 2) \quad \text{otherwise}$$

where

r is $|\text{residual}|/\sigma$.

σ is a measure of the scale of the error.

B   is a tuning constant (uses the example B=4.685).

The weighting function for the biweight is

$$w_i = (1 - (r_i / B)^2)^2 \quad \text{if } |r_i| \leq B$$

or

$$w_i = 0 \quad \text{if } |r_i| > B \quad .$$

The biweight estimator depends on both a measure of scale (like the standard deviation) and a tuning constant; results vary if these values are changed.

This example uses the same data as **Example 3** and produces **Output 23.5**:

```
*-----Beaton/Tukey Biweight by IRLS-----;
title 'TUKEY BIWEIGHT ROBUST REGRESSION USING IRLS';
proc nlin data=uspop nohalve;
    parms b0=20450.43 b1=-22.7806 b2=.0063456;
    model pop=b0+b1*year+b2*year*year;
    der.b0=1;
    der.b1=year;
    der.b2=year*year;
    resid=pop-model.pop;
    sigma=2;
    b=4.685;
    r=abs(resid / sigma);
    if r<=b then _weight_=(1-(r / b)**2)**2;
    else _weight_=0;
    output out=c r=rbi;
data c;
set c;
    sigma=2;
    b=4.685;
    r=abs(rbi / sigma);
    if r<=b then _weight_=(1-(r / b)**2)**2;
    else _weight_=0;
proc print;
run;
```

Output 23.5   Iteratively Reweighted Least Squares: PROC NLIN and
PROC PRINT

```
                           TUKEY BIWEIGHT ROBUST REGRESSION USING IRLS                          1

        Non-Linear Least Squares Iterative Phase    Dependent Variable POP    Method: Gauss-Newton
          Iter        B0              B1              B2          Weighted SS
            0    20450.430000    -22.780600        0.006346      57.264817
            1    20711.580896    -23.068940        0.006425      31.316348
            2    20889.771439    -23.263968        0.006478      19.794509
            3    20950.186053    -23.330292        0.006497      16.754875
            4    20966.814401    -23.348568        0.006502      16.057279
            5    20970.962721    -23.353129        0.006503      15.895348
            6    20971.960688    -23.354226        0.006503      15.857198
            7    20972.198207    -23.354487        0.006503      15.848167
            8    20972.254576    -23.354549        0.006503      15.846027
            9    20972.267943    -23.354563        0.006503      15.845520
           10    20972.271113    -23.354567        0.006503      15.845400
           11    20972.271864    -23.354568        0.006503      15.845371
           12    20972.272042    -23.354568        0.006503      15.845364
           13    20972.272084    -23.354568        0.006503      15.845363
           14    20972.272094    -23.354568        0.006503      15.845362
           15    20972.272097    -23.354568        0.006503      15.845362
NOTE: Convergence criterion met.

             Non-Linear Least Squares Summary Statistics    Dependent Variable POP

             Source              DF    Weighted SS      Weighted MS

             Regression           3    122571.96279     40857.32093
             Residual            16        15.84536         0.99034
             Uncorrected Total   19    122587.80815

             (Corrected Total)   18     59465.92678


             Parameter   Estimate     Asymptotic            Asymptotic 95 %
                                      Std. Error          Confidence Interval
                                                          Lower          Upper
                B0    20972.27210    309.61766746    20315.915225    21628.628969
                B1      -23.35457      0.32987833      -24.053875     -22.655261
                B2        0.00650      0.00008781        0.006317       0.006690


                              Asymptotic Correlation Matrix

             Corr                    B0              B1              B2
             ----------------------------------------------------------------
                B0              1      -0.999903521     0.9996131491
                B1      -0.999903521              1    -0.999902889
                B2       0.9996131491   -0.999902889              1
```

```
                           TUKEY BIWEIGHT ROBUST REGRESSION USING IRLS                          2

     OBS    POP      YEAR    YEARSQ      RBI       SIGMA     B        R       _WEIGHT_
      1     3.929    1790   3204100   -1.06728      2      4.685   0.53364   0.97422
      2     5.308    1800   3240000    0.38695      2      4.685   0.19347   0.99659
      3     7.239    1810   3276100    1.09250      2      4.685   0.54625   0.97300
      4     9.638    1820   3312400    0.96538      2      4.685   0.48269   0.97888
      5    12.866    1830   3348900    0.36659      2      4.685   0.18330   0.99694
      6    17.069    1840   3385600   -0.55787      2      4.685   0.27894   0.99292
      7    23.191    1850   3422500   -0.86400      2      4.685   0.43200   0.98307
      8    31.443    1860   3459600   -0.34080      2      4.685   0.17040   0.99736
      9    39.818    1870   3496900   -0.99528      2      4.685   0.49764   0.97756
     10    50.155    1880   3534400   -0.98842      2      4.685   0.49421   0.97787
     11    62.947    1890   3572100    0.17276      2      4.685   0.08638   0.99932
     12    75.994    1900   3610000    0.28827      2      4.685   0.14414   0.99811
     13    91.972    1910   3648100    2.03412      2      4.685   1.01706   0.90797
     14   105.710    1920   3686400    0.23929      2      4.685   0.11964   0.99870
     15   122.775    1930   3724900    0.47079      2      4.685   0.23539   0.99496
     16   131.669    1940   3763600   -8.76938      2      4.685   4.38469   0.01540
     17   151.325    1950   3802500   -8.54823      2      4.685   4.27411   0.02813
     18   179.323    1960   3841600   -1.28574      2      4.685   0.64287   0.96270
     19   203.211    1970   3880900    0.56608      2      4.685   0.28304   0.99271
```

The printout of the computed weights shows that the observations for 1940
and 1950 are highly discounted because of their large residuals.

The printout contains a note that missing values were propagated in thirty-two places. This happens when the last observation with a missing value for POP is handled. Since there are fifteen iterations plus an initial iteration and the program is executed twice for each iteration (for each observation), these propagations occurred thirty-two times.

Example 6: Maximum Likelihood for Binary Data

It is also possible to fit binary data models as described by Nelder and Wedderburn (1972). Maximum-likelihood estimates can be computed by iteratively reweighted least squares, where the weights are the reciprocals of the variances. In this case you maximize the binomial likelihood with a probit link function. The following statements produce **Output 23.6** and **23.7**:

```
%macro binomial(data=_last_,response=,number=,vars=);

/*-----------------------------------------------------------*/
/* Variable      Function                                    */
/* --------      --------                                    */
/*                                                           */
/* DATA          Input data set                             */
/* RESPONSE      Variable containing the number of respondents */
/* NUMBER        Variable containing the number in group    */
/* VARS          List of independent variables              */
/* P             Response prob as function of Z (=xb)        */
/* PHI           Derivative of p as a function of z and/or p */
/*                                                           */
/*-----------------------------------------------------------*/
/* response~bin(number,p)                                    */
/* e(response)=number*p                                      */
/* z=xb                                                      */
/* logit  link function  p=1/[1+exp[-z]]                     */
/* probit link function  p=probnorm[z]                       */
/* phi=derivative  p/wrt(z)                                  */
/* for logit  link phi=number*p*[1-p]                        */
/* for probit link phi=number*exp[-z*z/2]/sqrt(8*atan(1))    */
/* var(response)=number*p*(1-p)                              */
/* model response=number*p                                   */
/* _weight_=1/var(response)=1/(number*p*(1-p))               */
/* _loss_= (-response*log(p)-(number-response)*log(1-p))     */
/*               /_weight_                                    */
/* der.b=phi*der(z)/wrt(b)                                   */
/*                                                           */
/*-----------------------------------------------------------*/
   %let n=0;        /* SPLIT OUT INDIVIDUAL NAMES */
   %let old=;
   %do %while(%scan(&vars,&n+1)|=);
      %let n=%eval(&n+1);
      %let var&n=%scan(&vars,&n);
      %let old=&old _old&n;
      %end;

   /* DO MLE WITH NONLINEAR LEAST SQUARES */
```

```
proc nlin data=&data(rename=(
   %do i=1 %to &n;
      &&var&i=_old&i
   %end;));
   retain loglike 0;
   file print;

   /* START INITIAL VALUES AT ZERO */
   parms
      intercpt=0
      %do i=1 %to &n; &&var&i=0 %end; ;

   /* COMPUTE INNER PRODUCT */
   z=intercpt %do i=1 %to &n; + &&var&i*_old&i %end; ;

   /* MODEL RESPONSE PROBABILITY: CHANGE THIS FOR DIFFERENT MODEL */
   p=probnorm(z);      /*Probit regression*/
   *p=1/(1+exp(-z));   /*Logit  regression*/
   if _model_=1 then do;
      if _obs_=1 then do;
         put loglike=;
            loglike=0;
            end;
      loglike=loglike+&response*log(p)+(&number-&response)*log(1-p    );
      end;
   model &response=&number*p;
   _weight_=1/(&number*p*(1-p));
   _loss_=(-&response*log(p)-(&number-&response)*log(1-p))/_weight_;

   /* CHANGE THIS FOR DIFFERENT PROBABILITY MODEL */
   phi=&number*exp(-z*z/2)/sqrt(8*atan(1));  /* PROBIT REGRESSION */
   *phi=&number*p*(1-p);                     /* LOGIT  REGRESSION */
   der.intercpt=phi;
   %do i=1 %to &n;
      der.&&var&i=phi*_old&i;
      %end;
   %mend;

   /* RESPONSE DATA FROM FINNEY (1971, 104) */
data;
   input x n r group;
   g1=0; g2=0; g3=0; gx1=0; gx2=0; gx3=0;
   /* INDICATOR VARIABLES FOR GROUP */
   if group=1 then do;
      g1=1; gx1=x;
      end;
   else if group=2 then do;
      g2=1; gx2=x;
      end;
   else if group=3 then do;
      g3=1; gx3=x;
      end;
   cards;
.18 103 19 1
.48 120 53 1
```

```
.78 123 83 1
.18  60 14 2
.48 110 54 2
.78 100 81 2
-.12  90 31 3
.18  80 54 3
.48  90 80 3
.70  60 13 4
.88  85 27 4
1.0  60 32 4
1.18 90 55 4
1.30 60 44 4
;

title 'MLE ESTIMATES OF A PROBIT MODEL';
%binomial(response=r,number=n,vars=%str(g1 g2 g3 x gx1 gx2 gx3));
%binomial(data=data1,response=r,number=n,vars=%str(g1 g2 g3 x));
*--------------------Ingot Data----------------------------*
| Ingots are tested for readiness to roll after different  |
| treatments of heating time and soaking time.             |
| From Cox (1970, 67-68).                                  |
*----------------------------------------------------------* ;
data ingots;
   input heat soak nready ntotal @@;
   cards;
7 1.0  0 10    14 1.0  0 31    27 1.0  1 56    51 1.0  3 13
7 1.7  0 17    14 1.7  0 43    27 1.7  4 44    51 1.7  0  1
7 2.2  0  7    14 2.2  2 33    27 2.2  0 21    51 2.2  0  1
7 2.8  0 12    14 2.8  0 31    27 2.8  1 22
7 4.0  0  9    14 4.0  0 19    27 4.0  1 16    51 4.0  0  1
;
%binomial(response=nready,number=ntotal,vars=%str(heat soak));
run;
```

Output 23.6   Regression Analysis of Finney Data for Full Model: PROC NLIN and BINOMIAL Macro

```
                                   MLE ESTIMATES OF A PROBIT MODEL                                        1
LOGLIKE=0

                  Non-Linear Least Squares Iterative Phase     Dependent Variable R    Method: Gauss-Newton
   Iter    INTERCPT        G1              G2                  G3             X            GX1         GX2   Weighted loss
              GX3
     0        0            0               0                   0             0            0           0      853.264179
              0
LOGLIKE=-853.2641793
     1     -2.291055    1.143411        1.143308           2.219069      2.207843     -0.162484    0.228487  730.241254
           0.066690
LOGLIKE=-730.2412543
     2     -2.454065    1.192682        1.184646           2.390271      2.360510     -0.132282    0.341142  728.563960
           0.316393
LOGLIKE=-728.5639602
     3     -2.456342    1.191416        1.183428           2.393833      2.362557     -0.128990    0.347622  728.555294
           0.352295
```

(continued on next page)

(continued from previous page)

```
LOGLIKE=-728.5552941
     4      -2.456343      1.191396      1.183431      2.393848      2.362558      -0.128961      0.347643      728.555294
                0.352513
NOTE: Convergence criterion met.
```

Non-Linear Least Squares Summary Statistics   Dependent Variable R

Source	DF	Weighted SS	Weighted MS
Regression	8	2293.8098604	286.7262325
Residual	6	2.4899710	0.4149952
Uncorrected Total	14	2296.2998313	
(Corrected Total)	13	566.9510536	
Sum of Loss		728.5552938	

Parameter	Estimate	Asymptotic Std. Error	Asymptotic 95 % Confidence Interval Lower	Upper
INTERCPT	-2.456342881	0.23544554578	-3.0324577936	-1.8802279694
G1	1.191396006	0.26028055306	0.5545119761	1.8282800353
G2	1.183431127	0.27241817098	0.5168473950	1.8500148593
G3	2.393848179	0.24388724950	1.7970771473	2.9906192110
X	2.362557854	0.22607136385	1.8093807551	2.9157349524
GX1	-0.128960540	0.29959638837	-0.8620470222	0.6041259426
GX2	0.347642576	0.33301559124	-0.4672178091	1.1625029608
GX3	0.352512678	0.32697943346	-0.4475777498	1.1526031067

Asymptotic Correlation Matrix

Corr	INTERCPT	G1	G2	G3	X	GX1	GX2	GX3
INTERCPT	1	-0.9045837	-0.864279886	-0.965386859	-0.981826586	0.7408730014	0.6665239745	0.6788282465
G1	-0.9045837	1	0.7818134974	0.8732732172	0.8881443265	-0.924888007	-0.602926723	-0.614056967
G2	-0.864279886	0.7818134974	1	0.8343644446	0.8485729703	-0.640321633	-0.917003176	-0.5866976
G3	-0.965386859	0.8732732172	0.8343644446	1	0.9478424845	-0.71522906	-0.643453486	-0.746557653
X	-0.981826586	0.8881443265	0.8485729703	0.9478424845	1	-0.754586412	-0.6788612	-0.691393221
GX1	0.7408730014	-0.924888007	-0.640321633	-0.71522906	-0.754586412	1	0.5122594373	0.5217159305
GX2	0.6665239745	-0.602926723	-0.917003176	-0.643453486	-0.6788612	0.5122594373	1	0.4693600319
GX3	0.6788282465	-0.614056967	-0.5866976	-0.746557653	-0.691393221	0.5217159305	0.4693600319	1

Output 23.7   Regression Analysis of Finney Data for Restricted Model: PROC NLIN and BINOMIAL Macro

MLE ESTIMATES OF A PROBIT MODEL   2

```
LOGLIKE=0
```

	Non-Linear Least Squares Iterative Phase Dependent Variable R Method: Gauss-Newton					
Iter	INTERCPT	G1	G2	G3	X	Weighted loss
0	0	0	0	0	0	853.264179

```
LOGLIKE=-853.2641793
     1      -2.306052      1.070264      1.270400      2.243416      2.222591      730.788241
LOGLIKE=-730.7882414
     2      -2.561205      1.177738      1.413792      2.527750      2.465363      729.330438
LOGLIKE=-729.3304385
     3      -2.571850      1.182177      1.420036      2.541111      2.475476      729.327397
LOGLIKE=-729.3273974
     4      -2.571896      1.182203      1.420080      2.541202      2.475519      729.327397
NOTE: Convergence criterion met.
```

Non-Linear Least Squares Summary Statistics   Dependent Variable R

Source	DF	Weighted SS	Weighted MS
Regression	5	2197.9366418	439.5873284
Residual	9	4.0310449	0.4478939
Uncorrected Total	14	2201.9676867	
(Corrected Total)	13	547.1912375	
Sum of Loss		729.3273971	

(continued on next page)

(continued from previous page)

Parameter	Estimate	Asymptotic Std. Error	Asymptotic 95 % Confidence Interval Lower	Upper
INTERCPT	-2.571896252	0.12738015242	-2.8600526281	-2.2837398761
G1	1.182203043	0.08913326103	0.9805678823	1.3838382033
G2	1.420079950	0.09239180462	1.2110733893	1.6290865112
G3	2.541201896	0.12651919645	2.2549931541	2.8274106374
X	2.475519350	0.11589308720	2.2133487422	2.7376899582

Asymptotic Correlation Matrix

Corr	INTERCPT	G1	G2	G3	X
INTERCPT	1	-0.804451195	-0.774542435	-0.891373294	-0.930667693
G1	-0.804451195	1	0.6814039638	0.7282095963	0.6588340018
G2	-0.774542435	0.6814039638	1	0.701184132	0.6339464935
G3	-0.891373294	0.7282095963	0.701184132	1	0.8129698292
X	-0.930667693	0.6588340018	0.6339464935	0.8129698292	1

Output 23.8 Regression Analysis of Ingot Data: PROC NLIN and BINOMIAL Macro

MLE ESTIMATES OF A PROBIT MODEL   3

LOGLIKE=0

Non-Linear Least Squares Iterative Phase					
	Iter	INTERCPT	HEAT	SOAK	Weighted loss
	0	0	0	0	268.247959
LOGLIKE=-268.2479589					
	1	-1.353207	0.008697	0.002339	71.710426
LOGLIKE=-71.71042632					
	2	-2.053504	0.020274	0.007389	51.641219
LOGLIKE=-51.64121853					
	3	-2.581302	0.032626	0.018503	47.889468
LOGLIKE=-47.88946828					
	4	-2.838938	0.038763	0.030910	47.489236
LOGLIKE=-47.48923573					
	5	-2.890129	0.039889	0.035651	47.479967
LOGLIKE=-47.47996698					
	6	-2.893270	0.039953	0.036217	47.479945
LOGLIKE=-47.47994537					
	7	-2.893408	0.039955	0.036252	47.479945

NOTE: Convergence criterion met.

Non-Linear Least Squares Summary Statistics   Dependent Variable NREADY

Source	DF	Weighted SS	Weighted MS
Regression	3	13.011673421	4.337224474
Residual	16	13.850931733	0.865683233
Uncorrected Total	19	26.862605154	
(Corrected Total)	18	25.730010271	
Sum of Loss		47.479945327	

Parameter	Estimate	Asymptotic Std. Error	Asymptotic 95 % Confidence Interval Lower	Upper
INTERCPT	-2.893408210	0.46576916971	-3.8807898343	-1.9060265860
HEAT	0.039955339	0.01102232149	0.0165891777	0.0633215009
SOAK	0.036251825	0.13653295992	-0.2531836817	0.3256873321

Asymptotic Correlation Matrix

Corr	INTERCPT	HEAT	SOAK
INTERCPT	1	-0.795057798	-0.753827125
HEAT	-0.795057798	1	0.2959331155
SOAK	-0.753827125	0.2959331155	1

Example 7: Function Minimization

In some cases the NLIN procedure can be used to find the minimum of a function. The following example was taken from Kennedy and Gentle (1980). The use of arrays and METHOD=NEWTON is demonstrated. The following statements produce **Output 23.9**:

```
/*  10.6 OREN 1973                                        */
/* F(X)= sumi(sumj(((xj-1)*(xi-1))/(j+i+1))))            */
/* x=(1,1,1,1,....) x0(i)=4/i;                            */
/*                                                        */
/* minimize F(X)                                          */
/* taken from Kennedy and Gentle (1980)                   */


title 'Function Minimization Using Arrays and METHOD=NEWTON';
data oren;
   z=0;
run;


proc nlin method=newton g4 smethod=golden;
   parms x1=4 x2=2 x3=1.33333 x4=1;
   array x x1-x4;
   array dersum der.x1-der.x4;
   array der2 der.x1.x1
         der.x2.x1 der.x2.x2 der.x3.x1 der.x3.x2
         der.x3.x3 der.x4.x1 der.x4.x2 der.x4.x3 der.x4.x4;
   sum=0;
   ij=1;
   do i=1 to 4;
      dersum[i]=0;
         do j=1 to 4;
            sum=sum+((x[j]-1)*(x[i]-1)) / (j+i-1);
            dersum[i]=dersum[i]+(x[j]-1) / (j+i-1);
            end;
         dersum[i]=dersum[i]+(x[i]-1) / (i+i-1);
         do j=1 to i;
            if j<i then der2[ij]=1 / (i+j-1);
            else der2[ij]=2 / (i+i-1);
            ij=ij+1;
         end;
      end;
   model z=sum;
run;
```

Output 23.9   Function Minimization Using METHOD=NEWTON

```
                    Function Minimization Using Arrays and METHOD=NEWTON                    1

            Non-Linear Least Squares Iterative Phase    Dependent Variable Z    Method: Newton
        Iter        X1          X2              X3            X4  Sum of Squares
           0    4.000000    2.000000        1.333330      1.000000    173.946559
           1    0.986704    0.995568        0.998523      1.000000    0.0000000671
           2    1.000059    1.000020        1.000000      1.000000    2.5894167E-17
           3    1.000004    1.000001        0.999995      0.999991    2.4269235E-22
NOTE: Convergence criterion met.


              Non-Linear Least Squares Summary Statistics    Dependent Variable Z

              Source              DF  Sum of Squares    Mean Square

              Regression           4   -2.426923E-22    -6.067309E-23
              Residual            -3    2.4269235E-22              0
              Uncorrected Total    1               0

              (Corrected Total)    0               0


              Parameter     Estimate    Asymptotic              Asymptotic 95 %
                                        Std. Error         Confidence Interval
                                                          Lower         Upper
                    X1    1.000004386          0    1.0000043861  1.0000043861
                    X2    1.000000732          0    1.0000007318  1.0000007318
                    X3    0.999994647          0    0.9999946469  0.9999946469
                    X4    0.999991232          0    0.9999912319  0.9999912319


                            Asymptotic Correlation Matrix

      Corr              X1              X2              X3              X4
      ------------------------------------------------------------------------
            X1            1     -0.41981168    0.0854518691    0.3227266168
            X2  -0.41981168               1   -0.268808999    -0.250510084
            X3  0.0854518691   -0.268808999               1   -0.583127447
            X4  0.3227266168   -0.250510084   -0.583127447               1
```

REFERENCES

Bard, J. (1970), "Comparison of Gradient Methods for the Solution of the Nonlinear Parameter Estimation Problem," *SIAM Journal of Numerical Analysis*, 7, 157–186.

Bard, J. (1974), *Nonlinear Parameter Estimation*, New York: Academic Press, Inc.

Beaton, A.E. and Tukey, J.W. (1974), "The Fitting of Power Series, Meaning Polynomials, Illustrated on Band-Spectroscopic Data," *Technometrics*, 16, 147–185.

Charnes, A., Frome, E.L., and Yu, P.L. (1976). "The Equivalence of Generalized Least Squares and Maximum Likelihood Estimation in the Exponential Family," *Journal of the American Statistical Association*, 71, 169–172.

Cox, D.R. (1970), *Analysis of Binary Data*, London: Chapman and Hall.

Finney, D.J. (1971) *Probit Analysis*, 3d Edition, Cambridge: Cambridge University Press.

Gallant, A.R. (1975), "Nonlinear Regression," *American Statistician*, 29, 73–81.

Hartley, H.O. (1961), "The Modified Gauss-Newton Method for the Fitting of Non-Linear Regression Functions by Least Squares," *Technometrics*, 3, 269–280.

Holland, P.H. and Welsch, R.E. (1977), "Robust Regression Using Iteratively Reweighted Least-Squares," *Communications Statistics: Theory and Methods*, 6, 813–827.

Jennrich, R.I. (1969), "Asymptotic Properties of Nonlinear Least Squares Estimators," *Annals of Mathematical Statistics*, 40, 633–643.

Jennrich, R.I. and Moore, R.H. (1975), "Maximum Likelihood Estimation by Means of Nonlinear Least Squares," *American Statistical Association, 1975 Proceedings of the Statistical Computing Section*, 57–65.

Jennrich, R.I. and Sampson, P.F. (1968), "Application of Stepwise Regression to Non-Linear Estimation," *Technometrics*, 10, 63–72.

Judge, G.G., Griffiths, W.E., Hill, R.C., and Lee, Tsoung-Chao (1980), *The Theory and Practice of Econometrics*, New York: John Wiley & Sons, Inc.

Kennedy, W.J. and Gentle, J.E. (1980), *Statistical Computing*, New York: Marcel Dekker, Inc.

Marquardt, D.W. (1963), "An Algorithm for Least-Squares Estimation of Nonlinear Parameters," *Journal for the Society of Industrial and Applied Mathematics*, 11, 431–441.

Nelder, J.A. and Wedderburn, R.W.M. (1972), "Generalized Linear Models," *Journal of the Royal Statistical Society, Series A*, 135, 370–384.

Ralston, M.L. and Jennrich, R.I. (1978), "DUD, A Derivative-Free Algorithm for Nonlinear Least Squares," *Technometrics*, 20, 7–14.

Chapter 24

The NPAR1WAY
Procedure

ABSTRACT

The NPAR1WAY procedure performs analysis of variance on ranks, and it computes several statistics based on the empirical distribution function (EDF) and certain rank scores of a response variable across a one-way classification. NPAR1WAY is a nonparametric procedure for testing that the distribution of a variable has the same location parameter across different groups or, in the case of the EDF tests, that the distribution is the same across different groups.

INTRODUCTION

Most nonparametric tests are derived by examining the distribution of the rank scores of the response variable. The rank scores are simply functions of the ranks of the response variable, where the values are ranked from low to high.

NPAR1WAY calculates simple linear rank statistics based on Wilcoxon scores, median scores, Savage scores, and Van der Waerden scores. These statistics are used to test if the distribution of a variable has the same location parameter across different groups. These simple linear rank statistics computed by NPAR1WAY can also be computed by calculating the rank scores using PROC RANK and analyzing these rank scores with PROC ANOVA. **Table 24.1** shows the correspondence between NPAR1WAY Wilcoxon, Median, Van der Waerden, and Savage scores and various nonparametric tests.

Table 24.1   Comparison of NPAR1WAY with Nonparametric Tests

These NPAR1WAY scores . . .	correspond to these tests if data are classified in two levels, . . . *	correspond to these tests for a one-way layout or *k*-sample location test.**
Wilcoxon	Wilcoxon rank-sum test Mann-Whitney U test	Kruskal-Wallis test
Median	Median test for two samples	*k*-sample median test (Brown-Mood)
Van der Waerden	Van der Waerden test	*k*-sample Van der Waerden test
Savage	Savage test	*k*-sample Savage test

  * The tests are two-tailed. For a one-tailed test, transform the significance probability by $p/2$ or $(1-p/2)$.

  ** NPAR1WAY provides a chi-square approximate test.

In addition to the simple linear rank statistics discussed above, NPAR1WAY also calculates three statistics that are based on the empirical distribution of the sample. These are the Kolmogorov-Smirnov statistic, the Cramer-von Mises statistic, and, if there are only two levels of the classification variable, the Kuiper statistic. These statistics are used to test if the distribution of a variable is the same across different groups.

See **Simple Linear Rank Statistics** and **Statistics Based on the Empirical Distribution Function** in the **DETAILS** section for more information.

SPECIFICATIONS

The following statements are used in the NPAR1WAY procedure:

PROC NPAR1WAY *options*;
  CLASS *variable*;
  BY *variables*;
  VAR *variables*;

The CLASS statement is required. The BY, CLASS, and VAR statement descriptions follow the PROC NPAR1WAY statement description.

PROC NPAR1WAY Statement

PROC NPAR1WAY *options*;

The options below can be used in the PROC NPAR1WAY statement.

Data Set Options

DATA=*SASdataset*
   names the SAS data set containing the data to be analyzed. If the
   DATA= option is omitted, the most recently created SAS data set
   is used.

MISSING
   requests NPAR1WAY to interpret missing class values as nonmissing
   and to include them in calculations as valid class levels.

Options to Choose Analyses

These options can be specified in the PROC NPAR1WAY statement. If no options
are specified, then all six analyses are performed by default.

ANOVA
   requests a standard analysis of variance.

EDF
   requests that certain statistics based on the empirical distribution
   function be calculated. These always include the Kolmogorov-Smirnov
   and Cramer-von Mises statistics, and, if there are only two classification
   levels, the Kuiper statistic.

MEDIAN
   requests an analysis of the median scores. The median score is 1 for
   points above the median, 0 otherwise. For two samples, this produces a
   median test. For more than two samples, this is the Brown-Mood test.

SAVAGE
   requests that Savage scores be analyzed. These are the expected order
   statistics for the exponential distribution, with 1 subtracted to center the
   scores around 0. This test is appropriate for comparing groups of data
   with exponential distributions.

VW
   requests that Van der Waerden scores be analyzed. These are
   approximate normal scores derived by applying the inverse normal
   distribution function to the fractional ranks:

   $$\Phi^{-1}(R_i / (n + 1)) \quad .$$

   For two levels, this is the standard Van der Waerden test.

WILCOXON
   requests an analysis of the ranks of the data or the Wilcoxon scores.
   For two levels, this is the same as a Wilcoxon rank-sum test. For any
   number of levels, this is a Kruskal-Wallis test.

BY Statement

BY *variables*;

A BY statement can be used with PROC NPAR1WAY to obtain separate analyses
on observations in groups defined by the BY variables. When a BY statement

appears, the procedure expects the input data set to be sorted in order of the BY variables.

If your input data set is not sorted in ascending order, use the SORT procedure with a similar BY statement to sort the data, or, if appropriate, use the BY statement options NOTSORTED or DESCENDING. For more information, see the discussion of the BY statement in "SAS Statements Used in the PROC Step" in the *SAS Language Guide, Release 6.03 Edition.*

CLASS Statement

CLASS *variable;*

The CLASS statement, which is required, names one and only one classification variable.

VAR Statement

VAR *variables;*

The VAR statement names the response or dependent variables to be analyzed. If the VAR statement is omitted, all numeric variables in the data set are analyzed.

DETAILS

Missing Values

If an observation has a missing value for a response variable, that observation is excluded from the analysis. A missing value for the class variable is treated similarly unless the MISSING option is requested.

Limitations

The procedure must have

$$3 * n * (d + l) + nc * (d + l + 16 * c) + (nv + 2) * d$$

bytes of memory available to store the data. In the equation above,

d	is the number of bytes in a double-precision floating-point number.
l	is the number of bytes in a long integer.
c	is the number of bytes in a character.
n	is the number of nonmissing observations.
nc	is the number of nonempty classes.
nv	is the number of variables being processed for each BY group.

If the EDF option is requested, four temporary arrays, each of size $nc*d$ are allocated.

Resolution of Tied Values

Although the nonparametric tests were developed for continuous distributions, tied values do occur in practice. Ties are handled in all methods by assigning the average score for the different ranks corresponding to the tied values. Adjustments to variance estimates are performed in the manner described by Hajek

(1969, Chapter 7). Statistics based on the empirical distribution function are computed as usual from the definitions of the EDF. However, ties modify the exact distribution of the test statistics and may affect the quality of the large sample approximations of the probability values if they are numerous.

Simple Linear Rank Statistics

Statistics defined in the form

$$S = \Sigma_{j=1}^{n} \mathbf{c}_j a(R_j)$$

are called *simple linear rank statistics*, where

R_j is the rank of the *j*th observation.

$a(R_j)$ is the rank score.

$\mathbf{c}_j$ is an indicator vector denoting the class to which the *j*th observation belongs.

The NPAR1WAY procedure calculates simple linear rank statistics based on the following four scores.

Wilcoxon Scores

Wilcoxon scores are the ranks

$$a(R_j) = R_j$$

and are locally most powerful for location shifts of a logistic distribution.

Median Scores

Median scores are 1 for points above the median, 0 otherwise; that is,

$$
\begin{aligned}
a(R_j) &= 1 \quad \text{if } (R_j > (n + 1) / 2) \\
&= 0 \quad \text{if } (R_j \leq (n + 1) / 2) \quad .
\end{aligned}
$$

Median scores are locally most powerful for double exponential distributions.

Van der Waerden Scores

Van der Waerden scores are approximations of the expected values of the order statistics for a normal distribution

$$a(R_j) = \Phi^{-1}(R_j / (n + 1))$$

where Φ is the distribution function for the normal distribution. These scores are powerful for normal distributions.

Savage Scores

Savage scores are expected values of order statistics for the exponential distribution, with 1 subtracted to center the scores around 0:

$$a(R_j) = \Sigma_{i=1}^{R_j} 1 / (n - i + 1) - 1 \quad .$$

Savage scores are powerful for comparing scale differences in exponential distributions or location shifts in extreme value distributions (Hajek 1969, 83).

Statistics Based on the Empirical Distribution Function

The *empirical distribution function* (EDF) of a sample $\{x_j\}$, $j=1, 2, \ldots, n$, is defined as the following function:

$$F(x) = (1/n) \text{ (number of } x_j \leq x) = (1/n) \, \Sigma_{j=1}^n \, (x_j \leq x)$$

The NPAR1WAY procedure uses the subsample of values within the *i*th class level to generate an EDF, F_i. Let n_i be the number of values within the *i*th class level, and let n be the total number of values. Then the EDF for the pooled sample can also be written as

$$F = (1/n) \, \Sigma_i \, (n_i \, F_i) \quad .$$

The *k*-sample analogues of the Kolmogorov-Smirnov and Cramer-von Mises statistics used by NPAR1WAY are among those studied by Kiefer (1959).

Kolmogorov-Smirnov Statistic

As computed by NPAR1WAY, the Kolmogorov-Smirnov statistic is the value

$$KS = \max_j \sqrt{\Sigma_i \, (n_i \, / \, n)[F_i(x_j) - F(x_j)]^2} \quad \text{where } j = 1, 2, \ldots, n$$

which measures the maximum deviation of the EDF within the classes to the pooled EDF. The asymptotic statistic is

$$KSa = KS \sqrt{n}$$

The values of the F_i, the values $(F_i - F) \sqrt{n_i}$, the value of F at the maximum deviation, and the point where this maximum occurs are printed by NPAR1WAY, as well as the overall Kolmogorov statistic and the asymptotic statistic. If there are only two class levels, the two-sample Kolmogorov statistic

$$\max_j \, | \, F_1(x_j) - F_2(x_j) \, | \quad \text{where } j = 1, 2, \ldots, n$$

and the probability from the asymptotic distribution of observing a larger test statistic are also computed. The quality of this approximation has been studied by Hodges (1957).

Cramer-von Mises Statistic

The Cramer-von Mises statistic is defined as

$$\Sigma_i \, [(n_i/n^2) \, \Sigma_{j=1}^n \, (F_i(x_j) - F(x_j))^2]$$

which measures the integrated deviation of the EDF within the classes to the pooled EDF. The class-specific contributions to the sum are printed by the NPAR1WAY procedure together with the sum, which is the asymptotic value formed by multiplying the Cramer-von Mises statistic by the number of observations.

Kuiper Statistic

If there are only two class levels, the Kuiper statistic, a scaled value for the asymptotic distribution, and the probability from the asymptotic distribution of observing a larger test statistic, are also computed. In this case, the Kuiper statistic is computed as

$$K = \max_j (F_1(x_j) - F_2(x_j)) - \min_j (F_1(x_j) - F_2(x_j)) \quad \text{where } j = 1, 2, \ldots, n.$$

The asymptotic value is

$$Ka = K\sqrt{(n_1 n_2/n)} \quad .$$

Printed Output

If the ANOVA option is specified, NPAR1WAY prints the following:

1. the traditional Analysis of Variance table
2. the effect mean square reported as Among MS
3. the error mean square reported as Within MS.

(These are the same values that would result from using a procedure such as ANOVA or GLM.)

NPAR1WAY produces a table for each rank score and includes the following for each level in the classification:

4. the levels of the independent variable (the CLASS variable)
5. the number of observations in each level (N)
6. the Sum of Scores
7. the Expected sum of scores Under H0, the null hypothesis
8. the Std Dev Under H0, the standard deviation estimate of the sum of scores
9. the Mean Score.

For two or more levels, NPAR1WAY prints the following for each analysis of scores:

10. a chi-square statistic (CHISQ)
11. its degrees of freedom (DF)
12. Prob > CHISQ, the significance probability.

If there are only two levels, NPAR1WAY reports the following for each analysis of scores:

13. the sum of scores (S) corresponding to the smaller sample size
14. the ratio (S-expected)/(Std Dev) as Z, which is approximately normally distributed under the null hypothesis
15. Prob > |Z|, the probability of a greater observed Z value
16. T-Test approx., the significance level for the t test approximation.

NPAR1WAY produces a table for each statistic dependent on the empirical data function and includes the following for each level of classification:

17. the levels of the independent variable (the CLASS variable)
18. the number of observations in the level (N).

For the Kolmogorov-Smirnov statistic, the table includes

19. the EDF
20. the Deviation from Mean, that is, $(\sqrt{n_i})(F_i(x_j) - F(x_j))$
21. the total number of observations
22. the value F of the pooled EDF at the observation where the maximum occurs
23. the Kolmogorov-Smirnov statistic (KS), the value for the asymptotic distribution (KSa), where $KSa = KS\sqrt{n}$

24. if there are only two levels, the two-sample Kolmogorov statistic as D, where $D = \max_j | F_1(x_j) - F_2(x_j) |$.

For the Cramer-von Mises statistic, the table includes

25. the Summed Deviation from Mean $(n_i/n) \sum_{j=1}^{n} (F_i(x_j) - F(x_j))^2$
26. the Cramer-von Mises Statistic (CM) and the value for the asymptotic distribution (CMa), where $CMa = nCM$.

If there are only two classification levels, the table includes for the Kuiper statistic

27. Deviation from Mean, $\max_j(F_1(x_j) - F_2(x_j))$ and $\max_j(F_2(x_j) - F_1(x_j))$
28. the Kuiper 2-Sample Test statistic (K), the value for the asymptotic distribution (Ka), where $Ka = K\sqrt{(n_1 n_2/n)}$, and the probability of observing a larger Ka test statistic.

EXAMPLE

Weight Gains Data

The data are read in with a variable number of observations per record. In this example, NPAR1WAY first performs all six analyses on five levels of the class variable DOSE. Then the two lowest levels are output to a second data set to illustrate the two-sample tests. The following statements produce **Output 24.1**:

```
title 'Weight Gains with Gossypol Additive';
title3 'Halverson and Sherwood - 1932';
data g;
   input dose n;
   do i=1 to n;
      input gain @@;
      output;
      end;
   cards;
 0 16
   228 229 218 216 224 208 235 229 233 219 224 220 232 200 208 232
.04 11
   186 229 220 208 228 198 222 273 216 198 213
.07 12
   179 193 183 180 143 204 114 188 178 134 208 196
.10 17
   130  87 135 116 118 165 151  59 126  64  78  94 150 160 122 110 178
.13 11
   154 130 130 118 118 104 112 134  98 100 104
;
proc npar1way;
   class dose;
   var gain;
data g2;
   set g;
   if dose<=.04;
proc npar1way;
   class dose;
   var gain;
   title4 'Doses<=.04';
run;
```

Output 24.1   Two Separate Runs of PROC NPAR1WAY All CLASS Levels and
Two Levels Only

```
                      Weight Gains with Gossypol Additive                          1

                      Halverson and Sherwood - 1932

                      N P A R 1 W A Y   P R O C E D U R E

              ❶ Analysis of Variance for Variable GAIN
                   Classified by Variable DOSE
                                                      ❷              ❸
    DOSE          N            Mean              Among MS        Within MS
                                                  35020.7465      627.451597
    0            16       222.187500
    0.04         11       217.363636             F Value         Prob > F
    0.07         12       175.000000              55.814          0.0001
    0.1          17       120.176471
    0.13         11       118.363636
                   Average Scores were used for Ties
```

```
                      Weight Gains with Gossypol Additive                          2

                      Halverson and Sherwood - 1932

                      N P A R 1 W A Y   P R O C E D U R E

         Wilcoxon Scores (Rank Sums) for Variable GAIN
                   Classified by Variable DOSE
    ❹              ❺          ❻              ❼              ❽              ❾
                            Sum of        Expected        Std Dev         Mean
    DOSE           N        Scores        Under H0        Under H0        Score
    0            16       890.500000       544.0          67.9789655      55.6562500
    0.04         11       555.000000       374.0          59.0635883      50.4545455
    0.07         12       395.500000       408.0          61.1366221      32.9583333
    0.1          17       275.500000       578.0          69.3807412      16.2058824
    0.13         11       161.500000       374.0          59.0635883      14.6818182
                   Average Scores were used for Ties

         ❿ Kruskal-Wallis Test (Chi-Square Approximation)
            CHISQ= 52.666            ⓫ DF= 4        ⓬ Prob > CHISQ=    0.0001
```

```
                      Weight Gains with Gossypol Additive                          3

                      Halverson and Sherwood - 1932

                      N P A R 1 W A Y   P R O C E D U R E

         Median Scores (Number of Points above Median)
                     for Variable GAIN
                   Classified by Variable DOSE

                            Sum of        Expected        Std Dev         Mean
    DOSE           N        Scores        Under H0        Under H0        Score
    0            16        16.0           7.88059701      1.75790231      1.00000000
    0.04         11        11.0           5.41791045      1.52735508      1.00000000
    0.07         12         6.0           5.91044776      1.58096271      0.50000000
    0.1          17         0.0           8.37313433      1.79415153      0.00000000
    0.13         11         0.0           5.41791045      1.52735508      0.00000000
                   Average Scores were used for Ties
            Median 1-Way Analysis (Chi-Square Approximation)
            CHISQ= 54.176            DF= 4           Prob > CHISQ=    0.0001
```

Weight Gains with Gossypol Additive   4

Halverson and Sherwood - 1932

N P A R 1 W A Y   P R O C E D U R E

Van der Waerden Scores (Normal) for Variable GAIN
Classified by Variable DOSE

DOSE	N	Sum of Scores	Expected Under H0	Std Dev Under H0	Mean Score
0	16	16.1164737	0.0	3.32595675	1.00727961
0.04	11	8.3408986	0.0	2.88976066	0.75826351
0.07	12	-0.5766736	0.0	2.99118646	-0.04805613
0.1	17	-14.6889214	0.0	3.39454039	-0.86405420
0.13	11	-9.1917773	0.0	2.88976066	-0.83561612

Average Scores were used for Ties
Van der Waerden 1-Way (Chi-Square Approximation)
CHISQ= 47.297   DF= 4   Prob > CHISQ=   0.0001

Weight Gains with Gossypol Additive   5

Halverson and Sherwood - 1932

N P A R 1 W A Y   P R O C E D U R E

Savage Scores (Exponential) for Variable GAIN
Classified by Variable DOSE

DOSE	N	Sum of Scores	Expected Under H0	Std Dev Under H0	Mean Score
0	16	16.0743905	0.0	3.38527520	1.00464941
0.04	11	7.6930992	0.0	2.94129955	0.69937265
0.07	12	-3.5849578	0.0	3.04453428	-0.29874648
0.1	17	-11.9794882	0.0	3.45508203	-0.70467578
0.13	11	-8.2030437	0.0	2.94129955	-0.74573125

Average Scores were used for Ties
Savage 1-Way (Chi-Square Approximation)
CHISQ= 39.491   DF= 4   Prob > CHISQ=   0.0001

Weight Gains with Gossypol Additive   6

Halverson and Sherwood - 1932

N P A R 1 W A Y   P R O C E D U R E

Kolmogorov-Smirnov Test for Variable GAIN
Classified by Variable DOSE

⓱ DOSE	⓲ N	⓳ EDF at maximum	⓴ Deviation from Mean at maximum
0	16	0.0	-1.91044776
0.04	11	0.0	-1.58405960
0.07	12	0.3	-0.49979576
0.1	17	1.0	2.15386115
0.13	11	1.0	1.73256519
--------	㉑ 67	㉒ 0.5	------------

Maximum Deviation occurred at Observation   36
Value of GAIN   at maximum   178.000000

㉓ Kolmogorov-Smirnov Statistic (Asymptotic)
KS = 0.457928   KSa = 3.74830

```
                    Weight Gains with Gossypol Additive                        7

                      Halverson and Sherwood - 1932

                     N P A R 1 W A Y   P R O C E D U R E

                   Cramer-von Mises Test for Variable GAIN
                        Classified by Variable DOSE

                                                   25    Summed
                                                        Deviation
         DOSE                        N                   from Mean

         0                          16                 2.16521023
         0.04                       11                 0.91827966
         0.07                       12                 0.34822684
         0.1                        17                 1.49754164
         0.13                       11                 1.33574457


              26    Cramer-von Mises Statistic (Asymptotic)
                   CM = 0.093508          CMa  =  6.26500
```

```
                    Weight Gains with Gossypol Additive                        8

                      Halverson and Sherwood - 1932
                             Doses<=.04

                     N P A R 1 W A Y   P R O C E D U R E

                 Analysis of Variance for Variable GAIN
                      Classified by Variable DOSE

                                                    Among MS         Within MS
                                                    151.683712       271.479318
    DOSE          N            Mean
    0            16        222.187500                F Value          Prob > F
    0.04         11        217.363636                0.559            0.4617
                    Average Scores were used for Ties
```

```
                    Weight Gains with Gossypol Additive                        9

                      Halverson and Sherwood - 1932
                             Doses<=.04

                     N P A R 1 W A Y   P R O C E D U R E

                 Wilcoxon Scores (Rank Sums) for Variable GAIN
                        Classified by Variable DOSE

                         Sum of          Expected         Std Dev          Mean
    DOSE      N          Scores          Under H0         Under H0         Score

    0        16      253.500000            224.0        20.2215647     15.8437500
    0.04     11      124.500000            154.0        20.2215647     11.3181818
                       Average Scores were used for Ties
                   Wilcoxon 2-Sample Test (Normal Approximation)
                   (with Continuity Correction of .5)

        13  S= 124.500          14  Z= -1.43411          15  Prob > |Z| =   0.1515

        16  T-Test approx. Significance =    0.1635

                 Kruskal-Wallis Test (Chi-Square Approximation)
                 CHISQ=  2.1282            DF= 1             Prob > CHISQ=   0.1446
```

```
                    Weight Gains with Gossypol Additive                    10

                        Halverson and Sherwood - 1932
                                Doses<=.04

                        N P A R 1 W A Y   P R O C E D U R E

                 Median Scores (Number of Points above Median)
                            for Variable GAIN
                        Classified by Variable DOSE


                              Sum of        Expected        Std Dev          Mean
        DOSE        N         Scores        Under H0        Under H0         Score

        0          16          9.0         7.70370370      1.29999472     0.562500000
        0.04       11          4.0         5.29629630      1.29999472     0.363636364
                        Average Scores were used for Ties

                    Median 2-Sample Test (Normal Approximation)
                 S= 4.00000              Z= -.997155         Prob > |Z| =   0.3187

                    Median 1-Way Analysis (Chi-Square Approximation)
                 CHISQ= 0.99432           DF=  1             Prob > CHISQ=   0.3187
```

```
                    Weight Gains with Gossypol Additive                    11

                        Halverson and Sherwood - 1932
                                Doses<=.04

                        N P A R 1 W A Y   P R O C E D U R E

                 Van der Waerden Scores (Normal) for Variable GAIN
                        Classified by Variable DOSE


                              Sum of        Expected        Std Dev          Mean
        DOSE        N         Scores        Under H0        Under H0         Score

        0          16       3.34651962        0.0         2.32033631     0.209157476
        0.04       11      -3.34651962        0.0         2.32033631     -.304229056
                        Average Scores were used for Ties
                 Van der Waerden 2-Sample Test (Normal Approximation)
                 S= -3.34652             Z= -1.44226         Prob > |Z| =   0.1492

                    Van der Waerden 1-Way (Chi-Square Approximation)
                 CHISQ= 2.0801            DF=  1             Prob > CHISQ=   0.1492
```

```
                    Weight Gains with Gossypol Additive                    12

                        Halverson and Sherwood - 1932
                                Doses<=.04

                        N P A R 1 W A Y   P R O C E D U R E

                 Savage Scores (Exponential) for Variable GAIN
                        Classified by Variable DOSE

                              Sum of        Expected        Std Dev          Mean
        DOSE        N         Scores        Under H0        Under H0         Score

        0          16       1.83455386        0.0         2.40183886     0.114659616
        0.04       11      -1.83455386        0.0         2.40183886     -.166777623
                        Average Scores were used for Ties
                    Savage 2-Sample Test (Normal Approximation)
                 S= -1.83455             Z= -.763812         Prob > |Z| =   0.4450

                    Savage 1-Way (Chi-Square Approximation)
                 CHISQ= 0.58341           DF=  1             Prob > CHISQ=   0.4450
```

```
                    Weight Gains with Gossypol Additive                    13

                       Halverson and Sherwood - 1932
                              Doses<=.04

                      N P A R 1 W A Y   P R O C E D U R E

                  Kolmogorov-Smirnov Test for Variable GAIN
                        Classified by Variable DOSE


                                                                     Deviation
                                                    EDF               from Mean
        DOSE                        N           at maximum          at maximum

        0                            16                0.2          -.481481481
        0.04                         11                0.5           0.580688515
        --------                    ----        -----------
                                     27                0.4

                Maximum Deviation occurred at Observation     4
                Value of GAIN     at maximum   216.000000

                    Kolmogorov-Smirnov 2-Sample Test (Asymptotic)
                      KS = 0.145172             D = 0.295455       ㉔
                     KSa = 0.754337          Prob > KSa =   0.6199
```

```
                    Weight Gains with Gossypol Additive                    14

                       Halverson and Sherwood - 1932
                              Doses<=.04

                      N P A R 1 W A Y   P R O C E D U R E

                  Cramer-von Mises Test for Variable GAIN
                        Classified by Variable DOSE


                                                    Summed
                                                   Deviation
        DOSE                        N              from Mean

        0                            16           0.098638419
        0.04                         11           0.143474064


                Cramer-von Mises Statistic (Asymptotic)
                  CM = 0.008967            CMa = 0.242112
```

```
                    Weight Gains with Gossypol Additive                    15

                       Halverson and Sherwood - 1932
                              Doses<=.04

                      N P A R 1 W A Y   P R O C E D U R E

                  Kuiper Test for Variable GAIN
                        Classified by Variable DOSE

                                              ㉗ Deviation
        DOSE                        N           from Mean

        0                            16          0.090909091
        0.04                         11          0.295454545


                             Kuiper 2-Sample Test (Asymptotic)
      ㉘ K = 0.386364            Ka = 0.986440              Prob > Ka =   0.8383
```

REFERENCES

Conover, W.J. (1980), *Practical Nonparametric Statistics*, 2d Edition, New York: John Wiley & Sons, Inc.

Hajek, J. (1969), *A Course in Nonparametric Statistics*, San Francisco: Holden-Day.

Hodges, J.L. Jr. (1957),"The Significance Probability of the Smirnov Two-Sample Test," *Arkiv for Matematik*, 3, 469–486.

Kiefer, J. (1959), "K-Sample Analogues of the Kolmogorov-Smirnov and Cramer-von Mises Tests," *Annals of Mathematical Statistics*, 30, 420–447.

Lehmann, E.L. (1975), *Nonparametrics: Statistical Methods Based on Ranks*, San Francisco: Holden-Day.

Quade, D. (1966), "On Analysis of Variance for the *k*-Sample Problem," *Annals of Mathematical Statistics*, 37, 1747–1758.

Chapter 25

The ORTHOREG
Procedure

ABSTRACT

The ORTHOREG procedure performs regression using the Gentleman-Givens method. For ill-conditioned data, PROC ORTHOREG may produce noticeably more accurate estimates than other SAS procedures such as the REG and GLM procedures.

INTRODUCTION

The standard SAS regression procedures (REG and GLM) are very accurate for most problems. However, if you have very ill-conditioned data, the procedures can produce estimates that yield an error sum of squares very close to the minimum but still different from the exact least-squares estimates. Normally, this coincides with very high standard errors on the estimates. In other words, the numerical error is much smaller than the statistical standard error.

The ORTHOREG procedure can produce noticeably more accurate estimates than other regression procedures. Rather than collect crossproducts, ORTHOREG uses Gentleman-Givens transformations to collect and update a Cholesky root of the crossproducts, with special care for scaling (see Gentleman 1972a; 1972b). This method has the advantage over other special orthogonalization methods (for example, the QR method) of not requiring the data matrix to fit in memory.

SPECIFICATIONS

The following statements are used in PROC ORTHOREG:

PROC ORTHOREG *options*;
   MODEL *depvar=indepvars* / *modeloption*;
   WEIGHT *variable*;
   BY *variables*;

The PROC ORTHOREG and MODEL statements are required. The WEIGHT and BY statements are optional. The BY, MODEL, and WEIGHT statements are described after the PROC ORTHOREG statement.

PROC ORTHOREG Statement

   PROC ORTHOREG *options*;

The options in the PROC statement are

DATA=*SASdataset*
   specifies the input SAS data set to use. If the DATA= option is omitted, the most recently created SAS data set is used. The data set specified cannot be a TYPE=CORR, TYPE=COV, or TYPE=SSCP data set.

NOPRINT
   suppresses printing of the results.

OUTEST=*SASdataset*
   produces an output data set containing the parameter estimates, the BY variables, and the special variables _TYPE_ (value 'PARMS'), _NAME_ (blank), _RMSE_ (root mean squared error), and INTERCEP (intercept).

PRINT
   requests printing of the Cholesky root of the crossproducts matrix and its inverse.

BY Statement

   BY *variables*;

A BY statement can be used with PROC ORTHOREG to obtain separate analyses of observations in groups defined by the BY variables. When a BY statement appears, the procedure expects the input data set to be sorted in order of the BY variables.

   If your input data set is not sorted in ascending order, use the SORT procedure with a similar BY statement to sort the data, or, if appropriate, use the BY statement options NOTSORTED or DESCENDING. For more information, see the discussion of the BY statement in "SAS Statements Used in the PROC Step" in the *SAS Language Guide, Release 6.03 Edition*.

MODEL Statement

   MODEL *depvar=indepvars* / *modeloption*;

The MODEL statement names the dependent variable and the independent variables. The independent variables you specify in the MODEL statement must be variables in the data set being analyzed. In other words, independent variables of the form X1*X1 are not allowed. Only one MODEL statement is allowed. The following option can be used in the MODEL statement:

NOINT
   requests that no intercept term be included in the model.

WEIGHT Statement

WEIGHT *variable*;

A WEIGHT statement names a variable in the input data set whose values are relative weights for a weighted least-squares fit. If the weight value is proportional to the reciprocal of the variance for each observation, then the weighted estimates are the best linear unbiased estimates (BLUE). A more complete description of the WEIGHT statement can be found in the chapter on the GLM procedure.

DETAILS

Output Data Set

The OUTEST= option produces a TYPE=EST output SAS data set containing the BY variables, parameter estimates, and four special variables. For each BY group on the dependent variable, PROC ORTHOREG outputs an observation to the OUTEST= data set. The variables in the data set are as follows:

- parameter estimates for all variables listed in the MODEL statement
- the BY variables
- _TYPE_, a character variable with the value PARMS for every observation
- _NAME_, a character variable left blank for every observation
- _RMSE_, the root mean squared error, which is the estimate of the standard deviation of the true errors
- INTERCEP, the estimated intercept, unless the NOINT option is specified.

Printed Output

PROC ORTHOREG prints the parameter estimates and associated statistics. These include the following:

1. Sum of Squared Errors, the sum of squares for error in the model.
2. Degrees of Freedom associated with error.
3. Mean Squared Error is an estimate of σ^2, the variance of the true errors.
4. Root Mean Sqr Error is an estimate of the standard deviation of the true errors. It is calculated as the square root of the mean squared error.
5. R-square, a measure between 0 and 1 that indicates the portion of the total variation that is attributed to the fit.
6. Variables used as regressors, including the name INTERCEP, to identify the intercept parameter.
7. degrees of freedom (DF) for the variable. There is one degree of freedom unless the model is not full rank.
8. Parameter Estimate.
9. Std Error, the estimate of the standard deviation of the parameter estimate.
10. T-Ratio, the *t* test that the parameter is zero. This is computed as the parameter estimate divided by its standard error.
11. Prob>|t|, the probability that a *t* statistic would obtain a greater absolute value than that observed given that the true parameter is zero. This is the two-tailed significance probability.

EXAMPLES

The examples in this section apply both the ORTHOREG and GLM procedures to two sets of data noted for being ill-conditioned. (Portions of the printouts from GLM are not shown for the sake of brevity.) **The results from these examples will vary from machine to machine depending on floating-point configuration.** The particular results below were done on a Motorola 68881 floating-point processor.

Example 1: Longley Data

The first example is from Longley (1967). The estimates in the output compare very well with the best estimates available; for additional information, see Longley (1967) and also Beaton, Rubin, and Barone (1976). These statements produce **Output 25.1**:

```
data longley;
   input y x1 x2 x3 x4 x5 x6;
   cards;
60323  83.0 234289 2356 1590 107608 1947
61122  88.5 259426 2325 1456 108632 1948
60171  88.2 258054 3682 1616 109773 1949
61187  89.5 284599 3351 1650 110929 1950
63221  96.2 328975 2099 3099 112075 1951
63639  98.1 346999 1932 3594 113270 1952
64989  99.0 365385 1870 3547 115094 1953
63761 100.0 363112 3578 3350 116219 1954
66019 101.2 397469 2904 3048 117388 1955
67857 104.6 419180 2822 2857 118734 1956
68169 108.4 442769 2936 2798 120445 1957
66513 110.8 444546 4681 2637 121950 1958
68655 112.6 482704 3813 2552 123366 1959
69564 114.2 502601 3931 2514 125368 1960
69331 115.7 518173 4806 2572 127852 1961
70551 116.9 554894 4007 2827 130081 1962
;
proc orthoreg data=longley outest=longout;
   model y=x1-x6;
proc print data=longout;
   format _numeric_ 20.14;
proc glm data=longley;
   model y=x1-x6;
run;
```

Output 25.1   Results for Longley Example

```
                                        SAS                                               1

                          ORTHOREG Regression Procedure

Dependent Variable Y

Sum of Squared Errors 836424.05551
Degrees of Freedom                  9
Mean Squared Error     92936.006167
Root Mean Sqr Error     304.85407356
R-square                0.9954790046
```

(continued on next page)

(continued from previous page)

❻	❼	❽	❾	❿	⓫
Variable	DF	Parameter Estimate	Std Error	T-Ratio	Prob>|t|
INTERCEP	1	-3482258.63459581	890420.38361	-3.91	0.0036
X1	1	15.06187227137332	84.914925775	0.18	0.8631
X2	1	-0.03581917929259	0.0334910078	-1.07	0.3127
X3	1	-2.02022980381682	0.4883996817	-4.14	0.0025
X4	1	-1.03322686717359	0.2142741632	-4.82	0.0009
X5	1	-0.05110410565358	0.2260732001	-0.23	0.8262
X6	1	1829.15146461354	455.47849914	4.02	0.0030

```
                                        SAS
                                                                                        2
OBS    _TYPE_     _NAME_          _RMSE_             INTERCEP              X1               X2

 1     PARMS           304.85407356196400   -3482258.63459581000    15.06187227137320   -0.03581917929259

OBS           X3                  X4                  X5                  X6

 1    -2.02022980381682   -1.03322686717359   -0.05110410565358   1829.15146461354000
```

```
                                        SAS
                                                                                        3
                           General Linear Models Procedure

                           Number of observations in data set = 16
```

```
                                        SAS
                                                                                        4
                           General Linear Models Procedure
```

Dependent Variable: Y

Source	DF	Sum of Squares	Mean Square	F Value	Pr > F
Model	6	184172401.94450800	30695400.32408480	330.29	0.0001
Error	9	836424.05549113	92936.00616568		
Corrected Total	15	185008826.00000000			

	R-Square	C.V.	Root MSE		Y Mean
	0.995479	0.466730	304.85407356		65317.00000000

Source	DF	Type I SS	Mean Square	F Value	Pr > F
X1	1	174397449.77912500	174397449.77912500	1876.53	0.0001
X2	1	4787181.04445284	4787181.04445284	51.51	0.0001
X3	1	2263971.10981804	2263971.10981804	24.36	0.0008
X4	1	876397.16186042	876397.16186042	9.43	0.0133
X5	1	348589.39965127	348589.39965127	3.75	0.0848
X6	1	1498813.44960108	1498813.44960108	16.13	0.0030

Source	DF	Type III SS	Mean Square	F Value	Pr > F
X1	1	2923.97637581	2923.97637581	0.03	0.8631
X2	1	106306.25894371	106306.25894371	1.14	0.3127
X3	1	1590137.97175829	1590137.97175829	17.11	0.0025
X4	1	2160905.48182245	2160905.48182245	23.25	0.0009
X5	1	4748.94811877	4748.94811877	0.05	0.8262
X6	1	1498813.44960108	1498813.44960108	16.13	0.0030

Parameter	Estimate	T for H0: Parameter=0	Pr > |T|	Std Error of Estimate
INTERCEPT	-3482258.635	-3.91	0.0036	890420.38362
X1	15.062	0.18	0.8631	84.9149258
X2	-0.036	-1.07	0.3127	0.0334910
X3	-2.020	-4.14	0.0025	0.4883997
X4	-1.033	-4.82	0.0009	0.2142742
X5	-0.051	-0.23	0.8262	0.2260732
X6	1829.151	4.02	0.0030	455.4784991

Example 2: Wampler Data

This example is from Wampler (1970). For Y1, the true parameters are INTERCEP=−9999, X1=X2=X3=X4=X5=1, and Mean Squared Error=0. For Y2, the true parameters are INTERCEP=−999, X1=0.1, X2=0.01, X3=0.001, X4=0.0001, X5=0.00001, and Mean Squared Error=0. For Y3, the true parameters are INTERCEP=−9999, X1=X2=X3=X4=X5=1, and Mean Squared Error > 0. The ORTHOREG results are shown in **Output 25.2**, and the abbreviated GLM results are shown in **Output 25.3**.

```
data wampler;
   do x=0 to 20;
      input d @@;
      x1=x; x2=x*x; x3=x2*x; x4=x2*x2; x5=x3*x2;
      x1=x1+10000; x2=x2+10000; x3=x3+10000;
      x4=x4+10000; x5=x5+10000;
      y1=1+x+x2+x3+x4+x5;
      y2=1+.1*x+.01*x2+.001*x3+.0001*x4+.00001*x5;
      y3=y1+d; y4=y1+100*d; y5=y1+10000*d;
      output;
      end;
   cards;
759 -2048 2048 -2048 2523 -2048 2048 -2048 1838 -2048 2048
-2048 1838 -2048 2048 -2048 2523 -2048 2048 -2048 759
;
proc orthoreg data=wampler;
   model y1=x1 x2 x3 x4 x5;
proc orthoreg data=wampler;
   model y2=x1 x2 x3 x4 x5;
proc orthoreg data=wampler;
   model y3=x1 x2 x3 x4 x5;
proc glm data=wampler;
   model y1-y3 = x1-x5;
run;
```

Output 25.2   PROC ORTHOREG Results for Wampler Example

```
                                      SAS
                                                                              1
                          ORTHOREG Regression Procedure

         Dependent Variable Y1

         Sum of Squared Errors 1.671195E-19
         Degrees of Freedom            15
         Mean Squared Error     1.11413E-20
         Root Mean Sqr Error    1.055523E-10
         R-square                        1

Variable DF    Parameter Estimate    Std Error   T-Ratio Prob>|t|

INTERCEP  1    -9998.99999911426 7.6626468E-7   -9999.99   0.0001
X1        1     0.99999999987351 1.057047E-10    9999.99   0.0001
X2        1     1.00000000004521 3.485444E-11    9999.99   0.0001
X3        1     0.99999999999218 4.538271E-12    9999.99   0.0001
X4        1     1.00000000000054 2.524901E-13    9999.99   0.0001
X5        1     0.99999999999998 5.023485E-15    9999.99   0.0001
```

```
                                        SAS
                                                                                    2

                            ORTHOREG Regression Procedure

            Dependent Variable Y2

            Sum of Squared Errors  8.98666E-28
            Degrees of Freedom              15
            Mean Squared Error     5.991107E-29
            Root Mean Sqr Error    7.740224E-15
            R-square                         1

Variable DF    Parameter Estimate      Std Error    T-Ratio Prob>|t|

INTERCEP  1      -998.99999999999    5.61907E-11   -9999.99   0.0001
X1        1     0.09999999999999    7.751397E-15    9999.99   0.0001
X2        1                 0.01    2.5559E-15      9999.99   0.0001
X3        1     0.00099999999999    3.327945E-16    9999.99   0.0001
X4        1               0.0001    1.851527E-17    9999.99   0.0001
X5        1    9.9999999999998E-6   3.683755E-19    9999.99   0.0001
```

```
                                        SAS
                                                                                    3

                            ORTHOREG Regression Procedure

            Dependent Variable Y3

            Sum of Squared Errors       83554268
            Degrees of Freedom                15
            Mean Squared Error     5570284.5333
            Root Mean Sqr Error    2360.1450238
            R-square               0.999995559

Variable DF    Parameter Estimate      Std Error    T-Ratio Prob>|t|

INTERCEP  1    -9998.99999938427   17133638.649     -0.00    0.9995
X1        1     0.99999999991743   2363.5517347      0.00    0.9997
X2        1     1.00000000002504   779.34352433      0.00    0.9990
X3        1     0.99999999999569   101.47550755      0.01    0.9923
X4        1     1.00000000000028   5.6456651217      0.18    0.8618
X5        1     0.99999999999999   0.1123248547      8.90    0.0001
```

Output 25.3   PROC GLM Results for Wampler Example

```
                                        SAS

                            General Linear Models Procedure

Dependent Variable: Y1

Parameter                   Estimate        Parameter=0                      Estimate

INTERCEPT                 -9998.955713         -9999.99         0.0               0
X1                            0.999994          9999.99         0.0               0
X2                            1.000002          9999.99         0.0               0
X3                            1.000000          9999.99         0.0               0
X4                            1.000000          9999.99         0.0               0
X5                            1.000000          9999.99         0.0               0


                                                                (continued on next page)
```

(continued from previous page)

Dependent Variable: Y2

Parameter	Estimate	T for H0: Parameter=0	Pr > |T|	Std Error of Estimate
INTERCEPT	-999.0000274	-9999.99	0.0	0
X1	0.1000000	9999.99	0.0	0
X2	0.0100000	9999.99	0.0	0
X3	0.0010000	9999.99	0.0	0
X4	0.0001000	9999.99	0.0	0
X5	0.0000100	9999.99	0.0	0

Dependent Variable: Y3

Parameter	Estimate	T for H0: Parameter=0	Pr > |T|	Std Error of Estimate
INTERCEPT	-9998.955713	-0.00	0.9995	17133639.220
X1	0.999994	0.00	0.9997	2363.5518166
X2	1.000002	0.00	0.9990	779.34355091
X3	1.000000	0.01	0.9923	101.47551070
X4	1.000000	0.18	0.8618	5.64566528
X5	1.000000	8.90	0.0001	0.11232486

REFERENCES

Beaton, A.E., Rubin, D. B., and Barone, J.L. (1976), "The Acceptability of Regression Solutions: Another Look at Computational Accuracy," *Journal of the American Statistical Association, 71*, 158–168.

Gentleman, W. M. (1972a), "Basic Procedures for Large, Sparse or Weighted Least Squares Problems," Univ. of Waterloo Report CSRR-2068, Waterloo, Ontario, Canada.

Gentleman, W. M. (1972b), "Least Squares Computations by Givens Transformations without Square Roots," Univ. of Waterloo Report CSRR-2062, Waterloo, Ontario, Canada.

Lawson, C. L. and Hanson, R. J. (1974), *Solving Least Squares Problems*, Englewood Cliffs, NJ: Prentice-Hall, Inc.

Longley, J. W. (1967), "An Appraisal of Least Squares Programs for the Electronic Computer from the Point of View of the User," *Journal of the American Statistical Association, 62*, 819–41.

Wampler, R. H. (1970), "A Report of the Accuracy of Some Widely Used Least Squares Computer Programs," *Journal of the American Statistical Association, 65*, 549–563.

Chapter 26

The PLAN Procedure

ABSTRACT

The PLAN procedure constructs designs and randomizes plans for nested and crossed experiments.

INTRODUCTION

A cell in a factorial experiment can be indexed by the levels of the various *factors* associated with it. For example, in a randomized complete block design each cell is uniquely indexed by the block and treatment associated with the cell. In a factorial design, each cell is indexed by a combination of levels of the various factors. PROC PLAN generates designs by first generating a selection of the levels for the first factor. Then, for the second factor, PLAN generates a selection of its levels for each level of the first factor. In general, for a given factor, PLAN generates a selection of its levels for all combinations of levels for the factors that precede it. The selection can be done in three different ways:

- randomized selection, for which the levels are returned in a random order. In this case, the selection process is based on uniform pseudo-random variates generated as in the RANUNI function (see the *SAS Language Guide, Release 6.03 Edition*).
- ordered selection, for which the levels are returned in a standard order every time a selection is generated.
- cyclic selection, for which the levels returned are computed by cyclically permuting the levels of the previous selection.

The randomized mode of selection can be used to generate randomized plans. Also, by appropriate use of the facility for cyclic selection, any of the designs in the very wide class of generalized cyclic block designs (Jarrett and Hall 1978) can be generated.

There is no limit to the depth to which the different factors can be nested and any number of randomized plans can be generated.

You can also declare a list of factors to be selected simultaneously with the lowest (that is, the most nested) factor. The levels of the factors in this list can be seen as constituting the treatment to be applied to the cells of the design. For this reason, factors in this list are called *treatments*. With this list, you can generate and randomize plans in one run of PLAN. For example,

```
factors a b;
treatments drug;
```

produces a design with the DRUG *treatment* applied to the levels of *factor* B. The levels of B are nested within A.

Using PROC PLAN Interactively

PROC PLAN can be used interactively. After specifying a design with a FACTORS statement and running PLAN with a RUN statement, additional plans and output data sets can be generated without reinvoking PLAN.

The **SPECIFICATIONS** section describes which statements can be used interactively. These interactive statements can be executed singly or in groups by following the single statement or group of statements with a RUN statement.

If you use PLAN interactively, you can end the PLAN procedure with a DATA step, another PROC step, an ENDSAS statement, or with a QUIT statement. The syntax of this statement is

```
quit;
```

When you are using PLAN interactively, additional RUN statements do not end the procedure but tell PLAN to execute additional statements.

SPECIFICATIONS

The PLAN procedure is specified by the following statements:

   PROC PLAN *option*;
    FACTORS *requests* / *option*;
    TREATMENTS *requests* / *option*;
    OUTPUT OUT = *SASdataset* [**DATA** = *SASdataset*][*factor value settings*];

where brackets denote an optional specification. Include a FACTORS statement for each plan you want. Several FACTORS statements are permitted.

The PROC PLAN statement and at least one FACTORS statement must appear before the first RUN statement. The TREATMENTS statement, OUTPUT statement, and additional FACTORS statements can appear either before the first RUN statement or after it. The FACTORS, OUTPUT, and TREATMENTS statements are described after the PROC PLAN statement.

PROC PLAN Statement

PROC PLAN *option*;

The PROC PLAN statement invokes the PLAN procedure. Since input and output data sets are specified in the OUTPUT statement, there is neither a DATA= nor an OUT= option in the PROC PLAN statement. The following option can appear in the PROC PLAN statement:

SEED=*number*
> specifies a 5-, 6-, or 7-digit odd integer for PLAN to use to start the pseudo-random number generator for selecting factor levels randomly. The default is a value generated from reading the time of day from the computer's clock. However, in order to avoid the generation of artificial correlations, you should control the value of the seed explicitly rather than rely on the clock reading.

FACTORS Statement

FACTORS *requests / option*;

The FACTORS statement specifies the factors of the plan and generates the plan. The requests specify the plan to be generated. The form of *request* is

name=*m* [OF *n*][*selection type*]

where brackets denote an optional specification. More than one *request* can appear in the same FACTORS statement. The names in *request* must be valid SAS names. The *n* and *m* values must be positive integers.

A positive integer *m* appearing alone after the equal sign produces a random permutation of the integers 1, 2, . . . , *m*.

For the specification *m* OF *n*, *m* specifies the number of levels of the factor to select at a time, and *n* specifies the number of levels from which the chosen levels are selected. Thus, *n* is the number of possible levels the factor may take in the design, and *m* is essentially a block size (see **Specifying Factor Structures** later in this chapter). For example, the specification 5 OF 12 selects 5 integers from the integers 1, 2, 3, . . . , 12. The *m* value must be less than or equal to the *n* value.

The following *selection types* are allowed:

RANDOM
> specifies that the *m* levels of the factor are selected randomly without replacement from the integers 1, 2, . . . , *n*.

ORDERED
> specifies that the levels of the factor selected are the integers 1, 2, . . . , *m*, in that order.

CYCLIC [(*initial block*)][*increment number*]
> specifies that the levels of the factor are selected by cyclically permuting the integers 1, 2, . . . , *n*. For example, the specification

```
a=4 cyclic
```

> cyclically permutes the integers 1, 2, 3, and 4.

Optionally, you can specify an initial block of *m* integers, enclosed in parentheses. The default initial block is

$$(1\ 2\ 3\ \ldots\ m)\quad.$$

You can also specify an increment number for the cyclic permutation. This number must be a positive integer. The default increment number is 1.

For more detail, see **Specifying Factor Structures** later in this chapter.

The default *selection type* for the FACTORS statement is RANDOM.

The option below can appear in the FACTORS statement after the slash (/):

NOPRINT

suppresses printing of the plan when only an output data set is required.

For cases with more than one request in the same FACTORS statement, PROC PLAN constructs the design as follows:

1. PLAN first generates levels for the first request. These levels are permutations of integers (1, 2, and so on) appropriate for the selection type chosen. If you do not specify a selection type, PLAN uses the default (RANDOM).
2. For every integer generated for the first request, levels are generated for the second request. These levels are generated according to the specifications following the second equal sign.
3. This process is repeated until levels for all requests have been generated.

For example,

```
proc plan;
   factors one=4 two=3;
```

first generates a random permutation of the integers 1 to 4, and then for each of these, generates a random permutation of the integers 1 to 3. You can think of a factor TWO as being nested within factor ONE, where the levels of factor ONE are to be randomly assigned to 4 units.

As another example, six random permutations of the numbers 1, 2, 3 can be generated simply by specifying

```
factors a=6 ordered b=3;
```

For more on how to use the FACTORS statement to generate different designs, see **Specifying Factor Structures** later in this chapter.

OUTPUT Statement

OUTPUT OUT=*SASdataset* [DATA=*SASdataset*][*factor value settings*];

The OUTPUT statement applies only to the last plan generated. If you are using PLAN interactively, the OUTPUT statement for a given plan must be immediately preceded by the FACTORS statement (and the TREATMENTS statement, if appropriate) for the plan. Specifications in the OUTPUT statement are

OUT=*SASdataset*
DATA=*SASdataset*

The OUTPUT statement may be used both to output the last plan generated, and to use the last plan generated to randomize another SAS data set.

The first case is invoked by specifying only the OUT= option in the OUTPUT statement. This creates an output SAS data set. In this case, the output data set contains one variable for each factor in the plan and one observation for each cell in the plan. The value of a variable in a given observation is the level of the corresponding factor for that cell.

The second case is invoked by specifying both the DATA= and OUT= options in the OUTPUT statement. In this case, the output data set (OUT=) has the same form as the input data set (DATA=) but has modified values for the variables that correspond to factors (see **Output Data Sets** for details). Values for variables not corresponding to factors are transferred without change.

factor value settings

These may be used to specify the values which are to be input or output for the factors. The form for *factor value setting* is different when only an OUT= data set is specified, and when both OUT= and DATA= data sets are specified. Both forms are discussed below.

Factor Value Settings with Only an OUT= Data Set

The form for *factor value setting* specification in this case is

factorname [*values*][*association type*]

where

factorname   is a factor in the FACTORS statement that immediately precedes the OUTPUT statement.

values   is a list of values to be written to the output set for this factor. These values are

NVALS = (*list of n numbers*)

or

CVALS = (*list of n character strings*)

If neither NVALS nor CVALS is specified, the integers 1, 2, . . . , *n* are output. In other words, the default values specification is

NVALS = (1 2 . . . *n*)

For a CVALS list, a character string must be of length 40 or less and must be enclosed within quotes.

Warning: when output character values are specified using the CVALS= option, the variable created in the output data set has length equal to the length of the longest string given as a value; shorter strings are padded with trailing blanks. For example, the values output for the first level of a two-level factor with the two value specifications

```
CVALS=('String 1' 'String 2')
```

```
CVALS=('String 1' 'A longer string')
```

are not the same. The value output with the second specification is 'String 1' followed by seven blanks. In order to match two such values (for example, when merging two plans), you must use the TRIM function in the DATA step (see the *SAS Language Guide*).

association type   is either ORDERED or RANDOM and specifies how *values* are to be associated with the levels of a factor (the integers 1, 2, . . . , *n*). The default association type is ORDERED, for which the first value specified is output for a factor level setting of 1, the second value specified is output for a level of 2, and so on. You may also specify an association type of RANDOM, for which the levels are associated with the values in a random order. Specifying RANDOM is useful for randomizing crossed experiments (see **Randomizing Designs** later in this chapter).

Factor Value Settings with OUT= and DATA= Data Sets

If an input data set is specified, then PLAN assumes that each factor in the last plan generated corresponds to a variable in the input set. If the variable name is different from the name of the factor to which it corresponds, the two may be associated in the values specification by

input variable name = factorname

The NVALS= or CVALS= options can be used. In this case, use of NVALS or CVALS specifies the input values as well as the output values for the corresponding variable.

Note: because the collection of input factor variable values is assumed to constitute a plan position description (see **Output Data Sets**), the values must correspond to integers less than or equal to *m*, the number of values selected for the associated factor. If any input values do not correspond, then the collection does not define a plan position, and the corresponding observation is output as is, without changing the values of any of the factor variables.

TREATMENTS Statement

TREATMENTS *requests*;

The TREATMENTS statement specifies the *treatments* of the plan to generate, but it does not generate a plan. If several FACTORS and TREATMENTS statements are given before the first RUN statement, only the last TREATMENTS specification is used, and it is applied to the plans generated by each of the FACTORS statements. The TREATMENTS statement has the same form as the FACTORS statement. The individual *requests* also have the same form as in the FACTORS statement:

name=m [OF *n*][*selection type*]

Each *treatment* is generated simultaneously with the lowest (that is, the most nested) factor in the last FACTORS statement. The *m* value for each *treatment* must be at least as large as the *m* for the most-nested factor because this determines how many values are selected.

For example, if the FACTORS statement contains two factors to set up the rows and columns of a 3×3 square

```
factors r=3 ordered c=3 ordered;
```

then the subsequent augmentation of this design with two cyclic treatments

```
treatments a=3 cyclic
           b=3 cyclic 2;
```

produces the plan

```
      R    [C A B]
--------   -------+-------+-------+
      1    [1 1 1] [2 2 2] [3 3 3]

      2    [1 2 3] [2 3 1] [3 1 2]

      3    [1 3 2] [2 1 3] [3 2 1]
```

where the values for the column index C are given by the left-most number in each set of square brackets, the values for treatment factor A by the middle number, and the values for B by the right-most number. Notice how the values of R and C are ordered (1, 2, 3) as requested. Incidentally, in this example, the result is a 3×3 Graeco-Latin square, a type of design useful in main-effects factorial experiments.

DETAILS

Output Data Sets

The output facility for PROC PLAN may be used for either of the following:

- to specify a SAS data set to which to write the plan last generated
- to specify a SAS data set to randomize according to the plan last generated.

In order to see how to use PLAN to randomize an already-existing design, look at how the procedure represents a plan. A list of values, one for each factor, may define either the position of a cell within a plan (for example, the cell in row 3 and column 2) or the levels assigned to the factors for that cell. PLAN represents a plan as two series of such settings or lists of factor values: a position series, a typical element of which describes the position of the corresponding cell in the plan, and a value series, whose elements give the levels assigned to each factor for each cell.

If you specify only an output data set (OUT=), the value series is used by default. In other words, for each factor, the output data set contains a numeric variable with that factor's name; and the values of this numeric variable are the numbers of the successive levels selected for the factor in the plan (the corresponding elements of the value series). Alternatively, you may specify the values that are output for a factor (see the specifications for the OUTPUT statement earlier in this chapter). Also, you may specify that the internal values be associated with the output values in a random order, a facility useful for randomization of plans for crossed experiments (see **Randomizing Designs** later in this chapter.)

If you also specify an input data set (DATA=), each factor is associated with a variable in the DATA= data set. This occurs either implicitly by the factor and variable having the same name, or explicitly as described in the specifications for the OUTPUT statement. When both DATA= and OUT= data sets are specified, the values of variables that correspond to factors are interpreted as a plan position description. In this case, the values of the variables corresponding to the factors are first read and then interpreted as a plan position description. Then the respective values taken by the factors at that position are assigned to the variable in the OUT= data set. When the factors are random, this has the effect of randomizing the input data set in the same manner as the plan produced (see **Randomizing Designs** later in this chapter).

Specifying Factor Structures

By appropriately combining the different facilities of PLAN, a rich set of designs may be constructed. The basic tools are the factor selection specifications, which are used in both the FACTORS and TREATMENTS statements. The general form of the factor selection specifications is

   name = *selection specification*

The following are examples of different specifications and their actions:

- A positive integer *m* appearing alone after the equal sign produces a random permutation of the integers $1, 2, \ldots, m$.
- A positive integer *m* followed by the word ORDERED generates the list of integers $1, 2, \ldots, m$, in that order.
- The specification *m* OF *n* tells PROC PLAN to pick a random sample of *m* integers (without replacement) from the set of integers $1, 2, \ldots, n$ and to arrange the sample randomly.
- A positive integer *m* followed by the word CYCLIC specifies that the first selection of levels for this factor is the integers $1, 2, \ldots, m$, in that order; the second selection is the same list cyclically permuted one place to the right, that is, the integers $2, 3, \ldots, m-1, 1$; the third selection is $3, 4, \ldots, m-1, 1, 2$; and so on.
- An initial block and an increment number for a cyclic factor may also be specified. For example, the specification

   ```
   T=4 OF 30 CYCLIC (1 3 4 26) 2
   ```

generates the following selections for factor T:

```
1    3    4   26
3    5    6   28
5    7    8   30
7    9   10    2
9   11   12    4
         ·
         ·
         ·
```

The successive rows above constitute the generalized cyclic incomplete block design given in Example 1 of Jarrett and Hall (1978).
   In general, the statements

   ```
   treatments t=k of v cyclic (e₁ e₂ . . . eₖ) i;
   factors b=b p=k;
   ```

generate an appropriately randomized generalized cyclic incomplete block design for *v* treatments (given by the value of T) in *b* blocks (given by the value of B) of size *k* (with separate plots within blocks indexed by P) with initial block $(e_1 \, e_2 \ldots e_k)$ and increment number *i*.

Randomizing Designs

In many situations, proper randomization is crucial for the validity of any conclusions to be drawn from an experiment. Randomization is used both to neutralize the effect of any systematic biases that may be involved in the design as well as to provide a basis for the assumptions underlying the analysis. It is easy to use PLAN to randomize an already-existing design: one produced by a previous call to PLAN, perhaps, or a more specialized design taken from a standard reference such as Cochran and Cox (1957). The method is simply to call PLAN, specifying the appropriate block structure in the FACTORS statement and then to specify the data set in which the design is stored with the DATA= option of the OUTPUT statement.

Two sorts of randomization are provided for, corresponding to the RANDOM factor selection and association types in the FACTORS and OUTPUT statements, respectively. Designs in which factors are completely nested (for example, block designs) should be randomized by specifying that the selection type of each factor is RANDOM in the FACTORS statement, which is the default (see **Example 4**). On the other hand, if the factors are crossed (for example, row-and-column designs), they should be randomized by one random reassignment of their values for the whole design. To do this, specify that the association type of each factor is RANDOM in the OUTPUT statement (see **Example 5**).

Printed Output

The PLAN procedure prints

1. the m value for each factor, the number of values to be selected
2. the n value for each factor, the number of values to be selected from
3. the selection type for each factor, as specified in the FACTORS statement
4. the initial block and increment number for cyclic factors
5. the factor value selections making up each plan.

In addition, notes are printed on the log giving the starting and ending values of the random number seed for each call to PLAN.

EXAMPLES

Example 1: A Completely Randomized Design for Two Treatments

This first plan is appropriate for a completely randomized design with twelve experimental units, each to be assigned one of two treatments. Use a DATA statement to store the unrandomized design in a SAS data set and then call PLAN to randomize it by simply specifying one RANDOM factor of twelve levels. The following statements produce **Output 26.1**:

```
title 'COMPLETELY RANDOMIZED DESIGN';
data a;
   do unit=1 to 12;
      if (unit <= 6) then treat=1;
      else                treat=2;
      output;
      end;
proc plan seed=27371;
   factors unit=12;
   output data=a out=b;
```

```
proc sort;
   by unit;
proc print;
run;
```

Output 26.1 A Completely Randomized Design for Two Treatments:
                  PROC PLAN

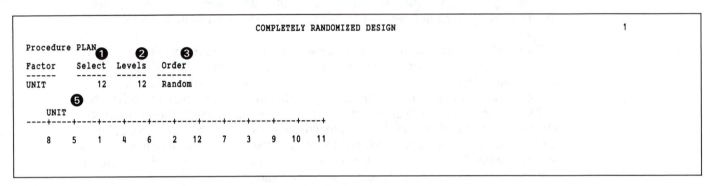

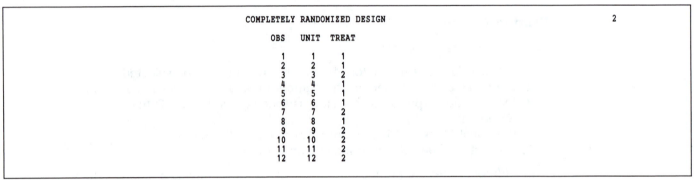

You can also generate the plan without using a DATA step to set up the unrandomized plan by using a TREATMENTS statement instead. The following code
generates the same plan as above:

```
proc plan seed=27371;
   factors unit=12;
   treatments treat=12 cyclic (1 1 1 1 1 1 2 2 2 2 2 2);
   output out=b;
run;
```

Example 2: A Split-Plot Design

The second plan is appropriate for a split-plot design with main plots forming a
randomized complete block design. In this example, there are three blocks, four
main plots per block, and two subplots per main plot. First, three random permutations (one for each of the blocks) of the integers 1, 2, 3, and 4 are produced.
The four integers correspond to the four levels of factor A; the permutation determines how the levels of A are assigned to the main plots within a block. For each
of these twelve numbers (4 numbers per block for 3 blocks), a random permutation of the integers 1 and 2 is produced. Each two-integer permutation determines

the assignment of the two levels of factor B to the subplots within a main plot. The following statements produce **Output 26.2**:

```
title 'SPLIT PLOT DESIGN';
proc plan seed=37277;
    factors block=3 ordered a=4 b=2;
run;
```

Output 26.2   A Split-Plot Design: PROC PLAN

```
                                    SPLIT PLOT DESIGN                                    1

Procedure PLAN

Factor    Select  Levels  Order
------    ------  ------  -----
BLOCK        3       3    Ordered
A            4       4    Random
B            2       2    Random


 BLOCK         A        B
--------  --------  ----+----+

    1         4      2   1

              3      2   1

              1      2   1

              2      2   1

    2         4      1   2

              3      1   2

              1      2   1

              2      1   2

    3         4      2   1

              2      2   1

              3      2   1

              1      2   1
```

Example 3: A Hierarchical Design

The third plan is appropriate for a hierarchical design. In this example, three plants are nested within four pots, which are nested within three houses. The FACTORS statement requests a random permutation of the numbers 1, 2, and 3 to choose houses randomly and a random permutation of the numbers 1, 2, 3, and 4 for each of those first three numbers. This second step randomly assigns pots to houses. Finally, the FACTORS statement requests a random permutation of 1, 2, and 3 for each of the twelve integers in the second set of permutations. This last step randomly assigns plants to pots. The following statements produce **Output 26.3**:

```
title 'HIERARCHICAL DESIGN';
proc plan seed=17431;
    factors houses=3 pots=4 plants=3;
run;
```

Output 26.3   A Hierarchical Design

```
                                    HIERARCHICAL DESIGN                                          1

Procedure PLAN

Factor    Select   Levels    Order
------    ------   ------    -------
HOUSES       3        3      Random
POTS         4        4      Random
PLANTS       3        3      Random


  HOUSES     POTS    PLANTS
--------  --------  ----+----+----+

     1        3        2    3    1

              1        3    1    2

              2        2    3    1

              4        3    2    1

     2        4        1    3    2

              2        2    1    3

              3        2    3    1

              1        2    3    1

     3        4        1    3    2

              1        3    2    1

              2        1    2    3

              3        3    2    1
```

Example 4: An Incomplete Block Design

Jarrett and Hall (1978) give an example of a generalized cyclic design with good efficiency characteristics. The design consists of two replicates of 52 treatments in 13 blocks of size 8. The following call to PROC PLAN generates this design in an appropriately randomized form and stores it in a SAS data set. PROC TABULATE is then used to print the randomized plan neatly. The following statements produce **Output 26.4**:

```
title 'GENERALIZED CYCLIC BLOCK DESIGN';
proc plan seed=33373;
   treatments trtmts=8 of 52 cyclic (1 2 3 4 32 43 46 49) 4;
   factors blocks=13 plots=8;
   output out=c;
quit;
proc tabulate;
   class blocks plots;
   var trtmts;
   table blocks, plots*(trtmts*f=8.) / rts=8;
run;
```

Output 26.4   A Generalized Cyclic Block Design (Jarrett and Hall, 1978, Example 4)

```
                        GENERALIZED CYCLIC BLOCK DESIGN                              1
Procedure PLAN

Plot Factors

Factor    Select   Levels   Order
------    ------   ------   -------
BLOCKS      13       13     Random
PLOTS        8        8     Random


Treatment Factors                  ❹

Factor    Select   Levels   Order    Initial block / Increment
------    ------   ------   -------   -------------------------
TRTMTS       8       52     Cyclic   (1 2 3 4 32 43 46 49) / 4


  BLOCKS [ PLOTS TRTMTS ]
  -------- -------+-------+-------+-------+-------+-------+-------+-------+
        10 [ 7  1] [ 4  2] [ 8  3] [ 1  4] [ 2 32] [ 3 43] [ 5 46] [ 6 49]

         8 [ 1  5] [ 2  6] [ 4  7] [ 3  8] [ 8 36] [ 6 47] [ 5 50] [ 7  1]

         9 [ 2  9] [ 5 10] [ 4 11] [ 7 12] [ 3 40] [ 1 51] [ 8  2] [ 6  5]

         6 [ 4 13] [ 2 14] [ 6 15] [ 8 16] [ 3 44] [ 7  3] [ 1  6] [ 5  9]

         7 [ 4 17] [ 7 18] [ 6 19] [ 3 20] [ 1 48] [ 2  7] [ 8 10] [ 5 13]

         4 [ 4 21] [ 8 22] [ 1 23] [ 5 24] [ 3 52] [ 6 11] [ 7 14] [ 2 17]

         2 [ 6 25] [ 2 26] [ 3 27] [ 8 28] [ 7  4] [ 5 15] [ 1 18] [ 4 21]

         3 [ 6 29] [ 2 30] [ 3 31] [ 1 32] [ 7  8] [ 4 19] [ 5 22] [ 8 25]

         1 [ 1 33] [ 2 34] [ 7 35] [ 8 36] [ 5 12] [ 6 23] [ 3 26] [ 4 29]

         5 [ 5 37] [ 7 38] [ 6 39] [ 8 40] [ 4 16] [ 3 27] [ 1 30] [ 2 33]

        12 [ 5 41] [ 8 42] [ 1 43] [ 4 44] [ 7 20] [ 3 31] [ 6 34] [ 2 37]

        13 [ 3 45] [ 5 46] [ 1 47] [ 8 48] [ 4 24] [ 2 35] [ 6 38] [ 7 41]

        11 [ 4 49] [ 1 50] [ 5 51] [ 2 52] [ 3 28] [ 8 39] [ 6 42] [ 7 45]
```

					PLOTS			
		1	2	3	4	5	6	7	8
		TRTMTS	TRTMTS	TRTMTS	TRTMTS	TRTMTS	TRTMTS	TRTMTS	TRTMTS
		SUM	SUM	SUM	SUM	SUM	SUM	SUM	SUM
BLOCKS									
1		33	34	26	29	12	23	35	36
2		18	26	27	21	15	25	4	28
3		32	30	31	19	22	29	8	25
4		23	17	52	21	24	11	14	22
5		30	33	27	16	37	39	38	40
6		6	14	44	13	9	15	3	16
7		48	7	20	17	13	19	18	10
8		5	6	8	7	50	47	1	36
9		51	9	40	11	10	5	12	2
10		4	32	43	2	46	49	1	3
11		50	52	28	49	51	42	45	39
12		43	37	31	44	41	34	20	42
13		47	35	45	24	46	38	41	48

Example 5: A Latin Square Design

The preceding examples have all dealt with designs with completely nested block structures, for which PROC PLAN was especially designed. However, by appropriate coordination of its facilities a much wider class of designs may be accommodated. A Latin square design is based on experimental units that have a row-and-column block structure. The following example uses the CYCLIC option for a treatment factor TMTS to generate a simple 4×4 Latin square. Randomizing a Latin square design involves randomly permuting the row, column, and treatment values independently. In order to do this, use the RANDOM option in the OUTPUT statement of PLAN. The example also shows the use of the value-setting option for the OUTPUT statement to make the output plan more easily interpretable. The following statements produce **Output 26.5**:

```
title 'LATIN SQUARE DESIGN';
proc plan seed=37430;
   factors rows=4 ordered cols=4 ordered / noprint;
   treatments tmts=4 cyclic;
   output out=g
          rows cvals=('Day 1' 'Day 2' 'Day 3' 'Day 4') random
          cols cvals=('Lab 1' 'Lab 2' 'Lab 3' 'Lab 4') random
          tmts nvals=(   0      100     250      450 ) random;
quit;
proc tabulate;
   class rows cols;
   var tmts;
   table rows, cols*(tmts*f=6.) / rts=8;
run;
```

Output 26.5   A Randomized Latin Square Design

```
                         LATIN SQUARE DESIGN                              1

             |      |            COLS              |
             |      |------------------------------|
             |      |Lab 1 |Lab 2 |Lab 3 |Lab 4 |
             |      |------+------+------+------|
             |      | TMTS | TMTS | TMTS | TMTS |
             |      |------+------+------+------|
             |      | SUM  | SUM  | SUM  | SUM  |
             |------+------+------+------+------|
             |ROWS  |      |      |      |      |
             |------|      |      |      |      |
             |Day 1 |    0 |  100 |  450 |  250 |
             |------+------+------+------+------|
             |Day 2 |  100 |  250 |    0 |  450 |
             |------+------+------+------+------|
             |Day 3 |  250 |  450 |  100 |    0 |
             |------+------+------+------+------|
             |Day 4 |  450 |    0 |  250 |  100 |
             --------------------------------------
```

REFERENCES

Cochran, W.G. and Cox, G.M. (1957), *Experimental Designs*, 2d Edition, New York: John Wiley & Sons, Inc.

Fishman, G.S. and Moore, L.R. (1982), "A Statistical Evaluation of Multiplicative Congruential Generators with Modulus ($2^{31}-1$)," *Journal of the American Statistical Association*, 77, 129–136.

Jarrett, R.G. and Hall, W.B. (1978), "Generalized Cyclic Incomplete Block Designs," *Biometrika*, 65, 397–401.

Chapter 27

The PRINCOMP
Procedure

ABSTRACT

The PRINCOMP procedure performs principal component analysis. As input you can use raw data, a correlation matrix, or a covariance matrix; either the correlation matrix or the covariance matrix can be analyzed. Output data sets containing eigenvalues, eigenvectors, and standardized or unstandardized principal component scores can be created.

INTRODUCTION

Principal component analysis is a multivariate technique for examining relationships among several quantitative variables. The choice between using factor analysis and principal component analysis depends in part upon your research objectives. You should use the PRINCOMP procedure if you are interested in summarizing data and detecting linear relationships. Plots of principal components are especially valuable tools in exploratory data analysis. Principal components can be used to reduce the number of variables in regression, clustering, and so on. Refer to Chapter 4, "Introduction to Multivariate Procedures," for a detailed comparison of the PRINCOMP and FACTOR procedures.

Background

Principal component analysis was originated by Pearson (1901) and later developed by Hotelling (1933). The application of principal components is discussed by Rao (1964), Cooley and Lohnes (1971), and Gnanadesikan (1977). Excellent statistical treatments of principal components are found in Kshirsagar (1972), Morrison (1976), and Mardia, Kent, and Bibby (1979).

Given a data set with p numeric variables, p principal components can be computed. Each principal component is a linear combination of the original variables, with coefficients equal to the eigenvectors of the correlation or covariance matrix. The eigenvectors are customarily taken with unit length. The principal components are sorted by descending order of the eigenvalues, which are equal to the variances of the components.

Principal components have a variety of useful properties (Rao 1964; Kshirsagar 1972):

- The eigenvectors are orthogonal, so the principal components represent jointly perpendicular directions through the space of the original variables.
- The principal component scores are jointly uncorrelated. Note that this property is quite distinct from the previous one.
- The first principal component has the largest variance of any unit-length linear combination of the observed variables. The jth principal component has the largest variance of any unit-length linear combination orthogonal to the first $j-1$ principal components. The last principal component has the smallest variance of any linear combination of the original variables.
- The scores on the first j principal components have the highest possible generalized variance of any set of unit-length linear combinations of the original variables.
- The first j principal components give a least-squares solution to the model

$$\mathbf{Y} = \mathbf{XB} + \mathbf{E}$$

  where $\mathbf{Y}$ is an $n \times p$ matrix of the centered observed variables; $\mathbf{X}$ is the $n \times j$ matrix of scores on the first j principal components; $\mathbf{B}$ is the $j \times p$ matrix of eigenvectors; $\mathbf{E}$ is an $n \times p$ matrix of residuals; and you want to minimize trace($\mathbf{E'E}$), the sum of all the squared elements in $\mathbf{E}$. In other words, the first j principal components are the best linear predictors of the original variables among all possible sets of j variables, although any nonsingular linear transformation of the first j principal components would provide equally good prediction. The same result is obtained if you want to minimize the determinant or the Euclidean (Schur, Frobenious) norm of $\mathbf{E'E}$ rather than the trace.
- In geometric terms, the j-dimensional linear subspace spanned by the first j principal components gives the best possible fit to the data points as measured by the sum of squared perpendicular distances from each data point to the subspace.

Principal component analysis can also be used for exploring polynomial relationships and for multivariate outlier detection (Gnanadesikan 1977) and is related to factor analysis, correspondence analysis, allometry, and biased regression techniques (Mardia, Kent, and Bibby 1979).

SPECIFICATIONS

You can invoke the PRINCOMP procedure with the following statements:

PROC PRINCOMP *options*;
  VAR *variables*;
  WEIGHT *variable*;
  FREQ *variable*;
  PARTIAL *variables*;
  BY *variables*;

Usually only the VAR statement is used in addition to the PROC PRINCOMP statement. The BY, FREQ, PARTIAL, VAR, and WEIGHT statements are described after the PROC PRINCOMP statement.

PROC PRINCOMP Statement

PROC PRINCOMP *options*;

The following options can appear in the PROC statement:

DATA=*SASdataset*
  names the SAS data set to be analyzed. The data set can be an ordinary SAS data set or a TYPE=CORR, COV, or SSCP data set (see Appendix 2, "Special SAS Data Sets"). If you omit the DATA= option, the most recently created SAS data set is used.

OUT=*SASdataset*
  names an output SAS data set that contains all the original data as well as the principal component scores. If you want to create a permanent SAS data set, you must specify a two-level name (see "SAS Files" in the *SAS Language Guide, Release 6.03 Edition* for information on permanent SAS data sets).

OUTSTAT=*SASdataset*
  names an output SAS data set that contains means, standard deviations, number of observations, correlations or covariances, eigenvalues, and eigenvectors. If the COV option is specified, the data set is TYPE=COV and contains covariances; otherwise, it is TYPE=CORR and contains correlations. If you want to create a permanent SAS data set, you must specify a two-level name (see "SAS Files" in the *SAS Language Guide* for information on permanent SAS data sets).

COVARIANCE
COV
  requests that the principal components be computed from the covariance matrix. If the COV option is not specified, the correlation matrix is analyzed. Use of the COV option causes variables with large variances to be more strongly associated with components with large eigenvalues and variables with small variances to be more strongly associated with components with small eigenvalues. The COV option should not be used unless the units in which the variables are measured are comparable or the variables have been standardized in some way.

N=*n*
  specifies the number of principal components to be computed. The default is the number of variables.

NOINT
  requests that the covariance or correlation matrix not be corrected for the mean, that is, that no intercept be used in the model. When you run

PRINCOMP with the NOINT option, the covariance matrix and hence the standard deviations are not corrected for the mean. If you are interested in the standard deviations corrected for the mean, get them from a procedure such as PROC MEANS.

NOPRINT

suppresses the printout.

PREFIX=*name*

specifies a prefix for naming the principal components. By default the names are PRIN1, PRIN2, . . . , PRIN*n*. If PREFIX=ABC is specified, the components are named ABC1, ABC2, ABC3, and so on. The number of characters in the prefix plus the number of digits required to designate the components should not exceed eight.

STANDARD

STD

requests that the principal component scores in the OUT= data set be standardized to unit variance. If the STANDARD option is not specified, the scores have variance equal to the corresponding eigenvalue.

VARDEF=*divisor*

specifies the divisor to be used in the calculation of variances and covariances. Possible values for *divisor* are N, DF, WEIGHT or WGT, and WDF. VARDEF=N requests that the number of observations (n) be used as the divisor. VARDEF=DF requests that the error degrees of freedom, $n-i$ (before partialling) or $n-p-i$ (after partialling) be used, where p is the number of degrees of freedom of the variables in the PARTIAL statement and i is 0 if the NOINT option is specified, 1 otherwise. VARDEF=WEIGHT or WGT requests that the sum of the weights (w) be used. VARDEF=WDF requests that $w-i$ (before partialling) or $w-p-i$ (after partialling) be used. The default value is DF.

BY Statement

BY *variables*;

You can use a BY statement with PROC PRINCOMP to obtain separate analyses on observations in groups defined by the BY variables. When a BY statement appears, the procedure expects the input data set to be sorted in order of the BY variables.

If your input data set is not sorted in ascending order, use the SORT procedure with a similar BY statement to sort the data, or, if appropriate, use the BY statement options NOTSORTED or DESCENDING. For more information, see the discussion of the BY statement in "SAS Statements Used in the PROC Step" in the *SAS Language Guide*.

FREQ Statement

FREQ *variable*;

If a variable in your data set represents the frequency of occurrence for the other values in the observation, include the variable's name in a FREQ statement. The procedure then treats the data set as if each observation appears n times, where n is the value of the FREQ variable for the observation. The total number of observations is considered equal to the sum of the FREQ variable.

The WEIGHT and FREQ statements have a similar effect except in the calculation of degrees of freedom.

PARTIAL Statement

> PARTIAL *variables*;

If you want to analyze a partial correlation or covariance matrix, specify the names of the numeric variables to be partialled out in the PARTIAL statement. PRINCOMP computes the principal components of the residuals from the prediction of the VAR variables by the PARTIAL variables. If an OUT= or OUTSTAT= data set is requested, the VAR variables should be distinguishable by the first six characters of their names so that the residual variables can be named by prefixing the characters R_.

VAR Statement

> VAR *variables*;

The VAR statement lists the numeric variables to be analyzed. If the VAR statement is omitted, all numeric variables not specified in other statements are analyzed.

WEIGHT Statement

> WEIGHT *variable*;

If you want to use relative weights for each observation in the input data set, place the weights in a variable in the data set and specify the name in a WEIGHT statement. This is often done when the variance associated with each observation is different and the values of the weight variable are proportional to the reciprocals of the variances.

DETAILS

Missing Values

Observations with missing values for any variable in the VAR, PARTIAL, FREQ, or WEIGHT statement are omitted from the analysis and are given missing values for principal component scores in the OUT= data set. If a correlation or covariance matrix is read, it can contain missing values as long as every pair of variables has at least one nonmissing entry.

Output Data Sets

OUT= Data Set

The OUT= data set contains all the variables in the original data set plus new variables containing the principal component scores. The N= option determines the number of new variables. The names of the new variables are formed by concatenating the value given by the PREFIX= option (or PRIN if PREFIX= is omitted) and the numbers 1, 2, 3, and so on. The new variables have mean 0 and variance equal to the corresponding eigenvalue, unless the STANDARD option is specified to standardize the scores to unit variance.

If a PARTIAL statement is used, the OUT= data set also contains the residuals from predicting the VAR variables from the PARTIAL variables. The names of the residual variables are formed by prefixing R_ to the names of the VAR variables and possibly truncating the last one or two characters to keep the name from exceeding eight characters.

An OUT= data set cannot be created if the DATA= data set is TYPE=CORR, COV, or SSCP.

OUTSTAT= Data Set

The OUTSTAT= data set is similar to the TYPE=CORR data set produced by the CORR procedure. The OUTSTAT= data set is TYPE=CORR unless the COV option is specified, in which case it is TYPE=COV.

The new data set contains the following variables:

- the BY variables, if any
- two new character variables, _TYPE_ and _NAME_
- either the variables analyzed, that is, those in the VAR statement, or, if there is no VAR statement, all numeric variables not listed in any other statement; or, if there is a PARTIAL statement, the residual variables as described under the OUT= data set.

Each observation in the new data set contains some type of statistic as indicated by the _TYPE_ variable. The values of the _TYPE_ variable are as follows:

TYPE	Contents
MEAN	mean of each variable. This observation is omitted if the NOINT option or the PARTIAL statement is specified.
STD	standard deviations. This observation is omitted if the COV option is specified, so the SCORE procedure does not standardize the variables before computing scores. If the PARTIAL statement is used, the standard deviation of a variable is computed as its root mean squared error as predicted from the PARTIAL variables.
N	number of observations on which the analysis is based. This value is the same for each variable. If the PARTIAL statement is used and the VARDEF= option is DF or unspecified, then the number of observations is decremented by the degrees of freedom for the PARTIAL variables.
SUMWGT	the sum of the weights of the observations. This value is the same for each variable. If the PARTIAL statement and VARDEF=WDF are specified, then the sum of the weights is decremented by the degrees of freedom for the PARTIAL variables. This observation is output only if the value is different from that in the observation with _TYPE_='N'.
CORR	correlations between each variable and the variable named by the _NAME_ variable. The number of observations with _TYPE_='CORR' is equal to the number of variables being analyzed. If the COV option is specified, no _TYPE_='CORR' observations are produced. If the PARTIAL statement is used, the partial correlations, not the raw correlations, are output.
COV	covariances between each variable and the variable named by the _NAME_ variable. _TYPE_='COV' observations are produced only if the COV option is specified. If the PARTIAL statement is used, the partial covariances, not the raw covariances, are output.
EIGENVAL	eigenvalues. If the N= option requested fewer than the maximum number of principal components, only the specified number of eigenvalues are produced, with missing values filling out the observation.

SCORE   eigenvectors. The _NAME_ variable contains the name of the corresponding principal component as constructed from the PREFIX= option. The number of observations with _TYPE_='SCORE' equals the number of principal components computed. The eigenvectors have unit length unless the STD option is used, in which case the unit-length eigenvectors are divided by the square roots of the eigenvalues to produce scores with unit standard deviations.

The data set can be used with the SCORE procedure to compute principal component scores, or it can be used as input to the FACTOR procedure specifying METHOD=SCORE to rotate the components. If you use the PARTIAL statement, the scoring coefficients should be applied to the residuals, not the original variables.

Computational Resources

Let

   n = number of observations
   v = number of VAR variables
   p = number of PARTIAL variables
   c = number of components.

- The minimum array space required is $232v + 120p + 48c + \max(8cv, 8vp + 4(v+p)(v+p+1))$ bytes.
- The time required to compute the correlation matrix is roughly proportional to $n(v+p)^2 + p(v+p)(v+p+1)/2$.
- The time required to compute eigenvalues is roughly proportional to v^3.
- The time required to compute eigenvectors is roughly proportional to cv^2.

Printed Output

The PRINCOMP procedure prints the following:

1. Simple Statistics, including the Mean and Std (standard deviation) for each variable, if the DATA= data set is not TYPE=CORR, COV, or SSCP.
2. the Correlation or, if the COV option is used, the Covariance Matrix unless the DATA= data set is TYPE=CORR, COV, or SSCP.

Items 3–5 are printed only if the PARTIAL statement is used.

3. Regression Statistics, giving the R-square and RMSE (root mean square error) for each VAR variable as predicted by the PARTIAL variables (not shown).
4. Standardized Regression Coefficients or, if the COV option is used, Regression Coefficients for predicting the VAR variables from the PARTIAL variables (not shown).
5. the Partial Correlation Matrix or, if the COV option is used, the Partial Covariance Matrix (not shown).
6. the Total Variance if the COV option is used.
7. Eigenvalues of the correlation or covariance matrix, as well as the Difference between successive eigenvalues, the Proportion of variance explained by each eigenvalue, and the Cumulative proportion of variance explained.
8. the Eigenvectors.

EXAMPLES

Example 1: January and July Temperatures

This example analyzes mean daily temperatures in selected cities in January and July. Both the raw data and the principal components are plotted to illustrate how principal components are orthogonal rotations of the original variables.

Note that since the COV option is used and JANUARY has a higher standard deviation than JULY, JANUARY receives a higher loading on the first component. The following statements produce **Output 27.1** through **Output 27.3**:

```
data temperat;
    title 'Mean Temperature in January and July for Selected Cities';
    input city $1-15 january july;
    cards;
Mobile          51.2 81.6
Phoenix         51.2 91.2
Little Rock     39.5 81.4
Sacramento      45.1 75.2
Denver          29.9 73.0
Hartford        24.8 72.7
Wilmington      32.0 75.8
Washington DC   35.6 78.7
Jacksonville    54.6 81.0
Miami           67.2 82.3
Atlanta         42.4 78.0
Boise           29.0 74.5
Chicago         22.9 71.9
Peoria          23.8 75.1
Indianapolis    27.9 75.0
Des Moines      19.4 75.1
Wichita         31.3 80.7
Louisville      33.3 76.9
New Orleans     52.9 81.9
Portland, ME    21.5 68.0
Baltimore       33.4 76.6
Boston          29.2 73.3
Detroit         25.5 73.3
Sault Ste Marie 14.2 63.8
Duluth           8.5 65.6
Minneapolis     12.2 71.9
Jackson         47.1 81.7
Kansas City     27.8 78.8
St Louis        31.3 78.6
Great Falls     20.5 69.3
Omaha           22.6 77.2
Reno            31.9 69.3
Concord         20.6 69.7
Atlantic City   32.7 75.1
Albuquerque     35.2 78.7
Albany          21.5 72.0
Buffalo         23.7 70.1
New York        32.2 76.6
Charlotte       42.1 78.5
Raleigh         40.5 77.5
Bismarck         8.2 70.8
```

```
Cincinnati      31.1 75.6
Cleveland       26.9 71.4
Columbus        28.4 73.6
Oklahoma City   36.8 81.5
Portland, OR    38.1 67.1
Philadelphia    32.3 76.8
Pittsburgh      28.1 71.9
Providence      28.4 72.1
Columbia        45.4 81.2
Sioux Falls     14.2 73.3
Memphis         40.5 79.6
Nashville       38.3 79.6
Dallas          44.8 84.8
El Paso         43.6 82.3
Houston         52.1 83.3
Salt Lake City  28.0 76.7
Burlington      16.8 69.8
Norfolk         40.5 78.3
Richmond        37.5 77.9
Spokane         25.4 69.7
Charleston, WV  34.5 75.0
Milwaukee       19.4 69.9
Cheyenne        26.6 69.1
;
proc plot;
   plot july*january=city / vpos=31;
proc princomp cov out=prin;
   var july january;
proc plot;
   plot prin2*prin1=city / vpos=19;
   title2 'Plot of Principal Components';
run;
```

Output 27.1   Plot of Raw Data: PROC PLOT

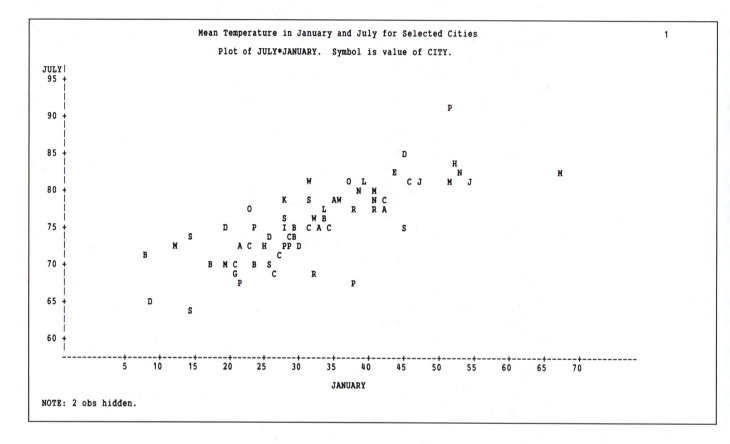

Output 27.2   Results of Principal Component Analysis: PROC PRINCOMP

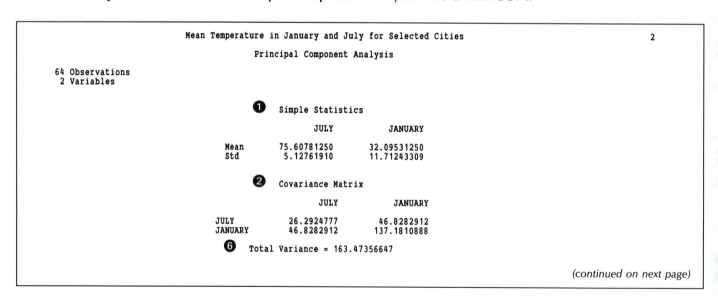

(continued on next page)

(continued from previous page)

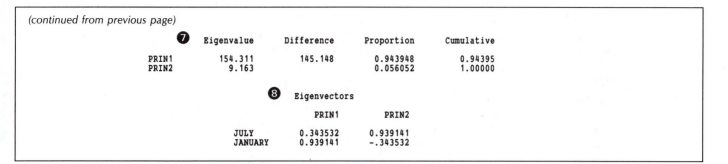

❼	Eigenvalue	Difference	Proportion	Cumulative
PRIN1	154.311	145.148	0.943948	0.94395
PRIN2	9.163		0.056052	1.00000

❽ Eigenvectors

	PRIN1	PRIN2
JULY	0.343532	0.939141
JANUARY	0.939141	-.343532

Output 27.3   Plot of Principal Components: PROC PLOT

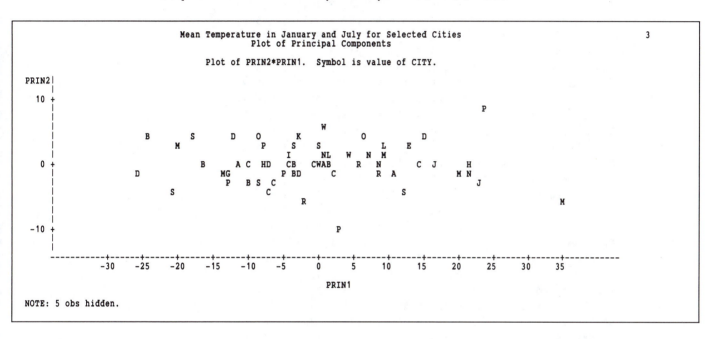

Mean Temperature in January and July for Selected Cities
Plot of Principal Components   3

Plot of PRIN2*PRIN1. Symbol is value of CITY.

NOTE: 5 obs hidden.

Example 2: Crime Rates

The data below give crime rates per 100,000 people in seven categories for each of the fifty states. Since there are seven variables, it is impossible to plot all the variables simultaneously. Principal components can be used to summarize the data in two or three dimensions and help to visualize the data. The following statements produce **Output 27.4**:

```
data crime;
    title 'Crime Rates per 100,000 Population by State';
    input state $1-15 murder rape robbery assault burglary larceny auto;
    cards;
Alabama          14.2 25.2  96.8 278.3 1135.5 1881.9 280.7
Alaska           10.8 51.6  96.8 284.0 1331.7 3369.8 753.3
Arizona           9.5 34.2 138.2 312.3 2346.1 4467.4 439.5
Arkansas          8.8 27.6  83.2 203.4  972.6 1862.1 183.4
California        11.5 49.4 287.0 358.0 2139.4 3499.8 663.5
Colorado          6.3 42.0 170.7 292.9 1935.2 3903.2 477.1
Connecticut       4.2 16.8 129.5 131.8 1346.0 2620.7 593.2
```

```
Delaware          6.0 24.9 157.0 194.2 1682.6 3678.4  467.0
Florida          10.2 39.6 187.9 449.1 1859.9 3840.5  351.4
Georgia          11.7 31.1 140.5 256.5 1351.1 2170.2  297.9
Hawaii            7.2 25.5 128.0  64.1 1911.5 3920.4  489.4
Idaho             5.5 19.4  39.6 172.5 1050.8 2599.6  237.6
Illinois          9.9 21.8 211.3 209.0 1085.0 2828.5  528.6
Indiana           7.4 26.5 123.2 153.5 1086.2 2498.7  377.4
Iowa              2.3 10.6  41.2  89.8  812.5 2685.1  219.9
Kansas            6.6 22.0 100.7 180.5 1270.4 2739.3  244.3
Kentucky         10.1 19.1  81.1 123.3  872.2 1662.1  245.4
Louisiana        15.5 30.9 142.9 335.5 1165.5 2469.9  337.7
Maine             2.4 13.5  38.7 170.0 1253.1 2350.7  246.9
Maryland          8.0 34.8 292.1 358.9 1400.0 3177.7  428.5
Massachusetts     3.1 20.8 169.1 231.6 1532.2 2311.3 1140.1
Michigan          9.3 38.9 261.9 274.6 1522.7 3159.0  545.5
Minnesota         2.7 19.5  85.9  85.8 1134.7 2559.3  343.1
Mississippi      14.3 19.6  65.7 189.1  915.6 1239.9  144.4
Missouri          9.6 28.3 189.0 233.5 1318.3 2424.2  378.4
Montana           5.4 16.7  39.2 156.8  804.9 2773.2  309.2
Nebraska          3.9 18.1  64.7 112.7  760.0 2316.1  249.1
Nevada           15.8 49.1 323.1 355.0 2453.1 4212.6  559.2
New Hampshire     3.2 10.7  23.2  76.0 1041.7 2343.9  293.4
New Jersey        5.6 21.0 180.4 185.1 1435.8 2774.5  511.5
New Mexico        8.8 39.1 109.6 343.4 1418.7 3008.6  259.5
New York         10.7 29.4 472.6 319.1 1728.0 2782.0  745.8
North Carolina   10.6 17.0  61.3 318.3 1154.1 2037.8  192.1
North Dakota      0.9  9.0  13.3  43.8  446.1 1843.0  144.7
Ohio              7.8 27.3 190.5 181.1 1216.0 2696.8  400.4
Oklahoma          8.6 29.2  73.8 205.0 1288.2 2228.1  326.8
Oregon            4.9 39.9 124.1 286.9 1636.4 3506.1  388.9
Pennsylvania      5.6 19.0 130.3 128.0  877.5 1624.1  333.2
Rhode Island      3.6 10.5  86.5 201.0 1489.5 2844.1  791.4
South Carolina   11.9 33.0 105.9 485.3 1613.6 2342.4  245.1
South Dakota      2.0 13.5  17.9 155.7  570.5 1704.4  147.5
Tennessee        10.1 29.7 145.8 203.9 1259.7 1776.5  314.0
Texas            13.3 33.8 152.4 208.2 1603.1 2988.7  397.6
Utah              3.5 20.3  68.8 147.3 1171.6 3004.6  334.5
Vermont           1.4 15.9  30.8 101.2 1348.2 2201.0  265.2
Virginia          9.0 23.3  92.1 165.7  986.2 2521.2  226.7
Washington        4.3 39.6 106.2 224.8 1605.6 3386.9  360.3
West Virginia     6.0 13.2  42.2  90.9  597.4 1341.7  163.3
Wisconsin         2.8 12.9  52.2  63.7  846.9 2614.2  220.7
Wyoming           5.4 21.9  39.7 173.9  811.6 2772.2  282.0
;
proc princomp out=crimcomp;
run;
```

Output 27.4   Results of Principal Component Analysis: PROC PRINCOMP

```
                       Crime Rates per 100,000 Population by State                    1
                            Principal Component Analysis

    50 Observations
     7 Variables


                                      Simple Statistics

              MURDER          RAPE       ROBBERY       ASSAULT      BURGLARY       LARCENY          AUTO

Mean    7.444000000   25.73400000   124.0920000   211.3000000   1291.904000   2671.288000   377.5260000
Std     3.866768941   10.75962995    88.3485672   100.2530492    432.455711    725.908707   193.3944175

                                      Correlation Matrix

              MURDER          RAPE       ROBBERY       ASSAULT      BURGLARY       LARCENY          AUTO

MURDER        1.0000        0.6012        0.4837        0.6486        0.3858        0.1019        0.0688
RAPE          0.6012        1.0000        0.5919        0.7403        0.7121        0.6140        0.3489
ROBBERY       0.4837        0.5919        1.0000        0.5571        0.6372        0.4467        0.5907
ASSAULT       0.6486        0.7403        0.5571        1.0000        0.6229        0.4044        0.2758
BURGLARY      0.3858        0.7121        0.6372        0.6229        1.0000        0.7921        0.5580
LARCENY       0.1019        0.6140        0.4467        0.4044        0.7921        1.0000        0.4442
AUTO          0.0688        0.3489        0.5907        0.2758        0.5580        0.4442        1.0000

                         Eigenvalue    Difference    Proportion     Cumulative

              PRIN1         4.11496       2.87624      0.587851        0.58785
              PRIN2         1.23872       0.51291      0.176960        0.76481
              PRIN3         0.72582       0.40938      0.103688        0.86850
              PRIN4         0.31643       0.05846      0.045205        0.91370
              PRIN5         0.25797       0.03593      0.036853        0.95056
              PRIN6         0.22204       0.09798      0.031720        0.98228
              PRIN7         0.12406                    0.017722        1.00000


                                       Eigenvectors

               PRIN1         PRIN2         PRIN3         PRIN4         PRIN5         PRIN6         PRIN7

MURDER      0.300279      -.629174      0.178245      -.232114      0.538123      0.259117      0.267593
RAPE        0.431759      -.169435      -.244198      0.062216      0.188471      -.773271      -.296485
ROBBERY     0.396875      0.042247      0.495861      -.557989      -.519977      -.114385      -.003903
ASSAULT     0.396652      -.343528      -.069510      0.629804      -.506651      0.172363      0.191745
BURGLARY    0.440157      0.203341      -.209895      -.057555      0.101033      0.535987      -.648117
LARCENY     0.357360      0.402319      -.539231      -.234890      0.030099      0.039406      0.601690
AUTO        0.295177      0.502421      0.568384      0.419238      0.369753      -.057298      0.147046
```

The eigenvalues indicate that two or three components provide a good summary of the data, two components accounting for 76 percent of the standardized variance and three components explaining 87 percent. Subsequent components contribute less than 5 percent each.

The first component is a measure of overall crime rate since the first eigenvector shows approximately equal loadings on all variables. The second eigenvector has high positive loadings on AUTO and LARCENY and high negative loadings on MURDER and ASSAULT. There is also a small positive loading on BURGLARY and a small negative loading on RAPE. This component seems to measure the preponderance of property crime over violent crime. The interpretation of the third component is not obvious.

A simple way to examine the principal components in more detail is to print the output data set sorted by each of the large components. These statements produce **Output 27.5**:

```
proc sort;
   by prin1;
proc print;
   id state;
   var prin1 prin2 murder rape robbery assault burglary larceny auto;
   title2 'States Listed in Order of Overall Crime Rate';
   title3 'As Determined by the First Principal Component';
proc sort;
   by prin2;
proc print;
   id state;
   var prin1 prin2 murder rape robbery assault burglary larceny auto;
   title2 'States Listed in Order of Property Vs. Violent Crime';
   title3 'As Determined by the Second Principal Component';
run;
```

Output 27.5   The OUT= Data Set Sorted by Principal Components: PROC PRINT

```
                      Crime Rates per 100,000 Population by State                                    1
                        States Listed in Order of Overall Crime Rate
                          As Determined by the First Principal Component

    STATE           PRIN1     PRIN2    MURDER   RAPE   ROBBERY   ASSAULT   BURGLARY   LARCENY   AUTO

    North Dakota   -3.96408   0.38767    0.9      9.0     13.3      43.8      446.1     1843.0   144.7
    South Dakota   -3.17203  -0.25446    2.0     13.5     17.9     155.7      570.5     1704.4   147.5
    West Virginia  -3.14772  -0.81425    6.0     13.2     42.2      90.9      597.4     1341.7   163.3
    Iowa           -2.58156   0.82475    2.3     10.6     41.2      89.8      812.5     2685.1   219.9
    Wisconsin      -2.50296   0.78083    2.8     12.9     52.2      63.7      846.9     2614.2   220.7
    New Hampshire  -2.46562   0.82503    3.2     10.7     23.2      76.0     1041.7     2343.9   293.4
    Nebraska       -2.15071   0.22574    3.9     18.1     64.7     112.7      760.0     2316.1   249.1
    Vermont        -2.06433   0.94497    1.4     15.9     30.8     101.2     1348.2     2201.0   265.2
    Maine          -1.82631   0.57878    2.4     13.5     38.7     170.0     1253.1     2350.7   246.9
    Kentucky       -1.72691  -1.14663   10.1     19.1     81.1     123.3      872.2     1662.1   245.4
    Pennsylvania   -1.72007  -0.19590    5.6     19.0    130.3     128.0      877.5     1624.1   333.2
    Montana        -1.66801   0.27099    5.4     16.7     39.2     156.8      804.9     2773.2   309.2
    Minnesota      -1.55434   1.05644    2.7     19.5     85.9      85.8     1134.7     2559.3   343.1
    Mississippi    -1.50736  -2.54671   14.3     19.6     65.7     189.1      915.6     1239.9   144.4
    Idaho          -1.43245  -0.00801    5.5     19.4     39.6     172.5     1050.8     2599.6   237.6
    Wyoming        -1.42463   0.06268    5.4     21.9     39.7     173.9      811.6     2772.2   282.0
    Arkansas       -1.05441  -1.34544    8.8     27.6     83.2     203.4      972.6     1862.1   183.4
    Utah           -1.04996   0.93656    3.5     20.3     68.8     147.3     1171.6     3004.6   334.5
    Virginia       -0.91621  -0.69265    9.0     23.3     92.1     165.7      986.2     2521.2   226.7
    North Carolina -0.69925  -1.67027   10.6     17.0     61.3     318.3     1154.1     2037.8   192.1
    Kansas         -0.63407  -0.02804    6.6     22.0    100.7     180.5     1270.4     2739.3   244.3
    Connecticut    -0.54133   1.50123    4.2     16.8    129.5     131.8     1346.0     2620.7   593.2
    Indiana        -0.49990   0.00003    7.4     26.5    123.2     153.5     1086.2     2498.7   377.4
    Oklahoma       -0.32136  -0.62429    8.6     29.2     73.8     205.0     1288.2     2228.1   326.8
    Rhode Island   -0.20156   2.14658    3.6     10.5     86.5     201.0     1489.5     2844.1   791.4
    Tennessee      -0.13660  -1.13498   10.1     29.7    145.8     203.9     1259.7     1776.5   314.0
    Alabama        -0.04988  -2.09610   14.2     25.2     96.8     278.3     1135.5     1881.9   280.7
    New Jersey      0.21787   0.96421    5.6     21.0    180.4     185.1     1435.8     2774.5   511.5
    Ohio            0.23953   0.09053    7.8     27.3    190.5     181.1     1216.0     2696.8   400.4
    Georgia         0.49041  -1.38079   11.7     31.1    140.5     256.5     1351.1     2170.2   297.9
    Illinois        0.51290   0.09423    9.9     21.8    211.3     209.0     1085.0     2828.5   528.6
    Missouri        0.55637  -0.55851    9.6     28.3    189.0     233.5     1318.3     2424.2   378.4
    Hawaii          0.82313   1.82392    7.2     25.5    128.0      64.1     1911.5     3920.4   489.4
    Washington      0.93058   0.73776    4.3     39.6    106.2     224.8     1605.6     3386.9   360.3
    Delaware        0.96458   1.29674    6.0     24.9    157.0     194.2     1682.6     3678.4   467.0
    Massachusetts   0.97844   2.63105    3.1     20.8    169.1     231.6     1532.2     2311.3  1140.1
    Louisiana       1.12020  -2.08327   15.5     30.9    142.9     335.5     1165.5     2469.9   337.7
    New Mexico      1.21417  -0.95076    8.8     39.1    109.6     343.4     1418.7     3008.6   259.5
    Texas           1.39696  -0.68131   13.3     33.8    152.4     208.2     1603.1     2988.7   397.6
    Oregon          1.44900   0.58603    4.9     39.9    124.1     286.9     1636.4     3506.1   388.9
```

(continued on next page)

(continued from previous page)

	PRIN1	PRIN2	MURDER	RAPE	ROBBERY	ASSAULT	BURGLARY	LARCENY	AUTO
South Carolina	1.60336	-2.16211	11.9	33.0	105.9	485.3	1613.6	2342.4	245.1
Maryland	2.18280	-0.19474	8.0	34.8	292.1	358.9	1400.0	3177.7	428.5
Michigan	2.27333	0.15487	9.3	38.9	261.9	274.6	1522.7	3159.0	545.5
Alaska	2.42151	0.16652	10.8	51.6	96.8	284.0	1331.7	3369.8	753.3
Colorado	2.50929	0.91660	6.3	42.0	170.7	292.9	1935.2	3903.2	477.1
Arizona	3.01414	0.84495	9.5	34.2	138.2	312.3	2346.1	4467.4	439.5
Florida	3.11175	-0.60392	10.2	39.6	187.9	449.1	1859.9	3840.5	351.4
New York	3.45248	0.43289	10.7	29.4	472.6	319.1	1728.0	2782.0	745.8
California	4.28380	0.14319	11.5	49.4	287.0	358.0	2139.4	3499.8	663.5
Nevada	5.26699	-0.25262	15.8	49.1	323.1	355.0	2453.1	4212.6	559.2

Crime Rates per 100,000 Population by State
States Listed in Order of Property Vs. Violent Crime
As Determined by the Second Principal Component

2

STATE	PRIN1	PRIN2	MURDER	RAPE	ROBBERY	ASSAULT	BURGLARY	LARCENY	AUTO
Mississippi	-1.50736	-2.54671	14.3	19.6	65.7	189.1	915.6	1239.9	144.4
South Carolina	1.60336	-2.16211	11.9	33.0	105.9	485.3	1613.6	2342.4	245.1
Alabama	-0.04988	-2.09610	14.2	25.2	96.8	278.3	1135.5	1881.9	280.7
Louisiana	1.12020	-2.08327	15.5	30.9	142.9	335.5	1165.5	2469.9	337.7
North Carolina	-0.69925	-1.67027	10.6	17.0	61.3	318.3	1154.1	2037.8	192.1
Georgia	0.49041	-1.38079	11.7	31.1	140.5	256.5	1351.1	2170.2	297.9
Arkansas	-1.05441	-1.34544	8.8	27.6	83.2	203.4	972.6	1862.1	183.4
Kentucky	-1.72691	-1.14663	10.1	19.1	81.1	123.3	872.2	1662.1	245.4
Tennessee	-0.13660	-1.13498	10.1	29.7	145.8	203.9	1259.7	1776.5	314.0
New Mexico	1.21417	-0.95076	8.8	39.1	109.6	343.4	1418.7	3008.6	259.5
West Virginia	-3.14772	-0.81425	6.0	13.2	42.2	90.9	597.4	1341.7	163.3
Virginia	-0.91621	-0.69265	9.0	23.3	92.1	165.7	986.2	2521.2	226.7
Texas	1.39696	-0.68131	13.3	33.8	152.4	208.2	1603.1	2988.7	397.6
Oklahoma	-0.32136	-0.62429	8.6	29.2	73.8	205.0	1288.2	2228.1	326.8
Florida	3.11175	-0.60392	10.2	39.6	187.9	449.1	1859.9	3840.5	351.4
Missouri	0.55637	-0.55851	9.6	28.3	189.0	233.5	1318.3	2424.2	378.4
South Dakota	-3.17203	-0.25446	2.0	13.5	17.9	155.7	570.5	1704.4	147.5
Nevada	5.26699	-0.25262	15.8	49.1	323.1	355.0	2453.1	4212.6	559.2
Pennsylvania	-1.72007	-0.19590	5.6	19.0	130.3	128.0	877.5	1624.1	333.2
Maryland	2.18280	-0.19474	8.0	34.8	292.1	358.9	1400.0	3177.7	428.5
Kansas	-0.63407	-0.02804	6.6	22.0	100.7	180.5	1270.4	2739.3	244.3
Idaho	-1.43245	-0.00801	5.5	19.4	39.6	172.5	1050.8	2599.6	237.6
Indiana	-0.49990	0.00003	7.4	26.5	123.2	153.5	1086.2	2498.7	377.4
Wyoming	-1.42463	0.06268	5.4	21.9	39.7	173.9	811.6	2772.2	282.0
Ohio	0.23953	0.09053	7.8	27.3	190.5	181.1	1216.0	2696.8	400.4
Illinois	0.51290	0.09423	9.9	21.8	211.3	209.0	1085.0	2828.5	528.6
California	4.28380	0.14319	11.5	49.4	287.0	358.0	2139.4	3499.8	663.5
Michigan	2.27333	0.15487	9.3	38.9	261.9	274.6	1522.7	3159.0	545.5
Alaska	2.42151	0.16652	10.8	51.6	96.8	284.0	1331.7	3369.8	753.3
Nebraska	-2.15071	0.22574	3.9	18.1	64.7	112.7	760.0	2316.1	249.1
Montana	-1.66801	0.27099	5.4	16.7	39.2	156.8	804.9	2773.2	309.2
North Dakota	-3.96408	0.38767	0.9	9.0	13.3	43.8	446.1	1843.0	144.7
New York	3.45248	0.43289	10.7	29.4	472.6	319.1	1728.0	2782.0	745.8
Maine	-1.82631	0.57878	2.4	13.5	38.7	170.0	1253.1	2350.7	246.9
Oregon	1.44900	0.58603	4.9	39.9	124.1	286.9	1636.4	3506.1	388.9
Washington	0.93058	0.73776	4.3	39.6	106.2	224.8	1605.6	3386.9	360.3
Wisconsin	-2.50296	0.78083	2.8	12.9	52.2	63.7	846.9	2614.2	220.7
Iowa	-2.58156	0.82475	2.3	10.6	41.2	89.8	812.5	2685.1	219.9
New Hampshire	-2.46562	0.82503	3.2	10.7	23.2	76.0	1041.7	2343.9	293.4
Arizona	3.01414	0.84495	9.5	34.2	138.2	312.3	2346.1	4467.4	439.5
Colorado	2.50929	0.91660	6.3	42.0	170.7	292.9	1935.2	3903.2	477.1
Utah	-1.04996	0.93656	3.5	10.2	68.8	147.3	1171.6	3004.6	334.5
Vermont	-2.06433	0.94497	1.4	15.9	30.8	101.2	1348.2	2201.0	265.2
New Jersey	0.21787	0.96421	5.6	21.0	180.4	185.1	1435.8	2774.5	511.5
Minnesota	-1.55434	1.05644	2.7	19.5	85.9	85.8	1134.7	2559.3	343.1
Delaware	0.96458	1.29674	6.0	24.9	157.0	194.2	1682.6	3678.4	467.0
Connecticut	-0.54133	1.50123	4.2	16.8	129.5	131.8	1346.0	2620.7	593.2
Hawaii	0.82313	1.82392	7.2	25.5	128.0	64.1	1911.5	3920.4	489.4
Rhode Island	-0.20156	2.14658	3.6	10.5	86.5	201.0	1489.5	2844.1	791.4
Massachusetts	0.97844	2.63105	3.1	20.8	169.1	231.6	1532.2	2311.3	1140.1

Another recommended procedure is to make scatter plots of the first few components. The sorted listings help to identify observations on the plots. The following statements produce **Output 27.6**:

```
proc plot;
   plot prin2*prin1=state / vpos=31;
   title2 'Plot of the First Two Principal Components';
proc plot;
   plot prin3*prin1=state / vpos=26;
   title2 'Plot of the First and Third Principal Components';
run;
```

Output 27.6   Plots of Principal Components: PROC PLOT

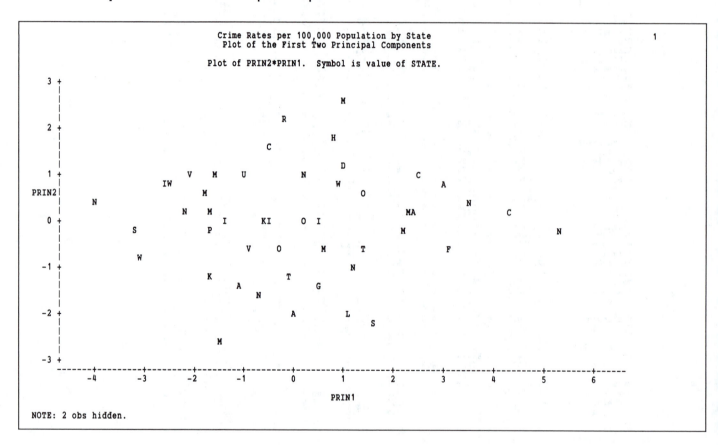

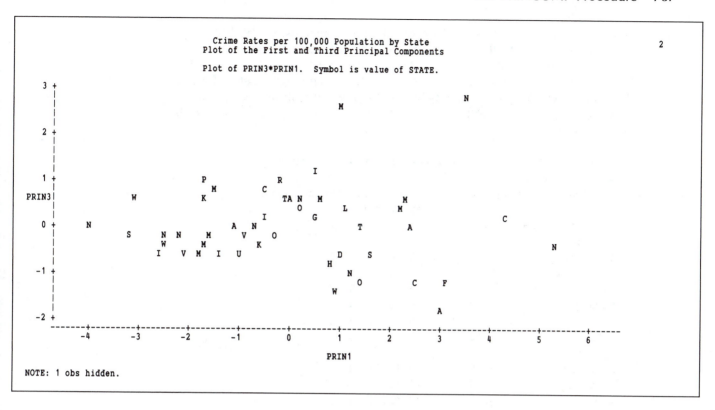

NOTE: 1 obs hidden.

It is possible to identify regional trends on the plot of the first two components. Nevada and California are at the extreme right, with high overall crime rates but an average ratio of property crime to violent crime. North and South Dakota are on the extreme left with low overall crime rates. Southeastern states tend to be in the bottom of the plot, with a higher-than-average ratio of violent crime to property crime. New England states tend to be in the upper part of the plot, with a greater-than-average ratio of property crime to violent crime.

The most striking feature of the plot of the first and third principal components is that Massachusetts and New York are outliers on the third component.

Example 3: Basketball Data

The data in this example are rankings of 35 college basketball teams. The rankings were made before the start of the 1985–86 season by 10 news services.

The purpose of the principal component analysis is to compute a a single variable that best summarizes all 10 of the pre-season rankings.

Note that the various news services rank different numbers of teams, varying from 20 through 30 (there is a missing rank in one of the variables, WASPOST). And, of course, each service does not rank the same teams, so there are missing values in these data. Each of the 35 teams is ranked by at least one news service.

PRINCOMP omits observations with missing values. To obtain principal component scores for all of the teams, it is necessary to replace the missing values. Since it is the best teams that are ranked, it is not appropriate to replace missing values with the mean of the nonmissing values. Instead, an ad hoc method is used that replaces missing values by the mean of the unassigned ranks. For example, if 20 teams are ranked by a news service, then ranks 21 through 35 are unassigned. The mean of the ranks 21 through 35 is 28, so missing values for that variable are replaced by the value 28. To prevent the method of missing-value replacement from having an undue effect on the analysis, each observation is weighted according to the number of nonmissing values it has.

Since the first principal component accounts for 78 percent of the variance, there is substantial agreement among the rankings. The eigenvector shows that all the news services are about equally weighted, so a simple average would work almost as well as the first principal component. The following statements produce **Output 27.7**:

```
title1 'Pre-Season 1985 College Basketball Rankings';
data bballm;
   input school $13. csn dursun durher waspost usatoda
         spormag insport upi ap sporill;
   format csn--sporill 5.1;
   cards;
```

school	csn	dursun	durher	waspost	usatoda	spormag	insport	upi	ap	sporill
Louisville	1	8	1	9	8	9	6	10	9	9
Georgia Tech	2	2	4	3	1	1	1	2	1	1
Kansas	3	4	5	1	5	11	8	4	5	7
Michigan	4	5	9	4	2	5	3	1	3	2
Duke	5	6	7	5	4	10	4	5	6	5
UNC	6	1	2	2	3	4	2	3	2	3
Syracuse	7	10	6	11	6	6	5	6	4	10
Notre Dame	8	14	15	13	11	20	18	13	12	.
Kentucky	9	15	16	14	14	19	11	12	11	13
LSU	10	9	13	.	13	15	16	9	14	8
DePaul	11	.	21	15	20	.	19	.	.	19
Georgetown	12	7	8	6	9	2	9	8	8	4
Navy	13	20	23	10	18	13	15	.	20	.
Illinois	14	3	3	7	7	3	10	7	7	6
Iowa	15	16	.	.	23	.	.	14	.	20
Arkansas	16	.	.	.	25	.	.	.	.	16
Memphis State	17	.	11	.	16	8	20	.	15	12
Washington	18	.	.	.	.	.	.	17	.	.
UAB	19	13	10	.	12	17	.	16	16	15
UNLV	20	18	18	19	22	.	14	18	18	.
NC State	21	17	14	16	15	.	12	15	17	18
Maryland	22	.	.	.	19	.	.	.	19	14
Pittsburgh	23	.	.	.	.	.	.	.	.	.
Oklahoma	24	19	17	17	17	12	17	.	13	17
Indiana	25	12	20	18	21	.	.	.	.	.
Virginia	26	.	22	.	.	18	.	.	.	.
Old Dominion	27	.	.	.	.	.	.	.	.	.
Auburn	28	11	12	8	10	7	7	11	10	11
St. Johns	29	.	.	.	.	14	.	.	.	.
UCLA	30	.	.	.	.	.	.	19	.	.
St. Joseph's	.	.	19	.	.	.	.	.	.	.
Tennessee	.	.	24	.	.	16	.	.	.	.
Montana	.	.	.	20	.	.	.	.	.	.
Houston	.	.	.	.	24	.	.	.	.	.
Virginia Tech	.	.	.	.	.	.	13	.	.	.

```
;
```

```
/* PROC MEANS is used to output a data set containing the maximum   */
/* value of each of the newspaper and magazine rankings.  The       */
/* output data set, maxrank, is then used to set the missing        */
/* values to the next highest rank plus thirty-six, divided by two  */
/* (that is, the mean of the missing ranks).  This ad hoc method of */
/* replacing missing values is based more on intuition than on      */
/* rigorous statistical theory.  Observations are weighted by the   */
/* number of nonmissing values.                                     */

proc means data=bballm;
   output  out=maxrank
           max=mcsn mdurs mdurh mwas musa mspom mins mupi map mspoi;
run;


/* The method of filling in missing values shown below is a  */
/* reasonable method for this specific example.  It would be */
/* inappropriate to use this method for other data sets.  In */
/* addition, any method of filling in missing                */
/* values can result in incorrect statistics. The choice of  */
/* whether to fill in missing values, and what method to use */
/* to do so, is the responsibility of the person performing  */
/* the analysis.                                             */

data bball;
   set bballm;
   if _n_=1 then set maxrank;
   array services{10} csn--sporill;
   array maxranks{10} mcsn--mspoi;
   keep  school csn--sporill weight;
   weight=0;
   do i=1 to 10;
      if services{i}=. then services{i}=(maxranks{i}+36) / 2;
      else weight=weight+1;
      end;
run;


/* Use the PRINCOMP procedure to transform the observed ranks. */
/* Use n=1 because the data should be related                  */
/* to a single underlying variable. Sort the data and print the */
/* resulting component.                                        */

proc princomp data=bball n=1 out=pcbball standard;
   var csn--sporill;
   weight weight;
run;

proc sort data=pcbball;
   by prin1;
proc print;
   var school prin1;
   title2 'College Teams as Ordered by PRINCOMP';
run;
```

Output 27.7   Basketball Rankings Using PROC PRINCOMP

```
                    Pre-Season 1985 College Basketball Rankings                    1

      N Obs  Variable   N      Minimum        Maximum         Mean       Std Dev
      ---------------------------------------------------------------------------
       35    CSN       30     1.0000000     30.0000000    15.5000000     8.8034084
              DURSUN    20     1.0000000     20.0000000    10.5000000     5.9160798
              DURHER    24     1.0000000     24.0000000    12.5000000     7.0710678
              WASPOST   19     1.0000000     20.0000000    10.4210526     6.0673607
              USATODA   25     1.0000000     25.0000000    13.0000000     7.3598007
              SPORMAG   20     1.0000000     20.0000000    10.5000000     5.9160798
              INSPORT   20     1.0000000     20.0000000    10.5000000     5.9160798
              UPI       19     1.0000000     19.0000000    10.0000000     5.6273143
              AP        20     1.0000000     20.0000000    10.5000000     5.9160798
              SPORILL   20     1.0000000     20.0000000    10.5000000     5.9160798
      ---------------------------------------------------------------------------
```

```
                    Pre-Season 1985 College Basketball Rankings                    2

                           Principal Component Analysis

     35 Observations
     10 Variables


                              Simple Statistics

                    CSN          DURSUN         DURHER         WASPOST        USATODA

       Mean    13.33640553    13.06451613    12.88018433    13.83410138    12.55760369
       Std     22.08036285    21.66394183    21.38091837    23.47841791    20.48207965


                    SPORMAG        INSPORT        UPI            AP             SPORILL

       Mean    13.83870968    13.24423963    13.59216590    12.83410138    13.52534562
       Std     23.37756267    22.20231526    23.25602811    21.40782406    22.93219584


                              Correlation Matrix

              CSN     DURSUN   DURHER   WASPOST  USATODA  SPORMAG  INSPORT   UPI      AP      SPORILL
    CSN     1.0000   0.6505   0.6415   0.6121   0.7456   0.4806   0.6558   0.7007   0.6779   0.6135
    DURSUN  0.6505   1.0000   0.8341   0.7667   0.8860   0.6940   0.7702   0.9015   0.8437   0.7518
    DURHER  0.6415   0.8341   1.0000   0.7035   0.8877   0.7788   0.7900   0.7676   0.8788   0.7761
    WASPOST 0.6121   0.7667   0.7035   1.0000   0.7984   0.6598   0.8717   0.6953   0.7809   0.5952
    USATODA 0.7456   0.8860   0.8877   0.7984   1.0000   0.7716   0.8475   0.8539   0.9479   0.8426
    SPORMAG 0.4806   0.6940   0.7788   0.6598   0.7716   1.0000   0.7176   0.6220   0.8217   0.7701
    INSPORT 0.6558   0.7702   0.7900   0.8717   0.8475   0.7176   1.0000   0.7920   0.8830   0.7332
    UPI     0.7007   0.9015   0.7676   0.6953   0.8539   0.6220   0.7920   1.0000   0.8436   0.7738
    AP      0.6779   0.8437   0.8788   0.7809   0.9479   0.8217   0.8830   0.8436   1.0000   0.8212
    SPORILL 0.6135   0.7518   0.7761   0.5952   0.8426   0.7701   0.7332   0.7738   0.8212   1.0000


                     Eigenvalues of the Correlation Matrix

                    Eigenvalue   Difference    Proportion    Cumulative

            PRIN1     7.88602                    0.788602      0.788602


                                Eigenvectors

                                    PRIN1

                    CSN          0.270205
                    DURSUN       0.326048
                    DURHER       0.324392
                    WASPOST      0.300449
                    USATODA      0.345200
                    SPORMAG      0.293881
                    INSPORT      0.324088
                    UPI          0.319902
                    AP           0.342151
                    SPORILL      0.308570
```

```
                Pre-Season 1985 College Basketball Rankings           3
                   College Teams as Ordered by PRINCOMP

          OBS        SCHOOL              PRIN1

            1        Georgia Tech       -0.58068
            2        UNC                -0.53317
            3        Michigan           -0.47874
            4        Kansas             -0.40285
            5        Duke               -0.38464
            6        Illinois           -0.33586
            7        Syracuse           -0.31578
            8        Lousiville         -0.31489
            9        Georgetown         -0.29735
           10        Auburn             -0.09785
           11        Kentucky            0.00843
           12        LSU                 0.00872
           13        Notre Dame          0.09407
           14        NC State            0.19404
           15        UAB                 0.19771
           16        Oklahoma            0.23864
           17        Memphis State       0.25319
           18        Navy                0.28921
           19        UNLV                0.35103
           20        DePaul              0.43770
           21        Iowa                0.50213
           22        Indiana             0.51713
           23        Maryland            0.55910
           24        Arkansas            0.62977
           25        Virginia            0.67586
           26        Washington          0.67756
           27        Tennessee           0.70822
           28        St. Johns           0.71425
           29        Virginia Tech       0.71638
           30        St. Joseph's        0.73492
           31        UCLA                0.73965
           32        Pittsburg           0.75078
           33        Houston             0.75534
           34        Montana             0.75790
           35        Old Dominion        0.76821
```

REFERENCES

Cooley, W.W. and Lohnes, P.R. (1971), *Multivariate Data Analysis*, New York: John Wiley & Sons, Inc.

Gnanadesikan, R. (1977), *Methods for Statistical Data Analysis of Multivariate Observations*, New York: John Wiley & Sons, Inc.

Hotelling, H. (1933), "Analysis of a Complex of Statistical Variables into Principal Components," *Journal of Educational Psychology*, 24, 417–441, 498–520.

Kshirsagar, A.M. (1972), *Multivariate Analysis*, New York: Marcel Dekker, Inc.

Mardia, K.V., Kent, J.T., and Bibby, J.M. (1979), *Multivariate Analysis*, London: Academic Press.

Morrison, D.F. (1976), *Multivariate Statistical Methods*, 2d Edition, New York: McGraw-Hill Book Co.

Pearson, K. (1901), "On Lines and Planes of Closest Fit to Systems of Points in Space," *Philosophical Magazine*, 6(2), 559–572.

Rao, C.R. (1964), "The Use and Interpretation of Principal Component Analysis in Applied Research," *Sankhya A*, 26, 329–358.

The REG
Procedure

ABSTRACT

The REG procedure fits linear regression models by least-squares. Subsets of independent variables that "best" predict the dependent or response variable can be determined by various model-selection methods.

INTRODUCTION

PROC REG is one of many regression procedures in the SAS System. REG is a general-purpose procedure for regression, while other SAS regression procedures have more specialized applications. Other SAS/STAT procedures that perform at least one type of regression analysis are CATMOD, GLM, NLIN, ORTHOREG, and RSREG. SAS/ETS procedures are specialized for applications in time-series or simultaneous systems. These other SAS/STAT and SAS/ETS regression procedures are summarized in Chapter 1, "Introduction to Regression Procedures," which also contains an overview of regression techniques and defines many of the statistics computed by REG and other regression procedures.

PROC REG

- handles multiple MODEL statements
- provides nine model-selection methods
- allows interactive changes both in the model and the data used to fit the model
- allows linear inequality restrictions on parameters
- tests linear hypotheses and multivariate hypotheses
- generates scatter plots of data and various statistics
- "paints" or highlights scatter plots
- produces partial regression leverage plots
- computes collinearity diagnostics
- prints predicted values, residuals, studentized residuals, confidence limits, and influence statistics and can output these items to a SAS data set
- can use correlations or crossproducts for input
- writes the crossproducts matrix to an output SAS data set.

Nine model-selection methods are available in PROC REG. The simplest method is also the default, where REG fits the complete model you specify. The other eight methods involve various ways of including or excluding variables from the model. These methods are specified with the SELECTION= option in the MODEL statement. The methods are identified below and explained in detail in **Model Selection Methods** later in this chapter.

NONE	no model selection. This is the default. The complete model specified in the MODEL statement is fit to the data.
FORWARD	forward selection. The method starts with no variables in the model and adds variables.
BACKWARD	backward elimination. The method starts with all variables in the model and deletes variables.
STEPWISE	stepwise regression. This is similar to FORWARD except that variables already in the model do not necessarily stay there.
MAXR	forward selection to fit the best one-variable model, the best two-variable model, and so on. Variables are switched so that R^2 is maximized.
MINR	similar to MAXR, except that variables are switched so that the increase in R^2 from adding a variable to the model is minimized.
RSQUARE	finds a specified number of models with the highest R^2 in a range of model sizes.
ADJRSQ	finds a specified number of models with the highest adjusted R^2 in a range of model sizes.
CP	finds a specified number of models with the lowest C_p in a range of model sizes.

Least-Squares Estimation

Suppose that a response variable Y can be predicted by a linear combination of some regressor variables X1 and X2. You can fit the β parameters in the equation

$$Y_i = \beta_0 + \beta_1 X1_i + \beta_2 X2_i + \varepsilon_i$$

for the observations $i = 1, \ldots, n$. To fit this model with the REG procedure, specify

```
proc reg;
   model y=x1 x2;
```

REG uses the principle of least squares to produce estimates that are the best linear unbiased estimates (BLUE) under classical statistical assumptions (Gauss 1809; Markov 1900).

You might use regression analysis to find out how well you can predict a child's weight if you know that child's height. Suppose you collect your data by measuring heights and weights of nineteen school children. You want to estimate the intercept β_0 and the slope β_1 of a line described by the equation

$$\text{WEIGHT} = \beta_0 + \beta_1 \text{ HEIGHT} + \varepsilon$$

where

WEIGHT	is the response variable.
β_0, β_1	are the unknown parameters.
HEIGHT	is the regressor variable.
ε	is the unknown error.

The data below produce **Output 28.1**, which shows a regression analysis and a plot of the data.

```
data class;
   input name $ height weight;
   cards;
Alfred  69.0 112.5
Alice   56.5  84.0
Barbara 65.3  98.0
Carol   62.8 102.5
Henry   63.5 102.5
James   57.3  83.0
Jane    59.8  84.5
Janet   62.5 112.5
Jeffrey 62.5  84.0
John    59.0  99.5
Joyce   51.3  50.5
Judy    64.3  90.0
Louise  56.3  77.0
Mary    66.5 112.0
```

```
        Philip  72.0 150.0
        Robert  64.8 128.0
        Ronald  67.0 133.0
        Thomas  57.5  85.0
        William 66.5 112.0
        ;
        proc reg;
           model weight = height;
           plot weight*height;
        run;
```

Output 28.1   Regression for Weight and Height Data

```
                                        SAS                                              1

Model: MODEL1
Dependent Variable: WEIGHT
                                 Analysis of Variance

                                 Sum of        Mean
       Source         DF        Squares       Square      F Value      Prob>F

       Model           1     7193.24912    7193.24912      57.076      0.0001
       Error          17     2142.48772     126.02869
       C Total        18     9335.73684

             Root MSE       11.22625     R-square       0.7705
             Dep Mean      100.02632     Adj R-sq       0.7570
             C.V.           11.22330

                                 Parameter Estimates

                       Parameter      Standard     T for H0:
       Variable  DF     Estimate         Error    Parameter=0      Prob > |T|

       INTERCEP   1   -143.026918    32.27459130       -4.432        0.0004
       HEIGHT     1      3.899030     0.51609395        7.555        0.0001
```

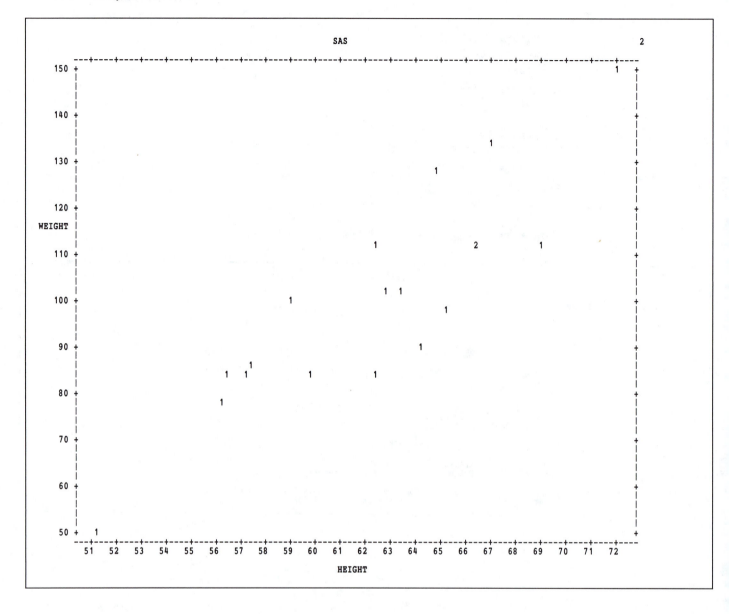

The *F* statistic for the overall model is significant, indicating that the model explains a significant portion of the variation in the data. From the parameter estimates, the fitted model is

WEIGHT = −143.0 + 3.9*HEIGHT   .

The output also contains the *t* statistics and the corresponding significance probabilities to test if each parameter is significantly different from zero. The significance probabilities, or *p* values, indicate that the intercept and HEIGHT parameter estimates are significant at the 95% significance level. For a complete regression analysis, you would want to try other models and, for each model, use various diagnostic techniques to examine the fit of the model. Techniques discussed later in this chapter include diagnostic plots, collinearity diagnostics, and influence statistics.

Regression is often used in an exploratory fashion to look for empirical relation-ships, such as the relationship between HEIGHT and WEIGHT. In this example, HEIGHT is not the cause of WEIGHT. You would need a controlled experiment to scientifically confirm the relationship. See **Comments on Interpreting Regres-sion Statistics** in Chapter 1, "Introduction to Regression Procedures," for more information.

Using PROC REG Interactively

REG can be used interactively. After you specify a model with a MODEL state-ment and run REG with a RUN statement, a variety of statements can be executed without reinvoking REG.

The **SPECIFICATIONS** section describes which statements can be used interac-tively. These interactive statements can be executed singly or in groups by follow-ing the single statement or group of statements with a RUN statement. Note that the MODEL statement can be repeated. This is an important difference from GLM, which allows only one MODEL statement.

If you use REG interactively, you can end the REG procedure with a DATA step, another PROC step, an ENDSAS statement, or with a QUIT statement. The syntax of the QUIT statement is

```
quit;
```

When you are using REG interactively, additional RUN statements do not end REG but tell the procedure to execute additional statements.

When a BY statement is used with PROC REG, interactive processing is not possible; that is, once the first RUN statement is encountered, processing pro-ceeds for each BY group in the data set, and no further statements are accepted by the procedure.

When using REG interactively, you may fit a model, perform diagnostics, then refit the model, and perform diagnostics on the refitted model. Most of the inter-active statements implicitly refit the model; for example, if you use the ADD state-ment to add a variable to the model, the regression equation is automatically recomputed. The two exceptions to this automatic recomputing are the PAINT and REWEIGHT statements. These two statements do not cause the model to be refitted. To do so, you can follow these statements either with a REFIT state-ment, which causes the model to be explicitly recomputed, or with another inter-active statement that causes the model to be implicitly recomputed.

SPECIFICATIONS

Although there are numerous statements and options available in REG, many analyses use only a few of them. Often you can find the features you need by looking at an example or by scanning through this section. The statements available in REG are

PROC REG *options*; }   required statement

label: **MODEL** *dependents* = *regressors* / *options*; }   required statement
for model fitting;
can be used interactively

BY *variables*;
FREQ *variable*;
ID *variable*;   must appear before
VAR *variables*;   the first **RUN** statement
WEIGHT *variable*;

ADD *variables*;
DELETE *variables*;
label: **MTEST** [*equation1*, . . . , *equationk* / *options*];   can appear
OUTPUT OUT = *SASdataset keyword* = *names* . . . ;   anywhere after
PAINT [*condition* | ALLOBS][/ *options*] | a **MODEL** statement
        [STATUS | UNDO];   and can be used
PLOT[*yvariable1**xvariable1][= *symbol1*]   interactively
        . . . [*yvariablek**xvariablek][= *symbolk*]
        [/ *options*];
PRINT [*options* ANOVA MODELDATA];
REFIT;
RESTRICT *equation1*, . . . , *equationk*;
REWEIGHT [*condition* | ALLOBS][/ *options*] |
        [STATUS | UNDO];
label: **TEST** *equation1*, . . . , *equationk* / *option*;

In the above list, brackets denote optional specifications, and vertical bars denote a choice of one of the specifications separated by the vertical bars. In all cases, *label* is optional.

The PROC REG statement is required. To fit a model to the data, the MODEL statement is required. If you only want to use the options available in the PROC REG statement, you do not need a MODEL statement, but you must use a VAR statement. (See the example in **Output Data Sets** later in this chapter.) Several MODEL statements can be used. In addition, several MTEST, OUTPUT, PAINT, PLOT, PRINT, RESTRICT, and TEST statements can follow each MODEL statement. The ADD, DELETE, and REWEIGHT statements are used interactively to change the regression model and the data used in fitting the model. The ADD, DELETE, MTEST, OUTPUT, PLOT, PRINT, RESTRICT, and TEST statements implicitly refit the model; changes made to the model are reflected in the printout from these statements. The REFIT statement is used to explicitly refit the model and is most helpful when it follows PAINT and REWEIGHT statements, which do not refit the model. The BY, FREQ, ID, VAR, and WEIGHT statements are optionally specified once for the entire PROC step and must appear before the first RUN statement.

When TYPE=CORR, TYPE=COV, or TYPE=SSCP data sets are used as input data sets to REG, statements and options that require the original data are not available. Specifically, the OUTPUT, PAINT, PLOT, and REWEIGHT statements, and the MODEL and PRINT statement options P, R, CLM, CLI, DW, INFLUENCE, and PARTIAL are disabled.

The statements used with the REG procedure in addition to the PROC REG statement are the following (in alphabetical order):

ADD	adds independent variables to the regression model.
BY	specifies variables to define subgroups for the analysis.
DELETE	deletes independent variables from the regression model.
FREQ	specifies a frequency variable.
ID	names a variable to identify observations in the printout.
MODEL	specifies the dependent and independent variables in the regression model, requests a model selection method, prints predicted values, and provides details on the estimates (according to which options are selected).
MTEST	performs multivariate tests across multiple dependent variables.
OUTPUT	creates an output data set and names the variables to contain predicted values, residuals, and other statistics.
PAINT	paints points in scatter plots.
PLOT	generates scatter plots.
PRINT	prints information about the model and can reset options.
REFIT	refits the model.
RESTRICT	places linear equality restrictions on the parameter estimates.
REWEIGHT	excludes specific observations from analysis or changes the weights of observations used. This statement replaces the DELOBS statement in Version 6.02 of SAS/STAT software.
TEST	performs an F test on linear functions of the parameters.
VAR	lists variables for which crossproducts are to be computed, variables that may be interactively added to the model, or variables to be used in scatter plots.
WEIGHT	declares a variable to weight observations.

PROC REG Statement

PROC REG *options*;

The PROC REG statement is required. If you want to fit a model to the data, you must also use a MODEL statement. If you only want to use the options described below, you do not need a MODEL statement, but you must use a VAR statement.

The following options can be specified in the PROC REG statement:

Data Set Options

COVOUT

outputs the covariance matrices for the parameter estimates to the OUTEST= data set. This option is valid only if the OUTEST= option is also specified. See **Output Data Sets** later in this chapter.

DATA=*SASdataset*

names the SAS data set to be used by PROC REG. The data set can be an ordinary SAS data set or a TYPE=CORR, TYPE=COV, or TYPE=SSCP data set. If one of these special TYPE= data sets is used, the OUTPUT, PAINT, PLOT, and REWEIGHT statements and some options in the MODEL and PRINT statements are not available. See Appendix 2, "Special SAS Data Sets," for more information on TYPE= data sets. If the DATA= option is not specified, REG uses the most recently created SAS data set.

OUTEST=*SASdataset*

requests that parameter estimates and optional statistics be output to this data set. See **Output Data Sets** later in this chapter for details. If you want to create a permanent SAS data set, you must specify a two-level name (see "SAS Files" in the *SAS Language Guide, Release 6.03 Edition* for more information on permanent SAS data sets).

OUTSSCP=*SASdataset*

requests that the sums of squares and crossproducts matrix be output to this TYPE=SSCP data set. See **Output Data Sets** for details. If you want to create a permanent SAS data set, you must specify a two-level name (see "SAS Files" in the *SAS Language Guide* for more information on permanent SAS data sets).

Printing and Miscellaneous Options

ALL

requests many printouts. Using ALL in the PROC REG statement is equivalent to specifying ALL in every MODEL statement. ALL also implies SIMPLE, USSCP, and CORR.

CORR

prints the correlation matrix for all variables listed in the MODEL or VAR statements.

NOPRINT

suppresses the printed output. Using this option in the PROC REG statement is equivalent to specifying NOPRINT in each MODEL statement.

SIMPLE

prints the sum, mean, variance, standard deviation, and uncorrected sum of squares for each variable used in REG.

SINGULAR=*n*

tunes the mechanism used to check for singularities. The default value is $1E-7$. This option is rarely needed. Singularity checking is described in **Computational Methods** later in this chapter.

USSCP

prints the uncorrected sums-of-squares and crossproducts matrix for all variables used in the procedure.

ADD Statement

ADD *variables*;

The ADD statement adds independent variables to the regression model. Only variables used in the VAR statement or used in MODEL statements before the first RUN statement can be added to the model. You can use the ADD statement interactively to add variables to the model or to include a variable that was previously deleted with a DELETE statement. See **Interactive Analysis** later in this chapter for an example.

BY Statement

BY *variables*;

A BY statement can be used with PROC REG to obtain separate analyses on observations in groups defined by the BY variables. When a BY statement appears, the procedure expects the input data set to be sorted in order of the BY variables.

If your input data set is not sorted in ascending order, use the SORT procedure with a similar BY statement to sort the data, or, if appropriate, use the BY statement options NOTSORTED or DESCENDING. For more information, see the discussion of the BY statement in "SAS Statements Used in the PROC Step" in the *SAS Language Guide*.

When a BY statement is used with PROC REG, interactive processing is not possible; that is, once the first RUN statement is encountered, processing proceeds for each BY group in the data set, and no further statements are accepted by the procedure. A BY statement that appears after the first RUN statement is ignored.

DELETE Statement

DELETE *variables*;

The DELETE statement deletes independent variables from the regression model. Use the DELETE statement to interactively delete variables from the model. The DELETE statement performs the opposite function of the ADD statement and is used in a similar manner. For an example of how the ADD statement is used (and how the DELETE statement can be used), see **Interactive Analysis** later in this chapter.

FREQ Statement

FREQ *variable*;

When a FREQ statement appears, each observation in the input data set is assumed to represent n observations, where n is the value of the FREQ variable. The analysis produced using a FREQ statement is the same as an analysis produced using a data set that contains n observations in place of each observation in the input data set. When the procedure determines degrees of freedom for significance tests, the total number of observations is considered to be equal to the sum of the values of the FREQ variable.

If the value of the FREQ variable is missing or is less than 1, the observation is not used in the analysis. If the value is not an integer, only the integer portion is used.

The FREQ statement must appear before the first RUN statement, or it is ignored.

ID Statement

> ID *variable*;

When one of the MODEL statement options CLI, CLM, P, R, or INFLUENCE is requested, the variable listed in the ID statement is printed on the output beside each observation. If the PARTIAL option is requested in the MODEL statement, the left-most nonblank character in the value of the ID variable is used as the plotting symbol. The ID variable can be used to identify each observation. If the ID statement is omitted, the observation number is used to identify the observations.

MODEL Statement

> *label*: MODEL *dependents=regressors / options*;

After the keyword MODEL, the dependent (response) variables are specified, followed by an equal sign and the regressor variables. Variables specified in the MODEL statement must be numeric variables in the data set being analyzed. For example, if you want to specify the quadratic term for X1 in the model, you cannot use X1*X1 in the MODEL statement but must create a new variable (say X1SQUARE=X1*X1) in a DATA step and use the new variable in the MODEL statement. The label in the MODEL statement is optional.

The following options are available in the MODEL statement after a slash (/):

Option for Model Selection

SELECTION=*name*

> specifies the method used to select the model, where *name* can be FORWARD (or F), BACKWARD (or B), STEPWISE, MAXR, MINR, RSQUARE, ADJRSQ, CP, or NONE (use the full model). The default method is NONE. See **Model-Selection Methods** for a description of each method. Only 1 method of selection may be specified for each MODEL statement.

Options to Specify Details of Model Selection

BEST=*n*

> is used with the RSQUARE, ADJRSQ, and CP model-selection methods. If SELECTION= CP or SELECTION=ADJRSQ is specified, the BEST= option specifies the maximum number of subset models to be printed or output to the OUTEST= data set. For SELECTION=RSQUARE, the BEST= option requests the maximum number of subset models for each size.
>
> If the BEST= option is used without the B option (printing estimated regression coefficients), the variables in each MODEL are listed in order of inclusion instead of the order in which they appear in the MODEL statement.
>
> If the BEST= option is omitted and the number of regressors is less than eleven, all possible subsets are evaluated. If the BEST= option is omitted and the number of regressors is greater than ten, the number of subsets selected is at most equal to the number of regressors. A small value of the BEST= option greatly reduces the CPU time required for large problems.

DETAILS
:   produces a table of statistics for entry and removal for each variable at each step in the model-building process. This option is available only in the BACKWARD, FORWARD, and STEPWISE methods. The statistics produced include the tolerance, R^2, and F statistic that results if each variable is added to the model, or the partial and model R^2 that results if the variable is deleted from the model.

GROUPNAMES='name1' 'name2' . . .
:   provides names for variable groups. This option is available only in the BACKWARD, FORWARD, and STEPWISE methods. The group name can be up to eight characters long. Subsets of independent variables listed in the MODEL statement can be designated as variable groups. This is done by enclosing the appropriate variables in braces. Variables in the same group are entered into or removed from the regression model at the same time. However, if the tolerance of a variable (see the TOL option below) in a group is less than the setting of the SINGULAR= option, then the variable is not entered into the model with the rest of its group. The group names GROUP1, GROUP2, . . . , are assigned as groups are encountered in the MODEL statement if the GROUPNAMES= option is not used. Variables not enclosed by braces are used as groups of a single variable.

    For example,

```
model y={x1 x2} x3 / selection=stepwise
   groupnames='x1 x2' 'x3';
```

As another example,

```
model y={ht wgt age} bodyfat / selection=forward
   groupnames='htwgtage' 'bodyfat';
```

INCLUDE=n
:   forces the first n independent variables listed in the MODEL statement to be included in all models. The selection methods are performed on the other variables in the MODEL statement. The INCLUDE= option is not available with SELECTION=NONE.

NOINT
:   suppresses the intercept term that is otherwise included in the model.

SLENTRY=value
SLE=value
:   specifies the significance level for entry into the model used in the FORWARD and STEPWISE methods. The defaults are 0.50 for FORWARD and 0.15 for STEPWISE.

SLSTAY=value
SLS=value
:   specifies the significance level for staying in the model for the BACKWARD and STEPWISE methods. The defaults are 0.10 for BACKWARD and 0.15 for STEPWISE.

START=s
:   is used to begin the comparing-and-switching process in the MAXR, MINR, and STEPWISE methods for a model containing the first s independent variables in the MODEL statement, where s is the START value. For these methods, the default value of START= is 0.

    For the RSQUARE, ADJRSQ, and CP methods, START=s specifies the smallest number of regressors to be reported in a subset model. For these methods, the default value of START= is 1.

The START= option cannot be used with model-selection methods other than the six described here.

STOP=s

causes REG to stop when it has found the "best" s-variable model, where s is the STOP value. For the RSQUARE, ADJRSQ, and CP methods, STOP=s specifies the largest number of regressors to be reported in a subset model. For the MAXR and MINR methods, STOP=s specifies the largest number of regressors to be included in the model.

The default setting for the STOP= option is the number of variables in the MODEL statement. This option can only be used with the MAXR, MINR, RSQUARE, ADJRSQ and CP methods.

Options Available Only in the RSQUARE, ADJRSQ, and CP Model-Selection Methods

The following statistics can be produced with the RSQUARE, ADJRSQ, and CP methods. Formulas for all of the statistics except B are given in **Table 28.1** below.

ADJRSQ

computes R^2 adjusted for degrees of freedom for each model selected (Darlington 1968; Judge et al. 1980).

AIC

computes Akaike's information criterion for each model selected (Akaike 1969; Judge et al. 1980).

B

computes estimated regression coefficients for each model selected.

BIC

computes Sawa's Bayesian information criterion for each model selected (Sawa 1978; Judge et al. 1980).

CP

computes Mallows' C_p statistic for each model selected (Mallows 1973; Hocking 1976).

GMSEP

computes the estimated mean square error of prediction assuming that both independent and dependent variables are multivariate normal (Stein 1960; Darlington 1969. Note that Hocking's formula (1976, eq. 4.20) contains a misprint: "$n-1$" should read "$n-2$.")

JP

computes J_p, the estimated mean square error of prediction for each model selected assuming that the values of the regressors are fixed and that the model is correct. The J_p statistic is also called the final prediction error (FPE) by Akaike (Nicholson 1948; Lord 1950; Mallows 1967; Darlington 1968; Rothman 1968; Akaike 1969; Hocking 1976; Judge et al. 1980).

MSE

computes the mean square error for each model selected (Darlington 1968).

PC

computes Amemiya's prediction criterion for each model selected (Amemiya 1976; Judge et al. 1980).

RMSE

prints the root mean square error for each model selected.

SBC
   computes the SBC statistic for each model selected (Schwarz 1978; Judge et al. 1980).

SIGMA=n
   specifies the true standard deviation of the error term to be used in computing CP and BIC (see above). If the SIGMA= option is not specified, an estimate from the full model is used.

SP
   computes the S_p statistic for each model selected (Hocking 1976).

SSE
   computes the error sum of squares for each model selected.

Table 28.1 Formulas and Definitions for Options Available Only with SELECTION=RSQUARE, or ADJRSQ, or CP

Option or Statistic	Definition or Formula
n	the number of observations
p	the number of parameters including the intercept
i	1 if there is an intercept, 0 otherwise
$\hat{\sigma}^2$	the estimate of pure error variance from the SIGMA= option or from fitting the full model
SST_0	the uncorrected total sum of squares for the dependent variable
SST_1	the total sum of squares corrected for the mean for the dependent variable
SSE	the error sum of squares
MSE	$SSE/(n-p)$
R^2	$1 - SSE/SST_i$
ADJRSQ	$1 - [((n-i)(1-R^2))/(n-p)]$
AIC	$(n)\ln(SSE/n) + 2p$
BIC	$(n)\ln(SSE/n) + 2(p+2)q - 2q^2$ where $q = \hat{\sigma}^2/(SSE/n)$
CP	$(SSE/\hat{\sigma}^2) + 2p - n$
GMSEP	$MSE(n+1)(n-2)/(n(n-p-1))$ $= SP(n+1)(n-2)/n$
JP	$(n+p)MSE/n$
PC	$(1-R^2)((n+p)/(n-p)) = JP(n/SST_i)$
RMSE	$\sqrt{MSE}$
SBC	$(n)\ln(SSE/n) + (p)\ln(n)$
SP	$MSE/(n-p-1)$

Options to Request Regression Calculations

I

prints the $(\mathbf{X'X})^{-1}$ matrix. The inverse of the crossproducts matrix is bordered by the parameter estimates and SSE matrices.

XPX

prints the $\mathbf{X'X}$ crossproducts matrix for the model. The crossproducts matrix is bordered by the $\mathbf{X'Y}$ and $\mathbf{Y'Y}$ matrices.

Options for Details on the Estimates

For the BACKWARD, FORWARD, MAXR, MINR, and STEPWISE model-selection methods, the statistics and analyses below are printed only for the final model. For the RSQUARE method, the statistics and analyses below are printed only for the full model. For the ADJRSQ and CP methods, these statistics and analyses are printed for the model with the optimal value of adjusted R^2 or C_p, respectively. For METHOD=NONE, these statistics and analyses are printed for the full model.

ACOV

prints the estimated asymptotic covariance matrix of the estimates under the hypothesis of heteroscedasticity. See **Testing for Heteroscedasticity** in the **DETAILS** section for more information.

COLLIN

requests a detailed analysis of collinearity among the regressors. This includes eigenvalues, condition indices, and decomposition of the variances of the estimates with respect to each eigenvalue. See **Collinearity Diagnostics** in the **DETAILS** section.

COLLINOINT

requests the same analysis as the COLLIN option with the intercept variable adjusted out rather than included in the diagnostics. See **Collinearity Diagnostics**.

CORRB

prints the correlation matrix of the estimates. This is the $(\mathbf{X'X})^{-1}$ matrix scaled to unit diagonals.

COVB

prints the estimated covariance matrix of the estimates. This matrix is $(\mathbf{X'X})^{-1}s^2$, where s^2 is the estimated mean squared error.

PCORR1

prints the squared partial correlation coefficients using Type I Sum of Squares (SS). This is calculated as SS/(SS+SSE), where SSE is the error Sum of Squares.

PCORR2

prints the squared partial correlation coefficients using Type II sums of squares. PCORR2 is calculated the same way as PCORR1, except that Type II SS are used instead of Type I SS.

SCORR1

prints the squared semi-partial correlation coefficients using Type I sums of squares. This is calculated as SS/SST, where SST is the corrected total SS. If NOINT is used, the uncorrected total SS is used in the denominator.

SCORR2

prints the squared semi-partial correlation coefficients using Type II sums of squares. This is calculated the same way as SCORR1, except that Type II SS are used instead of Type I SS.

SEQB

prints a sequence of parameter estimates as each variable is entered into the model. This is printed as a matrix where each row is a set of parameter estimates.

SPEC

performs a test that the first and second moments of the model are correctly specified. See **Testing for Heteroscedasticity** for more information.

SS1

prints the sequential sums of squares (Type I SS) along with the parameter estimates for each term in the model. See Chapter 9, "The Four Types of Estimable Functions," for more information on the different types of sums of squares.

SS2

prints the partial sums of squares (Type II SS) along with the parameter estimates for each term in the model. See also SS1 above.

STB

prints standardized regression coefficients. A standardized regression coefficient is computed by dividing a parameter estimate by the ratio of the sample standard deviation of the dependent variable to the sample standard deviation of the regressor.

TOL

prints tolerance values for the estimates. Tolerance for a variable is defined as $1 - R^2$, where R^2 is obtained from the regression of the variable on all other regressors in the model.

VIF

prints variance inflation factors with the parameter estimates. Variance inflation is the reciprocal of tolerance.

Options for Predicted and Residual Values

The options below are not available when data sets of TYPE=CORR, TYPE=COV, or TYPE=SSCP are used as input data sets to PROC REG. With these special data sets, the original observations needed to calculate predicted and residual values are not available.

For the BACKWARD, FORWARD, MAXR, MINR, and STEPWISE model-selection methods, the statistics and analyses below are printed only for the final model. For the RSQUARE method, the statistics and analyses below are printed only for the full model. For the ADJRSQ and CP methods, these statistics and analyses are printed for the model with the optimal value of adjusted R^2 or C_p, respectively. For the default method, NONE, these statistics and analyses are provided for the full model.

CLI

requests the 95% upper- and lower-confidence limits for an individual predicted value. The confidence limits reflect variation in the error, as well as variation in the parameter estimates. See **Predicted and Residual Values** in the **DETAILS** section for more information.

CLM

prints the 95% upper- and lower-confidence limits for the expected value of the dependent variable (mean) for each observation. This is not a prediction interval (see the CLI option) because it takes into account only the variation in the parameter estimates, not the variation in the error term. See **Predicted and Residual Values** for more information.

DW

calculates a Durbin-Watson statistic to test whether or not the errors have first-order autocorrelation. (This test is only appropriate for time series data.) The sample autocorrelation of the residuals is also printed. See **Autocorrelation in Time Series Data** in the **DETAILS** section.

INFLUENCE

requests a detailed analysis of the influence of each observation on the estimates and the predicted values. See **Influence Diagnostics** in the **DETAILS** section for more detail.

P

calculates predicted values from the input data and the estimated model. The printout includes the observation number, the ID variable (if one is specified), the actual and predicted values, and the residual. If CLI, CLM, or R is specified, P is unnecessary. See **Predicted and Residual Values** for more information.

PARTIAL

requests partial regression leverage plots for each regressor. See **Influence Diagnostics** for more information.

R

requests an analysis of the residuals. The printed output includes everything requested by the P option plus the standard errors of the predicted and residual values, the studentized residual, and Cook's D statistic to measure the influence of each observation on the parameter estimates. See **Predicted and Residual Values** for more information.

Printing and Miscellaneous Options

ALL

requests all these options: ACOV, CLI, CLM, CORRB, COVB, I, P, PCORR1, PCORR2, R, SCORR1, SCORR2, SEQB, SPEC, SS1, SS2, STB, TOL, VIF, and XPX.

NOPRINT

suppresses the printout of regression results.

MTEST Statement

label: MTEST *equation1, equation2, . . . , equationk / options*;
label: MTEST;

where each *equation* is a linear function composed of coefficients and variable names. *Label* is optional.

The MTEST statement is used to test hypotheses in multivariate regression models where there are several dependent variables fit to the same regressors. If no equations or options are specified, the MTEST statement tests the hypothesis that all estimated parameters except the intercept are zero.

These options are available in the MTEST statement:

CANPRINT
prints the canonical correlations for the hypothesis combinations and the dependent variable combinations. If you specify

```
mtest / canprint;
```

the canonical correlations between the regressors and the dependent variables are printed.

DETAILS
prints the **M** matrix and various intermediate calculations.

PRINT
prints the **H** and **E** matrices.

The hypotheses that can be tested with the MTEST statement are of the form

$$(\mathbf{L}\boldsymbol{\beta} - \mathbf{cj})\mathbf{M} = 0$$

where **L** is a linear function on the regressor side, $\boldsymbol{\beta}$ is a matrix of parameters, **c** is a column vector of constants, **j** is a row vector of ones, and **M** is a linear function on the dependent side. The special case where the constants are zero is

$$\mathbf{L}\boldsymbol{\beta}\mathbf{M} = 0 \quad .$$

See **Multivariate Tests** later in this chapter.

Each linear function extends across either the regressor variables or the dependent variables. If the equation is across the dependent variables, then the constant term, if specified, must be zero. The equations for the regressor variables form the **L** matrix and **c** vector in the formula above; the equations for dependent variables form the **M** matrix. If no equations for the dependent variables are given, REG uses an identity matrix for **M**, testing the same hypothesis across all dependent variables. If no equations for the regressor variables are given, REG forms a linear function corresponding to a test that all the nonintercept parameters are zero.

Examples of the MTEST Statement

In these statements

```
model y1 y2=x1 x2 x3;
mtest x1,x2;
```

the MTEST statement tests the hypothesis that the X1 and X2 parameters are zero for both Y1 and Y2. In addition, the statement

```
mtest y1-y2, x1;
```

tests the hypothesis that the X1 parameter is the same for both dependent variables. For the same model, the statement

```
mtest y1-y2;
```

tests the hypothesis that all parameters except the intercept are the same for both dependent variables.

OUTPUT Statement

```
OUTPUT OUT=SASdataset
     PREDICTED | P=names
     RESIDUAL | R=names
     L95M=names
     U95M=names
     L95=names
     U95=names
     STDP=names
     STDR=names
     STDI=names
     STUDENT=names
     COOKD=names
     H=names
     PRESS=names
     RSTUDENT=names
     DFFITS=names
     COVRATIO=names;
```

The OUTPUT statement creates an output data set containing statistics calculated for each observation. For each statistic, specify the keyword, an equal sign, and a variable name for the statistic in the output data set. If the model has several dependent variables, then a list of output variable names can be specified after each keyword to correspond to the list of dependent variables.

The OUTPUT statement cannot be used when a TYPE=CORR, TYPE=COV, or TYPE=SSCP data set is used as the input data set for PROC REG. See **Input Data Set** in the **DETAILS** section for more detail.

The output data set named with the OUT= option contains all the variables in the input data set (including any BY variables and the ID variable) and variables named in the OUTPUT statement that contain statistics. If the OUT= option is omitted, the output data set is created and given a default name using the DATA*n* convention.

For example, the SAS statements

```
proc reg data=a;
   model y z=x1 x2;
   output out=b
      p=yhat zhat
      r=yresid zresid;
```

create an output data set named B. In addition to the variables in the input data set, B contains the variable YHAT, whose values are predicted values of the dependent variable Y; ZHAT, whose values are predicted values of the dependent variable Z; YRESID, whose values are the residual values of Y; and ZRESID, whose values are the residual values of Z.

These statistics can be output to the new data set:

PREDICTED | P=*names*
   predicted values.

RESIDUAL | R=*names*
   residuals, calculated as ACTUAL minus PREDICTED.

L95M=*names*
   lower bound of a 95% confidence interval for the expected value (mean) of the dependent variable.

U95M=*names*

upper bound of a 95% confidence interval for the expected value (mean) of the dependent variable.

L95=*names*

lower bound of a 95% confidence interval for an individual prediction. This includes the variance of the error, as well as the variance of the parameter estimates.

U95=*names*

upper bound of a 95% confidence interval for an individual prediction.

STDP=*names*

standard error of the mean predicted value.

STDR=*names*

standard error of the residual.

STDI=*names*

standard error of the individual predicted value.

STUDENT=*names*

studentized residuals, which are the residuals divided by their standard errors.

COOKD=*names*

Cook's D influence statistic.

H=*names*

leverage, $x_i(\mathbf{X'X})^{-1}x_i'$.

PRESS=*names*

*i*th residual divided by $(1-h)$, where h is the leverage above, and where the model has been refit without the *i*th observation.

RSTUDENT=*names*

a studentized residual with the current observation deleted.

DFFITS=*names*

standard influence of observation on predicted value.

COVRATIO=*names*

standard influence of observation on covariance of betas, as discussed with INFLUENCE option.

See **Predicted and Residual Values** and **Influence Diagnostics** later in this chapter for details. Also, see Chapter 1, "Introduction to Regression Procedures," for definitions of these and other statistics.

PAINT Statement

PAINT [*condition* | ALLOBS][/ *options*];
PAINT [STATUS | UNDO];

where brackets denote optional specifications, and vertical bars denote a choice of one of the specifications separated by the vertical bars.

The PAINT statement selects observations to be *painted* or highlighted in a scatter plot. All observations that satisfy *condition* are painted using some specific symbol. The PAINT statement does not generate a scatter plot and must be followed by a PLOT statement, which does generate a scatter plot. However, several PAINT statements can be used before a PLOT statement. The requests from all previous PAINT statements are applied to all PLOT statements.

Unless the NOLIST statement is specified, the PAINT statement lists the observation numbers of the observations selected, the total number of observations selected, and the plotting symbol used to paint the points.

On a plot, paint symbols take precedence over all other symbols. If any print position contains more than one painted point, the paint symbol for the observation plotted last is used.

The PAINT statement cannot be used when a TYPE=CORR, TYPE=COV, or TYPE=SSCP data set is used as the input data set for PROC REG. Note that the syntax for the PAINT statement is the same as the syntax for the REWEIGHT statement. Also, note that PAINT is one of the two interactive statements that does *not* implicitly refit the model.

For detailed examples of painting scatter plots, see **Painting Scatter Plots** later in this chapter.

Specifying *Condition*

Condition is used to select observations to be painted. The syntax of *condition* is

       variable compare value

or

       variable compare value   logical   variable compare value

where

variable	is one of the following:
	• a variable name in the input data set.
	• OBS. which is the observation number.
	• *keyword.* where *keyword* is a keyword for a statistic requested in the OUTPUT statement. The keyword specification is applied to all dependent variables.
compare	is an operator which compares *variable* to *value*. *Compare* may be any one of the following: $<$, $<=$, $>$, $>=$, $=$, $\char94=$. The operators LT, LE, GT, GE, EQ, and NE can be used instead of the symbols above. See "SAS Expressions" in the *SAS Language Guide* for more information on comparison operators.
value	gives an unformatted value of *variable*. Observations are selected to be painted if they satisfy the condition created by *variable compare value*. *Value* can be a number or a character string. If *value* is a character string, it must be eight characters or less and must be enclosed in quotes. In addition, *value* is case-sensitive. In other words, the statements

        `paint name='henry';`

and

        `paint name='Henry';`

are not the same.

logical	is one of two logical operators. Either AND or OR can be used. To specify AND, use AND or the symbol &. To specify OR, use OR or the symbol |.

Examples of the *variable compare value* form are

```
paint name='Henry';
paint residual.>=20;
paint obs.=99;
```

Examples of the *variable compare value   logical   variable compare value* form
are

```
paint name='Henry'|name='Mary';
paint residual.>=20 or residual.<=20;
paint obs.>=11 and residual.<=20;
```

Note that in models with more than one dependent variable, the condition is
applied to all dependent variables.

Using ALLOBS

Instead of specifying *condition*, ALLOBS can be used to select all observations.
This is most useful when you want to unpaint all observations. For example,

```
paint allobs / reset;
```

resets the printing symbols for all observations.

Options in the PAINT Statement

The following options can be used when either a condition is specified, ALLOBS
is specified, or when nothing is specified before the slash. If only an option is
listed, the option applies to the observations selected in the previous PAINT
statement, *not* to the observations selected by reapplying the condition from the
previous PAINT statement. For example, with the statements

```
paint r.>0 / symbol='a';
reweight r.>0;
refit;
paint / symbol='b';
```

the second PAINT statement paints only those observations selected in the first
PAINT statement. No additional observations are painted even if, after refitting
the model, there are new observations that meet the condition in the first PAINT
statement. Note that options are not available when either UNDO or STATUS
is used.

The following options can be specified after a slash (/):

NOLIST
> suppresses printing the list of observation numbers selected. If NOLIST
> is not specified, a list of observations selected is printed on the log. The
> list includes the observation numbers and painting symbol used to paint
> the points. The total number of observations selected to be painted is
> also printed.

RESET
> changes the printing symbol to the current default symbol, effectively
> unpainting the observations selected. If you set the default symbol by
> using the SYMBOL= option in the PLOT statement, the RESET option in
> the PAINT statement changes the printing symbol to the symbol you
> specified. Otherwise, the default symbol of '1' is used.

SYMBOL = 'character'
> specifies a printing symbol. If the SYMBOL= option is omitted, the printing symbol is either the one used in the most recent PAINT statement or, if there are no previous PAINT statements, the symbol '@'. For example,

```
paint / symbol='#';
```

> changes the printing symbol for the observations selected by the most recent PAINT statement to '#'. As another example,

```
paint temp lt 22 / symbol='c';
```

> changes the printing symbol to 'c' for all observations with TEMP<22. In general, the numbers 1, 2, . . . , 9 and the asterisk are not recommended as painting symbols. These symbols are used as default symbols in the PLOT statement, where they represent the number of replicates at a point. If SYMBOL='' is used, no painting is done in the current plot. If SYMBOL=' ' is used, observations are painted with a blank and are no longer seen on the plot.

STATUS and UNDO

Instead of specifying *condition* or ALLOBS, you can use STATUS or UNDO as follows:

STATUS
> lists (on the log) the observation number and plotting symbol of all currently painted observations.

UNDO
> use this to undo changes made by the most recent PAINT statement. Observations may be, but are not necessarily, unpainted. For example,

```
paint obs. <=10 / symbol='a';
other interactive statements
paint obs.=1 / symbol='b';
other interactive statements
paint undo;
```

> The last PAINT statement changes the plotting symbol used for observation 1 back to 'a'. If the statement

```
paint / reset;
```

> had been used instead, observation 1 would have been unpainted.

PLOT Statement

PLOT [*yvariable1**xvariable1][=*symbol1*]
    [*yvariable2**xvariable2][=*symbol2*]
      .
      .
      .
    [*yvariablek**xvariablek][=*symbolk*] [/ *options*];

The PLOT statement prints scatter plots with *yvariables* on the vertical axes and *xvariables* on the horizontal axes. It uses *symbols* to mark points in the plots. The *yvariables* and *xvariables* can be any variables that appear in the VAR statement or in MODEL statements before the first RUN statement. *Yvariables* and *xvariables* can also be statistics available in the OUTPUT statement, or OBS, the observation number. The symbol can be specified as a single character enclosed in quotes or the name of any variable in the input data set.

The statement

```
plot;
```

is equivalent to respecifying the most recent PLOT statement without any options. However, the COLLECT, HPLOTS=, SYMBOL=, and VPLOTS= options (described below) apply across PLOT statements and remain in effect if they have been previously specified.

As with most other interactive statements, the PLOT statement implicitly refits the model. If a PLOT statement is preceded by a REWEIGHT statement, the model is recomputed, and the plot reflects the new model.

The PLOT statement cannot be used when TYPE=CORR, TYPE=COV, or TYPE=SSCP data sets are used as input to PROC REG.

Several PLOT statements can be specified for each MODEL statement, and more than one plot can be specified in each PLOT statement. For detailed examples of using the PLOT statement and its options, see **Producing Scatter Plots** in the **DETAILS** section.

Specifying *Yvariables*, *Xvariables*, and *Symbol*

To specify *yvariables* and *xvariables* when you are using variables in the data set, simply use the variable name. For statistics or OBS, use

> *keyword*.   where *keyword* is a statistic available in the OUTPUT statement, or OBS (the observation number). For example,
>
> ```
> plot residual.*predicted.;
> ```
>
> generates one scatter plot for each dependent variable in the model. The *keyword*. specification is applied to all dependent variables.

Yvariable and *xvariable* can be replaced by a set of variables and statistics enclosed in parentheses. When this occurs, all possible combinations of *yvariable* and *xvariable* are generated. For example,

```
plot (residual. student. rstudent.)*(age predicted.);
```

prints six scatter plots for each dependent variable in the model.

If a character variable is used for the symbol, the first (left-most) nonblank character in the formatted value of the variable is used as the plotting symbol. For unformatted character variables, the left-most nonblank character in the unformatted value is used as the plotting symbol. If a character in quotes is specified, that character becomes the plotting symbol. If a character is used as the plotting symbol, and if there are different plotting symbols needed at the same point, the symbol '?' is used at that point.

If an unformatted numeric variable is used for the symbol, the symbols '1', '2', . . . , '9' are used for variable values 1, 2, . . . , 9. For noninteger values, only the integer portion is used as the plotting symbol. For values of 10 or greater, the symbol '*' is used. For negative values, a '?' is used. If a numeric variable is used, and if there is more than one plotting symbol needed at the same point, the sum of the variable values is used at that point. If the sum exceeds 9, the symbol '*' is used.

If a symbol is not specified, the number of replicates at the point is printed. The symbol '*' is used if there are ten or more replicates.

Options in the PLOT Statement

The options below can be specified in the PLOT statement after a slash (/):

CLEAR
: clears any collected scatter plots before plotting begins but does not turn off the COLLECT option. Use this option when you want to begin a new collection with the plots in the current PLOT statement. For more information on collecting plots, see the COLLECT and NOCOLLECT options below.

COLLECT
: specifies that plots begin to be collected from one PLOT statement to the next, and that subsequent plots show an overlay of all collected plots. This option allows you to overlay plots before and after changes to the model or to the data used to fit the model. Plots collected before changes are unaffected by the changes and can be overlaid on later plots. You can request more than one plot with this option, and you do not need to request the same number of plots in subsequent PLOT statements. If you specify an unequal number of plots, plots in corresponding positions are overlaid. For example, the statements

```
plot residual.*predicted. y*x / collect;
run;
```

produce two plots. If these statements are then followed by

```
plot residual.*x;
run;
```

two plots are again produced. The first plot shows residual against X values overlaid on residual against predicted values. The second plot is the same as produced by the first PLOT statement.

Axes are scaled for the first plot or plots collected. The axes are not rescaled as more plots are collected.

Once specified, the COLLECT option remains in effect until the NOCOLLECT option is specified.

HPLOTS=*number*
: sets the number of scatter plots that can be printed across the page. The procedure begins with one plot per page. The value of the HPLOTS= option remains in effect until you change it in a later PLOT statement. See the VPLOTS= option for an example.

NOCOLLECT
: specifies that the collection of scatter plots end after adding the plots in the current PLOT statement. PROC REG starts with the NOCOLLECT option in effect. After specifying the NOCOLLECT option, any following PLOT statement produces a new plot that contains only the plots requested by that PLOT statement.

  For more information, see the COLLECT option above.

OVERLAY
: allows requested scatter plots to be superimposed. The axes are scaled so that points on all plots will be shown. If the HPLOTS= or VPLOTS= options are set to more than one, the overlaid plot occupies the first position on the page. OVERLAY is similar to COLLECT in that both options produce superimposed plots. However, OVERLAY superimposes only the plots in the associated PLOT statement; COLLECT superimposes plots across PLOT statements. OVERLAY may be used when COLLECT is in effect.

SYMBOL='*character'*

> changes the default plotting symbol used for all scatter plots produced in the current and in subsequent PLOT statements. Both SYMBOL='" and SYMBOL=' ' are allowed.
>
> If the SYMBOL= option has not been specified, the default symbol is '1' for positions with one observation, '2' for positions with two observations, and so on. For positions with more than 9 observations, '*' is used. The SYMBOL= option (or a plotting symbol) is needed to avoid any confusion caused by this default convention. Specifying a particular symbol is especially important when either the OVERLAY or COLLECT option is being used.
>
> If you specify the SYMBOL= option and use a number for *character*, that number is used for all points in the plot. For example, the statement

```
plot y*x / symbol='1';
```

> produces a plot with the symbol '1' used for all points.
>
> If you specify a plotting symbol and the SYMBOL= option, the plotting symbol overrides the SYMBOL= option. For example, in the statements

```
plot y*x y*v='.' / symbol='*';
```

> the symbol used for the plot of Y against X is '*', and a '.' is used for the plot of Y against V.
>
> If a paint symbol has been defined with a PAINT statement, the paint symbol takes precedence over both the SYMBOL= option and the default plotting symbol for the PLOT statement.

VPLOTS=*number*

> sets the number of scatter plots that can be printed down the page. The procedure begins with one plot per page. The value of the VPLOTS= option remains in effect until you change it in a later PLOT statement.
>
> For example, to specify a total of six plots per page, with two rows of three plots, use the HPLOTS= and VPLOTS= options as follows:

```
plot y1*x1 y1*x2 y1*x3 y2*x1 y2*x2 y2*x3 /
    hplots=3 vplots=2;
run;
```

PRINT Statement

PRINT [*options* ANOVA MODELDATA];

where brackets denote optional specifications. You can specify any combination of *options*, ANOVA, and MODELDATA.

The PRINT statement allows you to interactively print the MODEL statement options, print an *ANOVA* table, print the data for variables used in the current model, or reprint the options specified in a MODEL or a previous PRINT statement. In addition, like most other interactive statements in PROC REG, the PRINT statement implicitly refits the model; thus, effects of REWEIGHT statements are seen in the resulting printout.

The following specifications can appear in the PRINT statement:

options   interactively prints the MODEL statement options, where *option* is one or more of the following: ACOV, ALL, CLI, CLM, COLLIN, COLLINOINT, CORRB, COVB, DW, I, INFLUENCE, P, PARTIAL, PCORR1, PCORR2, R, SCORR1, SCORR2, SEQB, SPEC, SS1, SS2, STB, TOL, VIF, or XPX. See the section on the MODEL statement for a description of these options.

ANOVA   prints the *ANOVA* table associated with the current model. This is either the model specified in the last MODEL statement or the model that incorporates changes made by ADD, DELETE or REWEIGHT statements after the last MODEL statement.

MODELDATA   prints the data for variables used in the current model.

no options   Use the statement

```
print;
```

to reprint options in the most recently specified PRINT or MODEL statement.

Options that require original data values, such as R or INFLUENCE, cannot be used when a TYPE=CORR, TYPE=COV, or TYPE=SSCP data set is used as the input data set to REG. See **Input Data Set** in the **DETAILS** section for more detail.

REFIT Statement

REFIT;

The REFIT statement causes the current model and corresponding statistics to be recomputed immediately. No output is generated by this statement. REFIT is needed after one or more REWEIGHT statements to cause them to take effect before subsequent PAINT or REWEIGHT statements. This is sometimes necessary when you are using statistical conditions in REWEIGHT statements. For example, with these statements

```
paint student.>2;
plot student.*p.;
reweight student.>2;
refit;
paint student.>2;
plot student.*p.;
```

the second PAINT statement paints any additional observations that meet the condition after deleting observations and refitting the model. The REFIT statement is used because the REWEIGHT statement does not cause the model to be recomputed. In this particular example, the same effect could have been achieved by replacing the REFIT statement with a PLOT statement.

Most interactive statements can be used to implicitly refit the model; any plots or statistics produced by these statements reflect changes made to the model and changes made to the data used to compute the model. The two exceptions are the PAINT and REWEIGHT statements, which do not cause the model to be recomputed.

RESTRICT Statement

> RESTRICT *equation1, equation2, . . . , equationk*;

A RESTRICT statement is used to place restrictions on the parameter estimates in the MODEL preceding it. More than one RESTRICT statement can follow each MODEL statement. Each RESTRICT statement replaces any previous RESTRICT statement. To lift all restrictions on a model, submit a new MODEL statement. If there are several restrictions, separate them with commas. The statement

```
restrict equation1=equation2=equation3;
```

is equivalent to imposing the two restrictions

> *equation1=equation2*

and

> *equation2=equation3*

Each restriction is written as a linear equation. The form of an equation is

$$\pm term\ [\pm term\ . . .][\ =\ \pm term\ [\pm term\ . . .\ ]]$$

where *term* is a *variable*, a *number*, or a *number*variable*, and brackets indicate optional specifications.

When no equal sign appears, the linear combination is set equal to zero. Each variable name mentioned must be a variable in the MODEL statement to which the RESTRICT statement refers. The keyword INTERCEPT can also be used as a variable name and refers to the intercept parameter in the regression model.

Note that the parameters associated with the variables are restricted, not the variables themselves. Restrictions should be consistent and not redundant.

Examples of valid RESTRICT statements include the following:

```
restrict x1;
restrict a+b=1;
restrict a=b=c;
restrict a=b, b=c;
restrict 2*f=g+h, intercept+f=0;
restrict f=g=h=intercept;
```

The third and fourth statements in the list above produce identical restrictions. You cannot specify

```
restrict f-g=0,
         f-intercept=0,
         g-intercept=1;
```

because the three restrictions are not consistent. If these restrictions are included in a RESTRICT statement, one of the restrict parameters is zero and has zero degrees of freedom, indicating that REG is unable to apply a restriction.

The restrictions usually operate even if the model is not of full rank. Check to ensure that DF$=-1$ for each restriction. In addition, the Model DF should decrease by 1 for each restriction.

The parameter estimates are those that minimize the quadratic criterion (SSE) subject to the restrictions. If a restriction cannot be applied, its parameter value and degrees of freedom are listed as zero.

The method used for restricting the parameter estimates is to introduce a Lagrangian parameter for each restriction (Pringle and Raynor 1971). The estimates of these parameters are printed with test statistics. The Lagrangian parameter γ measures the sensitivity of the SSE to the restriction constant. If the restriction constant is changed by a small amount ε, the SSE is changed by $2\gamma\varepsilon$. The t ratio tests the significance of the restrictions. If γ is zero, the restricted estimates are the same as the unrestricted estimates, and a change in the restriction constant in either direction increases the SSE.

REWEIGHT Statement

    REWEIGHT [condition |ALLOBS][/ options];
    REWEIGHT [STATUS|UNDO];

where brackets denote optional specifications, and vertical bars denote a choice of one of the specifications separated by the vertical bars.

The REWEIGHT statement interactively changes the weights of observations that are used in computing the regression equation. REWEIGHT can change observation weights, or set them to zero, which causes selected observations to be excluded from the analysis. When a REWEIGHT statement sets observation weights to zero, the observations are not deleted from the data set. More than one REWEIGHT statement can be used. The requests from all REWEIGHT statements are applied to the subsequent statements.

The model and corresponding statistics are not recomputed after a REWEIGHT statement. For example, with the following statements

```
reweight r.>0;
reweight r.>0;
```

the second REWEIGHT statement does not exclude any additional observations since the model is not recomputed after the first REWEIGHT statement. Use either a REFIT statement to explicitly refit the model, or implicitly refit the model by following the REWEIGHT statement with any other interactive statement except a PAINT statement or another REWEIGHT statement.

The REWEIGHT statement cannot be used if a TYPE=CORR, TYPE=COV, or TYPE=SSCP data set is used as an input data set to REG. Note that the syntax used in the REWEIGHT statement is the same as the syntax for the PAINT statement.

The syntax of the REWEIGHT statement is described below. For detailed examples of using this statement see **Reweighting Observations in an Analysis** in the **DETAILS** section.

Specifying *Condition*

Condition is used to find observations to be reweighted. The syntax of condition is

        variable compare value

or

        variable compare value   logical   variable compare value

where

variable   is one of the following:

- a variable name in the input data set.
- OBS. which is the observation number.
- *keyword.* where *keyword* is a keyword for a statistic requested in the OUTPUT statement. The keyword specification is applied to all dependent variables in the model.

compare   is an operator which compares *variable* to *value*. *Compare* can be any one of the following: $<$, $<=$, $>$, $>=$, $=$, $^=$. The operators LT, LE, GT, GE, EQ, and NE can be used instead of the symbols above. See "SAS Expressions" in the *SAS Language Guide* for more information on comparison operators.

value   gives an unformatted value of *variable*. Observations are selected to be reweighted if they satisfy the condition created by *variable compare value*. *Value* can be a number or a character string. If *value* is a character string, it must be eight characters or less and must be enclosed in quotes. In addition, *value* is case-sensitive. In other words, the statements

```
reweight name='steve';
```

and

```
reweight name='Steve';
```

are not the same.

logical   is one of two logical operators. Either AND or OR can be used. To specify AND, use AND or the symbol &. To specify OR, use OR or the symbol | .

Examples of the *variable compare value* form are

```
reweight obs. le 10;
reweight temp=55;
reweight type='new';
```

Examples of the *variable compare value   logical   variable compare value* form are

```
reweight obs.<=10 and residual.<2;
reweight student.<-2 or student.>2;
reweight name='Mary' | name='Susan';
```

Using ALLOBS

Instead of specifying *condition*, you can use ALLOBS to select all observations. This is most useful when you want to restore the original weights of all observations. For example,

```
reweight allobs / reset;
```

resets weights for all observations and uses all observations in the subsequent analysis. Note that

```
reweight allobs;
```

specifies that all observations be excluded from analysis. Consequently, using ALLOBS is useful only if you also use one of the options discussed below.

Options in the REWEIGHT Statement

The following options can be used when either a condition, ALLOBS, or nothing is specified before the slash. If only an option is listed, the option applies to the observations selected in the previous REWEIGHT statement, not to the observations selected by reapplying the condition from the previous REWEIGHT statement. For example, with the statements

```
reweight r.>0 / weight=0.1;
refit;
reweight;
```

the second REWEIGHT statement excludes from the analysis only those observations selected in the first REWEIGHT statement. No additional observations are excluded even if there are new observations that meet the condition in the first REWEIGHT statement. Note that options are not available when either UNDO or STATUS is used.

NOLIST

    suppresses printing the list of observation numbers selected. If the NOLIST option is not specified, a list of observations selected is printed on the log.

RESET

    resets the observation weights to their original values as defined by the WEIGHT statement or to WEIGHT=1 if no WEIGHT statement is specified. For example,

```
reweight / reset;
```

    resets observation weights to the original weights in the data set. If previous REWEIGHT statements have been submitted, this REWEIGHT statement applies only to the observations selected by the previous REWEIGHT statement. Note that although RESET does reset observation weights to their original values, it does not cause the model and corresponding statistics to be recomputed.

WEIGHT = value

    changes observation weights to the specified nonnegative real number. If the WEIGHT= option is not specified, then the observation weights are set to zero, and observations are excluded from the analysis. For example,

```
reweight name='Alan';
other interactive statements
reweight / weight=0.5;
```

The first REWEIGHT statement changes weights to zero for all observations with NAME='Alan', effectively deleting these observations. The subsequent analysis would not include these observations. The second REWEIGHT statement applies only to those observations selected by the previous REWEIGHT statement, and changes the weights to 0.5 for all the observations with NAME='Alan'. Thus, the next analysis would include all original observations; however, those observations with NAME='Alan' would have their weights set to 0.5.

STATUS and UNDO

If *condition* or ALLOBS is not specified, then one of these two specifications may be specified:

STATUS
> lists on the log the observation's number and weight of all reweighted observations. If an observation's weight has been set to zero, it is reported as deleted. However, the observation is not deleted from the data set, only from the analysis.

UNDO
> use this to undo the changes made by the most recent REWEIGHT statement. Weights may be, but are not necessarily, reset. For example, in these statements

```
reweight student.>2 / weight=0.1;
reweight;
reweight undo;
```

> the first REWEIGHT statement sets the weights of observations that satisfy the condition to 0.1. The second REWEIGHT statement sets the weights of the same observations to zero. The third REWEIGHT statement undoes the second, changing the weights back to 0.1.

TEST Statement

> *label*:   TEST *equation1, . . . , equationk / option;*

The TEST statement tests hypotheses about the parameters estimated in the preceding MODEL statement. It has the same syntax as the RESTRICT statement except that it allows an option. Each equation specifies a linear hypothesis to be tested. The rows of the hypothesis are separated by commas.

Variable names must correspond to regressors, and each variable name represents the coefficient of the corresponding variable in the model. An optional label is useful to identify each test with a name. The keyword INTERCEPT can be used instead of a variable name to refer to the model's intercept.

One option can be specified in the TEST statement after a slash (/):

PRINT
> prints intermediate calculations. This includes $\mathbf{L(X'X)^-L'}$ bordered by $\mathbf{Lb-c}$, and $\mathbf{(L(X'X)^-L')^{-1}}$ bordered by $\mathbf{(L(X'X)^-L')^{-1}(Lb-c)}$.

REG performs an *F* test for the joint hypotheses specified in a single TEST statement. More than one TEST statement can accompany a MODEL statement. The numerator is the usual quadratic form of the estimates; the denominator is the mean squared error. If hypotheses can be represented by

$$\mathbf{L\beta = c,}$$

then the numerator of the *F* test is

$$\mathbf{Q = (Lb-c)'(L(X'X)^-L')^{-1}(Lb-c)}$$

divided by degrees of freedom, where $\mathbf{b}$ is the estimate of $\mathbf{\beta}$. For example,

```
        model y=a1 a2 b1 b2;
aplus:  test a1+a2=1;
b1:     test b1=0, b2=0;
b2:     test b1, b2;
```

The last two statements are equivalent; since no constant is specified, zero is assumed.

VAR Statement

> VAR *variables*;

The VAR statement is used to include numeric variables in the crossproducts matrix that are not specified in the first MODEL statement.

Variables not listed in MODEL statements before the first RUN statement must be listed in the VAR statement if you want the ability to add them interactively to the model with an ADD statement, to include them in a new MODEL statement, or to plot them in a scatter plot with the PLOT statement.

In addition, if you only want to use options in the PROC REG statement, and do not want to fit a model to the data (with a MODEL statement), you must use a VAR statement.

WEIGHT Statement

> WEIGHT *variable*;

A WEIGHT statement names a variable in the input data set whose values are relative weights for a weighted least-squares fit. If the weight value is proportional to the reciprocal of the variance for each observation, then the weighted estimates are the best linear unbiased estimates (BLUE).

Values of the weight variable must be non-negative. If an observation's weight is zero, the observation is deleted from the analysis. If a weight is negative or missing, it is set to zero, and the observation is excluded from the analysis. A more complete description of the WEIGHT statement can be found in the chapter on the GLM procedure.

Observation weights can be changed interactively with the REWEIGHT statement, described earlier in this chapter.

DETAILS

Missing Values

REG constructs only one crossproducts matrix for the variables in all regressions. If any variable needed for any regression is missing, the observation is excluded from all estimates. If you include variables with missing values in the VAR statement, the corresponding observations will be excluded from all analyses, even if you never include the variables in a model. PROC REG assumes that you may want to include these variables after the first RUN statement and deletes observations with missing values.

Input Data Set

REG does not compute new regressors. For example, if you want a quadratic term in your model, you should create a new variable when you prepare the input data. For example, the statement

```
model y=x1 x1*x1;
```

is not valid. Note that the MODEL statement above is valid in PROC GLM.

The input data set for most applications of PROC REG contains standard rectangular data, but special TYPE=CORR, TYPE=COV, or TYPE=SSCP data sets can also be used. TYPE=CORR and TYPE=COV data sets created by PROC CORR contain means and standard deviations. In addition, TYPE=CORR data sets contain correlations and TYPE=COV data sets contain covariances. TYPE=SSCP data sets created in previous runs of PROC REG that used the OUTSSCP= option contain the sums of squares and crossproducts of the variables. See Appendix 2, "Special SAS Data Sets," in this book and "SAS Files" in the *SAS Language Guide* for more information on special SAS data sets.

These summary files save CPU time. It takes nk^2 operations (where n=number of observations, k=number of variables) to calculate crossproducts; the regressions are of the order k^3. When n is in the thousands and k is in units, you can save 99 percent of the CPU time by reusing the SSCP matrix rather than recomputing it.

When you want to use a special SAS data set as input, PROC REG must determine the TYPE for the data set. PROC CORR and PROC REG automatically set the type for their output data sets. However, if you create the data set by some other means (such as a DATA step) you must specify its type with the TYPE= data set option. If the TYPE for the data set is not specified when the data set is created, you can specify TYPE= as a data set option in the DATA= option in the PROC REG statement. For example,

```
proc reg data=a(type=corr);
```

When TYPE=CORR, TYPE=COV, or TYPE=SSCP data sets are used with REG, statements and options that require the original data values have no effect. The OUTPUT, PAINT, PLOT, and REWEIGHT statements, and the MODEL and PRINT statement options P, R, CLM, CLI, DW, INFLUENCE, and PARTIAL are disabled. Since the original observations needed to calculate predicted and residual values are not present, the statements and options above are inoperative.

Example Using TYPE=CORR Data Set

Here is an example using PROC CORR to produce an input data set for PROC REG. The fitness data for this analysis can be found in **Example 2** at the end of this chapter.

```
proc corr data=fitness outp=r;
   var oxy runtime age weight runpulse maxpulse rstpulse;
proc print data=r;
proc reg data=r;
   model oxy=runtime age weight;
```

Since the OUTP= data set from PROC CORR is automatically set to TYPE=CORR, the TYPE= data set option is not required in the example above. The data set containing the correlation matrix is printed by the PRINT procedure as shown in **Output 28.2**. **Output 28.3** shows results from the regression using the TYPE=CORR data as an input data set.

Output 28.2   Output Created by PROC CORR

```
                              CORRELATION ANALYSIS                               1

          7 'VAR' Variables:   OXY     RUNTIME AGE     WEIGHT   RUNPULSE MAXPULSE RSTPULSE


                                   Simple Statistics

     Variable          N        Mean        Std Dev         Sum        Minimum       Maximum

     OXY              31      47.375806      5.327231    1468.650000    37.388000    60.055000
     RUNTIME          31      10.586129      1.387414     328.170000     8.170000    14.030000
     AGE              31      47.677419      5.211443    1478.000000    38.000000    57.000000
     WEIGHT           31      77.444516      8.328568    2400.780000    59.080000    91.630000
     RUNPULSE         31     169.645161     10.251986    5259.000000   146.000000   186.000000
     MAXPULSE         31     173.774194      9.164095    5387.000000   155.000000   192.000000
     RSTPULSE         31      53.451613      7.619443    1657.000000    40.000000    70.000000


              Pearson Correlation Coefficients / Prob > |R| under Ho: Rho=0 / N = 31

                  OXY        RUNTIME        AGE        WEIGHT     RUNPULSE      MAXPULSE      RSTPULSE

     OXY        1.00000     -0.86219     -0.30459     -0.16275     -0.39797     -0.23674     -0.39936
                0.0          0.0001       0.0957       0.3817       0.0266       0.1997       0.0260

     RUNTIME   -0.86219      1.00000      0.18875      0.14351      0.31365      0.22610      0.45038
                0.0001       0.0          0.3092       0.4412       0.0858       0.2213       0.0110

     AGE       -0.30459      0.18875      1.00000     -0.23354     -0.33787     -0.43292     -0.16410
                0.0957       0.3092       0.0          0.2061       0.0630       0.0150       0.3777

     WEIGHT    -0.16275      0.14351     -0.23354      1.00000      0.18152      0.24938      0.04397
                0.3817       0.4412       0.2061       0.0          0.3284       0.1761       0.8143

     RUNPULSE  -0.39797      0.31365     -0.33787      0.18152      1.00000      0.92975      0.35246
                0.0266       0.0858       0.0630       0.3284       0.0          0.0001       0.0518

     MAXPULSE  -0.23674      0.22610     -0.43292      0.24938      0.92975      1.00000      0.30512
                0.1997       0.2213       0.0150       0.1761       0.0001       0.0          0.0951

     RSTPULSE  -0.39936      0.45038     -0.16410      0.04397      0.35246      0.30512      1.00000
                0.0260       0.0110       0.3777       0.8143       0.0518       0.0951       0.0
```

```
                                                                                 2
     OBS    _TYPE_    _NAME_       OXY     RUNTIME     AGE      WEIGHT   RUNPULSE   MAXPULSE   RSTPULSE

      1     MEAN                 47.3758   10.5861   47.6774   77.4445   169.645    173.774    53.4516
      2     STD                   5.3272    1.3874    5.2114    8.3286    10.252      9.164      7.6194
      3     N                    31.0000   31.0000   31.0000   31.0000   31.000     31.000     31.0000
      4     CORR     OXY          1.0000   -0.8622   -0.3046   -0.1628   -0.398     -0.237     -0.3994
      5     CORR     RUNTIME     -0.8622    1.0000    0.1887    0.1435    0.314      0.226      0.4504
      6     CORR     AGE         -0.3046    0.1887    1.0000   -0.2335   -0.338     -0.433     -0.1641
      7     CORR     WEIGHT      -0.1628    0.1435   -0.2335    1.0000    0.182      0.249      0.0440
      8     CORR     RUNPULSE    -0.3980    0.3136   -0.3379    0.1815    1.000      0.930      0.3525
      9     CORR     MAXPULSE    -0.2367    0.2261   -0.4329    0.2494    0.930      1.000      0.3051
     10     CORR     RSTPULSE    -0.3994    0.4504   -0.1641    0.0440    0.352      0.305      1.0000
```

Output 28.3   Regression of Data Created by PROC CORR

```
Model: MODEL1                                                                    3
Dependent Variable: OXY
                                   Analysis of Variance

                                   Sum of          Mean
          Source          DF      Squares        Square     F Value     Prob>F

          Model            3     656.27095     218.75698      30.272     0.0001
          Error           27     195.11060       7.22632
          C Total         30     851.38154

                    Root MSE        2.68818     R-Square      0.7708
                    Dep Mean       47.37581     Adj R-Sq      0.7454
                    C.V.            5.67416

                                 Parameter Estimates

                          Parameter     Standard    T for H0:
          Variable   DF    Estimate       Error     Parameter=0    Prob > |T|

          INTERCEP    1    93.126150    7.55915630      12.320        0.0001
          RUNTIME     1    -3.140387    0.36737984      -8.548        0.0001
          AGE         1    -0.173877    0.09954587      -1.747        0.0921
          WEIGHT      1    -0.054437    0.06180913      -0.881        0.3862
```

Example Using TYPE=SSCP Data Set

The following is an example using the saved crossproducts matrix:

```
proc reg data=fitness outsscp=sscp;
   model oxy=runtime age weight runpulse maxpulse rstpulse;
proc print data=sscp;
proc reg data=sscp;
   model oxy=runtime age weight;
```

First, all variables are used to fit the data and create the SSCP data set. **Output 28.4** shows the PROC PRINT output for the SSCP data set. The SSCP data set is then used as the input data set for PROC REG, and a reduced model is fit to the data. **Output 28.4** also shows the PROC REG output for the reduced model. (For the PROC REG output for the full model, see **Output 28.13**.)

In the example above, the TYPE= data set option is not required since PROC REG sets the OUTSSCP= data set to TYPE=SSCP.

Output 28.4   Regression Using SSCP Matrix

```
                                                                                                           2
OBS   _TYPE_   _NAME_    INTERCEP   RUNTIME      AGE      WEIGHT    RUNPULSE   MAXPULSE   RSTPULSE      OXY

 1    SSCP     INTERCEP     31.00    328.17    1478.00    2400.78    5259.00    5387.00    1657.00    1468.65
 2    SSCP     RUNTIME     328.17   3531.80   15687.24   25464.71   55806.29   57113.72   17684.05   15356.14
 3    SSCP     AGE        1478.00  15687.24   71282.00  114158.90  250194.00  256218.00   78806.00   69767.75
 4    SSCP     WEIGHT     2400.78  25464.71  114158.90  188008.20  407745.67  417764.62  128409.28  113522.26
 5    SSCP     RUNPULSE   5259.00  55806.29  250194.00  407745.67  895317.00  916499.00  281928.00  248497.31
 6    SSCP     MAXPULSE   5387.00  57113.72  256218.00  417764.62  916499.00  938641.00  288583.00  254866.75
 7    SSCP     RSTPULSE   1657.00  17684.05   78806.00  128409.28  281928.00  288583.00   90311.00   78015.41
 8    SSCP     OXY        1468.65  15356.14   69767.75  113522.26  248497.31  254866.75   78015.41   70429.86
 9    N                     31.00     31.00      31.00      31.00      31.00      31.00      31.00      31.00
```

```
Model: MODEL1                                                                    3
Dependent Variable: OXY

                              Analysis of Variance

                                 Sum of          Mean
              Source       DF    Squares        Square     F Value    Prob>F

              Model         3   656.27095     218.75698     30.272    0.0001
              Error        27   195.11060       7.22632
              C Total      30   851.38154

                   Root MSE       2.68818     R-Square     0.7708
                   Dep Mean      47.37581     Adj R-Sq     0.7454
                   C.V.           5.67416

                              Parameter Estimates

                           Parameter     Standard    T for H0:
              Variable  DF   Estimate       Error   Parameter=0   Prob > |T|

              INTERCEP   1   93.126150    7.55915630    12.320      0.0001
              RUNTIME    1   -3.140387    0.36737984    -8.548      0.0001
              AGE        1   -0.173877    0.09954587    -1.747      0.0921
              WEIGHT     1   -0.054437    0.06180913    -0.881      0.3862
```

Output Data Sets

OUTEST= Data Set

The OUTEST= specification produces a TYPE=EST output SAS data set containing estimates and optional statistics from the regression models. For each BY group on each dependent variable occurring in each MODEL statement, REG outputs an observation to the OUTEST= data set. The variables are as follows:

- the BY variables, if any.
- _MODEL_, a character variable containing the label of the corresponding MODEL statement, or MODEL*n* if no label was specified, where *n* is 1 for the first MODEL statement, 2 for the second model statement, and so on.
- _TYPE_, a character variable with the value 'PARMS' for every observation.
- _DEPVAR_, the name of the dependent variable.
- _RMSE_, the root mean squared error or the estimate of the standard deviation of the error term.
- INTERCEP, the estimated intercept, unless NOINT is specified.
- all the variables listed in any MODEL statement. Values of these variables are the estimated regression coefficients for the model. A variable that does not appear in the model corresponding to a given observation has a missing value in that observation. The dependent variable in each model is given a value of −1.

If the COVOUT option is used, the covariance matrix of the estimates is output after the estimates; _TYPE_ is set to the value 'COV' and the names of the rows are identified by the 8-byte character variable, _NAME_.

For the RSQUARE, ADJRSQ, and CP methods, REG outputs one observation for each subset model selected. Additional variables are as follows:

- _IN_, the number of regressors in the model not including the intercept
- _P_, the number of parameters in the model including the intercept, if any
- _EDF_, the error degrees of freedom
- _SSE_, the error sum of squares, if the SSE option is specified
- _MSE_, the mean squared error, if the MSE option is specified

- _RSQ_, the R^2 statistic
- _ADJRSQ_, the adjusted R^2, if the ADJRSQ option is specified
- _CP_, the C_p statistic, if the CP option is specified
- _SP_, the S_p statistic, if the SP option is specified
- _JP_, the J_p statistic, if the JP option is specified
- _PC_, the PC statistic, if the PC option is specified
- _GMSEP_, the GMSEP statistic, if the GMSEP option is specified
- _AIC_, the AIC statistic, if the AIC option is specified
- _BIC_, the BIC statistic, if the BIC option is specified
- _SBC_, the SBC statistic, if the SBC option is specified.

The following is an example with a printout of the OUTEST= data set. This example uses the population data from **Example 1** at the end of this chapter. **Output 28.5** shows the regression equations and the resulting OUTEST= data set.

```
proc reg data=uspop outest=est;
m1:  model pop=year;
m2:  model pop=year yearsq;
proc print data=est;
```

Output 28.5   Regression with Printout of OUTEST= Data Set

```
Model: M1                                                                          1
Dependent Variable: POP
                                 Analysis of Variance

                             Sum of          Mean
        Source      DF       Squares        Square      F Value      Prob>F

        Model        1    66336.46923    66336.46923    201.873      0.0001
        Error       17     5586.29253      328.60544
        C Total     18    71922.76175

            Root MSE        18.12748    R-Square        0.9223
            Dep Mean        69.76747    Adj R-Sq        0.9178
            C.V.            25.98271

                              Parameter Estimates

                      Parameter      Standard     T for H0:
        Variable  DF   Estimate         Error    Parameter=0     Prob > |T|

        INTERCEP   1  -1958.366302   142.80454644    -13.714        0.0001
        YEAR       1      1.078795     0.07592765     14.208        0.0001
```

```
Model: M2                                                                          2
Dependent Variable: POP
                                 Analysis of Variance

                             Sum of          Mean
        Source      DF       Squares        Square      F Value      Prob>F

        Model        2    71799.01619    35899.50809   4641.719      0.0001
        Error       16      123.74557        7.73410
        C Total     18    71922.76175

            Root MSE         2.78102    R-Square        0.9983
            Dep Mean        69.76747    Adj R-Sq        0.9981
            C.V.             3.98613
```

(continued on next page)

(continued from previous page)

Parameter Estimates

Variable	DF	Parameter Estimate	Standard Error	T for H0: Parameter=0	Prob > |T|
INTERCEP	1	20450	843.47532634	24.245	0.0001
YEAR	1	-22.780606	0.89784904	-25.372	0.0001
YEARSQ	1	0.006346	0.00023877	26.576	0.0001

3

OBS	_MODEL_	_TYPE_	_DEPVAR_	_RMSE_	INTERCEP	YEAR	POP	YEARSQ
1	M1	PARMS	POP	18.1275	-1958.37	1.0788	-1	.
2	M2	PARMS	POP	2.7810	20450.43	-22.7806	-1	.0063456

Another example uses the RSQUARE method. This example requests only the "best" model for each subset size but asks for a variety of model selection statistics, as well as the estimated regression coefficients. An OUTEST= data set is created and printed. You can obtain plots of the statistics in the OUTEST= data set with PROC PLOT. See **Output 28.6** and **Output 28.7** for results.

```
proc reg data=fitness outest=est;
   model oxy=age weight runtime runpulse rstpulse maxpulse
           / selection=rsquare mse jp gmsep cp aic bic sbc b best=1;
proc print data=est;
```

Output 28.6 PROC REG Output for Physical Fitness Data: Best Models

N = 31   Regression Models for Dependent Variable: OXY   1

In	Rsq	C(p)	AIC	BIC	GMSEP	J(p)	MSE	SBC	Parameter Estimates Intercept MAXPULSE	AGE	WEIGHT	RUNTIME	RUNPULSE	RSTPULSE
1	0.7434	13.70	64.53	65.47	8.05	8.02	7.53	67.40	82.4218 .	.	.	-3.3106	.	.
2	0.7642	12.39	63.90	64.82	7.95	7.86	7.17	68.21	88.4623 .	-0.1504	.	-3.2040	.	.
3	0.8111	6.960	59.04	61.31	6.86	6.73	5.96	64.77	111.7 .	-0.2564	.	-2.8254	-0.1309	.
4	0.8368	4.880	56.50	60.40	6.40	6.21	5.34	63.67	98.1 0.2705	-0.1977	.	-2.7676	-0.3481	.
5	0.8480	5.106	56.30	61.57	6.46	6.18	5.18	64.90	102.2 0.3049	-0.2196	-0.0723	-2.6825	-0.3734	.
6	0.8487	7.000	58.16	64.07	6.99	6.58	5.37	68.20	102.9 0.3032	-0.2270	-0.0742	-2.6287	-0.3696	-0.0215

Output 28.7   PROC PRINT Output for Physical Fitness Data:
OUTEST= Data Set

```
                                                                                              1
OBS  _MODEL_  _TYPE_  _DEPVAR_  _RMSE_  INTERCEP   AGE      WEIGHT    RUNTIME  RUNPULSE  RSTPULSE  MAXPULSE

  1  MODEL1   PARMS    OXY     2.74478   82.422     .         .       -3.31056     .         .         .
  2  MODEL1   PARMS    OXY     2.67739   88.462  -0.15037     .       -3.20395     .         .         .
  3  MODEL1   PARMS    OXY     2.44063  111.718  -0.25640     .       -2.82538  -0.13091     .         .
  4  MODEL1   PARMS    OXY     2.31159   98.148  -0.19773     .       -2.76758  -0.34811     .       0.27051
  5  MODEL1   PARMS    OXY     2.27516  102.204  -0.21962  -0.072302  -2.68252  -0.37340     .       0.30491
  6  MODEL1   PARMS    OXY     2.31695  102.934  -0.22697  -0.074177  -2.62865  -0.36963  -0.021534  0.30322

OBS  OXY  _IN_  _P_  _EDF_   _MSE_    _RSQ_     _CP_     _JP_    _GMSEP_   _AIC_    _BIC_    _SBC_

  1   -1    1    2    29    7.53384  0.74338  13.6988  8.01990  8.05462  64.5341  65.4673  67.4021
  2   -1    2    3    28    7.16842  0.76425  12.3894  7.86214  7.94778  63.9050  64.8212  68.2069
  3   -1    3    4    27    5.95669  0.81109   6.9596  6.72530  6.85833  59.0373  61.3127  64.7733
  4   -1    4    5    26    5.34346  0.83682   4.8800  6.20531  6.39837  56.4995  60.3996  63.6694
  5   -1    5    6    25    5.17634  0.84800   5.1063  6.17821  6.45651  56.2986  61.5667  64.9025
  6   -1    6    7    24    5.36825  0.84867   7.0000  6.58043  6.98700  58.1616  64.0748  68.1995
```

OUTSSCP= Data Sets

The OUTSSCP= option produces a TYPE=SSCP output SAS data set containing sums of squares and crossproducts. A special row (observation) and column (variable) of the matrix called INTERCEP contain the number of observations and sums. Observations are identified by the 8-byte character variable _NAME_. The data set contains all variables used in MODEL statements. You can specify additional variables that you want included in the crossproducts matrix with a VAR statement.

The SSCP data set is used when a large number of observations are explored in many different runs. The SSCP data set can be saved and used for subsequent runs, which are much less expensive since REG never reads the original data again. If you run PROC REG once to only create a SSCP data set, you should list all the variables that you may need in a VAR statement or include all the variables that you may need in a MODEL statement.

The example below uses the fitness data from **Example 2** to produce an output data set with the OUTSSCP= option. The resulting output is shown in **Output 28.8**.

```
proc reg data=fitness outsscp=sscp;
   var oxy runtime age weight rstpulse runpulse maxpulse;
proc print data=sscp;
```

Since a model is not fit to the data and since the only request is to create the SSCP data set, a MODEL statement is not required in the example above. However, since the MODEL statement is not used, the VAR statement is required.

Output 28.8   SSCP Data Set Created with OUTSSCP= Option:
REG Procedure

```
                                                                                          1
OBS  _TYPE_   _NAME_    INTERCEP       OXY    RUNTIME        AGE     WEIGHT    RSTPULSE   RUNPULSE   MAXPULSE

 1   SSCP    INTERCEP     31.00    1468.65     328.17    1478.00    2400.78    1657.00    5259.00    5387.00
 2   SSCP    OXY        1468.65   70429.86   15356.14   69767.75  113522.26   78015.41  248497.31  254866.75
 3   SSCP    RUNTIME     328.17   15356.14    3531.80   15687.24   25464.71   17684.05   55806.29   57113.72
 4   SSCP    AGE        1478.00   69767.75   15687.24   71282.00  114158.90   78806.00  250194.00  256218.00
 5   SSCP    WEIGHT     2400.78  113522.26   25464.71  114158.90  188008.20  128409.28  407745.67  417764.62
 6   SSCP    RSTPULSE   1657.00   78015.41   17684.05   78806.00  128409.28   90311.00  281928.00  288583.00
 7   SSCP    RUNPULSE   5259.00  248497.31   55806.29  250194.00  407745.67  281928.00  895317.00  916499.00
 8   SSCP    MAXPULSE   5387.00  254866.75   57113.72  256218.00  417764.62  288583.00  916499.00  938641.00
 9   N                   31.00      31.00      31.00      31.00      31.00      31.00      31.00      31.00
```

Interactive Analysis

PROC REG allows you to interactively change both the model and the data used
to compute the model. See the **SPECIFICATIONS** section for information on
which statements may be used interactively. All interactive features will be disabled if there is a BY statement.

Other interactive features allow you to produce and highlight scatter plots.
These features are discussed in **Producing Scatter Plots** and **Painting Scatter Plots**
later in this chapter. In addition, a more detailed explanation of changing the data
used to compute the model is given in **Reweighting Observations in an Analysis**
later in this chapter.

The following example shows the usefulness of the interactive features. First
the full regression model is fit, and **Output 28.9** is produced.

```
data class;
    input name $ height weight age;
    cards;
Alfred   69.0 112.5 14
Alice    56.5  84.0 13
Barbara  65.3  98.0 13
Carol    62.8 102.5 14
Henry    63.5 102.5 14
James    57.3  83.0 12
Jane     59.8  84.5 12
Janet    62.5 112.5 15
Jeffrey  62.5  84.0 13
John     59.0  99.5 12
Joyce    51.3  50.5 11
Judy     64.3  90.0 14
Louise   56.3  77.0 12
Mary     66.5 112.0 15
Philip   72.0 150.0 16
Robert   64.8 128.0 12
Ronald   67.0 133.0 15
Thomas   57.5  85.0 11
William  66.5 112.0 15
;
proc reg;
    model weight=age height;
    id name;
run;
```

Output 28.9   Interactive Analysis: Full Model

```
Model: MODEL1                                                                    1
Dependent Variable: WEIGHT
                                    Analysis of Variance

                                    Sum of         Mean
             Source        DF       Squares        Square      F Value    Prob>F

             Model          2     7215.63710     3607.81855     27.228    0.0001
             Error         16     2120.09974      132.50623
             C Total       18     9335.73684

                   Root MSE       11.51114     R-Square      0.7729
                   Dep Mean      100.02632     Adj R-Sq      0.7445
                   C.V.           11.50811

                              Parameter Estimates

                          Parameter       Standard      T for H0:
             Variable  DF   Estimate         Error     Parameter=0    Prob > |T|

             INTERCEP   1  -141.223763    33.38309350     -4.230       0.0006
             AGE        1     1.278393     3.11010374      0.411       0.6865
             HEIGHT     1     3.597027     0.90546072      3.973       0.0011
```

Next, the regression model is reduced by the following statements, and **Output 28.10** is produced.

```
delete age;
print;
run;
```

Output 28.10   Interactive Analysis: Reduced Model

```
Model: MODEL1                                                                    2
Dependent Variable: WEIGHT
                                    Analysis of Variance

                                    Sum of         Mean
             Source        DF       Squares        Square      F Value    Prob>F

             Model          1     7193.24912     7193.24912     57.076    0.0001
             Error         17     2142.48772      126.02869
             C Total       18     9335.73684

                   Root MSE       11.22625     R-Square      0.7705
                   Dep Mean      100.02632     Adj R-Sq      0.7570
                   C.V.           11.22330

                              Parameter Estimates

                          Parameter       Standard      T for H0:
             Variable  DF   Estimate         Error     Parameter=0    Prob > |T|

             INTERCEP   1  -143.026918    32.27459130     -4.432       0.0004
             HEIGHT     1     3.899030     0.51609395      7.555       0.0001
```

Next, the following statements generate a scatter plot of the residuals against the predicted values from the full model. **Output 28.11** is produced. The scatter plot shows a possible outlier.

```
add age;
plot r.*p.;
run;
```

Output 28.11   Interactive Analysis: Scatter Plot

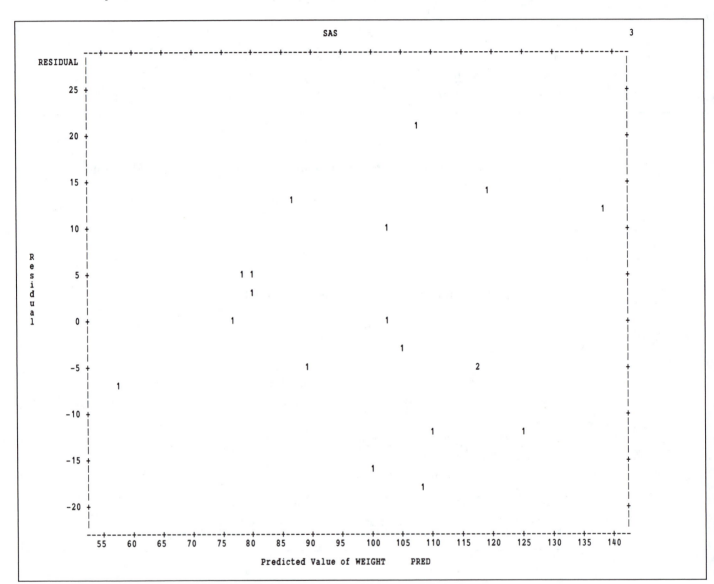

The following statements delete the observation with the largest residual, refit the regression model, and produce a scatter plot of residuals against predicted values for the refitted model. **Output 28.12** shows the new scatter plot.

```
reweight r.>20;
plot;
run;
```

Output 28.12   Interactive Analysis: Scatter Plot for Refitted Model

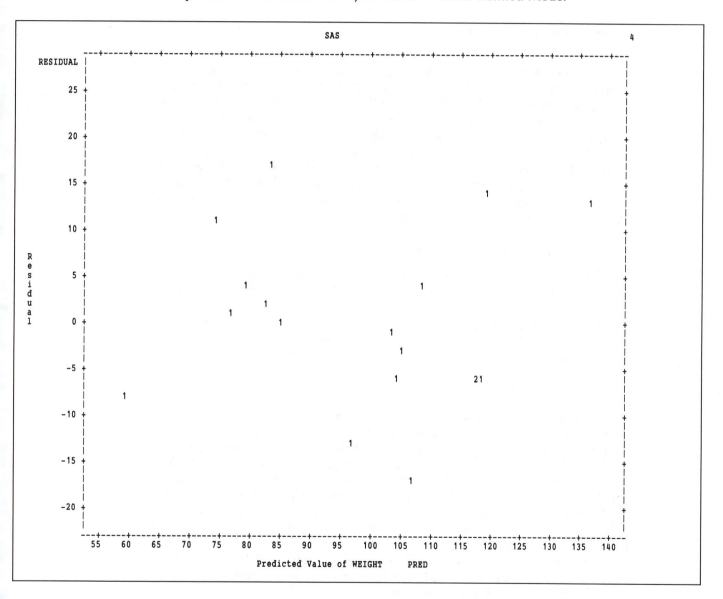

Model-Selection Methods

The nine methods of model selection implemented in PROC REG are specified with the SELECTION= option in the MODEL statement. Each method is discussed below.

Full Model Fitted (NONE)

This method is the default and provides no model selection capability. The complete model specified in the MODEL statement is used to fit the model. For many regression analyses, this may be the only method you need.

Forward Selection (FORWARD)

The forward-selection technique begins with no variables in the model. For each of the independent variables, FORWARD calculates F statistics that reflect the variable's contribution to the model if it is included. The p values for these F statistics are compared to the SLENTRY= value that is specified in the MODEL statement (or to 0.50 if the SLENTRY= option is omitted). If no F statistic has a significance level greater than the SLENTRY= value, FORWARD stops. Otherwise, FORWARD adds the variable that has the largest F statistic to the model. FORWARD then calculates F statistics again for the variables still remaining outside the model, and the evaluation process is repeated. Thus, variables are added one by one to the model until no remaining variable produces a significant F statistic. Once a variable is in the model, it stays.

Backward Elimination (BACKWARD)

The backward elimination technique begins by calculating statistics for a model, including all of the independent variables. Then the variables are deleted from the model one by one until all the variables remaining in the model produce F statistics significant at the SLSTAY= level specified in the MODEL statement (or at the 0.10 level if the SLSTAY= option is omitted). At each step, the variable showing the smallest contribution to the model is deleted.

Stepwise (STEPWISE)

The stepwise method is a modification of the forward-selection technique and differs in that variables already in the model do not necessarily stay there. As in the forward-selection method, variables are added one by one to the model, and the F statistic for a variable to be added must be significant at the SLENTRY= level. After a variable is added, however, the stepwise method looks at all the variables already included in the model and deletes any variable that does not produce an F statistic significant at the SLSTAY= level. Only after this check is made and the necessary deletions accomplished can another variable be added to the model. The stepwise process ends when none of the variables outside the model has an F statistic significant at the SLENTRY= level and every variable in the model is significant at the SLSTAY= level, or when the variable to be added to the model is the one just deleted from it.

Maximum R^2 Improvement (MAXR)

The maximum R^2 improvement technique does not settle on a single model. Instead, it tries to find the "best" one-variable model, the "best" two-variable model, and so forth, although it is not guaranteed to find the model with the largest R^2 for each size.

The MAXR method begins by finding the one-variable model producing the highest R^2. Then another variable, the one that yields the greatest increase in R^2, is added. Once the two-variable model is obtained, each of the variables in the model is compared to each variable not in the model. For each comparison, MAXR determines if removing one variable and replacing it with the other variable increases R^2. After comparing all possible switches, MAXR makes the switch that produces the largest increase in R^2. Comparisons begin again, and the process continues until MAXR finds that no switch could increase R^2. Thus, the two-variable model achieved is considered the "best" two-variable model the technique can find. Another variable is then added to the model, and the comparing-and-switching process is repeated to find the "best" three-variable model, and so forth.

The difference between the STEPWISE method and the MAXR method is that all switches are evaluated before any switch is made in MAXR. In the STEPWISE method, the "worst" variable may be removed without considering what adding the "best" remaining variable might accomplish. MAXR may require much more computer time than STEPWISE.

Minimum R^2 Improvement (MINR)

The MINR method closely resembles MAXR, but the switch chosen is the one that produces the smallest increase in R^2. For a given number of variables in the model, MAXR and MINR usually produce the same "best" model, but MINR considers more models of each size.

R^2 Selection (RSQUARE)

The RSQUARE method finds subsets of independent variables that best predict a dependent variable by linear regression in the given sample. You can specify the largest and smallest number of independent variables to appear in a subset and the number of subsets of each size to be selected. The RSQUARE method can efficiently perform all possible subset regressions and print the models in decreasing order of R^2 magnitude within each subset size. Other statistics are available for comparing subsets of different sizes. These statistics, as well as estimated regression coefficients, can be printed or output to a SAS data set.

The subset models selected by RSQUARE are optimal in terms of R^2 for the given sample, but they are not necessarily optimal for the population from which the sample was drawn or for any other sample for which you may want to make predictions. If a subset model is selected on the basis of a large R^2 value or any other criterion commonly used for model selection, then all regression statistics computed for that model under the assumption that the model is given a priori, including all statistics computed by REG, are biased.

While the RSQUARE method is a useful tool for exploratory model building, no statistical method can be relied on to identify the "true" model. Effective model building requires substantive theory to suggest relevant predictors and plausible functional forms for the model.

The RSQUARE method differs from the other selection methods in that RSQUARE always identifies the model with the largest R^2 for each number of variables considered. The other selection methods are not guaranteed to find the model with the largest R^2. RSQUARE requires much more computer time than the other selection methods, so a different selection method such as STEPWISE is a good choice when there are many independent variables to consider.

Adjusted R^2 Selection (ADJRSQ)

This method is similar to RSQUARE, except that the adjusted R^2 statistic is used as the criterion for selecting models, and the method finds the models with the highest adjusted R^2 within the range of sizes.

Mallows' C_p Selection (CP)

This method is similar to ADJRSQ, except that Mallow's C_p statistic is used as the criterion for model selection.

Additional Information on Model-Selection Methods

If PROC RSQUARE or PROC STEPWISE (as documented in *SAS User's Guide: Statistics, Version 5 Edition*) is requested, PROC REG with the appropriate model-selection method is actually used.

Reviews of model-selection methods by Hocking (1976) and Judge et al. (1980) describe these and other variable-selection methods.

Criteria Used in BACKWARD, FORWARD, and STEPWISE Model-Selection Methods

When many significance tests are performed, each at a level of, say 5 percent, the overall probability of rejecting at least one true null hypothesis is much larger than 5 percent. If you want to guard against including any variables that do not contribute to the predictive power of the model in the population, you should specify a very small significance level. In most applications many of the variables considered have some predictive power, however small. If you want to choose the model that provides the best prediction using the sample estimates, you need only guard against estimating more parameters than can be reliably estimated with the given sample size, so you should use a moderate significance level, perhaps in the range of 10 percent to 25 percent.

In addition to R^2, the C_p statistic is printed for each model generated in the model-selection methods. C_p was proposed by Mallows (1973) as a criterion for selecting a model. It is a measure of total squared error defined as

$$C_p = (\ SSE_p\ /\ s^2\ ) - (N\ - 2 {}^{*}p)$$

where s^2 is the MSE for the full model, and SSE_p is the sum-of-squares error for a model with p parameters including the intercept, if any. If C_p is plotted against p, Mallows recommends the model where C_p first approaches p. When the right model is chosen, the parameter estimates are unbiased, and this is reflected in C_p near p. For further discussion, see Daniel and Wood (1980).

The Adjusted R^2 statistic is an alternative to R^2 that is adjusted for the number of parameters in the model. The adjusted R^2 statistic is calculated as

$$ADJRSQ\ = 1 - [((n - i)(1 - R^2))\ /\ (n - p\ )]$$

where n is the number of observations used in fitting the model, and i is an indicator variable that is 1 if the model includes an intercept, and 0 otherwise.

Limitations in Model-Selection Methods

The use of model-selection methods can be time-consuming in some cases because there is no built-in limit on the number of independent variables, and the calculations for a large number of independent variables can be lengthy. The recommended limit on the number of independent variables for the MINR method is 20+*i*, where *i* is the value of the INCLUDE= option.

For the RSQUARE, ADJRSQ, or CP methods, with a large value of the BEST= option, adding one more variable to the list from which regressors are selected may significantly increase the CPU time. Also, the time required for the analysis is highly dependent on the data and on the values of the BEST=, START=, and STOP= options.

Parameter Estimates and Associated Statistics

The following example uses the fitness data from **Example 2**. **Output 28.13** shows the parameter estimates and the printout from the SS1, SS2, STB, COVB, and CORRB options:

```
proc reg data=fitness;
    model oxy=runtime age weight runpulse maxpulse rstpulse
        / ss1 ss2 stb covb corrb;
```

Output 28.13   Regression Using the SS1, SS2, STB, COVB, and CORRB Options

```
Model: MODEL1                                                                                      1
Dependent Variable: OXY

                                      Analysis of Variance

                                           Sum of          Mean
                    Source         DF     Squares        Square     F Value      Prob>F

                    Model           6    722.54361     120.42393      22.433      0.0001
                    Error          24    128.83794       5.36825
                    C Total        30    851.38154

                         Root MSE        2.31695      R-Square       0.8487
                         Dep Mean       47.37581      Adj R-Sq       0.8108
                         C.V.            4.89057

                                       Parameter Estimates

                     Parameter     Standard    T for H0:                                   Standardized
    Variable  DF      Estimate        Error   Parameter=0   Prob > |T|    Type I SS    Type II SS     Estimate

    INTERCEP   1    102.934479   12.40325810        8.299       0.0001        69578    369.728311    0.00000000
    RUNTIME    1     -2.628653    0.38456220       -6.835       0.0001   632.900100    250.822101   -0.68460149
    AGE        1     -0.226974    0.09983747       -2.273       0.0322    17.765633     27.745771   -0.22204052
    WEIGHT     1     -0.074177    0.05459316       -1.359       0.1869     5.605217      9.910588   -0.11596863
    RUNPULSE   1     -0.369628    0.11985294       -3.084       0.0051    38.875742     51.058058   -0.71132998
    MAXPULSE   1      0.303217    0.13649519        2.221       0.0360    26.826403     26.491424    0.52160512
    RSTPULSE   1     -0.021534    0.06605428       -0.326       0.7473     0.570513      0.570513   -0.03079918

                                     Covariance of Estimates

COVB            INTERCEP        RUNTIME           AGE         WEIGHT      RUNPULSE       MAXPULSE      RSTPULSE

INTERCEP    153.84081152    0.7678373769   -0.902049478   -0.178237818   0.280796516   -0.832761667   -0.147954715
RUNTIME       0.7678373769  0.1478880839   -0.014191688   -0.004417672  -0.009047784    0.0046249498  -0.010915224
AGE          -0.902049478  -0.014191688    0.009967521    0.0010219105  -0.001203914    0.0035823843   0.0014897532
WEIGHT       -0.178237818  -0.004417672    0.0010219105   0.0029804131   0.0009644683  -0.001372241    0.0003799295
RUNPULSE      0.280796516  -0.009047784   -0.001203914    0.0009644683   0.0143647273  -0.014952457   -0.000764507
MAXPULSE     -0.832761667   0.0046249498   0.0035823843  -0.001372241   -0.014952457    0.0186309364   0.0003425724
RSTPULSE     -0.147954715  -0.010915224    0.0014897532   0.0003799295  -0.000764507    0.0003425724   0.0043631674
```

CORRB	INTERCEP	RUNTIME	AGE	WEIGHT	RUNPULSE	MAXPULSE	RSTPULSE
			Correlation of Estimates				2
INTERCEP	1.0000	0.1610	-0.7285	-0.2632	0.1889	-0.4919	-0.1806
RUNTIME	0.1610	1.0000	-0.3696	-0.2104	-0.1963	0.0881	-0.4297
AGE	-0.7285	-0.3696	1.0000	0.1875	-0.1006	0.2629	0.2259
WEIGHT	-0.2632	-0.2104	0.1875	1.0000	0.1474	-0.1842	0.1054
RUNPULSE	0.1889	-0.1963	-0.1006	0.1474	1.0000	-0.9140	-0.0966
MAXPULSE	-0.4919	0.0881	0.2629	-0.1842	-0.9140	1.0000	0.0380
RSTPULSE	-0.1806	-0.4297	0.2259	0.1054	-0.0966	0.0380	1.0000

The output above first shows an Analysis of Variance table. The F statistic for the overall model is significant, indicating that the model explains a significant portion of the variation in the data.

The second portion of output shows Parameter Estimates and some associated statistics. First, the estimates are shown, followed by their Standard Errors. The next two columns of the table contain the t statistics and the corresponding probabilities for testing the null hypothesis that the parameter is not significantly different from zero. These probabilities are usually referred to as p values. For example, in the output above, the INTERCEP (or intercept) term in the model is estimated to be 102.9 and is significantly different from zero (at the 95% significance level). The next two columns of the table are the result of requesting the SS1 and SS2 options and show sequential and partial Sums of Squares (SS) associated with each variable. The Standardized Estimates (produced by the STB option) are the parameter estimates that result when all variables are standardized to a mean of 0 and a variance of 1. These estimates are computed by multiplying the original estimates by the standard deviation of the regressor (independent) variable, and then dividing by the standard deviation of the dependent variable.

The final two sections of output are produced as a result of requesting the COVB and CORRB options. These sections show the estimated covariance matrix of the parameter estimates, and the estimated correlation matrix of the estimates.

For further discussion of the parameters and statistics, see the **Printed Output** section later in this chapter, and **Parameter Estimates and Associated Statistics** and **Comments on Interpreting Regression Statistics** in Chapter 1, "Introduction to Regression Procedures."

Predicted and Residual Values

The printout of the predicted values and residuals is controlled by the P, R, CLM, and CLI options in the MODEL statement. The P option causes REG to print the observation number, the ID value (if an ID statement is used), the actual value, the predicted value, and the residual. The R, CLI, and CLM options also produce the items under the P option. Thus, P is unnecessary if you use one of the other options.

The R option requests more detail, especially about the residuals. The standard errors of the predicted value and the residual are printed. The studentized residual, which is the residual divided by its standard error, is both printed and plotted. A measure of influence, Cook's D, is printed. Cook's D measures the change to the estimates that results from deleting each observation. See Cook (1977, 1979). (This statistic is very similar to DFFITS.)

The CLM option requests that REG print the 95% lower and upper confidence limits for the predicted values. This accounts for the variation due to estimating the parameters only. If you want a 95% confidence interval for observed values, then you can use the CLI option, which adds in the variability of the error term.

You can use these statistics in PLOT and PAINT statements. This is useful in performing a variety of regression diagnostics. For definitions of the statistics produced by these options, see Chapter 1, "Introduction to Regression Procedures."

Here is an example using US population data found in **Example 1** later in this chapter. These statements produce **Output 28.14**:

```
proc reg data=uspop;
   id year;
   model pop=year yearsq / p r cli clm;
```

Output 28.14   Regression Using the P, R, CLI, and CLM Options

```
Model: MODEL1                                                                                          1
Dependent Variable: POP
                                          Analysis of Variance

                                       Sum of          Mean
                  Source         DF    Squares         Square      F Value      Prob>F

                  Model           2  71799.01619    35899.50809    4641.719     0.0001
                  Error          16    123.74557        7.73410
                  C Total        18  71922.76175

                      Root MSE       2.78102      R-Square      0.9983
                      Dep Mean      69.76747      Adj R-Sq      0.9981
                      C.V.           3.98613

                                       Parameter Estimates

                                    Parameter      Standard      T for H0:
                  Variable   DF      Estimate         Error     Parameter=0    Prob > |T|

                  INTERCEP   1        20450      843.47532634      24.245        0.0001
                  YEAR       1     -22.780606      0.89784904     -25.372        0.0001
                  YEARSQ     1       0.006346      0.00023877      26.576        0.0001
```

Obs	YEAR	Dep Var POP	Predict Value	Std Err Predict	Lower95% Mean	Upper95% Mean	Lower95% Predict	Upper95% Predict	Residual	Std Err Residual	Student Residual
1	1790	3.9290	5.0384	1.729	1.3734	8.7035	-1.9034	11.9803	-1.1094	2.178	-0.509
2	1800	5.3080	5.0389	1.391	2.0904	7.9874	-1.5528	11.6306	0.2691	2.408	0.112
3	1810	7.2390	6.3085	1.130	3.9122	8.7047	-0.0554	12.6723	0.9305	2.541	0.366
4	1820	9.6380	8.8472	0.957	6.8182	10.8761	2.6123	15.0820	0.7908	2.611	0.303
5	1830	12.8660	12.6550	0.872	10.8062	14.5037	6.4764	18.8335	0.2110	2.641	0.080
6	1840	17.0690	17.7319	0.858	15.9133	19.5504	11.5623	23.9015	-0.6629	2.645	-0.251
7	1850	23.1910	24.0779	0.884	22.2050	25.9509	17.8921	30.2637	-0.8869	2.637	-0.336
8	1860	31.4430	31.6931	0.920	29.7424	33.6437	25.4832	37.9029	-0.2501	2.624	-0.095
9	1870	39.8180	40.5773	0.949	38.5661	42.5885	34.3482	46.8064	-0.7593	2.614	-0.290
10	1880	50.1550	50.7307	0.959	48.6972	52.7642	44.4944	56.9670	-0.5757	2.610	-0.221
11	1890	62.9470	62.1532	0.949	60.1420	64.1644	55.9241	68.3823	0.7938	2.614	0.304
12	1900	75.9940	74.8448	0.920	72.8942	76.7955	68.6350	81.0547	1.1492	2.624	0.438
13	1910	91.9720	88.8056	0.884	86.9326	90.6785	82.6197	95.0	3.1664	2.637	1.201
14	1920	105.7	104.0	0.858	102.2	105.9	97.9	110.2	1.6746	2.645	0.633
15	1930	122.8	120.5	0.872	118.7	122.4	114.4	126.7	2.2406	2.641	0.848
16	1940	131.7	138.3	0.957	136.3	140.3	132.1	144.5	-6.6335	2.611	-2.540
17	1950	151.3	157.3	1.130	154.9	159.7	151.0	163.7	-6.0147	2.541	-2.367
18	1960	179.3	177.6	1.391	174.7	180.6	171.1	184.2	1.6770	2.408	0.696
19	1970	203.2	199.2	1.729	195.6	202.9	192.3	206.2	3.9895	2.178	1.831
20	1980	.	222.1	2.135	217.5	226.6	214.6	229.5	.	.	.
21	1990	.	246.2	2.602	240.7	251.7	238.1	254.3	.	.	.
22	2000	.	271.6	3.126	264.9	278.2	262.7	280.4	.	.	.

```
                                  Cook's                                              2
      Obs   YEAR       -2-1-0 1 2      D

        1   1790      |      *|       |    0.054
        2   1800      |       |       |    0.001
        3   1810      |       |       |    0.009
        4   1820      |       |       |    0.004
        5   1830      |       |       |    0.000
        6   1840      |       |       |    0.002
        7   1850      |       |       |    0.004
        8   1860      |       |       |    0.000
        9   1870      |       |       |    0.004
       10   1880      |       |       |    0.002
       11   1890      |       |       |    0.004
       12   1900      |       |       |    0.008
       13   1910      |       |**     |    0.054
       14   1920      |       |*      |    0.014
       15   1930      |       |*      |    0.026
       16   1940      | *****|        |    0.289
       17   1950      | ****|         |    0.370
       18   1960      |       |*      |    0.054
       19   1970      |       |***    |    0.704
       20   1980                      .
       21   1990                      .
       22   2000                      .

    Sum of Residuals               1.098623E-10
    Sum of Squared Residuals          123.7456
    Predicted Resid SS (Press)        188.5492
```

After printing the usual Analysis of Variance and Parameter Estimates tables, the procedure prints the results of requesting the options for predicted and residual values. For each observation, the requested information is shown. Note that the ID variable is used to identify each observation. Also, note that for observations with missing dependent variables, the predicted value, standard error of the predicted value, and confidence intervals for the predicted value are still available.

The plot of studentized residuals and the Cook's D statistics are printed as a result of requesting the R option. In the plot of studentized residuals, a large number of observations with absolute values greater than two indicates an inadequate model.

Producing Scatter Plots

The interactive PLOT statement available in REG allows you to look at scatter plots of data and diagnostic statistics. These plots can help you to evaluate the model and detect outliers in your data. Several options allow you to place multiple plots on a single page, superimpose plots, and collect plots to be overlayed by later plots. The PAINT statement can be used to highlight points on a plot. See **Painting Scatter Plots** later in this chapter for more information on painting.

The CLASS data set introduced in the **Interactive Analysis** section is used in the examples below.

You can superimpose several plots with the OVERLAY option. With the statements below, a plot of WEIGHT against HEIGHT is overlaid with plots of the predicted values and the 95% prediction intervals. The model on which the statistics are based is the full model including HEIGHT and AGE. These statements produce **Output 28.15**:

```
proc reg data=class;
   model weight=height age / noprint;
   plot (u95. l95. p.)*height='-' weight*height
        / overlay symbol='o';
run;
```

Output 28.15   Scatter Plot Showing Data, Predicted Values, and Confidence Limits

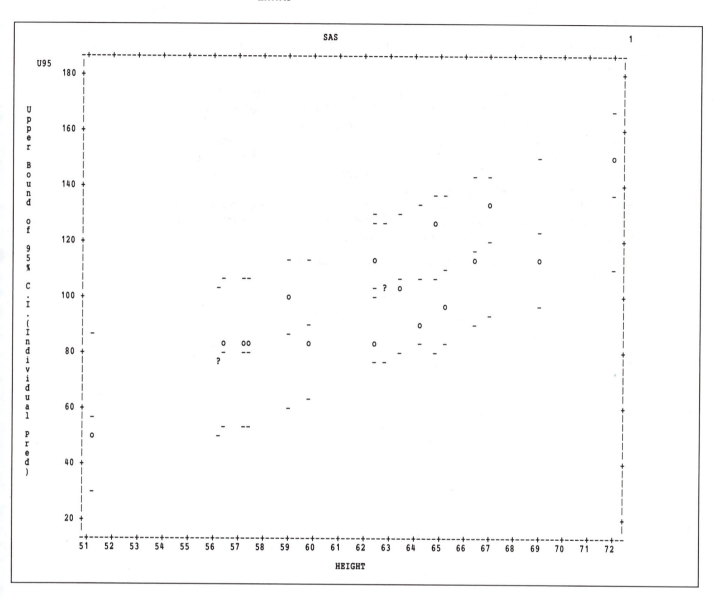

In this plot the data values are marked with the symbol 'o' and the predicted values and prediction interval limits are labeled with the symbol '-'. The plot is scaled to accommodate the points from all plots. This is an important difference from the COLLECT option, which does not rescale plots after the first plot or plots are collected. You could separate the overlaid plots above by using the following statements:

```
plot;
run;
```

This places each of the four plots on a separate page, while the statements

```
plot / overlay;
run;
```

would repeat the previous overlaid plot. In general, the statement

```
plot;
```

is equivalent to respecifying the most recent PLOT statement without any options. However, the COLLECT, HPLOTS=, SYMBOL=, and VPLOTS= options apply across PLOT statements and remain in effect.

The next example shows how you can overlay plots of statistics before and after a change in the model. For the full model involving HEIGHT and AGE, the ordinary residuals and the studentized residuals are plotted against the predicted values. The COLLECT option causes these plots to be collected or retained for redisplay later. HPLOTS=2 allows the two plots to appear side by side on one page. The symbol 'f' is used on these plots to identify them as resulting from the full model. The statements below produce **Output 28.16**:

```
plot r.*p. student.*p. / collect hplots=2 symbol='f';
run;
```

Output 28.16   Collecting Residual Plots for the Full Model

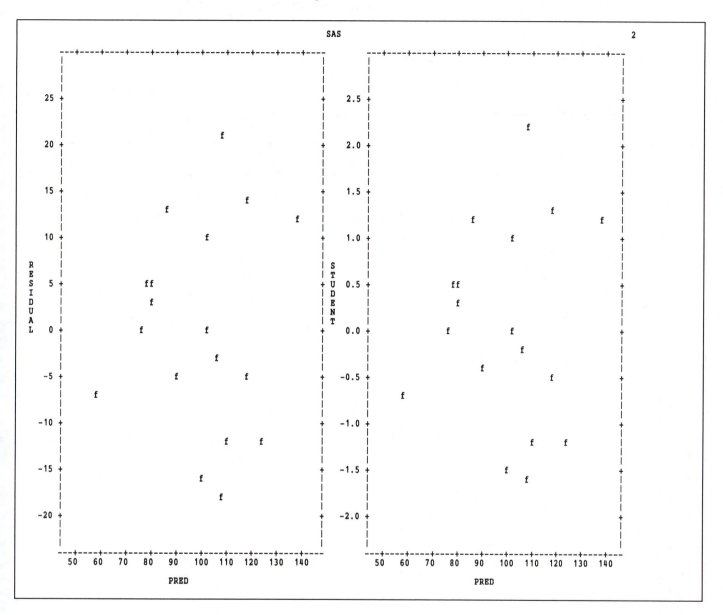

Note that these plots are not overlaid. The COLLECT option does not overlay the plots in one PLOT statement, but retains them so they can be overlaid by later plots. When the COLLECT option appears on a PLOT statement, the plots in that statement become the first plots in the collection.

Next, the model is reduced by deleting the AGE variable. The PLOT statement requests the same plots as before but labels the points with the symbol 'r' denoting the reduced model. The statements below produce **Output 28.17**:

```
delete age;
plot r.*p. student.*p. / symbol='r';
run;
```

Output 28.17   Overlaid Residual Plots for Full and Reduced Models

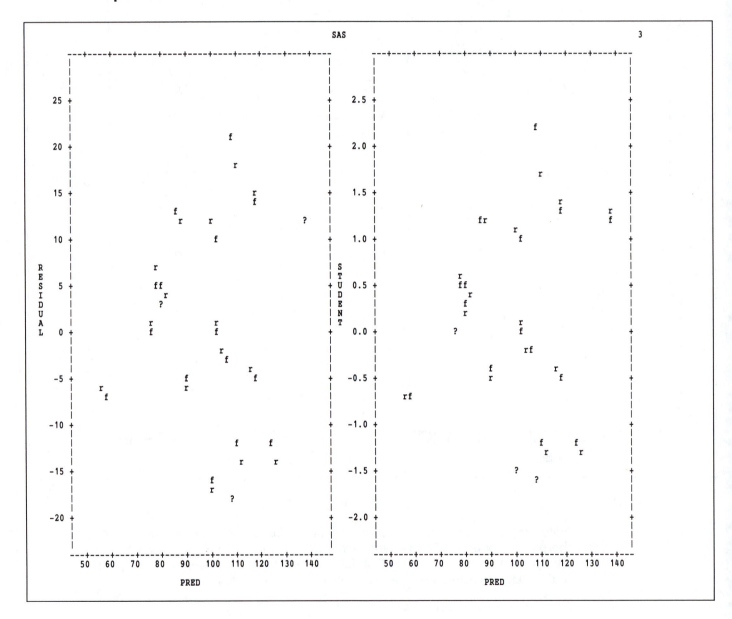

Notice that the COLLECT option caused the corresponding plots to be overlaid. The points labeled 'f' are from the full model, and points labeled 'r' are from the reduced model. Positions labeled '?' contain at least one point from each model. In this example, OVERLAY could not be used because all of the plots to be overlaid could not be specified in one PLOT statement. With the COLLECT option any changes to the model or the data used to fit the model do not affect plots collected before the changes. Collected plots are always reproduced exactly as they first appeared. (Similarly, a PAINT statement does not affect plots collected before the PAINT statement was issued.)

The previous example overlaid the residual plots for two different models. You may prefer to see them side by side on the same page. This can also be done with the COLLECT option by using a blank plot. Continuing from the last example, COLLECT, HPLOTS=2 and SYMBOL='r' are still in effect. In the PLOT statement below, the CLEAR option deletes the collected plots and allows the specified plot to begin a new collection. The plot created is the residual plot for the reduced model. The statements below produce **Output 28.18**:

```
plot r.*p. / clear;
run;
```

Output 28.18 Residual Plot for Reduced Model Only

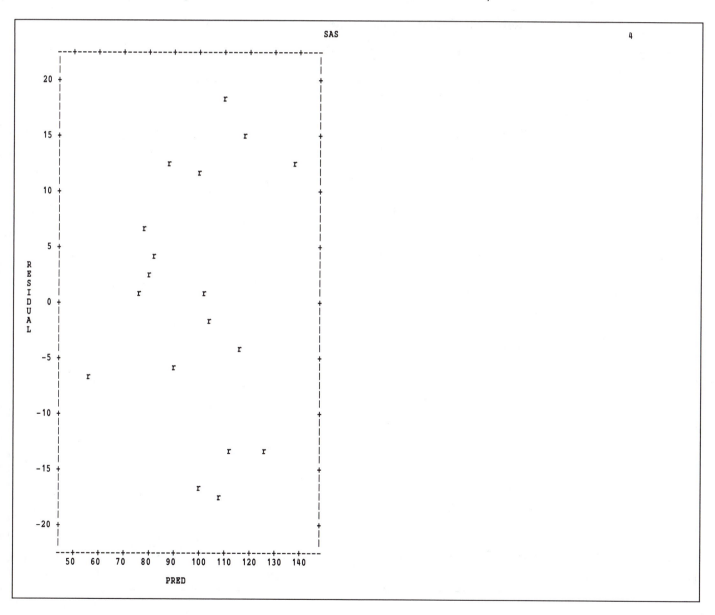

The next statements add AGE to the model and place the residual plot for the full model next to the plot for the reduced model. Notice that a blank plot is created in the first plot request by placing nothing between the quotes. Since COLLECT is in effect, this plot is superimposed on the residual plot for the reduced model. The residual plot for the full model is created by the second request. The result is the desired side-by-side plots. The NOCOLLECT option turns off the collection process after the specified plots are added and displayed. Any PLOT statements that follow show only the newly specified plots. These statements produce **Output 28.19**:

```
add age;
plot r.*p.='' r.*p.='f' / nocollect;
run;
```

Output 28.19   Side-by-Side Residual Plots for the Full and Reduced Models

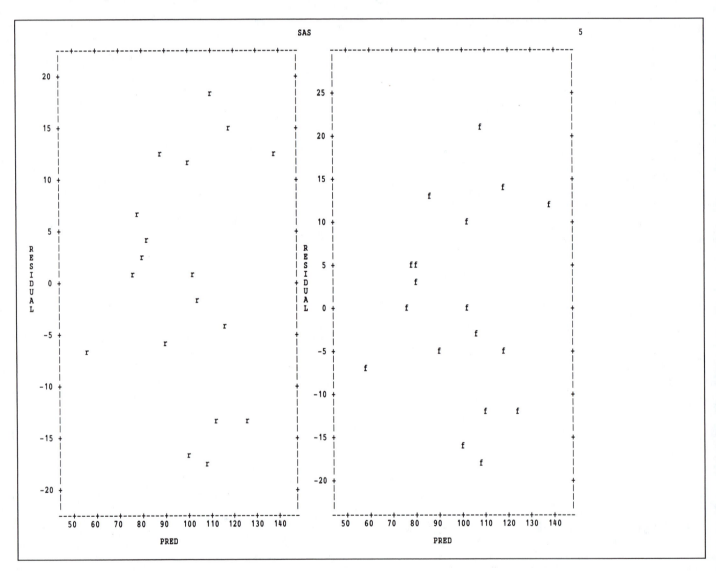

Frequently, when COLLECT is in effect you will want the current and following PLOT statements to show only the specified plots. To do this, use both the CLEAR and NOCOLLECT options in the current PLOT statement.

Painting Scatter Plots

Painting scatter plots is a useful interactive tool that allows you to mark points of interest in scatter plots. Painting can be used to identify extreme points in scatter plots or to reveal the relationship between two scatter plots. The CLASS data (from **Interactive Analysis** earlier in this chapter) is used to illustrate some of these applications. First, a scatter plot of the studentized residuals against the predicted values is generated. This plot is shown in **Output 28.20**.

```
proc reg data=class;
   model weight=age height / noprint;
   id name;
   plot student.*p.;
run;
```

Output 28.20   Plotting Studentized Residuals Against Predicted Values

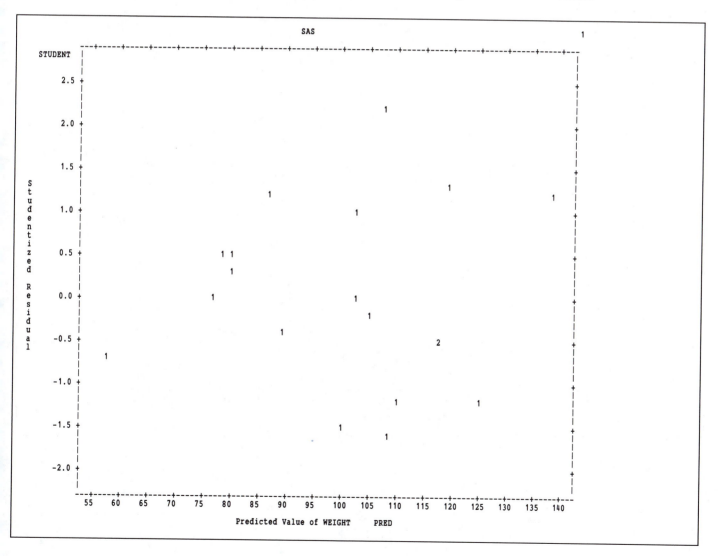

Then, the following statements identify the observation 'Henry' in the scatter plot
and produce **Output 28.21**:

```
paint name='Henry' / symbol = 'H';
plot;
run;
```

Output 28.21 Painting One Observation

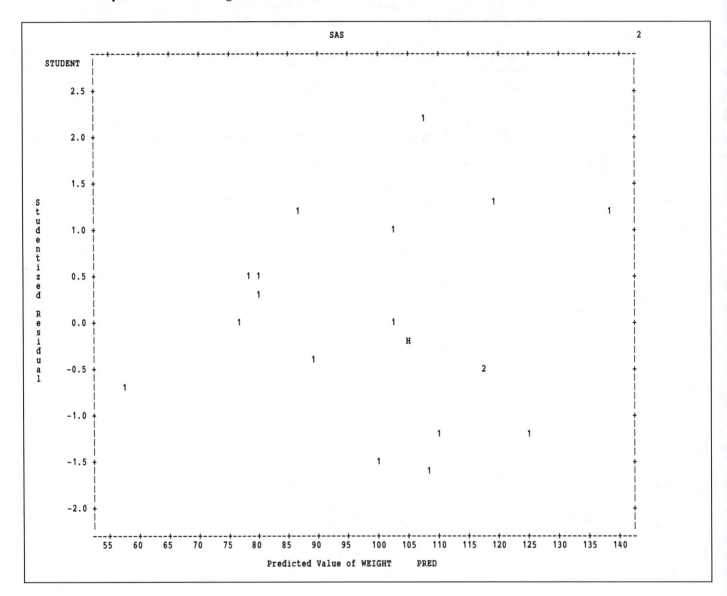

Then, use the following statements to identify observations with large absolute residuals:

```
paint student.>=2 or student.<=-2 / symbol='s';
plot;
run;
```

The log shows the observation numbers found with the above condition and gives the printing symbol and the number of observations found. Note that the previous PAINT statement is also used in the PLOT statement. **Output 28.22** shows the scatter plot produced by the statements above.

Output 28.22 Painting Several Observations

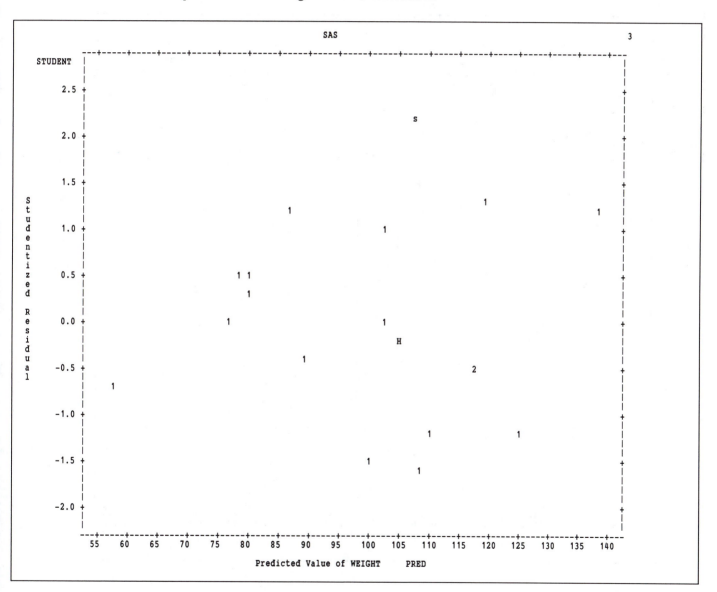

Use the following statements to relate two different scatter plots. These statements produce **Output 28.23**.

```
paint student.>=1 / symbol='p';
paint student.<1 and student.>-1 / symbol='s';
paint student.<=-1 / symbol='n';
plot student. * p. cookd. * h. / hplots=2;
run;
```

Output 28.23   Painting Observations on More than One Plot

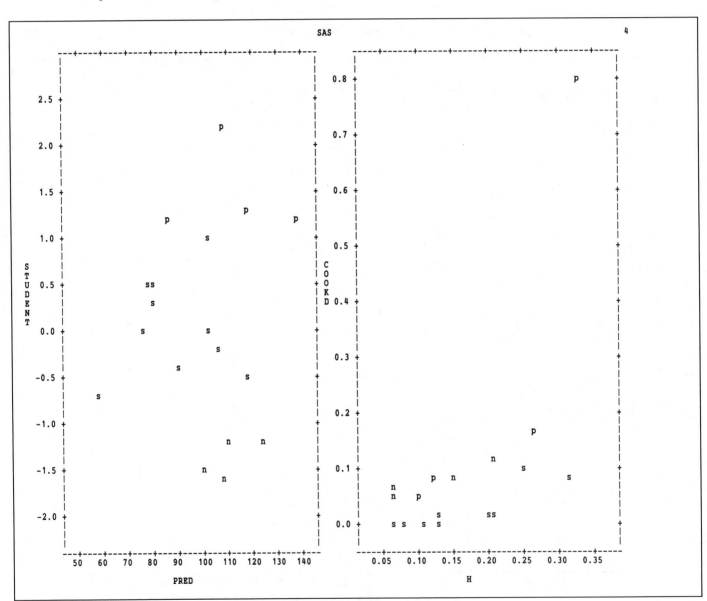

Models of Less than Full Rank

If the model is not full rank, there are an infinite number of least-squares solutions for the estimates. REG chooses a nonzero solution for all variables that are linearly independent of previous variables and a zero solution for other variables. This solution corresponds to using a generalized inverse in the normal equations, and the expected values of the estimates are the Hermite normal form of **X** multiplied by the true parameters:

$$E(\mathbf{b}) = (\mathbf{X}'\mathbf{X})^{-}(\mathbf{X}'\mathbf{X})\boldsymbol{\beta} \quad .$$

Degrees of freedom for the zeroed estimates are reported as zero. The hypotheses that are not testable have *t* tests printed as missing. The message that the model is not full rank includes a printout of the relations that exist in the matrix.

The example below uses the fitness data from **Example 2** later in this chapter. The variable DIF=RUNPULSE−RSTPULSE is created. When this variable is included in the model along with RUNPULSE and RSTPULSE, there is a linear dependency (or exact collinearity) between the dependent variables. **Output 28.24** shows how this problem is diagnosed.

```
data fit2;
   set fitness;
   dif=runpulse-rstpulse;
proc reg data=fit2;
   model oxy=runtime age weight runpulse maxpulse rstpulse dif;
run;
```

Output 28.24   Model That Is Not Full Rank: REG Procedure

```
Model: MODEL1                                                                               1
Dependent Variable: OXY
                                       Analysis of Variance

                             Sum of          Mean
       Source        DF      Squares        Square      F Value     Prob>F

       Model          6    722.54361     120.42393       22.433     0.0001
       Error         24    128.83794       5.36825
       C Total       30    851.38154


            Root MSE       2.31695     R-Square       0.8487
            Dep Mean      47.37581     Adj R-Sq       0.8108
            C.V.           4.89057
```

NOTE: Model is not full rank. Least squares solutions for the parameters are not unique. Some statistics will be
      misleading. A reported DF of 0 or B means that the estimate is biased.
      The following parameters have been set to 0, since the variables are a linear combination of other variables as
      shown.

```
   DIF     = +1.0000 * RUNPULSE -1.0000 * RSTPULSE
                                  Parameter Estimates

                        Parameter     Standard     T for H0:
       Variable   DF     Estimate        Error    Parameter=0    Prob > |T|

       INTERCEP   1    102.934479   12.40325810        8.299        0.0001
       RUNTIME    1     -2.628653    0.38456220       -6.835        0.0001
       AGE        1     -0.226974    0.09983747       -2.273        0.0322
       WEIGHT     1     -0.074177    0.05459316       -1.359        0.1869
       RUNPULSE   B     -0.369628    0.11985294       -3.084        0.0051
       MAXPULSE   1      0.303217    0.13649519        2.221        0.0360
       RSTPULSE   B     -0.021534    0.06605428       -0.326        0.7473
       DIF        0             0    0.00000000          .             .
```

Note that PROC REG prints a message informing you that the model is less than full rank. Parameters with DF=0 are not estimated, and parameters with DF=B are biased. In addition, the form of the linear dependency among the regressors is printed.

Collinearity Diagnostics

When a regressor is nearly a linear combination of other regressors in the model, the affected estimates are unstable and have high standard errors. This problem is called *collinearity* or *multicollinearity*. It is a good idea to find out which variables are nearly collinear with which other variables. The approach in PROC REG follows that of Belsley, Kuh, and Welsch (1980). REG provides several methods for detecting collinearity with the COLLIN, COLLINOINT, TOL, and VIF options.

The COLLIN option in the MODEL statement requests that a collinearity analysis be done. First, $X'X$ is scaled to have 1s on the diagonal. If COLLINOINT is specified, the intercept variable is adjusted out first. Then the eigenvalues and eigenvectors are extracted. The analysis in REG is reported with eigenvalues of $X'X$ rather than singular values of X. The eigenvalues of $X'X$ are the squares of the singular values of X.

The condition indices are the square roots of the ratio of the largest eigenvalue to each individual eigenvalue. The largest condition index is the condition number of the scaled X matrix. When this number is large, the data are said to be ill-conditioned. When this number is extremely large, the estimates may have a fair amount of numerical error (although the statistical standard error almost always is much greater than the numerical error).

For each variable, REG prints the proportion of the variance of the estimate accounted for by each principal component. A collinearity problem occurs when a component associated with a high condition index contributes strongly to the variance of two or more variables.

The VIF option in the MODEL statement provides the Variance Inflation Factors. These factors measure the inflation in the variances of the parameter estimates due to collinearities that exist among the regressor (dependent) variables. There are no formal criteria for deciding if a VIF is large enough to affect the predicted values.

The TOL option requests the tolerance values for the parameter estimates.

For a complete discussion of the methods discussed above, see Belsley, Kuh, and Welsch (1980). For a more detailed explanation of using the methods with PROC REG, see Freund and Littell (1986).

Here is an example using the COLLIN option on the fitness data found in **Example 2** later in this chapter. The statements below produce **Output 28.25**:

```
proc reg data=fitness;
   model oxy=runtime age weight runpulse maxpulse rstpulse
         / tol vif collin;
run;
```

Output 28.25   Regression Using the TOL, VIF, and COLLIN Options

```
Model: MODEL1                                                                      1
Dependent Variable: OXY
                              Analysis of Variance

                                   Sum of        Mean
              Source       DF     Squares      Square    F Value    Prob>F

              Model         6    722.54361   120.42393     22.433    0.0001
              Error        24    128.83794     5.36825
              C Total      30    851.38154

                  Root MSE        2.31695     R-Square      0.8487
                  Dep Mean       47.37581     Adj R-Sq      0.8108
                  C.V.            4.89057

                              Parameter Estimates

                   Parameter    Standard    T for H0:                            Variance
    Variable  DF    Estimate       Error   Parameter=0  Prob > |T|   Tolerance   Inflation

    INTERCEP   1   102.934479  12.40325810      8.299      0.0001       .        0.00000000
    RUNTIME    1    -2.628653   0.38456220     -6.835      0.0001    0.62858771  1.59086788
    AGE        1    -0.226974   0.09983747     -2.273      0.0322    0.66101010  1.51283618
    WEIGHT     1    -0.074177   0.05459316     -1.359      0.1869    0.86555401  1.15532940
    RUNPULSE   1    -0.369628   0.11985294     -3.084      0.0051    0.11852169  8.43727418
    MAXPULSE   1     0.303217   0.13649519      2.221      0.0360    0.11436612  8.74384843
    RSTPULSE   1    -0.021534   0.06605428     -0.326      0.7473    0.70641990  1.41558865

                              Collinearity Diagnostics

             Condition  Var Prop  Var Prop  Var Prop  Var Prop  Var Prop  Var Prop  Var Prop
 Number  Eigenvalue  Number  INTERCEP  RUNTIME  AGE    WEIGHT  RUNPULSE  MAXPULSE  RSTPULSE

    1   6.94991     1.00000   0.0000   0.0002   0.0002   0.0002   0.0000   0.0000   0.0003
    2   0.01868    19.29087   0.0022   0.0252   0.1463   0.0104   0.0000   0.0000   0.3906
    3   0.01503    21.50072   0.0006   0.1286   0.1501   0.2357   0.0012   0.0012   0.0281
    4   0.00911    27.62115   0.0064   0.6090   0.0319   0.1831   0.0015   0.0012   0.1903
    5   0.00607    33.82918   0.0013   0.1250   0.1128   0.4444   0.0151   0.0083   0.3648
    6   0.00102    82.63757   0.7997   0.0975   0.4966   0.1033   0.0695   0.0056   0.0203
    7  0.0001795  196.78560   0.1898   0.0146   0.0621   0.0228   0.9128   0.9836   0.0057
```

Influence Diagnostics

The INFLUENCE option requests the statistics proposed by Belsley, Kuh, and Welsch (1980) to measure the influence of each observation on the estimates. Influential observations are those that, according to various criteria, appear to have a large influence on the parameter estimates. Let $\mathbf{b}(i)$ be the parameter estimates after deleting the ith observation; let $s(i)^2$ be the variance estimate after deleting the ith observation; let $\mathbf{X}(i)$ be the $\mathbf{X}$ matrix without the ith observation; let $\hat{y}(i)$ be the ith value predicted without using the ith observation; let $r_i = y_i - \hat{y}_i$ be the ith residual; and let h_i be the ith diagonal of the projection matrix for the predictor space, also called the *hat matrix*:

$$h_i = \mathbf{x}_i(\mathbf{X'X})^{-1}\mathbf{x}_i' \quad .$$

Belsley, Kuh, and Welsch propose a cutoff of $2*p/n$, where n is the number of observations used to fit the model, and p is the number of parameters in the model. Observations with h_i values above this cutoff should be investigated.

For each observation, REG first prints the residual, the studentized residual, and the h_i. The studentized residual differs slightly from that in the previous section since the error variance is estimated by $s(i)^2$ without the ith observation, not by s^2. For example,

$$\text{RSTUDENT} = r_i / \left(s(i)\sqrt{(1-h_i)}\right) \quad .$$

Observations with RSTUDENT larger than 2 in absolute value may need some attention.

The COVRATIO statistic measures the change in the determinant of the covariance matrix of the estimates by deleting the ith observation:

$$\text{COVRATIO} = \det\left(s^2(i)(\mathbf{X}(i)'\mathbf{X}(i))^{-1}\right) / \det\left(s^2(\mathbf{X}'\mathbf{X})^{-1}\right) \quad .$$

Belsley, Kuh, and Welsch suggest observations with

$$|\,\text{COVRATIO} - 1\,| \geq 3p\,/\,n$$

where p is the number of parameters in the model, and n is the number of observations used to fit the model, are worth investigation.

The DFFITS statistic is a scaled measure of the change in the predicted value for the ith observation and is calculated by deleting the ith observation. A large value indicates that the observation is very influential in its neighborhood of the **X** space.

$$\text{DFFITS} = (\hat{y}_i - \hat{y}(i)) / \left(s(i)\sqrt{h_i}\right) \quad .$$

Large values of DFFITS indicate influential observations. A general cutoff to consider is 2; a size-adjusted cutoff recommended by Belsley, Kuh, and Welsch is $2\sqrt{p/n}$, where n and p are as defined above.

DFFITS is very similar to Cook's D, defined in **Predicted and Residual Values** earlier in this chapter.

DFBETAS are the scaled measures of the change in each parameter estimate and are calculated by deleting the ith observation:

$$\text{DFBETAS}_j = (b_j - b_j(i)) / \left(s(i)\sqrt{(\mathbf{X}'\mathbf{X})^{jj}}\right)$$

where

$$(\mathbf{X}'\mathbf{X})^{jj} \quad \text{is the } (j,\,j)\text{th element of } (\mathbf{X}'\mathbf{X})^{-1} \quad .$$

In general, large values of DFBETAS indicate observations that are influential in estimating a given parameter. Belsley, Kuh, and Welsch recommend 2 as a general cutoff value to indicate influential observations, and $2/\sqrt{n}$ as a size-adjusted cutoff.

Output 28.26 shows the portion of output produced by the INFLUENCE option for the population example (**Example 1**). See **Output 28.14** for the fitted regression equation.

```
proc reg data=uspop;
   model pop=year yearsq / influence;
run;
```

Output 28.26   Regression Using the INFLUENCE Option

Obs	Residual	Rstudent	Hat Diag H	Cov Ratio	Dffits	INTERCEP Dfbetas	YEAR Dfbetas	YEARSQ Dfbetas	1
1	-1.1094	-0.4972	0.3865	1.8834	-0.3946	-0.2842	0.2810	-0.2779	
2	0.2691	0.1082	0.2501	1.6147	0.0625	0.0376	-0.0370	0.0365	
3	0.9305	0.3561	0.1652	1.4176	0.1584	0.0666	-0.0651	0.0636	
4	0.7908	0.2941	0.1184	1.3531	0.1078	0.0182	-0.0172	0.0161	
5	0.2110	0.0774	0.0983	1.3444	0.0256	-0.0030	0.0033	-0.0035	
6	-0.6629	-0.2431	0.0951	1.3255	-0.0788	0.0296	-0.0302	0.0307	
7	-0.8869	-0.3268	0.1009	1.3214	-0.1095	0.0609	-0.0616	0.0621	
8	-0.2501	-0.0923	0.1095	1.3605	-0.0324	0.0216	-0.0217	0.0218	
9	-0.7593	-0.2820	0.1164	1.3519	-0.1023	0.0743	-0.0745	0.0747	
10	-0.5757	-0.2139	0.1190	1.3650	-0.0786	0.0586	-0.0587	0.0587	
11	0.7938	0.2949	0.1164	1.3499	0.1070	-0.0784	0.0783	-0.0781	
12	1.1492	0.4265	0.1095	1.3144	0.1496	-0.1018	0.1014	-0.1009	
13	3.1664	1.2189	0.1009	1.0168	0.4084	-0.2357	0.2338	-0.2318	
14	1.6746	0.6207	0.0951	1.2430	0.2013	-0.0811	0.0798	-0.0784	
15	2.2406	0.8407	0.0983	1.1724	0.2776	-0.0427	0.0404	-0.0380	
16	-6.6335	-3.1845	0.1184	0.2924	-1.1673	-0.1531	0.1636	-0.1747	
17	-6.0147	-2.8433	0.1652	0.3989	-1.2649	-0.4843	0.4958	-0.5076	
18	1.6770	0.6847	0.2501	1.4757	0.3954	0.2240	-0.2274	0.2308	
19	3.9895	1.9947	0.3865	0.9766	1.5831	1.0902	-1.1025	1.1151	
20	.	.	0.5893	.	.	.	.	.	
21	.	.	0.8753	.	.	.	.	.	
22	.	.	1.2632	.	.	.	.	.	

```
Sum of Residuals            1.098623E-10
Sum of Squared Residuals      123.7456
Predicted Resid SS (Press)    188.5492
```

In the output above, observations 16, 17, and 19 exceed the cutoff value of 2 for RSTUDENT. None of the observations exceeds the general cutoff of 2 for DFFITS or the DFBETAS, but observations 16, 17, and 19 exceed at least one of the size-adjusted cutoffs for these statistics. Observations 1 and 19 exceed the cutoff for the hat diagonals, and observations 1, 2, 16, 17, and 18 exceed the cutoffs for COVRATIO. Taken together, these statistics indicate looking first at observations 16, 17, and 19, and then perhaps investigating the other observations that exceeded a cutoff.

The PARTIAL option produces partial regression leverage plots. One plot is printed for each regressor in the full, current model. For example, plots are produced for regressors included by using ADD statements; plots are not produced for interim models in the various model-selection methods but only for the full model. If you use a model-selection method and the final model contains only a subset of the original regressors, the PARTIAL option still produces plots for all regressors in the full model.

For a given regressor, the partial regression leverage plot is the plot of the dependent variable and the regressor after they have been made orthogonal to the other regressors in the model. These can be obtained by plotting the residuals for the dependent variable against the residuals for the selected regressor, where the residuals for the dependent variable are calculated with the selected regressor omitted, and the residuals for the selected regressor are calculated from a model where the selected regressor is regressed on the remaining regressors. A line fit to the points has a slope equal to the parameter estimate in the full model.

In the plot, points are marked by the number of replicates appearing at one print position. The symbol '*' is used if there are ten or more replicates. If an ID statement is specified, the left-most nonblank character in the value of the ID variable is used as the plotting symbol.

The following statements use the fitness data in **Example 2** with the PARTIAL option to produce **Output 28.27**:

```
proc reg data=fitness;
    model oxy=runtime weight age / partial;
run;
```

Output 28.27   Regression Using the PARTIAL Option

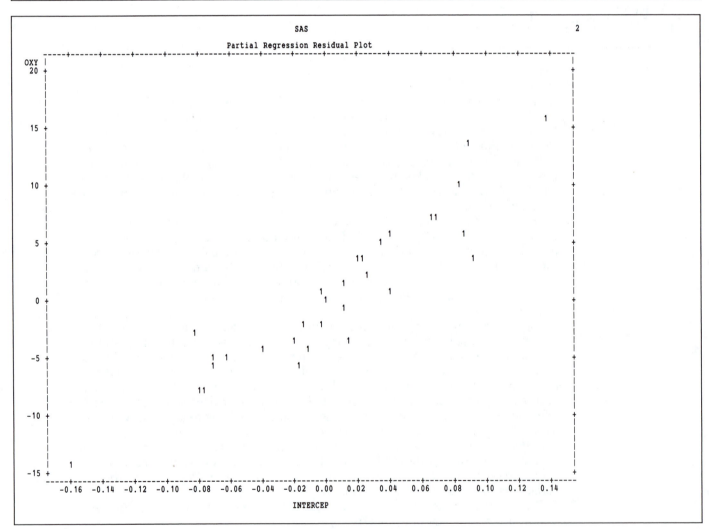

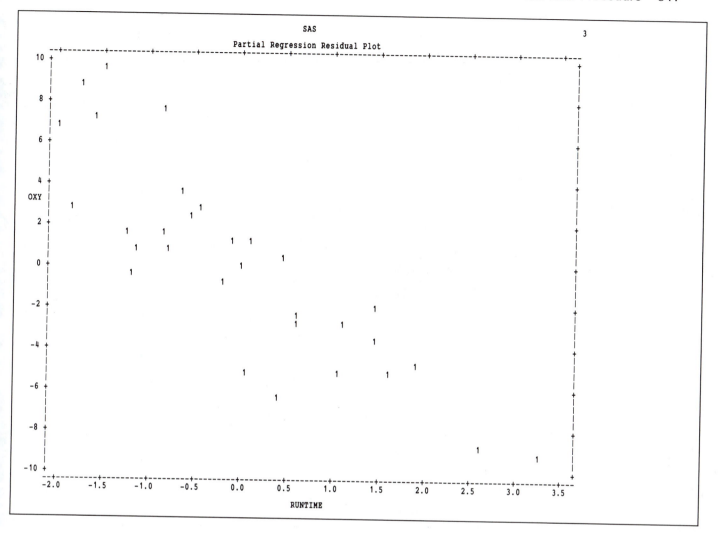

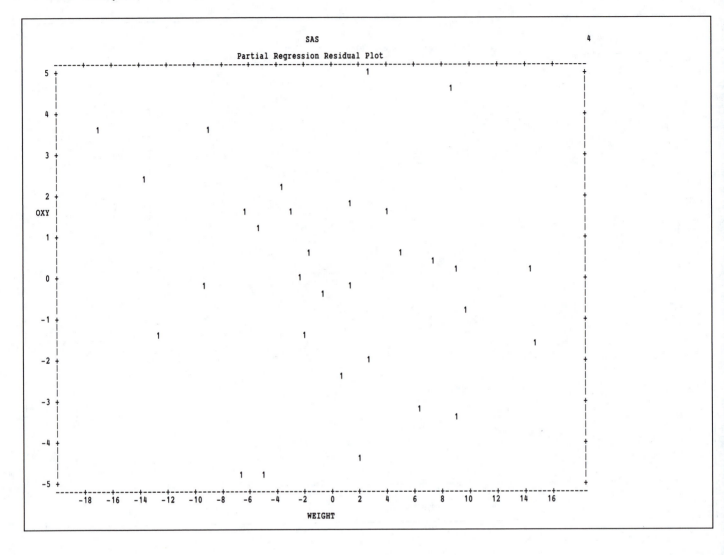

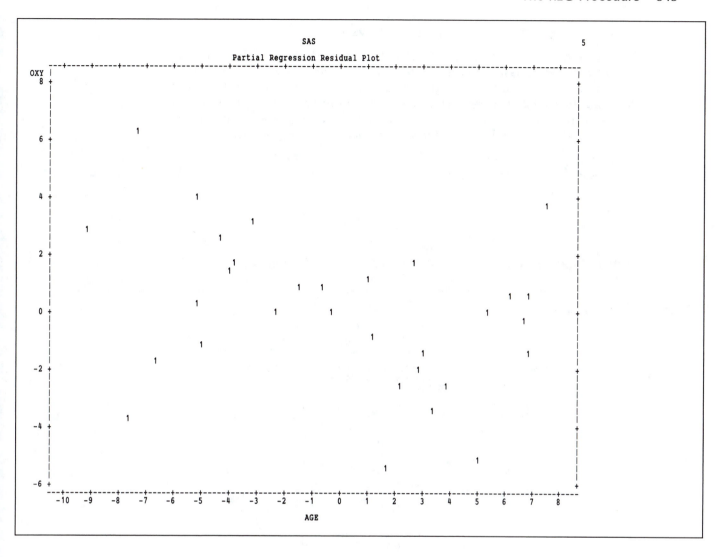

Reweighting Observations in an Analysis

Reweighting observations is an interactive feature of PROC REG that allows you to change the weights of observations used in computing the regression equation. Observations may also be deleted from the analysis (not from the data set) by changing their weights to zero. The CLASS data (from **Interactive Analysis** earlier in this chapter) are used to illustrate some of the features of REWEIGHT. First, the full model is fit, and the residuals are displayed in **Output 28.28**.

```
proc reg data=class;
   model weight=age height / p;
   id name;
run;
```

Output 28.28   Full Model for CLASS Data, Residuals Shown

```
Model: MODEL1                                                                         1
Dependent Variable: WEIGHT
                                      Analysis of Variance

                              Sum of          Mean
         Source        DF     Squares        Square      F Value      Prob>F

         Model          2   7215.63710    3607.81855      27.228      0.0001
         Error         16   2120.09974     132.50623
         C Total       18   9335.73684

              Root MSE      11.51114      R-Square       0.7729
              Dep Mean     100.02632      Adj R-Sq       0.7445
              C.V.          11.50811

                                   Parameter Estimates

                        Parameter       Standard     T for H0:
         Variable  DF    Estimate          Error    Parameter=0    Prob > |T|

         INTERCEP   1   -141.223763    33.38309350       -4.230       0.0006
         AGE        1      1.278393     3.11010374        0.411       0.6865
         HEIGHT     1      3.597027     0.90546072        3.973       0.0011


                                    Dep Var    Predict
                   Obs  NAME        WEIGHT       Value   Residual

                     1  Alfred       112.5       124.9   -12.3686
                     2  Alice        84.0000     78.6273    5.3727
                     3  Barbara      98.0        110.3   -12.2812
                     4  Carol       102.5        102.6    -0.0670
                     5  Henry       102.5        105.1    -2.5849
                     6  James        83.0000     80.2266    2.7734
                     7  Jane         84.5000     89.2191   -4.7191
                     8  Janet       112.5        102.8     9.7337
                     9  Jeffrey      84.0000    100.2    -16.2095
                    10  John         99.5         86.3415   13.1585
                    11  Joyce        50.5000     57.3660   -6.8660
                    12  Judy         90.0000    108.0    -17.9625
                    13  Louise       77.0000     76.6295    0.3705
                    14  Mary        112.0        117.2    -5.1544
                    15  Philip      150.0        138.2    11.7836
                    16  Robert      128.0        107.2    20.7957
                    17  Ronald      133.0        119.0    14.0471
                    18  Thomas       85.0000     79.6676    5.3324
                    19  William     112.0        117.2    -5.1544

Sum of Residuals             -6.6791E-13
Sum of Squared Residuals      2120.0997
Predicted Resid SS (Press)    3272.7219
```

Upon examining the data and residuals, you realize that observation 17 (Ronald) was mistakenly included in the analysis. Also, you would like to examine the effect of reweighting to 0.5 observations whose residuals have absolute values greater than or equal to 17.

```
reweight obs.=17;
reweight r. le -17 or r. ge 17 / weight=0.5;
print p;
run;
```

At this point, a message (on the log) appears that tells you which observations have been reweighted and what the new weights are. **Output 28.29** is produced:

Output 28.29   Model with Reweighted Observations

```
                                    Dep Var  Predict                               2
            Obs  NAME     Weight     WEIGHT    Value   Residual

              1  Alfred   1.0000    112.5     121.6     -9.1250
              2  Alice    1.0000     84.0000   79.9296   4.0704
              3  Barbara  1.0000     98.0      107.5     -9.5484
              4  Carol    1.0000    102.5      102.2      0.3337
              5  Henry    1.0000    102.5      104.4     -1.8632
              6  James    1.0000     83.0000   79.9762    3.0238
              7  Jane     1.0000     84.5000   87.8225    -3.3225
              8  Janet    1.0000    112.5      103.7      8.8111
              9  Jeffrey  1.0000     84.0000   98.8     -14.7606
             10  John     1.0000     99.5      85.3117   14.1883
             11  Joyce    1.0000     50.5000   58.6811    -8.1811
             12  Judy     0.5000     90.0000  106.9     -16.8740
             13  Louise   1.0000     77.0000   76.8377    0.1623
             14  Mary     1.0000    112.0      116.2     -4.2429
             15  Philip   1.0000    150.0      136.0     14.0312
             16  Robert   0.5000    128.0      103.5     24.4850
             17  Ronald        0    133.0      117.8     15.1879
             18  Thomas   1.0000     85.0000   78.1398    6.8602
             19  William  1.0000    112.0      116.2     -4.2429

Sum of Residuals          -1.38556E-12
Sum of Squared Residuals   1500.6119
Predicted Resid SS (Press)  2287.5762
NOTE: The statistics above use observation weights or frequencies.
```

The first REWEIGHT statement excluded observation 17 and the second reweighted observations 12 and 16 to 0.5. An important feature to note from this example is that the model was not refit until after the PRINT statement. REWEIGHT statements do not cause the model to be refit. This is so that multiple REWEIGHT statements can be applied to a subsequent model.

In this example, since the intent is to reweight observations with large residuals, first, the observation that was mistakenly included in the analysis should be deleted, then the model should be fit for those remaining observations, and then the observations with large residuals should be reweighted. To accomplish this, use the REFIT statement. These statements produce **Output 28.30**:

```
reweight obs.=17;
refit;
reweight r. le -17 or r. ge 17 / weight=.5;
print;
run;
```

Output 28.30   Observations Excluded from Analysis, Model Refitted and
Observations Reweighted

```
                                   Dep Var   Predict                              3
                 Obs  NAME   Weight WEIGHT    Value  Residual

                  1  Alfred  1.0000  112.5    121.0   -8.4716
                  2  Alice   1.0000  84.0000  79.5342  4.4658
                  3  Barbara 1.0000  98.0     107.1   -9.0746
                  4  Carol   1.0000  102.5    101.6    0.9319
                  5  Henry   1.0000  102.5    103.8   -1.2588
                  6  James   1.0000  83.0000  79.7204  3.2796
                  7  Jane    1.0000  84.5000  87.5443 -3.0443
                  8  Janet   1.0000  112.5    102.9    9.5533
                  9  Jeffrey 1.0000  84.0000  98.3   -14.3117
                 10  John    1.0000  99.5     85.0407 14.4593
                 11  Joyce   1.0000  50.5000  58.6253 -8.1253
                 12  Judy    1.0000  90.0000  106.3  -16.2625
                 13  Louise  1.0000  77.0000  76.5908  0.4092
                 14  Mary    1.0000  112.0    115.5   -3.4651
                 15  Philip  1.0000  150.0    135.0   15.0047
                 16  Robert  0.5000  128.0    103.2   24.8077
                 17  Ronald       0  133.0    117.0   15.9701
                 18  Thomas  1.0000  85.0000  78.0288  6.9712
                 19  William 1.0000  112.0    115.5   -3.4651

Sum of Residuals            -5.18696E-13
Sum of Squared Residuals     1637.8188
Predicted Resid SS (Press)   2473.8798
NOTE: The statistics above use observation weights or frequencies.
```

Notice that this results in a slightly different model than the previous set of
statements: only observation 16 is reweighted to 0.5.

Another important feature of REWEIGHT is the ability to nullify the effect of
a previous or all REWEIGHT statements. First, assume that you have several
REWEIGHT statements in effect and you want to restore the original weights of
all the observations. The following REWEIGHT statement accomplishes this and
produces **Output 28.31**:

```
REWEIGHT statements
possibly other statements
reweight allobs / reset;
print;
run;
```

Output 28.31   Restoring Weights of All Observations

```
                              Dep Var   Predict                               4
                 Obs  NAME    WEIGHT    Value  Residual

                  1  Alfred   112.5    124.9   -12.3686
                  2  Alice    84.0000  78.6273   5.3727
                  3  Barbara  98.0     110.3   -12.2812
                  4  Carol    102.5    102.6    -0.0670
                  5  Henry    102.5    105.1    -2.5849
                  6  James    83.0000  80.2266   2.7734
                  7  Jane     84.5000  89.2191  -4.7191
                  8  Janet    112.5    102.8     9.7337
                  9  Jeffrey  84.0000  100.2   -16.2095
                 10  John     99.5     86.3415  13.1585
                 11  Joyce    50.5000  57.3660  -6.8660
                 12  Judy     90.0000  108.0   -17.9625
                 13  Louise   77.0000  76.6295   0.3705
                 14  Mary     112.0    117.2    -5.1544
                 15  Philip   150.0    138.2    11.7836
```

(continued on next page)

```
(continued from previous page)
```

```
                              16  Robert      128.0    107.2   20.7957
                              17  Ronald      133.0    119.0   14.0471
                              18  Thomas    85.0000  79.6676    5.3324
                              19  William     112.0    117.2   -5.1544
Sum of Residuals              -6.6791E-13
Sum of Squared Residuals       2120.0997
Predicted Resid SS (Press)     3272.7219
```

The resulting model is identical to the original model specified at the beginning of this section. Note that the Weight column does not appear.

Now suppose you only want to undo the changes made by the most recent REWEIGHT statement. Use REWEIGHT UNDO for this. These statements produce **Output 28.32**:

```
reweight r. le -12 or r. ge 12 / weight=.75;
reweight r. le -17 or r. ge 17 / weight=.5;
reweight undo;
print;
run;
```

Output 28.32 Example of UNDO in REWEIGHT Statement

```
                                                Dep Var   Predict                      5
                    Obs  NAME     Weight        WEIGHT      Value   Residual

                     1   Alfred   0.7500        112.5       125.1  -12.6152
                     2   Alice    1.0000      84.0000     78.7691    5.2309
                     3   Barbara  0.7500         98.0       110.3  -12.3236
                     4   Carol    1.0000        102.5       102.9   -0.3836
                     5   Henry    1.0000        102.5       105.4   -2.8936
                     6   James    1.0000      83.0000     80.1133    2.8867
                     7   Jane     1.0000      84.5000     89.0776   -4.5776
                     8   Janet    1.0000        112.5       103.3    9.1678
                     9   Jeffrey  0.7500      84.0000       100.3  -16.2835
                    10   John     0.7500         99.5     86.2090   13.2910
                    11   Joyce    1.0000      50.5000     57.0745   -6.5745
                    12   Judy     0.7500      90.0000       108.3  -18.2622
                    13   Louise   1.0000      77.0000     76.5275    0.4725
                    14   Mary     1.0000        112.0       117.7   -5.6752
                    15   Philip   1.0000        150.0       138.9   11.0789
                    16   Robert   0.7500        128.0       107.0   20.9937
                    17   Ronald   0.7500        133.0       119.5   13.5319
                    18   Thomas   1.0000      85.0000     79.3061    5.6939
                    19   William  1.0000        112.0       117.7   -5.6752
Sum of Residuals              -8.49099E-13
Sum of Squared Residuals        1694.8711
Predicted Resid SS (Press)      2547.2275
NOTE: The statistics above use observation weights or frequencies.
```

The resulting model reflects changes made only by the first REWEIGHT statement since the third REWEIGHT statement negates the effect of the second REWEIGHT statement. Observations 1, 3, 9, 10, 12, 16, and 17 have their weights changed to 0.75.

Now suppose you want to reset the observations selected by the most recent REWEIGHT statement to their original weights. Use the REWEIGHT statement with the RESET option to do this. These statements produce **Output 28.33**:

```
reweight r. le -12 or r. ge 12 / weight=.75;
reweight r. le -17 or r. ge 17 / weight=.5;
reweight / reset;
print;
run;
```

Output 28.33   REWEIGHT Statement with RESET option

```
                                        Dep Var   Predict                            6
                 Obs  NAME      Weight   WEIGHT     Value    Residual

                   1  Alfred    0.7500   112.5     126.0    -13.5076
                   2  Alice     1.0000    84.0000   77.8727    6.1273
                   3  Barbara   0.7500    98.0      111.3   -13.2805
                   4  Carol     1.0000   102.5      102.5     0.0297
                   5  Henry     1.0000   102.5      105.1    -2.6278
                   6  James     1.0000    83.0000   80.2290    2.7710
                   7  Jane      1.0000    84.5000   89.7199   -5.2199
                   8  Janet     1.0000   112.5      102.0    10.4878
                   9  Jeffrey   0.7500    84.0000  100.7    -16.6507
                  10  John      0.7500    99.5       86.6828   12.8172
                  11  Joyce     1.0000    50.5000   56.7703   -6.2703
                  12  Judy      1.0000    90.0000  108.2    -18.1649
                  13  Louise    1.0000    77.0000   76.4327    0.5673
                  14  Mary      1.0000   112.0      117.2    -5.1975
                  15  Philip    1.0000   150.0      138.8    11.2419
                  16  Robert    1.0000   128.0      108.7    19.2984
                  17  Ronald    0.7500   133.0      119.1    13.9043
                  18  Thomas    1.0000    85.0000   80.3076    4.6924
                  19  William   1.0000   112.0      117.2    -5.1975

Sum of Residuals          -8.49099E-13
Sum of Squared Residuals   1879.0898
Predicted Resid SS (Press) 2959.5728
NOTE: The statistics above use observation weights or frequencies.
```

Note that observations that meet the condition of the second REWEIGHT statement (residuals with an absolute value greater than or equal to 17) now have weights reset to their original value of 1. Observations 1, 3, 9, 10, and 17 have weights of 0.75, but observations 12 and 16 (which met the condition of the second REWEIGHT statement) have their weights reset to 1.

Notice how the last three examples show three ways to change weights back to a previous value. In the first example, ALLOBS and the RESET option were used to change weights for all observations back to their original values. In the second example, the UNDO option was used to negate the effect of a previous REWEIGHT statement, thus changing weights for observations selected in the previous REWEIGHT statement to the weights specified in still another REWEIGHT statement. In the third example, the RESET option was used to change weights for observations selected in a previous REWEIGHT statement back to their original values.

Testing for Heteroscedasticity

The regression model is specified as $y_i = x_i\beta + \varepsilon_i$, where the ε_i's are identically and independently distributed: $E(\varepsilon) = 0$ and $E(\varepsilon'\varepsilon) = \sigma^2 I$. If the ε_i's are not independent or their variances are not constant, the parameter estimates are unbiased, but the estimate of the covariance matrix is inconsistent. In the case of heteroscedasticity, the ACOV option provides a consistent estimate of the covariance matrix. If the regression data are from a simple random sample, the ACOV option produces the covariance matrix. This matrix is

$$(\mathbf{X'X})^{-1}(\mathbf{X'}\mathrm{diag}(e_i^2)\mathbf{X})(\mathbf{X'X})^{-1}$$

where

$$e_i = y_i - \mathbf{x}_i\mathbf{b} \quad .$$

The SPEC option performs a test for heteroscedasticity. When the SPEC option has been specified, tests with both the usual covariance matrix and the heteroscedasticity consistent covariance matrix are performed. Tests performed with the consistent covariance matrix are asymptotic. For more information, see White (1980).

Both the ACOV and SPEC options can be specified in a MODEL or PRINT statement.

Multivariate Tests

The MTEST statement described above can test hypotheses involving several dependent variables in the form

$$(\mathbf{L}\boldsymbol{\beta} - \mathbf{cj})\mathbf{M} = 0$$

where $\mathbf{L}$ is a linear function on the regressor side, $\boldsymbol{\beta}$ is a matrix of parameters, $\mathbf{c}$ is a column vector of constants, $\mathbf{j}$ is a row vector of ones, and $\mathbf{M}$ is a linear function on the dependent side. The special case where the constants are zero is

$$\mathbf{L}\boldsymbol{\beta}\mathbf{M} = 0 \quad .$$

To test this hypothesis, REG constructs two matrices called $\mathbf{H}$ and $\mathbf{E}$ that correspond to the numerator and denominator of a univariate F test:

$$\mathbf{H} = \mathbf{M'}(\mathbf{LB} - \mathbf{cj})'(\mathbf{L}(\mathbf{X'X})^{-}\mathbf{L'})^{-1}(\mathbf{LB} - \mathbf{cj})\mathbf{M}$$

$$\mathbf{E} = \mathbf{M'}(\mathbf{Y'Y} - \mathbf{B'}(\mathbf{X'X})\mathbf{B})\mathbf{M} \quad .$$

These matrices are printed for each MTEST statement if the PRINT option is specified.

Four test statistics based on the eigenvalues of $\mathbf{E}^{-1}\mathbf{H}$ or $(\mathbf{E}+\mathbf{H})^{-1}\mathbf{H}$ are formed. These are Wilks' Lambda, Pillai's Trace, the Hotelling-Lawley Trace, and Roy's maximum root. These are discussed in Chapter 1, "Introduction to Regression Procedures."

The following statements perform a multivariate analysis of variance and produce **Output 28.34**:

```
* Manova Data from Morrison (1976, 190);
  data a;
     input sex $ drug $ a;
     do rep=1 to 4;
        input y1 y2 a;
        output;
        end;
     cards;
m a  5 6  5 4  9 9  7 6
m b  7 6  7 7  9 12  6 8
```

```
m c 21 15 14 11 17 12 12 10
f a  7 10  6  6  9  7  8 10
f b 10 13  8  7  7  6  6  9
f c 16 12 14  9 14  8 10  5
;
data b;
   set a;
   sexcode=(sex='m')-(sex='f');
   drug1=(drug='a')-(drug='c');
   drug2=(drug='b')-(drug='c');
   sexdrug1=sexcode*drug1;
   sexdrug2=sexcode*drug2;
proc reg;
   model y1 y2=sexcode drug1 drug2 sexdrug1 sexdrug2;
y1y2drug: mtest y1=y2, drug1,drug2;
drugshow: mtest drug1, drug2 / print canprint;
run;
```

Output 28.34   Multivariate Analysis of Variance: REG Procedure

```
Model: MODEL1                                                                              1
Dependent Variable: Y1
                                   Analysis of Variance

                                 Sum of        Mean
              Source      DF     Squares      Square      F Value      Prob>F

              Model        5   316.00000    63.20000       12.038      0.0001
              Error       18    94.50000     5.25000
              C Total     23   410.50000

                 Root MSE       2.29129     R-Square       0.7698
                 Dep Mean       9.75000     Adj R-Sq       0.7058
                 C.V.          23.50039

                                 Parameter Estimates

                          Parameter     Standard     T for H0:
              Variable  DF   Estimate       Error    Parameter=0    Prob > |T|

              INTERCEP   1   9.750000    0.46770717      20.846        0.0001
              SEXCODE    1   0.166667    0.46770717       0.356        0.7257
              DRUG1      1  -2.750000    0.66143783      -4.158        0.0006
              DRUG2      1  -2.250000    0.66143783      -3.402        0.0032
              SEXDRUG1   1  -0.666667    0.66143783      -1.008        0.3269
              SEXDRUG2   1  -0.416667    0.66143783      -0.630        0.5366
```

(continued on next page)

(continued from previous page)

Dependent Variable: Y2

Analysis of Variance

Source	DF	Sum of Squares	Mean Square	F Value	Prob>F
Model	5	69.33333	13.86667	2.189	0.1008
Error	18	114.00000	6.33333		
C Total	23	183.33333			

Root MSE	2.51661	R-Square	0.3782
Dep Mean	8.66667	Adj R-Sq	0.2055
C.V.	29.03782		

Parameter Estimates

Variable	DF	Parameter Estimate	Standard Error	T for H0: Parameter=0	Prob > |T|
INTERCEP	1	8.666667	0.51370117	16.871	0.0001
SEXCODE	1	0.166667	0.51370117	0.324	0.7493
DRUG1	1	-1.416667	0.72648316	-1.950	0.0669
DRUG2	1	-0.166667	0.72648316	-0.229	0.8211
SEXDRUG1	1	-1.166667	0.72648316	-1.606	0.1257
SEXDRUG2	1	-0.416667	0.72648316	-0.574	0.5734

Multivariate Test: Y1Y2DRUG   2

Multivariate Statistics and Exact F Statistics

S=1   M=0   N=8

Statistic	Value	F	Num DF	Den DF	Pr > F
Wilks' Lambda	0.28053917	23.0811	2	18	0.0001
Pillai's Trace	0.71946083	23.0811	2	18	0.0001
Hotelling-Lawley Trace	2.56456456	23.0811	2	18	0.0001
Roy's Greatest Root	2.56456456	23.0811	2	18	0.0001

Multivariate Test: DRUGSHOW   3

E, the Error Matrix

94.5	76.5
76.5	114

H, the Hypothesis Matrix

301	97.5
97.5	36.333333333

	Canonical Correlation	Adjusted Canonical Correlation	Approx Standard Error	Squared Canonical Correlation	Eigenvalue	Difference	Proportion	Cumulative
					Eigenvalues of INV(E)*H = CanRsq/(1-CanRsq)			
1	0.905903	0.899927	0.040101	0.820661	4.5760	4.5125	0.9863	0.9863
2	0.244371	.	0.210254	0.059717	0.0635	.	0.0137	1.0000

Test of H0: The canonical correlations in the current row and all that follow are zero

	Likelihood Ratio	Approx F	Num DF	Den DF	Pr > F
1	0.16862952	12.1991	4	34	0.0001
2	0.94028273	1.1432	1	18	0.2991

(continued on next page)

(continued from previous page)

```
                    Multivariate Statistics and F Approximations

                    S=2     M=-0.5     N=7.5

        Statistic                Value           F       Num DF    Den DF    Pr > F

        Wilks' Lambda           0.16862952    12.1991        4        34     0.0001
        Pillai's Trace          0.88037810     7.0769        4        36     0.0003
        Hotelling-Lawley Trace  4.63953666    18.5581        4        32     0.0001
        Roy's Greatest Root     4.57602675    41.1842        2        18     0.0001

               NOTE: F Statistic for Roy's Greatest Root is an upper bound.
                     NOTE: F Statistic for Wilks' Lambda is exact.
```

Autocorrelation in Time Series Data

When regression is done on time series data, the errors may not be independent. Often errors are autocorrelated; that is, each error is correlated with the error immediately before it. Autocorrelation is also a symptom of systematic lack of fit. The DW option provides the Durbin-Watson d statistic to test that the autocorrelation is zero:

$$d = \Sigma_{i=2}^{n} (e_i - e_{i-1})^2 / \Sigma e_i^2 \quad .$$

The value of d is close to 2 if the errors are uncorrelated. The distribution of d is reported by Durbin and Watson (1950, 1951). Tables of the distribution are found in most econometrics textbooks, such as Johnston (1972) and Pindyck and Rubinfeld (1976).

The sample autocorrelation estimate is shown after the Durbin-Watson statistic on the printout. The sample is computed as

$$r = \Sigma_{i=2}^{n} e_i \, e_{i-1} / \Sigma e_i^2 \quad .$$

This autocorrelation of the residuals may not be a very good estimate of the autocorrelation of the true errors, especially if there are few observations and the independent variables have certain patterns. If there are missing observations in the regression, these measures are computed as though the missing observations did not exist.

Positive autocorrelation of the errors generally tends to make the estimate of the error variance too small, so confidence intervals are too narrow and true null hypotheses are rejected with a higher probability than the stated significance level. Negative autocorrelation of the errors generally tends to make the estimate of the error variance too large, so confidence intervals are too wide and the power of significance tests is reduced. With either positive or negative autocorrelation, least-squares parameter estimates are usually not as efficient as generalized least-squares parameter estimates. For more details see Judge et al. (1985, Chapter 8) and the *SAS/ETS User's Guide, Version 5 Edition*.

The following SAS statements request the DW option for the US population data (see **Output 28.35**):

```
proc reg data=uspop;
   model pop=year yearsq / dw;
```

Output 28.35   Regression Using DW Option

```
Model: MODEL1                                                                    1
Dependent Variable: POP
                                 Analysis of Variance

                              Sum of          Mean
          Source      DF      Squares        Square      F Value     Prob>F

          Model        2   71799.01619   35899.50809    4641.719     0.0001
          Error       16     123.74557       7.73410
          C Total     18   71922.76175

                Root MSE      2.78102     R-Square     0.9983
                Dep Mean     69.76747     Adj R-Sq     0.9981
                C.V.          3.98613

                             Parameter Estimates

                         Parameter     Standard    T for H0:
          Variable   DF    Estimate       Error    Parameter=0    Prob > |T|

          INTERCEP    1       20450   843.47532634     24.245        0.0001
          YEAR        1   -22.780606     0.89784904    -25.372        0.0001
          YEARSQ      1     0.006346     0.00023877     26.576        0.0001

Durbin-Watson D              1.264
(For Number of Obs.)            19
1st Order Autocorrelation    0.299
```

Computational Methods

The REG procedure first composes a crossproducts matrix. The matrix can be calculated from input data, reformed from an input correlation matrix, or read in from an SSCP data set. For each model, the procedure selects the appropriate crossproducts from the main matrix. The normal equations formed from the crossproducts are solved using a sweep algorithm (Goodnight 1979). The method is accurate for data that are reasonably scaled and not too collinear.

The mechanism PROC REG uses to check for singularity involves the diagonal (pivot) elements of $X'X$ as it is being swept. If a pivot is less than SINGULAR*CSS, then a singularity is declared and the pivot is not swept (where CSS is the corrected sum of squares for the regressor, and SINGULAR is $1E-8$ or reset in the PROC statement).

The sweep algorithm is also used in many places in model-selection methods. The RSQUARE method uses the leaps and bounds algorithm by Furnival and Wilson (1974).

Computer Resources in Regression Analysis

The REG procedure is efficient for ordinary regression; however, requests for optional features can greatly increase the amount of time required.

The major computational expense in the regression analysis is the collection of the crossproducts matrix. For p variables and n observations, the time required is proportional to np^2. For each model run, REG needs time roughly proportional to k^3, where k is the number of regressors in the model. Add an additional nk^2 for one of the R, CLM, or CLI options and another nk^2 for the INFLUENCE option.

Most of the memory REG needs to solve large problems is used for crossproducts matrices. PROC REG requires $4p^2$ bytes for the main crossproducts matrix plus $4k^2$ bytes for the largest model. If several output data sets are requested, memory is also needed for buffers.

See **Input Data Set** earlier in this chapter for information on how to use TYPE=SSCP data sets to reduce computing time.

Printed Output

Many of the more specialized printouts are described in detail in the sections above. Most of the formulas for the statistics are in Chapter 1, "Introduction to Regression Procedures."

The analysis-of-variance table is printed and includes

1. the Source of the variation, Model for the fitted regression, Error for the residual error, and C Total for the total variation after correcting for the mean. The Uncorrected Total Variation is printed when the NOINT option is used.
2. the degrees of freedom (DF) associated with the source.
3. the Sum of Squares for the term.
4. the Mean Square, the sum of squares divided by the degrees of freedom.
5. the F Value for testing the hypothesis that all parameters are zero except for the intercept. This is formed by dividing the mean square for Model by the mean square for Error.
6. the Prob>F, the probability of getting a greater F statistic than that observed if the hypothesis is true. This is the significance probability.

Other statistics printed include the following:

7. Root MSE is an estimate of the standard deviation of the error term. It is calculated as the square root of the mean square error.
8. Dep Mean is the sample mean of the dependent variable.
9. C.V. is the coefficient of variation, computed as 100 times Root MSE divided by Dep Mean. This expresses the variation in unitless values.
10. R-Square is a measure between 0 and 1 that indicates the portion of the (corrected) total variation that is attributed to the fit rather than left to residual error. It is calculated as SS(Model) divided by SS(Total). It is also called the *coefficient of determination*. It is the square of the multiple correlation; in other words, the square of the correlation between the dependent variable and the predicted values.
11. Adj R-Sq, the adjusted R^2, is a version of R^2 that has been adjusted for degrees of freedom. It is calculated as

$$\bar{R}^2 = 1 - [((n - i)(1 - R^2)) / (n - p)]$$

where i is equal to 1 if there is an intercept, 0 otherwise; n is the number of observations used to fit the model; and p is the number of parameters in the model.

The parameter estimates and associated statistics are then printed, and they include the following:

12. the Variable used as the regressor, including the name INTERCEP to represent the estimate of the intercept parameter.
13. the degrees of freedom (DF) for the variable. There is one degree of freedom unless the model is not full rank.
14. the Parameter Estimate.
15. the Standard Error, the estimate of the standard deviation of the parameter estimate.
16. T for H0: Parameter=0, the t test that the parameter is zero. This is computed as the Parameter Estimate divided by the Standard Error.

17. the Prob > |T|, the probability that a *t* statistic would obtain a greater absolute value than that observed given that the true parameter is zero. This is the two-tailed significance probability.

If model-selection methods other than NONE, RSQUARE, ADJRSQ, or CP are used, the analysis-of-variance table and the parameter estimates with associated statistics are printed at each step. Also printed are

18. C(p), which is Mallows' C_p statistic
19. Bounds on the condition number of the correlation matrix for the variables in the model (Berk 1977).

After statistics for the final model have been printed, the following is printed when the method chosen is FORWARD, BACKWARD, or STEPWISE:

20. a Summary table listing Step number, Variable Entered or Removed, Partial and Model R**2, and C(p) and F statistics.

The RSQUARE method prints its results beginning with the model containing the fewest independent variables and producing the largest R^2. Results for other models with the same number of variables are then printed in order of decreasing R^2, and so on, for models with larger numbers of variables. The ADJRSQ and CP methods group models of all sizes together and print results beginning with the model having the optimal value of adjusted R^2 and C_p, respectively.

For each model considered, the RSQUARE, ADJRSQ, and CP methods print the following:

21. Number in Model or IN, the number of independent variables used in each model
22. R-Square or RSQ, the squared multiple correlation coefficient

If the B option is specified, RSQUARE, ADJRSQ, and CP print the following:

23. Parameter Estimates, the estimated regression coefficients (not shown).

If the B option is not specified, RSQUARE, ADJRSQ, and CP print the following:

24. Variables in Model, the names of the independent variables included in the model.

EXAMPLES

Example 1: Population Growth Trends

In the following example, the population of the United States from 1790 to 1970 is fit to linear and quadratic functions of time. Note that the quadratic term, YEARSQ, is created in the DATA step; this is done since polynomial effects such as YEAR*YEAR cannot be used in PROC REG. The statements below request options for predicted and residual values, add a variable to the model, and produce scatter plots. (Influence diagnostics and autocorrelation information for the full model are shown in **Output 28.26** and **Output 28.35** earlier in this chapter.) The statements shown below generate **Output 28.36** and **Output 28.37**:

```
data uspop;
   input pop @@;
   retain year 1780;
   year=year+10;
   yearsq=year*year;
   pop=pop/1000;
```

```
        cards;
3929 5308 7239 9638 12866 17069 23191 31443 39818 50155
62947 75994 91972 105710 122775 131669 151325 179323 203211
. . .
;
proc reg data=uspop;
    var yearsq;
    model pop=year / r cli clm;
    plot r.*p.;
    add yearsq;
    print;
    plot;
    plot pop*year='a' predicted.*year='p' u95.*year='u'
        195.*year='l' / overlay;
    run;
```

Output 28.36   Population Growth Trends: PROC REG

```
                                            SAS                                                    1

Model: MODEL1
Dependent Variable: POP

                                    Analysis of Variance

          ❶                ❷         ❸  Sum of      ❹  Mean       ❺            ❻
          Source           DF        Squares         Square      F Value      Prob>F

          Model            1    66336.46923    66336.46923     201.873      0.0001
          Error           17     5586.29253      328.60544
          C Total         18    71922.76175

                    ❼ Root MSE        18.12748  ❿ R-square      0.9223
                  ❽ Dep Mean          69.76747    Adj R-sq      0.9178
                  ❾ C.V.              25.98271  ⓫

                                    Parameter Estimates

          ⓬        ⓭      ⓮ Parameter   ⓯ Standard   ⓰ T for H0:           ⓱
          Variable  DF       Estimate       Error     Parameter=0     Prob > |T|

          INTERCEP  1    -1958.366302   142.80454644     -13.714        0.0001
          YEAR      1        1.078795     0.07592765      14.208        0.0001
```

```
                                            SAS                                                    2

          Dep Var   Predict   Std Err   Lower95%   Upper95%   Lower95%   Upper95%            Std Err   Student
     Obs    POP       Value    Predict     Mean       Mean     Predict    Predict  Residual  Residual  Residual

      1    3.9290   -27.3240    7.999    -44.2014   -10.4467   -69.1278    14.4797   31.2530   16.267    1.921
      2    5.3080   -16.5361    7.361    -32.0673    -1.0049   -57.8148    24.7426   21.8441   16.565    1.319
      3    7.2390    -5.7481    6.749    -19.9864     8.4901   -46.5579    35.0616   12.9871   16.824    0.772
      4    9.6380     5.0398    6.168     -7.9743    18.0539   -35.3592    45.4388    4.5982   17.046    0.270
      5   12.8660    15.8277    5.631      3.9476    27.7079   -24.2204    55.8758   -2.9617   17.231   -0.172
      6   17.0690    26.6157    5.150     15.7509    37.4805   -13.1430    66.3744   -9.5467   17.381   -0.549
      7   23.1910    37.4036    4.742     27.3996    47.4076    -2.1285    76.9358  -14.2126   17.496   -0.812
      8   31.4430    48.1916    4.427     38.8508    57.5323     8.8220    87.5611  -16.7486   17.579   -0.953
      9   39.8180    58.9795    4.227     50.0604    67.8987    19.7079     98.3   -19.1615   17.628   -1.087
     10   50.1550    69.7675    4.159     60.9934    78.5416    30.5285    109.0   -19.6125   17.644   -1.112
     11   62.9470    80.5554    4.227     71.6363    89.4746    41.2838    119.8   -17.6084   17.628   -0.999
     12   75.9940    91.3434    4.427     82.0026    100.7     51.9738    130.7   -15.3494   17.579   -0.873
     13   91.9720    102.1      4.742     92.1273    112.1     62.5992    141.7   -10.1593   17.496   -0.581
     14   105.7      112.9      5.150    102.1       123.8     73.1606    152.7    -7.2093   17.381   -0.415
     15   122.8      123.7      5.631    111.8       135.6     83.6591    163.8    -0.9322   17.231   -0.054
```

(continued on next page)

(continued from previous page)

16	131.7	134.5	6.168	121.5	147.5	94.0962	174.9	-2.8261	17.046	-0.166
17	151.3	145.3	6.749	131.0	159.5	104.5	186.1	6.0419	16.824	0.359
18	179.3	156.1	7.361	140.5	171.6	114.8	197.3	23.2520	16.565	1.404
19	203.2	166.9	7.999	150.0	183.7	125.1	208.7	36.3520	16.267	2.235
20	.	177.6	8.657	159.4	195.9	135.3	220.0	.	.	.
21	.	188.4	9.330	168.8	208.1	145.4	231.4	.	.	.
22	.	199.2	10.016	178.1	220.4	155.5	242.9	.	.	.

Obs	-2-1-0 1 2	Cook's D
1	| |*** |	0.446
2	| |** |	0.172
3	| |* |	0.048
4	| | |	0.005
5	| | |	0.002
6	| *| |	0.013
7	| *| |	0.024
8	| *| |	0.029
9	| **| |	0.034
10	| **| |	0.034
11	| *| |	0.029
12	| *| |	0.024
13	| *| |	0.012
14	| | |	0.008
15	| | |	0.000
16	| | |	0.002
17	| | |	0.010
18	| |** |	0.195
19	| |**** |	0.604
20		.
21		.
22		.

Sum of Residuals	1.861622E-12
Sum of Squared Residuals	5586.2925
Predicted Resid SS (Press)	7619.9035

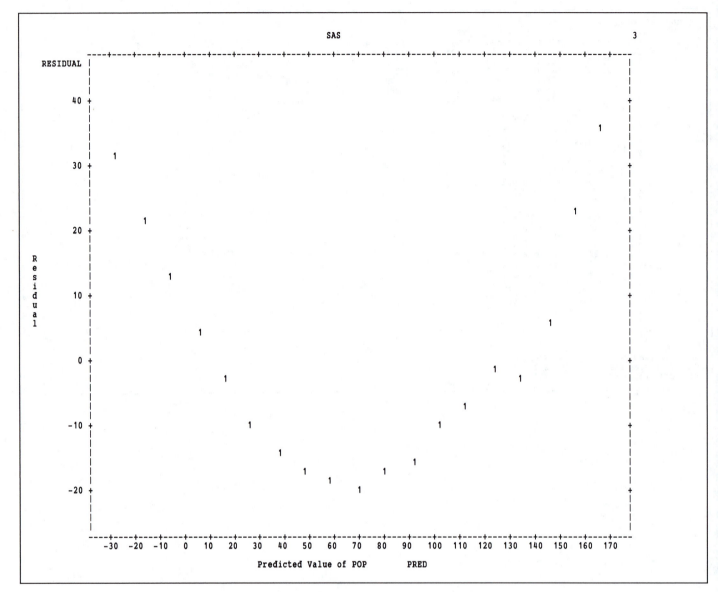

(continued on next page)

(continued from previous page)

Parameter Estimates

Variable	DF	Parameter Estimate	Standard Error	T for H0: Parameter=0	Prob > |T|
INTERCEP	1	20450	843.47532634	24.245	0.0001
YEAR	1	-22.780606	0.89784904	-25.372	0.0001
YEARSQ	1	0.006346	0.00023877	26.576	0.0001

SAS   5

Obs	Dep Var POP	Predict Value	Std Err Predict	Lower95% Mean	Upper95% Mean	Lower95% Predict	Upper95% Predict	Residual	Std Err Residual	Student Residual
1	3.9290	5.0384	1.729	1.3734	8.7035	-1.9034	11.9803	-1.1094	2.178	-0.509
2	5.3080	5.0389	1.391	2.0904	7.9874	-1.5528	11.6306	0.2691	2.408	0.112
3	7.2390	6.3085	1.130	3.9122	8.7047	-0.0554	12.6723	0.9305	2.541	0.366
4	9.6380	8.8472	0.957	6.8182	10.8761	2.6123	15.0820	0.7908	2.611	0.303
5	12.8660	12.6550	0.872	10.8062	14.5037	6.4764	18.8335	0.2110	2.641	0.080
6	17.0690	17.7319	0.858	15.9133	19.5504	11.5623	23.9015	-0.6629	2.645	-0.251
7	23.1910	24.0779	0.884	22.2050	25.9509	17.8921	30.2637	-0.8869	2.637	-0.336
8	31.4430	31.6931	0.920	29.7424	33.6437	25.4832	37.9029	-0.2501	2.624	-0.095
9	39.8180	40.5773	0.949	38.5661	42.5885	34.3482	46.8064	-0.7593	2.614	-0.290
10	50.1550	50.7307	0.959	48.6972	52.7642	44.4944	56.9670	-0.5757	2.610	-0.221
11	62.9470	62.1532	0.949	60.1420	64.1644	55.9241	68.3823	0.7938	2.614	0.304
12	75.9940	74.8448	0.920	72.8942	76.7955	68.6350	81.0547	1.1492	2.624	0.438
13	91.9720	88.8056	0.884	86.9326	90.6785	82.6197	95.0	3.1664	2.637	1.201
14	105.7	104.0	0.858	102.2	105.9	97.9	110.2	1.6746	2.645	0.633
15	122.8	120.5	0.872	118.7	122.4	114.4	126.7	2.2406	2.641	0.848
16	131.7	138.3	0.957	136.3	140.3	132.1	144.5	-6.6335	2.611	-2.540
17	151.3	157.3	1.130	154.9	159.7	151.0	163.7	-6.0147	2.541	-2.367
18	179.3	177.6	1.391	174.7	180.6	171.1	184.2	1.6770	2.408	0.696
19	203.2	199.2	1.729	195.6	202.9	192.3	206.2	3.9895	2.178	1.831
20	.	222.1	2.135	217.5	226.6	214.6	229.5	.	.	.
21	.	246.2	2.602	240.7	251.7	238.1	254.3	.	.	.
22	.	271.6	3.126	264.9	278.2	262.7	280.4	.	.	.

Obs	-2-1-0 1 2	Cook's D
1	| *| |	0.054
2	| | |	0.001
3	| | |	0.009
4	| | |	0.004
5	| | |	0.000
6	| | |	0.002
7	| | |	0.004
8	| | |	0.000
9	| | |	0.004
10	| | |	0.002
11	| | |	0.004
12	| | |	0.008
13	| |** |	0.054
14	| |* |	0.014
15	| |* |	0.026
16	|*****| |	0.289
17	|****| |	0.370
18	| |* |	0.054
19	| |***|	0.704
20		.
21		.
22		.

Sum of Residuals	1.098641E-10
Sum of Squared Residuals	123.7456
Predicted Resid SS (Press)	188.5492

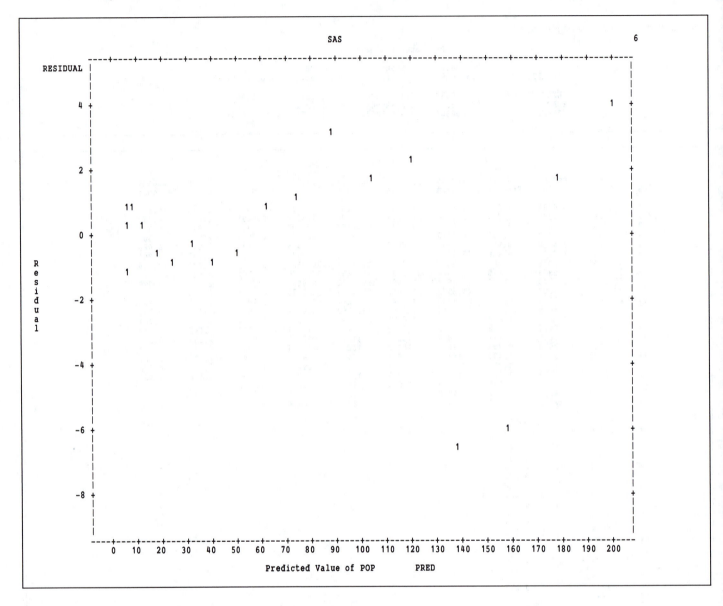

The fitted equation for the first model is

POP = −1958.37 + 1.079*YEAR

The first plot of residuals by predicted values indicates an inadequate model; perhaps additional terms (such as the quadratic) are needed, or perhaps the data need to be transformed before analysis. The second model adds the quadratic term. The fitted equation is

POP = 20450 − 22.78*YEAR + 0.0063*YEARSQ

The plot of residuals by predicted values is improved and no longer indicates the need for additional terms in the model. To complete an analysis of these data, you would want to examine influence statistics (and perhaps then refit the model), and, since the data are essentially time series data, examine the Durbin-Watson statistic. You might also want to examine other residuals plots, for example, the residuals plotted against the regressors.

Output 28.37   Overlaid Scatter Plot of Population Data: PROC REG

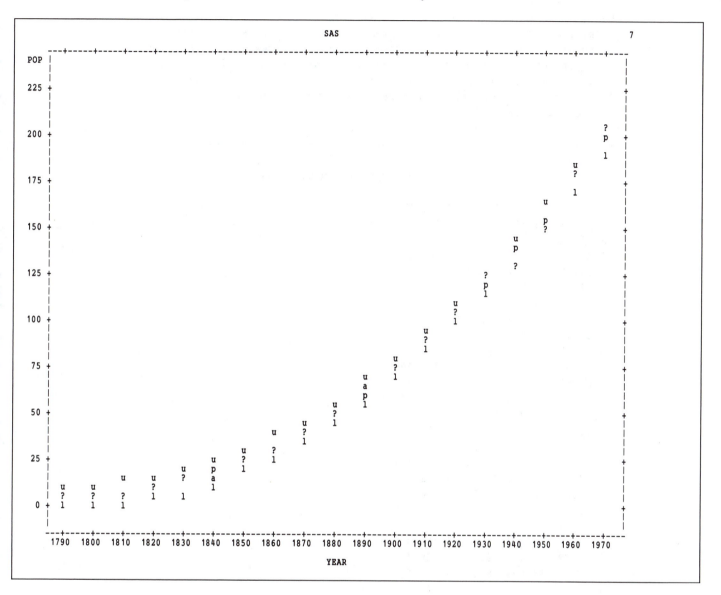

This plot shows the actual data as a's, the predicted values as p's, and the upper and lower 95% confidence limits for an individual value (sometimes called a *prediction interval*) as u's and l's, respectively.

Example 2: Aerobic Fitness Prediction

Aerobic fitness (measured by the ability to consume oxygen) is fit to some simple exercise tests. The goal is to develop an equation to predict fitness based on the exercise tests rather than on expensive and cumbersome oxygen consumption measurements. Three model-selection methods are used: forward selection, backward selection, and MAXR selection. The statements below produce **Output 28.38** through **Output 28.40**. (Collinearity diagnostics for the full model are shown in **Output 28.25** earlier in this chapter.)

```
*------------------------Data on Physical Fitness---------------------*
| These measurements were made on men involved in a physical fitness   |
| course at N.C.State Univ. The variables are age (years), weight (kg),|
| oxygen intake rate (ml per kg body weight per minute), time to run   |
| 1.5 miles (minutes), heart rate while resting, heart rate while      |
| running (same time oxygen rate measured), and maximum heart rate     |
| recorded while running.                                              |
| ***Certain values of maxpulse were changed for this analysis.        |
*--------------------------------------------------------------------*;
data fitness;
    input age weight oxy runtime rstpulse runpulse maxpulse;
    cards;
44 89.47   44.609 11.37 62 178 182
40 75.07   45.313 10.07 62 185 185
44 85.84   54.297  8.65 45 156 168
42 68.15   59.571  8.17 40 166 172
38 89.02   49.874  9.22 55 178 180
47 77.45   44.811 11.63 58 176 176
40 75.98   45.681 11.95 70 176 180
43 81.19   49.091 10.85 64 162 170
44 81.42   39.442 13.08 63 174 176
38 81.87   60.055  8.63 48 170 186
44 73.03   50.541 10.13 45 168 168
45 87.66   37.388 14.03 56 186 192
45 66.45   44.754 11.12 51 176 176
47 79.15   47.273 10.60 47 162 164
54 83.12   51.855 10.33 50 166 170
49 81.42   49.156  8.95 44 180 185
51 69.63   40.836 10.95 57 168 172
51 77.91   46.672 10.00 48 162 168
48 91.63   46.774 10.25 48 162 164
49 73.37   50.388 10.08 67 168 168
57 73.37   39.407 12.63 58 174 176
54 79.38   46.080 11.17 62 156 165
52 76.32   45.441  9.63 48 164 166
50 70.87   54.625  8.92 48 146 155
51 67.25   45.118 11.08 48 172 172
54 91.63   39.203 12.88 44 168 172
51 73.71   45.790 10.47 59 186 188
57 59.08   50.545  9.93 49 148 155
49 76.32   48.673  9.40 56 186 188
48 61.24   47.920 11.50 52 170 176
52 82.78   47.467 10.50 53 170 172
;
proc reg;
    model oxy=age weight runtime runpulse rstpulse maxpulse
          / selection=forward;
    model oxy=age weight runtime runpulse rstpulse maxpulse
          / selection=backward;
    model oxy=age weight runtime runpulse rstpulse maxpulse
          / selection=maxr;
    run;
```

Output 28.38 Forward Selection Method: PROC REG

```
                    Forward Selection Procedure for Dependent Variable OXY                    1
Step 1    Variable RUNTIME Entered    R-square = 0.74338010⑱ C(p) = 13.69884048

                         DF      Sum of Squares      Mean Square        F    Prob>F

           Regression     1        632.90009985      632.90009985    84.01   0.0001
           Error         29        218.48144499        7.53384293
           Total         30        851.38154484

                     Parameter        Standard         Type II
           Variable    Estimate          Error      Sum of Squares       F    Prob>F

           INTERCEP   82.42177268     3.85530378    3443.36654076    457.05   0.0001
⑲          RUNTIME    -3.31055536     0.36119485     632.90009985     84.01   0.0001

Bounds on condition number:        1,         1
----------------------------------------------------------------------------------------------

Step 2    Variable AGE Entered       R-square = 0.76424693   C(p) = 12.38944895

                         DF      Sum of Squares      Mean Square        F    Prob>F

           Regression     2        650.66573237      325.33286618    45.38   0.0001
           Error         28        200.71581247        7.16842187
           Total         30        851.38154484

                     Parameter        Standard         Type II
           Variable    Estimate          Error      Sum of Squares       F    Prob>F

           INTERCEP   88.46228749     5.37263885    1943.41070877    271.11   0.0001
           AGE        -0.15036567     0.09551468      17.76563252      2.48   0.1267
           RUNTIME    -3.20395056     0.35877488     571.67750579     79.75   0.0001

Bounds on condition number:    1.036941,    4.147763
----------------------------------------------------------------------------------------------

Step 3    Variable RUNPULSE Entered  R-square = 0.81109446   C(p) = 6.95962673

                         DF      Sum of Squares      Mean Square        F    Prob>F

           Regression     3        690.55085627      230.18361876    38.64   0.0001
           Error         27        160.83068857        5.95669217
           Total         30        851.38154484

                     Parameter        Standard         Type II
           Variable    Estimate          Error      Sum of Squares       F    Prob>F

           INTERCEP  111.71806443    10.23508836     709.69013814    119.14   0.0001
           AGE        -0.25639826     0.09622892      42.28867438      7.10   0.0129
           RUNTIME    -2.82537867     0.35828041     370.43528607     62.19   0.0001
           RUNPULSE   -0.13090870     0.05059011      39.88512390      6.70   0.0154

Bounds on condition number:    1.354763,    11.59745
----------------------------------------------------------------------------------------------
```

```
                                                                                             2
Step 4    Variable MAXPULSE Entered  R-square = 0.83681815   C(p) = 4.87995808

                         DF      Sum of Squares      Mean Square        F    Prob>F

           Regression     4        712.45152692      178.11288173    33.33   0.0001
           Error         26        138.93001792        5.34346223
           Total         30        851.38154484

                     Parameter        Standard         Type II
           Variable    Estimate          Error      Sum of Squares       F    Prob>F

           INTERCEP   98.14788797    11.78569002     370.57373243    69.35    0.0001
           AGE        -0.19773470     0.09563662      22.84231496     4.27    0.0488
           RUNTIME    -2.76757879     0.34053642     352.93569605    66.05    0.0001
           RUNPULSE   -0.34810795     0.11749917      46.90088674     8.78    0.0064
           MAXPULSE    0.27051297     0.13361978      21.90067065     4.10    0.0533

Bounds on condition number:    8.4182,    76.85135
----------------------------------------------------------------------------------------------
```

(continued on next page)

(continued from previous page)

Step 5   Variable WEIGHT Entered   R-square = 0.84800181   C(p) = 5.10627546

	DF	Sum of Squares	Mean Square	F	Prob>F
Regression	5	721.97309402	144.39461880	27.90	0.0001
Error	25	129.40845082	5.17633803		
Total	30	851.38154484			

Variable	Parameter Estimate	Standard Error	Type II Sum of Squares	F	Prob>F
INTERCEP	102.20427520	11.97928972	376.78934930	72.79	0.0001
AGE	-0.21962138	0.09550245	27.37429100	5.29	0.0301
WEIGHT	-0.07230234	0.05331009	9.52156710	1.84	0.1871
RUNTIME	-2.68252297	0.34098544	320.35967836	61.89	0.0001
RUNPULSE	-0.37340085	0.11714109	52.59623720	10.16	0.0038
MAXPULSE	0.30490783	0.13393642	26.82640270	5.18	0.0316

Bounds on condition number: 8.731225,   104.8254

No other variable met the 0.5000 significance level for entry into the model.

---

⑳   Summary of Forward Selection Procedure for Dependent Variable OXY   3

Step	Variable Entered	Number In	Partial R**2	Model R**2	C(p)	F	Prob>F
1	RUNTIME	1	0.7434	0.7434	13.6988	84.0076	0.0001
2	AGE	2	0.0209	0.7642	12.3894	2.4783	0.1267
3	RUNPULSE	3	0.0468	0.8111	6.9596	6.6959	0.0154
4	MAXPULSE	4	0.0257	0.8368	4.8800	4.0986	0.0533
5	WEIGHT	5	0.0112	0.8480	5.1063	1.8394	0.1871

The FORWARD model-selection method begins with no variables in the model, and adds RUNTIME, then AGE, then RUNPULSE, then MAXPULSE, and finally, WEIGHT. The final variable available to add to the model, RSTPLSE, is not added since it does not meet the 95% significance-level criterion for entry into the model.

Output 28.39   Backward Selection Method: PROC REG

Backward Elimination Procedure for Dependent Variable OXY   4

Step 0   All Variables Entered   R-square = 0.84867192   C(p) = 7.00000000

	DF	Sum of Squares	Mean Square	F	Prob>F
Regression	6	722.54360701	120.42393450	22.43	0.0001
Error	24	128.83793783	5.36824741		
Total	30	851.38154484			

Variable	Parameter Estimate	Standard Error	Type II Sum of Squares	F	Prob>F
INTERCEP	102.93447948	12.40325810	369.72831073	68.87	0.0001
AGE	-0.22697380	0.09983747	27.74577148	5.17	0.0322
WEIGHT	-0.07417741	0.05459316	9.91058836	1.85	0.1869
RUNTIME	-2.62865282	0.38456220	250.82210090	46.72	0.0001
RUNPULSE	-0.36962776	0.11985294	51.05805832	9.51	0.0051
RSTPULSE	-0.02153364	0.06605428	0.57051299	0.11	0.7473
MAXPULSE	0.30321713	0.13649519	26.49142405	4.93	0.0360

Bounds on condition number: 8.743848,   137.1345

(continued on next page)

(continued from previous page)

Step 1   Variable RSTPULSE Removed   R-square = 0.84800181   C(p) = 5.10627546

	DF	Sum of Squares	Mean Square	F	Prob>F
Regression	5	721.97309402	144.39461880	27.90	0.0001
Error	25	129.40845082	5.17633803		
Total	30	851.38154484			

Variable	Parameter Estimate	Standard Error	Type II Sum of Squares	F	Prob>F
INTERCEP	102.20427520	11.97928972	376.78934930	72.79	0.0001
AGE	-0.21962138	0.09550245	27.37429100	5.29	0.0301
WEIGHT	-0.07230234	0.05331009	9.52156710	1.84	0.1871
RUNTIME	-2.68252297	0.34098544	320.35967836	61.89	0.0001
RUNPULSE	-0.37340085	0.11714109	52.59623720	10.16	0.0038
MAXPULSE	0.30490783	0.13393642	26.82640270	5.18	0.0316

Bounds on condition number: 8.731225,   104.8254

Step 2   Variable WEIGHT Removed   R-square = 0.83681815   C(p) = 4.87995808

	DF	Sum of Squares	Mean Square	F	Prob>F
Regression	4	712.45152692	178.11288173	33.33	0.0001
Error	26	138.93001792	5.34346223		
Total	30	851.38154484			

Variable	Parameter Estimate	Standard Error	Type II Sum of Squares	F	Prob>F
INTERCEP	98.14788797	11.78569002	370.57373243	69.35	0.0001
AGE	-0.19773470	0.09563662	22.84231496	4.27	0.0488

5

Variable	Parameter Estimate	Standard Error	Type II Sum of Squares	F	Prob>F
RUNTIME	-2.76757879	0.34053642	352.93569605	66.05	0.0001
RUNPULSE	-0.34810795	0.11749917	46.90088674	8.78	0.0064
MAXPULSE	0.27051297	0.13361978	21.90067065	4.10	0.0533

Bounds on condition number: 8.4182,   76.85135

All variables in the model are significant at the 0.1000 level.

Summary of Backward Elimination Procedure for Dependent Variable OXY   6

Step	Variable Removed	Number In	Partial $R^{**}2$	Model $R^{**}2$	C(p)	F	Prob>F
1	RSTPULSE	5	0.0007	0.8480	5.1063	0.1063	0.7473
2	WEIGHT	4	0.0112	0.8368	4.8800	1.8394	0.1871

The BACKWARD model-selection method begins with the full model. RSTPLSE is the first variable deleted, followed by WEIGHT. No other variables are deleted from the model since the variables remaining (AGE, RUNTIME, RUNPULSE, and MAXPULSE) are all significant at the 90% significance level.

Output 28.40   Maximum R-Square Improvement Selection Method:
PROC REG

```
                    Maximum R-square Improvement for Dependent Variable OXY                    7

Step 1   Variable RUNTIME Entered   R-square = 0.74338010   C(p) = 13.69884048

                          DF      Sum of Squares      Mean Square       F    Prob>F

          Regression       1       632.90009985      632.90009985   84.01    0.0001
          Error           29       218.48144499        7.53384293
          Total           30       851.38154484

                       Parameter        Standard        Type II
          Variable      Estimate           Error    Sum of Squares       F    Prob>F

          INTERCEP    82.42177268      3.85530378    3443.36654076   457.05    0.0001
          RUNTIME     -3.31055536      0.36119485     632.90009985    84.01    0.0001

Bounds on condition number:        1,          1
-------------------------------------------------------------------------------------------

The above model is the best  1-variable model found.

Step 2   Variable AGE Entered       R-square = 0.76424693   C(p) = 12.38944895

                          DF      Sum of Squares      Mean Square       F    Prob>F

          Regression       2       650.66573237      325.33286618   45.38    0.0001
          Error           28       200.71581247        7.16842187
          Total           30       851.38154484

                       Parameter        Standard        Type II
          Variable      Estimate           Error    Sum of Squares       F    Prob>F

          INTERCEP    88.46228749      5.37263885    1943.41070877   271.11    0.0001
          AGE         -0.15036567      0.09551468      17.76563252     2.48    0.1267
          RUNTIME     -3.20395056      0.35877488     571.67750579    79.75    0.0001

Bounds on condition number:   1.036941,     4.147763
-------------------------------------------------------------------------------------------

The above model is the best  2-variable model found.

Step 3   Variable RUNPULSE Entered  R-square = 0.81109446   C(p) = 6.95962673

                          DF      Sum of Squares      Mean Square       F    Prob>F

          Regression       3       690.55085627      230.18361876   38.64    0.0001
          Error           27       160.83068857        5.95669217
          Total           30       851.38154484

                       Parameter        Standard        Type II
          Variable      Estimate           Error    Sum of Squares       F    Prob>F

          INTERCEP   111.71806443     10.23508836     709.69013814   119.14    0.0001
          AGE         -0.25639826      0.09622892      42.28867438     7.10    0.0129
          RUNTIME     -2.82537867      0.35828041     370.43528607    62.19    0.0001
          RUNPULSE    -0.13090870      0.05059011      39.88512390     6.70    0.0154

Bounds on condition number:   1.354763,     11.59745
```

```
------------------------------------------------------------------------------------------------------ 8
The above model is the best  3-variable model found.

Step 4   Variable MAXPULSE Entered  R-square = 0.83681815  C(p) = 4.87995808

                        DF        Sum of Squares      Mean Square        F     Prob>F

        Regression       4         712.45152692      178.11288173     33.33    0.0001
        Error           26         138.93001792        5.34346223
        Total           30         851.38154484

                      Parameter        Standard        Type II
        Variable       Estimate          Error       Sum of Squares      F     Prob>F

        INTERCEP     98.14788797       11.78569002    370.57373243     69.35    0.0001
        AGE          -0.19773470        0.09563662     22.84231496      4.27    0.0488
        RUNTIME      -2.76757879        0.34053642    352.93569605     66.05    0.0001
        RUNPULSE     -0.34810795        0.11749917     46.90088674      8.78    0.0064
        MAXPULSE      0.27051297        0.13361978     21.90067065      4.10    0.0533

Bounds on condition number:     8.4182,     76.85135
------------------------------------------------------------------------------------------------------
The above model is the best  4-variable model found.

Step 5   Variable WEIGHT Entered    R-square = 0.84800181  C(p) = 5.10627546

                        DF        Sum of Squares      Mean Square        F     Prob>F

        Regression       5         721.97309402      144.39461880     27.90    0.0001
        Error           25         129.40845082        5.17633803
        Total           30         851.38154484

                      Parameter        Standard        Type II
        Variable       Estimate          Error       Sum of Squares      F     Prob>F

        INTERCEP    102.20427520       11.97928972    376.78934930     72.79    0.0001
        AGE          -0.21962138        0.09550245     27.37429100      5.29    0.0301
        WEIGHT       -0.07230234        0.05331009      9.52156710      1.84    0.1871
        RUNTIME      -2.68252297        0.34098544    320.35967836     61.89    0.0001
        RUNPULSE     -0.37340085        0.11714109     52.59623720     10.16    0.0038
        MAXPULSE      0.30490783        0.13393642     26.82640270      5.18    0.0316

Bounds on condition number:     8.731225,    104.8254
------------------------------------------------------------------------------------------------------
The above model is the best  5-variable model found.

Step 6   Variable RSTPULSE Entered  R-square = 0.84867192   C(p) = 7.00000000

                        DF        Sum of Squares      Mean Square        F     Prob>F

        Regression       6         722.54360701      120.42393450     22.43    0.0001
        Error           24         128.83793783        5.36824741
        Total           30         851.38154484
```

```
                      Parameter        Standard        Type II                           9
        Variable       Estimate          Error       Sum of Squares      F     Prob>F

        INTERCEP    102.93447948       12.40325810    369.72831073     68.87    0.0001
        AGE          -0.22697380        0.09983747     27.74577148      5.17    0.0322
        WEIGHT       -0.07417741        0.05459316      9.91058836      1.85    0.1869
        RUNTIME      -2.62865282        0.38456220    250.82210090     46.72    0.0001
        RUNPULSE     -0.36962776        0.11985294     51.05805832      9.51    0.0051
        RSTPULSE     -0.02153364        0.06605428      0.57051299      0.11    0.7473
        MAXPULSE      0.30321713        0.13649519     26.49142405      4.93    0.0360

Bounds on condition number:     8.743848,    137.1345
------------------------------------------------------------------------------------------------------
The above model is the best  6-variable model found.

No further improvement in R-square is possible.
```

The MAXR method tries to find the "best" one-variable model, the "best" two-variable model, and so on. For the fitness data, the one-variable model contains RUNTIME; the two-variable model contains RUNTIME and AGE; and the three-variable model contains RUNTIME, AGE, and RUNPULSE. The four-variable model contains AGE, RUNTIME, RUNPULSE, and MAXPULSE. The five-variable model contains AGE, WEIGHT, RUNTIME, RUNPULSE, and MAXPULSE. Finally, the six-variable model contains all the variables in the MODEL statement.

Note that for all three of the above methods, RSTPULSE contributes least to the model. In the case of forward selection, it is not added to the model. In the case of backward selection, it is the first variable to be removed from the model. In the case of MAXR selection, RSTPULSE is included only for the full model.

Next, the RSQUARE model-selection method is used to request R^2 and C_p statistics for all possible combinations of the six independent variables. The statements below produce **Output 28.41**:

```
model oxy=age weight runtime runpulse rstpulse maxpulse
     / selection=rsquare cp;
title 'Physical fitness data: all models';
```

Output 28.41 All Models by the RSQUARE Method: PROC REG

Physical fitness data: all models   10

N = 31   Regression Models for Dependent Variable: OXY

㉑ Number in Model	㉒ R-square	C(p)	㉔ Variables in Model
1	0.74338010	13.69884	RUNTIME
1	0.15948531	106.30211	RSTPULSE
1	0.15838344	106.47686	RUNPULSE
1	0.09277653	116.88184	AGE
1	0.05604592	122.70716	MAXPULSE
1	0.02648849	127.39485	WEIGHT
2	0.76424693	12.38945	AGE RUNTIME
2	0.76142381	12.83718	RUNTIME RUNPULSE
2	0.74522106	15.40687	RUNTIME MAXPULSE
2	0.74493479	15.45227	WEIGHT RUNTIME
2	0.74353296	15.67460	RUNTIME RSTPULSE
2	0.37599543	73.96451	AGE RUNPULSE
2	0.30027026	85.97420	AGE RSTPULSE
2	0.28941948	87.69509	RUNPULSE MAXPULSE
2	0.25998174	92.36380	AGE MAXPULSE
2	0.23503072	96.32092	RUNPULSE RSTPULSE
2	0.18060672	104.95234	WEIGHT RSTPULSE
2	0.17403933	105.99390	RSTPULSE MAXPULSE
2	0.16685536	107.13325	WEIGHT RUNPULSE
2	0.15063534	109.70568	AGE WEIGHT
2	0.06751590	122.88807	WEIGHT MAXPULSE
3	0.81109446	6.95963	AGE RUNTIME RUNPULSE
3	0.80998844	7.13504	RUNTIME RUNPULSE MAXPULSE
3	0.78173017	11.61668	AGE RUNTIME MAXPULSE
3	0.77083060	13.34531	AGE WEIGHT RUNTIME
3	0.76734943	13.89741	AGE RUNTIME RSTPULSE
3	0.76189848	14.76190	RUNTIME RUNPULSE RSTPULSE
3	0.76182904	14.77292	WEIGHT RUNTIME RUNPULSE
3	0.74615485	17.25878	WEIGHT RUNTIME MAXPULSE
3	0.74522683	17.40596	RUNTIME RSTPULSE MAXPULSE
3	0.74511138	17.42427	WEIGHT RUNTIME RSTPULSE
3	0.46664844	61.58732	AGE RUNPULSE RSTPULSE
3	0.42227346	68.62501	AGE RUNPULSE MAXPULSE
3	0.40912553	70.71021	AGE WEIGHT RUNPULSE
3	0.39000680	73.74237	AGE RSTPULSE MAXPULSE
3	0.35684729	79.00132	AGE WEIGHT RSTPULSE
3	0.35377183	79.48908	RUNPULSE RSTPULSE MAXPULSE
3	0.32077932	84.72155	WEIGHT RUNPULSE MAXPULSE
3	0.29021246	89.56933	AGE WEIGHT MAXPULSE
3	0.24465116	96.79516	WEIGHT RUNPULSE RSTPULSE
3	0.18823207	105.74299	WEIGHT RSTPULSE MAXPULSE
4	0.83681815	4.87996	AGE RUNTIME RUNPULSE MAXPULSE

```
                    Physical fitness data: all models                          11

Number in     R-square          C(p)    Variables in Model
Model
    4        0.81649255      8.10351    AGE WEIGHT RUNTIME RUNPULSE
    4        0.81584902      8.20557    WEIGHT RUNTIME RUNPULSE MAXPULSE
    4        0.81167015      8.86832    AGE RUNTIME RUNPULSE RSTPULSE
    4        0.81040041      9.06970    RUNTIME RUNPULSE RSTPULSE MAXPULSE
    4        0.78622430     12.90393    AGE WEIGHT RUNTIME MAXPULSE
    4        0.78343214     13.34675    AGE RUNTIME RSTPULSE MAXPULSE
    4        0.77503285     14.67885    AGE WEIGHT RUNTIME RSTPULSE
    4        0.76225238     16.70578    WEIGHT RUNTIME RUNPULSE RSTPULSE
    4        0.74617854     19.25502    WEIGHT RUNTIME RSTPULSE MAXPULSE
    4        0.50339774     57.75904    AGE WEIGHT RUNPULSE RSTPULSE
    4        0.50245083     57.90921    AGE RUNPULSE RSTPULSE MAXPULSE
    4        0.47171966     62.78305    AGE WEIGHT RUNPULSE MAXPULSE
    4        0.42560710     70.09631    AGE WEIGHT RSTPULSE MAXPULSE
    4        0.38579687     76.41004    WEIGHT RUNPULSE RSTPULSE MAXPULSE
-----------------------------------------------------------------------
    5        0.84800181      5.10628    AGE WEIGHT RUNTIME RUNPULSE MAXPULSE
    5        0.83703132      6.84615    AGE RUNTIME RUNPULSE RSTPULSE MAXPULSE
    5        0.81755611      9.93484    AGE WEIGHT RUNTIME RUNPULSE RSTPULSE
    5        0.81608280     10.16850    WEIGHT RUNTIME RUNPULSE RSTPULSE MAXPULSE
    5        0.78870109     14.51112    AGE WEIGHT RUNTIME RSTPULSE MAXPULSE
    5        0.55406593     51.72328    AGE WEIGHT RUNPULSE RSTPULSE MAXPULSE
-----------------------------------------------------------------------
    6        0.84867192      7.00000    AGE WEIGHT RUNTIME RUNPULSE RSTPULSE MAXPULSE
-----------------------------------------------------------------------
```

The models in the output above are arranged first by the number of variables in the model, and second by the magnitude of R^2 for the model. Before making a final decision about which model to use, you would want to perform collinearity diagnostics. Note that since many different models have been fit and the choice of a final model is based on R^2, the statistics are biased and the p values for the parameter estimates are not valid.

Example 3: Predicting Weight by Height and Age

In this example, the weights of school children are modeled as a function of their heights and ages. Modeling is performed separately for boys and girls. The example shows the use of a BY statement with PROC REG; multiple MODEL statements; and the OUTEST= and OUTSSCP= options, which create data sets. Since the BY statement is used, interactive processing is not possible in this example; no statements can appear after the first RUN statement. The statements below produce **Output 28.42**:

```
*---------------Data on Age, Weight, and Height of Children----------*
|Age (months), height (inches), and weight (pounds) were recorded for|
|a group of school children. From Lewis and Taylor (1967).           |
*-------------------------------------------------------------------*;

data htwt;
   input sex $ age :3.1 height weight @@;
   cards;
f 143 56.3  85.0 f 155 62.3 105.0 f 153 63.3 108.0 f 161 59.0  92.0
f 191 62.5 112.5 f 171 62.5 112.0 f 185 59.0 104.0 f 142 56.5  69.0
f 160 62.0  94.5 f 140 53.8  68.5 f 139 61.5 104.0 f 178 61.5 103.5
f 157 64.5 123.5 f 149 58.3  93.0 f 143 51.3  50.5 f 145 58.8  89.0
f 191 65.3 107.0 f 150 59.5  78.5 f 147 61.3 115.0 f 180 63.3 114.0
f 141 61.8  85.0 f 140 53.5  81.0 f 164 58.0  83.5 f 176 61.3 112.0
f 185 63.3 101.0 f 166 61.5 103.5 f 175 60.8  93.5 f 180 59.0 112.0
f 210 65.5 140.0 f 146 56.3  83.5 f 170 64.3  90.0 f 162 58.0  84.0
f 149 64.3 110.5 f 139 57.5  96.0 f 186 57.8  95.0 f 197 61.5 121.0
```

```
f 169 62.3  99.5 f 177 61.8 142.5 f 185 65.3 118.0 f 182 58.3 104.5
f 173 62.8 102.5 f 166 59.3  89.5 f 168 61.5  95.0 f 169 62.0  98.5
f 150 61.3  94.0 f 184 62.3 108.0 f 139 52.8  63.5 f 147 59.8  84.5
f 144 59.5  93.5 f 177 61.3 112.0 f 178 63.5 148.5 f 197 64.8 112.0
f 146 60.0 109.0 f 145 59.0  91.5 f 147 55.8  75.0 f 145 57.8  84.0
f 155 61.3 107.0 f 167 62.3  92.5 f 183 64.3 109.5 f 143 55.5  84.0
f 183 64.5 102.5 f 185 60.0 106.0 f 148 56.3  77.0 f 147 58.3 111.5
f 154 60.0 114.0 f 156 54.5  75.0 f 144 55.8  73.5 f 154 62.8  93.5
f 152 60.5 105.0 f 191 63.3 113.5 f 190 66.8 140.0 f 140 60.0  77.0
f 148 60.5  84.5 f 189 64.3 113.5 f 143 58.3  77.5 f 178 66.5 117.5
f 164 65.3  98.0 f 157 60.5 112.0 f 147 59.5 101.0 f 148 59.0  95.0
f 177 61.3  81.0 f 171 61.5  91.0 f 172 64.8 142.0 f 190 56.8  98.5
f 183 66.5 112.0 f 143 61.5 116.5 f 179 63.0  98.5 f 186 57.0  83.5
f 182 65.5 133.0 f 182 62.0  91.5 f 142 56.0  72.5 f 165 61.3 106.5
f 165 55.5  67.0 f 154 61.0 122.5 f 150 54.5  74.0 f 155 66.0 144.5
f 163 56.5  84.0 f 141 56.0  72.5 f 147 51.5  64.0 f 210 62.0 116.0
f 171 63.0  84.0 f 167 61.0  93.5 f 182 64.0 111.5 f 144 61.0  92.0
f 193 59.8 115.0 f 141 61.3  85.0 f 164 63.3 108.0 f 186 63.5 108.0
f 169 61.5  85.0 f 175 60.3  86.0 f 180 61.3 110.5 m 165 64.8  98.0
m 157 60.5 105.0 m 144 57.3  76.5 m 150 59.5  84.0 m 150 60.8 128.0
m 139 60.5  87.0 m 189 67.0 128.0 m 183 64.8 111.0 m 147 50.5  79.0
m 146 57.5  90.0 m 160 60.5  84.0 m 156 61.8 112.0 m 173 61.3  93.0
m 151 66.3 117.0 m 141 53.3  84.0 m 150 59.0  99.5 m 164 57.8  95.0
m 153 60.0  84.0 m 206 68.3 134.0 m 250 67.5 171.5 m 176 63.8  98.5
m 176 65.0 118.5 m 140 59.5  94.5 m 185 66.0 105.0 m 180 61.8 104.0
m 146 57.3  83.0 m 183 66.0 105.5 m 140 56.5  84.0 m 151 58.3  86.0
m 151 61.0  81.0 m 144 62.8  94.0 m 160 59.3  78.5 m 178 67.3 119.5
m 193 66.3 133.0 m 162 64.5 119.0 m 164 60.5  95.0 m 186 66.0 112.0
m 143 57.5  75.0 m 175 64.0  92.0 m 175 68.0 112.0 m 175 63.5  98.5
m 173 69.0 112.5 m 170 63.8 112.5 m 174 66.0 108.0 m 164 63.5 108.0
m 144 59.5  88.0 m 156 66.3 106.0 m 149 57.0  92.0 m 144 60.0 117.5
m 147 57.0  84.0 m 188 67.3 112.0 m 169 62.0 100.0 m 172 65.0 112.0
m 150 59.5  84.0 m 193 67.8 127.5 m 157 58.0  80.5 m 168 60.0  93.5
m 140 58.5  86.5 m 156 58.3  92.5 m 156 61.5 108.5 m 158 65.0 121.0
m 184 66.5 112.0 m 156 68.5 114.0 m 144 57.0  84.0 m 176 61.5  81.0
m 168 66.5 111.5 m 149 52.5  81.0 m 142 55.0  70.0 m 188 71.0 140.0
m 203 66.5 117.0 m 142 58.8  84.0 m 189 66.3 112.0 m 188 65.8 150.5
m 200 71.0 147.0 m 152 59.5 105.0 m 174 69.8 119.5 m 166 62.5  84.0
m 145 56.5  91.0 m 143 57.5 101.0 m 163 65.3 117.5 m 166 67.3 121.0
m 182 67.0 133.0 m 173 66.0 112.0 m 155 61.8  91.5 m 162 60.0 105.0
m 177 63.0 111.0 m 177 60.5 112.0 m 175 65.5 114.0 m 166 62.0  91.0
m 150 59.0  98.0 m 150 61.8 118.0 m 188 63.3 115.5 m 163 66.0 112.0
m 171 61.8 112.0 m 162 63.0  91.0 m 141 57.5  85.0 m 174 63.0 112.0
m 142 56.0  87.5 m 148 60.5 118.0 m 140 56.8  83.5 m 160 64.0 116.0
m 144 60.0  89.0 m 206 69.5 171.5 m 159 63.3 112.0 m 149 56.3  72.0
m 193 72.0 150.0 m 194 65.3 134.5 m 152 60.8  97.0 m 146 55.0  71.5
m 139 55.0  73.5 m 186 66.5 112.0 m 161 56.8  75.0 m 153 64.8 128.0
m 196 64.5  98.0 m 164 58.0  84.0 m 159 62.8  99.0 m 178 63.8 112.0
m 153 57.8  79.5 m 155 57.3  80.5 m 178 63.5 102.5 m 142 55.0  76.0
m 164 66.5 112.0 m 189 65.0 114.0 m 164 61.5 140.0 m 167 62.0 107.5
m 151 59.3  87.0
;
```

```
title '-------- Data on age, weight, and height of children ---------';
proc reg outest=est1 outsscp=sscp1;
   by sex;
   eq1: model  weight=height;
   eq2: model  weight=height age;
proc print data=sscp1;
   title2 'SSCP type data set';
proc print data=est1;
   title2 'EST type data set';
run;
```

Output 28.42   Height and Weight Data: PROC REG

```
-------- Data on age, weight, and height of children ---------                                    1
-------------------------------------------------------- SEX=f ------------------------------------------------------

Model: EQ1
Dependent Variable: WEIGHT

                                     Analysis of Variance

                              Sum of         Mean
        Source        DF      Squares        Square       F Value      Prob>F

        Model          1    21506.52309   21506.52309     141.094      0.0001
        Error        109    16614.58502     152.42739
        C Total      110    38121.10811

               Root MSE       12.34615      R-Square       0.5642
               Dep Mean       98.87838      Adj R-Sq       0.5602
               C.V.           12.48620

                                     Parameter Estimates

                           Parameter      Standard     T for H0:
        Variable   DF       Estimate         Error    Parameter=0     Prob > |T|

        INTERCEP    1    -153.128910    21.24814273      -7.207        0.0001
        HEIGHT      1       4.163612     0.35052308      11.878        0.0001
```

```
-------- Data on age, weight, and height of children ---------                                    2
-------------------------------------------------------- SEX=f ------------------------------------------------------

Model: EQ2
Dependent Variable: WEIGHT

                                     Analysis of Variance

                              Sum of         Mean
        Source        DF      Squares        Square       F Value      Prob>F

        Model          2    22432.27243   11216.13621      77.210      0.0001
        Error        108    15688.83568     145.26700
        C Total      110    38121.10811

               Root MSE       12.05268      R-Square       0.5884
               Dep Mean       98.87838      Adj R-Sq       0.5808
               C.V.           12.18939

                                     Parameter Estimates

                           Parameter      Standard     T for H0:
        Variable   DF       Estimate         Error    Parameter=0     Prob > |T|

        INTERCEP    1    -150.596982    20.76729993      -7.252        0.0001
        HEIGHT      1       3.603780     0.40776801       8.838        0.0001
        AGE         1       1.907026     0.75542849       2.524        0.0130
```

```
                 -------- Data on age, weight, and height of children ---------                 3
--------------------------------------------------- SEX=m ------------------------------------------------------

Model: EQ1
Dependent Variable: WEIGHT

                                  Analysis of Variance

                               Sum of        Mean
         Source        DF       Squares      Square      F Value     Prob>F

         Model          1     31126.05991  31126.05991   206.239     0.0001
         Error        124     18714.35477    150.92222
         C Total      125     49840.41468

              Root MSE        12.28504     R-Square       0.6245
              Dep Mean       103.44841     Adj R-Sq       0.6215
              C.V.            11.87552

                                  Parameter Estimates

                         Parameter      Standard     T for H0:
         Variable   DF    Estimate        Error     Parameter=0    Prob > |T|

         INTERCEP    1   -125.698066    15.99362486    -7.859        0.0001
         HEIGHT      1      3.689771     0.25692946    14.361        0.0001
```

```
                 -------- Data on age, weight, and height of children ---------                 4
--------------------------------------------------- SEX=m ------------------------------------------------------

Model: EQ2
Dependent Variable: WEIGHT

                                  Analysis of Variance

                               Sum of        Mean
         Source        DF       Squares      Square      F Value     Prob>F

         Model          2     32974.75022  16487.37511   120.241     0.0001
         Error        123     16865.66447    137.11922
         C Total      125     49840.41468

              Root MSE        11.70979     R-Square       0.6616
              Dep Mean       103.44841     Adj R-Sq       0.6561
              C.V.            11.31945

                                  Parameter Estimates

                         Parameter      Standard     T for H0:
         Variable   DF    Estimate        Error     Parameter=0    Prob > |T|

         INTERCEP    1   -113.713465    15.59021361    -7.294        0.0001
         HEIGHT      1      2.680749     0.36809058     7.283        0.0001
         AGE         1      3.081672     0.83927355     3.672        0.0004
```

```
                 -------- Data on age, weight, and height of children ---------                 5
                                    SSCP type data set

  OBS   SEX   _TYPE_    _NAME_    INTERCEP     HEIGHT       WEIGHT        AGE

   1     f    SSCP     INTERCEP    111.0       6718.40     10975.50     1824.90
   2     f    SSCP     HEIGHT     6718.4     407879.32    669469.85   110818.32
   3     f    SSCP     WEIGHT    10975.5     669469.85   1123360.75   182444.95
   4     f    SSCP     AGE        1824.9     110818.32    182444.95    30363.81
   5     f    N                    111.00       111.00       111.00      111.00
   6     m    SSCP     INTERCEP    126.0       7825.00     13034.50     2072.10
   7     m    SSCP     HEIGHT     7825.0     488243.60    817919.60   129432.57
   8     m    SSCP     WEIGHT    13034.5     817919.60   1398238.75   217717.45
   9     m    SSCP     AGE        2072.1     129432.57    217717.45    34515.95
  10     m    N                    126.0       126.00       126.00      126.00
```

```
          -------- Data on age, weight, and height of children ---------                    6
                              EST type data set

   OBS  SEX  _MODEL_  _TYPE_  _DEPVAR_   _RMSE_   INTERCEP   HEIGHT   WEIGHT    AGE
    1    f    EQ1     PARMS   WEIGHT    12.3461  -153.129   4.16361    -1       .
    2    f    EQ2     PARMS   WEIGHT    12.0527  -150.597   3.60378    -1     1.90703
    3    m    EQ1     PARMS   WEIGHT    12.2850  -125.698   3.68977    -1       .
    4    m    EQ2     PARMS   WEIGHT    11.7098  -113.713   2.68075    -1     3.08167
```

For both females and males, the overall F statistics for both models are significant, indicating that the model explains a significant portion of the variation in the data. For females, the full model is

$$\text{WEIGHT} = -150.57 + 3.60 * \text{HEIGHT} + 1.91 * \text{AGE}$$

and, for males, the full model is

$$\text{WEIGHT} = -113.71 + 2.68 * \text{HEIGHT} + 3.08 * \text{AGE} \quad .$$

The OUTSSCP= data set is printed. Note how the BY groups are separated. Observations with _TYPE_='N' contain the number of observations in the associated BY group. Observations with _TYPE_='SSCP' contain the rows of the uncorrected sums of squares and crossproducts matrix. The observations with _NAME_='INTERCEP' contain crossproducts for the intercept.

The OUTEST= data set is printed, and again, the BY groups are separated. Observations with _MODEL_ contain the labels for models from MODEL statements. If no labels had been specified, the defaults MODEL1 and MODEL2 would appear as values for _MODEL_. Note that _TYPE_='PARMS' for all observations, indicating that all observations contain parameter estimates. _DEPVAR_ gives the dependent variable, and _RMSE_ gives the Root Mean Square Error for the associated model. INTERCEP gives the estimate for the intercept for the associated model, and variables with the same name as variables in the original data set (HEIGHT, AGE) give parameter estimates for those variables. Note that the dependent variable, WEIGHT, is shown with a value of -1.

REFERENCES

Akaike, H. (1969), "Fitting Autoregressive Models for Prediction," *Annals of the Institute of Statistical Mathematics*, 21, 243–247.

Allen, D.M. (1971), "Mean Square Error of Prediction as a Criterion for Selecting Variables," *Technometrics*, 13, 469–475.

Allen, D.M. and Cady, F.B. (1982), *Analyzing Experimental Data by Regression*, Belmont, CA: Lifetime Learning Publications.

Amemiya, T. (1976), "Selection of Regressors," Technical Report No. 225, Stanford, CA: Stanford University.

Belsley, D.A., Kuh, E., and Welsch, R.E. (1980), *Regression Diagnostics*, New York: John Wiley & Sons, Inc.

Berk, K.N. (1977), "Tolerance and Condition in Regression Computations," *Journal of the American Statistical Association*, 72, 863–866.

Bock, R.D. (1975), *Multivariate Statistical Methods in Behavioral Research*, New York: McGraw-Hill Book Co.

Box, G.E.P. (1966), "The Use and Abuse of Regression," *Technometrics*, 8, 625–629.

Cook, R.D. (1977), "Detection of Influential Observations in Linear Regression," *Technometrics*, 19, 15–18.

Cook, R.D. (1979), "Influential Observations in Linear Regression," *Journal of the American Statistical Association*, 74, 169–174.

Daniel, C. and Wood, F. (1980), *Fitting Equations to Data*, Revised Edition, New York: John Wiley & Sons, Inc.

Darlington, R.B. (1968), "Multiple Regression in Psychological Research and Practice," *Psychological Bulletin*, 69, 161–182.

Draper, N. and Smith, H. (1981), *Applied Regression Analysis*, 2d Edition, New York: John Wiley & Sons, Inc.

Durbin, J. and Watson, G.S. (1951), "Testing for Serial Correlation in Least Squares Regression," *Biometrika*, 37, 409–428.

Freund, R.J. and Littell, R.C. (1986), *"SAS System for Regression, 1986 Edition*, Cary, NC: SAS Institute Inc.

Furnival, G.M. and Wilson, R.W. (1974), "Regression by Leaps and Bounds," *Technometrics*, 16, 499–511.

Gauss, K.F. (1809), *Werke*, 4, 1–93.

Goodnight, J.H. (1979), "A Tutorial on the SWEEP Operator," *The American Statistician*, 33, 149–158. (Also available as *The Sweep Operator: Its Importance in Statistical Computing*, SAS Technical Report R-106.)

Grunfeld, Y. (1958), "The Determinants of Corporate Investment," Unpublished Thesis, Chicago, discussed in Boot, J.C.G. (1960), "Investment Demand: An Empirical Contribution to the Aggregation Problem," *International Economic Review*, 1, 3–30.

Hocking, R.R. (1976), "The Analysis and Selection of Variables in Linear Regression," *Biometrics*, 32, 1–50.

Johnston, J. (1972), *Econometric Methods*, New York: McGraw-Hill Book Co.

Judge, G.G., Griffiths, W.E., Hill, R.C., and Lee, T. (1980), *The Theory and Practice of Econometrics*, New York: John Wiley & Sons, Inc.

Judge, G.G., Griffiths, W.E., Hill, R.C., Lutkepohl, H., and Lee, T.C. (1985) "The Theory and Practice of Econometrics", 2d edition, New York: John Wiley & Sons, Inc.

Kennedy, W.J. and Gentle, J.E. (1980), *Statistical Computing*, New York: Marcel Dekker, Inc.

Lewis, T. and Taylor, L.R. (1967), *Introduction to Experimental Ecology*, New York: Academic Press, Inc.

Lord, F.M. (1950), "Efficiency of Prediction when a Progression Equation from One Sample is Used in a New Sample," Research Bulletin No. 50-40, Princeton, NJ: Educational Testing Service.

Mallows, C.L. (1967), "Choosing a Subset Regression," unpublished report, Bell Telephone Laboratories.

Mallows, C.L. (1973), "Some Comments on Cp," *Technometrics*, 15, 661–675.

Mardia, K.V., Kent, J.T., and Bibby, J.M. (1979), *Multivariate Analysis*, London: Academic Press, Inc.

Markov, A.A. (1900), *Wahrscheinlichkeitsrechnung*, Tebrer, Leipzig.

Morrison, D.F. (1976), *Multivariate Statistical Methods*, 2d Edition, New York: McGraw-Hill, Inc.

Mosteller, F. and Tukey, J.W. (1977), *Data Analysis and Regression*, Reading, MA: Addison-Wesley Publishing Co., Inc.

Neter, J. and Wasserman, W. (1974), *Applied Linear Statistical Models*, Homewood, IL: Irwin.

Nicholson, G.E., Jr. (1948), "The Application of a Regression Equation to a New Sample," unpublished Ph.D. dissertation, University of North Carolina at Chapel Hill.

Pillai, K.C.S. (1960), *Statistical Table for Tests of Multivariate Hypotheses*, Manila: The Statistical Center, University of the Philippines.

Pindyck, R.S. and Rubinfeld, D.L. (1981), *Econometric Models and Econometric Forecasts*, 2d Edition, New York: McGraw-Hill Book Co.

Pringle, R.M. and Raynor, A.A. (1971), *Generalized Inverse Matrices with Applications to Statistics*, New York: Hafner Publishing Company.

Rao, C.R. (1973), *Linear Statistical Inference and Its Applications*, 2d Edition, New York: John Wiley & Sons, Inc.

Rothman, D. (1968), Letter to the editor, *Technometrics*, 10, 432.

Sall, J.P. (1981), *SAS Regression Applications*, Revised Edition, SAS Technical Report A-102, Cary, NC: SAS Institute Inc.

Sawa, T. (1978), "Information Criteria for Discriminating Among Alternative Regression Models," *Econometrica*, 46, 1273–1282.

Schwarz, G. (1978), "Estimating the Dimension of a Model," *Annals of Statistics*, 6, 461–464.

Stein, C. (1960), "Multiple Regression," in *Contributions to Probability and Statistics*, eds. I. Olkin et al., Stanford, CA: Stanford University Press.

Timm, N.H. (1975), *Multivariate Analysis with Applications in Education and Psychology*, Monterey, CA: Brooks-Cole Publishing Co.

Weisberg, S. (1980), *Applied Linear Regression*, New York: John Wiley & Sons, Inc.

White, H. (1980), "A Heteroskedasticity-Consistent Covariance Matrix Estimator and a Direct Test for Heteroskedasticity," *Econometrica*, 48, 817–838.

ABSTRACT

The RSREG procedure fits the parameters of a complete quadratic response surface and analyzes the fitted surface to determine the factor levels of optimum response.

INTRODUCTION

Response Surface Experiments

Many industrial experiments are conducted to discover which values of factor variables optimize a response. If each factor variable is measured at three or more values, a quadratic response surface can be estimated by least-squares regression. The predicted optimal value can be found from the estimated surface if the surface is shaped like a simple hill or a valley. If the estimated surface is more complicated, or if the predicted optimum is far from the region of experimentation, then the shape of the surface can be analyzed to indicate the directions in which new experiments should be performed.

Suppose that a response variable y is measured at combinations of values of two factor variables, x_1 and x_2. The quadratic response-surface model for this variable is written:

$$y = \beta_0 + \beta_1 x_1 + \beta_2 x_2 + \beta_3 x_1^2 + \beta_4 x_2^2 + \beta_5 x_1 x_2 + \varepsilon \quad .$$

The steps in the analysis for such data are

1. model fitting and analysis of variance
2. canonical analysis to investigate the shape of the predicted response surface
3. ridge analysis to search for the region of optimum response.

Model Fitting and Analysis of Variance

The first task in analyzing the response surface is to estimate the parameters of the model by least-squares regression and to obtain information about the fit in the form of an analysis of variance. This is accomplished using the statements

```
proc rsreg;
   model y = x1 x2;
```

The estimated surface will typically be curved: a "hill" whose peak occurs at the unique estimated point of maximum response, a "valley," or a "saddle-surface" with no unique minimum or maximum. Use the results of this phase of the analysis to answer the questions:

- How much does each type of effect contribute to the statistical fit? (The types of effects are linear, quadratic, and crossproduct.)
- Is part of the residual error due to lack-of-fit? Does the quadratic response model adequately represent the true response surface?
- How much does each factor variable contribute to the statistical fit? Can the response be predicted as well if the variable is removed?
- For a grid of factor values, what are the predicted responses? (See **Plotting the Surface** and **Searching for Multiple Response Conditions** later in this chapter.)

Canonical Analysis

The second task in analyzing the response surface is to find the estimated stationary point and to examine the overall shape of the curve to see whether it is a maximum, a minimum, or a saddle-point. This canonical analysis of the response surface is performed by the PROC and MODEL statements above. The canonical analysis can be used to answer the following:

- Is the surface shaped like a hill, a valley, a saddle-surface, or a flat surface?
- If there is a unique optimum combination of factor values, where is it?
- To which factors is the predicted response most sensitive?

Because the eigenvalues and eigenvectors are based on parameter estimates from fitting the response to the coded data, they will in general be different from those computed by PROC RSREG in previous releases. (See **Coding the Factor Variables** below.)

Ridge Analysis

If the estimated surface is found to have a simple optimum well within the range of experimentation, the analysis performed by the two steps above may be sufficient. In more complicated situations, further search for the region of optimum response is required. The method of ridge analysis computes the estimated ridge of optimum response for increasing radii from the center of the original design. The ridge analysis answers the following question:

- If there is not a unique optimum of the response surface within the range of experimentation, in which direction should further searching be done in order to locate the optimum?

For example, after the model has been fit as above, the ridge of maximum response is computed using the additional statement:

```
ridge max;
```

Coding the Factor Variables

For the results of the canonical and ridge analyses to be interpretable, the values of different factor variables should be comparable. This is because the canonical and ridge analyses of the response surface are not invariant with respect to differences in scale and location of the factor variables. The analysis of variance is not affected by these changes. Although the actual predicted surface does not change, its parameterization does. The usual solution to this problem is to code each factor variable so that its minimum in the experiment is −1 and its maximum is 1 and to carry through the analysis with the coded values instead of the original ones. This practice has the added benefit of making 1 a reasonable boundary radius for the ridge analysis since 1 represents approximately the edge of the experimental region. By default, RSREG computes the linear transformation to perform this coding as the data are initially read in, and the canonical and ridge analyses are performed on the model fit to the coded data. The actual form of the coding operation for each value of a variable is

$$coded\ value = (original\ value - M)/S$$

where M is the average of the highest and lowest values for the variable in the design and S is half their difference.

Comparison to PROC GLM

Other SAS/STAT procedures can be used to fit the response surface, but PROC RSREG is more specialized. The MODEL statement for PROC RSREG

```
model y=x1 x2 x3;
```

is more compact than the MODEL statement for other regression procedures in SAS/STAT software. For example, the equivalent MODEL statement for PROC GLM is

```
model y=x1 x1*x1
        x2 x1*x2 x2*x2
        x3 x1*x3 x2*x3 x3*x3;
```

Terminology

Variables are used according to the following conventions:

factor variables
: independent variables used to construct the quadratic response surface. Variables must be numeric. For the necessary parameters to be estimated, each variable should have at least three distinct values in the data.

response variables
: the dependent variables to which the quadratic response surface are to be fit. They must be numeric.

covariates
: additional independent variables included in the regression but not used in the formation of the quadratic response surface. Variables must be numeric.

WEIGHT variable
: a variable for weighting the observations in the regression. WEIGHT variables must be numeric.

ID variables
: variables not in the above lists that are to be transferred to the output data set that contains statistics for each observation in the input data set. This data set is created using the OUT= option in the PROC RSREG statement. ID variables can be either character or numeric.

BY variables
: variables used to group observations. Separate analyses are obtained for each BY group. BY variables can be either character or numeric.

SPECIFICATIONS

The RSREG procedure allows one of each of the following statements:

PROC RSREG *options*;
 MODEL *responses=independents / options*;
 RIDGE *options*;
 WEIGHT *variable*;
 ID *variables*;
 BY *variables*;

The PROC RSREG and MODEL statements are required. The BY, ID, MODEL, RIDGE, and WEIGHT statements are described after the PROC RSREG statement below.

PROC RSREG Statement

PROC RSREG *options*;

The PROC RSREG statement can have the following options:

DATA=*SASdataset*
specifies the input SAS data set that contains the data to be analyzed. If the DATA= option is not specified, PROC RSREG uses the most recently created SAS data set.

NOPRINT
suppresses all printed results when only the output data set is required. For more information, see the description of the NOPRINT option in the MODEL and RIDGE statements.

OUT=*SASdataset*
names an output SAS data set to contain statistics specified by the user for each observation in the input data set. In particular, this data set will contain the BY variables, ID variables, the WEIGHT variable, variables in the MODEL statement, and the OUTPUT options requested in the MODEL statement. You must specify OUTPUT options in the MODEL statement. Otherwise, the output data set is created but contains no observations. If a permanent SAS data set is to be created, a two-level name must be specified (see "SAS Files" in the *SAS Language Guide, Release 6.03 Edition* for more information on permanent SAS data sets). For details on the data set created by PROC RSREG, see **Output Data Sets** later in this chapter.

BY Statement

BY *variables*;

A BY statement can be used with PROC RSREG to obtain separate analyses on observations in groups defined by the BY variables. When a BY statement appears, the procedure expects the input data set to be sorted in order of the BY variables.

If your input data set is not sorted in ascending order, use the SORT procedure with a similar BY statement to sort the data, or, if appropriate, use the BY statement options NOTSORTED or DESCENDING. For more information, see the discussion of the BY statement in "SAS Statements Used in the PROC Step" in the *SAS Language Guide*.

ID Statement

ID *variables*;

The ID statement names variables that are to be transferred to the data set created by the OUT= option in the PROC RSREG statement, which contains statistics for each observation in addition to variables mentioned in other statements.

MODEL Statement

MODEL *responses*=*independents* / *options*;

The MODEL statement lists response (dependent) variables followed by an equal sign and then lists independent variables, some of which may be covariates. Independent variables specified in the MODEL statement must be variables in the data set being analyzed. In other words, independent variables of the form

X1*X1 or X1(X2) are not valid. Any of the following options may be specified:

BYOUT
requests that only the first BY group be used to estimate the model. Subsequent BY groups have scoring statistics computed in the output data set only. The BYOUT option is used only when a BY statement is specified.

COVAR=n
declares that the first *n* variables on the independent side of the model are simple regressors (covariates) rather than factors in the quadratic response surface. If the COVAR= option is not specified, then PROC RSREG forms quadratic and crossproduct effects for all regressor variables in the MODEL statement.

LACKFIT
specifies that a lack-of-fit test is to be performed. If the LACKFIT option is specified, the data must first be sorted by the independent variables so that observations repeating the same values are grouped together.

NOANOVA
NOAOV
suppresses printing the analysis of variance and parameter estimates from the model fit.

NOCODE
specifies that the canonical and ridge analyses are to be carried out with the parameter estimates derived from fitting the response to the original values of the factors variables, rather than their coded values (see **INTRODUCTION** for details.) Use this option if the data are already stored in a coded form that does not have -1 and 1 as the lowest and highest values, respectively, for each factor variable. This is the case, for example, for some central composite designs (see Myers (1976)).

NOOPTIMAL
NOOPT
suppresses printing the canonical analysis for the quadratic response surface.

NOPRINT
suppresses printing both the analysis of variance and the canonical analysis.

PRESS
specifies that the predicted residual sum of squares (PRESS) statistic be computed and printed for each dependent variable in the model. The PRESS statistic is added to the summary information at the beginning of the analysis of variance, so if NOANOVA or NOPRINT is specified, this option has no effect.

Output Options

The following options to the MODEL statement control which types of statistics are output to the data set created using the OUT= option in the PROC RSREG statement. If none of the options are selected, the data set is created but contains no observations. The option keywords become values of the special variable _TYPE_ in the output data set.

ACTUAL
specifies the actual values from the input data set.

PREDICT
> specifies the values predicted by the model.

RESIDUAL
> specifies the residuals, calculated as ACTUAL−PREDICTED.

L95M
> specifies the lower bound of a 95% confidence interval for the expected value, or mean, of the dependent variable.

U95M
> specifies the upper bound of a 95% confidence interval for the expected value, or mean, of the dependent variable.

L95
> specifies the lower bound of a 95% confidence interval for an individual prediction. The variance used in calculating this bound includes the variance of the error, as well as the variance of the parameter estimates.

U95
> specifies the upper bound of a 95% confidence interval for an individual prediction.

D
> specifies Cook's D influence statistic.

RIDGE Statement

> RIDGE *options*;

A RIDGE statement specifies that the ridge of optimum response be computed. The ridge starts at a given point x_0, and the point on the ridge at radius r from x_0 is the collection of factor settings that optimizes the predicted response at this radius. You can think of the ridge as climbing or falling as fast as possible on the surface of predicted response. Thus, the ridge analysis can be used as a tool to help interpret an existing response surface or to indicate the direction in which further experimentation should be performed.

The default starting point, x_0, has each coordinate equal to the point midway between the highest and lowest values of the factor in the design. The default radii at which the ridge is computed are 0, 0.1, . . . , 0.9, 1. If, as usual, the ridge analysis is based on the response surface fit to coded values for the factor variables (see **INTRODUCTION** for details), then this results in a ridge that starts at the point with a coded zero value for each coordinate and extends toward, but not beyond, the edge of the range of experimentation. Alternatively, both the center point for the ridge and the radii at which it is to be computed may be specified.

The following options can be specified in the RIDGE statement:

CENTER=*uncoded factor values*
> specifies a list giving the coordinates of the point x_0 from which to begin the ridge. The list can take any of the forms described in the RADIUS= option below. The coordinates should be given in the original (uncoded) factor variable values. There must be as many coordinates specified as there are factors in the model, and the order of the coordinates must be the same as that used in the MODEL statement. If the number of coordinates in the list exceeds the number of factors in the model, the extra coordinates are ignored. This starting point should be well inside the range of experimentation. The default sets each coordinate equal to the value midway between the highest and lowest values for the associated factor.

MINIMUM

MIN

MAXIMUM

MAX

specifies the type of ridge to compute. Both the MIN and MAX options can be specified; at least one must be specified.

NOPRINT

suppresses printing the ridge analysis when only an output data set is required.

OUTR=*SASdataset*

names an output SAS data set in which to save the computed optimum ridge. For details, see **Output Data Sets** later in this chapter.

RADIUS=*coded radii*

specifies a list giving the distances from the ridge starting point at which to compute the optimum. The values in the list represent distances between coded points. The list can take any of the following forms or can be composed of mixtures of them:

$m_1, m_2, \ldots, m_n$ several values.

m TO n a sequence where m equals the starting value, n equals the ending value, and the increment equals 1.

m TO n BY i a sequence where m equals the starting value, n equals the ending value, and i equals the increment.

Mixtures of the above forms should be separated by commas. The default list runs from 0 to 1 by increments of 0.1.

WEIGHT Statement

WEIGHT *variable*;

The WEIGHT statement names a numeric variable in the input data set. The values are to be used as relative weights on the observations to produce weighted least-squares estimates. Specifying a weight variable changes the model for the variance of the errors, for if the weights are proportional to the reciprocals of the error variances, then the weighted least-squares estimates are best linear unbiased. In any case, when weights are specified, this is the error model assumed for all standard errors, confidence intervals, and tests that PROC RSREG computes. Because of the interpretation of the weights as reciprocals of variances, observations with zero or negative weights are ignored. A more complete description of the WEIGHT statement can be found in the chapter describing the GLM procedure.

DETAILS

Missing Values

If an observation has missing data for any of the variables used by the procedure, then that observation is not used in the estimation process. If one or more response variables are missing, but no factor or covariate variables are missing, then predicted values and confidence limits are computed for the output data set, but the residual and D statistic are missing.

Output Data Sets

Statistics for Each Observation

An output data set containing user-specified statistics for each observation in the input data set is created whenever the OUT= option is specified in the PROC RSREG statement. The data set contains the following variables:

- the BY variables.
- the ID variables.
- the WEIGHT variable.
- the independent variables in the MODEL statement.
- the variable _TYPE_, which identifies the observation type in the output data set. _TYPE_ is a character variable with a length of eight, and it takes on the values 'ACTUAL', 'PREDICT', 'RESIDUAL', 'U95M', 'L95M', 'U95', 'L95', and 'D'.
- the response variables containing special output values identified by the _TYPE_ variable.

All confidence limits use the two-tailed Student's t value.

The Optimum Response Ridge

If the OUTR= option is specified in the RIDGE statement, then an output data set is created to contain the optimum response ridge. The data set contains the following variables:

- the current values of the BY variables.
- a character variable _DEPVAR_ of length 8, containing the name of the dependent variable.
- a character variable _TYPE_ of length 8, identifying the type of ridge being computed, MINIMUM or MAXIMUM.
- a numeric variable _RADIUS_, giving the distance from the ridge starting point.
- the values of the model factors at the estimated optimum point at distance _RADIUS_ from the ridge starting point.
- a numeric variable _PRED_, the estimated expected value of the dependent variable at the optimum.
- a numeric variable _STDERR_, the standard error of the estimated expected value.

Lack-of-Fit Test

If the LACKFIT option is specified, the data should be sorted so that repeated observations appear together. If the data are not sorted, the procedure cannot find these repeats. Since all other test statistics for the model are tested by total error rather than pure error, you may want to hand-calculate the tests with respect to pure error if the lack-of-fit is significant.

Interpreting the Canonical Analysis

The eigenvalues and eigenvectors in the matrix of second-order parameters characterize the shape of the response surface. The eigenvectors point in the directions of principle orientation for the surface, and the signs and magnitudes of the associated eigenvalues give the shape of the surface in these directions. Positive eigenvalues indicate directions of upward curvature, and negative eigenvalues indicate directions of downward curvature. The larger an eigenvalue is in absolute value, the more pronounced is the curvature of the response surface in the associated direction. Often, all of the coefficients of an eigenvector except for one are relatively small, indicating that the vector points roughly along the axis associated with the factor corresponding to the single large coefficient. In this case, the canonical analysis can be used to determine the relative sensitivity of the predicted response surface to variations in that factor. (See **EXAMPLES** later in the chapter.)

Plotting the Surface

You can generate predicted values for a grid of points with the PREDICT option (see **Example 1** later in this chapter) and then use these values to create a contour plot of the response surface over a two-dimensional grid. Any two factor variables can be chosen to form the grid for the plot. Several plots can be generated by using different pairs of factor variables.

Searching for Multiple Response Conditions

Suppose you want to find the factor setting that produces responses in a certain region. For example, you want to find the values of x_1 and x_2 that maximize y_1 subject to $y_2 < 2$ and $y_3 < y_2 + y_1$. The exact answer is not easy to obtain analytically, but the following method can be applied. Approach the problem by checking conditions across a grid of values in the range of interest.

```
data b;
   set a end=eof;
   output;
   if eof then do;
      y1=.; y2=.; y3=.;
      do x1=1 to 5 by .1;
         do x2=1 to 5 by .1;
            output;
            end;
         end;
      end;
proc rsreg data=b out=c;
   model y1 y2 y3=x1 x2 / predict;
data d;
   set c;
   if y2<2;
   if y3<y2+y1;
proc sort data=d;
   by descending y1;
proc print;
```

Handling of the Covariates

Covariate regressors are added to a response surface model because they are believed to account for a sizable yet relatively uninteresting portion of the variation in the data. What the experimenter is really interested in is the response corrected for the effect of the covariates. A common example is the block effect in a block design. In the canonical and ridge analyses of a response surface, which estimate responses at hypothetical levels of the factor variables, the actual value of the predicted response is computed using the average values of the covariates. The estimated response values do optimize the estimated surface of the response corrected for covariates, but true prediction of the response requires actual values for the covariates.

Computational Method

For each response variable, the model can be written in the form:

$$y_i = x_i' A x_i + b' x_i + c' z_i + \varepsilon_i$$

where

y_i is the ith observation of the response variable.

$x_i = (x_{i1}, x_{i2}, \ldots, x_{ik})'$
   are the k factor variables for the ith observation.

$z_i = (z_{i1}, z_{i2}, \ldots, z_{iL})'$
   are the L covariates, including the intercept term.

A   is the $k \times k$ symmetrized matrix of quadratic parameters, with diagonal elements equal to the coefficients of the pure quadratic terms in the model and off-diagonal elements equal to half the coefficient of the corresponding cross-product.

b   is the $k \times 1$ vector of linear parameters.

c   is the $L \times 1$ vector of covariate parameters, one of which is the intercept.

ε_i is the error associated with the ith observation. Tests performed by RSREG assume that errors are independently and normally distributed with mean zero and variance σ^2.

The parameters in **A**, **b**, and **c** are estimated by least squares. To optimize y with respect to **x**, take partial derivatives, set them to zero, and solve:

$$\partial y / \partial x = 2x'A + b' = 0$$
$$x = -0.5 A^{-1} b \quad .$$

To determine if the solution is a maximum or minimum, find out if **A** is negative or positive definite by looking at the eigenvalues of **A**:

If eigenvalues	then solution is
are all negative	a maximum
are all positive	a minimum
have mixed signs	a saddle-point
contain zeros	in a flat area

The eigenvectors are also printed. The eigenvector for the largest eigenvalue gives the direction of steepest ascent from the stationary point, if positive, or steepest descent, if negative. The eigenvectors corresponding to small or zero eigenvalues point in directions of relative flatness.

The point on the optimum response ridge at a given radius R from the ridge origin is found by optimizing

$$(x_o + d)' A (x_o + d) + b' (x_o + d)$$

over $\mathbf{d}$ satisfying $\mathbf{d'd}=R^2$, where $\mathbf{x}_o$ is the $k\times1$ vector containing the ridge origin and $\mathbf{A}$ and $\mathbf{b}$ are as above. By the method of Lagrange multipliers, the optimal $\mathbf{d}$ has the form

$$\mathbf{d} = -(\mathbf{A} - \mu\mathbf{I})^{-1}(\mathbf{A}\mathbf{x}_o + 0.5\mathbf{b})$$

where $\mathbf{I}$ is the $k\times k$ identity matrix and μ is chosen so that $\mathbf{d'd}=R^2$. There may be several values of μ that satisfy this constraint; the right one depends on which sort of response ridge is of interest. If you are searching for the ridge of maximum response, then the appropriate μ is the unique one that satisfies the constraint and is greater than all the eigenvalues of $\mathbf{A}$. Similarly, the appropriate μ for the ridge of minimum response satisfies the constraint and is less than all the eigenvalues of $\mathbf{A}$. (See Myers (1976) for details.)

Printed Output

All estimates and hypothesis tests assume the model is correctly specified and the errors are distributed according to classical statistical assumptions.

The output for RSREG contains the following:

Estimation and Analysis of Variance

1. The actual form of the coding operation for each value of a variable is

   $$coded\ value = (original\ value - M)/S$$

   where M is the average of the highest and lowest values for the variable in the design and S is half their difference. The Subtracted off column contains the M values for this formula for each factor variable, and S is found in the Divided by column.
2. The Response Mean is the mean of the response variable in the sample.
3. The Root MSE estimates the standard deviation of the response variable and is calculated as the square root of the Total Error mean square.
4. The R-Square value is R^2, or the coefficient of determination. R^2 measures the proportion of the variation in the response that is attributed to the model rather than to random error.
5. The Coefficient of Variation is 100 times the ratio of the Root MSE to the Response Mean.
6. Terms are brought into the regression in four steps: (1) the intercept and any covariates in the model (not shown), (2) Linear terms like X1 and X2, (3) pure Quadratic terms like X1*X1 or X2*X2, and (4) Crossproduct terms like X1*X2.
7. The Degrees of Freedom should be the same as the number of corresponding parameters unless one or more of the parameters is not estimable.
8. Type I Sums of Squares, also called the sequential sums of squares, measure the reduction in the error sum of squares as sets of terms (Linear, Quadratic, and so forth) are added to the model.
9. These R-Squares measure the portion of total R^2 contributed as each set of terms (Linear, Quadratic, and so forth) is added to the model.
10. Each F-Ratio tests the null hypothesis that all parameters in the term are zero using the Total Error mean square as the denominator. This item is a test of a Type I hypothesis, containing the usual F test numerator, conditional on the effects of subsequent variables not being in the model.

11. Prob $>$ F is the significance value or probability of obtaining at least as great an F ratio given that the null hypothesis is true.
12. The Total Error Sum of Squares can be partitioned into Lack of Fit and Pure Error. When Lack of Fit is significant, there is variation in the model other than random error (such as cubic effects of the factor variables).
13. The Total Error Mean Square estimates σ^2, the variance.
14. The Parameter Estimates are the parameter estimates based on the *uncoded* values of the factor variables. If an effect is a linear combination of previous effects, the parameter for the effect is not estimable. When this happens, the degrees of freedom are zero, the parameter estimate is set to zero, and the estimates and tests on other parameters are conditional on this parameter being zero (not shown).
15. The Standard Error column contains the estimated standard deviations of the parameter estimates based on *uncoded* data.
16. The column headed T for H0: Parameter=0 contains t values of a test of the null hypothesis that the true parameter is zero when the *uncoded* values of the factor variables are used.
17. Prob $>$ |T| gives the significance value or probability of a greater absolute t ratio given that the true parameter is zero.
18. The Parameter Estimates from Coded Data are the parameter estimates based on the *coded* values of the factor variables. These are the estimates used in the subsequent canonical and ridge analyses.
19. The test on a Factor, say X1, is a joint test on all the parameters involving that factor. For example, the test for X1 tests the null hypothesis that the true parameters for X1, X1*X1, and X1*X2 are all zero.

Canonical Analysis

20. The Critical Values are the values of the factor variables that correspond to the stationary point of the fitted response surface. The critical values can be at a minimum, maximum, or saddle point.
21. The Eigenvalues and Eigenvectors are from the matrix of quadratic parameter estimates based on the coded data. They characterize the shape of the response surface. **Because the eigenvalues and eigenvectors are based on parameter estimates from fitting the response to the coded data, they will in general be different from those computed by PROC RSREG in previous releases.**

Ridge Analysis

22. The Coded Radius is the distance from the coded version of the associated point to the coded version of the origin of the ridge. The origin is given by the point at radius zero.
23. The Estimated Response is the estimated value of the response variable at the associated point. The Standard Error of this estimate is also given. This quantity is useful for assessing the relative credibility of the prediction at a given radius. Typically, this standard error increases rapidly as the ridge moves up to and beyond the design perimeter, reflecting the inherent difficulty of making predictions beyond the range of experimentation.
24. The Uncoded Factor Values are the values of the uncoded factor variables that give the optimum response at this radius from the ridge origin.

EXAMPLES

Example 1: A Response Surface with a Simple Optimum

This example uses the three-factor quadratic model discussed in John (1971). The objective is to minimize the unpleasant odor of a chemical. The following statements read the data and invoke PROC RSREG. These statements produce **Output 29.1**:

```
*----------------------------------------------------------------*
* Schneider and Stockett (1963) performed an experiment aimed at *
* reducing the unpleasant odor of a chemical product with several *
* factors. From John (1971).                                      *
*----------------------------------------------------------------*;

    data a;
       input y x1-x3 @@;
       label y="ODOR"
          x1="TEMPERATURE"
          x2="GAS-LIQUID RATIO"
          x3="PACKING HEIGHT";
       cards;
66 -1 -1  0      39  1 -1  0     43 -1  1  0     49  1  1  0
58 -1  0 -1      17  1  0 -1     -5 -1  0  1    -40  1  0  1
65  0 -1 -1       7  0  1 -1     43  0 -1  1    -22  0  1  1
-31 0  0  0     -35  0  0  0    -26  0  0  0
;
proc sort;
   by x1-x3;
proc rsreg;
   model y=x1-x3 / lackfit;
run;
```

Output 29.1 A Response Surface with a Simple Optimum, Using the
LACKFIT Option

```
                   Coding Coefficients for the Independent Variables                    1

                   Factor    Subtracted off    Divided by
              ❶    X1                    0       1.000000
                   X2                    0       1.000000
                   X3                    0       1.000000
```

❷❸ Response Mean   15.200000
❹ Root MSE   22.478508
❺ R-Square   0.8820
   Coef. of Variation   147.8849

❻ Regression	❼ Degrees of Freedom	❽ Type I Sum of Squares	❾ R-Square	❿ F-Ratio	⓫ Prob > F
Linear	3	7143.250000	0.3337	4.712	0.0641
Quadratic	3	11445	0.5346	7.550	0.0264
Crossproduct	3	293.500000	0.0137	0.194	0.8965
Total Regress	9	18882	0.8820	4.152	0.0657

Residual	Degrees of Freedom	Sum of Squares	Mean Square	F-Ratio	Prob > F
⓬ Lack of Fit	3	2485.750000	828.583333	40.750	0.0240
Pure Error	2	40.666667	20.333333		
Total Error	5	2526.416667	⓭ 505.283333		

Parameter	Degrees of Freedom	⓮ Parameter Estimate	⓯ Standard Error	⓰ T for H0: Parameter=0	⓱ Prob > |T|	⓲ Parameter Estimate from Coded Data
INTERCEPT	1	-30.666667	12.977973	-2.363	0.0645	-30.666667
X1	1	-12.125000	7.947353	-1.526	0.1876	-12.125000
X2	1	-17.000000	7.947353	-2.139	0.0854	-17.000000
X3	1	-21.375000	7.947353	-2.690	0.0433	-21.375000
X1*X1	1	32.083333	11.698187	2.743	0.0407	32.083333
X2*X1	1	8.250000	11.239254	0.734	0.4959	8.250000
X2*X2	1	47.833333	11.698187	4.089	0.0095	47.833333
X3*X1	1	1.500000	11.239254	0.133	0.8990	1.500000
X3*X2	1	-1.750000	11.239254	-0.156	0.8824	-1.750000
X3*X3	1	6.083333	11.698187	0.520	0.6252	6.083333

⓳ Factor	Degrees of Freedom	Sum of Squares	Mean Square	F-Ratio	Prob > F	
X1	4	5258.016026	1314.504006	2.602	0.1613	TEMPERATURE
X2	4	11045	2761.150641	5.465	0.0454	GAS-LIQUID RATIO
X3	4	3813.016026	953.254006	1.887	0.2510	PACKING HEIGHT

Canonical Analysis of Response Surface
(based on coded data)

3

Factor	⓴ Critical Value Coded	Uncoded	
X1	0.121913	0.121913	TEMPERATURE
X2	0.199575	0.199575	GAS-LIQUID RATIO
X3	1.770525	1.770525	PACKING HEIGHT

Predicted value at stationary point   -52.024631

㉑ Eigenvalues	Eigenvectors X1	X2	X3
48.858807	0.238091	0.971116	-0.015690
31.103461	0.970696	-0.237384	0.037399
6.037732	-0.032594	0.024135	0.999177

Stationary point is a minimum.

The canonical analysis indicates that the directions of principle orientation for the predicted response surface are along the axes associated with the three factors. The largest eigenvalue is associated with X2 and the next largest with X1. The third eigenvalue, associated with X3, is quite a bit smaller than the other two, indicating that the response surface is relatively insensitive to changes in this factor. The canonical analysis also finds a minimum for the estimated response surface when X1 and X2 are both near the middle of their respective ranges and X3 is relatively high. However, the lack-of-fit for the data is significant and further experimentation should be performed before firm statements are made concerning the underlying process. Since the data are stored in coded form, the coding operation within the procedure has no effect. The estimates based on coded and uncoded data are identical.

To plot the response surface with respect to two of the factor variables, first fix X3, the least significant factor variable, at its estimated optimum value and generate a grid of points for X1 and X2. To ensure that the grid data do not affect parameter estimates, the response variable (Y) is set to missing. (See **Missing Values** earlier in this chapter.) PROC RSREG computes the predicted values, which are output and plotted using the CONTOUR feature of PROC PLOT. The following statements produce **Output 29.2**:

```
data b;
   *-----GET THE ACTUAL VALUES-----;
   set a end=eof;
   output;
   *-----CREATE AN X1*X2 GRID FOR PLOTTING-----;
   if eof then do;
      y=.;
      x3=1.77;
      do x1=-1.5 to 1.5 by .1;
         do x2=-2 to 2 by .1;
            output;
            end;
         end;
      end;
proc rsreg data=b out=c noprint;
   model y=x1-x3 / predict;
data d;
   set c;
   if x3=1.77;
proc plot data=d;
   plot x1*x2=y / contour=6 hpos=100   vpos=36   hspace=10
                              haxis=-2     to 2    by .5
                              vaxis=-1.5   to 1.5 by .5;
   run;
```

Output 29.2 A Plot of the Response Surface using the PREDICT Option

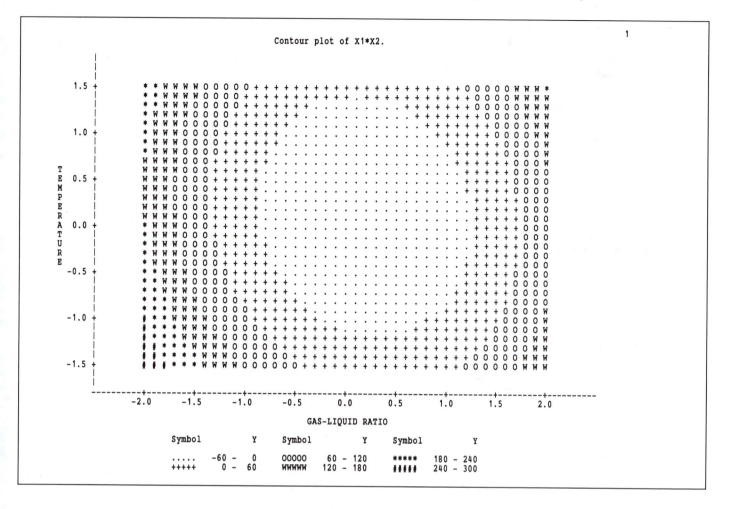

Example 2: A Saddle-Surface Response Using the Ridge Analysis

This is an example of a two-factor model in which the estimated surface does not have a unique optimum. A ridge analysis is used to determine the region in which the optimum lies. The objective is to find the settings of time and temperature in the processing of a chemical that maximize the yield. The following statements read the data and invoke PROC RSREG. These statements produce **Output 29.3**:

```
*------------------------------------------------------------------*
* Frankel (1961) reports an experiment aimed at maximizing the     *
* yield of mercaptobenzothiazole (MBT) by varying processing time  *
* and temperature.  From Myers (1976).                             *
*------------------------------------------------------------------*;

   data d;
     input time temp mbt;
     label
       time="REACTION TIME (HOURS)"
       temp="TEMPERATURE (DEGREES CENTIGRADE)"
        mbt="PERCENT YIELD MERCAPTOBENZOTHIAZOLE";
```

```
     cards;
     4.0    250    83.8
    20.0    250    81.7
    12.0    250    82.4
    12.0    250    82.9
    12.0    220    84.7
    12.0    280    57.9
    12.0    250    81.2
     6.3    229    81.3
     6.3    271    83.1
    17.7    229    85.3
    17.7    271    72.7
     4.0    250    82.0
    ;
proc sort;
   by time temp;
proc rsreg;
   model mbt=time temp / lackfit;
   ridge max;
run;
```

Output 29.3   A Saddle-Surface Response, with Ridge Analysis

Coding Coefficients for the Independent Variables			1

Factor	Subtracted off	Divided by
TIME	12.000000	8.000000
TEMP	250.000000	30.000000

Response Surface for Variable MBT: PERCENT YIELD MERCAPTOBENZOTHIAZOLE   2

Response Mean	79.916667
Root MSE	4.615964
R-Square	0.8003
Coef. of Variation	5.7760

Regression	Degrees of Freedom	Type I Sum of Squares	R-Square	F-Ratio	Prob > F
Linear	2	313.585803	0.4899	7.359	0.0243
Quadratic	2	146.768144	0.2293	3.444	0.1009
Crossproduct	1	51.840000	0.0810	2.433	0.1698
Total Regress	5	512.193947	0.8003	4.808	0.0410

Residual	Degrees of Freedom	Sum of Squares	Mean Square	F-Ratio	Prob > F
Lack of Fit	3	124.696053	41.565351	39.628	0.0065
Pure Error	3	3.146667	1.048889		
Total Error	6	127.842720	21.307120		

(continued on next page)

(continued from previous page)

Parameter	Degrees of Freedom	Parameter Estimate	Standard Error	T for H0: Parameter=0	Prob > |T|	Parameter Estimate from Coded Data
INTERCEPT	1	-545.867976	277.145373	-1.970	0.0964	82.173110
TIME	1	6.872863	5.004928	1.373	0.2188	-1.014287
TEMP	1	4.989743	2.165839	2.304	0.0608	-8.676768
TIME*TIME	1	0.021631	0.056784	0.381	0.7164	1.384394
TEMP*TIME	1	-0.030075	0.019281	-1.560	0.1698	-7.218045
TEMP*TEMP	1	-0.009836	0.004304	-2.285	0.0623	-8.852519

Factor	Degrees of Freedom	Sum of Squares	Mean Square	F-Ratio	Prob > F	
TIME	3	61.290957	20.430319	0.959	0.4704	REACTION TIME (HOURS)
TEMP	3	461.250925	153.750308	7.216	0.0205	TEMPERATURE (DEGREES CENTIGRADE)

Canonical Analysis of Response Surface   3
(based on coded data)

Factor	Critical Value Coded	Uncoded	
TIME	-0.441758	8.465935	REACTION TIME (HOURS)
TEMP	-0.309976	240.700718	TEMPERATURE (DEGREES CENTIGRADE)

Predicted value at stationary point   83.741940

Eigenvalues	Eigenvectors TIME	TEMP
2.528816	0.953223	-0.302267
-9.996940	0.302267	0.953223

Stationary point is a saddle point.

Estimated Ridge of Maximum Response for Variable MBT: PERCENT YIELD MERCAPTOBENZOTHIAZOLE   4

㉒ Coded Radius	㉓ Estimated Response	㉓ Standard Error	㉔ Uncoded Factor Values TIME	TEMP
0.0	82.173110	2.665023	12.000000	250.000000
0.1	82.952909	2.648671	11.964493	247.002956
0.2	83.558260	2.602270	12.142790	244.023941
0.3	84.037098	2.533296	12.704153	241.396084
0.4	84.470454	2.457836	13.517555	239.435227
0.5	84.914099	2.404616	14.370977	237.919138
0.6	85.390012	2.410981	15.212247	236.624811
0.7	85.906767	2.516619	16.037822	235.449230
0.8	86.468277	2.752355	16.850813	234.344204
0.9	87.076587	3.130961	17.654321	233.284652
1.0	87.732874	3.648568	18.450682	232.256238

The canonical analysis indicates that the predicted response surface is shaped like a saddle. The eigenvalue of 2.5 shows that the valley orientation of the saddle is less curved than the hill orientation, with eigenvalue of -9.99. The coefficients of the associated eigenvectors show that the valley is more aligned with TIME and the hill with TEMP. Because the canonical analysis resulted in a saddle point, the estimated surface does not have a unique optimum. However, the ridge analysis indicates that maximum yields will result from relatively high reaction times and low temperatures. Note from the analysis of variance for the model that the test for the time factor is not significant. If further experimentation is undertaken, it might be best to fix time at a moderate to high value and to concentrate on the effect of temperature. Finally, the lack of fit for the model is highly significant. The quadratic model does not fit the data very well, so firm statements about the underlying process should not be based only on the above analysis. In the actual experiment discussed here, extra runs were made that confirmed the above conclusions.

REFERENCES

Box, G.E.P. and Hunter, J.S. (1957), "Multifactor Experimental Designs for Exploring Response Surfaces," *Annals of Mathematical Statistics*, 28, 195–242.

Box, G.E.P. and Wilson, K.J. (1951), "On the Experimental Attainment of Optimum Conditions," *Journal of the Royal Statistical Society*, Ser. B, 13, 1–45.

Cochran, W.G. and Cox, G.M. (1957), *Experimental Designs*, 2d Edition, New York: John Wiley & Sons, Inc.

John, P.W.M. (1971), *Statistical Design and Analysis of Experiments*, New York: Macmillan Publishing Co., Inc.

Myers, R.H. (1976), *Response Surface Methodology*, Blacksburg, VA: Virginia Polytechnic Institute and State University.

Chapter 30

The SCORE
Procedure

ABSTRACT

The SCORE procedure multiplies values from two SAS data sets, one containing coefficients (for example, factor-scoring coefficients or regression coefficients) and the other containing raw data to be scored using the coefficients from the first data set. The result of this multiplication is a SAS data set containing linear combinations of the coefficients and the raw data values.

INTRODUCTION

Many statistical procedures output coefficients that PROC SCORE can apply to raw data to produce scores. The new score variable is formed as a linear combination of raw data and scoring coefficients. For each observation in the raw data set, PROC SCORE multiplies the value of a variable in the raw data set by the matching scoring coefficient from the data set of scoring coefficients. This multiplication process is repeated for each variable in the VAR statement. The resulting products are then summed to produce the value of the new score variable. This entire process is repeated for each observation in the raw data set. In other words, SCORE crossmultiplies part of one data set with another.

Raw Data Set

The raw data set can contain the original data used to calculate the scoring coefficients, or it can contain an entirely different data set. The raw data set must contain all the variables needed to produce scores. In addition, the scoring coefficients and the variables in the raw data set that are used in scoring must have the same names. See the **EXAMPLES** section for further illustration.

Scoring Coefficients Data Set

The data set containing scoring coefficients must contain two special variables: the _TYPE_ variable and the _NAME_ or _MODEL_ variable. The _TYPE_ variable identifies the observations that contain scoring coefficients. The _NAME_ or _MODEL_ variable provides a SAS name for the new score variable.

For example, PROC FACTOR produces an output data set that contains factor-scoring coefficients. In this output data set, the scoring coefficients are identified by _TYPE_='SCORE'. For _TYPE_='SCORE', the _NAME_ variable has values of 'FACTOR1', 'FACTOR2', and so forth. PROC SCORE gives the new score variables the names FACTOR1, FACTOR2, and so forth.

As another example, PROC REG produces an output data set that contains parameter estimates. In this output data set, the parameter estimates are identified by _TYPE_='PARMS'. The _MODEL_ variable contains the label used in the MODEL statement in PROC REG. This label is the name PROC SCORE gives to the new score variable.

Standardization of Raw Data

If the scoring coefficients data set contains observations with _TYPE_='MEAN' and _TYPE_='STD', then the raw data are standardized before scoring. If the scoring coefficients data set does not contain observations with _TYPE_='MEAN' and _TYPE_='STD', or if the NOSTD option is chosen, the raw data are not standardized. See the **EXAMPLES** section for further illustration.

SPECIFICATIONS

You can invoke PROC SCORE with the following statements:

    PROC SCORE *options*;
      VAR *variables*;
      ID *variables*;
      BY *variables*;

The only required statement is the PROC SCORE statement. The BY, ID, and VAR statements are described after the PROC SCORE statement below.

PROC SCORE Statement

    PROC SCORE *options*;

The options below can appear in the PROC SCORE statement:

DATA=*SASdataset*
    names the input SAS data set containing the raw data to score. This specification is required.

NOSTD
    suppresses centering and scaling of the raw data. Ordinarily, if PROC SCORE finds MEAN and STD observations in the SCORE= data set, the procedure uses these to standardize the raw data before scoring.

OUT=*SASdataset*
    specifies the name of the SAS data set created by PROC SCORE. If you want to create a permanent SAS data set, you must specify a two-level

name. (See "SAS Files" in the *SAS Language Guide, Release 6.03 Edition* for more information on permanent SAS data sets.) If the OUT= option is omitted, PROC SCORE still creates an output data set and automatically names it according to the DATA*n* convention, just as if you omitted a data set name in a DATA statement.

PREDICT

specifies that PROC SCORE should treat coefficients of −1 in the SCORE= data set as 0. In regression applications, the dependent variable is coded with a coefficient of −1. Applied directly to regression results, PROC SCORE produces negative residuals (see RESIDUAL below); the PREDICT option changes this so that predicted values are produced instead.

RESIDUAL

reverses the sign of each score. Applied directly to regression results, PROC SCORE produces negative residuals (predicted−actual); the RESIDUAL option produces positive residuals (actual−predicted) instead.

SCORE=*SASdataset*

names the data set containing the scoring coefficients. If the SCORE= option is omitted, the most recently created SAS data set is used. This data set must have two special variables: _TYPE_ and either _NAME_ or _MODEL_.

TYPE=*name*

specifies the observations in the SCORE= data set that contain scoring coefficients. The TYPE procedure option is unrelated to the data set parameter that has the same name. PROC SCORE examines the values of the special variable _TYPE_ in the SCORE= data set. When the value of _TYPE_ matches TYPE=*name*, the observation in the SCORE= data set is used to score the raw data in the DATA= data set. The default value of *name* is SCORE. When factor-scoring coefficients from PROC FACTOR are used, you want to select the observations in the SCORE= data set that have _TYPE_='SCORE'. Because the default for PROC SCORE is TYPE=SCORE, you need not specify TYPE= for factor scoring. When you use regression coefficients from PROC REG, specify TYPE=PARMS.

BY Statement

BY *variables*;

A BY statement can be used with PROC SCORE to obtain separate scoring for observations in groups defined by the BY variables. A BY statement can also be used to apply separate groups of scoring coefficients to the entire DATA= data set.

When a BY statement appears, the procedure expects the SCORE= input data set to be sorted in order of the BY variables. If your SCORE= data set is not sorted in ascending order, use the SORT procedure with a similar BY statement to sort the data, or, if appropriate, use the BY statement options NOTSORTED or DESCENDING. For more information, see the discussion of the BY statement in "SAS Statements Used in the PROC Step" in the *SAS Language Guide*.

If the DATA= data set does not contain any of the BY variables, the entire DATA= data set is scored by each BY group of scoring coefficients in the SCORE= data set.

If the DATA= data set contains some but not all of the BY variables, or if some BY variables do not have the same type or length in the DATA= data set as in the SCORE= data set, then PROC SCORE prints an error message and stops.

If all the BY variables appear in the DATA= data set with the same type and length as in the SCORE= data set, then each BY group in the DATA= data set is scored using scoring coefficients from the corresponding BY group in the SCORE= data set. The BY groups in the DATA= data set must be in the same order as in the SCORE= data set. All BY groups in the DATA= data set must also appear in the SCORE= data set. If you do not specify the NOTSORTED option, some BY groups can appear in the SCORE= data set but not in the DATA= data set; such BY groups are not used in computing scores.

ID Statement

ID *variables*;

The ID statement identifies variables from the DATA= data set to be included in the OUT= data set. If there is no ID statement, all variables from the DATA= data set are included in the OUT= data set. The ID variables can be character or numeric.

VAR Statement

VAR *variables*;

The VAR statement specifies the variables to be used in computing scores. These variables must be in both the DATA= and SCORE= input data sets and must be numeric. If no VAR statement is given, the procedure uses all numeric variables in the SCORE= data set. You should almost always use a VAR statement with PROC SCORE because you rarely want to score all the numeric variables.

DETAILS

Missing Values

If one of the variables in the DATA= data set has a missing value for an observation, all the scores have missing values for that observation. The exception to this criterion is if the PREDICT option is specified, the variable with a coefficient of -1 can tolerate a missing value and still produce a prediction score. Also, a variable with a coefficient of 0 can tolerate a missing value.

If a scoring coefficient in the SCORE= data set has a missing value for an observation, the coefficient is not used in creating the new score variable for the observation. In other words, missing values of scoring coefficients are treated as zeros. This treatment affects only the observation in which the missing value occurs.

Regression Parameter Estimates from PROC REG

When the SCORE= data set is an OUTEST= data set produced by PROC REG, and when TYPE=PARMS is specified, the interpretation of the new score variables depends on the PROC SCORE options chosen and the variables listed in the VAR statement. If the VAR statement contains only the independent variables used in a model in PROC REG, the new score variables give the predicted values. If the VAR statement contains the dependent variable and the independent variables used in a model in PROC REG, the interpretation of the new score variables depends on the PROC SCORE options chosen. If neither the PREDICT nor the RESIDUAL option is specified, the new score variables give negative residuals.

If the RESIDUAL option is chosen, the new score variables give positive residuals. If the PREDICT option is chosen, the new score variables give predicted values.

Unless you specify the NOINT option for PROC REG, the OUTEST= data set contains the variable INTERCEP. PROC SCORE uses the INTERCEP value in computing the scores.

Output Data Set

PROC SCORE produces an output data set but no printed output. The output OUT= data set contains the following:

- the ID variables, if any
- all variables from the DATA= data set, if no ID variables are specified
- the BY variables, if any
- the new score variables, named from the _NAME_ or _MODEL_ values in the SCORE= data set.

EXAMPLES

The following three examples use a subset of the FITNESS data set. The complete data set is given in the second example in the chapter on the REG procedure.

Example 1: Factor Scoring Coefficients

This example shows how to use PROC SCORE with factor scoring coefficients. First, PROC FACTOR produces an output data set containing scoring coefficients in observations identified by _TYPE_='SCORE'. These data, together with the original data set FITNESS, are supplied to PROC SCORE, resulting in a data set containing scores FACTOR1 and FACTOR2. These statements produce **Output 30.1** through **Output 30.3**:

```
* This data set contains only the first 12 observations from;
* the full data set used in the chapter on PROC REG.;

data fitness;
   input age weight oxy runtime rstpulse runpulse @@;
   cards;
44 89.47  44.609 11.37 62 178    40 75.07  45.313 10.07 62 185
44 85.84  54.297  8.65 45 156    42 68.15  59.571  8.17 40 166
38 89.02  49.874  9.22 55 178    47 77.45  44.811 11.63 58 176
40 75.98  45.681 11.95 70 176    43 81.19  49.091 10.85 64 162
44 81.42  39.442 13.08 63 174    38 81.87  60.055  8.63 48 170
44 73.03  50.541 10.13 45 168    45 87.66  37.388 14.03 56 186
;
proc factor data=fitness outstat=factout
            method=prin rotate=varimax score;
   var age weight runtime runpulse rstpulse;
   title 'FACTOR SCORING EXAMPLE';
proc print data=factout;
   title2 'Data Set from PROC FACTOR';
run;
```

```
proc score data=fitness score=factout out=fscore;
   var age weight runtime runpulse rstpulse;
proc print data=fscore;
   title2 'Data Set from PROC SCORE';
run;
```

Output 30.1 shows the PROC FACTOR output. The scoring coefficients for the two factors are shown at the end of the PROC FACTOR output.

Output 30.1   Creating an OUTSTAT= Data Set with PROC FACTOR

```
                                FACTOR SCORING EXAMPLE                                1

Initial Factor Method: Principal Components

                      Prior Communality Estimates: ONE

              Eigenvalues of the Correlation Matrix:  Total = 5  Average = 1

                           1          2          3          4          5
            Eigenvalue  2.309306   1.192200   0.882227   0.502567   0.113700
            Difference  1.117107   0.309972   0.379660   0.388867
            Proportion    0.4619     0.2384     0.1764     0.1005     0.0227
            Cumulative    0.4619     0.7003     0.8767     0.9773     1.0000

              2 factors will be retained by the MINEIGEN criterion.

                              Factor Pattern

                             FACTOR1    FACTOR2

                  AGE         0.29795    0.93675
                  WEIGHT      0.43282   -0.17750
                  RUNTIME     0.91983    0.28782
                  RUNPULSE    0.72671   -0.38191
                  RSTPULSE    0.81179   -0.23344

                  Variance explained by each factor

                             FACTOR1    FACTOR2
                             2.309306   1.192200


              Final Communality Estimates: Total = 3.501506

                  AGE      WEIGHT     RUNTIME   RUNPULSE   RSTPULSE
               0.966284   0.218834   0.928933   0.673962   0.713493
```

```
                                FACTOR SCORING EXAMPLE                                2

Rotation Method: Varimax

                         Orthogonal Transformation Matrix

                                    1          2

                          1      0.92536    0.37908
                          2     -0.37908    0.92536

                            Rotated Factor Pattern

                             FACTOR1    FACTOR2

                  AGE        -0.07939    0.97979
                  WEIGHT      0.46780   -0.00018
                  RUNTIME     0.74207    0.61503
                  RUNPULSE    0.81725   -0.07792
                  RSTPULSE    0.83969    0.09172

                  Variance explained by each factor

                             FACTOR1    FACTOR2
                             2.148775   1.352731
```

(continued on next page)

(continued from previous page)

Final Communality Estimates: Total = 3.501506

AGE	WEIGHT	RUNTIME	RUNPULSE	RSTPULSE
0.966284	0.218834	0.928933	0.673962	0.713493

Scoring Coefficients Estimated by Regression

Squared Multiple Correlations of the Variables with each Factor

FACTOR1	FACTOR2
1.000000	1.000000

Standardized Scoring Coefficients

	FACTOR1	FACTOR2
AGE	-0.17846	0.77600
WEIGHT	0.22987	-0.06672
RUNTIME	0.27707	0.37440
RUNPULSE	0.41263	-0.17714
RSTPULSE	0.39952	-0.04793

Output 30.2 lists the OUTSTAT= data set from PROC FACTOR. Note that observations 18 and 19 have _TYPE_='SCORE'. Observations 1 and 2 have _TYPE_='MEAN' and _TYPE_='STD', respectively. These four observations will be used by PROC SCORE.

Output 30.2   OUTSTAT= Data Set from PROC FACTOR Reproduced with PROC PRINT

```
                          FACTOR SCORING EXAMPLE                          3
                        Data Set from PROC FACTOR

OBS   _TYPE_    _NAME_      AGE    WEIGHT   RUNTIME  RUNPULSE  RSTPULSE

  1   MEAN                42.4167  80.5125  10.6483  172.917   55.6667
  2   STD                  2.8431   6.7660   1.8444    8.918    9.2769
  3   N                   12.0000  12.0000  12.0000   12.000   12.0000
  4   CORR     AGE         1.0000   0.0128   0.5005   -0.095   -0.0080
  5   CORR     WEIGHT      0.0128   1.0000   0.2637    0.173    0.2396
  6   CORR     RUNTIME     0.5005   0.2637   1.0000    0.556    0.6620
  7   CORR     RUNPULSE   -0.0953   0.1731   0.5555    1.000    0.4853
  8   CORR     RSTPULSE   -0.0080   0.2396   0.6620    0.485    1.0000
  9   COMMUNAL             0.9663   0.2188   0.9289    0.674    0.7135
 10   PRIORS              1.0000   1.0000   1.0000    1.000    1.0000
 11   EIGENVAL            2.3093   1.1922   0.8822    0.503    0.1137
 12   UNROTATE FACTOR1     0.2980   0.4328   0.9198    0.727    0.8118
 13   UNROTATE FACTOR2     0.9368  -0.1775   0.2878   -0.382   -0.2334
 14   TRANSFOR FACTOR1     0.9254  -0.3791     .         .         .
 15   TRANSFOR FACTOR2     0.3791   0.9254     .         .         .
 16   PATTERN  FACTOR1    -0.0794   0.4678   0.7421    0.817    0.8397
 17   PATTERN  FACTOR2     0.9798  -0.0002   0.6150   -0.078    0.0917
 18   SCORE    FACTOR1    -0.1785   0.2299   0.2771    0.413    0.3995
 19   SCORE    FACTOR2     0.7760  -0.0667   0.3744   -0.177   -0.0479
```

Since the PROC SCORE statement does not contain the NOSTD option, the data in FITNESS are standardized before scoring. For each variable specified in the VAR statement, the mean and standard deviation are obtained from FACTOUT. For each observation in FITNESS, the variables are then standardized. For example, for observation 1 in FITNESS, AGE is standardized to 0.5569 [(44−42.4167)/2.8431].

After the data in FITNESS are standardized, the standardized values of the variables in the VAR statement are multiplied by the matching coefficients in FACTOUT, and the resulting products are summed. This sum is output as a value of the new score variable.

Output 30.3 prints the FSCORE data set produced by PROC SCORE. This data set contains AGE, WEIGHT, OXY, RUNTIME, RSTPULSE, and RUNPULSE from FITNESS. It also contains FACTOR1 and FACTOR2, the two new score variables.

Output 30.3 OUT= Data Set from PROC SCORE Reproduced with PROC PRINT

```
                              FACTOR SCORING EXAMPLE                            4
                             Data Set from PROC SCORE

  OBS   AGE   WEIGHT    OXY    RUNTIME   RSTPULSE   RUNPULSE   FACTOR1    FACTOR2

   1    44    89.47   44.609    11.37      62         178      0.82129    0.35663
   2    40    75.07   45.313    10.07      62         185      0.71173   -0.99605
   3    44    85.84   54.297     8.65      45         156     -1.46064    0.36508
   4    42    68.15   59.571     8.17      40         166     -1.76087   -0.27657
   5    38    89.02   49.874     9.22      55         178      0.55819   -1.67684
   6    47    77.45   44.811    11.63      58         176     -0.00113    1.40715
   7    40    75.98   45.681    11.95      70         176      0.95318   -0.48598
   8    43    81.19   49.091    10.85      64         162     -0.12951    0.36724
   9    44    81.42   39.442    13.08      63         174      0.66267    0.85740
  10    38    81.87   60.055     8.63      48         170     -0.44496   -1.53103
  11    44    73.03   50.541    10.13      45         168     -1.11832    0.55349
  12    45    87.66   37.388    14.03      56         186      1.20836    1.05948
```

Example 2: Regression Parameter Estimates

In this example, PROC REG computes regression parameter estimates for the FITNESS data. (See **Example 1** to create the FITNESS data set.) The parameter estimates are output to a data set and used as scoring coefficients. For the first part of this example, PROC SCORE is used to score the FITNESS data, which are the same data used in the regression. In the second part of this example, PROC SCORE is used to score a new data set, FITNESS2. For PROC SCORE, the TYPE= specification is PARMS, and the names of the score variables are found in the variable _MODEL_, which gets its values from the label of a model. The following code produces **Output 30.4** through **Output 30.6**:

```
proc reg data=fitness outest=regout;
oxyhat: model oxy=age weight runtime runpulse rstpulse;
   title 'REGRESSION SCORING EXAMPLE';
proc print data=regout;
   title2 'OUTEST= Data Set from PROC REG';
run;
proc score data=fitness score=regout out=rscorep type=parms;
   var age weight runtime runpulse rstpulse;
proc print data=rscorep;
   title2 'Predicted Scores for Regression';
run;
proc score data=fitness score=regout out=rscorer type=parms;
   var oxy age weight runtime runpulse rstpulse;
proc print data=rscorer;
   title2 'Residual Scores for Regression';
run;
```

Output 30.4 shows the PROC REG output. The column labeled "Parameter Estimates" lists the parameter estimates. These estimates are output to the REGOUT data set.

Output 30.4   Creating an OUTEST= Data Set with PROC REG

```
                          REGRESSION SCORING EXAMPLE                          1

Model: OXYHAT
Dependent Variable: OXY

                          Analysis of Variance

                                  Sum of        Mean
        Source        DF        Squares       Square      F Value    Prob>F

        Model          5      509.62201    101.92440       15.802    0.0021
        Error          6       38.70060      6.45010
        C Total       11      548.32261

              Root MSE        2.53970     R-Square       0.9294
              Dep Mean       48.38942     Adj R-Sq       0.8706
              C.V.            5.24847

                          Parameter Estimates

                       Parameter       Standard     T for H0:
        Variable   DF   Estimate          Error    Parameter=0    Prob > |T|

        INTERCEP    1  151.915500    31.04737619          4.893    0.0027
        AGE         1   -0.630450     0.42502668         -1.483    0.1885
        WEIGHT      1   -0.105862     0.11868838         -0.892    0.4068
        RUNTIME     1   -1.756978     0.93844085         -1.872    0.1103
        RUNPULSE    1   -0.228910     0.12168627         -1.881    0.1090
        RSTPULSE    1   -0.179102     0.13005008         -1.377    0.2176
```

Output 30.5 lists the REGOUT data set. Notice that _TYPE_='PARMS' and _MODEL_='OXYHAT', the label in the MODEL statement in PROC REG.

Output 30.5   OUTEST= Data Set from PROC REG Reproduced with PROC PRINT

```
                          REGRESSION SCORING EXAMPLE                          2
                          OUTEST= Data Set from PROC REG

OBS  _MODEL_  _TYPE_  _DEPVAR_  _RMSE_  INTERCEP    AGE     WEIGHT   RUNTIME  RUNPULSE  RSTPULSE  OXY

 1   OXYHAT   PARMS    OXY      2.53970  151.916  -0.63045  -0.10586  -1.75698  -0.22891  -0.17910   -1
```

Output 30.6 lists the data sets created by PROC SCORE. Since the SCORE= data set does not contain observations with _TYPE_='MEAN' or _TYPE_='STD', the data in FITNESS are not standardized before scoring. The SCORE= data set contains the variable INTERCEP, so this intercept value is used in computing the score. To produce RSCOREP, the VAR statement in PROC SCORE includes only the independent variables from the model in PROC REG. As a result, OXYHAT gives predicted values. To produce RSCORER, the VAR statement in PROC SCORE includes both the dependent variable and the independent variables from the model in PROC REG. As a result, OXYHAT gives negative residuals. If the RESIDUAL option had been specified, OXYHAT would have given positive residuals. If the PREDICT option had been specified, OXYHAT would have given predicted values.

Output 30.6   Predicted and Residual Scores from the OUT= Data Set Created by PROC SCORE and Reproduced Using PROC PRINT

```
                           REGRESSION SCORING EXAMPLE                          3
                          Predicted Scores for Regression

        OBS   AGE   WEIGHT    OXY    RUNTIME   RSTPULSE   RUNPULSE   OXYHAT

          1    44    89.47   44.609   11.37       62        178     42.8771
          2    40    75.07   45.313   10.07       62        185     47.6050
          3    44    85.84   54.297    8.65       45        156     56.1211
          4    42    68.15   59.571    8.17       40        166     58.7044
          5    38    89.02   49.874    9.22       55        178     51.7386
          6    47    77.45   44.811   11.63       58        176     42.9756
          7    40    75.98   45.681   11.95       70        176     44.8329
          8    43    81.19   49.091   10.85       64        162     48.6020
          9    44    81.42   39.442   13.08       63        174     41.4613
         10    38    81.87   60.055    8.63       48        170     56.6171
         11    44    73.03   50.541   10.13       45        168     52.1299
         12    45    87.66   37.388   14.03       56        186     37.0080
```

```
                           REGRESSION SCORING EXAMPLE                          4
                          Residual Scores for Regression

        OBS   AGE   WEIGHT    OXY    RUNTIME   RSTPULSE   RUNPULSE   OXYHAT

          1    44    89.47   44.609   11.37       62        178    -1.73195
          2    40    75.07   45.313   10.07       62        185     2.29197
          3    44    85.84   54.297    8.65       45        156     1.82407
          4    42    68.15   59.571    8.17       40        166    -0.86657
          5    38    89.02   49.874    9.22       55        178     1.86460
          6    47    77.45   44.811   11.63       58        176    -1.83542
          7    40    75.98   45.681   11.95       70        176    -0.84811
          8    43    81.19   49.091   10.85       64        162    -0.48897
          9    44    81.42   39.442   13.08       63        174     2.01935
         10    38    81.87   60.055    8.63       48        170    -3.43787
         11    44    73.03   50.541   10.13       45        168     1.58892
         12    45    87.66   37.388   14.03       56        186    -0.38002
```

The second part of this example uses the parameter estimates to score a new data set. The following code produces **Output 30.7** and **Output 30.8**:

```
/* The FITNESS2 data set contains observations 13-16 from the
   FITNESS data set used in EXAMPLE 2 in the chapter on PROC REG.  */

data fitness2;
   input age weight oxy runtime rstpulse runpulse;
   cards;
45  66.45  44.754  11.12  51  176
47  79.15  47.273  10.60  47  162
54  83.12  51.855  10.33  50  166
49  81.42  49.156   8.95  44  180
;
proc print data=fitness2;
   title 'REGRESSION SCORING EXAMPLE';
   title2 'New Raw Data Set to be Scored';
run;
```

```
proc score data=fitness2 score=regout out=newpred type=parms nostd
          predict;
   var oxy age weight runtime runpulse rstpulse;
proc print data=newpred;
   title2 'Predicted Scores for Regression';
   title3 'for Additional Data from FITNESS2';
run;
```

Output 30.7 lists the FITNESS2 data set.

Output 30.7   FITNESS2 Data Set

```
                      REGRESSION SCORING EXAMPLE                           1
                      New Raw Data Set to be Scored

     OBS   AGE   WEIGHT    OXY    RUNTIME   RSTPULSE   RUNPULSE

      1    45    66.45   44.754   11.12       51        176
      2    47    79.15   47.273   10.60       47        162
      3    54    83.12   51.855   10.33       50        166
      4    49    81.42   49.156    8.95       44        180
```

PROC SCORE scores the FITNESS2 data set using the parameter estimates in REGOUT. These parameter estimates are from fitting a regression equation to FITNESS. The NOSTD option is specified, so the raw data are not standardized before scoring. (However, the NOSTD option is not necessary here. The SCORE= data set does not contain observations with _TYPE_='MEAN' or _TYPE_='STD', so standardization is not performed.) The VAR statement contains the dependent variable and the independent variables used in PROC REG. In addition, the PREDICT option is specified. This combination gives predicted values for the new score variable. The name of the new score variable is OXYHAT, from the value of _MODEL_ in the SCORE= data set. **Output 30.8** shows the data set produced by PROC SCORE.

Output 30.8   Predicted Scores from the OUT= Data Set Created by PROC
SCORE and Reproduced Using PROC PRINT

```
                      REGRESSION SCORING EXAMPLE                           2
                     Predicted Scores for Regression
                   for Additional Data from FITNESS2

   OBS   AGE   WEIGHT    OXY    RUNTIME   RSTPULSE   RUNPULSE   OXYHAT

    1    45    66.45   44.754   11.12       51        176      47.5507
    2    47    79.15   47.273   10.60       47        162      49.7802
    3    54    83.12   51.855   10.33       50        166      43.9682
    4    49    81.42   49.156    8.95       44        180      47.5949
```

Example 3: Custom Scoring Coefficients

This example uses a specially created custom scoring data set and produces **Output 30.9**. The first scoring coefficient creates a variable that is AGE—WEIGHT; the second evaluates RUNPULSE—RSTPULSE; and the third totals all six variables. Since the scoring coefficients data set (DATA=A) does not contain any observations with _TYPE_='MEAN' or _TYPE_='STD', the data in FITNESS are not standardized before scoring.

```
data a;
   input _type_ $ _name_ $
         age weight runtime runpulse rstpulse;
   cards;
SCORE   AGE_WGT   1 -1   0   0   0
SCORE   RUN_RST   0   0   0   1 -1
SCORE   TOTAL     1   1   1   1   1
;
proc print data=a;
   title 'CONSTRUCTED SCORING EXAMPLE';
   title2 'Scoring Coefficients';
run;
proc score data=fitness score=a out=b;
   var age weight runtime runpulse rstpulse;
proc print data=b;
   title2 'Scored Data';
run;
```

Output 30.9   Custom Scoring Data Set and Scored Fitness Data: PROC PRINT

```
                        CONSTRUCTED SCORING EXAMPLE                                    1
                           Scoring Coefficients

        OBS   _TYPE_   _NAME_   AGE   WEIGHT   RUNTIME   RUNPULSE   RSTPULSE

         1    SCORE    AGE_WGT    1     -1        0         0          0
         2    SCORE    RUN_RST    0      0        0         1         -1
         3    SCORE    TOTAL      1      1        1         1          1
```

```
                        CONSTRUCTED SCORING EXAMPLE                                    2
                              Scored Data

  OBS   AGE   WEIGHT    OXY    RUNTIME   RSTPULSE   RUNPULSE   AGE_WGT   RUN_RST   TOTAL

   1     44   89.47   44.609    11.37       62        178      -45.47     116    384.84
   2     40   75.07   45.313    10.07       62        185      -35.07     123    372.14
   3     44   85.84   54.297     8.65       45        156      -41.84     111    339.49
   4     42   68.15   59.571     8.17       40        166      -26.15     126    324.32
   5     38   89.02   49.874     9.22       55        178      -51.02     123    369.24
   6     47   77.45   44.811    11.63       58        176      -30.45     118    370.08
   7     40   75.98   45.681    11.95       70        176      -35.98     106    373.93
   8     43   81.19   49.091    10.85       64        162      -38.19      98    361.04
   9     44   81.42   39.442    13.08       63        174      -37.42     111    375.50
  10     38   81.87   60.055     8.63       48        170      -43.87     122    346.50
  11     44   73.03   50.541    10.13       45        168      -29.03     123    340.16
  12     45   87.66   37.388    14.03       56        186      -42.66     130    388.69
```

Chapter 31

The STEPDISC
Procedure

ABSTRACT

The STEPDISC procedure performs a stepwise discriminant analysis by forward selection, backward elimination, or stepwise selection of quantitative variables that can be useful for discriminating among several classes.

INTRODUCTION

The STEPDISC procedure selects a subset of quantitative variables to produce a good discrimination model using forward selection, backward elimination, or stepwise selection (Klecka 1980). The set of variables that make up each class is assumed to be multivariate normal with a common covariance matrix.

Variables are chosen to enter or leave the model according to one of two criteria:

1. the significance level of an F test from an analysis of covariance, where the variables already chosen act as covariates and the variable under consideration is the dependent variable, or

2. the squared partial correlation for predicting the variable under consideration from the CLASS variable, controlling for the effects of the variables already selected for the model.

In most applications, all variables considered have some discriminatory power, however small. To choose the model that provides the best discrimination using the sample estimates, all variables with corresponding parameters that can be reliably estimated should be included.

Costanza and Afifi (1979) use Monte Carlo studies to compare alternative stopping rules that can be used with the forward selection method in the two-group multivariate normal classification problem. Five different numbers of variables, ranging from 10 to 30, are considered in the studies. The comparison is based on conditional and estimated unconditional probabilities of correct classification. They conclude that the use of a liberal significance level, in the range of 10 percent to 25 percent, often performs better than the strict use of all variables.

Rencher and Larson (1980) show that, in stepwise selection, the order of selecting the variables considered for entry at each step depends on the data. Thus, the resulting F statistic for entry is biased. The bias can cause the inclusion of variables with poor discriminatory power in the model, especially in cases with a large number of variables and a relatively small sample size. If this should happen, a subset of variables chosen from the stepwise selection is not likely to be stable, and a different subset emerges from another repetition of the study. If you want to include only variables with significant contributions to the discriminatory power of the models rather than to maximize the probability of correct classification, you should specify a small significance level.

The significance level and the squared partial correlation criteria select variables in the same order, although they may select different numbers of variables. Increasing the sample size tends to increase the number of variables selected when using significance levels but has little effect on the number selected using squared partial correlations.

It is important to remember that when many significance tests are performed, each at a level of, for example, 5 percent, the overall probability of rejecting at least one true null hypothesis is much larger than 5 percent.

Forward selection begins with no variables in the model. At each step the variable is entered that contributes most to the discriminatory power of the model as measured by Wilks' lambda, the likelihood ratio criterion. When none of the unselected variables meets the entry criterion, the forward selection process stops.

Backward elimination begins with all variables in the model except those that are linearly dependent on previous variables in the VAR statement. At each step the variable that contributes least to the discriminatory power of the model as measured by Wilks' lambda is removed. When all remaining variables meet the criterion to stay in the model, the backward elimination process stops.

Stepwise selection begins like forward selection with no variables in the model. At each step the model is examined. If the variable in the model that contributes least to the discriminatory power of the model as measured by Wilks' lambda fails to meet the criterion to stay, then that variable is removed. Otherwise, the variable not in the model that contributes most to the discriminatory power of the model is entered. When all variables in the model meet the criterion to stay and none of the other variables meets the criterion to enter, the stepwise selection process stops.

It is important to realize that in the selection of variables for entry, only one variable can be entered into the model at each step. The selection process does not take into account the relationships between variables that have not yet been selected. Thus, some important variables could be excluded in the process.

The models selected by the STEPDISC procedure are not necessarily the best possible models, and Wilks' lambda may not be the best measure of discriminatory power for your application. However, if STEPDISC is used carefully, in combination with your knowledge of the data and careful cross-validation, it can be a valuable aid in selecting a discrimination model.

See Chapter 5, "Introduction to Discriminant Procedures," for more information on discriminant analysis.

SPECIFICATIONS

The following statements are used with the STEPDISC procedure:

PROC STEPDISC *options*;
   VAR *variables*;
   CLASS *variable*;
   FREQ *variable*;
   WEIGHT *variable*;
   BY *variables*;

The CLASS statement is required. The BY, CLASS, FREQ, VAR, and WEIGHT statements are described after the PROC STEPDISC statement.

PROC STEPDISC Statement

PROC STEPDISC *options*;

The options described in the following sections can appear in the PROC STEPDISC statement.

Data Set Option

DATA=*SASdataset*
names the data set to be analyzed. The data set can be an ordinary SAS data set or one of several specially structured data sets created by statistical procedures available with SAS/STAT software. These specially structured data sets include TYPE=CORR, COV, CSSCP, and SSCP. If the DATA= option is omitted, the most recently created SAS data set is used.

Method Selection Option

METHOD=FW | FORWARD
METHOD=BW | BACKWARD
METHOD=SW | STEPWISE
specifies the method used to select the variables in the model. METHOD=FORWARD requests forward selection, METHOD=BACKWARD requests backward elimination, and METHOD=STEPWISE requests stepwise selection. The default method is STEPWISE.

Selection Criterion Options

SLENTRY=p
SLE=p
> specifies the significance level for adding variables in the forward selection mode, where $0 \le p \le 1$. The default value is 0.15.

SLSTAY=p
SLS=p
> specifies the significance level for retaining variables in the backward elimination mode, where $0 \le p \le 1$. The default value is 0.15.

PR2ENTRY=p
PR2E=p
> specifies the partial R^2 for adding variables in the forward selection mode, where $p \le 1$.

PR2STAY=p
PR2S=p
> specifies the partial R^2 for retaining variables in the backward elimination mode, where $p \le 1$.

Selection Process Options

INCLUDE=n
> requests that the first n variables in the VAR statement be included in every model. The default value is 0.

MAXSTEP=n
> specifies the maximum number of steps. The default number is two times the number of variables in the VAR statement.

START=n
> specifies that the first n variables in the VAR statement be used to begin the selection process. The default value is 0 when METHOD=FORWARD or METHOD=STEPWISE is used and is the number of variables in the VAR statement when METHOD=BACKWARD is used.

STOP=n
> specifies the number of variables in the final model. The STEPDISC procedure stops the selection process when a model with n variables is found. This option applies only when METHOD=FORWARD or METHOD=BACKWARD is used. The default value is the number of variables in the VAR statement when METHOD=FORWARD is used and is 0 when METHOD=BACKWARD is used.

Singularity Option

SINGULAR=p
> specifies the singularity criterion for entering variables, where $0 < p < 1$. PROC STEPDISC precludes the entry of a variable if the squared multiple correlation of the variable with the variables already in the model exceeds $1 - p$. With more than one variable already in the model, STEPDISC also excludes a variable if it would cause any of the variables already in the model to have a squared multiple correlation (with the entering variable and the other variables in the model) exceeding $1 - p$. The default value is $1E-8$.

Printing Options

BCORR
: prints between-class correlations.

BCOV
: prints between-class covariances. The between-class covariance matrix equals the between-class SSCP matrix divided by $n(c-1)/c$, where n is the number of observations and c is the number of classes. The between-class covariances should be interpreted in comparison with the total-sample and within-class covariances, not as formal estimates of population parameters.

BSSCP
: prints the between-class SSCP matrix.

PCORR
: prints pooled within-class correlations (partial correlations based on the pooled within-class covariances).

PCOV
: prints pooled within-class covariances.

PSSCP
: prints the pooled within-class corrected SSCP matrix.

SIMPLE
: prints simple descriptive statistics for the total sample and within each class.

STDMEAN
: prints total-sample and pooled within-class standardized class means.

TCORR
: prints total-sample correlations.

TCOV
: prints total-sample covariances.

TSSCP
: prints the total-sample corrected SSCP matrix.

WCORR
: prints within-class correlations for each class level.

WCOV
: prints within-class covariances for each class level.

WSSCP
: prints the within-class corrected SSCP matrix for each class level.

ALL
: activates all of the printing options above.

SHORT
: suppresses the printout from each step.

BY Statement

BY *variables*;

You can use a BY statement with PROC STEPDISC to obtain separate analyses on observations in groups defined by the BY variables. When a BY statement appears, the procedure expects the input data set to be sorted in order of the BY variables.

If your input data set is not sorted in ascending order, use the SORT procedure with a similar BY statement to sort the data, or, if appropriate, use the BY statement options NOTSORTED or DESCENDING. For more information, see the discussion of the BY statement in "SAS Statements Used in the PROC Step" in the *SAS Language Guide, Release 6.03 Edition*.

CLASS Statement

CLASS *variable*;

The values of the CLASS variable define the groups for analysis. Class levels are determined by the formatted values of the CLASS variable. The CLASS variable can be numeric or character. A CLASS statement is required.

FREQ Statement

FREQ *variable*;

If a variable in the data set represents the frequency of occurrence for the other values in the observation, include the variable's name in a FREQ statement. The procedure then treats the data set as if each observation appears *n* times, where *n* is the value of the FREQ variable for the observation. The total number of observations is considered to be equal to the sum of the FREQ variable when the procedure determines degrees of freedom for significance probabilities.

If the value of the FREQ variable is missing or less than one, the observation is not used in the analysis. If the value is not an integer, the value is truncated to an integer.

VAR Statement

VAR *variables*;

The VAR statement specifies the quantitative variables eligible for selection. The default is all numeric variables not listed in other statements.

WEIGHT Statement

WEIGHT *variable*;

To use relative weights for each observation in the input data set, place the weights in a variable in the data set and specify the name in a WEIGHT statement. This is often done when the variance associated with each observation is different and the values of the WEIGHT variable are proportional to the reciprocals of the variances. If the value of the WEIGHT variable is missing or less than zero, then a value of zero for the weight is assumed.

The WEIGHT and FREQ statements have a similar effect except that the WEIGHT statement does not alter the degrees of freedom.

DETAILS

Missing Values

Observations containing missing values are omitted from the analysis.

Input Data Set

The input data set can be an ordinary SAS data set or one of several specially structured data sets created by statistical procedures available with SAS/STAT software. The BY variable in these data sets becomes the CLASS variable in PROC STEPDISC. These specially structured data sets include

- TYPE=CORR data sets created by PROC CORR using a BY statement
- TYPE=COV data sets created by PROC PRINCOMP using both the COV option and a BY statement
- TYPE=CSSCP data sets created by PROC CORR using the CSSCP option and a BY statement, where the OUT= data set is assigned TYPE=CSSCP with the TYPE= data set option
- TYPE=SSCP data sets created by PROC REG using both the OUTSSCP= option and a BY statement.

When the input data set is TYPE=CORR, TYPE=COV, or TYPE=CSSCP, STEPDISC reads the number of observations for each class from the observations with _TYPE_='N' and the variable means in each class from the observations with _TYPE_='MEAN'. STEPDISC then reads the within-class correlations from the observations with _TYPE_='CORR', the standard deviations from the observations with _TYPE_='STD' (data set TYPE=CORR), the within-class covariances from the observations with _TYPE_='COV' (data set TYPE=COV), or the within-class corrected sums of squares and crossproducts from the observations with _TYPE_='CSSCP' (data set TYPE=CSSCP).

When the data set does not include any observations with _TYPE_='CORR' (data set TYPE=CORR), _TYPE_='COV' (data set TYPE=COV), or _TYPE_='CSSCP' (data set TYPE=CSSCP) for each class, STEPDISC reads the pooled within-class information from the data set. In this case, STEPDISC reads the pooled within-class correlations from the observations with _TYPE_='PCORR', the pooled within-class standard deviations from the observations with _TYPE_='PSTD' (data set TYPE=CORR), the pooled within-class covariances from the observations with _TYPE_='PCOV' (data set TYPE=COV), or the pooled within-class corrected SSCP matrix from the observations with _TYPE_='PSSCP' (data set TYPE=CSSCP).

When the input data set is TYPE=SSCP, STEPDISC reads the number of observations for each class from the observations with _TYPE_='N', the sum of weights of observations from the variable INTERCEP in observations with _TYPE_='SSCP' and _NAME_='INTERCEP', the variable sums from the variable=*variablenames* in observations with _TYPE_='SSCP' and _NAME_='INTERCEP', and the uncorrected sums of squares and crossproducts from the variable=*variablenames* in observations with _TYPE_='SSCP' and _NAME_=*variablenames*.

Computational Resources

The amount of memory in bytes for temporary storage needed to process the data is

$$c(4v^2 + 28v + 3l + 4c + 72) + 16v^2 + 92v + 4t^2 + 20t + 4l$$

where

c = number of class levels
v = number of variables in the VAR list
l = length of the CLASS variable
t = $v+c-1$.

Additional temporary storage of 72 bytes at each step is also required to store the results.

Printed Output

The STEPDISC procedure prints the following output:

1. Class Level Information, including the values of the classification variable, the Frequency of each value, the Weight of each value, and its Proportion in the total sample.

Optional output includes

2. Within-Class SSCP Matrices for each group (not shown)
3. Pooled Within-Class SSCP Matrix (not shown)
4. Between-Class SSCP Matrix
5. Total-Sample SSCP Matrix
6. Within-Class Covariance Matrices for each group (not shown)
7. Pooled Within-Class Covariance Matrix (not shown)
8. Between-Class Covariance Matrix (not shown), equal to the between-class SSCP matrix divided by $n(c-1)/c$, where n is the number of observations and c is the number of classes
9. Total-Sample Covariance Matrix (not shown)
10. Within-Class Correlation Coefficients and Prob $> |R|$ to test the hypothesis that the within-class population correlation coefficients are zero (not shown)
11. Pooled Within-Class Correlation Coefficients and Prob $> |R|$ to test the hypothesis that the partial population correlation coefficients are zero (not shown)
12. Between-Class Correlation Coefficients and Prob $> |R|$ to test the hypothesis that the between-class population correlation coefficients are zero (not shown)
13. Total-Sample Correlation Coefficients and Prob $> |R|$ to test the hypothesis that the total population correlation coefficients are zero (not shown)
14. Simple descriptive Statistics (not shown) including N (the number of observations), Sum, Mean, Variance, and Standard Deviation for the total sample and within each class
15. Total-Sample Standardized Class Means (not shown), obtained by subtracting the grand mean from each class mean and dividing by the total-sample standard deviation
16. Pooled Within-Class Standardized Class Means (not shown), obtained by subtracting the grand mean from each class mean and dividing by the pooled within-class standard deviation.

At each step the following statistics are printed:

17. for each variable considered for entry or removal: (Partial) R**2, the squared (partial) correlation, the F statistic, and Prob $>$ F, the probability level, from a one-way analysis of covariance.
18. the minimum Tolerance for entering each variable. Tolerance for the entering variable is one minus the squared multiple correlation of the variable with the other variables already in the model. Tolerance for a variable already in the model is one minus the squared multiple correlation of the variable with the entering variable and other variables already in the model. A variable is entered only if its tolerance and the tolerances for variables in the model are greater than the value specified in the SINGULAR= option.

   The tolerance is computed using the total-sample correlation matrix. It is customary to compute tolerance using the pooled within-class correlation matrix (Jennrich 1977), but it is possible for a variable with excellent discriminatory power to have a high total-sample tolerance and a low pooled within-class tolerance. For example, PROC STEPDISC enters a variable that yields perfect discrimination (that is, produces a canonical correlation of one), but a program using pooled within-class tolerance does not.

19. the variable Label, if any.
20. the name of the variable chosen.
21. the variable(s) already selected or removed.
22. Wilks' Lambda and the associated F approximation with degrees of freedom and Prob < F, the associated probability level after the selected variable has been entered or removed. Wilks' lambda is the likelihood ratio statistic for testing the hypothesis that the means of the classes on the selected variables are equal in the population (see **Multivariate Tests** in Chapter 1, "Introduction to Regression Procedures"). Lambda is close to zero if any two groups are well separated.
23. Pillai's Trace and the associated F approximation with degrees of freedom and Prob > F, the associated probability level after the selected variable has been entered or removed. Pillai's trace is a multivariate statistic for testing the hypothesis that the means of the classes on the selected variables are equal in the population (see **Multivariate Tests** in Chapter 1, "Introduction to Regression Procedures").
24. Average Squared Canonical Correlation (ASCC). The ASCC is Pillai's trace divided by the number of groups minus 1. The ASCC is close to 1 if all groups are well separated and if all or most directions in the discriminant space show good separation for at least two groups.
25. A Summary is printed to give statistics associated with the variable chosen at each step. The Summary includes the following:

- Step number
- Variable Entered or Removed
- Number of variables In the model
- Partial R**2
- F Statistic for entering or removing the variable
- Prob > F, the probability level for the F statistic
- Wilks' Lambda
- Prob < Lambda based on the F approximation to Wilks' lambda
- Average Squared Canonical Correlation
- Prob > ASCC based on the F approximation to Pillai's trace
- the variable Label, if any.

EXAMPLE

Performing a Stepwise Discriminant Analysis

The iris data published by Fisher (1936) have been widely used for examples in discriminant analysis and cluster analysis. The sepal length, sepal width, petal length, and petal width were measured in millimeters on fifty iris specimens from each of three species: *Iris setosa, I. versicolor,* and *I. virginica.* A stepwise discriminant analysis is performed using stepwise selection.

In the PROC STEPDISC statement, the BSSCP and TSSCP options print the between-class SSCP matrix and the total-sample corrected SSCP matrix. By default, the significance level of an F test from an analysis of covariance is used as the selection criterion. The variable under consideration is the dependent variable, and the variables already chosen act as covariates. In Step 1, the tolerance is 1.0 for each variable under consideration because no variables have yet been in the model. Variable PETALLEN is selected because its F statistic, 1180.161, is the largest among all variables. In Step 2, with variable PETALLEN already in the model, PETALLEN is tested for removal before selecting a new variable for entry. Since PETALLEN meets the criterion to stay, it is used as a covariate in the analysis of covariance for variable selection. Variable SEPALWID is selected because its F statistic, 43.035, is the largest among all variables not in the model and its associated tolerance, 0.8164, meets the criterion to enter. The process is repeated in Steps 3 and 4. Variable PETALWID is entered in Step 3, and variable SEPALLEN is entered in Step 4. The following SAS statements produce **Output 31.1**:

```
proc format;
   value specname
      1='SETOSA    '
      2='VERSICOLOR'
      3='VIRGINICA ';
run;
data iris;
   title 'Fisher (1936) Iris Data';
   input sepallen sepalwid petallen petalwid species @@;
   format species specname.;
   label sepallen='Sepal Length in mm.'
         sepalwid='Sepal Width  in mm.'
         petallen='Petal Length in mm.'
         petalwid='Petal Width  in mm.';
   cards;
50 33 14 02 1 64 28 56 22 3 65 28 46 15 2 67 31 56 24 3
63 28 51 15 3 46 34 14 03 1 69 31 51 23 3 62 22 45 15 2
59 32 48 18 2 46 36 10 02 1 61 30 46 14 2 60 27 51 16 2
65 30 52 20 3 56 25 39 11 2 65 30 55 18 3 58 27 51 19 3
68 32 59 23 3 51 33 17 05 1 57 28 45 13 2 62 34 54 23 3
77 38 67 22 3 63 33 47 16 2 67 33 57 25 3 76 30 66 21 3
49 25 45 17 3 55 35 13 02 1 67 30 52 23 3 70 32 47 14 2
64 32 45 15 2 61 28 40 13 2 48 31 16 02 1 59 30 51 18 3
55 24 38 11 2 63 25 50 19 3 64 32 53 23 3 52 34 14 02 1
49 36 14 01 1 54 30 45 15 2 79 38 64 20 3 44 32 13 02 1
67 33 57 21 3 50 35 16 06 1 58 26 40 12 2 44 30 13 02 1
77 28 67 20 3 63 27 49 18 3 47 32 16 02 1 55 26 44 12 2
50 23 33 10 2 72 32 60 18 3 48 30 14 03 1 51 38 16 02 1
61 30 49 18 3 48 34 19 02 1 50 30 16 02 1 50 32 12 02 1
61 26 56 14 3 64 28 56 21 3 43 30 11 01 1 58 40 12 02 1
51 38 19 04 1 67 31 44 14 2 62 28 48 18 3 49 30 14 02 1
51 35 14 02 1 56 30 45 15 2 58 27 41 10 2 50 34 16 04 1
46 32 14 02 1 60 29 45 15 2 57 26 35 10 2 57 44 15 04 1
50 36 14 02 1 77 30 61 23 3 63 34 56 24 3 58 27 51 19 3
57 29 42 13 2 72 30 58 16 3 54 34 15 04 1 52 41 15 01 1
71 30 59 21 3 64 31 55 18 3 60 30 48 18 3 63 29 56 18 3
49 24 33 10 2 56 27 42 13 2 57 30 42 12 2 55 42 14 02 1
49 31 15 02 1 77 26 69 23 3 60 22 50 15 3 54 39 17 04 1
66 29 46 13 2 52 27 39 14 2 60 34 45 16 2 50 34 15 02 1
44 29 14 02 1 50 20 35 10 2 55 24 37 10 2 58 27 39 12 2
47 32 13 02 1 46 31 15 02 1 69 32 57 23 3 62 29 43 13 2
74 28 61 19 3 59 30 42 15 2 51 34 15 02 1 50 35 13 03 1
```

```
56 28 49 20 3 60 22 40 10 2 73 29 63 18 3 67 25 58 18 3
49 31 15 01 1 67 31 47 15 2 63 23 44 13 2 54 37 15 02 1
56 30 41 13 2 63 25 49 15 2 61 28 47 12 2 64 29 43 13 2
51 25 30 11 2 57 28 41 13 2 65 30 58 22 3 69 31 54 21 3
54 39 13 04 1 51 35 14 03 1 72 36 61 25 3 65 32 51 20 3
61 29 47 14 2 56 29 36 13 2 69 31 49 15 2 64 27 53 19 3
68 30 55 21 3 55 25 40 13 2 48 34 16 02 1 48 30 14 01 1
45 23 13 03 1 57 25 50 20 3 57 38 17 03 1 51 38 15 03 1
55 23 40 13 2 66 30 44 14 2 68 28 48 14 2 54 34 17 02 1
51 37 15 04 1 52 35 15 02 1 58 28 51 24 3 67 30 50 17 2
63 33 60 25 3 53 37 15 02 1
;
proc stepdisc data=iris bsscp tsscp;
   class species;
   var sepallen sepalwid petallen petalwid;
run;
```

Output 31.1   Iris Data: PROC STEPDISC

```
                           Fisher (1936) Iris Data                                     1

                          STEPWISE DISCRIMINANT ANALYSIS

            150 Observations           4 Variable(s) in the Analysis
              3 Class Levels           0 Variable(s) will be included

            The Method for Selecting Variables will be: STEPWISE

            Significance Level to Enter = 0.1500
            Significance Level to Stay  = 0.1500
                    ❶  Class Level Information

                    SPECIES      Frequency       Weight      Proportion

                    SETOSA          50          50.0000       0.333333
                    VERSICOLOR      50          50.0000       0.333333
                    VIRGINICA       50          50.0000       0.333333
```

```
                           Fisher (1936) Iris Data                                     2

                          STEPWISE DISCRIMINANT ANALYSIS
                    ❹  Between-Class SSCP Matrix

    Variable       SEPALLEN        SEPALWID        PETALLEN        PETALWID

    SEPALLEN      6321.21333     -1995.26667     16524.84000      7127.93333     Sepal Length in mm.
    SEPALWID     -1995.26667      1134.49333     -5723.96000     -2293.26667     Sepal Width  in mm.
    PETALLEN     16524.84000     -5723.96000     43710.28000     18677.40000     Petal Length in mm.
    PETALWID      7127.93333     -2293.26667     18677.40000      8041.33333     Petal Width  in mm.

                    ❺  Total-Sample SSCP Matrix

    Variable       SEPALLEN        SEPALWID        PETALLEN        PETALWID

    SEPALLEN     10216.83333      -632.26667     18987.30000      7692.43333     Sepal Length in mm.
    SEPALWID      -632.26667      2830.69333     -4911.88000     -1812.42667     Sepal Width  in mm.
    PETALLEN     18987.30000     -4911.88000     46432.54000     19304.58000     Petal Length in mm.
    PETALWID      7692.43333     -1812.42667     19304.58000      8656.99333     Petal Width  in mm.
```

```
                              Fisher (1936) Iris Data                               3
                          STEPWISE DISCRIMINANT ANALYSIS

Stepwise Selection:  Step 1

                                Statistics for Entry, DF = 2, 147
                      ⑰                                        ⑱       ⑲
           Variable   R**2        F        Prob > F    Tolerance    Label

           SEPALLEN   0.6187    119.265      0.0001      1.0000    Sepal Length in mm.
           SEPALWID   0.4008     49.160      0.0001      1.0000    Sepal Width  in mm.
           PETALLEN   0.9414   1180.161      0.0001      1.0000    Petal Length in mm.
           PETALWID   0.9289    960.007      0.0001      1.0000    Petal Width  in mm.
                      ⑳  Variable PETALLEN will be entered

                  ㉑ The following variable(s) have been entered:
                                      PETALLEN

                              Multivariate Statistics

              ㉒  Wilks' Lambda  = 0.05862828    F( 2, 147) = 1180.161    Prob > F = 0.0001
              ㉓  Pillai's Trace =  0.941372     F( 2, 147) = 1180.161    Prob > F = 0.0001

                  ㉔ Average Squared Canonical Correlation = 0.47068586
--------------------------------------------------------------------------------------------
Stepwise Selection:  Step 2
                                Statistics for Removal,  DF = 2, 147

              Variable   R**2        F        Prob > F    Label

              PETALLEN   0.9414   1180.161     0.0001    Petal Length in mm.


                           No variables can be removed

                           --------------------------

                           Statistics for Entry, DF = 2, 146

                        Partial
           Variable     R**2         F        Prob > F    Tolerance    Label

           SEPALLEN    0.3198     34.323      0.0001      0.2400    Sepal Length in mm.
           SEPALWID    0.3709     43.035      0.0001      0.8164    Sepal Width  in mm.
           PETALWID    0.2533     24.766      0.0001      0.0729    Petal Width  in mm.

                         Variable SEPALWID will be entered

                     The following variable(s) have been entered:
                              SEPALWID PETALLEN
```

```
                              Fisher (1936) Iris Data                               4
                          STEPWISE DISCRIMINANT ANALYSIS

Stepwise Selection:  Step 2
                              Multivariate Statistics

              Wilks' Lambda  = 0.03688411    F( 4, 292) =  307.105    Prob > F = 0.0001
              Pillai's Trace =  1.119908     F( 4, 294) =   93.528    Prob > F = 0.0001

                  Average Squared Canonical Correlation = 0.55995394
--------------------------------------------------------------------------------------------
Stepwise Selection:  Step 3
                                Statistics for Removal,  DF = 2, 146

                        Partial
              Variable   R**2         F        Prob > F    Label

              SEPALWID   0.3709     43.035      0.0001    Sepal Width  in mm.
              PETALLEN   0.9384   1112.954      0.0001    Petal Length in mm.

                           No variables can be removed

                           --------------------------
```

(continued on next page)

(continued from previous page)

```
                          Statistics for Entry, DF = 2, 145

                        Partial
           Variable      R**2         F        Prob > F    Tolerance    Label

           SEPALLEN      0.1447      12.268      0.0001      0.1323      Sepal Length in mm.
           PETALWID      0.3229      34.569      0.0001      0.0662      Petal Width  in mm.

                          Variable PETALWID will be entered

                  The following variable(s) have been entered:
                         SEPALWID PETALLEN PETALWID

                            Multivariate Statistics

          Wilks' Lambda  = 0.02497554     F( 6, 290) = 257.503     Prob > F = 0.0001
          Pillai's Trace =  1.189914      F( 6, 292) =  71.485     Prob > F = 0.0001

                 Average Squared Canonical Correlation = 0.59495691
```

```
                            Fisher (1936) Iris Data                              5
                          STEPWISE DISCRIMINANT ANALYSIS

Stepwise Selection:  Step 4

                          Statistics for Removal,  DF = 2, 145

                        Partial
           Variable      R**2         F        Prob > F    Label

           SEPALWID      0.4295      54.577      0.0001     Sepal Width  in mm.
           PETALLEN      0.3482      38.724      0.0001     Petal Length in mm.
           PETALWID      0.3229      34.569      0.0001     Petal Width  in mm.


                          No variables can be removed

                    ---------------------------

                          Statistics for Entry, DF = 2, 144

                        Partial
           Variable      R**2         F        Prob > F    Tolerance    Label

           SEPALLEN      0.0615      4.721       0.0103      0.0320      Sepal Length in mm.

                          Variable SEPALLEN will be entered

                        All variables have been entered

                            Multivariate Statistics

          Wilks' Lambda  = 0.02343863     F( 8, 288) = 199.145     Prob > F = 0.0001
          Pillai's Trace =  1.191899      F( 8, 290) =  53.466     Prob > F = 0.0001

                 Average Squared Canonical Correlation = 0.59594941
----------------------------------------------------------------------------------------------

Stepwise Selection:  Step 5

                          Statistics for Removal,  DF = 2, 144

                        Partial
           Variable      R**2         F        Prob > F    Label

           SEPALLEN      0.0615      4.721       0.0103     Sepal Length in mm.
           SEPALWID      0.2335     21.936       0.0001     Sepal Width  in mm.
           PETALLEN      0.3308     35.590       0.0001     Petal Length in mm.
           PETALWID      0.2570     24.904       0.0001     Petal Width  in mm.

                          No variables can be removed

No further steps are possible
```

```
                        Fisher (1936) Iris Data                                    6

                     STEPWISE DISCRIMINANT ANALYSIS

Stepwise Selection:  Summary ㉕

                Variable          Number   Partial      F        Prob >        Wilks'      Prob <
   Step    Entered    Removed       In      R**2     Statistic     F          Lambda      Lambda
   ------------------------------------------------------------------------------------------------
     1     PETALLEN                  1      0.9414    1180.161    0.0001      0.05862828    0.0001
     2     SEPALWID                  2      0.3709      43.035    0.0001      0.03688411    0.0001
     3     PETALWID                  3      0.3229      34.569    0.0001      0.02497554    0.0001
     4     SEPALLEN                  4      0.0615       4.721    0.0103      0.02343863    0.0001


                                            Average
                                            Squared
                Variable          Number   Canonical    Prob >
   Step    Entered    Removed       In     Correlation   ASCC     Label
   ------------------------------------------------------------------------------------------------
     1     PETALLEN                  1      0.47068586   0.0001    Petal Length in mm.
     2     SEPALWID                  2      0.55995394   0.0001    Sepal Width  in mm.
     3     PETALWID                  3      0.59495691   0.0001    Petal Width  in mm.
     4     SEPALLEN                  4      0.59594941   0.0001    Sepal Length in mm.
```

REFERENCES

Costanza, M.C. and Afifi, A.A. (1979), "Comparison of Stopping Rules in Forward Stepwise Discriminant Analysis," *Journal of the American Statistical Association*, 74, 777–785.

Fisher, R.A. (1936), "The Use of Multiple Measurements in Taxonomic Problems," *Annals of Eugenics*, 7, 179–188.

Jennrich, R.I. (1977), "Stepwise Discriminant Analysis," in *Statistical Methods for Digital Computers*, eds. K. Enslein, A. Ralston, and H. Wilf, New York: John Wiley & Sons, Inc.

Klecka, W.R. (1980), *Discriminant Analysis*, Sage University Paper Series on Quantitative Applications in the Social Sciences, Series No. 07-019, Beverly Hills: Sage Publications.

Rencher, A.C. and Larson, S.F. (1980), "Bias in Wilks's Λ in Stepwise Discriminant Analysis," *Technometrics*, 22, 349–356.

Chapter 32
The TREE
Procedure

ABSTRACT

The TREE procedure prints a tree diagram, also known as a dendrogram or pheno-gram, using a data set created by the CLUSTER or VARCLUS procedure. PROC TREE can also create an output data set identifying disjoint clusters at a specified level in the tree.

INTRODUCTION

The CLUSTER and VARCLUS procedures create output data sets giving the results of hierarchical clustering as a tree structure. The TREE procedure uses the output data set to print a diagram of the tree structure in the style of Johnson (1967), with the root at the top. Alternatively, the diagram can be oriented horizontally, with the root at the left. Any numeric variable in the output data set can be used to specify the heights of the clusters. PROC TREE can also create an output data set containing a variable to indicate the disjoint clusters at a specified level in the tree.

Trees are discussed in the context of cluster analysis by Duran and Odell (1974), Hartigan (1975), and Everitt (1980). Knuth (1973) provides a general treatment of trees in computer programming.

The literature on trees contains a mixture of botanical and genealogical terminology. The objects that are clustered are *leaves*. The cluster containing all objects is the *root*. A cluster containing at least two objects but not all of them is a *branch*. The general term for leaves, branches, and roots is *node*. If a cluster A is the union of clusters B and C, then A is the *parent* of B and C, and B and C are *children* of A. A leaf is thus a node with no children, and a root is a node with no parent. If every cluster has at most two children, the tree is a *binary tree*. The CLUSTER procedure always produces binary trees. The VARCLUS procedure can produce trees with clusters that have many children.

SPECIFICATIONS

The TREE procedure is invoked by the following statements:

> **PROC TREE** *options*;
>   **NAME** *variable*;
>   **HEIGHT** *variable*;
>   **PARENT** *variable*;
>   **BY** *variables*;
>   **COPY** *variables*;
>   **FREQ** *variable*;
>   **ID** *variable*;

If the input data set has been created by CLUSTER or VARCLUS, the only statement required is the PROC TREE statement. The BY, COPY, FREQ, HEIGHT, ID, NAME, and PARENT statements are described after the PROC TREE statement.

PROC TREE Statement

> PROC TREE *options*;

The following options can appear in the PROC TREE statement.

Data Set Options

DATA=*SASdataset*
> names the input data set defining the tree. If the DATA= option is omitted, the most recently created SAS data set is used.

DOCK=*n*
> in the OUT= data set, causes observations assigned to output clusters with a frequency of *n* or less to be given missing values for the output variables CLUSTER and CLUSNAME. If the NCLUSTERS= option is also specified, DOCK= also prevents clusters with a frequency of *n* or less from being counted toward the number of clusters requested by the NCLUSTERS= option. The default is DOCK=0.

LEVEL=*n*
> for the OUT= data set, specifies the level of the tree defining disjoint clusters. The LEVEL= option also causes only clusters between the root and a height of *n* to be printed. The clusters in the output data set are those that exist at a height of *n* on the tree diagram. For example, if the

HEIGHT variable is _NCL_ (number of clusters) and LEVEL=5 is specified, then the OUT= data set contains 5 disjoint clusters. If the HEIGHT variable is _RSQ_ (R^2) and LEVEL=0.9 is specified, then the OUT= data set contains the smallest number of clusters that yields an R^2 of at least 0.9.

NCLUSTERS=*n*
NCL=*n*
N=*n*
    specifies the number of clusters desired in the OUT= data set. The number of clusters obtained may not equal the number specified if (1) there are fewer than *n* leaves in the tree, (2) there are more than *n* unconnected trees in the data set, (3) a multi-way tree does not contain a level with the specified number of clusters, or (4) the DOCK= option eliminates too many clusters.

    The NCLUSTERS= option uses the _NCL_ variable to determine the order in which the clusters were formed. If there is no _NCL_ variable, the height variable (as determined by the HEIGHT statement or HEIGHT= option) is used instead.

OUT=*SASdataset*
    names an output data set that contains one observation for each object in the tree or subtree being processed and variables called CLUSTER and CLUSNAME showing cluster membership at any specified level in the tree. If the OUT= option is used, then either NCLUSTERS= or LEVEL= must be specified to define the output partition level. If you want to create a permanent SAS data set you must specify a two-level name (see "SAS Files" in the *SAS Language Guide, Release 6.03 Edition*).

ROOT='*name*'
    specifies the value of the NAME variable for the root of a subtree to be printed if you do not want to print the entire tree. If the OUT= option is also specified, the output data set contains only objects belonging to the subtree specified by the ROOT= option.

Options for the Variable to Specify Cluster Heights

For many situations, the only option you will need is the HEIGHT option below:

HEIGHT | H=*name*
    specifies certain conventional variables to be used for the height axis of the tree diagram. Valid values for *name* and their meanings are

HEIGHT	H	specifies the _HEIGHT_ variable.
LENGTH	L	causes the height of each node to be defined as its path length from the root. This can also be interpreted as the number of ancestors of the node.
MODE	M	specifies the _MODE_ variable.
NCL	N	specifies the _NCL_ variable.
RSQ	R	specifies the _RSQ_ variable.

    See also the HEIGHT statement, which can specify any variable in the input data set to be used for the height axis. In rare cases, you may need to use one of these two options:

DISSIMILAR
DIS

   implies that the values of the HEIGHT variable are dissimilarities; that is,
   a large height value means that the clusters are very dissimilar or far
   apart.

SIMILAR
SIM

   implies that the values of the HEIGHT variable are similarities; that is, a
   large height value means that the clusters are very similar or close
   together.

If neither the SIMILAR nor the DISSIMILAR option is specified, TREE attempts
to infer from the data whether the height values are similarities or dissimilarities.
If TREE cannot tell this from the data, it issues an error message and does not print
a tree diagram.

Option to Print Horizontal Trees

HORIZONTAL
HOR

   causes the tree diagram to be oriented with the height axis horizontal
   and the root at the left. If this option is not used, the height axis will be
   vertical, with the root at the top. If the tree takes up more than one
   page and will be viewed on a screen, horizontal orientation can make
   the tree diagram considerably easier to read.

Options Controlling the Height Axis

INC=n

   specifies the increment between tick values on the height axis. If the
   HEIGHT variable is _NCL_, the default is usually 1, although a different
   value can be used for consistency with other options. For any other
   HEIGHT variable, the default is some power of 10 times 1, 2, 2.5, or 5.

MAXHEIGHT=n
MAXH=n

   specifies the maximum value printed on the height axis.

MINHEIGHT=n
MINH=n

   specifies the minimum value printed on the height axis.

NTICK=n

   specifies the number of tick intervals on the height axis. The default
   depends on the values of other options.

PAGES=n

   specifies the number of pages over which the tree diagram (from root to
   leaves) is to extend. The default is chosen to make the diagram
   approximately square.

POS=n

   specifies the number of print positions on the height axis. The default
   depends on the value of the PAGES= option, the orientation of the tree
   diagram, and the values specified by the PAGESIZE= and LINESIZE=
   options.

SPACES=*s*
S=*s*

specifies the number of spaces between objects on the printout. The default depends on the number of objects, the orientation of the tree diagram, and the values specified by the PAGESIZE= and LINESIZE= options.

TICKPOS=*n*

specifies the number of print positions per tick interval on the height axis. The default value is usually between 5 and 10, although a different value may be used for consistency with other options.

Options to Control Characters Printed in Trees

FILLCHAR='*c*'
FC='*c*'

specifies the character to print between leaves that have not been joined into a cluster. The character should be enclosed in single quotes. The default is a blank.

JOINCHAR='*c*'
JC='*c*'

specifies the character to print between leaves that have been joined into a cluster. The character should be enclosed in single quotes. The default is X.

LEAFCHAR='*c*'
LC='*c*'

specifies a character to represent clusters having no children. The character should be enclosed in single quotes. The default is a period.

TREECHAR='*c*'
TC='*c*'

specifies a character to represent clusters with children. The character should be enclosed in single quotes. The default is X.

Miscellaneous Options

DESCENDING
DES

reverses the sorting order for the SORT option.

LIST

lists all the nodes in the tree, printing the height, parent, and children of each node.

NOPRINT

suppresses printing the tree if you only want to create an OUT= data set.

SORT

sorts the children of each node by the HEIGHT variable, in the order of cluster formation.

BY Statement

BY *variables*;

A BY statement can be used with PROC TREE to obtain separate analyses on observations in groups defined by the BY variables. When a BY statement appears, the procedure expects the input data set to be sorted in order of the BY variables.

If your input data set is not sorted in ascending order, use the SORT procedure with a similar BY statement to sort the data, or, if appropriate, use the BY statement options NOTSORTED or DESCENDING. For more information, see the discussion of the BY statement in "SAS Statements Used in the PROC Step" in the *SAS Language Guide*.

COPY Statement

COPY *variables*;

The COPY statement lists one or more character or numeric variables to be copied to the OUT= data set.

FREQ Statement

FREQ *variable*;

The FREQ statement lists one numeric variable that tells how many clustering observations belong to the cluster. If the FREQ statement is omitted, TREE looks for a variable called _FREQ_ to specify the number of observations per cluster. If neither the FREQ statement nor the _FREQ_ variable is present, each leaf is assumed to represent one clustering observation, and the frequency for each internal node is found by summing the frequencies of its children.

HEIGHT Statement

HEIGHT *variable*;

The HEIGHT statement specifies the name of a numeric variable to define the height of each node (cluster) in the tree. The height variable can also be specified by the HEIGHT= option in the PROC TREE statement. If both the HEIGHT statement and the HEIGHT= option are omitted, TREE looks for a variable called _HEIGHT_. If the data set does not contain _HEIGHT_, TREE looks for a variable called _NCL_. If _NCL_ is not found either, the height of each node is defined to be its path length from the root.

ID Statement

ID *variable*;

The ID variable is used to identify the objects (leaves) in the tree on the printout. The ID variable can be a character or numeric variable of any length. If the ID statement is omitted, the variable in the NAME statement is used instead. If both ID and NAME are omitted, TREE looks for a variable called _NAME_. If the _NAME_ variable is not found in the data set, TREE issues an error message and stops. The ID variable is copied to the OUT= data set.

NAME Statement

NAME *variable*;

The NAME statement specifies a character or numeric variable identifying the node represented by each observation. The NAME variable and PARENT variable jointly define the tree structure. If the NAME statement is omitted, TREE looks for a variable called _NAME_. If the _NAME_ variable is not found in the data set, TREE issues an error message and stops.

PARENT Statement

PARENT *variable*;

The PARENT statement specifies a character or numeric variable identifying the node in the tree that is the parent of each observation. The PARENT variable must have the same formatted length as the NAME variable. If the PARENT statement is omitted, TREE looks for a variable called _PARENT_. If the _PARENT_ variable is not found in the data set, TREE issues an error message and stops.

DETAILS

Missing Values

An observation with a missing value for the NAME variable is omitted from processing. If the PARENT variable has a missing value but the NAME variable is present, the observation is treated as the root of a tree. A data set can contain several roots and, hence, several trees.

Missing values of the HEIGHT variable are set to upper or lower bounds determined from the nonmissing values under the assumption that the heights are monotonic with respect to the tree structure.

Missing values of the FREQ variable are inferred from nonmissing values where possible; otherwise, they are treated as zero.

Output Data Set

The OUT= data set contains one observation for each leaf in the tree or subtree being processed. The variables are

- the BY variables, if any.
- the ID variable, or the NAME variable if the ID statement is not used.
- the COPY variables.
- a numeric variable CLUSTER taking values from 1 to c, where c is the number of disjoint clusters. The cluster to which the first observation belongs is given the number 1, the cluster to which the next observation belongs that does not belong to cluster 1 is given the number 2, and so on.
- a character variable CLUSNAME giving the value of the NAME variable of the cluster to which the observation belongs.

The CLUSTER and CLUSNAME variables are missing if the corresponding leaf has a nonpositive frequency.

Printed Output

The printed output from the TREE procedure includes the following:

1. the names of the objects in the tree.
2. the height axis.
3. the tree diagram. The root (the cluster containing all the objects) is indicated by a solid line of the character specified by TREECHAR= (the default character is X). At each level of the tree, clusters are shown by unbroken lines of the TREECHAR= symbol with the FILLCHAR= symbol (the default is a blank) separating the clusters. The LEAFCHAR= symbol (the default character is a period) represents single-member clusters.

By default, the tree diagram is oriented with the height axis vertical and the object names at the top of the diagram. If the HORIZONTAL option is used, then the height axis is horizontal and the object names are on the left.

EXAMPLES

Example 1: Mammals' Teeth

The data below give the numbers of different kinds of teeth for a variety of mammals. The mammals are clustered by average linkage using PROC CLUSTER. The first PROC TREE uses the average-linkage distance as the height axis, which is the default. The second PROC TREE sorts the clusters at each branch in order of formation and uses the number of clusters for the height axis. The third PROC TREE produces no printed output but creates an output data set indicating the cluster to which each observation belongs at the 6-cluster level in the tree; this data set is reproduced by PROC PRINT. The following statements produce **Output 32.1** through **Output 32.4**:

```
data teeth;
    title 'MAMMALS'' TEETH';
    input mammal $ 1-16 @21 (v1-v8) (1.);
    label V1='TOP INCISORS'
          V2='BOTTOM INCISORS'
          V3='TOP CANINES'
          V4='BOTTOM CANINES'
          V5='TOP PREMOLARS'
          V6='BOTTOM PREMOLARS'
          V7='TOP MOLARS'
          V8='BOTTOM MOLARS';
    cards;
BROWN BAT           23113333
MOLE                32103333
SILVER HAIR BAT     23112333
PIGMY BAT           23112233
HOUSE BAT           23111233
RED BAT             13112233
PIKA                21002233
RABBIT              21003233
BEAVER              11002133
GROUNDHOG           11002133
GRAY SQUIRREL       11001133
HOUSE MOUSE         11000033
PORCUPINE           11001133
WOLF                33114423
BEAR                33114423
RACCOON             33114432
MARTEN              33114412
WEASEL              33113312
WOLVERINE           33114412
BADGER              33113312
RIVER OTTER         33114312
SEA OTTER           32113312
JAGUAR              33113211
COUGAR              33113211
FUR SEAL            32114411
```

```
SEA LION          32114411
GREY SEAL         32113322
ELEPHANT SEAL     21114411
REINDEER          04103333
ELK               04103333
DEER              04003333
MOOSE             04003333
;
options pagesize=60 linesize=110;

proc cluster method=average std pseudo noeigen outtree=tree;
    id mammal;
    var v1-v8;

proc tree;

proc tree sort height=n;

proc tree noprint out=part nclusters=6;
    id mammal;
    copy v1-v8;

proc sort;
    by cluster;

proc print uniform;
    id mammal;
    var v1-v8;
    format v1-v8 1.;
    by cluster;
run;
```

Output 32.1   Clustering of Mammals: PROC CLUSTER

```
                              MAMMALS' TEETH                                              1

                        Average Linkage Cluster Analysis

              The data have been standardized to mean 0 and variance 1
              Root-Mean-Square Total-Sample Standard Deviation =       1
              Root-Mean-Square Distance Between Observations   =       4
```

Number of Clusters	Clusters Joined		Frequency of New Cluster	Pseudo F	Pseudo t**2	Normalized RMS Distance	Tie
31	BEAVER	GROUNDHOG	2	.	.	0.000000	T
30	GRAY SQUIRREL	PORCUPINE	2	.	.	0.000000	T
29	WOLF	BEAR	2	.	.	0.000000	T
28	MARTEN	WOLVERINE	2	.	.	0.000000	T
27	WEASEL	BADGER	2	.	.	0.000000	T
26	JAGUAR	COUGAR	2	.	.	0.000000	T
25	FUR SEAL	SEA LION	2	.	.	0.000000	T
24	REINDEER	ELK	2	.	.	0.0000.3	T
23	DEER	MOOSE	2	.	.	0.000000	
22	PIGMY BAT	RED BAT	2	281.19	.	0.228930	
21	CL28	RIVER OTTER	3	138.67	.	0.229221	
20	CL31	CL30	4	83.19	.	0.235702	T
19	BROWN BAT	SILVER HAIR BAT	2	76.71	.	0.235702	T
18	PIKA	RABBIT	2	73.24	.	0.235702	
17	CL27	SEA OTTER	3	67.37	.	0.246183	
16	CL22	HOUSE BAT	3	62.89	1.75	0.285937	

(continued on next page)

(continued from previous page)

15	CL21	CL17	6	47.42	6.81	0.332845
14	CL25	ELEPHANT SEAL	3	45.04	.	0.336177
13	CL19	CL16	5	40.83	3.50	0.367188
12	CL15	GREY SEAL	7	38.90	2.78	0.407838
11	CL29	RACCOON	3	38.02	.	0.422997
10	CL18	CL20	6	34.51	10.27	0.433918
9	CL12	CL26	9	30.01	7.27	0.507122
8	CL24	CL23	4	28.69	.	0.547281
7	CL9	CL14	12	25.74	6.99	0.566841
6	CL10	HOUSE MOUSE	7	28.32	4.12	0.579239
5	CL11	CL7	15	26.83	6.87	0.662106
4	CL13	MOLE	6	31.93	7.23	0.715610
3	CL4	CL8	10	30.98	12.67	0.879851
2	CL3	CL6	17	27.83	16.12	1.031622
1	CL2	CL5	32	.	27.83	1.193815

Output 32.2   Clustering of Mammals: PROC TREE

```
                                         MAMMALS' TEETH                                           2

                                   Average Linkage Cluster Analysis

                                   Name of Observation or Cluster

                 S                                                                              E
                 I                                                                              L
                 L                                 G                                            E
                 V                                 R           H                                P
                 E                                 A           O                R               H
        B     P     H           R                  Y    P      U                I            F  A
     ❶  R  H  I  O           R                  G  S  O  S     W  R          S  G         S  U  N
        O  A  G  U           E               G  R  Q  R  E     O  I       W  E  R      J  E  R  T
        W  I  M  S        M  I           M  A  O  U  B  U  M  R  L  V   W  A  O  A  G  C  L  E  S
        N  R  E  E     D  N        D  O  P  B  A  U  I  N  O  O  A  E  B  C  R  T  E  U  O  L  A  E
           Y  D        E  D     E  E  E  I  B  D  C  E  F  R  N  E  R  A  C  N  E  U  S  I  R  A  A
        B  B  B  B  M  O  D  E  O  P  E  I  V  H  R  I  P  S  E  E  R  L  R  L  R  L  N  O  I  N  L
        A  A  A  A  O  E  R  K  R  E  A  T  R  G  L  E  E  F  R  N  N  E  R  T  E  R  L  A  O  N  E
        T  T  T  T  L  R  K  R  E  A  T  R  G  L  E  E  F  R  N  N  E  R  T  E  R  L  A  O  N  E  L
   1.2 +XXXXXXXXXXXXXXXXXXXXXXXXXXXXXXXXXXXXXXXXXXXXX XXXXXXXXXXXXXXXXXXXXXXXXXXXXXXXXXXXXXXXXXXXXX
       |XXXXXXXXXXXXXXXXXXXXXXXXXXXXXXXXXXXXXXXXXXX  XXXXXXXXXXXXXXXXXXXXXXXXXXXXXXXXXXXXXXXXXXXXX
A      |XXXXXXXXXXXXXXXXXXXXXXXXXXXXXXXXXXXXXXXXXXX  XXXXXXXXXXXXXXXXXXXXXXXXXXXXXXXXXXXXXXXXXXXXX
v      |XXXXXXXXXXXXXXXXXXXXXXXXXXXXXXXXXXXXXXXXXXX  XXXXXXXXXXXXXXXXXXXXXXXXXXXXXXXXXXXXXXXXXXXXX
e      |XXXXXXXXXXXXXXXXXXXXXXXXXXXXXXXXXXXXXXXXXXX  XXXXXXXXXXXXXXXXXXXXXXXXXXXXXXXXXXXXXXXXXXXXX
r      |XXXXXXXXXXXXXXXXXXXXXXXXXXXXXXXXXXXXXXXXXXX  XXXXXXXXXXXXXXXXXXXXXXXXXXXXXXXXXXXXXXXXXXXXX
a   ❷  |XXXXXXXXXXXXXXXXXXXXXXXXXXXXXXXXXXXXXXXXXXX  XXXXXXXXXXXXXXXXXXXXXXXXXXXXXXXXXXXXXXXXXXXXX ❸
g    1 +XXXXXXXXXXXXXXXXXXXXXXXXX XXXXXXXXXXXXXXXXX  XXXXXXXXXXXXXXXXXXXXXXXXXXXXXXXXXXXXXXXXXXXXX
e      |XXXXXXXXXXXXXXXXXXXXXXXXX XXXXXXXXXXXXXXXXX  XXXXXXXXXXXXXXXXXXXXXXXXXXXXXXXXXXXXXXXXXXXXX
       |XXXXXXXXXXXXXXXXXXXXXXXXX XXXXXXXXXXXXXXXXX  XXXXXXXXXXXXXXXXXXXXXXXXXXXXXXXXXXXXXXXXXXXXX
D      |XXXXXXXXXXXXXXXXXXXXXXXXX XXXXXXXXXXXXXXXXX  XXXXXXXXXXXXXXXXXXXXXXXXXXXXXXXXXXXXXXXXXXXXX
i      |XXXXXXXXXXXXXXXXXXXXXXXXX XXXXXXXXXXXXXXXXX  XXXXXXXXXXXXXXXXXXXXXXXXXXXXXXXXXXXXXXXXXXXXX
s  0.8 +XXXXXXXXXXXXXXXXXX XXXXXX XXXXXXXXXXXXXXXXX  XXXXXXXXXXXXXXXXXXXXXXXXXXXXXXXXXXXXXXXXXXXXX
t      |XXXXXXXXXXXXXXXXXX XXXXXX XXXXXXXXXXXXXXXXX  XXXXXXXXXXXXXXXXXXXXXXXXXXXXXXXXXXXXXXXXXXXXX
a      |XXXXXXXXXXXXXXXXXX XXXXXX XXXXXXXXXXXXXXXXX  XXXXXXXXXXXXXXXXXXXXXXXXXXXXXXXXXXXXXXXXXXXXX
n      |XXXXXXXXXXXXXXXXXX XXXXXX XXXXXXXXXXXXXXXXX  XXXXXXXXXXXXXXXXXXXXXXXXXXXXXXXXXXXXXXXXXXXXX
c      |XXXXXXXXXXXX    .  XXXXXX XXXXXXXXXXXXXXXXX  XXXXXXXXXXXXXXXXXXXXXXXXXXXXXXXXXXXXXXXXXXXXX
e      |XXXXXXXXXXXX    .  XXXXXX XXXXXXXXXXXXXXXXX  XXXXXXX XXXXXXXXXXXXXXXXXXXXXXXXXXXXXXXXXXXXXX
  0.6  +XXXXXXXXXXXX    .  XXXXXX XXXXXXXXXXXXXXXXX  XXXXXXX XXXXXXXXXXXXXXXXXXXXXXXXXXXXXXXXXXXXXX
b      |XXXXXXXXXXXX    .  XXXXXX XXXXXXXXXXXXXXXXX  XXXXXXX XXXXXXXXXXXXXXXXXXXXXXXXXXXXXXXXXXXXXX
e      |XXXXXXXXXXXX    .  XXXXXX XXXXXXXXXXXXXXXXX  XXXXXXX XXXXXXXXXXXXXXXXXXXXXXXXXXXXX XXXXXXXX
t      |XXXXXXXXXXXX    .  XXXX  XXXX XXXXXXXXXXXXX  XXXXXXX XXXXXXXXXXXXXXXXXXXXXXXXXXXXX XXXXXXXX
w      |XXXXXXXXXXXX    .  XXXX  XXXX XXXXXXXXXXXXX  XXXX . XXXXXXXXXXXXXXXXXXXXXXXXX XXXX XXXXXXXX
  0.4  +XXXXXXXXXXXX    .  XXXX  XXXX  XXXX XXXXXXX  XXXX . XXXXXXXXXXXXXXXXXXXXXXXXX XXXX XXXXXXXX
e      |XXXXXXXXXXXX    .  XXXX  XXXX  XXXX XXXXXXX  XXXX . XXXXXXXXXXXXXXXXXXXXXXXXX XXXX XXXXXXXX
e      | XXXX XXXXXX    .  XXXX  XXXX  XXXX XXXXXXX  XXXX . XXXXXXXXXXXXXXXXX XXXXXXX XXXX XXXXXXXX
n      | XXXX XXXXXX    .  XXXX  XXXX  XXXX XXXXXXX  XXXX . XXXXXXX XXXXXXX . XXXX XXXX XXXX
       | XXXX XXXX  .      XXXX  XXXX  XXXX XXXXXXX  XXXX . XXXXXXX XXXXXXX . XXXX XXXX XXXX
C  0.2 +.   .   .  .      XXXX  XXXX  .  XXXX XXXX   XXXX .  XXXX . XXXX  .  XXXX XXXX
l      |.   .   .  .      XXXX  XXXX  .  XXXX XXXX   XXXX .  XXXX . XXXX  .  XXXX XXXX
u      |.   .   .  .      XXXX  XXXX  .  XXXX XXXX   XXXX .  XXXX . XXXX  .  XXXX XXXX
s      |.   .   .  .      XXXX  XXXX  .  XXXX XXXX   XXXX .  XXXX . XXXX  .  XXXX XXXX
t      |.   .   .  .      XXXX  XXXX  .  XXXX XXXX   XXXX .  XXXX . XXXX  .  XXXX XXXX
e      |.   .   .  .      XXXX  XXXX  .  XXXX XXXX   XXXX .  XXXX . XXXX  .  XXXX XXXX
r      |.   .   .  .      XXXX  XXXX  .  XXXX XXXX   XXXX .  XXXX . XXXX  .  XXXX XXXX
s    0 +.   .   .  .      XXXX  XXXX  .  XXXX XXXX   XXXX .  XXXX . XXXX  .  XXXX XXXX
```

Output 32.3 Clustering of Mammals: PROC TREE with SORT and HEIGHT= Options

```
                                          MAMMALS' TEETH                                          3

                                    Average Linkage Cluster Analysis

                                     Name of Observation or Cluster

                                                                                    S
                                                                                    I
                                                                                    L
                                                                                    V
                          E                                                         E
                          L                       R                 G               R
                          E                       I         H       R               B            H
                          P           G           V         O       A               R       H    O   P
                          H     F  S  R           E     W   U       Y               O       A    U   I
              R           A     U  E  E     J  C  Y     O   S    G  S               W   B    I    S   G   R
              A           N     R  A  Y     A  O        L   E    R  Q   P      R    N   R    R    E   M   E
              C     W  B  T     S  L  S     G  U  G  M  V   A  B  O  U   O   R  E    M   O    B    B   Y   D
              C     O  E  S  S  E  I  E  S  U  G  R  A  E   O  A  U  I   R   A  I    D   O  M  R    B   B   B
              O     O  A  E  S  A  O  A  E  A  A  E  R  R   T  D  N  R   C   B  N  D O  O  O  O    B   B   B
              O     L  A  A  E  L  N  A  I  R  R  Y  T  I   T  G  D  R   U   B  D  E O  S  L  W    B   B   B
              N     F  R  L  L  N  R  L  R  R  R  L  E  N   E  E  H  E   P   I  E  E M  E  E  N    T   T   T
   Number  1  +XXXXXXXXXXXXXXXXXXXXXXXXXXXXXXXXXXXXXXXXXXXXXXXXXXXXXXXXXXXXXXXXXXXXXXXXXXXXXXXX
   of      2  +XXXXXXXXXXXXXXXXXXXXXXXXXXXXXXXXXXXXXXXXXX XXXXXXXXXXXXXXXXXX XXXXXXXXXXXXXXXXXXXX
   Clusters 3  +XXXXXXXXXXXXXXXXXXXXXXXXXXXXXXXXXXXXXXXXXX XXXXXXXXXXXXXXXXXX XXXXXXXXXXXXXXXXXXXX
            4  +XXXXXXXXXXXXXXXXXXXXXXXXXXXXXXXXXXXXXXXXXX XXXXXXXXXXXXXXXXXX XXXXXXXXXXXXXXXXXXXX
            5  +XXXXXXXXXXXXXXXXXXXXXXXXXXXXXXXXXXXXXXXXXX XXXXXXXXXXXXXXXXXX XXXXXXXXXXXXXXXXXXXX
            6  +XXXXXX XXXXXXXXXXXXXXXXXXXXXXXXXXXXXXXXXXX XXXXXXXXXXXXXXXXXX XXXXXXXXXX . XXXXXXXXXX
            7  +XXXXXX XXXXXXXXXXXXXXXXXXXXXXXXXXXXXXXXXXX .  XXXXXXXXXXXXXXXX XXXXXXXXXX . XXXXXXXXXX
N           8  +XXXXXX XXXXXX XXXXXXXXXXXXXXXXXXXXXXXXXXXX .  XXXXXXXXXXXXXXXX XXXXXXXXXX . XXXXXXXXXX
u           9  +XXXXXX XXXXXX XXXXXXXXXXXXXXXXXXXXXXXXXXXX .  XXXXXXXXXXXXXXXX XXXXXXXXXX . XXXXXXXXXX
m          10  +XXXXXX XXXXXX XXXX XXXXXXXXXXXXXXXXXXXXXXX .  XXXXXXXXXXXXXXXX XXXX  XXXX . XXXXXXXXXX
b          11  +XXXXXX XXXXXX XXXX XXXXXXXXXXXXXXXXXXXXXXX .  XXXXXXXXXX XXXX  XXXX  XXXX . XXXXXXXXXX
e          12  +.  XXXX XXXXXX XXXX XXXXXXXXXXXXXXXXXXXXXXX .  XXXXXXXXXX XXXX  XXXX  XXXX . XXXXXXXXXX
r          13  +.  XXXX XXXXXX XXXX .  XXXXXXXXXXXXXXXXXXXX .  XXXXXXXXXX XXXX  XXXX  XXXX . XXXXXXXXXX
           14  +.  XXXX XXXXXX XXXX .  XXXXXXXXXXXXXXXXXXXX .  XXXXXXXXXX XXXX  XXXX  XXXX  XXXXXXXXXX
o          15  +.  XXXX . XXXX XXXX .  XXXXXXXXXXXXXXXXXXXX .  XXXXXXXXXX XXXX  XXXX  XXXX . XXXX XXXXXXXX
f          16  +.  XXXX . XXXX XXXX .  XXXXXXXX XXXXXXXX   .  XXXXXXXXXX XXXX  XXXX  XXXX . XXXX XXXXXXXX
           17  +.  XXXX . XXXX XXXX .  XXXXXXXX XXXXXXXX   .  XXXXXXXXXX XXXX  XXXX  XXXX . XXXX .  XXXX
C          18  +.  XXXX . XXXX XXXX .  XXXXXXXX .  XXXX   .  XXXXXXXXXX XXXX  XXXX  XXXX . XXXX .  XXXX
l          19  +.  XXXX . XXXX XXXX .  XXXXXXXX .  XXXX   .  XXXXXXXXXX .  .  XXXX  XXXX . XXXX .  XXXX
u          20  +.  XXXX . XXXX XXXX .  XXXXXXXX .  XXXX   .  XXXXXXXXXX .  .  XXXX  XXXX . .  .  .  XXXX
s          21  +.  XXXX . XXXX XXXX .  XXXXXXXX .  XXXX   .  XXXX  XXXX .  .  XXXX  XXXX . .  .  .  XXXX
t          22  +.  XXXX . XXXX XXXX .  .  XXXX  .  XXXX   .  XXXX  XXXX .  .  XXXX  XXXX . .  .  .  XXXX
e          23  +.  XXXX . XXXX XXXX .  .  XXXX  .  XXXX   .  XXXX  XXXX .  .  XXXX  XXXX .
r          24  +.  XXXX . XXXX XXXX .  .  XXXX  .  XXXX   .  XXXX  XXXX .  .  XXXX
s          25  +.  XXXX . XXXX XXXX .  .  XXXX  .  XXXX   .  XXXX  XXXX .  .
           26  +.  XXXX . .  .  XXXX .  .  XXXX .  XXXX   .  XXXX  XXXX .  .
           27  +.  XXXX . .  .  .  .  .  XXXX   .  XXXX   .  XXXX  XXXX
           28  +.  XXXX . .  .  .  .  .  XXXX   .  .  .   .  XXXX  XXXX
           29  +.  XXXX . .  .  .  .  .  .  .   .  .  .   .  XXXX  XXXX
           30  +.  .  . .  .  .  .  .  .  .     .  .  .   .  XXXX  XXXX
           31  +.  .  . .  .  .  .  .  .  .     .  .  .   .  XXXX
           32  +.  .  . .  .  .  .  .  .  .     .  .  .   .  .
```

Output 32.4   Clustering of Mammals: PROC PRINT

```
                              MAMMALS' TEETH                                    4
----------------------------------- CLUSTER=1 ----------------------------------

              MAMMAL          V1  V2  V3  V4  V5  V6  V7  V8

              BEAVER           1   1   0   0   2   1   3   3
              GROUNDHOG        1   1   0   0   2   1   3   3
              GRAY SQUIRREL    1   1   0   0   1   1   3   3
              PORCUPINE        1   1   0   0   1   1   3   3
              PIKA             2   1   0   0   2   2   3   3
              RABBIT           2   1   0   0   3   2   3   3
              HOUSE MOUSE      1   1   0   0   0   0   3   3


----------------------------------- CLUSTER=2 ----------------------------------

              MAMMAL          V1  V2  V3  V4  V5  V6  V7  V8

              WOLF             3   3   1   1   4   4   2   3
              BEAR             3   3   1   1   4   4   2   3
              RACCOON          3   3   1   1   4   4   3   2


----------------------------------- CLUSTER=3 ----------------------------------

              MAMMAL          V1  V2  V3  V4  V5  V6  V7  V8

              MARTEN           3   3   1   1   4   4   1   2
              WOLVERINE        3   3   1   1   4   4   1   2
              WEASEL           3   3   1   1   3   3   1   2
              BADGER           3   3   1   1   3   3   1   2
              JAGUAR           3   3   1   1   3   2   1   1
              COUGAR           3   3   1   1   3   2   1   1
              FUR SEAL         3   2   1   1   4   4   1   1
              SEA LION         3   2   1   1   4   4   1   1
              RIVER OTTER      3   3   1   1   4   3   1   2
              SEA OTTER        3   2   1   1   3   3   1   2
              ELEPHANT SEAL    2   1   1   1   4   4   1   1
              GREY SEAL        3   2   1   1   3   3   2   2


----------------------------------- CLUSTER=4 ----------------------------------

              MAMMAL          V1  V2  V3  V4  V5  V6  V7  V8

              REINDEER         0   4   1   0   3   3   3   3
              ELK              0   4   1   0   3   3   3   3
              DEER             0   4   0   0   3   3   3   3
              MOOSE            0   4   0   0   3   3   3   3

----------------------------------- CLUSTER=5 ----------------------------------

              MAMMAL          V1  V2  V3  V4  V5  V6  V7  V8

              PIGMY BAT        2   3   1   1   2   2   3   3
              RED BAT          1   3   1   1   2   2   3   3
              BROWN BAT        2   3   1   1   3   3   3   3
              SILVER HAIR BAT  2   3   1   1   2   3   3   3
              HOUSE BAT        2   3   1   1   1   2   3   3

----------------------------------- CLUSTER=6 ----------------------------------

              MAMMAL          V1  V2  V3  V4  V5  V6  V7  V8

              MOLE             3   2   1   0   3   3   3   3
```

To see how the tree diagram is interpreted, consider the first tree diagram, at the level of the tick mark labeled 0.6. The five BATs are in a cluster indicated by an unbroken line of Xs. The next cluster is represented by a period because it contains only one mammal, MOLE. REINDEER, ELK, DEER, and MOOSE form the next cluster, indicated by Xs again. The mammals PIKA through HOUSE MOUSE are in the fourth cluster. WOLF, BEAR, and RACCOON form the fifth cluster, while the last cluster contains MARTEN through ELEPHANT SEAL. The same clusters can be seen at the 6-cluster level of the second tree diagram, although they appear in a different order.

Example 2: Iris Data

Fisher's (1936) iris data are clustered by *k*th-nearest-neighbor density linkage using the CLUSTER procedure with K=8. Observations are identified by species in the tree diagram, which is oriented with the height axis horizontal. The following statements produce **Output 32.5** and **Output 32.6**:

```
data iris;
   title 'FISHER''S IRIS DATA';
   input sepallen sepalwid petallen petalwid spec_no @@;
   if spec_no=1 then species='SETOSA    ';
   else if spec_no=2 then species='VERSICOLOR';
   else if spec_no=3 then species='VIRGINICA ';
   cards;
50 33 14 02 1 64 28 56 22 3 65 28 46 15 2 67 31 56 24 3
63 28 51 15 3 46 34 14 03 1 69 31 51 23 3 62 22 45 15 2
59 32 48 18 2 46 36 10 02 1 61 30 46 14 2 60 27 51 16 2
65 30 52 20 3 56 25 39 11 2 65 30 55 18 3 58 27 51 19 3
68 32 59 23 3 51 33 17 05 1 57 28 45 13 2 62 34 54 23 3
77 38 67 22 3 63 33 47 16 2 67 33 57 25 3 76 30 66 21 3
49 25 45 17 3 55 35 13 02 1 67 30 52 23 3 70 32 47 14 2
64 32 45 15 2 61 28 40 13 2 48 31 16 02 1 59 30 51 18 3
55 24 38 11 2 63 25 50 19 3 64 32 53 23 3 52 34 14 02 1
49 36 14 01 1 54 30 45 15 2 79 38 64 20 3 44 32 13 02 1
67 33 57 21 3 50 35 16 06 1 58 26 40 12 2 44 30 13 02 1
77 28 67 20 3 63 27 49 18 3 47 32 16 02 1 55 26 44 12 2
50 23 33 10 2 72 32 60 18 3 48 30 14 03 1 51 38 16 02 1
61 30 49 18 3 48 34 19 02 1 50 30 16 02 1 50 32 12 02 1
61 26 56 14 3 64 28 56 21 3 43 30 11 01 1 58 40 12 02 1
51 38 19 04 1 67 31 44 14 2 62 28 48 18 3 49 30 14 02 1
51 35 14 02 1 56 30 45 15 2 58 27 41 10 2 50 34 16 04 1
46 32 14 02 1 60 29 45 15 2 57 26 35 10 2 57 44 15 04 1
50 36 14 02 1 77 30 61 23 3 63 34 56 24 3 58 27 51 19 3
57 29 42 13 2 72 30 58 16 3 54 34 15 04 1 52 41 15 01 1
71 30 59 21 3 64 31 55 18 3 60 30 48 18 3 63 29 56 18 3
49 24 33 10 2 56 27 42 13 2 57 30 42 12 2 55 42 14 02 1
49 31 15 02 1 77 26 69 23 3 60 22 50 15 3 54 39 17 04 1
66 29 46 13 2 52 27 39 14 2 60 34 45 16 2 50 34 15 02 1
44 29 14 02 1 50 20 35 10 2 55 24 37 10 2 58 27 39 12 2
47 32 13 02 1 46 31 15 02 1 69 32 57 23 3 62 29 43 13 2
74 28 61 19 3 59 30 42 15 2 51 34 15 02 1 50 35 13 03 1
56 28 49 20 3 60 22 40 10 2 73 29 63 18 3 67 25 58 18 3
49 31 15 01 1 67 31 47 15 2 63 23 44 13 2 54 37 15 02 1
56 30 41 13 2 63 25 49 15 2 61 28 47 12 2 64 29 43 13 2
51 25 30 11 2 57 28 41 13 2 65 30 58 22 3 69 31 54 21 3
54 39 13 04 1 51 35 14 03 1 72 36 61 25 3 65 32 51 20 3
61 29 47 14 2 56 29 36 13 2 69 31 49 15 2 64 27 53 19 3
68 30 55 21 3 55 25 40 13 2 48 34 16 02 1 48 30 14 01 1
45 23 13 03 1 57 25 50 20 3 57 38 17 03 1 51 38 15 03 1
55 23 40 13 2 66 30 44 14 2 68 28 48 14 2 54 34 17 02 1
51 37 15 04 1 52 35 15 02 1 58 28 51 24 3 67 30 50 17 2
63 33 60 25 3 53 37 15 02 1
;
```

```
options pagesize=60 linesize=110;

proc cluster data=iris method=twostage print=10 k=8 noeigen;
   var sepallen sepalwid petallen petalwid;
   copy species;

proc tree horizontal pages=1;
   id species;
run;
```

Output 32.5   Fisher's Iris Data: PROC CLUSTER with METHOD=DENSITY

```
                            FISHER'S IRIS DATA                                    1

                      Two-Stage Density Linkage Clustering

                                    K = 8

                Root-Mean-Square Total-Sample Standard Deviation = 10.69224

                                                        Maximum Density
                                                        in Each Cluster
    Number                              Frequency
      of                                 of New      Fusion
    Clusters    Clusters Joined          Cluster     Density     Lesser    Greater
       10       CL11      OB98              48       3.457E-6    1.776E-6    0.0001
        9       CL13      OB24              46       3.364E-6    2.408E-6   0.000042
        8       OB25      CL10              49       3.241E-6    1.647E-6    0.0001
        7       CL8       OB121             50       3.105E-6    1.647E-6    0.0001
        6       CL9       OB45              47       1.695E-6    9.992E-7   0.000042
        5       CL6       OB39              48       1.285E-6    7.261E-7   0.000042
        4       CL5       OB21              49       1.164E-6    6.495E-7   0.000042
        3       CL4       OB90              50       8.585E-7    4.441E-7   0.000042

                      3 modal clusters have been formed.

                                                        Maximum Density
                                                        in Each Cluster
    Number                              Frequency
      of                                 of New      Fusion
    Clusters    Clusters Joined          Cluster     Density     Lesser    Greater

        2       CL3       CL7              100       0.000032   0.000042    0.0001
```

Output 32.6   Fisher's Iris Data: PROC TREE with HORIZONTAL Option

```
                              FISHER'S IRIS DATA                                    2

                          Two-Stage Density Linkage Clustering

                                Cluster Fusion Density

          0       0.0001    0.0002    0.0003    0.0004    0.0005    0.0006    0.0007    0.0008  0.0009
          +---------+---------+---------+---------+---------+---------+---------+---------+---------+
S  SETOSA XX..................................................................................
P         XX
E  SETOSA XXX.................................................................................
C         XXX
I  SETOSA XXX.................................................................................
E         XXX
S  SETOSA XXXX................................................................................
          XXXX
   SETOSA XXXX................................................................................
          XXXX
   SETOSA XXXXXX..............................................................................
          XXXXXX
   SETOSA XXXXXX..............................................................................
          XXXXXX
   SETOSA XXXXXX..............................................................................
          XXXXXX
   SETOSA XXXXXX..............................................................................
          XXXXXX
   SETOSA XXXXXXX.............................................................................
          XXXXXXX
   SETOSA XXXXXXXXXXX.........................................................................
          XXXXXXXXXXX
   SETOSA XXXXXXXXXXX.........................................................................
          XXXXXXXXXXX
   SETOSA XXXXXXXXXXX.........................................................................
          XXXXXXXXXXX
   SETOSA XXXXXXXXXXXX........................................................................
          XXXXXXXXXXXX
   SETOSA XXXXXXXXXXXXXXX.....................................................................
          XXXXXXXXXXXXXXX
   SETOSA XXXXXXXXXXXXXXXXXXX.................................................................
          XXXXXXXXXXXXXXXXXXX
   SETOSA XXXXXXXXXXXXXXXXXXXXX...............................................................
          XXXXXXXXXXXXXXXXXXXXX
   SETOSA XXXXXXXXXXXXXXXXXXXXXXXXXX..........................................................
          XXXXXXXXXXXXXXXXXXXXXXXXXX
   SETOSA XXXXXXXXXXXXXXXXXXXXXXXXXXXXXXXXXXX.................................................
          XXXXXXXXXXXXXXXXXXXXXXXXXXXXXXXXXXX
   SETOSA XXXXXXXXXXXXXXXXXXXXXXXXXXXXXXXXXXXXXXX.............................................
          XXXXXXXXXXXXXXXXXXXXXXXXXXXXXXXXXXXXXXX
   SETOSA XXXXXXXXXXXXXXXXXXXXXXXXXXXXXXXXXXXXXXXXXXXXXXXXX...................................
          XXXXXXXXXXXXXXXXXXXXXXXXXXXXXXXXXXXXXXXXXXXXXXXXX
   SETOSA XXXXXXXXXXXXXXXXXXXXXXXXXXXXXXXXXXXXXXXXXXXXXXXXXXXXXXXXXXXXXXXXXXXXXXXXXXXXXXXXXXXXXXX
          XXXXXXXXXXXXXXXXXXXXXXXXXXXXXXXXXXXXXXXXXXXXXXXXXXXXXXXXXXXXXXXXXXXXXXXXXXXXXXXXXXXXXXX
   SETOSA XXXXXXXXXXXXXXXXXXXXXXXXXXXXXXXXXXXXXXXXXXXXXXXXXXXXXXXXXXXXXXXXXXXXXXXXXXXXXXXXXXXXXXX
          XXXXXXXXXXXXXXXXXXXXXXXXXXXXXXXXXXXXXXXXXXXXXXXXXXXXXXXXXXXXXXXXXXXXXXXXXXXXXXXXXXXXXX
   SETOSA XXXXXXXXXXXXXXXXXXXXXXXXXXXXXXXXXXXXXXXXXXXXXXXXXXXXXXXXXXXXXXXXXXXXXXXXXX...........
          XXXXXXXXXXXXXXXXXXXXXXXXXXXXXXXXXXXXXXXXXXXXXXXXXXXXXX
   SETOSA XXXXXXXXXXXXXXXXXXXXXXXXXXXXXXXXXXXXXXXXXXXXXXXXXXXXXX.......................
          XXXXXXXXXXXXXXXXXXXXXXXXXXXXXXXXXXXXXXXXXXXXXXXXXXXXXX
   SETOSA XXXXXXXXXXXXXXXXXXXXXXXXXXXXXXXXXXXXXXXXXXXXXXX..............................
          XXXXXXXXXXXXXXXXXXXXXXXXXXXXXXXXXXXXXXXXXXXXXXX
   SETOSA XXXXXXXXXXXXXXXXXXXXXXXXXXXXXXXXXXXXXXXXXXX..................................
          XXXXXXXXXXXXXXXXXXXXXXXXXXXXXXXXXXXXXXXXXXX
   SETOSA XXXXXXXXXXXXXXXXXXXXXXXXXXXXXXXXXXXXXXXX.....................................
          XXXXXXXXXXXXXXXXXXXXXXXXXXXXXXXXXXXXXXXX
   SETOSA XXXXXXXXXXXXXXXXXXXXXXXXXXXXXXXXXXXXX........................................
          XXXXXXXXXXXXXXXXXXXXXXXXXXXXXXXXXXXXX
   SETOSA XXXXXXXXXXXXXXXXXXXXXXXXXXXXXXXXXXX..........................................
          XXXXXXXXXXXXXXXXXXXXXXXXXXXXXXXXXXX
   SETOSA XXXXXXXXXXXXXXXXXXXXXXXXXXXXXXXXX............................................
          XXXXXXXXXXXXXXXXXXXXXXXXXXXXXXXXX
   SETOSA XXXXXXXXXXXXXXXXXXXXXXXXXXXXXXX..............................................
          XXXXXXXXXXXXXXXXXXXXXXXXXXXXXXX
   SETOSA XXXXXXXXXXXXXXXXXXXXXXXXXXXXX................................................
          XXXXXXXXXXXXXXXXXXXXXXXXXXXXX
   SETOSA XXXXXXXXXXXXXXXXXXXXXXXXXXX..................................................
          XXXXXXXXXXXXXXXXXXXXXXXXXXX
   SETOSA XXXXXXXXXXXXXXXXXXXXXXXXXX...................................................
          XXXXXXXXXXXXXXXXXXXXXXXXXX
   SETOSA XXXXXXXXXXXXXXXXXXXXXXXX.....................................................
          XXXXXXXXXXXXXXXXXXXXXXXX
```

(continued on next page)

(continued from previous page)

```
      SETOSA XXXXXXXXXXXXXXXXXXX.................................................
             XXXXXXXXXXXXX
      SETOSA XXXXXXXXXXXXX.......................................................
             XXXXXXXXXXXXX
      SETOSA XXXXXXXXXXXXX.......................................................
             XXXXXXX
      SETOSA XXXXXXX.............................................................
             XXXXXXX
      SETOSA XXXXXXX.............................................................
             XXXXXXX
      SETOSA XXXXXXX.............................................................
             XXXXXX
      SETOSA XXXXXX..............................................................
             XXXXX
      SETOSA XXXXX...............................................................
             XXX
      SETOSA XXX.................................................................
             XXX
      SETOSA XXX.................................................................
             XX
      SETOSA XX..................................................................
             X
      SETOSA X...................................................................

   VIRGINICA XXXX...............................................................
             XXXX
   VIRGINICA XXXXX..............................................................
             XXXXX
   VIRGINICA XXXXX..............................................................
             XXXXX
   VIRGINICA XXXXX..............................................................
             XXXXX
   VIRGINICA XXXXX..............................................................
             XXXXX
   VIRGINICA XXXXX..............................................................
             XXXXX
   VIRGINICA XXXXX..............................................................
             XXXX
   VIRGINICA XXXX...............................................................
             XXXX
  VERSICOLOR XXXXX..............................................................
             XXXXX
   VIRGINICA XXXXX..............................................................
             XXXX
   VIRGINICA XXXX...............................................................
             XXXX
   VIRGINICA XXXX...............................................................
             XXXX
   VIRGINICA XXXX...............................................................
             XXXX
   VIRGINICA XXXX...............................................................
             XXXX
   VIRGINICA XXXX...............................................................
             XXXX
   VIRGINICA XXXX...............................................................
             XXXX
   VIRGINICA XXXX...............................................................
             XXXX
  VERSICOLOR XXXX...............................................................
             XXXX
   VIRGINICA XXXX...............................................................
             XXXX
   VIRGINICA XXXX...............................................................
             XXXX
   VIRGINICA XXXX...............................................................
             XXXX
   VIRGINICA XXXX...............................................................
             XXXX
   VIRGINICA XXXX...............................................................
             XXX
   VIRGINICA XXX.................................................................
             XXX
   VIRGINICA XXX.................................................................
             XXX
   VIRGINICA XXX.................................................................
             XXX
   VIRGINICA XXX.................................................................
             XXX
   VIRGINICA XXX.................................................................
             XXX
   VIRGINICA XXX.................................................................
             XXX
   VIRGINICA XXX.................................................................
             XXX
   VIRGINICA XXX.................................................................
             XX
```

(continued on next page)

(continued from previous page)

```
   VIRGINICA XX.....................................................................
             XX
   VIRGINICA XX.....................................................................
             XX
   VIRGINICA XX.....................................................................
             XX
   VIRGINICA XX.....................................................................
             XX
   VIRGINICA XX.....................................................................
             XX
   VIRGINICA XX.....................................................................
             XX
  VERSICOLOR XX.....................................................................
             XX
   VIRGINICA XX.....................................................................
             XX
   VIRGINICA XX.....................................................................
             XX
   VIRGINICA XX.....................................................................
             XX
   VIRGINICA XX.....................................................................
             XX
   VIRGINICA XX.....................................................................
             X
   VIRGINICA X......................................................................
             X
   VIRGINICA X......................................................................
             X
   VIRGINICA X......................................................................
             X
   VIRGINICA X......................................................................
             X
   VIRGINICA X......................................................................
             X
   VIRGINICA X......................................................................
             X
   VIRGINICA X......................................................................
             X
   VIRGINICA X......................................................................
             X
  VERSICOLOR X......................................................................
             X
  VERSICOLOR X......................................................................
             X
  VERSICOLOR XX.....................................................................
             XX
  VERSICOLOR XXX....................................................................
             XXX
  VERSICOLOR XXX....................................................................
             XXX
  VERSICOLOR XXXX...................................................................
             XXXX
  VERSICOLOR XXXX...................................................................
             XXXX
  VERSICOLOR XXXX...................................................................
             XXXX
  VERSICOLOR XXXXX..................................................................
             XXXXX
  VERSICOLOR XXXXXX.................................................................
             XXXXXX
  VERSICOLOR XXXXXX.................................................................
             XXXXX
  VERSICOLOR XXXXX..................................................................
             XXXXX
  VERSICOLOR XXXXX..................................................................
             XXXXX
  VERSICOLOR XXXXX..................................................................
             XXXX
  VERSICOLOR XXXX...................................................................
             XXXX
   VIRGINICA XXXX...................................................................
             XXXX
  VERSICOLOR XXXXX..................................................................
             XXXXX
  VERSICOLOR XXXXX..................................................................
             XXXXX
  VERSICOLOR XXXXX..................................................................
             XXXXX
  VERSICOLOR XXXXX..................................................................
             XXXXX
  VERSICOLOR XXXXXXX................................................................
             XXXXXXX
  VERSICOLOR XXXXXXX................................................................
             XXXXXXX
```

(continued on next page)

(continued from previous page)

```
VERSICOLOR XXXXXXX.......................................................................
           XXXXXX
VERSICOLOR XXXXXXX.......................................................................
           XXXXXXX
VERSICOLOR XXXXXXXX......................................................................
           XXXXXXXX
VERSICOLOR XXXXXXXXX.....................................................................
           XXXXXXXXX
VERSICOLOR XXXXXXXXX.....................................................................
           XXXXXXXX
VERSICOLOR XXXXXXX.......................................................................
           XXXXXXXX
VERSICOLOR XXXXXXX.......................................................................
           XXXXXX
VERSICOLOR XXXXXX........................................................................
           XXXXXX
VERSICOLOR XXXXXXX.......................................................................
           XXXXX
VERSICOLOR XXXXX.........................................................................
           XXXXX
VERSICOLOR XXXXX.........................................................................
           XXXX
VERSICOLOR XXXX..........................................................................
           XXXX
VERSICOLOR XXXX..........................................................................
           XXXX
VERSICOLOR XXXX..........................................................................
           XXXX
VERSICOLOR XXXX..........................................................................
           XXX
VERSICOLOR XXX...........................................................................
           XXX
VERSICOLOR XXX...........................................................................
           XXX
VERSICOLOR XXX...........................................................................
           XXX
VERSICOLOR XXX...........................................................................
           XXX
VERSICOLOR XXX...........................................................................
           XXX
 VIRGINICA XXX...........................................................................
           XXX
VERSICOLOR XXX...........................................................................
           XXX
VERSICOLOR XXX...........................................................................
           XX
VERSICOLOR XX............................................................................
           X
VERSICOLOR X.............................................................................
           X
VERSICOLOR X.............................................................................
```

REFERENCES

Duran, B.S. and Odell, P.L. (1974), *Cluster Analysis*, New York: Springer-Verlag.

Everitt, B.S. (1980), *Cluster Analysis*, 2d Edition, London: Heineman Educational Books Ltd.

Fisher, R.A. (1936), "The Use of Multiple Measurements in Taxonomic Problems," *Annals of Eugenics*, 7, 179–188.

Hartigan, J.A. (1975), *Clustering Algorithms*, New York: John Wiley & Sons, Inc.

Johnson, S.C. (1967), "Hierarchical Clustering Schemes," *Psychometrika*, 32, 241–254.

Knuth, D.E. (1973), *The Art of Computer Programming, Volume 1, Fundamental Algorithms*, Reading, MA: Addison-Wesley Publishing Co., Inc.

Chapter 33

The TTEST Procedure

ABSTRACT

The TTEST procedure computes a t statistic for testing the hypothesis that the means of two groups of observations in a SAS data set are equal.

INTRODUCTION

Means for a variable are computed for each of the two groups of observations identified by levels of a classification or CLASS variable. The t test tests the hypothesis that the true means are the same. This analysis can be considered a special case of a one-way analysis of variance with two levels of classification.

PROC TTEST computes the t statistic based on the assumption that the variances of the two groups are equal, and it computes an approximate t based on the assumption that the variances are unequal (that is, for the Behrens-Fisher problem). For each t, the degrees of freedom and probability level are given; Satterthwaite's (1946) approximation is used to compute the degrees of freedom associated with the approximate t. In addition, you can request the Cochran and Cox (1950) approximation of the probability level for the approximate t. An F' (folded) statistic is computed to test for equality of the two variances (Steel and Torrie 1980).

The TTEST procedure was not designed for paired comparisons. See **Example 2** for a description of a method to get a paired-comparisons *t* test.

Note that the underlying assumption of the *t* test computed by the TTEST procedure is that the variables are normally and independently distributed within each group.

SPECIFICATIONS

The following statements are available in PROC TTEST:

PROC TTEST *options*;
    CLASS *variable*;
    VAR *variables*;
    BY *variables*;

No statement may be used more than once. There is no restriction on the order of the statements after the PROC statement. The CLASS statement is required.

PROC TTEST Statement

PROC TTEST *options*;

The following options can appear in the PROC TTEST statement:

COCHRAN
    requests the Cochran and Cox (1950) approximation of the probability level of the approximate *t* statistic for the unequal variance situation.

DATA=*SASdataset*
    names the SAS data set for the procedure to use. If the DATA= option is not given, PROC TTEST uses the most recently created SAS data set.

BY Statement

BY *variables*;

A BY statement can be used with PROC TTEST to obtain separate analyses on observations in groups defined by the BY variables. When a BY statement appears, the procedure expects the input data set to be sorted in order of the BY variables.

If your input data set is not sorted in ascending order, use the SORT procedure with a similar BY statement to sort the data, or, if appropriate, use the BY statement options NOTSORTED or DESCENDING. For more information see the discussion of the BY statement in "SAS Statements Used in the PROC Step" in the *SAS Language Guide, Release 6.03 Edition*.

CLASS Statement

CLASS *variable*;

A CLASS statement giving the name of the grouping variable must accompany the PROC TTEST statement. The grouping variable must have two, and only two, levels. PROC TTEST divides the observations into the two groups for the *t* test using the levels of this variable.

You can use either a numeric or a character variable in the CLASS statement. If you use a character variable longer than 16 characters, the values are truncated and a warning message is issued.

VAR Statement

VAR *variables*;

The VAR statement gives the names of the dependent variables whose means are to be compared. If the VAR statement is omitted, all numeric variables in the input data set (except a numeric variable appearing in the CLASS statement) are included in the analysis.

DETAILS

Missing Values

An observation is always omitted from the calculations if it has a missing value for either the CLASS variable or for the variable to be tested.

If more than one variable is listed in the VAR statement, an observation is included in calculations for all variables for which the observation has nonmissing values. In other words, if an observation has a missing value for one of the variables, the observation is omitted only from the calculations for that variable. The observation is still included in calculations for other variables.

Computational Method

The *t* Statistic

The usual t statistic for testing the equality of means $\bar{x}_1$ and $\bar{x}_2$ from two independent samples with n_1 and n_2 observations is

$$t = (\bar{x}_1 - \bar{x}_2) / \sqrt{s^2(1/n_1 + 1/n_2)}$$

where s^2 is the pooled variance

$$s^2 = [(n_1 - 1)s_1^2 + (n_2 - 1)s_2^2] / (n_1 + n_2 - 2)$$

and where s_1^2 and s_2^2 are the sample variances of the two groups. The use of this t statistic depends on the assumption that $\sigma_1^2 = \sigma_2^2$, where σ_1^2 and σ_2^2 are the population variances of the two groups.

The Folded Form *F* Statistic

You can use the folded form of the F statistic, F', to test the assumption that the variances are equal, where

$$F' = (\text{larger of } s_1^2, s_2^2) / (\text{smaller of } s_1^2, s_2^2) \quad .$$

A test of F' is a two-tailed F test since you do not specify which variance you expect to be larger. The printout value of Prob > F gives the probability of a greater F value under the null hypothesis that $\sigma_1^2 = \sigma_2^2$.

The Approximate *t* Statistic

Under the assumption of unequal variances, the approximate t statistic is computed as

$$t' = (\bar{x}_1 - \bar{x}_2) / \sqrt{w_1 + w_2}$$

where

$$w_1 = s_1^2 / n_1, \qquad w_2 = s_2^2 / n_2 \quad .$$

The Cochran and Cox Approximation

The Cochran and Cox (1950) approximation of the probability level of the approximate t statistic is the value of p such that

$$t' = (w_1 t_1 + w_2 t_2) / (w_1 + w_2)$$

where t_1 and t_2 are the critical values of the t distribution corresponding to a significance level of p and sample sizes of n_1 and n_2, respectively. The number of degrees of freedom is between $n_1 - 1$ and $n_2 - 1$. In general, the Cochran and Cox test tends to be conservative (Lee and Gurland 1975).

Satterthwaite's Approximation

The formula for Satterthwaite's (1946) approximation for the degrees of freedom for the approximate t statistic is as follows:

$$df = \frac{(w_1 + w_2)^2}{w_1^2 / (n_1 - 1) + w_2^2 / (n_2 - 1)}$$

Refer to Steel and Torrie (1980) or Freund, Littell, and Spector (1986) for more information.

Printed Output

For each dependent variable included in the analysis, the TTEST procedure prints the following statistics for each group:

1. the name of the dependent variable
2. the levels of the classification variable
3. N, the number of nonmissing values
4. the Mean or average
5. Std Dev, the standard deviation
6. Std Error, the standard error of the mean
7. the Minimum value, if the line size allows
8. the Maximum value, if the line size allows.

Under the assumption of unequal variances, the TTEST procedure prints

9. T, an approximate t statistic for testing the null hypothesis that the means of the two groups are equal.
10. DF, approximate degrees of freedom. The approximate degrees of freedom for Satterthwaite's approximation are always shown. If $n_1 = n_2$, then the approximate degrees of freedom for the Cochran and Cox approximation are shown.
11. Prob $> |T|$, the probability of a greater absolute value of t under the null hypothesis. This probability results from using Satterthwaite's approximation for the degrees of freedom. This is the two-tailed significance probability.
12. the Cochran and Cox approximation of Prob $> |T|$ if the COCHRAN option is specified. This is the two-tailed significance probability.

Under the assumption of equal variances, the TTEST procedure prints

13. T, the *t* statistic for testing the null hypothesis that the means of the two groups are equal.
14. DF, the degrees of freedom.
15. Prob > |T|, the probability of a greater absolute value of *t* under the null hypothesis. This is the two-tailed significance probability.

PROC TTEST then gives the results of the test of equality of variances:

16. the F' (folded) statistic (see **DETAILS**)
17. the degrees of freedom, DF, in each group
18. Prob > F', the probability of a greater *F* value.

Note that TTEST prints all the items in the list above. You need to decide which assumptions are appropriate for your data.

EXAMPLES

Example 1: Comparing Group Means

The data for this example consist of golf scores for a physical education class. You can use a *t* test to determine if the mean golf score for the men in the class differs significantly from the mean score for the women. The output is shown in **Output 33.1**.

The grouping variable is GENDER, and it appears in the INPUT statement and the CLASS statement.

The circled numbers on the sample output correspond to the statistics described above.

```
options linesize=110;
data scores;
   input gender $ score aa;
   cards;
f 75  f 76  f 80  f 77  f 80  f 77  f 73
m 82  m 80  m 85  m 85  m 78  m 87  m 82
;
proc ttest cochran;
   class gender;
   var score;
   title 'GOLF SCORES';
run;
```

Output 33.1   Comparing Group Means with PROC TTEST

```
                               GOLF SCORES                                    1
                             TTEST PROCEDURE

Variable: SCORE ❶
                        ❹                ❺              ❻            ❼              ❽
GENDER ❷    N ❸      Mean            Std Dev        Std Error     Minimum        Maximum
------------------------------------------------------------------------------------------
f           7     76.85714286      2.54483604     0.96185761    73.00000000    80.00000000
m           7     82.71428571      3.14718317     1.18952343    78.00000000    87.00000000

Variances       T     Method          DF    Prob>|T|
------------------------------------------------------------
Unequal ❾ -3.8288    Satterthwaite ❿ 11.5   0.0026 ⓫
                     Cochran      ⓬  6.0    0.0087 ⓬
Equal ⓭    -3.8288                ⓮ 12.0    0.0024 ⓯
For H0: Variances are equal, F' = 1.53 ⓱ DF = (6,6)    Prob>F' = 0.6189
        ⓰                             ⓲
```

The results from the test of equality of variances show that the assumption of equal variances is reasonable for these data. Thus, the appropriate test is the usual *t* test, which shows that the average golf scores for men and women are significantly different. The *p* value associated with this test is 0.0024.

Example 2: Paired Comparisons Using PROC MEANS

For paired comparisons, use PROC MEANS rather than PROC TTEST. You can create a new variable containing the differences between the paired variables, and use the T and PRT options of PROC MEANS to test whether the mean difference is significantly different from zero.

This is useful if you have a PRETEST and POSTTEST value for each observation in a data set and you want to test whether the average change between PRETEST and POSTTEST is significantly different from zero.

Following the INPUT statement in the DATA step is an assignment statement creating a new variable, DIFF, made by subtracting PRETEST from POSTTEST. Then PROC MEANS is used with the T and PRT options to get a *t* statistic and a probability value for the null hypothesis that DIFF's mean is equal to zero. This example produces **Output 33.2**.

```
data a;
   input id pretest posttest;
   diff=posttest-pretest;
   cards;
1   80    82
2   73    71
3   70    95
4   60    69
5   88   100
6   84    71
7   65    75
8   37    60
9   91    95
10  98    99
11  52    65
12  78    83
```

```
13  40  60
14  79  86
15  59  62
;
proc means mean stderr t prt;
   var diff;
   title 'PAIRED-COMPARISONS T TEST';
run;
```

Output 33.2   Making Paired Comparisons with PROC MEANS

```
                    PAIRED-COMPARISONS T TEST                              1

        Analysis variable : DIFF


        N Obs      Mean    Std Error        T  Prob>|T|
        ---------------------------------------------------------
          15  7.9333333   2.5643465  3.0937057    0.0079
        ---------------------------------------------------------
```

The results of the paired comparison show that the average DIFF is significantly different from zero. The associated *p* value is 0.0079.

REFERENCES

Cochran, W.G. and Cox, G.M. (1950), *Experimental Designs*, New York: John Wiley & Sons, Inc.

Lee, A.F.S. and Gurland, J. (1975), "Size and Power of Tests for Equality of Means of Two Normal Populations with Unequal Variances," *Journal of the American Statistical Association*, 70, 933–941.

Freund, R.J., Littell, R.C., and Spector, P.C. (1986), *SAS System for Linear Models, 1986 Edition*, Cary, NC: SAS Institute Inc.

Satterthwaite, F.W. (1946), "An Approximate Distribution of Estimates of Variance Components," *Biometrics Bulletin*, 2, 110–114.

Steel, R.G.D. and Torrie, J.H. (1980), *Principles and Procedures of Statistics*, 2d Edition, New York: McGraw-Hill Book Company.

948

Chapter 34

The VARCLUS Procedure

ABSTRACT

The VARCLUS procedure performs either disjoint or hierarchical clustering of variables based on a correlation or covariance matrix. The clusters are chosen to maximize the variation accounted for by either the first principal component or the centroid component of each cluster. An output data set containing the results of the analysis can be created and used with the SCORE procedure to compute cluster component scores. A second output data set can be used by the TREE procedure to draw a tree diagram of hierarchical clusters.

INTRODUCTION

The VARCLUS procedure divides a set of numeric variables into either disjoint or hierarchical clusters. Associated with each cluster is a linear combination of the variables in the cluster, which may be either the first principal component or the centroid component. PROC VARCLUS tries to maximize the sum across clusters of the variance of the original variables that is explained by the cluster components.

Either the correlation or the covariance matrix can be analyzed. If correlations are used, all variables are treated as equally important. If covariances are used, variables with larger variances have more importance in the analysis.

PROC VARCLUS creates an output data set that can be used with the SCORE procedure to compute component scores for each cluster. A second output data set can be used by the TREE procedure to draw a tree diagram of hierarchical clusters.

Background

The VARCLUS procedure attempts to divide a set of variables into non-overlapping clusters in such a way that each cluster can be interpreted as essentially unidimensional. For each cluster, VARCLUS computes a component that can be either the first principal component or the centroid component and tries to maximize the sum across clusters of the variation accounted for by the cluster components. VARCLUS is a type of oblique component analysis related to multiple group factor analysis (Harman 1976).

VARCLUS can be used as a variable-reduction method. A large set of variables can often be replaced by the set of cluster components with little loss of information. A given number of cluster components does not generally explain as much variance as the same number of principal components, but the cluster components are usually easier to interpret than the principal components, even if the latter are rotated.

For example, an educational test might contain fifty items. VARCLUS could be used to divide the items into, say, five clusters. Each cluster could be treated as a subtest, and the subtest scores would be given by the cluster components. If the cluster components were centroid components of the covariance matrix, each subtest score would simply be the sum of the item scores for that cluster.

By default, VARCLUS begins with all variables in a single cluster. It then repeats the following steps:

1. A cluster is chosen for splitting. Depending on the options specified, the selected cluster has either the smallest percentage of variation explained by its cluster component or the largest eigenvalue associated with the second principal component.
2. The chosen cluster is split into two clusters by finding the first two principal components, performing an orthoblique rotation (raw quartimax rotation on the eigenvectors), and assigning each variable to the rotated component with which it has the higher squared correlation.
3. Variables are iteratively reassigned to clusters to maximize the variance accounted for by the cluster components. The reassignment may be required to maintain a hierarchical structure.

The procedure stops when each cluster satisfies a user-specified criterion involving either the percentage of variation accounted for or the second eigenvalue of each cluster. By default, VARCLUS stops when each cluster has only a single eigenvalue greater than one, thus satisfying the most popular criterion for determining the sufficiency of a single underlying factor dimension.

The iterative reassignment of variables to clusters proceeds in two phases. The first is a nearest component sorting (NCS) phase, similar in principle to the nearest centroid sorting algorithms described by Anderberg (1973). In each iteration the cluster components are computed, and each variable is assigned to the component with which it has the highest squared correlation. The second phase involves a search algorithm in which each variable in turn is tested to see if assigning it to a different cluster increases the amount of variance explained. If a variable is reassigned during the search phase, the components of the two clusters involved are recomputed before the next variable is tested. The NCS phase is much faster than the search phase but is more likely to be trapped by a local optimum.

If principal components are used, the NCS phase is an alternating least-squares method and converges rapidly. The search phase is very time consuming for a large number of variables and is omitted by default. If the default initialization method is used, the search phase is rarely able to improve the results of the NCS phase. If random initialization is used, the NCS phase may be trapped by a local optimum from which the search phase can escape.

If centroid components are used, the NCS phase may not increase the amount of variance explained; therefore, it is limited to one iteration by default.

SPECIFICATIONS

The VARCLUS procedure is invoked by the following statements:

PROC VARCLUS *options*;
   VAR *variables*;
   SEED | SEEDS *variables*;
   PARTIAL *variables*;
   WEIGHT *variable*;
   FREQ *variable*;
   BY *variables*;

Usually only the VAR statement is used in addition to the PROC VARCLUS statement. The BY, FREQ, PARTIAL, SEED, VAR, and WEIGHT statements are described after the PROC VARCLUS statement.

PROC VARCLUS Statement

PROC VARCLUS *options*;

Data Set Options

DATA=*SASdataset*
   names the input data set to be analyzed. The data set can be an ordinary SAS data set or TYPE=CORR, COV, or FACTOR. If you do not specify the DATA= option, the most recently created SAS data set is used.

OUTSTAT=*SASdataset*
   names an output data set to contain statistics including means, standard deviations, correlations, cluster scoring coefficients, and the cluster structure. If you want to create a permanent SAS data set, you must specify a two-level name. See "SAS Files" in the *SAS Language Guide, Release 6.03 Edition* for more information on permanent SAS data sets.

OUTTREE=*SASdataset*
   names an output data set to contain information on the tree structure that can be used by the TREE procedure to print a tree diagram. The OUTTREE= option implies the HIERARCHY option. If you want to create a permanent SAS data set, you must specify a two-level name.

See "SAS Files" in the *SAS Language Guide* for more information on permanent SAS data sets.

Number of Clusters Options

MAXCLUSTERS=*n*
MAXC=*n*
: specifies the largest number of clusters desired. The default value is the number of variables.

MINCLUSTERS=*n*
MINC=*n*
: specifies the smallest number of clusters desired. The default value is 2 if INITIAL=RANDOM or INITIAL=SEED; otherwise, the procedure begins with one cluster and tries to split it in accordance with the PROPORTION= or MAXEIGEN= options.

MAXEIGEN=*n*
: specifies the largest permissible value of the second eigenvalue in each cluster. If you do not specify either the PROPORTION= or the MAXCLUSTERS= options, the default value is 1 if the correlation matrix is analyzed, or the average variance of the variables if the covariance matrix is analyzed. Otherwise, the default is 0. The MAXEIGEN= option cannot be used with the CENTROID option.

PROPORTION=*n*
PERCENT=*n*
: gives the proportion or percentage of variation that must be explained by the cluster component. Values greater than 1.0 are considered to be percentages, so PROPORTION=0.75 and PERCENT=75 are equivalent. If you specify the CENTROID option (see below), the default value is 0.75; otherwise, the default value is 0.

Cluster Formation Options

CENTROID
: uses centroid components rather than principal components. You should use centroid components if you want the cluster components to be (unweighted) averages of the standardized variables (the default) or the unstandardized variables (if you specify the COV option). It is possible to obtain locally optimal clusterings in which a variable is not assigned to the cluster component with which it has the highest squared correlation.

COVARIANCE
COV
: analyzes the covariance matrix rather than the correlation matrix.

HIERARCHY
HI
: requires the clusters at different levels to maintain a hierarchical structure.

INITIAL=*method*
: specifies the method for initializing the clusters. Values for the INITIAL= option can be RANDOM, SEED, INPUT, or GROUP. If the INITIAL= option is omitted and MINCLUSTERS= is greater than 1, the initial cluster components are obtained by extracting the required number of principal components and performing an orthoblique rotation. You can specify the following values for the INITIAL= option:

INITIAL=SEED

> initializes clusters according to the variables named in the SEED statement. Each variable listed in the SEED statement becomes the sole member of a cluster, and the other variables remain unassigned. If you do not specify the SEED statement, the first MINCLUSTERS= variables in the VAR statement are used as seeds.

INITIAL=INPUT

> can be used if the input data set is a TYPE=CORR, COV, or FACTOR data set, in which case scoring coefficients are read from observations where _TYPE_='SCORE'. Scoring coefficients from the FACTOR procedure or a previous run of VARCLUS can be used, or you can enter other coefficients in a DATA step.

INITIAL=GROUP

> can be used if the input data set is a TYPE=CORR, COV, or FACTOR data set. The cluster membership of each variable is obtained from an observation with _TYPE_='GROUP', which contains an integer for each variable ranging from one to the number of clusters. You can use a data set created either by a previous run of VARCLUS or in a DATA step.

INITIAL=RANDOM

> assigns variables randomly to clusters. If you specify INITIAL=RANDOM without the CENTROID option, it is recommended that you specify MAXSEARCH=5, although the CPU time required is substantially increased.

MAXITER=n

specifies the maximum number of iterations during the alternating least-squares phase. The default value is 1 if you specify CENTROID; the default is 10 otherwise.

MAXSEARCH=n

specifies the maximum number of iterations during the search phase. The default is 10 if you specify CENTROID; the default is 0 otherwise.

MULTIPLEGROUP

MG

performs a multiple group component analysis. The input data set must be TYPE=CORR, COV, or FACTOR and must contain an observation with _TYPE_='GROUP' defining the variable groups. Specifying MULTIPLEGROUP is equivalent to specifying all of the following options:

> MINC=1 MAXITER=0 MAXSEARCH=0 MAXEIGEN=0
> PROPORTION=0 INITIAL=GROUP

RANDOM=n

specifies a positive integer as a starting value for use with REPLACE=RANDOM. If you do not specify the RANDOM= option, the time of day is used to initialize the pseudo-random number sequence.

Output Options

CORR
C
  prints the correlation matrix.

NOPRINT
  suppresses the printout.

SHORT
  suppresses printing of the cluster structure, scoring coefficient, and intercluster correlation matrices.

SIMPLE
S
  prints means and standard deviations.

SUMMARY
  suppresses all default printout except the final summary table.

TRACE
  lists the cluster to which each variable is assigned during the iterations.

Miscellaneous Options

NOINT
  requests that no intercept be used; covariances or correlations are not corrected for the mean.

VARDEF=*divisor*
  specifies the divisor to be used in the calculation of variances and covariances. Possible values for *divisor* are N, DF, WEIGHT or WGT, and WDF.

VARDEF=N
                requests that the number of observations (n) be used as the divisor.

VARDEF=DF
                requests that the error degrees of freedom, $n-i$ (before partialling) or $n-p-i$ (after partialling), be used, where p is the number of degrees of freedom of the variables in the PARTIAL statement and i is 0 if the NOINT option is specified, 1 otherwise.

VARDEF=WEIGHT
VARDEF=WGT
                requests that the sum of the weights (w) be used.

VARDEF=WDF
                requests that $w-i$ (before partialling) or $w-p-i$ (after partialling) be used. The default value is DF.

BY Statement

  BY *variables*;

You can use a BY statement with PROC VARCLUS to obtain separate analyses on observations in groups defined by the BY variables. When a BY statement appears, the procedure expects the input data set to be sorted in order of the BY variables.

If your input data set is not sorted in ascending order, use the SORT procedure with a similar BY statement to sort the data, or, if appropriate, use the BY statement options NOTSORTED or DESCENDING. For more information, see the discussion of the BY statement in "SAS Statements Used in the PROC Step" in the *SAS Language Guide*.

FREQ Statement

FREQ *variable*;

If a variable in your data set represents the frequency of occurrence for the other values in the observation, include the variable's name in a FREQ statement. The procedure then treats the data set as if each observation appears *n* times, where *n* is the value of the FREQ variable for the observation. The total number of observations is considered equal to the sum of the FREQ variable.

PARTIAL Statement

PARTIAL *variables*;

If you want to base the clustering on partial correlations, list the variables to be partialled out in the PARTIAL statement.

SEED Statement

SEEDS *variables*;
SEED *variables*;

The SEED statement specifies variables to be used as seeds to initialize the clusters. It is not necessary to use INITIAL=SEED if the SEED statement is present, but if any other INITIAL= option is specified, the SEED statement is ignored.

VAR Statement

VAR *variables*;

The VAR statement specifies the variables to be clustered. If you do not specify the VAR statement, all numeric variables not listed in other statements (except the SEED statement) are processed.

WEIGHT Statement

WEIGHT *variable*;

If you want to use relative weights for each observation in the input data set, place the weights in a variable in the data set and specify the name in a WEIGHT statement. This is often done when the variance associated with each observation is different and the values of the weight variable are proportional to the reciprocals of the variances.

DETAILS

Missing Values

Observations containing missing values are omitted from the analysis.

Usage Notes

Default options for PROC VARCLUS often provide satisfactory results. If you want to change the final number of clusters, use the MAXCLUSTERS=, MAXEIGEN=, or PROPORTION= options. The MAXEIGEN= and PROPORTION= options usually produce similar results but occasionally cause different clusters to be selected for splitting. The MAXEIGEN= option tends to choose clusters with a large number of variables, while the PROPORTION= option is more likely to select a cluster with a small number of variables.

VARCLUS usually requires more computer time than principal factor analysis but can be faster than some of the iterative factoring methods. If you have more than thirty variables, you may want to reduce execution time by one or more of the following methods:

- Use the MINCLUSTERS= and MAXCLUSTERS= options if you know how many clusters you want.
- Use the HIERARCHY option.
- Use the SEED statement if you have some prior knowledge of what clusters to expect.

If you have sufficient computer time, you may want to try one of the following methods to obtain a better solution:

- Use the MAXSEARCH= option with principal components and specify a value of 5 or 10.
- Try several factoring and rotation methods with FACTOR to use as input to VARCLUS.
- Run VARCLUS several times specifying INITIAL=RANDOM.

Output Data Sets

OUTSTAT= Data Set

The OUTSTAT= data set is TYPE=CORR and can be used as input to the SCORE procedure or a subsequent run of VARCLUS. The variables it contains are

- BY variables
- _NCL_, a numeric variable giving the number of clusters
- _TYPE_, a character variable indicating the type of statistic the observation contains
- _NAME_, a character variable containing a variable name or a cluster name, which is of the form CLUS*n* where *n* is the number of the cluster
- the variables that were clustered.

The values of _TYPE_ are listed here:

TYPE	Contents
MEAN	means
STD	standard deviations
N	number of observations
CORR	correlations
MEMBERS	number of members in each cluster
VAREXP	variance explained by each cluster
PROPOR	proportion of variance explained by each cluster
GROUP	number of the cluster to which each variable belongs
RSQUARED	squared multiple correlation of each variable with its cluster component
SCORE	standardized scoring coefficients
STRUCTUR	cluster structure
CCORR	correlations between cluster components.

The observations with _TYPE_='MEAN', 'STD', 'N', and 'CORR' have missing values for _NCL_. All other values of _TYPE_ are repeated for each cluster solution, with different solutions distinguished by the value of _NCL_. If you want to use the OUTSTAT= data set with the SCORE procedure, you must use a DATA step to select observations with _NCL_ missing or equal to the desired number of clusters.

OUTTREE= Data Set

The OUTTREE= data set contains one observation for each variable clustered plus one observation for each cluster of two or more variables, that is, one observation for each node of the cluster tree. The total number of output observations is between n and $2n-1$, where n is the number of variables clustered.
   The variables in the OUTTREE= data set are

- the BY variables, if any.
- _NAME_, a character variable giving the name of the node. If the node is a cluster, the name is CLUSn where n is the number of the cluster. If the node is a single variable, the variable name is used.
- _PARENT_, a character variable giving the value of _NAME_ of the parent of the node.
- _NCL_, the number of clusters.
- _VAREXP_, the total variance explained by the clusters at the current level of the tree.
- _PROPOR_, the total proportion of variance explained by the clusters at the current level of the tree.
- _MINPRO_, the minimum proportion of variance explained by a cluster component.
- _MAXEIG, the maximum second eigenvalue of a cluster.

Computational Resources

The time required for VARCLUS to analyze a given data set varies greatly depending on the number of clusters requested, the number of iterations in both the alternating least-squares and search phases, and whether centroid or principal components are used.
   Let

n = number of observations
v = number of variables
c = number of clusters.

It is assumed that at each stage of clustering, the clusters all contain the same number of variables.
   The time required to compute the correlation matrix is roughly proportional to nv^2.
   Default cluster initialization requires time roughly proportional to v^3. Any other method of initialization requires time roughly proportional to cv^2.
   In the alternating least-squares phase, each iteration requires time roughly proportional to cv^2 if centroid components are used, or

$$(c + 5v/c^2)v^2$$

if principal components are used.
   In the search phase, each iteration requires time roughly proportional to v^3/c if centroid components are used, or v^4/c^2 if principal components are used. The HIERARCHY option speeds up each iteration after the first split by as much as $c/2$.

Interpreting VARCLUS Procedure Output

Because PROC VARCLUS is a type of oblique component analysis, its output is similar to the output from PROC FACTOR for oblique rotations. The scoring coefficients have the same meaning in both VARCLUS and FACTOR; they are coefficients applied to the standardized variables to compute component scores. The cluster structure is analogous to the factor structure containing the correlations between each variable and each cluster component. A cluster pattern is not printed because it would be the same as the cluster structure, except that zeros would appear in the same places that zeros appear in the scoring coefficients. The intercluster correlations are analogous to interfactor correlations; they are the correlations among cluster components.

VARCLUS also has a cluster summary and a cluster listing. The cluster summary gives the number of variables in each cluster and the variation explained by the cluster component. The latter is similar to the variation explained by a factor but includes contributions from only the variables in that cluster rather than from all variables, as in FACTOR. The proportions value is obtained by dividing the variance explained by the total variance of variables in the cluster. If the cluster contains two or more variables and the CENTROID option is not used, the second largest eigenvalue of the cluster is also printed.

The cluster listing gives the variables in each cluster. Two squared correlations are printed for each cluster. The column labeled Own Cluster gives the squared correlation of the variable with its own cluster component. This value should be higher than the squared correlation with any other cluster unless an iteration limit has been exceeded or the CENTROID option has been used. The larger the squared correlation is, the better. The column labeled Next Closest contains the next highest squared correlation of the variable with a cluster component. This value is low if the clusters are well separated. The column headed $1-R^{**}2$ Ratio gives the ratio of one minus the Own Cluster R^2 to one minus the Next Closest R^2. A small $1-R^{**}2$ Ratio indicates a good clustering.

Printed Output

The items described below are printed for each cluster solution unless NOPRINT or SUMMARY is specified. The CLUSTER SUMMARY table includes

1. the Cluster number.
2. Members, the number of members in the cluster.
3. Cluster Variation of the variables in the cluster.
4. Variation Explained by the cluster component. This statistic is based only on the variables in the cluster rather than all variables.
5. Proportion Explained, the result of dividing the variation explained by the cluster variation.
6. Second Eigenvalue, the second largest eigenvalue of the cluster. This is printed if the cluster contains more than one variable and the CENTROID option is not specified.

VARCLUS also prints

7. Total variation explained, the sum across clusters of the variation explained by each cluster
8. Proportion, the total explained variation divided by the total variation of all the variables.

The cluster listing includes

9. Variable, the variables in each cluster.
10. R-squared with Own Cluster, the squared correlation of the variable with its own cluster component; and R-squared with Next Closest, the next highest squared correlation of the variable with a cluster component. Own Cluster values should be higher than the R^2 with any other cluster unless an iteration limit has been exceeded or you specified the CENTROID option. Next Closest should be a low value if the clusters are well separated.
11. $1 - R^{**}2$ Ratio, the ratio of one minus the value in the Own Cluster column to one minus the value in the Next Closest column. The occurrence of low ratios indicates well-separated clusters.

If the SHORT option is not specified, VARCLUS also prints

12. Standardized Scoring Coefficients, standardized regression coefficients for predicting cluster components from variables
13. Cluster Structure, the correlations between each variable and each cluster component
14. Inter-Cluster Correlations, the correlations between the cluster components.

If the analysis includes partitions for two or more numbers of clusters, a final summary table is printed. Each row of the table corresponds to one partition. The columns include

15. Number of Clusters
16. Total Variation Explained by Clusters
17. Proportion of Variation Explained by Clusters
18. Minimum Proportion (of variation) Explained by a Cluster
19. Maximum Second Eigenvalue in a Cluster
20. Minimum R-squared for a Variable
21. Maximum $1 - R^{**}2$ Ratio for a Variable.

EXAMPLE

Correlations among Physical Variables

The data are correlations among eight physical variables as given by Harman (1976). The first VARCLUS run uses principal cluster components, the second uses centroid cluster components. The third analysis is hierarchical, and the TREE procedure is used to print a tree diagram. The following statements produce **Output 34.1** through **34.4**:

```
data phys8(type=corr);
   title 'Eight Physical Variables Measured on 305 School Girls';
   title2 'See Page 22 of Harman: Modern Factor Analysis, 3rd Ed';
   label height='height'
         arm_span='arm span'
         forearm='length of forearm'
         low_leg='length of lower leg'
         weight='weight'
         bit_diam='bitrochanteric diameter'
         girth='chest girth'
         width='chest width';
```

```
      input _name_ $ 1-8
            (height arm_span forearm low_leg weight bit_diam girth width)
            (8.);
      _type_='corr';
      cards;
height  1.0    .846   .805   .859   .473   .398   .301   .382
arm_span.846   1.0    .881   .826   .376   .326   .277   .415
forearm .805   .881   1.0    .801   .380   .319   .237   .345
low_leg .859   .826   .801   1.0    .436   .329   .327   .365
weight  .473   .376   .380   .436   1.0    .762   .730   .629
bit_diam.398   .326   .319   .329   .762   1.0    .583   .577
girth   .301   .277   .237   .327   .730   .583   1.0    .539
width   .382   .415   .345   .365   .629   .577   .539   1.0
;
proc varclus data=phys8;
proc varclus data=phys8 centroid;
proc varclus data=phys8 maxc=8 summary outtree=tree;
proc tree;
   height _propor_;
run;
```

Output 34.1   Principal Cluster Components: PROC VARCLUS

Eight Physical Variables Measured on 305 School Girls   1
See Page 22 of Harman: Modern Factor Analysis, 3rd Ed

Oblique Principal Component Cluster Analysis

10000 Observations   PROPORTION =   0
8 Variables   MAXEIGEN   =   1

Cluster summary for 1 cluster(s)

❶ Cluster	❷ Members	❸ Cluster Variation	❹ Variation Explained	❺ Proportion Explained	❻ Second Eigenvalue
1	8	8.00000	4.67288	0.5841	1.7710

❼ Total variation explained = 4.67288 Proportion = 0.5841 ❽

Cluster 1 will be split.

Eight Physical Variables Measured on 305 School Girls   2
See Page 22 of Harman: Modern Factor Analysis, 3rd Ed

Oblique Principal Component Cluster Analysis

Cluster summary for 2 cluster(s)

Cluster	Members	Cluster Variation	Variation Explained	Proportion Explained	Second Eigenvalue
1	4	4.00000	3.50922	0.8773	0.2361
2	4	4.00000	2.91728	0.7293	0.4764

Total variation explained = 6.426502 Proportion = 0.8033

❿ R-squared with

❾ Variable	Own Cluster	Next Closest	⓫ 1-R**2 Ratio	
Cluster 1				
HEIGHT	0.8777	0.2088	0.1545	height
ARM_SPAN	0.9002	0.1658	0.1196	arm span
FOREARM	0.8661	0.1413	0.1560	length of forearm
LOW_LEG	0.8652	0.1829	0.1650	length of lower leg

(continued on next page)

(continued from previous page)

```
Cluster   2-----------------------------------
          WEIGHT      0.8477   0.1974   0.1898   weight
          BIT_DIAM    0.7386   0.1341   0.3019   bitrochanteric diameter
          GIRTH       0.6981   0.0929   0.3328   chest girth
          WIDTH       0.6329   0.1619   0.4380   chest width
```

⑫   Standardized Scoring Coefficients

```
          Cluster          1          2
          -------------------------------------
          HEIGHT      0.266977   0.000000   height
          ARM_SPAN    0.270377   0.000000   arm span
          FOREARM     0.265194   0.000000   length of forearm
          LOW_LEG     0.265057   0.000000   length of lower leg
          WEIGHT      0.000000   0.315597   weight
          BIT_DIAM    0.000000   0.294591   bitrochanteric diameter
          GIRTH       0.000000   0.286407   chest girth
          WIDTH       0.000000   0.272710   chest width
```

⑬   Cluster Structure

```
          Cluster          1          2
          -------------------------------------
          HEIGHT      0.936881   0.456908   height
          ARM_SPAN    0.948813   0.407210   arm span
          FOREARM     0.930624   0.375865   length of forearm
          LOW_LEG     0.930142   0.427715   length of lower leg
          WEIGHT      0.444281   0.920686   weight
          BIT_DIAM    0.366201   0.859404   bitrochanteric diameter
          GIRTH       0.304779   0.835529   chest girth
          WIDTH       0.402430   0.795572   chest width
```

Eight Physical Variables Measured on 305 School Girls
See Page 22 of Harman: Modern Factor Analysis, 3rd Ed   3

Oblique Principal Component Cluster Analysis

⑭   Inter-Cluster Correlations

```
          Cluster          1          2

            1          1.00000    0.44513
            2          0.44513    1.00000
```

No cluster meets the criterion for splitting.

Eight Physical Variables Measured on 305 School Girls
See Page 22 of Harman: Modern Factor Analysis, 3rd Ed   4

Oblique Principal Component Cluster Analysis

⑮ Number of Clusters	⑯ Total Variation Explained by Clusters	⑰ Proportion of Variation Explained by Clusters	⑱ Minimum Proportion Explained by a Cluster	⑲ Maximum Second Eigenvalue in a Cluster	⑳ Minimum R-squared for a Variable	㉑ Maximum 1-R**2 Ratio for a Variable
1	4.672880	0.5841	0.5841	1.770983	0.3810	.
2	6.426502	0.8033	0.7293	0.476418	0.6329	0.4380

```
                  Eight Physical Variables Measured on 305 School Girls          5
                  See Page 22 of Harman: Modern Factor Analysis, 3rd Ed

                       Oblique Centroid Component Cluster Analysis

                  10000 Observations      PROPORTION  =    0.75
                      8 Variables         MAXEIGEN    =      0



                           Cluster summary for 1 cluster(s)

                                       Cluster    Variation   Proportion
                  Cluster    Members   Variation   Explained   Explained
                  -----------------------------------------------------------
                     1          8      8.00000     4.63100      0.5789

                  Total variation explained =     4.631 Proportion = 0.5789
```

Cluster 1 will be split.

Output 34.2   Centroid Cluster Components: PROC VARCLUS

```
                  Eight Physical Variables Measured on 305 School Girls          6
                  See Page 22 of Harman: Modern Factor Analysis, 3rd Ed

                       Oblique Centroid Component Cluster Analysis

                           Cluster summary for 2 cluster(s)

                                       Cluster    Variation   Proportion
                  Cluster    Members   Variation   Explained   Explained
                  -----------------------------------------------------------
                     1          4      4.00000     3.50900      0.8772
                     2          4      4.00000     2.91000      0.7275

                  Total variation explained =     6.419 Proportion = 0.8024


                               R-squared with
                               ------------------
                                Own      Next     1-R**2
                     Variable  Cluster  Closest   Ratio
           Cluster  1-----------------------------------------
                     HEIGHT    0.8778   0.2075    0.1543    height
                     ARM_SPAN  0.8994   0.1669    0.1208    arm span
                     FOREARM   0.8663   0.1410    0.1557    length of forearm
                     LOW_LEG   0.8658   0.1824    0.1641    length of lower leg
           Cluster  2-----------------------------------------
                     WEIGHT    0.8368   0.1975    0.2033    weight
                     BIT_DIAM  0.7335   0.1341    0.3078    bitrochanteric diameter
                     GIRTH     0.6988   0.0929    0.3321    chest girth
                     WIDTH     0.6473   0.1618    0.4207    chest width



                        Standardized Scoring Coefficients

                     Cluster         1          2
                     -----------------------------------
                     HEIGHT     0.266918   0.000000    height
                     ARM_SPAN   0.266918   0.000000    arm span
                     FOREARM    0.266918   0.000000    length of forearm
                     LOW_LEG    0.266918   0.000000    length of lower leg
                     WEIGHT     0.000000   0.293105    weight
                     BIT_DIAM   0.000000   0.293105    bitrochanteric diameter
                     GIRTH      0.000000   0.293105    chest girth
                     WIDTH      0.000000   0.293105    chest width
```

(continued on next page)

(continued from previous page)

Cluster Structure

Cluster	1	2	
HEIGHT	0.936883	0.455485	height
ARM_SPAN	0.948361	0.408589	arm span
FOREARM	0.930744	0.375468	length of forearm
LOW_LEG	0.930477	0.427054	length of lower leg
WEIGHT	0.444419	0.914781	weight
BIT_DIAM	0.366212	0.856453	bitrochanteric diameter
GIRTH	0.304821	0.835936	chest girth
WIDTH	0.402246	0.804574	chest width

Eight Physical Variables Measured on 305 School Girls
See Page 22 of Harman: Modern Factor Analysis, 3rd Ed

Oblique Centroid Component Cluster Analysis

Inter-Cluster Correlations

Cluster	1	2
1	1.00000	0.44484
2	0.44484	1.00000

Cluster 2 will be split.

Eight Physical Variables Measured on 305 School Girls
See Page 22 of Harman: Modern Factor Analysis, 3rd Ed

Oblique Centroid Component Cluster Analysis

Cluster summary for 3 cluster(s)

Cluster	Members	Cluster Variation	Variation Explained	Proportion Explained
1	4	4.00000	3.50900	0.8772
2	3	3.00000	2.38333	0.7944
3	1	1.00000	1.00000	1.0000

Total variation explained = 6.892333 Proportion = 0.8615

	Variable	Own Cluster	Next Closest	1-R**2 Ratio	
Cluster 1					
	HEIGHT	0.8778	0.1921	0.1513	height
	ARM_SPAN	0.8994	0.1722	0.1215	arm span
	FOREARM	0.8663	0.1225	0.1524	length of forearm
	LOW_LEG	0.8658	0.1668	0.1611	length of lower leg
Cluster 2					
	WEIGHT	0.8685	0.3956	0.2175	weight
	BIT_DIAM	0.7691	0.3329	0.3461	bitrochanteric diameter
	GIRTH	0.7482	0.2905	0.3548	chest girth
Cluster 3					
	WIDTH	1.0000	0.4259	0.0000	chest width

Standardized Scoring Coefficients

Cluster	1	2	3	
HEIGHT	0.26692	0.00000	0.00000	height
ARM_SPAN	0.26692	0.00000	0.00000	arm span
FOREARM	0.26692	0.00000	0.00000	length of forearm
LOW_LEG	0.26692	0.00000	0.00000	length of lower leg
WEIGHT	0.00000	0.37398	0.00000	weight
BIT_DIAM	0.00000	0.37398	0.00000	bitrochanteric diameter
GIRTH	0.00000	0.37398	0.00000	chest girth
WIDTH	0.00000	0.00000	1.00000	chest width

(continued on next page)

(continued from previous page)

Cluster Structure

Cluster	1	2	3	
HEIGHT	0.93688	0.43830	0.38200	height
ARM_SPAN	0.94836	0.36613	0.41500	arm span
FOREARM	0.93074	0.35004	0.34500	length of forearm
LOW_LEG	0.93048	0.40838	0.36500	length of lower leg
WEIGHT	0.44442	0.93196	0.62900	weight
BIT_DIAM	0.36621	0.87698	0.57700	bitrochanteric diameter
GIRTH	0.30482	0.86501	0.53900	chest girth
WIDTH	0.40225	0.65259	1.00000	chest width

Eight Physical Variables Measured on 305 School Girls
See Page 22 of Harman: Modern Factor Analysis, 3rd Ed   9

Oblique Centroid Component Cluster Analysis

Inter-Cluster Correlations

Cluster	1	2	3
1	1.00000	0.41716	0.40225
2	0.41716	1.00000	0.65259
3	0.40225	0.65259	1.00000

No cluster meets the criterion for splitting.

Eight Physical Variables Measured on 305 School Girls
See Page 22 of Harman: Modern Factor Analysis, 3rd Ed   10

Oblique Centroid Component Cluster Analysis

Number of Clusters	Total Variation Explained by Clusters	Proportion of Variation Explained by Clusters	Minimum Proportion Explained by a Cluster	Minimum R-squared for a Variable	Maximum 1-R**2 Ratio for a Variable
1	4.631000	0.5789	0.5789	0.4306	.
2	6.419000	0.8024	0.7275	0.6473	0.4207
3	6.892333	0.8615	0.7944	0.7482	0.3548

Output 34.3   Hierarchical Clusters: PROC VARCLUS Specifying the SUMMARY Option

Eight Physical Variables Measured on 305 School Girls
See Page 22 of Harman: Modern Factor Analysis, 3rd Ed   11

Oblique Principal Component Cluster Analysis

10000 Observations   PROPORTION =   1
8 Variables   MAXEIGEN   =   0

Number of Clusters	Total Variation Explained by Clusters	Proportion of Variation Explained by Clusters	Minimum Proportion Explained by a Cluster	Maximum Second Eigenvalue in a Cluster	Minimum R-squared for a Variable	Maximum 1-R**2 Ratio for a Variable
1	4.672880	0.5841	0.5841	1.770983	0.3810	.
2	6.426502	0.8033	0.7293	0.476418	0.6329	0.4380
3	6.895347	0.8619	0.7954	0.418369	0.7421	0.3634
4	7.271218	0.9089	0.8773	0.238000	0.8652	0.2548
5	7.509218	0.9387	0.8773	0.236135	0.8652	0.1665
6	7.740000	0.9675	0.9295	0.141000	0.9295	0.2560
7	7.881000	0.9851	0.9405	0.119000	0.9405	0.2093
8	8.000000	1.0000	1.0000	0.000000	1.0000	0.0000

Output 34.4   TREE Diagram: PROC TREE

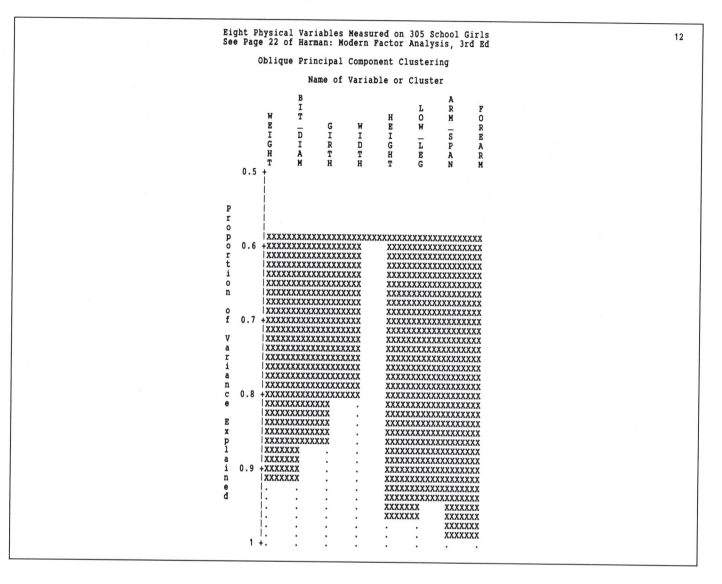

REFERENCES

Anderberg, M.R. (1973), *Cluster Analysis for Applications*, New York: Academic Press, Inc.

Harman, H.H. (1976), *Modern Factor Analysis*, 3d Edition, Chicago: University of Chicago Press.

The VARCOMP
Procedure

ABSTRACT

The VARCOMP procedure computes estimates of the variance components in a general linear model.

INTRODUCTION

The VARCOMP procedure is designed to handle models that have random effects. Random effects are classification effects where the levels of the effect are assumed to be randomly selected from an infinite population of possible levels. The goal of VARCOMP is to estimate the contribution of each of the random effects to the variance of the dependent variable. For more information on random effects and the kind of models that can be analyzed with PROC VARCOMP, see **Fixed and Random Effects** later in this chapter.

A single MODEL statement specifies the dependent variables and the effects: main effects, interactions, and nested effects. The effects must be composed of class variables; no continuous variables are allowed on the right side of the equal sign. See **Specification of Effects** in the chapter on the ANOVA procedure for information on how to specify effects in the MODEL statement.

You can specify certain effects as fixed (nonrandom) by putting them first in the MODEL statement and indicating the number of fixed effects with the FIXED= option. An intercept is always fitted and assumed fixed. Except for the effects specified as fixed, all other effects are assumed to be random, and their contribution to the model can be thought of as an observation from a distribution that is normally and independently distributed.

The dependent variables are grouped based on the similarity of their missing values. Each group of dependent variables is then analyzed separately. The columns of the design matrix **X** are formed in the same order as the effects are specified in the MODEL statement. No reparameterization is done. Thus, the columns of **X** contain only 0s and 1s.

Four methods of estimation are available, and each one is described below.

The Type I Method

This method (METHOD=TYPE1) computes the Type I sum of squares for each effect, equates each mean square involving only random effects to its expected value, and solves the resulting system of equations (Gaylor, Lucas, and Anderson 1970). The **X'X | X'Y** matrix is computed and adjusted in segments whenever memory is not sufficient to hold the entire matrix.

The MIVQUE0 Method

Based on the technique suggested by Hartley, Rao, and LaMotte (1978), the MIVQUE0 method (METHOD=MIVQUE0) produces estimates that are invariant with respect to the fixed effects of the model and are locally best quadratic unbiased estimates given that the true ratio of each component to the residual error component is zero. The technique is similar to TYPE1 except that the random effects are adjusted only for the fixed effects. This affords a considerable timing advantage over the TYPE1 method; thus, MIVQUE0 is the default method used in PROC VARCOMP. The **X'X | X'Y** matrix is computed and adjusted in segments whenever memory is not sufficient to hold the entire matrix. For more information, refer to Rao (1971, 1972).

The Maximum-Likelihood Method

The ML method (METHOD=ML) computes maximum-likelihood estimates of the variance components using the W-transformation developed by Hemmerle and Hartley (1973). Initial estimates of the components are computed using MIVQUE0. The procedure then iterates until the log-likelihood objective function converges.

The Restricted Maximum-Likelihood Method

Similar to the maximum-likelihood method is the REML method (METHOD=REML), but it first separates the likelihood into two parts: one that contains the fixed effects and one that does not (Patterson and Thompson 1971). Initial estimates are obtained using MIVQUE0, and the procedure iterates until convergence is reached for the log-likelihood objective function of the portion of the likelihood that does not contain the fixed effects.

SPECIFICATIONS

The following statements are used in the VARCOMP procedure:

PROC VARCOMP *options*;
   CLASS *variables*;
   MODEL *dependents*=*effects* / *option*;
   BY *variables*;

A MODEL statement and a CLASS statement are required with PROC VARCOMP. The CLASS statement must precede the MODEL statement, and only one MODEL statement is allowed. The BY, CLASS, and MODEL statements are described after the PROC VARCOMP statement.

PROC VARCOMP Statement

   PROC VARCOMP *options*;

The options below can appear in the PROC VARCOMP statement:

DATA=*SASdataset*
   names the SAS data set to be used by VARCOMP. If you do not specify the DATA= option, VARCOMP uses the most recently created SAS data set.

EPSILON=*number*
   specifies the convergence value of the objective function for METHOD=ML or REML. If you do not specify the EPSILON= option, its value is 1E−8.

MAXITER=*number*
   specifies the maximum number of iterations for METHOD=ML or REML. If you do not specify a value for the MAXITER= option, its value is set to 50.

METHOD=TYPE1
METHOD=MIVQUE0
METHOD=ML
METHOD=REML
   specifies which of the four methods (TYPE1, MIVQUE0, ML, or REML) the VARCOMP procedure should use. If you do not specify the METHOD= option, MIVQUE0 is the default.

BY Statement

   BY *variables*;

You can use a BY statement with PROC VARCOMP to obtain separate analyses on observations in groups defined by the BY variables. When a BY statement appears, the procedure expects the input data set to be sorted in order of the BY variables.

   If your input data set is not sorted in ascending order, use the SORT procedure with a similar BY statement to sort the data, or, if appropriate, use the BY statement options NOTSORTED or DESCENDING. For more information, see the discussion of the BY statement in the chapter "SAS Statements Used in the PROC Step" in the *SAS Language Guide, Release 6.03 Edition*.

CLASS Statement

CLASS *variables*;

The CLASS statement specifies the classification variables to be used in the analysis. All effects in the MODEL statement must be composed of effects that appear in the CLASS statement. Class variables may be either numeric or character; if they are character, their lengths must be sixteen or less.

Numeric class variables are not restricted to integers since a variable's format determines the levels. For more information, see the discussion of the FORMAT statement in the chapter "SAS Statements Used in the Proc Step" in the *SAS Language Guide*.

MODEL Statement

MODEL *dependents=effects / option*;

The MODEL statement gives the dependent variables and independent effects. If more than one dependent variable is specified, a separate analysis is performed for each one. The independent effects are limited to main effects, interactions, and nested effects; no continuous effects are allowed. All independent effects must be composed of effects that appear in the CLASS statement. Effects are specified in the VARCOMP procedure in the same way as described for the ANOVA procedure. Only one MODEL statement is allowed.

Only one option is available in the MODEL statement:

FIXED=*n*
> tells VARCOMP that the first *n* effects in the MODEL statement are fixed effects. The remaining effects are assumed to be random. If you do not specify the FIXED= option, VARCOMP assumes that all effects are random in the model. Keep in mind that if you use bar notation and, for example, specify Y=A | B / FIXED=2, then A*B is considered a random effect.

DETAILS

Fixed and Random Effects

Central to the idea of variance components models is the idea of fixed and random effects. Each effect in a variance components model must be classified as either a fixed or a random effect. Fixed effects arise when the levels of an effect constitute the entire population about which you are interested. For example, if a plant scientist is comparing the yields of three varieties of soybeans, then VARIETY would be a fixed effect, providing that the scientist was concerned about making inferences on only these three varieties of soybeans. Similarly, if an industrial experiment focused on the effectiveness of two brands of a machine, MACHINE would be a fixed effect only if the experimenter's interest did not go beyond the two machine brands.

On the other hand, an effect is classified as a random effect when you want to make inferences on an entire population, and the levels in your experiment represent only a sample from that population. Psychologists comparing test results between different groups of subjects would consider SUBJECT as a random effect. Depending on the psychologists' particular interest, the GROUP effect might be either fixed or random. For example, if the groups were based on the sex of the subject, then SEX would be a fixed effect. But if the psychologists were interested in the variability in test scores due to different teachers, then they might choose a random sample of teachers as being representative of the total population of teachers, and TEACHER would be a random effect. Note that, in the soybean example presented earlier, if the scientist were interested in making inferences on the entire population of soybean varieties and randomly chose three varieties for testing, then VARIETY would be a random effect.

If all the effects in a model (except for the intercept) are considered random effects, then the model is called a *random effects model*; likewise a model with only fixed effects is called a *fixed effects model*. The more common case, where some factors are fixed and others are random, is called a *mixed model*. In PROC VARCOMP, by default, effects are assumed to be random. You specify which effects are fixed by using the FIXED= option in the MODEL statement. In general, if an interaction or nested effect contains any effect that is random, then the interaction or nested effect should be considered as a random effect as well.

In the linear model, each level of a fixed effect contributes a fixed amount to the expected value of the dependent variable. What makes a random effect different is that each level of a random effect contributes an amount that is viewed as a sample from a population of normally distributed variables, each with mean 0, and an unknown variance, much like the usual random error term that is a part of all linear models. The estimate of the variance associated with the random effect is known as the *variance component* because it is measuring the part of the overall variance contributed by that effect. Thus, PROC VARCOMP estimates the variance of the random variables that are associated with the random effects in your model, and the variance components tell you how much each of the random factors contributes to the overall variability in the dependent variable.

A Note on Negative Variance Component Estimates

Because the variance components estimated by PROC VARCOMP are assumed to represent the variance of a random variable, they should always be positive. Nevertheless, when you are using METHOD=MIVQUE0 (the default) or METHOD=TYPE1, some estimates of variance components may become negative. (Due to the nature of the algorithms used for METHOD=ML and METHOD=REML, negative estimates are set to zero.) These negative estimates may arise for a variety of reasons:

- The variability in your data may be large enough to produce a negative estimate, even though the true value of the variance component is positive.
- Your data may contain outliers. See Hocking (1983) for a graphical technique for detecting outliers in variance components models using the SAS System.
- A different model for interpreting your data may be appropriate. Under some statistical models for variance components analysis, negative estimates are an indication that observations in your data are negatively correlated. See Hocking (1984) for further information about these models.

Assuming that you are satisfied that the model PROC VARCOMP is using is appropriate for your data, it is common practice to treat negative variance components as if they were zero.

Missing Values

If an observation has a missing value for any variable used in the independent effects, then the analyses of all dependent variables omit this observation. An observation will be deleted from the analysis of a given dependent variable if the observation's value for that dependent variable is missing. Note that a missing value in one dependent variable does not eliminate an observation from the analysis of the other dependent variables.

During processing, VARCOMP groups the dependent variables on their missing values across observations so that sums of squares and crossproducts can be computed in the most efficient manner.

Printed Output

VARCOMP prints the following items:

1. Class Level Information for verifying the levels and number of observations in your data.
2. for METHOD=TYPE1, an analysis-of-variance table with Source, DF, Type I SS, Type I MS, and Expected Mean Square.
3. for METHOD=MIVQUE0, the SSQ Matrix containing sums of squares of partitions of the $\mathbf{X'X}$ crossproducts matrix adjusted for the fixed effects. Each element (i,j) of this matrix is computed:

$$\mathbf{SSQ(X_i'MX_j)}$$

where

$$\mathbf{M = I - X_0(X_0'X_0)^- X_0'}$$

$\mathbf{X_0}$ is part of the design matrix for the fixed effects, $\mathbf{X_i}$ is part of the design matrix for one of the random effects, and $\mathbf{SSQ}$ is an operator that takes the sum of squares of the elements.

4. for METHOD=ML and METHOD=REML, the iteration history, including the objective function, as well as variance component estimates. The objective function for METHOD=ML is $\ln(|\mathbf{V}|)$, and for METHOD=REML, the function is $\ln(|\mathbf{MVM'}|)$ where

$$\mathbf{V} = \sigma_0^2 \mathbf{I} + \Sigma_{i=1}^{n_r} \sigma_i^2 \mathbf{X_i X_i'}$$

σ_0^2 is the residual variance, n_r is the number of random effects in the model, σ_i^2 represents the variance components, and $\mathbf{X_i}$ and $\mathbf{M}$ are defined as above.

5. for METHOD=ML and METHOD=REML, the estimated Asymptotic Covariance Matrix of the variance components.

EXAMPLES

Example 1: PROC VARCOMP for Four Estimation Methods

In this example, A and B are classification variables and Y is the dependent variable. A is declared fixed, and B and A*B are random. Note that the cell sizes are not all the same. VARCOMP is invoked four times, once for each of the estimation methods. The data are from Hemmerle and Hartley (1973). The following statements produce **Output 35.1**:

```
data a;
   input a b y @@;
   cards;
1 1 237 1 1 254 1 1 246
1 2 178 1 2 179
2 1 208 2 1 178 2 1 187
```

```
2 2 146 2 2 145 2 2 141
3 1 186 3 1 183
3 2 142 3 2 125 3 2 136
;
proc varcomp method=type1;
   class a b;
   model y=a|b / fixed=1;
proc varcomp method=mivque0;
   class a b;
   model y=a|b / fixed=1;
proc varcomp method=ml;
   class a b;
   model y=a|b / fixed=1;
proc varcomp method=reml;
   class a b;
   model y=a|b / fixed=1;
run;
```

Output 35.1 VARCOMP Procedure Invoked Once for Each Estimation Method

```
                              SAS                                        1
                Variance Components Estimation Procedure
              ❶        Class Level Information

                   Class    Levels    Values

                     A         3      1 2 3

                     B         2      1 2


           Number of observations in data set = 16
```

```
                              SAS                                        2
                  ❷  Variance Components Estimation Procedure

Dependent Variable: Y

Source          DF        Type I SS         Type I MS    Expected Mean Square

A                2    11736.43750000    5868.21875000    Var(Error) + 2.725 Var(A*B) + 0.1 Var(B) + Q(A)

B                1    11448.12564103   11448.12564103    Var(Error) + 2.6308 Var(A*B) + 7.8 Var(B)

A*B              2      299.04102564     149.52051282    Var(Error) + 2.5846 Var(A*B)

Error           10      786.33333333      78.63333333    Var (Error )

Corrected Total 15    24269.93750000



Variance Component              Estimate

Var(B)                       1448.37683150

Var(A*B)                       27.42658730

Var(Error)                     78.63333333
```

```
                                      SAS                                        3

                    Variance Components Estimation Procedure
                              Class Level Information

                         Class    Levels    Values

                         A          3       1 2 3

                         B          2       1 2


                    Number of observations in data set = 16
```

```
                                      SAS                                        4

                 MIVQUE(0) Variance Component Estimation Procedure

                              ❸ SSQ Matrix

        Source            B              A*B            Error              Y

        B          60.84000000      20.52000000     7.80000000     89295.38000000
        A*B        20.52000000      20.52000000     7.80000000     30181.30000000
        Error       7.80000000       7.80000000    13.00000000     12533.50000000

                                                 Estimate
                         Variance Component          Y

                              Var(B)            1466.12301587
                              Var(A*B)           -35.49170274
                              Var(Error)         105.73659674
```

```
                                      SAS                                        5

                    Variance Components Estimation Procedure
                              Class Level Information

                         Class    Levels    Values

                         A          3       1 2 3

                         B          2       1 2


                    Number of observations in data set = 16
```

```
                                      SAS                                        6

        ❹  Maximum Likelihood Variance Components Estimation Procedure

Dependent Variable: Y

        Iteration      Objective          Var(B)         Var(A*B)          Var(Error)

           0         78.38503712    1031.49069751  8.25905697094E-9       74.39097179
           1         78.27291305     794.73081143             0           76.56566052
           2         78.26385061     735.78408555             0           77.35118963
           3         78.26355058     724.94642106             0           77.51122694
           4         78.26354717     723.82414198             0           77.52810692
           5         78.26354712     723.68567767             0           77.53019360
           6         78.26354712     723.66831643             0           77.53045530

                              Convergence criterion met.

                 ❺  Asymptotic Covariance Matrix of Estimates

                              Var(B)        Var(A*B)        Var(Error)

        Var(B)         537833.41091             0          -107.3663357
        Var(A*B)                  0             0                     0
        Var(Error)       -107.3663357           0           858.71021425
```

```
                                    SAS                                         7
                    Variance Components Estimation Procedure
                            Class Level Information

                    Class     Levels     Values

                    A            3       1 2 3

                    B            2       1 2


              Number of observations in data set = 16
```

```
                                    SAS                                         8
            Restricted Maximum Likelihood Variance Components Estimation Procedure

Dependent Variable: Y


        Iteration     Objective        Var(B)          Var(A*B)       Var(Error)
            0        63.41341449    1269.52701231      0.00000001     91.55811913
            1        63.41285906    1274.06218033      0.00000006     91.52695138
            2        63.41233642    1278.46760636      0.00000039     91.49690480
            3        63.41184803    1282.71474020      0.00000246     91.46814787
            4        63.41138725    1286.84429407      0.00001527     91.44037695
            5        63.41095032    1290.85987878      0.00009504     91.41350988
            6        63.41052358    1294.76232525      0.00059136     91.38727924
            7        63.41003086    1298.53608905      0.00368041     91.36024796
            8        63.40900595    1302.06419710      0.02292164     91.32367959
            9        63.40454958    1304.59434704      0.14333359     91.22320277
           10        63.37851777    1301.30706353      0.91936326     90.71312389
           11        63.21813200    1257.57386963      7.12220390     87.31202881
           12        63.13163622    1248.18873174     48.32954677     76.11587489
           13        63.03332748    1494.12682156     24.36870376     79.37616688
           14        63.03118816    1456.21221616     26.57822509     78.97727508
           15        63.03113001    1462.37517647     26.86885449     78.87443012
           16        63.03112671    1463.90213561     26.93755228     78.84993342
           17        63.03112652    1464.25825754     26.95384207     78.84416193
           18        63.03112651    1464.34169199     26.95767589     78.84280590
           19        63.03112651    1464.36126988     26.95857643     78.84248750

                        Convergence criterion met.


                  Asymptotic Covariance Matrix of Estimates

                            Var(B)        Var(A*B)       Var(Error)

         Var(B)         4401632.150          1.258         -273.301
         Var(A*B)             1.258       3559.056         -502.849
         Var(Error)        -273.301       -502.849         1249.702
```

Example 2: Variance Components Analysis of the Cure Rate of Rubber

This example using data from Hicks (1973) is concerned with an experiment to determine the sources of variability in cure rates of rubber. The goal of the experiment was to find out if different laboratories had more of an effect on the variance of cure rates than did different batches of raw materials. This information would be useful in trying to control the cure rate of the final product because it would provide insights into the sources of the variability in cure rates. The rubber used was cured at three temperatures, which were taken to be fixed. Three laboratories were chosen at random, and three different batches of raw material were tested at each combination of temperature and laboratory.

The SAS statements to produce the data set and perform the restricted maximum-likelihood variance component analysis are given below. The output is shown in **Output 35.2**.

```
data cure;
   input lab temp batch $ cure aa;
   cards;
1 145 A 18.6    1 145 A 17.0    1 145 A 18.7    1 145 A 18.7
1 145 B 14.5    1 145 B 15.8    1 145 B 16.5    1 145 B 17.6
1 145 C 21.1    1 145 C 20.8    1 145 C 21.8    1 145 C 21.0
1 155 A  9.5    1 155 A  9.4    1 155 A  9.5    1 155 A 10.0
1 155 B  7.8    1 155 B  8.3    1 155 B  8.9    1 155 B  9.1
1 155 C 11.2    1 155 C 10.0    1 155 C 11.5    1 155 C 11.1
1 165 A  5.4    1 165 A  5.3    1 165 A  5.7    1 165 A  5.3
1 165 B  5.2    1 165 B  4.9    1 165 B  4.3    1 165 B  5.2
1 165 C  6.3    1 165 C  6.4    1 165 C  5.8    1 165 C  5.6
2 145 A 20.0    2 145 A 20.1    2 145 A 19.4    2 145 A 20.0
2 145 B 18.4    2 145 B 18.1    2 145 B 16.5    2 145 B 16.7
2 145 C 22.5    2 145 C 22.7    2 145 C 21.5    2 145 C 21.3
2 155 A 11.4    2 155 A 11.5    2 155 A 11.4    2 155 A 11.5
2 155 B 10.8    2 155 B 11.1    2 155 B  9.5    2 155 B  9.7
2 155 C 13.3    2 155 C 14.0    2 155 C 12.0    2 155 C 11.5
2 165 A  6.8    2 165 A  6.9    2 165 A  6.0    2 165 A  5.7
2 165 B  6.0    2 165 B  6.1    2 165 B  5.0    2 165 B  5.2
2 165 C  7.7    2 165 C  8.0    2 165 C  6.6    2 165 C  6.3
3 145 A 19.7    3 145 A 18.3    3 145 A 16.8    3 145 A 17.1
3 145 B 16.3    3 145 B 16.7    3 145 B 14.4    3 145 B 15.2
3 145 C 22.7    3 145 C 21.9    3 145 C 19.3    3 145 C 19.3
3 155 A  9.3    3 155 A 10.2    3 155 A  9.8    3 155 A  9.5
3 155 B  9.1    3 155 B  9.2    3 155 B  8.0    3 155 B  9.0
3 155 C 11.3    3 155 C 11.0    3 155 C 10.9    3 155 C 11.4
3 165 A  6.7    3 165 A  6.0    3 165 A  5.0    3 165 A  4.8
3 165 B  5.7    3 165 B  5.5    3 165 B  4.6    3 165 B  5.4
3 165 C  6.6    3 165 C  6.5    3 165 C  5.9    3 165 C  5.8
;
proc varcomp method=reml;
   class temp lab batch;
   model cure=temp|lab batch(lab temp) / fixed=1;
run;
```

Output 35.2   REML Analysis of Rubber Cure Data

```
                    Variance Components Estimation Procedure                    1
                          Class Level Information

                    Class    Levels    Values

                    TEMP       3       145 155 165

                    LAB        3       1 2 3

                    BATCH      3       A B C


             Number of observations in data set = 108
```

```
                    Restricted Maximum Likelihood Variance Components Estimation Procedure                        2
Dependent Variable: CURE


   Iteration         Objective            Var(LAB)        Var(TEMP*LAB)   Var(BATCH(TEMP*LAB))           Var(Error)
       0            13.45000603        0.50944643  6.4250662840678085E-11          2.40048886            0.57871852
       1            13.09863379        0.34714413                    0            2.11846698            0.59864919
       2            13.08979146        0.32113607                    0            2.08576691            0.60164589
       3            13.08933584        0.31796673                    0            2.07665523            0.60240517
       4            13.08931376        0.31769007                    0            2.07449971            0.60257381
       5            13.08931262        0.31762187                    0            2.07401261            0.60261212
       6            13.08931256        0.31760632                    0            2.07390147            0.60262087
       7            13.08931256        0.31760276                    0            2.07387607            0.60262286

                                        Convergence criteria met.


                                 Asymptotic Covariance Matrix of Estimates

                              Var(LAB)         Var(TEMP*LAB)   Var(BATCH(TEMP*LAB))            Var(Error)

Var(LAB)                  0.3245245707                    0         -0.049985597           -1.566904E-8
Var(TEMP*LAB)                        0                    0                    0                      0
Var(BATCH(TEMP*LAB))      -0.049985597                    0          0.4504308859           -0.002241803
Var(Error)               -1.566904E-8                    0         -0.002241803           0.0089667733
```

First, note that the variance of TEMP*LAB was set to zero after the first iteration, indicating that the variance component was initially less than zero, and set to a small positive number to begin the iterative process. In this case, the most likely interpretation would be that the variance contributed by the LAB*TEMP interaction is negligible. The results of the analysis show that the variance attributable to BATCH(TEMP*LAB) (with a variance component of 2.0739) is considerably larger than the variance attributable to LAB (0.3176). Therefore, attempts to reduce the variability of cure rates should concentrate on improving the homogeneity of the batches of raw material used rather than standardizing the practices or equipment within the laboratories. It is also of interest to note that since the BATCH(TEMP*LAB) variance is considerably larger than the experimental error (Var(Error)=0.6026), the BATCH(TEMP*LAB) variability plays an important part in the overall variability of the cure rates.

REFERENCES

Gaylor, D.W., Lucas, H.L., and Anderson, R.L. (1970), "Calculation of Expected Mean Squares by the Abbreviated Doolittle and Square Root Methods," *Biometrics*, 26, 641–655.

Goodnight, J.H. (1978), *Computing MIVQUE0 Estimates of Variance Components,* SAS Technical Report R-105. Cary, NC: SAS Institute Inc.

Goodnight, J.H. and Hemmerle, W.J. (1979), "A Simplified Algorithm for the W-Transformation in Variance Component Estimation," *Technometrics*, 21, 265–268.

Hartley, H.O., Rao, J.N.K., and LaMotte, L. (1978), "A Simple Synthesis-Based Method of Variance Component Estimation," *Biometrics*, 34, 233–242.

Hemmerle, W.J. and Hartley, H.O. (1973), "Computing Maximum Likelihood Estimates for the Mixed AOV Model Using the W-Transformation," *Technometrics*, 15, 819–831.

Hicks, C.R. (1973), *Fundamental Concepts in the Design of Experiments*, New York: Holt, Rinehart and Winston, Inc.

Hocking, R.R. (1983), "A Diagnostic Tool for Mixed Models with Applications to Negative Estimates of Variance Components," *SAS Users Group International Conference Proceedings*, Cary, NC: SAS Institute Inc., 711–716.

Hocking, R.R. (1984), *The Analysis of Linear Models*, Monterey, CA: Brooks-Cole Publishing Co.

Patterson, H.D. and Thompson, R. (1971), "Recovery of Inter-Block Information When Block Sizes Are Unequal," *Biometrika*, 58, 545–554.

Rao, C.R. (1971), "Minimum Variance Quadratic Unbiased Estimation of Variance Components," *Journal of Multivariate Analysis*, 1, 445–456.

Rao, C.R. (1972), "Estimation of Variance and Covariance Components in Linear Models," *Journal of the American Statistical Association*, 67, 112–15.

Changes and Enhancements to SAS/STAT™ Procedures

How to Use This Appendix

Use this appendix to get an overview of the changes and enhancements to procedures in Release 6.03 of SAS/STAT software. All of these changes and enhancements are incorporated into the chapters for the procedures. In all cases, the individual chapters contain more detail on the changes and enhancements. For information on a specific procedure, look at the table of contents at the beginning of the chapter for the procedure.

Release 6.03 of SAS/STAT software contains all the procedures that were documented in Release 6.02 and many that were not. Specifically, ANOVA, DISCRIM, FACTOR, FREQ, GLM, NPAR1WAY, REG, SCORE, and TTEST were available in Release 6.02. CATMOD, CANCORR, and ORTHOREG were available in Release 6.02 but with supplementary documentation (ORTHOREG and CANCORR were documented in SAS Technical Report P-161, *Additional SAS/STAT Procedures: CANCORR and ORTHOREG*; CATMOD documentation was available upon request). For each of these procedures, this chapter provides a summary of changes and enhancements from Release 6.02 to Release 6.03. The ACECLUS, CANDISC, CLUSTER, FASTCLUS, LIFEREG, NESTED, NLIN, PLAN, RSREG, STEPDISC, TREE, VARCLUS, and VARCOMP procedures were not available in Release 6.02 of SAS/STAT software. These procedures were previously documented in *SAS User's Guide: Statistics, Version 5 Edition*. For these procedures, this chapter provides a summary of changes and enhancements from Version 5 SAS software to Release 6.03 of SAS/STAT software. The NEIGHBOR procedure, documented in Version 5, is now part of PROC DISCRIM. The RSQUARE and STEPWISE procedures, documented in Version 5, are now part of PROC REG.

Interactive Procedures

In addition to the changes and enhancements described in this appendix, many of the Version 6 procedures can be run interactively. For example, you can submit a procedure, look at the output, and then submit additional statements for the procedure without reinvoking the procedure.

You can end an interactive procedure with a DATA step, by invoking another procedure, by submitting an ENDSAS statement, or by submitting a QUIT statement. The syntax of the QUIT statement is

```
quit;
```

You cannot end an interactive procedure by submitting additional RUN statements.

The ANOVA, CATMOD, GLM, PLAN, and REG procedures can be run interactively. In the chapters for these procedures, the **SPECIFICATIONS** section describes those statements that must appear before the first RUN statement and those that can appear after it.

Because of conflicts between BY group processing and interactivity, there are some limitations on using BY statements. For most interactive procedures, you cannot use both a BY statement and the interactive features of the procedure. In other words, in most cases, the BY statement must appear before the first RUN statement, and no additional statements are accepted after the first RUN statement. However, for CATMOD, the BY statement can appear after the first RUN statement, but, once it appears, the statements up to the subsequent RUN statement are executed, and CATMOD does not accept any additional statements.

ACECLUS Procedure

The default value for the converge criterion, CONVERGE=, is now 0.001.

ANOVA Procedure

PROC ANOVA Statement

Two new options have been added to the PROC ANOVA statement. The MANOVA option requests that ANOVA use the multivariate mode of eliminating observations with missing values. This option is useful if you are using ANOVA in interactive mode and will be performing a multivariate analysis. The MULTIPASS option requests that ANOVA reread the data set when necessary. While this option does decrease disk space usage, it is useful only in rare situations.

MANOVA Statement

An alternative form for entering a transformation matrix (M) in the M= specification of the MANOVA statement has been added. In addition to supplying the M matrix in equation form, you can input M directly by entering the elements of the matrix with commas separating the rows and enclosing the entire specification in parentheses. If you use this form of the M= specification, you must include as many entries in each row of the matrix as there are dependent variables.

MEANS Statement

Three new options for multiple comparison procedures have been added. These are the DUNNETT, DUNNETTL, and DUNNETTU options. These options perform Dunnett's tests to compare treatments to a control. The two-tailed test and both one-tailed tests are available. You can also specify which level of the effect is the control.

Using @ Notation

The @ notation is a new way to use bar notation to specify effects and control the number of effects generated. Specifically, the @ notation specifies the maximum number of variables involved in any effect that results from evaluation of bar notation. To use the @ notation, you specify the maximum number of variables after an @ sign at the end of the bar notation. For example, A | B | C | D@2 indicates that the effects to be included in the model are all the main effects and two-way interactions that can be formed from the variables A, B, C, and D.

CANCORR Procedure

Fourteen options for regression calculations have been added to PROC CANCORR. The VDEP option is useful if you want to do multiple regression analyses predicting your VAR variables with the variables specified in the WITH statement. Using the WDEP option, you can predict the variables in the WITH statement using the VAR statement variables. Other new options include T, requesting the t statistics; STB, requesting standardized regression coefficients; and SEB, requesting the standard errors of the regression coefficients. All new options are described in **Regression Options** in the chapter on the CANCORR procedure.

CANDISC Procedure

Six options have been added to the PROC CANDISC statement. The ANOVA option prints univariate statistics for testing the hypothesis that the class means are equal in the population for each variable. The SIMPLE option prints simple descriptive statistics for total sample and within each class. The ANOVA and SIMPLE options replace the Version 5 statistic UNIVARIATE. PSSCP prints the pooled within-class corrected SSCP matrix. In Version 5, this matrix was specified with the WSSCP option. PCORR and PCOV request the pooled within-class correlations and covariances, respectively. In Version 5, these options were specified with WCORR and WCOV. The DISTANCE option, replacing the Version 5 option MAHALANOBIS, prints squared Mahalanobis distances between the class means. The Version 5 options EDF=n and RDF=n are no longer available. The PROB statement is not available in Release 6.03.

TYPE=SSCP and CSSCP data sets can be used in addition to COV and CORR data sets as input data sets.

CATMOD Procedure

CATMOD is now an interactive procedure. There are two new statements, and several options or details to statements have been modified.

Interactivity

CATMOD is now totally interactive. Each statement replaces any previous occurrence of that statement, except for the CONTRAST and RESPONSE statements, which generate one analysis per statement.

New Statements

A new FACTORS statement allows you to identify the factors that distinguish certain response functions from others. The FACTORS statement can be used for repeated measurement factors and for log-linear model factors, but it is probably most useful for identifying factors based on independent variables when the response functions are read directly from the data set. In this case, the usual independent variables on the right-hand side of the MODEL statement are absent and therefore cannot generate any effects or statistical tests.

There is now a LOGLIN statement to facilitate the analysis of log-linear models.

Additional Enhancements

A TITLE option has been added to the RESPONSE, FACTORS, MODEL, LOGLIN, and REPEATED statements. This option causes the title to be printed at the top of certain pages of output that correspond to that statement.

In the MODEL, LOGLIN, FACTORS, and REPEATED statements, the maximum interaction level can now be specified for effects that use the bar operator. For example, A | B | C | D@2 indicates that the effects to be included in the model are all the main effects and two-way interactions that can be formed from the variables A, B, C, and D.

CATMOD now allows nested effects and nested-with-value effects in the REPEATED, LOGLIN, and FACTORS statements. Previously, these were allowed only in the MODEL statement.

CATMOD now allows you to specify the actual values of repeated measurement (or other) factors. This has two major advantages. First, it allows you to use nested-with-value effects in the REPEATED, LOGLIN, and FACTORS statements. Second, it allows the analysis of data from designs that are not full-factorial with respect to the factors of interest.

CATMOD now accepts direct input of a function vector and its covariance matrix. This allows the analysis of categorical data obtained from complex sampling methods, as well as the analysis of parameter estimates and predicted values obtained from previous analyses.

For log-linear models, the _RESPONSE_ matrix, which is essentially the "untransformed" design matrix, is now printed by default. This allows you to see exactly what parameterization is used since this information is not apparent from the usual transformed design matrix, X, used for log-linear models. The printing of this matrix can be suppressed with the NORESPONSE option in the MODEL statement.

The maximum-likelihood estimation algorithm was modified so that it now flags "infinite" parameters as it proceeds with the maximization. Previously, high collinearity among the parameters had the potential of resulting in an arithmetic overflow.

CLUSTER Procedure

The CLUSTER procedure has a new option, NOTIE, that prevents CLUSTER from checking for ties for minimum distance between clusters at each generation of the cluster history. If neither NOTIE nor METHOD=TWOSTAGE nor METHOD=DENSITY is specified, CLUSTER prints a column indicating where ties for minimum distance occur.

The CLUSTER procedure no longer requires that the data be stored in memory but allows the data to be stored either in memory or on disk. In addition, if the store distance or sorted distance algorithm is used, the distances are stored in memory or, if necessary, on disk. Previously, the distances could be stored only in memory.

DISCRIM Procedure

Enhancements to PROC DISCRIM include nonparametric methods of analysis, crossvalidation, and posterior probability error-rate estimates.

See the data set information in the **DETAILS** section of "The DISCRIM Procedure" for information on the input and output data sets. The output section has changed substantially in order to incorporate posterior probabilites, classification results, and group-specific density results.

Nonparametric Methods

Nonparametric discriminant methods are based on nonparametric estimates of group-specific probability densities. Either a kernel method or the *k*-nearest-neighbor method can be used to generate a nonparametric density estimate in each group and to produce a classification criterion. The kernel method uses uniform, normal, Epanechnikov, biweight, or triweight kernels in the density estimation.

PROC DISCRIM Statement

Fifteen new options have been added to the PROC DISCRIM statement. Specifically, the METHOD= option determines the method to use in deriving the classification criterion. The METRIC= option specifies the metric in which the computations of squared distances are performed.

Three new options concern the use of a nonparametric method (METHOD=NPAR). You can use the K= option to specify a k value for the k-nearest-neighbor rule. An observation **x** is classified into a group based on the information from the k nearest neighbors of **x**. Use the R= option to specify a radius r value for kernel density estimation. With the KERNEL= option, you can specify a kernel method for estimating the group-specific densities.

The SINGULAR= option is a new option used to specify the criterion for determining the singularity of a within-class covariance matrix or the pooled covariance matrix.

Several new options used for cross-validation are now available. The CROSSVALIDATE option is set when the CROSSLIST, CROSSLISTERR, or OUTCROSS= option is specified. When a parametric method is used, DISCRIM classifies each observation in the DATA= data set using a discriminant function computed from the other observations in the DATA= data set, excluding the observation being classified. When a nonparametric method is used, the pooled covariance (within-class covariance matrices) used to compute the distances is based on all observations in the data set and does not exclude the observation being classified. However, the observation being classified is excluded from the nonparametric density estimation (if the R= option is specified) or the k nearest neighbors (if the K= option is specified) of that observation. CROSSLIST prints the cross-validation classification results for each observation. CROSSLISTERR prints the cross-validation classification results for misclassified observations only.

The following are new options concerning canonical discriminant analysis. CANONICAL requests canonical discriminant analysis. NCAN=n specifies the number of canonical variables to be computed. CANPREFIX=$name$ specifies a prefix for naming the canonical variables.

One new option concerns error rate estimation. POSTERR prints the posterior probability error rate estimates of the classification criterion based on the classification results.

There are two new options to control printed output, STDMEAN and DISTANCE.

FACTOR Procedure

There are two new options in the PROC FACTOR statement. The RANDOM= option specifies a positive integer as the starting value for the pseudo-random-number generator for use with PRIORS=RANDOM. If you do not specify the RANDOM= option, the time of day is used to initialize the pseudo-random-number sequence. The VARDEF= option specifies the divisor to be used in the calculation of variances and covariances.

FASTCLUS Procedure

No changes have been made to the FASTCLUS procedure since Version 5.

FREQ Procedure

There are three new options to request statistical analysis and additional results for Fisher's exact test for 2×2 tables. In addition, the NOPERCENT option has a different effect for one-way frequencies or frequencies in list format. The ALPHA= option has been modified. Finally, the FREQ procedure now allows negative values for the weight variable (named in the WEIGHT statement).

Two of the new options concern the Cochran-Mantel-Haenszel statistics, which have been requested in previous versions with the CMH option. If the CMH option is specified, FREQ computes and prints three Cochran-Mantel-Haenszel summary statistics (the correlation statistic, the *ANOVA* statistic, and the general association statistic). The two new options allow some choice about which summary statistics are computed. The CMH1 option requests that only the first Cochran-Mantel-Haenszel statistic (the correlation statistic) is computed and printed. The CMH2 option requests that only the first two Cochran-Mantel-Haenszel statistics (the correlation and *ANOVA* statistics) are computed and printed.

The third new option, EXACT, provides Fisher's exact test for tables that are larger than 2×2.

For 2×2 tables, Fisher's exact test is performed if the CHISQ option is specified. In Release 6.03, both the left-tailed and right-tailed *p* values are produced. Previously, a single one-tailed *p* value was reported for the tail that produced the smaller *p* value.

The NOPERCENT option now has an effect for one-way frequencies and frequencies in list format. It suppresses printing of percentages and cumulative percentages.

The ALPHA= option allows values between 0.0001 and 0.9999. If you specify a value of 0, the limit of 0.0001 is actually used. See "The FREQ Procedure" for more detail.

GLM Procedure

PROC GLM Statement

Two new options have been added to the PROC GLM statement. The MANOVA option requests that GLM use the multivariate mode of eliminating observations with missing values. This option is useful if you are using GLM in interactive mode and will be performing a multivariate analysis. The MULTIPASS option requests that GLM reread the data set when necessary. While this option does decrease disk space usage, it is useful only in rare situations.

LSMEANS Statement

Several new options have been added to the LSMEANS statement, and you can now create an output data set containing the least-squares means and associated statistics.

Three of the new options concern the output data set. The OUT= option specifies the name of the output data set, which contains least-squares means and their standard errors. The COV option requests that covariances be included in the output data set. The NOPRINT option requests that the normal printed output from the LSMEANS statement be suppressed, which is helpful when you only want an output data set for the LSMEANS.

Another new option, TDIFF, requests that the *t* values for the hypotheses H_0: LSM(i)=LSM(j) be printed along with the corresponding probabilities.

For more information on the options and the contents of the OUT= data set, see the chapter on the GLM procedure.

MANOVA Statement

An alternative form for entering a transformation matrix (M) in the M= specification of the MANOVA statement has been added. In addition to supplying the M matrix in equation form, you can input M directly by entering the elements of the matrix with commas separating the rows and enclosing the entire specification in parentheses. If you use this form of the M= specification, you must include as many entries in each row of the matrix as there are dependent variables.

MEANS Statement

Three new options for multiple comparison procedures have been added. These are the DUNNETT, DUNNETTL, and DUNNETTU options. These options perform Dunnett's tests to compare treatments to a control. The two-tailed test and both one-tailed tests are available. You can also specify which level of the effect is the control.

OUTPUT Statement

The OUTPUT statement of PROC GLM has been expanded to provide a variety of diagnostic measures, similar to those available through PROC REG. Previously, only the OUT=, P=, and R= specifications were available. These specifications assigned a name to the data set and created new variables containing the predicted and residual values, respectively.

The fourteen new specifications allow you to create variables that contain many diagnostic measures. Specifically, U95M and L95M specify the upper and lower bounds of a 95% confidence interval for the mean of the dependent variable. U95 and L95 specify the upper and lower bounds of a 95% confidence interval for an individual prediction. STDP specifies the standard error of the mean predicted value, STDR specifies the standard error of the residual, and STDI specifies the standard error of the individual predicted value. STUDENT specifies the studentized residuals, and RSTUDENT specifies the studentized residuals with the current observation deleted. Other specifications are COOKD, H (leverage), DFFITS, COVRATIO, and PRESS.

RANDOM Statement

A new option has been added to the RANDOM statement of PROC GLM to provide appropriate tests for random and mixed model analysis of variance. The TEST option requests that hypothesis tests for each effect specified in the model be performed using appropriate error terms as determined by the expected mean squares.

If an exact test is possible, the TEST option performs one. In cases where an exact test is not possible, the TEST option uses Satterthwaite's approximation to construct an approximate test. For more detail, see **Expected Mean Squares for Random Effects** in the chapter on GLM.

Using @ Notation

The @ notation is a new way to use bar notation to specify effects and control the number of effects generated. Specifically, the @ notation specifies the maximum number of variables involved in any effect that results from evaluation of bar notation. To use the @ notation, you specify the maximum number of variables after an @ sign at the end of the bar notation. For example, A | B | C | D@2 indicates that the effects to be included in the model are all the main effects and two-way interactions that can be formed from the variables A, B, C, and D.

LIFEREG Procedure

This Version 5 procedure was not available in Release 6.02 of SAS/STAT software. LIFEREG now allows new censoring patterns and binomial response. A WEIGHT statement has been added. A new option, ORDER=, is available in the PROC LIFEREG statement and allows you to control the order in which the levels of the variables specified in the CLASS statement are to be sorted.

NESTED Procedure

The NESTED procedure is essentially unchanged from previous versions. This procedure was not available in Release 6.02 of SAS/STAT software. Several sections giving details on PROC NESTED have been added to the documentation.

NLIN Procedure

The NLIN procedure has several new options, a new iterative method, and several changes to the way the procedure interacts with the DATA step compiler. This procedure was not available in Release 6.02.

New Options

The SMETHOD= option in the PROC NLIN statement specifies the step-size search method NLIN uses. You can specify four values for this option, corresponding to step-halving, a golden section search, the Goldstein-Armijo method, and cubic interpolation.

The STEP= option in the PROC NLIN statement places a limit on the number of step-halvings.

The SAVE option in the PROC NLIN statement specifies that, when the iteration limit is exceeded (with either the default of 50 or with the value of the MAXITER= option), the parameter estimates from the final iteration are output to the OUTEST= data set.

The CONVERGE= option has been replaced by the CONVERGEOBJ= option, which performs the same function. If you have Version 5 programs that contain the CONVERGE= option, you do not need to change the option to CONVERGEOBJ= for Release 6.03. The new CONVERGEPARM= option specifies that the maximum change among parameter estimates be used as the convergence criterion. If both the CONVERGEOBJ= and CONVERGEPARM= options are used, NLIN uses both criteria to determine convergence.

The PLOT option that was available in Version 5 is not available.

New Method

The Newton iteration method is now available with NLIN. To use this method, specify METHOD=NEWTON. With this method, you need to specify the second derivatives of the model with respect to each parameter. The DER statement has been changed to allow you to specify second derivatives. Previously, only first derivatives could be specified with the DER statement.

PROC NLIN and the DATA Step Compiler

In Release 6.03, NLIN uses the DATA step compiler. As a result, the DATA step LAG and DIF functions are available. In addition, the DO OVER statement is now supported. Finally, you can now specify compound names as elements of an array in the ARRAY statement.

In Release 6.03, if you use the PUT statement, it writes to the log. To write to the output, you need to specify

```
file print;
```

before the PUT statement in your program.

NPAR1WAY Procedure

The NPAR1WAY procedure has a new option, EDF, that produces several statistics based on the Empirical Distribution Function (EDF). These statistics are used to test if the distribution of a variable is the same across different groups. The Kolmogorov-Smirnov and Cramer-von Mises statistics and the asymptotic values of these two statistics are always produced. If there are only two groups, the Kuiper statistic and its asymptotic value are also produced.

ORTHOREG Procedure

The ORTHOREG procedure is essentially unchanged from previous versions. This procedure was available in Release 6.02 of SAS/STAT software.

PLAN Procedure

The PLAN procedure has been substantially upgraded, and it now provides the ability to produce experimental designs, randomize a new or existing design, and output randomized plans to a data set.

FACTORS Statement

This statement specifies the factors of the plan and generates the plan. The form of a factor request has changed. Three selection types are now available. These allow you to choose how the levels of a factor are chosen. The RANDOM selection type specifies that the m levels of a factor are selected randomly without replacement from the integers $1, 2, \ldots, n$. The ORDERED selection type specifies that the levels of a factor are the integers $1, 2, \ldots, m$ in order. The CYCLIC selection type specifies that the levels of a factor are selected by cyclically permuting the integers $1, 2, \ldots, m$.

The FACTORS statement also allows a new option, NOPRINT, that suppresses printing of the experimental plan. This option is useful when you only want to create an output data set.

OUTPUT Statement

This statement can be used both to output an experimental plan and to use an experimental plan to randomize another SAS data set. In addition, you can specify the values that are to be input or output for the factors. For example, you can assign character strings to the levels of a factor.

TREATMENTS Statement

This statement is new and specifies the treatments of an experimental design. Essentially, the factors listed in the FACTORS statement form the cells of an experimental design; the TREATMENTS statement gives the treatments to be applied to the cells of the design. The enhancements to the FACTORS statement (described above) are also available for the TREATMENTS statement. Used alone, the TREATMENTS statement does not generate an experimental design.

PRINCOMP Procedure

The PRINCOMP procedure can output principal component scores when the PARTIAL statement is used. The VARDEF option has been added to the PROC PRINCOMP statement and is used to specify the divisor to be used in the calculation of variances and covariances.

REG Procedure

The REG procedure has several new statements and options. In addition, several options that were available in Version 5 but not in Release 6.02 are now available.

Two new model-selection methods, ADJRSQ and CP, are available. These two methods use the adjusted R^2 statistic and Mallow's C_p statistic, respectively, as the criterion for finding the "best" model within a range of sizes.

The REG procedure now accepts a TYPE=COV data set as input. See Appendix 2, "Special SAS Data Sets," and the chapter on the REG procedure for more information on this type of data set.

New Statements

The REWEIGHT, PLOT, PAINT, REFIT, and RESTRICT statements are new in Release 6.03. All of these statements can be used interactively. The function of each statement is discussed in the paragraphs below.

The new REWEIGHT statement replaces the DELOBS statement that was available in Release 6.02. This new statement excludes specific observations from the analysis or changes the weights of observations used in the analysis. In addition, several options and specifications can be used in various combinations to

- restore the original weights of some or all observations
- specify multiple conditions for excluding observations
- check the status of observation weights
- undo the changes made by the most recent REWEIGHT statement.

The new PLOT statement produces scatter plots. Variables in the input data set and diagnostic statistics can be plotted. Several options provide additional capabilities for

- overlaying several plots
- placing multiple plots on a single page
- collecting plots across PLOT statements and overlaying the plots
- specifying a plotting symbol or specifying that values of a variable be used as a plotting symbol.

The new PAINT statement highlights or "paints" points in scatter plots. In general, observations are painted if they meet the condition specified in the PAINT statement. Additional options and specifications can be used to

- unpaint all observations
- undo changes made by a previous PAINT statement
- specify or change the printing symbol used
- check the status of all painted observations
- suppress the list that is normally printed on the log.

The new REFIT statement causes the current model and corresponding statistics to be recomputed immediately. REFIT is most useful after one or more REWEIGHT statements and causes these statements to take effect before subsequent statements. Note that most interactive statements *implicitly* refit the model; the two exceptions are the PAINT and REWEIGHT statements. The REFIT statement *explicitly* refits the model.

The new RESTRICT statement places restrictions on the parameter estimates in the model. More than one RESTRICT statement can follow each MODEL statement. To lift all restrictions on a model, a new MODEL statement needs to be submitted.

New Options

In the MODEL statement, the METHOD= option has been replaced by the SELECTION= option. In addition, there are two new model-selection methods available, ADJRSQ and CP. These two new methods are similar to the RSQUARE method.

Also in the MODEL statement, the SELECT= option has been replaced by the BEST= option. The BEST= option is used with the RSQUARE, ADJRSQ, and CP model-selection methods.

The GROUPNAMES= option in the MODEL statement provides names for variable groups. Variables in the same group are entered into or removed from the model at the same time. The GROUPNAMES= option can be used with the BACKWARD, FORWARD, and STEPWISE model-selection methods.

The ACOV, PCORR1, PCORR2, SCORR1, SCORR2, SEQB, and SPEC options are now available for the MODEL and PRINT statements. These options were available in the MODEL statement for Version 5 but were not available in Release 6.02.

The new ANOVA and MODELDATA options in the PRINT statement print the *ANOVA* table associated with the current model and the data for variables used in the current model, respectively.

RSREG Procedure

The RSREG procedure has been expanded to perform ridge analysis. This analysis identifies the direction to search for the optimum response and is useful if the optimum response was not found to be in the experimental region. In addition to the ridge analysis, several detail sections on response surface analysis have been added to the documentation.

RIDGE Statement

This statement specifies that the ridge of optimum response be computed. Several options allow you to customize the search. You can request a minimum response ridge, a maximum response ridge, or both. You can also specify the coordinates from which to begin the ridge and the distances from the ridge starting point at which to compute the optimum. Additional options allow you to create an output data set that contains the optimum response ridge and to suppress printing the ridge analysis. This last option is useful when you only want to create an output data set for the ridge analysis.

SCORE Procedure

The BY and ID statements are now available in the SCORE procedure. The BY statement can be used to obtain separate scoring for observations in groups defined by the BY variables or to apply separate groups of scoring coefficients to the input data set. The ID statement identifies variables from the input data set that are to be included in the output data set.

STEPDISC Procedure

The options identifying the selection method (forward, backward, or stepwise) must now be specified in the METHOD= option in the PROC STEPWISE statement. In Version 5, each method was specified by a separate option (FORWARD, STEPWISE, or BACKWARD).

The PROB statement is not available in Release 6.03.

TYPE=SSCP and CSSCP data sets can be used in addition to COV and CORR data sets as input data sets.

Thirteen options have been added to PROC STEPDISC. Specifically, the START= option is used to specify that the first n variables in the VAR statement be used to begin the selection process. The STOP= option can be used to specify the number of variables in the final model. The STEPDISC procedure stops the selection process when a model with n variables is found. This option applies only when METHOD=FORWARD or METHOD=BACKWARD is used.

The following options are options regarding the printed output. WSSCP prints the within-class corrected SSCP matrix for each class level. PSSCP prints the pooled within-class corrected SSCP matrix. BSSCP prints the between-class SSCP matrix. TSSCP prints the total-sample corrected SSCP matrix. WCOV prints within-class covariances for each class level. PCOV prints pooled within-class covariances. BCOV prints between-class covariances. TCOV prints total-sample covariances. PCORR prints pooled within-class correlations (partial correlations based on the pooled within-class covariances). BCORR prints between-class correlations.

TREE Procedure

A new option, HORIZONTAL, in PROC TREE prints horizontal tree diagrams. If a tree takes up more than one page and will be viewed on a screen, horizontal orientation can make the tree diagram considerably easier to read.

TTEST Procedure

A new option, COCHRAN, in the PROC TTEST statement gives the Cochran and Cox approximation of the probability level for an approximate t test. This option provides another alternative test for the case of unequal variances for the two groups. Previously, only Satterthwaite's approximation for degrees of freedom was available.

VARCLUS Procedure

Several new options have been added to the PROC VARCLUS statement. The RANDOM= option allows you to specify a positive integer as a starting value for use with the REPLACE=RANDOM option. The VARDEF= option specifies the divisor to be used in the calculation of variances and covariances. The NOINT option requests that no intercept be used; covariances or correlations are not corrected for the mean.

VARCOMP Procedure

The VARCOMP procedure is essentially unchanged from previous versions. This procedure was not available in Release 6.02 of SAS/STAT software. An expanded introduction and **DETAILS** sections have been added to the documentation.

Special SAS® Data Sets

Introduction to Special SAS Data Sets

Many SAS/STAT procedures create SAS data sets containing various statistics. Some of these data sets are organized according to certain conventions that allow them to be read by a SAS/STAT procedure for further analysis. Such specially organized data sets are recognized by the TYPE= attribute of the data set.

For example, the CORR procedure can create a data set with the attribute TYPE=CORR containing a correlation matrix. This TYPE=CORR data set can be read by the REG or FACTOR procedures, among others. If the original data set is large, using a special SAS data set in this way can save a great deal of computer time by avoiding the recomputation of the correlation matrix in each of several analyses. (For a complete description of the CORR procedure, see the *SAS Procedures Guide, Release 6.03 Edition.*)

As another example, the REG procedure can create a TYPE=EST data set containing estimated regression coefficients. If you need to make predictions from new observations, you can have the SCORE procedure read both the TYPE=EST data set and a data set containing the new observations. PROC SCORE can then compute predicted values or residuals without repeating the entire regression analysis.

A special SAS data set may contain different kinds of statistics. A special variable called _TYPE_ is used to distinguish the various statistics. For example, in a TYPE=CORR data set, an observation in which _TYPE_='MEAN' contains the means of the variables in the analysis, and an observation in which _TYPE_='STD' contains the standard deviations. Correlations appear in observations with _TYPE_='CORR'. Another special variable, _NAME_, is needed to identify the row of the correlation matrix. Thus, the correlation between variables

X and Y would be given by the value of the variable X in the observation for which _TYPE_='CORR' and _NAME_='Y', or by the value of the variable Y in the observation for which _TYPE_='CORR' and _NAME_='X'.

You can create special SAS data steps directly in a DATA step. You must specify the data set TYPE= option in parentheses after the data set name in the DATA statement. Examples are given later in this appendix.

The special data sets created by SAS/STAT procedures can generally be used directly by other procedures without modification. However, if you create an output data set with PROC CORR and use the NOCORR option to omit the correlation matrix from the OUT= data set, you need to set the data set TYPE= option either in parentheses following the OUT= data set name in the PROC CORR statement, or in parentheses following the DATA= option in any other procedure that recognizes the special data set TYPE= attribute. In either case, the TYPE= option should be set to COV, CSSCP, or SSCP according to what type of matrix is stored in the data set and what data set types are accepted as input by the other procedures you plan to use. If you do not follow these steps, and you use the TYPE=CORR data set with no correlation matrix as input to another procedure, the procedure issues an error message indicating that the correlation matrix is missing from the data set.

If you use a DATA step with a SET statement to modify a special SAS data set, you must specify the TYPE= option in the DATA statement. The TYPE= of the data set in the SET statement is *not* automatically copied to the data set being created.

You can find out the TYPE= of a data set by using the CONTENTS procedure.

Table A2.1 summarizes the TYPE= data sets that may be used as input to SAS/STAT procedures and the TYPE= data sets that are created by SAS/STAT procedures. For output data sets, the statement that is used to create the data set is shown.

Table A2.1   SAS/STAT Procedures and Types of Data Sets

Procedure	Input Data Set TYPE= as shown*	Output Data Set(s) (TYPE=null or as shown)	Created by the Statement
ACECLUS	ACE, CORR, COV, SSCP	OUTSTAT=, TYPE=ACE OUT=	PROC ACECLUS
ANOVA		OUTSTAT=	PROC ANOVA
CANCORR	CORR, COV, SSCP	OUTSTAT=, TYPE=CORR OUT=	PROC CANCORR
CANDISC	CORR, COV, SSCP, CSSCP	OUTSTAT=, TYPE=CORR OUT=	
CATMOD	EST	OUT= OUTEST=, TYPE=EST	RESPONSE RESPONSE
CLUSTER	DISTANCE	OUTTREE=, TYPE=TREE	PROC CLUSTER
DISCRIM	CORR, COV, SSCP, CSSCP, LINEAR, QUAD, MIXED	OUTSTAT= and POOL=YES, TYPE=LINEAR OUTSTAT= and POOL=NO, TYPE=QUAD OUTSTAT= and POOL=TEST, TYPE=MIXED OUT=, OUTCROSS=, OUTD=, OUTTEST=, OUTTESTD=	PROC DISCRIM PROC DISCRIM PROC DISCRIM PROC DISCRIM PROC DISCRIM
FACTOR	CORR, COV, SSCP FACTOR	OUTSTAT=, TYPE=FACTOR OUT=	PROC FACTOR PROC FACTOR
FASTCLUS		OUT=, MEAN=	PROC FASTCLUS
FREQ		OUT=	TABLES
GLM		OUTSTAT= OUT= OUT=	PROC GLM LSMEANS OUTPUT
LIFEREG		OUTEST=, TYPE=EST OUT=	PROC LIFEREG OUTPUT
NESTED		none	
NLIN		OUTEST=, TYPE=EST OUT=	PROC NLIN OUTPUT
NPAR1WAY		none	
ORTHOREG		OUTEST=, TYPE=EST	PROC ORTHOREG
PLAN		OUT=	OUTPUT
PRINCOMP	CORR, COV, SSCP	OUTSTAT=, TYPE=CORR or COV OUT=	PROC PRINCOMP PROC PRINCOMP
REG	CORR, COV, SSCP	OUTEST=, TYPE=EST OUTSSCP=, TYPE=SSCP OUT=	PROC REG PROC REG OUTPUT
RSREG		OUT= OUTR=	PROC RSREG RIDGE
SCORE	FACTOR, EST	OUT=	PROC SCORE
STEPDISC	CORR, COV, SSCP, CSSCP	none	
TREE		OUT=	PROC TREE
TTEST		none	
VARCLUS	CORR, COV, SSCP, FACTOR	OUTSTAT=, TYPE=CORR OUTTREE=, TYPE=TREE	PROC VARCLUS
VARCOMP		none	

*If no TYPE= shown, the procedure accepts only TYPE=null data sets.

TYPE=CORR Data Sets

A TYPE=CORR data set usually contains a correlation matrix and possibly other statistics including means, standard deviations, and the number of observations in the original SAS data set from which the correlation matrix was computed.

Using PROC CORR with the OUT= option produces a TYPE=CORR data set. (For a complete description of the CORR procedure, see SAS Technical Report P-171). The CANCORR and PRINCOMP procedures can also create a TYPE=CORR data set with additional statistics.

A TYPE=CORR data set containing a correlation matrix can be used as input for CANCORR, CANDISC, FACTOR, PRINCOMP, REG, STEPDISC, VARCLUS, and other SAS/STAT procedures.

The variables in a TYPE=CORR data set are

- the BY variable(s), if a BY statement is used with the procedure.
- _TYPE_, a character variable of length eight whose values identify the type of statistic in each observation, such as MEAN, STD, N, and CORR.
- _NAME_, a character variable of length eight whose values identify the variable with which a given row of the correlation matrix is associated. _NAME_ is blank for observations in which a row name is not needed.
- the variables from the original data set that were analyzed by the CORR or other procedure.

The usual values of the _TYPE_ variable are as follows:

TYPE	Contents
MEAN	mean of each variable analyzed.
STD	standard deviation of each variable.
N	number of observations used in the analysis. PROC CORR records the number of nonmissing values for each variable unless the NOMISS option is used. If NOMISS is specified, or if the CANCORR or PRINCOMP procedures are used to create the data set, observations with one or more missing values are omitted from the analysis, so this value is the same for each variable and gives the number of observations with no missing values. If a FREQ statement was used with the procedure that created the data set, the number of observations is taken to be the sum of the relevant values of the variable in the FREQ statement. Procedures that read a TYPE=CORR data set use the smallest value in the observation with _TYPE_='N' as the number of observations in the analysis.
SUMWGT	sum of the observation weights if a WEIGHT statement was used with the procedure that created the data set. The values are determined analogously to those of the _TYPE_='N' observation.
CORR	correlations with the variable named by the _NAME_ variable.

There may be additional observations in a TYPE=CORR data set depending on the particular procedure and options used.

If you create a TYPE=CORR data set yourself, the data set need not contain the observations with _TYPE_='MEAN', 'STD', 'N', or SUMWGT'. Procedures assume that all of the means are 0.0 and that the standard deviations are 1.0 if this information is not in the TYPE=CORR data set. If _TYPE_='N' does not appear, the number of observations is taken to be 10,000; significance tests and other statistics that depend on the number of observations are, of course, meaningless.

A correlation matrix is symmetric; that is, the correlation between X and Y is the same as the correlation between Y and X. The CORR, CANCORR, and PRINCOMP procedures output the entire correlation matrix. If you create the data set yourself, you need to include only one of the two occurrences of the correlation between two variables; the other may be given a missing value.

If you create a TYPE=CORR data set yourself, the _TYPE_ and _NAME_ variables are also not necessary. If there is no _TYPE_ variable, then all observations are assumed to contain correlations. If there is no _NAME_ variable, the first observation is assumed to correspond to the first variable in the analysis, the second observation to the second variable, and so on. However, if you omit the _NAME_ variable, you will not be able to analyze arbitrary subsets of the variables or list the variables in a VAR or MODEL statement in a different order.

Example 1: A TYPE=CORR Data Set Produced by PROC CORR

See **Output A2.1** for an example of a TYPE=CORR data set produced by the following SAS statements:

```
title 'Five Socioeconomic Variables';
data socecon;
   title2 'see page 14 of Harman (1976), Modern Factor Analysis, 3rd ed';
   input pop school employ services house;
   cards;
5700    12.8    2500    270    25000
1000    10.9    600     10     10000
3400    8.8     1000    10     9000
3800    13.6    1700    140    25000
4000    12.8    1600    140    25000
8200    8.3     2600    60     12000
1200    11.4    400     10     16000
9100    11.5    3300    60     14000
9900    12.5    3400    180    18000
9600    13.7    3600    390    25000
9600    9.6     3300    80     12000
9400    11.4    4000    100    13000
;
proc corr noprint out=corrcorr;
proc print;
   title2 'A TYPE=CORR Data Set Produced by PROC CORR';
run;
```

Output A2.1   A TYPE=CORR Data Set Produced by PROC CORR

```
                           Five Socioeconomic Variables                          1
                        A TYPE=CORR Data Set Produced by PROC CORR

        OBS    _TYPE_    _NAME_      POP     SCHOOL    EMPLOY    SERVICES    HOUSE

         1     MEAN               6241.67   11.4417   2333.33    120.833   17000.00
         2     STD               3439.99    1.7865   1241.21    114.928    6367.53
         3     N                   12.00   12.0000     12.00     12.000      12.00
         4     CORR    POP          1.00    0.0098      0.97      0.439       0.02
         5     CORR    SCHOOL       0.01    1.0000      0.15      0.691       0.86
         6     CORR    EMPLOY       0.97    0.1543      1.00      0.515       0.12
         7     CORR    SERVICES     0.44    0.6914      0.51      1.000       0.78
         8     CORR    HOUSE        0.02    0.8631      0.12      0.778       1.00
```

Example 2: Creating a TYPE=CORR Data Set in a DATA Step

This example creates a TYPE=CORR data set by reading a correlation matrix in
a DATA step. **Output A2.2** shows the resulting data set.

```
data datacorr;
   infile cards missover;
   _type_='corr';
   input _name_ $ pop school employ services house;
   cards;
POP        1.00000
SCHOOL     0.00975   1.00000
EMPLOY     0.97245   0.15428   1.00000
SERVICES   0.43887   0.69141   0.51472   1.00000
HOUSE      0.02241   0.86307   0.12193   0.77765   1.00000
;
proc print;
   title2 'A TYPE=CORR Data Set Created by a DATA Step';
run;
```

Output A2.2   A TYPE=CORR Data Set Created by a DATA Step

```
                           Five Socioeconomic Variables                          1
                        A TYPE=CORR Data Set Created by a DATA Step

        OBS    _TYPE_    _NAME_      POP     SCHOOL    EMPLOY    SERVICES    HOUSE

         1     corr    POP        1.00000      .         .          .          .
         2     corr    SCHOOL     0.00975   1.00000      .          .          .
         3     corr    EMPLOY     0.97245   0.15428   1.00000       .          .
         4     corr    SERVICES   0.43887   0.69141   0.51472    1.00000       .
         5     corr    HOUSE      0.02241   0.86307   0.12193    0.77765       1
```

TYPE=COV Data Sets

A TYPE=COV data set is similar to a TYPE=CORR data set except that it has
TYPE='COV' observations containing covariances instead of or in addition
to _TYPE_='CORR' observations containing correlations. PROC PRINCOMP
creates a TYPE=COV data set if the COV option is used. You can also create
a TYPE=COV data set by using PROC CORR with the COV and NOCORR

options and specifying the data set option TYPE=COV in parentheses following the name of the OUT= data set.

TYPE=COV data sets are used by the same procedures that use TYPE=CORR data sets.

TYPE=SSCP Data Sets

A TYPE=SSCP data set contains an uncorrected sum of squares and crossproducts (SSCP) matrix. TYPE=SSCP data sets are produced by PROC REG when the OUTSSCP= option is specified in the PROC REG statement. You can also create a TYPE=SSCP data set by using PROC CORR with the SSCP option and specifying the data set option TYPE=SSCP in parentheses following the name of the OUT= data set. You can also create TYPE=SSCP data sets in a DATA step; in this case TYPE=SSCP must be specified as a data set option.

The variables in a TYPE=SSCP data set include those found in a TYPE=CORR data set. In addition there is a variable called INTERCEP that contains crossproducts for the intercept (sums of the variables). The SSCP matrix is stored in observations with _TYPE_='SSCP', including a row with _NAME_='INTERCEP'. PROC REG also outputs an observation with _TYPE_='N'. PROC CORR includes _TYPE_='MEAN' and 'STD' as well.

TYPE=SSCP data sets are used by the same procedures that use TYPE=CORR data sets.

Example 3: A TYPE=SSCP Data Set Produced by PROC REG

Output A2.3 shows a TYPE=SSCP data set produced by PROC REG from the SOCECON data set created in **Example 1**.

```
proc reg data=socecon outsscp=regsscp;
   model house=pop school employ services / noprint;
proc print;
   title2 'A TYPE=SSCP SAS Data Set Produced by PROC REG';
run;
```

Output A2.3 A TYPE=SSCP Data Set Produced by PROC REG

```
                              Five Socioeconomic Variables                                    1
                        A TYPE=SSCP SAS Data Set Produced by PROC REG

OBS   _TYPE_    _NAME_     INTERCEP        POP         SCHOOL       EMPLOY     SERVICES      HOUSE

 1    SSCP     INTERCEP       12.0        74900        137.30        28000        1450       204000
 2    SSCP     POP         74900.0    597670000     857640.00    220440000    10959000   1278700000
 3    SSCP     SCHOOL        137.3       857640       1606.05       324130       18152      2442100
 4    SSCP     EMPLOY      28000.0    220440000     324130.00     82280000     4191000    486600000
 5    SSCP     SERVICES     1450.0     10959000      18152.00      4191000      320500     30910000
 6    SSCP     HOUSE      204000.0   1278700000    2442100.00    486600000    30910000   3914000000
 7    N                       12.0           12         12.00           12          12           12
```

TYPE=EST Data Sets

A TYPE=EST data set contains parameter estimates. The CATMOD, LIFEREG, NLIN, ORTHOREG, and REG procedures create TYPE=EST data sets when the OUTEST= option is specified. A TYPE=EST data set produced by LIFEREG, ORTHOREG, or REG can be used with PROC SCORE to compute residuals or predicted values.

The variables in a TYPE=EST data set include

- the BY variables, if a BY statement is used.
- _TYPE_, a character variable of length eight, that indicates the type of estimate. The values depend on which procedure created the data set. Usually 'PARM' or 'PARMS' indicates estimated regression coefficients, and 'COV' or 'COVB' indicates estimated covariances of the parameter estimates. Some procedures, such as NLIN, have other values of _TYPE_ for special purposes.
- _NAME_, a character variable of length eight, appears if the procedure outputs the covariance matrix of the parameter estimates. The values are the names of the rows of the covariance matrix or are blank for observations that do not contain covariances.
- variables that contain the parameter estimates, usually the same variables that appear in the VAR statement or in any MODEL statement. For CATMOD and NLIN, the variable names are the names of the parameters.

Other variables may be included depending on the particular procedure and options used.

Example 4: A TYPE=EST Data Set Produced by PROC REG

Output A2.4 shows the TYPE=EST data set produced by the following PROC REG step:

```
proc reg data=socecon outest=regest covout;
    full:   model house=pop school employ services / noprint;
    empser: model house=employ services / noprint;
proc print;
    title 'A TYPE=EST Data Set Produced by PROC REG';
run;
```

Output A2.4 A TYPE=EST Data Set Produced by PROC REG

```
                         A TYPE=EST Data Set Produced by PROC REG                                    1

OBS  _MODEL_  _TYPE_  _NAME_    _DEPVAR_  _RMSE_      INTERCEP      POP      SCHOOL      EMPLOY    SERVICES  HOUSE

  1  FULL     PARMS             HOUSE     3122.03      -8074.21     0.65     2140.10      -2.92      27.81    -1
  2  FULL     COV     INTERCEP  HOUSE     3122.03  109408014.44  -9157.04  -9784744.54  20612.49  102764.89    .
  3  FULL     COV     POP       HOUSE     3122.03      -9157.04     2.32      852.86      -6.20      -5.20      .
  4  FULL     COV     SCHOOL    HOUSE     3122.03   -9784744.54   852.86   907886.36   -2042.24   -9608.59      .
  5  FULL     COV     EMPLOY    HOUSE     3122.03      20612.49    -6.20    -2042.24      17.44       6.50      .
  6  FULL     COV     SERVICES  HOUSE     3122.03     102764.89    -5.20    -9608.59       6.50     202.56      .
  7  EMPSER   PARMS             HOUSE     3789.96      15021.71       .        .         -1.94      53.88    -1
  8  EMPSER   COV     INTERCEP  HOUSE     3789.96    5824096.19       .        .      -1915.99   -1294.94      .
  9  EMPSER   COV     EMPLOY    HOUSE     3789.96      -1915.99       .        .          1.15      -6.41      .
 10  EMPSER   COV     SERVICES  HOUSE     3789.96      -1294.94       .        .         -6.41     134.49      .
```

TYPE=FACTOR Data Sets

A TYPE=FACTOR data set is created by PROC FACTOR when the OUTSTAT= option is specified. PROC FACTOR and PROC SCORE can use TYPE=FACTOR data sets as input. The variables are the same as in a TYPE=CORR data set. The statistics include means, standard deviations, sample size, correlations, eigenvalues, eigenvectors, factor pattern, residual correlations, scoring coefficients, and others depending on the options specified. See the chapter describing the FACTOR procedure for details.

TYPE=LINEAR Data Sets

A TYPE=LINEAR data set contains the coefficients of a linear function of the variables in observations with _TYPE_='LINEAR'.

The DISCRIM procedure stores linear discriminant function coefficients in a TYPE=LINEAR data set when OUTSTAT= and POOL=YES are specified; the data set can be used in a subsequent invocation of DISCRIM to classify additional observations. Many other statistics may be included depending on the options used. See the chapter describing the DISCRIM procedure for details.

TYPE=QUAD Data Sets

A TYPE=QUAD data set contains the coefficients of a quadratic function of the variables in observations with _TYPE_='QUAD'.

The DISCRIM procedure stores quadratic discriminant function coefficients in a TYPE=QUAD data set when OUTSTAT= and POOL=NO are specified; the data set can be used in a subsequent invocation of DISCRIM to classify additional observations. Many other statistics may be included depending on the options used. See the chapter describing the DISCRIM procedure for details.

TYPE=MIXED Data Sets

A TYPE=MIXED data set contains coefficients of either a linear or a quadratic function, or possibly both if there are BY groups.

The DISCRIM procedure produces a TYPE=MIXED data set when OUTSTAT= and POOL=TEST are specified. See the chapter describing the DISCRIM procedure for details.

Index

G

S

X

Z

2

Special Characters

Your Turn

If you have comments or suggestions about the *SAS/STAT User's Guide, Release 6.03 Edition* or SAS/STAT software, please send them to us on a photocopy of this page.

Please return the photocopy to the Publications Division (for comments about this book) or the Technical Support Department (for suggestions about the software) at SAS Institute Inc., SAS Campus Drive, Cary, NC 27513.